Fodor's Road Guide USA

Where to Stay with Your Pet

First Edition

Introduction and Pet Resources
by Andrea Arden

Fodor's Travel Publications
New York Toronto London Sydney Auckland
www.fodors.com

Fodor's Road Guide USA: Where to Stay with Your Pet

Fodor's Travel Publications
President: Bonnie Ammer
Publisher: Kris Kliemann
Executive Managing Editor: Denise DeGennaro
Editorial Director: Karen Cure
Director of Marketing Development: Jeanne Kramer
Senior Editor: Constance Jones
Director of Production and Manufacturing: Chuck Bloodgood
Creative Director: Fabrizio La Rocca

Contributors
Editor: Emmanuelle Morgen
Editorial Assistants: Jennifer LiButti, Andrew Beck
Production/Manufacturing: Yexenia (Jessie) Markland
Cover: Corbis (background photo), Bart Nagel (photo, illustration)
Andrea Arden is founder and director of the Manhattan Dog Training & Behavior Center. She's authored several books on dog training and has been the on-air animal trainer and field correspondent for Fox Cable Network's daily national pet show, *The Pet Department*, since its inception in June 1994. Andrea lives in Manhattan with her two dogs, Oliver and Meggie.

First Edition
ISBN 0–676–90207–3
ISSN 1534–0546

Special Sales
Fodor's Travel Publications are available at special discounts for bulk purchases for sales promotions or premiums. Special editions, including personalized covers, excerpts of existing guides, and corporate imprints, can be created in large quantities for special needs. For more information, contact your local bookseller or write to Special Markets, Fodor's Travel Publications, 280 Park Avenue, New York, NY 10017. Inquiries from Canada should be directed to your local Canadian bookseller or sent to Random House of Canada, Ltd., Marketing Department, 2775 Matheson Boulevard East, Mississauga, Ontario L4W 4P7. Inquiries from the United Kingdom should be sent to Fodor's Travel Publications, 20 Vauxhall Bridge Road, London SW1V 2SA, England.

PRINTED IN THE UNITED STATES OF AMERICA
10 9 8 7 6 5 4 3 2 1

CONTENTS

Happy Traveling with Your Pet

By Andrea Arden

Animals have been an important part of our family life for ages, so it's no surprise more and more people are making their pets a part of family travel. Pets can add to your travel adventures in many ways. Aside from the comfort they offer, pets also open the door to meeting new people. Animals are great conversation starters, and animal lovers are everywhere!

In return for companionship and fun, your pet will require much of your time, just as he does at home. In fact, if you elect to include him, your pet will probably be a major focus of your trip. Days must be planned keeping the pet's needs in mind. Often, this means you aren't as free to spend leisurely hours shopping or dining.

While the number of travelers accompanied by animals is growing, some hotels are still cautious to put out the welcome mat. In some areas of the country, finding decent accommodations that accept you and your pet can be a daunting task. Be prepared to spend extra time making travel plans.

Most importantly, if you don't think your pet will enjoy traveling, it is unfair to both him and yourself to make him do so needlessly. While most pets do have a remarkable ability to adapt to new situations, those that don't can become highly stressed and in some cases even ill.

Take Your Pet or Leave Him?

When deciding whether or not to travel with your pet, try not to let your emotions take precedence over practical concerns, such as your pet's age, temperament, and health. Consider your aspirations for the trip and how you will handle the responsibility of taking care of your pet on the road. If you think it will greatly hamper your enjoyment, then it may be unfair to you both to take her along. Instead, you might consider hiring a pet-sitter or finding a good kennel. Sending your dog to a doggie camp or bringing a dog-sitter along on your trip are other options.

The best candidates for travel are pets that are even-tempered, well behaved, sociable, and in good health. If your pet is anxious, aggressive, or is likely to be highly stressed, it is probably in his best interest to make alternative plans, such as finding him boarding or having a pet-sitter stay in your home.

While it is legal to transport an eight-week-old kitten or puppy by plane, it is advisable to wait until he or she is at least 12 weeks old. At eight weeks animals are susceptible to many more diseases because their immune systems are not fully developed. It's also important to control the environment of very young puppies and kittens so they don't have experiences that may frighten them. This is difficult to do while traveling.

Some trips are inappropriate for pets because of the environment, time of year, and nature of the journey. A friend of mine chose to take her six-year-old lab on a cross-country drive from New York to Arizona. She left at the end of June. By the time she reached the Grand Canyon it was mid-July. The heat was tough on her but almost unbearable for her dog. As a result she spent a lot of time worrying about her dog rather than sightseeing. If she had made the trip at a different time of year, it might have been a more pet-friendly adventure.

Who Should Stay and Who Should Go?

BRING	LEAVE
Calm pets	Anxious pets
Well-behaved pets	Noisy, boisterous, or un–house-trained pets
Friendly pets	Unfriendly pets
Pets who enjoy new experiences	Fearful pets
If your travel plans are pet-friendly	If your travel plans are not pet-friendly
If weather permits	If weather will be uncomfortable for your pet

Types of Travel with Pets

Around home. Most of the travel we do with our pets is around our hometown and often isn't pleasant for them. The destination is almost always a place they don't like, such as the veterinarian, groomer, or kennel. Try to make it a habit to take your pet on short trips and to places he likes around town so he learns to enjoy travel. You can drive your dog to the local park for a walk, or take your cat in its carrier to run an errand to the bank. When you get to your destination, give the animal a few treats, or better yet have a friendly person give a treat to your pet. This teaches your pet to enjoy travel by making it a more common and pleasant occurrence, and it will help the animal to be more comfortable with lots of different people and things in environments outside of your home.

Mostly-people destinations. Pets require a good part of your attention each day. If you are traveling to a place where there will be lot of people, be sure you are willing to devote a lot of time and attention to your pet. Trips to visit friends, relatives, or resorts can be fun, but often at these destinations your pet is likely to play second fiddle. If you are planning to do a lot of socializing, you may not want to devote your attention to your pet. In this case, you might consider leaving your pet at a kennel or with a pet-sitter at home.

Pet-friendly destinations. Campsites that allow dogs and cats can be very pet-friendly. Trips to this sort of destination are fun for both you and your pet and are relatively easy to plan. Dogs and cats should always be on-leash at a campsite.

Doggie destinations. There are vacations you can take with your dog that will be as much of an adventure for him as for you. Dog camps, seminars, and workshops are a terrific way to have fun with your pet and learn more about your canine companion. Some of the best sources for information on these sorts of trips are the Association of Pet Dog Trainers, Camp Gone to the Dogs, and Whiz Kid Dog Camp. For more information on these sources, *see* Pet Resources.

Traveling Happily with Your Pet

Before You Go/Preparing to Travel

Preparation is the key to successfully traveling with your pet. As when making any travel plans, the farther in advance you begin the better. This includes training your pet for travel and making reservations for accommodations.

Due to the fast-changing nature of the lodging industry, it is important to call ahead and confirm the pet-friendly status of your lodgings a few days prior to your departure. It's not uncommon for the policies of accommodations to change on short notice. After all, it can take just one irresponsible visitor with his or her pet to convince a manager that pets just aren't worth the trouble.

When confirming your reservation be sure to double-check the fees and restrictions of each lodging. Accommodations often have restrictions on the size and age of animals (puppies are often discouraged). Be prepared to leave a deposit (usually refundable) in case your animal damages the property.

Try to have a confirmation mailed or faxed to you prior to your departure. At the very least, take down the name and title of a contact person at each of your lodgings.

What to Pack

The following list may seem a bit daunting, but my friends with young children insist their lists are much longer when they pack for their kids! It's usually best to keep all of your pet's items in one easy-to-reach bag. You want to avoid fumbling around for something for your pet in an overhead bin or the back seat of your van.

One of the most important things to consider when traveling with your pet is to make sure your animal is wearing clear identification. The more methods of identification, the better the chances of recovery. The most common and traditional method is an ID tag. Your pet should wear two tags when traveling: one with your permanent address and telephone number and another with a way to contact you on the road. A trick is to staple a card or matchbook from your lodging to your pet's collar. You can also buy tags that can be changed by slipping in a new piece of paper. Also, keep a current photo of your pet on hand while traveling. Visual images are extremely helpful in locating lost pets. Consider having your pet tattooed or microchipped in addition to wearing traditional ID tags. Both processes are humane and effective for tracking pets. For more information on microchipping and tattooing, talk to your vet, and *see* Pet Resources.

HEALTH RECORDS AND METHODS OF IDENTIFICATION

- A leash and collar or harness with ID tags (an extra set is advisable).
- Health and vaccination records
- A lost-pet packet. Taking every imaginable precaution doesn't guarantee your pet won't get lost on your trip. As a safety measure, bring some current photos and a description of your pet in case you need to put up signs.
- A bell to attach to your pet's collar. This is a great backup safety measure if your pet gets loose in the woods.

FOOD AND WATER

- Bowls (paper plates and a collapsible water bowl are light to carry and easy to dispose of).
- Your pet's food. If it isn't a national brand and you suspect it may be difficult to find while traveling, be sure to bring enough for the whole trip. A sudden change in your dog's food could cause an upset stomach. If you usually add a bit of moist food to the dry food but prefer not to take heavy cans with you, bring a few packets of mild dry soup mix. Sprinkle a bit over the kibble and mix with warm water to make a tasty gravy.
- If you choose to bring canned food, don't forget an opener and a spoon.
- A container or two of water from your home. This is especially advisable if your pet has a sensitive stomach and may be affected by drinking new water.
- A spray bottle (to squirt water in your pet's mouth if necessary).

CLEANUP STUFF

- Plastic bags and/or newspaper.
- A lint and hair remover for yourself and to tidy up your lodgings.
- Room deodorizer.
- Baby wipes or towelettes for quick and easy clean ups of paws and hands.
- Old cloths and/or paper towels for lining the carrier and cleanup.
- Also, bring a supply of plastic bags for soiled towels and a spray bottle of cleaner.
- If you are traveling with a cat, don't forget a litter box, litter, a plastic bag to slip over the box, and a couple of large rubber bands to hold the bag in place.
- Grooming tools to keep your pet clean (and therefore more likely to be welcome).

SLEEPING

- A bed, blanket, or piece of carpet sample for your pet to sleep on (*see* What Should My Pet Be Trained to Do?).
- A relaxation tape (*see* Relaxing to Music).

TOYS

- Sterilized hollow white bones or Kong toys to stuff with meat, cheese, kibble or peanut butter (good for dogs and cats).
- Cat toys. The easiest and cheapest is a piece of crumpled paper or a square of cardboard tied to string. Pet stores sell all sorts of inexpensive, intriguing, safe toys.

MEDICAL STUFF

- Any medication prescribed by your veterinarian.
- A first-aid kit (Ask your vet for assistance, or contact Pet Pak, Inc. *See* Pet Resources).
- A slip-on muzzle, in case your pet or a stray has a medical emergency.
- Honey or hard candy to help alleviate car sickness (be sure to consult your vet first).
- Tweezers and scissors (for removing burs, ticks and other things).

EXTRAS

- Flashlight (for nighttime walks).
- A clip-on minifan for the hotel room or the car.

Stress and Traveling

Traveling is stressful for people, but for an animal it can be even more so. The best ways to alleviate stress for your pet are to teach her what you want and to control her environment. Most stress comes from not knowing how to act (*see* What Should My Pet Be Trained to Do, *below*). Be considerate of your pet's stress levels. Don't expect her to meet and greet too many people in one day, especially when under the stress of traveling. Even the most social animals can be overwhelmed if too many people say hello at once or if they are overtired from meeting too many new people. You should control who comes into contact with your pet and how often. Watch your pet for signs of stress (yawning, excessive panting, avoiding eye contact) and give her a place to relax quietly if she needs to. A crate or blanket is great for this purpose. Follow the guidelines set by the Delta Society (*see* Pet Resources), an organization that facilitates pet therapy programs in hospitals and nursing homes. They suggest that when an animal and owner team goes on a visit, they stay no more than one hour. Most pets should have no more than one hour of intense meeting and greeting a day.

Travel Petiquette

Training is what determines whether traveling with your pet will be easy and enjoyable or no fun at all. The best travel companion, whether two- or four-legged, is a well-behaved one. A calm, well-mannered pet is sure to be invited back for a second visit and will help to pave the way for future visits from other pets. Whether at home or on the road, an animal who likes to be around people and is calm and under control is a joy to be with. Dogs and cats are social animals who relish communication with their pack. Training helps your pet to communicate with you by putting human words to dog and cat behaviors. If you think your pet needs some travel training, plan on starting at least a few weeks before your trip to give both of you ample time. Have a travel-prep party to help you train your dog or cat to be an ambassador for canines and felines. Invite friends over to help your pet practice meeting people and coping in a hectic environment. James and Kenneth Publishers (*see* Pet Resources) is one of the best sources for training books, audios, and videos for both cats and dogs.

WHERE TO TRAIN

Most people just train their dogs at home and at a training club. But it's important to train your pet in a variety of places to optimize your pet's exposure to different people, places, and things. Visit local buildings and hotels where pets are welcome. These buildings should be climate-controlled, have good parking, and have carpeting, which makes for good traction. Think of this training as getting your pet ready at the "home game" before the big "away game."

WHAT SHOULD MY PET BE TRAINED TO DO?

Both cats and dogs should know how to be friendly with people and how to relax and calmly accept travel. They should know how to settle down in different situations, especially when left alone in a safe place. They should also be housetrained or litterbox trained. Dogs should know how to come to you when you call (cats can learn this too!), to walk politely on a leash, and to stop barking when asked.

GREETING PEOPLE

Start teaching your pet at home that meeting people is a safe and fun thing to do. The more good experiences your pet has with people, the more comfortable he will be around people. Take him to meet people all over town: at the local shopping mall, in the park, and on the streets. You should also teach him to sit to greet people. To do this, invite friends over and have each of them ready with a handful of treats. Have your dog on a leash and when they approach to greet him ask him to sit. While he is sitting they can give him a bit of food. Then have them vary from occasionally giving food to praise alone when he sits. He will learn that saying hello to people while sitting is a rewarding experience. For your cat, you can have people gently hold him and offer him a treat.

SETTLING DOWN

Your dog should be able to settle down at the drop of a hat. Start in your calm home environment by teaching him that the word down means to lay down and relax until you release him. Have a blanket, towel, or scrap of rug as the dog's settle-down spot. Ask him to lay down on it and use a bit of food in your hand to guide his head down, in which case his body will follow. When he is laying down, give him the treat and praise him. Let him know when he can get up by saying a word or phrase such as "all done" or "free dog." Start with very short periods of time and gradually build up. By repeating this you will be teaching him that laying quietly on that spot is the best way to get two of the things he likes most: your attention and a treat. Be sure to practice in different places—by your side, at the dinner table, while you're watching television or reading a book. Practice with the dog out of sight in a different room to prepare him for a time when you may need to leave him alone in his carrier while traveling.

When your dog will lay quietly in your home for a few moments, you should begin to use the settle-down command on walks. Stop every 25 yards or so to train him to quickly lay down and relax even when he is excited (most dogs are when going for a walk). Use praise and food the same way you did in your home. Offer him a bit to get him into the "down" position by using your hand with the food in it to guide his head to the floor. When he is laying down, occasionally give him the treat and praise him.

CARRIER/CRATE TRAINING

Crating allows you to relax while your pet is safe and secure. It also allows your pet to relax in a familiar place. The first step is to teach your pet to accept and even enjoy time spent in his or her carrier. I can't think of a better investment of a pet owner's time. If used properly, a carrier is a fantastic tool for training and helping your pet to feel at home anywhere. To begin, place the carrier near your pet's feeding and/or resting area. Let him investigate it on his own. A great little trick is to put a piece of food or your pet's dinner inside the crate and close the door with him outside the crate. When he shows a strong interest in the food, open the door and let him go in to get it. Then begin to have him spend time in the carrier by gently placing him in it and offering a food treat. Slowly increase the time your pet spends in the crate, from a few seconds to a few minutes. Make sure every encounter is a pleasant one and never use the carrier to punish your pet. Continue to have your pet spend time in his carrier doing things he enjoys (such as eating). To ensure that your pet sees his carrier as a safe place, don't let people bother him when he is in it.

How long should this take? Training puppies takes very little time. Older dogs and cats usually require a little more time. But it depends on your pet's temperament. The more laid back your pet, the quicker he'll respond. On average, it should take no more than a few weeks to teach your pet that his carrier is a pleasant place to spend a little time.

Choosing and maintaining the carrier. There are three main considerations to keep in mind when choosing a carrier: size, quality, and comfort. The carrier should be big enough for your pet to stand up, turn around and lay down in. Don't make the mistake of choosing one that gives your pet too much extra room. Animals are more likely to be injured in a carrier that is too big. There are many different brands of carriers on the market. Airline-approved carriers are a wise choice, because they can be used for both air and car travel and offer the best assurance of durability. For most pets you should line the carrier with a mat, towels, or shredded newspaper. However, if you are still house-training your dog, a liner may make him more likely to use the crate as a toilet. So until he is house-trained, keep the carrier floor bare.

RELAXING TO MUSIC

At home, play a tape of music every time you feed, stroke, or massage your pet. After a while he or she will begin to associate this tape with positive and calm experiences. Then you can bring the tape with you when you travel to help calm your pet. It's like bringing a bit of home with you.

SPEAKING AND SHUSHING

To teach your dog to be quiet on command, you first will have to get him or her to bark. Set up a situation that will get him to do so. Say "speak" and have a friend ring the doorbell. Praise him for barking once or twice, tell him to "shush" and waggle a treat in front of his nose. He will stop barking to sniff the treat. When he is quiet for just a moment give him the treat. Repeat this process a few times a day and he will start to understand that being quiet when you ask him to means he may get a reward. When he masters this exercise at home, practice at friends' homes so you have reliable control in many places.

WALKING NICELY ON A LEASH

Your dog should be able to walk calmly by your side, even in crowded areas. To teach this, start by walking her first in relatively quiet areas around your home and garden. Take one step, ask your dog to sit and reward her with a bit of food. Repeat this many times until your dog sits automatically when you stop. Now increase to two steps in between each sit, then three, four, and so on. Pretty soon your dog will be walking attentively by your side for many steps and sitting automatically when you stop. This is walking nicely on a leash. Most people think cats can't be trained to walk on a leash, but they can. If you plan on traveling with your cat it is a good idea to get her used to wearing a harness and leash for safety. You can teach your cat to enjoy wearing her harness by slowly acclimating her to it. To begin, put it on her for short periods of time. Each time she wears it give her a special food treat. In a short while she will associate wearing her harness with something great—food.

COMING WHEN CALLED

Make sure you've taught your dog to come to you when called. This is the most valuable emergency safety command. Imagine he's gotten loose and is headed toward a road. It's imperative that he knows to respond immediately when you call him. Unlike when training at home, where the objective is to phase out lures and rewards for obedience, it is a sound policy to always have a reward handy when on the road. Let your dog know he is highly likely to get a couple of treats and lots of praise when he comes when called. It is dangerous to have a dog who won't come when called while at home, but it is disastrous to lose your dog in an unfamiliar setting. Start teaching him to come when called by having your dog on a leash in a calm environment without too many distractions. Call him to you. When he turns your way, praise him, and give him a treat when he gets to you. You can also enlist friends and family to play recall games. Call your dog back and forth between you and a friend rewarding him lavishly each time. When he responds reliably at home, start to take him to new areas to train, but always keep him on a leash. You can use a longer leash and practice having him come when you call from a farther distance. With this reward system, your dog will learn that coming to you always results in something great: your praise and/or a treat. This means you shouldn't call your dog to you when you are going to do something to him he doesn't like, such as give him a bath. In those cases, go and get him. No matter how reliable a recall you teach, please try to keep your dog on a leash as much as possible when traveling. Remember, his attention and obedience will probably not be as dependable in unfamiliar places.

ELIMINATING

Whether you want your dog to go outside or on paper inside, training him or her to go on cue will make traveling much easier. "Pit stops" often are meant to be fast, and waiting for your dog to find just the right spot can delay your trip. With a small dog who goes on paper, the act of placing the paper on the floor usually is enough to get her to go. But larger dogs who eliminate outside are often taught to go for a long walk before they eliminate. Change things around: When you take your dog out, wait for her to eliminate before you walk around the block. When she begins to eliminate say something like "go potty" in a happy tone and praise her. This way she'll learn to go immediately on command and see the walk as the reward. For the first week or two this training may seem tedious (just standing in one spot), but it will be well worth the effort when you are on the road or when you must take your dog out on a rainy night.

SOCIALIZING

Take your pet out into the world and let him or her become accustomed to new sights, sounds, and people. Introduce him to people at your home, then take him with you on errands around town. Never push your pet into a situation where he feels uncomfortable. Bring along some treats and offer them as a way of praising your pet for calmly accepting new experiences. He will soon associate new experiences with good things.

CAR-TRAVEL TRAINING

Most pets only travel when going to the veterinarian, groomer or kennel, all of which are not much fun for your pet. In fact most pets, especially cats, only make three trips in the car (to the vet) before they are five months old. These experiences are not conducive to your pet enjoying travel. If your pet hasn't traveled much, you should dedicate at least a few weeks before your trip to getting him accustomed to car travel and carrier training. When your pet is calm and relaxed in the carrier at home, you can repeat the training process with the carrier placed in your car. After a few days take short trips in the car and make the destination a place that will please your pet. Most dogs will learn to love car rides if they believe they will sometimes bring them to play ball in the local park.

On the Road

CAR SAFETY

Travel by car is a far better option with your pet than travel by airplane. It is safer and less stressful for your pet. However, there are two major safety concerns for pets in the car: overheating and restraint.

Overheating. Leaving your pet in the car unsupervised is a dangerous proposition. Even in mild temperatures a car can heat up in minutes to a level that can cause heatstroke and even death. Opening the windows and parking in the shade will not prevent this from happening. Dogs and cats do not have good cooling systems, because they don't sweat very much through their skin, rather they rely on panting. In warm weather a damp towel draped over the carrier will help to cool the air circulating through the crate while you are in the car with your dog, but it will not do much good in a car that isn't moving.

Restraint. A loose animal in the car is a danger to himself and everyone else in the car. If you make a short stop or are involved in an accident, the animal could be badly injured or killed, or he could injure someone else. When loose, an animal is also likely to distract you and may get caught under the accelerator or brake pedal. Make sure your pet is restrained to avoid accidents and injury. Options for restraint are a carrier, a harness attached to a seatbelt or a regular leash tied to a stationary part of the car. If you choose to use a crate, make sure it is secured so it won't tip over if you make a sharp turn or stop. Don't allow your pet to keep his head out of the window when you are driving. It's common for animals to need veterinary care as a result of debris becoming embedded in their eyes. You can open the windows a bit to allow fresh air to circulate, but not enough to allow your pet to put his head out. If you want to open your windows fully consider installing window guards or restrain your pet so he can't put his head out.

CAR SICKNESS

Consult your vet if your pet has a history of severe car sickness. She may recommend medication. A holistic approach might also work well for your pet: Many people have had success with Rescue Remedy, which is a mix of flower essences. This option should also be discussed with your vet. Never give your pet any drugs, especially tranquilizers, without your veterinarian's approval.

LOSS OF APPETITE

Many animals suffer from a lack of appetite when they are traveling or under stress in general. It may be due to an existing chronic illness, in which case you should talk to a vet. But in most cases it is simply due to stress caused by travel. If you plan ahead, you can train your pet to eat in the car and/or his crate. Feed him in his crate in and out of the car for at least a few weeks prior to your trip. By doing so, you will train your pet to think of his crate as his portable dining room.

LEAVING YOUR PET IN THE CAR

It is dangerous to leave your pet unsupervised in the car. Animals are susceptible to heatstroke (even in mild weather) and are a target for theft. If you are traveling alone and must leave your pet in the car when you go to the restroom, an option is to leave the car running with the air-conditioning on (in warm weather). You'll need to have two sets of car keys with you so you can leave one in the ignition and lock up with the other. Be sure to keep your pet secured and away from the car's control panels, and remember that leaving your pet alone for even a moment leaves him susceptible to thieves. If you don't have air-conditioning, leave two windows open for circulation. But—and this point cannot be made often enough—if you leave your pet unsupervised in the car, you are taking an enormous risk with his life. If you want to stop and have a day of sightseeing in an area that does not allow pets, contact the local vet or boarding kennels and negotiate a day-rate for boarding.

BATHROOM ROUTINE

When on the road try to keep as close to your pet's normal routine as possible. When you stop for yourself, always be considerate of your pet and allow him time to stretch and relieve himself as well. How often you should stop depends on your pet's age and temperament. For very young or old animals, stops should be more frequent. Traveling can be stressful for even the calmest animals, and stress will make your pet more likely to need to eliminate. So allow your pet a few more opportunities to get out and eliminate than you would at home. At each rest stop offer your pet some water. Allowing him to exercise for a bit before you head off will make him more likely to sleep. Many rest stops have grassy areas appropriate for pets, but no matter how well trained your pet is, be sure to keep him on a leash at all times. You will find that pit stops will be much quicker if you've taught your dog to eliminate on command.

In the Air

Air travel can be a very stressful and sometimes dangerous experience for pets. This is especially true if they are in the excess baggage or cargo holds instead of in the cabin with you. The International Air Transport Association (IATA), which governs air travel for pets along with the United States Department of Agriculture (USDA), estimates half a million dogs and cats travel on commercial airlines in the United States each year. Of those, a reported 99 percent arrive at their destination without incident. However, that leaves approximately 5,000 airline mishaps a year—enough to make any pet owner very cautious of this mode of transportation. The best way to ensure your pet's safety is to ask lots of questions and be sure to get answers that sound right to you before you proceed. Just remember that each person you speak with is in some way responsible for the care of your pet, so be considerate!

Each airline has its own guidelines for travel. Reconfirm your plans 24 to 48 hours before flight departure, especially during peak flying times. If possible, get written confirmation of your arrangements from the airline. Most airlines have information regarding pet travel on their web sites (*see* Important Numbers and On-Line Info).

Pets who can fly by plane. Healthy animals over eight weeks old who have been issued a health certificate no more than ten days prior to flying are legally allowed to fly. However, it is advisable to wait until they are 12 weeks old. If your pet is under the care of a veterinarian for an existing medical condition, you should consult your vet on the pros and cons of air travel.

Pets who shouldn't travel by plane. If your pet is pregnant, ill, or under 12 weeks old she should not fly, because the stress can cause serious complications. According to the Animal Welfare Act, dogs and cats must be at least eight weeks old to travel by plane, but 12 weeks is a much safer age. Keep in mind that pug-nosed animals (such as Bulldogs, Pugs and Boston Terriers and Himalayan and Persian cats) may have difficulty breathing at high altitudes because of their short nasal passages. You should also consider an alternative method of travel or consult your vet if your pet does not handle new and stressful situations well.

Requirements to travel. To travel by plane, your pet will need an airline-approved carrier and a health certificate that has been issued no more than thirty days prior to the flight if he will be in the cabin and no more than ten days if he will be traveling via cargo.

WHEN TO TRAVEL

Best days to travel. Weekday flights are usually less hectic than weekend flights. Therefore, both you and your pet are more likely to receive attentive service during the week.

Best months to travel. If you must travel in the summer months, book flights only in the early morning or late evening when the temperatures are lowest. In the winter, midday flights are best because temperatures are usually higher than in the morning or evening. Remember, your pet may be waiting a bit to be loaded and unloaded from the plane.

Best routes to travel. Direct and nonstop flights are the best. Avoid bringing your pet on a flight with a stopover, especially flights that require passengers to change planes. These are the situations in which a mishap is most likely to occur because of scheduling changes or simple human error. If you are making a flight connection to a different airline, you will have to recheck your animal and pay another fee for excess baggage.

Weather requirements. Most airlines use the following guidelines regarding temperatures in which animals may be flown: No less than 32°F and no more than 85°F.

COST

The cost of flying your pet is determined by the individual airline and may be based on the size and weight of your animal as well as where and how (cabin, baggage or cargo) it is to be flown. Most airlines charge approximately $75 per pet. If you do not have your own carrier some airlines sell them, but they're usually quite a bit more expensive than carriers from a pet-supply catalog or store.

CRATE REQUIREMENTS

A crate must be big enough for your pet to stand up, turn around, and lay down in comfortably. It must be sturdy and well-ventilated and contain two plastic food and water dishes (these usually come with the crate). If your pet is traveling in the cabin with you, he can be carried in a Sherpa bag which is airline-approved. If you're traveling with two cats, you might consider using a slightly larger crate and letting the cats travel together.

TRANQUILIZERS

Most vets do not recommend tranquilizers because they can have adverse effects at high altitudes and may make the animal less able to right himself if his carrier is mishandled. Also, tranquilizers can adversely affect your pet's body temperature-regulation process. It is best to discuss this matter with your vet, who will consider your pet's age and temperament as well as the duration of the flight before advising you on the use of tranquilizers.

EXERCISE

Try to exercise your pet a bit before departure so he will be more likely to relax or even sleep.

FEEDING

In most cases it is advisable to avoid feeding your pet a large meal within two hours of departure time. It is usually best to feed dogs a small meal before you leave and then a larger meal upon arrival at your destination at the end of the day. Cats usually won't eat when they see you packing anyway, so when you get to your destination be sure to set up a quiet spot for your cat to eliminate and eat.

FLYING YOUR PET IN THE CABIN WITH YOU

Some airlines permit animals to travel in the cabin as long as they are kept in their carriers and the carrier fits under the seat. Usually, no more than two pets are allowed in a cabin per flight, so make reservations well in advance and double check the airline's regulations. As a general rule, pets permitted to travel in the cabin can weigh no more than 20 lbs. Most airlines charge between $50 and $75 one way for a pet in the cabin. When you arrive at the security gate, you will be required to remove your pet from its carrier and send the carrier through the X-ray machine. Be sure to have a collar or harness and leash attached to your pet. Most airlines have approved soft-sided carriers, such as the Sherpa bag, for cabin travel. To avoid delays, be sure to have your pet's health certificate and boarding pass ready when you approach the security gate.

CABIN NUMBER REQUIREMENTS

Airline	Animals allowed in 1st class/Main cabin
American	2/5
Continental	1/2
Delta	1/2
Northwest	1/1
TWA	1/2
United	1/2
USAir	1/1

FLYING YOUR PET AS BAGGAGE

To travel on your flight as excess baggage, the total weight of your pet and its carrier must not exceed 100 lbs. If the weight of the animal and carrier combined is greater than that, most airlines will only allow the pet to be shipped as cargo.

FLYING YOUR PET AS CARGO

If your pet and its carrier exceeds the maximum weight allowed to fly as excess baggage (100 lbs. in most cases), she may have to fly as cargo. When flying as cargo, airlines do not guarantee that your pet will be on the same flight as you. Pricing also changes: It will be based on the weight and/or the measurements of the kennel. Flying as cargo is one of the most hazardous ways to transport your pet. If it is your only option, you must be even more careful to question the airline on every aspect of your pet's journey.

CHECKING YOUR PET AS BAGGAGE OR CARGO

- The check-in process can take a bit of time, so get to the airport at least 1½ hours before flight time. Make sure you have all of your paperwork ready and be friendly to everyone at the airline: remember, they will be taking care of your pet.
- Bring a health certificate that has been issued no more than ten days before the flight.
- Have a carrier that is airline-approved and properly fitted to your pet. Approved crates will be marked as such, and appropriately sized crates should be big enough for your pet to stand up, turn around and lay down in with ease. If it is too large, your animal could be hurt because too much movement means he is more likely to be banged around. Don't include toys because they increase they possibility of choking. A piece of your old clothes or a blanket or towel from home may help to relax your pet a bit.
- Make sure the carrier is clearly identified and boldly marked so you can spot it from a distance. Tape a friendly note on the top of the crate with all relevant information regarding your pet. A sample might be: "Hi, my name is Frisky. I am a 7-year-old Labrador Retriever. I am going to St. Paul, MN, on Flight 5203. This is my first flight, so I am a little nervous. Thank you for taking good care of me."
- After you check your pet in, go to your gate and watch to make sure your pet is safely loaded (a brightly marked carrier will make it easy to spot your animal). If possible ask one of the airline employees to reconfirm with baggage personnel that your pet is aboard.
- If you must change planes at a stopover, check with airline personnel again to make sure your pet has made the connection. If there will be a long delay in the second flight departure, claim your pet, take him for a quick walk, etc. and then reboard him.
- After arrival your pet will be delivered to the baggage-claim area. Pick your pet up there.

When You Arrive at Your Lodging

Allowing pets to stay is a courtesy offered by hotels. Many places roll out the red carpet for travelers with pets, but they are also quick to roll the carpet up and put it away after just one or two bad encounters! You and your pet act as ambassadors for every person who travels with his or her pet, so please be on your best behavior. Make sure to adhere to some basic rules, such as cleaning up after your pet, as well as any specific rules posted by the manager. If no rules are posted, ask about them and follow them. Be understanding of people's concerns about pets.

Use the following general guidelines while in lodgings:

- Always clean up after your pet.
- Also, please clean up any other pet messes you see lying around. It is the only proper thing to do (anyway, someone might think your pet did it).
- Walk your pet in areas away from flower beds and other public areas.
- Ask the manager where he would prefer you to walk your pet.
- Always keep your pet on a leash or in its carrier.
- Never leave your pet alone in your room unless he is in his carrier and you are sure he will not disturb other guests. This is for the safety of your pet and the lodging employees. An employee might enter the room to clean and accidentally let your pet slip out of the room. For the safety of lodging employees, if you must leave your pet alone in a room, it is best to hang the DO NOT DISTURB sign on the door.
- If your pet damages any hotel property, immediately discuss the situation with the manager and agree to cover the cost.
- Request a ground-floor room, which is much more convenient for late-night potty runs.
- Be sure to wipe your dog's feet when you enter the room after a walk, and bring an extra towel or sheet if you intend to allow the dog on the furniture (which you shouldn't do anyway!)
- Bring a relaxation tape for your pet. Before you leave on your trip, play a music tape every time you feed him. He will begin to associate the tape with pleasant, calm experiences. When traveling, playing this tape will be like bringing a little bit of home with you.
- Cats should be secured on a leash and harness or in a carrier when transporting them from your room to the car. Put some newspaper under the litter box and put the box in the bathroom or in the bathtub so the cat is less likely to track litter on the carpet. If you know your cat has a tendency to scatter litter out of the box, be sure to clean it up.
- Control who comes into contact with your pet. Allowing too many people to say hello to him may add to his stress (and yours!). The stress of traveling can make even the most friendly animal behave abnormally.

POISONS

Be aware that many public areas and lodgings use poisons to get rid of insects and rodents. These are also poisonous to pets. When you register ask if any poisons are used, and always keep your pet leashed when in public areas.

Health and Safety Precautions

Health problems and emergencies when traveling with your pet are not much different from problems at home. If anything goes wrong, take your pet to the vet. If you have any questions or concerns about your pet's health, contact a vet. Following are some general tips on things to do before you leave.

KNOW YOUR PET'S "NORMALS"

You should know all your animal's normal vital signs, including temperature, heart rate, respiration rate and the frequency of eating, drinking, urinating and defecating. Consult your vet to help compile this list.

Any variation in your pet's normal heart rate, pulse, temperature, or urination or defecation may be an indication that something isn't right. Furthermore, you should take your pet to the vet in the case of persistent loose stool, vomit, blood in the stool or vomit, shortness of breath, excessive slobbering, abnormal body posture, loss of appetite, runny nose or eyes, or shaking.

COMPLETE PHYSICAL

Take your pet for a complete physical before you leave on your trip. The stress of travel can cause even the most minor health concern to turn into a more serious condition. Keep in mind that entry regulations for certain states require certain health certificates. A complete physical for your animal will identify any pre-existing conditions, ascertain your pet's "normals" and give you an opportunity to discuss your travel plans and concerns with your vet.

GET VET REFERRALS BEFORE YOU TRAVEL

Before you leave home ask your vet for veterinary referrals in any areas you plan to travel to. Alternatively contact the American Animal Hospital Association or the American Veterinary Medical Association (*see* Pet Resources).

FIRST-AID KIT

You should always have a first-aid kit whether at home or traveling. You can buy a pre-packed kit or make one on your own. At a minimum a first-aid kit should contain scissors, blunt tweezers, cotton gauze, antibiotic ointment, a rectal thermometer, 3% hydrogen peroxide, cotton swabs, panalog eardrops, Pepto-Bismol, kaopectate, and activated charcoal tablets.

BREED-SPECIFIC TRAVEL PROBLEMS

Breeds of animals with pug noses such as Boston Terriers, Pugs and Bulldogs, and Himalayan and Persian cats often have difficulty breathing at high altitudes, and some airlines advise against these animals being transported by air.

A to Z of Health Concerns

Following is a brief list of pet health concerns you may encounter while traveling. It is by no means meant to be a comprehensive list or treated as a substitute for good veterinary care.

Allergies. Many animals suffer from allergies, and traveling can make them worse. Be sure to discuss your travel plans with your vet prior to departure, so he can send you off fully prepared to deal with any allergic onsets.

Bites and Stings. *If your pet has been in a fight with another animal,* take him to a vet. On the way you should check for any wounds. If he is bleeding, try to stop it by applying pressure to the wound. *If your pet has been bitten by an insect,* you will most likely hear him yelp and see him begin to frantically lick the affected area. Have someone hold and in some cases muzzle him, and gently pull the stinger out, if there is one. Cool water, ice or rubbing alcohol is usually all that need be applied to the area. If you know your pet is allergic to certain insects, consult a veterinarian. *If you suspect your pet has been bitten by a snake*—symptoms of snakebites are swelling, vomiting, difficulty breathing, weakness and convulsion—get to a veterinarian immediately. Try not to let the animal walk. Do not attempt to capture the snake; in most cases clear identification of the type of snake is not necessary for the vet to treat the bite.

Bleeding. If your pet has been injured and blood is pumping out of the wound, slow or stop the bleeding as soon as possible and get him to a veterinarian immediately. As a temporary measure, try covering the wound with one hand while wrapping a finger and thumb around the limb to constrict blood flow. Release the finger and thumb every 15 seconds—do not close off blood flow for more than one minute at a time. If two people are available, one should drive while the other tends to the injured animal. If only one person is available, bandage the wound and get to the vet immediately.

Bloating. Bloat is especially dangerous in large breed dogs. The symptoms include a distended abdomen and whining or moaning sounds. Call a veterinarian immediately if you notice these symptoms.

Burns. Burns can be caused by heat, electric shock, or chemicals. A superficial burn is indicated by redness of the skin and in some cases mild swelling. Most burns should be looked at by a veterinarian because shock can set in quickly. In the meantime, for mild burns, apply cold water or an ice pack to cool the skin and ease the pain. Neosporin (a topical antibiotic) can be applied, and you may want to wrap the area in a light gauze to protect it until the vet can take a look.

Car accident. If your pet has been in a car accident, gently move him to a safe place, changing his position as little as possible. It's a good idea to leash the injured animal immediately following the accident and to tie the leash to a stationary object. Do not allow an injured and disoriented animal to jump up and run loose at an accident site.

Coughing. If coughing persists for more than a few moments, it may be due to an obstruction in the throat. Call your veterinarian immediately.

Dehydration. Dehydration can be caused by a lack of fluid intake, fever, prolonged vomiting and diarrhea. Symptoms are a dry mouth and lack of skin elasticity. When you pick up the fold of skin on your pet's back, it should spring back. If it doesn't, your pet might be dehydrated. Sunken eyes are also an indication of dehydration. If your pet is noticeably dehydrated, consult a vet immediately. In mild cases, fluids can be given.

Diarrhea. One loose stool is usually not enough to cause major concern. Loose stools are often caused by stress, overeating, or a deviation from the normal diet. However, if there is any blood in the stool, if the diarrhea is accompanied by any other symptoms, such as vomiting, or if it persists for more than 24 hours, call a veterinarian.

Drooling. Travel or motion sickness is a common cause of excessive drooling. Some drugs, especially tranquilizers, can also cause this. Foreign objects (for example, sticks) in the mouth can also cause drooling. If drooling persists, contact your vet.

Fever. Before you leave for your trip have your vet write down all of your pet's normal vital signs (body temperature, pulse, etc.). This record will serve as a baseline for comparison. If your pet is feverish, take him to a vet.

Heartworm. Heartworm is an infestation of the heart chambers by a parasitic worm. It is passed to your dog by mosquitoes. Every US state has reported cases of heartworm. If you haven't already, you should talk to your vet about putting your dog on preventative medication.

Heatstroke. If you suspect your pet is suffering from heatstroke, get her to a vet immediately. If possible, immerse the animal in cold water or an ice bath. Apply ice packs to her head and/or towels soaked in water around her body on the way to the vet. Symptoms of heatstroke are uncontrollable panting, foaming at the mouth and unconsciousness. The color of your pet's lips is an indication of her health. Normally, lips are a light pink, and if you press them the white spot caused by the pressure should fade back to pink with a couple of seconds. If the animal is suffering from heatstroke, the gums will be dark pink and it will take a bit longer for the white pressure spot to refill with color.

Hypothermia. Prolonged shivering is indicative of hypothermia. Hypothermia is especially serious if your dog or cat is wet. Vigorously rub her dry and keep her warm by wrapping her in a blanket and snuggling her close to you. Call a vet who will advise you whether or not to bring your pet in for emergency care.

Minor Cuts and Scrapes. Clean cuts and scrapes with peroxide and apply an over-the-counter antibacterial ointment (such as Neosporin) to prevent infection. If bleeding persists, apply direct pressure with a clean cloth. Seek veterinary care if the scrape is to the eye or if there is any discharge. Any wound inflicted by another animal should also be seen by a veterinarian.

Panting (excessive). Excessive panting can be due to overexertion or excitement. If fever, sneezing, racing pulse, vomiting, or diarrhea are also present, consult your vet. These symptoms can indicate a cold, fluid in the lungs, poisoning, or internal bleeding.

Paws (licking). If your pet is constantly licking his paw(s) it could be a sign of a foreign body (splinter, etc.) or other trauma to the paws. In some cases, persistent licking is a sign of an allergy or a behavioral disorder. In either case you should consult a vet.

Poisons. If you suspect your pet has been poisoned, contact a vet or the poison-control hot line immediately (*see* Pet Resources). The most obvious symptoms of poisoning are excessive/profuse salivation, vomiting, and convulsions. It is a good idea to keep activated charcoal tablets in your first-aid kit, which can be used to help absorb the poisons, if recommended by a vet. Some common poisons are car antifreeze, rat poison, and insecticides.

Pulse. The pulse is a reflection of the heartbeat. Have your pet stand or lay on his back and gently feel along the inside of the thigh or gently press along the rib cage just over the heart. Count the number of beats per minute. At rest, most dogs have a rate in the range of 60 to 160. Generally speaking, the smaller the dog the faster the heart rate.

Shock. Symptoms of shock are a racing pulse, fast breathing, a lower-than-normal temperature and in some cases a loss of consciousness. In cases of shock, lay the animal on its side and be sure the breathing passages are not obstructed. Do not give your pet anything to drink. Keep your pet warm and get him to a veterinarian immediately.

Skunks. If your pet has been sprayed by a skunk, soaking his coat in tomato juice may help to dilute the odor.

Staggering. If your pet shows prolonged difficulty getting up or laying down, or if he looks as if he has an aching back, you should contact a veterinarian immediately. This could indicate a herniated disc, damage to a joint, or any one of numerous neuro-logical conditions.

Stool (streaked with blood). Constipation is most often due to a lack of exercise and not enough water. In some cases it is due to an obstruction or stones in the bladder or urethra. Call your veterinarian if it persists for more than a day. If there is blood in the stool contact a vet immediately.

Ticks. Ticks can carry potentially dangerous diseases to both dogs and humans. If you find one on your pet—they usually attach near the neck and ears—drip a little rubbing alcohol on the tick and use tweezers to grab it as near to the head as possible and pull it out. After extracting the tick, soak the area with a bit of peroxide to clean the area. If infection occurs, consult your vet.

Urination (frequent). Frequent urination is most often a result of drinking large quantities of water after exertion. However, it may be a bladder infection or a sign of some sort of hormonal problem. If the condition persists, consult a vet.

Urine (blood in). Any sign of blood in the urine requires immediate attention from a vet.

Vomiting. Regurgitation—marked by repeated gulping sounds and production of a pile of semi-digested food—is normal for dogs. Vomiting, however, is much more violent and usually produces a yellow, viscous solution. If vomiting occurs more than once in a day or is accompanied by any other symptoms, consult a vet immediately. This is especially true if any blood is present in the vomit.

HOW TO USE THIS BOOK

Alphabetical organization should make it a snap to navigate through this book. Still, in putting it together, we've made certain decisions and used certain terms you need to know about.

LODGINGS

All are air-conditioned unless otherwise noted, and all permit smoking unless they're identified as "no-smoking."

AP: This designation means that a hostelry operates on the American Plan (AP)—that is, rates include all meals. AP may be an option or it may be the only meal plan available; be sure to find out.

Baths: You'll find private bathrooms with bathtubs unless noted otherwise.

Business services: If we tell you they're there, you can expect a variety on the premises.

Exercising: We note if there's "exercise equipment" even when there's no designated area; if you want a dedicated facility, look for "gym."

Facilities: We list what's available but don't note charges to use them. When pricing accommodations, always ask what's included.

Fodor's Choice: Stars denote hostelries that are Fodor's Choices—our editors' pick of the state's very best in a given price category.

Golf privileges: You may play at a nearby golf course, usually within 20 mi.

Hot tub: This term denotes hot tubs, Jacuzzis, and whirlpools.

MAP: Rates at these properties include two meals.

No smoking: Properties with this designation prohibit smoking.

Opening and closing: Assume that hostelries are open year-round unless otherwise noted.

Pets: We note whether or not some pets or all pets are welcome and whether there's a charge. Always call in advance to make sure that your four-legged (or winged) best friend will be welcome.

Pools: We say when a pool is available. If you're looking for an indoor pool, be sure to call and ask.

Prices: The price ranges listed are for a high-season double room for two, excluding tax and service charge.

Telephone and TV: Assume that you'll find them unless otherwise noted.

PETS IN THE NATIONAL PARKS

National parks protect and preserve the treasures of America's heritage, and they're always worth visiting whenever you're in the area. Many are worth a long detour. Generally, pets are allowed only in parks' developed areas, including drive-in campgrounds and picnic areas, but they must be kept on a leash at all times. With the exception of guide dogs, pets are not allowed inside buildings, and may be prohibited on trails, beaches, in the backcountry, and in areas controlled by concessionaires. Some parks have kennels, which charge a small daily fee. Be sure to inquire about restrictions on pets before taking yours to a park. If you will travel to many national parks, consider purchasing the National Parks Pass ($50), which gets you and your companions free admission to all parks for one year. (Camping and parking are extra.) A percentage of the proceeds from sales of the pass helps to fund important projects in the parks. Both the Golden Age Passport ($10), for those 62 and older, and the Golden Access Passport (free), for travelers with disabilities, entitle holders to free entry to all national parks, plus 50% off fees for the use of many park facilities and services. You must show proof of age and of U.S. citizenship or permanent residency (such as a U.S. passport, driver's license, or birth certificate) and, if requesting

Golden Access, proof of your disability. You must get your Golden Access or Golden Age passport in person; the former is available at all federal recreation areas, the latter at federal recreation areas that charge fees. You may purchase the National Parks Pass by mail or through the Internet. For information, contact the National Park Service (Department of the Interior, 1849 C St. NW, Washington, DC 20240-0001, 202/208–4747, *www.nps.gov*). To buy the National Parks Pass, write to 27540 Ave. Mentry, Valencia, CA 91355, call 888/GO–PARKS, or visit www.nationalparks.org.

IMPORTANT TIP

Although all prices, opening times, and other details in this book are based on information supplied to us at press time, changes occur all the time in the travel world, and Fodor's cannot accept responsibility for facts that become outdated or for inadvertent errors or omissions. **So always confirm information when it matters,** especially if you're making a detour to visit a specific place.

Let Us Hear from You

Keeping a travel guide fresh and up-to-date is a big job, and we welcome any and all comments. We'd love to have your thoughts on places we've listed, and we're interested in hearing about your own special pet-friendly finds, even the ones in your own backyard. If you know of a bed and breakfast that keeps a stash of doggie biscuits or catnip just for its four-legged guests, or if your hotel manager beamed animal love, do let us know. Our guides are thoroughly updated for each new edition, and we're always adding new information, so your feedback is vital. Contact us via e-mail in care of roadnotes@fodors.com (specifying the title of this book on the subject line) or via snail mail in care of the Road Guides Pet Editor at Fodor's, 280 Park Avenue, New York, NY 10017. We look forward to hearing from you. And in the meantime, have a wonderful road trip!

Important Numbers and On-Line Info

LODGINGS

Adam's Mark	800/444—2326	www.adamsmark.com
Baymont Inns	800/428—3438	www.baymontinns.com
Best Western	800/528—1234	www.bestwestern.com
	TDD 800/528—2222	
Budget Host	800/283—4678	www.budgethost.com
Clarion	800/252—7466	www.clarioninn.com
Comfort	800/228—5150	www.comfortinn.com
Courtyard by Marriott	800/321—2211	www.courtyard.com
Days Inn	800/325—2525	www.daysinn.com
Doubletree	800/222—8733	www.doubletreehotels.com
Drury Inns	800/325—8300	www.druryinn.com
Econo Lodge	800/555—2666	www.hotelchoice.com
Embassy Suites	800/362—2779	www.embassysuites.com
Exel Inns of America	800/356—8013	www.exelinns.com
Fairfield Inn by Marriott	800/228—2800	www.fairfieldinn.com
Fairmont Hotels	800/527—4727	www.fairmont.com
Forte	800/225—5843	www.forte-hotels.com
Four Seasons	800/332—3442	www.fourseasons.com
Friendship Inns	800/453—4511	www.hotelchoice.com
Hampton Inn	800/426—7866	www.hampton-inn.com
Hilton	800/445—8667	www.hilton.com
	TDD 800/368—1133	
Holiday Inn	800/465—4329	www.holiday-inn.com
	TDD 800/238—5544	
Howard Johnson	800/446—4656	www.hojo.com
	TDD 800/654—8442	
Hyatt & Resorts	800/233—1234	www.hyatt.com
Inns of America	800/826—0778	www.innsofamerica.com
Inter-Continental	800/327—0200	www.interconti.com
La Quinta	800/531—5900	www.laquinta.com
	TDD 800/426—3101	
Loews	800/235—6397	www.loewshotels.com
Marriott	800/228—9290	www.marriott.com
Master Hosts Inns	800/251—1962	www.reservahost.com
Le Meridien	800/225—5843	www.lemeridien.com
Motel 6	800/466—8356	www.motel6.com
Omni	800/843—6664	www.omnihotels.com
Quality Inn	800/228—5151	www.qualityinn.com
Radisson	800/333—3333	www.radisson.com
Ramada	800/228—2828	www.ramada.com
	TDD 800/533—6634	
Red Carpet/Scottish Inns	800/251—1962	www.reservahost.com
Red Lion	800/547—8010	www.redlion.com
Red Roof Inn	800/843—7663	www.redroof.com
Renaissance	800/468—3571	www.renaissancehotels.com
Residence Inn by Marriott	800/331—3131	www.residenceinn.com
Ritz-Carlton	800/241—3333	www.ritzcarlton.com
Rodeway	800/228—2000	www.rodeway.com

Sheraton	800/325—3535	www.sheraton.com
Shilo Inn	800/222—2244	www.shiloinns.com
Signature Inns	800/822—5252	www.signature-inns.com
Sleep Inn	800/221—2222	www.sleepinn.com
Super 8	800/848—8888	www.super8.com
Susse Chalet	800/258—1980	www.sussechalet.com
Travelodge/Viscount	800/255—3050	www.travelodge.com
Vagabond	800/522—1555	www.vagabondinns.com
Westin Hotels & Resorts	800/937—8461	www.westin.com
Wyndham Hotels & Resorts	800/996—3426	www.wyndham.com

AIRLINES

Air Canada	888/247—2262	www.aircanada.ca
Alaska	800/426—0333	www.alaska-air.com
American	800/433—7300	www.aa.com
America West	800/235—9292	www.americawest.com
British Airways	800/247—9297	www.british-airways.com
Canadian	800/426—7000	www.cdnair.ca
Continental Airlines	800/525—0280	www.continental.com
Delta	800/221—1212	www.delta.com
Midway Airlines	800/446—4392	www.midwayair.com
Northwest	800/225—2525	www.nwa.com
SkyWest	800/453—9417	www.delta.com
Southwest	800/435—9792	www.southwest.com
TWA	800/221—2000	www.twa.com
United	800/241—6522	www.ual.com
USAir	800/428—4322	www.usair.com

BUSES AND TRAINS

Amtrak	800/872—7245	www.amtrak.com
Greyhound	800/231—2222	www.greyhound.com
Trailways	800/343—9999	www.trailways.com

CAR RENTALS

Advantage	800/777—5500	www.arac.com
Alamo	800/327—9633	www.goalamo.com
Allstate	800/634—6186	www.bnm.com/as.htm
Avis	800/331—1212	www.avis.com
Budget	800/527—0700	www.budget.com
Dollar	800/800—4000	www.dollar.com
Enterprise	800/325—8007	www.pickenterprise.com
Hertz	800/654—3131	www.hertz.com
National	800/328—4567	www.nationalcar.com
Payless	800/237—2804	www.paylesscarrental.com
Rent-A-Wreck	800/535—1391	www.rent-a-wreck.com
Thrifty	800/367—2277	www.thrifty.com

Note: Area codes are changing all over the United States as this book goes to press. For the latest updates, check www.areacode-info.com.

Alabama

ANNISTON

Best Western Riverside Inn. Within easy access of the interstate, this beautifully landscaped two-story property is on Lake Logan Martin. It has a small pier and nearby marina. Restaurant. Cable TV. Pool, lake, wading pool. Boating, fishing. Laundry facilities. Some pets allowed. | 11900 U.S. 78, Riverside 35135 | 205/338–3381 | fax 205/338–3183 | 70 rooms | $79 | AE, D, DC, MC, V.

Lenlock Inn. Five miles from downtown, this brick-and-wood inn is just outside Fort McClellan. Refrigerators, in-room hot tubs in suites, cable TV, in-room VCRs. Pool. Sauna. Laundry facilities. Some pets allowed. | 6210 McClellan Blvd., 36206 | 256/820–1515 or 800/234–5059 | fax 256/820–1516 | 44 rooms, 4 suites | $36, $109 suites | AE, D, DC, MC, V.

ATHENS

Best Western. This two-story stucco hotel is 3 mi from downtown at Interstate 65 and U.S. 72. Picnic area, Complimentary Continental breakfast. In-room data ports, refrigerators, cable TV. Pool. Laundry facilities. Some pets allowed (fee). | 1329 U.S. 72 East | 256/233–4030 | fax 256/233–4554 | 83 rooms | $54–$64 | AE, D, DC, MC, V.

Mark Motel. This small family-run motel is a one-story brick building, on 4 acres, with some gardens. It is 2 mi from downtown Athens. Microwaves, refrigerators, cable TV. Free parking. Some pets allowed. | 210 U.S. Hwy. 31 South, 35611 | 256/232–6200 | 21 rooms | $35 | AE, D, MC.

ATMORE

Comfort Inn. This standard two-story hotel is convenient to Interstate 65 and near several restaurants, including a 24-hour eatery next door. Some microwaves, some refrigerators, cable TV. Pool. Business services. Some pets allowed (fee). | 198 Ted Bates Rd., Evergreen, 36401 | 334/578–4701 | fax 334/578–3180 | 60 rooms | $60–$80 | AE, D, DC, MC, V.

Days Inn. Just off Interstate 65, this standard motel is within walking distance of several fast-food restaurants. Complimentary Continental breakfast. Cable TV. No-smoking rooms. Some pets allowed (fee). | Rte. 2 (Box 389), Evergreen, 36401 | 334/578–2100 | fax 334/578–2100 | 40 rooms, 4 suites | $49, $59 suites | AE, D, DC, MC, V.

AUBURN

Auburn University Hotel and Conference Center. Auburn's only full-service six-story hotel is right on the university campus, just 3 mi from downtown. The redbrick, modern Georgian architecture blends right in with the campus; the light-filled lobby has hardwood floors and southern-style columns. Restaurant, bar. In-room data ports, microwaves in suites, refrigerators in suites, cable TV, in-room VCRs in suites. Pool. Gym. Business services. Some pets allowed. | 241 S. College St. | 334/821–8200 or 800/228–2876 | fax 334/826–8755 | auhotel@mail.auburn.edu | www.auhcc.com | 248 rooms, 3 suites | $49, $149 suites | AE, D, DC, MC, V.

Heart of Auburn. A tan, stucco two-story building across from Auburn University. Restaurant, bar. Kitchenettes, some in-room hot tubs, cable TV. Pool. Pets allowed. | 333 S. College St., 36830. | 334/887–3462 or 800/843–5634 | fax 334/887–5564 | 100 rooms | $45 | AE, D, V.

Quality Inn University Center. A standard brick motel between Interstate 85 and downtown Auburn. Restaurant, bar, complimentary Continental breakfast. In-room data ports, microwaves and refrigerators in suites, cable TV. Pool. Business services. Some pets allowed. | 1577 S. College St. | 334/821–7001 | fax 334/821–7001 | 122 rooms | $64 | AE, D, DC, MC, V.

BIRMINGHAM

AmeriSuites Birmingham Inverness. This hotel is in the center of the Inverness Business District, a suburb 15 mi from downtown Birmingham. You can walk to a number of restaurants, but the main attractions nearby are the Birmingham Zoo and Botanical Gardens (6 mi), and VisionLand Theme Park (16 mi). The Birmingham International Airport is 14 mi away. Complimentary Continental breakfast. In-room data ports, cable TV with VCR. Kitchenette with microwave, refrigerator. Pool. Exercise equipment. Video games. Laundry service. Business services. Free parking. Pets allowed. | 4686 Hwy. 280 East, 35242 | 205/995–9242 or 800/833–1516 | fax 205/995–2226 | www.amerisuites.com | 128 rooms | $59–$195 | AE, D, DC, MC.

AmeriSuites Birmingham Riverchase. This all-suites six-story building in Riverchase is 15 mi from downtown Birmingham, 16 mi from the airport, and just two blocks from Riverchase Galleria Mall (the largest mall in the Southeast). Complimentary Continental breakfast. In-room data ports, kitchenettes, microwaves, refrigerators, cable TV with VCR. Pool. Exercise equipment. Video games. Laundry service. Business services. Free parking. Pets allowed. | 2980 Hwy. 150, 35244 | 205/988–8444 or 800/833–1516 | fax 205/988–8407 | 128 rooms | $59–$195 | AE, D, DC, MC, V.

Days Inn. You'll find this standard motel just 1 mi south of Birmingham International Airport on Airport Boulevard. Complimentary Continental breakfast. Cable TV. Pool. Gym. Playground. Business services, airport shuttle. Some pets allowed. | 5101 Airport Blvd., 35212 | 205/592–6110 | fax 205/591–5623 | 138 rooms | $62 | AE, D, DC, MC, V.

Hawthorn Suites. Located on 17½ peaceful acres, this lushly landscaped property is only a 10-minute drive from the airport. Restaurant, bar, complimentary buffet breakfast, room service. In-room data ports, kitchenettes, cable TV. Pool. Gym. Laundry facilities, laundry service. Business services, airport shuttle. Some pets allowed (fee). | 5320 Beacon Dr., Irondale, 35210 | 205/951–1200 or 800/579–5464 | fax 205/951–1692 | 134 suites in 10 buildings | $65–$85 | AE, D, DC, MC, V.

Historic Redmont Hotel. Built in the 1920s, Birmingham's oldest-operating hotel reflects its Jazz Age heritage. A few years back, the building underwent a multimillion-dollar renovation. Restaurant, bar, room service. In-room data ports, refrigerators, cable TV. Laundry service. Business services, airport shuttle. Some pets allowed. | 2101 5th Ave. North, 35203 | 205/324–2101 | fax 205/324–0610 | 112 rooms | $79 | AE, D, DC, MC, V.

Hojo Inn. This inn is in a two-story building set off the road about 6 mi downtown. There are a number of restaurants within walking distance, and also nearby are a comedy club, the Botanical Gardens, Birmingham Zoo, a mall, and Samford University. Complimentary Continental breakfast. Cable TV. Pool. Exercise equipment. Laundry services. Pets allowed. | 275 Oxmoor Rd., 35209 | 205/942–0919 or 800/406–1411 | fax 205/942–1679 | www.hojo.com | 100 rooms | $39–$69 | AE, D, DC, MC, V.

Holiday Inn Airport. This recently renovated hotel is conveniently located just ¾ mi from Birmingham International Airport. Restaurant, bar, room service. In-room data ports, cable TV. Pool. Gym. Laundry service. Business services, airport shuttle. Some pets allowed (deposit). | 5000 10th Ave. North, 35212 | 205/591–6900 | fax 205/591–2093 | 226 rooms | $98 | AE, D, DC, MC, V.

Holiday Inn–Galleria South on the Lake. This three-story brick hotel is about 3 mi from the Galleria Mall. There is peaceful lake on the property where you are welcome to relax and fish. Restaurant, bar, picnic area, room service. In-room data ports, cable TV. Pool. Hot tub. Gym, volleyball. Laundry facilities. Business services. Some pets allowed (deposit). | 1548 Montgomery Hwy., 35216 | 205/822–4350 | fax 205/822–0350 | www.basshotels.com | 166 rooms in 2 buildings | $79 | AE, D, DC, MC, V.

La Quinta Motor Inn. This standard inn is about 4 mi west of downtown Birmingham, just a mile from Legion Field. Complimentary Continental breakfast. In-room data ports, some microwaves, some refrigerators, cable TV. Pool. Laundry facilities. Business services. Some pets allowed. | 905 11th Ct. West, 35204 | 205/324–4510 | fax 205/252–7972 | 106 rooms | $62 | AE, D, DC, MC, V.

Motel Birmingham. Just off Interstate 20, this motel is five minutes from the Birmingham International Airport, 2 mi from the Birmingham Race Course, and 6 mi from the Civil Rights District. Complimentary Continental breakfast. Some kitchenettes, cable TV. Pool. Playground. Laundry service. Business services, airport shuttle. Some pets allowed. | 7905 Crestwood Blvd., 35210 | 205/956–4440 or 800/338–9275 | fax 205/956–3011 | 242 rooms, 12 suites in 4 buildings | $61, $137 suites | AE, D, DC, MC, V.

Mountain Brook Inn. This comfortable, spacious inn is located in the exclusive Mountain Brook residential area, close to Brookwood Village Mall and a variety of shops and restaurants. Rooms range from bi-level suites to patio-level, poolside accommodations. Restaurant, bar (with entertainment). In-room data ports, no-smoking rooms and floors, cable TV. Pool. Laundry service. Business services, airport shuttle. Some pets allowed. | 2800 U.S. 280 South, Mountain Brook, 35223 | 205/870–3100 or 800/523–7771 | fax 205/414–2128 | www.mountainbrookinn.com | 162 rooms, 12 suites | $115 | AE, D, DC, MC, V.

Pickwick Hotel and Conference Center. This hotel with Art Deco furnishings is centrally located in the heart of the medical district and the historic Five Points South area. Complimentary Continental breakfast. In-room data ports, kitchenettes in suites, cable TV. Beauty salon. Business services, airport shuttle. Some pets allowed (fee). | 1023 20th St. South, 35205 | 205/933–9555 or 800/255–7304 | fax 205/933–6918 | 63 rooms, 28 suites | $99, $139 suites | AE, DC, MC, V.

Red Roof Inn. This sprawling three-story building is fronted by trees and built on top of a hill overlooking the town. Within a 10-mi radius are golf courses, downtown, Birmingham International Airport, Birmingham Zoo, Galleria Mall, and the Alabama State Fairgrounds. VisionLand Theme Park is about 19 mi away. There's complimentary morning coffee and newspaper. Cable TV. Video games. Free parking. Pets allowed. | 151 Vulcan Rd., 35209 | 205/942–9414 or 800/843–7663 | fax 205/942–9499 | www.redroof.com | 96 rooms | $45–$50 | AE, D, DC, MC, V.

Residence Inn by Marriott. This extended-stay hotel offers all the comforts of home and is located 2 mi from the Summit Mall. Complimentary Continental breakfast. In-room data ports, kitchenettes, cable TV. Pool. Hot tub. Basketball, gym, volleyball. Laundry facilities. Business services. Some pets allowed (fee). | 3 Greenhill Pkwy., Inverness, 35242 | 205/991-8686 | fax 205/991-8729 | www.marriott.com | 128 suites in 16 buildings | $85 | AE, D, DC, MC, V.

BOAZ

Key West Inn. This standard motel is downtown, just across the street from the Boaz Outlet Center. Complimentary Continental breakfast. Some microwaves and refrigerators, cable TV. Business services. Some pets allowed (fee). | 10535 Rte. 168, 35957 | 256/593-0800 | fax 256/593-9100 | www.keywestinn.net | 41 rooms | $54-$59 | AE, D, DC, MC, V.

Thunderbird Inn. An ex–Best Western, this is now a privately run two-story motel in the middle of town. There are not many amenities: this is a standard "drive up" motel. Complimentary Continental breakfast. Pool. Cable TV. Pets allowed. | 751 Hwy. 431 South, 35957 | 256/593-8410 | fax 256/593-8410 | 116 rooms | $43-$60 | AE, D, DC, MC, V.

CHILDERSBURG

Childersburg-Days Inn. This three-story brick hotel hotel is 5 mi from downtown Childersburg. There is a steak house next door. Nearby are Desoto Caverns, the Coosa River, and the Kymulga Grist Mill. Bar, complimentary Continental breakfast. In-room data ports, microwaves, refrigerators, cable TV. Pool. Laundry service. Free parking. Pets allowed. | 33669 U.S. Hwy. 280, 35044 | 256/378-6007 | fax 256/378-3575 | 40 rooms | $39-$60 | AE, D, DC, V.

CLANTON

Days Inn. About 3 mi from the heart of Clanton, this standard inn is near Peach Park, the Alabama Power Water Course, and fishing and recreational areas. Restaurant, bar. In-room data ports, cable TV. Pool, wading pool. Laundry service. Business services. Some pets allowed. | 2000 Holiday Inn Dr. | 205/755-0510 | fax 205/755-0510 ext. 316 | 100 rooms | $49-$60 | AE, D, DC, MC, V.

Key West Inn. This inn is just 1/4 mi from the interstate, across the street from the Alabama Power Museum and Peach Park and a fruit market with gardens. Complimentary Continental breakfast. In-room data ports, some microwaves and refrigerators, cable TV. Laundry facilities. Business services. Some pets allowed (fee). | 2045 7th St. South | 205/755-8500 or 800/833-0555 | fax 205/280-0044 | www.keywestinn.net | 43 rooms | $48-$55 | AE, D, DC, MC, V.

Shoney's Inn. This hotel is 5 mi away from the center of town. It is a two-story, L-shape hotel, built around a swimming pool. Shoney's steak-house restaurant is across the street, available for breakfast, lunch, and dinner. In-room data ports. Cable TV. Pool. Free parking. Pets allowed. | 946 Lake Mitchell Rd., 35045 | 205/280-0306 or 800/222-2222 | fax 205/755-8113 | 74 rooms | $57 | AE, D, DC, MC, V.

CULLMAN

Best Western Fairwinds Inn. This standard inn is located at Interstate 65, 4 mi from the Cullman Museum, antiques shops, and a golf course, and about 6 mi from Ave Maria Grotto. Complimentary Continental breakfast. In-room data ports, some microwaves, refrigerators, cable TV. Pool. Gym. Laundry facilities. Business services. Some pets allowed. | 1917 Commerce Ave., 35055 | 256/737-5009 or 888/559-0549 | fax 256/737-5009 | 50 rooms | $49-$69 | AE, D, DC, MC, V.

Comfort Inn Cullman. Standard two-story motel, 5 mi to downtown Cullman. Many chain restaurants are nearby. Complimentary Continental breakfast. In-room data ports, some microwaves, some refrigerators, cable TV. Pool. Gym. Business services. Some pets allowed. | 5917 SR 157 Northwest, 35058 | 256/734-1240 or 800/228-5150 | fax 256/734-3318 | 50 rooms | $55-$67 | AE, D, DC, V.

Days Inn. This standard inn is minutes away from Smith Lake, a popular fishing spot, and only 4 mi from Ave Maria Grotto. Restaurant, picnic area. In-room data ports, some microwaves, some refrigerators, cable TV. Pool. Business services. Some pets allowed (fee). | 1841 4th St. Southwest, 35055 | 256/739–3800 | fax 256/739–3800 | www.daysinn.com | 119 rooms | $40–$75 | AE, D, DC, MC, V.

Ramada Inn. Just off Interstate 65, this standard inn is about 8 mi from Wallace State College and a mile from Heritage Park. Restaurant, room service. In-room data ports, cable TV. Pool. Laundry facilities. Business services. Some pets allowed. | 1600 Rte. 437, 35056 | 256/734–8484 | fax 256/739–4126 | 126 rooms | $60 | AE, D, DC, MC, V.

DAUPHIN ISLAND

Gulf Breeze Motel. This family-owned motel has spacious rooms and two-bedroom efficiencies with fully equipped kitchens. It's located near the public beach and a boat launch on the bay side of the island. Refrigerators, cable TV. Some pets allowed (fee). | 1512 Cadillac Ave. | 334/861–7344 or 800/286–0296 | www.gulfinfo.com/gulfbreezemotel | 31 rooms, 6 apartments | $49–$59, $69 apartments | AE, D, MC, V.

DEMOPOLIS

River View Inn. A small independent property, this motel is on a marina and you can see the docked houseboats from every room. The banks of the Tombigbee River are an easy stroll from the motel. In-room data ports, microwaves, refrigerators, cable TV. Pets allowed. | 110 Yacht Basin Dr., 36732 | 334/289–0690 | 25 rooms | $45 | AE, DC, MC, V.

DOTHAN

Admiral Benbow Olympia Spa Golf Resort. About 4 mi south of Ross Clark Circle, this resort has a championship golf course and several affordable golf packages. Restaurant, bar, room service. Cable TV. Pool. Beauty salon, massage. 18-hole golf course. Laundry facilities. Business services. Some pets allowed (fee). | 7410 U.S. 231 South, 36301 | 334/677–3321 | fax 334/677–3321 | www.admiralbenbow.com | 93 rooms in 2 buildings | $59 | AE, D, DC, MC, V.

Comfort Inn. This award-winning inn, honored by its peers as one of the top five Comfort Inns in the nation, is between two malls and within walking distance from fast-food and fine-dining restaurants and from a movie theater. Complimentary Continental breakfast. In-room data ports, some microwaves, no-smoking floors, some refrigerators, cable TV. Pool. Gym. Business services. Some pets allowed. | 3593 Ross Clark Circle Northwest, 36303 | 334/793–9090 | fax 334/793–4367 | www.comfortinn.com | 122 rooms | $70 | AE, D, DC, MC, V.

Holiday Inn–South. A convenient stopping point for travelers en route to Florida via U.S. 231 South, this inn is located 2 mi from the historic downtown area and 7 mi from a Robert Trent Jones golf course. Restaurant, bar, complimentary breakfast, room service. In-room data ports, some microwaves, some refrigerators, cable TV. Pool. Gym. Laundry service. Business services. Some pets allowed. | 2195 Ross Clark Circle Southeast, 36301 | 334/794–8711 | fax 334/671–3781 | 144 rooms, 14 suites | $61, $71 suites | AE, D, DC, MC, V.

Holiday Inn–West. This standard inn is on the city's busy bypass, less than 2 mi from the Wiregrass Commons Mall and close to several restaurants. Restaurant, bar, room service. In-room data ports, microwaves in suites, refrigerators in suites, cable TV. Pool, wading pool. Laundry service. Business services. Some pets allowed. | 3053 Ross Clark Circle, 36301 | 334/794–6601 | fax 334/794–9032 | 102 rooms, 44 suites in 3 buildings | $65, $99 suites | AE, D, DC, MC, V.

Motel 6. This standard motel is just minutes from Wiregrass Commons Mall and Northside Mall, and it's also close to Water World and Landmark Park. In-room data ports, cable

TV. Pool. Some pets allowed. | 2907 Ross Clark Circle Southeast, 36301 | 334/793–6013 | fax 334/793–2377 | 101 rooms | $40 | AE, D, DC, MC, V.

Ramada Inn. This standard inn is on Dothan's bypass, close to several restaurants, a Robert Trent Jones golf course, and Water World. Restaurant, bar with entertainment, complimentary breakfast, room service. In-room data ports, cable TV. Pool, wading pool. Laundry service. Business services, airport shuttle. Some pets allowed. | 3011 Ross Clark Circle Southeast, 36302 | 334/792–0031 | fax 334/794–3134 | 114 rooms in 4 buildings | $62–$68 | AE, D, DC, MC, V.

Travelodge Dothan. A three-floor stone building, about 1½ mi outside of downtown Dothan, this Travelodge is distinguished by its "Sleepy Bear Den," a guest room designed for families with children. The rooms come with children's videos, toys, and "sleepy bear" decorations. Other than that, this is a standard chain motel. In-room data ports, microwaves, refrigerators, cable TV. Pool. Laundry service. Pets allowed. | 2901 Ross Clark Circle, 36301. | 334/793–5200 or 877/353–3311 | 99 rooms | $35–$45 | AE, D, DC, MC, V.

EUFAULA
Ramada Inn. Located on the Alabama/Georgia border, this inn is situated on beautiful Lake Eufaula. Restaurant, bar, room service. In-room data ports, cable TV. Pool, lake. Laundry service. Business services. Some pets allowed. | Barbour at Riverside Dr. | 334/687–2021 | fax 334/687–2021 | 96 rooms in 2 buildings | $49 | AE, D, DC, MC, V.

FLORENCE
Days Inn. This standard inn is about 2 mi from the Tennessee Valley Authority (TVA) reservation, 5 mi from the University of North Alabama, and across the street from a movie theater. Complimentary Continental breakfast. In-room data ports, cable TV. Pool. Some pets allowed (deposit). | 1915 Florence Blvd. | 256/766–2620 | fax 256/766–2620 | 77 rooms in 5 buildings | $55–$65 | AE, D, DC, MC, V.

Homestead Executive Inn. This standard inn is just ¼ mi from a new marina on the Tennessee River, five minutes from Regency Square Mall, and about 10 minutes from the Muscle Shoals Airport. Restaurant, bar, room service. Cable TV. Pool. Laundry facilities. Business services. Some pets allowed (fee). | 504 S. Court St. | 256/766–2331 | fax 256/766–3567 | 120 rooms | $54 | AE, D, DC, MC, V.

GADSDEN
Red Roof Inn. This standard motel is on the Coosa River, next door to the popular Top of the River restaurant and within walking distance from other eateries. Picnic area, complimentary Continental breakfast. Cable TV. Pool. Laundry facilities. Business services. Some pets allowed. | 1600 Rainbow Dr., 35901 | 256/543–1105 or 800/843–7663 | fax 256/543–7836 | 104 rooms in 3 buildings | $49–$115 | AE, D, DC, MC, V.

GULF SHORES/ORANGE BEACH
Lighthouse Resort Motel. On 630 ft of private beach, these motel rooms and apartments feature a gulf view. Some kitchenettes, refrigerators, cable TV. 3 pools. Hot tub. Beach. Business services. Some pets allowed (fee). | 455 E. Beach Blvd., 36542 | 334/948–6188 | fax 334/948–6100 | www.gulfcoastrooms.com | 219 rooms | $80–$159 | AE, D, DC, MC, V.

HUNTSVILLE
Baymont Inn and Suites. Completely renovated in 1999, this standard inn is one block from Madison Square Mall and 3 mi from the U.S. Space and Rocket Center. Kids under 18 stay free. Complimentary Continental breakfast. In-room data ports, microwaves in suites, refrigerators in suites, cable TV. Pool. Business services. Some pets allowed. No-smoking rooms. | 4890 University Dr. Northwest, 35816 | 256/830–8999 | fax 205/837–5720 | www.baymontinns.com | 102 rooms | $54–$99 | AE, D, DC, MC, V.

Guest House Suites. Each room in this conveniently located hotel features a fireplace and a private patio or balcony. Picnic area, complimentary Continental breakfast. In-room data ports, kitchenettes, cable TV. Pool. Hot tub. Tennis. Basketball. Laundry facilities, laundry service. Business services, airport shuttle. Some pets allowed. No-smoking rooms. | 4020 Independence Dr., 35816 | 256/837–8907 | fax 256/837–5435 | 112 suites in 12 buildings | $80–$105 | AE, D, DC, MC, V.

Hilton. This downtown historic district hotel is across the street from the Von Braun Center and near Big Springs Park. Several restaurants and a museum are nearby. Restaurant, bar (with entertainment). In-room data ports, cable TV. Pool. Hot tub. Gym. Business services, airport shuttle. Some pets allowed. No-smoking rooms. | 401 Williams Ave., 35801 | 256/533–1400 | fax 256/534–7787 | 277 rooms | $99–$129 | AE, D, DC, MC, V.

Holiday Inn–Space Center. Less than 2 mi from the U.S. Space and Rocket Center, this standard hotel is in a busy area near Madison Square Mall. Restaurant, bar, room service. In-room data ports, cable TV. Pool. Gym. Laundry facilities. Business services, airport shuttle. Some pets allowed. No-smoking rooms. | 3810 University Dr., 35816 | 256/837–7171 | fax 256/837–9257 | 112 rooms | $75 | AE, D, DC, MC, V.

La Quinta. Just 4 mi from the U.S. Space and Rocket Center, this standard motel is near many restaurants. Complimentary Continental breakfast. In-room data ports, cable TV. Pool. Laundry service. Business services. Some pets allowed. No-smoking rooms. | 3141 University Dr. Northwest, 35816 | 256/533–0756 | fax 256/539–5414 | 130 rooms | $59–$66 | AE, D, DC, MC, V.

MOBILE

Days Inn Airport. Renovated in 2000, this standard inn is found at Interstate 65 and Airport Boulevard. It's close to Springdale Mall, Bel Air Mall, and convenient to other shops and many restaurants. In-room data ports, some kitchenettes, cable TV. Pool. Laundry facilities. Business services. Some pets allowed (fee). No-smoking rooms. | 3650 Airport Blvd., 36608 | 334/344–3410 | fax 334/344–8790 | 162 rooms | $63 | AE, D, DC, MC, V.

Drury Inn. This inn is conveniently located at Interstate 65 and Airport Boulevard, next to a 24-hour restaurant, and close to Bel Air and Springdale malls. Complimentary Continental breakfast. In-room data ports, cable TV. Pool. Gym. Laundry facilities. Business services. Some pets allowed. No-smoking rooms. | 824 S. Beltline Hwy., 36609 | 334/344–7700 or 800/325–8300 | fax 334/344–7700 | 110 rooms | $72 | AE, D, DC, MC, V.

Lafayette Plaza. In the heart of downtown Mobile's business and historic districts, this hotel is within walking distance of the Museum of Mobile, Phoenix Fire Museum, Gulf Coast Exploreum, and more. The rooftop lounge offers breathtaking views of the city and the waterfront. Restaurants, bar. In-room data ports, cable TV. Pool. Beauty salon. Laundry service. Business services. Pets allowed. No-smoking rooms. | 301 Government St., 36602 | 334/694–0100 or 800/692–6662 | fax 334/694–0160 | 210 rooms | $59–$89 | AE, D, DC, MC, V.

La Quinta. This standard inn is along Interstate 65 at busy Airport Boulevard, just a mile from Bel Air and Springdale malls and close to many restaurants. Complimentary Continental breakfast. In-room data ports, cable TV. Pool. Laundry service. Business services. Some pets allowed. No-smoking rooms. | 816 S. Beltline Hwy., 36609 | 334/343–4051 or 800/531–5900 | fax 334/343–2897 | www.travelweb.com/laquinta.html | 122 rooms | $62–$69 | AE, D, DC, MC, V.

Red Roof Inn Mobile–South. In the Tillman's Corner area just off Interstate 10, this standard inn is about 18 mi from Bellingrath Gardens and Home, 10 mi from downtown Mobile, and 30 mi from Dauphin Island. In-room data ports, cable TV. Business services. Some pets allowed. No-smoking rooms. | 5450 Coca-Cola Rd., 36619 | 334/666–1044 | fax 334/666–1032 | 108 rooms | $41 | AE, D, DC, MC, V.

Shoney's Inn. This standard inn is along Interstate 10 in the Tillman's Corner area, just 2 mi from Mobile Greyhound Park, 10 mi from downtown Mobile, and 15 mi from Mobile Municipal Airport. Microwaves in suites, refrigerators in suites, cable TV. Pool. Business services. Some pets allowed (fee). No-smoking rooms. | 5472-A Inn Rd., 36614 | 334/660–1520 or 800/222–2222 | fax 334/666–4240 | 120 rooms, 15 suites | $54 rooms, $64 suites | AE, D, DC, MC, V.

MONTGOMERY

Baymont Inn and Suites. A convenient location for both shopping and sightseeing, this standard inn is located near Eastdale Mall and Montgomery Mall, 6 mi from downtown and the State Capitol. Kids under 18 stay free. Complimentary Continental breakfast. In-room data ports, microwaves in suites, refrigerators in suites, cable TV. Pool. Business services. Some pets allowed. No-smoking rooms. | 5225 Carmichael Rd., 36106 | 334/277–6000 | fax 334/279–8207 | 100 rooms, 8 suites | $59 rooms, $89 suites | AE, D, DC, MC, V.

Holiday Inn–East. This standard hotel is off Interstate 85, near Montgomery Mall, Montgomery Zoo, and the Alabama Shakespeare Festival. Bar, room service. In-room data ports, cable TV. Pool. Hot tub, sauna. Gym. Video games. Laundry facilities, laundry service. Business services. Some pets allowed (fee). No-smoking rooms. | 1185 Eastern Bypass, 36117 | 334/272–0370 | fax 334/270–0339 | 211 rooms in 3 buildings | $89 | AE, D, DC, MC, V.

Holiday Inn South/Airport. This four-story standard hotel is minutes away from Montgomery Mall and Montgomery Airport, near Interstate 65. Restaurant, bar, room service. In-room data ports, cable TV. Pool. Gym. Laundry facilities. Business services, airport shuttle. Some pets allowed. No-smoking rooms. | 1100 W. South Blvd., 36105 | 334/281–1660 | fax 334/281–1660 | 150 rooms | $59 | AE, D, DC, MC, V.

La Quinta. Just off Interstate 85, this standard motel is near the Alabama Shakespeare Festival and many restaurants and just 10 minutes from downtown. Complimentary Continental breakfast. In-room data ports, microwaves in suites, refrigerators in suites, cable TV. Pool. Business services. Some pets allowed. No-smoking rooms. | 1280 East Blvd., 36117 | 334/271–1620 | fax 334/244–7919 | 130 rooms, 2 suites | $59 rooms, $76–$82 suites | AE, D, DC, MC, V.

OPELIKA

Days Inn. At exit 62 off Interstate 85, this typical motel is less than five minutes from the USA Factory Outlet Stores and about 10 minutes from the Auburn University campus. Complimentary Continental breakfast. Microwaves, refrigerators, cable TV. Pool. Business services. Some pets allowed (fee). No-smoking rooms. | 1014 Anand Ave. | 334/749–5080 | fax 334/749–4701 | 44 rooms | $45–$50 | AE, D, DC, MC, V.

Travel Lodge. At Interstate 85 and U.S. 280, this standard motel is near several restaurants, the USA Factory Outlet Stores, and it's just 10 minutes from the Auburn University campus. Bar, complimentary Continental breakfast. In-room data ports, cable TV. Pool. Business services. Some pets allowed (fee). No-smoking rooms. | 1002 Columbus Pkwy. | 334/749–1461 | fax 334/749–1468 | 95 rooms in 3 buildings | $37–$99 | AE, D, DC, MC, V.

SCOTTSBORO

Days Inn. This standard motel is just off U.S. 72, approximately 10 minutes from Unclaimed Baggage, the famous store where you can shop for treasures retrieved from lost baggage from all over the country. There's a restaurant across the street and a movie theater is a five-minute drive. Complimentary Continental breakfast. In-room data ports, some microwaves, some refrigerators, cable TV. Pool. Business services. Some pets allowed. No-smoking rooms. | 23945 John T. Reid Pkwy. | 256/574–1212 | fax 256/574–1212 | 84 rooms | $46 | AE, D, DC, MC, V.

SELMA

Holiday Inn. This standard inn is about 3 mi from downtown Selma, near a variety of restaurants and about 45 minutes from Montgomery. Restaurant, bar, room service. In-room data ports, cable TV. Pool, wading pool. Business services. Some pets allowed. No-smoking rooms. | U.S. 80 West | 334/872–0461 | fax 334/872–0461 | 165 rooms in 3 buildings | $57 | AE, D, DC, MC, V.

SHEFFIELD

Ramada Inn. This standard inn is less than a mile from McFarland Park on the Tennessee River, which has a boat ramp, dock, and fishing. Restaurant, bar (with entertainment), room service. Microwaves in suites, some refrigerators, some in-room hot tubs, cable TV. Pool. Hot tub. Business services, airport shuttle. Some pets allowed (fee). No-smoking rooms. | 4205 Hatch Blvd. | 256/381–3743 | fax 256/386–7928 | 150 rooms, 3 suites | $55 rooms, $150–$200 suites | AE, D, DC, MC, V.

SYLACAUGA

Towne Inn. This locally owned inn is convenient to restaurants and shopping, and the Talladega Superspeedway is only 30 minutes away. Cable TV. Pool. Business services. Some pets allowed. No-smoking rooms. | 40860 U.S. 280 | 256/249–3821 | fax 256/249–4707 | 76 rooms | $42–$50 | AE, D, DC, MC, V.

TALLADEGA

Budget Inn. Located just 2 mi from Talladega Superspeedway, this motel is less than 5 mi from Talladega College, the Alabama School for the Deaf, and downtown Talladega. Restaurant, bar (with entertainment). Cable TV. Pool, wading pool. Business services. Some pets allowed. No-smoking rooms. | 65600 Rte. 77 North | 256/362–0900 | fax 256/362–0908 | 100 rooms in 2 buildings | $39–$80 | AE, D, DC, MC, V.

THEODORE

Holiday Inn. Designated the official hotel of Bellingrath Gardens and Home—over 60 acres of public gardens—this inn is about 20 minutes away in Theodore. Ask about their Bellingrath package rates. Restaurant, bar, room service. In-room data ports, cable TV. Pool. Hot tub. Gym. Laundry facilities. Business services, airport shuttle. Some pets allowed. No-smoking rooms. | 5465 U.S. 90 West, 36619 | 334/666–5600 | fax 334/666–2773 | 159 rooms | $69 | AE, D, DC, MC, V.

TUSCALOOSA

Ramada Inn. This standard inn is just ½ mi from McFarland Mall and about five minutes from the University of Alabama campus. Restaurant, bar (with entertainment). Cable TV. Pool. Business services. Some pets allowed. No-smoking rooms. | 631 Skyland Blvd. East, 35405 | 205/759–4431 | fax 205/758–9655 | 108 rooms in 3 buildings | $53 | AE, D, DC, MC, V.

Travel-Rite Inn. This standard motel is right across the street from the Jasper Mall, several restaurants, and about 1 mi from downtown. Cable TV. Some pets allowed. | 200 Mallway Dr., 35504 | 205/221–1161 | fax 205/221–1161 ext. 200 | 60 rooms | $39 | AE, D, DC, MC, V.

Arizona

AJO

Marine Resort Motel. This small family-owned motel offers very basic rooms 23 mi from Organ Pipe Cactus National Monument. Picnic area. Cable TV. Pets allowed. | 1966 N. 2nd Ave. | 520/387–7626 | fax 520/387–3835 | 22 rooms | $65 | AE, D, DC, MC, V.

ALPINE

Tal-Wi-Wi Lodge. Facing a lush meadow 4 mi north of Alpine on U.S. 191, this lodge's setting is unparalleled. Rooms are simple and clean; three have wood-burning stoves. The lodge saloon draws many locals on weekends and for sporting events shown on the big-screen satellite TV. The lodge restaurant is generally open from May to September. Restaurant, bar. No room phones, no TV. Hot tub. Pets allowed. | 40 County Rd. 2220, 85920 | 520/339–4319 | fax 520/339–1962 | www.talwiwilodge.com | 20 rooms | $65–$95 | AE, MC, V.

BENSON

Best Western Quail Hollow. This modern motel offers spacious and comfortable rooms just off Interstate 10 at exit 304. There are restaurants within walking distance but none on-premises. In-room data ports, some refrigerators, cable TV, some in-room VCRs. Pool. Hot tub. Laundry service. Some pets allowed. | 699 N. Octillo St. | 520/586–3646 | fax 520/586–7035 | www.bestwestern.com | 89 rooms | $60 | AE, D, DC, MC, V.

BISBEE

Bisbee Inn. The Bisbee Inn (sometimes called by its original name, Hotel La More) is a restored 1917 hotel in the Bisbee historic district. Regular rooms are basic, but furnished with period antiques, including the original oak dressers from the hotel. Suites are modern apartments with full kitchens and many extra amenities. Complimentary breakfast. In-room data ports, some kitchenettes, some refrigerators, some room phones, some in-room VCRs, no TV in some rooms, TV in common area. Laundry facilities. Pets allowed (fee). No smoking. | Box 1855, 45 Oak St., 85603 | 520/432–5131 or 888/432–5131 | fax 520/432–5343 | www.bisbeeinn.com | 20 rooms (4 with shared bath), 3 suites | $50–$80, $120–$165 suites | D, MC, V.

Calumet and Arizona Guest House. Most large rooms in this fully restored 1906 Mission-style home are furnished with antiques. It was originally a guest house for visiting mining executives. Complimentary breakfast. No room phones. Some pets allowed. No kids. No smoking. | 608 Powell St., 85603 | 520/432–4815 | 6 rooms (4 with shared bath) | $60–$70 | MC, V.

El Rancho Motel. This small chain motel offers basic amenities. There's also an RV park. Picnic area. Some kitchenettes, some microwaves, some refrigerators, cable TV. Laundry facilities. Pets allowed (fee). | 1104 Hwy. 92, 85603 | 520/432–2293 | fax 520/432–7738 | elranchomotelaz@aol.com | 39 rooms | $49 | AE, D, DC, MC, V.

Park Place Bed & Breakfast. This Mediterranean-style home built in 1910 has terraces overlooking Vista Park. The traditional decor includes antiques. Complimentary breakfast. No room phones, no TV in some rooms, TV in common area. Airport shuttle. Pets allowed. No smoking. | 200 E. Vista St., 85603 | www.theriver.com/parkplace | 520/432–3054 or 800/388–4388 | fax 520/459–7603 | 4 rooms (2 with shared bath), 2 suites | $50–$70 | MC, V.

San Jose Lodge. Only a couple of miles from the Mexican border, this one-level motel is also very close to downtown Bisbee. The local golf course is less than a mile away. There are also a number of full-service RV hookups. Restaurant, bar. Some kitchenettes, refrigerators, cable TV. Pool. Business services. Pets allowed (fee). | 1002 Naco Hwy. | 520/432–5761 | fax 520/432–4302 | www.sanjoselodge.com | 43 rooms | $65–$85 | AE, D, DC, MC, V.

BULLHEAD CITY

Best Western Bullhead City Inn. This well-maintained, two-story chain motel was built in 1992. Complimentary Continental breakfast. In-room safes, some microwaves, refrigerators, cable TV. Pool. Hot tub. Business services. Pets allowed (fee). | 2360 4th St., 86429 | 520/754–3000 or 800/634–4463 | fax 520/754–5234 | www.bestwestern.com | 88 rooms | $45–$75 | AE, D, DC, MC, V.

Bullhead City Super 8. This two-story chain motel offers basic rooms. Room service. Cable TV. Pool. Pets allowed. | 1616 Hwy. 95 | 520/763–1002 | fax 520/763–2984 | www.super8.com | 62 rooms | $40–$55 | AE, DC, MC, V.

Colorado River Resort. This two-story extended stay (by the week or month) resort still offers daily rates when rooms are available. It's right across the street from the Colorado River. The nearest restaurants are about 5 mi away. Kitchenettes, cable TV. Pool. Laundry facilities. Some pets allowed. | 434 River Glen Dr., 86429 | 520/754–4101 | fax 520/754–1033 | 32 rooms | $40–$60 | MC, V.

Lake Mohave Resort and Marina. Some rooms have lake views at this resort on spacious grounds about 10 mi north of Bullhead City off Highway 95. Restaurant, bar. Some kitchenettes. Water sports, boating, fishing. Business services. Some pets allowed (fee). | Katherine's Landing, 86430 | 520/754–3245 or 800/752–9669 | fax 520/754–1125 | www.sevencrown.com | 50 rooms | $70–$100 | D, MC, V.

CAMP VERDE

Comfort Inn of Camp Verde. This two-story motel is just off Interstate 17 at exit 287, 2 mi from Montezuma's Castle and 3 mi from the Cliff Castle Casino. Complimentary Continental breakfast. In-room data ports, cable TV. Pool. Hot tub. Pets allowed (fee). | 340 N. Industrial Dr. | 520/567–9000 | fax 520/567–1828 | www.comfortinn.com | 85 rooms | $75–$84 | AE, D, DC, MC, V.

Lodge at Cliff Castle. The two-story Cliff Castle Casino is located on a hill just behind this hotel, and its conference center was once part of the original casino. If you're feeling tired, there is a free shuttle to the casino just two blocks away. Restaurant. Some microwaves, some refrigerators, cable TV. Pool. Hot tub. Business services. Pets allowed (fee). | 333 Middle

Verde Rd., 86322 | 520/567–6611 or 800/524–6343 | fax 520/567–9455 | www.cliffcastle.com | 76 rooms, 6 suites | $64–$79, $89–$119 suites | AE, D, MC, V.

CAREFREE/CAVE CREEK

★ **Boulders Resort and Club.** Nestled among ancient boulders, this serene, secluded luxury resort is just outside Phoenix. The architecture is dramatic, with pueblo-style casitas built among the rocks. Each casita has a fireplace, patio, and huge bathroom. 5 restaurants, bar, room service. In-room data ports, refrigerators, cable TV, in-room VCRs. 2 pools. Hot tub, massage. Driving range, 2 18-hole golf courses, putting green, 6 tennis courts. Gym. Business services, airport shuttle. Some pets allowed (fee). | 34631 N. Tom Darlington Dr., Carefree, 85377 | 480/488–9009 or 800/553–1717 | fax 480/488–4118 | www.grandbay.com | 160 casitas | $545–$700 | AE, DC, MC, V.

Carefree Conference Resort. Accommodations here are in luxury rooms and casitas, each with either a balcony or patio and a view of the Continental Mountains or the main pool. Restaurant, 2 bars. Cable TV. Pool. Beauty salon, spa. Tennis. Bicycles. Pets allowed. | 37220 Mule Train Rd., Carefree, 85377 | 480/488–5300 or 800/227–7066 | fax 480/595–3795 | www.conferenceresorts.com/carefree | 216 rooms, 26 casitas, 4 suites | $290, $370 casitas, $450 suites | AE, D, DC, MC, V.

CHANDLER

Chandler Super 8. This two-story motel is 10 mi from Sky Harbor International Airport. Cable TV. Pool. Pets allowed. | 7171 Chandler Blvd. | 480/961–3888 | fax 480/961–3888 ext. 400 | www.super8.com | 75 rooms | $60–$79 | AE, D, DC, V.

Sheraton San Marcos Golf Resort and Conference Center. This contemporary resort has a particularly large, landscaped pool area. Most rooms have views of the golf course, which is one of Arizona's oldest. 2 restaurants, 2 bars, room service. Cable TV. Pool, wading pool. Barbershop, beauty salon, hot tub, massage. Driving range, 18-hole golf course, putting green, 2 tennis courts. Gym. Volleyball, bicycles. Shops. Business services. Pets allowed (fee). | 1 San Marcos Pl, 85224 | 480/963–6655 or 800/528–8071 | fax 480/963–6777 | www.sheraton.com | 287 rooms, 8 suites | $149–$179 | AE, D, DC, MC, V.

CLIFTON

Rode Inn Motel. Close to the Historical Society of Chase Creek, this motel attracts guests who want to bask in the clear country air. For those who enjoy fishing, the San Francisco River is directly across the street. Cable TV. Laundry facilities. Pets allowed (fee). | 186 S. Coronado Blvd. | 520/865–4536 | fax 520/865–2654 | 33 rooms | $54 | D, DC, MC, V.

COOLIDGE

Moonlite Motel. In the middle of town, this tiny motel is only ½ mi from the Casa Grande National Monument. Pets allowed. | 1087 N. Arizona Blvd. | 520/723–3475 | fax 520/723–3745 | 12 rooms | $45 | AE, D, DC, MC, V.

COTTONWOOD

Little Daisy Motel. A friendly staff and clean, comfortable rooms await guests at this locally owned motel. Some kitchenettes, cable TV. Pets allowed. | 34 S. Main St. | 520/634–7865 | fax 520/639–3447 | www.littledaisy.com | 23 rooms | $45 | AE, D, DC, MC, V.

FLAGSTAFF

Amerisuites. This all-suite chain hotel is less than a mile from the intersection of Interstate 17 and Interstate 40, ¼ mi from Northern Arizona University on the south side of Flagstaff. Off Interstate 17 North, exit 341. Complimentary Continental breakfast. In-room data ports, kitchenettes, microwaves, refrigerators, cable TV, in-room VCRs. Gym.

Pool. Hot tub. Laundry facilities. Business services, airport shuttle. Some pets allowed. | 2455 S. Beulah Blvd., 86001 | 520/774–8042 or 800/833–1516 | fax 520/774–5524 | www.amerisuites.com | 117 suites | $119–$159 | AE, D, DC, MC, V.

Arizona Mountain Inn. This Tudor-style inn borders the Coconino National Forest, 2 mi southeast of Flagstaff. Suites are in the main building, but most accommodations are in cabins (all with full kitchens and fireplaces) scattered around the 13-acre property. Off Interstate 17 North, exit 339 (Lake Mary Road), then 1 mi east. Picnic areas. No air-conditioning, full kitchens (in cabins), no room phones. Hiking, bicycles. Playground. Laundry facilities. Business services. Some pets allowed (fee). | 4200 Lake Mary Rd., 86001 | 520/774–8959 or 800/239–5236 | fax 520/774–8837 | www.arizonamountaininn.com | 3 suites, 17 cabins | $90–$110 suites, $110 cabins | D, MC, V.

Best Western Kings House Motel. Rooms at this two-story motel on the east side of Flagstaff are spacious and tidy. It's located on historic Route 66. Restaurant, bar, complimentary Continental breakfast. Cable TV. Pool. Some pets allowed. | 1560 E. Rte. 66 | 520/774–7186 | fax 520/774–7188 | www.bestwestern.com | 57 rooms | $69–$89 | AE, D, DC, MC, V.

Comfort Inn. This two-story motel is a mile north of Interstate 40 and just a few blocks from the University of Northern Arizona. Complimentary Continental breakfast. Cable TV. Pool. Some pets allowed. | 914 S. Milton Rd., 86001 | 520/774–7326 or 800/228–5150 | fax 520/774–7328 | www.comfortinn.com | 67 rooms | $69–$95 | AE, D, DC, MC, V.

Days Inn–Route 66. This large chain motel is 1 mi west of historic downtown, on old Route 66. Restaurant, bar, complimentary Continental breakfast. Cable TV. Pool. Laundry facilities. Business services. Some pets allowed. | 1000 W. Rte. 66 | 520/774–5221 or 800/422–4470 | fax 520/774–4977 | www.daysinn.com | 157 rooms | $45–$120 | AE, D, DC, MC, V.

Embassy Suites. This upscale, all-suite hotel is on the south side of Flagstaff, 1 mi north of Interstate 40, exit 195B, and less than 1 mi from Northern Arizona University. Each room has a private bedroom and two televisions. Picnic area, complimentary breakfast. In-room data ports, microwaves, refrigerators, cable TV. Pool. Hot tub. Gym. Business services. Some pets allowed. | 706 S. Milton Rd., 86001 | 520/774–4333 | fax 520/774–0216 | www.embassyflagstaff.com | 119 suites | $109–$164 suites | AE, D, DC, MC, V.

Flagstaff University/Grand Canyon Travelodge. This two-story motel is on the southwest side of Flagstaff, two blocks from Northern Arizona University and within walking distance of restaurants. Complimentary Continental breakfast. Cable TV. Hot tub, sauna. Business services. Some pets allowed. | 801 W. Rte. 66 | 520/774–3381 | fax 520/774–1648 | www.travelodge.com | 49 rooms | $89–$109 | AE, D, DC, MC, V.

Holiday Inn. This hotel is on the east side of Flagstaff, just off Interstate 40, exit 198. Restaurant, bar, room service. In-room data ports, cable TV. Pool. Hot tub. Gym. Laundry facilities. Airport shuttle. Pets allowed. | 2320 Lucky La., 86004 | 520/526–1150 or 800/533–2754 | fax 520/779–2610 | www.holiday-inn.com | 156 rooms, 1 suite | $59–$119, $150 suite | AE, D, DC, MC, V.

Hanford Hotel. This hotel is just 1½ mi from Northern Arizona State University, exit 198 off Interstate 40. Some of the rooms have views of the San Francisco Peak and there is an elegant two-story fireplace room which is ideal for spending a relaxing evening. Restaurant, bar, room service. Some refrigerators, cable TV. Pool. Hot tub, sauna. Video games. Business services, airport shuttle. Pets allowed (fee). | 2200 E. Butler Ave., 86004 | 520/779–6944 | fax 520/774–3990 | 83 rooms, 18 suites | $79, $99–$119 suites | AE, D, DC, MC, V.

Hotel Monte Vista. Over the years many Hollywood stars have stayed at this downtown hotel built in 1926. The lobby is appealing, but rooms and hallways are somewhat dark. Bar. Cable TV. Pets allowed (fee). | 100 N. San Francisco St. | 520/779–6971 or 800/545–3068 | fax 520/779–2904 | www.hotelmontevista.com/home.html | 48 rooms | $65–$125 | AE, D, DC, MC, V.

Ramada Limited West. This chain hotel is off Interstate 40, exit 195B, on the southwest side of Flagstaff. Its location less than a mile from Northern Arizona University makes it popular with NAU parents. Complimentary Continental breakfast. Microwaves, refrigerators, cable TV. Pool. Hot tub. Gym. Laundry facilities. Business services. Pets allowed (fee). | 2755 Woodland Village Blvd. | 520/773–1111 | fax 520/774–1449 | www.ramada.com | 87 suites | $59–$99 | AE, D, DC, MC, V.

Super 8. This two-story chain motel is on the east side of Flagstaff, off Interstate 40, exit 201. Cable TV. Business services. Pets allowed. | 3725 N. Kasper, 86004 | 520/526–0818 or 888/324–9131 | fax 520/526–8786 | www.super8.com | 90 rooms | $59–$69 | AE, D, DC, MC, V.

FLORENCE

Rancho Sonora Inn and RV Park. In this 1930s adobe the rooms open onto a walled courtyard, where the pool is. Picnic area, complimentary Continental breakfast. Some kitchenettes, some microwaves, some refrigerators, some room phones. Pool. Hot tub. Laundry facilities. Business services. Some pets allowed. No smoking. | 9198 N. Hwy. 79, 85232 | 520/868–8000 or 800/205–6817 | fax 520/868–8000 | florenceaz.org/ranchosonora | 9 rooms, 4 suites | $74, $75–$135 suites | AE, MC, V.

FREDONIA

Crazy Jug Motel. All the rooms at this basic motel are furnished with rustic log furniture and decorated in southwestern colors. Restaurant. Cable TV. Pets allowed. | 465 S. Main St. | 520/643–7752 | fax 520/643–7759 | www.xpressweb.com/crazyjug | 14 rooms | $35–$45 | AE, DC, MC, V.

GILA BEND

Best Western Space Age Lodge. An unusual-looking, single-level chain motel with an aeronautical theme. Photos of space travel decorate the basic rooms. Restaurant. Some refrigerators, cable TV. Pool. Hot tub. Pets allowed. | 401 E. Pima St., 85337 | 520/683–2273 | fax 520/683–2273 | www.bestwestern.com | 41 rooms | $65–$85 | AE, D, DC, MC, V.

GLENDALE

Rock Haven Motel. This basic motel is on Glendale's main thoroughfare, about a mile from the antiques district. Some kitchenettes, cable TV. Pets allowed. | 5120 N.W. Grand Ave. | 623/937–0071 | 44 rooms | $42 | AE, D, DC, MC, V.

Windmill Inn–Sun City West. This all-suite chain hotel with lovely grounds is 7 mi east of Glendale. Each room has a sleeper sofa. Complimentary Continental breakfast. Microwaves, refrigerators, cable TV. Pool. Hot tub. Gym, bicycles. Library. Laundry facilities. Business services. Pets allowed. | 12545 W. Bell Rd., Surprise, 85374 | 623/583–0133 or 800/547–4747 | fax 623/583–8366 | www.windmillinns.com | 127 suites | $116–$145 | AE, D, DC, MC, V.

GLOBE

Ramada Limited. This chain hotel is at the intersection of U.S. 60 and U.S. 70. It's 4 mi from Broad Street and a five-minute drive from the Apache Gold Casino. Picnic area, complimentary Continental breakfast. Refrigerators, cable TV. Pool. Hot tub. Laundry service. Business services. Some pets allowed. | 1699 E. Ash St., 85501 | 520/425–5741 or 800/256–8399 | fax 520/402–8466 | www.ramada.com | 77 rooms, 3 suites | $89–$99 | AE, DC, MC, V.

GRAND CANYON NATIONAL PARK

Rodeway Inn–Red Feather Lodge. This large, three-story motel was built in 1995. It's 1½ mi south of the South Rim park entrance. Restaurant. Cable TV. Gym. Business services.

Pets allowed (fee). | Hwy. 64, Tusayan, 86023 | www.redfeatherlodge.com | 520/638–2414 or 800/538–2345 | fax 520/638–9216 | 232 rooms | $100–$175 | AE, DC, MC, V.

GREER

Greer Mountain Resort. Nestled in a ponderosa pine forest 1½ mi south of Highway 260, these comfy cabin units appeal to budget travelers and families. Most of the cabins sleep up to six people, but one-bedroom pine studios are available for those seeking more intimate quarters. All have fully equipped kitchens and gas fireplaces, and a log cabin café on the premises serves hearty home-cooked breakfast and lunch dishes. Restaurant, picnic area. Kitchenettes, refrigerators, no room phones, no TVs. Hiking, horseback riding, fishing. Pets allowed (fee). | Hwy. 353 | 520/735–7560 | www.wmonline.com/greermountain | 4 cabins | $65–$90 | MC, V.

Molly Butler Lodge. One of Arizona's oldest guest lodges, which has been around since the turn of the 20th century, this is an inviting place, with simple accommodations and a well-regarded restaurant. Rooms are bright and carefully decorated with handmade quilts and wood furniture; many have views of the Little Colorado River and Greer Meadow. Fishing, hiking, and horseback riding can be arranged with local outfitters. Restaurant, bar. No room phones, no TV in rooms, TV in common area. Pets allowed. | 109 Main St. | 520/735–7226 | www.mollybutlerlodge.com | 11 rooms | $38–$65 | MC, V.

White Mountain Lodge. Built in 1892, the lodge is the oldest building in Greer. Rooms are all uniquely decorated with mostly southwestern and Mission-style furnishings. Separate cabins have wood-burning or gas-log fireplaces and full kitchens; many of them

HEADED FOR THE GRAND CANYON?

If Norman Rockwell had painted a scene featuring man's best friend, he might well have set it in the Grand Canyon. Just imagine it—you and your pooch, together, gazing out at America's greatest landmark. Fortunately, pets are welcome in the park, provided they're on a leash; the two of you can take in the stunning canyon view together from the paved 2.7-mi Rim Trail, which skirts the canyon's South Rim—the most popular vantage point for viewing the amazing scenery. The canyon walls are steep, so dogs are not permitted on the trails that descend down from there. They may be permitted on ranger-conducted walks and activities, at the discretion of the ranger in charge. Keep in mind that weather conditions at the Grand Canyon can reach extremes in both summer and winter, so be prepared. There and en route, remember that it's the desert, and both of you need plenty of water. Travel prepared. Contact: Grand Canyon National Park, Rte. 64, Grand Canyon AZ 86023, 520/638-7888.

have whirlpool tubs. Complimentary breakfast. Some in-room VCRs, no room phones, no TV in some rooms, TV in common area. Hot tub. Some pets allowed (fee). No smoking. | 140 Main St. | 520/735–7568 or 888/493–7568 | fax 520/735–7498 | www.wmlodge.com | 7 rooms, 6 cabins | $85–$105, $85–$195 cabins | D, DC, MC, V.

HOLBROOK

Best Western Arizonian Inn. The rooms in this chain motel are large and handsome. An all-night diner is just steps from the parking lot. Restaurant. Some microwaves, some refrigerators, cable TV. Pool. Some pets allowed. | 2508 E. Navajo Blvd., 86025 | 520/524–2611 or 877/280–7300 | fax 520/524–2611 | www.bestwestern.com | 70 rooms | $58–$72 | AE, D, DC, MC, V.

Comfort Inn. This chain motel is across the road from the Holbrook airport and 18 mi east of Petrified Forest National Park. Restaurant, complimentary Continental breakfast. Some microwaves, some refrigerators, cable TV. Pool. Laundry facilities. Business services. Some pets allowed. | 2602 E. Navajo Blvd., 86025 | 520/524–6131 or 800/228–5150 | fax 520/524–2281 | www.comfortinn.com | 60 rooms | $65 | AE, D, DC, MC, V.

Econo Lodge. This chain motel is ½ mi from Interstate 40 on the east side of Holbrook, next to the Comfort Inn. Restaurant, picnic area, complimentary Continental breakfast. Some refrigerators, cable TV. Pool. Laundry facilities. Pets allowed. | 2596 E. Navajo Blvd. | 520/524–1448 | fax 520/524–2281 | www.econolodge.com | 63 rooms | $50 | AE, D, DC, MC, V.

Holiday Inn Express. This chain hotel is at the intersection of Interstate 40 and Highway 60. Complimentary Continental breakfast. Some microwaves, some refrigerators, cable TV. Pool. Hot tub. Laundry service. Business services. Pets allowed. | 1308 E. Navajo Blvd., 86025 | 520/524–1466 | fax 520/524–1788 | www.hiexpress.com | 55 rooms, 4 suites | $89–$99, $109–$119 suites | AE, D, DC, MC, V.

Motel 6. This budget motel is on the east side of town at Interstate 40, exit 289. Cable TV. Pool. Laundry facilities. Some pets allowed. | 2514 Navajo Blvd. | 520/524–6101 | fax 520/524–1806 | www.motel6.com | 124 rooms | $35 | AE, D, DC, MC, V.

Ramada Limited. This standard chain motel is ½ mi off Interstate 40 on the east side of Holbrook. Restaurant. Cable TV. Some pets. | 2608 E. Navajo Blvd. | 520/524–2566 | fax 520/524–6427 | www.ramada.com | 41 rooms | $55–$65 | AE, D, DC, MC, V.

Wigwam Motel. This motel consists of concrete "teepees" built in the 1940s. There's a small museum of Native American artifacts and local history lore. Cable TV, no room phones. Pets allowed. | 811 W. Hopi Dr., 86025 | 520/524–3048 | www.nephi.com | 15 rooms | $33–$38 | MC, V.

JEROME

Surgeon's House Bed & Breakfast. Gorgeously restored and decorated with plants and handmade quilts, this Mediterranean-style home with hardwood floors and skylights offers knockout views, friendly service, and plenty of sun-filled nooks and crannies. A multi-course gourmet breakfast is prepared by innkeeper Andrea Prince from her own published cookbook. Complimentary breakfast. No room phones, no TVs. Some pets allowed (fee). | 101 Hill St. | 520/639–1452 | www.surgeonshouse.com | 3 suites | $100–$150 | MC, V.

KAYENTA

Goulding's Monument Valley Trading Post & Lodge. This historic trading post, about 20 mi northeast of Kayenta in Utah and 1 mi from Monument Valley Navajo Tribal Park, once served as a set for John Wayne films such as *Stagecoach* and *Fort Apache*. The original trading post houses a museum with movie memorabilia and a mutimedia show on Monument Valley. The two-story motel offers basic, comfortable rooms with spectacular views of

Monument Valley. Guided tours of the valley leave from here. Goulding's also runs a campground, a grocery store, and a convenience store. Restaurant, cafe. Refrigerators, in-room VCRs (and movies). Pool. Laundry facilities. Pets allowed. | Indian Hwy. 42, 84536 | 435/727-3231 or 800/874-0902 | fax 435/727-3344 | www.gouldings.com | 19 rooms in lodge, 41 rooms motel rooms, 2 cabins | $138 rooms, $150 cabins | AE, D, DC, MC, V.

KINGMAN

Best Western—A Wayfarer's Inn. This chain motel is on the motel strip in Kingman. It's a tad more upscale than many of the other motels in town. Microwaves, refrigerators, cable TV. Pool. Hot tub. Laundry facilities. Pets allowed. | 2815 E. Andy Devine Ave., 86401 | 520/753-6271 or 800/548-5695 | fax 520/753-9608 | www.bestwestern.com | 98 rooms, 3 suites | $67–$80, $90 suites | AE, D, DC, MC, V.

Brunswick Hotel. Antiques fill the rooms of this downtown hotel, which is a cut above the chains that line this strip. As you step into the lobby, the furnishings and decor will transport you back to the early 1900s. Restaurant, bar, complimentary Continental breakfast. Cable TV. Some kitchenettes. Laundry facilities. Pets allowed. | 315 E. Andy Devine Ave. | 520/718-1800. | fax 520/718-1801 | www.hotel-brunswick.com | 24 rooms | $65–$95 | AE, D, DC, MC, V.

Days Inn. This two-story budget motel is on the main strip in Kingman. Complimentary Continental breakfast. Kitchenettes, microwaves, refrigerators, cable TV. Pool. Hot tub. Laundry facilities. Business services. Pets allowed (fee). | 3023 E. Andy Devine Ave., 86401 | 520/753-7500 | fax 520/753-4686 | www.daysinn.com | 60 rooms | $55–$75 | AE, D, DC, MC, V.

Hill Top. An inexpensive independent motel with basic amenities. Some refrigerators, cable TV. Pool. Laundry facilities. Business services. Some pets allowed. | 1901 E. Andy Devine Ave., 86401 | 520/753-2198 | fax 520/753-5985 | 29 rooms | $32–$44 | D, MC, V.

Kingman Super 8 Motel. This two-story chain motel is at the northern end of the motel strip in Kingman. In-room data ports, cable TV. Pool. Hot tub. Pets allowed (fee). | 3401 E. Andy Devine Ave. | 520/757-4808 | fax 520/757-4808 | www.super8.com | 61 rooms | $45–$56 | AE, D, DC, MC, V.

Quality Inn. This chain motel has comfortable rooms and a spiffy coffee shop stocked with Route 66 memorabilia. Complimentary Continental breakfast. Some kitchenettes, some refrigerators. Cable TV. Pool. Hot tub, sauna. Gym. Business services, airport shuttle. Pets allowed. | 1400 E. Andy Devine Ave. | 520/753-4747 | fax 520/753-4747 | www.qualityinn.com | 98 rooms | $54–$69 | AE, D, DC, MC, V.

LAKE HAVASU CITY

Bridgeview Motel. Most of the southwestern-style rooms at this modern motel afford views of London Bridge and Lake Havasu. Accomodations are clean and simple, and the property is within walking distance of area restaurants and shops. Satellite TV. Pool. Some pets allowed. | 101 London Bridge Rd., 86403 | 520/855-5559 | fax 520/855-5564 | 37 rooms | $59–$145 | MC, V.

Havasu Springs Resort. Rooms here are in four motel buildings. There are also an RV park and houseboat rentals. Some of the motel rooms offer views of Lake Havasu, on which the houseboats are located. There are several houseboat models available; each sleeps from 10 to 12 people. Restaurant. Some kitchenettes, some microwaves, some refrigerators, cable TV. Laundry facilities. Pets allowed (fee). | 2581 Hwy. 95, Parker, 85344 | 520/667-3361 | fax 520/667-1098 | www.havasusprings.com | 44 rooms, 4 houseboat models | $85–$100 motel rooms, $901–$1,431 for 3 nights in houseboats (3-night minimum) | AE, D, MC, V.

Holiday Inn. This motel is about ½ mi from Lake Havasu, next to Lake Havasu State Park. Restaurant, bar, room service. In-room data ports, refrigerators, cable TV. Pool. Video games. Laundry facilities. Business services, airport shuttle. Some pets allowed. | 245 London Bridge Rd., 86403 | 520/855–4071 or 888/428–2465 | fax 520/855–2379 | www.holiday-inn.com | 157 rooms, 5 suites | $57–$84 | AE, D, DC, MC, V.

LITCHFIELD PARK

Best Western Phoenix Goodyear Inn. This motel in Goodyear, 3 mi south of Litchfield Park, is 5 mi from the Desert Sky Pavilion and 15 mi from Sky Harbor International Airport. Restaurant, bar. In-room data ports, cable TV. Pool. Laundry service. Business services. Some pets. | 55 N. Litchfield Rd., Goodyear, 85338. | 623/932–3210 | fax 623/932–3210 | www.bestwestern.com | 85 rooms | $89–$119 | AE, D, DC, MC, V.

Holiday Inn Express. This chain motel in Goodyear, 3 mi south of Litchfield Park, is 10 mi from Wildlife World and 17 mi west of downtown Phoenix. Complimentary Continental breakfast. In-room data ports, microwaves, refrigerators, some in-room hot tubs, cable TV. Pool. Hot tub. Gym. Video games. Laundry facilities. Business services. Pets allowed. | 1313 Litchfield Rd., Goodyear, 85338 | 602/535–1313 | fax 602/535–0950 | www.hiexpress.com | 60 rooms, 30 suites | $129, $149–$169 suites | AE, D, DC, MC, V.

The Wigwam. Built in 1918 as a retreat for executives of the Goodyear Company, this luxurious resort has two top-notch golf courses. Casita-style rooms are filled with local artwork, and in keeping with its origins, the business center is extensive and in a separate wing so as not to mix business with pleasure. Suites are breathtakingly large. Take Interstate 10, exit 128. 3 restaurants, 3 bars, room service. Some minibars, some refrigerators, cable TV. 2 pools. Barbershop, beauty salon, 2 hot tubs. 3 18-hole golf courses, putting greens, tennis courts. Basketball, gym, volleyball, bicycles. Library. Children's programs (ages 5–12), playground. Business services, airport shuttle. Some pets allowed. | 300 Wigwam Blvd., 85340 | 623/935–3811 or 800/327–0396 | fax 623/935–3737 | www.wigwamresort.com | 264 rooms in casitas, 67 suites | $330–$390, $390–$475 suites | AE, D, DC, MC, V.

MARBLE CANYON

Marble Canyon Lodge. This lodge opened in 1929 on the same day that Navajo Bridge was dedicated. You'll find historic rooms in the original lodge, more modern rooms in the newer motel across the street, and two-bedroom suites in a building from 1992. Popular with hikers, there are many trails within walking distance. It's ¼ mi west of Navajo Bridge. Restaurant, bar. Some kitchenettes. Laundry facilities. Business services. Pets allowed. | Hwy. 89A | 520/355–2225 or 800/726–1789 | 55 rooms, 7 suites | $55–$70, $134 suites | D, MC, V.

MESA

Arizona Golf Resort and Conference Center at Superstition Springs. This 150-acre resort, with a championship golf course and school, is very beginner-friendly. Many rooms have private balconies or patios. Restaurant, bar, picnic area. In-room safes, some kitchenettes, microwaves, refrigerators, cable TV. Pool. Driving range, 18-hole golf course, putting green, tennis courts. Gym. Laundry facilities. Business services. Pets allowed. | 425 S. Power Rd. | 480/832–3202 or 800/528–8282 | fax 480/981–0151 | www.azgolfresort.com | 89 rooms, 98 suites | $159, $259–$298 suites | AE, D, DC, MC, V.

Best Western Mesa Inn. This chain motel is less than a mile from the Mormon Temple. Complimentary Continental breakfast. In-room data ports, cable TV, in-room VCRs (and movies). Pool. Hot tub. Laundry facilities, laundry service. Pets allowed (fee). | 1625 E. Main St. | 480/964–8000 | fax 480/835–1272 | www.bestwestern.com | 100 rooms | $80–$99 | AE, D, DC, MC, V.

Gold Canyon Golf Resort. This resort 7 mi east of Mesa has great views of the Superstitious Mountains. Many rooms have fireplaces and private patios. The two golf courses here are considered very good by enthusiasts. Restaurant, bar, room service. In-room data ports, refrigerators, some in-room hot tubs, cable TV. Pool. Hot tub. Driving range, 2 18-hole golf courses, putting green, tennis courts. Bicycles. Business services. Pets allowed (fee). | 6100 S. Kings Ranch Rd., Gold Canyon, 85219 | 480/982–9090 or 800/624–6445 | fax 480/983–9554 | www.goldcanyongolfresort.com | 101 casitas | $160–$270 | AE, D, DC, MC, V.

Motel 6 Mesa Main. This chain motel in central Mesa is less than 1 mi from the Mormon Temple and 10 mi from Papago Park. Cable TV. Laundry facilities. Pool. Some pets allowed. | 630 W. Main St. | 480/969–8111 | fax 480/655–0747 | www.motel6.com | 102 rooms | $49 | AE, D, DC, MC, V.

Motel 6 Mesa South. Located in south Mesa, this chain motel is 1½ mi from the Fiesta Mall and ¼ mi from Golf Land Amusement Park. Cable TV. Some microwaves, some refrigerators. Pool. Laundry facilities. Some pets allowed. | 1511 S. Country Club Dr., 85210 | 480/834–0066 | fax 480/969–6313 | www.motel6.com | 91 rooms | $45 | AE, D, DC, MC, V.

Residence Inn Phoenix/Mesa. This three-story all-suite hotel is across the street from Fiesta Mall and 8 mi from Papago Park. Complimentary breakfast. In-room data ports, kitchenettes, microwaves, refrigerators, cable TV. Pool. Spa. Laundry service. Business services. Pets allowed (fee). | 941 W. Grove Ave. | 480/610–0100 | fax 480/610–6490 | www.residenceinn.com | 117 suites | $159–$199 | AE, D, DC, MC, V.

Sheraton Mesa Hotel and Conference Center. This 12-story hotel is 2 mi from the Fiesta Mall, 5 mi from Arizona State University. Restaurant, bar. Some refrigerators, cable TV. Pool. Hot tub. Driving range, putting green. Gym. Business services, airport shuttle. Some pets allowed (fee). | 200 N. Centennial Way, 85201 | 480/898–8300 or 800/456–6372 | fax 480/964–9279 | www.sheraton.com | 265 rooms, 8 suites | $119–$159, $225–$300 suites | AE, D, DC, MC, V.

NOGALES

Americana Motor Hotel. This motel less than 1 mi from the Mexican border has basic amenities. Restaurant, bar, room service. Some refrigerators, cable TV. Pool. Business services. Some pets allowed (fee). | 639 N. Grand Ave., 85621 | 520/287–7211 or 800/874–8079 | fax 520/287–5188 | 97 rooms | $55–$79 | AE, D, DC, MC, V.

Best Western Siesta Motel. This motel is 1 mi from the Mexican border. Complimentary Continental breakfast. In-room data ports, cable TV. Pool. Hot tub. Laundry service. Business services. Some pets allowed. | 673 N. Grand Ave. | 520/287–4671 | fax 520/287–9616 | www.bestwestern.com | 47 rooms | $80 | AE, D, DC, MC, V.

Nogales Days Inn. This chain motel about 2 mi from the Mexican border offers casual, unpretentious border flavor. The small-town service is friendly. Restaurant, bar, room service. Some refrigerators, cable TV. Pool. Hot tub. Laundry facilities, laundry service. Business services. Pets allowed (fee). | 884 N. Grand Ave. | 520/287–4611 | fax 520/287–0101 | www.daysinn.com | 98 rooms | $60–$65 | AE, D, DC, MC, V.

Rio Rico Resort and Country Club. Atop a mesa 12 mi north of Nogales with panoramic views of the surrounding landscape, this deluxe resort has one of the best golf courses in southern Arizona. There's entertainment on weekends and special events such as cookouts on a regular basis. It's off Interstate 17, exit 17. Restaurant, bar, room service. Cable TV. Pool. Beauty salon, hot tub. Driving range, 18-hole golf course, putting green, tennis courts. Gym, horseback riding. Business services, airport shuttle. Pets allowed. | 1069 Camino Caralampi, Rio Rico, 85648 | 520/281–1901 or 800/288–4746 | fax 520/281–7132 | www.rioricoresort.com | 181 rooms, 15 suites | $135–$175, $225–$700 suites | AE, D, DC, MC, V.

PAGE

Best Western Arizona Inn. This motel overlooks Glen Canyon Dam and Lake Powell. Some of the basic, southwestern-style rooms have views of the lake. Cable TV. Pool. Hot tub. Gym. Business services, airport shuttle. Pets allowed (fee). | 716 Rimview Dr., 86040 | 520/645-2466 or 800/826-2718 | fax 520/645-2053 | www.bestwestern.com | 101 rooms, 2 suites | $89-$113, $108-$128 suites | AE, D, DC, MC, V.

Best Western Weston Inn & Suites. This three-story motel overlooking the Glen Çanyon Dam has some nice views of Lake Powell. The large rooms are functional and comfortable. Complimentary Continental breakfast. In-room data ports, cable TV. Pool. Hot tub. Business services, airport shuttle. Pets allowed (fee). | 207 Lake Powell Blvd., 86040 | 520/645-2451 | fax 520/645-9552 | www.bestwestern.com | 99 rooms, 9 suites | $55-$170, $170-$180 suites | AE, D, DC, MC, V.

Canyon Colors Bed and Breakfast. Each room here has a unique theme: one features sunflower motifs, another mauve and rose paisley designs, and another is based on southwestern imagery. There is a view of the Vermillion Cliffs, which are about 20 mi away. Complimentary breakfast. Some in-room hot tubs, cable TV, in-room VCRs. Pool. Pets allowed. No smoking. | 225 S. Navajo Dr., 86040 | 800/536-2530 | fax 520/645-5979 | www.canyon-country.com/lakepowell/colors.htm | 3 rooms | $70-$90 | AE, D, DC, MC, V.

Lake Powell Motel. Rooms at this quaint and basic motor inn have views of canyon, cliffs, or Lake Powell. Guests here have access to all of the facilities at the Wahweap Lodge and Marina, which is down the hill from the motel. Cable TV. Airport shuttle. Pets allowed. | 2505 U.S. 89, 86040 | 520/645-2477, 800/528-6154 outside AZ | 24 rooms | $58-$79 | Closed Nov.–Mar. | AE, D, DC, MC, V.

Ramada Inn, Page–Lake Powell. This hotel offers standard rooms with views of the Vermilion Cliffs and the adjacent golf course. Restaurant, bar, picnic area, room service. Cable TV. Pool. Laundry facilities. Business services, airport shuttle. Pets allowed. | 287 N. Lake Powell Blvd., 86040 | 520/645-8851 | fax 520/645-2523 | www.ramada.com | 129 rooms | $99-$109 | AE, D, DC, MC, V.

★ **Wahweap Lodge and Marina.** This resort on the shores of Lake Powell offers basic rooms of various sizes, and can accommodate larger groups and families. Half of the southwestern-style rooms are lakeside, and all rooms have patios or balconies. Lake tours and boat rentals are available through the lodge's own marina. Restaurant, bar. Refrigerators, cable TV. 2 pools. Hot tub. Gym, boating. Laundry facilities. Business services, airport shuttle. Pets allowed. | 100 Lakeshore Dr., 86040 | 520/645-2433 or 800/528-6154 | fax 520/645-1031 | www.visitlakepowell.com | 369 rooms, 2 suites in 8 buildings | $79-$160, $227 suites | AE, D, DC, MC, V.

World Host Empire House. Larger-than-average rooms decorated in southwestern tones are available at this affordable two-story motor inn 2 mi from Lake Powell and across the street from Page's only shopping center. Tours of the lake and surroundings can be booked in the lobby. Restaurant, bar. Cable TV. Pool. Pets allowed (fee). | 107 S. Lake Powell Blvd. | 520/645-2406 or 800/551-9005 | fax 520/645-2647 | eh@pageamerica.net | 69 rooms | $72 | AE, D, MC, V.

PARKER

El Rancho Motel. You'll be right in the middle of downtown here, and you certainly can't beat the price. The small rooms feature southwestern motifs and paint schemes, and for the money they feature a lot of conveniences. Some kitchenettes, microwaves, refrigerators, cable TV. Pool. Pets allowed. | 709 California Ave., 85344 | 520/669-2231 | fax 520/669-2246 | 19 rooms | $35 | AE, D, MC, V.

PATAGONIA

Sonoita Inn. The owner of Secretariat used to own this home. The inn sits at the mile-high mark, with views of several mountain ranges, so the views of sunsets are great. The rooms are expansive with motifs ranging from florals to cowboys on bucking broncos. Complimentary Continental breakfast. Cable TV. Pets allowed (fee). No smoking. | 3243 Hwy. 82, 85624 | 520/455–5935 | fax 520/455–5069 | www.sonoitainn.com | 18 rooms | $99–$125 | AE, MC, V.

Stage Stop Inn. This rustic, family-owned and operated inn offers basic accommodations that surround a courtyard pool. Each room is individually named, and all are filled with western knickknacks and pictures of cowboys. Restaurant. Some kitchenettes, cable TV. Pool. Business services. Pets allowed. | 303 W. McKeown Ave., 85624 | 520/394–2211 or 800/923–2211 | fax 520/394–2211 | 54 rooms | $69–$125 | AE, D, DC, MC, V.

PAYSON

Best Western Paysonglo Lodge. Accommodations are typical motel-style rooms, except that you can also get a fireplace. Complimentary Continental breakfast. Refrigerators, cable TV. Pool. Hot tub. Laundry facilities. Business services. Some pets allowed. | 1005 S. Beeline Hwy., 85541 | 520/474–2382 | fax 520/474–1937 | www.bestwestern.com | 47 rooms | $72–$130 | AE, D, DC, MC, V.

Holiday Inn Express. This three-story chain hotel is 1 mi from the Payson Visitor's Information Center and 2 mi from the rodeo grounds. Complimentary Continental breakfast. Some microwaves, some refrigerators, cable TV. Pool. Hot tub. Laundry facilities. Business services. Pets allowed (fee). | 206 S. Beeline Hwy., 85541 | 520/472–7484 or 800/818–7484 | fax 520/472–6283 | www.hiexpress.com | 42 rooms, 2 suites | $99–$129, $129–$169 suites | AE, D, DC, MC, V.x

The Inn of Payson. This inn is surrounded by ponderosa pines. Each room has a patio or balcony and some rooms have a fireplace. Complimentary Continental breakfast. Refrigerators, some in-room hot tubs, cable TV. Pool. Hot tub. Gym. Business services. Pets allowed (fee). | 801 N. Beeline Hwy., 85541 | 520/474–3241 or 800/247–9477 | fax 520/472–6564 | www.innofpayson.com | 99 rooms | $49–$119 | AE, D, DC, MC, V.

Mountain Meadows Cabins. All the cabins at this place 27 mi east of Payson have porches with swings, pine-paneled interiors, and fireplaces. You'll enjoy a fine view of the mountains. Kitchenettes, some in-room hot tubs, no room phones, cable TV. Pets allowed (fee). | Hwy. 260, 85541 | 520/478–4415 | www.rimcountry.com/mmeadow.htm | 6 cabins | $55–$180 | MC, V.

PHOENIX

Best Western InnSuites. This all-suite hotel in north Phoenix is west of Squaw Peak, 5 mi from the Paradise Valley Mall and Biltmore Fashion Park. Picnic area, complimentary Continental breakfast. In-room data ports, some kitchenettes, microwaves, refrigerators, cable TV. Pool. Hot tub. Gym. Playground. Laundry facilities. Business services. Some pets allowed (fee). | 1615 E. Northern Ave. | 602/997–6285 | fax 602/943–1407 | www.bestwestern.com | 124 rooms | $119–$169 | AE, D, DC, MC, V.

Hampton Inn. This inexpensive motel is right off Interstate 17 in central Phoenix, 1 mi from the Metrocenter Mall and within walking distance of many restaurants. The newly remodeled rooms are clean, modern, and comfortable. Complimentary Continental breakfast. In-room data ports, cable TV. Pool. Hot tub. Business services. Some pets allowed. | 8101 N. Black Canyon Hwy. | 602/864–6233 | fax 602/995–7503 | www.hamptoninn.com | 147 rooms | $54–$94 | AE, D, DC, MC, V.

Holiday Inn Select–Airport. This 10-story hotel is seven minutes from Sky Harbor airport and has a 24-hour shuttle there. Restaurant, bar. In-room data ports, some microwaves, some refrigerators, cable TV. Pool. Hot tub. Gym. Laundry facilities. Business services, airport shuttle. Pets allowed. | 4300 E. Washington St. | 602/273–7778 | fax 602/275–5616 | www.holiday-inn.com | 301 rooms | $129–$139 | AE, D, DC, MC, V.

Hotel San Carlos. This seven-story boutique hotel in the center of Phoenix has been open for over 70 years; it was the first air-conditioned hotel in the Southwest. It prides itself on affordable luxury. It's done up in Italian Renaissance style, though rooms are not large. 2 restaurants, bar, complimentary Continental breakfast. In-room data ports, some refrigerators, cable TV. Pool. Laundry service. Pets allowed. | 22 N. Central Ave., 85004 | 602/253–4121 | fax 602/253–6668 | www.hotelsancarlos.com | 133 rooms | $140–$200 | AE, D, DC, MC, V.

La Quinta–Thomas Road. This two-story brick motel in central Phoenix is convenient to Interstate 17. The basic rooms are decorated in cream and hunter green, and are roomy and comfortable. Complimentary Continental breakfast. In-room data ports, some refrigerators, cable TV. Pool. Laundry facilities. Business services. Pets allowed. | 2725 N. Black Canyon Hwy. | 602/258–6271 | fax 602/340–9255 | www.laquinta.com | 139 rooms | $95–$110 | AE, D, DC, MC, V.

Lexington Hotel. This sports-themed hotel also gives you access to the huge, full-service City Square Sports Club in downtown Phoenix. Rooms range in size from average to small. Restaurant, bar. Some microwaves, cable TV. Pool. Barbershop, beauty salon, hot tub. Basketball, health club, racquetball. Business services. Some pets allowed. | 100 W. Clarendon Ave. | 602/279–9811 | fax 602/631–9358 | 180 rooms | $149–$169 | AE, D, DC, MC, V.

Premier Inn Phoenix. This large, southwestern-style motel is directly across from the Metro Center Mall and near Turf Paradise Race Track. Some refrigerators, cable TV. 2 pools, wading pool. Laundry facilities. Business services. Some pets allowed. | 10402 N. Black Canyon Hwy. | 602/943–2371 or 800/786–6835 | fax 602/943–5847 | www.premierinns.com | 249 rooms, 3 suites | $60–$90, $130 suites | AE, DC, MC, V.

Quality Hotel and Resort. With a 1½-acre lagoon ringed by palms and bamboo, this is one of central Phoenix's best bargains. The VIP floor has cabana suites and a private rooftop pool with skyline views. Restaurant, bar, picnic area. Refrigerators, cable TV. 4 pools, wading pool. Hot tub. Putting green, tennis court. Basketball, gym, volleyball. Video games. Playground, laundry facilities. Business services. Pets allowed (fee). | 3600 N. 2nd Ave. | 602/248–0222 | fax 602/265–6331 | www.qualityinn.com | 280 rooms, 33 suites | $79–$99, $210 suites | AE, D, DC, MC, V.

Quality Inn South Mountain. This four-story chain motel is in south Phoenix, 8 mi southeast of Sky Harbor International Airport. Restaurant. Some microwaves, some refrigerators, cable TV. Pool. Hot tub. Laundry facilities, laundry service. Business services. Pets allowed (fee). | 5121 E. La Puente Ave. | 480/893–3900 | fax 480/496–0815 | 189 rooms | $79–$129 | AE, D, DC, MC, V.

Sheraton Crescent. This large hotel in west Phoenix is next to the Metrocenter Mall, with a free shuttle there. Restaurant, bar, room service. Refrigerators, cable TV. Pool. Sauna, steam room. 2 tennis courts. Basketball, health club, volleyball. Business services. Some pets allowed (fee). | 2620 W. Dunlap Ave. | 602/943–8200 | fax 602/371–2857 | www.sheraton.com | 328 rooms, 14 suites | $59–$239, $500 suites | AE, D, DC, MC, V.

PINETOP/LAKESIDE

Lakeview Lodge. Antique furnishings, stone fireplaces, and rustic decor fill this quaint inn, which is the oldest guest lodge in Arizona, 8 mi east of Show Low. Outside, cobblestone walkways wind through the surrounding pine groves and gardens, and a private stocked lake is available for fishing. The main sitting area features a huge fireplace, leather chairs, and plush sofas, all under a two-story cathedral ceiling. Restaurant, picnic area. No room phones, no TV in some rooms, TV in common area. Fishing. Some pets allowed (fee). | Hwy. 260 | 520/368–5253 | www.dynexgroup.com/lakeview | 9 rooms | $65–$90 | MC, V.

Northwoods Resort. Surrounded by mountain pines, each of these home-style cabins has a full kitchen, covered porch, barbecue grill, and homey interior. Some cabins have in-room hot tubs, and two-story cabins can accommodate up to 18 people; accommodations are perfect for groups or families. Picnic area. Refrigerators, no in-room phones. Pool. Hot tub. Playground. Pets allowed (fee). | 165 E. White Mountain Blvd. | 520/367–2966 or 800/813–2966 | fax 520/367–2969 | www.northwoodsaz.com | 14 cabins | $79–$269 | D, DC, MC, V.

Whispering Pines Resort. These cabin-style accommodations come with double or king-size beds. Located at 7,200 ft and surrounded by a sea of conifers, you'll be soothed to sleep with the fresh smells of mountain air and evergreens. There's little traffic nearby, so you'll be assured a tranquil stay. Some kitchenettes, some microwaves, some refrigerators, some in-room hot tubs, cable TV, no room phones. Laundry facilities. Pets allowed (fee). | 237 E. Mountain Blvd., Pinetop, 85935 | 520/367–4386 or 800/840–3867 | fax 520/367–3702 | www.whisperingpinesaz.com | 33 cabins | $70–$240 | AE, D, MC, V.

PRESCOTT

Best Western Prescottonian. This well-kept, comfortable motel is in the heart of Prescott, on one of the main streets. Restaurant, bar. In-room data ports, refrigerators, cable TV. Pool. Hot tub. Laundry facilities. Business services. Pets allowed. | 1317 E. Gurley St. | 520/445–3096 | fax 520/778–2976 | www.bestwestern.com | 121 rooms, 3 suites | $79–$95, $125–$200 suites | AE, D, DC, MC, V.

Lynx Creek Farm. Very private, freestanding rooms overlook Lynx Creek. Call for directions, as the property is quite secluded and difficult to find. Picnic area, complimentary breakfast. Some kitchenettes, no room phones. Pool. Hot tub. Airport shuttle. Some pets allowed (fee). No smoking. | Mile marker 291 (Onyx Dr.) | 520/778–9573 | www.vacation-lodging.com | 6 rooms, 2 suites | $85–$180, $105–$165 suites | AE, D, MC, V.

SAFFORD

Ramada Inn Spa Resort. This hotel is fairly isolated, but the mountain views are splendid. The inn looks like a sprawling Mexican hacienda. The rooms have the ad hoc cheer of a beach house and will suffice for a good night's sleep. Restaurant. In-room data ports, microwaves, refrigerators, some in-room hot tubs, cable TV, in-room VCRs. Pool. Sauna. Gym. Pets allowed. | 420 E. U.S. 70, 85546 | 520/428–3288 | fax 520/428–3200 | www.ramadainn-sparesort.com | 102 rooms | $80–$150 | AE, D, DC, MC, V.

SCOTTSDALE

Four Seasons Scottsdale at Troon North. You'll enjoy a view of the acclaimed True North golf course from any room at this luxurious resort. Each room has a balcony or patio and extra touches like double vanity mirrors in the bathrooms. Suites have their own plunge pools. 3 restaurants. In-room data ports, in-room safes, some kitchenettes, minibars, cable TV, some in-room VCRs. Pool. Beauty salon, hot tub, massage, sauna, spa, steam room. 4 tennis courts. Health club, bicycles. Baby-sitting, children's programs (ages 5–17). Laundry service. Business services, airport shuttle. Some pets allowed. No smoking. | 10600 E. Crescent Moon Dr., 85255 | 480/515–5700 | fax 480/515–5599 | www.fourseasons.com/scottsdale | 187 rooms, 23 suites | $475–$625 rooms, $850–$3,500 suites | AE, D, DC, MC, V.

Hampton Inn Scottsdale-Old Town. This hotel is 1 mi north of Old Town and just a few blocks from the Fashion Square Mall. Complimentary Continental breakfast, room service. In-room data ports, cable TV. Pool. Laundry service. Business services. Pets allowed (fee). | 4415 N. Civic Center Plaza | 480/941–9400 | fax 480/675–5240 | www.hamptoninn.com | 126 rooms | $120–$150 | AE, D, DC, MC, V.

Holiday Inn Phoenix-Old Town Scottsdale. This hotel and conference center is right on the Civic Center Mall in Old Town Scottsdale. Restaurant, room service. In-room data ports, cable TV. Pool. Tennis court. Gym. Laundry service. Business services. Some pets allowed. | 7353 E. Indian School Rd. | 480/994–9203 or 800/695–6995 | fax 480/941–2567 | www.holiday-inn.com | 204 rooms, 2 suites | $145, $375 suites | AE, D, DC, MC, V.

Holiday Inn Hotel and Suites. This all-suite hotel is in north Scottsdale. All rooms have a pull-out couch in a separate living room, and some have great views of the McDowell Mountains. Restaurant, bar, complimentary Continental breakfast, room service. In-room data ports, kitchenettes, microwaves, refrigerators, cable TV. Pool. Hot tub. Gym. Laundry service. Business services. Some pets allowed. | 7515 E. Butherus Dr. | 480/951–4000 | fax 480/483–9046 | 120 suites | $149–$159 | AE, D, DC, MC, V.

Hospitality Suite Resort. This all-suite hotel is on the southern edge of Scottsdale. All rooms have full kitchens. Restaurant, bar, picnic area, complimentary breakfast, room service. Kitchenettes, microwaves, refrigerators, room service, cable TV. 3 pools. Hot tub. Tennis. Basketball. Laundry facilities. Business services, airport shuttle. Some pets allowed. | 409 N. Scottsdale Rd. | 480/949–5115 or 800/445–5115 | fax 480/941–8014 | www.hospitalitysuites.com | 210 suites in 3 buildings | $120–$169 | AE, D, DC, MC, V.

Hotel Waterfront Ivy. This hotel is made up primarily of suites and is located near 5th Avenue and the waterfront. Rooms are oversize with queen or king beds. Complimentary breakfast. In-room data ports, kitchenettes, microwaves, refrigerators, cable TV. 6 pools. Hot tub. 2 tennis courts. Basketball, gym. Laundry service. Pets allowed (fee). | 7445 E. Chapparal Rd., 85250 | 877/284–3489 or 480/994–5282 | fax 480/994–5625 | www.ivyfront.com | 35 rooms, 75 suites | $69–$369 | AE, D, DC, MC, V.

Inn at the Citadel. Antiques-filled rooms offer desert views at this luxurious B&B. Complimentary Continental breakfast, room service. Some minibars, cable TV. Business services. Pets allowed. | 8700 E. Pinnacle Peak Rd. | 480/585–6133 or 800/927–8367 | fax 480/585–3436 | 11 suites | $229–$259 suites | AE, D, DC, MC, V.

La Quinta Inn and Suites. This motel is in central Scottsdale, 15 mi from Sky Harbor airport. Complimentary Continental breakfast. In-room data ports, some microwaves, some refrigerators, cable TV. Pool. Hot tub. Gym. Laundry facilities. Business services. Some pets allowed. | 8888 E. Shea Blvd. | 480/614–5300 | fax 480/614–5333 | www.laquinta.com | 140 rooms | $89–$129 | AE, D, DC, MC, V.

Marriott's Camelback Inn Resort, Golf Club, and Spa. This historic 1930s resort set on 125 acres offers gracious service and has the best spa in Scottsdale. Rooms are notably spacious, some with fireplaces; a few suites have private pools. 5 restaurants, bar, room service. In-room data ports, minibars, microwaves, refrigerators, cable TV. 3 pools. Barbershop, beauty salon, hot tub, massage, spa. Driving range, 2 18-hole golf courses, putting greens, 6 tennis courts. Health club, hiking, bicycles. Children's programs (ages 3–12). Laundry facilities. Business services. Pets allowed. | 5402 E. Lincoln Dr. | 480/948–1700 or 800/24-CAMEL | fax 480/951–8469 | www.marriott.com | 394 rooms, 59 suites in casitas, 1 house | $409, $700–$950 1-bedroom suites, $980–$1,600 2-bedroom suites, $2,050 house | AE, D, DC, MC, V.

Renaissance Cottonwoods Resort. This 25-acre resort is across the street from the Borgata Shopping Center. The rooms are in adobe buildings spread out around the property; bathrooms are a bit small; villa suites, however, are grand in every way. Restaurant, bar, room service. Minibars, some microwaves, refrigerators, cable TV. 2 pools. Hot tub. Putting green, 4 tennis courts. Business services. Some pets allowed. | 6160 N. Scottsdale Rd. | 480/991–1414 | fax 480/951–3350 | 64 rooms, 107 suites | $285–$330, $345–$360 suites | AE, D, DC, MC, V.

Scottsdale Plaza Resort. This 40-acre Spanish-Mediterranean resort has an old-world charm. Some of the rooms are arranged around a courtyard pool, with Arizona's largest hot tub. 5 restaurants, bar, room service. Minibars, refrigerators, cable TV. 5 pools. Beauty salon. 5 tennis courts. Gym, racquetball, bicycles. Business services. Some pets allowed (fee). | 7200 N. Scottsdale Rd. | 480/948–5000 or 800/832–2025 | fax 480/998–5971 | www.scottsdaleplaza.com | res@tspr.com | 230 rooms, 174 suites | $350, $395–$445 suites | AE, D, DC, MC, V.

SEDONA

Best Western Inn of Sedona. Many rooms in this motel in West Sedona, which is ½ mi from the airport, have great views of the surrounding red rocks. Complimentary Continental breakfast. In-room data ports, some refrigerators, cable TV. Pool. Hot tub. Gym. Laundry service. Business services. Pets allowed (fee). | 1200 W. U.S. 89A | 520/282–3072 or 800/292–6344 | fax 520/282–7218 | www.innofsedona.com | 110 rooms | $115–$155 | AE, D, DC, MC, V.

Desert Quail Inn. This motel is about 6½ mi south of Sedona, and some rooms have views of the red-rock formations. Some microwaves, refrigerators, some in-room hot tubs, cable TV. Pool. Laundry facilities. Business services. Some pets allowed (fee). | 6626 Hwy. 179 | 520/284–1433 or 800/385–0927 | fax 520/284–0487 | www.desertquailinn.com | 40 rooms, 1 suite | $54–$89, $150 suite | AE, D, DC, MC, V.

Sky Ranch Lodge. This hotel near the top of Airport Mesa has the best views in Sedona. Some rooms have private patios or balconies, stone fireplace, or kitchenettes. The grounds are planted with flowers. Some kitchenettes, some refrigerators, cable TV. Pool. Hot tub. Laundry facilities. Business services. Some pets allowed (fee). | Airport Rd. | 520/282–6400 | fax 520/282–7682 | www.skyranchlodge.com | 94 rooms, 2 cottages | $75–$160, $180 cottages | AE, MC, V.

SELIGMAN

Comfort Lodge of Seligman. This small roadside motel in downtown Seligman offers basic 1980s-style rooms, and is within walking distance of convenience stores and restaurants. Restaurant, complimentary Continental breakfast. Cable TV. Pets allowed. | 114 E. Chino St. | 520/422–3255 or 800/700–5054 | fax 520/422–3600 | www.rentor.com/seligman-hotel.htm | 16 rooms | $27 | AE, D, DC, MC, V.

Romney Motel. This single-story motel is on historic Route 66. There are a handful of restaurants and a bar within walking distance. Some microwaves, some refrigerators, cable TV. Business services. Some pets allowed. | 122 Rte. 66 | 520/422–3700 | fax 520/422–3680 | 28 rooms | $28–$40 | AE, MC, V.

SHOW LOW

Best Western Paint Pony Lodge. Some of the rooms at this motel right in Show Low have fireplaces. Restaurant, bar, complimentary Continental breakfast, room service. In-room data ports, some microwaves, some refrigerators, cable TV. Business services. Pets allowed (fee). | 581 W. Deuce of Clubs Dr. | 520/537–5773 | fax 520/537–5766 | www.bestwestern.com | 50 rooms | $74–$84 | AE, D, DC, MC, V.

Days Inn. This motel is in the center of town. Restaurant. Microwaves, refrigerators, cable TV. Pool. Beauty salon. Laundry facilities. Business services, airport shuttle. Some pets allowed (fee). | 480 W. Deuce of Clubs | 520/537–4356 | fax 520/537–8692 | 122 rooms | $69–$74 | AE, D, DC, MC, V.

SIERRA VISTA

Baxter's at Thunder Mountain Inn. Although this hotel rests at the foot of the Huachuca Mountains, the view is rather modest. Rooms feature copper and turquoise colors. Guests get $5 off breakfast at the hotel's restaurant, so you'll probably eat free. Restaurant. In-room data ports, kitchenettes, some microwaves, cable TV. Pool. Hot tub. Pets allowed.

| 1631 S. Hwy. 92, 85635 | 520/458–7900 or 800/222–5811 | fax 520/458–7900 | 103 rooms, 2 suites | $55–$85 | AE, D, DC, MC, V.

Windemere Resort & Conference Center. This modern three-story hotel is right in town and a short drive from Ramsey Canyon. Restaurant, bar, complimentary breakfast, room service. Some refrigerators, cable TV. Pool. Hot tub. Laundry facilities. Business services, airport shuttle. Some pets allowed. | 2047 S. Hwy. 92 | 520/459–5900 or 800/825–4656 | fax 520/458–1347 | 148 rooms, 3 suites | $80 rooms, $150–$200 suites | AE, D, DC, MC, V.

SPRINGERVILLE-EAGAR

Reed's Lodge. This lodge in the foothills of the White Mountains offers interesting accommodations with a decent view. Rooms have individually made Navajo print bedspreads on either queen- or king-size beds, and southwestern color schemes. Some in-room data ports, some microwaves, some refrigerators, cable TV. Shop, video games. Pets allowed. | 514 E. Main St., Springerville, 85938 | 520/333–4323 | fax 520/333–5191 | 45 rooms, 5 suites | $40–$50 | AE, D, DC, MC, V.

TEMPE

Best Western Inn of Tempe. The rooms at this motel are bright and feature impressionist paintings of the desert. There is a Denny's on the grounds, but not much else of note within walking distance. Tempe's Old Town is a bit over a mile to the south. Restaurant. In-room data ports, cable TV. Pool. Hot tub. Gym. Some pets allowed. | 670 N. Scottsdale Rd., 85281 | 480/784–2233 | www.innoftempe.com | 103 rooms | $60–$130 | AE, D, DC, MC, V.

Holiday Inn Express. This hotel 5 mi south of Sky Harbor airport is 1 mi from Arizona Mills Mall and 5 mi from downtown Tempe. Complimentary breakfast. In-room data ports, some microwaves, some refrigerators, cable TV. Pool. Hot tub. Laundry service. Business services, airport shuttle. Pets allowed. | 5300 S. Priest Dr. | 480/820–7500 | fax 480/730–6626 | www.hiexpress.com | 160 rooms | $90–$140 | AE, D, DC, MC, V.

Innsuites Tempe/Airport. This all-suite hotel is at the intersection if Interstate 10 and Highway 60, next to the Arizona Mills Mall. Restaurant, complimentary Continental breakfast. In-room data ports, some kitchenettes, some microwaves, some refrigerators, cable TV. Pool. Hot tub. 2 tennis courts. Gym. Playground. Laundry facilities. Business services, airport shuttle. Pets allowed (fee). | 1651 W. Baseline Rd. | 480/897–7900 or 800/842–4242 | fax 480/491–1008 | www.innsuites.com | 251 suites | $89–$139 | AE, D, DC, MC, V.

La Quinta Inn Phoenix/Tempe Sky Harbor Airport. This three-story motel is southeast of Sky Harbor airport, a few blocks south of University Avenue, and 3 mi from ASU. Complimentary Continental breakfast. In-room data ports, cable TV. Pool. Putting green. Laundry service. Business services, airport shuttle. Some pets allowed. | 911 S. 48th St. | 480/967–4465 | fax 480/921–9172 | www.laquinta.co | 129 rooms, 3 suites | $99–$129 | AE, D, DC, MC, V.

Residence Inn Tempe. This all-suite hotel is less than a half mile from the Arizona Mills Outlet Mall and 4 mi from Sun Devil Stadium. Complimentary Continental breakfast. In-room data ports, kitchenettes, microwaves, refrigerators, cable TV. Pool. Hot tub. Tennis court. Basketball, gym. Laundry facilities, laundry service. Business services. Pets allowed (fee). | 5075 S. Priest Dr., 85282 | 480/756–2122 or 800/331–3131 | fax 602/345–2802 | www.residenceinn.com | 126 suites | $130–$180 | AE, D, DC, MC, V.

Tempe Mission Palms Hotel. Between the ASU campus and Old Town Tempe, this four-story courtyard hotel has a handsome lobby and an energetic young staff. It's next to Sun Devil Stadium, which is great if you are attending an ASU sports event. Restaurant, bar. In-room data ports, some refrigerators, some in-room hot tubs, cable TV. Pool. Hot tub. 3 tennis courts. Gym. Shops. Business services, airport shuttle. Pets allowed. | 60 E. 5th St. |

480/894–1400 or 800/547–8705 | fax 480/968–7677 | www.tempemissionpalms.com | 286 rooms, 17 suites | $189–$239, $395–$389 suites | AE, D, DC, MC, V.

Phoenix/Tempe-University Travelodge. This motel is near ASU, within walking distance of Sun Devil Stadium. Complimentary Continental breakfast. Some microwaves, some refrigerators, cable TV. 2 pools. Laundry facilities. Business services. Some pets allowed (fee). | 1005 E. Apache Blvd. | 480/968–7871 | fax 480/968–3991 | www.travelodge.com | 93 rooms | $49–$89 | AE, D, DC, MC, V.

TOMBSTONE

Best Western Lookout Lodge. Touches like Victorian-style lamps and locally made wooden clocks give these rooms more character than the typical motel. Views of the Dragoon Mountains are spectacular. Complimentary Continental breakfast. Cable TV. Pool. Business services. Some pets allowed (fee). | U.S. 80 W, 85638 | 520/457–2223 | fax 520/457–3870 | 40 rooms | $68–$84 | AE, D, DC, MC, V.

Tombstone Boarding House Bed & Breakfast. These two meticulously restored 1880s adobe homes sit side by side in a quiet residential neighborhood, away from the bustle of the main street. Rooms are spotless and are furnished with period antiques. Restaurant, complimentary breakfast. No room phones, TV in common area. Library. Some pets allowed. No smoking. | 108 N. 4th St., 85638 | 520/457–3716 | fax 520/457–3038 | 6 rooms, 1 cabin | $65–$80 rooms, $60 cabin | MC, V.

Tombstone Bordello B&B. The last remaining bordello in town moved to Allen Street in the 1920s. It's now a B&B decorated in a restrained Victorian style. It's charming, yet small, with views of the Dragoon Mountains from the porch and balcony. Complimentary breakfast. Cable TV, no room phones. Some pets allowed. | 101 W. Allen St., 85638 | 520/457–2394 | 2 rooms | $59–$69 | No credit cards.

Tombstone Motel. Right on the town's main street, this comfortable and well-run motel with basic rooms is catercorner from the offices of the *Tombstone Epitaph*. It will remind you of motor courts of years past. Some refrigerators, cable TV. Some pets allowed. | 502 E. Fremont St., 85638 | 520/457–3478 or 888/455–3478 | www.tombstonemotel.com | 12 rooms, 1 suite | $45–$70, $90–$120 suite | MC, V.

TUBA CITY

Quality Inn Tuba City. The standard rooms at this motel are spacious and well maintained. The Tuba City Trading Post is also here. It's fine for an overnight stop before or after a visit to the Hopi Mesas between Tuba City and Kayenta. Restaurant. Some in-room data ports, some in-room safes, cable TV. Laundry facilities. Business services. Pets allowed. | Main St. and Moenabe Rd., 86045 | 520/283–4545 or 800/644–8383 | fax 520/283–4144 | www.qualityinn.com | 80 rooms | $102 | AE, D, DC, MC, V.

TUCSON

Best Western Innsuites–Catalina Foothills. This all-suite hotel is in the foothills in northwest Tucson. Restaurant, bar, complimentary breakfast, room service. Kitchenettes, microwaves, refrigerators, some in-room hot tubs, cable TV. Pool. Hot tub. Tennis court. Gym. Video games. Laundry service. Business services. Some pets allowed. | 6201 N. Oracle Rd. | 520/297–8111 | fax 520/297–2935 | www.bestwestern.com | 159 rooms, 74 suites | $109–$129, $129–$179 suites | AE, D, DC, MC, V.

Doubletree Hotel at Reid Park. Only 8 mi from the airport and downtown, this midtown hotel is directly across from Reid Park. Some rooms have views of the park. Restaurant, bar, room service. In-room data ports, some kitchenettes, some minibars, some refrigerators, cable TV. Pool. Tennis court. Gym. Business services, airport shuttle. Some pets allowed (fee). | 445 S. Alvernon Way | 520/881–4200 | fax 520/323–5225 | www.doubletree.com | 288 rooms, 7 suites | $129, $150 suites | AE, D, DC, MC, V.

Embassy Suites Broadway. This reliable three-story all-suite hotel in midtown is 10 mi from the airport, 5 mi from downtown, and close to malls, theaters, and restaurants. All suites are two rooms and open onto an atrium lobby. Bar, complimentary breakfast. Kitchenettes, microwaves, refrigerators, cable TV. Pool. Hot tub. Laundry facilities. Some pets allowed (fee). | 5335 E. Broadway | 520/745–2700 | fax 520/790–9232 | www. embassysuites.com | 142 suites | $189 | AE, D, DC, MC, V.

Embassy Suites Hotel and Conference Center. This comfortable, three-story all-suite hotel is south of downtown, near the airport. Restaurant, bar, complimentary breakfast. Kitchenettes, microwaves, refrigerators, cable TV. Pool. Hot tub. Gym. Laundry facilities. Business services, airport shuttle. Pets allowed. | 7051 S. Tucson Blvd. | 520/573–0700 | fax 520/741–9645 | 204 suites | $139–$169 | AE, D, DC, MC, V.

Flamingo Hotel. This two-story pink motel is popular with families, who appreciate the affordable rates and proximity to downtown attractions. Complimentary Continental breakfast. Some refrigerators, cable TV. Pool. Hot tub. Laundry facilities. Business services. Some pets allowed. | 1300 N. Stone Ave. | 520/770–1910 | fax 520/770–0750 | 80 rooms | $50–$106 | AE, D, DC, MC, V.

Hawthorn Suites. This all-suite hotel in northeast Tucson is within walking distance of 30 restaurants. It's 6 mi from Saguaro National Park East. Complimentary breakfast. In-room data ports, some kitchenettes, some microwaves, some refrigerators, cable TV. Pool. Hot tub. Laundry facilities, laundry service. Business services. Pets allowed (fee). | 7007 E. Tanque Verde Rd. | 520/298–2300 | fax 520/298–6756 | www.hawthorn.com | 30 rooms, 60 suites | $100–$115, $120–$135 suites | AE, D, DC, MC, V.

La Quinta Hotel. This hotel on the east side of Tucson, built in 1975, is close to restaurants, a mall, and movie theaters. Complimentary Continental breakfast. Cable TV. Pool. Hot tub. Laundry facilities. Business services. Some pets allowed. | 6404 E. Broadway | 520/747–1414 | fax 520/745–6903 | www.laquinta.com | 144 rooms | $49–$129 | AE, D, DC, MC, V.

Presidio Plaza Hotel. This 14-story hotel is downtown, next to Tucson Convention Center. It's a five-minute walk to restaurants and museums. Restaurant, bar. Some microwaves, some refrigerators, cable TV. Pool. Gym. Business services. Some pets allowed. | 181 W. Broadway | 520/624–8711 | fax 520/623–8121 | 299 rooms, 10 suites | $99–$139, $185 suites | AE, D, DC, MC, V.

Rodeway Inn–Grant Road at I–10. This motel is 2 mi north of downtown, just off Interstate 10. Restaurant, bar, room service. Some refrigerators, cable TV. Pool. Hot tub. Laundry facilities, laundry service. Business services. Pets allowed (fee). | 1365 W. Grant Rd. | 520/622–7791 | fax 520/629–0201 | www.rodewayinn.com | 146 rooms | $60–$130 | AE, D, DC, MC, V.

Sheraton El Conquistador Resort and Country Club. This luxury resort at the base of the Catalina mountains 15 mi northwest of Tucson draws a large family contingent. Rooms are in the main hotel or private casitas. Some suites have kiva-style fireplaces. 4 restaurants, 2 bars, room service. Minibars, some microwaves, cable TV. 4 pools. Beauty salon, hot tub, massage, sauna. Driving range, 2 18-hole golf courses, putting green, 3 tennis courts. Basketball, gym, hiking, horseback riding, racquetball, volleyball, bicycles. Shops. Children's programs (ages 5–12). Laundry service. Business services, parking (fee). Some pets allowed. | 1000 N. Oracle Rd. | 520/544–5000 or 800/325–7832 | fax 520/544–1228 | www.sheraton.com | 328 rooms, 100 suites | $130–$300, $160–$850 suites | AE, D, DC, MC, V.

Wayward Winds Lodge. This ranch-style lodge with oversize rooms is north of downtown, off Interstate 10. Picnic area, complimentary Continental breakfast (in season). Some kitchenettes, some microwaves, some refrigerators, cable TV. Pool. Laundry facilities. Business services. Some pets allowed. | 707 W. Miracle Mile | 520/791–7526 or 800/791–9503 | fax 520/791–9502 | 40 rooms | $30–$99 | AE, D, DC, MC, V.

Westward Look Resort. This hotel in the foothills has excellent city, desert, and mountain views. Built in 1912, it was originally a private residence but became a resort in 1943. The rooms are done up with mission-style furnishings and leather chairs. 2 restaurants, bar, room service. In-room data ports, minibars, some refrigerators, cable TV. 3 pools. 3 hot tubs, massage. 8 tennis courts. Gym, horseback riding, bicycles. Business services. Some pets allowed. | 245 E. Ina Rd. | 520/297–1151 or 800/722–2500 | fax 520/297–9023 | www.westwardlook.com | 244 rooms | $169–$369 | AE, D, DC, MC, V.

Windmill Inn at St. Philip's Plaza. This all-suite hotel is in the St. Philip's Plaza shopping center in the foothills section of north Tucson. The suites all have sleeper sofas and two TVs. It's one of the better chain options in town, and, yes, there is a windmill on the front lawn. Complimentary Continental breakfast. Microwaves, refrigerators, cable TV. Pool. Hot tub. Bicycles. Library. Laundry facilities. Business services. Some pets allowed. | 4250 N. Campbell Ave. | 520/577–0007 or 800/547–4747 | fax 520/577–0045 | www.windmillinns.com | 122 suites | $65–$139 standard suites, $135–$395 king and deluxe suites | AE, D, DC, MC, V.

WICKENBURG

Americinn. At this family-run hotel you'll find small-town hospitality and affordable, basic rooms, some with patios. Restaurant, bar, room service. Some microwaves, some refrigerators, cable TV. Pool. Hot tub. Business services. Pets allowed (fee). | 850 E. Wickenburg Way | 520/684–5461 | fax 520/684–5461 | 29 rooms | $66–$82 | AE, D, DC, MC, V.

Best Western Rancho Grande. This stucco motel downtown has southwestern decor. Complimentary Continental breakfast. Some kitchenettes, some microwaves, some refrigerators, cable TV. Pool. Hot tub. Tennis. Playground. Business services, airport shuttle. Pets allowed. | 293 E. Wickenburg Way | 520/684–5445 | fax 520/684–7380 | 80 rooms, 10 suites | $66–$80, $88–$99 suites | AE, D, DC, MC, V.

WILLCOX

Best Western Plaza Inn. You'll have mountain views from this reliable motel 10 minutes from the Rex Allen Museum. Restaurant, bar, complimentary breakfast, room service. Some refrigerators, cable TV. Pool. Laundry facilities, laundry service. Business services. Some pets allowed (fee). | 1100 W. Rex Allen Dr. | 520/384–3556 | fax 520/384–2679 | 91 rooms | $59–$79 | AE, D, DC, MC, V.

Days Inn Willcox. This motel is right off Interstate 10 next to the Safeway shopping center. In-room data ports, cable TV. Pool. Laundry facilities. Business services. Some pets allowed. | 724 N. Bisbee Ave. | 520/384–4222 | fax 520/384–3785 | 73 rooms | $46–$65 | AE, D, DC, MC, V.

WILLIAMS

Holiday Inn. This family-friendly motel is three blocks from the Grand Canyon Railway Depot and a mile from Cataract Lake, which offers good fishing. Restaurant, bar, room service. Some refrigerators, cable TV. Pool. Hot tub. Gym. Laundry facilities, laundry service. Business services. Pets allowed. | 950 N. Grand Canyon Blvd. | 520/635–4114 | fax 520/635–2700 | 120 rooms, 12 suites | $79–$99, $99–$119 suites | AE, D, DC, MC, V.

Motel 6. This inexpensive motel is across the street from a Mexican restaurant and within walking distance of others on the west side of Williams. Cable TV. Pool. Hot tub. Laundry facilities. Business services. Pets allowed. | 831 W. Bill Williams Ave. | 520/635–9000 | fax 520/635–2300 | 52 rooms | $45–$69 | AE, D, DC, MC, V.

Mountainside Inn. This motel on 27 acres is one of the better maintained in town. There's a good steak house on the premises and country-and-western bands in summer. Hiking trails crisscross the property. Restaurant, bar, picnic area, room service. Some microwaves, some refrigerators, cable TV. Pool. Hot tub. Hiking. Some pets allowed (fee). | 642 E. Bill Williams Ave. | 520/635–4431 | fax 520/635–2292 | thegrandcanyon.com/mountainsideinn | 96 rooms | $86–$125 | AE, D, DC, MC, V.

Quality Inn Mountain Ranch and Resort. Just 6 mi east of town, this hotel is relatively convenient to Williams. Rooms are simple and predictable, but do offer views of the San Francisco Peaks. Restaurant, bar, complimentary Continental breakfast. Cable TV. Pool. Hot tub. 2 tennis courts. Horseback riding. Pets allowed (fee). | 6701 E. Mountain Ranch, 86046 | 520/635–2693 | fax 520/635–4188 | www.qualityinn.com | 73 rooms | $75–$110 | AE, D, MC, V.

WINSLOW

Best Western Adobe Inn. This motel is right off Interstate 40. Restaurant, bar, room service. Cable TV. Pool. Hot tub. Laundry facilities. Business services. Some pets allowed (fee). | 1701 N. Park Dr. | 520/289–4638 | fax 520/289–5514 | www.daysinn.com | 70 rooms, 2 suites | $55–$70, $80 suites | AE, D, DC, MC, V.

Econo Lodge at I–40. This motel is right off Interstate 40 at exit 253, on the northeast side of Winslow. Some microwaves, some refrigerators, cable TV. Pool. Laundry facilities. Business services. Pets allowed (fee). | 1706 N. Park Dr. | 520/289–4687 | fax 520/289–9377 | 72 rooms | $45–$69 | AE, D, DC, MC, V.

Winslow Inn. This motel is dirt cheap, rooms are downright institutional, and you may be awakened by the trains that churn by. Cable TV. Pets allowed. | 701 W. 3rd St., 86047. | 520/289–9389 | fax 520/289–9197 | 63 rooms | $30 | AE, D, DC, MC, V.

YUMA

Innsuites Yuma. This all-suite, low-rise hotel is close to the Colorado River Park and offers large rooms. It's one of the better chain options in Yuma. Complimentary Continental breakfast. In-room data ports, microwaves, refrigerators, cable TV. Pool. Hot tub. 2 tennis courts. Gym. Library. Laundry facilities, laundry service. Business services. Pets allowed. | 1450 Castle Dome Ave. | 520/783–8341 | fax 520/783–1349 | www.innsuites.com | 166 suites | $69–$139 | AE, D, DC, MC, V.

Interstate 8 Inn. This inexpensive, independent motel built in 1990 offers basic rooms within walking distance of several restaurants. It's right off Interstate 8. Picnic area. Some microwaves, refrigerators, cable TV. Pool. Hot tub. Laundry facilities. Business services. Some pets allowed. | 2730 S. 4th Ave. | 520/726–6110 or 800/821–7465 | fax 520/726–7711 | 120 rooms | $57 | AE, D, DC, MC.

Martinez Lake Resort. On Martinez Lake, 35 mi north of Yuma, this resort has spartan cabins, but people come here to waterski, fish for catfish, and spend time away from urban life rather than lounge about their rooms. The restaurant features live bands every Saturday. The resort is off U.S. 95, 13 mi down Martinez Drive, on the lake. Restaurant, bar. No room phones, no TV. Lake. Water sports, boating. Pets allowed (fee). | Martinez Dr., 85365 | 520/783–9589 or 800/876–7004 | fax 520/782–3360 | www.martinezlake.com | 8 cabins, 4 houses | $65 cabins, $135–$235 houses | D, MC, V.

Radisson Suites Inn. This upscale all-suite hotel is 2 mi from the airport and within walking distance of several restaurants. It's a sprawling hotel, with a well-manicured courtyard. Complimentary Continental breakfast. Microwaves, refrigerators, cable TV. Pool. Hot tub. Laundry facilities, laundry service. Business services, airport shuttle. Pets allowed. | 2600 S. 4th Ave. | 520/726–4830 | fax 520/341–1152 | 164 suites | $58–$119 | AE, D, DC, MC, V.

Shilo Inn Yuma. On the outskirts of Yuma, this quiet, secluded hotel has a tropical court-yard. Despite being a conference center, it's popular with leisure travelers. Restaurant, bar, complimentary breakfast. In-room data ports, some kitchenettes, some microwaves, some refrigerators, cable TV. Pool. Hot tub, sauna, steam room. Gym. Laundry facilities, laundry service. Business services. Pets allowed. | 1550 S. Castle Dome Rd. | 520/782–9511 | fax 520/783–1538 | www.shiloinn.com | 134 rooms | $89–$260 | AE, D, DC, MC, V.

Yuma Airport Travelodge. This two-story motel is near the Yuma airport, 3 mi from downtown. Restaurant, bar, picnic area, complimentary Continental breakfast. Some in-room data ports, some microwaves, some refrigerators, cable TV. Pool. Hot tub. Laundry facilities, laundry service. Business services. Some pets allowed. | 711 E. 32nd St. | 520/726–4721 | fax 520/344–0452 | 80 rooms | $62 | AE, D, MC, V.

Arkansas

ALTUS

Ozark's Motel. This cut-stone and shingled motel is at the foot of the Ozark Mountains less than 1 mi from the Arkansas River and the River Bridge. It sits amid the wildlife and wooded scenery of west Altus. Restaurant. In-room data ports, some microwaves, some refrigerators. Cable TV, room phones. Some pets allowed. | 1711 W. Commercial St. 72949 | 501/667–1500 | fax 501/667–1011 | 35 rooms | $36–$39 | AE, D, MC, V.

ARKADELPHIA

Best Western Continental Inn. This service-oriented hotel, a brick colonial style building, is about 4 mi from downtown, near Hot Springs and two universities, 5 mi from DeGray Lake, and ¼ mi from Caddo River. The inn is at exit 78 off I–30. Complimentary Continental breakfast. Cable TV. Pool. Playground. Laundry facilities. Pets allowed. | 136 Valley Rd. | 870/246–5592 | fax 870/246–3585 | www.bestwestern.com | 58 rooms | $39–$79 | AE, D, DC, MC, V.

Days Inn. Standard accommodations are what you'll find in this two-story motor hotel. DeGray Lake is 5 mi away and the Hot Springs horse track is 30 mi away. The inn is at the second Arkadelphia exit off I–30. Cable TV. Pool. Sauna, hot tub. Business services. Pets allowed. | 137 Valley St. | 870/246–3031 | fax 870/246–3743 | www.daysinn.com/ctg/cgi-bin/ DaysInn | 53 rooms | $45–$59 | AE, D, DC, MC, V.

Holiday Inn Express. This two-story hostelry is 4 mi from Lake DeGray. Complimentary Continental breakfast. In-room data ports, in-room safes, some microwaves, some refrigerators. Cable TV, room phones. Outdoor pool. Laundry facilities. Business services. Pets allowed. | 150 Valley St. 71923 | 870/230–1506 | fax 870/230–1015 | holiday@ezclick.net | www.holiday-inn.com | 100 rooms | $65–$69 | AE, D, DC, MC, V.

Quality Inn. On the interstate and close to restaurants, you can bowl at an alley 3 mi from this simple Quality Inn, and golf is just 7 mi away (but no guest privileges at the course). The inn is on I–30 at exit 78, just outside of town. Some in-room hot tubs. Cable TV. Pool. Laundry facilities. Pets allowed. | I–30 and Rte. 7 | 870/246–5855 | fax 870/246–8552 | 63 rooms | $55–$77 | AE, D, DC, MC, V.

BATESVILLE

Ramada Inn. This chain lodging is 1 mi from White River and 3–4 mi from the airport. The large brick building with a courtyard is right off Hwy. 167N, close to downtown. Restaurant, room service. Some refrigerators. Cable TV. Outdoor pool. Hot tub. Laundry facilities. Pets allowed. | 1325 N. St. Louis St. | 870/698–1800 | 124 rooms | $60–$70 | AE, D, DC, MC, V.

BENTON

Best Western Inn. This Best Western Inn is near Jerry Van Dyke's soda shop, a movie theater, and the location where the film *Sling Blade* was made. Restaurant. In-room data ports. Business services. Pets allowed. No smoking. | 17036 I–30 | 501/778–9695 | fax 501/776–1699 | 65 rooms | $45–$66 | AE, D, DC, MC, V.

BENTONVILLE

Best Western. This is a reliable chain option; the notable red-brick building is a short drive from several popular attractions, including the Country Music Show and the Great Eureka Springs Passion Play. The hotel is on Business 71, off Hwy 71 Bypass at exit 65, just 10 mi from the airport. In-room data ports, some refrigerators. Cable TV. Pool. Business services. Pets allowed. | 2307 S.E. Walton Blvd. | 501/273–9727 | fax 501/273–1763 | www.bestwestern.com/ | 55 rooms | $50–$58 | AE, D, DC, MC, V.

Super 8 Motel. This bungalow-type motel is 10 mi from the Northwest Regional Arkansas Airport and two blocks from a bus terminal, where there are several popular restaurants and clubs. The motel is off I–540, exit 85. Picnic area, complimentary Continental breakfast. Cable TV. Outdoor pool. Pets allowed (fee). | 2301 S.E. Walton Blvd. | 501/273–1818 | fax 501/273–5529 | 52 rooms | $50–$55 | AE, D, DC, MC, V.

BLYTHEVILLE

Days Inn. This typical motor hotel is close to shopping and a casino. Memphis, Tennessee, is 65 mi away, and it's just 4 mi to the Missouri state line. Complimentary Continental breakfast. Cable TV. Pool. Playground. Laundry facilities. Pets allowed (fee). | 200 S. Access Rd. 72315 | 870/763–1241 | fax 870/763–6696 | 122 rooms | $51–$62 | AE, D, DC, MC, V.

Hampton Inn. This standard chain accommodation off I–55 has an exterior stucco finish. The large lobby is warm and denlike, in cherry reds. The inn is next door to the Great Wall of China restaurant and within 2 mi of the industrial park and downtown shopping. You get discounts to the Ultimate Fitness Center less than 1 mi away. Picnic area, complimentary Continental breakfast. Cable TV, room phones. Outdoor pool. Pets allowed (fee). | 301 N. Access Rd. 72315 | 870/763–5220 or 800/426–7866 | fax 870/762–1397 | www.hampton-inn.com | 87 rooms | $63–$65 | AE, D, DC, V.

Holiday Inn Holidome. This brick and stucco Holiday Inn is in town, near Walker Park, where you can swim. Walker Park also has a picnic area and the county fair in September. The Holidome is full of plants, and used for parties and gatherings. You can rent a car at an on-site concierge desk. Restaurants, room service. Cable TV. Indoor-outdoor pools. Hot tub, steam room. Laundry facilities. Pets allowed. | 1121 E. Main St. | 870/763–5800 | fax 870/763–1326 | 153 rooms | $65–$68 | AE, D, DC, MC, V.

BULL SHOALS

Gaston's White River Resort. At this modern, family riverside fishing resort, there's no lack of outdoor activities. The single-story buildings are surrounded by lots of woods and other vegetation. The staff here will show you the hot spots and the kitchen will pack you a box lunch for your outing; or you can enjoy a picnic, a cookout, and the riverside walk. There are two nature trails. To get there, take Hwy. 178 to Bull Shoals dam. The resort is 1 1/2 mi beneath the dam on the river road. Bar, dining room, picnic area. In-room data ports, some kitchenettes, refrigerators. Cable TV. Pool. Tennis. Hiking. Dock, boating, fishing. Playground. Business services, airport shuttle. Pets allowed. | 1777 River Rd. Lakeview 72642 | 870/431–5202 | fax 870/431–5216 | 40 rooms, 35 cottages | $76–$120, $169 cottages | MC, V.

Mar-Mar Resort and Crooked Creek Tackle. This "mosquito-free" hotel in the Ozarks is two blocks from the Bull Shoals boat dock. It's a good place to go if you like to fish, or if you want to visit Bull Shoals State Park. The L-shaped, single-level resort, built in the 1950s, is in the middle of town on Hwy. 178, which becomes Central Blvd. Look for the big white marquee with the fisherman rocking in a boat. Some kitchenettes. Cable TV. Pets allowed. | 1512 Central Blvd. (U.S. 178) | 870/445–4444 | fax 870/445–7173 | www.marmarresort.com/ marmar/ | 13 rooms | $39 or $43 | AE, MC, V.

Rocky Hollow Lodge. These six stone and cedar cottages with hardwood floors and full kitchens have provided a Bull Shoals Lake–side experience since the 1950s. Within six blocks of Rocky Hollow there is a large marina with all types of watercraft rentals and a full service scuba shop. Picnic area. Kitchenettes, microwaves, refrigerators. Cable TV. Outdoor pool, lake. Volleyball. Dock, water sports, boating, fishing. Some pets allowed (fee). | 1306 Lake St. 72619 | 800/887–6259 or 870/445–4400 | rocky@southshore.com | www.bullshoals. com/rockyhollow | 6 rooms | $65–$90 | MC, V.

Shady Oaks. Guided fishing excursions and many other outdoor activities are available at this resort. Picnic area. Kitchenettes, microwaves, refrigerators. Pool, lake. Dock, water sports, boating, fishing. Video games. Playground. Laundry facilities. Pets allowed. | HC 62, Flippin 72634 | 870/453–8420 or 800/467–6257 | fax 870/453–7813 | 11 cottages | $60–$70 cottages | D, MC, V.

CONWAY

Best Western. This is a standard two-story brick building with simple conveniences, 5 mi from the Toadsuck Ferry Lock and Dam. It's on I-40 at exit 127. Restaurant. In-room data ports. Cable TV. Pool. Laundry facilities. Airport shuttle, free parking. Pets allowed. | 816 E. Oak St. | 501/329–9855 | fax 501/327–6110 | 70 rooms | $59–$69 | AE, D, DC, MC, V.

Comfort Inn. This two-level standard hotel is across from a sports center and atop a sloping rock formation on U.S. 65. From Little Rock, take I-40E, then take a right onto Hwy. 65. The inn is visible from the road. Complimentary Continental breakfast. Cable TV. Pool. Business services. Pets allowed. | 150 U.S. 65N | 501/329–0300 | fax 501/329–8367 | 58 rooms, 2 suites | $56–$59, $109 suites | AE, D, DC, MC, V.

Days Inn. Pink brick, with all outside access, this typical chain hotel is close to many area attractions. Go west on I-40, take a right on exit 127, and look for it from a block away. If coming east, take a left. Complimentary Continental breakfast. In-room data ports. Cable TV. Pool. Business services. Pets allowed (fee). | 1002 E. Oak St. | 501/450–7575 | fax 501/450–7001 | 58 rooms | $47–$55 | AE, D, DC, MC, V.

Ramada Inn. L-shaped, with exterior halls and a circular driveway, this hotel has catfish and trout fishing 2–3 mi away at Lake Conway. You can play tennis, soccer, and baseball in the nearby 5th Avenue Park. You can get there via I-40 to exit 127. Restaurant, room service. In-room data ports, some refrigerators. Cable TV. Pool. Business services. Pets allowed. | 815 E. Oak St. | 501/329–8392 | fax 501/329–0430 | 78 rooms | $50–$59 | AE, D, DC, MC, V.

EL DORADO

Best Western Kings Inn Conference Center. A big property, the landscape spreads out to hold three brick buildings. This chain hotel is 20 min from Big Sky Airport. There is a recreation facility and pool as well as a full-service restaurant. The hotel, which has a beautiful atrium, is close to golf, Moro Bay State Park, and local museums. The Conference Center is at the intersection of Hwy. "82 business" and Hwy. 167, on the southwest side of town. Restaurant, picnic areas, room service. Refrigerators. Cable TV. Indoor-outdoor pools, wading pool. Hot tub, sauna. Tennis court. Racquetball. Laundry facilities. Business services, airport shuttle, free parking. Pets allowed. | 1920 Junction City Rd. | 870/862–5191 | fax 870/863–7511 | www.bestwestern.com | 131 rooms | $57–$71 | AE, D, DC, MC, V.

Comfort Inn. This is a typical chain hotel 10 min from shopping, movie theaters, and restaurants downtown at "The Square," right off the bypass of "82 business" and Hwy. 167. Complimentary Continental breakfast. In-room data ports. Cable TV. Pool. Hot tub. Laundry facilities. Airport shuttle. Pets allowed. | 2303 Junction City Rd. | 870/863–6677 | fax 870/863–8611 | 70 rooms | $60–$71 | AE, D, DC, MC, V.

EUREKA SPRINGS

Alpen-Dorf. Alpen-Dorf is a family-owned hotel overlooking a nearby valley. The style is German-Swiss on the outside, contemporary on the inside. The view and the pleasantness of the people who run the place stay with you for a while. Alpen-Dorf is just outside of town, on Hwy. 62, 1 mi east of Passion Play Road. Complimentary Continental breakfast. Some kitchenettes. Cable TV. Pool. Hot tub. Playground. Pets allowed. | 6554 U.S. 62 | 501/253–9475 or 800/771–9876 (reservations) | fax 501/253–2928 | alpdorf@nwaft.com | www.eureka-usa.com | 30 rooms | $24–$125, seasonal | AE, D, MC, V.

Basin Park. The place is noted in *Ripley's Believe It or Not!* because each of its seven floors is a ground floor. Built in 1905, the Arts and Crafts–style hotel nestles against the side of a mountain, the only seven-story building downtown. Restaurant, bar, complimentary Continental breakfast. Some in-room hot tubs. Cable TV. Pool. Business services, free parking. Pets allowed. | 12 Spring St. | 501/253–7837 or 800/643–4972 | fax 501/253–6985 | www.basinpark.com | 61 rooms, including 3 honeymoon suites | $65–$175 | AE, D, MC, V.

Best Western Inn of the Ozarks. Many of the rooms here have views of the woods. The inn has standard accommodations in a two-story building. It's on Hwy. 62, the Eureka Springs exit, on the west side of town. Restaurant, picnic area. In-room data ports. Cable TV. Pool. Tennis court. Laundry facilities. Business services. Pets allowed. | 207 W. Van Buren | 501/253–9768 or 800/552–3785 | 122 rooms, including 4 suites | $59–$99, $129–$149 suites | AE, D, DC, MC, V.

Colonial Mansion Inn. A beautiful front greets you at this inn. Half of the rooms are in a Colonial mansion and half are in an adjacent inn on 6 wooded acres. Some of the rooms are oversized. The town trolley lets you off on Route 23 near the inn, which is also close to a magic show and country-western music. Although the inn is one block from Hwy. 62, it is quiet. Complimentary Continental breakfast. Cable TV. Pool. Business services. Pets allowed. | Rte. 23S | 501/253–7300 or 800/638–2622 | fax 501/253–7304 | 30 rooms, 1 suite | $32–$68, $85–$100 | AE, D, MC, V | Closed Dec. 15–Feb. 12.

Crescent Hotel. Built in 1886, this full-service, four-story Victorian hotel overlooks downtown Eureka Springs. It includes the New Moon Spa, where you'll find hydrotherapy, Vichy water-massage showers, homeopathic healing, and a workout and fitness area. To get there, take Hwy. 62 to the "historic loop," then follow Hwy. 62B to the hotel. 2 restaurants, room service. Cable TV. Pool. Pets allowed. | 75 Prospect Ave. | 501/253–9766 | fax 501/253–5296 | info@crescent-hotel.com | www.crescent-hotel.com | 68 rooms | $89–$145 | AE, D, DC, MC, V.

Dogwood Inn. A family-owned Victorian-style hotel, the place is homey and quiet, and just 1½ mi from downtown. You can take your coffee on a porch that includes a fireplace and overlooks dense woods. The inn is off Hwy. 62 on Hwy. 23S, and about 4 blocks from I-65. Complimentary Continental breakfast. In-room data ports. Cable TV. Pool. Hot tub. Playground. Business services. Pets allowed (fee). | 170 Huntsville Rd. | 501/253–7200 or 800/544–1884 | 33 rooms | $38–$68 | AE, D, MC, V.

Motel 6. This motel has a *Gone With the Wind* theme with pictures of Southern mansions, rooms named after the novel's characters, and other furnishings that recall mid-19th-century life. The Victorian-style establishment has steeples, Sheetrock walls, and pastel yellow siding; it is across from the Ozark Mountain Hoedown on the east side of town. Complimentary Continental breakfast. Microwaves, refrigerators, some in-room hot tubs. Cable TV, room phones. Outdoor pool. Pets allowed. | 3169 E. Van Buren St. 72632 | 501/253–5600 | fax 501/253–2110 | motel6@arkansas.net | 61 rooms, including 5 suites | $39–$119 | AE, D, MC, V.

Red Bud Manor B and B Inn. There are three rooms reserved for guests in this southern Victorian home (1891) on the "historic loop" downtown. It is shaded by an expanse of woods. The gourmet complimentary breakfast may include strawberry Romanoff, quiche, or soufflé. Complimentary breakfast. Refrigerators, in-room hot tubs. Cable TV. Laundry facilities. Pets allowed. | 7 Kings Hwy. | 501/253–9649 | 3 rooms | $90–$135 | D, MC, V.

Roadrunner Inn. This hilltop motel is on a peninsula extending into Beaver Lake. All the rooms have a view of the water. The marina, with boating, swimming, and park recreation, is 1 mi away. The inn is 10 mi west of town, but getting there can be a little tricky, so you may need to call for directions. Picnic area. Kitchenettes, refrigerators. Pets allowed. | 3034 Mundell Rd. | 501/253–8166 or 888/253–8166 (reservations) | 12 rooms | $29– $44 | AE, DC, MC, V | Closed mid-Nov.–mid-Mar.

Swiss Village. The Eureka trolley stops close to this hotel on U.S. 62; it's also near restaurants and the Opry music hall. The Swiss Village is in town, on the junction of Hwy. 62 and Hwy. 23, next door to the antiques mall. Picnic area, complimentary Continental breakfast. Some in-room hot tubs. Cable TV. Outdoor pool. Pets allowed. | 183 E. Van Buren St. | 501/253–9541 or 800/447–6525 | 38 rooms | $49–$69 | AE, D, MC, V.

Tradewinds. Some of this motor inn's rooms and cabins were built in the 1960s and some in the 1980s. It's ½ mi from downtown shopping and restaurants and is on Hwy. 62W, next door to the Chamber of Commerce. Picnic area. Some kitchenettes. Cable TV. Pool. Pets allowed. | 77 Kings Hwy. | 501/253–9774 or 800/242–1615 | 17 rooms | $42–$52 | AE, D, MC, V | Closed Jan., Feb.

FAYETTEVILLE

Best Western Windsor Suites. This two-story standard chain hotel has many conveniences and is six blocks from the University of Arkansas, 25 mi from Beaver Lake, and 60 mi from Eureka Springs. You can reach the hotel via U.S. Hwy. 71, exit 43; it's near the bypass of Hwy. 62 and 71. Complimentary Continental breakfast. In-room data ports, some refrigerators, some in-room hot tubs. Cable TV. Indoor pool. Hot tub. Exercise equipment. Laundry facilities. Business services. Some pets allowed. | 1122 S. Futrall Dr. | 501/ 587–1400 | 68 rooms, 37 suites | $60–$70, $130 suites | AE, D, DC, MC, V.

Days Inn. When you stay at this older Days Inn, built around 1963, you can show your hotel key at the Butcher Block restaurant next door and get a discount on all entrées, including the much-loved prime rib. You can shop at the Northwest Arkansas Mall, watch the Razorbacks play football at the University of Arkansas, or visit the Walton Art Center, each just 2 mi away. The inn is 2½ mi from exit 66 on I–540. Complimentary Continental breakfast. Cable TV. Pool. Laundry facilities. Business services. Some pets allowed (fee). | 2402 N. College Ave. | 501/443–4323 | 150 rooms, 6 suites | $50–$70, $100–$125 suites | AE, D, DC, MC, V.

Hilton. The tallest building downtown, this 15-story hotel has a splendid view of the Ozark Mountains and is only three blocks from the Walton Art Center. The University of Arkansas is ¼ mi away. The hotel is about 5 mi from Hwy. 71 Business. Restaurant, bar. Cable TV. Indoor-outdoor pool. Exercise equipment. Business services, airport shuttle. Some pets allowed. | 70 N. East Ave. | 501/442–5555 | fax 501/442–2105 | 235 rooms | $113–$125 | AE, D, DC, MC, V.

Motel 6. This typical chain motel is close to restaurants and shopping at the War Eagle Craft Fair and a 15-min drive from Fort Smith Regional Airport. You are 3 mi from the downtown antiques district and 8 mi from the Fort Smith Historic District. To get to the motel, take I–40 to exit 5. Cable TV. Pool. Some pets allowed. | 2980 N. College Ave. | 501/443–4351 | fax 501/444–8034 | 99 rooms | $35–$52 | AE, D, DC, MC, V.

Ramada Inn. All the rooms are reached from outside corridors at this two-story Ramada. The University of Arkansas and the Walton Art Center are both a quick 5-mi drive away. The inn is easy to get to; after you take U.S. 540 to Exit 67 (Hwy. Bus. 71), it's ½ mile away. Restaurant, complimentary breakfast, room service. Cable TV. Pool. Tennis. Playground. Business services, airport shuttle, free parking. Some pets allowed. | 3901 N. College Ave. | 501/443–3431 | fax 501/443–1927 | 120 rooms | $54–$63 | AE, D, DC, MC, V.

FORREST CITY

Best Western Colony Inn. This standard chain hotel between Little Rock and Memphis is 13 mi from Village Creek State Park and one block from Wal-Mart. Half the rooms are nonsmoking. The inn is right off exit 241A (Forrest City) on I–40. Pool. Hot tub. Some pets allowed. | 2333 N. Washington Ave., Forrest City 72335 | 870/633–0870 | fax 870/633–3252 | 104 rooms | $62–$76 | AE, D, DC, MC, V.

Best Western–Brinkley. Typical chain accommodations are what you'll find at this hotel off I–40, an hour away from Little Rock and Memphis. The convention center is three blocks away. The hotel is one block south of I–40, exit 216. Restaurant, picnic area, complimentary breakfast. Some in-room hot tubs. Cable TV. Pool. Exercise equipment. Playground. Some pets allowed. | 1306 N. Rte. 17, Brinkley 72021 | 870/734–1650 | fax 870/734–1657 | 100 rooms | $59–$69 | AE, D, DC, MC, V.

FORT SMITH/VAN BUREN

Comfort Inn. This two-story Comfort Inn with inside and outside corridors is about 2 mi from Van Buren. The inn is right off I–540, exit 2A. Complimentary Continental breakfast. In-room data ports. Cable TV. Pool. Laundry facilities. Some pets allowed. | 3131 Cloverleaf St., Van Buren 72956 | 501/474–2223 | fax 501/474–9049 | www.comfort.inn | 48 rooms | $65 | AE, D, DC, MC, V.

Days Inn. This chain with outside corridors is 5 mi from the Fort Smith airport, and three blocks from the Fort Smith Museum and downtown. The inn is 3½ mi from I–540, exit 6. Complimentary Continental breakfast. Cable TV. Pool. Airport shuttle. Some pets allowed (fee). | 1021 Garrison Ave., Fort Smith | 501/783–0548 | fax 501/783–0836 | www.daysinn.com | 53 rooms | $39–$49 | AE, D, DC, MC, V.

Four Points by Sheraton. This two-story hotel with outside corridors is two blocks from I–540, exit 8A and is near movie theaters and restaurants. The Central Mall is two blocks away, and you're 1½ mi from the tennis courts at Creekmore Park. Restaurant, complimentary breakfast, room service. In-room data ports, refrigerators. Cable TV. Pool, wading pool. Business services, airport shuttle. Some pets allowed. | 5711 Rogers Ave., Fort Smith | 501/452–4110 | fax 501/452–4891 | 151 rooms | $53, $90 suites | AE, D, DC, MC, V.

Holiday Inn Civic Center. This Holiday Inn four blocks from the Arkansas River is near downtown, parks, and shopping. You are 10 blocks from Fort Smith's historic district, and four blocks from the Judge Parker Museum and the Fort Smith Historical Museum. The nine-story inn, which has an atrium with a skylight, is 5 mi from I–540, exit 8A. Restaurant (with entertainment). In-room data ports. Cable TV. Indoor pool. Hot tubs. Exercise equipment. Business services. Airport shuttle. Some pets allowed. | 700 Rogers Ave. | 501/783–1000 | fax 501/783–0312 | hi426gm@sagehotel.com | 255 rooms | $79–$89 | AE, D, DC, MC, V.

Super 8 Motel. This two-story Super 8 with outside corridors is 1 mi from the Van Buren area, where you'll find a scenic train ride and antiques stores. The motel is right off exit 5 of I–540. Complimentary Continental breakfast. Cable TV. Pool. Hot tub. Laundry facilities. Some pets allowed (fee). | 106 N. Plaza Ct., Van Buren 72956 | 501/471–8888 | 46 rooms | $55–$68 | AE, D, DC, MC, V.

HARRISON

Ozark Mountain Inn. The Ozark Mountain Inn is on a hill overlooking the town of Harrison. Lake Harrison is 2 mi away. The large, spacious lobby has plenty of seating. Complimentary Continental breakfast. Cable TV. Pool, wading pool. Playground. Business services. Some pets allowed. | 1222 N. Main St. | 870/743–1949 | fax 870/743–2960 | 100 rooms | $38 | AE, D, DC, MC, V.

Super 8. This motor inn is right behind the Primetime shopping center and near the Catfish Wharf restaurant. Complimentary Continental breakfast. Some in-room hot tubs. Cable TV. Pool. Business services. Some pets allowed. | 1330 U.S. 62/65 N | 870/741–1741 | fax 870/741–8858 | 50 rooms | $48–$63 | AE, D, DC, MC, V.

HEBER SPRINGS

Budget Inn. Truck parking is available and fishing, boating, and camping are ½ mi away at Greers Ferry Lake. Cable TV. Pool. Some pets allowed. | 616 W. Main St. | 501/362–8111 or 888/297–7955 (reservations) | 25 rooms | $38–$60 | AE, D, DC, MC, V.

HELENA

Delta Inn. A free shuttle is available from this modern brick building to the Lady Luck Casino nearby. Complimentary Continental breakfast. Cable TV. Pool. Business services. Some pets allowed. | 1207 U.S. 49N, West Helena 72390 | 870/572–7915 or 800/748–8802 | fax 870/572–3757 | 100 rooms | $45–$89 | AE, D, DC, MC, V.

HOPE

Best Western. Standard chain accommodations right off I–30, exit 30. Refrigerators. Cable TV. Pool. Laundry facilities. Some pets allowed. | I–30 and Rte. 278 | 870/777–9222 | fax 870/777–9077 | 75 rooms | $45–$55 | AE, D, DC, MC, V.

Super 8. Standard accommodations on landscaped grounds right off exit 30 on I–30 and 2 mi from the Clinton sites. Complimentary Continental breakfast. Some refrigerators. Cable TV. Pool. Tennis. Playground. Laundry facilities. Business services. Some pets allowed. | 2000 Holiday Dr. | 870/777–8601 | fax 870/777–3142 | 100 rooms | $33–$39 | AE, D, DC, MC, V.

HOT SPRINGS

Avanelle Motor Lodge. The lodge is in the National Park with a view of the Hot Springs Mountains. It's ½ mi from the city, which is accessible by bus. Restaurant, room service. Some kitchenettes. Cable TV. Pool. Some pets allowed. | 1204 Central Ave. 71902 | 501/321–1332 or 800/225–1360 | 88 rooms | $42–$56 | AE, D, DC, MC, V.

Buena Vista Resort. These cottages and hotel units were built in the 1940s and overlook a lake and 10 acres of forest. Picnic area. Kitchenettes, refrigerators. Cable TV. Pool. Miniature golf, tennis court. Fishing. Playground. Laundry facilities. Business services. Some pets allowed. | 201 Aberina St. | 501/525–1321 or 800/255–9030 (reservations, outside AR) | fax 501/525–8293 | 32 rooms, 18 cottages | $50–$74, $82 cottages | MC, V.

Clarion Resort on the Lake. This resort on Lake Hamilton is 4 mi from the airport, and from the Oaklawn Thoroughbred Race Track. When you stay here, you are also 1 mi from the Hot Springs Mall, 7 mi from downtown, and 65 mi from Little Rock National Airport. Restaurant, bar. Some refrigerators. Cable TV. Pool. Tennis. Water sports, boating. Playground, laundry facilities. Business services. Some pets allowed. | 4813 Central Ave. 71913 | 501/525–1391 | fax 501/525–0813 | 149 rooms | $99–$149 | AE, D, MC, V.

Econo Lodge Inn and Suites. The hotel is located downtown near the Hot Springs Mall and several restaurants. Restaurant. Some microwaves, some refrigerators. Cable TV. Pool. Hot tub. Some pets allowed. | 4319 Central Ave. | 501/525–1660 | fax 501/525–7260 | 100 rooms | $55–$64 | AE, D, DC, MC, V.

Hampton Inn. Family suites are available in this hotel in downtown Hot Springs. Complimentary Continental breakfast. In-room data ports, microwaves in suites, refrigerators in suites, some in-room hot tubs. Cable TV. Pool. Laundry facilities. Some pets allowed. | 151 Temperance Hill Rd. 71913 | 501/525–7000 | fax 501/525–7626 | 83 rooms, 17 suites | $84–$91, $114–$121 suites | AE, D, DC, MC, V.

Lake Hamilton Resort. Every room at this resort is a suite with a balcony overlooking Lake Hamilton. Restaurant, bar, picnic area, room service. In-room data ports, refrigerators. Cable TV. indoor-outdoor pools. Hot tub, sauna. Tennis. Exercise equipment. Beach, dock, water sports, boating, fishing. Playground. Laundry facilities. Business services, airport shuttle. Kids under 18 free. Some pets allowed. | 2803 Albert Pike 71913 | 501/767–5511 or 800/426–3184 | fax 501/767–8576 | lhresort@direclynx.net | www.cabot-ar.com/hamilton/resort.htm | 104 suites | $79–$94 suites | AE, D, DC, MC, V | Closed Dec.

Quality Inn. The sides and back of this full-service motel overlook the mountains. Downtown Hot Springs is 1 mi away. Restaurant, bar, room service. In-room data ports, some refrigerators. Cable TV. Pool. Hot tub. Playground. Some pets allowed (fee). | 1125 E. Grand Ave. 71901 | 501/624–3321 | fax 501/624–5814 | 138 rooms | $59–$64 | AE, D, DC, MC, V.

Ramada Inn Tower. The hot springs are a short walk away, and so are a number of restaurants, including the Faded Rose. A cover band plays in the hotel lounge every weekend. Restaurant, bar (with entertainment). In-room data ports. Cable TV. Pool, wading pool. Business services. Some pets allowed. | 218 Park Ave. 71901 | 501/623–3311 | fax 501/623–8871 | 191 rooms | $67–$79 | AE, D, DC, MC, V.

Shorecrest Resort. This hotel on Lake Hamilton is just a few miles from downtown Hot Springs, art galleries, music, and shopping. Picnic area. Kitchenettes, refrigerators. Cable TV. Pool. Beach, fishing. Some pets allowed. | 360 Lakeland Dr. 71913 | 501/525–8113 or 800/447–9914 | 25 cottages | $52–$60 | D, MC, V.

JONESBORO

Best Western Inn. Chain accommodations 1 mi from Arkansas State University, 3 mi from the airport, and 90 mi from Memphis. Complimentary Continental breakfast. In-room data ports. Cable TV. Pool. Some pets allowed. | 2901 Phillips Dr. | 870/932–6600 | fax 870/935–1677 | 60 rooms | $50–$57 | AE, D, DC, MC, V.

Days Inn. Standard hotel off Rte. 463, a few blocks from a movie theater and the Regional Medical Center, 3 mi from the airport, and 5 mi from Cricket Forest Park. Complimentary Continental breakfast. Cable TV. Some pets allowed. | 2406 Phillips Dr. | 870/932–9339 or 800/227–9345 (reservations) | fax 870/931–5289 | 46 rooms | $47 | AE, D, MC, V.

Holiday Inn. The hotel is 2 mi from movie theaters, 3 mi from a mall, and 5 min from Cricket Forest Park. Restaurant, bar (with entertainment). Room service. Cable TV. Indoor pool. Hot tub. Exercise equipment. Laundry facilities. Business services. Some pets allowed. | 3006 S. Caraway Rd. | 870/935–2030 | fax 870/935–3440 | 179 rooms | $69 | AE, D, DC, MC, V.

Holiday Inn Express. The Jonesboro Bowling Center and a skating rink are across the bypass; Arkansas State University is 15 min away. Complimentary Continental breakfast. In-room data ports. Cable TV. Laundry facilities. Some pets allowed. | 2407 Phillips Dr. | 870/932–5554 | fax 870/932–2586 | 102 rooms | $65 | AE, D, DC, MC, V.

Motel 6. You're within walking distance of several restaurants; a bowling alley and a movie theater are also nearby. Restaurant. In-room data ports. Cable. Pool. Some pets allowed. | 2300 S. Caraway Rd. | 870/932–1050 | fax 870/935–3421 | 80 rooms | $36–$38 | AE, D, DC, MC, V.

Wilson Inn. This hotel is on the bypass at the edge of town, across the street from a multiplex theater and beside the Cracker Barrel restaurant. Complimentary Continental breakfast. Some kitchenettes, refrigerators. Cable TV. Business services. Some pets allowed. | 2911 Gilmore Dr. | 870/972–9000 | 108 rooms, 31 suites | $39–$59 | AE, D, DC, MC, V.

LITTLE ROCK AND NORTH LITTLE ROCK

Days Inn. Off the interstate, ½ mi from the airport, this hotel is next to a waffle restaurant. Complimentary Continental breakfast. In-room data ports, some kitchenettes, some refrigerators. Cable TV. Outdoor pool. Laundry facilities. Business services. Some pets allowed. | 3200 Bankhead Dr. 72206 | 501/490–2010 | fax 501/490–2229 | 108 rooms | $45–$50 | AE, D, DC, MC, V.

Holiday Inn Select. This five-story hotel caters to the corporate world in West Little Rock. It's 12 min from downtown and 7 mi from the Little Rock Zoo and War Memorial Stadium. The building is white stucco, with soaring floor-to-ceiling windows, and a drive-through, covered entrance. Restaurant, bar (with entertainment), room service. In-room data ports. Cable TV. Indoor-outdoor pool. Exercise equipment. Laundry facilities. Business services, airport shuttle, free parking. Some pets allowed. | 201 S. Shackelford Rd. 72211 | 501/223–3000 | fax 501/223–2833 | 246 rooms, 15 suites | $108, $150–$325 suites | AE, D, DC, MC, V.

La Quinta. This three-story hotel is made of white stucco and teal trim. The drive-through entrance has a Mexican-style shingled red clay roof. The hotel, formerly a Holiday Inn, is 7 mi west of downtown Little Rock, 8 mi from the airport, and close to Ryan's Family Steak House, the Dixie Café, and miniature golfing at Gator Golf. It's 8 mi to the Arkansas Arts Center and 14 mi to the Arkansas State Capitol. Restaurant, bar, complimentary Continental breakfast. In-room data ports. Cable TV. Pool. Laundry facilities. Business services, free parking. Some pets allowed. | 11701 I–30/430 72209 | 501/455–2300 | fax 501/455–5876 | 145 rooms | $65 | AE, D, DC, MC, V.

Motel 6. City buses stop near this three-story motel 10 mi west of downtown Little Rock. The Red Lobster restaurant is 2 mi away, the Steak Out is across the street, and live bands are at Smitty's one block from the motel. In-room data ports. Cable TV. Pool. Some pets allowed. | 10524 W. Markham St. 72205 | 501/225–7366 | fax 501/227–7426 | 146 rooms | $44–$49 | AE, D, DC, MC, V.

Red Roof Inn. The two-story motel is 7 mi from the airport, 3 mi south of downtown, and near the University of Arkansas and the Expo Center. In-room data ports. Cable TV. Business services. Some pets allowed. | 7900 Scott Hamilton Dr. 72209 | 501/562–2694 | fax 501/562–1723 | www.redroofinns.com | 108 rooms | $44–$48 | AE, D, DC, MC, V.

MAGNOLIA

Best Western Coachman's Inn. In the heart of town, this two-story brick Colonial-style building is next to the First Baptist Church and four blocks from the Greyhound bus terminal. You can enjoy country-style dining nearby at George's Steak House and seafood at the Old Feed House. Restaurant, complimentary Continental breakfast. In-room data ports, refrigerators. Cable TV. Pool. Business services. Some pets allowed. | 420 E. Main St. | 870/234–6122 | fax 870/234–1254 | magplace@magnolia-net.com | www.bestwestern.com | 84 rooms | $53–$69 | AE, D, DC, MC, V.

MORRILTON

Morrilton Days Inn. This two-story hotel is just off I–40, 2 mi from the Arkansas River Wildlife Management area, 16 mi from Petit Jean State Park, and 18 mi from the Antique Auto Museum. There's fishing at Lake Overcup 1 mi away. You can eat at Yesterday's bar and grill across the street. Restaurant. Some in-room data ports, some refrigerators. Cable TV. Pool. Hot tub. Pets allowed (fee). | 1506 N. Hwy. 95 72110 | 501/354–5101 | fax 501/354–8539 | 53 rooms | $52–$58 | AE, D, DC, MC, V.

Scottish Inn. This two-story motel is 18 mi from Petit Jean State Park and 1½ mi from downtown. Some microwaves, some refrigerators. Cable TV. Pool. Business services. Some pets allowed. | 356 Rte. 95 and I–40 | 501/354–0181 | fax 501/354–1458 | 55 rooms | $38–$52 | AE, D, DC, MC, V.

MOUNTAIN HOME

Best Western Carriage Inn. You can stroll around the pond in the landscaped garden at this two-floor hotel, which is near the center of Mountain Home; movie theaters, restaurants, and a shopping mall are within 2 mi. Restaurant, room service. Cable TV. Pool. Some pets allowed. | 963 U.S. 62E | 870/425–6001 | www.bestwesternmtnhome.com | 82 rooms | $49–$69 | AE, D, DC, MC, V.

Holiday Inn. You can listen to live country-western music in the Red Fox lounge at this two-story hotel in town. A new golf course is ½ mi away. Restaurant, room service. In-room data ports. Cable TV. Pool. Laundry facilities. Business services, airport shuttle. Some pets allowed. | 1350 U.S. 62 SW | 870/425–5101 | fax 870/425–5101 ext. 300 | 100 rooms | $58 | AE, D, DC, MC, V.

Scott Valley Ranch. You can go on guided horseback rides or take a peaceful walk through breathtaking meadows at this rustic ranch, nestled amid more than 600 acres in the Ozarks. The ranch is 7 mi south of Mountain Home. No room phones. No television, no TV in rooms, TV in common area. Pool. Hot tub. Tennis. Horseback riding, volleyball. Laundry facilities. Some pets allowed (fee). No smoking. | 223 Scott Valley Tr. 72653 | 870/425–5136 or 888/855–7747 | fax 870/424–5800 | www.scottvalley.com | 28 rooms, 1 cottage | $115–$145 | MC, V.

Teal Point. This resort on Lake Norfork's Teal Point and surrounded by the Ozark Mountains dates back to the 1950s and has both new and refurbished cottages. Teal Point is 5 mi east of Mountain Home. Picnic area. Kitchenettes, microwaves. Cable TV, no room phones. Pool. Boating, fishing. Playground. Laundry facilities. Some pets allowed (fee). | 715 Teal Point Rd. | 870/492–5145 | www.norfork.com/tealpoint | 18 cottages | $57–$220 cottages | MC, V.

Town and Country Motor Inn. This inn on Hwy. 62E just 1½ blocks from the center of town is within walking distance of Baxter County Courthouse square, which is ringed with restaurants and shops around a new veteran's memorial. The inn provides picnic tables and barbecue pits for outdoor dining, and you can spend evenings relaxing on the lighted porch in chairs and on swings. Some in-room data ports, microwaves, refrigerators. Cable TV. Some pets allowed. | 145 S. Main St. 72653 | 888/224–3323 | 40 rooms | $36 | AE, D, MC, V.

MOUNTAIN VIEW

Days Inn. This motor inn is at the junction of Routes 5, 9, and 14, at the only stoplight in town. The ground-floor motel is two blocks from the Hoe-Down and local fiddling attractions. Complimentary Continental breakfast. Pool. No smoking rooms. Hot tub. Some pets allowed (fee). | HC 72 | 870/269–3287 | fax 870/269–2807 | 71 rooms | $45–$85 | AE, D, DC, MC, V.

NEWPORT

Days Inn. Standard two-floor motor hotel in Newport with comfortable accommodations. Truck parking is available. Pool. Some pets allowed. | 101 Olivia Dr. | 870/523–6411 | fax 870/523–3470 | 40 rooms | $40–$65 | AE, D, DC, MC, V.

Park Inn International. This two-story motel is near the center of town, and 4 mi away from fishing and hiking in Jacksonport State Park. Restaurant, bar. Some refrigerators. Cable TV. Pool. Laundry facilities. Business services. Some pets allowed. | 901 Rte. 367N | 870/523–5851 | fax 870/523–9890 | 58 rooms | $49–$57 | AE, D, DC, MC, V.

PINE BLUFF

Best Western Inn. Regional Park, with its bass fishing, stratton javelin tournaments, and drag boat racing, is just 2 mi away from this standard two-story chain hotel. Restaurant. Cable TV. Pool. Some pets allowed (fee). | 2700 E. Harding Ave. | 870/535–8640 | fax 870/535–2648 | 116 rooms | $57–$61 | AE, D, DC, MC, V.

Ramada Inn. This five-floor, downtown hotel is 1 mi from Lake Pine Bluff and Regional Park. Restaurant, bar. In-room data ports, some microwaves, refrigerators. Cable TV. Indoor pool. Beauty salon, hot tub, sauna. Exercise equipment. Business services. Some pets allowed. | 2 Convention Center Plaza | 870/535–3111 | fax 870/534–5083 | 200 rooms, including 84 suites | $60–$100 | AE, D, DC, MC, V.

Super 7 Inn & Suites. Truck parking is allowed at this two-story hotel, 2 mi from boating, golfing, and fishing at Pine Bluff. Picnic area, complimentary Continental breakfast. Cable TV. Pool. Business services. Some pets allowed. | 210 N. Blake St. | 870/534–7222 | fax 870/534–5705 | 90 rooms | $59 | AE, D, DC, MC, V.

Super 8 Motel. Regional Park is 2 mi away, and the municipal airport is a 5-min drive from this standard two-story motel. Truck parking is available. Cable TV. Laundry facilities. Some pets allowed (fee). | 4101 W. Barraque St. | 870/534–7400 | fax 870/536–1201 | 53 rooms | $45 | AE, D, DC, MC, V.

ROGERS

Days Inn. This single-story, modern structure near the center of Rogers is a place where you can listen to country-western music in the hotel's Nice N' Easy lounge, go antiquing at several nearby shops, or drive 5 mi to Beaver Lake. Restaurant, bar, complimentary Continental breakfast. Pool. Some pets allowed (fee). Airport shuttle. | 2102 S. 8th St. | 501/636–3820 | fax 501/631–8952 | 55 rooms | $42–$100 | AE, D, DC, MC, V.

Ramada Inn. This two-story motel is 25 mi from the Northwest Mall in Rogers, with two movie theaters and a bowling alley, and it's 20 min from the War Eagle Craft Fair. You'll find live entertainment in the motel's lounge. Restaurant, bar (with entertainment), complimentary breakfast. Cable TV. Pool. Business services. Some pets allowed. | 1919 S. 8th St., U.S. 71B | 501/636–5850 | 127 rooms | $60–$85 | AE, D, DC, MC, V.

RUSSELLVILLE

Comfort Inn. This two-story hotel is 3 mi from Dardanelle Lake and 3 mi from Arkansas Technical University. In-room data ports, refrigerators, some in-room hot tubs. Cable TV. Pool. Some pets allowed. | 3019 E. Parkway Dr. | 501/967–7500 | fax 501/967–6314 | 61 rooms | $50 | AE, D, DC, MC, V.

Holiday Inn. This two-story modern hotel is 2 mi south of Russellville and 1½ mi from Arkansas Technical University. Fishing, boating, and camping are available at Dardanelle Lake, only one block away. Restaurant. In-room data ports, room service. Cable TV. Pool. Business services, airport shuttle. Some pets allowed. | 2407 N. Arkansas St. | 501/968–4300 | 149 rooms | $70 | AE, D, DC, MC, V.

Russellville Travelodge. All rooms at this hotel near I–40 and Hwy. 7 have a refrigerator, and pets are welcome to stay for an extra $10 a night. Guests can take advantage of the outdoor pool and free Continental breakfast. Complimentary Continental breakfast. In-room data ports, refrigerators. Cable TV, room phones. Outdoor pool. Pets allowed (fee). | 2200 N. Arkansas Ave. 72802 | 501/968–4400 | 45 rooms | $89–$179 | AE, DC, D, MC, V.

SEARCY

Best Western Inn. This two-story hotel is 8 mi from the Locomotion Family Fun Park and close to the Ozark Family Outlet Mall. There is a restaurant next door. In-room data ports. Cable TV. Some pets allowed (fee). | 1394 W. Sunset Ave. | 501/751–3100 | fax 501/756–2490 | 100 rooms | $52 | AE, D, DC, MC, V.

Comfort Inn. This two-story modern red-brick hotel is near the center of Searcy. Complimentary Continental breakfast. Cable TV. Pool. Some pets allowed. | 107 S. Rand St. | 501/279–9100 | 60 rooms | $60 | AE, D, DC, MC, V.

Hampton Inn. This chain hotel is 3 mi from Harding University. Restaurant, complimentary Continental breakfast, room service. Some refrigerators. Cable TV. Indoor-outdoor pool. Hot tub. Exercise equipment. Laundry facilities. Business services. Some pets allowed. | 3204 E. Race St. | 501/268–0654 | fax 501/278–5546 | tn009670@psinet.com | 106 rooms | $64–$69 | AE, D, DC, MC, V.

SPRINGDALE

Executive Inn. After enjoying a scenic tour of the Ozark Mountain region on the Arkansas Railway Association train, you can relax in the Rendezvous, the motel's lounge. Restaurant, bar. Some microwaves, some refrigerators. Cable TV. Outdoor pool. Laundry facilities. Some pets allowed. | 2005 U.S. 71B S | 501/756–6101 or 800/544–6086 | fax 501/756–6101, ext. 5 | 101 rooms | $49 | AE, D, DC, MC, V.

Hampton Inn. This three-story hotel is 20 min from the Northwest Arkansas Regional Airport and has a fireplace that glows in the lobby all winter long. There are restaurants and a movie theater nearby. Complimentary Continental breakfast. In-room data ports, some kitchenettes. Cable TV. Pool. Business services. Some pets allowed. | 1700 S. 48th St. | 501/756–3500 | fax 501/927–3500 | www.hamptonsuites.com/hisdocs/properties/ | 67 rooms, 35 suites | $69–$85, $106–$116 suites | AE, D, DC, MC, V.

Holiday Inn. This is a seven-story, atrium-style hotel with palm trees, vines, and a five-story waterfall. Some rooms overlook downtown. The inn is near the city's convention center. Restaurant, bar. In-room data ports. Cable TV. Indoor pool. Hot tub. Exercise equipment. Laundry facilities. Business services, airport shuttle. Some pets allowed. | 1500 S. 48th St. | 501/751–8300 | fax 501/751–4640 | 184 rooms, 22 suites | $59–109, $130–$150 suites | AE, D, DC, MC, V.

TEXARKANA

Baymont Inn. A golf course is 4 mi from this large, comfortable hotel, and Wright Patman Lake is 15 mi away. The four-story structure includes a lobby with a breakfast room, and an outdoor pool and lounge area. Restaurants are within walking distance. Complimentary Continental breakfast. In-room data ports, some microwaves, some refrigerators. Cable TV. Pool. Some pets allowed. | 5102 N. State Line Ave. | 870/773–1000 | www.baymontinns.com | fax 870/773–5000 | 104 rooms | $49–$64 | AE, D, DC, MC, V.

California

ALTURAS

Best Western Trailside Inn. This is the only lodging in town with a swimming pool. If you're looking for outdoor entertainment, this hotel is 2 mi north of Rachael Doris Park, 3 mi south of Devils Garden, and 5 mi north of Modoc Wildlife Reserve. It's also 5 blocks south of the Modoc County Museum. There is a courtesy car to and from Alturas Airport, 1 mi west. Cable TV. Some kitchenettes. Pool. Business services. Some pets allowed. | 343 N. Main St. | 530/233–4111 | fax 530/233–3180 | 38 rooms | $55–$75 | AE, DC, MC, V.

Hacienda. In the heart of farm country, this motel is marked with a large 19th-century wagon wheel out front. A gas station, fast-food restaurants, and a supermarket are all within 5 blocks. Cable TV. Some kitchenettes, some refrigerators. Pets allowed. | 201 E. 12th St. | 530/233–3459 | simcity@hdo.net | 20 rooms | $31–$49 | AE, D, DC, MC, V.

ANAHEIM

Anaheim Hilton and Towers. Next to the Anaheim Convention Center, this busy Hilton is the largest hotel in southern California; it even has its own post office. Rooms are bright, and you can either walk a few blocks or take a shuttle to Disneyland. 4 restaurants, 2 bars (with entertainment). Some refrigerators, room service, cable TV. 2 pools. Beauty salon, hot tub. Gym. Shops. Video games. Kids' programs. Business services. Parking fee. Some pets allowed. | 777 Convention Way 92802 | 714/750–4321 | fax 714/740–4460 | www.hilton.com | 1,567 rooms | $119–$179 | AE, D, DC, MC, V.

Quality Hotel Maingate. Three blocks south of Disneyland, this hotel offers a shuttle to the park. 2 restaurants, lounge. In-room data ports, room service, limited cable TV. Pool. Beauty salon. Video games. Laundry facilities. Business services. Parking (fee). Some pets allowed (fee). | 616 Convention Way 92802 | 714/750–3131 | fax 714/750–9027 | www.qualityinn.com | 284 rooms | $119 | AE, D, DC, MC, V.

APTOS

Apple Lane Inn. Set on a three-acre hillside and surrounded by apple orchards, flowerbeds, and a barn with livestock, this four-story 1870 farmhouse has an ocean view. Rooms have an eclectic country style, and are complemented by fresh flowers. The attic suite offers a view of the meadows. The wine cellar room has cedar paneling, a beamed ceiling, and a private entrance. Complimentary breakfast. Some pets allowed. No smoking. | 6265 Soquel

Dr. | 831/475–6868 or 800/649–8988 | fax 831/464–5790 | www.applelaneinn.com | 5 rooms | $110–$180 | AE, DC, D, MC, V.

ARCADIA

Residence Inn by Marriott. Many of the attractively decorated guest rooms have fireplaces. This hotel is 7 mi from Old Pasadena, 1 mi from Santa Anita Park and within walking distance of 12 restaurants. Pool. Hot tubs. Exercise equipment. Business services. Airport shuttle. Pets allowed (fee). | 321 E. Huntington Dr. 91006 | 626/446–6500 | fax 626/446–5824 | 120 rooms | $132–$158 | AE, D, DC, MC, V.

AUBURN

Best Western Golden Key. This chain hotel has a rose garden and flowerbeds in front of all rooms. Built in the 1960's on the outskirts of town, this two-story motel with exterior entrances is next door to Lou La Bonte's restaurant. Restaurant, picnic areas, complimentary Continental breakfast. Some refrigerators, room service, cable TV. Pool. Laundry facilities. Some pets allowed. | 13450 Lincoln Way | 530/885–8611 | fax 530/888–0319 | www.hotel-swest.com | 68 rooms | $56–$76 | AE, D, DC, MC, V.

AVALON (CATALINA ISLAND)

Edgewater Hotel. If you're lucky enough to snag a room at this family-run beachfront hotel, you'll get luxury with character. Rooms are all different, some with hot tubs, ocean views, swinging French doors, or fireplaces, all with light-oak furniture, candles, cheery bedspreads and curtains. Complimentary Continental breakfast. Microwaves, refrigerators, hot tub. Some pets allowed (fee). | 415 Crescent St. 90704 | 877/334–3728 or 310/510–0347 | edgewater@ispchannel.com | 8 rooms | $195–$395 | AE, D, MC, V.

BAKERSFIELD

Best Western Hill House. Catering primarily to business travelers, this property is in downtown Bakersfield, just across the street from the Convention Center and Centennial Garden. The courthouse and other government buildings are within easy walking distance of the hotel, as are the downtown area's restaurants and shopping opportunities. Restaurant, bar, complimentary Continental breakfast. Refrigerators, cable TV. Pool. Exercise equipment. Some pets allowed (fee). | 700 Truxton St. 93301 | 805/327–4064 | fax 805/327–1247 | 99 rooms | $50–$54 | AE, D, DC, MC, V.

La Quinta. Built to resemble an adobe Spanish Mission building, this three-story hotel 3 mi from the airport has a terra-cotta tiled roof, exposed wood beams, and a covered circular drive. Restaurant, complimentary Continental breakfast, cable TV. Pool. Business services. Airport shuttle. Some pets allowed. | 3232 Riverside Dr. 93308 | 661/325–7400 | fax 661/324–6032 | 129 rooms | $49–$65 | AE, D, DC, MC, V.

Oxford Inn. This modest motel is about 12 mi west of downtown Bakersfield, and the Kern County Airport complex is 3 mi away. Some guest rooms overlook the property's tropical courtyard. Refrigerators (in suites), cable TV. Pool. Laundry facilities. Business services. Airport shuttle. Some pets allowed (fee). | 4500 Buck Owens Blvd. 93308 | 661/324–5555 or 800/822–3050 (California) | fax 661/325–0106 | 208 rooms | $55 | AE, D, DC, MC, V.

BARSTOW

Days Inn. All the aquatic fun of Lake Dolores is within 5 mi of this motel, and there are more than a dozen popular restaurants within walking distace of your room. Cable TV. Pool. Some pets allowed. | 1590 Coolwater Ln. 92311 | 760/256–1737 | fax 760/256–7771 | www.daysinn.com | 113 rooms | $44–$54 | AE, D, DC, MC, V.

BEVERLY HILLS

Beverly Hills Plaza Hotel. Overstuffed sofas and lots of potted plants in the black-and-white lobby provide excellent screens for people-watchers. Guest suites are done in bright white with lots of light and glass. Restaurant, bar with entertainment. In-room data ports, safes, some kitchenettes, minibars, refrigerators, cable TV. Pool. Hot tub. Exercise equipment. Business services. Some pets allowed. | 10300 Wilshire Blvd. 90024 | 310/275–5575 or 800/800–1234 | fax 310/275–3257 | 116 suites | $160–$495 suites | AE, D, DC, MC, V.

Beverly Hilton. Celebrity-spotting is a popular pastime at this centrally located luxury hotel. The Hilton's marble-and-glass–filled public areas are in contrast to the guest rooms, which are decorated in warm desert colors. The Hilton stands in the heart of Beverly Hills, 2 blocks from Rodeo Drive's shops and galleries. Restaurant, 3 bars, room service. In-room data ports, refrigerators, cable TV. Pool, wading pool. Beauty salon. Exercise equipment. Shops. Business services. Some pets allowed. | 9876 Wilshire Blvd. 90210 | 310/274–7777 | fax 310/285–1313 | www.hilton.com | 581 rooms, 90 suites | $175–$395 rooms, suites $250–$1,100 | AE, D, DC, MC, V.

★ **Regent Beverly Wilshire.** Built in 1927, this landmark Italian Renaissance-style hotel is known for its exemplary service and celebrity clientele. Strategically located at the intersection of Rodeo Dr. and Wilshire Blvd., the hotel is within 2 blocks of dozens of fabulous shops, restaurants, and galleries. After a hard day of shopping, you can unwind with a beverage at a poolside cabana, or snooze in one of the Regent's famously comfortable beds. Restaurant, bar with entertainment, room service. In-room data ports, refrigerators, cable TV. Pool. Beauty salon, hot tub, massage. Gym. Business services. Some pets allowed. | 9500 Wilshire Blvd. 90212 | 310/275–5200 or 800/545–4000 | fax 310/274–2851 | www.rih.com | 395 rooms, 69 suites | $385–$545, $570–$750 suites | AE, D, DC, MC, V.

BIG BEAR LAKE

Eagle's Nest. This Ponderosa-pine log cabin B&B is just ½ mi from Snow Summit and 2 mi from Big Bear Mountain Ski Resort. Guest rooms are named after Western movies, and are decorated with Old West–themed antiques. Cottage suites have fireplaces, some with adjacent hot tubs. Complimentary breakfast for lodge guests. Microwaves (in cottages), refrigerators, cable TV. Some in-room hot tubs. Some pets allowed. | 41675 Big Bear Blvd. 93215 | 909/866–6465 | fax 909/866–8025 | www.bigbear.com/enbb | 5 rooms, 5 cottages | $85–$120 rooms, $130–150 cottages | AE, MC, V.

Wildwood Resort. Ideal for families or groups, the country-rustic cottages and rooms at Wildwood are uphill about four and a half blocks from several shops. Cottages have full kitchens, and the whole resort is just a ½ mi from the lake and nearby ski slopes. Most rooms and all cottages have fireplaces. Restaurant, picnic area. Kitchenettes (in cottages), cable TV. Pool. Hot tub. Playground. Some pets allowed (fee). | 40210 Big Bear Blvd./Rte. 18 93215 | 909/878–2178 or 888/294–5396 (for reservations) | fax 909/878–3036 | www.wildwoodresort.com | 5 rooms, 14 cottages | $75–$195 rooms, $100–$250 cottages | AE, D, MC, V.

BIG SUR

Big Sur Campground and Cabins. Rent a cabin, including three A-frame units in a tall stand of redwoods, a tent-cabin, or pitch your own tent at one of the camp sites with public restrooms and hot showers. The 13 cabins have heat and private bathrooms. RV sites with water and electric are available. Hot showers, telephones, fishing, playground, volleyball, basketball, beach and trail access within 10 mi drive. Pets allowed (fee) except in cabins. | Rte. 1 93920 | 831/667–2322 | www.caohwy.com/b/bigsurcg.htm | 81 camp sites, 4 tent-cabins, 13 cabins | $26 camp site, $50–$62 tent–cabins, $90–$235 cabins | AE, MC, V.

BISHOP

Best Western Holiday Spa Lodge. Anglers and nature enthusiasts often make this lodge their home base while taking advantage of the area (the hotel even offers fish cleaning services). There are fireplaces in the suites. Mammoth Mountain skiing areas are 45 mi northwest. Some microwaves, refrigerators, cable TV. Pool. Hot tub, spa. Laundry facilities. Some pets allowed. | 1025 N. Main St. 93514 | 760/873–3543 | fax 760/872–4777 | www.bestwestern.com | 89 rooms, 1 suite | $75–$82 rooms, $94 suite | AE, D, DC, MC, V.

Comfort Inn. Surrounded by the High Sierra, this Swiss-style motel is central to many hiking and fishing locales. Mammoth Mountain skiing resorts are 45 mi northeast. The hotel is ½ mi south of U.S. 6 and U.S. 395. Picnic area, complimentary Continental breakfast. Microwaves, refrigerators, cable TV. Pool. Hot tub. Laundry facilities. Some pets allowed. | 805 N. Main St. 93514 | 760/873–4284 | fax 760/873–8563 | www.comfortinn.com | 54 rooms | $79–$89 | AE, D, DC, MC, V.

Motel 6 Bishop. The motel is 15 mi from a water-skiing area and 45 mi from the Mammoth Mountain snow skiing area. Some kitchenettes, refrigerators, cable TV. Pool. Hot tub. Laundry facilities. Business services. Some pets allowed. | 1005 N. Main St. 93514 | 760/873–8426 | fax 760/873–8060 | www.motel6.com | 52 rooms | $59–$69 | AE, D, DC, MC, V.

Thunderbird. This is an economic choice if you wish to stay near the High Sierras. It's 45 mi from the Mammoth Mountain skiing and sports area. Refrigerators, cable TV. Some pets allowed. | 190 W. Pine St. 93514 | 760/873–4215 | fax 760/873–6870 | 23 rooms | $44–$80 | AE, D, DC, MC, V.

BLYTHE

Best Value Inn. This chain hotel is within walking distance of area fast food restaurants, movies and shopping. The quieter shores of the Colorado River are just 4 mi distant. Restaurant, bar, complimentary Continental breakfast. Cable TV. Pool. Some pets allowed (fee). | 850 W. Hobson Way 92225 | 760/922–5145 | fax 760/922–8422 | 50 rooms (34 with shower only) | $45–$49 | AE, D, DC, MC, V.

Best Western Sahara. Flanked by palm trees and topped with terra cotta tiles, this comfortable chain motel is 4 mi from the Colorado River and just 2 mi from recreational activities such as fishing, boating, skiing, and golfing. Restaurant, complimentary Continental breakfast. Microwaves, refrigerators, cable TV, in-room VCRs. Pool. Hot tub. Some pets allowed. | 825 W. Hobson Way 92225 | 760/922–7105 | fax 760/922–5836 | www.bestwestern.com | 46 rooms | $62 | AE, D, DC, MC, V.

Hampton Inn. In the town's hotel square area, this hotel allows easy access to various restaurants and stores and a movie theater. I–10 is little more than a block away. Restaurant, complimentary Continental breakfast. In-room data ports, microwaves, refrigerators, cable TV, in-room VCRs. Pool. Hot tub. Exercise equipment. Laundry facilities. Business services. Some pets allowed. | 900 W. Hobson Way 92225 | 760/922–9000 | fax 760/922–9011 | www.hampton-inn.com | 59 rooms | $65–$72 | AE, D, DC, MC, V.

Legacy Inn. Built in the 1950s, this moderate-size inn is right in the heart of the commercial district and is within walking distance to area restaurants and shops. Complimentary breakfast. Microwaves, cable TV. Pool. Some pets allowed. | 903 W. Hobson Way 92225 | 760/922–4146 | fax 760/922–8481 | 48 rooms | $54–$85 | AE, D, DC, MC, V.

BODEGA BAY

Inn at Occidental. Situated among grand redwoods atop a secluded knoll above the small village of Occidental, the original structure was built in 1877. With a nod to its Victorian design, the inn is filled with antiques, family heirlooms and works by local artists. Afternoons feature Sonoma wine and hors d'oeuvres. Complimentary breakfast. In-room hot tubs. Business services. Pets allowed in cottage. No kids under 12. No smoking. | 3657 Church St., Occidental 95465 | 707/874–1047 or 800/522–6324 | fax 707/

874–1078 | www.innatoccidental.com | 16 rooms, 2 suites | $175–$270 rooms, $270 suites | AE, D, MC, V.

BREA

Homestead Village. A modern three-story hotel with exterior corridors, this spot caters specifically to longer-staying guests—many of whom head straight to Disneyland, 10 mi away. Gym. Laundry service. Some pets allowed. | 3050 E. Imperial Hwy. 92821 | 714/528–2500 | fax 714/528–4900 | 133 rooms | $52–$89 | AE, D, MC, V.

Woodfin Suite Hotel. This all-suite hotel is divided among five two-story buildings. Complimentary shuttle service is provided to any destination within a 5 mi radius and also to Disneyland. All rooms have full kitchens. Complimentary breakfast. Pool. Gym. Laundry service. Business services. Some pets allowed (fee). | 3100 E. Imperial Hwy. 92821 | 714/579–3200 | fax 714/996–5984 | 88 suites | $79–$199 suites | AE, D, DC, MC, V.

BRIDGEPORT

Best Western Ruby Inn. Near the courthouse and in an area known for its prime angling, this motel offers fish cleaning and freezing facilities. Built in the early '60s, two single-story buildings rest in the high country valley of the eastern High Sierra. Cable TV. Some pets allowed. | 333 Main St. 93517 | 760/932–7241 | fax 760/932–7531 | 30 rooms | $80–$165 | AE, D, DC, MC, V.

Redwood Motel. In the Sierras just over 1 mi from many lakes and streams, this is a popular spot with anglers. Fish cleaning and freezing facilities are provided at this modest hotel built in the early 1950s. Bodie Ghost Town is 20 mi away; Yosemite is 45 mi east (when the passes are open; otherwise you will have to drive north almost as far as Lake Tahoe). Some pets allowed. | 425 Main St. 93517 | 760/932–7060 | 19 rooms | $75–$90 | AE, MC, V.

Silver Maple Inn. Next to the Mono County Courthouse (1880), this inn is centrally located in Bridgeport on attractive wooded grounds with views of the nearby Sierras. Built in the 1940s, the motel provides fish cleaning and freezing facilities and BBQ pits to cook your catch. Cable TV. Some pets allowed. | 310 Main St. 93517 | 760/932–7383 | 20 rooms | $70–$90 | AE, D, MC, V.

Walker River Lodge. Right in the center of Bridgeport, this hotel's lobby doubles as an antiques shop. Many of the rooms overlook the East Walker River. Picnic area. Pool, hot tub. Gym. Some pets allowed. | 100 Main St. 93517 | 760/932–7021 | fax 760/932–7914 | 36 rooms | $80–$125 | AE, D, DC, MC, V.

BUENA PARK

Red Roof Inn. Choose from standard rooms or larger suites at this chain hotel that sits 1 mi from Knott's Berry Farm and 6 mi from Disneyland. Restaurant, complimentary Continental breakfast. Cable TV. Pool. Hot tub. Business services. Some pets allowed. | 7121 Beach Blvd. 90620 | 714/670–9000 or 800/633–8300 | fax 714/522–7280 | www.redroof.com | 127 rooms | $50–$58 | AE, D, DC, MC, V.

Sheraton Cerritos at Towne Center. This large modern chain rises eight levels above the commercial center of town. Disneyland, by car or hotel shuttle, is 10 mi away, and Knott's Berry Farm is 4 mi away. Restaurant, bar. In-room data ports, some minibars, cable TV. Pool. Hot tub, spa. Exercise equipment. Shops. Business services. Some pets allowed. | 12725 Center Court Dr., Cerritos 90703 | 562/809–1500 | fax 562/403–2080 | 203 rooms | $79–$139 | AE, D, DC, MC, V.

BURBANK

Hilton–Burbank Airport. Right across from the Burbank-Glendale-Pasadena Airport, this eight-story hotel is geared towards the business traveler. Ask for a room with a mountain view—unless you would prefer to observe the airport activity. Courtesy shuttles will transport you 4 mi to Universal Studios and the Universal Ampitheatre, among other nearby attractions. Restaurant, bar, room service. Some in-room refrigerators, cable TV. 2 pools. Hot tub, sauna, spa. Exercise equipment. Laundry facilities. Business services. Airport shuttle. Some pets allowed. | 2500 Hollywood Way 91505 | 818/843–6000 | fax 818/842–9720 | 403 rooms, 83 suites | $159–$179 rooms, $180–$210 suites | AE, D, DC, MC, V.

CALISTOGA

Meadowlark Country House. A 20-acre country estate just north of downtown, this inn breeds and shows horses and lets guests feed them (carrots and apples provided). All rooms have breathtaking views. The main house, built in 1886, has a separate guest wing with flagstone terraces and French doors. The country-style rooms have four-poster beds and English country antiques. Complimentary breakfast. Cable TV, in-room VCRs. Pool. Hot tub, sauna. Business services. Some pets allowed. No smoking. | 601 Petrified Forest Rd. | 707/942–5651 or 800/942–5651 | fax 707/942–5023 | www.meadowlarkinn.com | 7 rooms | $185–$250 | AE, MC, V.

CAMBRIA

Cambria Shores Inn. From the central lawn of this waterside inn, you can enjoy spectacular ocean views, particularly at sunset. Complimentary Continental breakfast. No air-conditioning. Refrigerators, cable TV. Business services. Some pets allowed (fee). | 6276 Moonstone Beach Dr. | 805/927–8644 or 800/433–9179 (in CA) | fax 805/927–4070 | www.cambriashores.com | 24 rooms | $115–$135 | MC, V.

CARLSBAD

★ **Four Seasons Aviara.** This luxury hotel sits on 30 acres of coastline in a residential area, 5 mi from Legoland. Its rooms, with linen drapes and custom-designed bedding, have private balconies or landscaped terraces with views of the hotel's golf course, the lagoon or the mountains. Restaurants, bar (with entertainment), room service. In-room data ports, minibars, cable TV. Pool, wading pool. Beauty salon, hot tub, massage. Driving range, 18-hole golf course, putting green, tennis. Gym. Business services, airport shuttle. Some pets allowed. | 7100 Four Seasons Pt | 760/931–6672 or 800/332–3442 (for reservations) | fax 760/931–0390 | www.fourseasons.com | 276 rooms, 44 suites | $375–$485, $595–$645, $825–$4,100 suites | AE, DC, MC, V.

Inns of America. Some rooms have ocean views at this hotel within seven blocks of Carlsbad beach and accessible from the Poinsettia exit off of I–5. Restaurant, complimentary Continental breakfast. Cable TV. Pool. Laundry facilities. Business services. Some pets allowed. | 751 Raintree Dr. 92009 | 760/931–1185 | fax 760/931–0970 | www.innsofamerica.com | 126 rooms | $77–$82 | AE, MC, V.

CARMEL

Carmel Mission Inn. This modern inn on the edge of Carmel Valley has a lushly landscaped pool and hot tub area and an indoor pool. Some rooms have views of the valley. Restaurant, bar. In-room data ports, refrigerators, cable TV. Pool. Hot tubs. Laundry facilities. Business services. Some pets allowed (fee). No smoking. | 3665 Rio Rd. | 831/624–1841 or 800/348–9090 | fax 831/624–8684 | 163 rooms, 2 suites | $149–$189; $189–$359 suites | AE, D, DC, MC, V.

★ **Cypress Inn.** When Doris Day became part owner of this inn in 1988, she added her own touches, such as posters from her many movies and photo albums of her favorite canines. The 1929 inn, a block south of Main Street, has a courtyard with fireplaces and serves afternoon tea. Guests are greeted with complimentary sherry, fresh flowers, and a fruit basket. Bar, complimentary Continental breakfast. Some refrigerators, cable TV. Business services. Some pets allowed. | Lincoln St. and 7th Ave. | 831/624–3871 or 800/443–7443 |

fax 831/624–8216 | info@cypress-inn.com | www.cypress-inn.com | 34 rooms, 1 suite | $125–$350, $350 suite | AE, D, MC, V.

Highlands Inn/Park Hyatt Hotel. You may enjoy stunning views of the Pacific and coast from this luxury hotel, nestled in a Monterey Pine forest at the edge of Big Sur, on 12 wooded acres. The one- and two-bedroom suites have hot tubs, fireplaces, double spa baths, and ocean-view decks. 2 restaurants, bar (with entertainment). In-room data ports, some kitchenettes, minibars, cable TV, in-room VCRs. Pool. Exercise equipment. Bicycles. Business services. Airport shuttle. Baby-sitting. Some pets allowed (fee). | 120 Highland Dr. | 831/624–3801, 831/620–1234 or 800/682–4811 | fax 831/626–1574 | gm@highlands-inn.com | www.highlands-inn.com | 37 rooms, 106 suites | $315–$415, $450–$600 suites | AE, D, DC, MC, V.

Quail Lodge Resort and Golf Club. Five minutes from Carmel and the beach, this sprawling resort is practically surrounded by the golf course. Rooms are comfortable and pleasant with rattan armchairs, glass-topped tables, and floral drapes and spreads. 2 restaurants, bar (with entertainment). Cable TV. Two pools. Hot tub. Driving range, 18-hole golf course, putting greens, tennis. Baby-sitting. Business services. Pets allowed (fee). | 8205 Valley Greens Dr. | 831/624–2888 or 800/538–9516 | fax 831/624–3726 | info@quail-lodge-resort.com | www.quail-lodge-resort.com | 84 rooms, 15 suites | $295–$550, $395–$550 suites | AE, DC, MC, V.

Sunset House. A small B&B three blocks from Carmel Beach, this inn has cozy rooms with fireplaces and cathedral ceilings, and some with ocean views. Complimentary Continental breakfast. Refrigerators, some in-room hot tubs, no TV. Some pets allowed. | Camino Real near Ocean Ave. | 831/624–4884 | fax 831/624–4884 | www.sunset-carmel.com | 4 rooms | $150–$190 | AE, D, MC, V.

Vagabond's House Inn. Each room is uniquely furnished at this early-1900s inn, but all overlook the courtyard garden's flowers, oak tree, and waterfall. Many rooms have fireplaces. Complimentary Continental breakfast. Cable TV. No kids under 12. Some pets allowed (fee). | 4th Ave. at Dolores | 831/624–7738 or 800/262–1262 | fax 831/626–1243 | 11 rooms | $95–$165 | AE, MC, V.

Wayside Inn. This two-story motel is just one block off of Ocean Avenue. Perks include a picnic basket breakfast and a free newspaper delivered to your door every morning. Restaurant, complimentary Continental breakfast. Some kitchenettes, refrigerators, cable TV. Business services. Some pets allowed. | 7th Ave. and Mission St. | 831/624–5336 or 800/433–4732 | fax 831/626–6974 | www.webdzine.com/inns | 31 rooms | $99–$259 | AE, D, MC, V.

CATALINA ISLAND

Best Western Catalina Canyon Resort and Spa. In the foothills above Avalon Bay, this multi-level resort has a lush garden courtyard and Mediterranean-style architecture, minutes from downtown. Free shuttle to boating and shopping. Restaurant. Cable TV. Pool. Spa. Laundry service. Pets allowed (fee). | 888 Country Club Dr. 90704 | 310/510–0325 or 800/253–9361 | fax 310/510–0900 | www.catalina.com/canyon.html | 73 rooms | $161–$214 | AE, D, DC, MC, V.

CATHEDRAL CITY

Comfort Suites. Enjoy a complimentary barbecue every Wednesday here. The 3-story building has one, two, and three bedroom suites and has extended stay rates. Pool. Laundry service. Business services. Some pets allowed. | 69151 E. Palm Canyon Dr. 92234 | 760/324–5939 | fax 760/324–3034 | 97 suites | $95–$105 | AE, D, DC, MC, V.

CERRITOS

Sheraton Cerritos Hotel at Towne Center. Close to shopping, restaurants, and attractions, there is easy highway access from this hotel to Los Angeles and Orange County. The glass building is in park-like Towne Center, next to the Cerritos Center for Performing Arts. Cable TV. Pool. Gym. Video games. Laundry service. Business services. Some pets allowed. | 12725 Center Court Dr. 90703 | 562/809–1500 | fax 562/403–2080 | 203 rooms | $135–139 | AE, D, MC, V.

CHICO

Holiday Inn. The hotel is 2 mi from CSUC, the historic area downtown, Bidwell Park, Bidwell Mansion, and Sierra Nevada Brewery. Restaurant, bar (with entertainment), room service. In-room data ports, some refrigerators, cable TV. Pool. Hot tub. Video games. Laundry facilities. Business services. Airport shuttle. Free parking. Some pets allowed. | 685 Manzanita Ct | 530/345–2491 | www.holiday-inn.com | 171 rooms, 6 suites | $66–$85, $110–$150 suites | AE, D, DC, MC, V.

Vagabond Inn. This 1970s 2-story inn, designed with natural colors, is near restaurants, shopping, and historic homes. Complimentary Continental breakfast. Cable TV. Pool. Business services. Some pets allowed (fee). | 630 Main St. | 530/895–1323 | www.vagabondinns.com | 43 rooms | $50–$63 | AE, D, DC, MC, V.

CLAREMONT

Ramada Inn and Tennis Club. This 2-story motel is on seven landscaped acres, off "the 10" freeway. There's a free shuttle to the LA County Fairplex, Ontario International Airport, and all local colleges. You can walk to restaurants and shops. Complimentary Continental breakfast. Refrigerators, cable TV. Pool, wading pool. Hot tub. Tennis. Laundry facilities. Business services. Some pets allowed. | 840 S. Indian Hill Blvd. 91711 | 909/621–4831 | fax 909/621–0411 | www.ramadaclar.com | 122 rooms | $65–$89 | AE, D, DC, MC, V.

COALINGA

Big Country Inn. This inn is located right off I–5 on the west side of town. Four cottage-style, one-story buildings make up the inn complex. Pool. Some pets allowed. | 25020 W. Dorris Ave. 93210 | 559/935–0866 | fax 559/935–0644 | 48 rooms | $52–$86 | AE, D, DC, MC, V.

CORONA

Dynasty Suites. This two-story hotel of suites is 1 mi from the downtown civic center. Restaurant, complimentary Continental breakfast. Microwaves, refrigerators, some in-room hot tubs, cable TV, in-room VCRs (and movies) available. Pool. Hot tub. Business services. Some pets allowed (fee). | 1805 W. Sixth St. 91720 | 909/371–7185 or 800/842–7899 | fax 909/371–0401 | www.dynastysuites.com | 56 rooms | $59 | AE, D, DC, MC, V.

CORONADO

Loews Coronado Bay. You can dock your boat at the 80-slip marina here on the Silver Strand, 10 mi southwest of San Diego. All rooms have views of the bay, ocean, or marina. The lounge offers nightly entertainment. Its restaurant, Azzura Point, is known for its fresh seafood. 4 restaurants, bar (with entertainment), room service. In-room data ports, minibars, microwaves, cable TV. 3 pools. Beauty salon, hot tubs, massage. 5 tennis courts. Gym, beach, marina, water sports, boating, bicycles. Video games. Kids' programs. Laundry facilities. Business services. Some pets allowed. | 4000 Coronado Bay Rd. 92118 | 619/424–4000 or 800/235–6397 | fax 619/424–4400 | www.loewscoronadobay.com | 405 rooms, 33 suites | $209–$315 rooms, $300–$1,300, suites | AE, D, DC, MC, V.

COSTA MESA

Best Western Newport Mesa Inn. Near the center of the Irvine corporate business community is this three-story building, accessible by taking the Del Mar exit off of the 55. Complimentary Continental breakfast. Refrigerators, some in-room hot tubs, cable TV. Pool. Fitness center. Hot tub. Sauna. Laundry facilities. Business services. Some pets allowed. | 2642 Newport Blvd. 92627 | 949/650–3020 | fax 949/650–1220 | www.bestwestern.com | 97 rooms | $69–$149 | AE, D, DC, MC, V.

Doubletree Hotel. Near John Wayne Airport, this modern, spacious 7-story hotel has a glittering atrium lobby with glass elevators. Rooms have a contemporary feel and a warm sage and yellow color-scheme. The hotel is next to the South Coast Plaza shopping center. Restaurant, bar (with entertainment), room service. In-room data ports, refrigerators, cable TV. Pool. Beauty salon, hot tub, massage. Exercise equipment. Business services. Airport shuttle. Some pets allowed. | 3050 Bristol St. 92626 | 714/540–7000 | fax 714/540–9176 | www.doubletreehotels.com | 484 rooms | $89–$179 | AE, D, DC, MC, V.

Ramada Limited. In the business district, this simple 3-story hotel is one mi from Newport's attractive beaches and restaurants. Restaurant, complimentary Continental breakfast. Some microwaves, refrigerators, cable TV. Pool. Hot tub. Exercise equipment. Laundry facilities. Airport shuttle. Some pets allowed. | 1680 Superior Ave. 92627 | 949/645–2221 | fax 949/650–9125 | 140 rooms, 20 suites | $79–$109 rooms, $119–$169 suites | AE, D, DC, MC, V.

Vagabond Inn. The Costa Mesa branch of this western-based chain has lots of windows and lots of plants to make the interior cheery, and the rooms are spacious. Complimentary Continental breakfast. Microwaves, cable TV. Pool. Hot tub. Exercise equipment. Business services. Airport shuttle. Free parking. Some pets allowed (fee). | 3205 Harbor Blvd. 92626 | 714/557–8360 | fax 714/662–7596 | www.vagabondinn.com | 125 rooms | $63–$80 | AE, D, DC, MC, V.

Westin South Coast Plaza. This 16-story hotel is downtown, next to the South Coast Plaza Retail Center and Orange County Performing Arts Center. Restaurant, bar (with entertainment), room service. In-room data ports, minibars, cable TV. Pool. Tennis. Exercise equipment. Business services. Airport shuttle. Parking (fee). Some pets allowed. | 686 Anton Blvd. 92626 | 714/540–2500 | fax 714/662–6695 | www.westin.com | 390 rooms | $125–$275 | AE, D, DC, MC, V.

Wyndham Garden Hotel–Orange County Airport. Situated by a small lake in the center of the South Coast Metro area, this large, modern hotel is near many corporate offices and one block from the South Coast Retail Center and a shopping mall. It's directly across the street from the Orange County Performing Arts Center. The rooms are furnished with a Western style. Restaurant, bar. Microwaves, cable TV. Pool. Hot tub. Exercise equipment. Laundry facilities. Business services. Airport shuttle. Some pets allowed (fee). | 3350 Ave. of the Arts 92626 | 714/751–5100 | fax 714/751–0129 | www.wyndham.com | 238 rooms | $232–$262 | AE, D, DC, MC, V.

CRESCENT CITY

Super 8. Three blocks south of Cresent City, these affordable accommodations overlook the city and the marina. The large rooms in the two-story hotel have modern furnishings. Restaurant. Cable TV. Business services. Some pets allowed. | 685 U.S. 101 S | 707/464–4111 | fax 707/465–8916 | www.super8.com | 49 rooms | $66–$75 | AE, D, MC, V.

DANA POINT

Capistrano Seaside Inn. Across the Pacific Coast Highway from Capistrano Beach, this 1928, two-story inn offers small but cozy rooms at a good price for the location. Each room has a wood-burning fireplace and a balcony or small patio screened by shrubbery. Refrigerators, cable TV. Pets allowed (fee). | 34862 Pacific Coast Hwy., Capistrano Beach 92624 | 949/496–1399 or 800/252–3224 | 28 rooms | $99–$139 | AE, MC, V.

Marriott Laguna Cliffs Resort. On a hill overlooking Doheny State Beach, this 1985 property has attractive, comfortable rooms and first-rate service in one of the area's most scenic locations. The bar and deck area afford great views of the ocean and Orange County. Some rooms in the four-story hotel have a patio or balcony. 2 pools. Hot tub, sauna. 2 tennis courts. Health club. Pets allowed (fee). | 25135 Park Lantern 92629 | 949/661–5000 or 800/533–9748 | fax 949/661–3688 | 346 rooms | $179–$219 | AE, D, DC, MC, V.

DAVIS

Best Western University Lodge. This three-story lodge is a good place to stop if you have business at the university, which is one block away. Some kitchenettes, microwaves, refrigerators, cable TV. Spa. Exercise equipment. Some pets allowed. | 123 B St. | 530/756–7890 | fax 530/756–0245 | www.bestwestern.com | 53 rooms | $75–$99 | AE, D, DC, MC, V.

DEATH VALLEY NATIONAL PARK

Stove Pipe Wells Village. An aircraft landing strip is an unusual touch for an Old West-style motel, as is a heated mineral pool, but everything else here is pretty standard. There are, however, also some great panoramic views of mountains, the desert, and dunes. The property is 25 mi from Furnace Creek at the west end of Death Valley National Park. Restaurant, bar. No room phones. Pool. Some pets allowed (fee). | Rte. 190 92328 | 760/786–2387 | fax 760/786–2389 | 82 rooms in 5 buildings | $64–$83 | AE, D, MC, V.

DUNSMUIR

Cedar Lodge. This single-story lodge 6 mi away from Mount Shasta ski park is set on secluded, tree-shaded grounds near the Sacramento River. You'll find a large aviary with exotic birds on the premises. The lodge was built in the 1920s and has many wildlife photographs on the walls. Some rooms have wood-burning fireplaces or stoves. Picnic area. Some kitchenettes, cable TV, in-room VCRs. Some pets allowed (fee). | 4201 Dunsmuir Ave. 96025 | 530/235–4331 | fax 530/235–4000 | www.cedarlodgedunsmuir.com | 25 rooms | $40–$50 | AE, D, MC, V.

Railroad Park Resort. One of Dunsmuir's major attractions, this resort is a fitting tribute to the area's railroad legacy. You can stay in cabins or in restored antique cabooses that have been converted into wood-paneled guest rooms. The cabooses are loosely arranged in a semi-circle around a swimming pool and spa. The restaurant and lounge are in converted antique dining cars. On the grounds are a huge steam engine and a restored water tower from Dunsmuir's railroad days. Built in 1968, the resort is 1 mi north of Dunsmuir and within walking distance of the Sacramento River. RV hookups. Restaurant, bar, picnic area. Refrigerators, cable TV. Hot tubs. Laundry facilities. Some pets allowed (fee). | 100 Railroad Park Rd. 96025 | 530/235–4440 or 530/235–0430 (campground) | fax 530/235–4470 | rp@rrpark.com | www.rrpark.com | 27 rooms | $75–$80 | AE, D, MC, V.

EL CENTRO

El Dorado Motel. This two-story motel, built in the 1970s, is within walking distance of a fast-food restaurant and a Mexican restaurant. Restaurant, complimentary Continental breakfast. Some kitchenettes, some refrigerators, cable TV. Pool. Airport shuttle. Some pets allowed. | 1464 Adams Ave. 92243 | 760/352–7333 | 72 rooms | $49 | AE, D, DC, MC, V.

Executive Inn. This small, two-story motel is in the downtown area, near to shopping and movie theaters. Some of the rooms have views of the pool. Restaurant, complimentary Continental breakfast. Some kitchenettes, some microwaves, refrigerators, cable TV. Pool. Laundry facilities. Some pets allowed. | 725 State St. 92243 | 760/352–8500 | fax 760/352–1322 | 42 rooms | $30 | MC, V.

Ramada Inn. This two-story brick motel is in a residential neighborhood across from a medical center $1/4$ mi from I-8. Most of the basic rooms are accessed by interior corridors, and some rooms have pool views. It's only 11 mi from Mexicali. Restaurant, bar, room service. Cable TV. Pool. Hot tub. Gym. Laundry facilities. Airport shuttle. Some pets allowed. | 1455 Ocotillo Dr. 92243 | 760/352–5152 | fax 760/337–1567 | www.ramada.com | 147 rooms | $57–$70 | AE, D, DC, MC, V.

ELK

Elk Guest House. With over a mile of private beach access, you'll find seclusion as well as beautiful ocean views from every room in this guest house. One room has a fireplace and a feather bed beneath a skylight for stargazing. In the 60-acre gardens, you'll find a 200-ft waterfall, clear pools, and fern-filled grottos, and you can pick your own herbs, flowers, and vegetables. The guest house provides complimentary canoes and kayaks for paddling on the Navarro River. Some kitchenettes. Hot tub. Hiking. Beach. Pets allowed (fee). | 1900 Pacific Coast Hwy. 95432 | 707/877–3308 | www.elkguesthouse.com | 2 rooms, 2 cottages | $95 rooms, $195–$230 cottages.

Greenwood Pier Inn. On a rocky cliff 150 ft above sea level, these cottages guarantee spectacular ocean views. Each room is uniquely furnished with antiques, quilts, and original art. Some rooms have skylights, others have large spa tubs, fireplaces or wood-burning stoves. The lush garden is the source of the fresh flowers in every room, and there's an outdoor hot tub set on the cliff. Restaurant, complimentary breakfast. Refrigerators, no room phones, no TV. Hot tub. Some pets allowed. No smoking. | 5928 Rte. 1S 95432 | 707/877–9997 | fax 707/877–3439 | www.elkcoast.com or greenwoodpierinn.com | 13 cottages | $120–$235 | AE, MC, V.

ESCONDIDO

Quails Inn. This two-story 1970s inn on a mile-long lake is surrounded by a lush garden of pine trees, palms, flowering hibiscus, bougainvillea, and avocado groves. Some rooms have lake views. Restaurant, room service. Cable TV. 2 pools. Hot tub. Gym, boating. Some pets allowed (fee). | 1025 La Bonita Dr., Lake San Marcos 92069 | 760/744–0120 or 800/447–6556 | fax 760/744–0748 | www.quailsinn.com | 140 rooms | $99–$149 | AE, D, DC, MC, V.

Welk Resort Center. Built by bandleader Lawrence Welk in the 1960s, this resort covers more than 600 acres of rugged, oak-studded hillside and includes a hotel, condominiums, recreation facilities, and an entertainment complex that presents Broadway-style musicals year-round. A museum displays Welk memorabilia, and the rooms, decorated with a Southwestern flair, have golf-course views. Bar, dining room. In-room data ports, some refrigerators, cable TV. 2 pools. Beauty salon, hot tub, massage. 3 18-hole golf courses, putting green, 3 tennis courts. Exercise equipment. Children's programs. Some pets allowed. | 8860 Lawrence Welk Dr. 92026 | 760/749–3000 or 800/932–9355 | fax 760/749–5263 | www.welkresort.com | 133 rooms | $109–$119 | AE, D, DC, MC, V.

EUREKA

Eureka Inn. This large Tudor-style hotel was built in 1922 and named to the National Register of Historic Places in 1982. Its vast, high-ceilinged lobby with polished redwood beams, crystal chandeliers, and massive brick fireplace plays host to swing dances and a 22-ft Christmas tree. Past guests have included Winston Churchill, Robert F. Kennedy, J. D. Rockefeller, Cornelius Vanderbilt, Jr., Shirley Temple, Ronald Reagan, Bill Cosby, Steven Spielberg, and Mickey Mantle. 2 restaurants, 2 bars (1 with entertainment). Cable TV. Pool. Hot tub, saunas. Business services, airport shuttle. Some pets allowed. | 518 7th St. 95501 | 707/442–6441 or 800/862–4906 | fax 707/442–0637 | www.eurekainn.com | 95 rooms, 9 suites | $99–$145, $175–$289 suites | AE, D, DC, MC, V.

Eureka Red Lion Inn. This three-story inn, built in 1974, is located in downtown Eureka. Restaurant, bar (with entertainment), room service. In-room data ports, cable TV. Pool. Hot tub. Business services, airport shuttle, free parking. Some pets allowed. | 1929 4th St. | 707/445–0844 | fax 707/445–2752 | 178 rooms | $89–$109 | AE, D, DC, MC, V.

Eureka Travelodge. This two-story hotel was built in the early 1950s. Located in the center of downtown Eureka, it makes an economical option and is within walking distance of Old Town with its shops and restaurants. Complimentary Continental breakfast. Cable TV. Pool. Business services. Some pets allowed. | 4 4th St. 95501 | 707/443–6345 | fax 707/443–1486 | 46 rooms | $50–$74 | AE, D, DC, MC, V.

Quality Inn Eureka. This 2-story motel with exterior corridors is in the heart of downtown Eureka, right off U.S. 101. If you want a quiet room, ask for one in the back of the building. Complimentary Continental breakfast. Cable TV. Pool, wading pool. Hot tub, sauna. Business services. Some pets allowed. | 1209 4th St. 95501 | 707/443–1601 or 800/772–1622 | fax 707/444–8365 | www.qualityinn.com | 60 rooms | $68–$150 | AE, D, DC, MC, V.

Weaver's Inn. This B&B is in a quiet residential area a few blocks from downtown Eureka and 1 mi east of the Old Town area. It occupies a stately Colonial Revival house built in 1883. Special touches include overstuffed canopied beds and a Japanese Contemplation Garden. Complimentary breakfast. No room phones, TV in common area. Pets allowed. | 1440 B St. 95501 | 707/443–8119 or 800/992–8119 | fax 707/443–7923 | www.humboldt1.com/~weavrinn/weaversinn | 3 rooms, 1 suite | $75–$110, $125 suite | AE, D, DC, MC, V.

FAIRFIELD

Inns of America. At this contemporary chain motel adjacent to I–80, you'll be 5 mi from downtown Fairfield and 10 mi from Six Flags Marine World. In-room data ports, cable TV. Pool. Laundry facilities. Pets allowed. | 4376 Central Place, Suisun City 94585 | 707/864–1728 | fax 707/864–8226 | 101 rooms | $75–$130 | AE, MC, V.

FORT BRAGG

Colonial Inn. Built as a private residence in 1912 and converted to a hotel in the 1940s, this inn 4 blocks east of Main St. in a residential neighborhood is recognized as an architectural jewel of the Arts and Crafts Movement. The rooms, individually furnished in styles compatible with the Craftsman tradition, contain original art; two have wood-burning fireplaces. Cable TV, in-room VCRs, no room phones. Pets allowed (fee). | 533 E. Fir St. 95437 | 707/964–1384 or 877/964–1384 | innkeeper@colonialinnfortbragg.com | www.colonialinnfortbragg.com | 10 rooms | $80–$130 | No credit cards.

FREMONT

Best Western Garden Court Inn. Built in 1975, this three-story inn is situated on several acres of landscaped gardens in a suburban area. Restaurant, bar, complimentary Continental breakfast. Cable TV. Pool. Hot tub, sauna. Business services, free parking. Some pets allowed (fee). | 5400 Mowry Ave. 94538 | 510/792–4300 | fax 510/792–2643 | www.bestwestern.com | 122 rooms | $89–$149 | AE, D, DC, MC, V.

Residence Inn by Marriott. This two-story building on the east side of Fremont is next to New Port Mall, 2 mi from the local BART station, and 10 mi from Great America Theme Park. Suite-style rooms have separate living and sleeping areas, work desks, and fully equipped kitchens, perfect for business travelers and families. The inn is also within 7 mi of eight major companies. Restaurant, picnic area, complimentary Continental breakfast. Kitchenettes, cable TV. Pool. Hot tub. Laundry facilities. Business services, airport shuttle. Some pets allowed (fee). | 5400 Farwell Pl. 94536 | 510/794–5900 | fax 510/793–6587 | 80 suites | $149–$169 suites | AE, D, DC, MC, V.

FRESNO

Doubletree of Fresno. Formerly the Hilton of Fresno, this hotel is 4 blocks west of the convention center and 7 mi west of the airport. All rooms have an ironing board, coffee maker, and alarm clocks. Of the three restaurants on the property, one serves a casual breakfast, and one offers the only rooftop lounge in Fresno, with a great view of the city. 3 restaurants, bar. In-room data ports, cable TV. Pool. Hot tub. Airport shuttle. Some pets allowed. | 1055 Van Ness Ave. 93721 | 559/485–9000 | fax 559/485–7666 | www.doubletreehotels.com | 192 rooms | $55–$79 | AE, D, DC, MC, V.

Radisson Hotel and Conference Center. Eight stories high with an atrium and three-story waterfall, this brick hotel and conference center is 2 mi from the historic downtown Tower District. The spacious rooms have an elegant appearance, filled with dark wood furniture. The hotel is adjacent to Fresno's Convention center, and less than 10 mi to the airport, shopping and golf courses. Restaurant, Bar. In-room data ports, cable TV. Pool. Beauty salon, sauna. Shops, video games. Laundry service. Airport shuttle. Pets allowed. | 2233 Ventura 93721 | 559/268–1000 or 800/333–3333 | fax 559/441–2954 | www.radisson.com | 321 rooms | $79–$125 | AE, D, DC, MC, V.

FULLERTON

Marriott at California State University. This hotel is next to California State University Fullerton and 7 mi from Disneyland. Restaurants and the city's corporate center are within walking distance. All rooms are furnished with a work desk and the daily newspaper is complimentary. Restaurant, bar. In-room data ports, refrigerators, cable TV. Pool. Hot tub. Exercise equipment. Business services. Some pets allowed. | 2701 E. Nutwood Ave. 92831 | 714/738–7800 | fax 714/738–0288 | www.marriott.com/marriott/laxel | 224 rooms | $79–$125 | AE, D, DC, MC, V.

GARBERVILLE

Sherwood Forest. This one-story hotel is one of the few lodgings in central Garberville. The rustic setting, which includes 3 acres of pine and redwood trees, reflects the flavor of the town. Popular with tourists, the grounds also offer a flower garden and barbecue pits. Humbolt State Park is 10 mi to the north and Benbow Lake is 2 mi south. Restaurant, picnic area. Some refrigerators, cable TV. Pool. Hot tub. Fishing. Laundry facilities. Business services. Some pets allowed. | 814 Redwood Dr. | 707/923–2721 | fax 707/923–3677 | 32 rooms | $54–80 | AE, D, MC, V.

GLENDALE

Vagabond Inn. Rooms at this three-story hotel are equipped with work desks, ergonomic chairs, and other furnishings with business in mind. The hotel is in the commercial district, but there are also a number of tourist attractions nearby including Universal Studios, Dodger Stadium, and the Hollywood Rose Bowl. Restaurant, complimentary Continental breakfast. Some in-room data ports, some microwaves, refrigerators, cable TV. Pool. Some pets allowed (fee). | 120 W. Colorado St. 91204 | 818/240–1700 | fax 626/548–8428 | www.vagabondinn.com | 52 rooms | $89 | AE, D, DC, MC, V.

GLENDORA

Guest House Inn. This two-story building, in a commercial area, is only a five-minute walk from downtown. Complimentary breakfast. In-room modems, refrigerator, kitchenettes, cable TV. Pool. Hot tub, spa. Laundry service. Pets allowed. | 606 W. Alosta 91740 | 626/963–9361 | fax 626/914–2037 | 38 rooms | $74 | AE, D, DC, MC, V.

GUALALA

Gualala Country Inn. Situated on the Mendocino coastline, this inn affords views of the surf, the whales, and the breathtaking sunsets. Some rooms have wood-burning fireplaces and ocean views. The rooms each have their own country theme. Several beaches are within walking distance. Some pets allowed (fee). No smoking. | 47955 Center St. 95445 | 707/884–4343 or 800/564–4466 | fax 707/884–1018 | countryinn@gualala.com | www.gualala.com | 20 rooms | $89–$159 | AE, D, DC, MC, V.

HALF MOON BAY

Holiday Inn Express. This hotel is in downtown Half Moon Bay. Tennis and golf facilities are 2 mi away. You can go deep sea fishing at Princeton Harbor (4 mi), or hike in the Purisma

Redwoods (4 mi). Complimentary Continental breakfast. In-room data ports. Business services. Some pets allowed (fee). | 230 S. Cabrillo Hwy. | 650/726–3400 | fax 650/726–1256 | www.hiexpress.com/halfmoonbay | 52 rooms, 1 suite | $79–$149, $179 suite | AE, D, DC, MC, V.

HANFORD

Irwin Street. At this B&B inn you'll find four tree-shaded, restored Victorian homes that have been converted into rooms and suites. Most accommodations contain four-poster beds, leaded-glass windows, and dark wood detailing; bathrooms have marble basins, brass fixtures, and old-fashioned tubs. Restaurant, complimentary Continental breakfast. Cable TV. Pool. Some pets allowed. | 522 N. Irwin St. | 559/583–8000 or 888/583–8080 | fax 559/583–8793 | 33 rooms in 4 buildings | $69–$125 | AE, D, DC, MC, V.

HAYWARD

Executive Inn. This three-story hotel is downtown among restaurants, shopping, and the business district. A golf course and a movie theater are nearby. Restaurant, complimentary Continental breakfast. Refrigerators, cable TV. Pool. Exercise equipment. Laundry facilities. Business services, airport shuttle, free parking. Some pets allowed. | 20777 Hesperian Blvd. 94541 | 510/732–6300 or 800/553–5083 | fax 510/783–2265 | 168 rooms | $95–$109 | AE, D, DC, MC, V.

HEALDSBURG

Best Western Dry Creek Inn. The rooms in this Spanish-style building have king- or double queen-size beds. Upon arrival, you'll find a welcoming bottle of local wine. The three-story inn is on the north side of town. Complimentary Continental breakfast. In-room data ports, refrigerators, cable TV. Pool. Hot tub. Exercise equipment. Laundry facilities. Business services. Some pets allowed (fee). | 198 Dry Creek Rd. | 707/433–0300 or 800/222–5784 | fax 707/433–1129 | www.drycreekinn.com | 103 rooms | $69–$149 | AE, D, DC, MC, V.

HEMET

Best Western Hemet Motor Inn. On the west side of Hemet, this two-story inn built in the early 1980s provides some unique activities, such as shuffleboard. Palm trees dot the grounds. Only 90 minutes from beaches, Disneyland, and mountain resorts, this inn flourishes in the San Jacinto Valley. Some kitchenettes, refrigerators, cable TV. Pool. Hot tub. Laundry facilities. Business services. Some pets allowed. | 2625 W. Florida Ave. 92545 | 909/925–6605 | fax 909/925–7095 | www.bestwestern.com | 68 rooms | $46–$58 | AE, D, DC, MC, V.

Travelodge. A basic two-story lodge hotel built in 1990 has exterior corridors and nothing fancy. However you have a few more amenities here than you normally would see at this price. Complimentary Continental breakfast. Refrigerators, cable TV. Pool. Hot tub. Laundry facilities. Some pets allowed. | 1201 W. Florida Ave. 92543 | 909/766–1902 | www.travelodge.com | 46 rooms | $45–$75 | AE, D, DC, MC, V.

HOLLISTER

Cinderella Motel. See if you can spot the motel's namesake in its doll collection, on display in the lobby. The small, single-story lodging sits on the north side of town, about 2 blocks from downtown and 1 mi north of Route 25. Complimentary Continental breakfast. Refrigerators, cable TV. Pool. Pets allowed. | 110 San Felipe Rd. 95023 | 831/637–5761 | 20 rooms | $42–$85 | AE, D, DC, MC, V.

HOLLYWOOD (L.A.)

Best Western Hollywood Hills. In a residential area, two four-story buildings built in 1949 provide views of the Hollywood sign from a few of the rooms. Two miles from Universal

Studios and 2 blocks from Mann's Chinese Theater and the Hollywood Walk of Fame, this choice is all about location. Restaurant, room service. Some kitchenettes, refrigerators, cable TV. Pool. Business services. Some pets allowed (fee). | 6141 Franklin Ave. 90028 | 323/464–5181 | fax 323/962–0536 | www.bestwestern.com | 86 rooms | $99–$130 | AE, D, DC, MC, V.

HUNTINGTON BEACH

Hilton Waterfront Beach Resort. Practically on the beach, all rooms have an ocean view. The 12-story Mediterranean-style resort hotel was built in the early 1990s in a residential area, minutes from the Pier and the beach. Although it would appear that this hotel is best suited for those on vacation, there are also many amenities geared toward the business traveler. This resort prides itself in being able to accommodate your needs for a special event or a simple weekend getaway. Restaurant, bar (with entertainment). In-room data ports, minibars, cable TV. Pool. Hot tub. Tennis. Basketball, health club, volleyball. Beach, bicycles. Kids' programs (ages 2–8). Business services, airport shuttle. Pets allowed (fee). | 21100 Pacific Coast Hwy. 92648 | 714/960–7873 | fax 714/960–3791 | www.waterfrontbeachresort.hilton.com | 266 rooms, 24 suites | $179–$324, $369–$579 suites | AE, D, DC, MC, V.

IDYLLWILD

Cedar View Cottage. This 1920s gingerbread-style cottage was once owned by Dwight Taylor, author of *Top Hat* and other Fred Astaire films. Built of knotty pine and tucked into a woodsy corner of town, this housekeeping cottage, rented as a single unit, has a make-yourself-comfortable appeal, with a stereo and CD collection, lots of books and videos, espresso maker, popcorn popper, a gas grill on the back deck, fresh flowers, and a chocolate on your pillow at the end of the day. Downstairs there's a living room, fireplace, full kitchen, dining nook, queen-size bed and full bath. Upstairs, stretch out in a loft with 2 twin beds and ½-bath. Cable TV, in-room VCRs. Pets allowed (fee). | 25165 Cedar St. 92549 | 909/659–3339 (info) or 909/659–2966 (reservations) | www.towncrier.com/inns/cedarview.html | 1 cottage | $110–$125 | AE, D, MC, V.

Fireside. Nestled within the San Jacinto Mountains 3 blocks from the village center, you can sit back and feed the squirrels, birds, and raccoons from your front porch. If you're lucky, you may even see a black squirrel. Each cottage has a distinctive personality and rustic design, a fireplace, and sitting room; several have private porches and kitchens. Picnic area. Some refrigerators, some kitchenettes, cable TV, in-room VCRs, no room phones. Some pets allowed. No smoking. | 54540 N. Circle Dr. 92549 | 909/659–2966 | www.idyllwild.com/fireside.htm | 7 duplex cottages, 1 private | $60–$110 cottages | AE, D, MC, V.

Silver Pines Lodge and Creekside Cabins. Built in 1923 and an inn since the early 1950s, this rustic collection of free-standing cabins and rooms sits on 1½ acres of wooded pine forest overlooking Strawberry Creek, 2 blocks from the village. Overstuffed chairs in the 1,100-square-ft main lodge room invite you to sit a spell. Most lodge rooms have fireplaces; some also have kitchens. Or, use the gas grill on the lodge's back deck. Several of the larger cabins work well for families, and all of the rooms have porches. Refrigerators, cable TV. No room phones. Pets allowed (fee). No smoking. | 25955 Cedar St. 92549 | 909/659–4335 | www.silverpinesidyllwild.com | 6 cabins; 11 rooms | $55–$130 cabins; $55–$90 rooms | AE, D, MC, V.

INDIAN WELLS

Hyatt Grand Champions Resort. Expansive courtyards, sparkling fountains, formal gardens, and celebrated artwork can keep you occupied from the moment you cross the threshold, without even considering the golf course and tennis courts. The suites at this five-story Hyatt resort feature step-down parlors and a balcony or patio. There are also penthouse accommodations and garden villas. Built in 1988 on 35 acres at the foot of

California's San Jacinto mountains, the grounds include impeccably landscaped lawns with pristine views overlooking the golf course and pools, as well as the San Jacinto Mountains. This versatile resort, a mecca for business and vacation travelers, is 10 mi southeast of the Living Desert, the Desert Museum, and the Oasis Water Park; Palm Desert Business Center is 10 mi to the west, and downtown Palm Springs is 20 mi to the northwest. Guests have privileges to the public golf course. Restaurant. Pool. Steam room. Golf, tennis. Playground. Laundry service. Business services. Some pets allowed. | 44-600 Indian Wells La. 92210 | 760/341–1000 | fax 760/568–2236 | www.grandchampions. hyatt.com/champ/ | 338 suites | $290–$375 | AE, D, DC, MC, V.

Miramonte Resort. A retreat on 11 lush and landscaped acres at the base of the Santa Rosa Mountains in the heart of Indian Wells, Miramonte is a series of 12 two-story villas with plenty of outdoor lounging areas to relax and enjoy the warmth of the sun, or conduct business if you must. The Italianate design incorporates arches and columns, with stonework and wrought-iron touches. Each room has a private terrace and either a king-size bed or two queens, with marble baths and luxury bath products. Restaurant, room service. Pool. Spa. Gym. Laundry service. Business services. Some pets allowed. | 4500 Indian Wells La. 92210 | 760/341–2200 | fax 760/568–0541 | info@miramonteresort.com | www.miramonte-resort.com | 177 rooms, 45 suites | $239–$279 rooms; $299–$399 suites | AE, D, DC, MC, V.

INDIO

Best Western Date Tree. Surrounded by palm trees and cactus gardens, this two-story Best Western 2 mi north of downtown has adopted the unique landscape native to the area for its landscaping. It's less than 3 mi from virtually all of Indio's attractions. Suites with kitchenettes can accommodate you for an extended stay. Restaurant, picnic area, complimentary Continental breakfast. In-room data ports, refrigerators, cable TV. Pool. Hot tub. Exercise equipment. Video games. Playground. Laundry facilities. Business services. Some pets allowed. | 81-909 Indio Blvd. 92201 | 760/347–3421 or 800/292–5599 | fax 760/347–3421 | www.datetree.com | 119 rooms | $49–$109 | AE, D, DC, MC, V.

Quality Inn. Two blocks south of I-10 at the Monroe St. exit, this three-story inn received a facelift in 2000. Interior corridors and some handicap facilities make this hotel easily accessible. Free newspapers are a special morning treat along with your breakfast. Complimentary Continental breakfast. Some microwaves, refrigerators, cable TV. Pool. Hot tub. Business services. Pets allowed. | 43505 Monroe St. 92201 | 760/347–4044 | fax 760/347–1287 | www.comfortinn.com | 63 rooms | $49–$119 | AE, D, DC, MC, V.

Travelodge. Just off I-10 at the Washington St. exit, this dependable chain hotel consists of a two-story unit and is within 3 mi of golf courses and the Riverside Fairground, home to the annual Indio Date Festival. If you packed the racket, check out the on-site tennis court next to the pool. Cable TV. Pool, hot tub. Tennis court. Laundry service. Business services, free parking. Some pets allowed (fee). | 80651 Hwy. 111 92201 | 760/342–0882 or 888/515–6375 | fax 760/342–7560 | www.travelodge.com | 50 rooms | $39–$109 | AE, D, DC, MC, V.

INVERNESS

Manka's Inverness Lodge. Built in 1917, the lodge is surrounded by 8,000 acres of Point Reyes National Seashore, which has biking and hiking trails, gentle bay beaches, and wildlife. Vintage fishing gear and local artifacts decorate the rustic wood beams and evoke a hunting lodge aura. Deep red and black plaids reflect the warmth of the fireplaces. Rooms have log-framed beds and deep comfy reading chairs. Restaurant, complimentary breakfast. In-room data ports, some kitchenettes, refrigerators, cable TV, in-room VCRs. Some room phones. Hiking. Business services. Some pets allowed (fee). No smoking. | 30 Calendar Way | 415/669–1034 or 800/585–5634 | fax 415/669–1598 | www.mankas.com | 8 rooms (4 with shower only), 1 suite, 2 cabins | $215–$465 | MC, V.

IRVINE

Marriott. Four blocks northeast of the John Wayne Airport, this 17-story hotel, with its many meeting rooms and business services, is geared toward the business traveler. For those on vacation, Newport Beach and Balboa Island, the Orange County Performing Arts Center, and shopping are all within a few miles. A beauty salon and spa are across the street. Both Disneyland and Long Beach are within a half-hour's drive. 2 restaurants, bars (with entertainment). In-room data ports, refrigerators, microwaves, cable TV. Pool. Barbershop, beauty salon. Tennis. Exercise equipment, health club. Laundry facilities. Business services, airport shuttle, parking (fee). Some pets allowed. | 18000 Von Karman Ave. 92612 | 949/553–0100 | fax 949/261–7059 | www.marriott.com | 485 rooms, 10 suites | $189–$219 | AE, D, DC, MC, V.

JACKSON

Jackson Holiday Lodge. One eighth of a mile from the historic Kennedy Mines, 12 mi from local vineyards, and other town attractions, this motel ½ mi north of Jackson with simple rooms provides a quaint central home base from which to tour the area. Complimentary Continental breakfast. Some kitchenettes, cable TV. Pool. Some pets allowed. | 209/223–0486 | fax 209/223–2905 | kennedy.amadornet.net/travelers/lodging/holiday.html | 850 N. Rte. 49 | 36 rooms | $70–90 | AE, D, DC, MC, V.

JAMESTOWN

1859 Historic National Hotel. Brass beds, patchwork quilts, and lace curtains fill the rooms of this country inn in Jamestown, 3 mi south of Sonora via Route 108. Some rooms have private baths (with modern but funky looking pull-chain toilets) and some share baths fitted out with, among other things, antique wash basins. The 19th-century saloon has the orginal redwood bar. Dining room, complimentary breakfast, room service. No room phones, no TV in some rooms. Pets allowed (fee). No kids under 10. | 75 Main St. 95327 | 209/984–3446, 800/894–3446 from CA or 800/446–1333, Ext. 286 | fax 209/984–5620 | info@national-hotel.com | www.national-hotel.com | 9 rooms | $80–$120 | AE, D, DC, MC, V.

JOSHUA TREE NATIONAL PARK

Joshua Tree B&B. Housed in a 1930s hacienda-style building with a large swimming pool and a charming rose garden, all rooms here have private showers (no tubs), antiques and Old West memorabilia. Next to the Joshua Tree National Park. Dining room, picnic area, complimentary breakfast. In-room data ports, some microwaves, refrigerators, cable TV. Pool. Massage. Playground. Business services, airport shuttle. Some pets allowed. | 61259 Twentynine Palms Hwy., Joshua Tree 92252 | 760/366–1188 or 800/366–1444 | fax 760/366–3805 | joshuatreeinn@thegrid.net | www.joshuatreeinn.com | 8 rooms, 2 suites, 4 cottages (with shower only) | $85–$275 | AE, D, DC, MC, V.

Mojave Rock Ranch Cabins. If peace, solitude, and stunning desert views are what you seek, try one of these cabins near Joshua Tree National Park. The cabins, sitting on 120 acres of Mojave Desert land, are about 6 mi north of Highway 62 and 10 mi from either the east park entrance in Twentynine Palms, or the west entrance in Joshua Tree. Which to choose? Rock Ranch cabin has two bedrooms and a sleeping porch, great for star-gazing. The Bungalow has a hand-built stone-and-iron fireplace, outdoor dining on a covered patio, mesquite, and desert willow trees, and a pond. The Homesteader has authentic knotty pine paneling, antiques, and down pillows and comforters. All cabins have full kitchens, hammocks, and "Cowboy Spas" (private, outdoor hot tubs). There is a corral for your horses and dogs as well. If you need something to do, peruse the inn's library, or check-out a complimentary video. Cable TV. Hot tubs. Pets allowed (fee). No smoking. | Box 552 92252 | 760/366–8455 | fax 760/366–1996 | www.mojaverockranch.com | 4 cabins | $275–$325 | No credit cards.

JULIAN

Apple Tree Inn. Three miles west of downtown Julian in a residential country area, this homey single-story inn is convenient for those wanting to explore local shops and galleries. Rooms are unpretentious, but do have phones and satellite TV. Pool. Some pets allowed. | 4360 Rte. 78 92070 | 760/765–0222 | 16 rooms | $82–$87 | AE, D, MC, V.

Wikiup Bed and Breakfast. You won't be lonely here, not with a llama, dogs, cats, a donkey, sheep, goats, and assorted birds keeping you company at this rustic lodge. The contemporary cedar-and-brick structure, less than a mile east of Julian, has a relaxed, family appeal, with play equipment and, of course, the critters roaming across three wooded acres. Inside, high open-beam ceilings with sky lights, cedar paneling, and modern Danish furnishings set the tone in the common areas. Guest rooms have an eclectic flair, with names such as "Rose's Secret" (Victorian florals and cedar hot tub), "Dreamcatcher" (rustic, four-poster bed and two terra-cotta fireplaces), and "Willow Warren" (queen-size bed crowned by a canopy of willow branches). Complimentary breakfast. Refrigerators, microwaves, in-room hot tubs. Hot tub. TV in common area. Library. Pets allowed. | 1645 Whispering Pines Dr. 92036 | 760/765–1890 or 800/526–2725 | fax 760/765–1515 | www.wikiupbnb.com | 4 | $155–$175 | MC, V.

JUNE LAKE

Double Eagle Resort and Spa. These fully furnished, pine-paneled two-bedroom cabins have wood-burning stoves, fireplaces, overstuffed sofas and armchairs, and decks, and the spa's services are an unusual luxury in this forested location. Find the resort off Highway 158, within 1 mi of skiing areas. Restaurant. Kitchenettes, microwaves, refrigerators, cable TV. Beauty salon, spa. Gym, health club. Fishing. Business services. Pets allowed. No smoking. | Spa Rt. 3 | 760/648–7004 | fax 760/648–7017 | www.double-eagle-resort.com | 13 cabins | $153–$288 | AE, D, DC, MC, V.

KING CITY

Courtesy Inn. This modern all-suites hotel is right off U.S. 101 at the Broadway exit next to a family restaurant and several fast food chains, and 1 mi from town. Rooms are decorated in cool tones of blue and mauve. Restaurant, complimentary Continental breakfast. In-room data ports, microwaves, refrigerators, some in-room hot tubs, cable TV, in-room VCRs (and movies). Pool. Hot tub. Laundry facilities. Business services. Some pets allowed. | 4 Broadway Circle | 831/385–4646 or 800/350–5616 | fax 831/385–6024 | 63 suites | $85–$175 suites | AE, D, DC, MC, V.

LA JOLLA

Andrea Villa Inn. This two-story hotel is a 15-minute walk uphill to the Scripps Institute of Oceanography. Shops, golf, and the beaches are slightly further west, 1.5 mi from the hotel. Units are roomy and comfortable, and if you get hooked, the inn has weekly and monthly rates. Complimentary Continental breakfast. Some kitchenettes, cable TV. Pool. Hot tub. Laundry facilities. Business services. Pets allowed. | 2402 Torrey Pines Rd. | 858/459–3311 or 800/411–2141 | fax 858/459–1320 | www.andreavilla.com | 49 rooms | $119–$165 | AE, D, DC, MC, V.

Marriott. In the heart of La Jolla's Golden Triangle, a commercial district framed by I–5, I–805 and Rte. 52, this full-service 15-story hotel 3 mi east of downtown is geared toward the business traveler. A large shopping mall with movie theaters and an indoor ice rink are across the street. Restaurant, bar. In-room data ports, cable TV. Pool. Hot tub. Gym. Video Games. Laundry facilities. Business services, parking (fee). Some pets allowed. | 4240 La Jolla Village Dr. | 858/587–1414 | fax 858/546–8518 | www.marriott.com | 360 rooms | $189–$268 | AE, D, DC, MC, V.

Residence Inn by Marriott. If you want self-sufficiency for an extended stay this two-story hotel is a good bet. The large, comfortable suites have living rooms and full kitchens and some have fireplaces. Choose from a traditional suite, a penthouse suite, or a studio-style suite. Downtown is 4 mi away, beaches 3 mi. Complimentary Continental breakfast. In-room data ports, microwaves, refrigerators, cable TV. 2 pools. Hot tubs. Laundry facilities. Business services. Free parking. Some pets allowed. | 8901 Gilman Dr. | 858/587–1770 | fax 858/552–0387 | 288 suites | $179 suites | AE, D, DC, MC, V.

LAGUNA BEACH

Carriage House. Just two blocks from the beach and 1 mi south of downtown, this 1920s country-style inn is one of Laguna's architectural landmarks. Complimentary fresh fruit and wine, antique furniture, a garden courtyard, and large sitting rooms in the themed suites—Lilac Time has floral bedding, a brass bed, and French doors to the courtyard, Green Palms has white wicker furniture and netting over the bed—make the inn a local favorite. Complimentary breakfast. Pets allowed. | 1322 Catalina St. | 949/494–8945 | fax 949/494–6829 | crgehsebb@aol.com | www.carriagehouse.com | 6 suites | $125–$165 | AE, MC, V.

Vacation Village. With 300 ft of its own private beach, this hotel has stunning views of the ocean and Catalina Island. It's just two blocks from the center of town with plenty of shops, restaurants, and art galleries to explore. The casual tone makes this a good choice for families. Rooms are contemporary with light walls, red and black abstract patterned bedspreads, and dark carpeting; some have ocean views. Restaurant, bar. Kitchenettes, refrigerators, cable TV. 2 pools. Hot tub. Video games. Some pets allowed. Free parking. | 647 S. Coast Hwy. 92651 | 949/494–8566 or 800/843–6895 | fax 949/494–1386 | vvillage@earthlink.net | www.vacationvillage.com | 133 rooms, 70 suites in 5 buildings | $90–$204, $246–$324 suites | AE, D, DC, MC, V.

LAKE ARROWHEAD

Saddleback Inn. Constructed as the Raven Hotel in 1917, this Victorian inn later became a retreat for the Hollywood crowd. It sits at the entrance to Lake Arrowhead Village, surrounded by pines and a beautiful stone wall. Laura Ashley fabrics complement the country furnishings in rooms and cottages, many of which have fireplaces. Restaurant. Microwaves, refrigerators, cable TV, some in-room VCRs. Pool. Exercise equipment. Laundry facilities. Business services. Pets allowed in cottages. | 300 S. State Hwy. 173 | 909/336–3571 or 800/858–3334 | fax 909/336–6111 | www.saddlebackinn.com/ | 10 rooms in main bldg., 24 1-3 bdrm. cottages | $99–195 rooms, $99–185 cottages, $165–$294 1-bdrm. cottages, $144–$294 2-bdrm. cottages, $165–$294 3-bdrm. cottages with 2 bathrooms, $317–$533 3-bdrm. cottages with 3 bathrooms | AE, D, DC, MC, V.

LITTLE RIVER

Andiron Lodge. Each of the cottages at this lodge has a private deck that faces the ocean. Van Damme State Park is 1 mi to the north. Some kitchenettes, some refrigerators, cable TV, some in-room VCRs, no room phones. Business services. Some pets allowed. | 6051 Hwy. 1 | 707/937–1543 or 877/488–5332 | fax 707/937–1542 | reservations@andironlodge.com | www.andironlodge.com | 2 rooms, 5 cabins | $70, $150 cabins | MC, V.

Inn at Schoolhouse Creek. The farmhouse which now serves as the guest services center was constructed in 1862 by one of Little River's founders and most of the surrounding cottages were built in the 1890s. The inn is on eight acres of landscaped grounds and the ocean is across the street. Complimentary breakfast. In-room data ports, some kitch-enettes, some microwaves, some refrigerators, some in-room hot tubs, cable TV, in-room VCRs (and movies). Hot tub. Business services. Some pets allowed. No smoking. | 7051 Hwy. 1 | 707/937–5525 | fax 707/937–2012 | www.schoolhousecreek.com | 4 rooms, 2 suites, 9 cottages | $115–$225, $205–$240 suites, $140–$200 cottages | AE, D, MC, V.

Seafoam Lodge. A forested hillside provides the background scenery for this lodge, which is spread out over 6 acres of manicured lawns and pine trees. All rooms provide a panoramic view of the Pacific Ocean, which is across the street. Complimentary Continental breakfast. Some kitchenettes, refrigerators, cable TV, in-room VCRs (and movies). Hot tub. Pets allowed. | 6752 Hwy. 1 | 707/937–1827 | fax 707/937–0744 | info@seafoam-lodge.com | www.seafoamlodge.com | 24 rooms in 8 buildings | $95–$175 | AE, D, MC, V.

LONG BEACH

Hilton. An upscale hotel providing extensive business support services, this 14-story marble hotel has an L-shape tower of guest rooms above two floors of public spaces, with balconies facing the city and harbor. It is downtown, just four blocks from the Long Beach Aquarium. Built in 1992, your room will have modern furniture. Restaurant, bar. In-room data ports, minibars, cable TV. Pool. Hot tub. Gym. Business services, airport shuttle, parking (fee). Some pets allowed. | Two World Trade Center 90831 | 562/983–3400 | fax 562/983–1200 | www.hilton.com | 393 rooms | $119–$189 | AE, D, DC, MC, V.

Westin Long Beach. This 16-story hotel made of concrete and glass is next to the Long Beach Convention and Entertainment Center and one block from the beach. Rooms have contemporary furnishings; many have ocean views. If you are traveling on business, you'll like the rooms with ergonomic chairs and in-room laser printer/fax/copiers. You can also take advantage of the hotel's limousine service. Restaurant, bar, room service. In-room data ports, cable TV. Pool. Hot tub. Exercise equipment. Business services. Free parking. Some pets allowed. | 333 E. Ocean Blvd. 90802 | 562/436–3000 | fax 562/436–9176 | www.westin.com | 460 rooms | $218–$236 | AE, D, DC, MC, V.

LOS ANGELES

★ **Chateau Marmont.** This 1929 castle is a Hollywood landmark, the meeting place of legends like Jean Harlow and Clark Gable. Rooms, suites, and bungalows in beautifully maintained gardens have views of the city and the Hollywood Hills. It's 3 mi west of downtown. Restaurant, room service. In-room data ports, some kitchenettes. Cable TV, in-room VCRs. Pool. Gym. Laundry service. Business services, parking (fee). Some pets allowed. | 8221 Sunset Blvd. 90046 | 323/656–1010 | fax 323/655–5311 | chateaula@aol.com | 63 rooms | $220–$345 | AE, DC, MC, V.

Hilton and Towers Los Angeles Airport. This 5-story airport Hilton, 2 blocks north of the airport and 15 mi south of downtown, has a handsome lobby with a central staircase and chandelier and three gardens. Some rooms have bathrobes and lighted work desks. Restaurants, bar. In-room data ports. Cable TV. Pool. Hot tubs. Gym. Laundry facilities. Business services, airport shuttle, parking (fee). Some pets allowed. | 5711 W. Century Blvd. 90045 | 310/410–4000 | fax 310/410–6250 | 1,234 rooms | $188 | AE, D, DC, MC, V.

Holiday Inn Brentwood–Bel Air. In prestigious Brentwood, this 17-story tower is near the Getty Center Museum and ½ mi from UCLA, at I–405 and Sunset Blvd. Rooms have bright, geometric-print bedspreads and private balconies, most with a view of the city. Restaurant, bar. In-room data ports. Cable TV. Pool. Hot tub. Exercise equipment. Video games. Laundry facilities. Business services, parking (fee). Some pets allowed. | 170 N. Church La. 90049 | 310/476–6411 | fax 310/472–1157 | hibelair@deltanet.com | 211 rooms | $139–$250 | AE, D, DC, MC, V.

Holiday Inn City Center. This nine-story downtown hotel is accessible from all major freeways, next to the Staples Center. Business travelers and conventioneers are frequent guests. Restaurant, bar. Cable TV. Pool. Exercise equipment. Laundry facilities. Business services, parking (fee). Some pets allowed. | 1020 S. Figueroa St. 90015 | 213/748–1291 | fax 213/748–6028 | 195 rooms | $119–$179 | AE, D, DC, MC, V.

Hotel Del Capri. A tropical aquarium embellishes the lobby of this hotel built in 1954 and now almost hidden by high-rises; vine-covered walls surround the hotel garden. Rooms have vases of fresh flowers on tables and nightstands, and an airy, pastel color theme. The hotel is 5 blocks from the UCLA campus. Complimentary Continental breakfast. Some kitchenettes, refrigerators, some in-room hot tubs, cable TV. Pool. Exercise equipment. Laundry facilities. Business services, free parking. Pets allowed. | 10587 Wilshire Blvd. 90024 | 310/474–3511 or 800/44–HOTEL | fax 310/470–9999 | www.hoteldelcapri.com | 80 rooms, 46 suites | $105, $130 suites | AE, DC, MC, V.

Los Angeles Airport Marriott. This large business hotel ½ mi east of the airport is 4 mi northeast of El Segundo Golf Course and 16 mi southwest of downtown. Some rooms are designed for business travelers. 2 restaurants, bar, room service. In-room data ports, some refrigerators. Cable TV. Pool. Beauty salon, hot tub. Exercise equipment. Shops, video games. Laundry facilities. Business services, airport shuttle, parking fee. Some pets allowed. | 5855 W. Century Blvd. 90045 | 310/641–5700 | fax 310/337–5358 | www.marriotthotels.com | 1,010 rooms | $155 | AE, D, DC, MC, V.

Quality Hotel Los Angeles Airport. Rooms of this 10-story hotel 1.5 mi east of the airport and 4 mi west of Manhattan Beach were renovated in 2000 and have whitewashed furniture and turquoise carpeting. Restaurant, bar. Cable TV. Pool. Exercise equipment. Video Games. Business services, airport shuttle, parking (fee). Some pets allowed. | 5249 W. Century Blvd. 90045 | 310/645–2200 | fax 310/641–8214 | 278 room | $110–$140 | AE, D, DC, MC, V.

Travelodge LAX. This two-story hotel is just 1 mi east of the airport, and 20 mi southwest of central downtown. Some rooms have private terraces, and a tropical garden surrounds the pool. Restaurant, bar, room service. Cable TV. Pool. Exercise equipment. Video games. Laundry facilities. Airport shuttle, free parking. Some pets allowed. | 5547 W. Century Blvd.

SHOP CATS

They greet you at the door, swish a welcoming wave of their tails, perhaps nose up to whomever you have brought along, and then leave you to explore their store. Who are they? Why, they're almost their own breed: shop cats. Shop cats live at work, or rather keep businesses at their homes. No doubt you know some in your own home town. Californians have their own favorites.

Little Girl has kept Bodhi Tree bookstore (8585 Melrose Ave., 310/659–1733) in West Hollywood, California since 1987, when her predecessor Chubbs passed away. Little Girl particularly likes to go out to the parking lot to sniff her customers' tailpipes—that's where she gets the black mark that sometimes rings her nose. You can see a picture of her at www.bodhitree.com.

Head over to 4820 Vineland Ave., in North Hollywood, to the Iliad Book Shop (818/509–2665) and you will find Helga and her brother, Torquemada, both born in 1994. Helga is a sweetheart, but you may want to watch out for grim Torquemada, who was named after the head torturer of the Spanish Inquisition. If you get to Small World Books at Venice Beach early enough in the morning, you may see its manager, Esme, doing her excited morning exercises—she jumps up straight into the air with all of her fur standing on end. In the afternoon, Esme spends time in the attic doing inventory. The bookstore is at 1407 Ocean Front Walk, 310/399–2360, www.smallworldbooks.com.

In Napa, visit Volume One bookstore (1405 2nd St., 707/252–1466) and you can meet Jenny, who have been living there since 1992 and now has her own fan club.

90045 | 310/649–4000 | fax 310/649–0311 | www.travelodgelax.com | 147 rooms | $74–$110 | AE, D, DC, MC, V.

W Los Angeles. This all-suite hotel is in a quiet, tree-lined neighborhood. Rooms have attached parlor areas for working, relaxing, or socializing. The Avenue of the Stars and the 20th Century Fox studios are 2 mi to the west. 3 restaurants, bar with entertainment. In-room data ports, refrigerators, room service, cable TV. 2 pools. Massage. Exercise equipment. Business services. Pets allowed. | 930 Hilgard Ave. 90024 | 310/208–8765 or 800/421–2317 | fax 310/824–0355 | 257 suites | $225–$650 suites | AE, D, DC, MC, V.

★ **Westin L.A. Airport.** This 12-story hotel with floor-to-ceiling windows in the lobby is 4 blocks east of the airport, 4 mi west of Manhattan Beach and 15 mi southwest of central downtown. Some rooms have balconies and all have pool, garden or city views. Restaurant, bar, room service. In-room data ports, some minibars. Cable TV. Pool. Hot tub. Laundry facilities. Business services, airport shuttle, parking (fee). Some pets allowed. | 5400 W. Century Blvd. 90045 | 310/216–5858 | fax 310/645–8053 | www.westin.com | 720 rooms, 43 suites | $179 rooms, $229 suites | AE, D, DC, MC, V.

LOS GATOS

Los Gatos Lodge. The lodge is in a serene example of California landscaping, with plenty of trees on 8 acres. Floral patterns and dark, soothing colors predominate in the rooms. Studios with living room area are available. There's even a garden wedding chapel. In a residential area, 10 mi west of San Jose, the lodge has eight wooden buildings completed in 1958 that had extensive improvements made in 1999. Restaurant, bar (with entertainment), complimentary Continental breakfast. Some kitchenettes, cable TV. Pool. Hot tub. Putting green. Laundry facilities. Business services. Some pets allowed. No smoking. | 50 Saratoga Rd. 95032 | 408/354–3300 or 800/231–8676 | fax 408/354–5451 | www.losgatoslodge.com | 128 rooms | $135–$175 | AE, D, DC, MC, V.

MADERA

Super 8 Motel. This modest, no-frills lodging is right across the street from the Madera Fairgrounds. It's also within a mile of shopping and movie theaters. Restaurant, complimentary Continental breakfast. Cable TV. Pool. Laundry facilities. Some pets allowed. | 1855 W. Cleveland Ave. 93637 | 559/661–1131 | fax 559/661–0224 | www.super8.com | 80 rooms | $46–$60 | AE, MC, V.

MAMMOTH LAKES

Econo Lodge Wildwood Inn. You will have mountain views from some of the rooms at this downtown beige two-story wood hotel. Horseback riding, hiking, and fishing are within 5 mi. Complimentary Continental breakfast. No air-conditioning, some refrigerators, cable TV. Pool. Hot tub. Some pets allowed. | 3626 Main St. 93546 | 760/934–6855 or 800/845–8764 | fax 760/934–8208 | www.econolodge.com | 32 rooms | $59–$119 | AE, D, DC, MC, V.

Shilo Inn. With a rock exterior, this all mini-suites hotel has a fireplace in the lobby. An ice-skating rink is 1½ blocks away. Complimentary Continental breakfast. Refrigerators, cable TV. Pool. Exercise equipment. Laundry facilities. Business services, airport shuttle. Some pets allowed. | 2963 Main St./Rte. 203 93546 | 760/934–4500 | fax 760/934–7594 | www.shiloinn.com/California/mammoth_lakes.html | 70 rooms | $115–$150 | AE, D, DC, MC, V.

MANHATTAN BEACH

El Camino Motel. This no-frills motel is 1 mi east of the beach and less than ½ mi from two movie theaters. Cable TV, room phones. Pets allowed. | 3301 N. Sepulveda Blvd. 90266 | 310/546–5464 | 18 rooms | $60 | MC, V.

Embassy Suites. This Spanish Mission-style all-suites hotel has a sun deck, lobby atrium, and made-to-order breakfasts. It's near the beach, 16 mi west of downtown LA. Restaurant, bar, complimentary breakfast. In-room data ports, cable TV. Pool. Hot tub. Exercise equipment. Business services, airport shuttle, parking (fee). Some pets allowed. | 1440 E. Imperial Ave., El Segundo 90245 | 310/640–3600 | fax 310/322–0954 | www.embassy-suites.com | 350 suites | $159–$174 suites | AE, D, DC, MC, V.

Residence Inn by Marriott. All-suites hotel with studio (one-bedroom) and split-level penthouse suites (two-bedroom/two-bath), all with fully equipped kitchens, though you get breakfast and dinner as part of your stay. In a residential area 1 mi from Manhattan Beach pier. The hotel, built in 1985, has 22 two-story French-style wood buildings. There is a courtyard on the lush landscaped property. Complimentary Continental breakfast. In-room data ports, kitchenettes, refrigerators, cable TV, in-room VCRs. Pool. Exercise equipment, gym. Hot tub. Laundry service. Business services. Some pets allowed. | 1700 N. Sepulveda Blvd. 90266 | 310/546–7627 | fax 310/545–1327 | www.residenceinn.com/laxmh | 176 suites | $185–$195 | AE, D, DC, MC, V.

MARYSVILLE

Amerihost Inn Marysville. This modest motel off Highway 70 is 1 mi from downtown and 12 mi west of Beale Air Force Base. Complimentary Continental breakfast. Some microwaves, some refrigerators, some in-room hot tubs, cable TV, room phones. Pool. Hot tub. Laundry service. Business services. Pets allowed (fee). | 1111 N. Beale St. 95901 | 530/742–2700 | www.amerihost.com | 50 rooms, 12 suites | $69–$99, $99–$139 suites | AE, D, DC, MC, V.

Villager Lodge. Within 4 blocks of the Greyhound bus terminal, this 1939 lodge has four blue and lavender buildings. Complimentary Continental breakfast. Some kitchenettes, refrigerators, microwaves, cable TV. Some pets allowed (fee). | 545 Colusa Ave., Yuba City 95991 | 530/671–1151 or 800/593–4666 | 39 rooms | $65 | AE, D, MC, V.

MENDOCINO

McElroy's Cottage Inn. Gardens surround the house, water tower, and cottage that make up this early 1900s Craftsmen Period inn, which faces the ocean at the east end of the village of Mendocino. A ½ mi walk west will bring you to the other end of town. The beach is about three blocks away (down the cliffside via a staircase with safety railings); the headlands, where you can do some whale watching, are three blocks west. Two rooms have ocean views and two, garden views; all rooms have radios, games, books and puzzles, and flannel sheets and quilts on the beds. Breakfast includes homemade breads. Kids are welcome. Complimentary Continental breakfast. Some pets allowed. | 998 Main St. | 707/937–1734 | 4 rooms | $85–$125 | MC, V.

Mendocino Seaside Cottage. Quirky elements reflect the owner's taste for whimsy. Rooms are individually furnished. The wooden exterior of the building belies the marble interior; the cottage was built in 1997. You will have an ocean view, fireplace, and whirlpool tub. Some rooms have fireplaces and telescopes, so you can spot whales and other wildlife. Mendocino Headlands State Park is across the street. It's four blocks to the heart of the village's shopping area, and 3 mi north of the Point Cabrillo Lighthouse. No air-conditioning, microwaves, refrigerators, some kitchenettes, some minibars, some in-room hot tubs, cable TV, in-room VCRs. Some pets allowed. | 10940 Lansing Street | 707/485–0239 or 800/94–HEART | fax 707/485–9746 | romance@romancebythesea.com | www.romancebythesea.com | 4 rooms | $157–$301 | No credit cards.

★ **Stanford Inn by the Sea.** Extensive renovations that were underway in the fall of 2000 made this former motel-style lodge, located at the mouth of Big River, into a charming country inn. Big ocean-view rooms and 10 acres of landscaped property are two reasons to stay here; there is a certified organic farm on the property as well. It is 1 mi southeast of Mendocino Headlands State Park in a residential area. Complimentary full breakfast.

No air-conditioning, in-room data ports, some kitchenettes, refrigerators, cable TV, in-room VCRs (and movies). Pool. Hot tub, sauna. Exercise equipment. Boating, bicycles. Business services, airport shuttle. Some pets allowed. No smoking. | 44850 Comptche Rd. | 707/937–5615 or 800/331–8884 | fax 707/937–0305 | www.stanfordinn.com | 41 rooms | $242–$410 | AE, D, DC, MC, V.

MERCED

Best Western Sequoia Inn. A pink two-story building with exterior corridors, built in 1964, the inn is in a residential area 1 mi from downtown. Room service. Pool. Pets allowed. | 1213 V St. 95340 | 209/723–3711 | fax 209/722–8551 | www.bestwestern.com | 98 rooms | $64–$74 | AE, D, DC, MC, V.

Merced Days Inn. This one-story motel is ½ mi from the Wild Life Museum and 80 mi from Yosemite National Park. Restaurant, bar, complimentary Continental breakfast. In-room data ports, microwaves, refrigerators, cable TV, in-room VCRs. Pool. Spa. Tennis. Laundry service. Pets allowed. | 1199 Motel Dr. 95340 | 209/722–2726 or 800/544–8313 | fax 209/722–7083 | www.daysinnmerced.com | 24 rooms, 1 suite | $68–$78, $98–$150 suite | AE, D, DC, MC, V.

MODESTO

Doubletree Hotel Modesto. This 14-story luxury hotel 4 blocks south of downtown is just off Rte. 99 and less than 1 mi from St. Stans Brewery and factory outlet stores. There's an espresso cart in the lobby. 2 Restaurants, 1 bar (with entertainment), room service. In-room data ports, some refrigerators, cable TV, some in-room VCRs. Pool. Beauty salon, hot tub, spa, sauna. Exercise equipment. Shops. Laundry service. Business services, airport shuttle, free parking. Pets allowed. | 1150 9th St. 95354 | 209/526–6000 | fax 209/526–6096 | www.hilton.com | 258 rooms, 6 suites | $114–$158, $160–$250 suites | AE, D, DC, MC, V.

Vineyard View Bed and Breakfast. The owners here invite you to their quiet, country home filled with patchwork quilts. The inn sits on a bluff 4 mi west of town and overlooks 72 acres of vineyard. Complimentary breakfast. Room phones, TV in common area. Pets allowed. No smoking. | 2839 Michigan Ave. 95358 | 209/523–9009 | 3 rooms (with shared bath) | $70–$80 | AE, D, MC, V.

MONTEREY

Bay Park. In this 1917 hotel among the trees on Carmel Hill, rooms have bay views, a light beige and ivory color scheme, and plump chairs that make things cozy. It's 1 mi north of Pebble Beach. Restaurant, bar (with entertainment), room service. Refrigerators, cable TV. Pool. Hot tub. Business services. Pets allowed (fee). | 1425 Munras Ave. | 831/649–1020 or 800/338–3564 | fax 831/373–4258 | baypark@montereybay.com | 80 rooms | $105–$200 | AE, D, DC, MC, V.

Best Western Victorian Inn. All rooms have Victorian furnishings and gas fireplaces in two Victorian-style buildings (one dates from 1907, the other went up in 1986). A courtyard and garden are on the property. It's near Cannery Row, 2 blocks from the bay, 5 blocks east of the Monterey Bay Aquarium. Complimentary Continental breakfast. Refrigerators, cable TV, in-room VCRs (and movies). Hot tub. Business services. Pets allowed (fee). | 487 Foam St. | 831/373–8000 or 800/232–4141 | fax 831/373–4815 | 68 rooms | $249–$500 | AE, D, DC, MC, V.

Cypress Gardens Inn. The modern facade of this 1962 stucco building belies its old-fashioned interiors, done up with floral wallpaper, brass beds, and dark wood furniture. On landscaped grounds in a commercial area ½ mi south of downtown. Complimentary Continental breakfast. No air-conditioning, some kitchenettes, refrigerators, cable TV. Pool. Hot tub. Business services. Pets allowed. No smoking. | 1150 Munras Ave. | 831/373–2761 | 46 rooms, 1 suite | $99–$199, $269 suite | AE, D, MC, V.

El Adobe Inn. This stucco-faced building is between the Delmonte Shopping Center and downtown. Complimentary Continental breakfast. No air-conditioning, cable TV. Hot tub. Business services. Pets allowed. | 936 Munras Ave. | 831/372–5409 or 800/433–4732 | fax 831/375–7236 | www.montereyrooms.com | 26 rooms | $99–$169 | AE, D, MC, V.

MORRO BAY

Best Western El Rancho. This 1960s southwestern-style hotel just north of town consists of two stucco-faced buildings with bay views in some rooms. Restaurant. Refrigerators, cable TV, in-room VCRs (and movies). Pool. Laundry facilities. Business services. Pets allowed (fee). | 2460 Main St. | 805/772–2212 | fax 805/772–2212 | 27 rooms | $59–$99 | AE, D, DC, MC, V.

Days Inn Harbor House. In this two-story wooden building, some rooms have ocean views and some have wood-burning fireplaces. It's downtown, 3 blocks from the Embarcadero. Complimentary Continental breakfast. No air-conditioning, in-room data ports, refrigerators, cable TV. Hot tub. Business services. Pets allowed (fee). | 1095 Main St. | 805/772–2711 or 800/247–5076 | fax 805/772–2711 | thrturk@aol.com | www.daysinn.com | 46 rooms, 1 suite | $69–$145, $125–$199 suite | AE, D, DC, MC, V.

The Villager. In a commercial area, this wood-framed, Southwestern-style building was built in 1973. It's 2½ blocks from the bay. Cable TV. Hot tub. Pets allowed (fee). | 1098 Main St. 93942 | 805/772–1235 | fax 805/772–1236 | www.villager-morrobay.com | 22 rooms | $119–$129 | AE, D, DC, MC, V.

MT. SHASTA

Best Western Tree House Motor Inn. This chain motel has landscaped grounds, views of Mt. Shasta, pleasant rooms, and a spacious lobby with a large fireplace. It's near skiing and bike trails. The three wooden buildings, built in 1974, are 3 mi from downtown. Restaurant, bar. Cable TV. Pool. Business services. Pets allowed. | 111 Morgan Way | 530/926–3101 or 800/545–7164 | fax 530/926–3542 | www.bestwestern.com | 98 rooms | $79–$149 | AE, D, DC, MC, V.

Finlandia. Choose from regular or deluxe rooms, some with lake or mountain views, at this 1969 European-style wood building with a stucco finish. The motel is 3 mi west of Lake Siskiyou. Picnic area. No air-conditioning in some rooms, some kitchenettes, cable TV. Sauna. Business services. Pets allowed. | 1612 S. Mt Shasta Blvd. | 530/926–5596 | finlandia@snowcrest.net | 22 rooms | $34–$75 | AE, D, DC, MC, V.

Swiss Holiday Lodge. This two-story southwestern-style wood building has quiet, affordable rooms overlooking Mt. Shasta. The lodge is 1½ mi from downtown. Picnic area, complimentary Continental breakfast. Some kitchenettes, cable TV. Pool. Hot tub. Pets allowed. | 2400 S. Mt. Shasta Blvd. | 530/926–3446 | fax 530/926–3091 | 21 rooms, 1 suite | $46–$54, $95 suite | AE, D, DC, MC, V.

MOUNTAIN VIEW

Residence Inn by Marriott. Business travelers are the primary clients of this particular Marriott, which has one- and two-bedroom suites. The grounds of the contemporary stucco building are landscaped, with three courtyards. The hotel is 1 mi from downtown. Complimentary Continental breakfast. Kitchenettes, refrigerators, cable TV. Pool. Hot tub. Laundry facilities. Business services, free parking. Pets allowed (fee). | 1854 W. El Camino Real 94040 | 650/940–1300 | fax 650/969–4997 | www.residence.com | 112 suites | $149–$329 | AE, D, DC, MC, V.

NAPA

Beazley House. Two Victorian wood houses built in 1902 are the site of Napa's first B&B, which is ideal for couples seeking a romantic getaway downtown. The carriage house behind the main mansion has six rooms with fireplaces. Afternoon tea is served in the guest living room. Extensive gardens include a 200-year-old oak tree. Dining room, complimentary breakfast, some in-room hot tubs. Library. Business services. Pets allowed. No smoking. | 1910 1st St. 94559 | 707/257–1649 or 800/559–1649 | fax 707/257–1518 | www.beazleyhouse.com | 11 rooms | $125–$275 | AE, MC, V.

NEEDLES

Best Western Colorado River Inn. This 2-story rural stucco motel built in 1993 is 1½ mi west of downtown. Restaurant. Refrigerators, microwaves. Sauna. Pool. Pets allowed. | 2371 W. Broadway 92363 | 760/326–4552 | fax 760/326–4562 | www.bestwestern.com | 63 rooms | $60–$70 | AE, D, DC, MC, V.

Best Western Royal Inn. This 1990 wood and stucco 2-story motel is 1½ mi northwest of downtown. In-room data ports, cable TV. Pool. Hot tub, spa. Laundry facilities. Pets allowed (fee). | 1111 Pashard St. 92363 | 760/326–5660 | fax 760/326–4002 | www.bestwestern.com | 60 rooms | $60–$70 | AE, D, DC, MC, V.

Days Inn. Rooms surround a courtyard pool at this 2-story motel built in 1985, just off I–40 at the J street exit, 25 mi northwest of Lake Havasu. Complimentary Continental breakfast. In-room data ports, some microwaves, some refrigerators, cable TV. Pool. Pets allowed. | 1215 Hospitality Lane | 760/326–5836 | fax 760/326–4444 | www.daysinn.com | 121 rooms | $90–$119 | AE, D, MC, V.

River Valley Motor Lodge. One mile east of downtown, this motel, built in 1978, is a very affordable option. Cable TV. Refrigerators. Pool. Pets allowed. | 1707 W. Broadway 92363 | 760/326–3839 | fax 760/326–3881 | 26 rooms | $23–$29 | AE, D, DC, MC, V.

Super 8 Motel of Needles. This two-story peach motel on the edge of Needles off I–40 is near golf and fishing. It offers standard rooms, with basic amenities. Cable TV. Pool. Laundry services. Pets allowed. | 1102 E. Broadway 92363 | 760/326–4501 or 800/800–8000 | fax 760/326–2054 | 30 rooms | $50–$60 | AE, D, DC, MC, V.

NEVADA CITY

Outside Inn. This is a 1940s motel in a residential area, 2 blocks from downtown Nevada City. Rooms are individually appointed, many with knotty pine paneling and hardwood floors. Some kitchenettes, some refrigerators. Cable TV. Pool. Pets allowed. | 575 E. Broad St. | 530/265–2233 | fax 530/265–2236 | manager@outsideinn.com | www.outsideinn.com | 11 rooms | $60–$125 | AE, MC, V.

NEWPORT BEACH

★ **Four Seasons Hotel.** This 20-story contemporary marble-and-stucco building has tropically landscaped grounds and caters to couples, families, and business travelers. It's across the street from Fashion Island. Restaurants, bar (with entertainment), room service. In-room data ports, refrigerators, cable TV. Pool. Beauty salon, spa, hot tub, massage. Tennis. Gym, bicycles. Business services, airport shuttle. Pets allowed. | 690 Newport Center Dr. 92660 | 949/759–0808 or 800/332–3442 | fax 949/759–0568 | www.fourseasons.com | 285 rooms, 92 suites | $340–$465, $400–$3900 suites | AE, D, DC, MC, V.

Hyatt Newporter. These three three-story Spanish-style stucco buildings are ideal for families. The hotel is on 26 acres of tropical landscaped property; across the street is the Fashion Island Shopping Center. Bar (with entertainment), dining room, room service. In-room data ports, cable TV. Refrigerators. 3 pools. 3 spas. 9-hole golf course. Exercise equipment, bicycles. Baby-sitting. Laundry facilities, laundry services. Business services, airport shuttle. Pets allowed. | 1107 Jamboree Rd. 92660 | 949/729–1234 | fax 949/644–

1552 | www.hyattnewporter.com | 405 rooms, 11 suites | $190–$275, $350 suites | AE, D, DC, MC, V.

Marriott Hotel and Tennis Club. Tennis enthusiasts will enjoy their stay at this 1975 contemporary 16-story hotel across the street from Fashion Island and 2 mi from the beach. Restaurant, bar, room service. In-room data ports, cable TV. 2 pools. Hot tub. 8 tennis courts. Gym. Laundry facilities. Business services. Pets allowed. | 900 Newport Center Dr. 92660 | 949/640–4000 | fax 949/640–5055 | 570 rooms | $250–$305 | AE, D, DC, MC, V.

OAKLAND

Clarion Suites Lake Merritt. Echoing the 1930s, this six-story Art Deco hostelry is by Lake Merritt and most guest rooms have water views. A popular spot for visiting musicians, the lounge has live jazz on Thursday nights. Restaurant, bar, complimentary Continental breakfast. In-room data ports, kitchenettes, minibars, microwaves, refrigerators, cable TV. Business services. Pets allowed (fee). | 1800 Madison 94612 | 510/832–2300 or 800/933–4683 | fax 510/832–7150 | 51 rooms, 38 suites | $259, $189–$259 suites | AE, D, DC, MC, V.

Hilton Airport. Five three-story buildings sit on 10 acres at this chain hotel with a large conference facility. The Oakland Coliseum is 2 mi north. 2 restaurants, bar (with entertainment), room service. In-room data ports, cable TV. Pool. Exercise equipment. Business services, airport shuttle. Pets allowed (fee). | 1 Hegenberger Rd. 94621 | 510/635–5000 | fax 510/729–0491 | www.hilton.com | 363 rooms | $165–$215 | AE, D, DC, MC, V.

OCEANSIDE

Ramada Limited Oceanside. This four-story chain hotel is 1½ mi from the beach and entrance to Oceanside Harbor west of I–5. Complimentary Continental breakfast. In-room data ports, some microwaves, refrigerators, cable TV. Laundry facilities. Pets allowed. | 1440 Mission Ave. 92054 | 760/967–4100 | fax 760/439–5546 | ramada@ramada-oceanside.com | www.ramada-oceanside.com | 67 rooms | $69–$99 | AE, D, DC, MC, V.

OJAI

Best Western Casa Ojai. Surrounded by mountains, this southwestern-style building is 1 mi east of downtown Complimentary Continental breakfast. In-room data ports, some refrigerators, cable TV. Pool. Hot tub. Business services. Pets allowed. | 1302 E. Ojai Ave. 93023 | 805/646–8175 | fax 805/640–8247 | www.bestwestern.com | 45 rooms | $119–$199 | AE, D, DC, MC, V.

Blue Iguana Inn. Local artists run this 1930s Mission-style hotel, with arched entrances and terra cotta-tiled roofs. The fountain in the inn's central courtyard is iguana-shaped, and Mexican-style domed ceilings, sandblasted wood beams, murals, and works by local painters and artisans fill the rooms. All rooms have private outdoor patios. In-room data ports, some kitchenettes, microwaves, refrigerators, cable TV. Pool. Hot tub. Business services. Pets allowed. | 11794 N. Ventura Ave. 93023 | 805/646–5277 | fax 805/646–8078 | innkeeper@blueiguanainn.com | www.blueiguanainn.com | 4 rooms, 7 suites | $95–$125, $129–$189 suites | AE, D, DC, MC, V.

ONTARIO

Best Western Airport. This stucco hostelry is in a residential area 3 mi west of Ontario Mills Mall and just 2 blocks north of the airport. Complimentary Continental breakfast. Refrigerators, cable TV. Pool. Hot tub. Laundry facilities. Airport shuttle. Pets allowed. | 209 N. Vineyard Ave. 91764 | 909/937–6800 | fax 909/937–6815 | www.bestwestern.com | 150 rooms | $72 | AE, D, DC, MC, V.

Motel 6. This reasonably priced chain hostelry is close to fast-food restaurants and 2 mi from Ontario International Airport. Cable TV. Pool. Pets allowed (fee). | 1560 E. 4th St. 91764 | 909/984–2424 | fax 909/984–7326 | www.motel6.com | 69 rooms | $56 | AE, D, DC, MC, V.

ORANGE

Residence Inn by Marriott. Three mi west of downtown near Anaheim Stadium, this 1988 property is 2 blocks from the Block At Orange shopping district. Landscaped walkways encourage leisurely strolling on the grounds. Picnic area, complimentary Continental breakfast. Kitchenettes, microwaves, cable TV. Pool. Hot tub. Basketball, volleyball. Laundry facilities. Business services, airport shuttle. Pets allowed. | 3101 W. Chapman Ave. 92868 | 714/978–7700 | fax 714/978–6257 | 104 rooms | $92–$114 | AE, D, DC, MC, V.

OROVILLE

Best Inn and Suites. Near the Oroville Dam boating and fishing area, the hotel is near two casinos. Built in 1989 in a largely residential area, the property caters to business travelers. Complimentary Continental breakfast. In-room data ports, refrigerators, cable TV. Pool. Hot tub. Exercise equipment. Laundry facilities. Business services. Pets allowed (fee). | 1470 Feather River Blvd. 95965 | 530/533–9673 | fax 530/533–5862 | 54 rooms, 8 suites | $66–$89, $80–$130 suites | AE, D, DC, MC, V.

Lake Oroville Bed and Breakfast. This 1990 inn reflects French Provincial style with covered porches. Most of the rooms have a view of the lake. Picnic area, complimentary breakfast. Some in-room hot tubs, in-room VCRs. Hiking. Business services. Pets allowed. No smoking. | 240 Sunday Dr., Berry Creek 95916 | 530/589–0700 or 800/455–5253 (for reservations) | fax 530/589–4761 | lakeinn@cncnet.com | www.lakeoroville.com | 6 rooms | $75–$145 | AE, D, MC, V.

Motel 6. This two-story motel has the usual amenities of this dependable chain, with the added bonus of being within walking distance to Feather River. You can try your hand at fishing, or just relax and watch life float by. The Feather River Casino is 5 mi south. Restaurant. Cable TV. Laundry facilities. Business services. Pets allowed. | 505 Montgomery St. | 530/532–9400 | fax 530/534–7653 | www.motel6.com | 102 rooms | $51–$61 | AE, D, DC, MC, V.

Travelodge. This one-story motel, built in 1960, sits squarely in the middle of town, with plenty of restaurants within walking distance. Oroville Dam is 8 mi north. Picnic area. Complimentary breakfast. Microwaves, refrigerators, cable TV. Pool. Laundry services. Business services. Pets allowed. | 580 Oro Dam Blvd. 95965 | 530/533–7070 | fax 530/532–0402 | www.travelodge.com | 70 rooms | $55–$65 | AE, D, DC, MC, V.

OXNARD

Best Western Oxnard Inn. This chain offers lots of services, making it an easy stop for families or business travelers. If you're not in the mood for a dip in the pool, consider a jaunt to Point Hueneme Beach, 4 mi northwest. Complimentary Continental breakfast. In-room data ports, some microwaves, some refrigerators, some in-room hot tubs, cable TV. Pool. Hot tub, spa. Exercise equipment. Laundry facilities. Business services. Pets allowed. | 1156 S. Oxnard Blvd. 93030 | 805/483–9581 or 800/469–6273 | fax 805/483–4072 | www.bestwestern.com | 99 rooms, 3 suites | $79–$89, $169 suites | AE, D, DC, MC, V.

Casa Sirena Resort. This modest motor inn is 6 mi from downtown on the Channel Islands Harbor, with views of the marina from many rooms. The four Spanish-style wood buildings were constructed in 1962. The grounds are landscaped and a park is next to the property. Restaurant, bar, room service. No air-conditioning in some rooms, in-room data ports, some kitchenettes, refrigerators, cable TV. Pool. Beauty salon, hot tub. Putting green. Tennis. Exercise equipment. Video games. Playground. Business services, airport shuttle, free parking. Pets allowed. | 3605 Peninsula Rd. | 805/985–6311 or 800/228–6026 | fax 805/985–4329 | www.casasirenahotel.com | 261 rooms, 12 suites | $99–$148, $168 suites | AE, D, DC, MC, V.

Vagabond Inn Oxnard. Less than 2 mi from the Carnegie Cultural Arts Center, this is next door to a 24-hour eatery. Complimentary Continental breakfast. In-room data ports, some refrigerators, cable TV. Pool. Business services. Pets allowed (fee). | 1245 N. Oxnard Blvd. 93030 | 805/983–0251 or 800/522–1555 | fax 805/988–9638 | www.vagabondinns.com | 69 rooms | $59–$69 | AE, D, DC, MC, V.

PACIFIC GROVE

Lighthouse Lodge and Suites. Really two lodgings in one, with economical, motel-style rooms in a building on one side of the street, a roomier, all-suite facility on the other. The Pacific Ocean is one block away and there are a number of eateries within walking distance. Complimentary breakfast. Microwaves, refrigerators, some in-room hot tubs, cable TV. Pool. Hot tub. Business services. Pets allowed (fee). | 1150 and 1249 Lighthouse Ave. 93950 | 831/655–2111 or 800/858–1249 | fax 831/655–4922 | www.lhls.com | 68 rooms, 31 suites | $149–$171, $219–$288 suites | AE, D, DC, MC, V.

PALM DESERT

Comfort Suites of Palm Desert. Built in 2000, this all-suite hotel of the familiar chain is off I–10 at the Washington Street exit. A good bet if you're a golfer, the lodging has several courses within a 5-mi radius. There's also a restaurant within walking distance, so you can work up an appetite, or work off that dessert. Complimentary Continental breakfast. In-room data ports, in-room safes, microwaves, refrigerators, some in-room hot tubs, cable TV. Pool. Hot tub. Gym. Laundry facilities. Business services. Pets allowed (fee). | 39585 Washington St. 92211 | 760/360–3337 or 800/517–4000 | fax 760/360–5496 | www.palmdesertcomfort.com | 72 suites | $95–$145 | AE, D, DC, MC, V.

Deep Canyon Inn. Completely remodeled in 1999, this inn has a small pond and waterfall. The 1965 three-story stucco building is in a residential area a bit more than a mile from the El Paseo shopping area. Complimentary Continental breakfast. Some kitchenettes, refrigerators, cable TV. Pool. Hot tub. Business services. Pets allowed. | 74470 Abronia Trail 92260 | 760/346–8061 or 800/253–0004 (for reservations) | fax 760/341–9120 | innkper@aol.com | www.inn-adc.com | 32 rooms | $119–$219 | AE, D, MC, V.

Desert Patch Inn. The ubiquitous palm trees sway and exotic flowers scent the air of this one-story inn. Pottery and pastel hues give the rooms a Southwestern look; all have views of the landscaped grounds. The El Paseo area (fine shops, restaurants) is one block away. Complimentary Continental breakfast. Some kitchenettes, some microwaves, refrigerators, cable TV, in-room VCRs. Pool. Hot tub. Business services. Pets allowed. No smoking. | 73785 Shadow Mountain Dr. 92260 | 760/346–9161 or 800/350–9758 | fax 760/776–9661 | desertpatch@earthlink.net | www.desertpatch.com | 11 rooms, 3 suites | $59–$89, $104 suites | AE, D, MC, V.

Residence Inn of Palm Desert. This all-suite option, built in 1999, aims to have a low-key, neighborhood feel, with lodgings (studios and two bedroom suites) spread out among several two-story buildings. All rooms have views of the Santa Rosa Mountains or the adjacent Desert Willow Golf Resort. The Children's Discovery Museum of the Desert is 6 mi away and there are a number of restaurants within a short drive. Complimentary Continental breakfast. In-room data ports, in-room safes, kitchenettes, microwaves, refrigerators, cable TV, in-room VCRs (and movies). Pool. Hot tub. 1 tennis court. Gym. Laundry facilities, laundry service. Business services. Pets allowed (fee). | 38305 Cook St. 92211 | 760/776–0050 | fax 760/776–1806 | www.residenceinn.com | 130 suites | $159–$259 | AE, D, DC, MC, V.

PALM SPRINGS

Casa Cody. Founded in the 1920s, this B&B in the San Jacinto Mountains captures the look and feel of the Southwest. Take off the evening chill with your own fireplace. The acclaimed Palm Springs Desert Museum is a short walk. Dining room, complimentary Continental breakfast. In-room data ports, some kitchenettes, some microwaves, some refrigerators, cable TV, some in-room VCRs. 2 pools. Hot tub. Business services. Pets allowed. | 175 S. Cahuilla Rd. 92262 | 760/320–9346 or 800/231–2639 | fax 760/325–8610 | 14 rooms, 8 suites, 1 house | $79–$149, $159–$189 suites, $249–$349 house | AE, D, DC, MC, V.

Coyote Inn. Don't be surprised if you get dive-bombed by a hummingbird in the flower-filled courtyard of this sheltered, Spanish Mission-style inn. The peaceful courtyard makes a pleasant retreat from the bustling shops, restaurants, and museums of downtown, 4 blocks away. Kitchenettes, microwaves, refrigerators, cable TV, in-room VCRs. Pool. Hot tub. Laundry facilities. Pets allowed. No kids under 14. | 234 S. Patencio Rd. 92262 | 760/327–0304 or 888/334–0633 | fax 760/327–4304 | info@gardeninns.com | www.coyoteinn.gardeninns. com | 5 rooms, 2 suites | $109–$139, $159–$189 suites | AE, MC, V.

Hilton. Catering to the upscale crowd, this full-service, three-story hotel sits in the heart of downtown across the street from the action of the Spa Casino. Restaurant. In-room data ports, refrigerators, cable TV. Pool. Hot tub. 6 tennis courts. Exercise equipment. Kids' programs. Business services, airport shuttle. Pets allowed. | 400 E. Tahquitz Canyon Way 92262 | 760/320–6868 | fax 760/320–2126 | pshilton@aol.com | www.palmsprings.hilton.com | 260 rooms | $159–$235 | AE, D, DC, MC, V.

★ **Merv Griffin's Resort Hotel and Givenchy Spa.** This spa aims to capture the ambience of the Givenchy spa in Versailles, France, right down to the manicured rose gardens and Empire-style decor. Private patios with mountain or garden views enhance most rooms. Pamper yourself with an array of spa services—from traditional facials to marine mud wraps and aromatherapy. The 4,200-sq-ft, four-bedroom Grand Suite has a grand piano in the living room. 2 restaurants, room service. Some minibars, cable TV, some in-room VCRs. 2 pools. Hot tub, barber shop, beauty salon, spa. 6 tennis courts. Gym. Laundry services. Business services. Pets allowed. | 4200 E. Palm Canyon Dr., 92264 | 760/770–5000 or 800/ 276–5000 | fax 760/324–6104 | info@merv.com | www.merv.com/hotel/givenchy_ spa/default.asp | 103 rooms, villas, and suites | $290–$350, $400 suite, $600–$1,150 villa, $4,000 Grand Suite | AE, D, DC, MC, V.

Motel 6. This economical chain is a three-story building opened in 1990, is in the heart of downtown, and close to shops and restaurants. Cable TV. Pool. Laundry facilities. Business services. Pets allowed. | 660 S. Palm Canyon Dr. 92264 | 760/327–4200 or 800/ 466–7356 | fax 760/320–9827 | www.motel6.com | 148 rooms (shower only) | $51–$57 | AE, D, DC, MC, V.

Place in the Sun. The oldest, and one of the most charming, lodgings in Palm Springs, this collection of 1948 bungalows has gardens, gazebos, and a putting green for the kids (or the kids at heart). The all-suite lodgings have cathedral ceilings and private patios. It's ½ mi southeast to both the downtown area and the shopping district. Restaurant. Kitchenettes, microwaves, refrigerators, cable TV. Pool. Laundry facilities. Pets allowed (fee). | 754 San Lorenzo Rd. 92264 | 760/325–0254 or 800/779–2254 | fax 760/237–9303 | www.palmsprings.com/placeinthesun | placeinthesun@yahoo.com | 16 bungalows | $79–$139 | AE, MC, V.

Ramada Resort. This 3-story hotel, built in 1980, has rooms with handmade wood furniture from Mexico. Rooms also have a private patio or balcony, with views of the mountains or the hotel's enormous pool. It's in a quiet area 2 mi south of the Palm Canyon Dr. shopping/entertainment district. Restaurant, bar (with entertainment). In-room data ports, refrigerators. Pool. Hot tubs. Exercise equipment. Laundry facilities. Free airport shuttle. Pets allowed. | 1800 E. Palm Canyon Dr. 92264 | 760/323–1711 or 800/245–6907 (outside CA), 800/245–6904 (in CA) | fax 760/322–1075 | www.ramada.com | 254 rooms | $89–$119, $99–$109 suites | AE, D, DC, MC, V.

Riviera Resort and Racquet Club. Another Palm Springs classic, this large complex, built in 1958, consists of eight wooden buildings on 23 acres of landscaped grounds. The resort is 2 mi north of downtown. Restaurant, bar (with entertainment), room service. In-room data ports, refrigerators, cable TV. 2 pools. Hot tubs, massage. Tennis. Exercise equipment. Airport shuttle. Pets allowed. | 1600 N. Indian Canyon Dr. 92262 | 760/327–8311 or 800/444–8311 | fax 760/327–4323 | psriviera.com | 477 rooms | $219 | AE, D, DC, MC, V.

PALO ALTO

Hyatt Rickeys. Families and couples enjoy this resort-style hotel in the heart of Silicon Valley. The lodging's 16 acres have gardens, fountains, and a gazebo. The Mediterranean-style complex is 2 mi south of downtown. Restaurant, bar. In-room data ports, cable TV. Pool. Putting green. Exercise equipment. Business services. Pets allowed (fee). | 4219 El Camino Real 94306 | 650/493–8000 | fax 650/424–0836 | 336 rooms, 14 suites | $204–$300, $350–$375 suites | AE, D, DC, MC, V.

Sheraton Palo Alto. At the entrance to Stanford University—a convenient option for visiting families or business travelers—this hotel has a resort-like setting, with flower gardens, ponds, fountains, and a pool. The four-story Mediterranean-style stucco building has guest rooms that overlook a water garden and the pool. Downtown shops and restaurants are one block east. Restaurant, bar, room service. Some kitchenettes, in-room hot tubs, cable TV. Pool. Exercise equipment. Laundry facilities. Business services. Pets allowed (fee). | 625 El Camino Real 94301 | 650/328–2800 | fax 650/327–7362 | www.sheraton.com | 346 rooms | $229–$299 | AE, D, DC, MC, V.

PASADENA

★ **Ritz-Carlton Huntington.** A mansion among mansions, this legendary hotel is situated on 23 acres of old gardens in a quiet residential area 2 mi south of Colorado Boulevard. It's shaded by centuries-old oak trees, boasts California's first Olympic-sized swimming pool, and has a tranquil Japanese garden. Although the hotel dates back to 1906, it suffered extensive damage in a 1987 earthquake necessiting a total reconstruction; local pressure forced the builders to "put it back exactly the way it was." Rooms have been updated and lavishly appointed with marble, thick carpeting and original art on the walls. The Huntington Library and Cal Tech are 2 mi northeast of the hotel. Restaurants, bar (with entertainment), room service. Cable TV. Pool. Beauty salon, spa, hot tub, massage. Tennis. Gym, bicycles. Kids' programs. Business services. Parking (fee). Pets allowed (fee). | 1401 S. Oak Knoll Ave. 91106 | 626/568–3900 | fax 626/568–3700 | www.ritzcarlton.com | 387 rooms, 8 cottages | $235–$310, $395–$595 cottages | AE, D, DC, MC, V.

PEBBLE BEACH

★ **Lodge at Pebble Beach.** This 1919 lodge is surrounded by four golf courses. Luxurious rooms are in the main and 11 adjacent buildings. They have fireplaces, and balconies or patios with wonderful views. Guests have privileges at the Inn at Spanish Bay. Nature trails lead to ocean vistas, an ancient Indian village, and S. F. B Morse Botanical Reserve. 4 restaurants, bar. In-room data ports, microwaves, cable TV. Pool, wading pool. Beauty salon, hot tub, massage. 2 driving ranges, 4 18-hole golf courses, putting green, tennis. Gym, horseback riding, beach. Shops, video games. Kids' programs. Business services. airport shuttle. Pets allowed. | 2790 17-Mile Dr. | 831/624–3811 or 800/654–9300 | fax 831/625–8598 | www.pebble-beach.com | 151 rooms, 10 suites | $450–$600, $1100–$2125 suites | AE, D, DC, MC, V.

PISMO BEACH

Oxford Suites Resort. This hotel, 1 mi from the beach, has a tree-shaded courtyard and a rose garden. Complimentary breakfast. Microwaves, refrigerators, cable TV, in-room VCRs (and movies). Pool, wading pool. Hot tub. Laundry facilities. Business services. Pets allowed (fee). | 651 Five Cities Dr. 93449 | 805/773–3773 or 800/982–7848 | fax 805/773–5177 | www.oxfordsuites.com | 133 suites | $69–$129 suites | AE, D, DC, MC, V.

Spyglass Inn. Landscaped grounds with palm trees overlook the ocean at this hotel on a bluff. Rooms have a nautical theme. There are ocean views from the outdoor pool and from a heated ocean view deck. Restaurant, bar. Refrigerators, cable TV. Pool. Hot tub. Business services. Pets allowed (fee). | 2705 Spyglass Dr. 93449 | 805/773–4855 or 800/824–2612 | fax 805/773–5298 | www.spyglassinn.com | 82 rooms | $79–$199 | AE, D, DC, MC, V.

PLEASANTON

Crowne Plaza Hotel. You'll find reasonably priced rooms at this 6-story hotel 5 mi northwest of downtown. Restaurant, bar. In-room data ports, some refrigerators, cable TV. Pool. Hot tub. Exercise equipment. Laundry facilities. Business services. Pets allowed (fee). | 11950 Dublin Canyon Rd. 94588 | 925/847–6000 | fax 925/463–2585 | 244 rooms | $70–$135 | AE, D, DC, MC, V.

Hilton Pleasanton at the Club. Spacious guest rooms and suites cater to business travelers. Restaurant, bar. In-room data ports, some refrigerators, cable TV. Pool. Beauty salon. Tennis. Gym. Business services. Pets allowed. | 7050 Johnson Dr. 94588 | 925/463–8000 | fax 925/463–3801 | 290 rooms, 4 suites | $169–$179, $400–$600 suites | AE, D, DC, MC, V.

POMONA

Sheraton Suites Fairplex. This hotel ½ mi east of Pomona has landscaped grounds with rose bushes. It's directly adjacent to the LA County Fairgrounds. Restaurant. In-room data ports, minibars, microwaves, refrigerators, cable TV. Pool. Exercise equipment. Laundry facilities. Business services. Pets allowed. | 601 W. McKinley Ave. 91768 | 909/622–2220 | fax 909/622–3577 | 247 rooms | $189 | AE, D, DC, MC, V.

Shilo Hotel–Pomona. This hotel, across the street from the Shilo Hilltop Suites Pomona, also has mountain views, but is slightly more affordable. It has a new fitness center with a spa. Restaurant, room service. In-room data ports, microwaves, refrigerators, cable TV. Pool. Exercise equipment. Laundry facilities. Business services, airport shuttle. Pets allowed. | 3200 Temple Ave. 91768 | 909/598–0073 | fax 909/594–5862 | 160 rooms | $72–$114 | AE, D, DC, MC, V.

PORTERVILLE

Best Western Porterville Inn. Rooms at this hotel have views of the rosebush courtyard, or the mountains. Restaurant, complimentary breakfast, room service. In-room data ports, refrigerators, cable TV. Pool. Hot tub. Exercise equipment. Laundry facilities. Business services. Pets allowed. | 350 W. Montgomery Ave. 93257 | 559/781–7411 | fax 559/781–8910 | www.bestwestern.com | 116 rooms | $70 | AE, D, DC, MC, V.

RANCHO BERNARDO

La Quinta Inn. This attractive and reasonably priced four-story chain motel is in a suburban area near shopping. Complimentary Continental Breakfast. Cable TV. Pool. Video games. Pets allowed. | 10185 Paseo Montril 92129 | 858/484–8800 | fax 858/538–0476 | 120 rooms | $75–$85 | AE, D, DC, MC, V.

Radisson Suite Hotel. Its proximity to the commercial district makes this three-story hotel 20 min north of San Diego a favorite of business travelers. Restaurant, bar, complimentary Continental breakfast, room service. In-room data ports, minibars, cable TV. Pool. Exercise equipment. Laundry facilities. Business services. Pets allowed. | 11520 W. Bernardo Ct. 92127 | 858/451–6600 | fax 858/592–0253 | 181 suites | $109–$129 | AE, D, DC, MC, V.

Rancho Bernardo Travelodge. This simple motel is centered in a corporate area, and offers affordable rates. Microwaves, refrigerators, cable TV. Pool. Pets allowed. | 16929 W. Bernardo Dr. 92127 | 858/487–0445 | fax 858/673–2062 | www.travelodge.com | 49 rooms | $60–$135 | AE, D, DC, MC, V.

RANCHO CORDOVA

Best Inn and Suites. Built in the 1980s, this hotel is 12 mi east of Sacramento, and a ½ mi from Mather Field Air Force Base. At U.S. 50, exit at Mather Field. Complimentary Continental breakfast. Some refrigerators, cable TV. Pool. Hot tub. Laundry facilities. Free parking. Pets allowed (fee). | 3240 Mather Field Rd. 95670 | 916/363–3344 | fax 916/362–0903 | 95 rooms, 15 suites | rooms $69–$89, suites $89–$129 | AE, D, DC, MC, V.

Inns of America. Surrounded by commercial Rancho Cordova, this Spanish-style stucco hotel was built in 1988 at Route 50 off Hazel Avenue. Aerojet is adjacent to the property; Folsom Lake is 2 mi south. Complimentary Continental breakfast. Cable TV. Pool. Pets allowed. | 12249 Folsom Blvd. 95670 | 916/351–1213 | fax 916/351–1817 | www.innsofamerica.com | 124 rooms | $70 | AE, MC, V.

RANCHO MIRAGE

Westin Mission Hills. Lush gardens and meandering streams characterize the grounds of this 360-acre Spanish-Moorish golf resort. Rooms and suites are housed in 16 two-story pavilions that surround patios and fountains; guest quarters have terra-cotta tile floors and private patios or balconies, and fine linens cover the king-size beds. There are 10 championship golf courses within 3 mi and two on the property. 2 restaurants, bar (with entertainment), room service. In-room data ports, minibars, cable TV. 3 pools. Hair salon, hot tub, massage. 2 18-hole golf courses, 6 putting greens, 7 tennis courts. Basketball, gym, volleyball, bicycles. Video games. Kids' programs, playground. Laundry services. Business services. Some pets allowed. | 71333 Dinah Shore Dr. 92270 | 760/328–5955 | fax 760/321–2955 | www.westin.com | 512 rooms, 41 suites | $289–$309 rooms, $300–$1,100 suites | AE, D, DC, MC, V.

RANCHO SANTA FE

Inn at Rancho Santa Fe. Built in 1923, this 20-acre property's center is the main lodge, an adobe-style building with one floor and a domed roof. The cottages are made of wood and stucco and have outdoor patios. Landscaped grounds with eucalyptus trees and pines surround the area. The San Diego Wild Animal Park is 12 mi to the southwest and seven golf courses are within 3 mi. (Guests here have privileges at the Rancho Santa Fe Country Club golf course.) Restaurant, bar, room service. Some refrigerators, some in-room hot tubs, cable TV. Heated pool. Massage. Tennis. Exercise equipment. Business services. Pets allowed. | 5951 Linea del Cielo | 858/756–1131 or 800/654–2928 | fax 858/759–1604 | www.theinnatranchosantafe.com | 89 rooms, 21 cottages | $110–220 rooms, $350–$650 cottages | AE, DC, MC, V.

Rancho Valencia. The views of the valley below from this resort's elevated location are incredible. You can stay in a duplex suite with whitewashed beams, cathedral ceilings, stucco walls, and private terraces. European massages, beauty treatments, and aromatherapy are offered at the sleek spa. The Farm at Rancho Santa Fe Golf Course is across the street and two wineries are 9 mi to the northeast. Restaurant, bar, picnic area, room service. In-room data ports, refrigerators, cable TV, in-room VCRs. Pool. Massage, sauna, spa. Golf privileges, 17 tennis courts. Exercise equipment, hiking. Laundry facilities. Business services. Pets allowed ($75 fee). | 5921 Valencia Cir | 858/756–1123 or 800/548–3664 | fax 858/756–0165 | www.ranchovalencia.com | 43 suites | $425–$695 suites | AE, DC, MC, V.

REDDING

La Quinta Inn. The rooms of this white three-story hotel face a garden of flowers and trees in the courtyard. It's in central Redding's commercial district among a host of restaurants and shops. Complimentary Continental breakfast. In-room data ports, cable TV. Pool. Hot tub. Laundry facilities. Business services, free parking. Pets allowed. | 2180 Hilltop Dr. 96002 | 530/221–8200 | fax 530/223–4727 | 141 rooms | $69–$76 | AE, D, DC, MC, V.

Red Lion Hotel. The restaurants and businesses of central Redding are within walking distance of this two-story hotel. Restaurant, bar (with entertainment), complimentary breakfast, room service. In-room data ports, cable TV. Pool, wading pool. Hot tub. Business services, airport shuttle, free parking. Pets allowed. | 1830 Hilltop Dr. 96002 | 530/221–8700 | fax 530/221–0324 | www.redlion.com | 192 rooms | $84–$114 | AE, D, DC, MC, V.

River Inn. This hotel is across from the Redding Convention Center and a ¹/₂ mi west of the I–5 and Route 299 junction. You can borrow a fishing pole from the hotel to fish in the nearby lake. Restaurant, bar, picnic area. Refrigerators, some in-room hot tubs, cable TV. Pool. Hot tub, sauna. Business services. Pets allowed ($6 fee). | 1835 Park Marina Dr. 96001 | 530/241–9500 or 800/995–4341 | fax 530/241–5345 | www.reddingriverinn.com | 79 rooms | $46–$80 | AE, D, DC, MC, V.

RIVERSIDE

Dynasty Suites. Only ¹/₂ mi from the UC Riverside, this two-story suites hotel built in 1990 is about 14 mi from Ontario International Airport and 41 mi from Lake Arrowhead. The guest rooms use a lot of dark woods in kitchenettes and furnishings, and all suites have sofabeds and two-line speaker phones. Complimentary Continental breakfast. In-room data ports, kitchenettes, cable TV. Pool. Business services, free parking. Pets allowed (fee). | 3735 Iowa Ave. 92507 | 909/369–8200 or 800/842–7899 | fax 909/341–6486 | info@dynasty-suites.com | www.dynastysuites.com | 34 rooms | $59 | AE, D, DC, MC, V.

RUTHERFORD/ST. HELENA

El Bonita. This family-run, two-story motel on Route 29 in downtown St. Helena has rooms with terraces or balconies. Picnic area, complimentary Continental breakfast. Some kitchenettes, microwaves, refrigerators, some in-room hot tubs, cable TV. Pool. Hot tub, sauna. Business services. Pets allowed (fee). | 195 Main St. | 707/963–3216 or 800/541–3284 | fax 707/963–8838 | www.elbonita.com | 41 rooms in 3 buildings | $85–$199 | AE, D, DC, MC, V.

Harvest Inn. An English Tudor-style inn, this lodging has rooms in the main building and cottages, some with elaborate brick fireplaces and antiques. Complimentary Continental breakfast. In-room data ports, refrigerators, cable TV. 2 pools. Hot tubs. Business services. Pets allowed, (fee). | 1 Main St. | 707/963–9463 or 800/950–8466 | fax 707/963–4402 | www.harvestinn.com | 54 rooms | $229–$649 | AE, D, DC, MC, V.

SACRAMENTO

Best Western Expo Inn. This two-story hotel next to Cal Expo and 3 mi from downtown has two-room executive suites with sitting areas, ceiling fans, and computer work areas. Complimentary Continental breakfast. Some kitchenettes, some microwaves, some refrigerators, cable TV. Pool. Spa. Business services, airport shuttle, free parking. Pets allowed (fee). | 1413 Howe Ave. | 916/922–9833 or 800/643–4422 | fax 916/922–3384 | 127 rooms, 20 suites | $65, $90–$120 suites | AE, D, DC, MC, V.

Best Western Harbor Inn. Guest rooms at this hotel have balconies and views of downtown Sacramento, just ¹/₂ mi away. Complimentary Continental breakfast. Some refrigerators, in-room hot tubs, cable TV. Pool. Hot tubs. Business services, airport shuttle, free parking. Pets allowed (fee). | 1250 Halyard Dr., West Sacramento | 916/371–2100 or 800/371–2101 | fax 916/373–1507 | 138 rooms, 19 suites | $79, $89 suites | AE, D, DC, MC, V.

Clarion. Ivy covers the two buildings of this hotel, which takes up an entire city block just across the street from the Governor's Mansion, near the Convention Center and the Capitol. Restaurant, bar, room service. In-room data ports, some refrigerators, cable TV. Pool. Business services, airport shuttle, free parking. Pets allowed. No smoking. | 700 16th St. | 916/444–8000 | fax 916/442–8129 | 238 rooms | $114–$139 | AE, D, DC, MC, V.

Doubletree. Redwoods adorn the grounds of this hotel, and you can admire them from the paths that run through the 22-acre property. Two restaurants, bar, complimentary breakfast, room service. In-room data ports, some refrigerators, some in-room hot tubs. Pool. Exercise equipment. Business services, airport shuttle, free parking. Pets allowed.

| 2001 Point West Way | 916/929–8855 or 800/222–2733 | fax 916/924–4913 | 448 rooms in 6 buildings | $149–$159 | AE, D, DC, MC, V.

La Quinta. This three-story hotel is near Old Sacramento, the Capitol, and the Arco Arena. I–5, exit Richards Boulevard. Complimentary Continental breakfast. In-room data ports, cable TV. Pool. Exercise equipment. Laundry facilities. Business services, airport shuttle. Pets allowed. | 200 Jibboom St. | 916/448–8100 | fax 916/447–3621 | 165 rooms | $69–$135 | AE, D, DC, MC, V.

La Quinta. This three-story hotel 8 mi west of downtown sits on attractive, landscaped grounds. At business I–80, take Madison Avenue exit. Complimentary Continental breakfast. In-room data ports, cable TV. Pool. Laundry facilities. Business services. Pets allowed. | 4604 Madison Ave. | 916/348–0900 | fax 916/331–7160 | 127 rooms | $65–$82 | AE, D, DC, MC, V.

Radisson. There's a lake on the grounds of this two-story hotel, 2 mi west of downtown. There are also picnic tables and a courtyard. Restaurant, bar (with entertainment), room service. In-room data ports, some refrigerators, cable TV. Pool, lake. Exercise equipment, boating, bicycles. Business services, free parking. Pets allowed (fee). | 500 Leisure Lane | 916/922–2020 or 800/333–3333 | fax 916/649–9463 | sales@radisson.com | www.radisson.com/sacramentoca | 307 rooms | $129–$169 | AE, D, DC, MC, V.

Red Lion Sacramento Inn. This large hotel near Arden Fair shopping and cinema has spacious grounds. Restaurant, bar (with entertainment), room service. Refrigerators, in-room hot tubs, cable TV. 3 pools, wading pool. Putting green. Exercise equipment. Laundry facilities. Airport shuttle. Pets allowed (fee). | 1401 Arden Way | 916/922–8041 or 800/733–5466 | fax 916/922–0386 | 376 rooms | $95–$119 | AE, D, DC, MC, V.

Vagabond Inn. This three-story hotel is near downtown and Cal Expo. Take Business I–80 to Rte. 99 north. Complimentary Continental breakfast. Cable TV. Pool. Spa. Free parking. Pets allowed (fee). | 1319 30th St. | 916/454–4400 | fax 916/736–2812 | 83 rooms | $65–$85 | AE, D, DC, MC, V.

Vagabond Inn. This three-story hotel is eight blocks from the Capitol, near the Chinese Cultural Center and Old Sacramento. I–5, exit J Street. Restaurant, complimentary Continental breakfast. Some refrigerators, cable TV. Pool. Airport shuttle, free parking. Pets allowed (fee). | 909 3rd St. | 916/446–1481 or 800/522–1555 | fax 916/448–0364 | 108 rooms | $86–$98 | AE, D, DC, MC, V.

SAN BERNARDINO

La Quinta. You'll find more than a dozen restaurants in the area around this turquoise-and-brown structure with the red tile roof. Built in 1983, the three-story motel is 3 mi from San Bernardino International Airport and 3 mi south of downtown. Complimentary Continental breakfast. Cable TV. Pool. Business services. Pets allowed. | 205 E. Hospitality Ln. 92408 | 909/888–7571 | fax 909/884–3864 | www.laquinta.com | 153 rooms | $65 | AE, D, DC, MC, V.

SAN CLEMENTE

Holiday Inn. You'll find some ocean views from the balconies of this three-story Mediterranean-style motel built in the early '90s with new furnishings in 2000. On a small hill two blocks from the ocean, it's 29 mi from John Wayne Airport, 4 mi from San Juan Capistrano Mission, and 30 mi from Disneyland. Restaurant, bar, room service. In-room data ports, refrigerators, cable TV. Pool. Business services, free parking. Pets allowed (fee). | 111 S. Ave. de Estrella 92672 | 949/361–3000 or 800/469–1161 | fax 949/361–2472 | holidaysc@aol.com | www.holiday-inn.com | 72 rooms, 20 suites | $139–$149 | AE, D, DC, MC, V.

SAN DIEGO

Doubletree Carmel Highland Golf and Tennis Resort. Set back in the rolling green hills surrounding San Diego, 18 mi from downtown, this resort offers grand vistas and lots of exercise and sporting possibilities. The rooms are decorated in beiges and blues and overlook the golf fairways, hills, and the bay beyond. Dining room, bar, room service. In-room data ports, cable TV. 2 pools. Beauty salon, hot tub. 18-hole golf course, putting green, 5 tennis courts. Gym. Business services. Kids' programs. Pets allowed (fee). | 14455 Penasquitos Dr. 92129 | 858/672–9100 | fax 858/672–9187 | carmel@highland.doubletreehotels.com | www.highland.doubletreehotels.com | 166 rooms, 6 suites | $139–$179, $250–$350 suites | AE, D, DC, MC, V.

Doubletree Mission Valley. An 11-story modern tower on beautifully landscaped grounds, the hotel has light-filled public areas with Italian marble and extravagant flower arrangements. Rooms are spacious, decorated in earth tones and brass fittings, with marble bathrooms. It's close to Route 163, I–8, and a San Diego Trolley station, with stops at the Gaslamp District and the convention center, is within walking distance. It's also near Fashion Valley Shopping Center and next door to Hazard Center with its seven-screen movie theater and major restaurants, and within 5 mi of San Diego airport, Old Town, and Balboa Park. Restaurant, bar (with entertainment). In-room data ports, cable TV. 2 pools. Hot tub. Tennis. Exercise equipment. Laundry Services. Business servicesm, airport shuttle. Pets allowed. | 7450 Hazard Center Dr. 92108 | 619/297–5466 | fax 619/297–5499 | dbltreemv@aol.com | www.doubletreehotels.com | 284 rooms, 16 suites | $149–$169, $295–$495 suites | AE, D, DC, MC, V.

Good Nite Inn. This two-story motel is set around a central courtyard with a pool, and makes up in price and location what it lacks in charm. The no-frills rooms are small. It's 8 mi northeast of downtown, and within walking distance of shops, movie theaters, and restaurants. Microwaves, cable TV. Pool. Laundry facilities. Pets allowed. | 4545 Waring Rd. 92120 | 619/286–7000 or 800/648–3466 | fax 619/286–8403 | www.good-nite.com | 94 rooms | $65 | AE, D, DC, MC, V.

Hanalei Hotel. This is a tropical-themed eight-story hotel with lush gardens in Mission Bay, within 5 mi of Sea World, the Zoo, and Lindbergh Airport. Rooms are decorated in subtle beiges and creams with tropical flourishes, and each room has a private balcony or patio. 2 restaurants, bar, room service. In-room data ports, some refrigerators, cable TV. Pool. Hot tub. Excercise equipment. Video Games. Laundry facilities. Business services. Pets allowed (fee). | 2270 Hotel Cir. N 92108 | 619/297–1101 or 800/882–0858 | fax 619/297–6049 | www.hanaleihotel.com | 402 rooms, 14 suites | $129–$149, $250–$350 suites | AE, D, DC, MC, V.

Hilton Beach and Tennis Resort. An eight-floor Hacienda-style highrise surrounded by 18 acres of bi-level villas, lush tropical flowers, and a private beach on Mission Bay, rooms here are large and bright, with Polynesian accents, and private balconies or patios. Referred to as "Hawaii on the Mainland," this sprawling resort has so many activities that it would attract guests even without its excellent location. The hotel is 8 mi from Lindbergh Airport, 3 mi from Sea World, and 4 mi from downtown. 2 restaurants, 2 bars (with entertainment). In-room data ports, refrigerators, cable TV. Pool, wading pool. Hot tub, massage, spa. Putting green, tennis. Health club, beach, dock, boating. Kids' programs, playground. Laundry facilities. Business services, airport shuttle. Pets allowed (fee). | 1775 E. Mission Bay Dr. 92109 | 858/276–4010 | fax 858/275–8944 | contact@hilton-sandiego.com | www.hiltonsandiego.com | 357 rooms | $155–$195; $229 and up for suites and bungalows | AE, D, DC, MC, V.

Hilton Mission Valley. Directly facing I–8, the hotel has soundproof rooms, and the lush greenery and rolling hills at the back will help you forget the closeness of the highway. There's a business center with leather executive chairs and a helpful concierge, making it an attractive spot for business travelers. Rooms are decorated in a bright, contemporary style. Restaurant, bar. In-room data ports, refrigerators, cable TV. Pool. Hot tub.

Exercise equipment. Laundry services. Business Services. Pets allowed (fee). | 901 Camino del Rio S 92108 | 619/543–9000 | fax 619/543–9358 | www.hilton.com | 341 rooms, 9 suites | $189–$209, $250–$450 suites | AE, D, DC, MC, V.

Holiday Inn on the Bay. This 14-story, triple-towered Holiday Inn is located on the Embarcadero and overlooks San Diego Bay. It has an outside glass-enclosed elevator. Rooms are spacious and comfortable with furnished balconies, and many have excellent bay views. The cruise ship terminal is across the street and both of San Diego's airports and the Amtrak station are within 6 mi. Restaurant, bar, room service. In-room data ports, refrigerators, cable TV. Pool. Exercise equipment. Laundry service. Business services, airport shuttle. Pets allowed (fee). | 1355 N. Harbor Dr. 92101 | 619/232–3861 | fax 619/232–4924 | www.holiday-inn.com | 600 rooms, 17 suites | $159–$199, $229 suites | AE, D, DC, MC, V.

La Quinta Penasquitos. This four-story hotel has whitewashed walls, Spanish tiles, and semi-tropical landscaping. Its rooms are bright and airy in green and floral prints. It's 10 mi from the San Diego Wild Animal Preserve and 25 mi from Lindbergh Airport. Complimentary Continental breakfast. In-room data ports, cable TV. Pool. Pets allowed. | 10185 Paseo Montril 92129 | 858/484–8800 | fax 858/538–0476 | www.laquinta.com | 112 rooms, 8 suites | $86, $115 suites | AE, D, DC, MC, V.

Marriott Hotel and Marina. Built in 1988, this luxurious hotel sits on the bay in downtown San Diego, adjoining the convention center and Seaport Village. Two 25-story glass towers house the spacious, elegant rooms, all of which open onto spectacular views of the private marina. A variety of water sports are offered, and you can walk to shopping and entertainment. It's 2 mi north of the Lindbergh Airport. Restaurant, bar (with entertainment), room service. In-room data ports, refrigerators, some in-room hot tubs, cable TV. Pool. Beauty salon, hot tub. 6 tennis courts. Basketball, gym, boating. Video Games. Laundry services. Business services. Pets allowed. | 333 W. Harbor Dr. 92101 | 619/234–1500 | fax 619/234–8678 | www.sdmarriott.com | 1,302 rooms, 52 suites | $245–$270, $450+ suites | AE, D, DC, MC, V.

Marriott Suites–Downtown. All accommodations are suites in this hotel with a lobby on the 12th floor of the modern Symphony Towers, above Symphony Hall. It's near Balboa Park and the financial district, within walking distance of restaurants, shopping, and the beach, and 3 mi south of Lindbergh Airport. There are some good views of downtown, but no harbor views. Restaurant, bar. In-room data ports, refrigerators, cable TV. Pool. Hot tub. Exercise equipment. Baby-sitting. Laundry service. Business services. Pets allowed (fee). | 701 A St. 92101 | 619/696–9800 | fax 619/696–1555 | www.marriott.com | 264 suites | $250–$310 suites | AE, D, DC, MC, V.

Old Town Inn. This central inn has three separate structures: a three-story building with deluxe rooms and two one-story budget and economy wings. Even the deluxe rooms are small, but the location, across the street from Old Town and the trolley stop, can't be beat. It's 2 mi north of the San Diego Airport. Complimentary Continental breakfast. No air-conditioning in some rooms, in-room data ports, cable TV. Pool. Laundry facilities. Pets allowed (fee). | 4444 Pacific Hwy. 92110 | 619/260–8024 or 800/643–3025 | fax 619/296–0524 | 84 rooms (41 with shower only) | $65–$115 | AE, D, DC, MC, V.

Paradise Point Resort. This single-story, lanai bungalow–style resort opened in 1962 occupies a private island about 1 mi from Sea World and 7 mi northeast of downtown. All rooms are done comfortable and beachy (but with marble bathrooms) and have patios that look out to the private beach, the lagoon, or one of the pools. Pathways wind through the lush grounds, inhabited by friendly ducks and landscaped with more than 600 different kinds of tropical plants. If you're interested, ask about jet ski, sailboat, and kayak rentals. Restaurants, bars (with entertainment), room service. In-room data ports, some refrigerators, cable TV. 5 pools, wading pool. Sauna. Putting green, tennis. Gym, beach, boating, bicycles. Video games. Kids' programs. Laundry facilities. Business services. Pets allowed. | 1404 W. Vacation Rd. 92109 | 858/274–4630 or 800/344–2626 | fax 858/581–5929

| reservations@paradisepoint.com | www.paradisepoint.com | 462 rooms, 153 suites | $195–$350 rooms, $360–$550 suites | AE, D, MC, V.

Radisson. Seven miles north of downtown and a 10-min walk to the beach, this 13-story modern tower has easy access to I–8 and comfortable accomodations with special amenities for business travelers. Rooms have full desks, fuchsia and plum color schemes, and views of Mission Valley. The top two floors are "executive level," with complimentary cocktails and hors d'oeuvres, balconies, and spacious rooms. Restaurant, bar. In-room data ports, cable TV. Pool. Hot tub. Exercise equipment. Laundry service. Business services, airport shuttle. Pets allowed (fee). | 1433 Camino del Rio S 92108 | 619/260–0111 | fax 619/ 497–0853 | sand@radisson.com | www.radisson.com | 248 rooms, 12 suites | $129, $209 suites | AE, D, DC, MC, V.

Radisson Suite. This three-story Spanish-style hotel has suites overlooking the landscaped central courtyard, with fountains and vine-covered walkways. The lobby has an arched entryway with Italian marble, and plants and flowers. The suites are studio-style, with semi-separate bedrooms in dark Spanish patterns with fresh cut flowers and overstuffed couches, and many suites have faxes. It's 10 mi north of the airport and a 15-min drive to the city's attractions. Plus, there are four wineries, the Wild Animal Park, and 15 golf courses within 5 mi. Restaurant, bar, complimentary breakfast. In-room data ports, microwaves, cable TV, in-room VCRs (and movies). Pool. Hot tub. Exercise equipment. Laundry facilities. Business services. Pets allowed. | 11520 W. Bernardo Ct. 92127 | 858/451–6600 | fax 858/592–0253 | www.radisson.com | 181 suites | $129 | AE, D, DC, MC, V.

U.S. Grant. This classic hotel was built in 1910 by the grandson of Ulysses S. Grant; Franklin D. Roosevelt and Charles Lindbergh have stayed here. Declared a National Historic Site and fully restored in the early 1990's, the lobby, with marble pillars, tapestries, and crystal chandeliers, and the rooms, with high ceilings, ornamental moldings, and Queen Anne–style furnishings, are a transporting experience. An English high tea is served in the lobby every afternoon. In downtown and close to Old Town, it's a great match of luxury and convenience. Restaurant, bar (with entertainment). Cable TV. Massage. Gym. Laundry services. Business services, airport shuttle. Pets allowed. | 326 Broadway 92101 | 619/232– 3121 or 800/237–5029 | fax 619/232–3626 | www.grandheritage.com | 280 rooms, 60 suites | $165–$245, $275–$1500 suites | AE, D, DC, MC, V.

Vagabond Inn. Built in 1959 and renovated in 1993, this motel has the standard, landscaped central courtyard design. The white and baby-blue color scheme and ranch-style design with slanted roofs evoke yesteryear, but its inexpensive rates and good location make it a choice for today's budget traveler. About 3 mi north of downtown and 6 mi east of Sea World. Complimentary Continental breakfast. In-room data ports, cable TV. 2 pools. Hot tub. Business services. Pets allowed (fee). | 625 Hotel Cir. S 92108 | 619/297–1691 | fax 619/692–9009 | www.vagabondinn.com | 88 rooms | $87 | AE, D, DC, MC, V.

SAN FRANCISCO

★ **Campton Place.** This 18-floor luxury hotel showcases a unique European/Asian design scheme. The lobby has a carved Buddha statue, Japanese screens, and French furniture from the Chippendale and Louis XVI periods. Rooms have minimal Japanese furniture, fresh-cut flowers, and subtle, natural color schemes. There's also a landscaped rooftop patio with views of Union Square half a block away. Restaurant, bar, room service. In-room data ports, cable TV (and movies). Some pets allowed (fee). | 340 Stockton St. 94108 | 415/ 781–5555 or 800/235–4300 | fax 415/955–5536 | reserve@campton.com | www.campton-place.com | 110 rooms; 9 suites | $295 –$415 rooms, $520 and up for suites | AE, DC, MC, V.

The Clift. Built for the 1915 Panama-Pacific Exposition, this elegant hotel towers over the Theater District, two blocks away. The opulent lobby has hand-carved balustrades, crystal chandeliers, and arched redwood ceilings and columns. Rooms have high ceilings, decorative moldings, carved woodwork, and marble bathrooms. You can have a cocktail in the dramatic Art Deco Redwood Room lounge. Restaurant, bar (entertainment), room service.

In-room data ports, refrigerators, cable TV. Exercise equipment. Laundry service. Business services, parking (fee). Some pets allowed. | 495 Geary St. 94102 | 415/775–4700 | fax 415/441–4621 | 301 rooms; 25 suites | $285–$385 rooms, $440 and up for suites | AE, D, DC, MC, V.

Hotel Beresford. In the heart of San Francisco, this seven-story hotel, built in 1913, has Victorian furniture and an authentic English tavern off the lobby. Each floor is unique, with different floral wallpapers, crown moldings and faux antiques. It's a short walk to shops, theaters, Chinatown, and the Financial District, two blocks to Union Square and cable cars to Telegraph Hill, Fisherman's Wharf, and Pier 39. Restaurant, bar, complimentary Continental breakfast. No air conditioning, in-room data ports, refrigerators, cable TV. Business services, parking (fee). Some pets allowed. | 635 Sutter St. 94102 | 415/673–9900 or 800/533–6533 | fax 415/474–0449 | beresfordsfo@delphi.com | www.beresford.com | 114 rooms | $135 | AE, D, DC, MC, V.

Hotel Beresford Arms. Near its sister hotel, the Beresford Hotel, this place has kitchens and large rooms. The lobby has a worn, regal atmosphere with columns, crown moldings, lush red carpeting, and crystal chandeliers. It's three blocks from Union Square and the cable cars. Complimentary Continental breakfast. No air conditioning, in-room data ports, refrigerators, cable TV, in-room VCR (and movies). Some hot tubs. Some pets allowed. | 701 Post St. 94109 | 415/673–2600 or 800/533–6533 | fax 415/533–5349 | beresfordsfo@delphi.com | www.beresford.com | 86 rooms, 40 kitchenettes, 13 suites | $139 rooms, $160 kitchenettes, $195 suites | AE, D, DC, MC, V.

Holiday Inn–Fisherman's Wharf. Completely renovated in 1993, this five-story, late-'50s, concrete and brick hotel is within walking distance of Fisherman's Wharf and both

FROM AFFENPINSCHER TO SHAR PEI

In June 1993, dog lovers and struggling entrepreneurs Craig Alan Lerner and Roland Turner moved their pet business to smart Ghirardelli Square at the western end of Fisherman's Wharf and had huge success by doing something nearly impossible. Their store, Beastro by the Bay, is stocked with breed-specific dog- and cat-related merchandise featuring virtually every kind of dog and cat in the world. No generic dogs here: Instead, every item contains a representation of a specific animal. Balinese Avalon and Slavic Tchouvatch, Italian spinone and Shar Pei, Afghan hound and Walker hound, Corgi and Akita, vizsla and pure white boxers with uncropped ears; they're all here, along with terriers and spaniels of all kinds, Westies and Yorkies, and much more. Some breeds are depicted in all their various colors as well—springer spaniel wares represent liver-and-whites and black-and-whites, whippet items show the dogs in white, tan, black, and white with tan, brindle, fawn, or gray. There are ceramic tiles, wooden items, mugs, coasters, notecards, mousepads, clay figurines, bronzes, mailboxes, street signs, Christmas decorations, calendars, clay figurines, T-shirts, totes, and more. Keychains are available representing 120 different breeds of dogs (and cats, too). The collars are leather, studded with nickel-plated brass hearts and animal profiles. You can also arrange to have your pet's numerological profile done, suitable for framing. The shop stays open seven days a week and until 9 PM on Friday and Saturday. 900 N. Point St., Ghirardelli Sq., San Francisco, CA 94109, 415/346–1010 or 888/BEASTRO, beastro.citysearch.com.

cable car lines. Rooms are reasonably spacious, with balconies and patios that overlook the Cannery and the bay. It's a good choice for families. Restaurants, bar, and room service. In-room data ports. Cable TV. Pool. Exercise facility. Laundry facility. Business service, parking (fee). Pets allowed (fee). | 1300 Columbus Ave. 94133 | 415/771–9000 | fax 415/771–7006 | www.hiwharf.com | 577 rooms, 7 suites | $190–$212 rooms, $350–$525 suites | AE, D, DC, MC, V.

Holiday Inn Select–Union Square. One block from Union Square, this centrally located hotel rises 30 stories, allowing great views of downtown and the bay. The lobby has a Mediterranean flair, with Italian marble and mixed wood inlays. Rooms are spacious with large desks and earth-tone color schemes. You can catch a free shuttle to the Financial District. Restaurant, bar. In-room data ports, some refrigerators, cable TV. Exercise equipment. Laundry service. Business services, parking (fee). Pets allowed (fee). | 480 Sutter St. 94108 | 415/398–8900 | fax 415/989–8823 | www.basshotels.com/crowneplaza | 350 rooms, 51 suites | $199–$279 rooms, $329–$779 suites | AE, D, DC, MC, V.

Hotel Triton. The lobby has whimsical curved gold chairs, purple ottomans, and a large mural of the god Triton. At night, it's the scene of wine reception and tarot card readings. Walls in the small-but-cheery guest rooms are adorned with work by local artists and craftspeople. The hotel regularly hosts bigwigs in the fashion, entertainment, music, and film industries. It's across the street from Chinatown's "Dragon Gates" and three blocks from Union Square. Restaurant, bar, complimentary snacks. In-room data ports, cable TV. Exercise equipment. Laundry service. Business services, parking (fee). Some pets allowed (fee). | 342 Grant Ave. 94108 | 415/394–0500 or 800/433–6611 | fax 415/394–0555 | sales@hotel-tritonsf.com | www.hotel-tritonsf.com | 134 rooms, 6 suites | $209–$239 rooms, $339 suites | AE, D, DC, MC, V.

Inn San Francisco. You can take in the panoramic view of the city or relax in the library or an English garden at this 1872 Victorian mansion in the Mission District. Rooms have Victorian antiques and feather beds; some have private hot tubs and fireplaces. Public transportation is a few blocks away. Complimentary breakfast. No air conditioning, in-room data ports, refrigerators, cable TV. Hot tub. Laundry service. Parking (fee). Pets allowed (fee). | 943 S. Van Ness Ave. 94110 | 415/641–0188 or 800/359–0913 | fax 415/641–1701 | www.innsf.com | 21 rooms, 2 with shared bath | $85–$235 | AE, D, DC, MC, V.

Jackson Court. Built in 1900, this three-story brownstone mansion in Pacific Heights has comfortable, luxurious rooms. The clientele would just as soon keep the bed and breakfast a well-kept secret but it's too late for that. Homey rooms have antiques and private baths. The hotel is just two blocks to public transportation. Complimentary breakfast and afternoon tea. No air conditioning, in-room data ports, cable TV. Laundry service. Business services. Pets allowed (fee). No smoking. | 2198 Jackson St. 94115 | 415/929–7670 | fax 415/929–1405 | www.sftrips.com | 10 rooms, shower only | $150–$215 | AE, MC, V.

Marriott Fisherman's Wharf. This four-story modern concrete hotel is two blocks from Fisherman's Wharf and cable cars. Rooms are somewhat generic but spacious and you can catch a free shuttle to the Financial District. Restaurant, bar, mini-bars in some rooms. In-room data ports, cable TV. Exercise equipment. Laundry service. Business services, parking (fee). Pets allowed (fee). | 1250 Columbus Ave. 94133 | 415/775–7555 | fax 415/474–2099 | www.marriott.com | 285 rooms; 16 suites | $269 rooms, $349 and up for suites | AE, D, DC, MC, V.

★ **Monaco.** You can take part in the wine and cheese reception held each evening in this four-star, four-diamond property's sumptuous lobby or dine in its dramatic French restaurant. Rooms have canopy beds and bamboo writing desks. You can take a free shuttle to the Financial District. Restaurant, bar, room service. In-room data ports. Video games. Exercise facility. Cable TV. Spa. Laundry service. Business services, parking (fee). Pets allowed (fee). | 501 Geary St. 94102 | 415/292–0100 or 800800/214–4220 | fax 415/292–0111 | www.monaco-sf.com | 201 rooms, 34 suites | $239–$299 rooms, $329–$429 suites | AE, D, DC, MC, V.

Pan Pacific. This contemporary tower blends Asian and American elements in a 17-story glass and brass atrium with fountain sculptures. Asian simplicity predominates in the rooms too, with muted colors, granite desks, and arched windows. It's two blocks from Union Square. Restaurant, bar, room service. In-room data ports, in-room safes, cable TV. Some saunas. Exercise equipment. Laundry service. Business services, parking (fee). Some pets allowed (fee). | 500 Post St. 94102 | 415/771–8600 or 800/533–6465 | fax 415/398–0267 | www.panpac.com | 330 rooms | $325–$425 | AE, D, DC, MC, V.

Park Hyatt. This 24-floor contemporary tower in the center of the Financial District connects to the Federal Building. The lobby has extravagant flower arrangements, inlaid wood accents and a library. Neo-Classical rooms have black granite bathrooms. Some have balconies with bay views. Restaurant, bar (entertainment), afternoon snacks, room service. Cable TV (and movies). Exercise equipment. Laundry service. Business services. Some pets allowed. | 333 Battery St. 94111 | 415/392–1234 | fax 415/421–2433 | 360 rooms, 37 suites | $445–$520 rooms, $520–$545 suites | AE, D, DC, MC, V.

Tuscan Inn at Fisherman's Wharf. One of the nicest hotels on Fisherman's Wharf, this four-story, brick-and-wood hotel, built in the 1980s, has a lobby that feels like a clubroom with fireplace and nightly wine reception. Rooms have country furnishings, fresh flowers, and mirrored walls and there's a free shuttle to the Financial District. Restaurant, bar, room service. In-room data ports, refrigerators, cable TV. Laundry service. Business services. Parking (fee). Pets allowed (fee). | 425 North Point St. 94133 | 415/561–1100 or 800/648–4626 | fax 415/561–1199 | www.tuscaninn.com | 221 rooms, 12 suites | $230–$278 rooms, $308 and up for suites | AE, D, DC, MC, V.

Westin St. Francis. A Union Square landmark, this massive 32-story hotel, built in 1904, has exterior glass elevators and an exquisite, rosewood-panel, gilded, and thoroughly ornate lobby. Rooms range from simple hardwood furnishings and baby-blue hues to club-like accommodations with chandeliers, French antique desks, and overstuffed chairs. 2 restaurants, bar (with entertainment), room service. In-room data ports, microwaves, refrigerators, cable TV. Beauty salon. Exercise equipment. Laundry service. Business services, parking (fee). Some pets allowed. | 335 Powell St. 94102 | 415/397–7000 or 800/228–3000 | fax 415/774–0124 | www.westin.com | 1,192 rooms, 84 suites | $195–$315 rooms, $450–$2,000 suites | AE, D, DC, MC, V.

SAN JOSE

Doubletree. This multi-level hotel with two high-rise towers is downtown, ½-mi from the San Jose Airport, and a 45-min drive from San Francisco Airport. Restaurant. In-room data ports, refrigerators, cable TV. Pool. Hot tub, sauna. Gym. Business services, airport shuttle. Pets allowed. | 2050 Gateway Pl. 95110 | 408/453–4000 | fax 408/437–2898 | www.doubletree.com | 505 rooms, 10 suites | $89–$275 | AE, D, DC, MC, V.

Residence Inn by Marriott. The apartment-style suites in this two-story hotel have living rooms and dining areas, and some have fireplaces. In-room data ports, kitchenettes, microwaves, refrigerators, cable TV. Pool. Bicycles. Laundry service. Business services, airport shuttle. Pets allowed. | 2761 S. Bascom Ave. 95008 | 408/559–1551 | fax 408/371–9808 | residenceinn.com | 80 suites | $79–$135 suites | AE, D, DC, MC, V.

Summerfield Suites. This all-suite hotel with red-tile roof is off I–880 at U.S. 101, and 1 mi south of San Jose International Airport. Picnic area, complimentary Continental breakfast. Kitchenettes, cable TV, in-room VCRs. Pool. Hot tub. Gym. Laundry service. Business services, airport shuttle, free parking. Pets allowed (fee). | 1602 Crane Ct. 95112 | 408/436–1600 or 800/833–4353 | fax 408/436–1075 | www.summerfieldsuites.com | 114 suites | $99–$299 | AE, D, DC, MC, V.

SAN JUAN CAPISTRANO

Best Western Capistrano Inn. This two-story hotel overlooks Capistrano Valley, and is ¼-mi east of Mission San Juan Capistrano. Complimentary breakfast. In-room data ports, cable TV. Pool. Hot tub. Business services. Pets allowed. | 27174 Ortega Hwy. 92675 | 949/493–5661 | fax 949/661–8293 | www.bestwestern.com | 108 rooms | $79–$99 | AE, D, DC, MC, V.

SAN MATEO

Marriott San Mateo. This six-floor, white stucco building with a red-tile roof curves around this lodging's landscaped parking lot and grounds. The hotel, at the intersection of U.S. 101 and Route 92, is 7 mi south of San Francisco International Airport. Restaurant, bar, room service. Some refrigerators, cable TV. Pool. Exercise equipment. Laundry facilities, laundry service. Airport shuttle. Pets allowed (fee). | 1770 S. Amphlett Blvd. 94401 | 650/573–7661 or 800/843–6664 (outside CA), 800/238–6339 (CA) | fax 650/573–0533 | www.marriott.com | 316 rooms | $105–$145 | AE, MC, V.

Villa Hotel–Airport South. Restaurants, shopping, and entertainment are within 4 mi of this hotel, 8 mi south of San Francisco's airport. Restaurant, bar (with entertainment), room service. Some refrigerators, cable TV. Pool. Beauty salon. Exercise equipment. Business services, airport shuttle. Pets allowed. | 4000 S. El Camino Real 94403 | 650/341–0966 | fax 650/573–0164 | www.villahotel.com | 285 rooms | $89–$119 | AE, D, DC, MC, V.

SAN PEDRO

Vagabond Inn. This four-story, exterior corridor hotel is 1 mi west of Ports O' Call Village. Complimentary Continental breakfast. Cable TV. Pool. Pets allowed. | 215 S. Gaffey St. 90731 | 310/831–8911 | fax 310/831–2649 | www.vagabondinns.com | 72 rooms | $65–$80 | AE, D, DC, MC, V.

SAN RAFAEL

Panama Hotel. Built in 1910, this two-story Victorian sports a flamboyant collection of past and present antiques mingling with garage-sale finds. It's kind of a "Key West meets Queen Victoria" look, with rooms ranging from the elegant Venetian Room (French doors opening onto a private balcony and claw-foot tub in the bath) to Ken's Safari, where mosquito netting drapes the queen bed and a ceiling fan slowly spins. Mimi's is a separate bungalow. The hotel, five blocks west of downtown, is in a quiet, leafy neighborhood. Some rooms have balconies or patios. The adjacent restaurant has live jazz Tues. and Thurs., and Sunday brunch. Restaurant. Complimentary Continental breakfast. Kitchenettes, some microwaves, refrigerators. Pets allowed. | 4 Bayview St. 94901 | 415/457–3993 or 800/899–3993 | www.panamahotel.com | 17 suites | $75–$160 | AE, MC, V.

SAN YSIDRO

Economy Motel. This two-story motel is 1 mi from the Mexican border. Cable TV. Pool. Pets allowed. | 230 Via de San Ysidro 92173 | 619/428–6191 | fax 619/428–0068 | 120 rooms | $39–$47 | AE, D, MC, V.

International Motor Inn. This motor inn is 1 mi from the Mexican border. Some kitchenettes, refrigerators, cable TV. Pool. Hot tub. Laundry facilities. Business services. Pets allowed. | 190 E. Calle Primera 92173 | 619/428–4486 | fax 619/428–3618 | 127 rooms, 35 suites | $65, $75 suites | AE, D, DC, MC, V.

Ramada Limited. This three-story standard hotel has a shopping center adjacent, and Mexican and fast-food restaurants ½-mi away. In-room data ports, cable TV. Pool. Exercise equipment. Laundry facilities. Pets allowed (fee). | 930 W. San Ysidro Blvd. 92173 | 619/690–2633 or 888/298–2054 | fax 619/690–1360 | www.ramada.com | 68 rooms | $60–$90 | AE, D, DC, MC, V.

Travelodge. This four-story chain hotel is 11 mi from San Diego airport, 7 mi from Tijuana airport, just off I–5. Cable TV. Laundry service. Pets allowed (fee). | 643 E. San Ysidro Blvd. 92173 | 619/428–2800 or 888/515–6375 | fax 619/428–8136 | www.travelodge.com | 68 rooms | $40–$60 | AE, D, DC, MC, V.

SANTA BARBARA

Casa del Mar Inn. Terra-cotta tile roofs and a leafy courtyard highlight this inn, a half-block from the beach and harbor and two blocks from Stearns Wharf. Lodgings include some family-size units with fireplaces and kitchens. Complimentary Continental breakfast. In-room data ports, some kitchenettes, cable TV. Hot tub. Business services. Pets allowed (fee). | 18 Bath St. 93101 | 805/963–4418 or 800/433–3097 | fax 805/966–4240 | www.casadelmar.com | 21 rooms | $119–$249 | AE, D, DC, MC, V.

Days Inn. This one-story chain motel is one block north of West Beach, the yacht harbor and wharf, three blocks from the State Street shopping district. Complimentary Continental breakfast. Cable TV. Hot tub. Laundry facilites. Pets allowed. | 116 Castillo St. 93101 | 805/963–9772 or 800/329–7466 | fax 805/963–6699 | www.daysinn.com | 25 rooms | $85–$160 | AE, D, DC, MC, V.

Fess Parker's Doubletree Resort. Surrounded by the Santa Ynez Mountains, this two-story hotel, where suites have patios or decks overlooking the ocean, is on 24 acres eight blocks east of the downtown area. Restaurants, bar (with entertainment), room service. In-room data ports, cable TV. Pool. Beauty salon, massage. Putting green, tennis. Basketball, exercise equipment. Laundry facilities. Business services, airport shuttle, free parking. Pets allowed. | 633 E. Cabrillo Blvd. 93103 | 805/564–4333 | fax 805/564–4964 | www.fpdtr.com | 337 rooms, 23 suites | $235–$285 rooms, $455–$855 suites | AE, D, DC, MC, V.

★ **Four Seasons Biltmore.** Adobe archways and terra-cotta roofs characterize the Spanish Colonial architecture of this 1927 hotel, on 23 acres of gardens and palm trees, where some rooms have ocean views. 3 restaurants, bar (with entertainment), room service. No air-conditioning, in-room data ports, cable TV, in-room VCRs. 2 pools, wading pool. Beauty salon, hot tub, massage. Putting green, tennis. Gym, bicycles. Kids' programs. Business services, airport shuttle. Pets allowed. | 1260 Channel Dr. 93108 | 805/969–2261 | fax 805/969–4682 | www.fshr.com | 234 rooms | $450–$610 | AE, DC, MC, V.

Motel 6. This two-story motel is a half-block from the beach. Cable TV. Pool. Laundry facilities. Pets allowed. | 443 Corona del Mar 93103 | 805/564–1392 or 800/466–8356 | fax 805/963–4687 | 51 rooms | $60–$80 | AE, D, DC, MC, V.

Ocean Palms Hotel. This ocean-front property, with red tile roof, patios, and flowering courtyards is across the street from the beach, and two blocks from shops, and restaurants. Complimentary breakfast. No air conditioning, some kitchenettes, some microwaves, some refrigerators, cable TV. Pool. Spa. Beach. Laundry service. Pets allowed. | 232 W. Cabrillo Blvd. 93101 | 805/966–9133 or 800/350–2326 | fax 805/965–7882 | www.ocean-palms.com | $55–$185 | AE, D, MC, V.

Pacifica Suites. Among 7 acres of exotic gardens, this inn is off U.S. 101, near the Patterson Avenue exit. All suites have one bedroom with a separate living room. Complimentary breakfast. In-room data ports, microwaves, refrigerators, cable TV, in-room VCRs (and movies). Pool. Hot tub. Business services, airport shuttle, free parking. Pets allowed. | 5490 Hollister Ave. 93111 | 805/683–6722 or 800/338–6722 | fax 805/683–4121 | www.pacificasuites.com | 87 suites | $139–$169 suites | AE, D, DC, MC, V.

★ **San Ysidro Ranch.** The views across 500 acres of orange groves and west to the sea and Channel Islands were enough to entice John and Jackie Kennedy here on their honeymoon. You, too, can enjoy luxury fit for a future president in this 1893 lodge, with rooms warmed by wood stoves or fireplaces. Dining room, bar (with entertainment), room service. In-room data ports, refrigerators, some in-room hot tubs, cable TV, in-room VCRs (and movies). Pool, wading pool. Massage. Driving range, tennis. Gym, hiking. Playground. Business services. Pets allowed (fee). | 900 San Ysidro La. 93108 | 805/969–5046 or 800/ 368–6788 | fax 805/565–1995 | www.sanysidroranch.com | 23 rooms, 15 suites | $375– $575, $675–1750 suites | AE, DC, MC, V.

Santa Barbara Holiday Inn. Off U.S. 101, this two-floor hotel, where rooms overlook the pool, is less than 1 mi northeast of the Santa Barbara Municipal Airport. Restaurant, room service. In-room data ports, cable TV. Pool. Shops. Business services, airport shuttle, free parking. Pets allowed. | 5650 Calle Real, Goleta 93117 | 805/964–6241 | fax 805/964–8467 | www.holiday-inn.com | 160 rooms | $120–$137 | AE, D, DC, MC, V.

SANTA MONICA

Days Inn Santa Monica. This three-story chain hotel, 1 mi from the beach, sits in the middle of the city near popular restaurants. Complimentary Continental breakfast. Cable TV. Hot tub. Exercise equipment. Laundry facilities. Pets allowed. | 3007 Santa Monica Blvd. 90404 | 310/829–6333 or 800/591–5995 | fax 310/829–1983 | www.smdaysinn.com | 68 rooms | $79–$115 | AE, D, MC, V.

Georgian. Marble floors and arched entry ways complement the Art Deco facade of this 1931 landmark, across the street from the ocean. Rooms, many with views of the water, are appointed with custom-made furnishings. Restaurant. In-room data ports, cable TV. Business services. Pets allowed. | 1415 Ocean Ave. 90401 | 310/395–9945 or 800/538–8147 | fax 310/451–3374 | sales@georgianhotel.com | www.georgianhotel.com | 84 rooms, 28 suites | $210–$260, $325–$475 suites | AE, DC, MC, V.

Holiday Inn. Sand hues dominate the rooms, suggestive of the beach one block from the hotel. Restaurant, bar, room service. In-room data ports, some refrigerators, cable TV. Pool. Exercise equipment. Laundry facilities. Pets allowed (fee). | 120 Colorado Ave. 90401 | 310/ 451–0676 | fax 310/393–7145 | www.holidayinnsm.com | 132 rooms | $179–$219 | AE, D, DC, MC, V.

SANTA NELLA

Best Western Andersen's Inn. This two-story, Danish-style inn with a real windmill overlooks a landscaped courtyard and pool. Restaurant, bar, complimentary Continental breakfast. Pool. Laundry service. Pets allowed. | 12367 S. Rte. 33 | 209/826–5534 | fax 209/ 826–4353 | www.bestwestern.com | 94 rooms | $61–$79 | AE, D, DC, MC, V.

Holiday Inn Express. This attractive, two-story Mission-style hotel surrounds a landscaped courtyard with fountain. Complimentary Continental breakfast. Refrigerators, cable TV. Pool. Spa. Laundry facilities. Pets allowed. | 28976 W. Plaza Dr. | 209/826–8282 | www.holidayinn.com | 100 rooms | $59–$79 | AE, D, DC, MC, V.

SANTA ROSA

Best Western Garden Inn. Attractively landscaped grounds surround this hotel east of U.S. 101 and less than 1 mi from the Sonoma County Fairgrounds and Luther Burbank Gardens. Some refrigerators, cable TV. 2 pools. Laundry facilities. Business services. Pets allowed (fee). | 1500 Santa Rosa Ave. 95404 | 707/546–4031 or 800/929–2771 | fax 707/526– 4903 | www.bestwestern.com | 78 rooms | $80–$180 | AE, D, DC, MC, V.

Los Robles Lodge. Five acres of landscaped grounds surround this two-story lodge off U.S. 101. Restaurant, bar (with entertainment), room service. In-room data ports, refrigerators, cable TV. Pool, wading pool. Hot tub, steam room. Exercise equipment. Laundry facilities. Business services, airport shuttle. Pets allowed. | 1985 Cleveland Ave. 95401 | 707/ 545–6330 or 800/255–6330 | fax 707/575–5826 | www.losrobleslodge.com | 104 rooms | $96–$150 | AE, D, DC, MC, V.

SEAL BEACH

Radisson Inn of Seal Beach. This three-story hotel is two blocks from the beach. Pool. Exercise equipment. Laundry facilities. Business services, airport shuttle. Pets allowed. | 600 Marina Dr. 90740 | 562/493–7501 | fax 562/596–3448 | 71 rooms | $118–$125 | AE, D, DC, MC, V.

SELMA

Best Western John Jay Inn. This Federalist-style, three-story hotel is on landscaped grounds across the highway from convenience stores. Pool. Hot tub, sauna. Exercise equipment. Laundry facilities. Pets allowed. | 2799 Floral Ave. 93662 | 559/891–0300 | fax 559/891–1538 | 57 rooms | $50–$95 | AE, D, DC, MC, V.

Microtel Inn and Suites. The Selma branch of this fast-growing chain is 3 mi from the Sun-Maid raisin factory. A trimmed-down approach keeps room rates down. In-room data ports, cable TV. Laundry facilities. Pets allowed (fee). | 2527 Highland Ave. 93662 | 888/771–7171 | www.microtelinn.com | 62 rooms | $55–$75, $69–$99 suites | AE, D, DC, MC, V.

Super 8 Motel. This one-story motel sits across from fast-food eateries. Pool. Pets allowed. | 3142 S. Highland Ave. 93662 | 559/896–2800 | fax 559/896–7244 | 40 rooms | $49 | AE, D, DC, MC, V.

SOLVANG

Country Inn and Suites. The loft spaces and Mission-style furniture in these spacious rooms give this hotel more character than the typical chain hotel. Complimentary breakfast. Microwaves, in-room refrigerators, cable TV, in-room VCRs. Pool. Hot tub. Business services. Some pets allowed (fee). | 1455 Mission Rd. 93463 | 805/688–2018 | fax 805/688–1156 | cisolvang@rimcorp.com | www.countryinns.com | 82 rooms | $99–$110 rooms, $139 suites | AE, D, DC, MC, V.

Econo Lodge. One of the two buildings has interior entrances and the other has exterior at this motel 3 mi west of town. Some microwaves, cable TV. Laundry facilities. Business services. Pets allowed. | 630 Ave. of Flags, Buellton 93427 | 805/688–0022 | fax 805/688–7448 | www.econolodge.com | 60 rooms | $64–$80 | AE, D, DC, MC, V.

SONORA

Best Western Sonora Oaks. The larger rooms of this hotel off Route 108 on the east side of Sonora have outside sitting areas, and the suites have fireplaces, whirlpool tubs, and hillside views. (Rooms fronting the highway can be noisy.) Restaurant. Some in-room data ports, cable TV. Pool. Hot tub. Laundry service. Business services. Pets allowed (fee). | 19551 Hess Ave. 95370 | 209/533–4400 or 800/532–1944 | fax 209/532–1964 | www.bestwestern.com | 96 rooms, 4 suites | $74–$84, $94 suites | AE, D, DC, MC, V.

Days Inn. This 1896 Victorian hotel furnished in antique reproductions is downtown. Some refrigerators, cable TV. Pool. Pets allowed. | 160 S. Washington St. 95370 | 209/532–2400; 800/580–4667 from CA | fax 209/532–4542 | becky@sonoradaysinn.com | www.sonora-daysinn.com | 64 rooms | $69–$79 | AE, D, DC, MC, V.

SOUTH LAKE TAHOE

Sorensen's Resort. In business since 1926, this resort is on 165 wooded acres at an elevation of 7000 ft 20 mi south of South Lake Tahoe. It's a great family place, with lots to do for every member of the family. In winter, everybody cross-country skis on the resort's network of trails or goes downhilling and snowboarding at Kirkwood ski area, 15 mi away. Cabins have wood furnishings and most have wood-burning stoves. Restaurant. Some kitchenettes, some microwaves, some refrigerators, some room phones, no TV. Sauna. Fishing. Cross-country skiing. Pets allowed. No smoking. | 14255 Hwy. 88, Hope Valley 96120

| 530/694–2203 or 800/423–9949 | fax 530/694–2271 | sorensensresort@yahoo.com | www.sorensensresort.com | 33 cabins | $105–$215 | AE, MC, V.

TAHOE VISTA

Rustic Cottages. Detached 1920s clapboard cottages encircle a central lawn across the road from Lake Tahoe; many have kitchenettes and fireplaces. No air-conditioning, some kitchenettes. Some pets allowed (fee). | 7449 N. Lake Blvd. 96148 | 530/546–3523 or 888/778–7842 | fax 530/546–0146 | www.rusticcottages.com | 18 cottages | $59–$95, $95–$189 suites | AE, D, DC, MC, V.

TEHACHAPI

Resort at Stallion Springs. You enter the resort, surrounded by an ancient oak forest at 4,000 ft, through a covered bridge across a small lake, then up to the lodge and its sweeping mountain views. Some of the cottages overlook the golf course and all have fireplaces. Dining room, bar with entertainment. Some kitchenettes, cable TV. Pool. Hot tub. Driving range, 18-hole golf course, putting green, tennis. Exercise equipment, hiking, bicycles. Kids' programs, playground. Pets allowed. | 18100 Lucaya Way 93561 | 805/822–5581 or 800/244–0864 | fax 805/822–4055 | www.stallionsprings.com | 63 rooms, 19 cottages | $75–$85, $160–$205 cottages | AE, D, DC, MC, V.

THREE RIVERS

Best Western Holiday Lodge. The lobby of this two-story stucco lodge 8 mi from Sequoia National Park and 4 mi from Lake Kaweah has a stone fireplace and Navajo-print fabrics. Complimentary Continental breakfast. Refrigerators, cable TV. Pool. Hot tub. Playground. Pets allowed. | 40105 Sierra Dr. 93271 | 559/561–4119 | fax 559/561–3427 | www.bestwestern.com | 54 rooms | $85–$105 | AE, D, DC, MC, V.

Lazy J Ranch Motel. Some rooms in this single-story motel in the foothills of the Sierra Nevada have fireplaces, and the cabins are fully equipped. Picnic area. Refrigerators, cable TV. Pool. Cross-country skiing. Playground. Laundry facilities. Pets allowed. | 39625 Sierra Dr. 93271 | 559/561–4449 or 800/341–8000 | fax 559/561–4885 | www.bestvalueinn.com | 11 rooms, 7 cottages | $70–$78, $95–$160 cottages | AE, D, DC, MC, V.

Sierra Lodge. This lodge with mountain views and a small library is near the entrance to Sequoia National Park, as well as Lake Kaweah. Complimentary Continental breakfast. Some kitchenettes, refrigerators, cable TV. Pool. Library. Business services. Pets allowed (fee). | 43175 Sierra Dr. 93271 | 559/561–3681 or 800/367–8879 | fax 559/561–3264 | 22 rooms, 5 suites | $68–$82, $110–$150 suites | AE, D, DC, MC, V.

TORRANCE

Residence Inn Torrance–Redondo Beach. All the rooms have fireplaces, and there are some two-bedroom, two-story rooms at this motorlodge 2 mi south of downtown. Complimentary Continental breakfast. Some kitchenettes, microwaves, refrigerators, cable TV. Pool. Hot tub. Exercise equipment. Baby-sitting. Laundry service. Business services. Pets allowed. | 3701 Torrance Blvd. 90503 | 310/543–4566 or 800/331–3131 | fax 310/543–3026 | www.marriott.com | 247 suites | $109–$259 suites.

Summerfield Suites. Choose from a one- or two-bedroom suite, each with its own work area and kitchen. Picnic area, complimentary Continental breakfast. Kitchenettes, microwaves, cable TV. Pool. Hot tub. Exercise equipment. Laundry facilities. Airport shuttle. Pets allowed. | 19901 Prairie Ave. 90503 | 310/371–8525 or 800/833–4353 | fax 310/542–9628 | www.wyndham.com/AboutWyndham/summerfield.cfm | 144 suites | $148–$178 suites | AE, D, DC, MC, V.

VACAVILLE

Best Western Heritage Inn. This simple two-story motel is at the Monte Vista exit off Interstate 80. Complimentary breakfast. Pets allowed. | 1420 E. Monte Vista Ave. 95688 | 707/448–8453 or 800/552–2124 | fax 707/447–8649 | www.bestwestern.com | 41 rooms | $66–$80 | AE, MC, V.

Quality Inn Vacaville. This well-landscaped two-story hotel is at the Leisure Town Road exit off Interstate 80. Complimentary breakfast. In-room data ports, cable TV. Hot tub. Laundry facilities. Business services. Pets allowed (fee). | 950 Leisure Town Rd. 95687 | 707/446–8888 | fax 707/449–0109 | www.qualityinn.com | 120 rooms | $54–$99 | AE, D, DC, MC, V.

VALLEJO

Ramada Inn. Easily recognizable with its gray-and-burgundy exterior, this three-story hotel is in the middle of a shopping mall, close to Six Flags, and within walking distance of restaurants. Room service. Some in-room safes, some minibars, microwaves, refrigerators. Pool. Laundry facilities, laundry service. Pets allowed. | 1000 Admiral Callaghan La. | 707/643–2700 | fax 707/642–1148 | www.ramada.com | 130 rooms | $78–$145 | AE, D, MC, V.

WALNUT CREEK

Walnut Creek Motor Lodge. One block from a rapid transit station, this two-story motel has some rooms with kitchenettes. It's at the Ygnacio Valley Road exit off I–680. In-room data ports, refrigerators, cable TV, in-room VCRs (and movies). Hot tub. Pets allowed. No smoking. | 1960 N. Main St. | 925/932–2811 | fax 925/932–5989 | wcmotorlodge@hotmail.com | 71 rooms | $69–$79 | AE, DC, MC, V.

WEAVERVILLE

49er Gold Country Inn. A dozen rooms in this one-story motel have whirlpools and gas fireplaces, and the grounds include a re-creation of a 49er cabin and gold mining machinery. It's in the center of town, within walking distance of restaurants. Complimentary Continental breakfast. Some microwaves, refrigerators, some in-room hot tubs, cable TV. Pool. Pets allowed. | 718 Main St. | 530/623–4937 | www.49ermotel.random.net | 25 rooms | $61–$85 | AE, D, MC, V.

Weaverville Hotel. This Old West survivor—a hotel since 1861—is in the heart of town, across the street from the courthouse and next to the town bandstand. The hotel's simplicity and faded charm (and the sporting goods store downstairs) make it a popular destination for European backpackers. There are full baths in all rooms, two with antique claw-foot tubs. No room phones. Pets allowed. No smoking. | 201 Main St. | 530/623–3121 | 8 rooms | $39.50–$42.50 | MC, V.

WEST HOLLYWOOD

Le Parc Hotel. A tree-bordered residential street is the setting for this hotel. Accommodations are all roomy suites, with sunken living rooms, fireplaces, high ceilings, and eclectic furnishings. CBS Television City is 1 mi east and Rodeo Drive 2 mi southwest. Pool. Hot tub. Tennis. Exercise equipment. Business services, airport shuttle. Pets allowed. | 733 N.W. Knoll Dr. 90069 | 310/855–8888 | fax 310/659–7812 | 44 suites | $225–$275 suites | AE, D, DC, MC, V.

Le Montrose Suite Hôtel de Grand Luxe. A contemporary exterior leads into the Art Nouveau lobby of this hotel noted for its excellent service. You can take in a game of tennis or relax by the pool, on the rooftop, five stories up. Rooms have sunken living rooms and fireplaces; suites have upgraded amenities such as fax machines, copiers, printers, and furnishings, and the lobby displays an elaborately polished marble floor. Restaurant, room service. In-room data ports, kitchenettes, refrigerators, cable TV. Pool. Hot tub, massage. Tennis. Gym. Business services. Some pets allowed. | 900 Hammond St., West Hollywood

90069 | 310/855–1115 or 800/776–0666 | fax 310/657–9192 | www.lemontrose.com | 132 suites | $260–$390 suites | AE, DC, MC, V.

Summerfield Suites. A courtyard with a landscaped outdoor dining area is a focal point of this six-story all-suites. All units have a fireplace and a balcony. It's 11 mi west of downtown. Complimentary Continental breakfast. In-room data ports, kitchenettes. Cable TV, in-room VCRs (and movies). Pool. Exercise equipment. Laundry facilities. Some pets allowed. Parking (fee). | 1000 Westmount Dr. 90069 | 310/657–7400 or 800/833–4353 | fax 310/854–6744 | www.summerfieldsuites.com | 111 suites | $155–$258 | AE, D, DC, MC, V.

WHITTIER

Vagabond Inn. This three-story property is built around a sparkling outdoor pool surrounded by live palm trees and faux-tropical rock outcroppings. Complimentary Continental breakfast. Cable TV. Pool. Pets allowed (fee). | 14125 E. Whittier Blvd. 90605 | 562/698–9701 | fax 562/698–8716 | www.vagabondinn.com | 49 rooms | $60–$70 | AE, D, DC, MC, V.

WOODLAND

Cinderella Motel Woodland. The basic rooms at this two-story motel have combination or shower baths. Refrigerators, cable TV, in-room VCRs (and movies). Pool. Hot tub. Pets allowed (fee). No smoking. | 99 W Main St. | 530/662–1091 | fax 530/662–2804 | 30 rooms | $49–$58 | AE, D, DC, MC, V.

YOSEMITE NATIONAL PARK

Camping in Yosemite. There are lots of sites in Yosemite (nearly 2,000 in summer, 400 year-round)—but there are also lots of people who want them. Reservations at most of Yosemite's campgrounds are required, especially in summer. Most of the park's 15 campgrounds are in Yosemite Valley and along the Tioga Road (Route 120). Glacier Point and Wawona have one each. None of the campgrounds has water or electric hookups, but there are dump stations and shower facilities in the valley area year-round. You can sometimes find a site on the spur of the moment by stopping at the Campground Reservations Office in Yosemite Valley, but don't bank on it. Summer reservations are strongly recommended for Tuolumne Meadows, Hogdon Meadows, Wawona, Crane Flat, Lower Pines, North Pines, and Upper Pines campgrounds. On the 15th of each month you can reserve a site up to five months in advance. Sites at the Sunnyside campground in the valley are available on a first-come basis year-round. Pets allowed. | Box 1600, Cumberland, MD 21502 | 800/436–7275 | reservations.nps.gov/ | $6–$15 per site | D, MC, V | Reservations office 7–7, PST.

Tenaya Lodge At Yosemite. You could hang a canoe from the four-story, vaulted lobby and lounge area of this hotel—and, in fact, that's exactly what's up there. This contemporary take on the High Sierra lodge has rustically upscale touches—iron chandeliers, exposed timbers, and a huge stone fireplace with plenty of soft seating nearby. Native American rugs add warm earth tones to the mix. The main lodge and wing of rooms and suites looks out across heavily wooded parklands. This lodge books a lot of corporate conferences off-season. In summer, it's a prime spot for families, especially for touring Yosemite's southern sites—the Mariposa Grove and Glacier Point. A nearby stable leads trail rides through the mountain terrain (ask for details at the Activity Desk, in the lobby.) The hotel is 2 mi south of Yosemite's South Gate entrance. 2 restaurants, bar. In-room data ports, room service. Cable TV. 2 pools. Hot tub. Exercise equipment, hiking, horseback riding, water sports, boating, bicycles. Cross-country skiing, downhill skiing. Kids' programs (ages 3–12). Laundry facilities. Business services. Pets allowed (fee). | 1122 Rte. 41, Fish Camp 93623 | 559/683–6555 or 800/635–5807 | fax 559/683–8684 | www.tenayalodge.com | 244 rooms, 20 suites | $159–$279, $409–$529 suites | AE, D, DC, MC, V.

YREKA

Amerihost Inn Yreka. This 1997 hostelry is off I–5 on the south edge of town. Complimentary breakfast. Some in-room hot tubs, cable TV. Pool. Sauna. Business services. Pets allowed. | 148 Moonlit Oaks Ave. | 530/841–1300 or 800/434–5800 | fax 530/841–0399 | ameri-hostyreka@snowcrest.net | www.amerihostinn.com | 61 rooms | $64–139 | AE, D, MC, V.

Wayside Inn. This single-story white brick motel, 1/2 mi south of downtown, was built in the 1950s and remodeled in 1988. The lawn behind the motel is available for picnicking. Some kitchenettes, refrigerators, cable TV. Pool. Hot tub. Pets allowed (fee). | 1235 S. Main St. | 530/842–4412 or 800/795–7974 | 44 rooms | $45–$78 | AE, D, MC, V.

YUCCA VALLEY

Oasis of Eden Inn and Suites. An unusual inn 1/2 mi from the Joshua Tree National Park, 14 of the rooms here with in-room spas have names like Orient, Ancient Rome, Deep South, New York New York, and Persian. The "Safari" has a big four-poster bed with gauzy canopy and huge urns filled with palm fronds. Complimentary Continental breakfast. Some kitchenettes, refrigerators, some in-room hot tubs, cable TV, in-room VCRs (and movies). Pool. Hot tub. Business services. Pets allowed. | 56377 Twentynine Palms Hwy. 92284 | 760/365–6321 or 800/606–6686 | fax 760/365–9592 | www.desertgold.com/eden/eden.html | 20 rooms | $70–$200 | AE, D, DC, MC, V.

Super 8 Motel. This hotel is 14 mi west of Twentynine Palms and 10 mi north of Desert Hot Springs. Restaurant. Pool. Pets allowed. | Rte. 62 at Barberry Ave. 92284 | 760/228–1773 | fax 760/365–7799 | 48 rooms | $44–$56 | AE, D, DC, MC, V.

Colorado

ALAMOSA

Holiday Inn. Located less than a mile from downtown Alamosa, this well-kept motor lodge is a Holidome and also has conference facilities. Restaurant, bar. In-room data ports, room service, some microwaves, cable TV. Pool. Hot tub, sauna. Video games. Laundry facilities. Business services. Airport shuttle. Pets allowed. | 333 Santa Fe Ave. | 719/589–5833 | fax 719/589–4412 | www.holiday-inn.com | 127 rooms, 3 suites | $86–$96 | AE, D, DC, MC, V.

ASPEN

The Beaumont. Just four blocks from downtown Aspen, the Beaumont has a casual lounge where you can have dinner and drinks in front of the fireplace. Some rooms are rustic, with German antiques, while others are more modern. Complimentary breakfast. In-room data ports, cable TV, some in-room VCRs (and movies). Pool. Hot tub. Laundry facilities. Business services. Some pets allowed (fee). | 1301 E. Cooper Ave. | 970/925–7081 or 800/344–3853 | fax 970/925–1610 | www.thebeaumont.com | 30 rooms | $140–$285 | AE, D, DC, MC, V.

★ **Hotel Jerome.** A Gold Rush–era grand dame that's Victorian to the core, with lavishly patterned wallpaper and appropriately ornate guest rooms. 3 restaurants, 2 bars. In-room data ports, refrigerators, room service, some in-room hot tubs, cable TV, in-room VCRs (and movies). Pool. Hot tubs, massage. Gym. Business services. Airport shuttle. Pets allowed (fee). | 330 E. Main St. | 970/920–1000 or 800/331–7213 | fax 970/925–2784 | www.hoteljerome.com | 93 rooms, 16 suites | $485–$575, $885–$950 suites | AE, DC, MC, V.

Limelite Lodge. Located next to Wagner Park in the heart of Aspen, the Limelite Lodge offers traditionally furnished rooms and one- and two-bedroom apartments at reasonable prices. Complimentary Continental breakfast. No air-conditioning in some rooms, in-room data ports, refrigerators, cable TV, some in-room VCRs. 2 pools. 2 hot tubs, sauna. Laundry facilities. Pets allowed. | 228 E. Cooper Ave. | 970/925–3025 or 800/433–0832 | fax 970/925–5120 | www.limelite.net | 63 rooms, 9 apartments | $68–$350, $250–$350 apartments | AE, D, DC, MC, V.

★ **Little Nell.** Colorado's only five-star, five-diamond property. Rooms are luxuriously furnished and have gas fireplaces; all the large bathrooms have a separate tub and shower; most have balconies. The hotel also has a ski concierge. Restaurant, bar (with entertainment).

In-room data ports, in-room safes, minibars, refrigerators, room service, cable TV, in-room VCRs (and movies). Pool. Hot tub, massage. Health club. Shops. Business services. Airport shuttle. Pets allowed. | 675 E. Durant Ave. | 970/920–4600 or 800/843–6355 | fax 970/920–4670 | www.thelittlenell.com | 77 rooms, 14 suites | $550–$700, $1,025–$4,100 suites | AE, D, DC, MC, V.

Silvertree Hotel. A full-service slopeside hotel in the Snowmass Village Mall decorated in a contemporary mountain style and loaded with recreational facilities and amenities. Restaurant, bar (with entertainment). No air-conditioning, in-room data ports, refrigerators, room service, some in-room hot tubs. Cable TV. 2 pools. Beauty salon, 2 hot tubs, massage. Gym. Bicycles. Shops. Playground, laundry facilities. Business services. Airport shuttle, free parking. Pets allowed. | 100 Elbert La., Snowmass Village | 970/923–3520 or 800/525–9402 | fax 970/923–5192 | www.silvertreehotel.com | 247 rooms, 14 suites | $265–$435, $775–$1,680 suites | AE, D, DC, MC, V.

★ **St. Regis at Aspen.** A luxury hotel that is memorable even by Aspen standards, from the overstuffed leather chairs in the lobby lounge to the rich dark woods and muted colors of the guest rooms. It's also close by the ski slopes. Restaurant, 2 bars. In-room data ports, in-room safes, minibars, room service, cable TV, some in-room VCRs (and movies). Pool. Beauty salon, hot tubs, massage, sauna, spa, steam room. Health club, hiking. Bicycles. Shops. Baby-sitting, children's programs (ages 3–16). Business services. Parking (fee). Pets allowed. | 315 E. Dean St. | 970/920–3300 | fax 970/925–8998 | www.stregisaspen.com | 257 rooms, 27 suites | $500–$600, $775–$1,000 suites | AE, D, DC, MC, V.

Wildwood Lodge. This rustic Snowmass ski lodge is 60 yards from the slopes overlooking the village mall. Some rooms have fireplaces, and you have access to the health club at the Silvertree Hotel, its sister property. Restaurant, bar, complimentary Continental breakfast. In-room data ports, some microwaves, refrigerators, room service, cable TV, some in-room VCRs. Pool. Hot tub. Laundry facilities. Business services. Airport shuttle, free parking. Pets allowed. | 40 Elbert La., Snowmass Village (mailing address: Box 5009) | 970/923–3550 or 800/525–9402 | fax 970/923–5192 | www.wildwood-lodge.com | 148 rooms, 6 suites | $69–$229, $89–$259 suites | Closed late Apr.–early May | AE, D, DC, MC, V.

BEAVER CREEK

Inn at Riverwalk. These comfortable rooms and condominiums are quite affordable. All have a queen- or king-size bed, and some have balconies with great views. The inn also offers ski and bicycle storage. Just 4 mi from Beaver Creek in Edwards. Restaurant, bar. Complimentary Continental breakfast. In-room data ports, some kitchenettes, some microwaves, some refrigerators, cable TV, some in-room VCRs (and movies). Pool. Hot tub. Gym. Laundry service. Pets allowed (fee). | 27 Main St., Edwards | 970/926–0606 or 888/926–0606 | fax 970/926–0616 | www.vail.net/riverwalk | 60 rooms, 14 condos | $150–$250, $500–$700 condos | AE, D, DC, MC, V.

BOULDER

Broker Inn. This small hotel three blocks from the campus of the University of Colorado at Boulder offers many of the amenities of a larger, more expensive hostelry. Rooms are modern, but decorated in a Victorian motif. Restaurant, bar (with entertainment), complimentary Continental breakfast. In-room data ports, room service, cable TV. Pool. Hot tub. Business services. Airport shuttle. Pets allowed. | 555 30th St. 80303 | 303/444–3330 or 800/338–5407 | fax 303/444–6444 | www.boulderbrokerinn.com | 116 rooms, 4 suites | $120–$130, $160–$195 suites | AE, D, DC, MC, V.

★ **Foot of the Mountain Motel.** This collection of wood cabin–style units is just a few minutes' walk from downtown Boulder and across the street from a city park with bike path. Each cabin has a mountain or stream view. Refrigerators, cable TV. Pets allowed (fee). | 200 Arapahoe Ave. 80302 | 303/442–5688 | 18 rooms | $65–$75 | AE, D, MC, V.

Residence Inn by Marriott. Spacious rooms in this modern, all-suite property feature separate sleeping and living areas and fully equipped kitchens. Picnic area, complimentary Continental breakfast. In-room data ports, kitchenettes, microwaves, refrigerators, cable TV. Pool. Hot tub. Playground. Laundry facilities. Business services. Pets allowed (fee). | 3030 Center Green Dr. 80301 | 303/449–5545 | fax 303/449–2452 | www.residenceinn.com | 128 suites | $139–$199 | AE, D, DC, MC, V.

BRECKENRIDGE

Great Divide. Located just 50 yards from the base of Peak 9 and two blocks from Main Street, this is one of the few full-service hotels in Breckenridge. Offers especially large guest rooms, some with private balconies, as well as meeting facilities. Bar. In-room data ports, refrigerators, cable TV. Pool. Hot tub, massage. Gym. Video games. Business services, airport shuttle. Pets allowed. | 550 Village Rd. 80424 | 970/453–4500 or 800/321–8444 | fax 970/453–0212 | www.greatdividelodge.com | 208 rooms | $150–$225 | AE, D, DC, MC, V.

Lodge at Breckenridge. The lodge is on a cliff surrounded by trees, 2.2 mi from town. Some rooms have gas fireplaces or private balconies with stunning views of the mountains. Be sure to pamper yourself with an appointment at the full-service spa. Restaurant, complimentary Continental breakfast. Pool. 2 indoor hot tubs, spa. Health club, racquetball. Shops. Some pets allowed (fee). | 112 Overlook Dr. 80424 | 970/453–9300 or 800/736–1607 | fax 970/453–0625 | www.thelodgeatbreck.com | 45 rooms | $190–$340 | AE, D, DC, MC, V.

BUENA VISTA

Topaz Lodge. This small motel is next to downtown Buena Vista, near a park and a launch point for white-water rafting trips on the Arkansas River. No air-conditioning, cable TV. Some pets allowed. | 115 U.S. 24 N | 719/395–2427 | 18 rooms, 1 two-bedroom apartment | $65–$110 | AE, D, DC, MC, V.

BURLINGTON

Budget Host Chaparral Motor Inn. A budget motel located one block from the intersection of Interstate 70 (exit 437) and U.S. 385, near several restaurants. Cable TV. Pool. Hot tub. Playground. Some pets allowed. | 405 S. Lincoln St. | 719/346–5361 | fax 719/346–8502 | 39 rooms | $45 | AE, D, DC, MC, V.

CAÑON CITY

Cañon Inn. A two-story motel just 8 mi from Royal Gorge Bridge. Spacious rooms abound in this comfortable motel. Conveniently located just off of Highway 50. Restaurant, bar. Some microwaves, some refrigerators, room service, cable TV. Pool. 6 hot tubs. Laundry facilities. Business services, airport shuttle. Pets allowed (fee). | 3075 E. U.S. 50 | 719/275–8676, 800/525–7727 in Colorado | fax 719/275–8675 | www.canoninn.com | 152 rooms | $65–$100 | AE, D, DC, MC, V.

COLORADO SPRINGS

Doubletree World Arena. Conveniently located across from a shopping mall and the World Arena, this upscale chain hotel has large, comfortable rooms. Restaurant, bar (with entertainment). In-room data ports, room service, cable TV. Pool. Hot tub. Gym. Business services. Airport shuttle. Pets allowed. | 1775 E. Cheyenne Mountain Blvd. 80906 | 719/576–8900 or 800/222–8733 | fax 719/576–4450 | www.doubletree.com | 299 rooms, 6 suites | $109–$498, $299 suites | AE, D, DC, MC, V.

Drury Inn. This reasonably priced chain motel is on the north side of Colorado Springs, near a shopping mall and the Air Force Academy. Complimentary Continental breakfast. In-room data ports, some microwaves, some refrigerators, cable TV, some in-room VCRs. Indoor-outdoor pool. Hot tub. Gym. Laundry facilities. Business services. Some pets allowed. | 8155 N. Academy Blvd. (I–25, exit 150) 80920 | 719/598–2500 or 800/378–7946 | fax 719/598–2500 | www.drury-inn.com | 118 rooms | $74–$109 | AE, D, DC, MC, V.

Fireside Suites. Have all the comforts of home while you travel. Each suite has a living/dining area, a spacious work station, a bedroom with a king- or queen-size bed, a kitchen, a closet, and a bath. Some of the suites have a private balcony/patio with views of Pikes Peak. Complimentary Continental breakfast. In-room data ports, kitchenettes, microwaves, refrigerators, cable TV, in-room VCRs. Outdoor pool. Gym. Laundry facilities. Pets allowed (fee). | 620 N. Murray | 719/597–6207 | fax 719/597–7483 | www.firesidesuites.com | 70 rooms | $79–$149 | AE, D, MC, V.

Maple Lodge. Set on 2 acres ¼ mile from the Garden of the Gods, this small lodge offers traditional suites and separate two-room units. Picnic area. Some kitchenettes, some microwaves, refrigerators, cable TV. Pool. Miniature golf. Pets allowed. | 9 El Paso Blvd. | 719/685–9230 | www.colorado-springs.com | 17 rooms | $30–$159 | AE, D, MC, V.

Radisson Inn North. This upscale chain hotel near the Air Force Academy offers above-average facilities and amenities. Restaurants, bar. In-room data ports, some microwaves, room service, cable TV, some in-room VCRs. Pool. Hot tub, sauna. Gym. Laundry facilities. Business services. Airport shuttle. Some pets allowed. | 8110 N. Academy Blvd. (I–25, exit 150) 80920 | 719/598–5770 or 800/333–3333 | fax 719/598–3434 | www.radisson.com | 188 rooms, 12 suites | $144–$154, $159–$259 suites | AE, D, DC, MC, V.

Radisson Inn and Suites–Airport. Near the airport, reasonably priced suites make this a good choice for business travelers. Restaurant, bar, complimentary breakfast. In-room data ports, some microwaves, room service, cable TV. Pool. Hot tub. Gym. Video games. Laundry facilities. Business services. Airport shuttle. Some pets allowed (fee). | 1645 Newport Dr. 80916 | 719/597–7000 or 800/333–3333 | fax 719/597–4308 | www.radisson.com | 200 rooms, 44 suites | $100–$140, $160 suites | AE, D, DC, MC, V.

Ramada Inn North. This full-service budget hotel is just off Interstate 25, one exit south of Garden of the Gods. Restaurant, bar. In-room data ports, room service, cable TV, Pool. Video games. Laundry facilities. Airport shuttle. Pets allowed. | 3125 Sinton Rd. 80907 | 719/633–5541 or 888–298–2054 | fax 719/633–3870 | www.ramada.com | 220 rooms, 4 suites | $99–$109, $175–$225 suites | AE, D, DC, MC, V.

Residence Inn by Marriott–North. An all-suite hostelry near the Air Force Academy, with fireplaces in some units. Complimentary Continental breakfast. In-room data ports, kitchenettes, microwaves, refrigerators, cable TV, some in-room VCRs. Pool. Hot tub. Laundry facilities. Business services. Airport shuttle. Some pets allowed (fee). | 3880 N. Academy Blvd. (I–25, exit 146) 80917 | www.residenceinn.com | 719/574–0370 or 800/228–9290 | fax 719/574–7821 | 96 suites | $127–$185 | AE, D, DC, MC, V.

Residence Inn by Marriott–South. An all-suite hostelry near downtown Colorado Springs, across from the World Arena. Some units have fireplaces. Complimentary Continental breakfast. In-room data ports, kitchenettes, microwaves, refrigerators, cable TV, some in-room VCRs. Pool. Hot tub. Gym. Laundry facilities. Business services. Some pets allowed (fee). | 2765 Geyser Dr. 80906 | 719/576–0101 or 800/228–9290 | fax 719/576–4848 | www.residenceinn.com | 72 suites | $119–$195 | AE, D, DC, MC, V.

Sheraton Colorado Springs Hotel. This upscale chain hotel is just 4 mi from Seven Falls and has several recreational facilities. Restaurant, bars (with entertainment). In-room data ports, some microwaves, some refrigerators, room service, cable TV, some in-room VCRs (and movies). 2 pools (1 indoor), wading pool. Hot tub, sauna, steam room. Putting green, 2 tennis courts. Basketball, gym. Video games. Playground. Business services. Airport shuttle. Pets allowed. | 2886 S. Circle Dr. (I–25, exit 138) 80906 | 719/576–5900 or 800/981–4012 | fax 719/576–7695 | www.asgusa.com/scsh | 500 rooms, 16 suites | $105–$155, $250 suites | AE, D, DC, MC, V.

CORTEZ

Anasazi Motor Inn. This motor inn with large rooms is a mile from the intersection of U.S. Highways 160 and 666. Restaurant, bar (with entertainment). Room service, cable TV, some in-room VCRs. Pool. Hot tub. Business services. Airport shuttle. Pets allowed. | 640 S. Broadway | 970/565–3773, 800/972–6232 outside CO | fax 970/565–1027 | iyp.uswestdex.com/anasazimotorinn/ | 87 rooms | $57–$71 | AE, D, DC, MC, V.

Best Western Turquoise Inn and Suites. This chain motel is 10 mi from Mesa Verde National Park. Complimentary Continental breakfast. In-room data ports, microwaves, some refrigerators, cable TV. Pool. Hot tub. Laundry facilities. Business services. Airport shuttle. Some pets allowed. | 535 E. Main St. | 970/565–3778 or 800/547–3376 | fax 970/565–3439 | www.cortezbestwestern.com | 46 rooms, 31 suites | $79–$150, $99–$129 suites | AE, D, DC, MC, V.

Comfort Inn. This mid-priced motel is on Cortez's east side. Complimentary Continental breakfast. In-room data ports, some in-room hot tubs, satellite TV. Pool. Hot tub. Laundry facilities. Pets allowed. | 2321 E. Main St. | 970/565–3400 | fax 970/564–9768 | www.comfortinn.com | 148 rooms | $89–$99 | AE, D, DC, MC, V.

Holiday Inn Express. This clean and comfortable chain motel is on the outskirts of Cortez, about 9 mi from Mesa Verde National Park. Complimentary Continental breakfast. In-room data ports, cable TV. Pool. Hot tub. Gym. Business services. Airport shuttle. Some pets allowed. | 2121 E. Main St. | 970/565–6000 | fax 970/565–3438 | www.holiday-inn.com | 100 rooms | $48–$109 | AE, D, DC, MC, V.

CRAIG

Holiday Inn Hotel and Suites. This full-service hotel 1 mi south of town center is the only place to stay between Steamboat Springs and the state line. Restaurant, bar. Some microwaves, room service, cable TV, some in-room VCRs. Pool. Hot tub. Gym. Video games. Laundry facilities. Business services. Pets allowed. | 300 S. Colorado Hwy. 13 | 970/824–4000 | fax 970/824–3950 | www.holidayinn.com | 152 rooms, 20 suites | $69–$89, $84–$109 suites | AE, D, DC, MC, V.

CRIPPLE CREEK

Victor Hotel. A former bank 6 mi from Cripple Creek is an historic landmark built in 1899, though guest rooms have a more modern feel. Many guests claim that there is a ghost residing in the hotel. Restaurant, complimentary Continental breakfast. Cable TV. Business services. Pets allowed. | 4th St. and Victor Ave., Victor 80860 | 719/689–3553 or 800/748–0870 | fax 719/689–3979 | www.indra.com/fallline/vh/vh.htm | 30 rooms | $89–$99 | D, MC, V.

CUCHARA

Yellow Pine Guest Ranch. Hidden in the pine groves just north of Cuchara, these 1920s cabins are a true getaway; only the lulling sound of nearby Cuchara River intrudes on your quiet. The cabins are on spacious, private lots, have full kitchens, and are individually decorated in country fashion. Many have fireplaces and porches and some can accommodate up to eight guests. Kitchenettes, refrigerators. No room phones, no TV. Horseback riding. Fishing. Laundry facilities. Pets allowed (fee). | 15880 Rte. 12 81055 | 719/742–3528 | www.coloradodirectory.com/yellowpineranch | 9 cabins | $75–$120 | Closed Nov.–Apr. | AE, MC, V.

DELTA

Best Western Sundance. This chain motel is centrally located near the heart of town. Restaurant, bar, complimentary breakfast. In-room data ports, room service, cable TV. Outdoor pool. Hot tub. Gym. Laundry facilities. Business services. Pets allowed. | 903 Main St. | 970/

874–9781 or 800/626–1994 | fax 970/874–5440 | www.bestwestern.com | 41 rooms | $55–$70 | AE, D, DC, MC, V.

DENVER

Best Western Executive. One of the closest properties to Denver International Airport, this chain motel is geared for business travelers. Restaurant, bar. In-room data ports, room service, cable TV, some in-room VCRs. Pool. Gym. Laundry facilities. Business services. Free parking. Some pets allowed (fee). | 4411 Peoria Way 80239 | 303/373–5730 or 800/848–4060 | fax 303/375–1157 | www.bestwestern.com | 186 rooms, 12 suites | $80–$85, $99 suites | AE, D, DC, MC, V.

Burnsley All Suite Hotel. This all-suite boutique hotel is near the state capitol in a residential area. Since the hotel was originally an apartment building, all rooms have full kitchens. Restaurant, bar. Kitchenettes, microwaves, room service, cable TV. Pool. Business services. Some pets allowed (fee). | 1000 Grant St. (I–25, exit 6th St.) 80203 | 303/830–1000, 800/231–3915 outside CO | fax 303/830–7676 | www.burnsley.com | 82 suites | $159–$189 | AE, DC, MC, V.

Doubletree Denver. This large upscale chain hotel is across from the former Stapleton Airport, between downtown Denver and Denver International Airport. Some rooms have views of the Rocky Mountains. Restaurant, bar. In-room data ports, some refrigerators, room service, cable TV, some in-room VCRs. Pool. Hot tub. Gym. Business services. Airport shuttle, free parking. Pets allowed. | 3203 Quebec St. 80207 | 303/321–3333 | fax 303/329–5233 | www.doubletree.com | 557 rooms, 6 suites | $169, $350–$500 suites | AE, D, DC, MC, V.

Drury Inn–Denver East. The rooms in this inexpensive chain motel, 12 mi from downtown Denver and 15 mi from Denver International Airport, are quiet and comfortable and have a desk with chair and an in-room coffee machine. Complimentary breakfast. In-room data ports, some microwaves, some refrigerators, cable TV. Indoor-outdoor pool. Hot tub. Gym. Laundry facilities, laundry service. Business services. Free parking. Pets allowed. | 4400 Peoria St. | 303/373–1983 or 800/378–7946 | fax 303/373–1983 | www.druryinn.com | 138 rooms | $70–$80 | AE, D, DC, MC, V.

Holiday Chalet. A B&B in an 1896 Victorian brownstone in the Wyman neighborhood north of Capitol Hill, a few blocks south of City Park. Complimentary Continental breakfast. Kitchenettes, some microwaves, in-room data ports, cable TV, in-room VCRs (and movies). Library. Pets allowed. No smoking. | 1820 E. Colfax Ave. 80218 | 303/321–9975 or 800/626–4497 | fax 303/377–6556 | www.bbonline.com/co/holiday/index.html | 10 suites | $94–$160 | AE, D, DC, MC, V.

Hotel Monaco. In the completely renovated 1917 Railway Exchange Building in downtown Denver, this upscale and elegant boutique hotel offers such extra amenities as in-room fax machines and pet treats (if you are traveling with Rover). Each evening there is a wine and cheese reception. Restaurant, bar. In-room data ports, minibars, some in-room hot tubs, cable TV. Beauty salon, spa. Gym. Laundry service. Business services. Pets allowed. | 1717 Champa St. | 303/296–1717 or 800/397–5380 | fax 303/296–1818 | www.monaco-denver.com | 189 rooms | $185–$990 | AE, D, DC, MC, V.

La Quinta Airport–South. A chain hotel on the east side of Denver, just north of Aurora, about 15 mi from both the airport and downtown. Complimentary Continental breakfast. In-room data ports, microwaves, some refrigerators, cable TV. Pool. Laundry facilities. Business services. Airport shuttle, parking (fee). Some pets allowed. | 3975 Peoria Way (I–70, exit 281) 80239 | 303/371–5640 or 800/687–6667 | fax 303/371–7015 | www.laquinta.com | 112 rooms | $69–$89 | AE, D, DC, MC, V.

La Quinta–Downtown. This economical chain motel with simply furnished yet comfortable rooms is on the northwest side of downtown Denver. Complimentary Continental breakfast. In-room data ports, cable TV. Pool. Business services. Free parking. Pets allowed.

| 3500 Park Ave. W (I–25, exit 213) 80216 | 303/458–1222 or 800/687–6667 | fax 303/433–2246 | www.laquinta.com | 105 rooms | $70–$85 | AE, D, DC, MC, V.

★ **Loews Giorgio.** This 12-story luxury hotel is modern on the outside but has an unexpected Italian Baroque interior. Restaurant, bar. Minibars, some refrigerators, cable TV, some in-room VCRs (and movies). Gym. Library. Business services. Free parking. Some pets allowed. | 4150 E. Mississippi Ave. 80246 | 303/782–9300 or 800/235–6397 | fax 303/758–6542 | www.loewshotels.com | 183 rooms, 19 suites | $199–$249, $259–$1,000 suites | AE, D, DC, MC, V.

Marriott–City Center. A large chain hotel in downtown Denver is a block from the 16th Street Mall and 1.5 mi from Coors Field. Restaurant, bar. In-room data ports, some refrigerators, room service, cable TV, some in-room VCRs. Pool. Hot tub. Gym. Shops. Business services. Some pets allowed. | 1701 California St. 80202 | 303/297–1300 or 800/321–2211 | fax 303/298–7474 | www.marriott.com | 615 rooms, 20 suites | $169–$179, $550–$680 suites | AE, D, DC, MC, V.

Marriott–Denver Tech Center. A large chain hotel, south of downtown, near the Denver Tech Center. 4 restaurants, bar. In-room data ports, refrigerators, room service, cable TV, some in-room VCRs. 2 pools (1 indoor). Barbershop, beauty salon, hot tub. Gym. Shops. Laundry service. Business services. Free parking. Pets allowed. | 4900 S. Syracuse St. 80237 | 303/779–1100 or 800/321–2211 | fax 303/740–2523 | www.marriott.com | 614 rooms, 12 suites | $87–$169, $260–$500 suites | AE, D, DC, MC, V.

Marriott–Southeast. Located immediately east of Interstate 25 in south Denver, this chain hotel has rooms with balconies and a luxury level. Restaurant, bar. In-room data

PETS A-OK

Denver's Hotel Monaco, in the renovated 1917 Railway Exchange Building downtown, is near the Colorado Convention Center and other attractions. Service is first class, and rooms superbly equipped with everything from data ports and CD players to mini bars and coffee makers. There's a full-service spa and a fine Italian restaurant serving three meals a day to satisfy other needs. But for pet-lovers, the best news is that you'll never spend a night alone. The hotel may well be the most pet-friendly hotel in the country. Lily, the hotel's Jack Russell terrier, greets you in the lobby. The hotel has welcomed dogs, cats, birds, turtles, and other animal friends—all pets are welcome, without size or weight limit. There's no extra charge, and no deposit is required. Every pet gets a special treat on check-in. In fact, even if you arrive without a pet but would like company in your room, just tell the folks at the desk and they'll send up a goldfish. If you do plan to bring your own, you'll be glad to learn that dog walking and sitting services are available, and there's an exercise area within walking distance. Just in case, the hotel also can provide a list of veterinarians with offices nearby if you need one. Just be sure to give the hotel a heads-up, so they'll be ready for the two of you. Contact the hotel at 1717 Champa St., Denver CO 80202, 303/296–1717 or 800/397–5380, www.monaco-denver.com.

ports, some refrigerators, cable TV. 2 pools (1 indoor). Barbershop, beauty salon, hot tub. Gym. Video games. Shops. Laundry facilities. Business services. Airport shuttle. Some pets allowed. | 6363 E. Hampden Ave. (I–25, exit Hampden Ave.) 80222 | 303/758–7000 or 800/321–2211 | fax 303/691–3418 | www.marriott.com | 280 rooms, 10 suites | $59–$154, $250–$450 suites | AE, D, DC, MC, V.

Quality Inn and Suites. This northeast Denver chain hotel provides easy access to Interstate 70, 1 mi away, and the airport, 16 mi away. Restaurant, bar. In-room data ports, room service, cable TV. Outdoor pool. Hot tub. Gym. Laundry service. Business services. Airport shuttle, free parking. Pets allowed. | 4590 Quebec St. (I–70, exit 278) 80216 | 303/320–0260 or 800/228–5151 | fax 303/320–7595 | www.qualityinn.com | 164 rooms, 18 suites | $75–$85, $89–$135 suites | AE, D, DC, MC, V.

Quality Inn South. This chain hotel is 2 mi from the Denver Tech Center and 12 mi south of downtown. Bar, picnic area, complimentary Continental breakfast. In-room data ports, some refrigerators, cable TV. Pool. Hot tub, gym. Laundry facilities. Business services. Pets allowed (fee). | 6300 E. Hampden Ave., at I–25 80222 | 303/758–2211 or or 800/228–5151 | fax 303/753–0156 | www.qualityinn.com | 185 rooms | $75–$120 | AE, D, DC, MC, V.

Quality Inn West. A reasonably priced chain motel 13 mi west of downtown Denver on Tabor Lake in Wheat Ridge. Restaurant, bar. Room service, cable TV. Gym. Business services. Some pets allowed (fee). | 12100 W. 44th Ave., Wheat Ridge 80033 | 303/467–2400 or 800/228–5151 | fax 303/467–0198 | www.qualityinn.com | 108 rooms | $54–$79 | AE, D, DC, MC, V.

Ramada Inn–Airport. A chain motel 5 mi from downtown Denver and 17 mi from Denver International Airport. Restaurant, bar. In-room data ports, some refrigerators, room service, cable TV. Pool. Gym. Laundry facilities. Business services. Airport shuttle, free parking. Pets allowed (deposit). | 3737 Quebec St. (I–70, exit 278) 80207 | 303/388–6161 or 888/298–2054 | fax 303/388–0426 | www.ramada.com | 148 rooms | $87–$145 | AE, D, DC, MC, V.

Residence Inn by Marriott–Downtown. In this all-suite motor hotel in downtown Denver, many rooms have fireplaces. Complimentary Continental breakfast. Kitchenettes, microwaves, refrigerators, cable TV, some in-room VCRs. Outdoor pool. Hot tub. Gym. Business services. Free parking. Pets allowed (fee). | 2777 Zuni St. (I–25, exit Speer Blvd.) 80211 | 303/458–5318 or 800/321–2211 | fax 303/458–5318 | www.residenceinn.com | 156 suites | $89–$155 suites | AE, D, DC, MC, V.

The Warwick. This stylish hotel on the east side of downtown is three blocks northeast of the state capitol. The large rooms are furnished with antique reproductions. Restaurant, bar, complimentary Continental breakfast. In-room data ports, some microwaves, some refrigerators, room service, cable TV. Pool. Business services. Airport shuttle, parking (fee). Some pets allowed. | 1776 Grant St. 80203 | 303/861–2000 or 800/525–2888 | fax 303/832–0320 | www.warwickhotels.com | 220 rooms, 49 suites | $165–$175, $200–$800 suites | AE, D, DC, MC, V.

★ **Westin Tabor Center.** This large, sleek high-rise hotel downtown is next to the 16th Street Mall. Restaurant, bar. In-room data ports, minibars, refrigerators, room service, cable TV, some in-room VCRs. Indoor-outdoor pool. Hot tub. Gym. Shops. Business services. Some pets allowed. | 1672 Lawrence St. 80202 | 303/572–9100 or 800/325–3589 | fax 303/572–7288 | www.westin.com | 417 rooms, 13 suites | $222–$237, $390–$1285 suites | AE, D, DC, MC, V.

DILLON

Best Western Ptarmigan Lodge. This chain motel on the west side of town overlooks Lake Dillon. Complimentary Continental breakfast. No air-conditioning, some kitchenettes, some microwaves, cable TV. Hot tub, sauna. Boating. Business services. Pets allowed (fee). | 652 Lake Dillon Dr. | 970/468–2341 or 800/842–593 | fax 970/468–6465 | ptarmiganlodge@colorado.net | 69 rooms | $110–$140 | AE, D, DC, MC, V.

Silverthorne Days Inn. This chain motel is just off I–70. Some rooms have fireplaces. Complimentary Continental breakfast. Some kitchenettes, some microwaves, cable TV. Wading pool. Hot tub, sauna. Laundry facilities. Business services. Pets allowed (fee). | 580 Silverthorne La., Silverthorne 80498 | 970/468–8661 | fax 970/468–1421 | www.daysinn.com | 73 rooms | $139–$229 | AE, D, DC, MC, V.

DINOSAUR

Four Queens Motel. Rooms are small in this spartan motel 18 mi from Dinosaur. Refrigerators, cable TV. Laundry facilities. Pets allowed. | 206 E. Main, Rangely 81648 | 970/675–5035 | fax 970/675–5037 | 32 rooms | $40–$48 | AE, D, DC, MC, V.

Hi Vu Motel. This low-priced family motel is in downtown Dinosaur and has a picnic barbecue area. No room phones, cable TV. Pets allowed. | 122 E. Brontosaurus Blvd. | 970/374–2267 or 800/374–5332 | fax 970/374–2249 | www.cmn.net/~whtrvn | 8 rooms | $28–$36 | AE, MC, V.

DOLORES

Dolores Mountain Inn. Located right in the heart of downtown Dolores, this mountain inn, which consists of three separate buildings, offers comfortable accommodations at an affordable price. Cable TV, some kitchenettes. Pets allowed (fee). No smoking. | 701 Railroad Ave. | 970/882–7203 or 800/842–8113 | fax 970/882–7011 | www.dminn.com | 14 rooms, 16 suites. | $68 | AE, D, MC, V.

DURANGO

Alpine Motel. This small motel is on the north side of Durango, 2½ mi north of the center near several restaurants and grocery stores. Some microwaves, cable TV. Some pets allowed. | 3515 N. Main Ave. | 970/247–4042 or 800/818–4042 | fax 970/385–4489 | 25 rooms | $74–$84 | AE, D, DC, MC, V.

Best Western Purgatory. In this chain motel just 150 yards from the Purgatory ski lift you stay either in a suite or in traditional motel rooms. Restaurant, bar, picnic area, complimentary Continental breakfast. Some kitchenettes, cable TV, some in-room VCRs (and movies). Pool. Hot tub. Gym. Business services. Pets allowed (fee). | 49617 Hwy. 550 N, Purgatory | 970/247–9669 | fax 970/247–9681 | www.purgatorylodge.com | 31 rooms, 18 suites | $99–$109, $119–$129 suites | AE, D, DC, MC, V.

Doubletree Durango. This upscale, full-service chain hotel is located one block from downtown, next to the Animas River, an easy walk from the train station and the shopping and dining districts. Restaurant, bar. In-room data ports, room service, cable TV. Pool. Beauty salon, hot tub. Gym. Laundry facilities. Business services. Airport shuttle. Pets allowed. | 501 Camino Del Rio | 970/259–6580 | fax 970/259–4398 | www.doubletree.com | 157 rooms, 2 suites | $119–$154, $300 suites | AE, D, DC, MC, V.

Iron Horse Inn. This property on the north edge of town has many two-story suites with fireplaces, making it a great choice for larger families. Restaurant. Some refrigerators, cable TV. Pool. Hot tub, sauna. Video games. Laundry facilities. Business services. Airport shuttle. Pets allowed. | 5800 N. Main Ave. | 970/259–1010 or 800/748–2990 | fax 970/385–4791 | www.durango.com/ironhorseinn/ | 144 suites | $99–$129 suites | AE, D, DC, MC, V.

★ **New Rochester Hotel.** Many films have been made in these parts, and the rooms in this small, 19th-century hotel take their cue from the moviemakers' vision, from their names to the artifacts inside. Strives for a chic but funky atmosphere, with mismatched furniture and wagon-wheel chandeliers. Complimentary breakfast. Some kitchenettes, refrigerators, cable TV, some in-room VCRs (and movies). Business services. Some pets allowed (fee). No smoking. | 726 E. 2nd Ave. | 970/385–1920 or 800/664–1920 | fax 970/385–1967 | www.rochesterhotel.com | 12 rooms, 3 suites | $139–$179, $179–$199 suites | AE, D, DC, MC, V.

ENGLEWOOD

Hampton Inn–Denver Southeast. Easy access to Interstate 25, the Denver Tech Center, and Fiddler's Green. Complimentary Continental breakfast. In-room data ports, cable TV. Pool. Gym. Laundry facilities. Business services. Some pets allowed. | 9231 E. Arapahoe Rd. 80112 | 303/792–9999 or 800/426–7866 | fax 303/790–4360 | www.hamptoninn.com | 152 rooms | $89–$99 | AE, D, DC, MC, V.

Residence Inn by Marriott–South. This all-suite chain hotel provides easy access to the Denver Tech Center. All suites have full kitchens; many rooms have fireplaces. Complimentary Continental breakfast. In-room data ports, kitchenettes, microwaves, refrigerators, cable TV. Pool. Hot tub. Laundry facilities. Business services. Pets allowed (fee). | 6565 S. Yosemite 80111 | 303/740–7177 or 800/331–3131 | fax 303/741–9426 | www.residenceinn. com | 128 suites | $129–$165 | AE, D, DC, MC, V.

ESTES PARK

Columbine Inn. This friendly, old-fashioned mountain inn caters to senior citizens. It is 1 mi east of Lake Estes Marina and within walking distance of golfing and horseback riding. Some kitchenettes, some refrigerators, cable TV. Outdoor hot tub. Some pets allowed. | 1540 Big Thompson Ave. | 970/586–4533 or 800/726–9049 | fax 970/586–4363 | www.estes-park.com/columbine | 19 rooms | $81–$98 | MC, V.

Estes Park Center/YMCA of the Rockies. Both the lodge rooms and the 200 cabins are simple, clean, and attractive, and all are constructed of sturdy oak. This property is so huge it has its own zip code. Restaurant. Some kitchenettes. Pool. Basketball, gym. Playground. Some pets allowed. | 2515 Tunnel Rd. | 970/586–3341 | 730 rooms | $64–$92 | No credit cards.

Machin's Cottages in the Pines. These cottages nestled within a shady pine forest, with big windows, porches, patios, and fireplaces, are on private property within the boundaries of Rocky Mountain National Park. Picnic area. Kitchenettes, microwaves, cable TV. Hiking. Playground. Some pets allowed. | 2450 Eagle Cliff Rd. 80517 | 970/586–4276 | www.estes-park.com/machins | 17 1- to 3-bedroom cottages | $82–$178 | Closed Oct.–late May | AE, MC, V.

FORT COLLINS

Holiday Inn Fort Collins–I–25. This reliable, mid-priced chain hotel is just east of downtown Fort Collins. Restaurant, bar, room service. Cable TV, some in-room VCRs. Pool, wading pool. Hot tub, sauna. Gym. Video games. Laundry facilities. Business services. Pets allowed. | 3836 E. Mulberry St. 80524 | 970/484–4660 or 800/465–4329 | fax 970/484–2326 | www.holiday-inn.com | 197 rooms | $89–$99 | AE, D, DC, MC, V.

Residence Inn Fort Collins. Rooms at this all-suite chain hotel are comfortable and spacious. It is ideal for business travelers and there is a meeting room. Complimentary breakfast. In-room data ports, kitchenettes, refrigerators, cable TV. Pool. Gym. Laundry service. Business services. Pets allowed (fee). | 1127 Oakridge Dr. | 970/223–5700 | fax 970/266–9280 | www.residenceinn.com | 78 suites | $89–$109 | AE, D, DC, MC, V.

FORT MORGAN

Best Western Park Terrace. This simple chain motel is four blocks south of Interstate 76. Picnic area. In-room data ports, cable TV. Pool. Hot tub. Pets allowed (fee). | 725 Main St. 80701 | 970/867–8256 or 888/593–5793 | fax 970/867–8256 | www.bestwestern.com | 24 rooms | $49–$70 | AE, D, DC, MC, V.

Central Motel. This independently owned budget motel is in downtown Fort Morgan. Microwaves, refrigerators, cable TV, some in-room VCRs. Some pets allowed. | 201 W. Platte Ave. | 970/867–2401 | fax 970/867–2401 | 13 rooms, 6 suites | $40–$55, $60 suites | AE, D, DC, MC, V.

FRISCO

New Summit Inn. One of the more economical places to stay in Frisco, it is relatively quiet and offers many amenities. Close to Lake Dillon and downtown, almost everything is a walk away. Complimentary Continental breakfast. Some microwaves, cable TV. Hot tub, sauna. Gym. Laundry facilities. Pets allowed (fee). | 1205 N. Summit Blvd. 80443 | 970/668–3220 or 800/745–1211 | fax 970/668–0188 | www.newsummitinn.com | 31 rooms | $99–$109 | AE, D, DC, MC, V.

GLENWOOD SPRINGS

Avalanche Ranch. Many of the cozy, carpeted, pine-paneled cabins have lofts and fireplaces at this ranch on the Crystal River about 30 mi south of Glenwood Springs. Each cabin has its own yard with a picnic table and charcoal grill as well as a full kitchen. Down comforters on all the beds keep you warm and comfortable. Picnic area. No air-conditioning, kitchenettes, some in-room VCRs, no room phones, TV in common area. Hot tub. Playground. Business services. Some pets allowed (fee). No smoking. | 12863 Hwy. 133, Redstone 81623 | 970/963–2846 or 877/963–9339 | fax 970/963–3141 | www.avalancheranch.com | 12 cabins, 1 3-bedroom ranch house | $95–$175 cabins, $395 ranch house (3–night minimum stay in summer) | D, MC, V.

Hotel Colorado. The exterior of this building is simply exquisite, with graceful sandstone colonnades and Italian campaniles. In its halcyon days everybody from Doc Holliday to Al Capone stayed here. Rooms are decorated in somewhat updated period fashion. Restaurant, bar. Cable TV. Beauty salon. Gym. Pets allowed (fee). | 526 Pine St. | 970/945–6511 or 800/544–3998 | fax 970/945–7030 | www.hotelcolorado.com | 128 rooms, 32 suites | $122–$178 | AE, D, DC, MC, V.

Hotel Denver. Although this hotel was originally built in 1806, its most striking features are the numerous Art Deco touches throughout. The rooms are neat and comfortable, ranging in size from small to quite large. Restaurant, bar. Some kitchenettes, cable TV. Beauty salon. Gym. Pets allowed. | 402 7th St. | 970/945–6565 or 800/826–8820 | fax 970/945–2204 | www.thehoteldenver.com | 60 rooms | $89–$129 | AE, D, DC, MC, V.

GOLDEN

Denver-Days Inn & Suites West/Golden. Tucked away in the foothills of the Rockies, this Days Inn is just west of downtown Denver. Restaurant, room service. In-room data ports, cable TV. Pool. Hot tub. Gym. Laundry services. Some pets allowed (fee). | 15059 W. Colfax Ave. | 303/277–0200 | fax 303/279–2812 | www.daysinn.com | 133 rooms, 24 suites | $79–$119, $109–$179 suites | AE, D, DC, MC, V.

La Quinta. A reliable, mid-priced chain motel 4 mi east of downtown Golden. Complimentary Continental breakfast. In-room data ports, cable TV. Pool. Laundry facilities. Business services. Pets allowed. | 3301 Youngfield Service Rd. 80401 | 303/279–5565 or 800/687–6667 | fax 303/279–5841 | www.laquinta.com | 129 rooms | $79–$99 | AE, D, DC, MC, V.

GRANBY

Casa Milagro B&B. In Parshall, 15 mi south of Granby, this modern log building is situated amid the pine trees above the Williams Fork Road. Various packages including recreational activities are offered. Complimentary breakfast. Some in-room hot tubs, cable TV, some room phones, in-room VCRs (and movies). Outdoor hot tub. Business services. Some pets allowed (fee). | 13628 County Rd. 3, Parshall 80468 | 970/725–3640 or 888–632–8955 | fax 970/725–3617 | www.casamilagro.com. | 4 rooms | $145–$220 | AE, D, DC, MC, V.

Homestead Motel. This small, economical motel offers a significant money-saving opportunity in winter, since it is less than 5 mi from activities such as snowboarding, ice fishing, and ice biking. Some refrigerators, cable TV. Some pets allowed. | 851 W. Agate Ave. | 970/887–3665 or 800/669–3605 | fax 970/887–2426 | 10 rooms | $57–$65 | AE, D, DC, MC, V.

Inn at Silver Creek. This large inn is located next to the Silver Creek ski area, about 2 mi south of Granby. Most rooms have a fireplace and private patio. Seasonal hot-air balloon rides can be arranged at the front desk. Bar. No air-conditioning, in-room data ports, some kitchenettes, refrigerators, in-room hot tubs, cable TV. Pool. Hot tub. Tennis. Gym, racquetball. Fishing, bicycles. Downhill skiing, sleigh rides. Shops. Laundry facilities. Pets allowed (fee). | 62927 U.S. 40, Silver Creek | 970/887–2131 or 800/926–4386 | fax 970/887–4083 | www.innatsilvercreek.com | 342 rooms | $89–$299 | AE, D, DC, MC, V.

Trail Riders. A small, economical motel just off of U.S. 40 in Granby. Microwaves, refrigerators, cable TV. Airport shuttle. Some pets allowed. | 215 E. Agate Ave. 80446 | 970/887–3738 | 11 rooms, 5 suites | $35–$45, $49–$75 suites | AE, D, MC, V.

GRAND JUNCTION

Best Western Horizon Inn. Some of the rooms at this chain motel offer exquisite views of Grand Mesa and Colorado National Monument. Complimentary Continental breakfast. In-room data ports, cable TV. Pool. Hot tub. Playground. Laundry services. Business services. Pets allowed. | 754 Horizon Dr. | 970/245–1410 | fax 970/245–4039 | www.bestwestern.com | 99 rooms | $59–$72 | AE, D, DC, MC, V.

Days Inn. Rooms at this Days Inn are spacious and bright. The hotel restaurant, Good Pastures, is a popular local spot in Grand Junction. Restaurant. In-room data ports, cable TV. Pool. Laundry services. Airport shuttle. Some pets allowed. | 733 Horizon Dr. | 970/245–7200 or 800/790–2661 | fax 970/243–6709 | www.daysinn.com | 104 rooms, 4 suites | $64–$71, $85–$103 suites | AE, D, DC, MC, V.

Grand Vista Hotel. This hotel, while mid-priced, offers upscale amenities and service. Rooms have old-fashioned charm and are decorated in dark mountain colors. The hotel is convenient to Interstate 70. Restaurant, bar, room service. In-room data ports, cable TV. Pool. Hot tub. Business services, airport shuttle. Pets allowed. | 2790 Crossroads Blvd. 81506 | 970/241–8411 or 800/800–7796 | fax 970/241–1077 | 158 rooms, 19 suites | $89–$99, $109–$119 suites | AE, D, DC, MC, V.

Holiday Inn–Grand Junction. This mid-priced chain motel, just south of Walker Field Airport, is reliably clean and comfortable. Restaurant, bar (with entertainment), room service. Cable TV, some in-room VCRs. 2 pools. Hot tub. Gym. Video games. Laundry facilities. Airport shuttle. Pets allowed. | 755 Horizon Dr. 81502 | 970/243–6790 or 888/489–9796 | fax 970/243–6790 | www.holiday-inn.com | 292 rooms, 9 suites | $74–$79, $83–$89 suites | AE, D, DC, MC, V.

Ramada Inn. Less than a mile south of Walker Field Airport, this chain motel has rooms with private patios or balconies. Restaurant. In-room data ports, some microwaves, cable TV, some in-room VCRs (and movies). Pool. Laundry facilities. Business services, airport shuttle. Pets allowed (fee). | 752 Horizon Dr. 81506 | 970/243–5150 or 888/298–2054 | fax 970/242–3692 | www.ramada.com | 100 rooms | $54–$91 | AE, D, DC, MC, V.

West Gate Inn. An economical motel on the western edge of Grand Junction. Restaurant, bar. Cable TV. Pool. Laundry facilities. Business services. Pets allowed. | 2210 U.S. 6 81505 | 970/241–3020 or 800/453–9253 | fax 970/243–4516 | www.gj.net/wgi | 100 rooms | $49–$76 | AE, D, DC, MC, V.

GRAND LAKE

Waconda Motel. This small, two-story motel provides a serene setting and a respite from hectic city life. "Waconda" translated is a Kansas Sioux name for running water; the Lake and public beach are only two blocks away. Restaurant, bar. Cable TV. Hot tub. Pets allowed (fee). | 725 Grand Ave. | 970/627–8312 | fax 970/627–8312 | www.grandlakecolorado.com/waconda | 10 rooms | $50–$80 | AE, D, DC, MC, V.

GREELEY

Best Western Ramkota Inn. This mid-priced motel is the closest place to stay near the University of Northern Colorado campus. Restaurant, bar, room service. Cable TV. Pool. Video games. Business services. Pets allowed. | 701 8th St. 80631 | 970/353–8444 | fax 970/353–4269 | www.bestwestern.com | 144 rooms, 4 suites | $69–$104, $135–$195 suites | AE, D, DC, MC, V.

Fairfield Inn Greeley. This chain hotel is less than 2 mi from the University of Northern Colorado. There are many restaurants within walking distance. Complimentary Continental breakfast. In-room data ports, cable TV. Pool. Laundry service. Business services. Some pets allowed. | 2401 W. 29th St. | 970/339–5030 | fax 970/339–5030 | www.marriot.com. | 62 rooms, 8 suites | $71–$74, $85 suites | AE, D, DC, MC, V.

Motel 6. This budget motel is located 2 mi south of Greeley on U.S. 85. Cable TV. Pool. Pets allowed. | 3015 8th Ave., Evans 80620 | 970/351–6481 or 800/466–8356 | www.motel6.com | 94 rooms | $32–$40 | AE, D, DC, MC, V.

GUNNISON

Days Inn Gunnison. This Days Inn was renovated in 1998 and offers clean and modern rooms. Room service. In-room data ports, microwaves, refrigerators, cable TV. Hot tub. Laundry services. Business services. Pets allowed (fee). | 701 W. U.S. 50 | 970/641–0608 or 888/641–0608 | fax 970/641–2854 | www.bestwestern.com | 45 rooms | $69–$79 | AE, D, DC, MC, V.

Hylander Motel. This small, basic motel is next to the City Park and across the street from miniature golf. All the rooms are decorated with intricate handmade quilts. Cable TV. Some pets allowed. | 412 E. Tomichi Ave. | 970/641–0700 | 24 rooms | $58–$78 | AE, D, DC, MC, V.

LA JUNTA

Best Western Bent's Fort Inn. This chain motel is in the tiny berg of Las Animas, 20 mi east of La Junta via U.S. 50. Restaurant, bar, room service. Cable TV. Pool. Business services, airport shuttle. Some pets allowed. | 719/456–0011 | fax 719/456–2550 | www.bestwestern.com | 38 rooms | $49–$59 | AE, D, DC, MC, V.

Quality Inn. Located on La Junta's east side, offering reliable chain motel amenities. Restaurant, bar, room service. Some refrigerators, cable TV, some in-room VCRs (and movies). Indoor-outdoor pool. Hot tub. Gym. Business services, airport shuttle. Some pets allowed. | 1325 E. 3rd St. 81050 | 719/384–2571 or 800/228–5151 | fax 719/384–5655 | www.qualityinn.com | 60 rooms, 16 suites | $59–$89, $89–$95 suites | AE, D, DC, MC, V.

Stagecoach Motel. This economical roadside motel is on the western outskirts of La Junta. In-room data ports, cable TV. Pool. Pets allowed. | 905 W. 3rd St. | 719/384–5476 | fax 719/384–9091 | 31 rooms | $35–$65 | AE, D, DC, MC, V.

LAKE CITY

Matterhorn Motel. This small motel is in the majestic San Juan Mountains and just two blocks from the Lake City Historical District. Rooms are comfortable and affordable. Some kitchenettes, some refrigerators, cable TV. Some pets allowed. No smoking. | 409 N. Bluff | 970/944–2210 | 12 rooms, 2 cabins | $65–$80 | MC, V.

LAKEWOOD

Comfort Inn–Southwest Denver. This upper-budget motel is located just north of a thriving retail area. Complimentary Continental breakfast. Microwaves, refrigerators, cable TV. Pool. Hot tub. Gym. Laundry facilities. Business services. Pets allowed (fee). | 3440 S. Vance St. 80227 | 303/989–5500 or 800/228–5150 | fax 303/989–2981 | www.comfortinn.com | 123 rooms, 4 suites | $72–$83, $117 suites | AE, D, DC, MC, V.

LAMAR

Best Western–Cow Palace Inn. This mid-priced motel has several hunting-themed events a year. Restaurant, bar, room service. Cable TV, some in-room VCRs. Pool. Barbershop, beauty salon. Hot tub. Driving range. Business services, airport shuttle. Pets allowed. | 1301 N. Main St. 81052 | 719/336–7753 or 800/678–0344 | fax 719/336–9598 | www.bestwestern.com | 102 rooms | $75–$95 | AE, D, DC, MC, V.

Blue Spruce. An inexpensive roadside motel across the street from Lamar College on the south side of town. Complimentary Continental breakfast. Cable TV. Pool. Airport shuttle. Pets allowed. | 1801 S. Main St. 81052 | 719/336–7454 | fax 719/336–4729 | 30 rooms | $32–$44 | AE, D, DC, MC, V.

LIMON

Best Western–Limon Inn. This reliable chain motel is just west of the town center, convenient to area highways. Complimentary Continental breakfast. In-room data ports, cable TV. Pool. Pets allowed (fee). | 925 T Ave. (I–70, exit 359) 80828 | 719/775–0277 | fax 719/775–2921 | www.bestwestern.com | 48 rooms | $50–$75 | AE, D, MC, V.

Preferred Motor Inn. In eastern Limon, this motel is next to restaurants and a market. Cable TV. Pool. Hot tub. Airport shuttle. Pets allowed. | 158 E. Main St. 80828 | 719/775–2385 | fax 719/775–2901 | 57 rooms, 2 suites | $28–$62, $65–$100 suites | AE, D, DC, MC, V.

Safari Motel. A small one- and two-story downtown motel. In-room data ports, cable TV. Pool. Playground. Laundry facilities. Pets allowed (fee). | 637 Main St. 80828 | 719/775–2363 | fax 719/775–2316 | 28 rooms, 2 suites | $36–$58, $68 suites | AE, D, DC, MC, V.

LONGMONT

Raintree Plaza Hotel Suites and Conference Center. This full-service two-story hotel also houses the largest conference center in northern Colorado. All rooms feature small sitting areas with a couch and/or chairs. Restaurant, bar, complimentary Continental breakfast, room service. Some kitchenettes, refrigerators, cable TV. Pool. Gym. Laundry service. Business services, airport shuttle. Pets allowed. | 1900 Ken Pratt Blvd. 80501 | 303/776–2000 or 800/843–8240 | fax 303/678–7361 | www.raintree.com | 211 rooms, 84 suites | $89–$265, $109–$265 suites | AE, D, DC, MC, V.

MANITOU SPRINGS

Red Wing. This small motel is one block from the entrance to the Garden of the Gods. Some kitchenettes, microwaves, refrigerators, cable TV. Pool. Playground. Some pets allowed. | 56 El Paso Blvd. 80829 | 719/685–5656 or 800/733–9547 | fax 719/685–9547 ext. 42 | 27 rooms | $49–$120 | AE, D, DC, MC, V.

MESA VERDE NATIONAL PARK

Far View Lodge. This lodge in Mesa Verde National Park, 15 mi south of the park entrance, boasts a spectacular view of Shiprock Canyon and offers educational programs, campsites, trailer facilities, and Mesa Verde tours. The lodge is operated by Aramark, the official park concessionaire. Restaurant, bar, dining room, picnic area. No air-conditioning, no room phones, no TV. Hiking. Laundry facilities. Some pets allowed. | Chapin Mesa Rd. | 970/529–4421 or 800/449–2288 | fax 970/533–7831 | www.visitmesaverde.com | 150 rooms | $96–$106 | Closed mid-Oct.–mid-Apr. | AE, D, DC, MC, V.

MONTE VISTA

Best Western–Movie Manor. From May through September, guests at this motel about 2½ mi from the Monte Vista town center enjoy a view of a drive-in movie screen from their rooms; most rooms have speakers for the movies' sound. Restaurant, bar. Cable TV. Gym. Playground. Business services. Pets allowed (fee). | 2830 W. Hwy. 160 | 719/852–5921 or 800/771–9468 | fax 719/852–0122 | www.bestwestern.com | 60 rooms | $77–$95 | AE, D, DC, MC, V.

Comfort Inn. Chain motel on the east side of town, just off U.S. 160. Complimentary Continental breakfast. In-room data ports, cable TV. Pool. Hot tub. Business services. Pets allowed. | 1519 Grand Ave. 81144 | 719/852–0612 or 800/228–5150 | fax 719/852–3585 | www.comfortinn.com | 45 rooms | $60–$90 | AE, D, DC, MC, V.

MONTROSE

Black Canyon Motel. This inexpensive motel is named after the nearby Black Canyon of the Gunnison National Park and is on the east side of Montrose. Rooms are large, clean, and modern. Complimentary Continental breakfast. Some microwaves, cable TV. Pool. Hot tub. Business services. Some pets allowed. | 1605 E. Main (U.S. 550) 81401 | 970/249–3495 or 800/348–3495 | fax 970/249–0990 | www.innfinders.com/blackcyn | 49 rooms, 5 suites | $45–$75, $95 suites | AE, D, DC, MC, V.

Holiday Inn Express–Hotel and Suites. The fireplace in the lobby lets you know that this is not your ordinary chain motel. Some of the spacious rooms and suites have fireplaces. There are many amenities for business travelers and families at this limited-service motor hotel. Enjoy the oversize lap pool and the sundeck. Bar, complimentary Continental breakfast. In-room data ports, some microwaves, some refrigerators, some in-room hot tubs, cable TV. Pool. 2 hot tubs. Gym. Laundry facilities, laundry service. Business services, airport shuttle. Pets allowed. | 970/240–1800 | fax 970/240–9093 | www.holidayinnexpmontrose.com | 122 rooms, 25 suites | $99–$149 | AE, D, DC, MC, V.

San Juan Inn. This inexpensive motel is located on the south side of Montrose. Some microwaves, cable TV. Pool. Hot tub. Playground. Airport shuttle. Pets allowed. | 1480 S. Townsend Ave. 81401 | 970/249–6644 | fax 970/249–9314 | www.sanjuaninns.com | 51 rooms | $48–$61 | AE, D, DC, MC, V.

Uncompahgre Bed and Breakfast. This B&B 5½ mi south of Montrose was once a country schoolhouse, built in 1904 in Frank Lloyd Wright's prairie style. Enjoy your breakfast in the dining room that has space for 50, or sit around the fireplace. Complimentary breakfast. Some microwaves, some in-room hot tubs, cable TV, some in-room VCRs (and movies). Gym. Laundry facilities. Pets allowed. No smoking. | 21049 Uncompahgre Rd. | 970/240–4000 or 800/318–8127 | fax 970/249–5124 | www.uncbb.com | 7 rooms | $75–$95 | AE, D, MC, V.

NEDERLAND

Nederhaus Hotel. Just to the south of downtown Nederland, this quaint little hotel offers affordable rooms uniquely decorated with antiques and collectibles. A wonderful alpine backyard with goldfish ponds faces the Great Divide. There's a free shuttle service to nearby ski areas during ski season and to local casinos in summer. Restaurant. Cable TV, in-room VCRs. Pets allowed. | 686 Rte. 119 80466 | 303/258–3585 | fax 303/258–3850 | 9 rooms, 1 apartment, 2 suites | $55–$85, $85–$100 apartment and suites | AE, D, MC, V.

NORWOOD

Back Narrows Inn & Lodge. Inexpensive accommodations in a 100-year-old inn in downtown Norwood. The modern, six-room lodge has private baths and more amenities, such as room phones and TVs. Restaurant, bar. Some room phones, cable TV in some rooms. Pets allowed. | 1515 Grand Ave. | 970/327–4417 or 970/327–4260 | www.norwoodcolorado.com/bnarrows.html | 13 rooms (7 with shared bath) | $25–$60 | Restaurant closed Sept. | AE, D, DC, MC, V.

OURAY

Ouray Victorian Inn. On the Uncompaghre River, this pretty and inviting two-story motel offers year-round comfortable rooms. Packages offer half-price Telluride lift tickets. Picnic area. No air-conditioning, cable TV. Hot tub. Playground. Business services. Some pets allowed. | 50 3rd Ave. | 970/325–7222 or 800/443–7361 | fax 970/325–7225 | www.ouraylodging.com | 38 rooms, 4 suites | $84–$89, $95 suites | AE, D, DC, MC, V.

PAGOSA SPRINGS

Fireside Inn. This "inn" actually provides accommodations in 15 private cabins with gas fireplaces, along the San Juan River, 1 mi from downtown Pagosa Springs. The property has horse corrals so you can bring your own horses. No air-conditioning, in-room data ports, kitchenettes, microwaves, refrigerators, cable TV, some in-room VCRs. Hot tub. Laundry facilities. Pets allowed (fee). | 1600 E. Hwy. 160 | 970/264–9204 or 888/264–9204 | fax 970/264–9204 | www.websites.pagosa.net/firesideinn | 15 cabins | $99–$159 | AE, D, MC, V.

Pagosa Springs Inn. A comfortable motel on the western side of Pagosa Springs. Some microwaves, refrigerators, some in-room hot tubs, cable TV. Pool. Hot tub. Video games. Business services. Pets allowed. | 3565 U.S. 160 W | 970/731–3400 or 888/221–8088 | fax 970/731–3402 | 97 rooms | $80–$99 | AE, D, DC, MC, V.

PUEBLO

Best Western Inn at Pueblo West. This chain motel is just off U.S. 50 in Pueblo West, a small town 8½ mi west of Pueblo. Restaurant. Cable TV. Pool. Gym. Business services. Some pets allowed (fee). | 201 S. McCulloch Blvd., Pueblo West 81007 | 719/547–2111 or 800/448–1972 | fax 719/547–0385 | www.bestwestern.com | 80 rooms | $64–$84 | AE, D, DC, MC, V.

RIFLE

Buckskin Inn. A quiet country inn surrounded by a tree-lined lawn with picnic tables and outdoor grills just west of Rifle. Some rooms are decorated in knotty pine, some in country wallpaper. In-room data ports, some kitchenettes, microwaves, refrigerators, cable TV. Laundry facilities. Pets allowed. | 101 Ray Ave. 81650 | 970/625–1741 or 877/282–5754 | fax 970/625–4325 | www.buckskininn.com | 24 rooms | $40–$65 | AE, MC, V.

Red River Inn. A simple motel just south of Interstate 70, across the street from McDonald's. Complimentary donuts in the morning, hot beverages throughout the day in the lobby. In-room data ports, some kitchenettes, some microwaves, some refrigerators, cable TV. Some pets allowed. | 718 Taughenbaugh Blvd. | 970/625–3050 or 800/733–3152 | fax 970/625–0848 | www.redriverinnmotel.com | 65 rooms | $40–$85 | AE, D, MC, V.

Rusty Cannon Motel. A clean, basic motel just south of Interstate 70 next to McDonald's. In-room data ports, some refrigerators, cable TV. Pool. Sauna. Laundry facilities. Some pets allowed (fee). | 701 Taughenbaugh Blvd. | 970/625–4004 or 800/341–8000 | fax 970/625–3604 | www.imalodging.com | 88 rooms | $44–$92 | AE, D, MC, V.

SALIDA

Travelodge. An economical highway-side motel just west of Salida, with both cabins and rooms. Complimentary Continental breakfast. Some in-room hot tubs. Cable TV. Pool. Hot tub. Business services. Some pets allowed. | 7310 U.S. 550 W | 719/539–2528 or 800/515–6375 | fax 719/539–2528 | www.travelodge.com | 27 rooms (10 with shower only), 3 cottages | $65–$79, $75–$97 cottages | AE, D, DC, MC, V.

SILVERTON

Alma House. Victorian furnishings decorate this 1898 mountain inn one block west of the Silverton train depot. Complimentary breakfast. Cable TV, no room phones. Business services. Some pets allowed. No smoking. | 220 E. 10th St. 81433 | 970/387–5336 or 800/267–5336 | fax 970/387–5974 | www.subee.com/alma/home.html | 10 rooms (2 with shared bath), 2 suites | $69–$99, $119–$129 suites | Closed Nov.–May | AE, MC, V.

SOUTH FORK

South Fork Lodge. This lodge property includes cabins with full kitchens and separate bedrooms. The main lodge has a recreation room with two pianos, one of which is a player piano. There are also 27 RV sites. All of this is located 300 yards from the Hungry Logger restaurant. Kitchenettes, some microwaves, refrigerators, cable TV, TV in common area. Outdoor hot tub. Playground. Laundry facilities. Pets allowed (fee). | 0364 Hwy. 149 | 719/873–5303 or 877/354–2345 | fax 719/873–5305 | 12 cabins | $50–$75 | AE, MC, V.

Wolf Creek Ranch Ski Lodge. This roadside lodge is 18 mi east of the Wolf Creek Ski Area, on the eastern side of Wolf Creek Pass. Some rooms have mountain views. Bar. Some kitchenettes, some microwaves, cable TV. Hot tub. Hiking, fishing. Playground. Business services. Pets allowed. | 31042 U.S. 160 W | 719/873–5371 or 800/522–WOLF | www.wolfcreekco.com/ranch | 8 rooms, 6 cabins | $40–$70, $50–$125 cabins | AE, D, DC, MC, V.

STEAMBOAT SPRINGS

Alpiner Lodge. An economical motel 3 mi west of the ski slopes. In-room data ports, some microwaves, cable TV. Business services. Pets allowed. | 424 Lincoln Ave. | 970/879–1430 or 800/538–7519 | fax 970/879–0054 | www.steamboat-lodging.com/alpiner_ph2.html | 33 rooms | $70–$100 | AE, D, DC, MC, V.

Best Western Ptarmigan Inn. Many rooms at this ski-in, ski-out property have balconies that offer great views of Mt. Wernery. Restaurant, bar, room service. No air-conditioning in some rooms, in-room data ports, refrigerators, cable TV. Pool. Hot tub, sauna. Laundry facilities. Business services. Pets allowed (fee). | 2304 Apres Ski Way 80477 | 970/879–1730 or 800/538–7519 | fax 970/879–6044 | www.bestwestern.com | 77 rooms | $179–$209 | Closed early Apr.–late May | AE, D, DC, MC, V.

★ **Harbor Hotel and Condominiums.** This completely refurbished 1940s hotel is in the middle of Steamboat's historic district, and filled with period artifacts, such as the old switchboard. Each room is individually decorated with antique furnishings and most have views of the surrounding mountains. The property also runs an adjacent motel and condo complex. Restaurant, bar. In-room data ports, some kitchenettes, some microwaves, some refrigerators, cable TV. Hot tub, sauna, steam room. Laundry facilities. Pets allowed (fee). | 703 Lincoln Ave. | 970/879–1522 or 800/543–8888 | fax 970/543–8888 | 113 rooms | $100–$200 | AE, D, DC, MC, V.

Holiday Inn. This chain motel can be found just southeast of the town of Steamboat Springs. It offers many amenities and facilities for skiers. Restaurant, bar, room service. In-room data ports, some microwaves, some refrigerators, cable TV. Pool, wading pool. Hot tub. Gym. Video games. Laundry facilities. Business services. Some pets allowed (fee). | 3190 S. Lincoln Ave. | 970/879–2250 or 800/654–3944 | fax 970/879–0251 | www.holiday-inn.com | 82 rooms | $99–$159 | AE, D, DC, MC, V.

Scandinavian Lodge. You can ski-in and ski-out at this lodge. The rooms on the lower level have views of the valley, and other rooms have views of the woods. In-room data ports, kitchenettes, microwaves, refrigerators, cable TV, in-room VCRs. Pool. Hot tub, sauna. Laundry facilities. Pets allowed (fee). No smoking. | 2883 Burgess Creek Rd. | 970/879–0517 | fax 970/879–0943 | www.steamboat-springs.com | 21 rooms | $89–$699 | AE, D, MC, V.

STERLING

Best Western Sundowner. This chain motel is immediately off Interstate 76, across the South Platte River from Sterling. Picnic area, complimentary Continental breakfast. In-room data ports, cable TV. Pool. Hot tub. Gym. Laundry facilities. Business services. Pets allowed. | 125 Overland Trail St. 80751 | 970/522–6265 or 800/848–4060 | fax 970/522–6265 | www.bestwestern.com | 30 rooms | $74–$94 | AE, D, DC, MC, V.

Colonial Motel. This quiet roadside motel sits four blocks west of downtown Sterling. Some microwaves, some refrigerators, cable TV. Pets allowed. | 915 S. Division Ave. 80751 | 970/522–3382 or 888/522–2901 | fax 888/522–2901 | 14 rooms | $32–$44 | AE, D, MC, V.

Crest Motel. You'll receive friendly, thoughtful treatment at this small, inexpensive motel. The rooms are simple and have full-size beds. Microwaves, refrigerators, cable TV. Laundry facilities. Pets allowed. | 516 Division Ave. | 970/522–3753 | 8 rooms | $25–$35 | AE, D, DC, MC, V.

Oakwood Inn. This small motel has clean, quiet rooms that have oak furnishings and queen or full-size beds. It is in a quiet area of town, three blocks from downtown Sterling. Some kitchenettes, microwaves, refrigerators, cable TV. Pets allowed (fee). | 810 S. Division Ave. | 970/522–1416 | fax 970/521–0759 | 15 rooms | $40–$50 | AE, D, DC, MC, V.

Ramada Inn. Immediately next to Interstate 76, this mid-priced chain motel offers basic amenities. Restaurant, bar. Cable TV. Pool. Hot tub. Gym. Video games. Business services. Some pets allowed. | 22246 E. Hwy. 6 | 970/522–2625 or 888/298–2054 | fax 970/522–1321 | www.ramada.com | 102 rooms | $60–$81 | AE, D, DC, MC, V.

TELLURIDE

Wyndham Peaks Resort and Golden Door Spa. In Telluride Mountain Village, this ski-in, ski-out property offers a wide variety of luxury accommodations. Some rooms have balconies with a view of either the village or the Wilson Mountain Range. This resort also has the only golf course in Telluride. Restaurant, bar, room service. In-room data ports, minibars, some microwaves, refrigerators, cable TV, in-room VCRs (and movies). 2 pools (1 indoor-outdoor). Hot tub. Driving range, 18-hole golf course, putting green, tennis. Gym, hiking. Children's programs (ages 8 weeks–12 years). Business services, airport shuttle, parking (fee). Some pets allowed. | 136 Country Club Dr. 81435 | 970/728–6800 or 800/789–2220 | fax 970/728–6175 | www.thepeaksresort.com | 174 rooms, 28 suites | $385–$435, $685–$785 suites | AE, DC, MC, V.

TRINIDAD

Best Western Trinidad Inn. The rooms at this mid-priced chain motel, four blocks from the downtown historic district and museums, are comfortable and clean; some connecting rooms are available. Restaurant, bar. In-room data ports, microwaves, refrigerators, cable TV. Pool. Hot tub. Gym. Laundry facilities. Pets allowed. | 900 W. Adams St. | 719/846–2215 | fax 719/846–2480 | www.bestwestern.com | 55 rooms | $79–$99 | AE, D, DC, MC, V.

Budget Host. This economical chain motel 2 mi south of downtown is home to a local landmark: a 107-ft oil derrick. Picnic area. Some microwaves, some refrigerators, cable TV. Hot tub. Pets allowed (fee). | 10301 Santa Fe Trail Dr. 81082 | 719/846–3307 or 800/283–4678 | fax 719/846–3309 | www.budgethost.com | 26 rooms | $50–$70 | AE, D, MC, V.

Budget Summit Inn. An economical roadside hotel south of Trinidad, immediately off Interstate 25. Complimentary Continental breakfast. In-room data ports, some microwaves, some refrigerators, cable TV. Hot tub. Laundry facilities. Business services. Pets allowed (fee). | 9800 Santa Fe Trail Dr. | 719/846–2251 | fax 719/846–2251 ext. 30 | 39 rooms (21 with shower only) | $40–$80 | AE, DC, MC, V.

Chicosa Canyon Bed and Breakfast. This century-old stone home is on 64 acres of land, 12 mi from Trinidad. Enjoy the great solarium, the hot tub, or curl up with a book near the central fireplace. The rooms are generously sized and the cabin has a wood-burning stove and canyon views. Complimentary breakfast. Some kitchenettes, some microwaves, some refrigerators, no room phones, no TV in some rooms, TV in common area. Hot tub.

Hiking. Pets allowed. No smoking. | 32391 County Rd. 40 | 719/846–6199 | fax 719/846–6199 | www.bbonline.com/co/chicosa | 3 rooms (2 with shared bath), 1 cabin | $88–$128 | MC, V.

Holiday Inn–Trinidad. Located just north of the Raton Pass, this chain motel offers a variety of amenities on the edge of a wooded area, 2 mi south of downtown Trinidad. Restaurant, bar, room service. Some microwaves, refrigerators, cable TV, some in-room VCRs. Pool. Video games. Laundry facilities. Business services. Some pets allowed. | 3125 Toupal Dr. 81082 | 719/846–4491 or 800/465–4329 | fax 719/846–2440 | www.holiday-inn.com | 113 rooms | $89–$119 | AE, D, DC, MC, V.

WALSENBURG

Best Western Rambler. This small chain motel is less than 2 mi north of Walsenburg, near Lathrop State Park. Restaurant. Cable TV, some in-room VCRs. Pool. Some pets allowed. | I–25 (exit 52) | 719/738–1121 | fax 719/738–1093 | www.bestwestern.com | 32 rooms | $62–$87 | AE, D, DC, MC, V.

WINTER PARK

High Mountain Lodge. This simple but comfortable lodge with dark paneling and beams is perched on a hill overlooking 40 wooded acres with great sunset views of the Rockies. Rooms come with either a pool or mountain view. Take U.S. 40 to County Rd. 5. Bar, picnic area, complimentary breakfast. Microwaves, refrigerators, cable TV in common area. Pool. Hot tub, massage, sauna. Library. Gym. Laundry facilities. Some pets allowed. | 425 County Rd. 5001, Fraser | 970/726–5958 or 800/772–9987 | fax 970/726–9796 | www.himtnlodge.com | 14 rooms | $79–$99 per person | Closed May | MAP (ski season) | D, MC, V.

Viking Lodge. In the middle of Winter Park, within walking distance to the area's restaurants and nightlife, this lodge offers everything from small economy rooms to deluxe suites and condos. Complimentary Continental breakfast. Some kitchenettes, cable TV. Hot tub, sauna. Pets allowed. | Hwy. 40 and Vasquez Rd. | 970/726–8885 or 800/421–4013 | 22 rooms, 3 condos | $60–$595 | AE, D, MC, V.

The Vintage Hotel. Despite the name, this is a contemporary lodge located right at the main entrance to the Winter Park Ski Resort. One of the most upscale properties in the area, the hotel offers large rooms with upscale features. Restaurant, bar (with entertainment), picnic area, complimentary Continental breakfast (summer only), room service. In-room data ports, some kitchenettes, cable TV. Pool. Hot tub, sauna. Gym. Cross-country skiing, downhill skiing. Video games. Laundry facilities. Business services. Pets allowed. | 100 Winter Park Dr. 80482 | 970/726–8801 or 800/472–7017 | fax 970/726–9230 | 118 rooms, 30 suites | $90–$185, $310–$525 suites | AE, D, DC, MC, V.

Connecticut

AVON

Avon Old Farms Hotel. At the foot of Talcott Mountain and across the street from a golf course, this hotel is housed in a redbrick Colonial-style building. There is a garden gazebo and a wooden bridge on the grounds. Restaurant, bar, complimentary Continental breakfast, room service. In-room data ports, cable TV. Pool. Sauna. Gym. Laundry service. Business services. Pets allowed. | 279 Avon Mountain Rd. 06001 | 860/677–1651 or 800/ 836–4000 | fax 860/677–0364 | www.avonoldfarmshotel.com | 160 rooms | $170–$311 | AE, D, DC, MC, V.

BRANFORD

Days Inn and Conference Center. Rooms at this two-story hotel are decorated mostly in blues and have wood furniture. I-95 runs right behind the hotel. Complimentary Continental breakfast, room service. Some kitchenettes, cable TV. Pool. Gym. Laundry facilities. Business services. Pets allowed (fee). | 375 E. Main St. 06405 | 203/488–8314 | fax 203/483–6885 | 78 rooms, 3 suites | $130–$150; $175 suites | AE, D, DC, MC, V.

BRIDGEPORT

Holiday Inn. Two blocks from the train and bus stations, this nine-floor hotel is in the center of Bridgeport. 2 restaurants, bar, room service. In-room data ports, cable TV. Indoor and outdoor pool. Gym. Laundry services. Business services. Small pets allowed. | 1070 Main St. 06604 | 203/334–1234 | fax 203/367–1985 | 234 rooms, 6 suites | $129–$139; $350 suites | AE, D, DC, MC, V.

CHESTER

The Inn at Chester This 18th century clapboard inn was once a farmhouse for a local family, the Parmalees. The rooms are furnished with Eldred Wheeler antique reproductions. There is a billiard room and on-site massages can be arranged. 2 restaurants, complimentary breakfast. Sauna. Tennis court. Gym. Library. Baby-sitting. Pets allowed (fee). | 318 W. Main St. 06412 | 860/526–9541 or 800/949–7829 | fax 860/526–4387 | www.innatchester.com | 41 rooms, 1 suite | $105–$215 | MC, V.

CORNWALL

Cornwall Inn. One of the two buildings that comprise this inn dates back to 1871. Some rooms have strip cedar bed frames and most of them are done in light pastel colors. Restaurant, complimentary Continental breakfast (weekends only). In-room hot tubs, no room phones, TV in common area. Pool. Pets allowed. | 270 Kent Rd. | 860/672–6884 or 800/786–6884 | fax 860/672–0352 | 14 rooms in 2 buildings | $89–$169 | AE, D, MC, V.

DANBURY

Danbury Hilton and Towers. Danbury's most luxurious hotel opened in 1981 and is 3 mi from Danbury Airport, off I–84, and near I–684. Suites have kitchenettes and sitting area. There's a common room with pool table, and a free local shuttle. Restaurant, bar, room service. In-room data ports, cable TV. Indoor pool. Saunas, hot tub. 2 tennis courts. Gym. Laundry facilities, laundry service. Business services. Pets allowed. | 18 Old Ridgebury Rd. | 203/794–0600 | fax 203/830–5188 | www.danburyhilton.com | 242 rooms | $109–$199 | AE, D, DC, MC, V.

Holiday Inn. The Danbury Railway museum and the Danbury Fair Mall are 5 mi from this four-story hotel. Rooms have wood furniture. Restaurant, bar, room service. In-room data ports, cable TV. Pool. Laundry service. Business services. Pets allowed. | 80 Newtown Rd. | 203/792–4000 | fax 203/797–0810 | 114 rooms | $100–$139 | AE, D, DC, MC, V.

Ramada Inn. The two-story main building and five-story tower at this hotel have traditional decor with earth tones. Suites include full size pullout sofabeds. The bus line, Danbury train station, and the downtown area are five minutes away. The hotel is one of the few in the country that boasts the Outback Steak House on its premises. Restaurant, bar, room service. In-room data ports, cable TV. Indoor pool. Laundry service. Business services. Pets allowed. | 116 Newtown Rd. | 203/792–3800 | fax 203/730–1899 | 171 rooms, 10 suites | $139–$175 | AE, D, DC, MC, V.

ENFIELD

Red Roof Inn. There are two two-story buildings that make up this modern, standard hotel. It is within walking distance of Enfield's shops and restaurants. In-room data ports. Pets allowed. | 5 Hazard Ave. | 860/741–2571 | fax 860/741–2576 | 108 rooms | $52–$96 | AE, D, DC, MC, V.

ESSEX

Griswold Inn. A 1776 inn with a mix of Colonial, Federal, and Victorian decor that is in downtown Essex, near the Connecticut River. The inn is a main hub of the town's social life. Some of the rooms have fireplaces and most are furnished with period antiques. Restaurant, bar, complimentary Continental breakfast. TV in common area. Some pets allowed (fee). No smoking. | 36 Main St. | 860/767–1776 | fax 860/767–0481 | www.griswoldinn.com | 16 rooms, 15 suites | $95–$125, $150–$200 suites | AE, MC, V.

FAIRFIELD

Fairfield Motor Inn. A two-story, upscale motor lodge. Restaurant, bar. In-room data ports, refrigerators, cable TV. Pool. Business services. Pets allowed (fee). | 417 Post Rd. | 203/255–0491 | fax 203/255–2073 | 80 rooms | $80–$100 | AE, D, DC, MC, V.

FARMINGTON

Centennial Inn. This all-suites inn is on 12 wooded acres and has large rooms decorated in a Colonial style. There's a playground on the property. Complimentary Continental breakfast. In-room data ports, kitchenettes, cable TV, in-room VCRs. Pool. Hot tub. Gym. Laundry facilities, laundry service. Business services. Pets allowed. No smoking. | 5 Spring La. | 860/677–4647 or 800/852–2052 | fax 860/676–0685 | www.centennialinn.com | 112 suites | $129–$219 | AE, DC, MC, V.

GREENWICH

Howard Johnson. This standard chain hotel is less than 1 mi from town in a residential area of Riverside. Restaurant. Cable TV. Outdoor pool. Pets allowed. | 1114 Post Rd., Riverside 06878 | 203/639–3691 | 104 rooms | $99 | AE, D, DC, MC, V.

GROTON

Clarion Inn. A comfortable, family-oriented inn that is right across from Wal-Mart. The suites have a living room with pull-out couch. Restaurant, bar, room service. Cable TV. Indoor pool. Barber shop, beauty salon, hot tub. Gym. Laundry facilities. Business services. Pets allowed (deposit). | 156 Kings Hwy. | 860/446–0660 | fax 860/445–4082 | 69 rooms, 2 suites | $169–$209 | AE, D, MC, V.

HARTFORD

Crowne Plaza Hartford Downtown. A chain option that is convenient to downtown attractions. Restaurant, bar, room service. In-room data ports, cable TV. Pool. Gym. Laundry service. Business services. Pets allowed. | 50 Morgan St. | 860/549–2400 | fax 860/527–2746 | 350 rooms, 4 suites | $109–$189 | AE, D, DC, MC, V.

★ **The Goodwin.** The facade of this grand city hotel—and registered historic landmark—dates back to 1881, but the rest of the building was completely rebuilt from top to bottom in the 1980s. Restaurant, bar, room service. In-room data ports, cable TV. Gym. Laundry service. Business services. Pets allowed. | 1 Haynes St. 06103 | 860/246–7500 or 800/922–5006 | fax 860/247–4576 | www.goodwinhotel.com | 111 rooms, 13 suites | $99–$239 | AE, D, DC, MC, V.

Holiday Inn. A chain option in East Hartford that is within five minutes of downtown Hartford. Restaurant, bar, room service. Cable TV. Indoor pool. Gym. Laundry facilities, laundry service. Business services. Pets allowed. | 363 Roberts St., East Hartford 06108 | 860/528–9611 | fax 860/289–0270 | 130 rooms | $100–$130 | AE, D, MC, V.

Ramada Inn-Capitol Hill. This glass-front chain hotel is in downtown Hartford and right across the street from Bushnell Park. Restaurant, bar, complimentary Continental breakfast. In-room data ports, cable TV. Business services. Pets allowed (fee). | 440 Asylum St. | 860/246–6591 | fax 860/728–1382 | 96 rooms | $87–$97 | AE, D, DC, MC, V.

LAKEVILLE

Inne at Iron Masters. The grounds of this motel contain English country gardens and several gazebos. In colder weather, you can warm yourself by the fireplace in the common area. Guest rooms are individually appointed and have sitting areas. Restaurant, bar, complimentary Continental breakfast. Cable TV. Pool. Pets allowed. | 229 Main St. | 860/435–9844 | fax 860/435–2254 | www.innatironmasters.com | 28 rooms | $75–$135 | AE, D, DC, MC, V.

Interlaken Inn. A conference and business retreat complex that is also appropriate for families. You have a choice of the main building, English Tudor house or Victorian-style building with wraparound porch. The rooms are modern American. Restaurant, room service. Cable TV. Pool, lake. Sauna. 2 tennis courts. Gym, beach, water sports. Fishing. Laundry service. Business services. Pets allowed (fee). | 74 Interlaken Rd. 06039 | 860/435–9878 | fax 860/435–2980 | www.interlakeninn.com | 73 rooms, 7 suites | $149–$189, $289–$319 suites | AE, MC, V.

Wake Robin Inn. This Georgian Colonial–Revival inn was built in 1898 as a girls' school. Inside the rooms have period furnishings, some with fireplaces. Sharing the 12-acre site is a small motel with a more modern look. Complimentary Continental breakfast. Cable TV. Business services. Pets allowed (fee). | Rte. 41 06039 | 860/435–2515 | fax 860/435–2000 | www.wakerobininn.com | 24 rooms in inn, 15 in motel | $95–$175, $225 suites | AE, D, MC, V.

LEDYARD

Abbey's Lantern Hill Inn. No two rooms here are alike and each has its own name (such as Downeast and Southwest) to reflect its personality. What the rooms share is warmth and coziness; each has polished wood floors with throw rugs, large beds with quilts, and outside sitting areas with views of the surrounding countryside. Two have fireplaces and one has its own private courtyard (they say this one is perfect for pets). Complimentary breakfast. Some in-room hot tubs. Pets allowed. | 780 Lantern Hill Rd. 06339 | 860/572–0483 | fax 860/572–0518 | www.abbeyslanternhill.com | 8 rooms | $79–$140 | AE, MC, V.

Applewood Farms Inn. This 1826 center-chimney, Colonial farmhouse is on the State and National Register of Historic Landmark properties. It has 33 acres (the inn shares a border with Nature Conservancy land as well) with paths to walk and great birdwatching. Guests can also practice their "short game" on a USGA chipping and putting green. The rooms have views of the surrounding countryside and are furnished with antiques; four have fireplaces. Complimentary breakfast. Hot tub. Putting green. Pets allowed. No kids under 10. | 528 Colonel Ledyard Hwy. 06339 | 860/536–2022 or 800/717–4262 | fax 860/536–6015 | www.visitmystic.com/applewoodfarmsinn | 6 rooms | $105–$290 | AE, MC.

MADISON

Madison Beach Hotel. This hotel overlooks Long Island Sound and has a lobby with white wicker furniture and a water view. Most of the rooms have wicker furniture and some have balconies. Two-night minimum stay on weekends. 2 restaurants, bar, complimentary Continental breakfast. Cable TV. Beach. Laundry service. Business services. Pets allowed (fee). | 944 W. Wharf Rd. | 203/245–1404 | fax 203/245–0410 | 29 rooms, 6 suites | $115–$225 | Closed Jan.–Feb. | AE, D, MC, V.

MANCHESTER

Clarion Suites Inn. This all-suites chain hotel is within easy commuting distance of Hartford (it's just off I–84) and is close to the University of Connecticut. The rooms are set up for long term stays, and relocations. Buffet dining room, bar, complimentary breakfast. In-room data ports, kitchenettes, cable TV. Pool. Hot tub, sauna. Tennis court. Gym. Laundry facilities, laundry service. Business services, airport shuttle. Pets allowed (fee). | 191 Spencer St. | 860/643–5811 or 800/992–4004 | 104 suites | $107–$161 | Dinner included Mon.–Thurs. | AE, D, DC, MC, V.

MIDDLETOWN

Comfort Inn. A comfortable, central inn that is near I–84, I–91, and Routes 2, 3, and 9. It is also close to West Farm Malls, Wesleyan, Trinity, Goodspeed Opera House, and steamboat rides. It is 10 minutes' drive north of Middletown. Complimentary Continental breakfast. Cable TV. Pets allowed. | 111 Berlin Rd., Cromwell 06416 | 860/635–4100 | fax 860/632–9546 | 77 rooms | $79–$94 | AE, MC, V.

Holiday Inn. This three-story chain option has traditional furnishings. The rooms are done in navy and neutral colors and have corporate art and bright lighting. Restaurant, bar, room service. In-room data ports, refrigerators, in-room hot tubs, cable TV. Indoor pool. Sauna. Gym. Laundry service. Business services. Pets allowed. | 4 Sebethe Dr., Cromwell 06416 | 860/635–1001 | fax 860/635–0684 | 143 rooms, 2 suites | $139; $179 suites | AE, D, DC, MC, V.

Middletown Motor Inn. This is your basic no-frills motel that is comfortable and convenient. Service is friendly and the price makes its a good place to hang your hat for the night. Cable TV. Some pets allowed (fee). | 988 Washington St. 06457 | 860/346–9251 | 41 rooms | $50–$65 | AE, MC, V.

MYSTIC

★ **Inn at Mystic.** The three buildings here include a turn-of-the-century inn, a gatehouse, and a motor lodge spread over 15 hilltop acres that overlook the harbor, which include gardens and 1¼ mi of walking trails. All the rooms have antiques and period reproductions. Half of them also have fireplaces, canopy beds, private balconies or patios. Restaurant, bar, room service. In-room hot tubs, cable TV. Pool. Putting green, tennis court. Boating. Business services. Pets allowed. No smoking. | U.S. 1 and Rte. 27 | 860/536–9604 or 800/237–2415 | fax 860/572–1635 | www.innatmystic.com | 67 rooms | $125–$275 | AE, D, DC, MC, V.

Residence Inn Mystic. This three-story inn-style hotel is just ½ mi from the Mystic Aquarium and Olde Mistick Village and one mi from the Mystic Seaport. Rooms have sleek, contemporary furniture in neutral colors. Complimentary Continental breakfast. In-room data ports. Laundry facilities, laundry service. Business services. Pets allowed (charge may apply). | 40 Whitehall Ave. 06355 | 860/536–5150 or 800/331–3131 | fax 860/572–4724 | www.residenceinn.com | 128 suites | $110–$199 | AE, MC, V.

NEW BRITAIN

Ramada Inn. This four-story hotel was built in 1973. It is geared toward the business traveler—there are eight meeting rooms and it is near I–84 (15 minutes west of Hartford) and 28 mi from Bradley Airport. Guest rooms are comfortable and done in neutral and dark colors. Restaurant, bar, room service. Outdoor pool. Laundry facilities, laundry services. Business services. Pets allowed (fee). | 400 New Britain Ave., Plainville 06062 | 860/747–6876 or 888/298–2054 | fax 860/747–9747 | www.ramada.com | 106 rooms | $60–$210 | AE, D, DC, MC, V.

NEW HAVEN

New Haven Grande Chalet. This eight-story chain hotel was renovated in 1998 and is just off I–95 at Exit 46. Many of the rooms have views of the New Haven Harbor. Complimentary Continental breakfast. In-room data ports, cable TV. Pool. Gym. Laundry service. Business services. Pets allowed. | 400 Sargent Dr. | 203/562–1111 | 153 rooms | $70–$90 | AE, D, DC, MC, V.

Residence Inn by Marriott. The only all-suite hotel in New Haven is off I–95 at Exit 46. It's close to the downtown area, and the water, and the summer port of the *Amistad* is just across the highway. Restaurant. Kitchenettes, cable TV. Pool. Hot tub. Laundry service. Business services. Pets allowed (fee). | 3 Long Wharf Dr. | 203/777–5337 | www.residence.com | 112 suites | $145–$180 | AE, D, MC, V.

NEW LONDON

Red Roof Inn. A good budget alternative, this hotel is 20 minutes from Foxwoods, 10 minutes from Mystic Seaport, and just eight minutes from Ocean Beach. It has grounds filled with flowers and trees. Picnic area. Some in-room data ports, cable TV. Pets allowed. | 707 Colman St. | 860/444–0001 | fax 860/443–7154 | www.redroof.com | 108 rooms in 2 buildings | $69–$99 | AE, D, DC, MC, V.

NEW PRESTON

Atha House. One mile south of New Preston, this Cape Cod cottage stands among many trees and landscaped lawns on 3 acres. You can lounge in the living room with the fireplace and grand piano, or relax on the patio watching horses graze in a pasture. Complimentary breakfast. No air-conditioning, TV in common area. Pets allowed. No smoking. | Wheaton Rd. 06777 | 860/355–7387 or 860/355–7307 | 2 rooms | $90–$110 | AE, DC, D, MC, V.

OLD LYME

Old Lyme. This two-story, white clapboard 1850s inn is on 2 acres in Old Lyme's historic district. It's filled with Empire and Victorian furnishings, and a maple spiral staircase leads to the rooms. Restaurant, bar, complimentary Continental breakfast. Cable TV. Business services. Pets allowed (as long as the pet is not in the room when guest is not there). | 85 Lyme St. | 860/434–2600 or 800/434–5352 | fax 860/434–5352 | www.oldlymeinn.com | 13 rooms | $99–$160 | AE, D, DC, MC, V.

OLD SAYBROOK

Sandpiper Motor Inn. This three-story simple motel is ideal for families. The rooms have standard double beds and private baths. Complimentary Continental breakfast. Cable TV. Pool. Pets allowed. | 1750 Boston Post Rd. | 860/399–7973 or 800/323–7973 | fax 860/399–7387 | 44 rooms | $75–$135 | AE, D, DC, MC, V.

PUTNAM

King's Inn. A country inn overlooking a pond that is within walking distance of downtown. The rooms have either cream colored walls or floral wallpaper and all have wood furniture. Complimentary Continental breakfast. Cable TV. Pool. Business services. Pets allowed. | 5 Heritage Rd. | 860/928–7961 or 800/541–7304 | fax 860/963–2463 | 40 rooms, 1 suite | $60–$120 | AE, D, DC MC, V.

SALISBURY

White Hart Inn. This rambling country inn overlooks the Salisbury village green and has an expansive front porch. The rooms are filled with Thomasville furniture and Waverly wall coverings. Two-night minimum stay on weekends. 2 restaurants, bar. Cable TV. Laundry service. Business services. Pets allowed. | 15 Under Mountain Rd. | 860/435–0030 or 800/932–0041 | fax 860/435–0040 | www.whitehartinn.com | 26 rooms | $115–$235 | AE, D, DC, MC, V.

SOUTHINGTON

Ramada Inn. This representative of the chain is oriented toward business travelers and is 5 mi south of Southington. Restaurant, bar, complimentary Continental breakfast, room service. Cable TV. Indoor pool. Gym. Laundry Service. Business services. Pets allowed. | 275 Research Pkwy., Meriden 06450 | 203/238–2380 | fax 203/238–3172 | 150 rooms | $139–$149 | AE, D, DC, MC, V.

STAMFORD

Budget Hospitality Inn. Rising seven stories above Stamford's business district, this hotel is north of I–95. The rooms are basic with floral patterned bedspreads and burgundy carpets. Some of the rooms have ocean views. Restaurant, room service, complimentary Continental breakfast. In-room data ports, cable TV. Pool. Gym. Laundry service. Business services, free parking. Some pets allowed (fee). | 19 Clark's Hill Ave. | 203/327–4300 | www.budgethospitalityinn.com | 86 rooms | $60–$159 | AE, D, DC, MC, V.

Grand Chalet Stamford. This eight-story chain hotel stands just south of I–95 (at Exit 6) on Stamford's western edge and caters to the business traveler. Complimentary Continental breakfast. In-room data ports, cable TV. Pool. Gym. Laundry facilities. Free parking. Pets allowed. | 135 Harvard Ave. | 203/357–7100 | 158 rooms | $75–$95 | AE, MC, V.

Holiday Inn Select. A chain option in downtown Stamford. The rooms are lime green and maroon and have either king-size beds or two double beds. The rooms with king-size beds have sofas and all rooms have a desk and chairs. Restaurant, bar, room service. In-room data ports, cable TV. Indoor pool. Gym. Laundry service. Business services. Pets allowed. | 700 Main St. | 203/358–8400 | fax 203/358–8872 | www.holiday-inn.com | 383 rooms | $205–$215 | AE, D, DC, MC, V.

STRATFORD

Ramada Inn. A chain option near I–95 that has clean, standard rooms. Restaurant, bar, room service. Indoor pool. Business services. Pets allowed. | 225 Lordship Blvd. | 203/375–8866 | fax 203/375–2482 | 145 rooms | $99–$109 | AE, D, MC, V.

WATERBURY

House on the Hill. An 1888, three-story Victorian mansion is home to this inn, which has an English-style garden. You can relax on the huge porch with wicker furniture or in the mahogany library or cherry wood parlor. The rooms are individually decorated, filled with antiques and have sitting areas. The beds are brass, iron, or pencil-post canopy and have handmade Ohio quilts. Some of the bathrooms have original bathtubs with marble surrounds and pedestal sinks. Two-night minimum stay on weekends. Complimentary breakfast. No air-conditioning in some rooms, cable TV. Pets allowed. No smoking. | 92 Woodlawn Terr | 203/757–9901 | 4 suites | $125–$175 | Closed mid-Dec.–mid-Jan. | AE, D, DC, MC, V.

Sheraton Waterbury. This standard chain hotel has rooms with either two double beds or a king-size bed. Restaurant, bar, room service. In-room data ports, cable TV. Indoor pool. Hot tub, sauna. Gym, racquetball. Laundry service. Business services. Pets allowed. | 3580 E. Main St. | 203/573–1000 | fax 203/573–1349 | 279 rooms | $115–$129 | AE, D, DC, MC, V.

Tucker Hill Inn. A New England Colonial-style inn built in 1923 that is close to downtown Middlebury, 3 mi west of Waterbury. The inn was originally a tearoom at a trolley stop on the way to Waterbury. The rooms have country-style antiques and furnishings. Complimentary breakfast. No air-conditioning in some rooms, cable TV, no room phones. Pets allowed (no fee). No smoking. | 96 Tucker Hill Rd., Middlebury | 203/758–8334 | fax 203/598–0652 | 4 rooms | $90–$140 | AE, MC, V.

WATERFORD

Oakdell Motel. This two-story motel, 2 mi north of I–95, has been family-owned and operated since 1972. A gazebo crowns the broad lawns that encircle the pool; there is space to relax and enjoy what wildlife creeps from the woods. Two penthouse rooms have private balconies overlooking the pool. Complimentary Continental breakfast, picnic area. Some kitchenettes, microwaves, refrigerators, cable TV. Pool. Pets allowed. | 983 Rte. 85 | 860/442–9446 | www.oakdellmotel.com | 22 rooms | $55–$135 | AE, D, DC, MC, V.

WETHERSFIELD

Ramada Inn. This four-story, spacious chain option is near I–91 and has rooms with either king or double beds. Complimentary Continental breakfast, room service. Cable TV. Laundry service. Business services. Pets allowed. | 1330 Silas Deane Hwy. | 860/563–2311 | 111 rooms | $66–$89 | AE, D, DC, MC, V.

WINDSOR LOCKS

Residence Inn by Marriott. A chain option near both I–91 and the airport and 9 mi south of Windsor Locks. The rooms have two double beds, a table and chairs. Complimentary Continental breakfast. Cable TV. Pool. Hot tub. Business services, airport shuttle. Pets allowed. | 100 Dunfey La., Windsor 06095 | 860/688–7474 | 96 suites | $149–$179 | AE, D, DC, MC, V.

WOODBURY

Hilton. A three-story, full-service hotel in a quiet setting and ½ mi south of Woodbury. The rooms are filled with Ethan Allan furniture and were renovated in 2000. Restaurant, bar, room service. Cable TV. Indoor pool. Hot tub, sauna. Gym. Laundry service. Business services. Pets allowed. | 1284 Strongtown Rd., Southbury 06488 | 203/598–7600 | fax 203/598–0837 | 198 rooms | $105–$155 | AE, D, DC, MC, V.

Delaware

DOVER

Comfort Inn. This two-story motel is 5 blocks from historic Dover, just south of town. Complimentary Continental breakfast. Some refrigerators, cable TV. Pool. Exercise equipment. Some pets allowed. | 222 S. DuPont Hwy. (U.S. 13) | 302/674–3300 | fax 302/674–3300, ext. 190 | 94 rooms | $55–$69 | AE, D, DC, MC, V.

NEW CASTLE

Ramada Inn. The location might not sound appealing—near the graveyard and state hospital—but this full-service hotel is a good value. Restaurant, bar, room service. In-room data ports, cable TV. Pool. Business services. Some pets allowed. | I–295 and Rte. 13, Manor Branch | 302/658–8511 | fax 302/658–3071 | 131 rooms| $72–$90 | AE, D, DC, MC, V.

Rodeway Inn. The DuPont family built this Dutch-theme bungalow-style motel with Colonial furnishings. Historic New Castle is 2 mi away, and the Christiana Mall, with 260 stores, is a five-minute drive. Cable TV. Business services. Some pets allowed. | 111 S. DuPont Hwy. | 302/328–6246 | fax 302/328–9493 | 40 rooms | $59–$74 | AE, D, DC, MC, V.

NEWARK

Comfort Inn. This reasonably priced motel is 2 mi from the University of Delaware and close to the New Castle County airport. Wilmington's waterfront area is 7 mi away. Restaurant, bar, complimentary Continental breakfast. In-room data ports, some refrigerators, cable TV. Pool. Business services. Some pets allowed. | 1120 S. College Ave. (Rte. 896) 19713 | 302/368–8715 | fax 302/368–6454 | 102 rooms | $63–$90 | AE, D, DC, MC, V.

Howard Johnson. These standard motel accommodations are 3 mi from the racetrack and 2 mi south of the University of Delaware. Complimentary Continental breakfast. In-room data ports, cable TV. Pool. Business services. Free parking. Some pets allowed. | 1119 S. College Ave. (Rte. 896) 19713 | 302/368–8521 | fax 302/368–9868 | 142 rooms | $65–$125 | AE, D, DC, MC, V.

REHOBOTH BEACH

Sea'esta Motel Inn. All rooms in this three-story motel have balconies looking onto the bay; the ocean is a block away. There is covered parking; the Rusty Rudder restaurant is across the street. Kitchenettes, cable TV. Beach. Some pets allowed (fee). | 1409 Rte. 1, Dewey Beach | 302/227–4343 or 302/227–7299 | 33 units | $33–$129 | Closed Nov.–Mar. | AE, D, DC, MC, V.

WILMINGTON

Best Western Brandywine Valley Inn. This hotel, a few miles from historic downtown, is just off I–95. A restaurant with cocktail lounge and kid's menu is next door. In-room data ports, some kitchenettes, cable TV. Hot tub. Pool, wading pool. Exercise equipment. Business services. Free parking. Some pets allowed. | 1807 Concord Pike (U.S. 202) 19803 | 302/656–9436 | fax 302/656–8564 | www.brandywineinn.com | 98 rooms, 12 suites | $63–$95 | AE, D, DC, MC, V.

Holiday Inn–North. In north Wilmington, near Longwood Gardens, museums, and shopping, this two-story motel is 5 mi from downtown. Restaurant, bar, room service. In-room data ports, cable TV. Pool. Laundry facilities. Business services. Some pets allowed. | 4000 Concord Pike (U.S. 202) 19803 | 302/478–2222 | fax 302/479–0850 | www. holiday-inn.com | 138 rooms | $94–$135 | AE, D, DC, MC, V.

Wyndham Garden Hotel. About 25 minutes south of Philadelphia, this nine-story hotel in the center of downtown is near museums, the Grand Opera, and the baseball stadium. The University of Delaware is 15 minutes away. Restaurant, bar. In-room data ports, cable TV. Indoor pool. Beauty salon. Hot tub. Exercise equipment. Business services. Some pets allowed. | 700 King St. 19801 | 302/655–0400 | fax 302/655–5488 | 217 rooms | $99–$142 | AE, D, DC, MC, V.

District of Columbia

Best Western. This all-suite representative of the chain is six blocks from the White House and two blocks from the Metro. The hotel provides à la carte service from the many neighborhood eateries. Complimetary Continental breakfast. Microwaves, refrigerators. Cable TV. Parking (fee). Some pets allowed. | 1121 New Hampshire Ave. NW | 202/457–0565 or 800/762–3777 | fax 202/331–9421 | www.bestwestern.com | 76 suites| $169 | AE, D, DC, MC, V.

Days Inn Gateway. This chain property is 4 mi away from the White House, the Capitol, and the Vietnam Memorial, 2 mi north of Howard University, and 3 mi northeast of Union Station. Restaurant. Cable TV. Outdoor pool. Exercise equipment. Laundry facilities, laundry service. Free parking. Some pets allowed. | 2700 New York Ave. NE 20002 | 202/832–5800 or 800/544–8313 | fax 202/269–4317 | www.daysinn.com | 193 | $49–$99 | AE, D, DC, MC, V.

Four Seasons Hotel. This brick hotel at the east end of Georgetown overlooks Rock Creek Park from the back. The restaurant is superb, the lobby is inviting and comfortable, and the rooms are spacious and bright. Some have sunken tubs and all have an extensive array of amenities. Restaurant, bar, room service. In-room data ports, minibars. Cable TV. Indoor pool. Spa. Gym. Business services, parking (fee). Some pets allowed. | 2800 Pennsylvania Ave. NW 20007 | 202/342–0444 | fax 202/944–2076 | www.fourseasons.com | 260 rooms | $410 | AE, D, DC, MC, V.

★ **Hay-Adams.** At this stately, historical, luxury property, with antiques and renaissance art, the motto is "Nothing is overlooked but the White House." The architecture is vintage Italian, and the rooms have elaborately carved moldings and marble bathrooms. The downtown spot is a favorite of visiting dignitaries. Restaurant, bar, room service. In-room data ports, minibars, some refrigerators. Cable TV. Business services, parking (fee). Some pets allowed. | 800 16th St. NW 20006 | 202/638–6600 or 800/424–5054 | fax 202/638–2716 | www.hayadams.com | 143 rooms, 42 suites | $375–$570 | AE, D, DC, MC, V.

Henley Park. Reminiscent of an English country house, this hotel is quaint and small and promises everything you need at your fingertips. It's eight blocks from the Smithsonian Museums, five blocks from the MCI Sports Arena. Restaurant, bar with entertainment, room service. In-room data ports, minibars (in suites), refrigerators. Cable TV. Business services, parking (fee). Some pets allowed. | 926 Massachusetts Ave. NW 20001 | 202/638–

5200 or 800/222–8474 | fax 202/638–6740 | www.henleypark.com | 96 rooms, 10 suites | $195, $245 suites | AE, D, DC, MC, V.

Hotel Harrington. Family-owned and operated since 1914, this downtown hotel is in an older brick building with a cozy, contained lobby and is ideal for families and students. 3 restaurants, bar. Cable TV. Laundry facilities. Business services, parking (fee). Some pets allowed. | 436 11th St. NW 20004 | 202/628–8140 or 800/424–8532 | fax 202/343–3924 | reservations@hotel-harrington.com | www.hotel-harrington.com | 250 rooms, 40 deluxe rooms (2 adjoining rooms) | $85–$125 | AE, D, DC, MC, V.

Hotel Sofitel. This chain property, in a tastefully refurbished 1904 apartment building, sits at the juncture of upper downtown and the tony Kalorama neighborhood. Restaurant, bar, room service. In-room data ports, minibars. Cable TV. Exercise equipment. Business services, parking (fee). Some pets allowed (fee). | 1914 Connecticut Ave. NW 20009 | 202/797–2000 or 800/424–2464 | fax 202/462–0944 | www.sofitel.com | 104 rooms, 40 suites | $99–$159, $119–$259 suites | AE, D, DC, MC, V.

Hotel Tabard Inn. Three Victorian town houses make up this quaint, popular hotel in Dupont Circle, with old Victorian and American Empire furniture, fireplaces, and outdoor patio. Rooms vary in size, and some share bathrooms. Restaurant. In-room data ports, no TV in some rooms. Business services, parking (fee). Some pets allowed. | 1739 N St. NW 20036 | 202/785–1277 | fax 202/785–6173 | www.tabardinn.com/home.htm | 40 rooms, 25 with bath | $140–$175 | AE, D, DC, MC, V.

WHERE TO PLAY WITH YOUR DOG

You already know how to play with your dog. But when you take her on the road with you, where to go to play becomes a question. The world is an obstacle course of community groups, of pro-dog and anti-dog forces. Sometimes, in some places, the dog-lovers hold sway, and a corner of a pretty park is designated for off-leash frolics. The next year, the same park is off limits to six-legged couples who are not conjoined by a leash. What's a traveler to do? Before you hit the road, detailed guidance is helpful. Ask at your hotel—many staff in pet-friendly hostelries keep abreast of these things. And, before you go, check the internet. Some sites, like doortosummer.com, cover a specific area—Florida, in this case. Others travel nationwide—among them, dogpark.com, which lists dog-friendly parks and hotels, covers dog trivia and news that appeals to dogs and their folks, and describes dog walk-a-thons and other events that you might want to attend with your dog—things that are designed just for dogs and their people. Both doggonefun.com and dogfriendly.com can give you ideas about having fun on the road, just the two of you, from a National Capital Air Canines Frisbee Disc Dog Club event (near Washington, DC) to the Bark and Whine Ball in San Francisco to Yappy Hour in Jefferson, Louisiana. Happy tails!

★ **Hotel Washington.** This historic downtown property dating from 1918, has a popular rooftop bar with extensive views and is within walking distance of most major attractions. Rooms have various color schemes, but all have painted walls and mahogany furniture. Restaurant, bar. In-room data ports. Cable TV. Exercise equipment. Business services, parking (fee). Some pets allowed. | 515 15th St. NW 20004 | 202/638–5900 or 800/424–9540 | fax 202/638–4275 | www.hotelwashington.com | 344 rooms, 16 suites | $205 | AE, D, DC, MC, V.

Lincoln Suites. A modern studio-suite hotel with a quaint lobby, it's centrally located downtown. A king or two double beds are available. In-room data ports, some kitchenettes, microwaves, refrigerators. Cable TV. Business services, parking (fee). Some pets allowed (fee). | 1823 L St. NW 20036 | 202/223–4320 or 800/424–2970 | fax 202/223–8546 | www.lincolnhotels.com | 99 rooms | $109–$179 | AE, D, DC, MC, V.

Loews L'Enfant Plaza. Amid some government and private sector offices—and close to other Federal agencies—this French-themed hotel, in the center of L'Enfant Plaza, is within walking distance of the scenic Tidal Basin. The plaza's underground shops, eateries, and Metro add to the convenience. The rooms, on the top four floors, have views of monuments, the Potomac, or the Capitol. Amenities include 2 double beds or a king, hair dryers, irons and ironing boards, and coffeemakers. Restaurant, bar, room service. In-room data ports, minibars, refrigerators. Cable TV. Indoor/outdoor pool. Gym. Business services, parking (fee). Some pets allowed. | 480 L'Enfant Plaza SW 20024 | 202/484–1000 | fax 202/646–4456 | www.loewshotels.com/lenfanthome.html | 370 rooms, 21 suites | $259, $375 suites | AE, D, DC, MC, V.

Marriott Wardman Park Hotel. This three-building compound, part of the chain, sits on a rolling hill in Woodley Park, between the National Zoo and downtown. There are some modernized rooms but a number of antique-style rooms remain. Restaurant, bar. Some refrigerators. Cable TV. Outdoor pool. Exercise equipment. Business services, parking (fee). Some pets allowed. | 2660 Woodley Rd. NW 20008 | 202/328–2000 | fax 202/234–0015 | www.marriotthotels.com | 1,206 rooms, 125 suites | $139, $350 suites | AE, D, DC, MC, V.

Omni Shoreham. This elegant 11-acre grand dame has hosted the rich and famous since 1930. In Woodley Park, it's a 10-minute walk to downtown. Traditional guest rooms have cherry furniture and floral bedspreads, and some rooms overlook Rock Creek Park. Amenities include hair dryers, irons and ironing boards, and coffeemakers. Restaurant, bar, room service. Cable TV. Indoor pool. Health Club. Business services, parking (fee). Shops. Some pets allowed. | 2500 Calvert St. NW 20008 | 202/234–0700 | fax 202/332–1373 | www.omnishoreham.com | 834 rooms, 60 suites | $209, $399 suites | AE, D, DC, MC, V.

Renaissance Washington. It's a convention hotel, big, bright and airy, located directly across the street from the Convention Center's main entrance. Rooms are individually furnished, some in antique style, some modern; all the furniture is custom-made. Restaurant, bar, room service. In-room data ports, minibars. Cable TV. Indoor pool. Hot tub. Gym. Business services, parking (fee). Some pets allowed. | 999 9th St. NW 20001 | 202/898–9000 | fax 202/289–0947 | www.renaissancehotel.com | 801 rooms, 14 suites | $199, $229 suites | AE, D, DC, MC, V.

River Inn. Filled with old country art and furnishings, this quaint all-suite boutique hotel is in a quiet townhouse-lined neighborhood close to Georgetown and George Washington University, only a short Metro ride from downtown. King and queen beds are available. All suites (some efficiency, some one-bedroom) have full kitchens. Restaurant, bar. In-room data ports, microwaves. Cable TV. Health club. Business services, parking (fee). Some pets allowed (fee). | 924 25th St. NW 20037 | 202/337–7600 or 800/424–2741 | fax 202/337–6520 | riverinn@erols.com | www.theriverinn.com | 126 suites | $175–$245 | AE, DC, MC, V.

St. Regis Hotel. This elegant luxury hotel, near the White House, is among the city's preferred spots for the business elite and visiting dignitaries. There's a roomy lobby, and the rooms, with desk and chair, have antique furniture and Italian marble bathrooms. Restaurant, bar, complimentary afternoon tea, room service. In-room data ports, minibars, refrigerators. Cable TV. Exercise equipment. Business services, parking (fee). Some pets allowed. | 923 16th St. NW 20006 | 202/638–2626 | fax 202/638–4231 | www.starwood.com | 194 rooms, 14 suites | $460, $800 suites | AE, D, DC, MC, V.

Swissotel Washington–The Watergate. Rising up from the banks of the Potomac River, this hotel is part of the fashionable shopping district in Georgetown and is next to the Kennedy Center. The luxurious rooms, furnished in modern European style, have marble baths, irons and ironing boards, coffeemakers, and hair dryers. Restaurant, bar (with entertainment), room service. In-room data ports, minibars. Cable TV. Indoor pool. Beauty salon, hot tub, massage. Gym. Business services, parking (fee). Some pets allowed. | 2650 Virginia Ave. NW 20037 | 202/965–2300 or 800/424–2736 | fax 202/337–7915 | www.swissotel.com | 250 rooms, 89 suites | $400, $475 suites | AE, D, DC, MC, V.

Washington Hilton and Towers. This chain property, with a grand, spacious lobby adorned with chandeliers and modern carpeting, hosts numerous conventions, large meetings, and banquets. It's a true full-service hotel, a few blocks north of Dupont Circle. Restaurant, bar with pianist. In-room data ports, some minibars. Cable TV. Outdoor pool, wading pool. 3 outdoor tennis courts. Gym. Business services, parking (fee). Some pets allowed. | 1919 Connecticut Ave. NW 20009 | 202/483–3000 | fax 202/232–0438 | www.washington-hilton.com | 1,103 rooms, 15 suites | $175–$250, $350 suites | AE, D, DC, MC, V.

Washington Monarch Hotel. A high-ceilinged atrium with massive windows and sunken lounge area greets you at this upscale hotel (formerly the Ana), two blocks from downtown. It's a frequent site of major industry conferences. Restaurant, bar (with entertainment), room service. In-room data ports, minibars, some refrigerators. Cable TV. Indoor pool. Hot tub, massage. Gym, racquetball, squash. Business services, parking (fee). Some pets allowed. | 2401 M St. NW 20037 | 202/429–2400 or 877/222–2266 | fax 202/457–5010 | 406 rooms, 9 suites | $289, $600 suites | AE, D, DC, MC, V.

Washington Suites Georgetown. Between Georgetown and downtown, nine blocks from the White House and a few blocks from the heart of the business district, this all-suite hotel has a small, cozy lobby decorated with photos of D.C. monuments and the C&O Canal. In-room data ports, microwaves. Cable TV. Business services, Parking (fee). Some pets allowed (fee). | 2500 Pennsylvania Ave. NW 20037 | 202/333–8060 | fax 202/338–3818 | www.washingtonsuiteshotel.com | 124 kitchen suites | $129–$219 | AE, D, DC, MC, V.

★ **Willard Inter-Continental.** Two blocks from the Mall and the White House, in the heart of the downtown government area, this stately, grand hotel is a specimen of turn-of-the-20th-century architecture, with huge marble columns and opulent comfort. Rooms have king or two double beds, writing desks, lounge chairs, sofas, marble baths, bathrobes, hair dryers, and in-room video games. Restaurant, bar, room service. In-room data ports, minibars, some microwaves. Cable TV. Gym. Business services, parking (fee). Some pets allowed. | 1401 Pennsylvania Ave. NW 20004 | 202/628–9100 | fax 202/637–7326 | www.interconti.com | 265 rooms, 38 suites | $425, $550 junior suites, $1,000 suites | AE, D, DC, MC, V.

Florida

ALTAMONTE SPRINGS

La Quinta Orlando North. This is a pretty hacienda-style motel 19 miles from the Orlando Airport, 18 miles from SeaWorld, and 28 mi from Walt Disney World. Some rooms feature sofa beds and recliners. Complimentary Continental breakfast. In-room data ports, some microwaves, some refrigerators. Cable TV. Outdoor pool. Business services. Pets allowed. | 150 S. Westmonte Dr. 32714 | 407/788–1411 | fax 407/788–6472 | www.laquinta.com | 115 rooms | $69–$99 | AE, D, DC, MC, V.

Residence Inn Orlando-Altamonte Springs. Every room in this all-suites hotel has a sofa bed and a full kitchen; some even have fireplaces. Every Monday and Thursday there is a complimentary dinner, which includes free beer and wine. Walt Disney World is about 30 mi away; Universal Studios and SeaWorld are about 20 mi away. Complimentary Continental breakfast. In-room data ports, kitchenettes, microwaves, refrigerators. Cable TV. Pool. Hot tub. Laundry service. Business services. Pets allowed (fee). | 270 Douglas Ave. 32714 | 407/788–7991 | fax 407/869–5468 | www.marriott.com | 128 suites | $145–$169 | AE, D, DC, MC, V.

AMELIA ISLAND/FERNANDINA BEACH

The Florida House Inn. Ulysses S. Grant is among those who have spent the night in this inn, built in 1857, which is Florida's oldest surviving hotel. Listed on the National Register of Historic Places, it has second-story verandas, gleaming hardwood floors, and comfortable period antiques. Ten rooms have working fireplaces; five have hot tubs. The inn is especially dog-friendly. Restaurant, bar, complimentary breakfast. Some in-room hot tubs. Cable TV. Laundry facilities. Business services. Pets allowed (fee). | 22 S. 3rd St., Fernandina Beach 32034 | 904/261–3300 or 800/258–3301 | fax 904/277–3831 | www. floridahouseinn.com | 15 rooms | $69–$169 | AE, D, DC, MC, V.

The Inn at Fernandina Beach. Located less than 100 yards from the beach, this two-story motel is adjacent to a Shoney's restaurant. Other restaurants and shopping are within easy walking distance. Restaurant, bar, picnic area. Some kitchenettes, some microwaves, some refrigerators. Cable TV. Pool. Beauty salon, hot tub. Tennis court. Volleyball. Laundry facilities. Pets allowed (fee). | 2707 Sadler Rd., Fernandina Beach | 904/277–2300 | 134 rooms | $49–$89 | AE, D, DC, MC, V.

ARCADIA

Best Western Arcadia Inn. This simple, single-story motel is right next to the rodeo, and 20 mi from Solomon's Castle. Complimentary Continental breakfast. Refrigerators, microwaves, some in-room hot tubs. Cable TV. Outdoor pool. Laundry facilities. Business services. Some pets allowed. | 504 S. Brevard Ave. 34266 | 863/494–4884 | fax 863/494–2006 | www.bestwestern.com | 38 rooms | $59–$69 | AE, D, DC, MC, V.

BARTOW

El Jon Motel. This motel is popular with golfers because greens fees for two people at the Bartow Golf Course are included in the nightly rates. The rooms here all come with Direct TV. Refrigerators, cable TV. Outdoor pool. Golf privileges, golf course. Some pets allowed. | 1460 E. Main St. 33830 | 863/533–8191 | 42 rooms | $41–$69 | AE, D, DC, MC, V.

BELLE GLADE

Okeechobee Inn. This basic, two-story blue motel offers simple rooms with balconies overlooking the pool. Be glad you have a car because Lake Okeechobee is almost 2 mi away. No air-conditioning in some rooms. Laundry facilities. Pets allowed (fee). | 265 N. U.S 27, South Bay 33493 | 561/996–6517 | 115 rooms | $45–$75 | MC, V.

BOCA RATON

Boca Raton Radisson Suite Hotel. Six mi from the beach, this attractive hotel is in a Mediterranean-style business center built around an atrium with tropical gardens and fountains. All the rooms are suites and feature two TVs and VCRs. Complimentary Conti-

INNOPET PARK

It was in 1992 that Coral Springs' veterinarian Dr. Steven G. Paul got the idea for this innovative park. At a Boston veterinary conference, he saw dogs frolicking on the Boston Common. Why couldn't Florida pets enjoy such a space, he thought? Back home in Coral Springs (15 mi from Boca Raton), Dr. Paul embarked on the arduous task of making his vision a reality. City Commissioners and other politicos had to be persuaded. Local citizens had to be won over. Red tape had to be unsnarled and snipped. And funds had to be raised. Four years later, and with the financial support of InnoPet Brands Dog Food, the City of Coral Springs finally opened a two-acre minipark inside the Sportsplex Regional Park Complex for the exclusive use of the dogs and their owners. Today, you'll find a paved running path along with leash posts. Dog statues punctuate special landscaping. And waste collection bag dispensers and trash barrels are strategically located. Pets can hone their agility on special equipment. The watering area and the dog shower are especially welcome on hot days. Annual events are numerous as well. For more information, contact Dr. Paul at 8008 Wiles Road, Coral Springs, FL 33067-2059, (954) 752-1879.

nental breakfast. Some in-room data ports, microwaves. Cable TV, VCRs. Outdoor pool, lake. Hot tub. Gym. Some pets allowed. | 7920 Glades Rd. 33434 | 561/483–3600 | fax 561/479–2280 | 200 rooms | $135–$245 | AE, D, DC, MC, V.

Doubletree Guest Suites. All units are suites in this appealing hotel with a lovely courtyard. Two mi from the beach, and in the heart of the business district, all rooms have two TVs and window views of the courtyard or the pool. Restaurant, room service. In-room data ports, microwaves, refrigerators. Cable TV. Pool. Hot tubs. Laundry facilities. Business services. Some pets allowed (fee). | 701 N.W. 53rd St. 33487 | 561/997–9500 | fax 561/994–3565 | www.doubletree.com | 182 suites | $149–$189 | AE, D, DC, MC, V.

Radisson Suite Hotel. This all-suites hotel is on a lake and features a landscaped lobby with pine trees. Each room has a private balcony and living room. Bar, complimentary breakfast. In-room data ports, kitchenettes, minibars, microwaves, refrigerators. Cable TV, some in-room VCRs (and movies). Pool. Hot tub. Exercise equipment. Laundry facilities. Business services. Some pets allowed (fee). | 7920 Glades Rd. 33434 | 561/483–3600 or 800/333–3333 | fax 561/479–2280 | www.radisson.com | 200 suites | $130–$170 | AE, D, DC, MC, V.

Ramada Inn. This contemporary four-floor hotel has nice public zones, like the palm-landscaped pool area. Some rooms have balconies. Restaurant, bar, complimentary Continental breakfast. In-room data ports, kitchenettes, some microwaves. Cable TV, some in-room VCRs. Pool. Hot tub. Laundry services. Business services. Some pets allowed (fee). | 2901 N. Federal Hwy. 33431 | 561/395–6850 | fax 561/368–7964 | www.ramada.com | 97 rooms | $105–$135 | AE, D, DC, MC, V.

Residence Inn by Marriott. This two-story hotel 2 mi from Delray Beach has volleyball and basketball courts, an outdoor pool, and two whirlpools. All rooms have full kitchens. Picnic areas, complimentary Continental breakfast. In-room data ports, kitchenettes, microwaves, refrigerators. Cable TV, some in-room VCRs (and movies). Pool. Hot tubs. Driving range, putting green. Basketball, gym, volleyball. Baby-sitting. Laundry facilities. Business services. Some pets allowed (fee). | 525 N.W. 77th St. 33487 | 561/994–3222 | fax 561/994–3339 | www.marriott.com | 120 rooms | $149–$199 | AE, D, DC, MC, V.

BOYNTON BEACH

Ann Marie Motel. This motel offers standard rooms and efficiencies with full kitchens. There's a heated pool outside that has a covered area at one end with a barbecue grill. Say hello to the two parrots in the lobby. Picnic area, complimentary Continental breakfast. In-room data ports, some kitchenettes, some microwaves, refrigerators. Cable TV, in-room VCRs (and movies). Pool. Library. Business services. Pets allowed (fee). | 911 S. Federal Hwy. 33435 | 561/732–9283 or 800/258–8548 | www.annmariemotel.com | 16 rooms | $79–$99 | AE, D, DC, MC, V.

BRADENTON

Best Western Inn Ellenton. This hotel is 5 mi north of Bradenton and 15 miles west of gulf beaches. All standard rooms have a king- or two queen-size beds. Suites with lounging areas are also available. The pool is landscaped with a patio and several palm trees. Restaurant, complimentary Continental breakfast. Some in-room data ports, some microwaves, some refrigerators. Cable TV, some in-room hot tubs. Pool. Gym. Laundry service. Business services. Pets allowed. | 5218 17th St. E, Ellenton 34222 | 941/729–8505 | fax 941/729–1110 | $80–$90 | 73 rooms | AE, D, DC, MC, V.

Econo Lodge Airport. This hotel is ideal if you need to access the Sarasota–Bradenton Airport, which is 2 mi away. All rooms have double or king-size beds. Complimentary Continental breakfast. Some microwaves, some refrigerators. Cable TV. Pool. Business services. Pets allowed. | 6727 14th St. W 34207 | 941/758–7199 or 800/553–2666 | fax 941/751–4947 | www.econolodge.com | 78 rooms | $66–$86 | AE, D, DC, MC, V.

Howard Johnson Express. This two-story, limited-service motel on U.S. 41 is 8 mi from Bradenton Beach, 5 mi from Lido Beach, and 3½ miles north of the Sarasota–Bradenton Airport. Complimentary Continental breakfast. In-room data ports, some kitchenettes, some microwaves, some refrigerators. Cable TV. Laundry service. Business service. Pets allowed. | 6511 14th St. W 34207 | 941/756–8399 or 800/446–4656 | fax 941/755–1387 | www.hojo.com | 50 rooms | $85–$90 | AE, D, DC, MC, V.

Luxury Inn. The beach is 12 mi away from this inexpensive motel, which caters to families and businesspeople alike. Complimentary Continental breakfast. Cable TV. Pool. Laundry facilities. Business services. Pets allowed (fee). | 668 67th St. Circle 34208 | 941/745–1876 | fax 941/747–5046 | 105 rooms | $40–$65 | AE, D, DC, MC, V.

Park Inn Club and Breakfast. This hotel offers packages such the the "Couch Potato," which includes a pizza delivered to your door and two movie tickets for the theater directly behind. Shopping and restaurants are also within walking distance; the beach is 6 mi away. Complimentary Continental breakfast. Some microwaves, some refrigerators, some in-room hot tubs. Cable TV. Pool. Hot tub. Business services. Some pets allowed. | 4450 47th St. W 34210 | 941/795–4633 | fax 941/795–0808 | 110 rooms, 20 suites | $104–$134 | AE, D, DC, MC, V.

BROOKSVILLE

Best Western Heritage Inn. This modern two-story motel has a tropical pool and a cascading waterfall. Otherwise, the rooms are very modern and simple and only an hour's drive from Walt Disney World, and Universal Studios. Restaurant, bar. Pool. Golf. Laundry service. Pets allowed (fee). | 6320 Windmere Rd. 34602 | 352/796–9486 | fax 352/754–8721 | www.bestwestern.com | 118 rooms | $60–$75 | AE, D, DC, MC, V.

Holiday Inn. This hotel is 10 mi from downtown Brooksville and one block from Croom Motor Park. Several golf courses are nearby, including World Woods, 18 mi from the property. Restaurant, bar, complimentary breakfast, room service. In-room data ports, some microwaves, some refrigerators. Cable TV. Pool, wading pool. 2 tennis courts. Playground. Laundry facilities, laundry service. Business services. Some pets allowed (fee). | 30307 Cortez Blvd. 34602 | 352/796–9481 or 800/465–4329 | fax 352/799–7595 | www.holiday-inn.com | 122 rooms | $79–$105 | AE, D, DC, MC, V.

CAPE CORAL

Quality Inn Nautilus. This tropically decorated five-story hotel has a poolside tiki bar and guest rooms with balconies. It is 15 mi from S.W. Florida Regional Airport, 10 mi from Fort Myers Beach, and 20 mi from Captiva Island. Restaurant, bar. Cable TV. Pool. Laundry facilities. Business services. Pets allowed (fee). | 1538 Cape Coral Pkwy. 33904 | 941/542–2121 | fax 941/542–6319 | 144 rooms | $100–$150 | AE, D, DC, MC, V.

CAPTIVA ISLAND

Tween Water Inn. Luxury has a casual, breezy style at this sprawling island resort. The rooms are each different, but all represent the Old Florida look and comfort. Though some of the cottages are originals from the 1930s, most of the inn is more modern like the fitness center. You have your choice of several dining options, from casual to classy. 4 restaurants, complimentary Continental breakfast. Some kitchenettes, some microwaves, some refrigerators, in-room safes. Pool, wading pool. Massage. Tennis. Gym. Water sports, kayaking, boating, fishing, beach, dock. Laundry facilities. Pets allowed (fee). | 15951 Captiva Dr. 33924 | 941/472–5161 or 800/223–5865 | fax 941/472–0249 | www.tween-waters.com | 137 units | $105–$235 | AE, D, MC, V.

CEDAR KEY

Gulf Side Motel. Some of the rooms at this single-story motel have views of the Gulf of Mexico. You can fish off the 180-ft pier or use the deck swing in the cool Gulf breeze. Restaurants, shops, and the historic downtown district are within walking distance. Some kitchenettes, some microwaves, some refrigerators. Cable TV. Fishing. Pets allowed (fee). | 552 1st St. 32625 | 352/543–5308 or 888/364–0477 | www.gulfsidemotel.com | 9 rooms | $50–$60 | D, MC, V.

CHATTAHOOCHEE

Admiral Benbow Morgan Lodge. This single-story lodge off Highway 90 has a 24-hr restaurant next door. Lake Seminole is just minutes away. Microwaves available, refrigerators available. Cable TV. Pets allowed (fee). | 116 E. Washington St. 32324 | 850/663–4336 or 800/451–1986 | fax 850/663–4336 | www.admiralbenbow.com | 43 rooms | $50–$55 | AE, MC, V.

CHIEFLAND

Best Western Suwannee Valley Inn. You'll know you're at this motel when you see the broad blue roof. It's 6 mi from Suwannee River and Manatee State Park, 26 mi from the Gulf of Mexico. Complimentary Continental breakfast. Some microwaves, some refrigerators. Pool. Laundry service. Some pets allowed. | 1125 N. Young Blvd. 32626 | 352/493–0663 | fax 352/493–0663 | www.bestwestern.com | 60 rooms | $55–$75 | AE, D, MC, V.

Manatee Springs Motel. This single-story motel is 5 mi from Manatee Springs State Park. A number of eateries are within walking distance. Some kitchenettes, microwaves, refrigerators. Cable TV. Some pets allowed. | 2226 Young Blvd. 32626 | 352/493–2991 | fax 352/493–2991 | 18 rooms | $40–$45 | AE, D, MC, V.

CHIPLEY

Holiday Inn Express. This motel is about 3 mi east of downtown Chipley. In-room data ports, refrigerators, some in-room hot tubs. Cable TV. Outdoor pool. Business services. Pets allowed (fee). | 1700 A Main St., #A, 32428 | 850/638–3996 or 800/465–4329 | fax 850/638–4569 | www.hiexpress.com | 48 rooms, 2 suites | $62–$81 | AE, D, DC, MC, V.

CLEARWATER

Holiday Inn Express. In the heart of the Clearwater business district, this hotel offers both standard rooms and suites that feature king-size beds and sleeper sofas. The gulf beaches are 10 mi away. Complimentary Continental breakfast. In-room data ports, some microwaves, some refrigerators. Cable TV. Pool. Hot tub. Business services. Some pets allowed. | 13625 ICOT Blvd., Clearwater 33760 | 727/536–7275 or 800/465–4329 | fax 727/530–3053 | www.holiday-inn.com | 127 rooms | $110–$135 | AE, D, DC, MC, V.

La Quinta Clearwater Airport. This Spanish-style, three-story hotel is a mile from the St. Petersburg/Clearwater Airport, 11 mi from the beaches. All suites have two queen-size beds. There is a second-floor deck where you can relax in a lounge chair. Complimentary Continental breakfast. In-room data ports, refrigerators. Cable TV. Pool. Hot tub, sauna. Gym. Laundry service. Business services, airport shuttle. Some pets allowed. | 3301 Ulmerton Rd., Clearwater 34622 | 727/572–7222 or 800/531–5900 | fax 727/572–0076 | www.laquinta.com | 118 rooms | $79–$110 | AE, D, DC, MC, V.

Residence Inn by Marriott. This hotel has studios, suites, and loft units. Every room has a full kitchen and a fireplace. Gulf beaches are 8 mi away; the Airco and Feather Sound golf courses are within 4 mi. Complimentary Continental breakfast. In-room data ports, kitchenettes, microwaves, refrigerators. Cable TV. Pool. Hot tub. Laundry facilities, laundry service. Business services. Some pets allowed (fee). | 5050 Ulmerton Rd., Clearwater 34620 | 727/573–4444 or 800/331–3131 | fax 727/572–4446 | www.residenceinn.com | 88 rooms | $135–$149 | AE, D, DC, MC, V.

Safety Harbor Resort and Spa. The spa and hotel were originally built over natural hot springs on the western shore of Tampa Bay in 1926, but now it's much more modern, with on-site golf and tennis academies. But beside the 22 acres of sports and recreation facilities and luxury accommodations, visitors flock to experience the therapeutic effects of this resort's five natural mineral springs and the 50,000-square-ft spa. A few pleasant hours can be spent exploring the main street of Safety Harbor, a pleasant little hamlet with interesting gift shops and cafés. Restaurant, bar, room service. In-room data ports, some refrigerators. Cable TV. 3 pools. Beauty salon, 2 hot tubs, massage, sauna, spa, steam room. Driving range, putting green, 9 tennis courts. Basketball, gym, volleyball, bicycles. Shops. Laundry facilities, laundry services. Business services. Pets allowed. | 105 N. Bayshore Dr., Safety Harbor 34695 | 727/726–1161 or 888/237–8722 | fax 727/726–4268 | www.safetyharborspa.com | 194 rooms | $119–$189 | AE, D, DC, MC, V.

COCOA

Best Western Cocoa Inn. This hotel has a covered deck with grills by the pool. Cocoa Village is 4 mi away. Picnic area, bar, complimentary Continental breakfast. Microwaves available, refrigerators available. Cable TV. Pool. Video games. Laundry facilities. Pets allowed (fee). | 4225 W. King St. 32926 | 407/632–1065 | fax 407/631–3302 | www.bestwestern.com | 120 rooms | $69–$79 | AE, D, DC, MC, V.

Cocoa Beach/Kennedy Space Center Super 8 Motel. This basic two-story motel is at exit 76 off I–95, 12 mi from the Kennedy Space Center and Cocoa Beach. Restaurant, picnic area, room service. In-room data ports, some microwaves, some refrigerators. Cable TV. Outdoor pool. Pets allowed (fee). | 900 Friday Rd. 32926 | 321/631–1212 or 800/800–8000 | fax 321/636–8661 | www.super8.com | 53 rooms | $62–$69 | AE, D, DC, MC, V.

Days Inn Space Coast. This simple two-story drive-up motel is 18 mi from Kennedy Space Center. Some microwaves, some refrigerators. Cable TV. Pool. Laundry service. Pets allowed (fee). | 5600 Hwy. 524 32926 | 407/636–6500 or 800/544–8313 | fax 407/631–0513 | www.daysinn.com | 121 rooms | $75–$85 | AE, D, DC, MC, V.

Ramada Inn Cocoa-Kennedy Space Center. This hotel is on a 17-acre plot, with a private fishing lake and a jogging trail. Kennedy Space Center is 9 mi away. Restaurant, bar, room service. In-room data ports, microwaves, refrigerators. Cable TV. Pool, lake. Fishing. Laundry facilities. Pets allowed. | 900 Friday Rd. 32926 | 407/631–1210 | fax 407/636–8661 | www.ramada.com | 98 rooms | $79–$89 | AE, D, DC, MC, V.

COCOA BEACH

Best Western Ocean Inn. Only one block from the beach and the Cocoa Beach Pier, this moderately priced two-story motel offers tropical decor in comfortable rooms. Some units have patios, balconies, and kitchenettes. Picnic area. In-room data ports, microwaves, some refrigerators. Cable TV. Pool. Gym. Laundry facilities. Some pets allowed. | 5500 N. Atlantic Ave. 32931 | 321/784–2550 or 877/233–9330 | fax 321/868–7124 | www.bestwestern.com | 103 rooms | $80–$90 | AE, D, DC, MC, V.

Days Inn Oceanfront. Just steps away from the Cocoa Beach Pier, this hotel has clean, bright rooms and suites in two complexes: an off-ocean two-story building and an oceanfront seven-story tower. The former has 120 rooms around a courtyard with hibiscus and palm trees, plus a two-level sundeck around the pool. All 60 rooms in the oceanfront tour have private balconies overlooking the Atlantic. In-room data ports, microwaves. Cable TV. Pool. Gym. Beach. Playground. Laundry facilities. Business services. Pets allowed. | 5600 N. Atlantic Ave. 32931 | 321/783–7621 or 800/962–0028 | fax 321/799–4576 | www.daysinn.com | 180 rooms | $89–$239 | AE, D, DC, MC, V.

Surf Studio Beach Resort. This friendly family-owned oceanfront motel in southern Cocoa Beach has a large sundeck facing quiet beaches with more local surfers than tourists. Rooms are small but clean and well-kept. In-room data ports, some kitchenettes, microwaves, refrigerators. Cable TV, in-room VCRs available. Pool. Beach, water sports, fishing, bicycles. Laundry facilities. Pets allowed (fee). | 1801 S. Atlantic Ave. 32931 | 321/783–7100 | fax 321/783–2695 | 11 rooms | $50–$145 | AE, D, DC, MC, V.

COCONUT GROVE

Hotel Sofitel Miami. Part of the French chain, the hotel is 15 minutes from downtown, near the Vizcaya Museum and various golf courses. Glass dominates the 15-story high-rise, while the furnishings and amenities aim for a French tone. You will find fresh-cut flowers and handmade French soaps, as well as French music playing throughout the building. Many rooms have views of the Blue Lagoon, a pool with a waterfall, or the Miami skyline. Restaurant, bar (with entertainment). In-room data ports, refrigerators, cable TV, in-room VCRs (and movies). Pool. Tennis courts. Gym. Laundry facilites. Business services, free parking, airport shuttle. Pets allowed. | 5800 Blue Lagoon Dr. 33126 | 305/264–4888 | fax 305/262–9049 | 281 rooms | $170–$235 room, $220–$465 suite | AE, D, DC, MC, V.

Mayfair House Hotel. This European-style luxury hotel is within the upscale Streets of Mayfair complex. Rooms are decorated in fluid Art Nouveau patterns and feature either a Japanese hot tub on the balcony or a Roman tub inside. Restaurant, bar, room service. In-room data ports, minibars, in-room hot tubs. Cable TV, in-room VCRs. Outdoor pool. Outdoor hot tub, sauna. Laundry services. Business services. Some pets (fee). | 3000 Florida Ave. 33133 | 305/441–0000 or 800/433–4555 | fax 305/447–9173 | www. mayfairhousehotel.com | 179 suites | $269–$800 | AE, D, DC, MC, V.

CORAL GABLES

Quality Inn, South. Official host of the Miami Metro Zoo, this two-story stucco motel has cozy, well-appointed rooms. It's 14 mi from downtown, but less than 10 mi from such attractions as the Miami Museum of Science, Monkey Jungle, and major shopping centers featuring Bloomingdale's and Macy's. Restaurant, bar. In-room data ports, microwaves, refrigerators, cable TV. Pool. Gym. Laundry facilites. Business services. Free parking. Pets allowed. | 14501 S. Dixie Rte. 33176 | 305/251–2000 or 800/228–5151 | fax 305/235–2225 | 100 rooms | $75–$125 | AE, D, DC, MC, V.

CRESTVIEW

Jameson Inn. This southeastern chain—which is found mostly in small towns—has hotels designed after elegant southern colonial mansions. Choose from one- and two-bedroom suites. From I–10, take exit 12 and follow Highway 85 south to Cracker Barrel Dr. Complimentary Continental breakfast. In-room data ports, some kitchenettes, some microwaves, some refrigerators. Cable TV, some in-room VCRs. Outdoor pool. Gym. Laundry facilities. Pets allowed. | 151 Cracker Barrel Dr. 32536 | 850/683–1778 or 800/526–3766 | fax 850/683–1779 | www.jamesoninns.com | 55 rooms | $59–$89 room, $159 suite | AE, D, DC, MC, V.

Crestview Holiday Inn. You'll find this simple stucco-and-sandstone motel at the intersection of Highway 85 and I–10. And you'll know you're in Florida when you see the shell-shape ceramic lamps, seashell-print bedspreads, and ocean-theme art on the walls. Restaurant, bar, room service. In-room data ports. Cable TV. Outdoor pool. Gym. Laundry facilities. Pets allowed (fee). | 4050 S. Ferdon Blvd. 32536 | 850/682–6111 or 800/465–4329 | fax 850/689–1189 | www.holiday-inn.com | 120 rooms | $74 | AE, D, DC, MC, V.

CRYSTAL RIVER

Best Western Crystal Resort. Directly on King's Bay, a spring-fed bay that leads into the Crystal River, this resort hotel offers rooms and efficiencies. It sits in the middle of Florida's "Nature Coast," a 150-mi stretch of coast along the state's western edge where eco-tourism dominates. The hotel is near the Crystal River Shopping Mall. Bar, picnic area. Some kitchenettes, some refrigerators. Cable TV. Pool. Hot tub. Dock, water sports, boating. Shops. Laundry facilities. Business services. Pets allowed (fee). | 614 N.W. Hwy. 19 34428 | 352/795–3171 or 800/435–4409 | fax 352/795–3179 | 114 rooms | $78–$110 | AE, D, DC, MC, V.

Comfort Inn Crystal River. This three-story Comfort Inn is 3 mi east of the beaches and 10 mi south of Homosassa Springs Nature World. The Crystal River Mall is 1 mi south. Picnic area, complimentary Continental breakfast. In-room data ports. Cable TV. Pool. Tennis court. Laundry facilities. Business services. Pets allowed (fee). | 4486 N. Suncoast Blvd. | 352/563–1500 | fax 352/563–5426 | 66 rooms | $54–$65 | AE, D, DC, MC, V.

Crystal River Days Inn. This single-story Days Inn is off Highway 19. The on-site restaurant is open 24 hours. You can fish off the boat ramp. Restaurant. Some in-room hot tubs. Cable TV. Outdoor pool. Dock, fishing. Laundry services. Pets allowed (fee). | 2380 Suncoast Blvd. (Hwy. 19) 34428 | 352/795–2111 or 800/962–0028 | fax 352/795–4126 | www.daysinn.com | 107 rooms | $60–$70 | AE, D, DC, MC, V.

Econo Lodge. This simple, affordable single-story motel offers free local calling and has a restaurant and lounge next door. Complimentary Continental breakfast. Refrigerators available. Cable TV. Outdoor pool. Laundry facilities. Business services. Pets allowed (fee). | 2575 Suncoast Blvd. (Hwy. 19) 34428 | 352/795–9447 or 800/553–2666 | fax 352/795–6431 | www.econolodge.com | 44 rooms | $50–$65 | AE, D, DC, MC, V.

DANIA BEACH

Sheraton Fort Lauderdale Airport Hotel. You enter this hotel via a courtyard, which has a large stone fountain. The hotel is located just off I–95, 1½ miles from the airport terminals. The beach is 7 mi east. Restaurant, bar. In-room data ports, some refrigerators. Cable TV. Pool. Hot tub, sauna. Tennis court. Gym. Laundry service. Business services, airport shuttle. Some pets allowed (fee). | 1825 Griffin Rd. 33004 | 954/920–3500 or 800/325–3535 | fax 954/927–2808 | www.sheraton.com | 250 rooms | $129–$149 | AE, D, DC, MC, V.

DAVENPORT

Comfort Inn Maingate South. This motel is off U.S. 27, only 5 mi from Walt Disney World, and allows visitors to avoid much of the traffic that surrounds the local attractions. There are two fast-food eateries within walking distance. Complimentary Continental breakfast. Some refrigerators. Cable TV. Outdoor pool, outdoor hot tub. Video games. Playground. Business services. Pets allowed (fee). | 5510 U.S. 27 N 33837 | 863/424–2811 | fax 863/424–1723 | www.comfortinn.com | 150 rooms | $59–$79 | AE, D, DC, MC, V.

Days Inn South of Magic Kingdom. This two-story inn is just 7 mi south of Walt Disney World. The heated pool is surrounded by palm trees. There are a handful of eateries within walking distance. In-room data ports, refrigerators. Cable TV. Outdoor pool. Outdoor hot tub. Video games. Laundry facilities. Business services. Pets allowed (fee). | 2524 Frontage Rd. 33837 | 863/929–3577 or 800/424–1880 | fax 863/420–8717 | www.daysinn.com | 122 rooms | $70 | AE, D, DC, MC, V.

DAVIE

Homestead Village Guest Studios. This hotel chain designs rooms with extended stays in mind. Studio rooms, which are tidy and modern, come equipped with kitchens and phones with both voice mail and data ports. In-room data ports, kitchenettes, microwaves, refrigerators. Cable TV. Gym. Laundry facilities, laundry service. Pets allowed (fee). | 7550 State Rd. 84 33317 | 954/476–1211 | fax 954/476–0026 | www.stayhsd.com | 125 rooms | $60–$70 | AE, D, DC, MC, V.

DAYTONA BEACH

Aruba Inn. This clean, modern two-story, Mediterranean-style facility has modest prices for its beachfront location. Rooms are modern, and most have terrific views of the beach. Picnic area. Some kitchenettes, some refrigerators. Cable TV. Pool. Beach. Laundry facilities. Pets allowed. | 1254 N. Atlantic Ave. 32118 | 904/253–5643 or 800/241–1406 | fax 904/248–1279 | www.arubainn.com | 32 rooms | $60–$75 | AE, D, MC, V.

Best Western Aku Tiki Inn. This Best Western inn, 1½ mi from the Daytona International Speedway, once sported a Polynesian theme. While no longer exotic-minded, it is still beachfront, and all rooms have balconies overlooking the Atlantic, and the large pool. Restaurant, bar (with entertainment), picnic area, room service. Some kitchenettes, some microwaves, refrigerators. Cable TV. Pool, pond, wading pool. Basketball. Beach. Shops, video games. Laundry facilities. Business services. Pets allowed. | 2225 S. Atlantic Ave. 32118 | 904/252–9631 or 800/258–8454 | fax 904/252–1198 | www.bestwestern.com | 132 rooms | $110–$120 | AE, D, DC, MC, V.

Days Inn Speedway. This three-story hotel is 4 mi from the beach and less than a mile from the Speedway. Prices skyrocket during race weeks. Restaurant. In-room data ports. Cable TV. Outdoor pool. Laundry services. Business services. Pets allowed (fee). | 2900 International Speedway Blvd. 32124 | 904/255–0541 or 800/544–8313 | fax 904/253–1468 | www.daysinn.com | 180 rooms | $69–$79 | AE, D, DC, MC, V.

Super 8 Speedway. Sitting just west of I–95, off exit 87, this two-story motel is 1½ mi west of the speedway and the airport, and 6 mi from the beach. Bar, complimentary Continental breakfast. Cable TV. Pool. Laundry facilities. Pets allowed. | 2992 W. International Speedway Blvd. (Hwy. 92) 32124 | 904/253–0643 or 800/800–8000 | fax 904/238–7764 | www.super8.com | 112 rooms | $45–$155 | AE, D, DC, MC, V.

DE FUNIAK SPRINGS

Best Western Crossroads Inn. Surrounded by eight acres of pecan groves, this motel sits halfway between Tallahassee and Pensacola at the junction of I–10 and Highway 331. Restaurant, bar, complimentary breakfast, room service. Cable TV. Pool. Pets allowed. | 2343 Freeport Rd. 32433 | 850/892–5111 | fax 850/892–2439 | www.bestwestern.com | 100 rooms | $59–$79 | AE, D, DC, MC, V.

DEERFIELD BEACH

Comfort Suites Deerfield Beach. This hotel, located next to the Quality Suites in the Newport Center Corporate Park (just west of I–95 at exit 36C), is just 4 miles west of the beaches and 15 mi north of Fort Lauderdale Airport. Flower beds and well-maintained lawns add a colorful touch to this chain, which offers spacious rooms with separate sitting areas. Complimentary cocktails are offered in the evenings. Restaurant, bar, complimentary Continental breakfast. In-room data ports, refrigerators. Cable TV. Pool. Hot tub. Laundry facilities. Business services, free parking. Pets allowed. | 1040 E. Newport Center Dr. 33442 | 954/570–8887 or 800/538–2777 | fax 954/570–5346 | www.sunbursthospitality.com | 101 suites | $109–$179 suites | AE, D, DC, MC, V.

Wellesley Inn Deerfield Beach. This four-story hotel with spacious rooms is 3 mi from the beach, among several office parks. Manicured lawns and many oak and palm trees help to add color to the corporate landscape. The hotel is just west of I–95, off exit 37. Complimentary Continental breakfast. In-room data ports, some microwaves, some refrigerators. Cable TV. Pool. Laundry facilities. Pets allowed. | 100 S.W. 12th Ave. 33442 | 954/428–0661 | fax 954/427–6701 | 79 rooms | $120–$145 | AE, D, DC, MC, V.

DELAND

Holiday Inn. This six-story hotel sits 2 mi north of downtown and Stetson University. Blue Spring State Park is 5 mi south. Restaurant, bar. In-room data ports, some microwaves, some refrigerators. Cable TV. Pool. Hot tub. Business services. Pets allowed (fee). | 350 E. International Speedway Blvd. 32724 | 904/738–5200 | fax 904/734–7552 | www.holiday-inn.com | 149 rooms | $80–$180 | AE, D, DC, MC, V.

Quality Inn. Just off I–4 at exit 56 (on Highway 44), this two-story motel sits 4 mi east of DeLand and 1 mi west of the Volusia County Fairgrounds. The Daytona Speedway is 15 mi to the east. Restaurant, bar (with entertainment), complimentary Continental breakfast, room service. In-room data ports, some microwaves, some refrigerators. Cable TV. Pool, wading pool. Gym. Laundry facilities. Business services. Pets allowed (fee). | 2801 E. New York Ave. 32724 | 904/736–3440 | fax 904/736–7484 | www.qualityinn.com | 113 rooms | $50–$95 | AE, D, DC, MC, V.

University Inn. Across the street from Stetson University and about a mile away from downtown DeLand, the University Inn provides quality service and a few surprises in its traditional two-story building, including eco-conscious rooms (with air and water filters) called Evergreen Rooms, and a nicely landscaped courtyard. Breakfast is served in the lobby. You can get your hair or nails done at the full-service salon. Complimentary Continental breakfast. Some microwaves, some refrigerators. Cable TV. Gym. Pool. Pets allowed (fee). | 644 N. Woodland Blvd. 32720 | 904/734–5711 or 800/345–8991 | fax 904/734–5716 | 60 rooms | $50–$60 | AE, D, DC, MC, V.

ENGLEWOOD
Days Inn. This two-story motel sits 2 mi north of Englewood Beach and the gulf, in a quiet area off Route 776. Complimentary Continental breakfast. Some in-room data ports, some kitchenettes, some microwaves, some refrigerators. Cable TV. Pool. Playground. Laundry facilities. Business services. Pets allowed (fee). | 2540 S. McCall Rd./Hwy. 776 34224 | 941/474–5544 800/887–5412 | fax 941/475–2124 | 84 rooms | $89–$99 | AE, D, DC, MC, V.

Veranda Inn of Englewood. Located on the Intracoastal Waterway, 2 mi north of the beach, this two-story hotel (with elevator) has basic accommodations. The veranda on the second floor is furnished with chairs for lounging and offers full views of the waterway. In-room data ports. Cable TV. Pool. Laundry facilities. Pets allowed (fee). | 2073 S. McCall Rd./Hwy. 776 34224 | 941/475–6533 or 800/633–8115 | 38 rooms | $85–$95 | AE, D, DC, MC, V.

EVERGLADES CITY
On the Banks of the Everglades. The name of this spacious B&B is a pun. The teal neo-classical facade reveals the teal inn to be the first bank in Collier County, built by Barron Collier in 1923. The inn keeps some original artifacts from the bank, including an old safe. A complimentary breakfast is served in the old vault. Picnic area, complimentary breakfast. No air-conditioning in some rooms, some kitchenettes, some microwaves, some refrigerators. Cable TV, TV in common area. Fishing, bicycles. Playground. Some pets allowed (fee). | 201 W. Broadway 34139 | 941/695–3151 or 888/431–1977 | fax 941/695–3335 | www.banksoftheeverglades.com | 10 rooms (5 with shared bath) | $55–$180 | Closed June–Oct. | A, DC, MC, V.

EVERGLADES NATIONAL PARK
Flamingo Lodge. The only home-away-from-home within Everglades National Park, this simple motel has the backdrop of grumbling alligators, raccoons, and a variety of chirping birds. The cottages are in a wooded area and can accommodate up to six guests. Florida Bay is nearby, but most rooms do not look out onto it. Reservations are mandatory in the winter. Restaurant (seasonal), bar, complimentary Continental breakfast (May–Oct.). Some kitchenettes, some refrigerators. No TV in some rooms. Pool. Gift shop. Laundry facilities. Some pets allowed. | 1 Flamingo Lodge Hwy. 33034 | 941/695–3101 or 800/600–3813 | fax 941/695–3921 | www.flamingolodge.com | 102 rooms, 24 cottages | $65–$95 lodge room, $115–$135 cottage | AE, D, DC, MC, V.

FLORIDA CITY
Everglades Motel. This simple, single-story motel is 2 mi south of Homestead; it's decorated with bright colors. Many restaurants are within walking distance. Cable TV. Outdoor pool. Laundry facilities. Pets allowed (fee). | 605 S. Krome Ave., Florida City 33030 | 305/247–4117 | 14 rooms | $32–$37 | AE, D, DC, MC, V.

Gateway to the Keys. This modern two- and three-story motel across the street from outlet stores and restaurants, was built in 1994. The tidy courtyard area has a pool and spa. It's 1 mi south of Homestead, and the Keys are 20 mi away. Complimentary Continental breakfast. In-room data ports, some microwaves, some refrigerators. Cable TV. Pool. Outdoor hot tub. Laundry facilities, laundry service. Business services. Pets allowed (fee). No smoking. | 411 S. Krome Ave. 33034 | 305/246–5100 or 800/528–1234 | fax 305/242–0056 | www.bestwestern.com | 74 rooms, 40 suites | $89–$99 room, $94–$114 suite | AE, D, DC, MC, V.

Hampton Inn. If you can't make it all the way to the Keys, try this two-story motel on the corner of U.S. 1, which was built in 1990. Complimentary Continental breakfast. In-room data ports. Cable TV. Outdoor pool. Pets allowed. | 124 E. Palm Dr. 33034 | 305/247–8833 or 800/426–7866 | fax 305/247–6456 | www.hampton-inn.com | 123 rooms | $110 | AE, D, DC, MC, V.

FORT LAUDERDALE

Best Western Oceanside Inn. This five-story hotel is just south of the Bahia Mar Marina, 1 mi north of the Broward Convention Center, and two blocks from the Jungle Queen. Rooms here have wonderful views of the water from private balconies. Restaurant, bar, complimentary breakfast. In-room data ports, in-room safes, refrigerators. Cable TV. Pool. Beach. Laundry facilities. Business services. Pets allowed. | 1180 Seabreeze Blvd. 33316 | 954/525–8115 | fax 954/527–0957 | 101 rooms | $99–$139 | AE, D, DC, MC, V.

Doubletree Guest Suites. Towering 14 stories above the Intracoastal Waterway, this all-suites hotel is two blocks west of the beaches. The Galleria Mall, with its many boutiques, is next door. All rooms have full kitchens and views of either the Atlantic, the waterway, or the skyline. Restaurant, bar, room service. Kitchenettes, microwaves, refrigerators. Cable TV. Pool. Hot tub. Gym. Dock. Laundry facilities. Business services. Pets allowed (fee). | 2670 E. Sunrise Blvd. 33304 | 954/565–3800 | fax 954/561–0387 | www.doubletree.com | 239 suites | $189–$209 | AE, D, DC, MC, V.

La Quinta Inn-Cypress Creek. This four-story motel, not even a mile west of I–95, stands on the northeast corner of the Fort Lauderdale Executive Airport. It is 9 mi north of downtown and 2 mi west of the beaches. In-room data ports, refrigerators. Cable TV. Pool. Hot tub. Gym. Laundry facilities. Business services. Pets allowed. | 999 W. Cypress Creek Rd. 33309 | 954/491–7666 | fax 954/491–7669 | 144 rooms | $119–$134 | AE, D, DC, MC, V.

Motel 6 Fort Lauderdale. Just east of I–95 at exit 27, this two-story motel is 3 mi north of the Fort Lauderdale International Airport and 3 mi west of the Broward Convention Center. Cable TV. Pool. Laundry facilities. Pets allowed. | 1801 Hwy. 84 33315 | 954/760–7999 | fax 954/832–0653 | 106 rooms | $48–$65 | AE, D, DC, MC, V.

Radisson Resort Coral Springs. This golf resort is 24 mi northwest of Fort Lauderdale, a 10-min drive from the Sawgrass Mills Mall, and 20 min from the beach. The seven-story hotel has a sunlit atrium in the center and a tropical garden, complete with bright, fresh flowers. Golfers will be impressed with Heron Bay Golf Club, on the premises. Restaurant, bar. In-room data ports, some minibars. Cable TV. Pool, hot tub, 2 saunas. 18-hole golf course. Gym. Video games. Laundry facilities, laundry service. Some pets allowed (fee). | 11775 Heron Bay Blvd., Coral Springs 33076 | 954/753–5598 | fax 954/753–5598 | wwww.radisson.com | 224 rooms, 6 suites | $129–$189 room, $219 suite | AE, D, MC, V.

Residence Inn Plantation. Two mi west of the Florida Turnpike and 15 min west of downtown Fort Lauderdale, this Residence Inn is composed of two four-story, L-shape buildings. All units have full kitchens; the two-bedroom units have fireplaces. Bar, complimentary breakfast, room service. In-room data ports, kitchenettes, microwaves, refrigerators. Cable TV. Pool. Hot tub. Gym. Laundry facilities. Business services. Pets allowed (fee). | 130 N. University Dr., Plantation 33324 | 954/723–0300 | fax 954/474–7385 | www.marriott.com | 138 suites | $139–$159 | AE, D, DC, MC, V.

Wellesley Inn and Suites. Three mi west of the Fort Lauderdale Executive Airport and less than a mile east of the Sabal Palm Golf Club, this all-suites hotel is easily accessed from the highways. I–95 is 3 mi to the east (take exit 32), and the Florida Turnpike is less than 1 mi to the west (take exit 62). Complimentary Continental breakfast. In-room data ports, some microwaves, some refrigerators. Cable TV. Pool. Laundry facilities. Business services. Pets allowed (fee). | 5070 N St. Hwy. 7 33319 | 954/484–6909 or 800/444–8888 | fax 954/731–2374 | 100 rooms | $79–$89 | AE, D, DC, MC, V.

The Westin, Fort Lauderdale. This 15-story hotel, just east of I–95 at exit 33A, towers above a three-acre lagoon around which you can jog. The hotel is just 1½ mi east of the Fort Lauderdale Executive Airport. Restaurant, bar, room service. In-room data ports, in-room safes, minibars, some microwaves. Cable TV. Pool. Hot tub, sauna. Gym, boating. Business services. Pets allowed. | 400 Corporate Dr. 33334 | 954/772–1331 or 800/937–8461 | fax 954/772–6867 | 293 rooms | $155–$225 | AE, D, DC, MC, V.

FORT MYERS

Baymont Inn Fort Myers. This four-story, salmon-colored building is right in central Fort Myers. Rooms are designed in early American style, with maplewood furniture, contrasting with the Floridian lobby's pastels and tropical plants. A light breakfast is brought to your room each morning. Continental breakfast. Some in-room data ports, some microwaves, some refrigerators. Pool. Golf. Boating, fishing. Laundry service. Pets allowed (fee). | 2717 Colonial Blvd. 33907 | 941/275–3500 or 800/428–3438 | fax 941/275–5426 | www. baymontinn.com | 123 rooms | $60–$117 | AE, D, DC, MC, V.

Comfort Suites Airport. This simple, economic two-story motel is off I–75 at exit 21, 1 mi west of the airport and 2 mi east of the Minnesota Twins spring training site. Bar, complimentary Continental breakfast. In-room data ports, microwaves, refrigerators. Cable TV. Pool. Hot tub. Gym. Laundry facilities. Business services. Airport shuttle. Some pets allowed. | 13651 Indian Paint La. 33912 | 941/768–0005 | fax 941/768–5458 | www. comfortsuites.com | 65 rooms | $54–$89.

La Quinta Inn Fort Myers. This two-story chain hotel has a white exterior with teal trim and a Southwestern architecture. It is 10 mi west of the airport. Complimentary Continental breakfast. In-room data ports. Cable TV, some in-room VCRs (and movies). Pool. Video games. Laundry services. Business services. Free parking. Some pets allowed. | 4850 Cleveland Ave. 33907 | 941/275–3300 or 800/531–5900 | fax 941/275–6661 | www.laquinta.com | 130 rooms | $95–$115 | AE, D, DC, MC, V.

Radisson Inn Sanibel Gateway. This Radisson hotel uses Southwestern color schemes and artwork; the lobby has dark tiles and a fountain. The three-story inn is just across the bridge from Sanibel Island, in south Fort Myers. The Olympic-size pool has an underwater music system. Restaurant, bar, room service. In-room data ports, refrigerators. Cable TV. Pool. Hot tub. Laundry facilities. Bicycles (in season). Business services. Some pets allowed (fee). | 20091 Summerlin Rd. 33908 | 941/466–1200 or 800/333–3333 | fax 941/466–3797 | www.radisson.com | 158 rooms | $109–$199 | AE, D, DC, MC, V.

Ta Ki-Ki. This relaxed motel has a private fishing pier with a covered pavilion on the Caloosahatchee River. It is within walking distance of downtown's historic district. Picnic area. Some kitchenettes. Cable TV. Pool. Dock, boating. Some pets allowed. | 2631 First St. 33916 | 941/334–2135 | fax 941/332–1879 | www.cyberstreet.com/takiki | 28 rooms | $42–$80 | AE, D, DC, MC, V.

Wellesley Inn and Suites. The portico and fountain at the entrance provide a stylish welcome to this four-story hotel 4 mi from downtown. There is a landscaped courtyard surrounding the heated pool, and barbecue grills. Continental breakfast. In-room data ports, some kitchenettes, some microwaves, some refrigerators. Cable TV. Pool. Golf, tennis. Health club. Laundry facilities, laundry service. Some pets allowed (fee). | 4400 Ford St. 33916 |

941/278–3949 or 800/444–8888 | fax 941/278–3670 | www.wellesleyinnandsuites.com | 105 rooms | $107–$119 | AE, D, DC, MC, V.

FORT MYERS BEACH

Best Western Beach Resort. The white exterior of this five-story hotel blends with the beach beside it. All rooms have Gulf views from private balconies and tropical prints. Picnic area, complimentary Continental breakfast. Kitchenettes, microwaves, refrigerators. Cable TV. Pool. Water sports. Playground. Laundry facilities. Business services. Some pets allowed (fee). | 684 Estero Blvd. 33931 | 941/463–6000 or 800/336–4045 | fax 941/463–3013 | www.bestwestern.com | 75 rooms | $199–$209 | AE, D, DC, MC, V.

FORT PIERCE

Comfort Inn. This Comfort Inn is 4 mi from the beach and 1½ mi from downtown. There are a number of restaurants within walking distance. Complimentary Continental breakfast. In-room data ports, some kitchenettes. Cable TV. Outdoor pool. Outdoor hot tub. Laundry facilities. Business services. Some pets (fee). | 3236 S. U.S. 1 34982 | 561/461–2323 or 800/228–5150 | fax 561/464–5151 | www.comfortinn.com | 60 rooms | $69–$159 | AE, D, DC, MC, V.

Days Inn. This two-story motel is 8 mi from the beach. While there is no restaurant on property, there are many restaurants within a mile of the property. The motel is right off I–95 at exit 65. In-room data ports, some refrigerators, some microwaves. Cable TV. Outdoor pool. Laundry facilities. Business services. Pets allowed (fee). | 6651 Darter Ct. 34945 | 561/466–4066 or 800/544–8313 | fax 561/468–3260 | www.daysinn.com | 125 rooms | $55–$60 | AE, D, DC, MC, V.

Garden State Motel. This single-story motel is on the southern tip of Fort Pierce, near Port St. Lucie. There is a shuffleboard court. At night the tall palm and oak trees are lit up. Some kitchenettes, microwaves, refrigerators. Cable TV, no room phones. Outdoor pool. Some pets allowed. | 5220 S. U.S. 1 34982 | 561/461–7031 | fax 561/595–8896 | 17 rooms | $55–$70 | AE, D, MC, V.

Holiday Inn Express. This two-story motel is in the western part of town. The beach is 8 mi away and Fort Pierce Jai Alai is 1 mi away. There are restaurants within walking distance. Complimentary Continental breakfast. Cable TV. Pool, wading pool. Laundry facilities. Business services. Some pets allowed. | 7151 Okeechobee Rd. 34945 | 561/464–5000 or 800/664–7775 | fax 561/461–9573 | www.holiday-inn.com | 103 rooms | $69–$79 | AE, D, DC, MC, V.

FORT WALTON BEACH

Days Inn. This two-story motel is in the middle of Fort Walton Beach, 2 mi from the beach. There is a restaurant next door. Complimentary Continental breakfast. Refrigerators, microwaves. Cable TV. Outdoor pool. Some pets allowed. | 135 Miracle Strip Pkwy. 32548 | 850/244–6184 or 800/544–8313 | fax 850/244–5764 | www.daysinn.com | 62 rooms | $68–$74 | AE, D, DC, MC, V.

Marina Motel. This motel across the street from Choctawhatchee Bay offer many rooms with excellent ocean views. Restaurants are within walking distance. Complimentary Continental breakfast. Some kitchenettes, microwaves, refrigerators. Cable TV. Outdoor pool. Docks, boating, fishing. Laundry facilities. Pets allowed (fee). | 1345 Miracle Strip Pkwy. 32548 | 850/244–1129 | fax 850/243–6063 | 36 rooms, 2 suites | $50–$125 | AE, D, DC, MC, V.

GAINESVILLE

Best Western Gateway Grand. Built in 1998, this three-story hotel has a tranquil setting on a hill overlooking corn fields. There's a restaurant nearby, and the downtown Gainesville historic district is 12 mi away. Complimentary Continental breakfast. In-room data ports, some refrigerators, some microwaves. Cable TV. Pool. Outdoor hot tub. Gym. Laundry service.

Business services. Some pets. | 4200 N.W. 97th Blvd. 32606 | 352/331–3336 | fax 352/331–3337 | www.bestwestern.com | 152 rooms | $79–$89 | AE, D, DC, MC, V.

Econo Lodge. This inexpensive motel is six blocks from the University of Florida and 6 miles from the Gainesville Raceway. There are many restaurants within walking distance. In-room data ports. Cable TV. Pool. Pets allowed. | 2649 S.W. 13th St. 32608 | 352/373–7816 | fax 352/372–9099 | www.econolodge.com | 53 rooms | $47–$57 | AE, D, DC, MC, V.

La Quinta. Just 12 mi from the airport, this chain motel is across the street from a mall with shops and restaurants. Complimentary Continental breakfast. In-room data ports, some microwaves, some refrigerators. Cable TV. Pool. Pets allowed. | 920 N.W. 69th Terr. 32605 | 352/332–6466 | fax 352/332–7074 | www.laquinta.com | 131 rooms, 4 suites | $65–$69, $89–$99 suites | AE, D, DC, MC, V.

Magnolia Plantation Bed & Breakfast. This Second Empire Victorian home dates to 1885. The mansard roof, in addition to ten original fireplaces, contributes to the inn's elegance. Wine and snacks are served nightly. Complimentary breakfast. Refrigerators. Some in-room VCRs, some room phones, no TV in some rooms. Massage. Pets allowed (restrictions). No smoking. | 309 S.E. 7th St. 32601 | 352/375–6653 | fax 352/338–0303 | www.magnoliabnb.com | 5 rooms, 3 cottages | $90–$105, $135–$165 cottages | AE, MC, V.

Ramada Limited–Gainesville. This charming Ramada Inn is spread out over 4 wooded acres, next to I–75. A movie theater, shopping center, and restaurants are within walking distance. Complimentary Continental breakfast. In-room data ports. Cable TV. Pool. Business services. Pets allowed (fee). | 4021 S.W. 40th Blvd. 32608 | 352/373–0392 | fax 352/336–7855 | www.ramada.com | 114 rooms | $64–$74 | AE, D, DC, MC, V.

Residence Inn by Marriott. This luxurious hotel is ideally located, 4 mi from the university and 7 mi from the airport. Also, most local attractions are within 10 mi, and the Bivens Arm Nature Park is a half-mile away. Complimentary Continental breakfast. Kitchenettes, microwaves, refrigerators. Cable TV. Pool. Hot tub. Laundry service. Business services. Airport shuttle. Some pets allowed (fee). | 4001 S.W. 13th St. 32608 | 352/371–2101 or 888/236–2427 | fax 352/371–2247 | www.residenceinn.com | 80 suites | $90–$125 suites | AE, D, DC, MC, V.

GULF BREEZE

Holiday Inn Gulf Breeze Bay Beach. This hotel comprises three two-story buildings on Pensacola Bay. It's 6 mi from Pensacola Beach, and 5 mi from the zoo. Restaurant. In-room data ports, some microwaves, some refrigerators. Cable TV. Pool, wading pool. Laundry service. Business services. Pets allowed (fee). | 51 Gulf Breeze Pkwy. 32561 | 850/932–2214 | fax 850/932–0932 | www.holiday-inn.com | 160 rooms, 8 suites in 3 buildings | $89–$109, $129 suites | AE, D, DC, MC, V.

HAINES CITY

Best Western Lake Hamilton. Built in 1994 and just off U.S. 27, this Best Western has a quiet country setting and is surrounded by three fields. The famed Southern Dunes Championship Golf Course is only 3 mi away. Complimentary Continental breakfast. Some microwaves, some refrigerators. Cable TV. Pool. Tennis court. Laundry facilities. Business services. Pets allowed. | 605 B. Moore Rd. 33844 | 863/421–6929 | fax 863/422–0409 | www.bestwestern.com | 45 rooms, 5 suites | $55–$65, $75 suites | AE, D, DC, MC, V.

Howard Johnson–Haines City. This hotel was built in 1973 and remodeled in 1998. On U.S. 27, this two-story property is 20 mi from Walt Disney World. Restaurant, bar. Some microwaves, some refrigerators available. Cable TV. Pool. Laundry service. Business services. Some pets (fee). | 1504 U.S. 27 S 33844 | 863/422–8621 or 800/406–1411 | fax 863/421–4745 | www.hojo.com | 120 rooms | $59–$89 | AE, D, DC, MC, V.

HOLLYWOOD

Days Inn Airport South. This seven-story motel was renovated in 2000. The Ft. Lauderdale/Hollywood International Airport is minutes away, as are Hollywood Beach (3 mi) and the Broward County Convention Center. There is a handful of eateries within walking distance. Bar. Complimentary Continental breakfast. In-room data ports, some microwaves, some refrigerators. Cable TV. Pool. Outdoor hot tub. Gym. Laundry facilities. Business services, airport shuttle. Pets allowed (fee). | 2601 N. 29th Ave. 33020 | 954/923–7300 | fax 954/921–6706 | www.daysinn.com | 114 rooms | $89–$129 | AE, D, DC, MC, V.

Holiday Inn. This Holiday Inn is convenient to Fort Lauderdale–Hollywood International Airport, I–95, and the Tri-Rail station. Hollywood Beach is 3 mi away, and fast-food restaurants a short walk. Restaurant, bar. In-room data ports, some microwaves, some refrigerators. Cable TV. Pool. Outdoor hot tub. Gym. Laundry facilities. Business services, airport shuttle. Some pets allowed. | 2905 Sheridan St. 33020 | 954/925–9100 | fax 954/925–5512 | www.holidayinnfll.com | 140 rooms, 10 suites | $159–$170, $175–$250 suites | AE, D, DC, MC, V.

HOMESTEAD

Homestead Days Inn. Every aspect of this motel has been updated in the past few years after it was ravaged by Hurricane Andrew. The lobby is a warm environment with comfy couches and is usually filled with guests reading newspapers. Rooms are bright with tropical colors on the bedspreads. Some rooms in the two-story building look out to the pool courtyard. Everglades National Park is 15 mi west. Bar, complimentary Continental breakfast. In-room data ports, refrigerators. Cable TV. Pool. Laundry facilities. Business services. Some pets allowed. | 51 S. Homestead Blvd. 33030 | 305/245–1260 | fax 305/247–0939 | www.daysinn.com | 100 rooms | $89–$109 | AE, D, DC, MC, V.

Ramada Limited Homestead. This Ramada is 2 mi south of the famed Coral Castle and 4 mi from the Miami-Dade Homestead Motorsports Complex. Restaurants are across the street. Complimentary Continental breakfast. In-room data ports, some refrigerators. Cable TV. Pool. Laundry facilities. Business services. Some pets allowed. | 990 N. Homestead Blvd. 33030 | 305/247–7020 | fax 305/247–7020 | www.ramada.com | 148 rooms | $69–$99 | AE, D, DC, MC, V.

HOMOSASSA SPRINGS

The Crown Hotel. This beautiful Victorian hotel dates to the early 1900s. The opulence is full-blown here, from the huge chandelier in the lobby to the elegant circular staircase. Replicas of England's famed Crown Jewels are in the lobby. It's 17 mi east of Homosassa Springs via Hwy. 44. Restaurant, bar, complimentary Continental breakfast. Cable TV. Pool. Business services. Some pets allowed (fee). | 109 N. Seminole Ave., Inverness 34450 | 352/344–5555 | fax 352/726–4040 | www.thecrownhotel.com | 34 rooms | $50–$80 | AE, MC, V.

Ramada Inn. This two-story Ramada Inn was built in 1970 and is adjacent to the Homosassa Springs State Wildlife Park. Restaurant, bar, room service. In-room data ports, some refrigerators. Cable TV. Pool. Tennis Court. Playground. Business services, airport shuttle. Some pets allowed. | U.S. 19 at Hwy. 490A 34446 | 352/628–4311 or 888/298–2054 | fax 352/628–4311 | www.ramada.com | 103 rooms, 1 suite | $59–$69, $139 suite | AE, D, DC, MC, V.

ISLAMORADA

Sands of Islamorada. Spectacular sunrises, an extremely friendly staff, and macaws await you at this oceanfront resort. Some of the rooms have wraparound porches. Picnic area. In-room data ports, some kitchenettes, microwaves, refrigerators. Cable TV. Pool. Outdoor hot tub. Dock, boating, fishing. Pets allowed (fee). | 80051 Overseas Hwy. 33036

| 305/664–2791 | fax 305/664–2886 | www.florida-keys.fl.us/sandsislamorada | 9 rooms | $115–$185 | MC, V.

White Gate Court. Far from the crowds of Islamorada's business district, this resort consists of five wooden cottages laid out on 3 pretty, landscaped acres along 200 ft of white-sand beach. Barbecue grills and big palm trees contribute to the relaxing mood. Picnic area. Kitchenettes, microwaves, refrigerators. Cable TV. Beach, dock, boating, bicycles. Laundry facilities. Business services. Pets allowed. | 76010 Overseas Hwy. 33036 | 305/664–4136 or 800/645–4283 | fax 305/664–9746 | www.whitegatecourt.com | 7 rooms | $105–$180 | MC, V.

JACKSONVILLE

Amerisuites. This six-story hotel is right off Baymeadows Road, 11 mi from Jacksonville Beach. All accommodations are one- and two-bedroom suites. There's no restaurant in the hotel, but there are several within walking distance. Complimentary Continental breakfast. In-room data ports, microwaves, refrigerators, some in-room hot tubs. Cable TV, in-room VCRs. Pool. Gym. Laundry facilities. Business services. Pets allowed. | 8277 Western Way Cir. 32256 | 904/737–4477 | fax 904/739–1649 | 112 suites | $79–$99 suites | AE, D, DC, MC, V.

Best Inns of America. This two-story chain hotel is a beacon to budget travelers. Restaurants are a short walk away. Picnic area, complimentary Continental breakfast. In-room data ports, some refrigerators. Cable TV. Pool. Business services. Some pets allowed. | 8220 Dix Ellis Tr. 32256 | 904/739–3323 | fax 904/739–3323 | 61 rooms | $51–$60 | AE, D, DC, MC, V.

Comfort Suites Baymeadows. Suites decorated in hues often described as 'tropical' are a feature of this hotel built in 1988. Offices of many corporations are based in the Baymeadows suburb, so this spot may be a good option for those on business trips. Complimentary Continental breakfast. In-room data ports, refrigerators, some microwaves. Cable TV, some in-room VCRs. Pool. Outdoor hot tub. Laundry facilities. Business services. Pets allowed. | 8333 Dix Ellis Tr. 32256 | 904/739–1155 | fax 904/731–0752 | www.comfortinn.com | 128 suites | $89–$119 | AE, D, DC, MC, V.

Days Inn South. This two-story Days Inn was built in 1998 and is just off I–95 which may make it a convenient choice for you if you're touring the area's far-flung attractions or planning business meetings in several locations. Palm trees shade a swimming pool and you'll find restaurants just a short distance away. In-room data ports. Cable TV. Pool. Business services. Some pets allowed. | 5649 Cagle Rd. 32216 | 904/733–3890 | fax 904/636–9841 | www.daysinn.com | 120 rooms | $65 | AE, D, DC, MC, V.

Holiday Inn Baymeadows. This four-story Holiday Inn in the office park area of Jacksonville gets you in the tropical mood right in the lobby where tropical plants fill big urns and colorful fish zip about in large saltwater and freshwater aquariums. You'll find the hotel on the south side of Jacksonville about 10 mi from downtown. Restaurant, bar, room service. In-room data ports, some microwaves, some refrigerators. Cable TV, some in-room VCRs. Pool. Gym. Video games. Laundry facilities. Business services. Pets allowed. | 9150 Baymeadows Rd. 32256 | 904/737–1700 | www.holiday-inn.com | fax 904/737–0207 | 240 rooms, 9 suites | $69–$89, $79–$119 suites | AE, D, DC, MC, V.

Holiday Inn Express Hotel & Suites. This four-story hotel offers Holiday Inn amenities but no restaurant, although the hotel treats you to a complimentary breakfast that's a bit more extensive than the bagel and brew offered by some hotels. Just off I–95, it's a popular stop with passing-through travelers, and parents of University of North Florida students often settle in here to visit their offspring—the university is 8 mi away. In-room data ports, some microwaves, some refrigerators. Cable TV. Pool. Gym. Laundry facilities. Business services. Some pets. | 4675 Salisbury Rd. 32256 | 904/332–9500 or 888/610–3555 | fax 904/332–9222 | www.holiday-inn.com | 50 rooms, 38 suites | $109, $129 suites | AE, D, DC, MC, V.

Homewood Suites Jacksonville-Baymeadows. You'll find one- and two-bedroom suites here, some with fireplaces, which is definitely an unusual feature in a Florida hostelry. A number of restaurants are within walking distance; Jacksonville beaches are a short drive. Complimentary Continental breakfast. In-room data ports, kitchenettes, microwaves, refrigerators. Cable TV, in-room VCRs (and movies). Pool. Outdoor hot tub. Gym. Laundry facilities. Business services. Some pets allowed (fee). | 8737 Baymeadows Rd. 32256 | 904/733–9299 | fax 904/448–5889 | www.homewood-suites.com | 116 suites | $119–$175 suites | AE, D, DC, MC, V.

Inns of America. This three-story motel has a landscaped pool area with a pretty gazebo. The beach is 10 mi away, and there are a number of restaurants within 2 mi. Complimentary Continental breakfast. Some refrigerators, some microwaves. Cable TV. Pool. Laundry facilities. Some pets allowed. | 4300 Salisbury Rd. N 32216 | 904/281–0198 | fax 904/296–3580 | 124 rooms | $45–$55 | AE, MC, V.

La Quinta Orange Park. Built in 1980, this two-story chain hotel has a 24-hr restaurant next door and is in the Orange Park area, home to a variety of restaurants and shops. The Orange Park Greyhound Track is just a mile to the east. Complimentary Continental breakfast. In-room data ports, microwaves available, refrigerators. Pool. Laundry facilities. Business services. Some pets allowed. | 8555 Blanding Blvd. 32244 | 904/778–9539 | fax 904/779–5214 | www.laquinta.com | 121 rooms, 1 suite | $59–$77, $125 suite | AE, D, DC, MC, V.

La Quinta Baymeadows. This two-story La Quinta is in the suburban Baymeadows area where many corporations have headquarters in office parks. Beaches are 12 mi to the east; restaurants are nearby. Complimentary Continental breakfast. In-room data ports, some microwaves, some refrigerators. Cable TV. Pool. Laundry facilities, laundry service. Business services. Pets allowed. | 8255 Dix Ellis Tr. 32256 | 904/731–9940 | fax 904/731–3854 | www.laquinta.com | 104 rooms, 2 suites | $76–$93, $99–$106 suites | AE, D, DC, MC, V.

Motel 6 Southeast. This single-story motel is a likely spot for budget travelers. Jacksonville Landing is 8 mi and Jacksonville International Airport 20 mi. Cable TV. Pool. Laundry facilities. Some pets allowed. | 8285 Dix Ellis Tr. 32256 | 904/731–8400 | fax 904/730–0781 | www.motel6.com | 109 rooms | $41–$51 | AE, D, DC, MC, V.

Omni Jacksonville Hotel. This smart, 16-story hotel smack in the middle of downtown Jacksonville has a luxuriously decorated, four-story atrium lobby and a rooftop pool and sundeck overlooking the St. Johns River. Many rooms have attractive views of the city. Restaurant, bar, room service. In-room data ports, minibars. Cable TV. Pool. Gym. Laundry facilities. Business services, parking (fee). Pets allowed (fee). | 245 Water St. 32202 | 904/355–6664 | fax 904/791–4863 | www.omnihotels.com | 348 rooms | $159–$179 | AE, D, DC, MC, V.

Quality Inn & Suites. Alltel Stadium is 8 mi from this two-story property, making this a popular spot for sports fans. Both hotel rooms and small suites are available here. Picnic area. Complimentary Continental breakfast. In-room data ports, some microwaves, some refrigerators. Cable TV. Pool. Gym. Business services, airport shuttle. Pets allowed (fee). | 1153 Airport Rd. 32218 | 904/741–4600 | fax 904/741–4424 | www.qualityinn.com | 199 rooms, 25 suites in four buildings | $50–$55, $75–$80 suites | AE, D, DC, MC, V.

Ramada Inn Mandarin. This two-story property in the nearby town of Mandarin, which was once the home of author Harriet Beecher Stowe, was built in 1985. Today, the Comedy Zone resides here, luring comedians from across the nation. Restaurant, bar (with entertainment), complimentary breakfast, room service. In-room data ports, some microwaves, some refrigerators. Cable TV. Pool, wading pool. Laundry facilities. Business services. Some pets allowed (fee). | 3130 Hartley Rd. 32257 | 904/268–8080 | fax 904/262–8718 | www.ramada.com | 149 rooms, 3 suites | $67–$80, $135–$150 suites | AE, D, DC, MC, V.

Ramada Inn Jacksonville Downtown. Built in 1984, this big hotel sprawls over 19 attractively landscaped acres. During football season, it's often packed with fans attending the games at Alltel Stadium, just steps away. Restaurant, bar, room service. In-room data ports, some microwaves, some refrigerators. Cable TV. Pool. Outdoor hot tub. Tennis court. Laundry service. Business services. Pets allowed (fee). | 5865 Arlington Expressway 32211 | 904/724–3410 | fax 904/727–7606 | www.ramada.com | 270 rooms in 5 buildings | $49–$89 | AE, D, DC, MC, V.

Red Roof Inn. This two-story motel is 17 mi southwest of downtown Jacksonville, off I-295. Several chain restaurants are a short distance away. In-room data ports. Cable TV. Pool. Business services. Some pets allowed. | 6099 Youngerman Cir. 32244 | 904/777–1000 | fax 904/777–1005 | www.redroof.com | 108 rooms | $65–$75 | AE, D, DC, MC, V.

Residence Inn by Marriott. In this two-story Residence Inn on the south side of Jacksonville, 28 of the units have lofts and/or fireplaces, a cozy touch on cool winter nights here. You'll find several restaurants nearby and the hotel offers complimentary area transportation. Complimentary Continental breakfast. In-room data ports, kitchenettes, microwaves, refrigerators. Cable TV. Pool. 3 outdoor hot tubs. Laundry facilities, laundry service. Business services. Pets allowed (fee). | 8365 Dix Ellis Tr. 32256 | 904/733–8088 or 888/236–2427 | fax 904/731–8354 | 112 suites | $130–$175 suites | AE, D, DC, MC, V.

JENSEN BEACH

Hutchinson Island Marriott Beach Resort. This 200-acre resort attracts many families, with its many recreational activities, restaurants, swimming pool, and complimentary tram service to get around the sprawl. Many of the rooms are in three four-story buildings built around a central courtyard. The rest are in apartments tucked here and there throughout the property. 4 Restaurants, 2 bars. In-room dataports, some kitchenettes, some microwaves, refrigerators, cable TV. 4 pools. Hot tub. 18-hole golf course, putting green, 13 tennis courts. Health club, beach, water sports, dock, boating, fishing, bicycles. Babysitting, children's programs (ages 5–11), playground. Laundry facilities, laundry service. Business services. Pets allowed (fee). | 555 N.E. Ocean Blvd., Hutchinson Island, Stuart 34996 | 561/225–3700 or 800/775–5936 | fax 561/225–0033 | www.marriott.com | 298 rooms, 72 suites, 150 condos | $209–$219 room, $259–$299 suite, $349–$399 condo | AE, DC, MC, V.

River Palm Cottages & Fish Camp On the western bank of Indian River Lagoon, this 7¼-acre tropical spread has cottages, bungalows, and houses. You can fish in the ocean or go bird-watching on eco-tours, or simply relax in a *chickee* hut or hammock. Picnic area. Some kitchenettes, some microwaves, some refrigerators, cable TV. Pool. Fishing, boating, dock. Playground. Laundry facilities. Pets allowed (fee). | 2325 N.E. Indian River Dr., Jensen Beach 34957 | 561/334–0401 or 800/305–0511 | fax 561/334–0527 | www.riverpalmcottages.com | 25 units | $125–$159 | AE, D, DC, MC, V.

JUPITER

Wellesley Inn. Adjacent to the Fisherman's Wharf Shopping Center, this three-story hotel is just 5 mi from the region's popular Jonathan Dickinson Park, where sports opportunities include canoeing and cycling. Complimentary Continental breakfast. In-room data ports. Cable TV. Pool. Laundry facilities. Business services. Pets allowed. | 34 Fisherman's Wharf 33477 | 561/575–7201 or 800/444–8888 | fax 561/575–1169 | www.wellesleyinnandsuites.com | 93 rooms, 11 suites | $109–179, $129–$189 suites | AE, D, DC, MC, V.

KEY LARGO

Howard Johnson Resort. Just a short distance from John Pennekamp Coral Reef State Park, this hotel is right on the ocean, has a private beach and fishing and snorkeling equipment. Restaurant, bar. In-room data ports, some microwaves, refrigerators. Cable TV.

Pool. Beach, dock, fishing. Laundry facilities. Business services. Some pets allowed. | MM 102 on U.S. 1 33037 | 305/451–1400 or 800/406–1411 | fax 305/451–3953 | www.hojo.com | 100 rooms | $189–$249 | AE, D, DC, MC, V.

KEY WEST

Center Court Historic Inn & Cottages. Only a block away from the touristy Duval street is this sprawling array of intimate lodgings. Each unit is uniquely designed with ceiling fans and some even have their own pools or Jacuzzis. The landscaped gardens complement the main Inn that was given an award by the Key West Historical Preservation Society. There are hammocks and a complimentary happy hour for proper relaxation, not to mention the love-seat within one of the pools for cuddling and sipping your drink surrounded by the tropical foliage. The attentive concierge can arrange anything from baby-sitting to bicycle deliveries—anything that will make your stay more pleasant. Complimentary breakfast. Some in-room data ports, in-room safes, some kitchenettes, some refrigerators. Cable TV. 2 pools. Outdoor hot tubs. Health club. Beach, bicycles. Laundry facilities. Pets allowed (fee). | 915 Center St. 33040 | 305/296–9292 or 800/797–8787 | fax 305/294–4104 | www.centercourtkw.com | 5 rooms, 17 cottages, 1 house | $138–$188 room, $188–$348 cottage, $358 house | AE, D, MC, V.

Cuban Club Suites (and La Casa de Luces). These two lodgings make up a private complex of rooms and town house–style suites overlooking Duval Street. The full concierge is able to set you up with tours, sports, you name it. With the beach only 3 blocks away and the 20-ft vaulted ceilings with skylights, you're sure to have a sunny disposition. The original building, built in 1860 as a social club for Cuban cigar makers, was later used as a

A DOG'S BEACH

Where, oh, where can your little dog go? Dogs love the beach. They can kick up sand, chase frisbees and gulls, and jump over the waves; swimming in the water off a causeway, they can catch waves from passing boats. Throughout Florida, pet policy varies radically from one area to another—from one park to another, from one beach to another, and from coast to coast. At some beaches, dogs are permitted off-leash; more often they must be leashed or at least obedient to voice commands. Sometimes permits are required; sometimes not. Some parks prohibit pets altogether; some provide plastic bags for life's little accidents—or more: InnoPet Park in Coral Springs (*see* Boca Raton, above) even has doggie showers, and Naples' Veterans Park has a doggie drinking fountain. In Key West, where everyone seems to have a dog, many a pooch is walked on the strand locals know as Dog Beach, next to Louie's Back Yard Restaurant near the southernmost point. St. Augustine has Paws Park, on Wildwood Road between Route 1 and Route 207, off I–95. A part of Treaty Park, it's completely fenced and full of shade trees. There's even a special area just for smaller pups. And no leashes are allowed. Throughout the state, be alert for alligators in fresh water and pygmy rattlesnakes in wooded areas in summer. Many of the legalities are discussed in www.doortosummer.com, a website devoted to life in the tropics; reader updates keep you abreast of current regulations.

gentlemen's club. After a fire in 1983, the building was rebuilt with modern luxuries including tiled counters, French doors, and balconies wrapping around the building in New Orleans style. Some units come with washer and dryer. Some in-room safes. Cable TV. Hot tub. Free parking. Pets allowed. | 1108 Duval St. (lobby at 422 Amelia St.) 33040 | 305/296–0465 or 800/432–4849 | fax 305/293–7669 | www.keywestcubanclub.com | 8 suites | $79–$349 | AE, MC, V.

Curry Mansion Inn. Nestled alongside the original 1899 Curry Mansion, this B&B has elegant rooms appointed with wicker furniture and handmade quilts. The pool is surrounded by lush foliage. Complimentary breakfast. Refrigerators. Cable TV. Pool. Beach. Library. Laundry facilities. Business services. Some pets allowed. No smoking. | 511 Caroline St. 33040 | 305/294–5349 or 800/253–3466 | fax 305/294–4093 | www.currymansion.com | 28 rooms | $180–$325 | AE, D, DC, MC, V.

Frances Street Bottle Inn. This B&B in an 1875 Conch house is named for the collection of rare antique bottles and marine articles scattered throughout the rooms. The porches of some rooms and the brick patio are shaded by poinciana trees—perfect places for spending a relaxing evening. Picnic area, complimentary Continental breakfast. Some refrigerators. Cable TV, no room phones. Outdoor hot tub. Bicycles. Business services. Pets allowed. No smoking. | 535 Frances St. 33040 | 305/294–8530 or 800/294–8530 | fax 305/294–1628 | www.bottleinn.com | 7 rooms | $135–$165 | AE, MC, V.

Holiday Inn, La Concha. This seven-story hotel in the heart of Old Town dates back to the 1930s and is Key West's tallest building. The observation deck provides a panoramic view of the island. 3 restaurants, bar, room service. In-room data ports. Cable TV. Pool. Laundry service. Business services. Pets allowed. | 430 Duval St. 33040 | 305/296–2991 | fax 305/294–3283 | www.holiday-inn.com | 146 rooms, 14 suites | $179–$450, $525 suites | AE, D, DC, MC, V.

Key Lodge. This single-story lodge in Old Town is near Hemingway House. Rooms are basic motel. The Atlantic Ocean is within walking distance. Complimentary Continental breakfast. Some kitchenettes, refrigerators. Cable TV. Pool. Pets allowed (fee). | 1004 Duval St. 33040 | 305/296–9915 or 800/458–1296 | fax 305/292–5222 | www.keylodge.com | 22 rooms | $165–$180 | AE, D, MC, V.

Pelican Landing. This four-story condominium complex is on Garrison Bight. Rooms are fully furnished and equipped. Tennis privileges across the street at Bayview Park are included. Picnic area. In-room data ports, in-room safes, kitchenettes, microwaves, refrigerators. Cable TV, in-room VCRs. Pool. Dock, boating. Laundry facilities. Business services. Pets allowed. | 915 Eisenhower Dr. 33040 | 305/293–9730 | fax 305/296–7792 | www.centercourthideaways.com | 16 units | $189–$324 | AE, D, MC, V.

Speakeasy Inn. With a rich history of rum-running and cigars, this inn has some of the most spacious and relaxing rooms in town. The Saltillo-tiled rooms and oak floors provide a cool refuge from the heat, but the bright artwork and throw rugs spice it up. The house was formerly owned by Raul Vasquez, who smuggled liquor in from Cuba during Prohibition. The current owner, Thomas Favelli, runs the small Key West Havana Cigar Company in the front lobby, the only place to smoke in the inn. The full concierge can arrange massages, water sport activities, or rooms at their other facility, the Casa 325 Suites, just down the block, with more classy rooms and a pool. Some microwaves, some refrigerators. Some room phones. Parking. Some pets allowed (fee). | 117 Duval St. 33040 | 305/296–2680 or 800/217–4884 | fax 305/296–2608 | www.keywestcigar.com | 15 rooms in 2 buildings | $85–$250 | AE, D, MC, V.

KISSIMMEE

Comfort Suites Main Gate Resort. The suites at this three-story all-suites hotel are actually one oversized room with a separate sitting area and two queen-size or one king-size bed. Many have double sofa beds, allowing you to sleep six—great if you've got more than two kids. Free Disney shuttle. It's 10 mi from Walt Disney World. I–4 exit 25B, west 3 mi on U.S. 192. Complimentary Continental breakfast. In-room data ports, in-room safes, microwaves, refrigerators. Cable TV. Pool, wading pool. Beauty salon, hot tub. Video games. Laundry facilities. Business services. Pets allowed. | 7888 U.S. 192W (Irlo Bronson Memorial Hwy.) 34747 | 407/390–9888 or 800/228–5150 | fax 407/390–0981 | www.choicehotels.com | 150 rooms | $69–$139 | AE, D, DC, MC, V.

Days Suites. Dense tropical vegetation and waterfalls highlight this two-story family resort 2½ mi from Walt Disney World and adjacent to Old Town shopping and entertainment complex. The apartment-style suites, done in beige with burgundy carpeting, have living rooms, dining areas, and kitchens with a dishwasher, stove, dishes, and utensils. Three pools and an expansive barbecue and picnic area give you plenty of room to spread out. All suites have a balcony or patio and sleep six. In-room safes, kitchenettes, microwaves, refrigerators. Cable TV. Pools. Video games. Playground. Laundry facilities. Business services. Pets allowed (fee). | 5820 U.S. 192W (Irlo Bronson Memorial Hwy.) 34746 | 407/ 396–7900 or 800/327–9126 | fax 407/396–1789 | 603 rooms | $79–$149 | AE, D, DC, MC, V.

Econo Lodge Maingate–Hawaiian Resort. This property is 1 mi from Walt Disney World. The two-story pink and blue building surrounds a large courtyard and pool. Rooms have two double beds and white walls, blue carpet, and blue floral bedding. The pool bar and grill is open seasonally. Rollaway beds are available. I–4 exit 25B, 2 mi west on U.S. 192. Free Disney shuttle. Restaurant, bar. In-room data ports. Cable TV. Pool. Hot tub. Video games. Laundry facilities. Business services. Pets allowed (fee). | 7514 U.S. 192W (Irlo Bronson Memorial Hwy.) 34747 | 407/396–2000 or 800/365–6935 | fax 407/396–2832 | www.enjoyfloridahotels.com | 445 rooms | $59–$109 | AE, D, DC, MC, V.

Fantasy World Club Villas. Pink stucco villas, trimmed in green, make up this resort complex 3 mi from Walt Disney World. The two-story units have two bedrooms, a screened porch, a fully equipped kitchen, and a washer and dryer. Each sleeps up to six. Free Disney shuttle. Bar. In-room data ports, in-room safes, microwaves, refrigerators. Cable TV, in-room VCRs (and movies). 3 pools. Hot tub. Tennis. Volleyball. Playground. Laundry facilities. Business services. Airport shuttle. Pets allowed. | 2935 Hart Ave. 34746 | 407/396– 1808 or 800/874–8047 | fax 407/396–6737 | 300 villas | $195 | AE, D, DC, MC, V.

Holiday Inn Hotel and Suites, Main Gate East. This family-friendly resort is 3 mi from Walt Disney World next to the Old Town shopping and entertainment complex. Standard rooms are done in shades of blue and mauve and overlook the pool courtyard or parking lot. Each has two double beds. Sleeping bags and rollaway beds are available. Standard rooms can be upgraded to a Kidsuite, a theme room inside the parents' room with bunk beds, Nintendo, CD player, phone, TV, and VCR. Complimentary tuck-in service is offered by the hotel's mascot—Holiday Hound. Free Disney shuttle. Restaurant, bar. In-room data ports, in-room safes, microwaves, refrigerators. Cable TV, in-room VCRs (and movies). Pool, wading pool. Hot tubs. Tennis court. Basketball, volleyball. Video games. Playground. Laundry facilities. Airport shuttle. Pets allowed. | 5678 U.S. 192W (Irlo Bronson Memorial Hwy.) 34746 | 407/396–4488 or 800/465–4329 | fax 407/396–1296 | www.holiday-inn.com | 614 rooms in 8 buildings | $109–$139 | AE, D, DC, MC, V.

Ramada Inn Resort Maingate. This shady property spread out under a hammock of palm trees is 1 mi from Walt Disney World. The two-story pink-and-blue hotel's amenities include two tropical outdoor heated swimming pools, fitness center, and a game room. Rooms sleep up to 4, or 5 with a rollaway bed for an extra fee. Kids under 10 eat free. I–4 exit 25B. Free Disney shuttle. Restaurant, bar, room service. In-room data ports, in-room safes, microwaves, refrigerators. Cable TV. Pool, wading pool. Putting green, tennis court. Basketball, gym. Video games. Playground. Laundry facilities. Business services. Pets allowed (fee). | 2950 Reedy Creek Blvd. 34747 | 407/396–4466 or 800/365–6935 | fax 407/ 396–6418 | www.enjoyfloridahotels.com | 391 rooms, 3 suites | $69–$139 | AE, D, DC, MC, V.

Ramada Plaza Hotel and Inns, Gateway. The exterior and interior of this two-story hotel 1 mi west of Walt Disney World are pink and blue. Room have contemporary furnishings and tropical patterns. Rollaway beds. I–4 exit 25B. Free Disney shuttle. Restaurant, bar, room service. In-room data ports, microwaves, refrigerators. Cable TV. 2 Pools. Putting green. Basketball, gym. Video games. Playground. Laundry facilities. Business services. Pets allowed (fee). | 7470 U.S. 192W (Irlo Bronson Memorial Hwy.) 34747 | 407/396–4400 or 800/ 327–9170 | fax 407/397–4481 | 500 rooms | $55–$65 | AE, D, DC, MC, V.

Red Roof Inn. This three-floor hotel is close to it all. Near theme parks, this hotel is also near the training camp for the Houston Astros and the Citrus Bowl. Rooms are standard, but the pool is landscaped in a nice tropical style. Free shuttle to Disney World. Continental breakfast. Pool. Hot tub. Laundry facilities. Pets allowed. | 4970 Kyng's Heath Rd. 34746 | 407/396–0065 or 800/843–7663 | fax 407/396–0245 | www.redroof.com | 102 rooms | $36–$89 | AE, D, DC, MC, V.

Summerfield Resort. This resort has two-story blue town house–style units accommodating up to eight people each. The two-story units have two bedrooms, two baths, a washer and dryer, and fully equipped kitchens. The site has a swimming pool, club house, hot tub, wood sun deck, picnic tables, gas grills, and two equipped playground areas. I–4 exit 25A, east on U.S. 192. Kitchenettes, microwaves. Cable TV, in-room VCRs (and movies). Pool. Hot tub. Playground. Laundry facilities, laundry service. Business services. Pets allowed. | 2422 Summerfield Pl. 34741 | 407/847–7222 | fax 407/847–6774 | 37 units | $59–$179 | AE, D, DC, MC, V.

LAKE BUENA VISTA

Comfort Inn at Lake Buena Vista. This five-story white hotel on 23 acres less than 1 mi from Walt Disney World has a large, shady pool area. Rooms have two double beds, blue carpet, and blue floral bedding. Family suites sleep up to five and have bunk beds for kids and a queen-size bed for the adults. I–4 exit 27. Restaurant, bar. In-room safes, some microwaves, some refrigerators. Cable TV. 2 pools. Video games. Laundry facilities. Business services. Pets allowed (fee). | 8442 Palm Pkwy. 32836 | 407/239–7300 or 800/999– 7300 | fax 407/239–7740 | www.comfortinnorlando.com | 640 rooms | $85–$110 | AE, D, MC, V.

Days Inn Lake Buena Vista Village. This eight-story brick motel is near International Drive and SeaWorld, 3 mi from Walt Disney World. Rooms are pink and blue and have large windows. Standard rooms sleep four. Connecting rooms and rollaway beds available. Free Disney shuttle. I–4 exit 27. Restaurant, bar. Microwaves, refrigerators. Cable TV, in-room VCRs (and movies). Pool, wading pool. Video games. Playground. Laundry facilities. Business services. Pets allowed. | 12490 Apopka-Vineland Rd. 32820 | 407/239–4646 or 800/521–3297 | fax 407/239–8469 | 203 rooms | $49–$125 | AE, D, MC, V.

Holiday Inn SunSpree Resort. Kids have their own check-in area where they get a goodie bag upon arrival at this six-story hotel 1 mi from Walt Disney World. They also have their own dining area where they can eat with other kids and watch cartoons and movies. Camp Holiday has a free child-care center with magic shows, clowns, and arts and crafts. Half of the guest units include themed kid suites that sleep three or four kids, and have a semi-private divider wall, color TV, VCR, CD player, and Nintendo. The adult side has one or two queen-size beds and a kitchenette. Rooms have green carpet and blue and pink floral bedding. I–4 exit 27. Restaurant, bar, room service. In-room data ports, minibars, kitchenettes, microwaves, refrigerators. Cable TV, in-room VCRs (and movies). Pool, wading pool. Hot tub. Gym. Video games. Children's programs (ages 3–12). Laundry facilities. Business services. Some pets allowed. | 13351 Rte. 535 32821 | 407/239–4500 or 800/465–4329 | fax 407/239–7713 | www.kidsuites.com | 507 rooms | $89–$173 | AE, D, MC, V.

Residence Inn by Marriott, Lake Buena Vista. All of the one-and two-bedroom apartments in this hotel on 50 wooded acres 1 mi from Walt Disney World have a kitchen; some have washers and dryers. Suites sleep six and have large living rooms and country furnishings. Guests have privileges at the Orlando World Center Marriott. Free Disney shuttle. I–4 exit 27. Complimentary breakfast. In-room data ports, in-room safes, kitchenettes. Cable TV, in-room VCRs (and movies). Pool. Hot tub. Tennis courts. Basketball, volleyball. Video games. Laundry facilities. Business services. Pets allowed. | 8800 Meadow Creek Dr. 32821 | 407/239–7700 or 888/236–2427 | fax 407/239–7605 | 688 apartments | $199–$239 | AE, D, MC, V.

LAKE CITY

Lake City Knights Inn. This two-story motel is 1 mi from the Florida Sports Hall of Fame and local shopping. Fishing and area springs are nearby. Continental breakfast, picnic area. Cable TV. Pool. Putting green. Business services, free parking. Pets allowed. | Rte. 13, Box 201 32055 | 904/752–7720 or 800/418–8977 | fax 904/752–7720 | www.knightsinn.com | 100 rooms, 3 suites | $40–$70 | AE, D, DC, MC, V.

LAKE PLACID

Ramada Inn Lake Placid Conference. This motel has a poolside tiki bar and grill, and an 18-hole golf course. The area's freshwater lakes are ideal for water-skiing, boating, and sailing. Bar, restaurant. Cable TV. Pool. Golf, tennis. Dock, fishing. Pets allowed. | 2165 U.S. 27S 33852 | 941/465–3133 | fax 941/465–3354 | www.ramada.com | 100 rooms | $60–$140 | AE, D, DC, MC, V.

LAKELAND

Wellesley Inn and Suites. This six-story hotel is near the Lakeland Square Mall and restaurants. Standard rooms have a king-size or two double beds. Complimentary Continental breakfast. Some microwaves, refrigerators (in suites). Cable TV. Pool. Laundry facilities. Business services. Pets allowed (fee). | 3520 U.S. 98N 33809 | 863/859–3399 | fax 863/859–3483 | 106 rooms, 24 suites | $82–$92 | AE, D, DC, MC, V.

LIVE OAK

Suwannee River Inn. This basic chain motel is 4 mi from the famed Suwannee River and the Spirit of Suwannee Music Park. Tubing and scuba diving activities are 25 mi away. Complimentary Continental breakfast. Cable TV. Pool. Pets allowed (fee). | 6819 U.S. 129 32060 | 904/362–6000 | fax 904/364–1309 | 64 rooms | $60 | AE, D, DC, MC, V.

LONGBOAT KEY

Riviera Beach Motel. Lush, landscaped walkways add intimacy to this waterfront motel. Garden on premises. Studio, 1-bedroom, or 2-bedroom apartments with full kitchens, living area, and dining room table. Most with 2 beds. Some price breaks for weekly rentals. Microwaves, refrigerators. Cable TV. Beach. Some pets allowed (fee). | 5451 Gulf of Mexico Dr. 34228 | 941/383–2552 | fax 941/383–2245 | 11 rooms | $113–$160 | AE, MC, V.

MADEIRA BEACH

Lighthouse B&B Motel. The three buildings were built around 1948 and are set around a common courtyard, secluding the goldfish pond and gazebo from the public. The main one, shaped like a lighthouse, is where a full breakfast is served and has several of the carpeted rooms. Each room is individually designed with floral to tropical patterns and tiled kitchen areas. They are only 2 blocks from the beach and 5 blocks from John's Path boardwalk. Complimentary breakfast. Some kitchenettes, some refrigerators, some microwaves. Cable TV, no phones in rooms. Bicycles. Laundry facilities. Some pets allowed (fee). | 13355 2nd St. E 33708 | 727/391–0015 or 800/241–0334 | fax 727/393–7285 | lighthousebb@aol.com | bedandbreakfast.com | 6 rooms | $60–$95 | AE, D, MC, V.

MARATHON

Faro Blanco Marine Resort. Loyal guests return season after season to this resort with a topnotch and accommodating staff. You can stay in three-bedroom condominiums, cottages, and guest rooms. The guest rooms, like the condos and cottages, all have kitchens or kitchenettes. The condos, individually decorated, have wraparound screen porches; many have views of the water. 3 restaurants. Kitchenettes, microwaves, refrigerators. Cable TV. Pool. Dock, boating. Pets allowed. | 1996 Overseas Hwy. 33050 | 305/743–9018 | 100 units | $89–$327 | AE, MC, V.

Marathon Wellesley Inn and Suites. This two-story resort is on the beach. In business since 1974, the owners completed major renovations in 2000. Rooms have one king-size or two double beds, with a desk. Nintendo is available. The restaurant next door is convenient. In-room data ports, microwaves, refrigerators. Cable TV, some in-room VCRs (and movies). Pool. Beach, water sports, boating. Laundry facilities. Business services. Some pets allowed. | 13351 Overseas Hwy. 33050 | 305/743–8550 | fax 305/743–8832 | www.wellesleyinnand-suites.com | 80 rooms | $129–$200 | AE, D, MC, V.

MARCO ISLAND

The Boathouse. For a great location at a good price, check into this modest but appealing motel at the north end of Marco Island. The two-story, white building trimmed in turquoise is on a canal very close to the mouth of the Gulf. Units are light and bright and furnished with natural wicker and print fabrics. Each room has a balcony or terrace, and some have great water views. You can fish from the boat docks. Picnic area. Some microwaves. Cable TV. Pool. Dock. Laundry facilities. Business services. Some pets allowed (fee). | 1180 Edington Pl. 34145 | 941/642–2400 or 800/528–6345 | fax 941/642–2435 | www.theboathousemotel.com | 20 rooms | $93–$105 | MC, V.

Lakeside Inn. The most affordable lodgings on the island, this two-story hotel sits on Marco Lake, 1 mi east of the beaches. Each unit has a private, screened-in porch with a view of the lake. Kitchenettes, refrigerators, microwaves. Cable TV. Pool. Shops. Laundry facilities. Pets allowed. | 155 First Ave. 34145 | 941/394–1161 | www.lakesideinnmarco.com | 12 suites, 26 efficiencies | $89–$119 | AE, D, DC, MC, V.

MARIANNA

Comfort Inn. Just off I–10 at Exit 21, this two-story motor inn is 4 mi south of Marianna. You're close to several restaurants and to the Florida Caverns State Park. Complimentary Continental breakfast. Cable TV. Pool. Laundry service. Business services. Pets allowed. | 2175 Hwy. 71 32446 | 850/526–5600 | fax 850/482–7899 | www.comfortinn.com | 80 rooms | $45–$54 | AE, D, DC, MC, V.

MATLACHA

Bayview B&B. You might glimpse manatees or dolphins from the 70-ft-long pier of this B&B in the historic fishing village of Matlacha. Rooms reflect the natural tropical setting with bright colors and wicker furniture. The staff is helpful with knowledge of area tours and especially bird-watching information. After you try the watermelon cake here, you might want to take home the recipe. Complimentary Continental breakfast. Some kitchenettes, refrigerators, some microwaves. Cable TV. Dock, boating, watersports, fishing. Some pets allowed (fee). | 12251 Shoreview Dr. 33993 | 941/283–7510 | www.webbwiz.com/bayviewbb | 4 rooms | $79–$149 | No credit cards.

The Sun and the Moon Inn. The rooms in the two stilt houses that make up this inn each have private decks or patios with views of the water and islands. The interiors are equally lovely, with four-poster beds and down pillows and comforters. You can use the inn's canoe and rowboat to look for wildlife from the Matlacha waters. Complimentary Continental breakfast. Refrigerators. Cable TV, no room phones. Pool. Hot tub. Beach, dock, boating. Pets allowed. No kids under 18. No smoking. | 3962 N.W. Pine Island Rd. 33993 | 941/283–3192 or 888/321–3192 | fax 941/283–6042 | www.sunandmoon.net | 6 rooms | $99–$250 (minimum stay may be required) | AE, D, MC, V.

MIAMI

La Quinta Inn. This well-furnished and affordable three-story pseudo-southwestern stucco motel is noted for its clean guest rooms. You're a few minutes away from the International Mall, Mall of America, and the Doral Golf Resort. Kids under 18 free. Complimentary Continental breakfast. In-room data ports, some microwaves, refrigerators. Cable TV. Pool. Gym. Laundry facilities. Business services, airport shuttle, free parking. Pets allowed. | 7401 N.W. 36th St. 33166 | 305/599–9902 | fax 305/594–0552 | 165 rooms | $69–$119 | AE, D, DC, MC, V.

MIAMI BEACH

Brigham Gardens. More than 100 tropical plants, a fountain, and colorful birds set the mood at this small hotel one block from the beach. Although the hotel is not immaculate, it offers functional rooms suited for budget travelers who need to dine in. Each room has a minifridge, microwave, and coffee maker; one-bedroom apartments have fully-equipped kitchens. Some in-room data ports, some kitchenettes, microwaves, refrigerators. Cable TV. Laundry facilities. Parking (fee). Pets allowed (fee). | 1411 Collins Ave. 33139 | 305/531–1331 | fax 305/538–9898 | www.brighamgardens.com | 9 rooms, 11 studios, 2 1-bedroom apartments | $100 room, $125 studio, $145 apartment | AE, MC, V.

Casa Grande. A Balinese theme dominates the luxury suites of this hotel: dhurrie rugs, Indonesian fabrics and artifacts, and two-poster beds. All rooms also have large baths (a rarity in the Art Deco District) and full kitchens; some include ocean views and terraces. Restaurant. In-room safes, kitchenettes, microwaves, refrigerators. Cable TV, in-room VCRs. Beach. Shops. Laundry service. Business services. Pets allowed. | 834 Ocean Dr. 33139 | 305/672–7003 or 800/688–7678 | fax 305/673–3669 | www.islandoutpost.com | 34 suites | $295–$1,500 | AE, D, DC, MC, V.

Cavalier. This is one of Chris Blackwell's six Island Outpost hotels (the others are Casa Grande, Kent, Leslie, Marlin, and the Tides). Rooms include a TV/VCR/CD player, queen-size bed, batik fabrics, requisite Deco-style furniture, vintage black-and-white photos, and access to the pool at the Tides. Suites get an ocean view and a king-size bed. 2 restaurants, 1 bar, room service. In-room data ports, in-room safes, minibars, refrigerators, some hot tubs. Cable TV, in-room VCRs. Pool. Massage. Shops. Laundry service. Business services, parking (fee). Some pets allowed. | 1320 Ocean Dr. 33139 | 305/604–5064 or 800/688–7678 | fax 305/672–5611 | www.thecavalierhotel.com | 45 rooms, 3 suites | $185–$210 room, $350–$395 suite | AE, D, DC, MC, V.

Days Inn Convention Center. Nothing flashy and nothing trashy, this chain hotel inhabits a happy middle ground. The lobby is bright and floral, with a fountain and a gift shop. Deluxe rooms have impressive views of the ocean. It's literally seconds from the beach, the boardwalk, and the new arts complex containing the Miami City Ballet and the Bass Museum. Restaurant, bar. In-room data ports, in-room safes, some refrigerators. Cable TV. Pool. Shops. Laundry facilities, laundry services. Parking (fee). Some pets allowed. | 100 21st St. 33139 | 305/538–6631 or 800/451–3345 | fax 305/674–0954 | www.daysinn.com | 172 rooms | $119–$149 | AE, D, DC, MC, V.

Fisher Island Club. William Vanderbilt's former mansion is the centerpiece of this ultra-exclusive resort hotel reachable only by ferry, and only for those with reservations. The resort features a top nine-hole golf course, the Spa Internazionale (an island market), two deep-water marinas, and a mile-long private beach with Bahamian sand. There are suites, villas, and cottages. 6 restaurants, 3 bars, picnic area, room service. In-room data ports, in-room safes, kitchenettes, minibars, microwaves, refrigerators, some in-room hot tubs. Cable TV, in-room VCRs. 2 pools. Barber shop, beauty salon, hot tub, massage, sauna, spa, steam room. Driving range, 9-hole golf course, 18 tennis courts. Exercise equipment, gym, health club, beach. Dock, water sports, boating, bicycles. Shops. Baby-sitting, children's programs (ages 4–12), playground. Laundry services. Free parking. Some pets allowed. | 1 Fisher Island Dr. 33109 | 305/535–6000 or 800/537–3708 | fax 305/535–6003 | www.fisherisland-florida.com | 30 rooms, 27 suites, 3 cottages | $385–$765 room, $765–$1,265 suite, $950–$1530 cottage | AE, D, DC, MC, V.

Fontainebleau Hilton Resort and Towers. Perhaps the most recognizable landmark on the beach, the Fontainebleau Hilton Resort is on 20 lush tropical acres. Every president since Eisenhower has stayed here, as have many entertainers, some of whom performed here: Frank Sinatra, Elvis Presley, Bob Hope, Sammy Davis, Jr., and Lucille Ball. All the rooms are spacious and elegant; some are furnished in 1950s style, others are ultracontemporary. The half-acre lagoon-style rock-grotto pool with cascading waterfalls is surrounded by greenery; you can play night tennis on the seven lighted tennis courts. The 2-mi seaside boardwalk leads to the Art Deco District. Restaurants, bars. In-room data ports, some minibars, microwaves, some refrigerators. Cable TV. Pools. Barbershop, beauty salon, hot tub. 7 tennis courts. Gym. Dock, water sports, boating. Shops. Children's programs. Laundry service. Business services, airport shuttle. Some pets allowed. | 4441 Collins Ave. 33140 | 305/538–2000 | fax 305/531–9274 | www.hilton.com | 1,146 rooms, 60 suites | $240–$345 | AE, D, DC, MC, V.

★ **Hotel Impala.** This small Mediterranean Revival–style hotel has a tropical garden courtyard and rooms with Italian saturnier stone floors, and Spanish surrealist art. Ocean Drive is a block away, but it feels a lot further. Rooms are stocked with mineral water, CDs, and videos. Restaurant, bar, room service. In-room data ports, some refrigerators, some minibars. Cable TV, in-room VCRs (and movies). Laundry service. Business services. No kids under 15. Pets allowed. | 1228 Collins Dr. 33139 | 305/673–2021 or 800/646–7252 | fax 305/673–5984 | www.hotelimpalamiamibeach.com | 17 rooms | $215–$400 | AE, DC, MC, V.

Hotel Ocean. This luxury hotel is reminiscent of the French Riviera, complete with a shaded, bougainvillea-draped courtyard and complimentary breakfast at the hotel's brasserie. The comfortable rooms are highlighted by soft beds, authentic 1930s Art Deco pieces, large fold-out couches, and clean, spacious baths. Also offered are wet bars with refrigerators, TV/VCR/CD players, and two phone lines with data-port access, and well as soundproof windows. Restaurant, 1 bar, complimentary Continental breakfast, room service. In-room safes, minibars, refrigerators, some hot tubs. Cable TV, in-room VCRs. Shops. Baby-sitting. Laundry services. Parking (fee). Pets allowed. | 1230-38 Ocean Dr. 33139 | 305/672–2579 or 800/783–1725 | fax 305/672–7665 | www.hotelocean.com | 4 rooms, 23 suites | $215–$255 room, $275–$325 suite | AE, D, DC, MC, V.

Marlin Hotel. This is one of the most photographed of South Beach hotels. Fun Jamaican art complements striking hand-painted furniture, woven grass rugs, batik-like shades, and rattan and mahogany furniture at this Island Outpost property. Every room is different; some have kitchenettes, but all are complete with VCRs, minibars, and orchid-theme embellishments. Each room also has Web-TV. Larger suites here are like villas. The Marlin Bar downstairs, a very hip spot, serves Jamaican appetizers like jerk chicken and coconut shrimp. Restaurant, bar. In-room data ports, in-room safes, minibars, kitchenettes. Cable TV, in-room VCRs. Laundry service. Parking (fee). Some pets allowed (fee). | 1200 Collins Ave. 33139 | 305/604–5063 or 800/688–7678 | fax 305/673–9609 | www.islandoutpost.com | 13 suites | $280–$395 | AE, D, DC, MC, V.

Raleigh Hotel. Thick tropical foliage hides one of the nicest hotels in South Beach, with Victorian features. The hotel is popular among fashion photographers and production crews for its spacious and state-of-the-art accommodations. A breath-taking fleur-delis swimming pool and 300-ft beach give you ample room for swimming. The lobby has a coffee bar, martini bar, and restaurant. Restaurant, room service. In-room data ports, in-room safes, refrigerators. Cable TV, in-room VCRs. Pool. Massage. Gym. Beach. Laundry service. Business services. Pets allowed. | 1775 Collins Ave. 33139 | 305/534–6300 or 800/848–1775 | fax 305/538–8140 | www.raleighhotel.com | 107 rooms | $256–$1,500 | AE, D, DC, MC, V.

Seacoast Suites. An elegant all-suites, apartment-style hotel right on the beach, this place has spacious living and dining rooms and its own mini-market. The suites' terraces overlook the Atlantic or the exciting skyline of Miami. You're 15 minutes from the Bal Harbour shops, the Bayside Marketplace, and the Art Deco District. A private bus service runs from South Beach to Aventura Mall. Restaurant, bar. Minibars. Cable TV. Pool. Tennis court. Gym. Beach. Laundry facilities. Parking (fee). Pets allowed. | 5101 Collins Ave. 33140 | 305/865–5152 | fax 305/868–4090 | 73 1- to 2-bedroom suites | $119–$179 1–bedroom, $269–$359 2–bedroom | AE, D, DC, MC, V.

Taft. Renovated and reopened in 1998, this hotel is part of the Park Washington Resort, an entire block of Art Deco accommodations. This one is furnished Deco style. You can lounge by a pool, drink at the tiki bar, and exchange stories with fellow guests. Bar, complimentary Continental breakfast. Refrigerators. Cable TV. Pool. Pets allowed. | 1020–1050 Washington Ave. 33139 | 305/532–1930 or 888/424–1930 | fax 305/534–6597 | www.parkwashingtonresort.com | 30 rooms | $159 | AE, MC, V.

Villa Paradiso. Less than a block from the beach, this place has studios and one-bedrooms that open onto a lush, tropical courtyard. Rooms all have full-size kitchens and living rooms with French doors and polished hardwood floors. The owners are friendly and accommodating. Kitchenettes, microwaves, refrigerators. Cable TV. Laundry facilities. Pets allowed. | 1415 Collins Ave. 33139 | 305/532–0616 | fax 305/673–5874 | www.villaparadisohotel.com | 14 studios, 3 1-bedrooms | $100–$125 | AE, DC, MC, V.

MICANOPY

Herlong Mansion. Four two-story Corinthian columns pierce the wide veranda of this stately Greek Revival–style B&B. The classical touches were part of a 1910 renovation of a two-story 1845 Victorian house, still surrounded by old oak trees. Inside are 10 working fireplaces, mahogany inlaid oak floors, and suites decorated with period furniture, Oriental rugs, and armoires. Dining room, picnic area, complimentary breakfast. Some kitchenettes, some refrigerators, some in-room hot tubs. Some in-room VCRs, no TV in some rooms. Library. Some pets allowed. | 402 Cholokka Blvd. 32667 | 352/466–3322 or 800/437–5664 | fax 352/466–3322 | www.herlong.com | 5 rooms, 4 suites, 2 cottages | $80–$179 | AE, MC, V.

NAPLES

Hotel Escalante. Opened in 2000, this hotel is really a compound of different buildings, the rooms of which encircle four separate courtyards. Around the compound stands a row of well-maintained bushes. Rooms have a Spanish-Colonial appearance with dark wood furnishings and light-colored walls. Shuttle service is provided to 5th Avenue shops and restaurants. The hotel is very up to date and even rents laptops. Bar, complimentary Continental breakfast, room service. In-room data ports, in-room safes, minibars, refrigerators. Cable TV. Pool. Hot tub, spa. Laundry service. Business services. Pets allowed. | 290 5th Ave. S 34102 | 941/659–3466 or 877/GULF–INN | fax 941/262–8748 | www.hotelescalante.com | 65 rooms | $250–$600 | AE, D, DC, MC, V.

NEW SMYRNA BEACH

Coquina Warf B&B. This 1903 Dutch Colonial overlooking the Intercoastal Waterway is decorated with a combination of antiques and tasteful contemporary furnishings. Lace curtains and antique plates ornament the guest rooms, while the living room has a fireplace and pine floors. You can lounge on the two porches. Complimentary breakfast. Cable TV. Dock. Pets allowed. | 704 S. Riverside Dr. 32168 | 904/428–9458 | fax 904/409–9077 | www.coquinawarf.com | 3 rooms, 1 cottage | $75–$200 | No credit cards.

OCALA

Days Inn. This two-story motel is ½ mi from Silver Springs. The lobby and rooms are simple and unassuming. Microwaves, refrigerators. Cable TV, in-room VCRs (and movies). Pool. Playground. Laundry facilities. Pets allowed. | 5001 E. Silver Springs Blvd. (Hwy. 40) 34488 | 352/236–2891 | fax 352/236–3546 | 56 rooms | $45–$75 | AE, D, MC, V.

Holiday Inn Silver Springs. Directly across the highway from the entrance to Silver Springs, this single-story property has drive-up rooms and polyester curtains. The motel has a 24-hr restaurant. Restaurant, bar. In-room data ports, microwaves, refrigerators. Cable TV, in-room VCRs. Pool. Business services. Pets allowed. | 5751 E. Silver Springs Blvd. (Hwy. 40) 34488 | 352/236–2575 or 800/465–4329 | fax 352/236–2575 | www.holiday-inn. com | 104 rooms | $65–$90 | AE, D, DC, MC, V.

Ocala Silver Springs Hilton. A tree-lined road leads to this nine-story pink hotel in a forested area near the intersection of Highway 200 and I–75, a few minutes from downtown. The marble-floor lobby, with a piano bar, greets you before you reach the guest rooms, decorated in contemporary colors and prints. Restaurant, bar, room service. Some minibars, some refrigerators, some in-room hot tubs. Cable TV. Pool. Hot tub. Putting green, 2 tennis courts. Volleyball. Laundry service. Business services. Pets allowed. | 3600 SW 36th Ave. 34474 | 352/854–1400 | fax 352/854–4010 | 197 rooms | $89–$129 | AE, D, DC, MC, V.

OKEECHOBEE

Budget Inn. Rooms are basic and economic at this single-story building surrounded by trees and shrubs. There are restaurants within walking distance. Complimentary Continental breakfast. Microwaves, refrigerators. Cable TV. Pool. Business services. Pets allowed (fee). | 201 S. Parrott Ave. 34974 | 863/763–3185 | fax 863/763–3185 | 23 rooms | $49–$89 | AE, D, DC, MC, V.

Holiday Inn Express. This two-story chain motel is ¼ mi north of Lake Okeechobee and within walking distance of shops and restaurants. Complimentary Continental breakfast. In-room data ports, microwaves, refrigerators. Cable TV, some in-room hot tubs. Outdoor pool. Laundry facilities. Business services. Pets allowed (fee). | 3975 U.S. 441S 34974 | 863/357–3529 | fax 863/357–3529 | www.holiday-inn.com | 43 rooms | $125–$150 | AE, D, DC, MC, V.

ORLANDO

Baymont Inn. Rooms at this motel are comfortably modern and have little extras like in-room coffeemakers and radios. It's 6 mi from Universal Orlando and 13 mi from Walt Disney World. Complimentary Continental breakfast. In-room data ports, microwaves, refrigerators. Cable TV. Pool. Laundry facilities. Business services. Pets allowed. Take I–4 exit 28. | 2051 Consulate Dr. 32837 | 407/240–0500 or 800/789–4103 (reservations) | fax 407/240–5194 | www.baymontinn.com | 128 rooms | $53–$75 | AE, D, DS, MC, V.

Crosby's Motor Inn. This pleasant, two-story rural motel is off the beaten path in a small town 10 mi north of Orlando. Walt Disney World is about 35 mi away, and Universal Studios is only 25 mi away. Each room is uniquely decorated—most with antique mirrors, pink and green carpeting, and upholstery. Picnic area. In-room data ports, some kitchenettes, refrigerators. Pool. Laundry facilities. Some pets allowed. | 1440 W. Orange Blossom Trail (Hwy. 441N), Apopka 32712 | 407/886–3220 or 800/821–6685 | fax 407/886–7458 | 75 rooms | $50–$70 | AE, D, MC, V.

La Quinta Inn Airport. This hotel has three stories with a bright, new look that goes beyond the crisp white exteriors, including all new landscaping and lobbies. Rooms feature contemporary decor, floor-length draperies, built-in closets, ceiling moldings, and rich wood furniture. Expanded bathrooms have ceramic tile floors, designer vanities, and enhanced lighting. You'll also find an oversized workdesk and a data-port phone in every room. Walt Disney World and Universal Orlando are 20 mi from the hotel. Complimentary Continental breakfast. In-room data-ports, refrigerators. Cable TV. Pool. Gym. Laundry facilities. Airport shuttle. Pets allowed. | 7931 Daetwyler Dr. 32812-4809 | 407/857–9215 | fax 407/857–0877 | 128 rooms | $84–$116 | AE, D, MC, V.

La Quinta Inn, Orlando International Drive. This hotel features rooms with floor-length draperies, built-in closets, and expanded bathrooms. They have enhanced lighting, large desks and computer-friendly data-port telephones. There is a free shuttle to Universal Studios. Complimentary Continental breakfast. In-room data-ports, microwaves, refrigerators. Cable TV. Pool. Laundry facilities. Pets allowed. | 8300 Jamaican Ct. 32819 | 407/351–1660 | fax 407/351–9264 | 200 rooms | $84–$109 | AE, D, MC, V.

Quality Inn, Plaza. Close to restaurants along International Drive, this motel offers rooms spread among five-, six-, and seven-story buildings. All rooms have two double beds. Built in 1983, the property is clean, but its furnishings are the bare minimum. Walt Disney World is 7 mi and Universal Orlando is 4 mi from the hotel. Restaurant, bar. In-room safes, refrigerators. Cable TV. Pool, wading pool. Hot tub. Kids programs (ages 2–12). Laundry facilities. Business services. Pets allowed. | 9000 International Dr. 32819 | 407/996–8585 or 800/999–8585 (reservations) | fax 407/996–6839 | www.tamarinns.com | 1,020 rooms | $35–$89 | AE, D, MC, V.

Residence Inn Orlando International Drive. Units in this two-story all-suites hotel accommodate up to five people, offering home-away-from-home comfort for families. Suites include full kitchen and living rooms. Most units have fireplaces and two full bathrooms. Walt Disney World is 9 mi, Universal Orlando is 2 mi. Free Walt Disney World shuttle. Complimentary Continental breakfast. In-room data ports, in-room safes, microwaves, refrigerators. Cable TV. Pool. Hot tub. Basketball, volleyball. Laundry facilities. Pets allowed. | 7975 Canada Ave. 32819 | 407/345–0117 or 888/236–2427 | fax 407/352–2689 | marriottresidenceinn.com | 176 rooms | $95–$205 | AE, D, MC, V.

Wyndham Orlando Resort. After a $36 million expansion, this hotel opened a children's entertainment center and an upscale shopping court. The most important fact, however, is its stone's throw-proximity to the new $2.6 billion Universal Orlando complex; 8 mi Disneyland and 3½ to Universal. There is a free shuttle to Universal Orlando, SeaWorld, and Wet 'n' Wild. 3 restaurants, 2 bars, room service. In-room dataports, in-room safes, some refrigerators, some in-room hot tubs. Cable TV. 3 pools, 2 wading pools. Outdoor hot tub, sauna, steam room. 4 tennis courts. Basketball, gym, volleyball. Video games, shops. Children's programs (ages 2–14), playground. Laundry facilities, laundry service. Free parking. Some pets allowed (fee). | 8001 International Dr. 32819 | 407/351–2420 or 800/996–3426 | fax 407/351–5016 | www.wyndham.com | 1,064 rooms | $99–$159 | AE, D, DC, MC, V.

ORMOND BEACH

Comfort Inn Interstate. At exit 89 off I–95, this two-story motel is set back in the woods of Tomoka State Park, 7 mi northwest of the beach. There are 10 restaurants within walking distance. Complimentary Continental breakfast. In-room data ports, some microwaves, some refrigerators. Cable TV. Pool. Laundry facilities. Business services. Some pets allowed (fee). | 1567 U.S. 1N 32174 | 904/672–8621 | fax 904/677–9107 | www.comfortinn.com | 75 rooms | $70–$160 | AE, D, DC, MC, V.

Comfort Inn on the Beach. This four-story motel is, as the name boasts, right on the beach, with shopping, miniature golf, and tennis courts within a mile. The heart of Daytona Beach is 4 mi south. There are three one-bedroom apartments that sleep up to six, and standard rooms, which sleep four. Complimentary Continental breakfast. In-room data ports, in-room safes, some kitchenettes, microwaves, refrigerators. Cable TV. Pool, wading pool. Beach. Some pets allowed (fee). | 507 S. Atlantic Ave. 32176 | 904/677–8550 | fax 904/673–6260 | www.comfortinn.com | 49 rooms | $75–$165 | AE, D, DC, MC, V.

Jameson Inn of Ormond Beach. This white-columned, three-story chain has motel rooms and one-bedroom suites. It is just off I–95 at exit 88. Complimentary Continental breakfast. In-room data ports, some minibars, some microwaves, some refrigerators. Cable TV. Pool. Gym. Laundry service. Business services. Pets allowed. | 175 Interchange Blvd. 32174 | 904/672–3675 | 67 rooms | $65–$71 | AE, D, MC, V.

Makai Lodge Beach Resort. A Polynesian theme dominates the lobby of this owner-operated lodge, a mile north of the BelAir Shopping Plaza. Motel rooms, lodge rooms, and efficiencies are available; all are outfitted with new dark mahogany furniture. Half the units face the ocean. In-room data ports, in-room safes, some kitchenettes, some microwaves, refrigerators. Cable TV. Pool, wading pool. Hot tub. Beach. Video games. Laundry facilities. Business services. Pets allowed. | 707 S. Atlantic Ave. 32176 | 904/677–8060 or 800/799–1112 | www.makailodge.com | 110 rooms | $33–$130 | AE, D, DC, MC, V.

PALM BEACH

The Chesterfield Hotel. Two blocks from Worth Avenue is this elegant four-story, white stucco Mediterranean palace cum boutique hotel. Rooms are individually decorated in rich colors, with marble bathrooms, antique desks, and potted plants. The pool is surrounded by lush foliage and all public areas, from the library to the dining room, exhibit extravagant luxury. Restaurant, bar (with entertainment), room service. In-room data ports, in-room safes, some refrigerators. Cable TV, some in-room VCRs. Pool. Hot tub. Library. Laundry service. Business services, free parking. Pets allowed (fee). | 363 Cocoanut Row 33480 | 561/659–5800 or 800/243–7871 | fax 561/659–6707 | 55 rooms, 12 suites | $229–$329 room, $429–$529 1–bedroom suite, $699–$799 2–bedroom suite | AE, D, DC, MC, V.

The Four Seasons Resort. This six-acre beachside hotel at the south end of town has a serene atmosphere buoyed by marble, art, fanlight windows, swagged drapes, chintz, and palms. Every guest room has a private balcony and full marble bathroom. A number of poolside and beachfront restaurants add to the sense of luxurious relaxation. 3 restaurants, bar (with entertainment), room service. In-room data ports, in-room safes, minibars, some microwaves, some refrigerators. Cable TV, some in-room VCRs (and movies). Pool. Beauty salon, hot tub, massage, sauna, spa, steam room. 3 tennis courts. Gym. Beach, water sports, boating, fishing, bicycles. Baby-sitting, children's programs (ages 3–13). Laundry service. Business services, parking (fee). Pets allowed. | 2800 S. Ocean Blvd. 33480 | 561/582–2800 or 800/432–2335 | fax 561/547–1374 | www.fourseasons.com | 197 rooms, 13 suites | $375–$695 | AE, D, DC, MC, V.

Heart of Palm Beach Hotel. This European-style hotel is three blocks north of Worth Avenue and a 3-min walk from the beach. The two low, pink buildings date from 1960 and 1975. Rooms are spacious and sunny, with private balconies and terraces. A garden pavilion is the ideal place for drinks or outdoor dining. Restaurant, 2 bars. Refrigerators. Cable TV. Pool. Bicycles. Laundry facilities. Business services. Pets allowed. | 160 Royal Palm Way 33480 | 561/655–5600 or 800/523–5377 | fax 561/832–1201 | 88 rooms | $259 | AE, D, MC, V.

Palm Beach Hawaiian Ocean Inn. This two-story wood motel attracts families with reasonable prices and a beachfront location. The staff is laid-back and knowledgeable. A wide wooden sundeck surrounds the free-form pool and looks out to the sand, where you can rent umbrellas and rafts. An adjoining restaurant includes a bar and patio, and has live music most of the week. Restaurant, bar, room service. In-room data ports, in-room safes, some kitchenettes, some microwaves, refrigerators. Cable TV, some in-room VCRs. Pool. Beach, fishing. Laundry facilities, laundry service. Free parking. Some pets allowed. | 3550 South Ocean Blvd. 33480 | 561/582–5631 | fax 561/582–5631 | www.palmbeachhawaiian.com | 50 rooms, 8 suites | $150–$160 room, $180–$320 | AE, D, DC, MC, V.

Palm Beach Historic Inn. Tucked behind Town Hall and a seaside residential block, you'll be surprised to discover this delightful B&B in the heart of downtown. Built in 1923 in a Victorian style, the inn is just a block from the beach and two blocks from Worth Avenue. The two-story building is built around a garden courtyard. Guest rooms tend toward the frilly, with lots of lace, ribbons, and scalloped edges; there are Victorian antiques and reproductions throughout. Complimentary Continental breakfast. Refrigerators. Cable TV, in-room VCRs. Beach. Laundry service. Business services, free parking. Pets allowed (fee). No smoking. | 365 S. County Rd. 33480 | 561/832–4009 | fax 561/832–6255 | www.palmbeachhistoricinn.com | 9 rooms, 4 suites | $185–$275 | AE, D, DC, MC, V.

Plaza Inn. The three-story 1939 Art Deco building that houses this B&B-style hotel is fronted in pale pink stucco with light green trim. It is a block from the beach, and four blocks north of Worth Avenue. The French- and Italian-style rooms come with antique and high-quality reproduction furniture. Some have four-poster beds, hand-blown Murano glass chandeliers and French draperies. At the back is a secret garden, tropical plants set around a fountain, and the outdoor pool and Jacuzzi with waterfalls and plenty of room for sunbathing. Bar, complimentary breakfast. In-room data ports, refrigerators. Cable TV, some in-room VCRs. Pool. Hot tub. Laundry service. Business services, free parking. Pets allowed. | 215 Brazilian Ave. 33480 | 561/832–8666 or 800/233–2632 | fax 561/835–8776 | www.plazainnpalmbeach.com | 50 rooms | $205–$305 | AE, MC, V.

PANAMA CITY

Bayside Inn. One mi from the heart of Panama City and 8 mi from Gulf beaches, this motel has rooms that look out over St. Andrew's Bay. There is a private beach with a sand volleyball court. Rooms are designed in a nuevo-Caribbean style with brightly colored prints and island art work on the walls; most have patios that lead right out to the water. Restaurant, bar. In-room data ports, some kitchenettes. Cable TV. Pool. Volleyball, fishing, dock. Playground. Laundry facilities, laundry service. Free parking. Pets allowed (fee). | 711 West Beach Dr. 32401 | 850/763–4622 or 800/900–7047 | fax 850/747–9522 | www.bestwesternbaysideinn.com | 97 rooms, 3 suites | $75–$115 | AE, D, DC, MC, V.

La Quinta Inn and Suites. Three-quarters of the guests at this motel are business travellers, attracted by the location in the middle of the business district and reasonable prices. The six-story stucco building has modern and comfortably furnished rooms. Panama City Beach is 10 mi away, and Panama City Mall is next door. In-room data ports, some microwaves, some refrigerators. Cable TV. Pool. Exercise equipment. Laundry facilities. Business services. Pets allowed. | 1030 E. 23rd St. 32405 | 850/914–0022 or 800/687–6667 | fax 850/914–0027 | 119 rooms | $74–$109 | AE, D, DC, MC, V.

PANAMA CITY BEACH

Dolphin Inn Motel at Pineapple Beach. Part of Pineapple Resorts, along with its sister property Pineapple Villas, the three-story Dolphin Inn is right on the beach with a Tiki bar, sun deck, and barbecue and picnic areas beside the beachfront pool. All rooms have ocean views. Kitchenettes, microwaves, refrigerators. Cable TV, some in-room VCRs. Pool. Beach, watersports. Laundry facilities. Free parking. Pets allowed (fee). | 19935 Front Beach Rd. (Hwy. 98) 32413 | 850/234–1788 or 800/234–1788 | www.pineapplebeachresort.com | 30 rooms | $49–$125 | AE, D, MC, V.

PENSACOLA

Civic Inn. This white-stucco building with grey columns and royal blue doors had its origins as a 1950's travel lodge. It is a 10-min walk to Pensacola's historic district, and convenient to the trolley system, which you can use to get to museums and sights. Some refrigerators, some microwaves. Cable TV. Pool. Laundry facilities. Free parking. Some pets allowed (fee). | 200 N. Palafox St. 32501 | 850/432–3441 | fax 850/438–5956 | 48 rooms | $40–$68 | AE, D, MC, V.

Comfort Inn N.A.S.-Corry. This three-building motel is the entrance to Corry Field military base. The airport is 7 mi away, and the Historic District is 3 mi away. There are nearby hiking and jogging trails, fishing, and tennis facilities. Bar (with entertainment), complimentary Continental breakfast. In-room data ports, microwaves, refrigerators. Cable TV. Pool. Laundry facilities. Business services. Pets allowed (fee). | 3 New Warrington Rd. 32506 | 850/455-3233 or 800/554-3206 | fax 850/453-3445 | www.comfortinn.com | 101 rooms | $70 | AE, D, DC, MC, V.

Days Inn. This motel was renovated in 2000. It's an easy walk to restaurants, museums, art galleries, and shops and two blocks from the trolley stop. Restaurant, bar, room service. In-room data ports. Outdoor pool. Beauty parlor. Baby-sitting. Laundry service. Pets allowed. | 710 N. Palafox St. 32501 | 850/438-4922 or 800/544-8313 | fax 850/438-7999 | 146 rooms | $58-$100 | AE, MC, V.

Econo Lodge. This small motel is 10 mi from the beach, 2 mi from University Mall, and 5 miles from the University of West Florida. Rooms, decorated in a contemporary style, come with either a queen or king bed. Complimentary Continental breakfast. Cable TV. Pool. Laundry facilities. Free parking. Some pets allowed (fee). | 7194 Pensacola Blvd. 32505 | 850/479-8600 or 800/553-2666 | fax 850/479-8600 | 60 rooms | $30-$49 | AE, MC, V.

Howard Johnson Inn. This motel is a step up in comfort from the Howard Johnson Express in town. Some guest rooms come with kitchenettes and pool views. The motel is ¼ mi south of I-10, off exit 3A, about 12 mi from the beach. Restaurant, complimentary Continental breakfast, room service. In-room data ports, in-room safes, microwaves, refrigerators. Cable TV. Pool. Laundry service. Free parking. Pets allowed (fee). | 6911 Pensacola Blvd. 32505 | 850/479-3800 or 800/406-1411 | www.hojo.com | 97 rooms, 24 suites | $45-$70 | AE, D, DC, MC, V.

La Quinta Inn. Like most properties in the La Quinta chain, this three-story motel has a white exterior with teal trim, and a sharp, vaguely southwestern-style look. The beach and Historic District are 7-8 mi away; the airport is 3 mi from the motel. Complimentary Continental breakfast. In-room data ports, some microwaves, some refrigerators. Cable TV. Pool. Laundry facilities. Pets allowed. | 7750 N. Davis Hwy. 32514-7557 | 850/474-0411 or 800/531-5900 | fax 850/474-1521 | www.laquinta.com | 128 rooms, 2 suites | $59-$72 | AE, D, DC, MC, V.

Pensacola Grand Hotel. You enter this downtown hotel through the restored 1912 Louisville & Nashville train depot. The hotel still has old railway signs, ticket and baggage counters. Twenty-first century rooms are in the attached 15-story modern tower; some have huge picture windows and wooden spiral staircases. Restaurant, bars. In-room data ports, some refrigerators. Cable TV. Pool. Exercise equipment. Library. Laundry facilities. Business services, airport shuttle. Pets allowed (fee). | 200 E. Gregory St. 32501 | 850/433-3336 or 800/348-3336 | fax 850/432-7572 | www.pensacolagrandhotel.com | 201 rooms, 11 suites | $90-$100 | AE, D, DC, MC, V.

Ramada Inn Bayview. This hotel, off I-10 at exit 6, 5 mi from downtown, contains several buildings surrounding a landscaped courtyard with a pool and gazebo. The hotel, on a cliff overlooking the bay, offers Atlantic views from the restaurant and lounge. Rooms do not have views. Restaurant, bar (with entertainment). Complimentary Continental breakfast. In-room data ports, some microwaves, some refrigerators. Cable TV. Pool. Hot tub. Exercise equipment. Laundry facilities, laundry service. Business services, airport shuttle. Pets allowed. | 7601 Scenic Hwy. 32504 | 850/477-7155 or 800/212-1212 | fax 850/477-7198 | www.ramada.com | 150 rooms | $70-$78 | AE, D, DC, MC, V.

Shoney's Inn and Suites. This motel curls around a pool courtyard. There are rooms and two kinds of suites, which come with a refrigerator and microwave. It is 8 mi from downtown, off I-10 at exit 5, within walking distance of University Mall. A Shoney's restaurant is next door. Complimentary Continental breakfast. In-room data ports, some microwaves, some refrigerators. Cable TV. Pool. Laundry facilities, laundry service. Airport shuttle. Pets allowed (fee). | 8080 N. Davis Hwy. 32514 | 850/484–8070 or 800/222–2222 | fax 850/484–3853 | www.shoneysinn.com | 111 rooms, 4 suites | $67–$79 | AE, D, DC, MC, V.

The Yacht House Bed & Breakfast. This B&B is just west of downtown, across from the prestigious Pensacola Yacht Club, and a 5-min walk to Sanders Beach. Each of the three upper level rooms—the Shanghai, Nairobi, and Sahara suites—has an outdoor hot tub on a private deck. Guests can borrow a telescope for stargazing, or test their fortune with a daily tarot reading. Complimentary Continental breakfast. In-room data ports, in-room safes, some refrigerators, in-room hot tubs. Cable TV, some in-room VCRs. Pond. Gym. Laundry facilities. Pets allowed (fee). | 1820 Cypress St. 32501 | 850/433–3634 | www.yachthouse.com | 6 rooms | $65–$125 suites | AE, D, MC, V.

PERRY

Perry Days Inn. This small two-story motel is in the center of rural Perry and is a popular place to stay if you're in the area for fishing or hunting. Some in-room data ports, in-room safes, some microwaves, some refrigerators. Cable TV. Pool. Laundry facilities, laundry service. Some pets allowed (fee). | 2277 S. Byron Butler Pkwy. 32347 | 850/584–5311 or 800/544–8313 | www.daysinn.com | 60 rooms | $40–$70 | AE, D, DC, MC, V.

Villager Lodge. This basic motel is surrounded by fast-food chains and a retail area with a huge laundromat. This two-story red brick building takes up only a portion of the 4 acres it owns, so there is a touch of nature around. While not big on charm, you can't beat the price. Complimentary Continental breakfast. Some kitchenettes, some microwaves, some refrigerators. Cable TV. Pool. Pets allowed (fee). | 2238 S. Byron Butler Pkwy. 32347 | 850/584–4221 | fax 850/838–1718 | 66 rooms | $40 | AE, MC, V.

PORT CHARLOTTE

Days Inn of Port Charlotte. This is an affordable, simple three-story motel, off U.S. 41 at exits 31 and 32. It is in a commercial area, across the street from several strip malls, and next door to a restaurant. There are century-old oak trees covered in Spanish Moss nearby. In-room data ports, refrigerators, some microwaves. Cable TV. Pool. Exercise equipment. Laundry facilities. Business services. Some pets allowed (fee). | 1941 Tamiami Trail (U.S. 41) 33948 | 941/627–8900 or 800/329–7466 | fax 941/743–8503 | www.daysinn.com | 122 rooms, 4 suites | $99–$109 | AE, D, DC, MC, V.

Litchfield Inn. Across from Promenades Mall in downtown Port Charlotte is this complex of three two-story, landscaped buildings. Most of the rooms overlook a central garden-filled courtyard, and others have exterior entrances for easy unloading from the car. Many of the rooms have small, separate living room areas and some have bars. Restaurant, bar (with entertainment). Some microwaves, some refrigerators. Cable TV. Pool. Laundry facilities, laundry service. Business services. Pets allowed (fee). | 3400 Tamiami Tr. (U.S. 41) 33952 | 941/625–4181 or 800/933–9987 | fax 941/629–1740 | 104 rooms, 13 suites | $59–$149 | AE, D, DC, MC, V.

PUNTA GORDA

Best Western Waterfront. A great pool area looks out over a few palm trees to Charlotte Harbor. Adjacent to the hotel is Gilchrist Park, with tennis courts, bicycle paths, and playgrounds. Fishermen's Village is just 1 mi away. The hotel restaurant is on a large covered deck 3 ft from the water. Restaurant, bar. In-room data ports, some microwaves, some refrigerators. Cable TV. Pool. Exercise equipment. Dock, fishing. Laundry facilities. Business services. Pets allowed (fee). | 300 W. Retta Esplanade 33950 | 941/639–1165 or 800/525–1022 | fax 941/639–8116 | www.bestwestern.com | 176 rooms, 7 suites | $89–$145 | AE, D, DC, MC, V.

Holiday Inn Harborside. This centrally located motel is next to the bridge over the Peace River. Fishermen's Village, the nearest attraction, is 2 mi away. Restaurant, bar (with entertainment), room service. In-room data ports, some kitchenettes, some refrigerators.

Cable TV. Pool. Gym. Dock, fishing. Laundry facilities, laundry service. Business services. Some pets allowed (fee). | 33 Tamiami Trail (U.S. 41) 33950 | 941/639–2167 or 877/639–9399 | fax 941/639–1707 | www.holiday-inn.com | 100 rooms | $67–$109 | AE, MC, V.

Motel 6. This one-story, no-frills motel is clean, comfortable, and inexpensive. There are several restaurants within a mile. In-room data ports. Cable TV. Pool. Laundry facilities. Some pets allowed. | 9300 Knights Dr. | 941/639–9585 or 800/466–8356 | fax 941/639–6820 | www.motel6.com | 114 rooms | $35–$50 | AE, MC, V.

ST. AUGUSTINE BEACH

Best Western Ocean Inn. This two-story hotel is near beautiful beaches, 3 mi from the St. Augustine Alligator Farm, and 10 mi from Marineland of Florida. Restaurant, complimentary Continental breakfast. Cable TV. Outdoor pool. Laundry facilities. Business services. Pets allowed. | 3955 Hwy. A1A S 32084 | 904/471–8010 or 888/879–3578 (reservations) | fax 904/460–9124 | www.bestwestern.com | 33 rooms, 2 suites | $99–$149, $119–$169 suites | AE, D, DC, MC, V.

Holiday Inn, St. Augustine Beach. Built in the late 1960s, this five-story motel offers guests access to a private beach. Restaurant, bar. In-room data ports. Cable TV. Outdoor pool. Exercise equipment. Beach. Video games. Laundry facilities. Business services. Some pets allowed. | 860 A1A Beach Blvd. 32084 | 904/471–2555 or 800/626–7263 | fax 904/461–8710 | www.holiday-inn.com | 151 rooms | $110–$130 | AE, D, DC, MC, V.

ST. PETERSBURG

La Quinta Inn. This two-story hotel is built around a courtyard. St. Petersburg Beach is just 10 mi away and there is a 24-hr restaurant across the street. Complimentary Continental breakfast. In-room data ports. Cable TV. Pool. Exercise equipment. Laundry facilities. Business services. Some pets allowed. | 4999 34th St. N 33714 | 727/527–8421 | fax 727/527–8851 | www.laquinta.com | 120 rooms | $69–$110 | AE, D, DC, MC, V.

St. Petersburg Bayfront Hilton. Rooms have a view of Tampa Bay in this 15-story hotel on exit 9 of I–275. The St. Petersburg-Clearwater Airport is 20 min away. Restaurant, bar. In-room data ports, some refrigerators. Cable TV. Outdoor pool. Outdoor hot tub. Gym. Laundry facilities. Business services. Pets allowed (fee). | 333 1st St. S 33701 | 727/894–5000 or 800/916–2221 (reservations) | fax 727/894–7655 | www.hilton.com | 315 rooms, 18 suites | $189, $190–$315 suites | AE, D, DC, MC, V.

SANFORD

Best Western Marina Hotel and Conference Center. Set on its own small, man-made island, this two-story hotel is just 2 mi from the Central Florida Zoological Park. The River-ship *Romance* tour boat departs from here. 2 restaurants, bar. In-room data ports, some microwaves. Cable TV. Outdoor pool, lake. Dock, water sports, boating, fishing. Laundry facilities. Business services. Pets allowed (fee). | 530 N. Palmetto Ave. 32771 | 407/323–1910 or 800/290–1910 | fax 407/322–7076 | www.bestwestern.com | 96 rooms | $79–$89 | AE, D, DC, MC, V.

Days Inn. This two-story motel is across the street from the Seminole Towne Center Mall. There's a 24-hr restaurant on premises and several additional eateries within walking distance. In-room data ports, some refrigerators. Cable TV. Outdoor pool. Laundry facilities. Business services. Pets allowed. | 4650 Hwy. 46W 32771 | 407/323–6500 or 800/544–8313 | fax 407/323–2962 | www.daysinn.com | 119 rooms | $60–$105 | AE, D, DC, MC, V.

SANIBEL ISLAND

Brennen's Tarpon Tale Inn. Built in the early 1960s, this B&B offers five charming attached bungalows and—two blocks away—a cottage with two units (each with full gourmet kitchens). Accommodations are decorated in whitewash wicker and rattan and have antique oak furniture. Complimentary Continental breakfast (for inn guests). Some kitchenettes, microwaves, refrigerators. Cable TV, in-room VCRs (and movies), some room phones. Bicycles. Library. Laundry facilities. Some pets allowed. | 367 Periwinkle Way 33957 | 941/472–0939 | fax 941/472–6202 | www.tarpontale.com | 5 rooms, 2 cottage units | $159–$289, $209–$299 cottages | D, MC, V.

Driftwood Inn. These fully stocked, light-pink and hot-pink efficiency cottages with turquoise doors, have two bedrooms and two bathrooms units, plus multiple beds and pull-out couches—it's ideal for groups of friends traveling together. Each cottage has a full kitchen, dining, and living room areas, as well as a screened-in porch, complete with dining-room table for eating alfresco. Most amenities including sheets, beach chairs, and umbrellas are included; you just provide your own beach towels. Microwaves, refrigerators. Beach, water sports. Pets allowed. | 711 Donax St. 33957 | 941/395–8874 | fax 941/472–6935 | www.driftwoodsanibel.com | 4 units | $150–$175 | MC, V.

Signal Inn Beach and Racquetball Club. Each of these elevated, bedecked cottages has cross ventilation and lets in plenty of sunlight. The upscale accommodations range from one- to four-bedroom units. The resort is eco-friendly—the pool and each unit's water is solar-heated. The beach is famous for shelling. Kitchenettes. In-room VCRs. Hot tub, sauna. Hiking, racquetball. Beach, water sports. Laundry facilities. Some pets allowed (fee). | 1811 Olde Middle Gulf Dr. 33957 | 941/472–4690 or 800/992–4690 | fax 941/472–3988 | www.signalinn.com | 19 cottages | $195–$395 (7–night minimum) | AE, MC, V.

Waterside Inn on the Beach. Accommodations at the Waterside are in clusters and consist of condo units, beach cottages, and efficiencies. Rooms are in an airy, island motif; some have a private patio. There are two outdoor pools, and the property fringes the gulf. Some kitchenettes, some microwaves, some refrigerators, some in-room hot tubs. 2 outdoor pools. Beach, water sports, boating, fishing. Laundry facilities. Some pets allowed. | 3033 W. Gulf Dr. 33957 | 941/472–1345 or 800/741–6166 | fax 941/472–2148 | www.watersideinnonthebeach.com | 4 rooms, 10 efficiencies, 8 cottages | $218–$346 | AE, D, MC, V.

SARASOTA

Quayside Inn. A B&B atmosphere prevails here at this downtown property. Rooms in this two-story building are adorned with standard motel furnishings, such as matching bedside and sitting-area tables. Light-wood furnishings and soft colors help brighten things up. Some refrigerators, some microwaves. Outdoor pool. Pets allowed. | 270 N. Tamiami Trail 34236 | 941/366–0414 or 877/294–3265 | fax 941/954–3379 | www.quaysideinn.com | 26 rooms | $65–$85 | AE, D, MC.

Wellesley Inn. This independently run motel is a dependable choice for basic, no-frills accommodations. It has interior corridors, an elevator to the second floor, connecting rooms, and is about 5 mi from local museums and restaurants. Complimentary Continental breakfast. In-room data ports, microwaves, refrigerators. Cable TV. Pool. Business services, airport shuttle. Pets allowed. | 1803 N. Tamiami Trail 34234 | 941/366–5128 or 800/444–8888 | fax 941/953–4322 | 106 rooms | $60–$130 | AE, D, MC, V.

SEBRING

Chateau Elan Hotel and Spa. The Chateau is close to Sebring International Raceway, with a number of guest rooms and all the meeting areas overlooking the action. An on-site spa offers beauty treatments and massages. Restaurant, bar. Microwaves, refrigerators. Cable TV, in-room VCRs. Pool. Hot tub, massage, spa. Exercise equipment. Laundry facilities. Business services. Pets allowed. | 150 Midway Dr. 33870 | 863/655–6252 | fax 863/655–6303 | 161 rooms | $88–$125 | AE, D, MC, V.

SIESTA KEY

Turtle Beach Resort. This is a small, cozy waterfront property—on Siesta Key's less-touristy southern tip—consisting of eight private cottages themed differently (Victorian, Caribbean, etc.) and with hot tubs and beach chairs. Ophelia's on the Bay restaurant is next door. Microwaves, refrigerators, in-room hot tubs. Cable TV, in-room VCRs. Pool. Laundry facilities. Pets allowed. | 9049 Midnight Pass Rd. 34242 | 941/349–4554 | 10 units | $155–$315 | AE, MC, V.

STARKE

Best Western Motor Inn. This simple, two-story motel has basic rooms but rather bleak grounds. Complimentary Continental breakfast. Refrigerators. Cable TV. Pets allowed. | 1290 N. Temple Ave. 32091 | 904/964–6744 | fax 904/964–3355 | 51 rooms | $53–$115 | AE, D, MC, V.

Starke Days Inn. This basic motel has a tropical courtyard, large airy rooms, and a Denny's restaurant and Winner's Pub. Pets allowed. | 1101 N. Temple Ave. 32091 | 904/964–7600 or 800/544–8313 | fax 904/964–5201 | www.daysinn.com | 100 rooms | $49–$99 | AE, DC, D, MC, V.

SUGARLOAF KEY

Sugarloaf Lodge. All rooms at this resort face the sparkling blue-green waters off the keys. Rooms in the older building have a fishing-lodge feel with dark-wood paneling and bright bedspreads. The rooms in the new building have light walls and light-wood furniture. Restaurant, bar (with entertainment), room service. Some kitchenettes, some refrigerators, cable TV. Pool. 2 tennis courts, miniature golf. Dock, water sports, boating, fishing, bicycles. Laundry facilities. Pets allowed (fee). | MM 17, Overseas Hwy. 33043 | 305/745–3211 or 800/553–6097 | www.sugarloaflodge.com | 55 rooms | $130 | AE, D, DC, MC, V.

Sugarloaf Key KOA Resort. Camp at the southernmost KOA in the US, 20 mi from Key West. You can hang out on the beach, boat, swim, and all the rest. New RV efficiency rentals are available with kitchenettes and air-conditioning. Great snorkeling, diving, and fishing are available nearby. Some sites are beachfront. Bar. Pool. Outdoor hot tub. Miniature golf. Volleyball. Beach, boating, fishing, bicycles. Playground. Laundry facilities. Pets allowed. | MM 20, cross Bow channel bridge, immediately on left 33042 | 305/745–3549 or 800/KOA–7731 | fax 305/745–9889 | sugarloaf@koa.net | www.koa.com | 200 sites plus tent area | $43–$83 | AE, D, MC, V.

SUN CITY CENTER

Sun City Center Inn. Tropical plants and a putting green might drive you to dance to the oldies with some older golf-lovers in the bar. This motel is 9 mi from the boating activities on the bay and about 25 mi to the Gulf beach. Rooms have two double beds, and some open directly onto the pool patio. Restaurant, bar (with entertainment). Cable TV. Pool. Putting green, tennis. Business services. Pets allowed. | 1335 Rickenbacker Dr. 33573 | 813/634–3331 or 800/237–8200 | fax 813/634–2053 | 100 rooms | $49–$79 | AE, MC, V.

TALLAHASSEE

Holiday Inn, Northwest. This two-story hotel has a covered drive and pale stucco exterior. Rooms are done in dark pine greens and earthy browns. It's within walking distance of shops and restaurants and 5 mi from the Governor's Square Mall. Restaurant, bar. In-room data ports, microwaves, refrigerators. Cable TV. Pool. Laundry facilities. Business services, free parking. Pets allowed. | 2714 Graves Rd. | 850/562–2000 | fax 850/562–8519 | www.holiday-inn.com | 179 rooms | $66–$89 | AE, D, MC, V.

La Quinta Inn-North. Rooms in this three-story motel in a colonnaded Mission-style building have large, white-tiled bathrooms with huge mirrors. Most have comfortable sitting areas with tables and love seats. In-room data ports, microwaves, refrigerators. Cable TV. Pool. Laundry facilities. Business services, free parking. Some pets allowed. | 2905 N. Monroe St. 32303-3636 | 850/385–7172 | fax 850/422–2463 | www.laquinta.com | 154 units | $76–$96 | AE, D, MC, V.

La Quinta Inn, Tallahassee South. This motel has a crisp, white exterior with teal trim and well-maintained grounds. The outdoor pool has an expansive deck area with chaise longues for sunbathing and umbrellaed tables for shade. Rooms are basic but comfortable. In-room data ports, refrigerators. Cable TV. Pool. Laundry facilities. Business services, free parking. Some pets allowed. | 2850 Apalachee Pkwy. 32301-3608 | 850/878–5099 | fax 850/ 878–6665 | www.laquinta.com | 134 rooms | $72–$92 | AE, D, MC, V.

Ramada Inn, North. Situated on 13 acres of landscaped grounds, this motel has a pleasant lobby with high ceilings. Rooms are done in mauve. Restaurant, bar. Microwaves, refrigerators. Cable TV, in-room VCRs (and movies). Pool. Business services, airport shuttle, free parking. Pets allowed. | 2900 N. Monroe St. 32303 | 850/386–1027 | fax 850/422–1025 | www.ramada.com | 200 rooms | $79–$102 | AE, D, MC, V.

Shoney's Inn. The central courtyard is filled with fountains and a huge moss-covered oak tree. Rooms are done in Spanish-mission style with autumn colors and views of the courtyard. Your breakfast is served at the adjacent Shoney's restaurant. Complimentary Continental breakfast. In-room data ports, some microwaves, some refrigerators, some in-room hot tubs. Cable TV. Pool. Laundry facilities. Free parking. Pets allowed. | 2801 N. Monroe St. 32303 | 850/386–8286 | fax 850/422–1074 | www.shoneysinn.com | 112 rooms | $67–$99 | AE, D, DC, MC.

TownePlace Suites Marriott. These roomy town house–style Marriott suites come in studio, one-bedroom, and two-bedroom varieties. Rooms are beige with green carpet. All have full kitchens. The hotel is 5 mi from the Capitol and the Tallahassee Museum of History and Natural Science, and 20 mi from Wakulla Springs State Park. Pool. Exercise room. Laundry facilities. Business services. Pets allowed. | 1876 Capital Circle, NE 32308 | 850/219–0122 | fax 850/219–0133 | www.towneplace.com | 95 suites | $84–$110.

TAMPA

Amerisuites. This all-suites property has accommodations with large sleeping and sitting areas and mini-kitchens. Busch Gardens and the University of South Florida campus are less than 1 mi away. Picnic area, complimentary Continental breakfast. In-room data ports, microwaves, refrigerators. Cable TV, in-room VCRs (and movies). Pool. Gym. Laundry facilities. Business services, free parking. Pets allowed. | 11408 N. 30th St. 33612-6446 | 813/ 979–1922 or 800/833–1516 (reservations) | fax 813/979–1926 | www.amerisuites. com | 128 suites | $79–$109 | AE, D, MC, V.

Amerisuites, Tampa Airport. This all-suites hotel is 2 mi from Raymond James Stadium and 5 mi from the Tampa Performing Arts Center, the Florida Aquarium, and the Convention Center. Picnic area, complimentary Continental breakfast. In-room data ports, microwaves, refrigerators. Cable TV, in-room VCRs (and movies). Pool. Gym. Laundry facilities. Business services, airport shuttle, free parking. Pets allowed. | 4811 W. Main St. 33607 | 813/282–1037 or 800/833–1516 (reservations) | fax 813/282–1148 | www.amerisuites.com | 126 suites | $129–$189 | AE, D, MC, V.

Baymont Inn, Tampa/Busch Gardens. This well-maintained property is 2 mi west of Busch Gardens' main gate. The three-story inn is finished in pale, cream-colored stucco with white trim. The rooms have large windows. Complimentary Continental breakfast. In-room data ports, in-room safes, microwaves, refrigerators. Cable TV. Pool. Business services, free parking. Pets allowed. | 9202 30th St. N 33612 | 813/930–6900 or 800/789–4103 (reservations) | fax 813/930–0563 | www.baymontinn.com | 149 rooms | $56–$96 | AE, D, MC, V.

Baymont Inn, Tampa Fairgrounds. This chain motel across from the state fairgrounds has large rooms. It's 7 mi from downtown. Complimentary Continental breakfast. In-room data ports, microwaves, refrigerators. Cable TV. Pool. Business services, free parking. Pets allowed. | 4811 U.S. 301 N 33610 | 813/626–0885 or 800/789–4103 (reservations) | fax 813/623–3321 | www.baymontinn.com | 102 rooms | $54–$90 | AE, D, MC, V.

Baymont Inn, Tampa Southeast. This lodging is within 2 mi of a dozen popular chain restaurants. The rooms are large. Complimentary Continental breakfast. In-room data ports, microwaves, refrigerators. Cable TV. Pool. Laundry service. Business services, free parking. Pets allowed. | 602 S. Falkenburg Rd. 33619 | 813/684–4007 or 800/789–4103 (reservations) | fax 813/681–3042 | www.baymontinn.com | 102 rooms | $57–$82 | AE, D, MC, V.

Best Western Weeki Wachee Resort. This motel is across from the Weeki Wachee Springs and Buccaneer Bay water parks. Rooms in the two-story building have bright, tropical prints, balconies, and floor-to-ceiling windows. The resort can set you up with golf packages at area courses. Local nature paths offer good hiking and biking. Picnic area, complimentary Continental breakfast. Pool, wading pool. Cable TV. Business services, free parking. Some pets allowed. | 6172 Commercial Way, Weeki Wachee 34606 | 352/596–2007 | fax 352/596–0667 | www.bestwestern.com | 122 rooms | $65–$78 | AE, D, DC, MC, V.

Comfort Inn. This motel angles around an outdoor pool area. Rooms are done in pale colors, and all have whirlpool baths. There are more than 25 restaurants within 4 mi of the motel, and the Florida Aquarium and Fairgrounds are within 6 mi. Refrigerators. Cable TV. Pool. Business services, free parking. Some pets allowed. | 9373 Cortez Blvd., Weeki Wachee 34613 | 352/596–9000 or 800/228–5150 | fax 352/597–4010 | www.comfortinn.com | 68 rooms | $55–$70 | AE, D, MC, V.

Days Inn Airport Stadium. Raymond James Stadium and the Yankees' spring training facility are within walking distance of this two-story motel. The building wraps around a central courtyard with two pools. The motel has a Hawaiian theme, with a tropical fish–garden and a palms-and-hyacinths motif in the lobby and rooms. Complimentary Continental breakfast. Pools. Cable TV. Laundry facilities. Business services, free parking. Pets allowed. | 2522 N. Dale Mabry Hwy. 33607 | 813/877–6181 or 800/448–4373 | fax 813/875–6171 | www.daysinn.com | 285 rooms | $70–$84 | AE, D, MC, V.

Embassy Suites Hotel, Tampa/Airport/Westshore. This white tower looms over the adjacent pool area. Most rooms look out into the multistory atrium, which is full of live plants and fountains. All rooms have dark wood antique reproductions. Restaurant, bar, complimentary full breakfast. In-room data ports, minibars, microwaves, refrigerators. Cable TV, in-room VCRs (and movies). Pool. Hot tub, saunas. Exercise equipment. Laundry facilities. Airport shuttle, free parking. Pets allowed. | 555 N. Westshore Blvd. 33609 | 813/875–1555 | fax 813/287–3664 | www.embassysuites.com | 221 rooms | $129–$199 | AE, D, MC, V.

Holiday Inn Busch Gardens. This hotel's lobby area has Crayola-bright color schemes in the lobby and rooms. Kids' Suites have separate sleeping areas for kids, cordoned off from the main room by screens emblazoned with wildlife images. The minirooms have three-tiered bunkbeds, TVs, and pay-per-play video games. It's next to Busch Gardens and across from Tampa's largest shopping mall. Restaurant. In-room data ports, minibars, microwaves, refrigerators. Cable TV, in-room VCRs (and movies). Pool. Exercise equipment. Laundry facilities. Business services, free parking. Pets allowed. | 2701 E. Fowler Ave. 33612 | 813/971–4710 | fax 813/977–0155 | www.holiday-inn.com | 395 rooms | $90–$109 | AE, D, MC, V.

Holiday Inn Express. The rooms here are basic but pleasant, with modular, wood-veneer furnishings and a muted, mauve-and-teal color scheme. Complimentary Continental breakfast. In-room data ports, microwaves, refrigerators. Cable TV. Pool, wading pool. Laundry facilities. Business services, free parking. Pets allowed. | 100 E. Bears Ave. 33613 | 813/961–1000 | fax 813/961–5704 | www.holiday-inn.com | 154 rooms | $80–$100 | AE, D, MC, V.

La Quinta Inn Airport. Mission-style architecture characterizes this motel, with its clay tiles and arches. The airport generates some noise. Rooms are comfortable. In-room data ports, microwaves, refrigerators. Cable TV. Pool. Exercise equipment. Laundry service. Free parking. Pets allowed. | 4730 Spruce St. 33607-1497 | 813/287-0440 | fax 813/286-7399 | www.laquinta.com | 122 rooms | $84-$119 | AE, D, MC, V.

La Quinta Inn State Fair. The State Fairgrounds and Expo Park are directly across the highway, and Busch Gardens is about 5 mi away. The rooms have a Southwestern theme with floral bedspreads. In-room data ports, microwaves, refrigerators. Cable TV. Pool. Laundry service. Pets allowed. | 2904 Melbourne Blvd. 33605-2457 | 813/623-3591 | fax 813/620-1375 | www.laquinta.com | 128 rooms | $49-$76 | AE, D, MC, V.

La Quinta Inn and Suites USF. This motel sports La Quinta's hallmark Hacienda-style architecture—vanilla stucco, terra-cotta tiles, and palm trees. Rooms are sedate with lots of cream and teal accents in both the sleeping and sitting areas, which are separated by arched doorways. In-room data ports, microwaves, refrigerators. Cable TV. Pool. Exercise equipment. Laundry service. Free parking. Pets allowed. | 3701 E. Fowler Ave. 33612 | 813/910-7500 | fax 813/910-7600 | www.laquinta.com | 109 rooms | $99-$109, $129 suites | AE, D, MC, V.

Tahitian Inn. This smallish motel bills itself as "the last independently owned and operated motel in the Tampa area." The service is personal and the accommodations are non-generic. The pool area has deck chairs shaded by thatched awnings. Rooms have understated furnishings, track-lighting, and patio/courtyard views via glass sliding doors. The Tahitian is quiet and pleasantly removed from the crowded tourist areas. In-room data ports, refrigerators. Cable TV. Pool. Exercise equipment. Laundry facilities. Business services, free parking. Pets allowed. | 601 S. Dale Mabry Hwy. 33609 | 813/877-6721 or 800/876-1397 (reservations) | fax 813/877-6218 | www.tahitianinn.com | 79 rooms | $55-$61 | AE, D, MC, V.

TAVARES

Inn on the Green. This motel has a man-made lake behind the property and a 3-hole chipping and putting green. The rooms are done in earth tones and have king-size beds and walk-in closets. Some have lake views. Picnic area. Microwaves, refrigerators. Cable TV, in-room VCRs (and movies). Volleyball. Laundry facilities. Pets allowed. | 700 E. Burleigh Blvd. 32778 | 352/343-6373 or 800/935-2935 | fax 352/343-7216 | www.innonthegreen.net | 77 rooms, 4 suites | $79 | AE, D, DC, MC, V.

TITUSVILLE

Best Western Space Shuttle Inn. This two-story motel is on the Indian River. The pool has a large screened porch adjacent to the pool area. There's also a picnic/barbecue area and a fishing dock. Rooms have king-size or two double beds, light wood furnishings, a lounge chair, and a balcony. Evergreen Rooms are odor- and allergen-free and have purified water. I-95 exit 79. Restaurant, bar, complimentary Continental breakfast. Picnic area. In-room data ports, microwaves, refrigerators. Cable TV. Pool. Sauna. Basketball, exercise equipment, volleyball. Fishing. Playground. Laundry facilities, laundry service. Children's programs (up to age 12). Business services. Pets allowed. | 3455 Cheney Hwy. 32780 | 321/269-9100 | fax 321/383-4674 | www.spaceshuttleinn.com | 125 rooms | $59-$99 | AE, D, MC, V.

Days Inn, Kennedy Space Center. Rooms are done in yellow, green, and pink with floral bedding and have queen- or king-size beds and a sitting area. The two-story motel sits on the Indian River. Restaurant, bar. Microwaves, refrigerators. Cable TV. Pool, wading pool. Hot tub. Laundry facilities. Pets allowed. | 3755 Cheney Hwy. 32780 | 321/269-4480 | fax 321/383-0646 | www.daysinn.com | 150 rooms | $54-$69 | AE, D, MC, V.

Holiday Inn, Kennedy Space Center. The Titusville outpost of this chain overlooks the Kennedy Space Center launch pads from across the Indian River. Rooms in the two-story hotel are comfortable with balconies overlooking the river or pool. Restaurant, bar (with entertainment), room service. In-room data ports, refrigerators. Cable TV. Pool. Gym, volleyball. Beach, fishing. Laundry facilities. Business services. Pets allowed. | 4951 S. Washington Ave. 32780 | 407/269–2121 or 800–HOLIDAY | fax 407/267–4739 | www.holiday-inn.com | 118 rooms | $69–$129 | AE, D, MC, V.

Riverside Inn. This motel with views of the Indian River is nothing fancy, but has a small pool area with lounge chairs and sparse tropical landscaping. Rooms, which are small and show some wear, have wood furnishings and dark hues of maroons and blues. I–95 exit 80. Restaurant, bar. Microwaves, refrigerators. Cable TV, in-room VCRs (and movies). Pool. Exercise equipment. Dock. Laundry facilities. Business services. Pets allowed. | 1829 Riverside Dr. 32780 | 321/267–7900 | fax 321/267–7080 | 119 rooms | $45–$79 | AE, D, MC, V.

VENICE

Days Inn. This motel is less than 3 mi from Venice Beach and 2 mi from I–75. Rooms are basic motel. Restaurant. Microwaves, refrigerators. Cable TV. Pool. Laundry service. Business services. Pets allowed. | 1710 S. Tamiami Trail 34293 | 941/493–4558 or 800/DAYS–INN | fax 941/493–1593 | info@daysinnvenice.com | 72 rooms | $56–$99 | AE, D, MC, V.

VERO BEACH

Great American Inn & Suites. The hotel is ½ mi away from Outlet Mall and Indian River Mall, 8 mi west of Vero Beach, and near fishing, boating, and wildlife areas. It has a restaurant that serves breakfast and an outdoor pool. Cable TV. Laundry service. Pets allowed. | 8800 20th St. 32966 | 561/562–9991 or 800/960–7707 (reservations) | fax 561/562–0716 | 225 rooms, 4 suites | $57–$69 | AE, D, DC, MC, V.

WEST PALM BEACH

Blossom's Otahiti. After a summer 2000 renovation, this B&B has a casual dining area, a bright family room, and an elegant living room. There is a screened-in pool and patio area, a lush garden, and a pond with water lilies and tropical fish. Complimentary breakfast, dining room. TV in common area. Laundry facilities. Some pets allowed (fee). | 3169 Horseshoe Circle W 33417 | 561/640–9295 | fax 561/640–9542 | www.blossoms-otahiti.com | 4 rooms | $95 | AE, MC, V.

Comfort Inn. This six-story budget motel is 3 mi south of West Palm Beach International Airport, and 20 min from the beaches. Most of the rooms have patios or balconies that overlook the pool area. A new in-house restaurant opens in 2001, but there are plenty within walking distance. You can also hit the gym at a nearby health club with which the motel is affiliated. Complimentary Continental breakfast. In-room data ports, in-room safes, some microwaves, some refrigerators, cable TV. Pool. Video games. Laundry facilities, laundry service. Business services. Pets allowed (fee). | 1901 Palm Beach Lakes Blvd. 33409 | 561/689–6100 or 800/228–5150 | fax 561/686–6177 | www.comfortinn.com | 162 rooms | $120 | AE, D, DC, MC, V.

Days Inn West Palm Beach/Airport North. A lush tropical courtyard garden creates a colorful tropical atmosphere at this motel. Rooms are basic, but have balconies. Restaurant. Some in-room data ports, in-room safes, some microwaves, some refrigerators. Cable TV. Pool. Outdoor hot tub. Laundry facilities. Airports shuttles. Pets allowed (fee). | 2300 45th St. 33407 | 561/689–0450 or 800/544–8313 | fax 561/686–7439 | www.daysinn.com | 214 rooms | $52–$70 | AE, D, DC, MC, V.

Hibiscus House. Built in 1922 by Mayor David Dunkle during the Florida land boom, this Cape Cod–style B&B began the beautification trend that landed the neighborhood on the National Register of Historic Places. Rooms are individually decorated with antiques the owner collected during his career as an interior designer. Each room of this residential B&B has a terrace view of the attractive poolside covered in tropical Florida foliage. Complimentary breakfast. In-room data ports, microwaves. Cable TV. Pool. Airport shuttle. Pets allowed. | 501 30th St. 33407 | 561/863–5633 or 800/203–4927 | fax 561/863–5633 | www. hibiscushouse.com | 5 rooms, 2 suites, 1 apartment, 1 cottage | $95–$170 | AE, D, MC, V.

Red Roof Inn. This chain motel is 20 min from the beach and Palm Beach Mall. Rooms are basic with pastel walls and wood furniture, but the pool area and the landscaping around the building are lush, with tropical foilage and blooming flowers. In-room data ports, some microwaves, some refrigerators, cable TV. Pool. Some pets allowed (fee). | 2421 Metro Center Blvd. E 33407 | 561/697–7710 or 800/843–7663 | fax 561/697–1728 | www.redroof.com | 129 rooms | $84 | AE, D, DC, MC, V.

Wellesley Inn. This six-story building is 4 mi from the beach. Standard rooms come with views of the city. Complimentary Continental breakfast. In-room data ports, refrigerators. Cable TV. Pool. Laundry service. Business services. Pets allowed. | 1910 Palm Beach Lakes Blvd. 33409 | 561/689–8540 or 800/444–8888 | fax 561/687–8090 | www.wellesley.com | 93 rooms, 13 suites | $67–$110 | AE, D, MC, V.

WHITE SPRINGS

Suwannee Valley Campground. Located on the high banks of the Suwannee River, this scenic and tranquil site offers fully equipped cabins, in addition to campsites. Each cabin sleeps four, and has air-conditioning, a microwave, a refrigerator, and a porch. Hiking trails run through the property. Pool. TV in common area. Hiking. Dock, water sports, fishing. Playground. Laundry facilities. Pets allowed. | Rt. 1 Box 1860 32096 | 904/397–1667 | fax 904/397–1560 | www.isgroup.net/camping | 12 cabins | Cabin $39.

WINTER HAVEN

Best Western Admiral's Inn. Adjacent to Cypress Gardens, and 1 mi from Lake Eloise, this luxury hotel has a heated Olympic-size pool, and a lounge with a comedy club. Restaurant, bar, complimentary Continental breakfast. Refrigerators. Cable TV. Pool. Beauty salon. Business services, airport shuttle. Pets allowed. | 5665 Cypress Gardens Blvd. (Hwy. 540) 33884 | 863/324–5950 or 888/879–3578 | fax 941/324–2376 | www.bestwestern.com | 157 rooms | $95–$105 | AE, D, DC, MC, V.

Budget Host Driftwood. This budget motel is 1½ mi from Cypress Gardens, and ¼ mi from the Cleveland Indians' spring training facility. Complimentary Continental breakfast. Refrigerators. Cable TV. Pool. Pets allowed. | 970 Cypress Gardens Blvd. (Hwy. 540) 33880 | 863/294–4229 or 800/283–4678 | fax 863/293–2089 | 23 rooms | $38–$68 | AE, DC, MC, V.

Cypress Motel. This family retreat, 2 mi east of Cypress Gardens on a quiet side road, has a 50-ft pool surrounded by two acres of lush greenery. The rooms are basic, but tastefully decorated, with views of the pool and garden. There are four mobile homes behind the motel, and eight efficiencies. Lake Fox is 200 yards away. Picnic area, complimentary Continental breakfast. In-room data ports, some kitchenettes, some microwaves, some refrigerators. Cable TV, some in-room VCRs (with movies). Pool. Playground. Laundry facilities. Pets allowed. | 5651 Cypress Gardens Blvd. (Hwy. 540) 33884 | 863/324–5867 or 800/729–6706 | fax 941/324–5867 | www.cypressmotel.com | 21 rooms | $70–$80 | AE, D, DC, MC, V.

Holiday Inn Cypress Gardens, Winter Haven. This hotel is 1 mi west of Lake Shipp, in a quiet area with fishing, waterskiing, and boating. There is a Country Kitchen restaurant on the premises which serves breakfast, and a courtyard with a heated outdoor pool and a lounge area. Restaurant, room service. In-room data ports, refrigerators. Cable TV. Pets allowed. | 1150 3rd St. SW (Hwy. 17) 33880 | 863/294–4451 or 800/465–4329 | fax 863/293–9829 | www.holiday-inn.com | 223 rooms, 2 suites | $119–$139 | AE, D, DC, MC, V.

Georgia

ALBANY

Holiday Inn Express. This typical chain hotel is convenient to Albany State University and the Convention and Visitors Bureau. It is one of the minimum-service branches of the Holiday Inn chain, but has many amenities. Complimentary Continental breakfast. In-room data ports, microwaves, refrigerators. Cable TV. Pool. Business services, airport shuttle. Pets allowed (fee). | 911 E. Oglethorpe Blvd., 31705 | 912/883–1650 | fax 912/883–1163 | www.holiday-inn.com | 151 rooms | $59–$69 | AE, D, DC, MC, V.

Ramada Inn. This colonial-style chain hotel with attractive landscaping is built around an atrium, over which some rooms have balconies. It is convenient to the medical center and business district, as well as to shops and sports facilities; the Hugh Mills Stadium is 5 min away, and a putting green is across the street. Restaurant, bar. In-room data ports, in-room safes. Cable TV. Pool, wading pool. Putting green. Basketball. Business services, airport shuttle. Pets allowed. | 2505 N. Slappey Blvd., 31701-1095 | 912/883–3211 | fax 912/439–2806 | www.ramada-albany.com | 158 rooms | $50 | AE, D, DC, MC, V.

AMERICUS

Pathway Inn. This Victorian-era home (1906) has the wide verandas, rockers, and colorful gardens associated with that period. All the rooms are furnished with antiques, and each is decorated individually—some have painted ceilings, some have rose wallpaper. Complimentary breakfast. Some in-room hot tubs. Cable TV, in-room VCRs. Pets allowed. No smoking. | 501 S. Lee St., 31709 | 912/928–2078 or 800/889–1466 | fax 912/928–2078 | www.1906pathwayinn.com | 5 rooms (2 with shower only) | $85–$115 | AE, D, MC, V.

ATHENS

Holiday Inn. Step out your door and you are on UGA's North Campus or in the midst of Athens's bustling downtown business district. The facilities mix motel-style lodging with newer rooms in an attached tower. You know what to expect from this type of chain hotel— floral bedspread, dismal curtains, peculiar artwork on the walls. However, there is a certain comfort in knowing in advance, and it makes this a reliable choice. Restaurant, bar. In-room data ports, some minibars, some microwaves, some refrigerators. Cable TV, some in-room VCRs. Indoor pool. Exercise equipment. Business services. Pets allowed.

| 197 E. Broad St., 30603 | 706/549–4433 | www.hdayn@hi-athens.com | 308 rooms | $84–$104 | AE, D, DC, MC, V.

Magnolia Terrace. In the historic Cobbham neighborhood, this 1912 colonial-style inn is within walking distance of shops and restaurants along Prince Avenue. The cozy, plush Phinizy Parlor and the large front porch with comfortable wicker furniture provide welcoming common areas. Each bedroom is furnished in its own unique style with antiques and houseplants, making Magnolia Terrace a home away from home. The trimmings—fireplaces and fine linen—add luxury and comfort. Complimentary Continental breakfast (full on weekends). In-room data ports. Cable TV. Pets allowed. No smoking. | 277 Hill St., 30601 | 706/548–3860 | fax 706/369–3439 | www.bbonline.com/ga/magnoliaterrace | 8 rooms | $95–$115 | AE, MC, V.

ATLANTA

Beverly Hills Inn. Each of the rooms in this pleasant inn has a balcony. The inn itself is tucked away on a residential side street just off Peachtree. Well-equipped for business travelers, this European-style spot is a wonderful alternative to the nearby high-rise hotels. Complimentary Continental breakfast. In-room data ports. Cable TV. Business services. Pets allowed. | 65 Sheridan Dr., 30305 | 404/233–8520 | fax 404/233–8659 | www.beverlyhillsinn.com | 18 rooms | $120–$160 | AE, D, DC, MC, V.

Days Inn Peachtree. Once known as the York Hotel, this somber, brick-fronted hostelry is directly across the street from the Fox Theatre, making it the perfect choice for concert- and theatergoers. Decorated like a 19th-century men's club, the property displays a charm rarely, if ever, associated with a Days Inn. Complimentary Continental breakfast. In-room safes. Cable TV. Pets allowed. | 683 Peachtree St., 30308 | 404/874–9200 | fax 404/873–4245 | www.daysinn.com | 132 rooms | $99 | AE, D, DC, MC, V.

Four Seasons Hotel. A sweeping staircase leads up to a welcoming, refined bar and Park 75, the hotel's main restaurant. Rose-hue marble gives the public spaces a sense of warmth. Marble bathrooms, pale lemon or celadon color schemes, and polished brass chandeliers are among the guest-room appointments. Pets are allowed and even welcomed—a special pet menu is available. Restaurant, bar (with entertainment). In-room data ports, in-room safes. Cable TV, some in-room VCRs. Indoor pool. Beauty salon, massage, sauna. Health club. Laundry services. Business services, parking (fee). Pets allowed. | 75 Fourteenth St., 30309 | 404/881–9898 | fax 404/873–4692 | www.fourseasons.com | 244 rooms | $175–$370 | AE, D, DC, MC, V.

Grand Hyatt Hotel. This 25-story postmodern skyscraper was built by a Japanese concern before being taken over by Hyatt. There's still a dash of the Orient about the place, as evidenced by the Japanese rock garden just beyond the lobby. Rooms are appointed with such luxuries as marble bathrooms. 3 restaurants. In-room data ports, minibars, some refrigerators. Cable TV. Pool. Sauna. Health club. Laundry services. Business services, parking (fee). Pets allowed (fee). | 3300 Peachtree Rd., 30305 | 404/365–8100 | fax 404/233–5686 | www.hyatt.com | 438 rooms | $220 | AE, D, DC, MC, V.

★ **Ritz-Carlton, Buckhead.** Decorated with the Ritz's signature 18th- and 19th-century antiques and art, this elegant gem bids a discreet welcome. Shoppers from nearby Lenox Mall and Phipps Plaza often revive here over afternoon tea or cocktails in the richly paneled Lobby Lounge. The Dining Room is one of the city's finest restaurants. The spacious rooms are furnished with traditional reproductions and have luxurious white-marble baths. From the hotel's club floors you get a view of Buckhead and an understanding of why Atlanta is known as a city of trees. Weekend musical performances are a delight. 2 restaurants, bar. In-room data ports, in-room safes, minibars. Cable TV, some in-room VCRs. Pool. Hot tub, massage, sauna. Gym. Laundry services. Business services, parking (fee). Pets allowed (fee). | 3434 Peachtree Rd., 30326 | 404/237–2700 or 800/241–3333 | fax 404/239–0078 | www.ritzcarlton.com | 553 rooms | $230–$255 | AE, D, DC, MC, V.

Sheraton at Colony Square Hotel. Theatricality and opulence are epitomized by the dimly lit lobby with overhanging balconies, piano music, and fresh flowers. Rooms are modern, with muted tones; those on higher floors have city views. The hotel is two blocks from MARTA's Art Center station and two blocks from the Woodruff Arts Center and the High Museum of Art; it anchors the Colony Square complex of office, residential, and retail buildings. Restaurant, bar. In-room data ports. Cable TV. Pool. Exercise equipment. Laundry service. Business services, parking (fee). Pets allowed. | 188 14th St., 30361 | 404/892–6000 or 800/325–3535 | fax 404/872–9192 | www.sheraton.com | 467 rooms | $129–$195 | AE, D, DC, MC, V.

Swissôtel. Sleek and efficient, this stunner boasts a chic, modern exterior of glass and white tile, with curved walls and Biedermeier-style interiors. Convenient to Lenox Square Mall, a prime location for shopping and dining, the hotel is a favorite with business travelers. The restaurant, the Palm, is noted for its steaks. The full-service fitness center has everything from facials to fitness trainers. Restaurant, bar. In-room data ports, in-room safes, minibars. Cable TV. Indoor pool. Beauty salon, massage. Gym. Laundry facilities. Business services, parking (fee). Pets allowed. | 3391 Peachtree Rd., 30326 | 404/365–0065 or 888/737–9477 | fax 404/365–8787 | www.swissotel.com | 365 rooms | $149–$289 | AE, D, DC, MC, V.

Westin Peachtree Plaza. One of the tallest hotels in the world, this steel-and-glass tower has more than 1,000 rooms and a five-floor atrium lobby that bustles with activity. The Sun Dial bar and restaurant, 73 stories up, offers an amazing view of the Atlanta skyline. Restaurant, 2 bars (with entertainment). In-room data ports, in-room safes, minibars. Cable TV. Indoor-outdoor pool. Massage, sauna. Exercise equipment. Business services. Pets allowed. | 210 Peachtree St. NW, 30083 | 404/659–1400 | fax 404/589–7424 | www.westin.com | 1,086 rooms | $235–$255 | AE, D, DC, MC, V.

AUGUSTA

Augusta Sheraton. The rooms in this typical chain hotel are furnished with writing desks. The rooms are spacious with various sizes of bed. Restaurant, bar, Continental breakfast. In-room data ports, some microwaves, refrigerators. Cable TV, in-room VCRs (in suites). 2 pools (1 indoor). Laundry facilities. Business services, airport shuttle. Pets allowed. | 2651 Perimeter Pkwy., 30909 | 706/855–8100 or 800/325–3535 | fax 706/860–1720 | 179 rooms | $99–$159 | AE, D, DC, MC, V.

Amerisuites. This chain hotel offers living room area/bedroom combination suites. The kitchen area has dishes and silverware. Picnic area, complimentary Continental breakfast. In-room data ports, microwaves, refrigerators, cable TV. Pool. Exercise equipment. Laundry facilities. Business services. Pets allowed ($30 fee). | 1062 Claussen Rd., 30907 | 706/733–4656 or 800/833–1516 | fax 706/736–1133 | www.amerisuites.com | 111 suites | $59–$79 suites | AE, D, DC, MC, V.

Holiday Inn Gordon Hwy. This renovated chain hotel is convenient to Fort Gordon, Bush Field Airport, and Augusta Mall. The rooms are spacious and nicely decorated. Restaurant, bar. In-room data ports, microwaves. Cable TV. Gym. Laundry facilities. Business services, airport shuttle, free parking. Pets allowed ($35 fee). | 2155 Gordon Hwy., 30909 | 706/737–2300 or 800/465–4329 | fax 706/737–0418 | aghigm@shanerhotels.com | www.holiday-inn.com | 150 rooms | $72–$350 | AE, D, DC, MC, V.

Radisson Riverfront. Augusta's swankest hotel has more than 200 rooms, many of which have sweeping views of the Savannah River below. If you're planning to explore the downtown area, it just doesn't get any more convenient than this—the Morris Museum of Art is literally next door. The spacious rooms have beautiful furniture. Restaurant, bar. In-room data ports, some refrigerators. Cable TV. Pool. Driving range, putting green. Exercise equipment. Business services. Pets allowed (fee). | 2 Tenth St., 30901 | 706/722–8900 or 800/333–3333 | fax 706/823–6513 | www.radisson.com/augustagariverfront | 234 rooms | $119–$149 | AE, D, DC, MC, V.

Radisson Suites Inn. A typical chain hotel; the room furnishings include writing desks. Restaurant, bar, complimentary breakfast, room service. In-room data ports, some microwaves, refrigerators, cable TV. Pool. Laundry facilities. Pets allowed (fee). | 3038 Washington Rd., 30907 | 706/868–1800 or 800/333–3333 | fax 706/868–9300 | www.radisson.com | 176 suites | $99–$129 | AE, D, DC, MC, V.

DARIEN
Open Gates. Right in the center of Darien sits this comfortable white-frame Victorian house dating from 1876. Fine antiques fill the public spaces and guest rooms. Breakfast specialties include fresh fig preserves, plantation pancakes (puffed pancakes), and Hunter's casserole (a baked egg strata). Innkeeper Carolyn Hodges guides guests on tours of the Altamaha River. Complimentary breakfast. Cable TV. Pool. Pets allowed. | 301 Franklin St., 31305 | 912/437–6985 | fax 912/437–8211 | 4 bedrooms (3 with shared bath) | $80–$90 | No credit cards.

DUBLIN
Holiday Inn. This typical chain hotel underwent major renovations in early 2000. The rooms are those familiar from chain hotels, with a writing desk in every one. Restaurant, bar (with entertainment), complimentary breakfast, room service. In-room data ports. Cable TV. Pool. Exercise equipment. Business services, free parking. Pets allowed. | 2190 U.S. 441 S, 31021 | 912/272–7862 or 800/465–4329 | fax 912/272–1077 | dbnga@nlamerica.com | 124 rooms | $64–$79 | AE, D, DC, MC, V.

JEKYLL ISLAND
Comfort Inn Island Suites. Most suites in this hotel have beautiful beach views; golf courses and bike trails are a few strides away. Complimentary Continental breakfast. Outdoor hot tub. Playground. Some pets allowed (fee). | 711 N. Beachview Dr., 31527 | 800/204–0202 | www.motelproperties.com | 180 rooms | $149 | AE, D, DC, MC, V.

MACON
Holiday Inn Express. A renovated Holiday Inn offering complimentary newspaper and free local calls. Complimentary Continental breakfast. In-room data ports, some microwaves, refrigerators, cable TV. Pool. Business services. Free parking. Pets allowed (fee). | 2720 Riverside Dr., 31298 | 912/743–1482 or 800/465–4329 | fax 912/745–3967 | www.holiday-inn.com | 94 rooms | $55–$63 | AE, D, DC, MC, V.

Rodeway Inn. A well-maintained hotel 1 mi off I–475 at Exit 3. Queen- and king-sized beds. Complimentary Continental breakfast. Microwaves, refrigerators, cable TV (and movies). Pool. Laundry facilities. Business services. Pets allowed (fee). | 4999 Eisenhower Pkwy., 31206 | 912/781–4343 or 800/228–2000 | fax 912/784–8140 | www.rodeway.com | 56 rooms | $45 | AE, D, DC, MC, V.

Scottish Inn I–475 Corner. Like those in many other Macon lodgings, the rooms at Scottish Inn have full kitchens with ovens, stovetops, and coffeemakers. Kitchenettes, microwaves, refrigerators. Pool. Pets allowed (fee). | I–475 and U.S. 80 31210 | 912/474–2665 | 80 rooms | $35 | AE, D, MC, V.

PERRY
New Perry Hotel. The main building is a mint-green concrete take on a colonial-style mansion, with simple, clean rooms. Out back, there's a motel court. Rooms are basic and affordable, with far more charm than you'd find at a similarly priced chain motel. Restaurant. Cable TV. Pool. Pets allowed (fee). | 800 Main St., 31069 | 912/987–1000 | 56 rooms in 2 buildings | $39–$49 | AE, MC, V.

SAVANNAH

Holiday Inn. This Holiday Inn, 9 miles away from the airport, is within walking distance to the mall and dining. Restaurant. In-room data ports. Cable TV. Pool. Gym. Laundry service. Business services. Pets allowed. | I–95 and GA 204, 31419 | 912/925–2770 | fax 912/925–2770 | 176 rooms | $77 | AE, D, DC, MC, V.

Marshall House. This restored hotel, with original pine floors, woodwork, and bricks, caters to business travelers while providing the intimacy of a bed-and-breakfast inn. Different spaces reflect different parts of Savannah's history, from its founding to the Civil War. Restaurant, bar. In-room data ports. Pets allowed (fee). | 123 E. Broughton St., 31401 | 912/644–7896 or 800/589–6304 | fax 912/234–3334 | www.marshallhouse.com | 68 rooms, 3 suites | $159–$209 | AE, D, MC, V.

STATESBORO

Georgia's B&B. You may want the Eggs Benedict for breakfast at this 1893 Victorian, where rooms are individually decorated and children are welcome. Bright colors and hospitality abound; the owner stresses that "this is a home." Cable TV. Pets allowed. | 123 S. Zetterower | 912/489–6330 | 4 rooms | $75 | No credit cards.

THOMASVILLE

Evans House B&B. Lee and John Puskar, the hospitable owners of this antiques-filled Victorian, believe in the little touches. After dinner liqueurs, pillow sweets, homemade cookies, and nightcaps are a few of the extras you can expect. Breakfasts vary, and have included fresh squeezed orange juice, peach crepes, bananas and strawberries in cream, and apple cinnamon muffins. Paradise Park is directly across the street; downtown Thomasville is just ¼ mile away. All rooms with private bath and/or shower. Library. Pets allowed. No smoking. | 725 S. Hansell St., 31792 | 800/344–4717 | fax 912/226–0653 | 4 rooms | $75–$90 | No credit cards.

TIFTON

Econo Lodge Tifton. With restaurants, shopping, tennis, and cinemas nearby, Econo Lodge Tifton is a family-friendly place. Complimentary Continental breakfast. Microwaves. Cable TV. Playground. Pets allowed. | 1025 W. 2nd St. | 912/382–0280 | fax 912/386–0316 | $41–$56 | AE, D, DC, V.

VALDOSTA

Best Western King of the Road. This chain hotel is convenient to the Valdosta Mall. Restaurant, bar (with entertainment), complimentary Continental breakfast, room service. Some microwaves, refrigerators. Cable TV. Pool. Playground. Business services, airport shuttle. Pets allowed. | 1403 N. St. Augustine Rd., 31601 | 912/244–7600 or 800/528–1234 | fax 912/245–1734 | www.bestwestern.com | 137 rooms, 5 suites, in 2 buildings | $48–$55 | AE, D, DC, MC, V.

Comfort Inn. A typical chain hotel, convenient to the Valdosta Mall and outlet malls, the university, Moody Air Force Base, and Wild Adventure. The rooms have either two double beds or one king-size bed. The rooms also have ironing boards. Bar, complimentary Continental breakfast. Microwaves, refrigerators. Cable TV. Pool. Laundry facilities. Business services, airport shuttle, free parking. Pets allowed. No smoking. | 2101 W. Hill Ave., 31603 | 912/242–1212 or 800/228–5150 | fax 912/242–2639 | www.hotelchoice.com | 138 rooms, 12 suites, in 3 buildings | $55–$65, $99–$129 suites | AE, D, DC, MC, V.

Ramada Inn. A standard chain hotel convenient to Wild Adventure and Valdosta State University. The standard rooms have two double beds and a desk. Complimentary Continental breakfast. Cable TV. Pool. Pets allowed (fee). | 2008 W. Hill Ave., 31601 | 912/242–1225 or 800/272–6232 | fax 912/247–2755 | 103 rooms | $42 | AE, D, DC, MC, V.

Idaho

ARCO

DK Motel. Very reasonable rates and a convenient location two blocks from the town center make this older motel a good stopping point. Rooms are well maintained and clean. Picnic area. No-smoking rooms. Cable TV. Laundry facilities. Business services. Pets allowed. | 316 S. Front St. | 208/527–8282 or 800/231–0134 | www.atcnet.net/~dkm | 24 rooms, 6 suites | $28–$49, $35–$65 suites | AE, D, MC, V.

BELLEVUE

Come on Inn. This cluster of individual log cabins with homey country furnishings is near the center of town and close to Sun Valley and Ketchum. You can walk to downtown Bellevue. Kitchenettes, no room phones. Cable TV. Laundry facilities. Pets allowed. | 414 N. Main St. | 208/788–0825 | 5 cabins | $50–$65 | AE, D, MC, V.

BLACKFOOT

Best Western Blackfoot Inn. Modern accommodations in a newer motel. Complimentary Continental breakfast. In-room data ports. Cable TV. Pool. Hot tub. Gym. Business services, Pets allowed. | 750 Jensen Grove Dr. | 208/785–4144 or 800/528–1234 | fax 208/785–4304 | 60 rooms | $40–$85 | AE, D, MC, V.

BOISE

Best Western Safari. An older hotel in downtown's Old Boise area, this is within walking distance of the Convention Center and government offices. Complimentary Continental breakfast. Refrigerators. Cable TV. Pool. Hot tub, sauna. Business services. Laundry services. Airport shuttle. Pets allowed. | 1070 Grove St. | 208/344–6556 | fax 208/344–7240 | www.safari@bigplanet.com | 103 rooms | $59–$85 | AE, D, DC, MC, V.

Doubletree. This downtown high-rise hotel has contemporary furnishings and an upbeat feel. Restaurant, bar, room service. Cable TV. Pool. Exercise equipment. Downhill skiing. Business services. Airport shuttle, pets allowed (fee). Free parking. | 1800 Fairview Ave. | 208/344–7691 | fax 208/336–3652 | www.hiltonhonors.com | 182 rooms | $69–$104 | AE, D, DC, MC, V.

Doubletree-Riverside. A mile from downtown and overlooking the Boise River. Guest rooms are decorated in dark rose with floral fabrics and blue-gray carpeting. Restaurant, bar. In-room data ports, some refrigerators, room service. Cable TV. Pool, wading pool. Hot tub. Exercise equipment. Business services. Airport shuttle. Some pets allowed (fee). | 2900 Chinden Blvd. | 208/343–1871 | fax 208/344–1079 | 264 rooms, 40 suites | $79–$159 rooms, $145–$395 suites | AE, D, DC, MC, V.

Holiday Inn. Near the airport, with a Holidome recreation center featuring a 25-ft video wall. Rooms are newly redecorated in light rose and blue floral upholstery and light-wood contemporary furniture. Restaurant, bar, room service. Cable TV. Indoor pool. Hot tub. Exercise equipment. Laundry facilities. Business services. Airport shuttle. Pets allowed. | 3300 Vista Ave. | 208/344–8365 | fax 208/343–9635 | www.bhr.com | 266 rooms | $79–$99 | AE, D, DC, MC, V.

Owyhee Plaza Hotel. One of the original big hotels downtown was built in 1910 and has since been renovated. Guest rooms have stylish, brightly painted walls, dark floral spreads, and warm copper-color carpeting. 2 restaurants, bar (with entertainment), room service. In-room data ports. Cable TV. Pool. Beauty salon. Business services. Laundry services. Airport shuttle. Pets allowed (fee). Free parking. | 1109 Main St. | 208/343–4611, 800/233–4611 (outside Idaho), or 800/821–7500 | fax 208/336–3860 | www.owyheeplaza.com | 100 rooms | $59–$132 | AE, MC, V.

Quality Inn Airport Suites. An older motel next to the airport, this has dark green plush carpeting and floral spreads accented with dark wood, brass lamps in guest rooms, and a pool surrounded by trees for a seclusion. Complimentary Continental breakfast. Many kitchenettes, refrigerators. Cable TV. Pool. Laundry facilities. Airport shuttle. Some pets allowed (fee). | 2717 Vista Ave. | 208/343–7505 | fax 208/342–4319 | 79 suites | $58–$70 suites | AE, D, DC, MC, V.

Residence Inn by Marriott. An all-suites hotel with fully equipped kitchens and living rooms, most with brick fireplaces. Studio, one- and two-bedroom, and two-bath units; contemporary upholstered wood furniture, framed Western prints, and warm earth-tone carpeting make the loft suites with fireplaces especially warm and comfortable. Picnic area. Refrigerators. Cable TV. Pool. Hot tub. Laundry facilities, dry cleaning. Business services. Airport shuttle. Some pets allowed ($10 fee). | 1401 Lusk Ave. | 208/344–1200 | fax 208/384–5354 | www.residenceinn.com/boiio | 104 suites | $105–$135 suites | AE, D, DC, MC, V.

Shilo Inn Airport. This is a relatively new hotel near the airport. The rooms are comfortable and the amenities standard. Complimentary Continental breakfast. Some refrigerators. Cable TV. Pool. Hot tub. Exercise equipment. Laundry facilities. Business services. Airport shuttle. Pets allowed. | 4111 Broadway | 208/343–7662 | fax 208/344–0318 | 126 rooms | $60–$71 | AE, D, DC, MC, V.

Shilo Inn Riverside. In a parklike setting on the bank of the Boise River and close to downtown. There is a free shuttle, and the driver will take people anywhere in the area. Complimentary Continental breakfast. Microwaves and refrigerators in every room. Cable TV. Indoor pool. Exercise equipment. Laundry facilities. Business services. Airport shuttle. Pets allowed (fee). | 3031 Main St. | 208/344–3521 or 800/222–2244 | fax 208/384–1217 | www.shiloinn.com | 112 rooms | $55–$95 | AE, D, DC, MC, V.

Super 8 Lodge–Boise Airport. Standard chain accommodations at the airport. Snack shop. Cable TV. Pool. Laundry facilities. Business services. Airport shuttle. Some pets allowed (fee). | 2773 Elder St. | 208/344–8871 | fax 208/344–8871 ext. 444 | www.super8.com | 108 rooms | $55–$65 | AE, D, DC, MC, V.

BURLEY

Best Western Burley Inn. A playground and volleyball court make this very well maintained hotel a good choice for families. Rooms overlook the pool and a shady courtyard. There is a small shopping mall nearby. Restaurant, bar, room service. Cable TV, some in-room VCRs. Pool. Volleyball. Playground. Laundry facilities. Business services. Pets allowed. | 800 N. Overland Ave., I–84 Exit 208 | 208/678–3501 | fax 208/678–9532 | 126 rooms | $60–$80 | AE, D, DC, MC, V.

CALDWELL

Best Inn and Suites. Just off I–84, with coffee and cookies in the evening and a 24-hour recreation facility including an indoor pool. Natural stone accents against yellowish tan siding, planters with flowers, and old wagon wheels resting against a split rail fence give the hotel a rustic flavor. Picnic area, complimentary Continental breakfast. Minibars, some refrigerators. Cable TV. Indoor pool. Hot tub. Exercise equipment, health club privileges. Laundry facilities. Pets allowed ($10 deposit). | 901 Specht Ave. | 208/454–2222 | fax 208/454–9334 | bestinn@cyberhighway.net | 65 rooms | $58–$100 | AE, D, DC, MC, V.

Sundowner Motel. This older, independent motel downtown is close to everything and has spacious rooms. Complimentary Continental breakfast. Some refrigerators. Cable TV. Pool. Pets allowed (fee). | 1002 Arthur St., I–84 Exit 28 | 208/459–1585 or 800/454–9487 | fax 208/454–9487 | 67 rooms | $40–$100 | AE, D, DC, MC, V.

CHALLIS

Northgate Inn. A large, older, well-maintained motel on the north end of town, this place is close to both the Salmon River and to restaurants and shopping. Both rates and the amenities are basic. Satellite TV. Pets allowed (fee). | HC 63, Box 1665 | 208/879–2490 | fax 208/879–5767 | 56 rooms | $34–$51 | AE, D, MC, V.

Village Inn. A modern hotel with a restaurant, air-conditioned rooms, and a large hot tub. Restaurant. Some kitchenettes, some refrigerators. Cable TV. Hot tub. Pets allowed. | U.S. 93 | 208/879–2239 | fax 208/879–2813 | 54 rooms | $34–$68 | AE, D, DC, MC, V.

COEUR D'ALENE

Best Western Templin's Resort. Older and well maintained, this hotel is good if you plan to do a lot of hiking. It's a five-minute walk from the Centennial Trail, which runs from Coeur d'Alene to Spokane. On the bank of the Spokane River, many rooms overlook the marina and private beach. Restaurant, bar (with entertainment), picnic area, room service. In-room data ports, some refrigerators. Cable TV. Indoor pool. Hot tub. Tennis. Exercise equipment, beach, dock, marina, boating. Business services. Laundry facilities. Some pets allowed [fee]. | 414 E. 1st Ave., Post Falls, I–90 Exit 5 | 208/773–1611 | fax 208/773–4192 | www.bestwestern.com | 167 rooms | $84–$139 | AE, D, DC, MC, V.

Coeur D'Alene Inn and Conference Center. The room furnishings are striking at this new hotel—dark fabrics against light-wood contemporary furniture and short looped-pile carpet. The reasonably priced inn is five minutes from downtown and close to the interstate. Restaurant, bar (with entertainment), room service. In-room data ports, some refrigerators and microwaves. Cable TV. Pool. Business services. Laundry services. Pets allowed (fee). | 414 W. Appleway St. | 208/765–3200 or 800/251–7829 | fax 208/664–1962 | www.cdainn.com | 122 rooms | $59–$119 | AE, D, DC, MC, V.

Days Inn. A well-maintained older inn off I–90 and near the center of downtown. Complimentary Continental breakfast. Cable TV, in room-VCRs available. Hot tub, sauna. Exercise equipment. Pets allowed ($25 deposit). | 2200 Northwest Blvd. | 208/667–8668 | fax 208/765–0933 | www.the.daysinn.com/coeurdalene06805 | 61 rooms | $50–$107 | AE, D, DC, MC, V.

Hawthorne Inn and Suites. A very child-friendly place that's just off the interstate, this inn has some spa rooms, some kitchenettes, and an indoor pool. The freshly baked cookies served in the evening make it even nicer. Wednesday night socials have free hors d'oeuvres. Complimentary full breakfast. Some microwaves, some refrigerators. Cable TV. Indoor pool. Sauna. spa. Laundry facilities. Pets allowed. | 2209 E. Sherman Ave., I–90 Exit 15 | 208/667–6777 | fax 208/769–7332 | www.nwhotels.com | 62 rooms | $50–$100 | AE, D, DC, MC, V.

Holiday Inn Express, Post Falls. You can get microwaves and refrigerators on request here, a nice amenity if you're traveling with a family. The newly remodeled hotel is close to the lake with a convenient location off the interstate but near downtown. Complimentary Continental breakfast. Microwaves and refrigerators available upon request. Health club privileges. Pool privileges. laundry services. Pets allowed (deposit). | 3105 E. Seltice Way, Post Falls | 208/773–8900 or 800/779–7789 | fax 208/773–0890 | 47 rooms | $60–$110 | AE, D, DC, MC, V.

DRIGGS

Best Western Teton West. Only 30 mi from Grand Targhee resort, this is a good alternative to the high-priced resort-area accommodations. There's a ski-wax room on the premises. Rooms are furnished with dark-rose floral spreads and carpet and dark-wood furniture. Most have views of the Grand Tetons. Complimentary Continental breakfast. Cable TV. Indoor pool. Hot tub. Pets allowed (deposit). | 476 N. Main St. | 208/354–2363 | fax 208/354–2962 | 40 rooms | $48–$79 | AE, D, DC, MC, V | Closed Oct.–Dec.

★ **Pines Motel Guest Haus.** The big stucco and cedar-shingled cottage looks as though it would be right at home in the Bavarian Alps and is surrounded by 1 acre of shady lawn. Guest rooms are comfortable, with country-style furnishings and quilts. You're one block from the center of town and 12 mi from Grand Targhee. Room phones. Cable TV. Hot tub. Pets allowed ($10 fee). | 105 S. Main | 208/354–2774 or 800/354–2778 | www.travelassist.com | 8 rooms | $40–$50 | AE, D, DC, MC, V.

★ **Teton Ridge Ranch.** Built of lodgepole pine in 1984, this luxuriously rustic ranch lodge west of the Tetons accommodates just 12 guests. The 10,000-square-ft lodge has beamed cathedral ceilings, stone fireplaces, an inviting lounge, and a library with comfy sofas. Forty-five minutes from Grand Targhee resort, the lodge is on 4,000 acres atop a 6,800-ft knoll, with majestic views. Suites—five in the main lodge, two in a cabin—have woodstoves, hot tubs, and steam showers. You decide what you want to do with your time: hiking on 14 mi of marked trails, horseback riding with an experienced wrangler, fishing at two spring-fed stocked ponds, cycling, and shooting at two sporting clay courses. Sleigh rides are also offered. In-room hot tubs. TV in common area. Hiking, horseback riding. Fishing. Library. Laundry facilities. No kids under 6. Some pets allowed. | 200 Valley View Rd., Tetonia | 208/456–2650 | fax 208/456–2218 | www.ranchweb/teton | 7 suites | $450–$550 | MC, AE, V | Closed Nov.–Dec., Apr.–May | AP.

GLENN'S FERRY

Redford Motel. Room sizes vary from small to large enough for two king-size beds here at this non-chain motel in the downtown area. Some have kitchens. Some kitchenettes. Cable TV, air-conditioning. Pets allowed. | 11 rooms | $28–$65.

HAGERMAN

Hagerman Valley Inn. An all-cedar, homey motel in the Frog's Landing retail and commercial complex has spacious guest rooms that open onto a grassy picnic area and two large decks. Restaurant nearby, picnic area. Cable TV. Pets allowed (fee). | 661 Frogs Landing | 208/837–6196 | www.northrim.net¢hvimotel | 16 rooms | $46 | AE, MC, V.

IDAHO FALLS

Best Western Cottontree Inn. With newly remodeled rooms and conveniently located off I–15, this inn is within walking distance of both the falls and restaurants. Complimentary Continental breakfast. Some kitchenettes, some in-room hot tubs. Cable TV. Indoor pool. Hot tub. Exercise equipment. Laundry facilities. Business services. Airport shuttle. Pets allowed ($25 deposit). | 900 Lindsay Blvd., I–15 Exit 119 | 208/523–6000 or 800/662–6886 | fax 208/523–0000 | 94 rooms | $74–$145 | AE, D, DC, MC, V.

Best Western Driftwood Inn. Landscaped with flower gardens and overlooking a grassy lawn, this hotel is 34 steps from the Snake River and the falls. Nicely renovated guest rooms have coffeemakers, and some rooms are actually fireplace suites. You're ¼ mi from downtown. Restaurant. Complimentary full breakfast. Some kitchenettes, microwaves, refrigerators. Cable TV. Pool. Hot tub. Fishing. Bicycles. Pets allowed ($10 fee). | 575 River Pkwy. | 208/523–2242 or 800/939–2242 | fax 208/523–0316 | 60 rooms | $55–$109 | AE, D, DC, MC, V.

Littletree Inn. An older, well-maintained motel with rooms that overlook a landscaped courtyard in a quiet setting across from a golf course. You can walk to some shops and department stores. Restaurant, complimentary Continental breakfast. Cable TV, in-room VCRs on request. Pool. Hot tub, sauna. Gym. Laundry facilities. Pets allowed ($25 deposit). | 888 N. Holmes Ave. | 208/523–5993 or 800/521–5993 | fax 208/523–7104 | 92 rooms | $49–$59 | AE, D, DC, MC, V.

Shilo Inn. A big hotel that overlooks the Snake River and has spacious suites. It's close to Idaho Falls and to shopping areas. Restaurant, bar, complimentary breakfast, room service. In-room data ports, microwaves, refrigerators. Cable TV. Indoor pool. Hot tub. Exercise equipment. Laundry facilities. Business services. Airport shuttle. Some pets allowed. | 780 Lindsay Blvd. | 208/523–0088 or 800/222–2244 | fax 208/522–7420 | www.shiloinns.com | 161 suites | $69–$119 suites | AE, D, DC, MC, V.

West Coast Idaho Falls Hotel. Some of the rooms in this high-rise hotel overlook the Snake River, some are pool-side. Restaurant, lounge, complimentary full breakfast. Some refrigerators. Some microwaves. Cable TV. Pool. Hot tub, sauna. Gym. Pets allowed. | 475 River Pkwy. | 208/523–8000 or 800/325–4000 | fax 208/529–9610 | www.westcoast hotels.com | 138 rooms, 1 suite | $89–$109, $350 suite | AE, D, DC, MC, V.

JEROME

Best Western Sawtooth Inn and Suites. River-rock details against tan siding make the exterior of this hotel distinctive. The interior is contemporary in style. Complimentary Continental breakfast. Microwaves (in suites), some refrigerators. Cable TV. Indoor pool. Hot tub. Exercise equipment. Laundry facilities. Business services. Some pets allowed ($50 deposit). | 2653 S. Lincoln Ave. | 208/324–9200 | fax 208/324–9292 | 57 rooms, 12 suites | $69–$79, $79–$100 suites | AE, D, MC, V MC.

Days Inn. Just off I–84 and U.S. 93, this three-story white inn is within walking distance of the town. In-room data ports. Cable TV, in room VCRs and movies. Hot tub. Laundry facilities. Business services. Pets allowed ($15 fee and $100 deposit). | 1200 Centennial Spur Rd. | 208/324–6400 | fax 208/324–9207 | 73 rooms | $49–$65 | AE, D, DC, MC, V.

KELLOGG

Silverhorn. This big multistory hotel has shutters and window boxes that make it resemble an Old World inn. And it's less than ½ mi from Silver Mountain base gondola. The gift shop features Native American crafts. Restaurant, room service. Cable TV. Hot tub. Cross-country and downhill skiing. Laundry facilities. Business services. Pets allowed. | 699 W. Cameron Ave., I–90 Exit 49 | 208/783–1151 or 800/437–6437 | fax 208/784–5081 | sminn@rand.nidlink.com | 40 rooms | $48–$56 | AE, D, DC, MC, V.

KETCHUM

Heidelberg Inn. An older hotel set back off the road about 1 mi from Ketchum on Warm Springs Road, en route to the Sun Valley base day lodge and lifts. Rooms have been updated and redecorated. Complimentary Continental breakfast, picnic area. Some kitchenettes, microwaves, refrigerators. Cable TV, in-room VCRs and movies. Pool. Hot tub, sauna. Laundry facilities. Pets allowed. | 1908 Warm Springs Rd. | 208/726–5361 or 800/ 284–4863 | fax 208/726–2084 | 30 rooms | $100–$150 | AE, D, DC, MC, V.

LEWISTON

Howard Johnson. An older, low-slung motel with a small pool in downtown. Complimentary Continental breakfast. Some kitchenettes, refrigerators. Cable TV. Pool. Laundry facilities. Airport shuttle. Pets allowed. | 1716 Main St. | 208/743–9526 or 800/634–7669 | fax 208/ 746–6212 | 66 rooms | $55–$99 | AE, D, DC, MC, V.

Riverview Hotel. A large, multistory hotel with newly decorated rooms 2 mi from I–95. Complimentary Continental breakfast. Cable TV. Pool. Pets allowed. | 1325 Main St. | 208/ 746–3311 or 800/806–7666 | fax 208/746–7955 | 75 rooms | $38–$48 | AE, D, DC, MC, V.

Sacajawea Select Inn. An older motel with well maintained rooms in a quiet setting 1mi from I–15 and near downtown. The motel's restaurant, the Helm, serves simple, well prepared food. Restaurant, bar. Refrigerators. Cable TV. Pool. Hot tub. Exercise equipment. Laundry facilities. Airport shuttle. Some pets allowed. | 1824 Main St. | 208/746–1393 or 800/333– 1393 | fax 208/746–3625 | 90 rooms | $50 | AE, D, DC, MC, V.

Super 8. Just off I–95, this is a good choice if you're only stopping for the night. Rates are very reasonable. Refrigerators (in suites). Cable TV. Laundry facilities. Pets allowed ($25 deposit). | 3120 North-South Hwy. | 208/743–8808 | fax 208/743–8808 | 62 rooms | $39– $49 | AE, D, DC, MC, V.

MCCALL

Bear Creek Lodge. Among pine trees in a wooded mountain meadow, this rustic yet elegantly furnished lodge also has luxurious cabins, set on 65 acres next to Bear Creek, 4 mi west of town. Restaurant. Room phones. Laundry facilities. Pets allowed ($100 deposit). | 3492 Rte. 55 | 208/634–3551 | fax 208/634–7699 | 9 lodge rooms, 4 cabins | $120, $125–$200 cabins | AE, D, DC, MC, V.

Best Western. A new hotel with light brick and white trim, this place is two blocks from Payette Lake and near downtown. In-room data ports, refrigerators, microwaves. Cable TV. Indoor pool. Hot tub. Exercise equipment. Laundry facilities. Business services. Some pets allowed. | 415 3rd St. | 208/634–6300 or 800/528–1234 | fax 208/634–2967 | 79 rooms | $74–$105 | AE, D, DC, MC, V.

MONTPELIER

Best Western Clover Creek Inn. A nice redbrick hotel featuring wide windows for sunny guest rooms. There's a restaurant nearby. Complimentary Continental breakfast. In-room data ports, some refrigerators. Cable TV. Hot tub. Exercise equipment. Business services. Some pets allowed. | 243 N. 4th St. | 208/847–1782 | fax 208/847–3519 | 65 rooms | $62– $70 | AE, D, DC, MC, V.

MOSCOW

Best Western—University Inn. This big, newer hotel on the Washington state line is at the west end of the University of Idaho campus. Rooms are decorated with light blue and tan floral spreads, light wood furniture, and tan walls. 2 restaurants, bar, room service. Some refrigerators. Cable TV. Indoor pool, wading pool. Hot tub, sauna. Business services. Laundry services. Airport shuttle. Pets allowed ($10 fee). | 1516 Pullman Rd. | 208/ 882–0550 | fax 208/883–3056 | 173 rooms | $85–$105 | AE, D, DC, MC, V.

Hillcrest. An older strip motel downtown has modest rooms that are well maintained. You're close to restaurants and shopping, and the rates are very modest. Some refrigerators. Cable TV. Business services. Laundry facilities. Pets allowed ($5 fee). | 706 N. Main St. | 208/882–7579 or 800/368–6564 | fax 208/882–0310 | hillcrest@moscow.com | 35 rooms | $36 | AE, MC, V.

MOUNTAIN HOME

Best Western—Foothills Motor Inn. Just off I–84, this tan brick building has remodeled rooms and good amenities. Complimentary Continental breakfast. Cable TV. Pool. Hot tub. Gym. Business services. Laundry facilities. Pets allowed ($50 deposit). | 1080 U.S. 20, I–84 Exit 95 | 208/587–8477 | fax 208/587–5774 | 76 rooms | $65–$125 | AE, D, DC, MC, V.

Hilander Motel and Steak House. A small, older strip motel is 4 mi from I–84 near the center of town. Some rooms have kitchenettes, and the fee for pets is unusually low. Restaurant, bar, room service. Some kitchenettes. Cable TV. Pets allowed ($4 fee). | 615 S. 3rd W, I–84 Exit 90 | 208/587–3311 | fax 208/580–2152 | 34 rooms | $35–$39 | AE, D, DC, MC, V.

Sleep Inn. A newer motel near I–84, on a strip of highway with other chain motels. Complimentary Continental breakfast. In-room data ports, refrigerators. Cable TV, in-room VCRs. Business services. Pets allowed ($50 deposit). | 1180 U.S. 20 | 208/587–9743 | fax 208/587–7382 | 60 rooms (with shower only) | $53–$74 | AE, D, DC, MC, V.

NAMPA

Shilo Inn. The older of the two Shilo Inns, this is a basic motel with modest rooms that's convenient to downtown, 3/4 mi from the Nampa Physics Center and 3 mi from the Idaho Center. Complimentary Continental breakfast. Cable TV. Pool. Hot tub, sauna, steam room. Laundry facilities. Airport shuttle. Pets allowed ($7 fee). | 617 Nampa Blvd., I–84 Exit 35 | 208/466–8993 | fax 208/465–3239 | www.shiloinns.com | 61 rooms | $69 | AE, D, DC, MC, V.

Shilo Inn Nampa Suites. The newer of the two Shilos, this multistory contemporary-styled hotel features minisuites with tan walls, blue, green, and burgundy print spreads, and framed prints. It's located just off I–84. Restaurant, room service. Some kitchenettes, refrigerators. Cable TV. Indoor pool. Hot tub. Exercise equipment. Laundry facilities. Airport shuttle. Pets allowed ($10 fee). | 1401 Shilo Dr., I–84 Exit 36 | 208/465–3250 | fax 208/465–5929 | www.shiloinns.com | 83 suites | $79–$89 suites | AE, D, DC, MC, V.

POCATELLO

Comfort Inn. The suites are a good value at this chain that's off I–15 in the lodging district and set back off an access road. Complimentary Continental breakfast. Cable TV. Indoor pool. Hot tub. Pets allowed. | 1333 Bench Rd., I–15 Exit 71 | 208/237–8155 | fax 208/237–5695 | 52 rooms, 14 suites | $56, $66 suites | AE, D, DC, MC, V.

Holiday Inn. This property is in the motel strip off I–15. Some rooms are poolside and overlook a putting green. Restaurant, bar, complimentary Continental breakfast, room service. Cable TV. Indoor pool. Hot tub. Putting green. Exercise equipment. Laundry facilities. Business services. Airport shuttle. Some pets allowed. | 1399 Bench Rd., I–15 Exit 71 | 208/237–1400 | fax 208/238–0225 | 202 rooms | $79 | AE, D, DC, MC, V.

Super 8. A new multistory hotel in the lodging district just off I–15. Some rooms have hot tubs, microwaves, and refrigerators. The fee for pets is unusually low. Complimentary Continental breakfast. Cable TV, in-room VCRs on request. Laundry service. Some pets allowed ($2 fee). | 1330 Bench Rd., I–15 Exit 71 | 208/234–0888 | fax 208/232–0347 | 80 rooms | $56–$70 | AE, D, DC, MC, V.

West Coast Pocatello Hotel. This is one of the original hotels along the interstate lodging strip. It has a steak-house restaurant and 24-hour coffee shop in a redbrick Colonial-style building with white trim and traditional furnishings. Restaurant, bar, room service. Cable TV. Indoor pool, wading pool. Hot tub. Exercise equipment. Laundry facilities. Business services. Airport shuttle. Some pets allowed. | 1555 Pocatello Creek Rd., I–15 Exit 71 | 208/233–2200 | fax 208/234–4524 | www.westcoasthotels.com | 150 rooms | $59–$89 | AE, D, DC, MC, V.

PRIEST LAKE AREA

Elkin's. A secluded rustic and elegant cabin resort at Reeder Bay on the west side of Priest Lake. Restaurant, bar, picnic area. No air-conditioning, kitchenettes. Cross-country skiing. Beach, boating. Pets allowed ($10 fee). | West shore of Priest Lake | 208/443–2432 | fax 208/ 443–2527 | 30 cottages | $75–$100 cottages | D, MC, V.

Hill's Resort. A long-time resort with a central lodge and cabins spread along the shore-line and among the trees on Luby Bay. These are family-oriented lodgings with ample recreation options. Bar, dining room, picnic area. No air-conditioning, some kitchenettes. Driving range, putting green, tennis. Beach, water sports, boating. Bicycles. Cross-country skiing, snowmobiling, tobogganing. Laundry facilities. Business services. Pets allowed ($10 fee). | West shore of Priest Lake via Rte. 57 to Luby Bay Rd. | 208/443–2551 | fax 208/ 443–2363 | 30 cabins, 25 condos | $900–$2,500/wk, $1,200–$2,600/wk condos (7-day minimum stay in summer) | D, MC, V.

REXBURG

Best Western Cottontree. The motel is in the center of town at a main highway inter-section. Some rooms have balconies, and all are well equipped for business travelers. Restau-rant. In-room data ports, some microwaves, some refrigerators. Cable TV. Indoor pool. Hot tub. Health club privileges. Gym. Laundry facilities. Laundry services. Business services. Pets allowed. | 450 W. 4th S | 208/356–4646 or 800/662–6886 | fax 208/356–7461 | 99 rooms | $50–$70 | AE, D, DC, MC, V.

Comfort Inn. This mid-sized, family hotel is outside of town, in suburban surroundings. The suites are well equipped for families. Complimentary Continental breakfast. Microwaves (in suites), refrigerators (in suites). Cable TV. Indoor pool. Hot tub. Exercise equipment. Business services. Pets allowed. | 1565 W. Main St. | 208/359–1311 | fax 208/ 359–1387 | 52 rooms | $62–$120 | AE, D, DC, MC, V.

SANDPOINT

Lakeside Inn. Overlooking the lake, in a parklike wooded setting, this motel is one block from downtown. Picnic area, complimentary Continental breakfast. Some kitchenettes. Cable TV. Hot tub, sauna. Laundry facilities. Airport shuttle. Some pets allowed ($5 fee). | 106 Bridge St. | 208/263–3717 or 800/543–8126 | fax 208/265–4781 | 60 rooms | $54–$79 | AE, D, DC, MC, V.

STANLEY

Mountain Village Lodge. At a highway intersection in the tiny town, the rustic wood-sided building resembles a strip motel but features recently remodeled guest rooms with contemporary decor in shades of brown, tan, and dark green. It has its own private hot springs. Restaurant, bar (with entertainment). Cable TV. Laundry facilities. Business services. Airport shuttle. Pets allowed ($12 fee and $25 deposit). | Rtes. 75 and 21 | 208/774– 3661 or 800/843–5475 | fax 208/774–3761 | 60 rooms | $63–$74 | AE, D, DC, MC, V.

SUN VALLEY AREA

Sun Valley's Elkhorn Resort and Golf Club. This is Sun Valley's "other" resort, a large hotel and restaurant complex nestled next to a sage-covered mountainside and surrounded by condominiums. The resort and top-ranked golf course are just over the mountain from the Sun Valley Resort. Elkhorn's hotel has fully appointed rooms with modern decor and refrigerators. Upgraded rooms have fireplaces, kitchens, and hot tubs. The resort offers a variety of year-round activities, including jazz concerts under the stars on the complex's center terrace and surrounding lawn area. The Robert Trent Jones–designed golf course challenges even the best golfers. 2 restaurants, 3 bars, dining rooms, room service. No air-conditioning, in-room data ports, some kitchenettes, some in-room hot tubs. Cable TV, in-room VCRs. 2 pools. Hot tub, massage. Driving range, 18-hole golf course, putting green, 18 tennis courts. Exercise equipment. Fishing. Bicycles. Downhill skiing. Shops. Children's programs (ages 6–12). Business services. Airport shuttle. Some pets allowed ($25 fee). | Elkhorn Rd. (Box 6009) 3 mi from Ketchum on Sun Valley Rd. to Dollar, then Elkhorn | 208/622–4511 or 800/355–4676 | fax 208/622–3261 | 124 rooms, 7 suites, 90 condos | $128–$228, $248–$299 suites, $120–$425 condos | AE, D, DC, MC, V.

TWIN FALLS

Best Western Apollo Motor Inn. This smaller motel offers clean, reliable rooms but no restaurant or lounge. A breakfast is served in the lobby, and restaurants are a short walk away. Complimentary Continental breakfast. In-room phones. Pool. Hot tub. Small pets allowed. | 296 Addison Ave. W | 208/733–2010 or 800/528–1234 | fax 208/734–0748 | www.bestwesterninns.com | 50 rooms | $56–$85 | AE, D, DC, MC, V.

Best Western Cavanaughs Canyon Springs. Dark-brown stained-wood siding on units gives the hotel a residential feel. Diamondfield Jack's serves homestyle fare amid turn-of-the-century decor. Within walking distance of a mall and laundry facilities. Restaurant, bar, room service. Cable TV. Pool. Spa, sauna. Exercise equipment. Gym. Airport shuttle. Pets allowed. | 1357 Blue Lakes Blvd. N | 208/734–5000 | fax 208/733–3813 | 112 rooms | $60–$112 | AE, D, DC, MC, V.

Comfort Inn. Across from the Magic Valley Mall about 1 mi from I–84 and on the edge of town, this inn is also within walking distance of mall stores and restaurants. Complimentary Continental breakfast. Cable TV. Indoor pool. Hot tub. Health club privileges. Laundry services. Pets allowed. | 1893 Canyon Springs Rd. | 208/734–7494 | fax 208/735–9428 | www.choicehotels.com | 52 rooms, 15 suites | $64–$79, $90–$130 suites | AE, D, DC, MC, V.

Shilo Inn. A big new multistory hotel with suites is off I–84 and popular with business travelers. You can walk to restaurants and the Valley Mall. Complimentary Continental breakfast. In-room data ports, microwaves, refrigerators. Cable TV. Indoor pool. Hot tub. Exercise equipment. Laundry facilities. Business services. Some pets allowed ($10 fee). | 1586 Blue Lakes Blvd N | 208/733–7545 | fax 208/736–2019 | 128 suites | $75–$140 suites | AE, D, DC, MC, V.

WALLACE

Stardust. This economy lodging is well maintained and clean, in the center of town. No air-conditioning (in some rooms). Cable TV. Cross-country and downhill skiing. Airport shuttle. Pets allowed. | 410 Pine St. | 208/752–1213 | fax 208/753–0981 | 42 rooms | $47 | AE, D, DC, MC, V.

Illinois

ALTON

Days Inn. This standard motel has a "fundome," with an indoor pool, sauna, jacuzzi, putting green, and video games, to help you loosen up; and it's just 5 mi from the Alton Belle Casino, where you can try your luck. Restaurant, bar, complimentary Continental breakfast. Cable TV. Indoor pool. Video games. Pets allowed (fee). | 1900 Homer Adams Pkwy. | 618/463-0800 | fax 618/463-4397 | www.daysinn.com | 115 rooms | $59–$75 | AE, DC, D, MC, V.

Holiday Inn. Thirty minutes from downtown St. Louis, this motel has a Holidome indoor recreation center, where you can relax in the sauna, play video games, or use the tanning beds. Restaurant, bar (with entertainment), room service. In-room data ports, cable TV, in-room VCRs (and movies). Indoor pool. Hot tub. Exercise equipment. Video games. Business services, airport shuttle. Pets allowed. | 3800 Homer Adams Pkwy. | 618/462-1220 | fax 618/462-0906 | www.basshotels.com | 137 rooms | $75–$100 | AE, D, DC, MC, V.

ANTIOCH

Best Western Regency Inn. Only a half mile from downtown, where you can shop and dine, this inn overlooks Lake Antioch. Bar, complimentary Continental breakfast. In-room data ports, some refrigerators, some minibars, cable TV, in-room VCRs. Indoor pool. Hot tub. Business services. Some pets allowed (fee). | 350 Rte. 173 | 847/395-3606 | 68 rooms, 24 suites | $71–$114 | AE, D, DC, MC, V.

ARLINGTON HEIGHTS

Amerisuites. This six-story all-suites hotel is in the business district, 1 mi off I-90, 10 mi from the Chicago O'Hare airport, and 1½ mi from Woodfield Mall. Complimentary Continental breakfast. Refrigerators, cable TV. Hot tub. Exercise equipment. Business services, free parking. Some pets allowed. | 2111 S. Arlington Heights Rd. | 847/956-1400 | fax 847/956-0804 | www.amerisuites.com | 114 suites | $69–$129 | AE, D, DC, MC, V.

Arlington Park Sheraton Conference Center. Best-known for its conference facilities, this large hotel is 16 mi from Chicago O'Hare, within 5 mi of I-290, I-294, and I-90, and 2 mi from Woodfield Mall. Restaurant, bar. In-room data ports, cable TV. Indoor pool. Hot tub, massage. Tennis. Gym. Business services. Some pets allowed. | 3400 W. Euclid Ave. 60005 | 847/394-2000 | fax 847/394-2095 | www.sheraton.com | 428 rooms | $69–$209 | AE, D, DC, MC, V.

La Quinta. This four-story motel is 4 mi north of downtown, 2 mi from the Arlington Park Race Track and 15 mi from the Chicago O'Hare airport. It is right off of I–290, on the Dundee Rd Exit. Complimentary Continental breakfast. In-room data ports, cable TV, in-room VCRs. Pool. Business services. Some pets allowed. | 1415 W. Dundee Rd. | 847/253–8777 | fax 847/818–9167 | www.laquinta.com | 123 rooms | $59–$89 | AE, D, DC, MC, V.

Radisson. You can lounge on the sundeck at this six-story hotel 2 mi from downtown Arlington Heights and 8½ mi from Chicago O'Hare. Restaurant, bar (with entertainment). In-room data ports, some refrigerators, cable TV. Indoor pool. Hot tub. Exercise equipment. Business services, airport shuttle. Some pets allowed. | 75 W. Algonquin Rd. | 847/364–7600 | fax 847/364–7665 | www.radisson.com | 201 rooms, 10 suites | $79–$169, $175–$210 suites | AE, D, DC, MC, V.

BARRINGTON

Days Inn. This inn is right next to Lageschulte Park and its pool, golf, tennis, and playground facilities, which you can appreciate whether you are visiting on business or for pleasure. Restaurant, bar. Kitchenettes, some refrigerators, cable TV. Gym. Laundry facilities. Business services. Pets allowed (fee). | 405 W. Northwest Hwy. | 847/381–2640 | fax 847–381–6208 | www.daysinn.com | 57 rooms | $69–$74 | AE, D, DC, MC, V.

BENTON

Days Inn. This standard motel is just 5 mi from Rend Lake. Just off I-57. Restaurant, bar (with entertainment). Cable TV. Business services. Pets allowed. | 711 W. Main St. | 618/439–3183 | www.daysinn.com | 113 rooms | $55 | AE, D, DC, MC, V.

BLOOMINGTON AND NORMAL

Best Inns of America. This motel is 2 mi from the Illinois Wesleyan campus and 5 mi from Illinois State University. Complimentary Continental breakfast. In-room data ports, cable TV. Pool. Business services. Pets allowed. | 1905 W. Market St., Bloomington 61701 | 309/827–5333 | fax 309/827–5333 | www.bestinn.com | 106 rooms | $46–$66 | AE, D, DC, MC, V.

Holiday Inn. This motel and its approximately 14,000 square ft of conference space are one mile from downtown Bloomington and Illinois State University. Restaurant, bar, room service. Cable TV, in-room VCRs (and movies). Indoor pool. Hot tub. Exercise equipment. Video games. Business services, airport shuttle, free parking. Pets allowed. | 8 Traders Cir., Normal 61761 | 309/452–8300 | fax 309/454–6722 | www.holiday-inn.com | 160 rooms | $81 | AE, D, DC, MC, V.

Jumer's Chateau. This five-story Old World–style hotel has an opulent lobby and is furnished with antiques. Restaurant, bar (with entertainment). Refrigerators, some in-room minibars, cable TV. Indoor pool. Hot tub, sauna. Exercise equipment. Business services, airport shuttle. Pets allowed. | 1601 Jumer Dr., Bloomington 61704 | 309/662–2020 or 800/285–8637 | fax 309/662–2020, ext. 617 | www.jumers.com | 180 rooms, 26 suites | $98–$158; $135–$175 suites | AE, D, DC, MC, V.

Ramada Empire Inn. This motel is known for its indoor recreation center, which is the largest in the area. Restaurant, bar, room service. Cable TV. Indoor pool. Hot tub. Miniature golf. Exercise equipment. Video games. Laundry facilities. Business services, airport shuttle. Pets allowed. | 1219 Holiday Dr., Bloomington 61704 | 309/662–5311 | fax 309/663–1732 | www.empire.com | 209 rooms | $59 | AE, D, DC, MC, V.

CAIRO

Days Inn. On Rural Route 1 near downtown Cairo, this motel is 3 mi from the Custom House Museum, 5 mi from the Mississippi and Ohio rivers and 7 mi from Fort Defiance. Rooms with wheelchair access available. Restaurant, complimentary Continental breakfast.

Cable TV. Pool. Pets allowed. | RR 1, 62914 | 618/734–0215 | fax 618/734–1754 | www.daysinn.com | 38 rooms | $32–$60 | AE, D, DC, MC, V.

CARBONDALE

Best Inn. This standard motel is close to Giant City State Park and Crab Orchard National Wildlife Refuge and only 3 mi from Southern Illinois University. Complimentary Continental breakfast, cable TV. Pool. Pets allowed. | 1345 E. Main St. 62901 | 618/529–4801 | fax 618/529–7212 | www.bestinn.com | 86 rooms | $50–$60 | AE, D, DC, MC, V.

Holiday Inn. You are 2 mi from the Southern Illinois University campus, 3 mi from Crab Lake, and 5 mi from Shawnee National Forest at this motel. Restaurant, complimentary Continental breakfast, room service. In-room data ports, refrigerators, some in-room VCRs, cable TV. Indoor pool. Video games. Laundry facilities, laundry service. Business services, airport shuttle. Some pets allowed. | 800 E. Main St. | 618/529–1100 | fax 618/457–0292 | www.basshotels.com | 95 rooms, 1 suite | $74; $135 suite | AE, D, DC, MC, V.

Super 8. This motel offers standard accommodations just across the way from University Mall and 3 mi from Crab Orchard Lake. Complimentary Continental breakfast. Cable TV. Pets allowed. | 1180 E. Main St. | 618/457–8822 | fax 618/457–4186 | www.super8.com | 63 rooms | $46–$51 | AE, D, DC, MC, V.

CHAMPAIGN AND URBANA

Best Western Paradise Inn. Five miles south of Urbana in Savoy, this motel is 2 mi from Willard Airport. Complimentary breakfast. In-room data ports, cable TV. Pool, wading pool. Playground. Laundry facilities. Business services, airport shuttle. Some pets allowed. | 1001 N. Dunlap Ave., Savoy 61874 | 217/356–1824 | www.bestwestern.com | 62 rooms | $44–$70 | AE, D, DC, MC, V.

Clarion Hotel. The property of this large seven-story hotel in Champaign includes a 20,000-square-ft convention center. Restaurant, bar, complimentary Continental breakfast. In-room data ports, some microwaves, cable TV. 2 pools, wading pool. Hot tub. Exercise equipment. Business services, airport shuttle. Pets allowed. | 1501 S. Neil St., Champaign 61820 | 217/352–7891 | fax 217/352–8108 | www.clarion.com | 224 rooms | $49–$99 | AE, D, DC, MC, V.

Comfort Inn. These standard accommodations are 3 mi north of the University of Illinois campus. Complimentary Continental breakfast. Some microwaves, some refrigerators, cable TV. Indoor pool. Hot tub. Business services. Some pets allowed. | 305 W. Marketview Dr., Champaign 61821 | 217/352–4055, ext. 329 | fax 217/352–4055 | www.hotelchoicece.com | 66 rooms | $59–$79 | AE, D, DC, MC, V.

Eastland Suites. This hostelry in Urbana is a 10-minute drive from the University of Illinois and serves a complimentary breakfast buffet during the week. Bar, complimentary Continental breakfast. Some refrigerators, microwaves, some in-room VCRs, cable TV. Indoor pool. Exercise equipment. Business services, airport shuttle. Pets allowed. | 1907 N. Cunningham Ave., Urbana 61802 | 217/367–8331 | fax 217/384–3370 | www.eastland-suitesurbana.com | 105 rooms, 48 suites | $59–$150; $95–$130 suites | AE, D, DC, MC, V.

Jumer's Castle Lodge. This restored 1924 hotel in downtown Urbana, a mile south of I–74, recalls Old World Bavaria with its German decor, many antiques, and woodwork of cherry and oak. Restaurant, bar, room service. In-room data ports, cable TV. Indoor pool. Hot tub, sauna. Shops. Business services, airport shuttle. Some pets allowed (fee). | 209 S. Broadway, Urbana 61801 | 217/384–8800 or 800/285–8637 | fax 217/384–9001 | www.jumers.com | 127 rooms | $82–$143 | AE, D, DC, MC, V.

La Quinta. Across the street from the Market Place mall, which has a food court in the shopping area, this motel is also within 2 mi of more than 20 restaurants and 6 mi from Willard Airport. Complimentary Continental breakfast. In-room data ports, cable TV. Pool. Laundry facilities. Free parking. Some pets allowed. | 1900 Center Dr., Champaign

61820 | 217/356–4000 | fax 217/352–7783 | www.laquinta.com | 122 rooms | $59–$62 | AE, D, MC, V.

Red Roof Inn. Just a mile north of downtown Champaign, this motel is 3 mi from the University of Illinois, and within 2 mi of more than 20 restaurants. Cable TV. Business services. Pets allowed. | 212 W. Anthony Dr., Champaign 61820 | 217/352–0101 | fax 217/352–1891 | www.redroof.com | 112 rooms | $29–$51 | AE, D, DC, MC, V.

CHARLESTON

Best Western Worthington Inn. Convenient to Eastern Illinois University, this motel is also close to Town Square and 8 mi from the Lincoln Log Cabin. Restaurant. Some microwaves, refrigerators, cable TV. Pool. Business services, airport shuttle. Some pets allowed. | 920 W. Lincoln Hwy. | 217/348–8161 | fax 217/348–8165 | www.bestwestern.com | 67 rooms | $56–$116 | AE, D, DC, MC, V.

CHICAGO

Chicago Marriott. Rooms in this 46-story Michigan Avenue motel right on the Magnificent Mile have views of Lake Michigan. Restaurant, bar. In-room data ports, some microwaves, some in-room VCRs, cable TV. Indoor pool. Barbershop, beauty salon, hot tub, massage. Basketball, gym. Shops, video games. Business services. Pets allowed. | 540 N. Michigan Ave. 60611 | 312/836–0100 | fax 312/836–6139 | www.marriott.com | 1,172 rooms | $189–$449 | AE, D, DC, MC, V.

Claridge. Limousines are available every morning to take you wherever you want to go within a 2-mi radius when you stay at this quiet, elegant hotel on the Gold Coast. Restaurant, bar, complimentary Continental breakfast. Minibars, cable TV. Business services. Some pets allowed. | 1244 N. Dearborn Pkwy. 60610 | 312/787–4980 or 800/245–1258 | fax 312/266–0978 | www.claridge.com | 162 rooms | $139–$250 | AE, D, DC, MC, V.

★ **Four Seasons Hotel.** This hotel is on floors 30–46 in the the Nine-Hundred Building, which also houses Bloomingdale's and other upscale shops and restaurants. It's across the street from Water Tower Place and the John Hancock Center, and three blocks from Lake Michigan. The lobby has Italian marble floors and reception desks, chandeliers, and large assortments of fresh flowers, all of which can make you feel like royalty. Restaurant, bar (with entertainment), room service. In-room data ports, minibars, some in-room VCRs (and movies), cable TV. Indoor pool. Barbershop, beauty salon, hot tub, massage. Gym. Shops. Business services, parking (fee). Pets allowed. | 120 E. Delaware Pl. 60611 | 312/280–8800 | fax 312/280–1748 | www.fourseasons.com | 186 rooms, 157 suites | $380–$425; $535–$3,000 suites | AE, D, DC, MC, V.

Holiday Inn–Mart Plaza. This full-facilities hotel is on the 16th through 23rd floors of the Apparel Center, next to the Merchandise Mart, where you could easily spend your entire visit to Chicago. Restaurant, bar. In-room data ports. Some refrigerators, cable TV. Indoor pool. Exercise equipment. Shops. Laundry facilities. Some pets allowed. | 350 N. Orleans St. 60654 | 312/836–5000 | fax 312/222–9508 | www.basshotels.com | 526 rooms | $179–$225 | AE, D, DC, MC, V.

Hotel Monaco. You are offered free pet goldfish to keep you company during your stay at this downtown hotel, overlooking the Chicago River that's a block from Michigan Avenue. Restaurant, bar, room service. In-room data ports, minibars, cable TV, some VCRs. Gym. Video games. Laundry service. Business services. Parking (fee). Pets allowed. | 225 N. Wabash Ave. | 312/960–8500 | fax 312/960–1883 | 170 rooms, 22 suites | $185–$230; $325–$425 suites | AE, D, DC, MC, V.

Palmer House Hilton. In the heart of the Loop, this grand old hotel has lavish lobbies and public areas. 3 restaurants, 3 bars (with entertainment). In-room data ports, minibars, some refrigerators, cable TV. Indoor pool. Barbershop, beauty salon, hot tub, massage. Gym. Shops. Business services, parking (fee). Some pets allowed. | 17 E. Monroe St. 60603

| 312/726–7500 | fax 312/917–1707 | www.hilton.com | 1,640 rooms | $159–$479 | AE, D, DC, MC, V.

Radisson Hotel and Suites. Just off Michigan Avenue and one block east of the Northwestern University medical complex and law school, this large hotel is just two blocks from such stores as Bloomingdale's, Tiffany's, Hammacher Schlemmer, Godiva, and Water Tower Place. Restaurant, bar, room service. In-room data ports, minibars, some microwaves, some refrigerators, some in-room VCRs, cable TV. Pool. Barbershop. Exercise equipment. Business services. Some pets allowed. | 160 E. Huron St. 60611 | 312/787–2900 | fax 312/787–5158 | www.radisson.com | 350 rooms, 100 suites | $239; $279 suites | AE, D, DC, MC, V.

★ **Renaissance.** You can ask for a room with a view of the Chicago River at this hotel with a lavish lobby, complete with high ceilings, a marble floor, and chandeliers. The rooms are simple and classic. 2 restaurants, bar, room service. In-room data ports, minibars, cable TV. Indoor pool. Hot tub, massage. Gym. Shops. Business services. Some pets allowed. | 1 W. Wacker Dr. 60601 | 312/372–7200 | fax 312/372–0093 | www.renaissancehotels.com | 553 rooms | $179–$350 | AE, D, DC, MC, V.

Residence Inn by Marriott. This 19-story hostelry is 2 blocks away from Oak Street Beach, north of the Loop, and provides complimentary evening refreshments—salad, buffalo wings, and other appetizers. Complimentary Continental breakfast. In-room data ports, kitchenettes, microwaves, cable TV. Exercise equipment. Business services. Some pets allowed (fee). | 201 E. Walton Pl. 60611 | 312/943–9800 | fax 312/943–8579 | www.marriott.com | 221 rooms | $169–$315 | AE, D, DC, MC, V.

The Ritz-Carlton. The lobby of this hotel is two-stories high and made comfortable by its intimate groupings of wicker chairs, potted palms, and grand floral arrangements. Guest rooms are richly decorated in deep colors like burgundy, navy blue, and dark green. The hotel is within two blocks of the Magnificent Mile's most popular stores. Pet kennels are available. Restaurant, bar, room service. In-room data ports, minibars, some refrigerators, some in-room VCRs, cable TV. Hot tub, massage. Gym. Business services. Pets allowed. | 160 E. Pearson St. 60611 | 312/266–1000 or 800/621–6906 (except IL) | fax 312/266–1194 | www.fourseasons.com | 347 rooms, 88 suites | $400–$475; $435–$1,050 suites | AE, D, DC, MC, V.

Sutton Place Hotel. This hotel is in a prime shopping location—just one block east of Magnificent Mile. Restaurant, bar, room service. In-room data ports, minibars, cable TV, in-room VCRs (and movies). Exercise equipment. Business services, airport shuttle. Some pets allowed (fee). | 21 E. Bellevue Pl. 60611 | 312/266–2100 or 800/606–8188 | fax 312/266–2103 | 206 rooms, 40 suites | $199–$240; $240–$360 suites | AE, D, DC, MC, V.

Westin. Across the street from the John Hancock Center, this hotel is just a block from the Water Tower Place shopping mall. Restaurant, bar, room service. In-room data ports, minibars, some microwaves, cable TV. Massage. Exercise equipment. Business services. Some pets allowed. | 909 N. Michigan Ave. 60611 | 312/943–7200 | fax 312/397–5580 | www.westin.com | 751 rooms | $189–$214 | AE, D, DC, MC, V.

Westin River North Chicago. The gleaming black lacquer, mahogany, and granite in this 20-story River North tower create clean, contemporary lines and surfaces in common areas of this hotel, where the guest rooms are either traditional or contemporary in design. Restaurant, bar, room service. In-room data ports, minibars, cable TV. Massage. Gym. Business services. Some pets allowed. | 320 N. Dearborn St. 60610 | 312/744–1900 | fax 312/527–2650 | www.westinrivernorth.com | 424 rooms | $399 | AE, D, DC, MC, V.

The Willows Hotel. This small Lincoln Park hotel has a 19th-century French countryside feeling that borders on being overdone, complete with large, frilly sitting rooms adorned with chandeliers and columns. Complimentary Continental breakfast, room service. In-room data ports, cable TV. Pets allowed (fee). | 555 W. Surf St. 60657 | 773/528–8400 or 800/787–3108 | fax 773/528–8483 | www.cityinns.com | 55 rooms | $109–$200 | AE, D, DC, MC, V.

CHICAGO O'HARE AIRPORT AREA

Hotel Sofitel. Although this is a 10-story high rise, the lobby and guest rooms have details and furnishings reminiscent of France, just 2½ mi from Chicago O'Hare, in Rosemont. Two restaurants, bar, room service. In-room data ports, minibars, some refrigerators, cable TV. Indoor pool. Exercise equipment. Business services, airport shuttle. Some pets allowed. | 5550 N. River Rd., Rosemont 60018 | 847/678–4488 | fax 847/678–4244 | www.sofitel.com | 300 rooms | $235 | AE, D, DC, MC, V.

La Quinta. This representative La Quinta's standard accommodations are 8 mi from Chicago O'Hare and 4 mi from the Allstate Arena. Complimentary Continental breakfast. In-room data ports, some refrigerators, cable TV. Pool. Business services, airport shuttle, free parking. Some pets allowed. | 1900 Oakton St., Elk Grove Village 60007 | 847/439–6767 | fax 847/439–5464 | www.laquinta.com | 142 rooms | $109–$135 | AE, D, DC, MC, V.

Marriott Suites. In Rosemont, a five-minute drive from the Chicago O'Hare airport, this all-suites hotel also has meeting spaces. Restaurant, bar. In-room data ports, some microwaves, some refrigerators, some in-room VCRs, cable TV. Indoor pool. Hot tub. Exercise equipment. Business services, airport shuttle. Pets allowed. | 6155 N. River Rd., Rosemont 60018 | 847/696–4400 | fax 847/696–2122 | www.marriott.com | 256 suites | $234–$389 | AE, D, DC, MC, V.

Residence Inn by Marriott. This all-suites hotel is in Schiller Park, a five-minute shuttle ride to O'Hare. Restaurant, picnic area, complimentary Continental breakfast. In-room data ports, kitchenettes, microwaves, refrigerators, cable TV. Pool. Laundry facilities. Business services, airport shuttle, free parking. Pets allowed (fee). | 9450 W. Lawrence Ave., Schiller Park 60176 | 847/725–2210 | fax 847/725–2211 | www.residenceinn.com | 171 suites | $129–$350 | AE, D, DC, MC, V.

Sheraton Suites. This all-suites hotel is in Elk Grove Village, 8 mi from Chicago O'Hare and 3 mi to Woodfield Mall. Restaurant, bar. In-room data ports, some microwaves, refrigerators, some in-room VCRs, cable TV. Outdoor pool, indoor pool. Hot tub. Exercise equipment. Laundry facilities. Business services. Some pets allowed (fee). | 121 Northwest Point Blvd., Elk Grove Village 60007 | 847/290–1600 | fax 847/290–1129 | www.sheraton.com | 253 suites | $79–$219 | AE, D, DC, MC, V.

CLINTON

Days Inn. You are just 7 mi from Clinton Lake at this motel, where you can picnic, barbecue, and play basketball on the motel's grounds. Complimentary Continental breakfast, picnic area. Some microwaves, some refrigerators, some in-room hot tubs, some in-room VCRs, cable TV. Gym, basketball. Video games. Playground. Laundry facilities. Business services. Some pets allowed. | U.S. 51 Bypass and Kleeman Dr. 61727 | 217/935–4140 or 800/544–8313 | fax 217/935–4140 | www.daysinn.com | 46 rooms, 4 suites | $38–$68; $80–$130 suites | AE, D, DC, MC, V.

COLLINSVILLE

Days Inn. You can see St. Louis and the Mississippi River valley from rooms in this motel, which is convenient to downtown Collinsville. Restaurant, bar (with entertainment). Complimentary Continental breakfast. Some in-room data ports, microwaves, refrigerators, cable TV. Pool. Laundry services. Business services. Some pets allowed. | 1803 Ramada Blvd. 62234 | 618/345–8100 or 800/544–8313 | fax 618/345–8110 | www.daysinn.com | 57 rooms, 2 suites | $40–$75; $100–$150 suites | AE, D, DC, MC, V.

Howard Johnson Express Inn. Just one block from exit 11 off I–70, this modest motel with its standard accommodations is two blocks from the Gateway Convention Center. Restaurant, bar. Cable TV. Pool, wading pool. Laundry facilities. Business services. Some pets allowed. | 301 N. Bluff Rd. 62234 | 618/345–1530 or 800/406–1411 | fax 618/345–1321 | www.hojo.com | 88 rooms | $30–$70 | AE, D, DC, MC, V.

Maggie's Bed and Breakfast. On two rural landscaped acres 1 mi north of Collinsville, this house, built around 1900, is filled with period furnishings. Complimentary breakfast. Cable TV, in-room VCRs (and movies). Hot tub. Some pets allowed. No smoking. | 2102 N. Keebler Rd. 62234 | 618/344–8283 | 5 rooms | $55–$100 | No credit cards.

CRYSTAL LAKE

Super 8 Motel–Crystal Lake. This motel is 1½ mi from downtown Crystal Lake in a business area. Complimentary Continental breakfast. In-room data ports, microwaves, some refrigerators, some in-room VCRs, cable TV. Laundry facilities. Business services. Pets allowed (fee). | 577 Crystal Point Dr. 60014 | 815/455–2388 or 800/800–8000 | fax 815/455–2388 | www.super8.com | 54 rooms, 5 suites | $41–$59; $76–$96 suites | AE, D, DC, MC, V.

DANVILLE

Comfort Inn. Maroon and blue accents in the rooms at this motel 3 mi from the center of the town are picked up in the floral bedding and curtains. The suites include couches that convert into queen-size beds. Complimentary Continental breakfast. Some microwaves, some refrigerators, cable TV. Indoor pool. Hot tub. Business services. Pets allowed. | 383 Lynch Dr. 61834 | 217/443–8004 or 800/228–5150 | fax 217/443–8004 | 42 rooms, 14 suites | $65–$75 | AE, D, DC, MC, V.

Ramada Inn. Just off exit 220 of I–74, in the farm country along the highway, this motel has wide-screen TVs in its lounge so that you can catch the afternoon and evening off-track betting broadcasts. Restaurant, bar. Some minibars, cable TV. Pool. Exercise equipment. Laundry facilities. Business services, airport shuttle. Some pets allowed. | 388 Eastgate Dr. 31834 | 217/446–2400 or 888/298–2054 | fax 217/446–3878 | www.ramada.com | 131 rooms | $55–$76 | AE, D, DC, MC, V.

Regency Inn. This motel is 5 mi east of downtown Danville, and right next to Big Boy Restaurant. In-room data ports, microwaves, refrigerators, cable TV. Indoor pool. Hot tub. Exercise equipment. Pets allowed (fee). | 360 Eastgate Dr. 61834 | 217/446–2111 | fax 217/446–2444 | 36 rooms, 6 suites | $62–$68; $95–$115 suites | AE, D, MC, V.

DECATUR

Baymont Inn. You are just 6 mi north of the civic center and Millikin University's campus when you stay at this motel. Complimentary Continental breakfast. In-room data ports, microwaves, some refrigerators, cable TV. Business services. Pets allowed. | 5100 Hickory Point Frontage Rd. 62526 | 217/875–5800 | fax 217/875–7537 | www.baymontinns.com | 105 rooms | $49–$69 | AE, D, DC, MC, V.

Days Inn. Convenient to U.S. Route 36, this motel is also close to area restaurants. Complimentary Continental breakfast. Cable TV. Pets allowed. | 333 N. Wyckles Rd. 62522 | 217/422–5900 or 800/325–2525 | www.daysinn.com | 62 rooms, 4 suites | $38–$62 | AE, D, DC, MC, V.

Holiday Inn Select Conference Hotel. Two miles west of Millikin University's campus and just a few blocks from the Scovill Golf Course, this six-story business-class hotel has a Holidome recreation center. Three restaurants, bar (with entertainment), room service. In-room data ports, cable TV. Indoor pool. Hot tub. Exercise equipment. Video games. Laundry service. Business services, airport shuttle. Pets allowed. | U.S. 36 and Wyckles Rd. 62522 | 217/422–8800 or 800/HOLIDAY | fax 217/422–9690 | www.basshotels.com | 383 rooms | $65–$120 | AE, D, DC, MC, V.

DEKALB

Best Western DeKalb Inn and Suites. When you stay at this motel, you are 3 mi from downtown DeKalb and right next to NIU's stadium, which means all campus facilities are just down the road. Complimentary Continental breakfast. Some kitchenettes, cable

TV. Pool. Exercise equipment. Laundry facilities, laundry services. Business services. Free parking. Some pets allowed. | 1212 W. Lincoln Hwy. 60115 | 815/758–8661 or 800/528–1234 | fax 815/758–0001 | www.bestwestern.com | 95 rooms | $69–$130 | AE, D, DC, MC, V.

DIXON

Best Western Brandywine Lodge. Five state parks, including White Pines Forest, Castle Rock, and Lowden, where you can hike and bike the trails, are within 30 mi of this redbrick lodge in the rural Rock River Valley. Restaurant, bar, room service. In-room data ports, some in-room VCRs (and movies), cable TV. Pool. Hot tub. Exercise equipment. Business services. Pets allowed (fee). | 443 Rte. 2 61021 | 815/284–1890 or 800/528–1234 | fax 815/284–1174 | www.bestwestern.com | 91 rooms | $59–$80 | AE, D, DC, MC, V.

DOWNERS GROVE

Amerisuites. Surrounded by malls, movie theaters, and restaurants, this hotel offers high-speed Internet access and Nintendo in its rooms. Complimentary Continental breakfast. In-room data ports, microwaves, refrigerators, cable TV, in-room VCRs. Indoor pool. Exercise equipment. Business services. Some pets allowed. | 2340 Fountain Square Dr. 60148 | 630/932–6501 | fax 630/932–6502 | 151 suites | $49–$152 | AE, D, DC, MC, V.

Red Roof Inn. This standard motel is close to Good Samaritan Hospital and College of DuPage. In-room data ports, cable TV. Business services. Pets allowed. | 1113 Butterfield Rd. 60515 | 630/963–4205 or 800/843–7663 | fax 630/963–4425 | www.redroof.com | 135 rooms | $42–$79 | AE, D, DC, MC, V.

EDWARDSVILLE

The Innkeeper. This modest motel is 7 mi north of Edwardsville on Route 157. Some microwaves, some refrigerators, cable TV. Pets allowed (fee). | 401 E. State St., Hamel 62046 | 618/633–2111 | fax 618/633–1965 | 23 rooms | $40–$50 | AE, D, MC, V.

EFFINGHAM

Abe Lincoln Motel. This small motel is a basic mom-and-pop operation with no frills in downtown Effingham. Cable TV. Pets allowed. | 1108 Edgar St. 62401 | 217/342–4717 | 18 rooms | $30 | AE, D, MC, V.

Holiday Inn Express. You take exit 160 off of I–57 to reach this motel, which was previously the Baymont Inn. Complimentary Continental breakfast. Cable TV. Indoor pool. Laundry facilities. Business services. Some pets allowed (fee). | 1103 Ave. of Mid America | 217/342–2525 | fax 217/347–7341 | www.basshotels.com | 122 rooms, 14 suites | $75–$85 | AE, D, DC, MC, V.

Best Inns of America. Shopping and restaurants are within a mile of this motel, which is 2 mi north of the Amtrak station. Complimentary Continental breakfast. Cable TV. Pool. Some pets allowed. | 1209 N. Keller Dr. 62401 | 217/347–5141 or 877/877–6810 | www.bestinn.com | 83 rooms | $31–$50 | AE, D, DC, MC, V.

Comfort Suites. This all-suites hotel a mile from the Amtrak station. Complimentary Continental breakfast. In-room data ports, microwaves, refrigerators, cable TV. Indoor pool. Sauna. Laundry facilities. Business services. Pets allowed. | 1310 W. Fayette Rd. 62401 | 217/342–3151 | fax 217/342–3555 | www.comfortsuites.com | 65 suites | $53–$99 | AE, D, DC, MC, V.

Days Inn. Just off I–57/70, this motel is within 2 mi of factory outlet shopping and a mall. Restaurant, complimentary Continental breakfast. Cable TV. Pool. Laundry services. Pets allowed. | W. Fayette Ave. 62401 | 217/342–9271 or 800/544–8313 | www.daysinn.com | 109 rooms | $34–$49 rooms, $65–$80 suites | AE, D, DC, MC, V.

Hampton Inn. Just a mile from downtown, this motel is off I–57/70. Complimentary Continental breakfast. Microwaves, some refrigerators, cable TV. Indoor pool. Laundry services. Business services. Pets allowed. | 1509 Hampton Dr. 62401 | 217/342–4499 or 800/HAMPTON | fax 217/347–2828 | www.hamptoninn.com | 62 rooms | $62–$82 | AE, D, DC, MC, V.

Howard Johnson. It's too bad this HoJo didn't retain its futuristic styling of the 1950s, when it was built, but its refurbishing assures contemporary accommodations, just a mile from a large outlet mall. Complimentary Continental breakfast. In-room data ports, cable TV, in-room VCRs (and movies). Indoor pool. Pets allowed (fee). | 1606 W. Fayette Ave. 62401 | 217/342–4667 or 800/446–4656 | fax 217/342–4645 | 50 rooms | $55–$70 | AE, D, DC, MC, V.

Paradise Inn. This plainly appointed motel is just two blocks from downtown and four blocks from a favorite local's haunt, Niemerg's Steak House. Cable TV. Pets allowed (fee). | 1000 W. Fayette Ave. 62401 | 217/342–2165 | fax 217/347–3373 | 33 rooms | $33–$39 | AE, D, DC, MC, V.

Ramada Inn–Thelma Keller Convention Center. The premises of this motel complex include a bowling alley, where you can also try your luck at off-track betting, and a ballroom in the convention center. Restaurant, bar, complimentary Continental breakfast, room service. Cable TV. Indoor pool, outdoor pool. Hot tubs. Miniature golf. Bowling, exercise equipment. Video games. Playground. Some pets allowed. | 1202 N. Kellar Dr. | 217/342–2131 | fax 217/347–8757 | www.ramada.com | 169 rooms; 8 condo units | $69–$95 | AE, D, DC, MC, V.

Super 8. You can walk to the factory outlet mall from these standard chain accommodations. Complimentary Continental breakfast. Cable TV. Some pets allowed. | 1400 Thelma Keller Ave. 62401 | 217/342–6888 or 800/800–8000 | fax 217/347–2863 | www.super8.com | 49 rooms | $43–$55 | AE, D, DC, MC, V.

Super 8. This motel is in Altamont, 14 mi southwest of Effingham. Cable TV. Playground. Laundry facilities. Pets allowed (fee). | Rte. 2, Altamont 62401 | 618/483–6300 or 800/800–8000 | fax 618/483–3323 | www.super8.com | 25 rooms | $46–$51 | AE, D, DC, MC, V.

ELGIN

Days Inn. Just off of I–90, the standard accommodations of this motel are 2 mi northeast of the Grand Victoria Riverboat casino. In-room data ports, cable TV. Indoor pool. Some hot tubs. Pets allowed. | 1585 Dundee Ave. 60120 | 847/695–2100 or 800/544–8313 | fax 847/697–9114 | www.daysinn.com | 96 rooms | $54–$149 | AE, D, DC, MC, V.

ELMHURST

Amerisuites Elmhurst. You can really spread out and stretch your legs here, as all accommodations are suites with full sitting rooms. Complimentary Continental breakfast. Kitchenettes, microwaves, refrigerators, cable TV, in-room VCRs. Indoor pool. Business services. Pets allowed. | 410 W. Lake St. 60126 | 630/782–6300 | fax 630/782–6303 | www.amerisuites.com | 128 suites | $79–$131 | AE, D, DC, MC, V.

Holiday Inn. Just 7 mi southeast of Chicago O'Hare and 2 mi from Elmhurst College, this chain hotel has a Holidome recreation center, and a putting green. Restaurant, bar, room service. In-room data ports, cable TV. Indoor pool. Hot tub. Putting green. Exercise equipment. Game room. Laundry facilities, laundry service. Business services, airport shuttle. Some pets allowed. | 624 N. York Rd. 60126 | 630/279–1100 or 800/707–7070 | fax 630/279–4038 | www.basshotels.com | 238 rooms | $99–$129 | AE, D, DC, MC, V.

Holiday Inn Hillside and Convention Center. In Hillside, 3 mi south of Elmhurst, these chain accommodations and convention facilities are 10 mi south of Chicago O'Hare Airport. Restaurant, bar, room service. In-room data ports, cable TV. Pool. Exercise equipment. Laundry facilities, laundry service. Business services, free parking. Pets allowed. | 4400 Frontage Rd., Hillside 60162 | 708/544–9300 | fax 708/544–9310 | www.basshotels.com | 248 rooms | $99–$119 | AE, D, DC, MC, V.

EVANSTON

The Homestead. This is a sprawling 1927 Colonial. An inn since its inception, the Homestead's rooms are furnished with period pieces. Complimentary parking at a garage half a block away. Restaurant, complimentary Continental breakfast. Some kitchenettes, some microwaves, some refrigerators, cable TV. Pets allowed. | 1625 Hinman Ave. 60201 | 847/475–3300 | fax 847/570–8100 | www.thehomestead.net | 30 rooms, 30 suites, 30 apartments | $120 rooms; $175 suites; $200–$290 apartments | AE, D, DC, MC, V.

FREEPORT

Ramada Inn Freeport. A 10-minute drive from downtown, this Ramada is on the eastern edge of Freeport, near Route 20. Restaurant, bar, complimentary breakfast, room service. In-room data ports, some microwaves, some refrigerators, cable TV. Indoor pool. Hot tub. Gym. Video games. Laundry service. Business services. Pets allowed (fee). | 1300 E. South St. 61032 | 815/297–9700 | fax 815/297–9701 or 800/2RAMADA | www.ramada.com | 90 rooms | $56–$86 | AE, D, DC, MC, V.

Stephenson Hotel. This eight-story brick hotel in the center of the Freeport business district has both standard rooms and suites and serves its complimentary Continental breakfast weekends only. Restaurant, bar. In-room data ports, some refrigerators, cable TV, some VCRs. Exercise equipment. Laundry service. Business services. Some pets allowed (fee). | 109 S. Galena Ave. 61032 | 815/233–0300 or 888/320–7820 | fax 815/233–1599 | 73 rooms | $55; $125–$150 suites | AE, D, DC, MC, V.

GALENA

Best Western Quiet House Suites. The all-suites accommodations here include specialty suites with themes and fireplaces. Downhill skiing is 8 mi away. In-room data ports, some microwaves, some refrigerators, some in-room hot tubs, cable TV. Indoor-outdoor pool. Exercise equipment. Business services. Some pets allowed (fee). | 9923 U.S. 20 W 61036 | 815/777–2577 | fax 815/777–0584 | www.bestwestern.com | 42 suites | $91–$190 | AE, D, DC, MC, V.

Palace Motel. These accommodations are in a complex made up of a standard motel and two late-19th-century homes with period details and furnishings. Cable TV, some room phones. Hot tub. Some pets allowed. | 11383 U.S. 20 W | 815/777–2043 | fax 815/777–2625 | 51 rooms | $85–$175 | AE, D, MC, V.

GALESBURG

Comfort Inn. This motel has standard rooms and suites; it's 4 mi northwest of downtown Galesburg and Knox College. Complimentary Continental breakfast. Some in-room VCRs, cable TV. Business services. Pets allowed. | 907 W. Carl Sandburg Dr. | 309/344–5445 | www.comfortinn.com | 46 rooms, 6 suites | $58–$74 | AE, D, DC, MC, V.

Jumer's Continental Inn. On the east edge of town, this two-story motel's interior is appointed with such elegant details as dark-wood paneling. Restaurant, bar (with entertainment), room service. Some in-room VCRs, cable TV. Indoor pool. Hot tubs, sauna. Putting green. Laundry facilities. Business services, airport shuttle. Pets allowed. | 260 S. Soangetaha St. 61401 | 309/343–7151 or 800/285–8637 | fax 309/343–7151 | www.jumers.com | 147 rooms | $50–$88 | AE, D, DC, MC, V.

Ramada Inn. You can request a room with a balcony at this seven-story motel in downtown Galesburg, four blocks from the historic district of Seminary Street and Knox College. Restaurant, bar. Some in-room VCRs (and movies), cable TV. Indoor pool. Hot tub. Business services. Pets allowed. | 29 Public Sq. 61401 | 309/343–9161 or 888/298–2054 | fax 309/343–0157 | www.ramada.com | 96 rooms | $40–$75 | AE, D, DC, MC, V.

Super 8. This modest accommodation is 5 mi east of downtown Galesburg, just off of I–74. Complimentary Continental breakfast. Indoor pool. Cable TV. Business services. Pets allowed (fee). | 737 Rte. 10 61401 | 309/289–2100 or 800/800–8000 | fax 309/289–2132 | www.super8.com | 47 rooms | $46–$61 | AE, D, DC, MC, V.

GLEN ELLYN

Best Western Inn. This two-story motel is within two blocks of the nearest golf course. Complimentary Continental breakfast. In-room data ports, some in-room hot tubs, cable TV. Indoor pool. Exercise equipment. Laundry service. Business services. Pets allowed (fee). | 675 Roosevelt Rd. 60137 | 630/469–8500 or 800/448–1190 | fax 630/469–6731 | www.bestwestern.com | 122 rooms, 7 studios | $65–$175 | AE, D, DC, MC, V.

Holiday Inn. On Route 38, 2 mi south of the station for the commuter train to Chicago, this motel is within 5 mi of the campuses of College of DuPage and Wheaton College. Restaurant, bar, room service. In-room data ports, cable TV. Pool. Laundry facilities, laundry service. Business services. Pets allowed. | 1250 Roosevelt Rd. 60137 | 630/629–6000 | fax 630/629–0025 | www.basshotels.com | 121 rooms | $99–$111 | AE, D, DC, MC, V.

GLENVIEW

Baymont Inn and Suites. This three-story motel is on the northwest border of Glenview, nearly in Northbrook and close to the Pal-Waukee Airport, just off of I–294. Complimentary Continental breakfast. In-room data ports, microwaves, some refrigerators, cable TV. Laundry facilities. Business services. Free parking. Some pets allowed. | 1625 Milwaukee Ave. 60025 | 847/635–8300 | fax 847/635–8166 | www.baymontinns.com | 142 rooms | $62–$94 | AE, D, DC, MC, V.

Motel 6. This motel, typical of the chain known for its practicality and simplicity, is 6 mi north of town. Cable TV. Pets allowed. | 1535 Milwaukee Ave. 60025 | 847/390–7200 | fax 847/390–0845 | www.motel6.com | 111 rooms | $51–$57 | AE, D, DC, MC, V.

GREENVILLE

Best Western Country View Inn. These standard accommodations are 3 mi southeast of Greenville College, at the junction of I–70 and Route 127. Complimentary Continental breakfast. Cable TV. Pool. Hot tub. Exercise equipment. Business services. Some pets allowed (fee). | RR 4, Box 163, Rte. 127 at I–70 62246 | 618/664–3030 | www.bestwestern.com | 83 rooms | $38–$52 | AE, D, DC, MC, V.

Budget Host Inn Greenville. To reach this Budget Host, take exit 45 off of I–70, 1 mi south of Greenville College. Complimentary Continental breakfast. In-room data ports, kitchenettes, some refrigerators, cable TV. Pool. Playground. Laundry facilities. Business services, airport shuttle. Pets allowed (fee). | 1525 S St. | 618/664–1950 or 800/283–4678 | fax 618/664–1960 | www.budgethost.com | 48 rooms | $28–$69 | AE, D, MC, V.

GURNEE

Baymont Inn and Suites. This motel is adjacent to Six Flags Great America and ½ mi from Gurnee Mills Mall. Complimentary Continental breakfast. In-room data ports, some microwaves, refrigerators, cable TV. Laundry facilities. Business services. Pets allowed. | 5688 N. Ridge Rd. 60031 | 847/662–7600 | fax 847/662–5300 | www.baymontinns.com | 103 rooms, 4 suites | $69–$94; $124 suites | AE, D, DC, MC, V.

Country Inn and Suites-Gurnee. Entertainment and shopping are practically outside your door at this hotel, which is across the street from Six Flags Great America and three blocks from Gurnee Mills Mall. All rooms offer the same amenities, though suites have a sitting room with a hide-a-bed couch in them. Complimentary Continental breakfast. In-room data ports, microwaves, refrigerators, cable TV. Indoor pool. Hot tub. Laundry facilities, laundry service. Pets allowed. | 5420 Grand Ave. 60031 | 847/625–9700 or 800/456–4000 | fax 847/625–4251 | 56 rooms, 12 suites | $125–$135 | AE, D, DC, MC, V.

HINSDALE

Baymont Inn and Suites. In Willowbrook, 4 mi southwest of Hinsdale, this hotel is one in a cluster of four, surrounded by several Italian restaurants, 12 mi south of Midway Airport and the Brookfield Zoo. Complimentary Continental breakfast. Some refrigerators, cable TV. Business services. Some pets allowed. | 855 79th St., Willowbrook | 630/654–0077 | fax 630/654–0181 | 134 rooms | $79–$89 | AE, D, DC, MC, V.

Red Roof Inn. This standard three-story motel is 15 mi southwest of Midway Airport, in Willowbrook, which is 4 mi southwest of Hinsdale. In-room data ports, cable TV. Business services. Some pets allowed. | 7535 S. Kingery Hwy., Willowbrook 60521 | 630/323–8811 | fax 630/323–2714 | www.redroof.com | 109 rooms | $61–$82 | AE, D, DC, MC, V.

ITASCA

Holiday Inn. You'll find this standard motel at the intersection of Irving Park and Rowhling roads. There are several golf courses 2 mi from the motel, and the Arlington Race Track is 7 mi away. Room service. In-room data ports, cable TV. Indoor pool. Hot tub, sauna. Exercise equipment. Video games. Laundry facilities, laundry service. Pets allowed. | 860 W. Irving Park Rd. | 630/773–2340 | fax 630/773–1077 | www.basshotels.com | 156 rooms, 4 suites | $109–$159 | AE, D, DC, MC, V.

JACKSONVILLE

Holiday Inn. On the south edge of town, just off U.S. 67, this hotel with a Holidome recreation center is less than a mile from both Illinois and Mac Murray colleges. Restaurant, bar, room service. In-room data ports, microwaves, some refrigerators, cable TV. Indoor pool. Hot tub. Video games. Business services, free parking. Pets allowed. | 1717 W. Morton Ave. 62650 | 217/245–9571 or 800/HOLIDAY | fax 217/245–0686 | 116 rooms | $69–$100 | AE, D, DC, MC, V.

JOLIET

Comfort Inn–North. This Comfort Inn is 5 mi northwest of downtown Joliet, near the Louis Joliet shopping mall, 5 mi northeast of the riverboat casinos. Complimentary Continental breakfast. Some refrigerators, cable TV. Indoor pool. Hot tub. Pets allowed. | 3235 Norman Ave. 60435 | 815/436–5141 or 800/228–5150 | www.comfortinn.com | 64 rooms | $58–$72 | AE, D, DC, MC, V.

Comfort Inn–South. It is just under 2 mi to Rialto Square Theater from this Comfort Inn, which is 3 mi southwest of the heart of Joliet and offers shuttle service to the riverboat casinos and several nearby restaurants. Complimentary Continental breakfast. Some refrigerators, cable TV. Indoor pool. Hot tub. Business services. Pets allowed. | 135 S. Larkin Ave. 60436 | 815/744–1770 or 800/228–5150 | www.comfortinn.com | 67 rooms | $57–$104 | AE, D, DC, MC, V.

Manor Motel. These modest accommodations are in Channahon, 10 mi southeast of Joliet, just off of I-55. Cable TV. Pool. Business services. Pets allowed. | 23926 W. Eames Rd., Channahon 60410 | 815/467–5385 | fax 815/467–1617 | 77 rooms | $45–$53 | AE, D, DC, MC, V.

Motel 6. You take the Larkin Avenue exit, 130-B, off of I-80 to reach this standard motel. Cable TV. Laundry facilities. Business services. Some pets allowed. | 1850 McDonough Rd. 60436 | 815/729–2800 | fax 815/729–9528 | www.motel6.com | 132 rooms | $48–$53 | AE, D, DC, MC, V.

KEWANEE

Kewanee Motor Lodge. This standard motel is one of the newer hostelries in town. Some refrigerators, cable TV. Business services. Pets allowed (fee). | 400 S. Main St. 61443 | 309/853–4000 | 29 rooms | $42–$52 | AE, D, DC, MC, V.

LIBERTYVILLE

Best Inns Of America. Thirty miles north of downtown Chicago and 6 mi from Lake Michigan, this motel is just on the edge of Libertyville. Complimentary Continental breakfast. Some refrigerators, cable TV. Pool. Pets allowed. | 1809 N. Milwaukee Ave. 60048 | 847/816–8006 | www.bestinn.com | 90 rooms | $72–$78 | AE, D, DC, MC, V.

LINCOLN

Comfort Inn. These standard accommodations are 1 mi west of the Logan County fairgrounds and 3 mi west of the Amtrak station. Complimentary Continental breakfast. Microwaves, some refrigerators, some in-room VCRs, cable TV. Indoor pool. Video games. Laundry service. Business services. Pets allowed. | 2811 Woodlawn Rd. | 217/735–3960 | fax 217/735–3960 | www.comfortinn.com | 52 rooms, 6 suites | $44–$55; $60–$65 suites | AE, D, DC, MC, V.

Lincoln Super 8 Motel. These standard accommodations are just off I–55 on a stretch of road lined with fast food restaurants. Lincoln College is 2 mi away. Complimentary Continental breakfast. In-room data ports, cable TV. Indoor pool. Pets allowed. | 2809 Woodlawn Rd. 62656 | 217/732–8886 or 800/800–8000 | fax 217/732–8886 | www.super8.com | 45 rooms | $66–$101 | AE, D, DC, MC, V.

LISLE

Radisson. You take the Naperville Road exit off of I–88 to reach this hotel, which includes 20,000 square ft of meeting space for workshops, banquets, and business conventions. Restaurant, bar, room service. In-room data ports, some microwaves, some in-room VCRs, cable TV. Indoor pool. Hot tub, massage. Gym. Video games. Laundry service. Business services. Some pets allowed. | 3000 Warrenville Rd. 60532 | 630/505–1000 | fax 630/505–1165 | www.radisson.com | 242 rooms | $99–$184 | AE, D, DC, MC, V.

MACOMB

Days Inn. This standard two-story motel is only two blocks from Western Illinois University. Restaurant, bar, complimentary Continental breakfast. In-room data ports, some microwaves, refrigerators, some in-room VCRs, cable TV. Pool, wading pool. Playground. Laundry services. Pets allowed. | 1400 N. Lafayette St. 61455 | 309/833–5511 or 800/544–8313 | fax 309/836–2926 | www.daysinn.com | 144 rooms | $45–$98; $85–$196 suites | AE, D, DC, MC, V.

MARION

Best Western Airport Inn. The 1991 brown-brick chain hotel remains quiet even though it's conveniently two blocks from the Williamson County Airport and a mile from the nearby mall and restaurants. There's also a golf course a mile away. Complimentary Continental breakfast. Refrigerators, some microwaves, some in-room hot tubs, some in-room VCRs, cable TV. Pool. Business services, airport shuttle. Pets allowed (fee). | 8101 Express Dr. 62959 | 618/993–3222 | fax 618/993–8868 | www.bestwestern.com | 34 rooms, 10 suites | $55; $65–$70 suites | AE, D, DC, MC, V.

Days Inn. Four blocks from town center on a well traveled business strip, this hotel comprising two 1970s brick buildings is 12 mi from Rend Lake and five minutes from the State Farm Rail Classic Golf Course. Complimentary Continental breakfast. Some refrigerators, cable TV. Pets allowed (fee). | 1802 Bittle Pl. 62959 | 618/997–1351 | fax 618–997–2770 | www.daysinn.com | 70 rooms | $60 | AE, D, MC, V.

MATTOON

Ramada Inn and Conference Center. Cross County Mall and restaurants are within walking distance of this two-story hotel off I–57. Restaurant, bar. Cable TV. Indoor and outdoor pools. Hot tub, sauna. Laundry facilities. Business services. Pets allowed. | 300 Broadway Ave. E 61938 | 217/235–0313 or 888/MATTOON | fax 217/235–6005 | www.ramada.com | 124 rooms, 2 suites | $76; $105 suite | AE, D, DC, MC, V.

METROPOLIS

Best Western Metropolis Inn. On U.S. 45 just off I–24, this 1980s brick building lies close to restaurants and shops, and is a 10-minute drive from the commerce of Paducah, Kentucky. The Superman Museum and Fort Massac State Park are less than 2 mi away. Complimentary Continental breakfast. Some kitchenettes, some in-room refrigerators, cable TV. Indoor pool. Pets allowed. | 2119 E. 5th St. 62960 | 618/524–3723 or 800/577–0707 | fax 618/524–2480 | www.bestwestern.com | 57 rooms | $64 | AE, D, DC, MC, V.

Comfort Inn. This standard chain property is east of downtown, a short drive from the Superman Museum and Player's Island casino. Complimentary Continental breakfast. In-room data ports, some in-room microwaves, some in-room refrigerators, some in-room hot tubs, cable TV. Indoor pool. Laundry facilities. Business services. Pets allowed (fee). | 2118 E. 5th St. 62960 | 618/524–7227 or 800/228–5150 | fax 618/524–9708 | www.comfortinn.com | 49 rooms, 3 suites | $75; $85 suites | AE, D, DC, MC, V.

MOLINE

Best Western Airport Inn. This two-story stucco chain property lies close to Moline International Airport, a mall, and restaurants; it's 3 mi south of downtown. Complimentary Continental breakfast. Some refrigerators, some microwaves, cable TV. Indoor pool. Hot tub. Business services. Some pets allowed (fee). | 2550 52nd Ave. 61265 | 309/762–9191 or 800/528–1234 | www.bestwestern.com | 50 rooms | $89–$99 | AE, D, DC, MC, V.

Hampton Inn. This early 1980s property faces Quad City Airport and is 5 mi from downtown. Complimentary Continental breakfast. In-room data ports, cable TV. Pool. Business services, airport shuttle. Pets allowed. | 6920 27th St. 61265 | 309/762–1711 | fax 309/762–1788 | www.hampton-inn.com | 138 rooms | $85 | AE, D, DC, MC, V.

La Quinta Inn. Adjacent to the Moline International Airport and convenient to nearby Snowstar Ski Area, this Spanish-style motel sits atop a bluff overlooking Rock River. Many casinos and paddlewheelers are close by. Bender's Restaurant, just next door, is known for ribs. Complimentary Continental breakfast. In-room data ports, some refrigerators, cable TV. Pool. Laundry facilities. Business services, airport shuttle. Pets allowed. | 5450 27th St. 61265 | 309/762–9008 or 800/531–5900 | fax 309/762–2455 | www.laquinta.com | 126 rooms, 4 suites | $69–$79; $89 suites | AE, D, DC, MC, V.

MONMOUTH

Meling's Motel. Seven blocks north of downtown and a 15-minute drive from Monmouth College, the stone-faced early '70s building remains independently owned. The full-scale restaurant here is known for its buffet of American favorites and homemade cakes and pies. Restaurant, bar. Cable TV. Laundry facilities. Business services. Pets allowed (fee). | 1129 N. Main St. 61462 | 309/734–2196 | fax 309/734–2127 | eva@naplecity.com | 34 rooms | $46 | AE, D, DC, MC, V.

MORRIS

Comfort Inn. This redbrick two-story motel is less than a block from I–80, and 1½ mi north of town. R Place restaurant is within walking distance. Complimentary Continental breakfast. Some microwaves, some refrigerators, cable TV. Pool. Hot tub. Laundry service. Business services. Pets allowed. | 70 W. Gore Rd. | 815/942–1433 or 800/222–1212 | fax 815/942–1433 | www.comfortinn.com | 50 rooms | $79 | AE, D, DC, MC, V.

Holiday Inn–Morris. A mile from Grundy County Fairgrounds, this late '70s property is just off exit 112 of I–80. There's a movie theater within walking distance. Restaurant, bar.

In-room data ports, cable TV. Pool. Business services. Some pets allowed. | 200 Gore Rd. | 815/942–6600 or 800/HOLIDAY | fax 815/942–8255 | www.basshotels.com | 120 rooms | $77 | AE, D, DC, MC, V.

MT. VERNON

Best Inns of America. Close to Jent Factory Outlet Mall, these accommodations are 1½ mi west of the town center in a small business district. Complimentary Continental breakfast. Cable TV. Pool. Some pets allowed. | 222 S. 44th St. 62864 | 618/244–4343 | fax 618/244–4343 | www.bestinn.com | 153 rooms | $47.99 | AE, D, DC, MC, V.

Drury Inn. Just half a block east of I–57 and I–64 this three-story 1970s concrete-and-brick structure is 2 mi from downtown. Complimentary Continental breakfast. Some microwaves, some refrigerators, cable TV. Pool. Pets allowed. | 145 N. 44th St. 62864 | 618/244–4550 or 800/378–7946 | 81 rooms | $64.99–$70.99 | AE, D, DC, MC, V.

Holiday Inn. There's a sundeck and three-story atrium at this 1984 hotel 1 mi west of downtown, and it's within walking distance of the Casey Creek Golf Course. Shopping is available at the nearby Jent Factory Outlet Mall. Two restaurants, bar, room service. In-room data ports. Cable TV. Indoor pool. Hot tub, sauna. Exercise equipment. Video games. Airport shuttle. Free parking. Some pets allowed. | 222 Potomac Blvd. 62864 | 618/244–7100 or 800/243–7171 | fax 618/242–8876 | www.basshotels.com | 236 rooms | $71 | AE, D, DC, MC, V.

Villager Premier. Guests at this four-story redbrick hostelry with extensive meeting space can enjoy a recreation atrium, complete with inside pool, exercise equipment, games, and landscaping. Restaurants are within walking distance and a shopping mall within a half mile. Restaurant, bar. In-room data ports, cable TV. Indoor pool. Hot tub. Exercise equipment. Pool table. Miniature golf. Business services. Pets allowed (fee). | 405 S. 44th St. 62864 | 618/244–3670 | fax 618/244–6904 | 135 rooms, 27 suites | $65; $99–$129 suites | AE, D, DC, MC, V.

NAPERVILLE

Chicago/Naperville Red Roof Inn. This standard three-story beige-stone chain accommodation is close to I–88, with easy access to rail transit into Chicago; it's 5 mi northwest of downtown and a 40-minute drive from Chicago. In-room data ports, cable TV. Business services. Pets allowed. | 1698 W. Diehl Rd. 60563 | 630/369–2500 or 800/REDROOF | fax 630/369–9987 | www.redroof.com | 119 rooms | $78.99 | AE, D, DC, MC, V.

Exel Inn. Next to Naperville Corporate Center, this three-story redbrick late 1980s building lies within walking distance of restaurants and corporate offices. Complimentary Continental breakfast. In-room data ports, some microwaves, cable TV. Video games. Laundry facilities. Business services. Pets allowed (fee). | 1585 N. Naperville-Wheaton Rd. 60563 | 630/357–0022 or 800/367–3935 | fax 630/357–9817 | www.exelinns.com | 123 rooms | $64 | AE, D, DC, MC, V.

NORTHBROOK

Marriott Suites. This all-suites hotel is in a corporate park, less than 1 mi west of I–294 and 4 mi west of Northbrook. Restaurants and shopping are 2 mi away. Restaurant, bar. In-room data ports, microwaves, refrigerators, cable TV, some in-room VCRs. Indoor-outdoor pool. Hot tub. Exercise equipment. Laundry facilities. Business services. Some pets allowed. | 2 Parkway N, Deerfield 60015 | 847/405–9666 or 800/228–9290 | fax 847/405–0354 | 248 suites | $94–$189 | AE, D, DC, MC, V.

Red Roof Inn–Northbrook. You can find this standard chain motel north of Dundee and south of Lakecook at the Deerfield end of Northbrook along I-94. The surrounding area is fairly commercial and there is a restaurant just across the street. Some in-room data ports, some microwaves, some refrigerators, some in-room hot tubs, cable TV. Pets allowed. | 340 Waukegan Rd. 60062 | 847/205–1755 or 800/843–7663 | fax 847/205–1891 | 117 rooms, 1 suite | $45–$110 | AE, D, DC, MC, V.

Residence Inn by Marriott–Deerfield. An extended-stay hotel with 17 two-story town houses is in a quiet corporate park ¾ mi west of Northbrook. The property is geared to business training and relocation, plus family travel. Restaurants and shopping are within 2 mi; rooms have separate entries and fully equipped kitchens, and most have fireplaces. In-room data ports, cable TV. Pool. Hot tub. Tennis. Basketball, gym, volleyball. Laundry facilities, laundry service. Business services. Free parking. Pets allowed (fee). | 530 Lake Cook Rd., Deerfield 60015 | 847/940–4644 or 800/331–3131 | fax 847/940–7639 | www.marriott.com | 128 suites | $164–$204 | AE, D, DC, MC, V.

OAK BROOK

La Quinta. This three-story business hotel offers free local transportation weekdays to destinations within a 3-mi radius. Yorktown and Oak Brook shopping malls are 1 mi away. Complimentary Continental breakfast. In-room data ports, cable TV. Pool. Exercise equipment. Business services. Some pets allowed. | 1S666 Midwest Rd., Oakbrook Terrace 60181 | 630/495–4600 or 800/687–6667 | fax 630/495–2558 | www.laquinta.com | 150 rooms, 1 suite | $99 | AE, D, DC, MC, V.

Oak Brook Hills Resort and Conference Center. This state-of-the-art, 45,000-square-ft conference center on sweeping, landscaped grounds is designed for business meetings. The interior is dark wood and marble. Oak Brook Center is 6 mi away. Restaurant, bar, room service. In-room data ports, cable TV. Indoor–outdoor pools. Barbershop/beauty salon, hot tubs, saunas. 18-hole golf course. Cross-country skiing. Shops. Business services. Some pets allowed. | 3500 Midwest Rd. 60523 | 630/850–5555 or 800/445–3315 | fax 630/850–5569 | www.dolce.com | 340 rooms, 44 suites | $199; suites $450 | AE, D, DC, MC, V.

Residence Inn by Marriott. This all-suites hotel consists of 18 two-story town homes on landscaped grounds; all units have private outside entrances and full kitchens. It is two blocks from Yorktown Mall and 2 mi west of Oak Brook. A spa and health club are nearby. Picnic area, complimentary breakfast. In-room data ports, microwaves, refrigerators, cable TV. Pool. Hot tub. Gym. Laundry facilities. Pets allowed (fee). | 2001 S. Highland Ave., Lombard 60148 | 630/629–7800 or 800/331–3131 | fax 630/629–6987 | www.marriott.com | 108 studios, 36 suites | $144; suites $174 | AE, D, DC, MC, V.

OAK LAWN

Baymont Inn. Midway airport is 8 mi and the Metra station is 3 mi from this three-story hotel. Four suites have hot tubs. Complimentary Continental breakfast. In–room data ports, some refrigerators, some in-room hot tubs, cable TV. Business services. Pets allowed. | 12801 S. Cicero Ave., Alsip 60803 | 708/597–3900 or 800/301–0200 | fax 708/597–3979 | www.baymont.net/alsip.com | 95 rooms, 6 suites | $70–$85; suites $85–$160 | AE, D, DC, MC, V.

Exel Inn. This standard brick motel is about 5 mi west of Oak Lawn in the industrial area of Bridgeview. Restaurants are one block, Chicago Ridge Mall is 1 ½ mi. Complimentary Continental breakfast. Some microwaves, some refrigerators, cable TV. Exercise equipment. Video games. Laundry facilities. Business services. Some pets allowed. | 9625 S. 76th Ave., Bridgeview 60455 | 708/430–1818 or 800/367–3935 | fax 708/430–1894 | www.exelinns.com | 113 rooms | $79 | AE, D, DC, MC, V.

Hampton Inn. This brick, four-story hotel is 3 mi south of Oak Lawn. Complimentary Continental breakfast. In-room data ports, some in-room hot tubs, cable TV. Indoor pool. Exercise equipment. Business services, airport shuttle. Some pets allowed. | 13330 S. Cicero Ave., Crestwood 60445 | 708/597–3330 or 800/HAMPTON | fax 708/597–3691 | www.hampton-inn.com | 115 rooms, 8 suites | $95; $150 suites | AE, D, DC, MC, V.

Radisson Hotel–Alsip. This brick hotel in the heart of Alsip 5 mi southeast of Oak Lawn has landscaped grounds with trees, a courtyard, and a bocci ball court. It's 8 mi south of Midway. Free shuttle to bus station. Restaurant, bar, room service. In–room data ports, some microwaves, cable TV. Indoor pool. Gym. Video games. Laundry facilities. Business services. Airport shuttle. Pets allowed. | 5000 W. 127th St., Alsip 60803 | 708/371–7300 or 800/333–3333 | fax 708/371–9949 | www.radisson.com | 188 rooms, 5 suites | $139; suites $200 | AE, D, DC, MC, V.

OTTAWA
Holiday Inn Express. This three-story motel is 10 mi from Starved Rock State Park, walking distance to restaurants. Complimentary Continental breakfast. In-room data ports, some microwaves, some refrigerators, cable TV. Indoor pool. Hot tub. Laundry facilities. Business services. Some pets allowed. | 120 W. Stevenson Rd. 61350 | 815/433–0029 or 800/ HOLIDAY | fax 815/433–0382 | www.basshotels.com | 70 rooms, 10 suites | $85; suites $100 | AE, D, DC, MC, V.

PEORIA
Comfort Suites. An all-suites brick hotel next to I–74, 8 minutes northwest of downtown and 8 mi to Par-A-Dice Riverboat Casino. Complimentary pass to local health club. Complimentary Continental breakfast. In-room data ports, cable TV. Indoor pool. Hot tub. Business services. Some pets allowed. | 4021 N. War Memorial Dr. 61614 | 309/688–3800 or 800/228–5150 | www.comfortinn.com | 66 suites | $80 | AE, D, DC, MC, V.

Holiday Inn City Centre. This lavishly renovated nine-story tower, one of Peoria's tallest buildings, has a convention center that accommodates up to 1,400 people. Because it's geared to business travelers, an Avis car rental and six meeting rooms are on site. Caterpillar and the civic center are a block away. Restaurant, bar. In-room data ports, some kitchenettes, cable TV. Indoor pool. Barbershop. Exercise equipment, hot tub. Video games. Business services. Airport shuttle. Pets allowed. | 500 Hamilton Blvd. 61602 | 309/ 674–2500 or 800/474–2501 | fax 309/674–1205 | www.basshotels.com | 306 rooms, 21 suites | $108; suites $150–$250 | AE, D, DC, MC, V.

Jumer's Castle Lodge Hotel. Elaborate woodwork and European paintings grace the lobby of this four-story, half-timber hostelry, just west of town. Some rooms have fireplaces, four-poster beds, and tapestries. Restaurant, bar. In-room data ports, cable TV, in-room VCRs. Indoor pool. Sauna, hot tub. Gym. Business services. Airport shuttle. Pets allowed. | 117 N. Western Ave. 61604 | 309/673–8040 or 800/285–8637 | fax 309/673–9782 | www.jumers.com | 175 rooms | $85–$95 | AE, D, DC, MC, V.

Red Roof Inn. This standard two-story motel is 3 mi west of town and 3 mi from Bradley University. Two restaurants are within walking distance. Free pass to local health club. Cable TV, some in-room VCRs. Laundry service. Business services. Some pets allowed. | 4031 N. War Memorial Dr. 61614 | 309/685–3911 or 800/REDROOF | fax 309/685–3941 | www.redroof.com | 108 rooms | $58 | AE, D, DC, MC, V.

Ruth's Bed and Breakfast. On 1 acre in the farmland just outside of Peoria proper, this country-style lace-curtained B&B has two rooms upstairs that share a bath, while the downstairs room has its own; there are flower gardens in the yard. Complimentary Continental breakfast. Some microwaves, no room phones, no TV. Laundry facilities. Pets allowed. | 10205 Eva La. 61615 | 309/243–5977 | 3 rooms (2 share a bath) | $45 | No credit cards.

Sleep Inn. A three-story motel with indoor entrances is geared to the business traveler. Northwoods Mall is across the street. Complimentary Continental breakfast. In-room data ports, some in-room hot tubs, cable TV. Indoor pool. Gym. Laundry facilities. Airport shuttle. Pets allowed. | 4244 Brandywine Dr. | 309/682–3322 | 72 rooms | $58–$128 | AE, D, DC, MC, V.

PERU

Econolodge. Right off I–80 is this two-story motel ¼ mile north of Peru. Restaurant. Some kitchenettes, cable TV. Indoor pool. Video games. Laundry facilities. Business services. Free parking. Pets allowed (fee). | 1840 May Rd. 61354 | 815/224–2500 or 800/55ECONO | fax 815/224–3693 | 104 rooms | $60 | AE, D, DC, MC, V.

Super 8. This motel is 10 mi from Starved Rock and Matthiessen state parks and 3 mi north of downtown Peru. Complimentary Continental breakfast. Some refrigerators, some microwaves, cable TV, in-room movies. Laundry facilities. Pets allowed (fee). | 1851 May Rd. 61354 | 815/223–1848 or 800/800–8000 | 61 rooms, 2 suites | $57.99, $67.99 suites | AE, D, DC, MC, V.

PRINCETON

Princeton Days Inn. Also in the northern part of town, this motel is 1 mi from Sherwood Antique Mall and 3 mi from the Hennepin Canal State Park. Bar, complimentary Continental breakfast. Some microwaves, some refrigerators, cable TV. Pool. Laundry facilities. Business services. Pets allowed (fee). | 2238 N. Main St. 61356 | 815/875–3371 or 800/DAYSINN | fax 815/872–1600 | www.daysinn.com | 85 rooms, 2 suites | $60, $89 suites | AE, D, DC, MC, V.

Yesterday's Memories Bed & Breakfast. This 1852 home is three blocks from Main Street where you can peruse many of Princeton's antique stores. These Victorian accommodations include the Coach House Suite with its countrified furnishings and a private bath, and the innkeepers here share organic produce from their garden with you. Complimentary breakfast. Microwave, refrigerator, no TV in some rooms. No smoking. Pets allowed. | 303 E. Peru St. 61356 | 815/872–7753 | 2 room (with shared bath), 1 suite | $65 | No credit cards.

QUINCY

Quincy Holiday Inn. Right next to the convention center, this hotel also has views of the Mississippi. Restaurant, 2 bars, complimentary breakfast, room service. In-room data ports, microwaves, refrigerators, cable TV, in-room VCRs. Indoor pool. Hot tub. Gym. Volleyball. Video games. Laundry facilities. Business services, airport shuttle. Pets allowed (fee). No-smoking rooms. | 201 S. 3rd St. 62301 | 217/222–2666 or 800/HOLIDAY | fax 217/222–3238 | www.basshotels.com | 151 rooms, 2 suites | $89.50, $139.50 suites | AE, D, DC, MC, V.

Quincy Riverside Days Inn. This downtown motel is across from the convention center and perched on a bluff overlooking the Mississippi. Restaurant, bar, complimentary breakfast. In-room data ports, some refrigerators, microwaves, cable TV. Pool. Laundry facilities. Business services. Pets allowed (fee). No-smoking rooms. | 200 Maine St. | 217/223–6610 or 800/329–7466 | fax 217/223–DAYS | www.daysinn.com | 121 rooms | AE, D, DC, MC, V.

Travelodge. This motel a block from the Civic Center is on a bluff overlooking the Mississippi River. Complimentary Continental breakfast. Some microwaves, some refrigerators, cable TV. Pool. Laundry facilities. Business services. Pets allowed (fee). | 200 S. 3rd St. 62301 | 217/222–5620 or 800/578–7878 | fax 217/224–2582 | www.travelodge.com | 67 rooms | $58 | AE, D, DC, MC, V.

RANTOUL

Best Western Heritage Inn. A mile from Chanute Aerospace Museum, this motel is also 1 mi west of Rantoul and close to restaurants. Complimentary Continental breakfast. Cable TV. Pool. Hot tub, sauna. Pets allowed. | 420 S. Murray Rd. 61866 | 217/892–9292 or 800/528–1234 | fax 217/892–4318 | www.bestwestern.com | 46 rooms, 2 suites | $72.98, $88.98 suites | AE, D, DC, MC, V.

Days Inn. This motel in downtown Rantoul is close to restaurants. Bar. Cable TV. Indoor pool. Pets allowed (fee). | 801 W. Champaign St. 61866 | 217/893–0700 or 800/329–7466 | www.daysinn.com | 80 rooms, 1 suite | $49–$58, $70 suite | AE, D, DC, MC, V.

RICHMOND

Days Inn. Within a few blocks of antiques shopping, this motel is in the northern part of town. It's also 5 mi to fishing, golfing, skiing, and other recreation in Chain O'Lakes and Lake Geneva. Complimentary Continental breakfast. Satellite TV. Pool. Some pets allowed (fee). | 11200 N. U.S. 12 60071 | 815/678–4711 or 800/DaysInn | fax 815/678–4623 | www.daysinn.com | 60 rooms | $75–$110 | AE, D, DC, MC, V.

ROCKFORD

Best Western Colonial Inn. Next to Rockford College, this motel is 4 mi east of downtown. Some refrigerators, some microwaves, some in-room hot tubs, cable TV. Indoor pool. Hot tub. Exercise equipment. Business services. Pets allowed (fee). | 4850 E. State St. 61108 | 815/398–5050 or 800/528–1234 | fax 815/398–8180 | www.bestwestern.com | 84 rooms, 10 suites | $96, $105–$170 suites | AE, D, DC, MC, V.

Comfort Inn. About 10 mi east of downtown, this motel is 3 mi to the Cherry Vale shopping mall and close to restaurants. Complimentary Continental breakfast. In-room data ports. Some microwaves, some refrigerators, cable TV. Indoor pool. Hot tub. Business services. Some pets allowed. | 7392 Argus Dr. 61107 | 815/398–7061 or 800/228–5150 | www.comfortinn.com | 54 rooms, 10 suites | $79, $89 suites | AE, D, DC, MC, V.

Exel Inn. About 10 mi east of downtown, this motel is also 3 mi from Cherry Valley Mall and 2 mi from Magic Waters Water Park. Complimentary Continental breakfast. In-room data ports, microwaves (fee), refrigerators (fee), cable TV. Gym. Laundry facilities. Business services. Some pets allowed. | 220 S. Lyford Rd. 61108 | 815/332–4915 or 800/367–3935 | fax 815/332–4843 | www.exelinns.com | 100 rooms, 1 suite | $65, $125 suite | AE, D, DC, MC, V.

Red Roof Inn. This motel is 2 mi north of Magic Waters Water Park and 7 mi east of downtown. Some in-room data ports, some microwaves, some refrigerators, cable TV. Business services. Pets allowed. | 7434 E. State St. 61108 | 815/398–9750 or 800/REDROOF | fax 815/398–9761 | www.redroof.com | 108 rooms | $55.99–$65.99 | AE, D, DC, MC, V.

Residence Inn by Marriott. One block west of I–90, this all-suite hotel is 7 mi east of downtown and about a mile from shopping and restaurants. Complimentary Continental breakfast. In-room data ports, kitchenettes, cable TV. Indoor pool. Hot tub. Exercise equipment. Laundry facilities. Business services. Pets allowed (fee). | 7542 Colosseum Dr. 61107 | 815/227–0013 or 800/331–3131 | fax 815/227–0013 | www.residenceinn.com | 94 rooms | $94–$135 | AE, D, DC, MC, V.

Sweden House Lodge. Just 3 mi west of I–90, this motel 4 mi east of downtown is along the Rock River. Complimentary Continental breakfast. In-room data ports, cable TV. Indoor pool. Hot tub. Exercise equipment. Business services. Some pets allowed (fee). | 4605 E. State St. 61108 | 815/398–4130 or 800/886–4138 | fax 815/398–9203 | www.sweden-houselodge.com | 105 rooms, 2 suites | $51–$61 | AE, D, DC, MC, V.

SCHAUMBURG

Holiday Inn. On the north side of Schaumburg, this hostelry is a half-hour from O'Hare International Airport. Restaurant. Bar. Complimentary Continental breakfast, room service. In-room data ports, microwaves, refrigerators, cable TV. Pool. Exercise room. Laundry service. Business services. Some pets allowed. | 1550 N. Roselle Rd. 60195 | 847/310–0500 or 877/289–8443 | fax 847/312–0579 | www.holidayinnschaumburg.com | 141 rooms, 2 suites | $159.95, $199.95 suites | AE, D, DC, MC, V.

Homewood Suites. This extended-stay hotel is where visitors to local corporations make their home. It's 1 mi west of Woodfield Mall and 13 mi west of O'Hare International Airport. Picnic area, complimentary Continental breakfast. In-room data ports, kitchenettes, microwaves, cable TV, in-room VCRs (and movies). Pool. Hot tub. Basketball, exercise equipment. Laundry facilities. Business services. Some pets allowed (fee). | 815 E. American La. 60173 | 847/605-0400 or 800/CALLHOME | fax 847/619-0990 | www.homewood-suites.com | 108 suites | $159 | AE, D, DC, MC, V.

La Quinta Motor Inn. One block west of I-290, this stucco motel is in south Schaumburg and 3 blocks north of downtown. Complimentary Continental breakfast. In-room data ports, cable TV. Outdoor pool. Laundry services. Pets allowed. | 1730 E. Higgins Rd. 60173 | 847/517-8484 or 800/687-6667 | fax 847/517-4477 | www.laquinta.com | 127 rooms | $109 | AE, D, DC, MC, V.

Marriott. This 14-story tower is 1 mi south of Woodfield Mall; a shuttle to the mall is provided. Restaurant, bar. In-room data ports. microwaves, refrigerators, cable TV, in-room VCRs (fee). Indoor-outdoor pool. Pond. Hot tub. Exercise equipment. Laundry facilities. Business services. Some pets allowed. | 50 N. Martingale Rd. 60173 | 847/240-0100 or 800/228-9290 | fax 847/240-2388 | www.marriott.com | 394 rooms, 4 suites | $99-$174 | AE, D, DC, MC, V.

Red Roof Inn. Located in Hoffman Estates, this motel is 3 mi northwest of Schaumburg. In-room data ports, some microwaves, some refrigerators, cable TV. Business services. Pets allowed. | 2500 Hassell Rd., Hoffman Estates 60195 | 847/885-7877 or 800/REDROOF | fax 847/885-8616 | www.redroof.com | 118 rooms | $65.99-$68.99 | AE, D, DC, MC, V.

SKOKIE

Holiday Inn North Shore. The Holidome and Recreational Center at this hotel 12 mi from downtown Chicago has all sorts of sports activities and expansive meeting spaces. Restaurant, bar, room service. In-room data ports, microwaves, refrigerators, cable TV. Indoor pool. Hot tub. Sauna. Exercise equipment. Video games. Laundry facilities. Some pets allowed. | 5300 W. Touhy Ave. 60077 | 847/679-8900 or 888/221-1298 | fax 847/679-7447 | www.basshotels.com | 243 rooms | $99-$179 | AE, D, DC, MC, V.

Howard Johnson Hotel–Skokie. This hotel in northern Skokie is a block from the North Shore Center for Performing Arts and two blocks from Old Orchard shopping mall. Restaurant, bar, complimentary breakfast buffet. In-room data ports, microwaves, refrigerators, cable TV. Indoor pool. Hot tub. Sauna. Exercise equipment. Business services. Pets allowed. | 9333 Skokie Blvd. 60077 | 847/679-4200 or 800/654-2000 | fax 847/679-4218 | www.hojo.com | 134 rooms | $133 | AE, D, DC, MC, V.

SPRINGFIELD

Best Inns of America. This motel is 10 mi south of Capital Airport. Complimentary Continental breakfast. In-room data ports, cable TV, in-room VCRs. Pool. Laundry facilities. Some pets allowed. | 500 N. 1st St. 62702 | 217/522-1100 or 800/237-8466 | fax 217/753-8589 | www.bestinn.com | 91 rooms | $48-$64 | AE, D, DC, MC, V.

Comfort Inn. This hotel is 8 mi southwest of downtown Springfield. Complimentary Continental breakfast. In-room data ports, some microwaves, some refrigerators, cable TV. Indoor pool. Hot tub. Some pets allowed. | 3442 Freedom Dr. 62704 | 217/787-2250 or 800/228-5150 | www.comfortinn.com | 51 rooms, 15 suites | $59, $72 suites | AE, D, DC, MC, V.

Days Inn. Just two blocks west of Lake Springfield is this modern motel in the southeast section of town. It has free shuttle service to Capital Airport and the train station. Picnic area, complimentary Continental breakfast. Some in-room data ports, some microwaves, some refrigerators, cable TV. Pool. Laundry services. Business services, airport shuttle. Pets allowed (fee). | 3000 Stevenson Dr. 62703 | 217/529–0171 or 800/DAYSINN | fax 217/529–9431 | www.daysinn.com | 153 rooms | $68 | AE, D, DC, MC, V.

Ramada Inn–South Plaza. This hotel is in a quiet, old residential neighborhood 2 mi south of downtown. Restaurant, bar. In-room data ports, some microwaves, some refrigerators (in suites), cable TV. Pool. Laundry facilities. Business services. Airport shuttle. Parking (fee). Some pets allowed (fee). | 625 E. St. Joseph St. 62703 | 217/529–7131 or 877/529–7131 | fax 217/529–7160 | www.ramada.com | 108 rooms, 6 suites | $62, $150 suites | AE, D, DC, MC, V.

Red Roof Inn. This motel is 2 mi east of downtown and 3 mi north of Lake Springfield. In-room data ports, cable TV. Business services. Pets allowed. | 3200 Singer Ave. 62703 | 217/753–4302 or 800/THEROOF | fax 217/753–4391 | www.redroof.com | 108 rooms | $55.99 | AE, D, DC, MC, V.

Super 8–South. These basic accommodations are 4 mi south of downtown. Some microwaves, some refrigerators, cable TV. Laundry facilities. Business services. Some pets allowed. | 3675 S. 6th St. 62703 | 217/529–8898 | fax 217/529–4354 | 122 rooms | $36–$65 | AE, D, DC, MC, V.

VANDALIA

Days Inn. This motel is 2 mi north of downtown and convenient to area golf courses (Vandalia Country Club is 3 mi away) and antiques shopping (5 mi from town). Complimentary Continental breakfast. In-room data ports, some microwaves, some refrigerators, cable TV. Pool. Video games. Pets allowed. | 1920 Kennedy Blvd. 62471 | 618/283–4400 or 800/DAYSINN | fax 618/283–4240 | www.daysinn.com | 83 rooms, 10 suites | $57.95 | AE, D, DC, MC, V.

Jay's. This family-run, two-story hostelry a block southwest of I–70 has a restaurant and bar next door. Some microwaves, refrigerators. Cable TV. Pets allowed. | 720 Gochenour St. 62471 | 618/283–1200 | fax 618/283–4588 | 21 rooms | AE, D, DC, MC, V.

Ramada Limited. Two miles west of downtown, this hostelry is next to I–70. Complimentary breakfast, room service (from adjacent restaurant). In-room data ports, some microwaves, some refrigerators, cable TV. Pool. Exercise equipment. Laundry service. Business services. Pets allowed. | 2707 Veterans Ave. 62471 | 618/283–1400 or 800/2RAMADA | fax 618/283–3465 | www.ramada.com | 55 rooms, 5 suites | $62.95, $87.95 suites | AE, D, DC, MC, V.

Travelodge. This stucco motel is 1 mi north of downtown and has truck and RV parking. Complimentary Continental breakfast. In-room data ports, some microwaves, some refrigerators. Cable TV. Pool. Playground. Business services. Airport shuttle. Pets allowed (fee). | 1500 N. 6th St. 62471 | 618/283–2363 or 800/578–7878 | fax 618/283–2363 | www.travelodge.com | 48 rooms | $59.95 | AE, D, DC, MC, V.

VERNON HILLS

Homestead Guest Studios. Designed with the extended stay traveler in mind, each suite has a full-size kitchen and separate workspace with oversized desk. Fourteen miles from Six Flags America and 3 mi from Cuneo Museum. In-room data ports, cable TV. Laundry facilities. Business services. Pets allowed (fee). | 675 Woodland Pkwy. 60061 | 847/955–1111 or 800/888–STAYHSB | fax 847/955–0446 | $89 | AE, D, DC, MC, V.

WAUKEGAN

Best Inns of America. This motel is 12 blocks east of downtown. Complimentary Continental breakfast. In-room data ports, some microwaves, some refrigerators, cable TV. Pool. Some pets allowed (fee). | 31 N. Green Bay Rd. 60085 | 847/336–9000 or 800/BESTINN | fax 847/336–9000 | www.bestinn.com | 89 rooms | $78.99–$89.99 | AE, D, DC, MC, V.

Super 8. This standard motel is 3 mi west of downtown. Complimentary Continental breakfast. Some in-room data ports. Some microwaves, some refrigerators. Cable TV. Laundry facilities. Business services. Pets allowed (fee). | 630 N. Green Bay Rd. 60085 | 847/249–2388 or 800/800–8000 | fax 847/249–0975 | 59 rooms, 2 suites | $77.99, $139.99 suites | AE, D, DC, MC, V.

WHEELING

Exel Inn. This motel is a half mile south of downtown Wheeling. Complimentary Continental breakfast. In-room data ports, microwaves, refrigerators, cable TV. Video games. Laundry facilities. Business services. Some pets allowed. | 540 N. Milwaukee Ave., Prospect Heights 60070 | 847/459–0545 or 800/367–3935 | fax 847/459–8639 | www.exelinns.com | 121 rooms, 2 suites | $65, $90 suites | AE, D, DC, MC, V.

Hawthorn Suites. This all-suite hotel is 5 mi south of Wheeling in Lincolnshire. There's a free light dinner buffet Mon.–Thurs. Complimentary breakfast. Kitchenettes, microwaves, cable TV. Indoor pool. Hot tub. Exercise equipment. Laundry facilities. Business services. Some pets allowed (fee). | 10 Westminster Way, Lincolnshire 60069 | 847/945–9300 or 800/527–1133 | fax 847/945–0013 | www.hawthorn.com | 125 suites | $139 | AE, D, DC, MC, V.

Marriott's Lincolnshire Resort. A 900-seat theater-in-the-round that mounts musical comedies anchors this sprawling resort 3 mi south of downtown Wheeling. Some rooms have a view of the lake. Two restaurants, bars (with entertainment), room service. Some microwaves, refrigerators. Cable TV. Two pools (1 indoor). Hot tub, massage. 18-hole golf course, putting green. Tennis. Gym, boating. Video games. Playground. Laundry facilities. Business services. Some pets allowed (fee). | 10 Marriott Dr., Lincolnshire 60069 | 847/634–0100 or 800/228–9290 | fax 847/634–1278 | www.marriott.com | 384 rooms, 6 suites | $133–$209, $325 suites | AE, D, DC, MC, V.

Indiana

ANDERSON

Best Inns of America. This two-story motel built in 1986 is ¼ mi from I-69, exit 26 (Anderson), along a motel strip, 5 mi south of town. An indoor corridor leads to guest rooms. Complimentary Continental breakfast. Cable TV. Some pets allowed. | 5706 Scatterfield Rd. 46013 | 765/644-2000 or 800/237-8466 | fax 765/644-2000 | 93 rooms | $52 | AE, D, DC, MC, V.

Comfort Inn. This two-story motel is on the motel strip ½ mi from I-69, exit 26 (Anderson), at the south end of town. Complimentary Continental breakfast. Microwaves (in suites), refrigerators (in suites). Cable TV. Indoor pool. Hot tub. Some pets allowed (with fee). | 2205 E. 59th St. 46013 | 765/644-4422 | fax 765/644-4422 | 56 rooms, 14 suites | $66 rooms, $71 suites | AE, D, DC, MC, V.

AUBURN

Holiday Inn Express. In this hotel built in 1996, guest rooms have hair dryers, coffeemakers, irons, and ironing boards. The three-story building is in western Auburn, off I-69, exit 129 (Auburn/Garrette), and is 12 blocks from downtown. Complimentary Continental breakfast. In-room data ports, some microwaves, refrigerators. Cable TV. Indoor pool. Laundry facilities. Some pets allowed. | 404 Touring Dr. | 219/925-1900 | fax 219/927-1138 | cndmgment@aol.com | cmphotels.com | 70 rooms | $87-$108 | AE, D, DC, MC, V.

BEDFORD

Bedford Super 8 Motel. This two-story motel opened in 2000 on the south end of town near Leatherwood Creek, 3 mi from the Blue Springs Caverns and 10 mi from Spring Mill State Park. One suite has a hot tub. Complimentary Continental breakfast. In-room data ports. Refrigerators. Cable TV. Indoor pool. Indoor hot tub. Laundry facilities. Business services. Pets allowed ($10). | 501 Bell Back Rd. 47421 | 812/275-8881 or 800/800-8000 | fax 812/275-8881 | www.super8.com | 47 rooms, 10 suites | $50-$70, suites $89-$109 | AE, D, MC, V.

Holiday Inn Express. There are at least four restaurants within a mile of this three-story hotel with interior corridors and rooms with one double bed, two queen beds, one king, or suites. It's 1³⁄₁₀ mi from the Antique Auto and Race Car Museum, and 2½ mi from Blue

Springs Caverns. Some microwaves, some refrigerators. Cable TV. Pool. Hot tub. Exercise equipment. Business services. Some pets allowed ($20). | 2800 Express Ln., at Rte. 37 47421 | 812/279–1206 or 877/838–6434 | fax 812/279–1496 | www.hiexpress.com | 64 rooms | $74–$84 rooms, $84–$124 suites | AE, D, DC, MC, V.

Mark III. Built in the 1970s and constructed with stone, this small, family-owned two-story motel is four blocks from downtown. Cable TV. Some pets allowed. | 1709 M St. | 812/275–5935 | 21 rooms | $38 | AE, D, DC, MC, V.

BLOOMINGTON

Best Western Fireside Inn. On the east side of town just 2 mi from Indiana University, and 5 mi from Lake Monroe, this two-story hotel was refurbished in 1995. Complimentary Continental breakfast. Cable TV. Pool. Laundry facilities. Some pets allowed. | 4501 E. 3rd St. 47401 | 812/332–2141 or 800/528–1234 | www.bestwestern.com | 96 rooms | $51–$84 | AE, D, DC, MC, V.

Hampton Inn. On the outskirts of town, in a row of newer motels, this big, new four-story hotel has bright, airy rooms with dark wood furniture. Some rooms have exercise equipment. There are 25″ TVs and voicemail in all rooms. Complimentary Continental breakfast. In-room data ports, some in-room hot tubs. Cable TV. Indoor pool. Gym. Business services. Some pets allowed. | 2100 N. Walnut St. 47401 | 812/334–2100 | fax 812/334–8433 | www.hamptoninn.com | 131 rooms | $63–$149 | AE, D, DC, MC, V.

CRAWFORDSVILLE

Holiday Inn. Rooms overlook the outdoor pool at this completely renovated Holiday Inn built in 1996. It's 2 mi from downtown. Restaurant, bar (with entertainment). In-room data ports, some microwaves, room service, cable TV. Pool. Video games. Laundry facilities. Business services. Some pets allowed. | 2500 Lafayette Rd. | 765/362–8700 | fax 765/362–8700 | 150 rooms | $66–$166 | AE, D, DC, MC, V.

ELKHART

Econo Lodge. In town at I–80/90, exit 92 (Elkhart), this small older motel on two floors has been maintained but not renovated. Complimentary Continental breakfast. Cable TV. Laundry facilities. Business services. Some pets allowed. | 3440 Cassopolis St. (Rte. 19) 46514 | 219/262–0540 | 35 rooms | $65 | AE, D, DC, MC, V.

Elkhart Super 8 Motel. This two-story motel was built in 1986 and has been updated. It's ¼ mi from I–80/90, exit 92 (Elkhart). Some microwaves. Some refrigerators. Cable TV. Free parking. Pets allowed. | 345 Windsor Ave. 46514 | 219/264–4457 or 800/800–8000 | fax 219/264–4457 | www.super8.com | 62 rooms | $39–$99 | AE, D, DC, MC, V.

Hampton Inn Elkhart. A shopping mall is 5 mi from this Hampton Inn, which opened in 1997. Museums are 4 mi away. The motel is off I–80/90, exit 92 (Elkhart). Cable TV. Pool. Hot tub. Exercise equipment. Business services. | 215 North Point Blvd. 46514 | 219/264–2525 or 800/426–7866 | fax 219/264–9164 | www.hamptoninn.com | $80 | AE, D, DC, MC, V.

Knights Inn. This 1987 addition to Elkhart's lodging roster is a well-maintained one-story place. It's at I–80/90, exit 92 (Elkhart). Guest rooms have an antique look. In-room data ports, some kitchenettes, some microwaves, some refrigerators, cable TV. Pool. Business services. Some pets allowed (deposit). | 3252 Cassopolis St. (Rte. 19) 46514 | 219/264–4262 or 800/843–5644 | fax 219/264–4262 | 62 rooms | $33–$42 | AE, D, DC, MC, V.

Red Roof Inn. This two-story motel is off Route 19 N, 4 mi north of town. Cable TV. Some pets allowed. | 2902 Cassopolis St. (Rte. 19) 46514 | 219/262–3691 | fax 219/262–3695 | 80 rooms | $72 | AE, D, DC, MC, V.

EVANSVILLE

EvansvilleSuper 8 Motel. Wesselman Park Nature Center is across the street from this three-story, brick motel that opened in 1989. It's near I-164, exit 9 (Morgan Ave.), on Route 62. Complimentary Continental breakfast. Some microwaves, some refrigerators. Cable TV. Pets allowed. | 4600 Morgan Ave. 47715 | 812/476-4008 or 800/800-8000 | www.super8.com | 62 rooms | $46-$64 | AE, D, DC, MC, V.

Drury Inn–Evansville North. Built in 1983, this family-owned four-story motel in the northern section of town is 3½ mi south of the airport. Some rooms have a desk and recliner, and the hotel has a complimentary cocktail hour from Monday through Thursday night. Complimentary Continental breakfast. In-room data ports. Cable TV. Indoor pool. Hot tub. Exercise equipment. Laundry facilities. Business services. Free parking. Some pets allowed. | 3901 U.S. 41 N 47711 | 812/423-5818 or 800/378-7946 | www.drury-inn.com | 151 rooms | $73 | AE, D, DC, MC, V.

Radisson Hotel. This downtown 10-story new hotel is across the street from the city's convention center and six blocks from the riverboat casino. Restaurant. Cable TV. Indoor pool. Sauna. Health club. Business services. Some pets allowed. | 600 Walnut St. | 812/424-8000 or 800/333-3333 | fax 812/424-8999 | www.radisson.com | 471 rooms | $69 | AE, D, DC, MC, V.

FISHERS

Holiday Inn Express. When you stay at this two-building motel built in 1983, you're 2 mi from Geist Reservoir and 6 mi to the State Fairgrounds. One building has two stories and the second building is three stories. There is a Bennigan's Restaurant in the hotel. Restaurant. Complimentary Continental breakfast, room service. In-room data ports. Refrigerators. Cable TV. Indoor pool. Hot tub. Exercise equipment. Business services. Some pets allowed. | 9790 North by Northeast Blvd. 46038 | 317/578-2000 | fax 317/578-1111 | www.basshotels.com | 140 | $84-$104 | AE, D, DC, MC, V.

FORT WAYNE

Days Inn–East. A well-maintained, older, property 2 mi east of downtown. Restaurant, pub. Some refrigerators. Cable TV. Outdoor pool. Business services. Some pets allowed. | 3730 E. Washington Blvd. 46803 | 219/424-1980 | fax 219/422-6525 | 120 rooms | $40 | AE, D, DC, MC, V.

Hampton Inn and Suites–Ft. Wayne North. Built in 1996, this four-story motel is on the north side of town close to the Glenbrook Mall and Memorial Coliseum. Complimentary Continental breakfast. Refrigerators. Cable TV. Pool. Hot tub. Exercise equipment. Laundry facilities, laundry services. Business services. Pets allowed. | 5702 Challenger Pkwy. 46818 | 219/489-0908 | fax 219/489-9295 | www.hamptoninn.com | 90 rooms | $69, suites $109-$119 | AE, D, DC, MC, V.

Fort Wayne Marriott. Shades of brown with Western and rustic accents distinguish the guest rooms of this newer six-story hotel on the north side. The Red River Steaks and BBQ restaurant features Western cooking. Restaurant, bar, picnic area. In-room data ports, some refrigerators, room service. Cable TV. Indoor-outdoor pool. Hot tub. Putting green. Exercise equipment. Free parking. Laundry facilities. Business services. Airport shuttle. Some pets allowed. | 305 E. Washington Center Rd. 46825 | 219/484-0411 | www.marriott.com | fax 219/483-2892 | 223 rooms | $109 | AE, D, DC, MC, V.

Residence Inn by Marriott. This all-suites hotel with fully equipped kitchens and fireplaces is on the north side of town set back one block off I-69, exit 111A (Lima Road). There are 10, two-story buildings on this property. Complimentary Continental breakfast. Kitchenettes, microwaves. Cable TV. Pool. Playground. Some pets allowed (fee). | 4919 Lima Rd. 46808 | 219/484-4700 | fax 219/484-9772 | 80 suites | $99-$159 | AE, D, DC, MC, V.

GREENFIELD

Lees Inn. This two-story redbrick motel is off I–70, exit 104. Complimentary Continental breakfast. Cable TV. Free parking. Some pets allowed. | 2270 N. State St. 46140 | 317/462–7112 | fax 317/462–9801 | greenfield@leesinn.com | www.leesinn.com/greenfield.htm | 100 rooms | $59 | AE, D, DC, MC, V.

HAMMOND

Holiday Inn Chicago Southeast–Hammond. This four-story motel is off I–80/94, exit 912 (Cline Avenue). It is 20 mi from downtown Chicago. Restaurant, bar, room service. In-room data ports. Cable TV. Pool. Exercise equipment. Laundry facilities. Business services, free parking. Some pets allowed. | 3830 179th St. 46323 | 219/844–2140 | fax 219/845–7760 | www.holiday-inn.com | 154 rooms | $90–$96 | AE, D, DC, MC, V.

INDIANAPOLIS

Comfort Inn South. This three-story motel is off I–465, exit 2B (East Street), 2 mi from downtown. Complimentary Continental breakfast. Some refrigerators. Cable TV. Pool. Business services, free parking. Some pets allowed. | 5040 S. East St. 46227 | 317/783–6711 | fax 317/787–3065 | 94 rooms | $79 | AE, D, DC, MC, V.

Hampton Inn–East. This four-story motel is on the east side of town in an older, busy commercial strip off I–70, exit 89 (Shadeland Ave.), $1/2$ mi west of I–465, exit 42 (Washington St.). Complimentary Continental breakfast. In-room data ports. Cable TV. Indoor pool. Hot tub. Business services. Some pets allowed. | 2311 N. Shadeland Ave. 46219 | 317/359–9900 | fax 317/359–1376 | www.hampton-inn.com | 125 rooms | $80 | AE, D, DC, MC, V.

Hampton Inn Indianapolis–Northwest. This four-story chain is off the highway in Park 100, one of the state's largest corporate/industrial areas, $1/2$ mi from I–465, exit 21 (71st St.), and 3 mi from I–65, exit 124 (71st St.). Complimentary Continental breakfast. In-room data ports. Cable TV. Indoor pool. Hot tub. Exercise equipment. Business services, free parking. Some pets allowed. | 7220 Woodland Dr. 46278 | 317/290–1212 | fax 317/291–1579 | www.hampton-inn.com | 124 rooms | $119 | AE, D, DC, MC, V.

Holiday Inn–East. Car racing collectibles adorn the lobby of this motel. It's 8 mi from downtown, off I–70, exit 89 (Shadeland Ave.). Restaurant, bar, complimentary breakfast, room service. In-room data ports, cable TV. Indoor pool. Hot tub. Exercise equipment. Laundry facilities. Business services, free parking. Some pets allowed. | 6990 E. 21st St. 46219 | 317/359–5341 | fax 317/351–1666 | www.holiday-inn.com | 184 rooms | $99 | AE, D, DC, MC, V.

Homewood Suites. This three-story all-suites hostelry has apartment-style accommodations with outside entrances, bay windows, and fireplaces. Although it's tucked in the trees in a suburban residential area on the northeast side of town, there's easy access from the highway. Homewood is about $1 1/2$ mi from I–465, exit 33 (Keystone). Complimentary Continental breakfast. In-room data ports, microwaves, refrigerators. Cable TV, in-room VCRs. Pool. Hot tub. Exercise equipment. Laundry facilities. Business services, free parking. Some pets allowed (fee). | 2501 E. 86th St. 46240 | 317/253–1919 | fax 317/255–8223 | homewoodnd@genhotels.com | www.homewoodsuites.com | 116 suites | $124 | AE, D, DC, MC, V.

Indianapolis Marriott. Minutes from the downtown area, this five-story chain is known for its restaurant, Durbin's, which has a railroad theme. Restaurant, bar, room service. In-room data ports. Cable TV. Indoor-outdoor pool, wading pool. Hot tub. Putting green. Exercise equipment. Laundry facilities. Business services, free parking. Some pets allowed. | 7202 E. 21st St. 46219 | 317/352–1231 | fax 317/352–9775 | www.marriott.com | 253 rooms | $111–$180 | AE, D, DC, MC, V.

JASPER

Jasper–Days Inn. This two-story motel is at the intersection of two main highways, Routes 162 and 164. Golf packages are available at a golf course ½ mi away. Complimentary Continental breakfast. Some refrigerators. Cable TV. Pool. Laundry facilities. Business services, free parking. Some pets allowed (fee). | 272 Brucke Strasse Rd. 47546 | 812/482–6000 | fax 812/482–7207 | www.daysinn.com | 84 rooms | $58–$77 | AE, D, DC, MC, V.

JEFFERSONVILLE

Best Western Greentree Inn. This suburban property, with a curved drive-through entrance and appealing gardens in front, is 4 mi from downtown Louisville at I–65, exit 4 (Clarksville). Malls and restaurants are within ½ mi, and a health club is next door. All rooms are on the ground floor. In-room data ports. Cable TV. Pool. Business services. Some pets allowed. | 1425 Broadway St., Clarksville 47129 | 812/288–9281 | fax 812/288–9281 | www.bestwestern.com | 107 rooms | $69 | AE, D, DC, MC, V.

Ramada Inn–Riverside. The 10-story hostelry on the west side of town is along the Ohio River with a view of the Louisville skyline. It is 1½ mi from the Howard Steamboat Museum. Bar. Cable TV. Pool. Video games. Business services, airport shuttle. Some pets allowed. | 700 W. Riverside Dr. 47130 | 812/284–6711 or 800/537–3612 | fax 812/283–3686 | RamadaRVR@aol.com | 186 rooms, 20 suites | $65–$105, $145 suites | AE, D, DC, MC, V.

KOKOMO

Comfort Inn Kokomo. This contemporary two-story hotel is off U.S. 31 S and less than 2 mi from several restaurants, a golf course, and two shopping malls. Downtown Kokomo is about 1 mi away. Complimentary Continental breakfast. Microwaves, some in-room refrigerators, cable TV, in-room VCRs. Indoor pool. Hot tub. 18-hole golf course, tennis. Business services, free parking. Some pets allowed (fee). | 522 Essex Dr., 46901 | 765/452–5050 | www.comfortinn.com | 47 rooms, 16 suites | $52–$69, $54–$75 suites | AE, D, DC, MC, V.

Motel 6. This two-story motel is off U.S. 31 on the south side of town. Restaurant. Cable TV. Laundry facilities. Some pets allowed. | 2808 S. Reed Rd. 46902 | 765/457–8211 | fax 765/454–9774 | 93 rooms | $46 | AE, D, DC, MC, V.

LAFAYETTE

Holiday Inn. This four-story brick building is one of the few motels close to the Purdue University campus. There are small gardens in front and out back. Restaurant, bar, room service. Cable TV. Indoor pool. Sauna. Video games. Laundry service. Business services. Some pets allowed. | 5600 Rte. 43 N 47906 | 765/567–2131 | fax 765/567–2511 | www.holiday-inn.com | 150 rooms | $115 | AE, D, DC, MC, V.

Homewood Suites. A three-story all-suites hostelry with traditional English country-style furnishings, this chain is on the east side of Lafayette off I–65, exit 172, across from restaurants and shopping, 7 mi from Purdue University. Complimentary Continental breakfast. In-room data ports, kitchenettes, microwaves. Cable TV, in-room VCRs (and movies). Pool. Hot tub. Exercise equipment. Laundry facilities. Business services, airport shuttle. Some pets allowed. | 3939 Rte. 26 E 47905 | 765/448–9700 | fax 765/449–1297 | www.homewoodsuites.com | 84 suites | $95–$155 | AE, D, DC, MC, V.

Radisson Inn. A geometric, hatlike roof shades the entrance to this chain. It's off I–65, exit 172 (State Rd. 26 E), 8 mi from downtown Lafayette and 10 mi from Purdue University. Restaurant, bar with entertainment, room service. In-room data ports, refrigerators. Cable TV. Indoor pool. Hot tub, sauna. Laundry facilities. Free parking. Some pets allowed. | 4343 State Rd. 26 E 47905 | 765/447–0575 | fax 765/447–0901 | www.radisson.com/lafayettein | 124 rooms | $79–$99 | AE, D, DC, MC, V.

MERRILLVILLE

Radisson Hotel at Star Plaza. This big four-story hostelry and conference center is at the Star Plaza Theatre complex, a half hour's drive from downtown Chicago off I–65, exit 253 (Merrillville), and U.S. 30. Tropical plants fill its atrium. Restaurant, bar with entertainment. In-room data ports, some refrigerators, in-room hot tubs. Cable TV. 2 pools (1 indoor). Beauty salon, sauna. Exercise equipment. Video games. Playground. Laundry facilities. Business services. Some pets allowed. | 800 E. 81st Ave. 46410 | 219/769–6311 | fax 219/793–9025 | www.radisson.com | 347 rooms | $109–$169 | AE, D, DC, MC, V.

MICHIGAN CITY

Red Roof Inn–Michigan City. This two-story motel is in a commercial area 7 mi southwest of downtown Michigan City and 1/4 mi from I–94, exit 34B. In-room data ports. Cable TV. Business services. Some pets allowed. | 110 W. Kieffer Rd. 46360 | 219/874–5251 | fax 219/874–5287 | www.redroofinn.com | 79 rooms | $79–$85 | AE, D, DC, MC, V.

MUNCIE

Muncie Days Inn Ball State University. This two-story chain motel is about 1 mi from Ball State, 7 mi east of I–69, exit 41. Complimentary Continental breakfast. Some in-room safes, some microwaves, some refrigerators. Pets allowed (fee). | 3509 N. Everbrook Ln. 47304 | 765/288–2311 | fax 765/288–0485 | www.daysinn.com | 62 room | $48–$58 | AE, D, DC, MC, V.

Lee's Inn Muncie. This place is on the north side of town, with rooms in warm hues and contemporary furnishings. There's a hot breakfast buffet every day. Minibars, complimentary Continental breakfast. Cable TV. Pool. Some pets allowed. | 3302 N. Everbrook Ln., 47304 | 765/282–7557 or 800/733–5337 | fax 765/282–0345 | 87 rooms, 30 suites, 3 presidential suites | $74–$159 | AE, D, MC, V.

Radisson Hotel Roberts. This 1920s hotel 11 blocks from Ball State hotel offers luxury behind its period facade. Restaurant, bar (with entertainment), room service. Cable TV. Indoor pool. Hot tub. Business services. Some pets allowed. | 420 S. High St. 47305 | 765/741–7777 | fax 765/747–0067 | www.radisson.com | 130 rooms, 28 suites | $69–$99 | AE, D, DC, MC, V.

Ramada Inn. Room access is via outdoor walkways at this chain hostelry on the south side of town. Charlie's Lounge is popular for dinner. Restaurant, bar (with entertainment), complimentary Continental breakfast, room service. Cable TV. Pool. Laundry facilities. Business services. Some pets allowed. | 3400 S. Madison St. 47302 | 765/288–1911 | fax 765/282–9458 | 148 rooms | $45–$99 | AE, D, DC, MC, V.

RICHMOND

Comfort Inn. This chain motel is at I–70, exit 151, on the east side of town. Microwaves (in suites), refrigerators (in suites). Indoor pool. Hot tub. Some pets allowed. | 912 Mendelson Dr. | 765/935–4766 | fax 765/935–4766 | 52 rooms, 10 suites | $59–$89 | AE, D, DC, MC, V.

Lees Inn. Along motel row, this place is just off I–70, exit 156A, on the northeast side of town. Complimentary Continental breakfast. Microwaves in some rooms, some in-room hot tubs. Cable TV. Business services. Some pets allowed. | 6030 National Rd. E | 765/966–6559 or 800/733–5337 | fax 765/966–7732 | 91 rooms, 12 suites | $64–$94 | AE, D, DC, MC, V.

Philip W. Smith Bed and Breakfast. An 1890 Queen Anne brick home with ornately carved woodwork, stained glass, and guest rooms furnished in antique traditional furniture faces Glen Miller Park on the east side of town. Cable TV. Some pets allowed. | 2039 E. Main St. | 800/966–8972 | 4 rooms | $60–$75 | MC, V.

ROCKVILLE

Billie Creek Inn. Designed in the style of clapboard 19th-century buildings this place is modestly decorated in contemporary and traditional wing-back chairs in dark wood. It's next to Billie Creek Village and overlooks two covered bridges. Complimentary Continental breakfast. Outdoor pool. Pets allowed. | U.S. 36 47872 | 765/569–3430 | fax 765/569–3582 | www.billiecreek.org | 31 rooms, 9 suites | $49–$69, $89–$119 suites | AE, D, MC, V.

SANTA CLAUS

Motel 6. I–64, exit 57 (Dale Huntingburg), leads to this three-story motel. Some microwaves, some refrigerators. Outdoor pool. Small pets allowed. | 20840 N. U.S. 231 47523 | 812/937–2294 | fax 812/937–2495 | 62 rooms | $53 | AE, D, DC, MC, V.

SOUTH BEND

Best Inns of America. Lobby and rooms here are traditonally furnished in warm colors at this hostelry 1½ mi from the University of Notre Dame. Complimentary Continental breakfast. Cable TV. Some pets allowed. | 425 Dixie Hwy. 46637 | 219/277–7700 or 800/237–8466 | fax 219/277–7700, ext. 113 | www.bestinns.com | 93 rooms | $40–$62 | AE, D, DC, MC, V.

Holiday Inn–University Area. A Holidome recreation center is the focal point of this motel ½ mi north of Notre Dame. Restaurant, bar, picnic tables, complimentary Continental breakfast and room service. Cable TV. 2 pools (1 indoor), wading pool. Hot tub. Exercise equipment. Laundry facilities. Business services. Complimentary airport shuttle. Some pets allowed. | 515 Dixie Hwy. 46637 | 219/272–6600 | fax 219/272–5553 | www.usahotel-guide.com/states/indiana/southbend/hinn_southbend.html | 220 rooms | $89–$99 | AE, D, DC, MC, V.

Oliver Inn Bed and Breakfast. South Bend's largest bed-and-breakfast, the huge gabled 1886 Victorian home rests on a wooded acre with a carriage house next door. Fireplaces and porches add quiet charm. It's ½ mi from Notre Dame Stadium. Picnic area, complimentary Continental breakfast. Cable TV. Putting green. Business services. Some pets allowed. No smoking. | 630 W. Washington St. 46601 | 219/232–4545 or 888/697–4466 (reservations) | fax 219/288–9788 | oliver@michiana.org | www.lodging-south-bend.com | 9 rooms, 2 share bath | $95–$149 | AE, D, MC, V.

Residence Inn by Marriott. The all-suites hotel is in a quiet area 1 mi from the Notre Dame campus. Complimentary Continental breakfast. Kitchenettes, microwaves. Cable TV. Pool. Hot tub. Exercise equipment. Playground. Laundry facilities. Business services. Some pets allowed (fee). | 716 N. Niles Ave. 46617 | 219/289–5555 | fax 219/288–4531 | www.marriott.com | 80 suites | $89–$199 | AE, D, DC, MC, V.

TERRE HAUTE

Holiday Inn. A Holidome recreation center is the focal point of this hostelry on motel row off I–70, exit 7 (U.S. 41 S). Restaurant, bar. In-room data ports, room service. Cable TV. Indoor pool. Hot tub. Exercise equipment. Laundry service. Laundry facilities. Business services. Free parking. Some pets allowed. | 3300 U.S. 41 S 47802 | 812/232–6081 | fax 812/238–9934 | www.holiday-inn.com/terrehautein | 230 rooms | $79–$89 | AE, D, DC, MC, V.

VINCENNES

Inn of Old Vincennes. One and a half miles from the George Rogers Clark National Historical Park and 2 mi from downtown Vincennes, this two-story brick motel has large rooms. Complimentary Continental breakfast, refrigerators, some in-room hot tubs. Outdoor pool. Exercise equipment. Pets allowed. | 1800 Old Decker Rd. 47591 | 812/882–2100 | fax 812/882–2100 | www.bestwestern.com | 40 rooms | $60–$70 | AE, D, DC, MC, V.

WARSAW

Ramada Plaza Hotel, Restaurant and Entertainment Complex. The Ramada Plaza is a large, newly renovated, full-service hotel on the east side of town right off U.S. 30. Restaurant, bar, room service. In-room data ports. Cable TV. Indoor-outdoor pool. Hot tub. Gym, exercise equipment. Laundry facilities. Business services. Free parking. Some pets allowed. | 2519 E. Center St. | 219/269–2323 | fax 219/269–2432 | 156 rooms | $89–$159 | AE, D, DC, MC, V.

White Hill Manor. This former country estate on the east side of town, built of brick in Tudor style in 1932, is surrounded by lawn and trees and filled with traditional furnishings. Picnic area, complimentary breakfast. In-room data ports. TV. No kids under 12. Business services. Some pets allowed. No smoking. | 2513 E. Center St. | 219/269–6933 | fax 219/268–1936 | 8 rooms (2 with shower only) | $86–$159 | AE, D, DC, MC, V.

Iowa

AMANA COLONIES

Best Western Quiet House Suites. Fifteen miles southwest of Amana and directly across from the Tanger outlet mall, this hotel looks like a rambling, multilevel house. The spacious guest rooms have large windows and each is decorated with a different local or area theme. Complimentary Continental breakfast. Cable TV. Indoor-outdoor pool. Hot tub. Exercise equipment. Business services. Pets allowed (fee). | 1708 N. Highland St., Williamsburg 52361 | 319/668–9777 or 800/528–1234 | fax 319/668–9770 | www.bestwestern.com | 33 rooms, 7 suites | $101, $145 suites | AE, D, DC, MC, V.

Die Heimat Country Inn. Built in 1854, this former stagecoach stop in Homestead incorporates hand-pieced quilts as decoration and also as very practical covers on the inn's four-poster canopy beds. Complimentary breakfast. Some refrigerators, in-room TVs. Some pets allowed (fee). | 4430 V St., Homestead 52236 | 319/622–3937 | 18 rooms | $70–$100 | D, MC, V.

Holiday Inn. Next to Little Amana and an Iowa Welcome Center, this hotel is just 7 mi from the Colonies and 18 mi from Iowa City. The hotel boasts a large lobby with vaulted ceilings and a dozen or so couches and chairs for lounging and instead of generic, modular motel furnishings, the rooms here are decorated with antique reproductions in a variety of fine woods. Restaurant, bar, room service. Cable TV. Pool. Hot tub. Exercise equipment. Playground. Laundry facilities. Business services. Pets allowed. | 2211 U Ave., Williamsburg 52361 | 319/668–1175 or 800/465–4329 | fax 319/668–2853 | www.amanaholidayinn.com | 155 rooms | $65–$100 | AE, D, DC, MC, V.

Super 8. This standard motel is in Williamsburg, within sight of the Tanger Outlet Mall and 15 mi from the Amana Colonies. Complimentary Continental breakfast. Cable TV. Business services. Some pets allowed (fee). | 2228 U Ave., Williamsburg 52361 | 319/668–2800 or 800/800–8000 | fax 319/668–2800 | www.super8.com | 63 rooms | $57 | AE, D, DC, MC, V.

AMES

Baymont Inn and Suites. This chain hotel on the south edge of town less than 5 mi from the interstate and Iowa State University prides itself on fast, cheerful service and spacious rooms. A convenience store and deli are within walking distance and several restaurants and shopping areas are just a short drive away. Complimentary Continental breakfast. Some refrigerators, cable TV. Pool. Hot tub. Exercise equipment. Pets allowed. | 2500 Elwood Dr. | 515/296–2500 | fax 515/296–2874 | www.baymontinns.com | 88 rooms | $72 | AE, D, DC, MC, V.

Best Western Starlite Village. This hotel is in a rural area 1 mi east of Ames off I-35. All rooms look out onto an indoor pool/atrium area, either through sliding deck-level glass doors or from railed balconies. Restaurant, bar, room service. Cable TV, in-room VCRs available. Pool. Hot tub. Free parking. Pets allowed. | 2601 E. 13th St. | 515/232–9260 or 800/903–0009 | fax 515/232–9260 | www.bestwestern.com | 130 rooms | $64 | AE, D, DC, MC, V.

Comfort Inn. Visible from the interstate, this motel in the middle of a corporate park in southeast Ames is still a quiet haven after a day visiting the ISU campus or shouting yourself hoarse at a Cyclones game. The motel is just 4 mi east of ISU and is within walking distance of several restaurants and other hotels. Complimentary Continental breakfast. Some refrigerators, cable TV. Pool. Hot tub. Business services. Pets allowed (fee). | 1605 S. Dayton Ave. | 515/232–0689 or 800/221–2222 | fax 515/232–0689 | www.choicehotels. com | 52 rooms, 6 suites | $55–$85 | AE, D, DC, MC, V.

ATLANTIC

Econo Lodge. This basic motor inn with reasonably spacious rooms surrounding a pool is in a rural area 8 mi north of town off I-80 at exit 60. There's a Country Kitchen Restaurant within walking distance. Cable TV. Pool. Pets allowed. | 64968 Boston Rd. 50022 | 712/243–4067 | fax 712/243–1713 | www.hotelchoice.com | $28 | AE, D, DC, MC, V.

AVOCA

Capri. This simple motel offers small but well-maintained rooms in a quiet rural setting less than a mile north of downtown. Cable TV. Pets allowed. | 110 E. Pershing St. 51521 | 712/343–6301 | 26 rooms | $41–$55 | AE, D, MC, V.

BETTENDORF

Econo Lodge-Quad Cities. This chain motel is within 5 mi of both the Duck Creek and North Park malls in a commercial area with plenty of shopping and restaurants within walking distance. Complimentary Continental breakfast. Cable TV. Pool. Playground. Business services. Some pets allowed. | 2205 Kimberly Rd. 52722 | 319/355–6471 | fax 319/359–0559 | www.hotelchoice.com | 65 rooms | $60–80 | AE, D, DC, MC, V.

Jumer's Castle Lodge. This massive stone hotel with a nine-story tower section and sharply pitched roof looks like a European castle set down on the banks of the Mississippi. And the opulent, medieval feel isn't just on the outside: guest rooms are finished in custom-made woodwork with deep marble fireplaces, one-of-a-kind tapestries, scores of rich oil paintings, and heavily draped four-poster oak beds. Restaurant, 2 bars (with entertainment). Cable TV. 2 pools. Hot tub. Putting green. Exercise equipment. Playground. Business services, airport shuttle. Some pets allowed (fee). | 900 Spruce Hills Dr. 52722 | 319/359–7141 or 800/285–8637 | fax 319/359–5537 | www.jumers.com | 161 rooms, 49 suites | $91, $94–$140 suites | AE, D, DC, MC, V.

BURLINGTON

Best Western Pizazz Motor Inn. Burlington's only full-service hotel is in the northwest corner of town, just north of U.S. 34 and U.S. 61. Most guest rooms are either poolside or have balconies overlooking the three-story indoor pool atrium, which encloses a heated swimming pool and two attached hot tubs. There's also a game room. Restaurant, bar (with entertainment), complimentary Continental breakfast, room service. In-room data ports, cable TV, in-room VCR, and movies. Pool. Barbershop, beauty salon, hot tub. Exercise equipment. Laundry facilities. Business services, airport shuttle. Pets allowed. | 3001

Winegard Dr. | 319/753–2223 or 800/528–1234 | fax 319/753–2224 | www.bestwestern.com | 151 rooms | $72 | AE, D, DC, MC, V.

Comfort Inn. This quiet, unassuming chain motel is on a commercial street only 2 mi east of Snake Alley and the Mississippi River with plenty of shops and restaurants within walking distance. Complimentary Continental breakfast. In-room data ports, cable TV. Pool. Business services. Pets allowed. | 3051 Kirkwood | 319/753–0000 or 800/221–2222 | fax 319/753–0000 ext. 301 | www.comfortinn.com | 52 rooms | $46 | AE, D, DC, MC, V.

CEDAR FALLS

Holiday Inn University Plaza. Within sight of the University of Northern Iowa campus, this hotel often hosts UNI parents or those in town for UNI sporting events. Restaurant, bar, room service. Cable TV. Pool. Hot tub, sauna. Exercise equipment. Laundry facilities. Business services, airport shuttle. Pets allowed. | 5826 University Ave. | 319/277–2230 or 800/465–4329 | fax 319/277–0364 | www.holidayinn.com | 182 rooms | $65–$120 | AE, D, DC, MC, V.

CEDAR RAPIDS

Best Western Cooper's Mill. This downtown chain motel is within walking distance of the convention center, Paramount Theater, and the federal building. Restaurant, bar, room service. In-room data ports, cable TV. Pool. Hot tub. Business services. Laundry services. Pets allowed (fee). | 100 F Ave. NW 52401 | 319/366–5323 or 800/858–5511 | fax 319/366–5323 | www.bestwestern.com | 86 rooms | $70 | AE, D, DC, MC, V.

Cedar Rapids Inn and Convention Center. This independently run horseshoe-shape hotel is 3 mi from the interstate and the airport and encloses a "fun dome" with a pool, hot tub, and playground facility. Some rooms face outward with a view of the surrounding buildings and countryside, and others look out onto the dome area. Restaurant, bar, room service. In-room data ports, cable TV. Pool. Hot tub, sauna. Laundry facilities. Business services, airport shuttle, free parking. Pets allowed. | 2501 Williams Blvd. SW | 319/365–9441 | fax 319/365–0255 | 184 rooms | $65–$75 | AE, D, DC, MC, V.

Comfort Inn–North. Rooms are spacious and have large windows at this chain motel north of downtown next to Noelridge Park. Lindale Mall is a mile away. Complimentary Continental breakfast. In-room data ports, some refrigerators, cable TV. Exercise equipment. Business services, free parking. Some pets allowed. | 5055 Rockwell Dr. 52401 | 319/393–8247 or 800/221–2222 | fax 319/393–8247 | www.comfortinn.com | 59 rooms | $76 | AE, D, DC, MC, V.

Comfort Inn–South. Slightly more removed from the thick of things than its northern counterpart, the Comfort Inn South is about 5 mi from downtown, but has easy access to Interstate 380 and is a quieter place to stay. Complimentary Continental breakfast. Cable TV. Exercise equipment. Free parking. Pets allowed. | 390 33rd Ave. SW | 319/363–7934 or 800/221–2222 | fax 319/363–7934 | www.comfortinn.com | 60 rooms | $60 | AE, D, DC, MC, V.

Days Inn. This motel is about 5 mi southwest of downtown and 3 mi from Interstate 380 and the airport, in a commercial area with plenty of shops and restaurants. The lobby is done in a country-home theme, with wooden chairs, Formica dinette tables, and sprays of dried wildflowers on the walls. Complimentary Continental breakfast. In-room data ports, some refrigerators, cable TV. Pool. Hot tub. Business services, airport shuttle, free parking. Pets allowed (fee). | 3245 Southgate Pl. SW | 319/365–4339 or 800/325–2525 | fax 319/365–4339 | www.daysinn.com | 40 rooms, 8 suites | $60 | AE, D, DC, MC, V.

Econo Lodge. This standard motel, built in 1992, is 6 mi south of downtown in a commercial area with plenty of shopping and places to eat within walking distance. Complimentary Continental breakfast. Cable TV. Pool. Laundry facilities. Free parking. Pets allowed. | 622

33rd Ave. SW | 319/363–8888 | fax 319/363–7504 | www.choicehotels.com | 50 rooms | $65 | AE, D, DC, MC, V.

Exel Inn. This cream-and-mint-green building is 5 mi south of downtown in a commercial area with many other hotels and restaurants nearby. Complimentary Continental breakfast. In-room data ports, cable TV. Laundry service. Business services, free parking. Pets allowed (fee). | 616 33rd Ave. SW | 319/366–2475 | fax 319/366–5712 | www.exelinns.com | 120 rooms | $42 | AE, D, DC, MC, V.

Sheraton Four Points. This elegant hotel is about halfway between the airport and the downtown area in a commercial neighborhood with plenty of restaurants within walking distance. The lobby sets the tone here with its marble floors, 16-ft ceilings, crystal chandeliers, and large fireplace. Restaurant, bar (with entertainment), room service. In-room data ports, cable TV. Pool. Hot tub, sauna. Exercise equipment. Business services, airport shuttle, free parking. Pets allowed. | 525 33rd Ave. SW | 319/366–8671 | fax 319/362–1420 | www.sheraton.com | 153 rooms, 4 suites | $119 | AE, D, DC, MC, V.

CHARLES CITY

Hartwood Inn. This quiet lodging with basic rooms overlooks the Cedar River and is within easy walking distance of a park. Complimentary Continental breakfast. Cable TV. Pool. Laundry facilities. Some pets allowed. | 1312 Gilbert St. | 515/228–4352 or 800/972–2335 | fax 515/228–2672 | www.imalodging.com | 35 rooms | $45 | AE, D, DC, MC, V.

CLEAR LAKE

Best Western Holiday Lodge. The immediate surroundings are nothing special here, but this hotel is just a mile from downtown and the lake. Inside you'll find a brass-and-oak bar and lounge and guest rooms with upholstered wing chairs and well-lit work areas. Restaurant, bar, complimentary Continental breakfast, room service. Cable TV. Pool. Hot tub, sauna. Airport shuttle. Pets allowed. | 2023 7th Ave. N | 515/357–5253 or 800/528–1234 | fax 515/357–8153 | www.bestwestern.com | 136 rooms | $55–$62 | AE, D, DC, MC, V.

Budget Inn. This basic motor inn is within a mile of the lake in a commercial area with several fast food establishments within walking distance. Complimentary Continental breakfast. Cable TV. Pool. Playground. Pets allowed. | 1306 N. 25th St. | 515/357–8700 | fax 515/357–8811 | 60 rooms | $50 | AE, D, DC, MC, V.

Lake Country Inn. This is a mom-and-pop drive-up-to-your-room motel with friendly, small-town service. Many of Clear Lake's most popular restaurants are less than $\frac{1}{2}$ mi away. Complimentary breakfast. Some kitchenettes, cable TV. Pets allowed. | 518 Hwy. 18 W | 641/357–2184 | loopsia@aol.com | www.netmation.com/lci | 28 rooms | $40 | AE, D, MC, V.

CLINTON

Best Western Frontier Motor Inn. This motel is in an industrial area in the southwestern part of town 3 mi from the airport, and caters to business travelers, with large work surfaces and lots of light in guest rooms. Restaurant, bar, room service. Some refrigerators, cable TV. Pool. Hot tub. Exercise equipment. Business services. Some pets allowed. | 2300 Lincolnway | 319/242–7112 or 800/528–1234 | fax 319/242–7117 | www.bestwestern.com | 117 rooms | $58 | AE, D, DC, MC, V.

Travelodge. This chain hotel is just two blocks from the river and three blocks from Clinton's downtown shopping and dining. Some rooms have river views. Complimentary breakfast. Some refrigerators, cable TV. Pool. Pets allowed. | 302 6th Ave. S | 319/243–4730 | fax 319/243–4732 | www.travelodge.com | 51 rooms | $48–$60 | AE, DC, MC, V.

COUNCIL BLUFFS

Best Western-Metro Inn and Suites. This chain hotel is 1 mi from downtown Omaha and 5 mi from such Council Bluff sites as the Golden Spike and General Dodge House. Rooms have beamed ceilings, work spaces, and partially separated sleeping areas. Restaurant, complimentary Continental breakfast. In-room data ports, microwaves in suites, refrigerators, cable TV. Pool. Video games. Business services, airport shuttle. Pets allowed. | 3537 W. Broadway | 712/328–3171 or 800/528–1234 | fax 712/328–2205 | www.bestwestern.com | 89 rooms, 43 suites | $68 rooms, $79 suites | AE, D, DC, MC, V.

DAVENPORT

Best Western Steeplegate Inn. Many rooms in this centrally located chain hotel look out onto an atrium with an indoor pool, a hot tub, a lounge with umbrellas and bistro seating, and a pool table. Restaurant, bar (with entertainment), room service. Some refrigerators and microwaves, cable TV. Pool. Hot tub. Exercise equipment. Business services, airport shuttle. Pets allowed (fee). | 100 W. 76th St. | 319/386–6900 or 800/528–1234 | fax 319/388–9955 | www.bestwestern.com | 121 rooms | $75–$85 | AE, D, DC, MC, V.

Comfort Inn. On the western edge of Davenport, away from the river but close to Interstate 80, this chain motel caters primarily to business travelers and those just passing through town. Complimentary Continental breakfast. Microwaves available, in-room VCRs available. Exercise equipment. Business services. Some pets allowed. | 7222 Northwest Blvd. | 319/391–8222 or 800/221–2222 | fax 319/391–1595 | www.comfortinn.com | 89 rooms | $54–$60 | AE, D, DC, MC, V.

Davenport Country Inn and Suites. Popular with business travelers, this hotel is in a commerical area off Highway 61, 10 mi north of downtown. Complimentary Continental breakfast. In-room data ports, some microwaves, some refrigerators, cable TV. Pool. Pets allowed. | 140 E. 55th St. 52806 | 319/388–6444 | www.countryinns.com | 49 rooms, 15 suites | $79–$99, $105–$125 suites | D, DC, MC, V.

Days Inn. You can reach Davenport's river casinos or the huge Northpark Mall in five minutes from this chain motel. Most rooms have comfy recliners and some overlook the pool area. Complimentary Continental breakfast. Cable TV. Pool. Beauty salon, hot tub, spa. Exercise room. Laundry service. Business services. Some pets allowed. | 3202 E. Kimberly Rd. | 319/355–1190 or 800/325–2525 | fax 319/355–1190 | www.daysinn.com | 65 rooms | $58 | AE, D, DC, MC, V.

Hampton Inn. Rooms are basic, but some have views of the city at this chain hotel on the western edge of town 3 mi from the riverfront. Complimentary Continental breakfast. In-room data ports, cable TV. Pool. Exercise equipment. Business services, airport shuttle. Some pets allowed. | 3330 E. Kimberly Rd. | 319/359–3921 or 800/426–7866 | fax 319/359–1912 | www.hamptoninn.com | 132 rooms | $55 | AE, D, DC, MC, V.

Super 8. This no-frills motel is across the street from the Northpark Mall and within 5 mi of Davenport's river casinos. Complimentary Continental breakfast. Microwaves available, cable TV. Business services. Pets allowed. | 410 E. 65th St. | 319/388–9810 or 800/800–8000 | fax 319/388–9810 | www.super8.com | 61 rooms | $54 | AE, D, DC, MC, V.

DECORAH

Super 8. This basic facility is within easy walking distance of Decorah's dining and nightlife destinations. Complimentary Continental breakfast. In-room data ports, cable TV, in-room VCRs available. Laundry facilities. Business services. Pets allowed. | 810 Hwy. 9 E | 319/382–8771 or 800/800–8000 | fax 319/382–8771 | www.super8.com | 60 rooms | $45–$56 | AE, D, DC, MC, V.

DENISON

Ho-Hum Motel. All of the rooms at this small motel six blocks southwest of downtown contain 19th-century antiques. Some microwaves, some refrigerators, cable TV. Pets allowed. | 916 4th Ave. S (Hwy. 30) 51442 | 712/263–3843 | 12 rooms | $32–$34 | AE, D, MC, V.

DES MOINES

Airport Comfort Inn. This chain hotel is near the airport, on the south side of town, about 3 mi from downtown. Complimentary Continental breakfast. In-room data ports, refrigerator in suites, cable TV. Pool. Hot tub. Business services, airport shuttle. Some pets allowed. | 5231 Fleur Dr. | 515/287–3434 | fax 515/287–3434 | www.comfortinn.com | 55 rooms, 16 suites | $65 rooms, $75 suites | AE, D, DC, MC, V.

Airport Inn. This motel is on a commercial strip 2 mi from the airport, 4 mi from Interstate 35, and 6 mi from Interstate 80. Complimentary Continental breakfast. Cable TV. Pool. Laundry facilities. Business services, airport shuttle, free parking. Pets allowed. | 1810 Army Post Rd. | 515/287–6464 | fax 515/287–5818 | 145 rooms | $65–$77 | AE, D, DC, MC, V.

Archer Motel. This motel off Highway 65 is within 1 mi of Adventureland and Prairie Meadows Racetrack and Casino, and about 8 mi northeast of downtown. Cable TV. Pool. Pets allowed. | 4965 Hubbell Ave. (Hwy. 65, exit 141) 50309 | 515/265–0368 | 29 rooms | $36–$50 | AE, D, DC, MC, V.

Best Inn. Locally themed art prints dominate the lobby of this chain motel 2 mi from Merle Hay Mall and 12 mi from the heart of downtown. Rooms are basic but spacious. Complimentary Continental breakfast. Microwaves available, cable TV. Pool. Hot tub. Business services. Pets allowed. | 5050 Merle Hay Rd., Johnston 50131 | 515/270–1111 or 800/237–8466 | fax 515/331–2142 | www.bestinns.com | 92 rooms, 14 suites | $63 rooms, $77 suites | AE, D, DC, MC, V.

Best Western Starlite Village. This chain hotel is about 10 mi north of downtown in the town of Ankeny, almost halfway to Ames and Iowa State University. It's just off I–35 in a commercial area among other hotels and several restaurants. Restaurant, bar. Cable TV. Business services. Some pets allowed. | 133 S.E. Delaware, Ankeny 50021 | 515/964–1717 | fax 515/964–8781 | www.bestwestern.com | 116 rooms | $63–$68 | AE, D, DC, MC, V.

Chase Suites. This hotel is on the outskirts of town, off Interstate 80 in the residential suburbs of West Des Moines and you'll need your car when you are exploring local attractions. There's a Thursday-night poolside barbecue from June to September and free beverages in the lobby on weeknights. Picnic area, complimentary Continental breakfast. In-room data ports, kitchenettes, microwaves available, cable TV. Pool. Hot tub. Exercise equipment. Laundry facilities. Business services, free parking. Pets allowed (fee). | 11428 Forest Ave., Clive 50325 | 515/223–7700 | fax 515/223–7222 | 112 suites | $64 | AE, D, DC, MC, V.

Des Moines Marriott. This hotel in the heart of the downtown financial district is connected to Des Moines's skywalks. It caters mostly to those in town for business, but the large rooms and commanding view of downtown make it a nice choice for anyone. 4 restaurants, bar. Cable TV, in-room VCRs available. Pool. Barbershop, beauty salon, hot tub. Exercise equipment. Business services, airport shuttle, free parking. Some pets allowed. | 700 Grand | 515/245–5500 | fax 515/245–5567 | www.marriott.com | 415 rooms | $79–$169 | AE, D, DC, MC, V.

Fort Des Moines. Built in 1919, this downtown hotel has played host to some of the world's most noted dignitaries, among them Nikita Khrushchev and Woodrow Wilson. Elvis Presley spent a night here on his way through town, and eccentric musician Tiny Tim made the hotel his home for 34 years. The hotel's history and guest list earned it a place on the National Register of Historic Places. Walnut and marble figure largely in both the lobby and guest rooms. Restaurant, bar. In-room data ports, refrigerators in some suites, cable TV. Pool. Hot tub. Exercise equipment. Business services, airport shuttle. Pets allowed. | 1000 Walnut St. | 515/243–1161 or 800/532–1466 | fax 515/243–4317 | www.hotelfortdesmoines.com | 242 rooms, 56 suites | $109–$159 rooms, $130–$350 suites | AE, D, DC, MC, V.

Heartland Inn. This motel is on the west side of town about 5 min from the Valley West Mall and is surrounded by restaurants. Rooms are done in what could be called "motor inn traditional"—which is to say, somewhat nondescript, faux-wood furniture, bedside wall-bracket lamps, and floral bedspreads. Complimentary Continental breakfast. Microwaves available, cable TV. Hot tub, sauna. Business services. Some pets allowed (fee). | 11414 Forest Ave. | 515/226–0414 | fax 515/226–9769 | 87 rooms | $55 | AE, D, DC, MC, V.

Hotel Savery. This stately downtown hotel was built in 1919 and now boasts a day spa and a link to the downtown skywalk system. Most of the lobby's furnishings are original, including the gas lights, antique mirrors, and front desk. 2 restaurants, bar, room service. Some kitchenettes, cable TV. Pool. Beauty salon, hot tub. Exercise equipment. Airport shuttle. Some pets allowed. | 401 Locust St. | 515/244–2151 or 800/798–2151 | fax 515/244–1408 | 224 rooms | $119–$145 | AE, D, DC, MC, V.

Inn at Merle Hay. This hotel, on a quiet suburban road near a commercial strip with a wide variety of chain and fast-food restaurants, is 12 mi northwest of downtown in Johnston. It boasts a small library in the lobby and an adjacent retro diner with bright lime, yellow, and orange furnishings (accessible via the hotel lobby and from the street). Restaurant, bar. Microwaves available, cable TV. Pool. Hot tub. Business services, airport shuttle. Pets allowed (fee). | 5055 Merle Hay Rd., Johnston 50131 | 515/276–5411 or 800/643–1197 | fax 515/276–0696 | knapp@dwx.com | www.knapphotels.com | 146 rooms | $59–$71 | AE, D, DC, MC, V.

Motel 6-East. This chain motel is 10 mi east of downtown, and 5 mi east of the Adventureland Park and Prairie Meadows Racetrack in Altoona. Cable TV. Pool. Business services. Pets allowed. | 3225 Adventureland Dr., Altoona 50009 | 515/967–5252 | fax 515/957–8637 | www.motel6.com | 116 rooms | $48–$58 | AE, D, DC, MC, V.

Sheraton Four Points. Trees and flowering bushes surround this upscale hotel in the suburbs 20 mi west of downtown. Restaurant, bar, room service. In-room data ports, cable TV. Pool, wading pool. Hot tub, sauna. Laundry facilities. Business services, airport shuttle, free parking. Pets allowed. | 11040 Hickman Rd. | 515/278–5575 | fax 515/278–4078 | www.sheratoninns.com | 161 rooms | $69 | AE, D, DC, MC, V.

Sleep Inn at Living History Farms. This hotel is 5 mi west of downtown right next to the Living History Farms, which you can see from the lobby. The large indoor pool and whirlpool are in a two-story atrium, and there's a recreation room with pool tables. Complimentary Continental breakfast. Some microwaves, some refrigerators, cable TV. Pool. Hot tub. Laundry facilities. Pets allowed (fee). | 11211 Hickman Rd. (I-80/I-35, exit 125), Urbandale 50332 | 515/270–2424 | fax 515/270–2424 | www.hoari.com | 107 rooms, 3 suites, 2 two-bedroom conference suites | $69–$89 rooms, $99–$119 suites, $149–$179 conference suites | AE, D, DC, MC, V.

University Park Holiday Inn. Frequented by business travelers, this hotel is 6 mi west of downtown, near the financial district. Restaurant, bar. In-room data ports, some in-room hot tubs, cable TV. Pool. Sauna. Gym. Laundry facilities, laundry service. Business services, airport shuttle, free parking. Pets allowed (fee). | 1800 50th St. (I-80, exit 126), West Des Moines 50266 | 515/223–1800 or 800/HOLIDAY | 226 rooms, 62 suites | $89–$99 rooms, $99–$109 suites | AE, D, DC, MC, V.

DUBUQUE

Best Western Midway. Rooms are comfortable but unremarkable at this hotel just 1½ mi from the Mississippi. Restaurant, bar, picnic area, complimentary breakfast weekdays, room service. In-room data ports, some refrigerators, cable TV, in-room VCRs (and movies). Pool. Hot tub. Exercise equipment. Business services, airport shuttle. Some pets allowed. | 3100 Dodge St. | 319/557–8000 | fax 319/557–7692 | www.bestwestern.com | 151 rooms | $75–$99 | AE, D, DC, MC, V.

Comfort Inn. This smallish hotel on Dubuque's main drag does a brisk business with tourists on weekends and is primarily filled with businesspeople during the week. It's only a half mile to the Kennedy Mall and less than 3 mi to the big riverboat casinos. Rooms have large work areas for business travelers. Complimentary Continental breakfast. In-room data ports, refrigerators and microwaves in suites, cable TV. Pool. Hot tub. Business services. Pets allowed. | 4055 Dodge St. | 319/556–3006 | fax 319/556–3006 | www.comfortinn.com | 52 rooms, 14 suites | $50 rooms, $65 suites | AE, D, DC, MC, V.

Days Inn. Built against the limestone cliffs of the Mississippi River, this motel has pleasant, unassuming rooms with great water views. Restaurant, bar, picnic area, complimentary Continental breakfast. Refrigerators and microwaves in suites, in-room VCRs available. Pool. Exercise equipment. Business services, airport shuttle. Pets allowed. | 1111 Dodge St. | 319/583–3297 | fax 319/583–5900 | www.daysinn.com | 154 rooms | $55–$75 | AE, D, DC, MC, V.

Holiday Inn. A freestanding fireplace dominates the spacious lobby of this downtown hotel. Some rooms have excellent views of city and the area's surrounding bluffs. Restaurant, bar, room service. Some refrigerators, cable TV. Pool. Hot tub. Exercise equipment. Business services, airport shuttle. Some pets allowed. | 450 Main St. | 319/556–2000 | fax 319/556–2303 | www.basshotels.com/holiday-inn | 173 rooms | $89–$145 | AE, D, DC, MC, V.

Super 8. This simple but adequate motel is on the west edge of town, away from the river and closer to Interstate 80. Complimentary Continental breakfast. Cable TV. Business services. Some pets allowed. | 2730 Dodge St. | 319/582–8898 | fax 319/582–8898 | www.super8.com | 61 rooms | $45–$56 | AE, D, DC, MC, V.

DYERSVILLE

Comfort Inn Dyersville. This chain hotel is in a commercial area right off Highway 20 at exit 294 about 1 mi south of downtown. Complimentary Continental breakfast. Some in-room data ports, some microwaves, some refrigerators, cable TV. Pool. Hot tub. Gym. Video games. Laundry facilities. Pets allowed (fee). | 527 16th Ave. SE 52040 | 319/875–7700 or 800/228–5150 | www.comfortinnhotels.com | 46 rooms, 4 suites | $60–$87 rooms, $80–$148 suites | AE, D, DC, MC, V.

EMMETSBURG

Lucky Charm Motel. This single-story motel is 500 yards of the Des Moines River and seven blocks from Five Island Lake. For hunters there's a game room in back. Some refrigerators, some in-room hot tubs, cable TV. Laundry facilities. Pets allowed. | 3681 450th Ave. 50536 | 712/852–3640 | 12 rooms | $34 | AE, D, MC, V.

FAIRFIELD

Best Western. This basic lodging is centrally located between the area's largest parks. It's 2 mi from Jefferson County Park, 15 mi from Lake Darling, and 20 mi from Lacey-Keosauqua State Park. Restaurant, complimentary Continental breakfast. Cable TV. Pool. Hot tub. Some pets allowed. | 2200 W. Burlington St. | 515/472–2200 | fax 515/472–7642 | www.bestwestern.com | 52 rooms | $62–$75 | AE, D, DC, MC, V.

FORT DODGE

Budget Host Inn Ft. Dodge. This chain hotel is next to the Fort Dodge Museum, off Highway 169, 2 mi east of downtown. Restaurant. In-room data ports, some microwaves, some refrigerators, some in-room hot tubs. Pool. Hot tub. Gym. Video games. Laundry facilities, laundry service. Pets allowed. | 116 Kenyon Rd. 50501 | 515/955–8501 | www.budgethostinn.com | 109 rooms, 1 suite | $47–$55 rooms, $90 suite | AE, D, DC, MC, V.

Towers Motel. This single-story motel is 2 mi west of downtown, ½ mi east of the Ft. Dodge Museum, and 1½ mi north of the Ft. Dodge Fairgrounds. Refrigerators, cable TV. Laundry facilities. Pets allowed (fee). | 324 Kenyon Rd. (Hwy. 20 W) 50501 | 515/955–8575 | 50 rooms | $32 | AE, D, MC, V.

FORT MADISON

Madison Inn. The owners' vacation photos adorn this homey mom-and-pop motel with pine furnishings and all queen-size beds 1½ mi east of downtown. Complimentary Continental breakfast. In-room data ports, cable TV. Business services. Some pets allowed (fee). | 3440 Ave. L | 319/372–7740 or 800/728–7316 | fax 319/372–1315 | www.madisoninn.com | 20 rooms | $45–$50 | AE, D, DC, MC, V.

GARNER

R-Motel. This two-building motel at the junction of Highways 18 and 69, in a commercial district less than a mile from downtown, is the only lodging in town. It is 7 mi west of the closest point of Clear Lake. Cable TV. Pets allowed. | 785 Hwy. 18 W 50438 | 641/923–2823 | 21 rooms | $30–$45 | AE, D, MC, V.

GRINNELL

Days Inn. This white stucco hotel with a red-tile roof is just off Interstate 80, on a commercial strip 2 mi south of town. Complimentary Continental breakfast. Cable TV. Pool. Pets allowed (fee). | 1902 West St. | 515/236–6710 | fax 515/236–5783 | www.daysinn.com | 41 rooms | $55 | AE, D, DC, MC, V.

Super 8. Another chain motel just off Interstate 80 2 mi south of town. Complimentary Continental breakfast. Cable TV. Some pets allowed. | 2111 West St. S | 515/236–7888 | fax 515/236–7888 | www.super8.com | 53 rooms | $58–$62 | AE, D, DC, MC, V.

HAMPTON

Gold Key. This single-story brick motel is 2 mi north of downtown in a rural farming area. Restaurant. Cable TV. Pets allowed. | 1570 B Hwy. 65 | 515/456–2566 | fax 515/456–3622 | 20 rooms | $44 | AE, D, DC, MC, V.

HUMBOLDT

Corner Inn. This small hotel, with its meticulously kept flower beds out front, is right on the town's main intersection. The lobby and guest rooms are simply furnished. Cable TV. Pets allowed. | 1004 N. 13th St. | 515/332–1672 | 22 rooms | $36–$40 | AE, D, MC, V.

Super 8 Humboldt. This chain motel 2 mi northwest of downtown has some suites with fold-out couches. Complimentary Continental breakfast. Some microwaves, some refrigerators, cable TV. Pets allowed (fee). | 1520 10th Ave. N 50548 | 712/476–9389 or 800/800–8000 | 28 rooms, 5 suites | $52–$67 rooms, $57–$74 suites | AE, D, DC, MC, V.

IOWA CITY

Bella Vista. This B&B is on the historic north side overlooking the Iowa River and the university's Hancher Auditorium. The 1920s-era house is filled with antiques and international artifacts collected by the globe-trotting innkeeper. Complimentary breakfast. Cable TV. Some pets allowed. | 2 Bella Vista Pl | 319/524–3888 | 2 rooms (with shared bath), 3 suites | $70–$125 | AE, MC, V.

Ramada Westfield Inn. This Coralville chain hotel is 4 mi north of downtown right across from the Coral Ridge Mall, the largest mall in Iowa. In the dome-enclosed recreational area you can sit poolside, play pool, or soak in the hot tub. Restaurant, bar, complimentary breakfast. In-room data ports, cable TV. Pool. Hot tub. Gym. Video games. Laundry facilities. Business services. Pets allowed (fee). | 2530 Holiday Rd., Coralville 52241 | 319/337–9002 or 800/2–RAMADA | 155 rooms | $50–$79 | AE, D, DC, MC, V.

LE MARS

Amber Inn. This basic one-story motel is just off Highway 75 about 2 mi south of town. Complimentary Continental breakfast. Cable TV. Business services. Pets allowed. | 635 8th

Ave., SW | 712/546–7066 or 800/338–0298 | fax 712/548–4058 | www.geocities.com/amberinn | 70 rooms | $45 | AE, D, MC, V.

MARSHALLTOWN

Comfort Inn. This no-frills lodging is 3 mi south of downtown and the same distance from several antiques shopping malls and the Meskwaki Casino. Complimentary Continental breakfast. Cable TV. Pool. Hot tub. Business services. Pets allowed (fee). | 2613 S. Center St. | 515/752–6000 | fax 515/752–8762 | www.comfortinn.com | 62 rooms | $55 | AE, D, DC, MC, V.

MASON CITY

Days Inn. This modest chain hotel is within walking distance of the lake, which may afford you some pleasant views around sunset. Complimentary Continental breakfast. Cable TV. Business services. Pets allowed. | 2301 4th St. SW | 515/424–0210 | fax 515/424–0210 | www.daysinn.com | 58 rooms | $48 | AE, D, DC, MC, V.

MISSOURI VALLEY

Days Inn. This motel is off Interstate 29 at exit 75, 1 mi east of downtown Missouri Valley. You'll find several restaurants and shops nearby. Complimentary Continental breakfast. Some refrigerators, in-room TVs. Pool. Hot tub. Gym. Pets allowed (fee). | 1967 Rte. 30 51555 | 712/642–4788 | fax 712/642–3813 | www.daysinn.com | 48 rooms | $60–$85 | AE, D, DC, MC, V.

MOUNT PLEASANT

Heartland Inn. Photos and framed newspaper clippings line the lobby and hallways of this motel 2 mi north of town. Complimentary Continental breakfast. Cable TV. Pool. Hot tub, sauna. Business services. Pets allowed. | Hwy. 218 N | 319/385–2102 | fax 319/385–3223 | 59 rooms | $57–$65 | AE, D, DC, MC, V.

MUSCATINE

Holiday Inn. This hotel 5 mi northeast of town is built around a central atrium with a waterfall and a miniature pond. There are several restaurants within a mile. Restaurant, bar, room service. In-room data ports, some refrigerators, cable TV. Pool, wading pool. Hot tub, sauna. Exercise equipment. Laundry facilities. Business services. Pets allowed (fee.). | 2915 N. U.S. 61 | 319/264–5550 | fax 319/264–0451 | www.basshotels.com/holiday-inn | 112 rooms | $68–$89 | AE, D, DC, MC, V.

NEWTON

Best Western Newton Inn. Immediately south of Interstate 80, this motel is known for its indoor family recreation area which boasts a junior-Olympic-size indoor pool, an oversize whirlpool, two cedar-wood saunas, indoor putting green and picnic area, Ping-Pong tables, and a video-game arcade. There's also a sundeck on the roof. Restaurant, bar. Cable TV, in-room VCRs available. Pool. Hot tub. Putting green. Gym. Business services. Pets allowed. | 2000 W. 18th St. S | 515/792–4200 | fax 515/792–0108 | www.bestwestern.com | 118 rooms | $65 | AE, D, DC, MC, V.

Days Inn. This hotel is 2 mi south of town near the interstate but surrounded by cornfields. Guest rooms are spacious and very quiet. Complimentary Continental breakfast. Cable TV. Business services. Pets allowed. | 1605 W. 19th St. S | 641/792–2330 | fax 641/792–1045 | www.daysinn.com | 59 rooms | $50–$75 | AE, D, DC, MC, V.

OKOBOJI

Country Club Motel. Rooms are simple at this one-story, L-shape motel centered around a pool and surrounded on three sides by trees, but you'll be just half a block from Lake Okoboji and a public boat ramp. Picnic area. Some kitchenettes, cable TV. Pool. Business services. Pets allowed. | 1107 Sanborn Ave. | 712/332–5617 or 800/831–5615 | fax 712/332–7705 | 40 rooms, 13 suites | $60–$99 rooms, $119 suites | AE, D, DC, MC, V.

Fillenwarth Beach. This resort on West Okoboji Lake caters to outdoor enthusiasts. Wood-frame buildings are nestled into a wooded hillside, and all rooms have balconies with lake views. The resort also offers lake cruises, boat trips, and a host of other, nonwatery, activities. Picnic area. Cable TV, in-room VCRs. Indoor-outdoor pool. Tennis. Beach, dock, water sports, boating. Business services, airport shuttle. Children's programs (ages 2 and up), playground. Pets allowed. | 87 Lake Shore Dr., Arnold's Park 51331 | 712/332–5646 | fax 712/332–5646 | www.fillenwarthbeach.com | 15 cottages (fit up to 18 people), 75 apartments | $88–$480 cottages, $120–$216 apartments | No credit cards | Closed Oct.–Apr.

Four Seasons Resort. A nautical motif dominates this resort on West Okoboji Lake—there's lots of brass, sea blue, seashells, and lighthouses. The property has its own boating jetties, beach, marina, and lakefront walking paths. Some rooms have balconies with lake views. Restaurant, bar, picnic area. Cable TV. Beach. Pets allowed. | 3333 U.S. 71, Arnold's Park 51331 | 712/332–2103 or 800/876–2103 | 32 rooms | $75–$115 | AE, MC, V.

Village East Resort. This resort on Lake Okoboji offers fine lake and golf course views. Guest rooms have antique reproduction furnishings. Two restaurants are adjacent to the resort. Restaurant, bar. Cable TV, in-room VCRs available. 2 pools. Beauty salon, hot tub, sauna. 18-hole golf course, tennis. Gym. Cross-country skiing. Playground. Business services. Pets allowed. | 1405 Hwy. 71 | 712/332–2161 or 800/727–4561 | fax 712/332–7727 | 95 rooms, 4 suites | $149–$164 rooms, $225 suites | AE, D, DC, MC, V.

ONAWA

Super 8. This chain hotel is 2 mi west of Onawa in a commercial area; several restaurants are within walking distance. Picnic area. Cable TV. Pets allowed. | 22868 Filbert Ave. | 712/423–2101 | fax 712/423–3480 | www.super8.com | 80 rooms | $40 | AE, D, DC, MC, V.

OSKALOOSA

Red Carpet Inn. Large flower beds welcome you to this motel on 3 acres of well-tended grounds 2 mi north of downtown. Complimentary Continental breakfast. Cable TV. Pool. Basketball. Pets allowed. | 2278 U.S. 63 N | 515/673–8641 | fax 515/673–4111 | www.reservahost.com | 41 rooms | $46 | AE, D, MC, V.

SHENANDOAH

Country Inn. Though independently run, this motel 3 blocks west of downtown has something of a chain-property feel and caters primarily to business travelers and those just passing through. Restaurant, bar, complimentary Continental breakfast, room service. Cable TV. Pool. Business services, airport shuttle. Pets allowed. | 1503 Sheridan Ave. | 712/246–1550 | fax 712/246–4773 | 65 rooms | $50 | AE, D, DC, MC, V.

SIOUX CITY

Best Western City Center. Local art fills the bright, spacious lobby in this downtown hotel. Guest rooms are primarily equipped for business travelers—they're soundproof and spacious with large work spaces. Bar, complimentary breakfast. Cable TV. Pool. Laundry facilities. Business services, airport shuttle. Some pets allowed. | 130 Nebraska St. | 712/277–1550 | fax 712/277–1120 | www.bestwestern.com | 114 rooms | $59 | AE, D, DC, MC, V.

Palmer House. This simple, independent motel is just outside of town. Restaurant, complimentary Continental breakfast. Cable TV. Pool. Laundry facilities. Business services. Pets allowed. | 3440 E. Gordon Dr. | 712/276–4221 or 800/833–4221 | fax 712/276–9535 | 60 rooms | $43–$60 | AE, D, DC, MC, V.

Super 8. This standard chain hotel is less than 1 mi from Western Iowa Tech and Morningside College and within 4 mi of the Sioux City Arts and Public Museums. Complimentary Continental breakfast. Cable TV. Pets allowed. | 4307 Stone Ave. | 712/274–1520 | fax 712/274–1520 | www.super8.com | 60 rooms | $36–$65 | AE, D, DC, MC, V.

SPENCER

AmericInn. Like others of its ilk, this motel is a no-fuss overnight option. Rooms here are big enough to accommodate a rollaway bed or two, and you'll be just 5 min from the Clay County Fairgrounds. In-room data ports, cable TV. Pool, hot tub. Laundry services. Business services. Pets allowed. | 1005 13th St. SW | 712/262–7525 | fax 712/262–7514 | 46 rooms | $59–$122 | AE, D, DC, MC, V.

WALNUT

Walnut Super 8 Motel. This basic chain motel is just off Interstate 80 at exit 46. Kids 12 and under stay free. In-room data ports, some in-room hot tubs, cable TV. Pool. Laundry facilities. Some pets allowed. | 2109 Antique City Dr. | 712/784–2221 | fax 712/784–3961 | 51 rooms | $39–$60 | AE, D, DC, MC, V.

WATERLOO

Best Western Starlite Village. This 11-story tower 2 blocks from downtown rises like a skyscraper in an otherwise uninterrupted landscape of fields, barns, and homes. Rooms are spacious but basic, and all enjoy an excellent view of the city. Restaurant, bar. In-room data ports, cable TV. Pool. Business services, airport shuttle. Pets allowed. | 214 Washington St. | 319/235–0321 | fax 319/235–6343 | www.bestwestern.com | 215 rooms | $88 | AE, D, DC, MC, V.

Fairfield Inn by Marriott. This pink- and white-brick hotel 5 mi south of downtown is right next to a shopping center. Rooms have work spaces and sitting areas separated from the sleeping area by low, wood-trimmed partitions. Complimentary Continental breakfast. Cable TV. Pool. Hot tub. Some pets allowed. | 2011 La Porte Rd. | 319/234–5452 | fax 319/234–5452 | www.marriott.com | 57 rooms | $72 | AE, D, DC, MC, V.

Grand Hotel Waterloo. A dozen brightly colored flags mark the front of this downtown hotel. Guest rooms are full of light from large, ground-floor windows. Complimentary Continental breakfast. In-room data ports, cable TV. Pool. Exercise equipment. Laundry services. Business services. Pets allowed. | 300 W. Mullan Ave. | 319/234–7791 or 877/928–3756 | grandhotel@earthdome.com | www.grandhotelwaterloo.com | fax 319/234–1727 | 96 rooms | $45 | AE, D, MC, V.

Heartland Inn. The standard chain hotel is in a commercial area near the Crossroads Mall 3 mi from downtown. There are several restaurants and fast-food establishments within walking distance. Complimentary Continental breakfast. In-room data ports, cable TV. Exercise equipment. Business services. Pets allowed (fee). | 1809 LaPorte Rd. | 319/235–4461 or 800/334–3277 | fax 319/235–0907 | 118 rooms | $62 | AE, D, DC, MC, V.

Holiday Inn-Convention Center. This 10-story high-rise hotel with a soaring glass atrium in the lobby is right in the center of Waterloo, and a skywalk connects the inn to an adjacent parking garage. Rooms have large work spaces. Restaurant, dining room, bar (with entertainment). In-room data ports, some refrigerators, cable TV. Pool. Hot tub. Airport shuttle. Pets allowed. | 205 W. 4th St. | 319/233–7560 | fax 319/236–9590 | www.basshotels.com/holiday-inn | 229 rooms | $85–$105 | AE, D, DC, MC, V.

Quality Inn. This chain hotel is just 1½ blocks from the Waterloo Convention Center. Bar, complimentary Continental breakfast. In-room data ports, microwaves, refrigerators, some in-room hot tubs, cable TV. Laundry service. Business services. Pets allowed. | 226 W. 5th St. | 319/235–0301 or 800/228–5151 | fax 319/234–4837 | www.qualityinn.com | 50 rooms, 17 suites | $60–$72 rooms, $80–$144 suites | AE, D, DC, MC, V.

Super 8. This brown-and-white, faux-exposed-timber chain hotel is adjacent to the Crossroads Shopping Center 2 mi from the center of town. Complimentary Continental breakfast. Cable TV. Some pets allowed. | 1825 LaPorte Rd. | 319/233–1800 | fax 319/233–1800 | www.super8.com | 62 rooms | $46–$50 | AE, D, DC, MC, V.

WEBSTER CITY

Best Western Norseman Inn. Rooms are spacious enough to sleep a family comfortably at this small, brick motel. Bar, complimentary Continental breakfast. Cable TV. Pets allowed. | 3086 220th St., Williams 50271 | 515/854–2281 | fax 515/854–2447 | www.bestwestern.com | 33 rooms | $50 | AE, D, DC, MC, V.

Super 8. This motel is 1 mi west of the center of town at the junction of U.S. 20 and U.S. 27, a few minutes' drive from several restaurants. In-room data ports, cable TV. Pool. Laundry facilities. Business services. Pets allowed. | 305 Closz Dr. | 515/832–2000 | fax 515/832–2000 | www.super8.com | 44 rooms | $43–$58 | AE, D, DC, MC, V.

WEST BEND

West Bend Motel. This humble, single-story motel is proud of its down-home friendly service at the desk and is right in town about a block from the Grotto. Cable TV. Pets allowed. | 13 4th Ave. | 515/887–3611 | 18 rooms | $36 | D, MC, V.

WEST BRANCH

Econo Lodge Motel. A basic motel just off Interstate 80 at exit 259 in West Liberty, about 5 mi from West Branch. Kids stay free. Complimentary Continental breakfast. Cable TV. Pool. Some pets allowed. | 1943 Garfield Ave., West Liberty 52776 | 319/627–2171 or 888/589–5007 | fax 319/627–4982 | 35 rooms | $48–$55 | AE, D, DC, MC, V.

Presidential Motor Inn. Pictures of Herbert Hoover hang in each room of this basic motel. Microwaves available, refrigerators, cable TV. Laundry facilities. Some pets allowed. | 711 S. Downey Rd. 52358 | 319/643–2526 | fax 319/643–5166 | 38 rooms | $42 | AE, D, DC, MC, V.

WINTERSET

Village View Motel. This white-sided motel on the north edge of town provides guests with maps of the county's famous bridges. Rooms are small and basic, but the motel is within easy walking distance of the town square. Cable TV, in-room VCRs available. Pets allowed. | 711 E. Hwy. 92 | 515/462–1218 or 800/862–1218 | fax 515/462–1231 | www.madisoncounty.com | 16 rooms | $43 | AE, D, DC, MC, V.

Kansas

ABILENE

Diamond. In a calm, quiet setting, this country Victorian structure is about ½ mi from the local Abilene airport (where jets can land), about 2 mi from the Eisenhower Center, and five blocks from Eisenhower Park. Refrigerators, cable TV, some pets allowed. | 1407 N.W. 3rd St. | 785/263–2360 | fax 785/263–2186 | 30 rooms | $27–$37 | D, MC, V.

Holiday Inn Express Hotel and Suites. Opened in August 2000, this two-story hotel is right off I–70, Exit 275. A cozy fireplace can be found in the lobby. Complimentary Continental breakfast, in-room data ports, microwaves, refrigerators, cable TV, pool, hot tub, sauna, exercise equipment, laundry facilities, business services, pets allowed (fee). | 110 E. Lafayette Ave. 67410 | 785/263–4049 | fax 785/263–3201 | www.holiday-inn.com | 61 rooms, 15 suites | $69–$79, $89–$99 suites | AE, D, DC, MC, V.

Spruce House. This 1882 Italianate home has an eclectic decor and original art by the innkeeper, who is a founder of the Great Plains Theater Festival. The rooms are named after Jean Harlow, Doris Day, and Roy Rogers. Facilities vary in availability and pets are allowed, but you must call ahead of time. This B&B accepts long-term guests; minimum stay is two nights. | 604 N. Spruce | 785/263–3900. Some pets allowed, no smoking. | 3 rooms | $100 (2–night minimum stay) | No credit cards.

Super 8. This three-story motel is on the southeast side of I–70. Rooms are no-frills and reasonably priced. Complimentary Continental breakfast, cable TV, business services, some pets allowed (fee). | 2207 N. Buckeye Ave. | 785/263–4545 | fax 785/263–7448 | www.super8.com | 62 rooms | $46 | AE, D, DC, MC, V.

ARKANSAS CITY

Crestview Motel. The epitome of a place to rest your head for the night, this strip motel offers few frills, and only economical rooms. Some kitchenettes, some refrigerators, cable TV, pets allowed. | 2401 N. Summit St. 67005 | 316/442–6229 | 23 rooms | $30–$35 | AE, D, MC, V.

Hallmark Inn. This single story motel was built in the 1970s. A shopping center and numerous restaurants are within walking distance. Complimentary Continental breakfast, cable TV, pool, business services, pets allowed. | 1617 N. Summit St. | 316/442–1400 | fax 316/442–4729 | 47 rooms | $55 | AE, D, DC, MC, V.

Regency Court Inn. Floral/faunal arrangements and oil paintings by local artists are found in the atrium lobby of this moderately priced, two-story motel. Restaurant, cable TV, indoor pool, outdoor hot tub, video games, business services, pets allowed (fee). | 3232 N. Summit St. | 316/442–7700 or 800/325–9151 | fax 316/442–1218 | 86 rooms | $62 | AE, D, DC, MC, V.

Victorian Inn. Established in 1998, this inn has a bright Victorian exterior, with lacy curtains, winding stairways, and elegant furnishings inside. Complimentary Continental breakfast, cable TV, pets allowed. | 3228 N. Summit St. | 316/442–8880 | fax 316/442–8885 | 36 rooms | $57 | AE, DC, D, MC, V.

ASHLAND
Wallingford Inn Bed and Breakfast. Built at the turn of the twentieth century, this Victorian mansion has period furnishings, and the grounds include an English garden. Complimentary breakfast, some in-room data ports, pets allowed. | 712 Main | 316/635–2129 | fax 316/635–4358 | 4 rooms (3 with shared bath) | $60–$65 | MC, V.

ATCHISON
Comfort Inn. This three-story hotel next to a mini-golf course is 2 mi from Amelia Earhart's home and 5 mi from her airport. Bar, picnic area, complimentary Continental breakfast, cable TV, pets allowed. | 509 S. 9th St. | 913/367–7666 | fax 913/367–7566 | www.comfortinn.com | 45 rooms, 10 suites | $48; $54–$64 suites. | AE, D, DC, MC, V.

BELLEVILLE
Best Western Bel Villa. This single-story motel is on five acres of landscaped grounds. Restaurant, bar, in-room data ports, cable TV, pool, playground, business services, airport shuttle, some pets allowed. | 215 U.S. 36 | 785/527–2231 | fax 785/527–2572 | www.bestwestern.com | 40 rooms | $43 | AE, D, DC, MC, V.

Plaza Motel. This brick motel is just off Rte. 36 and K St. Rooms have white walls, matching bedspreads and draperies, and recliners and ceiling fans. Some microwaves, some refrigerators, cable TV, some in-room VCRs, pool, business services, pets allowed. | 901 28th St. 66935 | 785/527–2228 or 800/466–9605 | fax 785/527–2333 | dfranceis@mckcn.com | 22 rooms, 1 apartment | $34–$41, $45 apartment | AE, D, MC, V.

BELOIT
Super 8. This two-story off-white stucco building opened in May 1997. Rooms are simple, but reliably clean and economical. For a small fee, you can swim at North Central Technical College across the street. Complimentary Continental breakfast, in-room data ports, some in-room hot tubs, cable TV, laundry facilities, business services, pets allowed. | 205 Rte. 24W 67420 | 785/738–4300 or 800/800–8000 | fax 785/738–2777 | 33 rooms, 7 suites | $50–$55, $65–$77 suites | AE, D, DC, MC, V.

COFFEYVILLE
Apple Tree Inn. Native sandstone was used to construct this two-story building, which includes a 40-ft oak cathedral ceiling in the lobby. Complimentary Continental breakfast, in-room data ports, some refrigerators, in-room hot tubs (in some suites), cable TV, indoor pool, outdoor hot tub, business services, pets allowed (fee). | 820 E. 11th St. | 316/251–0002 | fax 316/251–1615 | 64 rooms, 21 suites | $57 | AE, D, DC, MC, V.

Super 8. This two-story budget hotel is in the middle of town and offers discounted rates for seniors and truck drivers. You can request a room with king-size or double bed. Restaurant nearby, cable TV, pool, business services, pets allowed (fee). | 104 W. 11th St. 67337 | 316/251–2250 | fax 316/215–3846 | 91 rooms | $45–$67 | AE, D, DC, MC, V.

COLBY

Best Western Crown. This cozy, one-story hotel is only one block from I–70. In-room data ports, cable TV, pool, business services, airport shuttle, pets allowed. | 2320 S. Range Ave. | 785/462–3943 | www.bestwestern.com | 29 rooms | $50 | AE, D, DC, MC, V.

Desert Rose Inn. This spacious B&B is housed in a rambling ranch-style home and has a secluded patio overlooking Villa High Park and Pond, which are within walking distance. Each room is individually decorated with a different "rose" theme, incorporating contemporary and antique pieces. Alcohol is not served on the property. 2 dining rooms, complimentary breakfast, cable TV, no room phones, hot tub, laundry facilities, business services, pets allowed, no smoking. | 1060 Villa Vista Dr. 67701 | 785/462–7189 | 4 rooms | $65–$70 | No credit cards.

CONCORDIA

Best Western Thunderbird Motor Inn. Attractions such as the sports complex and rodeo arena, as well as the public library, are only 2 mi away. Restaurant, cable TV, pool, outdoor hot tub, laundry facilities, business services, some pets allowed. | 89 N. Lincoln | 785/243–4545 | fax 785/243–4545, ext. 137 | www.bestwestern.com | 50 rooms | $65 | AE, D, DC, MC, V.

COUNCIL GROVE

Cottage House. Each guest room in this Prairie Victorian building is individually decorated with antiques. Complimentary Continental breakfast, in-room data ports, some refrigerators, some in-room hot tubs, cable TV, outdoor hot tub, business services, some pets allowed (fee). | 25 N. Neosho | 316/767–6828 or 800/727–7903 | fax 316/767–6414 | 40 rooms | $68 | AE, D, DC, MC, V.

DODGE CITY

Best Western Silver Spur Lodge. You'll find pleasant but undistinguished rooms at this sprawling complex, just 5 minutes from Front St. and the downtown district. Restaurant, bar, cable TV, pool, business services, airport shuttle, free parking, some pets allowed (fee). | 1510 W. Wyatt Earp Blvd. 67801 | 316/227–2125 | fax 316/227–2030 | www.bestwestern.com | 120 rooms | $55–$60 | AE, D, DC, MC, V.

Super 8. Basic, economical rooms are available at this chain hotel, 2 mi west of the Boot Hill Museum. Complimentary Continental breakfast, cable TV, pool, pets allowed. | 1708 W. Wyatt Earp Blvd. | 316/225–3924 | fax 316/225–5793 | www.super8.com | 64 rooms | $48–52 | AE, D, DC, MC, V.

EL DORADO

Best Western Red Coach Inn. Built in the mid-1970s, this brick building with red shingles is 25 blocks from downtown El Dorado, and 30 minutes from the Wichita airport. Restaurant, 1 kitchenette, room service, some in-room hot tubs, cable TV, indoor pool, hot tub, exercise equipment, video games, business services, some pets allowed. | 2525 W. Central St. | 316/321–6900 | fax 316/321–6900, ext. 208 | www.bestwestern.com | 73 rooms | $69 | AE, D, DC, MC, V.

Sunset Inn. This single-story inn may seem like any other basic Midwestern roadside motel, but thoughtful touches like a newspaper and thermos bottle of hot coffee at your door in the morning will make your stay that much more enjoyable. Picnic area, complimentary Continental breakfast, some microwaves, refrigerators, cable TV, laundry service, business services, pets allowed (fee). | 1901 W. Central Ave. 67042 | 316/321–9172 or 800/233–6355 | fax 316/322–7316 | 36 rooms | $46 | AE, D, MC, V.

EMPORIA

Best Western Hospitality House. The town's largest facility has a brick exterior, larger than average rooms, and a spacious, open lobby. It's 1½ mi from the National Teachers Hall of Fame, and 2 mi from Emporia State University. Restaurant, complimentary Continental breakfast, in-room data port, room service, cable TV, indoor pool, hot tub, sauna, exercise equipment, video games, laundry service, business services, pets allowed. | 3021 W. U.S. 50 | 316/342–7587 | fax 316/342–9271 | www.bestwestern.com | 143 rooms | $55 | AE, D, DC, MC, V.

Days Inn. This brick-facade building has medium-sized, economically priced rooms just two blocks from I–35. Complimentary Continental breakfast, in-room data ports, cable TV, indoor pool, outdoor hot tub, business services, some pets allowed. | 3032 W. U.S. 50 Business | 316/342–1787 | fax 316/342–2292 | www.daysinn.com | 39 rooms | $48 | AE, D, DC, MC, V.

EUREKA

Blue Stem Lodge. Named for the wild prairie flowers of this region, this comfortable lodge offers good service and clean rooms. In-room data ports, cable TV, pool, business services, some pets allowed. | 1314 E. River St. | 316/583–5531 | fax 316/583–6427 | 27 rooms | $41 | AE, D, DC, MC, V.

Carriage House Motel. This basic strip motel is sufficient for short stays, and the price is very economical. Request a room with a king-size bed, and get on the road in the morning with a cup of complimentary coffee. Some microwaves, some refrigerators, cable TV, laundry service, business services, pets allowed. | 201 S. Main St. 67045 | 316/583–5501 | 16 rooms | $33 | AE, D, MC, V.

FORT SCOTT

Best Western Fort Scott Inn. Rooms are slightly larger than usual at this motel, across the street from the Fort Scott National Historic Site. Restaurant, picnic area, complimentary Continental breakfast, cable TV, pool, hot tub, sauna, exercise equipment, laundry facilities, business services, pets allowed (fee). | 101 State St. | 316/223–0100 | fax 316/223–1746 | www.bestwestern.com | 78 rooms | $61 | AE, D, DC, MC, V.

GARDEN CITY

Best Western Wheat Lands Motor Inn. Local shopping, the business district, and the zoo are within 2–3 mi of this strip motel. Bar (with entertainment), complimentary breakfast, in-room data ports, some refrigerators, cable TV, pool, barbershop, beauty salon, exercise equipment, laundry facilities, business services, airport shuttle, pets allowed. | 1311 E. Fulton | 316/276–2387 | fax 316/276–4252 | www.bestwestern.com | 107 rooms | $68 | AE, D, DC, MC, V.

Plaza Inn. Exterior entrances lead to comfortable rooms with warm, soft color schemes and pleasing amenities. Restaurant, bar (with entertainment), complimentary Continental breakfast, room service, cable TV, indoor pool, hot tub, video games, business services, airport shuttle, pets allowed. | 1911 E. Kansas Ave. | 316/275–7471 or 800/875–5201 | fax 316/275–4028 | www.plazainn.com | 109 rooms | $68 | AE, D, DC, MC, V.

GOODLAND

Best Western Buffalo Inn. Exterior entrances lead to simple rooms with reasonable prices. The High Plains Museum is a ½ mi from this brick motel. Restaurant, bar, cable TV, indoor pool, wading pool, hot tub, playground, laundry facilities, guest laundry, business services, airport shuttle, some pets allowed. | 830 W. U.S. 24 | 785/899–3621 or 800/436–3621 | fax 785/899–5072 | www.bestwestern.com | 93 rooms | $52 | AE, D, DC, MC, V.

Comfort Inn. Convenience and dependability meet at this brick and stucco hotel with green awnings, which opened in July 1997. Its location right off I–70 and Rte. 27 makes it a good choice for those passing through. A gas station and a variety of fast food choices are just down the road. Complimentary Continental breakfast, in-room data ports, some microwaves, some refrigerators, some in-room hot tubs, cable TV, pool, hot tub, video games, laundry facilities, business services, pets allowed (fee). | 2519 Enterprise Rd. 67735 | 785/899–7181 | fax 785/899–7183 | www.comfortinn.com | 49 rooms | $57–$99 | AE, D, DC, MC, V.

Howard Johnson. Interior halls lead to guest rooms at this chain hotel, right off I–70. A recreation dome houses pool tables, Ping-Pong, and much more. RV hookups are available for campers. Restaurant, bar, room service, cable TV, indoor pool, hot tub, miniature golf, putting green, exercise equipment, video games, playground, laundry facilities, business services, airport shuttle, pets allowed. | 2218 Commerce Rd. | 785/899–3644 | fax 785/899–3646 | www.hojo.com | 79 rooms | $64–69 | AE, D, DC, MC, V.

GREAT BEND

Best Western Angus Inn. Recreational activities are housed under the hotel's "Fun Dome," and sunshine can be enjoyed via the sundeck or open roof. Restaurant, cable TV, indoor pool, hot tub, exercise equipment, video games, business services, airport shuttle, some pets allowed. | 2920 10th St. | 316/792–3541 | fax 316/792–8621 | www.bestwestern.com | 90 rooms | $60 | AE, D, DC, MC, V.

Holiday Inn. This full-service hotel has a glass-domed recreation area, a lounge for relaxation, and is within a 30-minute drive of such local attractions as Fort Larned and Barton County Historical Museum. Restaurant, bar, room service, cable TV, indoor pool, hot tub, laundry facilities, business services, airport shuttle, pets allowed. | 3017 W. 10th St. | 316/792–2431 | fax 316/792–5561 | www.holiday-inn.com | 174 rooms, 1 suite | $65–$72, $75–$90 suites | AE, D, DC, MC, V.

GREENSBURG

Kansan Motel. There are a handful of renovated rooms at this blond-brick-with-brown-trim strip motel. A town park with a playground and gazebo is across the street. Some in-room data ports, some microwaves, some refrigerators, cable TV, pool, laundry facilities, business services, pets allowed. | 800 E. Kansas Ave. 67054 | 316/723–2141 or 800/535–2141 | fax 316/723–2774 | 29 rooms | $42–$49 | AE, D, DC, MC, V.

HAYS

Best Western Vagabond. Fort Hays State Historic Site is about 3 mi from this motel, which has king- and queen-size beds and pleasing amenities at reasonable prices. Restaurant, bar, in-room data ports, cable TV, pool, hot tub, business services, pets allowed. | 2524 Vine St. | 785/625–2511 | www.bestwestern.com | 92 rooms | $54 | AE, D, DC, MC, V.

Budget Host Villa Inn. This two-story motel is 2½ mi from I–70 and the Sternberg Museum of Natural History. Three restaurants are within walking distance, and the downtown area is eight blocks away. Picnic area, cable TV, pool, business services, airport shuttle, some pets allowed. | 810 E. 8th St. | 785/625–2563 | fax 785/625–3967 | www.budgethost.com | 49 rooms | $45 | AE, D, DC, MC, V.

Hampton Inn. Near I–70 at the north end of town, this motel has exterior room entrances and is 1 mi from the center of town. Complimentary Continental breakfast, in-room data ports, cable TV, business services, airport shuttle, pets allowed. | 3801 Vine St. | 785/625–8103 | fax 785/625–3006 | www.hampton-inn.com | 117 rooms | $69 | AE, D, DC, MC, V.

Holiday Inn. Comfortable rooms have king-size or double beds. Hays Municipal Airport is 5 mi away. Restaurant, in-room data ports, room service, cable TV, indoor pool, hot tub, business services, airport shuttle, pets allowed. | 3603 Vine St. | 785/625–7371 | fax 785/625–7250 | www.holiday-inn.com | 190 rooms | $79 | AE, D, DC, MC, V.

HUTCHINSON

Astro Motel. Clean, basic, and economical rooms are available in this centrally located, two-story, L-shaped motel. Some refrigerators, cable TV, pool, business services, pets allowed. | 15 E. Fourth St. 67501-6912 | 316/663–1151 | fax 316/663–7169 | 30 rooms | $40.

Comfort Inn. Rooms are basic and reasonably priced. Both Amtrak and the Hutchinson Municipal Airport are within 2 mi of the motel. Complimentary Continental breakfast, in-room data ports, cable TV, pool, hot tub, business services, pets allowed. | 1621 Super Plaza | 316/663–7822 | fax 316/663–1055 | www.comfortinn.com | 63 rooms | $73 | AE, D, DC, MC, V.

Quality Inn City Center. This strip motel is 4 mi from the Hutchinson Municipal Airport and less than 1 mi from the Amtrak and bus depot stations. Restaurant, bar, in-room data ports, room service, cable TV, pool, business services, some pets allowed. | 15 W. 4th St. | 316/663–1211 or 800/228–5151 | fax 316/663–6636 | www.qualityinn.com | 98 rooms | $50 | AE, D, DC, MC, V.

★ **Ramada Inn Hutchinson.** Rooms in the "minidome" section of this busy convention hotel look out onto a quiet, landscaped courtyard. "Maindome" rooms open onto a recreation area with a swimming pool. Restaurant, bar, room service, in-room data ports, microwaves (in suites), refrigerators (in suites), cable TV, pool, hot tub, exercise room, laundry facilities, business services, some pets allowed (fee). | 1400 N. Lorraine St. 67501 | 316/669–9311 or 800/362–5018 | fax 316/669–9830 | www.ramada.com | 220 rooms, 6 suites | $74–$90, $100–$375 suites | AE, D, DC, MC, V.

INDEPENDENCE

Apple Tree Inn. This two-story building is made with native sandstone, and its lobby includes a 40-ft oak cathedral ceiling. Complimentary Continental breakfast, in-room data ports, some refrigerators, cable TV, indoor pool, hot tub, business services, pets allowed. | 201 N. 8th St. | 316/331–5500 | fax 316/331–0641 | 64 rooms | $60 | AE, D, DC, MC, V.

Best Western Prairie Inn. A single-story motel, this Best Western is 5 mi from the Little House on the Prairie log cabin. Complimentary Continental breakfast, cable TV, pool, business services, some pets allowed (fee). | 3222 W. Main St. | 316/331–7300 | fax 316/331–8740 | www.bestwestern.com | 41 rooms | $52–$56 | AE, D, DC, MC, V.

Microtel Inn and Suites. This three-story hotel opened in March 2000 and is 2½ mi from Riverside Park and the city zoo. All rooms have queen-size beds and window seats, and suites have additional sofa sleepers and amenities that are useful for longer stays. Complimentary Continental breakfast, in-room data ports, some microwaves, some refrigerators, cable TV, business services, pets allowed. | 3021 W. Main St. 67301 | 316/331–0088 or 888/771–7171 | fax 316/331–5777 | www.microtel.com | 45 rooms, 22 suites | $50–$55, $61 suites | AE, D, DC, MC, V.

IOLA

Crossroads Motel. The redbrick facade matches the fireplace bricks in an exceptionally warm and spacious lobby. Complimentary Continental breakfast, cable TV, pool, pets allowed. | 14 N. State St. | 316/365–2183 | fax 316/365–2183 | 54 rooms | $42 | AE, D, DC, MC, V.

JUNCTION CITY

Best Western Jayhawk. Rooms in this modern building are comfortable and reasonably priced. The Junction City/Manhattan Airport is 12 mi away. Picnic area, complimentary Continental breakfast, some kitchenettes, some refrigerators, cable TV, pool, pets allowed.

| 110 E. Flint Hills Blvd. | 785/238–5188 | fax 785/238–7585 | www.bestwestern.com | 48 rooms | $48 | AE, D, DC, MC, V.

Days Inn. Just off I–70, this Days Inn has the largest indoor pool of a motel in the city. Milford Lake, great for boating, fishing, and waterskiing, is 3 mi from the motel. Bar, complimentary Continental breakfast, cable TV, 2 pools (1 indoor), outdoor hot tub, video games, laundry facilities, business services, some pets allowed. | 1024 S. Washington St. | 785/762–2727 | fax 785/762–2751 | www.daysinn.com | 108 rooms | $46 | AE, D, DC, MC, V.

Holiday Inn Express. Built in 1997, this two-story motel is just off I–70, Exit 298. Complimentary Continental breakfast, in-room data ports, microwaves, refrigerators, cable TV, pool, hot tub, sauna, exercise equipment, laundry facilities, business services, pets allowed (fee). | 120 N. East St. 66441 | 785/762–4200 | fax 785/762–4219 | holidayinnexpress@oz-online.net | www.holiday-inn.com | 60 rooms, 5 suites | $69–$79, $89–$99 suites | AE, D, DC, MC, V.

Super 8. Here you'll find basic rooms 2 mi from Fort Riley and local shopping. Restaurant, bar, picnic area, complimentary Continental breakfast, in-room data ports, some refrigerators, room service, cable TV, pool, laundry facilities, business services, some pets allowed. | 1001 E. 6th St. | 785/238–8101 | fax 785/238–7470 | www.super8.com | 97 rooms | $50 | AE, D, DC, MC, V.

KANSAS CITY

Best Western Inn and Conference Center. Built in the early 1980s, this two-story motel is 2 mi from downtown Kansas City. A handful of restaurants are within two blocks of the motel. Restaurant, bar, complimentary Continental breakfast, in-room data ports, room service, cable TV, pool, sauna, exercise equipment, laundry facilities, business services, airport shuttle. Some pets allowed. | 501 Southwest Blvd. | 913/677–3060 or 800/368–1741 | fax 913/362–0540 | www.bestwestern.com | 113 rooms | $69–$79 | AE, D, MC, V.

LARNED

Best Western Townsman Inn. Basic rooms and amenities can be found at this motel, 2 mi from the Santa Fe Trail Center and 6 mi from Ft. Larned. Complimentary Continental breakfast, in-room data ports, cable TV, pool, business services, pets allowed. | 123 E. 14th St. | 316/285–3114 | fax 316/285–7139 | www.bestwestern.com | 44 rooms | $48–$59 | AE, D, DC, MC, V.

LAWRENCE

Best Western Hallmark Inn. Just 2 mi from both downtown Lawrence and the University of Kansas, this motel is within walking distance of local restaurants and entertainment. Complimentary Continental breakfast, in-room data ports, cable TV, pool, laundry facilities, business services, some pets allowed. | 730 Iowa St. (U.S. 59) | 785/841–6500 | fax 785/841–6612 | www.bestwestern.com | 60 rooms | $95 | AE, D, DC, MC, V.

Days Inn. This motel is adjacent to the University of Kansas and 5 mi from the downtown area. Complimentary Continental breakfast, in-room data ports, cable TV, pool, hot tub, laundry facilities, business services, some pets allowed. | 2309 Iowa St. (U.S. 59) 66046 | 785/843–9100 | fax 785/843–1572 | www.daysinn.com | 101 rooms | $80 | AE, D, DC, MC, V.

Holiday Inn. This motel has exterior entrances and is 2 mi from downtown and the University of Kansas. Restaurant, bar, room service, cable TV, pool, hot tub, exercise equipment, video games, laundry facilities, business services, pets allowed. | 200 McDonald Dr. 66044 | 785/841–7077 | fax 785/841–2799 | www.holiday-inn.com | 192 rooms, 12 suites | $90–$102 | AE, D, DC, MC, V.

Westminster Inn. This comfortable brick and stucco inn has a warm lobby with cathedral ceilings and heavy-wood beams. Cable TV, pool, pets allowed. | 2525 W. 6th St. 66049

| 785/841–8410 or 888/937–8646 | fax 785/841–1901 | 60 rooms, 12 suites | $63, $73 suites | AE, D, DC, MC, V.

LEAVENWORTH

Ramada Inn. This motel in the heart of downtown Leavenworth has exterior entrances and is 1 mi southeast of Fort Leavenworth. Restaurant, bar, room service, cable TV, pool, business services, some pets allowed. | 101 S. 3rd St. | 913/651–5500 | fax 913/651–6981 | www.ramada.com | 97 rooms | $64 | AE, D, DC, MC, V.

LIBERAL

Gateway Inn. For a rather small town, this inn has very modern, high-tech facilities for meetings and conferences. Restaurant, bar, picnic area, in-room data ports, cable TV, pool, tennis, laundry facilities, business services, airport shuttle, some pets allowed. | 720 E. Pancake Blvd. (U.S. 54) | 316/624–0242 or 800/833–3391 | fax 316/624–1952 | 101 rooms | $46 | AE, D, DC, MC, V.

Liberal Inn. This two-story stone building was built in the mid 1960s and is across the street from Dorothy's House. Restaurant, picnic area, in-room data ports, room service, cable TV, pool, hot tub, laundry facilities, airport shuttle, pets allowed. | 603 E. Pancake Blvd. (U.S. 54) | 316/624–7254 or 800/458–4667 | fax 316/624–7254 | 123 rooms | $48–$53 | AE, D, DC, MC, V.

LUCAS

Lucas Country Inn. This two-story inn was built in the early 1900s. Most of its guests are hunters and anglers who spend the day at Lake Wilson, which is 8 mi away. Two cafés are within walking distance. No room phones, no TV in some rooms. Pets allowed. | 229 S. Main St. 67648 | 785/525–6358 | 12 rooms | $30 | No credit cards.

MANHATTAN

Days Inn. Clean, comfortable rooms are found at this strip motel. Picnic area, complimentary Continental breakfast, in-room data ports, some refrigerators, cable TV, pool, playground, laundry facilities, business services, pets allowed. | 1501 Tuttle Creek Blvd. | 785/539–5391 | fax 785/539–0847 | www.daysinn.com | 119 rooms | $62 | AE, D, DC, MC, V.

Holiday Inn. This Holidome hotel has an atrium, comfortably sized rooms, and recreational equipment. 2 restaurants, bar, in-room data ports, room service, cable TV, indoor pool, wading pool, hot tub, sauna, video games, airport shuttle, laundry facilities, business services, pets allowed. | 530 Richards Dr. | 785/539–5311 | fax 785/539–8368 | www.holiday-inn.com | 197 rooms, 5 suites | $76–$86, $169–$189 suites | AE, D, DC, MC, V.

Ramada Inn. Across from Kansas State University, this Ramada is less than 5 minutes from area shopping, dining, entertainment, and attractions. Restaurant, bar, in-room data ports, refrigerators, room service, cable TV, pool, business services, airport shuttle, pets allowed. | 17th and Anderson | 785/539–7531 | fax 785/539–3909 | www.ramada.com | 115 rooms, 4 suites | $89–$149 | AE, D, DC, MC, V.

MANKATO

Crest-Vue. This friendly inn is renowned for its clean, spacious rooms. Picnic area, cable TV, pets allowed. | U.S. 36 E 66956 | 785/378–3515 | 12 rooms | $30–$38 | AE, D, MC, V.

Dreamliner Motel. An older gray strip motel in need of room renovation, there's nothing to entice you here except the price. Cable TV, pets allowed. | W. Rte 36 66956 | 785/378–3107 | 28 rooms | $32–$48 | AE, MC, V.

MARYSVILLE

Best Western Surf. This Best Western has comfortable, affordable rooms. Complimentary Continental breakfast, refrigerators, cable TV, exercise equipment, playground, laundry facilities, business services, some pets allowed. | 2105 Center St. | 785/562–2354 | fax 785/562–2354 | www.bestwestern.com | 52 rooms | $58 | AE, D, DC, MC, V.

Oak Tree Inn. Built in 1999, this inn is nestled on the edge of town along the fabled Pony Express Highway. You'll find many modern conveniences, as well as an authentic 1950s-style diner with chrome toasters and hearty helpings of traditional American favorites. In-room data ports, some minibars, microwaves, refrigerators, cable TV, hot tub, gym, laundry facilities, pets allowed (fee), free parking. | 1127 Pony Express Hwy. | 785/562–1234 | fax 785/562–1100 | 104 rooms | $42 | AE, D, DC, MC, V.

Thunderbird Motel. Sitting high on a hill west of town, this motel is in a quiet residential area. The lobby has Pony Express memorabilia from the manager's drive along the trail in the 1960s. RV hook-ups are available. Complimentary Continental breakfast, in-room data ports, microwaves, refrigerators, cable TV, some pets allowed. | 819 Pony Express Hwy. (U.S. 36 W) | 785/562–2373 or 800/662–2373 | fax 785/562–2531 | 21 rooms | $37–$43 | AE, D, DC, MC, V.

MCPHERSON

Best Western Holiday Manor. Drive right up to your door at this two-story strip motel, 2 mi from the McPherson Museum. Restaurant, room service, cable TV, 2 pools (1 indoor), hot tub, business services, some pets allowed. | 2211 E. Kansas Ave. (U.S. 56) | 316/241–5343 | fax 316/241–8086 | www.bestwestern.com | 110 rooms | $55–$72 | AE, D, DC, MC, V.

Red Coach Inn. This two-story strip motel is surrounded by fast-food restaurants. Restaurant, in-room data ports, cable TV, in-room VCRs (and movies), pool, hot tub, miniature golf, playground, business services, some pets allowed. | 2111 E. Kansas Ave. (U.S. 56) | 316/241–6960 or 800/362–0072 (outside KS) | fax 316/241–4340 | 88 rooms | $60–$65 | AE, D, DC, MC, V.

Super 8 Motel. This motel is off I–135, Exit 60. Complimentary Continental breakfast, cable TV, business services, free parking, pets allowed (fee). | 2110 E. Kansas | 316/241–8881 | fax 316/241–8853 | www.super8.com | 42 rooms | $50 | AE, D, MC, V.

MEADE

Dalton's Bedpost. Clean and inexpensive rooms are available in this small, unassuming, one-story motor lodge. Cable TV, pets allowed. | 519 E. Carthage Hwy. | 316/873–2131 | 12 rooms | $35 | AE, D, MC, V.

MEDICINE LODGE

Copa Motel. This strip motel with exterior entrances is just 1 mi from a fishing lake and down the hill from the Medicine Lodge Stockade. Rooms are basic and economical. Picnic area, cable TV, pool, pets allowed. | 401 W. Fowler Ave. | 316/886–5673 or 800/886–2672 | fax 316/886–5241 | 54 rooms | $40–$47 | AE, D, DC, MC, V.

Lodge Inn. A two-story drive-up motel, this mom-and-pop is about 1 mi from the town center. In-room data ports, some refrigerators, cable TV, laundry service, pets allowed. | U.S. 281 North | 316/886–3080 | fax 316/886–3812 | 29 rooms | $34 | AE, MC, V.

NEWTON

Best Western Red Coach Inn. Right off Exit 31 of I–135, this two-story motel is 8 mi from the Kauffman Museum and less than 30 mi from numerous other attractions. A few restaurants are within walking distance. Restaurant, room service, cable TV, pool, outdoor hot tub, exercise equipment, video games, airport shuttle, some pets allowed. | 1301 E. 1st St.

| 316/283–9120 or 800/777–9120 | fax 316/283–4105 | www.bestwestern.com | 81 rooms | $52–$109 | AE, D, DC, MC, V.

NORTON

The Rose of Sharon Inn. This elegant Victorian B&B dates back to 1880. The guest rooms, fitted with regional antiques, are ideal for honeymoons, romantic getaways, or family vacations. (This region is known for its rich hunting and fishing, as well as hiking, swimming, and other outdoor pursuits). For a fee, lunch and dinner are available upon request. Complimentary full breakfast, pets allowed, no smoking. | 603 East Main St. | 785/877–3010 | 3 rooms | $65–$75 | D, MC, V.

OAKLEY

Annie Oakley Motel. Built in 1949, this one-story, sandy brick building is on the town's main thoroughfare, just blocks from the town center, the cinema, and the Fick Fossil and History Museum. Rooms have floral accents and queen or double beds. Some kitchenettes, cable TV, laundry facilities, pets allowed. | 428 Center St. | 785/672–3223 | 26 rooms | $40 | AE, MC, V.

First Interstate Inn. Rooms have nature-themed murals on the walls in this two-story inn across the highway from a Greyhound bus depot. Cable TV, business services, pets allowed. | 1006 U.S. 40 67748 | 785/672–3203 or 800/462–4667 | fax 785/672–3330 | 29 rooms | $55 | AE, D, DC, MC, V.

OBERLIN

Frontier Motel. A little ways out of town you'll find this one-story motel, which is adjacent to several other roadside businesses, including Janey's Frontier Restaurant. Some rooms have views of the pool and courtyard. Restaurant nearby, some refrigerators, cable TV, pool, pets allowed. | 207 E. Frontier Pkwy. | 785/475–2203 | 28 rooms | $49 | AE, D, MC, V.

OSAWATOMIE

Landmark Motel. There aren't a lot of frills at this independently owned motel/restaurant, but you're sure to receive genuine hospitality and reasonable rates. Restaurant. Cable TV, pool, pets allowed. | 304 E. Gate | 913/755–3051 | 39 rooms | $49 | AE, D, MC, V.

OTTAWA

Best Western Hallmark Inn. Rooms have pastel colors and pictures of country scenes at this two-story motel 3 mi from downtown Ottawa. Complimentary Continental breakfast, cable TV, pool, business services, laundry facilities, some pets allowed (fee). | 2209 S. Princeton Rd. (U.S. 59) | 785/242–7000 | fax 785/242–8572 | www.bestwestern.com | 60 rooms | $74 | AE, D, DC, MC, V.

Village Inn Motel. A one-story, exterior corridor motel on the edge of town, just off Exit 182B of I–35. Picnic area, some kitchenettes, some microwaves, refrigerators, cable TV, pool, volleyball, pets allowed. | 2520 S. Main | 785/242–4433 | fax 785/242–3087 | ottawamotel@usa.net | www.ottcom.org/villagemotel/ | 18 rooms | $36 | AE, D, DC, MC, V.

OVERLAND PARK

Amerisuites. Built in the mid 1990s, this six-story hotel is 38 mi from the airport, 17 mi from Kansas City, and within 2 mi of several restaurants. Complimentary Continental breakfast, in-room data ports, microwaves, refrigerators, cable TV, in-room VCRs (and movies), pool, exercise equipment, laundry facilities, business services, some pets allowed. | 6801 W. 112th St. 66211 | 913/451–2553 or 800/833–1516 | fax 913/451–3098 | www.amerisuites.com | 126 suites | $99–$119 | AE, D, DC, MC, V.

Doubletree Hotel. This 18-story hotel is adjacent to two major highways, a business park, and a scenic public jogging trail. A bowling alley and tennis courts are less than 2 mi away, and a shopping mall is 4 mi away. Restaurants, bar, in-room data ports, some refrigerators, cable TV, pool, outdoor hot tub, gym, business services, airport shuttle, some pets allowed. | 10100 College Blvd. | 913/451–6100 | fax 913/451–3873 | mcidt@aol.com | www.doubletreehotels.com | 357 rooms | $139–$144 | AE, D, DC, MC, V.

Drury Inn. Built in the early 1980s, this four-story hotel is about 10 mi from one of the largest malls in the state and within walking distance of area restaurants. Complimentary Continental breakfast, in-room data ports, cable TV, pool, business services, some pets allowed. | 10951 Metcalf Ave. 66210 | 913/345–1500 | fax 913/345–1500 | www.drury-inn.com | 55 rooms | $83 | AE, D, DC, MC, V.

Homestead Village. A strip of restaurants is nine blocks from this three-story extended-stay hotel. In-room data ports, kitchenettes, microwaves, refrigerators, cable TV, laundry facilities, pets allowed (deposit). | 5401 W. 110th St. | 913/661–7111 | fax 913/661–4744 | www.stayhsd.com | 132 rooms | $59–$75 | AE, D, DC, MC, V.

Parks Lodge. A number of restaurants are within walking distance of this modest two-story motel. Some in-room data ports, cable TV, pool, pets allowed. | 7508 Shawnee Mission Pkwy. | 913/262–9600 | 86 rooms | $39 | AE, D, DC, MC, V.

White Haven. This motel has a white-brick facade, white wrought-iron balconies, and leaded-glass windows. Some kitchenettes, refrigerators, cable TV, pool, business services, some pets allowed. | 8039 Metcalf Ave. 66204 | 913/649–8200 or 800/752–2892 | fax 913/901–8199 | 79 rooms | $43–$85 | AE, D, DC, MC, V.

PARSONS

Super 8 Motel. A number of restaurants are across the highway from this two-story motel on the east side of town. Complimentary Continental breakfast, some microwaves, refrigerators, some in-room hot tubs, cable TV, pool, laundry facilities, pets allowed (deposit). | 229 East Main | 316/421–8000 | fax 316/421–8228 | www.super8.com | 48 rooms | $55 | AE, D, DC, MC, V.

Townsman. Attractive, modern rooms in this white-brick motel have mirrors and pictures throughout. The lobby has a miniature house owned by the manager and decorated for all seasons. Restaurant, cable TV, business services, some pets allowed. | 1830 South U.S. 59 67357 | 316/421–6990 or 800/552–4008 | fax 316/421–4767 | 38 rooms | $37 | AE, D, DC, MC, V.

PHILLIPSBURG

Cottonwood Inn. Some rooms at this modern, attractive, two-story motel have a view of the 18-hole golf course across the street. Cable TV, pool, gym, pets allowed. | Jct. E. U.S. 36 and 183 | 800/466–7332 | fax 785/543–5432 | 40 rooms | $55 | AE, D, DC, MC, V.

PRATT

Best Western Hillcrest. Each room has modern furnishings and pictures of country settings in this motel 1 mi from a golf course and the Pratt County Historical Society Museum. Complimentary Continental breakfast, in-room data ports, refrigerators, cable TV, pool, business services, pets allowed. | 1336 E. 1st St. | 316/672–6407 | fax 316/672–6707 | www.bestwestern.com | 42 rooms | $42 | AE, D, DC, MC, V.

RUSSELL

Bonnie's Cottage Inn. Built in 1890, this authentic Victorian home has much of its original detail intact. The proprietors live across the street, so you'll have the eight-room home to yourself. Regional antiques can be found throughout, and Main St., where you'll find antique and gift shops, a cultural center, and more, is just one block away. Complimentary full breakfast, laundry facilities, pets allowed, no smoking. | 223 W. 7th | 785/483–5837 | 3 rooms | $80 | No credit cards.

SALINA

Best Western Heart of America Inn. Rooms have contemporary furnishings in this hotel just off I–35. The family suite accommodates up to six people. 2 restaurants nearby, bar, in-room data ports, cable TV, pool, hot tub, sauna, pets allowed. | 632 Westport Blvd. | 785/827–9315 | fax 785/827–4119 | www.bestwestern.com | 100 rooms, 1 suite | $58; $100 suite | AE, D, DC, MC, V.

Best Western Mid-America Inn. Modern guest rooms have large couches at this motel 2 mi from the Bicentennial Center and the Smoky Hill Museum. Restaurant, bar, complimentary Continental breakfast, in-room data ports, room service, cable TV, indoor-outdoor pool, hot tub, business services, some pets allowed. | 1846 N. 9th | 785/827–0356 | fax 785/827–7688 | www.bestwestern.com | 108 rooms | $42–$64 | AE, D, DC, MC, V.

Budget Host Vagabond II. Bright, colorful rooms have modern furnishings and scenic pictures of mountains and landscapes on the walls. Cable TV, pool, business services, pets allowed. | 217 S. Broadway (U.S. 81 Bus.) | 785/825–7265 | fax 785/825–7003 | www.budgethost.com | 45 rooms | $34–$45 | AE, D, DC, MC, V.

Comfort Inn. Contemporary rooms have warm, pastel colors and comfortable beds and recliners. Complimentary Continental breakfast, in-room data ports, some refrigerators, cable TV, indoor pool, hot tub, business services, some pets allowed. | 1820 W. Crawford | 785/826–1711 | fax 785/827–6530 | www.comfortinn.com | 60 rooms | $59–$89 | AE, D, DC, MC, V.

Ramada Inn. This two-story hotel is 6 mi from the Central Mall, where you can take care of all your shopping needs. Restaurant, bar, complimentary Continental breakfast, room service, cable TV, pool, business services, pets allowed (fee). | 1949 N. 9th St. | 785/825–8211 | fax 785/823–1048 | www.ramada.com | 103 rooms | $48–$68 | AE, D, DC, MC, V.

Red Coach Inn. This two-story motel is recognizable by the big red stage coach outside. A mall and a movie theater are 5 mi away. Restaurant, complimentary Continental breakfast, in-room data ports, some refrigerators, room service, cable TV, some in-room VCRs, indoor pool, hot tub, miniature golf, playground, laundry facilities, business services, some pets allowed. | 2020 W. Crawford | 785/825–2111 | fax 785/825–6973 | 114 rooms | $49–$120 | AE, D, DC, MC, V.

SENECA

Seneca Motel. Clean rooms and hospitable service are what you'll find here. Some refrigerators, cable TV, some pets allowed. | 1106 North St. (U.S. 36) | 785/336–6127 | 12 rooms | $38 | AE, D, DC, MC, V.

Starlite. The lobby is home to the owner's doll collection, and perennials brighten the picket fence and windmill in warm weather. Cable TV, some pets allowed. | 410 North St. (U.S. 36) | 785/336–2191 | 16 rooms | $37 | AE, D, DC, MC, V.

SMITH CENTER

Prairie Winds Motel. This two-story motel is across the highway from a fast food restaurant and four blocks from both a café and the Old Dutch Mill. Complimentary Continental breakfast. Some kitchenettes, some microwaves, some refrigerators, cable TV. Pets allowed. | U.S. 36 E 66967 | 785/282–6608 | 17 rooms | $38 | MC, V.

STOCKTON

Midwest Motel. Chuck and Linda Williams own and operate this one-story brick motel, built in 1954. In the parlor you'll find Mrs. Williams's porcelain doll collection competing for space with her husband's extensive barbed-wire collection. Complimentary Continental breakfast, cable TV, laundry facilities, pets allowed. | 1401 Main | 785/425–6706 | 13 rooms | $32 | D, MC, V.

TOPEKA

Days Inn. Modern rooms have queen- or king-size beds and a large sofa. Complimentary Continental breakfast, some refrigerators, cable TV, pool, hot tub, business services, pets allowed. | 1510 S.W. Wanamaker Rd. 66604 | 785/272–8538 | fax 785/272–8538 | www.daysinn.com | 62 rooms, 6 suites | $69, $79 suites | AE, D, DC, MC, V.

The Plaza Inn. Rooms have modern furnishings in this hotel just off Topeka Blvd., the main strip where many restaurants and shops can be found. It's just 5 mi from the Expo Center and Heartland Park raceway. Restaurant, bar, dance club, in-room data ports, cable TV, pool, business services, laundry facilities, free parking, some pets allowed. | 3802 S. Topeka Blvd. (U.S. 75) 66609 | 785/266–8880 | fax 785/267–3311 | 150 rooms | $75–$80 | AE, D, DC, MC, V.

Ramada Inn. This is the largest hotel in Kansas. Its executive tower has rooms overlooking the city. Restaurants, bar, some refrigerators, room service, cable TV, pool, barbershop, beauty salon, exercise equipment, laundry facilities, business services, airport shuttle, free parking, some pets allowed. | 420 E. 6th St. | 785/234–5400 | fax 785/233–0460 | www.ramada.com | 361 rooms, 22 suites | $68–$85, $95–$125 suites | AE, D, DC, MC, V.

WICHITA

Hampton Inn Wichita–East. Spacious rooms have contemporary furnishings in this hotel 7 mi from downtown Wichita. Complimentary Continental breakfast, some microwaves, some refrigerators, cable TV, indoor pool, indoor hot tub, business services, pets allowed. | 9449 E. Corporate Hills Dr. 67207 | 316/686–3576 or 800/426–7866 | www.hampton-inn.com | 81 rooms | $59–$69 | AE, D, DC, MC, V.

Holiday Inn Airport. Rooms are modern and reasonably priced at this hotel 2 mi from Mid-Continent Airport. Restaurant, bar, room service, cable TV, pool, hot tub, laundry facilities, business services, airport shuttle, free parking, pets allowed (fee). | 5500 W. Kellogg St. (U.S. 54) 67209 | 316/943–2181 | fax 316/943–6587 | www.holiday-inn.com | 152 rooms | $69–$89 | AE, D, DC, MC, V.

La Quinta Inn. Rooms are simple, with double beds and a desk. The lobby has a Southwestern flair and a lovely mock fireplace. Complimentary Continental breakfast, in-room data ports, cable TV, pool, business services, some pets allowed. | 7700 E. Kellogg St. 62707 | 316/681–2881 | fax 316/681–0568 | www.laquinta.com | 122 rooms | $69–$90 | AE, D, DC, MC, V.

Residence Inn by Marriott–East. This all-suite hotel has studios and penthouses, all with a country atmosphere. Some suites have a view of the courtyard and pool area. Complimentary Continental breakfast, in-room data ports, kitchenettes, refrigerators, cable TV, pool, outdoor hot tub, laundry facilities, business services, pets allowed (fee). | 411 S. Webb Rd. 67207 | 316/686–7331 | fax 316/686–2345 | www.marriott.com | 64 suites | $103–$123 suites | AE, D, DC, MC, V.

Sheraton Four Points. Views of both the countryside and the city can be enjoyed from this ten-story high-rise hotel. Restaurant, bar, in-room data ports, cable TV, in-room VCRs available, pool, business services, airport shuttle, pets allowed (fee). | 549 S. Rock Rd. 67207 | 316/686–7131 | fax 316/686–0018 | 260 rooms, 8 suites | $59–$129; $175–$300 suites | AE, D, DC, MC, V.

WINFIELD

Quail Ridge Comfort Inn. Each room has a king-size bed in this hotel at the south end of town. Nice views are available of the adjacent 18-hole golf course. Restaurant nearby, complimentary Continental breakfast, in-room data ports, some in-room safes, some microwaves, some refrigerators, cable TV, pool, gym, laundry facilities, pets allowed. | U.S. 77 at Quail Ridge | 316/221–7529 | fax 316/221–0821 | www.comfortinn.com | 51 rooms | $64 | AE, D, DC, MC, V.

YATES CENTER

Townsman Motel. This two-story motel was built in 1963, and an additional section was added in 1980. The motel is very popular with hunters and anglers who plan on spending the day at Toronto Lake, which is 12 mi west of town. Cable TV. Business services. Some pets allowed. | 609 W. Mary St. 66783 | 316/625–2131 | fax 316/625–2133 | 32 rooms | $34–$39 | AE, D, DC, MC, V.

Kentucky

ASHLAND

Days Inn–Ashland. This two-story no-frills outlet of the motel chain is a modern stucco building situated 8 mi from downtown Ashland. Picnic area, complimentary Continental breakfast. In-room data ports; some microwaves and refrigerators. Cable TV. Outdoor pool. Fitness room. Laundry facilities. Business facilities. Free parking and ample truck parking. Pets allowed (fee). | 12700 Rte. 180 | 606/928–3600 or 800/329–7466 | fax 606/928–6515 | ash@musselmanhotels.com | www.daysinn.com/kentucky/ashland | 63 rooms | $45–$66; high–season rack rate $55.55 plus tax | AE, D, DC, MC, V.

Holiday Inn Express–Ashland. This inn is located 2 mi from downtown, convenient to the Paramount Arts Center, Kentucky Highland Museum, and many shops and restaurants. It is 9 mi from the Tri-State Airport in Huntington, WV. Complimentary Continental breakfast. Cable TV. Indoor pool. Some in-room hot tubs. Pets allowed (restrictions). | 4708 Winchester Ave. 41105 | 606/325–8989 or 800/465–4329 | fax 606/465–8989 | aslky@worldnet.att.net | www.exonline.com | 50 rooms, 5 hot tub suites | $58–$97 | AE, D, DC, MC, V.

Knights Inn. The Knights Inn is just 5 mi from downtown Ashland surrounded by 3 woody acres. A half dozen one-story stucco buildings comprise the motel. Parking spaces are by the room doors. Complimentary Continental breakfast. Refrigerators. Cable TV. Pool. Laundry facilities. Business services. Free parking. Some pets allowed (fee). | 7216 U.S. 60 41102 | 606/928–9501 or 800/497–7560 | fax 606/928–4436 | 122 rooms in 6 buildings | $38–$43 | AE, D, DC, MC, V.

BARDSTOWN

Bardstown Parkview. Its name evokes the views from the rooms which have traditional American furnishings. The stone colonial inn has horse prints on the walls and is just across the street from My Old Kentucky Home State Park. Restaurant, bar, complimentary Continental breakfast. Some kitchenettes. Cable TV. Pool. Laundry facilities. Some pets allowed. Free parking. | 418 E. Stephen Foster Ave. 40004 | 502/348–5983 or 800/732–2384 | fax 502/349–6973 | 38 rooms | $70 | AE, D, MC, V.

Holiday Inn. This is a typical roadside Holiday Inn with modern decor dominated by blues, greens, and mauves. Restaurant, bar. In-room data ports. Cable TV. Pool. Driving range, 9-hole golf course. Exercise equipment. Playground. Video games. Business services. Free parking. Some pets allowed. | 1875 New Haven Rd. 40002 | 502/348–9253 or 800/HOLIDAY | fax 502/348–5478 | 101 rooms | $89–$95 | AE, D, DC, MC, V.

Ramada Inn. Stately white columns, large maple trees, and southern hospitality welcome you to this motel in the historic district. Continental breakfast. Cable TV. In-room data ports. Pool, hot tub, some in-room hot tubs. Pets allowed. | 523 N. 3rd St. 40004 | 502/349–5979 | www.ramada-inn.com | 40 rooms | $48–$75 | AE, D, MC, V.

BEREA
Days Inn. You'll easily spot this familiar example of the national chain when you exit the interstate. The southern-style stucco motel has arts and crafts in the lobby and hallway. | Take exit 77 off I–75. TV. Pool. Mini-golf. Business services. Pets allowed (fee). | 1202 Walnut Meadow Rd. 40403 | 859/986–7373 or 800/329–7466 | fax 859/986–3144 | 60 rooms | $45–$51 | AE, D, DC, MC, V.

Holiday Inn Express, Berea. Opened in December 1998, this two-story hotel is near Berea College and the old town craft section. The adjacent Columbia Steakhouse has free delivery. Free deluxe Continental breakfast. Cable TV. Indoor pool, hot tubs. Fitness equipment. Meeting rooms. Pets allowed. | 108 Peggy Flats Rd. 40403 | 859/985–1901 or 800/465–4329 | fax 859/985–8095 | spurlockgm@aol.com | www.basshotels.com | 52 rooms, 4 suites | $53–$89 | AE, D, MC, V.

BOWLING GREEN
Days Inn. Situated along a 2-mi strip of shops, antique stores, and restaurants, you may not want to venture far. But this Days Inn is also central to points of interest like Mammoth Cave, the Kentucky Museum, Shakertown, the Hobson House Historical Landmark, and Barren River State Park. RV and truck parking is available. Restaurant, complimentary breakfast. Pool. Pets allowed. | 4617 Scottsville Rd. 42104 | 270/781–6470 | fax 270/781–0546 | www.daysinn.com | 65 rooms | $37–$65 | AE, D, DC, MC, V.

Holiday Inn I–65. This familiar favorite has modern appointments and a floral-print lobby carpet are echoed in the two floors of rooms with pleasant pink and green bedspreads. | Take exit 22 off I–65. The motel is ½ mi from Greenwood Mall and 6 mi from the National Corvette Museum. Restaurant, bar, picnic area. In-room data ports. Cable TV. Pool, wading pool. Exercise equipment. Playground. Business services. Small pets allowed. | 3240 Scottsville Rd. 42104 | 270/781–1500 | fax 270/842–0030 | 107 rooms | $49–$89 | AE, D, DC, MC, V.

Ramada Inn–Bowling Green. The familiar chain delivers on its reputation. This large facility has spacious rooms—some are suites with king-size beds, and others have queen-size beds. Many rooms have patios on the poolside. Restaurant, complimentary breakfast. Outdoor pool. Exercise room. Playground. Business services. Pets allowed. | 4767 Scottsville Rd. 42104. | 502/781–3000 | fax 502/782–2591 | www.ramada.com | 118 rooms | $45–$75 | AE, D, DC, MC, V.

University Plaza Hotel. This upscale hotel has a seven-floor atrium, waterfall, and a garden with a pool and fountains. It is connected to the Bowling Green/Warren County Convention Center, which has 28,000 square ft of meeting space. Restaurant. Cable TV. Indoor pool. Hot tub, sauna. Exercise equipment. Meeting space. Pets allowed. | 1021 Wilkerson Trace 42104 | 270/745–0088 or 800/801–1777 or 888/294–6491 | 186 rooms, 19 Suites | $89–$129 | AE, D, DC, MC, V.

BRANDENBURG

Otter Creek Park. Rough it in a rustic cabin in the middle of this 2,600-acre park stretching along the Ohio River. Nature lovers and adventure-seekers can hike, bike, rock-climb (summers only), or just kick back in front of the fireplace. Pool, playground. Pets allowed (restrictions). | 850 Otter Creek Park Rd. | 270/583–3577 | fax 270/583–9035 | ottercreek@louky.org | www.ottercreekpark.org | 20 rooms, 10 Cabins | $50–90 rooms, $65–150 cabins | MC, V.

CADIZ

Holiday Inn Express. At the gateway to the Lake Barclay area, this Holiday Inn is near Murray State University, Ft. Campbell, and the Arrowhead and Boots Randolph golf courses. Nostalgic downtown Main Street, 7 mi away, has antique malls and the 1867 Cadiz Log Cabin Museum and Visitor Center. Opened in 1998, this motel is two stories. Complimentary Continental breakfast. Cable TV. Some microwaves, some refrigerators. Some in-room hot tubs. Indoor pool. Laundry facilities. Business services. Pets allowed. | 153 Broadbent Blvd. 42211 | 270/522–3600 | fax 270/522–0636 | holidayinncadiz@ziggycom.net | www.basshotels.com | 48 rooms, 4 hot tub suites | $60–$79 | AE, D, DC, MC, V.

Super 8 Motel. Built in 1991, this 2-story motel is located 10 mi from the Land Between the Lakes National Recreational Area. | Take I–24 to exit 65. The motel is 5 mi from Cadiz and 10 mi east of Land Between the Lakes Resort. Complimentary Continental breakfast. Cable TV. Pool. Business services. Some pets allowed (fee). | 154 Hospitality Lane 42211 | 270/522–7007 or 800/800–8000 | fax 270/522–3893 | 48 rooms | $45–$65 | AE, D, DC, MC, V.

Knights Inn. You'll appreciate this southern, contemporary motel with its beige and teal color scheme. The single-story layout will be welcome, too. Complimentary Continental breakfast. Some pets allowed. | 5698 Hopkinsville Rd. 42211 | 270/522–9395 | fax 270/522–4150 | www.theknightsinn.com | 25 rooms | $44–$64 | AE, D, DC, MC, V.

CARROLLTON

Holiday Inn Express. Just 3 mi from Carrollton and 13 mi from the Kentucky Speedway, this familiar favorite has a modern lobby and rooms with cherry wood furniture. | Take I–71 to exit 44 to the motel. Complimentary Continental breakfast. In-room data ports. Cable TV. Business service (fee). Free parking. Some pets (dogs, cats, birds) allowed. | 141 Inn Rd. 41008 | 502/732–6661 or 800–HOLIDAY | fax 502/732–6661 | www.basshotels.com/hiexpress | 62 rooms | $59–$69 (except for special events) | AE, D, DC, MC, V.

CAVE CITY

Comfort Inn, Cave City. This two-story motel with connecting buildings overlooks a section of Mammoth Cave National Park's 52,830 acres of woodlands. The park's entrance is located 5 mi from the hotel. The Wildlife Museum is only 2 ½ mi away, and the Corvette Museum is 30 mi away. Complimentary deluxe Continental breakfast. Cable TV, free local phone calls. In-room microwave and refrigerator. Outdoor heated pool. Hot tub in some rooms. Iron/ironing board. Playground. Pets allowed. | 801 Mammoth Cave St. 42127 | 270/773–2030 or 800/221–2222 | 65 rooms, 1 suite | $36–90 | AE, D, MC, V.

Days Inn. This moderately priced redbrick motel has modern, streamlined rooms. The lobby is modern with cream and brown appointments and floral prints. You'll be 10 minutes from Cave City's restaurant area and Mammoth Cave National Park. | Take exit 53 off I–65 to Highways 70 and 90. Restaurant. Cable TV. Pool, wading pool. Game room. Laundry facilities. Business services. Small pets allowed (fee). | 822 Mammoth Cave Rd. 42127 | 270/773–2151 | fax 270/773–2151 | 110 rooms | $32–$76 | AE, D, DC, MC, V.

CORBIN

Baymont Inn. Modern motel decor is the rule at this chain. Some rooms have king-size beds; some rooms also have recliners. There's a modern burgundy and green lobby with a fireplace. The four floors have modern architecture and lots of plants. Complimentary Continental breakfast. Some refrigerators. Cable TV. Pool. Spa. Business services. Some pets allowed. | 174 Adams Rd. 40701 | 606/523–9040 | fax 606/523–0072 | 95 rooms | $50–$60 | AE, D, DC, MC, V.

Super 8 Motel of Corbin/Cumberland Falls. Stone pillars mark the entrance to the glass-encased lobby of this motel. Shopping addicts can check out the adjacent Past Times Antique Mall before heading out to nearby Cumberland Falls State Park, home of the only moonbow. Parking for RVs is available. Complimentary Continental breakfast. Cable TV. Some in-room hot tubs. Laundry facilities. Pets allowed. | 171 W. Cumberland Gap Pkwy. 40701 | 606/528–8888 or 800/800–8000 | motel@gte.net | home1@gte.net | 34 rooms | $39–$79, $69–$106 suites | AE, D, DC, MC, V.

COVINGTON (CINCINNATI AIRPORT AREA)

Carneal House. This beautiful redbrick antebellum mansion in Covington's historic district was built in 1815. The inn is furnished with period antiques, a patio, and sun room overlook the Licking River. Complimentary breakfast. Some pets allowed. | 405 E. 2nd St. 41011 | 859/431–6130 | fax 859/581–6041 | 6 rooms | $90–$130 | Closed Jan.–Feb. | AE, MC, V, D.

The Clarion Hotel Riverview. This landmark cylindrical hotel dominates the western edge of the skyline and overlooks the river which is 2½ blocks away. There's a great view of the river from the 18th-floor revolving restaurant. The elegant lobby is rust-colored marble and mahogany. There are florals and cherry wood in the hallways, too. 2 restaurants, bar. In-room data ports. Some suites have hot tubs. Cable TV. Indoor-outdoor pool. Hot tub. Exercise equipment. Free laundry. Business services. Airport shuttle. Some pets allowed. | 668 W. 5th St. 41011 | 859/491–1200 or 800/292–2079 | fax 859/491–0326 | www.clarioninn.com | 236 rooms | $89–$225 | AE, D, DC, MC, V.

DANVILLE

Holiday Inn Express. You'll find a standard stucco and brick structure. The lobby has an equestrian theme—horse prints and fabric. It's 2 mi from Centre College. Some larger rooms have sleeper sofas. Complimentary Continental breakfast. Cable TV. Outdoor pool. Hot tub. Laundry facilities. Free parking. Pets allowed ($50 deposit). | 96 Daniel Dr. 40422 | 859/236–8600 or 800–HOLIDAY | fax 859/236–4299 | 63 rooms | $66–$89 | AE, D, DC, MC, V.

Super 8 Motel. You'll find a familiar favorite with a modern brick style. The lobby has a purple color scheme, paintings, plants and flowers, and cherry wood furniture. There are cheerful, contemporary rooms and a landscaped lawn. Some refrigerators. Cable TV. Free Continental breakfast. Laundry room. Business services. Free parking. Some pets allowed. | 3663 U.S. 150 Bypass 40422 | 859/236–8881 or 800/800–8000 | fax 859/236–8881, ext. 301 | 49 rooms | $50–$65 | AE, D, DC, MC, V.

ELIZABETHTOWN

Best Western Cardinal Inn. This one won't remind you of a typical chain. The brick exterior and columns evoke a Southern colonial style. It has the look and ambience of a B&B rather than a motel chain. The quiet spot is ½ mi from the highway; described as off the beaten path. The inn has a one-acre back lawn with cookout grills, shuffleboard, and swings. | You'll find it at the junction of I-65N and I-65S at Exit 91. Cable TV. Pool. Playground. Laundry facilities. Some pets allowed (fee). | 642 E. Dixie 42701 | 270/765–6139 | fax 270/737–9944 or 800/528–1234 | 55 rooms | $59–$79 | AE, D, DC, MC, V.

Holiday Inn. In the heartland of Kentucky between Louisville and Bowling Green, this motel is 2 mi from downtown Elizabethtown. The glistening white-washed building has two floors. All rooms have either two double beds or one king-size bed. Restaurant. Cable TV. In-room data ports. Pool. Laundry facilities. Pets allowed (restrictions). | 1058 N. Mulberry St. 42701 | 270/769–2344 | fax 270/737–2850 | holiday@ne.infi.net | www.basshotels.com | 150 rooms | $65–$69 | AE, D, DC, MC, V.

Red Roof Inn. "Business king rooms" are what you'll find at this motel—Internet hookup, office furniture (including desk and lighted hutch); king-size bed, and a recliner. This place is also family-friendly. It's reported to have the biggest rooms of all the motels/hotels on the Interstate. Two of the suites have a jacuzzi, a queen-size sofa bed, and a king-size bed. There's an area for barbecuing and a gated pool. The lobby has high ceilings with fans and lots of windows where breakfast is served. | The inn is 25–30 minutes from Fort Knox and 30 minutes from Louisville; take I–65 to exit 94. Complimentary Continental breakfast. In-room data ports. Cable TV and free Showtime. Pool. Business services. Free parking. Some pets allowed (fee), with advanced notice. | 2009 N. Mulberry St. 42701 | 270/765–4166 | fax 270/769–9396 | 106 rooms | $46.99–$99.99 | AE, D, DC, MC, V.

Super 8. It's a no-frills modern motel for the budget-minded. You'll like the fact that it's just 1½ mi to old Elizabethtown. | Take I–65 to exit 94 to the motel. Complimentary Continental breakfast. Pool. Some pets allowed. Free parking. | 2028 N. Mulberry St. 42701 | 270/737–1088 | fax 270/737–1098 | 59 rooms, 1 suite | $35 | AE, D, MC, V.

FLORENCE

Knights Inn. The rooms and lobby are in bright, pastel colors. There's complimentary coffee, juice, and doughnuts every day. | Take exit 180 off I–75. Some kitchenettes, some microwaves. Cable TV. Pool. Business services. Some pets allowed. | 8049 Dream St. 41042 | 859/371–9711 | fax 859/371–4325 | knightsinnflorenceky.com | 115 rooms | $35–$62 | AE, D, MC, V.

FRANKFORT

Bluegrass Inn. Free *USA Today* and free Continental breakfast await you at this contemporary motel. The stucco and brick building has a courtyard and outdoor pool. Some rooms have king-size beds. | Take I–64 to exit 58. Some refrigerators. Cable TV and free HBO. Pool. Free parking. Pets allowed (fee). | 635 Versailles Rd. | 502/695–1800 or 800/322–1802 | fax 502/695–1800, ext. 333 | 61 rooms | $36–$58 | AE, D, DC, MC, V.

GILBERTSVILLE

Early American. This one-story motel, located 1½ mi from the town center, features modern rooms with a choice of double or king-sized beds. Picnic area. Some kitchenettes. Cable TV. Pool. Playground. Some pets allowed. | 16749 U.S. 68, Aurora 42048 | 270/474–2241 | 18 rooms | $45–$65 | AE, D, MC, V.

Moors Resort & Marina. This year-round resort on Kentucky Lake has a log cabin lodge with fireplace and one-, two-, three-, and four-bedroom lakeside cottages. Their restaurant has "down home cooking." The full service marina has boat and houseboat rentals, fishing licenses, and guide service. You'll find RV sites and primative camping sites, too. Restaurant. Pool. Golf privileges, miniature golf. Beach, boating, fishing. Video games. Playground. Pets allowed. | 570 Moors Rd. 42044 | 270/362–8361 or 800/626–5472 | fax 270/362–8172 | www.moorsresort.com | 24 rooms in lodge; 30 cottages | $79 | AE, D, MC, V.

Ramada Inn Resort. Located 1½ mi from Kentucky Dam Village State Resort Park, this 45-year-old hotel features three stories of rooms decorated in earth tones. Restaurant, complimentary breakfast. Pool. Hot tub. Playground. Some pets allowed. | 2184 U.S. 62 42044 | 270/362–4278 | fax 270/362–9845 | 95 rooms, 4 suites | $45–$55 | AE, D, MC, V.

GLASGOW

Houston Inn. Chain-style basic, this two-story, family-owned establishment is 10 mi from Barren River Lake. Restaurant. Cable TV. Pool. Some pets allowed (fee). | 1003 W. Main St. 42141 | 270/651–5191 or 800/452–7469 | fax 270/651–9233 | 78 rooms | $35–$45 | AE, D, DC, MC, V.

HARRODSBURG

Best Western. A typical chain accommodation, this motel offers basic rooms with modern amenities. It's 3 mi south of downtown. Complimentary Continental breakfast. Some refrigerators. Cable TV. Pool. Business services. Some pets allowed. | 1680 Danville Rd. 40330 | 859/734–9431 | fax 859/734–5559 | www.bestwestern.com | 69 rooms | $60–$65 | AE, D, DC, MC, V.

HAZARD

Hazard–Days Inn. This three-story motel with outside corridors is adjacent to a 24 hour restaurant and has 24-hour free coffee in lobby. The refurbished rooms have two double beds. Kids, 17 and under, stay free with parent. Fishing is close by at Buckhorn and Carrfork Lakes. Some microwaves, some refrigerators. Cable TV. Pets allowed ($6). | 359 Morton Blvd. 41701 | 606/436–4777 | 60 rooms | $42–$59 | AE, D, DC, V.

HENDERSON

Scottish Inn. Offering basic accommodations in a quiet setting near downtown, this motel is located 1½ mi from Audubon State Park, and 1 mi from Ellis Park Race Track. A restaurant and lounge are within walking distance. Cable TV. Pool, wading pool. Business services. Some pets allowed (fee). | 2820 U.S. 41N 42420 | 270/827–1806 or 800/251–1962 | fax 270/827–8192 | 60 rooms | $40–$45 | AE, D, DC, MC, V.

HOPKINSVILLE

Best Western Hopkinsville. This three-story motel with inside corridors and elevators is 2 mi south of town on U.S. 41. Some in-room coffeemakers and suites are available. Bar, complimentary Continental breakfast. Some in-room data ports. Cable TV. Pool. Pets allowed ($5). | 4101 Fort Campbell Blvd. 42240 | 270/886–9000 | fax 270/886–9000 | ccook@commercecenter.org | 107 rooms | $59 | AE, D, DC, MC, V.

Holiday Inn. The motel lobby includes a lounge with complimentary coffee, fruit, or cookies (depending upon the time of day) and an entertainment area for kids, which offers G-rated videos. Restaurant, bar. In-room data ports. Cable TV. Indoor pool. Sauna. Exercise equipment. Business services. Free parking. Some pets allowed. | 2910 Fort Campbell Blvd., Hopkinsville 42241 | 270/886–4413 | fax 270/886–4413 | 101 rooms | $60–$80 | AE, D, DC, MC, V.

HORSE CAVE

Budget Host Inn. This property is located 2½ mi from downtown Horse Cave, and 14 mi from Mammoth Cave. You have a choice of rooms with double, queen, and king beds; family rooms have fold-out sleeper couches. Restaurant. Cable TV. Pool. Free parking. Some pets allowed. | Rte. 218 (Box 332) 42749 | 270/786–2165 | fax 270/786–2168 | 80 rooms | $30–$47 | AE, D, DC, MC, V.

LEXINGTON

Days Inn. Budget accommodations are available at this standard chain motel, located just off U.S. 75, at exit 104. Complimentary Continental breakfast. In-room data ports, some microwaves. TV. Business services. Some pets allowed. | 5575 Athens-Boonesboro Rd. 40509 | 859/263–3100 | fax 859/263–3120 | 56 rooms | $45–$65 | AE, D, DC, MC, V.

Holiday Inn–North. This large chain hotel, located 2 mi north of downtown, features the Bluegrass region's largest Holidome recreation facility with indoor pool, sauna, and hot tub. The climate-controlled Holidome also has an array of exercise equipment. Restaurant, bar with entertainment. In-room data ports, microwaves, some refrigerators. Cable TV. Indoor pool. Hot tub, sauna. Exercise equipment. Video games. Laundry facilities. Business services. Free parking. Some pets allowed. | 1950 Newtown Pike 40511 | 859/233–0512 | fax 859/231–9285 | www.holidayinn.com.ru/holiday-inn?_franchisee=lexno | 302 rooms | $110 | AE, D, DC, MC, V.

Holiday Inn–South. This stucco-and-brick hotel is just off U.S. 75, at exit 104, south of the city. Sports fans can request one of the two rooms decorated with the blue and white colors of the University of Kentucky Wildcats. Restaurant, bar with entertainment. In-room data ports. Cable TV. Pool. Exercise equipment. Laundry facilities. Business services. Free parking. Some pets allowed. | 5532 Athens-Boonesboro Rd. 40509 | 859/263–5241 | fax 859/263–4333 | 149 rooms | $60–$80 | AE, D, DC, MC, V.

La Quinta Inn. You'll find modern rooms and a small lobby with a bubbling fountain. The facility is located 3 mi from downtown, off U.S. 75 at exit 115. Complimentary Continental breakfast. In-room data ports. Cable TV. Pool. Business services. Free parking. Some pets allowed. | 1919 Stanton Way 40511 | 859/231–7551 | fax 859/281–6002 | www.laquinta.com | 130 rooms | $70 | AE, D, DC, MC, V.

★ **Marriott's Griffin Gate Resort.** Located near major highways 3½ mi north of downtown, this resort boasts a two-story atrium lounge with waterfalls. Equestrian art figures prominently in the decor. Bar, dining room, picnic area. In-room data ports, refrigerators (in suites). Cable TV. 2 pools (1 indoor). Beauty salon. Hot tub. 18-hole golf course, putting green, tennis. Gym. Laundry facilities. Business services. Airport shuttle. Free parking. Some pets allowed. | 1800 Newtown Pike Rte. 922 40511 | 859/231–5100 | fax 859/288–6245 | www.marriott.com/lex | 409 rooms, 9 suites | $130–$170, $195–$250 suites | AE, D, DC, MC, V.

Quality Inn–Northwest. Cherry veneer furniture accents these guest rooms, some of which are equipped with desks, speaker phones, and recliner chairs. The motel is located just off the highway, 3 mi northwest of downtown. Complimentary Continental breakfast. Some microwaves. Cable TV. Pool. Playground. Business services. Free parking. Some pets allowed. | 1050 Newtown Pike Rte. 922 40511 | 859/233–0561 | fax 859/231–6125 | 109 rooms | $45–$78 | AE, D, DC, MC, V.

Red Roof Inn. Similar to other motels in the chain, this establishment offers no-frills accommodation at budget prices. The facility is located 5 mi from downtown and about ½ mi off U.S. 75. Cable TV. Business services. Some pets allowed. | 1980 Haggard Court 40505 | 859/293–2626 | fax 859/299–8353 | 107 rooms | $53–$73 | AE, D, DC, MC, V.

LONDON

Budget Host–Westgate Inn. This small motel, located on the highway 1 mi north of downtown, is well-kept, and the decor is warmer than that of most chain hotels. Cable TV. Pool. Some pets allowed. | 254 W. Daniel Boone Pkwy. (Rte. 80) 40741 | 606/878–7330 | fax 606/878–7330 | mail@budgethost.com | www.budgethost.com | 46 rooms | $47 | AE, D, DC, MC, V.

Holiday Inn Express–London. This comfortable two-story motel, with outside corridors, has a spacious sitting area in the lobby with a small selection of games and books. The rooms feature king- or queen-size beds, desk, movies, coffeemakers, hair dryers, irons and boards. A deluxe Continental breakfast is offered with homemade breads and Belgian waffles made to order. Near I–75 exit 41 at the junction of Hwy 80. Complimentary Continental breakfast. In-room data ports. Cable TV. Indoor–outdoor pool. Hot tub. Pets allowed (small). | 400 GOP St. 40741 | 606/878–7678 or 800/831–3958 | fax 606/878–7654 | www.londonky.com/holidayinnexpress/ | $75 | AE, D, DC, MC, V.

LOUISVILLE

Aleksander House Bed & Breakfast. Listed on the National Register of Historic Places, the three-story, 1882 Victorian Italianate brick home, features 12-foot ceilings, original hardwood floors and moldings and five fireplaces. The five spacious guest rooms (with a suite available) are decorated in antique French furnishings. Two rooms each have a private bath. In the heart of Historic "Old Louisville," special antiquing, theater and Mystery Weekend Packages are available. A full, made-from-scratch breakfast is served to include Belgian waffles and quiche, and cater to special diets. | It's near I–65 at St. Catherine St. exit 135. Complimentary breakfast, some refrigerators. In-room TV/VCRs. Pets allowed. | 1213 S. First St. | 502/637–4985 | fax 502/635–1398 | www.bbonline/ky/ aleksander | 5 rooms | $85–$149 | AE, D, MC, V.

Breckinridge Inn. Spacious rooms are tucked away in this distinguished white-brick and board colonial structure, situated near the Watterson Expressway interchange. Restaurant, bar. Cable TV. 2 pools (1 indoor). Barbershop. Tennis. Exercise equipment. Business services. Airport shuttle. Free parking. Some pets allowed (fee). | 2800 Breckinridge La. | 502/456–5050 | fax 502/451–1577 | 123 rooms | $65–$95 | AE, D, DC, MC, V.

Executive West. This facility is an annex to the Executive Inn next door; together they form the state's largest motor inn complex. Six Flags Over Kentucky Kingdom Amusement Park is within walking distance. Restaurant, bar with entertainment. In-room data ports, refrigerators (in suites). Cable TV. Indoor-outdoor pool. Beauty salon. Business services. Airport shuttle. Some pets allowed. | 830 Phillips La. | 502/367–2251 or 800/626–2708 (outside KY) | fax 502/363–2087 | exwest@iglou.com | 611 rooms, 50 suites | $74–$125, $105–$240 suites | AE, D, DC, MC, V.

Holiday Inn Airport. Located very near the airport, this hotel is convenient to major highways going both downtown and toward suburbs. Restaurant, bar. Complimentary breakfast. In-room data ports. Cable TV. Pool. Tennis. Exercise equipment. Video games. Laundry facilities. Business services. Airport shuttle. Free parking. Some pets allowed. | 4000 Gardiner Point Dr. | 502/452–6361 | fax 502/451–1541 | 200 rooms | $98 | AE, D, DC, MC, V.

Holiday Inn–Downtown. This typical chain hotel is located at the southern end of the business district, near the theaters on Broadway. Restaurant, bar. In-room data ports, minibars, some refrigerators. Cable TV. Indoor pool. Business services. Airport shuttle. Some pets allowed. | 120 W. Broadway | 502/582–2241 | fax 502/584–8591 | 287 rooms, 2 suites | $103–$125, $280–$355 suites | AE, D, DC, MC, V.

Red Roof Inn. The rooms are small but clean at this budget-priced motel, located close to two shopping malls, 8 mi east of downtown. In-room data ports. Cable TV. Business services. Free parking. Some pets allowed. | 9330 Blairwood Rd. | 502/426–7621 | fax 502/ 426–7933 | 108 rooms | $45–$80 | AE, D, DC, MC, V.

★ **Seelbach Hilton.** Listed on the National Register of Historic Places, this 1905 hotel boasts murals by Arthur Thomas that tell the story of settlers and Native Americans of the area. Guest rooms feature four-poster beds and and marble baths. You'll enjoy pool privileges at a nearby facility. The hotel is the site of Tom and Daisy Buchanan's wedding in F. Scott Fitzgerald's famous book, *The Great Gatsby,* and is located three blocks from the convention center. Restaurants, bar with entertainment. In-room data ports. Cable TV. Business services. Airport shuttle. Parking (fee). Some pets allowed for a fee. | 500 4th Ave. | 502/ 585–3200 or 800/333–3399 | fax 502/585–9239 | 321 rooms, 36 suites | $180–$230, $210–$510 suites | AE, D, DC, MC, V.

The Inn at Woodhaven. This 1853 yellow-and-white Gothic Revival house is located near the junction of U.S. 64 and U.S. 71. The carriage house and octagonal Rose Cottage are all decorated in the style of the period. Complimentary breakfast. No smoking. Cable TV. Business services. Some pets allowed. | 401 S. Hubbards La. | 502/895–1011 or 888/895–1011 | www.bbonline.com/ky/woodhaven/index.html | fax 502/895–1011 | 7 rooms | $75–$175 | AE, D, MC, V.

MADISONVILLE

Best Western Pennyrile Inn. Two-story accommodations are 6 mi from Madisonville and 15 mi from Pennyrile State Park. There's an adjacent campground. Take Pennyrile Pkwy. to Exit 37. Restaurant, complimentary breakfast buffet. Some refrigerators. Cable TV. Pool. Tennis. Exercise equipment. Laundry facilities. Business services. Airport shuttle. Pets allowed. | Pennyrile Pkwy., Mortons Gap 42440 | 270/258–5201 | fax 270/258–9072 | www.bestwestern.com | 60 rooms | $40–$50 | AE, D, DC, MC, V.

Days Inn. Large rooms and a comfortable lobby are 3 mi from downtown Madisonville. Restaurant, complimentary Continental breakfast, some room service. Cable TV. Indoor pool. Sauna. Exercise equipment. Laundry facilities. Laundry service. Business services. Some pets allowed. | 1900 Lantaff Blvd. 42431 | 270/821–8620 or 800/544–8313 | fax 270/825–9282 | www.daysinn.com | 143 rooms, 4 suites | $49–$75, $80–$100 suites | AE, D, DC, MC, V.

MAMMOTH CAVE NATIONAL PARK

Mammoth Cave Hotel. You'll have your choice of rustic or modern accommodations at this hotel inside the national park. An arched bridge leads from the main building to the Mammoth Cave Park Visitor Center. 2 restaurants. Some Cable TV. Tennis. Laundry facilities (summer). Business services (winter). Some pets allowed. | Hwy. 70, Mammoth Cave 42259 | 270/758–2225 | fax 270/758–2301 | www.mammothcavehotel.com | 110 rooms | $62–$68; $72 motor lodge; $45–$52 cottages | AE, DC, MC, V.

MAYFIELD

Super 8. Just off the Purchase Pkwy., the motel is 2 mi from the Mayfield airport and 25 mi from the Paducah airport. The rooms were renovated in 1998. Complimentary Continental breakfast. Some refrigerators. Cable TV. Free parking. Some pets allowed. | 1100 Links La. 42066 | 270/247–8899 or 800/800–8000 | fax 270/247–8899 | www.super8.com | 47 rooms, 4 suites | $42–$71 | AE, MC, V.

MIDWAY

Scottwood Bed and Breakfast. This circa 1795 Federal home is listed on Bluegrass Trust. All rooms have queen-size beds and two rooms share a bath. Landscaped with gardens and hemlocks, the B&B is on the scenic South Elkhorn Creek renowned for its widemouth bass fishing. You'll find a canoe there. Telephone is available in the common area. Complimentary breakfast. No in-room telephones. Cable TV, VCRs. Fishing. Pets (ask). | 2004 Leestown Rd. 40347 | 859/846–5037 or 877/477–0778 | fax 859/846–4887 | www.scottwoodbb.com | 4 rooms | $95–$125 | MC, V.

MONTICELLO

Anchor Motel. This is a modern, independently-owned motel in the downtown area. The rooms are basic with contemporary furnishings. The adjacent Anchor Restaurant serves standard American fare. Downtown shopping areas are just a few minutes away. Restaurant. Some refrigerators. Cable TV. Pool. Laundry facilities. Business services. Pets allowed. | 1077 N. Main St. 42633 | 606/348–8441 | fax 606/348–5118 | 50 rooms | $35 | AE, D, MC, V.

MOUNT VERNON

Econo Lodge. Renfro Valley is just a 1/2 mi from this facility, and downtown just 1 1/2 mi. Cable TV. Pool. Some pets allowed. | 1630 Richmond St. 40456 | 606/256–4621 | fax 606/256–4622 | www.econolodge.com | 35 rooms | $36–$40 | AE, D, DC, MC, V.

Kastle Inn. Weekly and monthly rates are available at this two-story inn, situated 3 mi south of downtown, and 3 mi from Renfro Valley. Restaurant. Cable TV. Pool. Some pets allowed. | I–75 and U.S. 25 40456 | 606/256–5156 | fax 606/256–5156 | 50 rooms | $56 | AE, D, DC, MC, V.

MURRAY

Days Inn. Murray State University is ½ mi from this facility. Complimentary Continental breakfast. Some kitchenettes, microwaves, refrigerators, some in-room hot tubs. Cable TV. Pool. Business services. Some pets allowed (fee). | 517 S. 12th St. 42071 | 270/753–6706 or 800/544–8313 | fax 270/753–6708 | www.daysinn.com | 33 rooms, 6 suites | $43–$54, $105–$125 suites | AE, D, DC, MC, V.

Plaza Court. Weekly rates are available here, only five blocks from Murray State University. Cable TV. Free parking. Some pets allowed. | 502 S. 12th St. 42071 | 270/753–2682 | 40 rooms | $36–$39 | AE, D, MC, V.

Shoney's Inn. With room colors on the bright side, the motel is ½ mi from both Murray State University and Murray State Events Center. Kentucky Lake Recreation Area is 10 mi away. In-room data ports, some microwaves, some refrigerators. Cable TV. Pool. Business services. Some pets allowed (fee). | 1503 N. 12th St. 42071 | 270/753–5353 | fax 270/753–5353 | www.shoneysinn.com | 67 rooms | $49–$61, $80 suites | AE, D, DC, MC, V.

OLIVE HILL

Travelodge. Surrounded by trees, this two-story motel supplies lovely green views. The rooms, too, are decorated in hunter-green with accents of burgundy. Right off I–64, the motel is near several restaurants and a Kmart. Complimentary Continental breakfast. In-room data ports, in-room safes, some kitchenettes, some in-room hot-tubs. Cable TV. Pool. Business services. Pets allowed (fee). | 205 U.S. 1947, Grayson 41143 | 606/474–7854 or 877/750–1222 | fax 606/474–8425 | www.travelodge.com | 60 rooms | $55 | AE, D, DC, MC, V.

OWENSBORO

Days Inn. Catering to business travelers, this motel is on the outskirts of town. Restaurant. Complimentary breakfast. Room service. In-room data ports. Pool. Business services. Some pets allowed. | 3720 New Hartford Rd. 42303 | 270/684–9621 or 800/544–8313 | fax 270/684–9626 | www.daysinn.com | 122 rooms | $32–$43 | AE, D, DC, MC, V.

Holiday Inn. Downtown Owensboro is 1 mi from this hotel. Nearby attractions include Ben Hawes State Park (3 mi), Summitt golf course (9 mi), the Owensboro Museum of Fine Art (3 mi). Restaurant, bar with entertainment Tues.–Sat., complimentary breakfast. In-room data ports. Cable TV. Indoor pool. Hot tub, sauna. Putting green. Exercise equipment. Playground. Business services. Airport shuttle. Some pets allowed. | 3136 W. 2nd St. 42303 | 270/685–3941 | fax 270/926–2917 | 145 rooms, 4 suites | $53–$69, $95 suites | AE, D, DC, MC, V.

WeatherBerry Bed & Breakfast. Wide porches, rooms furnished with antiques, and several 12-ft mirrors characterize this 1840 house, situated on seven acres next to a city park. Complimentary breakfast. Some pets allowed. | 2731 2nd Street W. 42301 | 270/684–8760 | fax 270/684–8760 | weatherber@aol.com | www.bbonline.com/ky/weatherberry/index.html | 3 rooms | $65–$80 | AE, MC, V.

PADUCAH

Drury Inn. An atrium lobby graces this facility, which is 5 mi from Barkley airport and 2 mi from Bluegrass Downs Racetrack. Complimentary breakfast. Data ports. Cable TV. Indoor pool. Hot tub. Some pets allowed. | 3975 Hinkleville Rd. 42001 | 270/443–3313 or 800/378–7946 | fax 270/443–3313 | www.drury-inn.com | 118 rooms, 14 suites | $80–$105, $85–$115 suites | AE, D, DC, MC, V.

1857 Bed & Breakfast. This Federalist-style B&B is in the heart of downtown Paducah. Simplicity dominates the interior; high ceilings and contemporary furnishings provide for an uncluttered look. Restaurant. Complimentary Continental breakfast, room service. Some in-room data ports. Cable TV, VCRs. Pool. Hot tub. Gym. Laundry facilities. Business services. Some pets allowed. | 127 Market House Sq. 42001 | 270/444–3690 or 800/264–5604 | fax 270/444–6309 | 3 rooms | $75–$85 | AE, MC, V.

Holiday Inn Express. Rooms in this downtown hotel are all equipped with desks and data ports. Restaurant, picnic area, complimentary Continental breakfast. Minibars, microwaves, refrigerators. Cable TV. Indoor pool. Hot tub. Laundry facilities. Business services. Some pets allowed. | 3994 Hinkleville Rd. 42001 | 270/442–8874 | fax 270/443–3367 | pahex@apex.net | www.basshotels.com | 76 rooms | $76–$150 | AE, D, DC, MC, V.

Quality Inn. Situated near railroad tracks, the hotel is 1½ mi from downtown, and 1 mi from the location for the Miss Kentucky Beauty Pageant. Complimentary Continental breakfast. Cable TV. Pool. Laundry facilities. Business services. Some pets allowed. | 1380 Irvin Cobb Dr. 42003 | 270/443–8751 | fax 270/442–0133 | www.qualityinn.com | 101 rooms | $49–$59 | AE, D, DC, MC, V.

Westowne Inn. This contemporary hotel is within ¼ mile of the Kentucky Oak Mall. Carpeted rooms have desks, dressers, and vanities. Take Exit 4 from I–24. In-room data ports. Cable TV. Pool. Pets allowed (fee). | 3901 Hinkleville Rd. 42001 | 270/442–5666 | www.westowneinn.com | 44 rooms | $41 | AE, D, DC, MC, V.

PARIS

Crockett's Colonial Motel. Built in the 1950s, this motel on the southern edge of downtown has an art-deco interior and mahogany furnishings. Some in-room refrigerators. Cable TV. Playground. Business services. Some pets allowed (fee). | 1493 S. Main St. 40361 | 859/987–3250 | 8 rooms | $35 | No credit cards.

PIKEVILLE

Landmark Inn. Efficiency suites as well as regular rooms are available at this four-story hotel in downtown Pikeville, 25 mi from Breaks Park. Restaurant, bar with entertainment. Cable TV. Pool. Laundry facilities. Some pets allowed. | 146 S. Mayo Trail 41502 | 606/432–2545 or 800/831–1469 | fax 606/432–2545 | 103 rooms, 2 suites | $65, $89 suites | AE, D, DC, MC, V.

PRESTONSBURG

Days Inn. Downtown Pineville is 5 mi from this two-story motel. Complimentary Continental breakfast. Some in-room hot tubs. Cable TV. Pool. Exercise equipment. Business services. Some pets allowed. | 512 S. Mayo Trail, Paintsville 41240 | 606/789–3551 or 800/544–8313 | fax 606/789–9299 | www.daysinn.com | 72 rooms | $45–$65 | AE, D, DC, MC, V.

Holiday Inn. This motel is 3 mi from downtown, 2 mi from the Mountain Art Center, and 7 mi from Jenny Wiley State Park. Restaurant, bar with entertainment. In-room data ports. Cable TV. Pool. Hot tub, sauna. Exercise equipment. Laundry facilities. Business services. Some pets allowed. | 1887 N. U.S. Hwy. 23 41653 | 606/886–0001 | fax 606/886–9850 | hipburg@itiseasy.com | www.basshotels.com | 117 rooms | $58–$85 | AE, D, DC, MC, V.

Super 8 Motel. This is a modern motel located ¼ mile from downtown. Complimentary Continental breakfast. Some in-room hot tubs. Cable TV. Business services. Pets allowed (fee). | 550 S. U.S. Hwy. 23 41653 | 606/886–3355 | www.super8.com | 80 rooms | $52 | AE, D, DC, MC, V.

RICHMOND

Days Inn. Situated on the edge of town, this three-story motel is within a few miles of a mall and a golf course. Room service. Cable TV. Pool. Laundry service. Business services. Some pets allowed (fee). | 2109 Belmont Dr. 40475 | 859/624–5769 or 800/544–8313 | fax 859/624–1406 | www.daysinn.com | 70 rooms | $50–$56 | AE, D, DC, MC, V.

Econo Lodge. This lodge is less than 1 mi from Eastern Kentucky University. Richmond's main shopping area and Fort Boonesborough State Park are also nearby. Complimentary Continental breakfast. Some in-room microwaves, refrigerators. Cable TV. Pool. Laundry facilities. Business services. Pets allowed (fee). | 230 Eastern Bypass 40475 | 859/623–8813 | fax 859/624–3482 | www.econolodge.com | 100 rooms | $48 | AE, D, DC, MC, V.

Super 8. Queen-size rooms are available at this two-story motel, 1 mi from Eastern Kentucky University and 4 mi from the Hummel Planetarium and a public golf course. Complimentary Continental breakfast. Cable TV. Business services. Some pets allowed (fee). | 107 N. Keeneland 40475 | 859/624–1550 or 800/800–8000 | fax 859/624–1553 | www.super8.com | 63 rooms | $34–$68 | AE, D, DC, MC, V.

SHELBYVILLE
Best Western Shelbyville Lodge. Reclining chairs occupy many rooms of this well-landscaped motel, which is 2 mi from downtown Shelbyville, and 3 mi from Wakefield Science Galleries. Cable TV. Pool. Exercise equipment, gym. Laundry service. Some pets allowed. | 115 Isaac Shelby Dr. 40065 | 502/633–4400 | fax 502/633–6818 | www.bestwestern.com | 79 rooms | $55–$60 | AE, D, DC, MC, V.

SHEPHERDSVILLE
Best Western–South. Just outside of Shepherdsville town center (1 mi), this two-story facility is 6 mi from Bernheim Forest and Jim Beam Distillery. A golf course is 1 mi away. Restaurant, bar with entertainment, some room service. Cable TV, in-room VCRs. Pool, wading pool. Business services. Free parking. Some pets allowed. | 211 S. Lakeview Dr. 40165 | 502/543–7097 | fax 502/543–2407 | www.bestwestern.com | 85 rooms | $60–$70 | AE, D, DC, MC, V.

SOMERSET
Somerset Lodge. The motor lodge is 8 mi from Burnside State Park and 5 mi from Lake Cumberland. Renfro Valley is 45 mi away. Complimentary Continental breakfast. Cable TV. Pool. Business services. Free parking. Some pets allowed (fee). | 725 S. U.S. 27 42501 | 606/678–4195 | fax 606/679–3299 | 100 rooms | $36–$50 | AE, D, DC, MC, V.

VERSAILLES
Tyrone Pike Bed & Breakfast. This contemporary gray house on a sunny lot features eclectic decor. One room has a canopy bed, another a sleigh bed, and a special honeymoon suite is available. You can visit a horse farm abutting the property, which is located in a small town outside Lexington. Picnic area, complimentary breakfast. Some kitchenettes, some refrigerators. TV. Some pets allowed. | 3820 Tyrone Pike 40383 | 859/873–2408 or 800/736–7722 | tyronebb@uky.campus.mci.net | www.innsite.com/inns/a000708.html | 2 rooms (1 with shower only, 1 shares bath), 1 suite, 1 efficiency suite | $98–$115, $135 suite | MC, V.

WILLIAMSBURG
Super 8. Housed in three separate buildings (two 2-story and one 3-story), the motel is next door to the Briar Creek City Park and 20 mi from Cumberland Falls State Park. Complimentary Continental breakfast. In-room data ports. Cable TV. Pool. Business services. Free parking. Some pets allowed. | 30 Rte. 92W 40769 | 606/549–3450 or 800/800–8000 | fax 606/549–8161 | www.super8.com | 100 rooms | $51–$65 | AE, D, DC, MC, V.

Williamsburg Motel. This 2-story motel is off I–75 at Exit 11. Rooms have double beds and are done in mauve, pink, and beige. BJ's Steak House is a block away. Complimentary breakfast. In-room data ports, some refrigerators. Cable TV. Pool. Business services. Pets allowed. | 50 Balltown Rd. 40769 | 606/549–2300 or 800/426–3267 | fax 606/549–8279 | 87 rooms | $43 | AE, D, MC, V.

WILLIAMSTOWN

Days Inn. Just off highways 75 and 36, this three-story motel has blue-green carpeting and blond wood furniture. Restaurant. Cable TV. Pool. Free parking. Some pets allowed. | 211 W. Rte. 36 41097 | 859/824–5025 or 800/544–8313 | fax 859/824–5028 | www.daysinn.com | 50 rooms | $35–$70 | AE, D, DC, MC, V.

Howard Johnson Express Inn. This motel is off I–75, 15 minutes from downtown. The Sterling Family Restaurant is next door, and the Dry Ridge Outlet Mall is about 5 mi away. Some microwaves, refrigerators. Cable TV, room phones. Pool. Business services. Pets allowed (fee). | 10 Williamstown Dr. 41097 | 859/824–7177 | fax 859/824–7177 | www.hojo.com | 40 rooms | $38–$48 | AE, D, DC, MC, V.

WINCHESTER

Best Western Country Square. You'll find king-size, queen-size, and double beds at this standard, economic motel. Fort Boonesborough is a few miles away, and several shops and restaurants are within 1/2 mi of the motel. Complimentary Continental breakfast. Some kitchenettes, some microwaves, refrigerators. Cable TV. Pool. Business services. Pets allowed (fee). | 1307 W. Lexington Ave. 40391 | 859/744–7210 | fax 859/744–7210 | www.bestwestern.com | 46 rooms | $69 | AE, D, DC, MC, V.

Holiday Inn. Rooms with king beds also have recliner chairs at this hotel. It's 10 mi from Fort Boonesborough State Park. Restaurant, complimentary Continental breakfast. Data ports, some refrigerators. Cable TV. Pool. Hot tub. Laundry facilities. Business services. Free parking. Some pets allowed. | 1100 Interstate Dr. 40391 | 859/744–9111 | fax 859/745–1369 | nmcwinchester@qx.net | www.basshotels.com | 64 rooms | $62–$75, $110 suites | AE, D, DC, MC, V.

Louisiana

ALEXANDRIA

Best Western of Alexandria. This up-to-date motel is about 5 mi north of the historic district, museums, and the arts center. Rooms are oversize and decorated in southwest Aztec or garden themes. Bar, picnic area. In-room data ports, microwaves, some refrigerators. Cable TV. Indoor pool, wading pool. Hot tub. Exercise equipment. Business services, airport shuttle, free parking. Some pets allowed. | 2720 W. MacArthur Dr. 71303 | 318/445–5530, 800/528–1234, 888/338–2008 | fax 318/445–8496 | www.beswesalex.com | 155 rooms | $67–$127 | AE, D, DC, MC, V.

Rodeway Inn. This motel is 5 mi north of shopping at the Alexandria Mall. Cable TV. Pool, wading pool. Business services. Some pets allowed (deposit). | 742 MacArthur Dr. 71301 | 318/448–1611, 800/228–2000 | fax 318/473–2984 | www.hotelchoice.com | 121 rooms | $45–$56 | AE, D, DC, MC, V.

BATON ROUGE

La Quinta. This two-story hotel with white exterior, teal trim, and lush landscaping is south of Southern University, east of LSU, and close to many restaurants. T.J. Ribs Restaurant and Lounge is across the street, Lonestar Steakhouse and Outback Steakhouse are ¼ mi south, and a 24-hour Denny's is adjacent to the hotel. The Louisiana Art and Science Center is 3 mi southwest, the New State Capitol is 4 mi northwest, and the U.S.S. *Kidd* and Naval War Museum are 3 mi northwest. Complimentary Continental breakfast. In-room data ports. Cable TV. Pool. Laundry facilities. Business services, airport shuttle, free parking. Some pets allowed. | 2333 S. Acadian Thruway, Exit 157B off I–10 70808 | 225/924–9600, 800/531–5900 | fax 225/924–2609 | www.laquinta.com | 140 rooms, 2 suites | $69–$76, $125 suite | AE, D, DC, MC, V.

Shoney's Inn and Suites. This family-oriented motel is next to Celebration Station Family Entertainment Center and 3 mi from historic plantation homes. There's a Shoney's next door (no relation) and several family-style chain and steak restaurants at the adjacent Cortana Mall. Both standard and oversize rooms are available in this two-story motel. Complimentary Continental breakfast. In-room data ports. Cable TV. Pool. Business services. Some pets allowed. | 9919 Gwenadele Dr. 70816 | 225/925–8399, 800/222–2222 | fax 225/927–1731 | www.shoneysinn.com | 196 rooms | $63–$76 | AE, D, DC, MC, V.

BOSSIER CITY

Residence Inn by Marriott. Rooms are oversized and some have fireplaces at this popular member of the Marriott chain. The riverfront in downtown Shreveport is 2 mi west, and the Louisiana Downs racetrack is 3 mi east. Picnic area, complimentary Continental breakfast. In-room data ports, kitchenettes, some refrigerators. Cable TV. Pool. Hot tub. Business services. Some pets allowed (fee). | 1001 Gould Dr. 71111 | 318/747–6220 | fax 318/747–3424 | www.marriott.com | 72 rooms | $105–$159 | AE, D, DC, MC, V.

LAFAYETTE

Bois Des Chenes. The former Charles Mouton Plantation House, built in 1820, is a raised Creole cottage. It is shaded by 300-year-old oak trees on two acres in the downtown historic district. The rooms are decorated in regional antiques and period furnishings, and several open onto deep porches. A nature guide is on site. Complimentary breakfast. Refrigerators. Cable TV. Airport shuttle. Some pets allowed. | 338 N. Sterling St. 70501 | 337/233–7816 | fax 337/233–7816 | www.members.aol.com/boisdchene/bois.html | 5 rooms, 3 suites | $85–$125, $100–$200 suites | AE, MC, V.

La Quinta. This modern motel on I–10 offers a good central location for swamp tours and exploring Cajun Country towns and attractions. Acadian Village is 6 mi to the southwest, Vermilionville is 6 mi southeast. Heymann Convention Center is 4 mi away, and University of South Louisiana is 3 mi to the southwest. Complimentary Continental breakfast. In-room data ports. Cable TV. Pool. Business services. Pets allowed. | 2100 Evangeline Thruway NE 70501 | 337/233–5610, 800/687–6667 | fax 337/235–2104 | www.laquinta.com | 140 rooms | $59–$69 | AE, D, DC, MC, V.

Red Roof Inn. The swamps and other delights of Cajun Country can be reached easily from this motel, which is 4 mi northwest of downtown Lafayette. Cajun Dome is just 3 mi away, Pelican Park and Vermilionville are each within 5 mi, and Acadian Village is 12 mi away. Cable TV. Business services, free parking. Pets allowed. | 1718 N. University Ave. 70507 | 337/233–3339, 800/843–7663 | fax 337/233–7206 | www.redroof.com | 108 rooms | $63–$87 | AE, D, DC, MC, V.

LAKE CHARLES

Days Inn. A family-friendly chain hotel 3 mi west of the riverboat casinos. Complimentary Continental breakfast. Pool. Some pets allowed. No smoking. | 1010 N. Martin Luther King/Hwy. 171 70601 | 337/433–1711, 800/544–8313 | fax 337/491–9753 | www.daysinn.com | 147 rooms. | $45–$55 | AE, D, DC, MC, V.

MANY

Lakeview Lodge Resort. All of these comfortable cabins are directly on the lake in a rustic setting 9 mi from Many with lots of trees for shade. Professional fishing guides are available, as well as golf packages for play at the Cypress Bend Resort course. One-bedroom cabins sleep up to 4, 2-bedroom cabins up to 8 people. There is a banquet room with catering. Kitchenettes, microwaves, refrigerators. Cable TV. Pool, lake. Boating. Playground. Pets allowed (fee). | 1558 Matthews Lodge Rd. 71449 | 318/256–9261, 888/445–9266 | www.lakeviewldg.com | 9 cabins | $65–$100 | MC, V.

METAIRIE

La Quinta. In-room VCRs at this three-story motel offer Nintendo games. Near I–10's exit 225, the hotel is 5 mi from the airport and several restaurants and 15 min from downtown New Orleans. Esplanade Mall and Treasure Chest Casino are 4 mi east. Complimentary Continental breakfast. In-room data ports. Cable TV. Pool. Laundry service. Business services, airport shuttle, free parking. Some pets allowed. | 5900 Veterans Memorial Blvd. 70003 | 504/456–0003, 800/687–6667 | fax 504/885–0863 | www.laquinta.com | 153 rooms | $79–$99 | AE, D, DC, MC, V.

Quality Hotel. This contemporary high-rise on I-10 at exit 228 is a 10-min drive from downtown New Orleans (there's also a shuttle to the French Quarter). Restaurants and the Lakeside Shopping Mall are 1/2 mi from hotel, and the Causeway is right next to it. The Jazz Festival and the Fairgrounds are 5 mi southeast. Restaurant, bar, room service. In-room data ports, some microwaves. Cable TV. Pool. Exercise equipment. Laundry facilities. Business services, airport shuttle, free parking. Some pets allowed. | 2261 N. Causeway Blvd. 70001 | 504/833-8211, 800/228-5151 | fax 504/833-8213 | www.qualityinn.com | 204 rooms | $79-$129 | AE, D, DC, MC, V.

MINDEN

Best Western Minden Inn. This two-story hotel opened in 1997. It's 2 mi from downtown at the intersection of I-20 and Hwy. 7 (Exit 47). A 24-hr restaurant is across the street. Complimentary Continental breakfast. In-room data ports, some microwaves, some refrigerators. Pool. Hot tub. Exercise equipment. Laundry facilities. Business services. Some pets allowed. | 1411 Sibley Rd. 71055 | 318/377-1001 | www.bestwestern.com | 40 rooms | $55-$73 | AE, D, DC, MC, V.

MONROE/WEST MONROE

Baymont Inn and Suites. This three-story inn opened in 1999. Follow exit 114 (Thomas Road) off I-20. It's 3 mi from the Civic Center and 5 mi from Louisiana Purchase Gardens & Zoo and Pecanland Mall. There is no onsite restaurant but there are several restaurant choices within 1/4 mi of the inn. Complimentary Continental breakfast. Some in-room data ports, some microwaves, some refrigerators. Cable TV. Pool. Pets allowed. | 503 Constitution Dr., W. Monroe 71292 | 318/387-2711, 800/301-0200 | fax 318/324-1143 | www.baymontinn.com | 68 rooms, 9 suites | $55-$65, $75-$85 suites | AE, D, DC, MC, V.

Best Western Airport Inn. This two-story hotel with a peach-colored exterior and outside entrances is 1 mi from the Monroe airport, 2 mi from Northeastern University, and 1 mi from Pecanland Mall. Restaurants are just across the Interstate. Complimentary Continental breakfast. In-room data ports, microwaves, refrigerators. Cable TV. Pool. Hot tub. Laundry facilities, laundry service. Pets allowed (fee). | 1475 Gerratte Rd., Monroe 71202 | 318/345-4000 | fax 318/345-4455 | www.bestwestern.com | 50 rooms | $54-$70 | AE, D, DC, MC, V.

Courtyard by Marriott. This three-story hotel got input on its design from frequent business travelers. It opened in January 2000 at the Pecanland Mall, off I-20, exit 120, about 2 mi from the airport and 3 mi from the Civic Center. In-room data ports, some in-room hot tubs. Cable TV. Indoor pool. Exercise equipment. Free parking. Pets allowed. | 4915 Pecanland Mall Dr., Monroe 71203 | 318/388-0034, 800/321-2211 | fax 318/388-1450 | www.courtyard.com | 90 rooms | $79-$129 | AE, D, DC, MC, V.

Days Inn. This two-story hotel, off I-20 at Exit 120 and across from the Pecanland Mall, opened in the mid-1980s. Chain restaurants are about 1/4 mi away. Complimentary Continental breakfast. In-room data ports, microwaves, refrigerators. Cable TV. Pool. Business services. Pets allowed. | 5650 Frontage Rd., Monroe 71202 | 318/345-2220, 800/544-8313 | fax 318/343-4098 | www.daysinn.com | 58 rooms | $43-$58 | AE, D, DC, MC, V.

La Quinta Inn and Suites. This two-story inn is 3 mi from the airport and next door to a 24-hr restaurant. Complimentary Continental breakfast. In-room data ports. Cable TV. Pool. Laundry service. Business services, airport shuttle. Pets allowed. | 1035 U.S. 165 Bypass South, Monroe 71203 | 318/322-3900 | fax 318/323-5537 | www.laquinta.com | 130 units | $64-$71 | AE, D, DC, MC, V.

Red Roof Inn. This three-story hotel with white exterior is 9 mi from the airport, 3 mi southwest of downtown Monroe, at exit 114 off I-20. Cable TV. Business services. Pets allowed. | 102 Constitution Dr., West Monroe 71292 | 318/388-2420, 800/843-7663 | fax 318/388-2499 | 97 rooms | $49 | AE, D, DC, MC, V.

Travelodge. This one-story hotel in a park setting 1 mi east of downtown welcomes both business travelers and families. It was built in 1958. There is a large grass courtyard where children can play. From I–20, take the Bastrop Exit for 165 North. Restaurant, bar, complimentary Continental breakfast. Cable TV. Pool. Laundry service. Business services. Pets allowed. | 2102 Louisville Ave., Monroe 71201 | 318/398–0129, 318/325–5851, 888/515–6375 | fax 318/323–3808 | www.travelodge.com | 98 rooms | $40–$48 | AE, D, DC, MC, V.

MORGAN CITY

Ramada Inn. Only 3 mi from the downtown historic district and a few blocks away from Swamp Gardens, this hotel built in 1975 is a two-story building with exterior corridors. Restaurant, bar, room service. Cable TV. Pool. Laundry service. Pets allowed. | 7408 Hwy. 182, 70380 | 504/384–5750, 888/298–2054 | fax 504/385–0224 | www.ramada-inn.com | 150 rooms, 3 suites | $65–$70, $85–$90 suites | AE, D, DC, MC, V.

NATCHITOCHES

Cloutier Townhouse. This B&B is a turn-of-the-20th-century, 12-room town house, furnished with a collection of antiques dating mostly from the Louisiana Empire and Victorian periods. The purchase of two early 19th-century four-poster beds that had been in the old St. Mary's Convent in Natchitoches inspired the Nun Suite. The master suite has a four-poster queen-size bed, an embroidered bedspread, and wing chairs. In the heart of the historic district, and ½ block from the Front Street shops and restaurants. Complimentary breakfast. In-room hot tubs (in master suite). Cable TV and in-room VCR (in master suite). Pets allowed. No children. No smoking. | 416 Jefferson St. 71457 | 318/352–5242, 800/351–7666 | www.cloutierbandb.com | 2 suites | $95–$110 | AE, MC, V.

Comfort Inn. This hotel with exterior entranceways is near the intersection of I–49 and Hwy. 6 on the west side of town, about 4 mi from historic sites. Complimentary Continental breakfast. In-room data ports, microwaves, refrigerators. Cable TV. Pool. Business services. Pets allowed. | 5362 Hwy. 6 71457 | 318/352–7500, 800/228–5150 | www.comfortinn.com | 59 rooms | $60–$75 | AE, D, DC, MC, V.

Tante Huppé. Robert "Bobby" DeBlieux (pronounced dub-you), a former mayor of Natchitoches, restored, and now lives in, this 1830 Creole house in the historic district. Most of the furnishings and family heirlooms are original to the house. His library contains the state's oldest collection of 18th-century Creole books. A candlelit breakfast, made from recipes in a 1745 Creole cookbook, is served in the formal dining room. Two suites are in the restored, detached former servants' quarters, each with bedroom, parlor, full kitchen, private entrance, patio, and modern tile bath. A third suite in the main house, a former slave's quarters, has exposed, old brick walls, beamed ceilings, and a bedroom as well as a loft bed. Complimentary breakfast. Some kitchenettes. Cable TV, VCRs. Pets allowed. No children under 13. No smoking. | 424 Jefferson St. 71457 | 318/352–5342, 800/482–4276 | www.tantehuppe.com | 3 suites | $95 | AE, MC, V.

NEW IBERIA

Holiday Inn. Convenient to the historic district, this motel was built circa 1978 and has two stories with exterior entranceways. Restaurant, bar, room service. In-room data ports. Cable TV. Pool. Exercise equipment. Playground. Laundry facilities. Business services. Pets allowed. | 2915 Hwy. 14 70560 | 337/367–1201, 800/465–4329 | fax 337/367–7877 | www.basshotels.com | 177 rooms | $62 | AE, D, DC, MC, V.

NEW ORLEANS

Ambassador Hotel. Exposed brick walls, ceiling fans, and hardwood floors, as well as four-poster iron beds and armoires in the guest rooms, add to the character of this hotel composed of three pre-Civil War renovated warehouses. It's on the border of the Central Business District and the Arts and Warehouse District, three blocks from the

Convention Center, Riverwalk, and the French Quarter. Restaurant, bar, room service. In-room data ports. Cable TV. Exercise equipment. Business services, airport shuttle, parking (fee). Some pets allowed (deposit). | 535 Tchoupitoulas St. 70130 | 504/527–5271, 888/527–5271 | fax 504/599–2110 | www.neworleans.com/ambassador | 73 rooms | $119–$189 | AE, D, DC, MC, V.

Chimes. A butterfly garden separates the guest annex from a friendly family home. These lodgings are in a tranquil residential area, two blocks off St. Charles streetcar line and a couple of blocks from shops and the galleries of Magazine Street. Rooms in the main house and carriage house overlook with shaded brick courtyard and have antique furnishings, high ceilings, and hardwood or slate floors, all with private entranceways. English, French, Arabic, and Spanish are spoken in the house. Complimentary Continental breakfast. Cable TV. Pets allowed. No smoking. | 1146 Constantinople St. 70115 | 504/488–4640, 800/729–4640 | fax 504/899–9858 | www.historiclodging.com | 5 rooms (2 with shared bath) | $85–$140 | AE, MC, V.

Claiborne Mansion. Enormous rooms with high ceilings, canopy or four-poster beds, polished hardwood floors, spacious marble baths, and rich fabrics are features of this handsome 1859 mansion in Faubourg Marigny on the fringe of the French Quarter. The house overlooks Washington Square Park and has a lush rear courtyard and pool. Enjoy complimentary evening cocktails and gourmet breakfasts. Vases of fresh flowers accent the contemporary furnishings. Complimentary breakfast. Cable TV. In-room VCRs (and movies). Pool. Business services, free parking. Pets allowed (with advance notice). No smoking. | 2111 Dauphine St. 70116 | 504/949–7327 | fax 504/949–0388 | 2 rooms, 4 suites | $150–$185 rooms, $210–$300 suites | AE, D, MC, V.

BLUE DOG MAN

Artist George Rodrigue is the Blue Dog Man. He was born in New Iberia, Louisiana, in the heart of Cajun Country, and spent the first 20 years of his professional life painting the scenes and faces of the remote, isolated, melancholic region of Spanish-moss hung live oaks and mysterious, alligator filled swamps. In 1984, while illustrating a book of Cajun ghost stories, he was struck by the traditional story of the loup-garou, the ghostly red-eyed werewolf dog that looks blue in moonlight. Using as a model his recently deceased terrier spaniel Tiffany, he painted his first portrait of the Blue Dog. Five years later, after opening a gallery in the French Quarter of New Orleans, he placed another picture of Blue Dog in the window and his career almost instantly turned in a new direction, winning him fame as a master of pop art. Today the Blue Dog is as well known as any modern icon. The image is owned by such notables as Whoopi Goldberg, Hillary Rodham Clinton, and Tom Brokaw (who wrote the foreword for one of Rodrigue's popular books); it hangs on the set of television's popular Friends series; and it has been featured on CNN, "The Today Show," the Wall Street Journal and the New York Times, and advertising for Absolut Vodka and Xerox. Rodrigue's Blue Dog, with the white chest, the round yellow eyes, and the quizzical look, is everywhere these days. Rodrigue Studio displays and sells the artist's silkscreens ($2,000 and up) and paintings ($20,000 and up); between 40 and 60 works are available at any given time, along with occasional bronzes and sculpture. Want to acquire the image but can't afford something framed? You can also buy Rodrigue's books here. There are two galleries behind St. Louis Cathedral in the French Quarter in New Orleans (721 Royal St., 504/581-4244) and the other in Carmel, California (6th Ave., between Lincoln St. and Dolores St., Carmel CA 93923, 831/626-4444). You can see pictures at www.bluedogart.com.

Columns Hotel. This impressive, white-columned 1883 Victorian-style hotel, listed on the National Register of Historic Places, was the setting for the film *Pretty Baby*. The wide veranda, set with cloth-covered tables for outdoor dining or cocktails, is very inviting, as are the two period-furnished parlors. The dark, intimate lounge with two wood-burning fireplaces is a favorite with locals and has excellent live progressive jazz on Tuesdays and Thursdays. There's also a Sunday jazz brunch. An impressive staircase leads to large, somewhat sparsely furnished rooms. Breakfast is served either in the dining room or on the veranda. Bar with entertainment. Complimentary Continental breakfast. No TV. Some pets allowed. | 3811 St. Charles Ave. 70115 | 504/899–9308, 800/445–9308 | fax 504/899–8170 | 20 rooms | $100–$170 | AE, MC, V.

French Quarter Courtyard. The rooms in this two-story hotel with balconies overlook a landscaped courtyard with fountains and a pool. Rooms, some with original fireplaces, have four-poster beds and hardwood and brick flooring. It's across Rampart Street from the French Quarter, three blocks from Bourbon Street. Bar, complimentary Continental breakfast. Cable TV. Pool. Laundry service. Business services, parking (fee). Pets allowed. | 1101 N. Rampart 70116 | 504/522–7333, 800/290–4233 | fax 504/522–3908 | www.neworleans.com/fqch | 51 rooms, 10 suites | $159–$189, $219 suites | AE, D, DC, MC, V.

Rathbone Inn. Built in 1850 as a private family mansion, the inn's antebellum decor includes an ornamental cast-iron fence. The two-story front porch is supported by columns. The high-ceilinged rooms vary in size. It's just two blocks from the French Quarter, four blocks from Bourbon St. Complimentary Continental breakfast. Kitchenettes, microwaves, refrigerators. Cable TV. Hot tub. Laundry facilities. Business services. Some pets allowed. | 1227 Esplanade Ave. 70116 | 504/947–2100, 800/947–2101 | fax 504/947–7454 | www.rathboneinn.com | 9 rooms, 3 suites | $90–$165, $100–$175 suites | AE, D, DC, MC, V.

OPELOUSAS

Best Western Opelousas. This motel, built in 1996 on I–49, is convenient for visits to local Cajun prairie towns and the Evangeline Downs racetrack. Complimentary Continental breakfast. Cable TV. Pool. Business services. Pets allowed (fee). | 5791 I–49 Service Road S 70570 | 337/942–5540, 888/942–5540 | fax 318/942–5540 | www.bestwestern.com | 46 rooms | $63–$83 | AE, D, DC, MC, V.

RUSTON

Maxwell's Inn and Conference Center. This one-story, brick hotel with exterior corridors and parking right outside the door was built in 1962. It sits in the heart of the downtown Ruston area, close to plenty of shopping and fast food restaurants. Restaurant, room service. In-room data ports. Cable TV. 2 pools, wading pool. Playground. Laundry facilities. Free parking. Pets allowed. | 318/255–5901 | fax 318/255–3729 | 140 rooms | $69–$79 | AE, D, DC, MC, V.

ST. FRANCISVILLE

Butler Greenwood. Shaded by huge oak trees dripping with Spanish moss, writer Anne Butler's two-story frame house with a wraparound veranda was built in the early 1800s and is still the center of a working plantation, 2 mi North of St. Francisville on Hwy. 61. Seven cottages spread over 50 landscaped acres. Each cottage is unique, some with exposed brick walls and beams, fireplaces, claw-foot tubs, and skylights. One cottage has a front porch with rocking chairs, another has a three-level rear deck overlooking the bluffs. All have either a full kitchen or a kitchenette. Guided nature/birdwatching walks are available. Complimentary Continental breakfast. Kitchenettes. Some in-room hot tubs. Cable TV. Pool. Some pets allowed. | 8345 U.S. Hwy. 61 70775 | 225/635–6312 | fax 225/635–6370 | www.butlergreenwood.com | 7 cottages | $110 | AE, MC, V.

SHREVEPORT

Holiday Inn Downtown. This six-story hotel is in the heart of downtown, two blocks from Harrah's casino and close to the entertainment district. Restaurant, bar. In-room data ports. Cable TV. Pool. Exercise equipment. Laundry service. Business services, airport shuttle. Pets allowed (fee). | 102 Lake St. 71101 | 318/222–7717, 800/465–4329 | fax 318/221–5951 | www.basshotels.com | 185 rooms | $69–$94 | AE, D, DC, MC, V.

Ramada Inn. This Ramada Inn is made up of two brick buildings, one with two floors, the other with four. It is on I–20 at Exit 13, two blocks from the airport and handy to all areas of the surrounding Art-La-Tex. Landscaped atrium with plants and waterfalls has a sauna, car rentals, and a gift shop. There is also an outdoor garden. Restaurant, bar (with entertainment), room service. Cable TV. Pool. Hot tub. Exercise equipment. Business services, airport shuttle. Pets allowed. | 5116 Monkhouse Dr. 71109 | 318/635–7531 | fax 318/635–1600 | www.ramada.com | 255 rooms | $59–$72 | AE, D, DC, MC, V.

Remington Suite. This former pharmaceutical warehouse was renovated and opened as an all-suites hotel in 1986 in the heart of the downtown area. The first two floors house the hotel and floors three through five are offices. Restaurant, complimentary Continental breakfast. Refrigerators, in-room hot tubs. Cable TV. Indoor pool. Steam room. Exercise equipment, racquetball. Laundry services. Airport shuttle, free parking. Pets allowed. | 220 Travis St. 71101 | 318/425–5000, 800/444–6750 | 22 suites | $110–$175 | AE, D, DC, MC, V.

SLIDELL

La Quinta. Built in 1960, this two-story brick hotel is right off I–10 in a commercial area. It's 10 mi from Honey Island Swamp Tours, 1½ mi from I–12 and I–59, and about 45 min from downtown New Orleans. Bar, complimentary Continental breakfast. In-room data ports. Cable TV. Pool. Laundry facilities. Business services. Pets allowed. | 794 E I–10 Service Rd. 70461 | 504/643–9770, 800/531–5900 | fax 504/641–4476 | www.laquinta.com | 172 rooms | $65 | AE, D, DC, MC, V.

THIBODAUX

Howard Johnson. Built in 1972, this motel is in downtown Thibodaux near Civic Center. It's a good location for exploring swamp tours, bayou plantations, scenic drives, and antique shops. Restaurant, bar (with entertainment), room service. Refrigerators. Cable TV. Pool. Tennis. Exercise equipment. Video games. Business services, free parking. Pets allowed (fee). | 201 N. Canal Blvd. 70301 | 504/447–9071, 800/952–2968 | fax 504/447–5752 | www.hojo.com | 118 rooms | $65–$100 | AE, D, DC, MC, V.

Maine

AUGUSTA

Best Western Senator Inn. This standard hotel is just off the turnpike and near the state capitol and government offices. Restaurant, bar, picnic area, complimentary breakfast, room service. In-room data ports, some refrigerators, cable TV, in-room VCRs (and movies) available. 2 pools. Massage. Indoor putting green. Gym. Laundry facilities. Some pets allowed (deposit). | 284 Western Ave. | 207/622–5804 | fax 207/622–8803 | www.senatorinn.com | 103 rooms | $89–$139 | AE, D, DC, MC, V.

Edwards House Inn. This 1872 Victorian home overlooking the Kennebec River is a pure slice of Americana with a shady front porch and restored period antiques. Rooms have wall-to-wall carpeting. Dining room, complimentary Continental breakfast. No room phones, cable TV. Pets allowed. | 53 Water St., 04330 | 207/622-2691 or 207/622-3617 evenings and weekends | fax 207/622-2824 | river@ctell.net | www.ctell.net/~ninnian | 16 rooms (16 rooms share 4 baths) | $55–$85 | D, MC, V.

Motel 6. This two-story chain offering, next to several state government offices, is one of the newest hotels in the area. Cable TV. Laundry facilities. Some pets allowed. | 18 Edison Dr. | 207/622-0000 | fax 207/622-1048 | 70 rooms | $52 | AE, D, DC, MC, V.

Travel Lodge. This standard hotel is near the state capitol, government offices, and turnpike. Restaurant, bar, complimentary Continental breakfast. Some microwaves, cable TV. Pool, wading pool. Laundry facilities. Business services. Pets allowed. | 390 Western Ave. | 207/622–6371 | fax 207/621–0349 | www.travellodge.com | 98 rooms | $80 | AE, D, DC, MC, V.

BAILEY ISLAND/ORR'S ISLAND

Driftwood Inn and Cottages. This classic 1910 getaway has stood the test of time, and hasn't changed much throughout the years. Secluded and private, the rooms have bare original wood and furnishings and overlook the coastline. The saltwater pool and patio are nice places to relax in the sun. Dining room. No air-conditioning, no room phones, TV in common area. Pool. Pets allowed (no fee). No smoking. | 81 Washington Ave., Bailey Island, 04003 | 207/833–5461 | www.midcoastmaine.com | 24 rooms (10 with half bath, 14 share 6 baths), 6 cottages | $80–$90 | Closed mid-Oct.–late May | No credit cards.

BANGOR

Best Inn. This downtown inn near the Civic Center has been well maintained. The restaurant features homemade baked goods and pastries. Restaurant, bar. Cable TV. Business services. Pets allowed. | 570 Main St. | 207/947–0566 | fax 207/945–3309 | 50 rooms, 1 suite | $75–$120 | AE, D, DC, MC, V.

Best Western White House Inn. This standard, chain hotel is near the civic center. Bar, picnic area, complimentary Continental breakfast. In-room data ports, refrigerators, cable TV, in-room VCRs (and movies). Pool. Sauna. Laundry facilities. Business services. Pets allowed. | 155 Littlefield Ave., Hampden | 207/862–3737 | fax 207/862–6465 | 64 rooms | $45–$89 | AE, D, DC, MC, V.

Comfort Inn. This standard hotel is near the interstate, airport, and shopping malls. Restaurant, complimentary Continental breakfast. Pool. Video games. Business services, airport shuttle. Pets allowed (fee). | 750 Hogan Rd. | 207/942–7899 | fax 207/942–6463 | 96 rooms | $55–$90 | AE, D, DC, MC, V.

Days Inn. This is a typical chain motel. Complimentary Continental breakfast. Cable TV. Pool. Hot tub. Video games. Business services, airport shuttle. Pets allowed (fee). | 250 Odlin Rd. | 207/942–8272 | fax 207/942–1382 | www.daysinn.com | 101 rooms | $50–$80 | AE, D, DC, MC, V.

Econo Lodge. This standard chain is near the interstate and shopping malls. In-room data ports, cable TV. Laundry facilities. Business services. Pets allowed. | 327 Odlin Rd. | 207/945–0111 or 800/393–0111 | fax 207/942–8856 | 128 rooms | $50–$85 | AE, D, DC, MC, V.

Four Points Sheraton. This standard chain at the airport is near shopping. An enclosed walkway connects the hotel to the airport. Restaurant, bar. In-room data ports, cable TV. Pool. Exercise equipment. Business services. Pets allowed. | 308 Godfrey Blvd. | 207/947–6721 | fax 207/941–9761 | www.fourpoints.com/bangor | 103 rooms | $125 | AE, D, DC, MC, V.

Holiday Inn. This standard chain offering is near the airport and 3 mi west of Bangor on Interstate 395. Restaurant, bar with entertainment, room service. In-room data ports, microwaves, some refrigerators, cable TV, some in-room VCRs. 2 pools. Hot tub. Video games. Laundry facilities. Business services, airport shuttle, free parking. Pets allowed. | 404 Odlin Rd. | 207/947–0101 | fax 207/947–7619 | bgror@aol.com | 207 rooms | $72–$92 | AE, D, DC, MC, V.

Holiday Inn–Civic Center. This standard chain, near the Civic Center, is across the street from the Paul Bunyan statue. Restaurant, bar with entertainment, room service. In-room data ports, cable TV. Pool. Laundry facilities. Business services, airport shuttle, free parking. Pets allowed. | 500 Main St. | 207/947–8651 | fax 207/942–2848 | www.holidayinn.com | 122 rooms | $69–$89 | AE, D, DC, MC, V.

Main Street Inn. This older, typical inn across from the Civic Center is well priced, near a variety of restaurants, and provides basic amenities. Complimentary Continental breakfast. Cable TV. Business services. Pets allowed. | 480 Main St. | 207/942–5281 or 800/928–9877 | fax 207/947–8733 | 64 rooms | $49–$59 | AE, D, DC, MC, V.

Phenix Inn at West Market Square. This inn occupies a late-19th-century building that's on the National Register of Historic Places. Complimentary Continental breakfast. Some microwaves, some refrigerators, cable TV, some in-room VCRs. Gym. Laundry service. Business services. Pets allowed. | 20 Broad St. | 207/947–0411 | fax 207/947–0255 | www.maineguide.com/bangor/phenixinn | 32 rooms | $85–$169 | AE, D, DC, MC, V.

Ranger Inns. This family-owned, clean, efficient, and modern inn is near the airport and shopping. Bar. No air-conditioning, some kitchenettes. Laundry facilities. Pets allowed (fee). | 1476 Hammond St. | 207/945–2934 | fax 207/945–3456 | www.rangerinn.com | 90 rooms | $49–$59 | AE, D, MC, V.

Rodeway Inn. This standard chain inn is near the airport and shopping. Restaurant, picnic area. Cable TV. Business services, airport shuttle. Pets allowed (fee). | 482 Odlin Rd. | 207/942–6301 | fax 207/941–0949 | 98 rooms | $42–$70 | AE, D, DC, MC, V.

BAR HARBOR

Ledgelawn Inn. This beautiful three-story, 1904 summer cottage–style mansion has a historic air. Rooms are elegantly furnished, and many have fireplaces, porches, and canopy beds. Complimentary Continental breakfast. No air-conditioning in some rooms, some in-room hot tubs, cable TV. Pool. Pets allowed (fee). No smoking. | 66 Mount Desert St., 04609 | 207/288–4596 or 800/274–5334 | fax 207/288–9968 | www.barharborvacations.com | 33 rooms | $125–$275 | Closed mid-Oct.–Apr. | AE, D, MC, V.

BATH

Holiday Inn. This standard chain hotel is near U.S. 1 and downtown. Restaurant, bar with entertainment. In-room data ports, some refrigerators, cable TV. Pool. Hot tub. Exercise equipment. Business services, free parking. Pets allowed. | 139 Richardson St. | 207/443–9741 | fax 207/442–8281 | hibath@aol.com | www.holidayinn.com/bathme | 141 rooms | $79–$129 | AE, D, DC, MC, V.

The Inn at Bath. This beautiful 1810 Greek Revival home is in Bath's Historic District. It's filled with antiques yet polished off with modern amenities. Rooms are elegant but comfortable; some have wood-burning fireplaces and private terraces. Four rooms can be converted into two suites for families. Complimentary breakfast. In-room data ports. Some in-room hot tubs, cable TV, in-room VCRs. Laundry facilities. Business services. Pets allowed. No smoking. | 969 Washington St., 04530 | 207/443–4294 | fax 207/443–4295 | innkeeper@innatbath.co | www.innatbath.com | 8 rooms, 1 suite | $85–$145, $185–$370 suites | AE, D, MC, V.

BELFAST

Belfast Bay Meadows. This turn-of-the-20th-century country inn on 10 acres has a view of Penobscot Bay. It's richly decorated with antiques, but retains a relaxed atmosphere. There's outdoor dining on the deck and views of the bay. You'll find many activities nearby, including whale-watching boat trips, steam-train excursions, tennis, golf, hiking, biking, and winter sports. Complimentary breakfast. Some refrigerators, no TV in some rooms, cable TV in common area. Business services. Pets allowed. No smoking. | 192 Northport Ave. | 207/338–5320 or 800/335–2370 | fax 207/338–5715 | bbmi@baymeadowinn.com | www.baymeadowsinn.com | 20 rooms | $85–$165 | AE, D, MC, V.

Belfast Harbor Inn. This family-style inn and motel sits on 6 acres overlooking Penobscot Bay. You'll find excellent views of the bay and the historic port of Belfast from here. Picnic area, complimentary Continental breakfast. Cable TV. Pool. Business services. Pets allowed (fee). | U.S. 1 | 207/338–2740 or 800/545–8576 | fax 207/338–5205 | stay@belfastharborinn.com | www.belfastharborinn.com | 61 rooms | $84–$119 | AE, D, MC, V.

Belhaven Bed and Breakfast. This 1851 Victorian inn is in the heart of town. Rooms are filled with lace and country antiques and furnishings. The efficiency suite has a fully equipped kitchen, sundeck, and private entrance and is suitable for families. Dining room, complimentary breakfast. No air-conditioning, no room phones, TV in common area. Library. Pets allowed (fee). No smoking. | 14 John St., 04915 | 207/338–5435 | stay@belhaveninn.com. | www.belhaveninn.com | 4 rooms (3 with shared bath), 1 suite | $65–$105 | MC, V.

Gull Motel. This small family motel with a bay view is 3 mi north of Belfast. Cable TV. Pets allowed (fee). | U.S. 1 | 207/338–4030 | 14 rooms | $65–$79 | MC, V.

Wonderview Cottages. On the property's own Penobscot Bay beach, 3 mi northeast of Belfast, these cottages have screened-in porches and fireplaces. Picnic area. No air-conditioning, kitchenettes, cable TV. Playground. Pets allowed. | Searsport Ave. 04915 | 207/338–1455 | wondercottages@acadia.net | www.maineguide.com/belfast/wonderview | 20 1–3 bedroom cottages | $485–$860 (7-day minimum stay) | Closed mid-Oct.–mid-May | D, MC, V.

BETHEL

Bethel Inn and Country Club. An elegant country inn (circa 1913) on the town square, the Bethel has its own golf course and is tucked in the Mahoosuc. Dining room, bars with entertainment. No air-conditioning in some rooms, cable TV, some in-room VCRs. Pool. Hot tub. Driving range, 18-hole golf course, putting green, tennis. Exercise equipment, boating. Cross-country skiing. Children's programs (June–Labor Day, ages 4–12). Business services. Pets allowed. | 1 Broad St. | 207/824–2175 or 800/654–0125 | fax 207/824–2233 | connorsa@nxi.com | www.bethelinn.com | 60 rooms in 5 buildings, 40 condominiums | $109–$199, $119–$189 condominiums | MAP | AE, D, DC, MC, V.

Briar Lea Inn and Restaurant. This 1850s farmhouse filled with antiques is 1 mi north of town. Restaurant, complimentary breakfast. Hiking, cross-country skiing. Some pets allowed. | 150 Mayville Rd. | 207/824–4717 or 888/479–5735 | fax 207/824–7121 | briarlea@megalink.net | www.briarleainnrestaurant.com | 6 rooms (3 with shower only) | $73–$103 | AE, D, MC, V.

Chapman Inn. This 1865 colonial inn, named for the 19th-century composer William Chapman, is right on Bethel's town square. Guest rooms are simply furnished with antiques and local art. Dormitory bunk accommodations are available in the barn and are perfect for those on a modest budget, or for the kids. Dining room, complimentary breakfast. In-room data ports. Hot tub. Sauna. Exercise equipment, bicycles. Ice-skating. Laundry facilities. Business services. Pets allowed (fee). No smoking. | Bethel Town Common 04217 | 207/824–2657 or 877/359–1498 | fax 207/824–7152 | info@chapmaninn.com | www.chapmaninn.com | 7 rooms (2 with shared bath), 1 suite, 24 dorm beds | $45–$119, $119 suites, $25–$30 dorm | AE, D, MC, V.

L'Auberge Country Inn. The Auberge is a charming, white 1880s converted carriage house on 5 wooded acres, just off the town common. Rooms are large and sunlit, and have king-size beds and antiques. Dining room, complimentary breakfast. No air-conditioning, no room phones, TV in common area. Library. Laundry facilities. Business services. Pets allowed (no fee). No smoking. | 32 Mill Hill Rd., 04217 | 207/824–2774 or 800/760–2774 | fax 207/824–0806 | reservations@laubergecountryinn.com | www.laubergecountryinn.com | 7 rooms | $79–$129 | MAP available | AE, D, MC, V.

BIDDEFORD-SACO

Classic Motel. The Classic is convenient to Old Orchard Beach and other beaches. Picnic area. In-room data ports, some kitchenettes, refrigerators, cable TV. Pool. Some pets allowed. | 21 Ocean Park Rd., (Rte. 5), Saco, 04072 | 207/282–5569 or 800/290–3909 | www.classicmotel.com | 17 rooms | $55–$85 | AE, D, MC, V.

Crown 'n Anchor Inn. Steeped in local lore, this grand Federal inn listed on the National Register of Historic Places consists of two distinct homes built in 1760 and 1827. The guest rooms are filled with antiques and contain memorabilia from the local historical figures and events for which they were named. On three acres. Dining room, complimentary breakfast. No air-conditioning, in-room hot tubs, cable TV, TV in common area. Library. Pets allowed (no fee). No smoking. | 121 North St., 04072 | 207/282–3829 or 800/561–8865 | 6 rooms | $75–$120 | AE, MC, V.

BINGHAM

Bingham Motor Inn and Sports Complex. This family motel 1 mi north of town caters to hunters and fishermen and has downhill skiing 5 mi away. Picnic area. Some kitchenettes, some refrigerators, cable TV. Pool. Hot tub. Basketball, hiking, volleyball. Cross-country skiing, snowmobiling. Pets allowed (no fee). | Rte. 201 | 207/672–4135 | fax 207/672–4138 | www.ctel.net/~bmisc | 20 rooms | $61 | AE, MC, V.

BOOTHBAY HARBOR

Hillside Acres Cabins and Motel. This old-style motel with cabins on a hill is just outside Boothbay. Picnic area. No air-conditioning, some kitchenettes, cable TV, no room phones. Pool. Pets allowed in cottages. | Adams Pond Rd., 04537 | 207/633–3411 | fax 207/633–2295 | hillside@clinic.net | www.gwi.net/~hillside | 14 rooms (2 with shared bath), 7 cabins | $54–$75 | MC, V.

Lawnmeer Inn. This historic inn 2 mi south of Boothbay Harbor is on a quiet inlet, but near shopping, galleries, and boat rides. Restaurant, bar. No air-conditioning in some rooms, cable TV. Dock. Pets allowed (fee). | Southport Island, West Boothbay Harbor, 04575 | 207/633–2544 or 800/633–7645 | fax 207/633–7198 | cooncat@lawnmeerinn.com | www.lawnmeerinn.com | 35 rooms | $95–$150 | Closed mid-Oct.–mid-May | MC, V.

The Pines. This hotel's spacious rooms offer views of the harbor. It's 1¼ mi southeast of Boothbay Harbor and welcomes families. Refrigerators, cable TV. Pool. Tennis. Playground. Pets allowed. | Sunset Rd. | 207/633–4555 | 29 rooms | $80 | Closed late Oct.–early May | D, MC, V.

Smugglers Cove Inn. This inn, 4¼ mi east of Boothbay Harbor, has a wooded location and is on the ocean. You'll even find a swimming beach nearby. Restaurant, bar, complimentary Continental breakfast. No air-conditioning, some kitchenettes, cable TV. Pool. Business services. Some pets allowed. | Rte. 96, East Boothbay, 04544 | 207/633–2800 or 800/633–3008 | fax 207/633–5926 | www.smugglerscovemotel.com | 60 units | $99–$149 | Closed mid-Oct.–late May | AE, D, MC, V.

Welch House Inn. This 1873 home is on peaceful McKown Hill with a great view of Boothbay Harbor. Rooms are filled with an eclectic array of antiques like four-poster beds and oriental rugs; most have water views. Breakfast is served on a glassed-in patio overlooking the harbor. Dining room, complimentary breakfast. No room phones, cable TV. Library. Pets allowed (fee). No kids under 8. No smoking. | 56 McKown St., 04538 | 207/633–3431 or 800/279–7313 | fax 207/633–3752 | welchhouse@wiscasset.net | www.welchhouse.com | 16 rooms | $80–$145 | Closed Dec.–Mar. | MC, V.

BRUNSWICK

Atrium Inn and Convention Center. This business and traveler's hotel is convenient to the Naval Air Station and Bowdoin College. Restaurant, bar, room service. Refrigerators, cable TV, some in-room VCRs (and movies). Pool, wading pool. Hot tub. Exercise equipment. Video games. Laundry facilities. Business services. Pets allowed. | 21 Gurnet Rd., (Rte. 24) | 207/729–5555 | fax 207/729–5149 | 186 rooms | $74–$125 | AE, D, DC, MC, V.

BUCKSPORT

Best Western Jed Prouty Motor Inn. This hotel is convenient to coastal areas on the Penobscot River. In-room data ports, cable TV. Business services. Some pets allowed. | 53 Main St., 04428 | 207/469–3113 | fax 207/469–3113 | 40 rooms | $89–$99 | AE, D, DC, MC, V.

Bucksport Motor Inn. This standard roadside motel is convenient to coastal areas. Cable TV. Pets allowed. | 151 Main St., 04416 | 207/469–3111 or 800/626–9734 | 24 rooms | $72 | AE, D, MC, V.

River Inn Bed and Breakfast. This 1793 colonial home was built by the founder of Bucksport and overlooks the Penobscot River and Fort Knox. Some rooms have fireplaces. Many have views of the fort. Complimentary breakfast. Cable TV, no room phones. Library. Business services. Pets allowed (fee). No smoking. | 210 Main St., 04416 | 207/469–3575 | fax 207/469–0008 | stngry22@aol.com | 7 rooms (3 with shared bath) | $50–$75 | AE, D, MC, V.

CALAIS

Downeaster Motel. This simple, red, single-story stopover spot with large rooms overlooks the water. Rooms are furnished with standard motel fixtures. No air-conditioning, no room phones, cable TV. Pets allowed (fee). No smoking. | Rte. 1, 04619 | 207/454–3376 or 800/899–3376 | cwing@calais-maine.com | www.calais-maine.com/downeast | 7 rooms | $45. | Closed Nov.–Apr. | D, MC, V.

CAMDEN

Blue Harbor House. An antiques-filled 1810 house. Complimentary breakfast. No air-conditioning in some rooms, some kitchenettes, no TV in some rooms. Some pets allowed. No kids under 12. No smoking. | 67 Elm St. | 207/236–3196 or 800/248–3196 | fax 207/236–6523 | balidog@midcoast.com | www.blueharborhouse.com | 8 rooms, 2 suites | $95–$165, $165 suites | AE, D, MC, V.

CAPE ELIZABETH

Inn by the Sea. This all-suites inn has excellent views of Crescent Beach and Kettle Cove. All units have a private porch or deck with ocean view, full kitchen, and living room. Rooms are fully furnished with many amenities; some have fireplaces. Suitable for families. Restaurant, dining room, room service. No air-conditioning, in-room data ports, cable TV, in-room VCRs. Pool. Tennis court. Beach, boating, bicycles. Pets allowed (no fee). No smoking. | 40 Bowery Beach Rd., 04107 | 207/799–3134 or 800/888–4287 | fax 207/799–4779 | innmaine@aol.com | www.innbythesea.com | 25 suites, 18 cottage units | $269–$549 | AE, D, MC, V.

CASTINE

Castine Harbor Lodge. This stately 1893 mansion inn is right on the harbor. Though it can be grand, it's still a good choice for families. Rooms are comfortable and filled with an eclectic mix of antiques and modern pieces. The efficiency cottage is a fully furnished studio right on the water's edge. Nine of the rooms have water views. Complimentary Continental breakfast. No air-conditioning, no room phones, TV in common area. Pets allowed (fee). No smoking. | 147 Perkins St., 04421 | 207/326–4335 | fax 207/326–0900 | chl@acadia.net | www.castinemaine.com | 15 rooms (6 with shared bath), 1 cottage | $75–$175 | D, DC, MC, V.

CHEBEAGUE ISLANDS

Chebeague Orchard Bed and Breakfast Inn. This beautiful Greek Revival home is on 2 acres with ocean views. The 3-acre property across the road has an apple orchard and organic vegetable and flower garden. Rooms are simply done with period antiques, hardwood dressers, and beautiful quilts. Complimentary breakfast. No air-conditioning, no room phones, no TV. Bicycles. Library. Pets allowed (winter only, no fee). No smoking. | 453 North Rd., 04017 | 207/846–9488 | orchard@nlis.net | www.chebeague-orchard.com | 5 rooms (2 with shared bath) | $75–$125 | MC, V.

CRANBERRY ISLES

Braided Rugs Inn. This white clapboard home was built in 1892 and has been occupied by the same family ever since. It's popular with bird enthusiasts who come to see the island's migratory species. Rooms are simple, filled with period antiques. As there are few places to eat on the island, ask about receiving home-cooked meals. Complimentary breakfast. No air-conditioning. No room phones, TV in common area. Pets allowed. No smoking. | 1892 Main St., Islesford, 04646 | 207/244–5943 | 3 rooms (all with shared bath) | $75 | MC, V.

DAMARISCOTTA

Brannon-Bunker Inn. This antiques-filled charmer, 4½ mi south of Damariscotta, occupies a couple of early 19th-century structures on the river. Complimentary Continental breakfast. No air-conditioning, some kitchenettes, no room phones, TV in common area. Some pets allowed (fee). No smoking. | 349 State Rte. 129, Walpole 04573 | 207/563–5941 or 800/563–9225 | brnbnkinn@lincoln.midcoast.com | 8 rooms (2 with shared bath) | $60–$75 | Closed Dec. 1–Apr. 1 | AE, MC, V.

EASTPORT

Milliken House. This ornate, well-preserved 1846 Victorian inn is two blocks from the Eastport waterfront. Marble-topped furnishings, books, and antiques are remnants from Benjamin Milliken, a shipbuilder and the home's founder. Rooms are filled with Victorian and Eastlake furniture, and with fresh flowers in season. Complimentary breakfast. No air-conditioning, no room phones, TV in common area. Library. Pets allowed (no fee). No smoking. | 29 Washington St., 04631 | 207/853–2955 | millikenhouse@eastport-inn.com | www.eastport-inn.com | 5 rooms (2 with shared bath) | $50–$65 | AE, D, MC, V.

Todd House. This vintage New England charmer, a few hundred feet from the ocean, is filled with antiques and has fine views of the bay. Picnic area, complimentary Continental breakfast. No air-conditioning, some kitchenettes, no room phones, cable TV in some rooms. Pets allowed. | 1 Capen Ave. | 207/853–2328 | fax 207/853–2328 | 8 rooms (6 with shared bath) | $55–$80 | MC, V.

ELLSWORTH

Colonial Travel Lodge. This efficient, modern motel is on the way to Bar Harbor. Restaurant, picnic area, complimentary Continental breakfast (May–Oct.). Some kitchenettes, some refrigerators, cable TV. Pool. Hot tub. Business services. Pets allowed. | 321 High St., 04605 | 207/667–5548 | fax 207/667–5549 | colonial@acadia.net | www.acadia.net/colonial | 69 rooms, 3 suites | $88–$108, $139 suites | AE, D, MC, V.

Twilite. This old-style roadside motel is 1 mi west of town and convenient to downtown, Acadia, and the ferry to Yarmouth, Nova Scotia. All rooms have individual decks. Picnic area, complimentary Continental breakfast. No air-conditioning in some rooms, some refrigerators, cable TV. Pets allowed (fee). | U.S. 1 (Rte. 3) | 207/667–8165 or 800/395–5097 | fax 207/667–0289 | twilite@downeast.net | www.twilitemotel.com | 23 rooms | $40–$78 | AE, D, MC, V.

FREEPORT

Freeport Inn and Cafe. This inn is on 25 acres and has canoeing nearby. Restaurant, picnic area. Some refrigerators, cable TV. Pool. Business services, free parking. Some pets allowed. | 31 U.S. 1 S, 04032 | 207/865–3106 or 800/998–2583 | fax 207/865–6364 | www.freeportinn.com | 80 rooms | $110 | AE, D, DC, MC, V.

Maple Hill Bed & Breakfast. The owners of this B&B emphasize a warm family-friendly environment; the cheery golden retriever will even welcome you into the home. Formerly a farmhouse, Maple Hill's barn and garden preserve the traditions of its rural heritage. Complimentary breakfast. Cable TV. Pets allowed. No smoking. | 18 Maple Ave., 04032 | 207/865–3730 or 800/867–0478 | www.web-knowledge.com/maplehill | 3 rooms | $110–$150 | AE, D, MC, V.

FRYEBURG

Jockey Cap Motel. This affordable motel is within reach of rock climbing, skiing, golf, and other activities. There is also a well-stocked country store on the premises. Restaurant, complimentary Continental breakfast. Some microwaves, some refrigerators, cable TV. Hiking. Snowmobiling. Shops. Pets allowed. | 16 Bridgton Rd., 04037 | 207/935–2306 | fax 207/935–2351 | www.jockeycapmotel.com | 7 rooms | $42–$56 ($87–$97 during Fryeburg Fair) | AE, D, MC, V.

GREENVILLE

Chalet Moosehead Motel. Most rooms here have lake views, and some have private balconies and Jacuzzis. Beds are either double or queen, and paddleboats and canoes are available at no charge. Squaw Mountain is 5 mi to the north. Picnic area. No air-conditioning, in-room data ports, some kitchenettes, some refrigerators, some in-room hot tubs, cable TV. Lake. Dock, boating. Shops. Some pets allowed (fee). | Rte. 15 Greenville Junction | 207/695–2950 | www.mooseheadlodge.com | 27 rooms | $68–$105 | AE, D, MC, V.

Greenwood Motel. This is a family-owned and well-maintained motel near Moosehead Lake, 3 mi northwest of town. Picnic area, complimentary Continental breakfast. Refrigerators, cable TV. Pool. Hiking. Business services. Pets allowed (fee). | Rte. 6 and 15, Rockwood Little Squaw 04442 | 207/695–3321 or 800/477–4386 | fax 207/695–2122 | grenqoos@moosehead.net | www.mooseheadlake.net | 16 rooms | $65–$75 | AE, D, DC, MC, V.

Kineo View Motor Lodge. This modern motel with spectacular views of Moosehead Lake and mountains is on 55 acres of unspoiled landscape 2 mi south of Greenville. Picnic area. Hot tub. Cross-country skiing. Pets allowed (fee). | Rte. 15 04441 | 207/695–4470 or 800/659–8439 | fax 207/695–4656 | www.kineoview.com | 12 rooms, 1 suite | $55–$65 | AE, MC, V.

Lakeview House. The view of Moosehead Lake is as stunning here as it is at more expensive lodges. This quiet bed-and-breakfast is only 3 mi from Greenville. Complimentary breakfast. In-room VCRs, no room phones. Some pets allowed. No smoking. | Lily Bay Rd. 04441 | 207/695–2229 | fax 207/695–8951 | www.lakeview.com | 2 rooms, 1 suite | $110–$150 | MC, V.

HANCOCK–HANCOCK POINT

Le Domaine. The French-country-style rooms, sprawling 95 wooded acres, and top-shelf dining will transport you to Provence, the region of France on which this bed-and-breakfast is modeled. Luxurious rooms, a superb wine collection, and extensive gardens are some of the other treats you will encounter. Restaurant, complimentary breakfast. Pond. Hiking, fishing. Pets allowed (fee). | U.S. 1 04640 | 207/422–3395 or 800/554–8498 | fax 207/422–2316 | www.ledomaine.com | 3 rooms, 2 suites | $110–$135 | AE, D, MC, V.

HOULTON

Scottish Inns. This chain option 1 mi south of Houlton is near businesses, U.S. 1, and the interstate. Some refrigerators, cable TV. Business services. Pets allowed (fee). | 239 Bangor St. | 207/532–2236 | fax 207/532–9893 | 43 rooms | $40–$80 | AE, D, MC, V.

Stardust Motel. Extensively renovated in 2000, this small motel will appeal to you if you prefer a no-frills, inexpensive room. Pets allowed (fee). | 672 North St., 04730 | 207/532–6538 or 800/437–8406 | fax 207/532–4143 | 11 rooms | $50 | AE, D, MC, V.

KENNEBUNKPORT

Captain Jefferds Inn. Kennebunkport has many Federal-style sea captains' homes-turned-inns and this is a good one with its solarium and antique furnishings. Rooms have fresh flowers, down-filled comforters, working fireplaces, private porches, oversize showers, and CD players. Complimentary breakfast. In-room hot tubs, no room phones, TV in common area. Pets allowed (fee). No smoking. | 5 Pearl St., 04046 | 207/967–2311 or 800/839–6844 | fax 207/967–0721 | captjeff@captainjefferdsinn.com | www.captainjefferdsinn.com | 15 rooms | $135–$285 | AE, MC, V.

Colony Hotel. A family-operated resort on a peninsula, with a surf beach and organic gardens. Bar, dining room, complimentary breakfast, room service. No air-conditioning, no TV in some rooms. Pool. Putting green. Beach, bicycles. Business services. Pets allowed (fee). No smoking. | 140 Ocean Ave. | 207/967–3331 or 800/552–2363 | fax 207/967–8738 | info-me@thecolonyhotel.com | www.thecolonyhotel.com/maine | 123 rooms in 3 buildings | $175–$425 | Closed mid-Oct.–mid-May | AE, MC, V.

Seaside Inn. This beachside hotel and cottages complex designed for family vacations is ³/₄ mi south of Kennebunkport. No air-conditioning, some kitchenettes, refrigerators, cable TV. Beach. Playground. Laundry facilities. Some pets allowed (fee). | Gooch's Beach 04046 | 207/967–4461 | fax 207/967–1135 | www.kennebunkbeach.com | 22 rooms, 10 cottages | $179–$199, $975–$1,295/wk cottages | Cottages closed Nov.–Apr. | AE, MC, V.

KINGFIELD

Herbert Inn. Built by the Carrabassett River in 1917, this inn has antiques, ornate woodwork, and marble terrazzo floors. Dining room, complimentary Continental breakfast. No air-conditioning in some rooms, in-room hot tubs, no room phones, no TV in some rooms, TV in common area. Massage. Pets allowed. | Main St. (Rte. 27) | 207/265–2000 or 800/843–4372 | fax 207/265–4594 | herbert@somtel.com | www.mainemountaininn.com | 27 rooms, 4 suites | $99–$119, $119–$149 suites | AE, D, DC, MC, V.

LEWISTON-AUBURN

Coastline Inn. This thoroughly modern facility is most notable for its location in the heart of Auburn. Complimentary Continental breakfast. In-room data ports, some microwaves, some refrigerators, cable TV. Laundry facilities. Pets allowed. | 170 Center St., 04210 | 207/784–1331 or 800/470–9494 | fax 207/786–2286 | www.coastlineinnmaine.com | 69 rooms, 3 suites | $72–$85 | AE, D, MC, V.

LINCOLN

Briarwood Motor Inn. A standard motel by Interstate 95 and 1 mi south of Lincoln that is convenient to stores and services. Refrigerators available, cable TV. Pets allowed. | U.S. 2 and Rte. 6, on Outer W. Broadway | 207/794–6731 | 24 rooms | $65 | AE, D, MC, V.

Dunloggin' Bed and Breakfast. All the rooms in this 1980 home 12 mi east of Lincoln have a view of Mattakeunk Lake, and you can borrow the Dunloggin's boat to paddle across the water. In addition to breakfast, the inn offers High Teas every Wednesday from mid-June to mid-October. Complimentary breakfast. Some room phones. Dock. Pets allowed. No smoking. | Just off Rte. 6 at Silver Lake, 04457 | 207/738–5014 | www.dunlogbnb.com | 3 rooms | $60 | D, MC, V.

LUBEC

Eastland Motel. A small, family-oriented motel in the country, set back from the highway. It's minutes from Quoddy Head State Park, the home of the famous candy-stripe lighthouse that has guided Down East mariners for generations. Complimentary Continental breakfast. Cable TV. Some pets allowed. | Rte. 189 04652 | 207/733–5501 | fax 207/733–2932 | eastland@nemaine.com | www.nemaine.com/eastland | 20 rooms | $54–$64 | AE, D, MC, V.

MACHIAS

Bluebird Motel. A rural motel 1 mi west of Machias that is near both downtown and the ocean. Cable TV. Pets allowed. | U.S. 1 04654 | 207/255–3332 | 40 rooms | $60 | AE, MC, V.

Maineland Motel. This basic roadside motel is 1 mi east of town and near ocean and downtown. Picnic area. No air-conditioning in some rooms, some refrigerators, microwaves available, cable TV. Some pets allowed. | U.S. 1, East Machias, 04630 | 207/255–3334 | maineland@memaine.com | www.freeyellow.com/members8/visitmaine | 30 rooms | $48–$53 | AE, D, DC, MC, V.

MILLINOCKET

Best Western Heritage Motor Inn. This chain motel is convenient to Baxter State Park and local industry, as well as snowmobiling and rafting. Restaurant, bar, complimentary Continental breakfast. Cable TV. Hot tubs. Exercise equipment. Business services. Some pets allowed. | 935 Central St., 04462 | 207/723–9777 | fax 207/723–9777 | 49 rooms | $89 | AE, D, DC, MC, V.

Katahdin Inn. A business and tourist hotel that is near both Baxter State Park and Millinocket's paper mills. Bar, complimentary Continental breakfast. Some microwaves, some refrigerators, cable TV, some in-room VCRs. Pool, wading pool. Hot tub. Exercise equipment. Playground. Laundry facilities. Pets allowed. | 740 Central St., 04462 | 207/723–4555 | fax 207/723–6480 | 72 rooms, 10 suites | $65–$70, $90 suites | AE, D, DC, MC, V.

MONHEGAN ISLAND

Trailing Yew. This inn reflects the island's undeveloped condition; only one building has electricity, kerosene lamps provide the lighting, and only one room has its own bath. Restaurant, complimentary breakfast and dinner. No room phones, no TV. Pets allowed. No smoking. | 8 Lobster Cove Rd., Monhegan Island, 04852 | 207/596–0440 or 800/592–2520 | 37 (36 with shared bath) | $60 per person | Closed mid-Oct.–mid-May | No credit cards.

NORWAY

Goodwin's Motel. This downtown South Paris motel is ½ mi west of Norway. Microwaves, cable TV. Cross-country skiing, downhill skiing. Pets allowed. | 191 Main St., (Rte. 26), South Paris, 04281 | 207/743–5121 or 800/424–8803 outside ME | fax 207/743–5121 | 25 rooms | $52 | AE, D, DC, MC, V.

Waterford Inn. A converted 1825 farmhouse on 25 secluded acres that is 8 mi west of Norway. Dining room, complimentary breakfast. No room phones. Cross-country skiing. Library. Pets allowed (fee). | 258 Chadbourne Rd., Waterford, 04088 | 207/583–4037 | inne@gwi.net | 9 rooms (2 with shared bath) | $75–$110 | AE.

OLD ORCHARD BEACH

Alouette Beach Resort. This friendly establishment is great for families. With four types of accommodations to choose from, you'll find a good fit. Just 10 minutes from downtown, and within walking distance to the beach, you can have an apartment or cottage with full kitchen and private porch or balcony. The main 100-year-old cottage has a dining room, two baths, and full kitchen, and sleeps eight. The motel-style rooms have kitchenettes and sleep four. Restaurant, bar, picnic area. No air-conditioning in some rooms, kitchenettes, some microwaves, cable TV. Beach. Pets allowed (fee). | 91 E. Grand Ave., 04064 | 207/934–4151 or 800/565–4151 | fax 207/934–9464 | info@alouettebeachresort.com | www.alouettebeachresort.com | 75 rooms | $77–$138, $116–$175 cottages and apartments | AE, DC, MC, V.

Deluxe Oceanfront Motel of Cottages. Families come here to relax on the beach, barbecue, and picnic. The center of town is a 15-minute walk so you are away from the hustle and bustle of it all. Some rooms have private porches or balconies. Pets allowed. | 187 E. Grand Ave. | 207/934–2460 | 12 rooms, 13 cottages | $135–$150 | MC, V.

Flagship Motel. Just across the street from the ocean, near downtown attractions, this motel has small but pleasant knotty-pine rooms. Picnic area. Refrigerators, cable TV. Pool.

Beach. Some pets allowed. | 54 W. Grand Ave., (Rte. 9) 04064 | 207/934–4866 or 800/486–1681 | www.flagshipmotel.com | 27 rooms, 8 suites, 1 cottage | $89–$109, $99–$119 suites, $675–$875/wk cottage | Closed mid-Oct.–mid-May | AE, D, MC, V.

ORONO

Best Western Black Bear Inn. Three miles from downtown Orono, this inn isn't within walking distance of anything. All rooms have two queen beds, and generally accommodate families visiting students at the University of Maine Orono. Less than half a mile from Interstate 95. Restaurant, complimentary Continental breakfast. Some microwaves, cable TV. Exercise equipment. Pets allowed. | 4 Godfrey Dr., 04473 | 207/866–7120 | fax 207/866–7433 | www.bestwestern.com | 68 rooms | $70–$99 | AE, D, DC, MC, V.

Milford Motel. A riverfront motel in a small town, northwest of Orono picnic area. Kitchenettes, cable TV. Laundry facilities. Pets allowed. | 154 Main St., (U.S. 2), Milford, 04461 | 207/827–3200 or 800/282–3330 | milford@mint.net | www.mint.net/milford.motel | 22 rooms (2 with shower only), 8 suites | $59–$84 | AE, D, MC, V.

University Motor Inn. This motel is within walking distance of the University and downtown. Complimentary Continental breakfast. Cable TV. Pool. Business services. Pets allowed. | 5 College Ave., 04473 | 207/866–4921 or 800/321–4921 | fax 207/866–4550 | www.universitymotorinn.com | 48 rooms | $56–$59 | AE, D, DC, MC, V.

PORTLAND

Best Western Merry Manor Inn. This chain option is near the airport, the Maine Mall, and U.S. 1, and is 3½ mi south of the city. Restaurant. In-room data ports, some microwaves, some refrigerators, cable TV, some in-room VCRs. Pool. Laundry facilities. Business services. Free parking. Pets allowed. | 700 Main St., South Portland, 04106 | 207/774–6151 | fax 207/871–0537 | www.bestwestern.com | 151 rooms | $107–$130 | AE, D, DC, MC, V.

The Eastland. A refurbished older hotel in the arts district, with an excellent view of the city, harbor, and mountains from the lounge. Restaurant, bar with entertainment. Cable TV. Exercise equipment. Business services, airport shuttle. Pets allowed (deposit). | 157 High St., 04101 | 207/775–5411 | fax 207/775–2872 | 204 rooms | $169–$239 | AE, D, DC, MC, V.

Howard Johnson. Near the turnpike and West Portland businesses. Restaurant, bar, room service. Some microwaves, some in-room hot tubs, cable TV. Pool. Hot tub. Exercise equipment. Video games. Laundry facilities. Business services, airport shuttle, free parking. Pets allowed (deposit). | 155 Riverside St. | 207/774–5861 | fax 207/774–5861 | www.hojoportland.com | 119 rooms | $110–$130 | AE, D, DC, MC, V.

Inn at St. John. An old-world turn-of-the-20th-century inn. Complimentary Continental breakfast. No air-conditioning in some rooms. Some microwaves, some refrigerators, cable TV. Laundry facilities. Business services, airport shuttle. Pets allowed. | 939 Congress St., 04102-3031 | 207/773–6481 or 800/636–9127 | fax 207/756–7629 | www.innatstjohn.com | 37 rooms (15 with shared bath, 15 with shower only) | $55–$160 | AE, D, DC, MC, V.

Inn by the Sea. A deluxe inn on the ocean with a swimming beach nearby, it's 6 mi southeast of Portland. Restaurant, picnic area, room service. No air-conditioning, in-room data ports, kitchenettes, microwaves, cable TV, in-room VCRs. Pool. Bicycles. Tennis. Beach. Business services. Pets allowed. No smoking. | 40 Bowery Beach Rd., Cape Elizabeth, 04107 | 207/799–3134 or 800/888–4287 | fax 207/799–4779 | innmaine@aol.com | www.innbythesea.com | 43 suites | $269–$549 | AE, D, MC, V.

Marriott at Sable Oaks. Near the airport and Maine Mall businesses, on golf course. Restaurant, bar, room service. In-room data ports, cable TV, some in-room VCRs. Pool. Hot tub. Exercise equipment. Business services, free parking. Some pets allowed. | 200 Sable Oaks Dr., South Portland, 04106 | 207/871–8000 | fax 207/871–7971 | www.marriott.com | 227 rooms | $149 | AE, D, DC, MC, V.

PRESQUE ISLE

Northern Lights Motel. This family-run motel is business and family friendly. You can picnic and barbecue on the lawn outside. Picnic area. In-room data ports, microwaves, refrigerators, cable TV, some in-room VCRs. Laundry facilities. Business services. Pets allowed. | 72 Houlton Rd., 04769 | 207/764–4441 | northernlightsmotel@yahoo.com | www.northernlightsmotel.com | 13 rooms | $40–$50 | AE, D, MC, V.

ROCKLAND

Navigator Motor Inn. This downtown hotel is near the ocean and close to state ferries. Restaurant, bar, room service. Some kitchenettes, refrigerators, cable TV. Laundry facilities. Business services. Pets allowed. | 520 Main St., 04841 | 207/594–2131 or 800/545–8026 | fax 207/594–7763 | 81 rooms | $75–$110 | AE, D, DC, MC, V.

ROCKWOOD

Birches Resort. A log cabin resort on an 11,000-acre preserve along Moosehead Lake. Canoeing trips and moose-watching cruises are offered. Bar, dining room. No air-conditioning, some kitchenettes. Hot tub, sauna. Beach, boating, fishing, bicycles. Cross-country skiing, snowmobiling. Business services. Pets allowed (fee). | Birches Rd. 04478 | 207/534–7305 or 800/825–9453 | fax 207/534–8835 | wwld@aol.com | www.birches.com | 4 rooms (all with shared bath) in lodge, 20 cottages | $45–$75, $95–$185 cottages | AE, D, MC, V.

RUMFORD

Andover Guest House. An 18th-century colonial home with Shaker-style furnishings that is popular with budget travelers and hikers. There's a dorm room with solid wood beds and ceiling fans and a large common room with a Ping-Pong table, darts, and a wood-burning stove. The kitchen is open for guest use. Dormers, bring your own blankets. The Andover Playground is across the street, with a picnic area and convenience store. Dining room. No air-conditioning, no room phones, TV in common area. Hiking. Cross-country skiing. Pets allowed. No smoking. | 28 S. Main St., Andover, about 15 mi from Rumford 04216 | 207/392–1209 | fax 508/653–7723 | info@andoverguesthouse.com | www.andoverguesthouse.com | 7 rooms, 1 dorm with 10 beds | $40–$55 rooms, $15 bunks | D, MC, V.

Coos Canyon Cabins. This large, duplex cabin has two modern, fully equipped units with electricity, kitchen, satellite TV, and a loft and can sleep up to seven people. The property, 13 mi north of Rumford, is along the Swift River where you can pan for gold or jump off 32-ft cliffs into swimming holes. It is close to hiking, snowmobiling, skiing, and the Appalachian Trail. No air-conditioning, cable TV. Cross-country skiing, snowmobiling. Pets allowed. No smoking. | Byron Village Rd., Byron, 04275 | 207/364–7446 | fax 207/369–9332 | coos_cabins@yahoo.com | www.geocities.com/coos_cabins/cooscanyoncabins | 2 units | $70 | No credit cards.

SEARSPORT

Captain A. V. Nickels Inn. This 1874 early Victorian inn on 6½ acres is on the National Register of Historic Places. Named after a sea captain of great renown who raised his family on the property, the inn has two large parlors, a TV room, and a porch looking out over Penobscot Bay. Rooms are filled with period antiques. The apartment unit has a full kitchen, French doors opening to a porch, and can sleep four to five adults. Dining room, complimentary breakfast. No room phones, TV in common area. Pets allowed. No smoking. | 127 E. Atlantic Coast Hwy., 04974 | 207/548–6691 or 800/343–5001 | www.captavseaside.com | 9 rooms (4 with shared bath) | $55–$105 | Closed Nov.–Apr. | AE, D, MC, V.

SEBAGO LAKE

Suburban Pines Motel. A motel close to the lake that is 5 mi south of Sebago Lake and on U.S. 302. It has beautiful landscaped gardens. Picnic area. Some kitchenettes, cable TV. Laundry facilities. Pets allowed (deposit). | 322 Roosevelt Trail, Windham, 04062 | 207/892–4834 | 18 rooms, 1 suite | $70–$80, $150 suite | D, MC, V.

SKOWHEGAN

Lovley's Motel. Centrally located, en route to Greenville and near I–95. Picnic area. Some kitchenettes, cable TV. Pool. Hot tub. Laundry facilities. Business services. Pets allowed. | Rte. 2, Newport, 04953 | 207/368–4311 or 800/666–6760 | 63 rooms | $59–$100 | AE, D, MC, V.

WATERVILLE

Best Western Inn. This chain option is near I–95, but also has a wooded area at rear. Restaurant, bar. Some microwaves, refrigerators, cable TV, some in-room VCRs. Pool. Hot tub. Video games. Business services, free parking. Pets allowed. | 356 Main St. | 207/873–3335 | fax 207/873–3335 | bwwtun@mint.com | www.bestwestern.com/thisco/bw/20018/20018_b.html | 86 rooms | $85–$140 | AE, D, DC, MC, V.

Budget Host Inn. The clean, efficient rooms at this inn, as well as its proximity to local attractions, makes this a good choice. There's a diner on site remodeled in a 1950s style. Restaurant, picnic area, Continental breakfast. Cable TV. Laundry facilities. Pets allowed. | 400 Kennedy Memorial Dr., 04901 | 207/873–3366 or 800/283–4678 | www.budgethost.com | 45 rooms | $80–$100 | AE, D, MC, V.

Holiday Inn. A chain hotel with amenities for families that is near the interstate and Colby College. Restaurant, bar, room service. In-room data ports, refrigerators, cable TV. Pool. Hot tub. Exercise equipment. Video games. Laundry facilities. Business services. Pets allowed. | 375 Main St., 04901 | 207/873–0111 | fax 207/872–2310 | hiwlume@mint.net | www.acadia.net/hiwat-cm | 138 rooms | $95–$105 | AE, D, DC, MC, V.

THE YORKS

York Commons Inn. This inn is on U.S. 1 and is near beaches and shopping. It has modern, landscaped grounds. Complimentary Continental breakfast. Some refrigerators, cable TV. Pool. Business services. Some pets allowed. | 362 U.S. 1, 03909 | 207/363–8903 or 800/537–5515 New York and New England | fax 207/363–1130 | 90 rooms | $95–$120 | AE, D, DC, MC, V.

Maryland

ABERDEEN

Budget Inn. The motel is 1½ mi south of downtown Aberdeen, on Rte. 40 near a shopping center and fast-food restaurants. | 24 rooms. Complimentary Continental breakfast. Cable TV. Business services. Some pets allowed. | 1112 S. Philadelphia Blvd. 21001 | 410/272–2401 | fax 410/297–8906 | $35–$50 | AE, D, DC, MC, V.

Days Inn. The motel is in a quiet suburban area, 3 mi west of downtown Aberdeen, 2 mi from the Cal Ripken Museum and 3 mi from Aberdeen Proving Ground. | 49 rooms. Complimentary Continental breakfast. Cable TV. Pool. Pets allowed (fee). | 783 W. Bel Air Ave. 21001 | 410/272–8500 | fax 410/272–5782 | www.daysinn.com | $53–$60 | AE, D, DC, MC, V.

Holiday Inn–Chesapeake House. This hotel is 2 mi east of the Aberdeen Proving Grounds and downtown Aberdeen. | 122 rooms. Restaurant, bar. Cable TV. Indoor heated pool. Gym. Some pets allowed. | 1007 Beards Hill Rd. 21001 | 410/272–8100 | fax 410/272–1714 | www.basshotels.com/holiday-inn | $104–$114 | AE, D, DC, MC, V.

ANNAPOLIS

Historic Days Inn & Suites. This suburban Days Inn is close to Annapolis Mall and 3 mi west of downtown. | 68 rooms. Complimentary Continental breakfast. Cable TV. Business services. Some pets allowed. | 2451 Riva Rd. | 410/224–4317 | fax 410/224–6010 | www.daysinn.com | $75–$109 | AE, DC, MC, V.

Loews Annapolis Hotel. Four stories of redbrick surround an atrium at this luxury chain hotel six blocks from busy City Dock. The top two floors have a view of the water. Each suite has a private balcony. Parking (fee). | 217 rooms, 11 suites. Restaurant, bar. In-room data ports, minibars, refrigerators, cable TV. Beauty salon. Gym. Business services. Some pets allowed. Gift shop. Complimentary local shuttle. | 126 West St. 21401 | 410/263–7777 | fax 410/263–7813 | info@loewsannapolis.com | www.loewsannapolis.com | $109–$209 | AE, D, DC, MC, V.

Radisson. You can walk from the Radisson to the nearby Annapolis Mall and restaurants, ½ mi north of the hotel. | 219 rooms. Restaurant, bar, room service. In-room data ports, cable TV. Pool. Gym. Business services. Some pets allowed. | 210 Holiday Ct. | 410/224–3150 | fax 410/571–1123 | www.radisson.com/annapolis | $79–$179 | AE, D, DC, MC, V.

BALTIMORE

★ **Admiral Fell Inn.** In Fells Point near the busy nightlife, this hotel consists of eight buildings dating back to the 1700s and 1800s. The rooms are furnished with 19th-century Federal pieces as well as antique reproductions. | 80 rooms. 3 restaurants, 3 bars, complimentary Continental breakfast. In-room data ports, some in-room hot tubs, cable TV. Business services. Free parking. Pets allowed. | 888 S. Broadway 21231 | 410/522–7377 or 800/292–4667 (outside MD) | fax 410/522–0707 | info@admiralfell.com | www.admiralfell.com | $139–$199 | AE, DC, MC, V.

Best Inn And Suites. Directly across the street from a mall full of stores and restaurants, this chain hotel is 7 mi from the Inner Harbor. | 147 rooms. Cable TV. Pool. Hot tub, sauna. Laundry facilities. Business services. Pets allowed (fee). | 5701 Baltimore National Pk. (Rte. 40) 21228 | 410/747–8900 | fax 410/744–3522 | $73–$83 | AE, D, DC, MC, V.

Christlen. This no-frills, family-owned motel built in 1965 is 7 mi east of downtown. The look is quite simple with basic furniture in each room and white wallpapered walls. | 28 rooms. Cable TV. Pets allowed. | 8733 Pulaski Hwy. (U.S. 40) 21237 | 410/687–1740 | fax 410/391–1847 | $51–$60 | AE, D, DC, MC, V.

Comfort Inn–Airport. The motel, 8 mi south of downtown, is 3 mi from the airport and light rail. | 188 rooms. Restaurant, bar, complimentary breakfast. In-room data ports, cable TV. Sauna. Gym. Video games. Business services, airport shuttle. Some pets allowed. | 6921 Baltimore-Annapolis Blvd. (Rte. 648) 21225 | 410/789–9100 or 800/228–5150 | fax 410/355–2854 | www.comfortinn.com | $89–$109 | AE, D, DC, MC, V.

Doubletree Inn at the Colonnade. The Victorian-influenced building is across the street from Johns Hopkins University and 3½ mi north of the Inner Harbor. | 125 rooms, 31 suites. Restaurant, bar, room service. In-room data ports, cable TV. Indoor pool. Beauty salon, hot tub. Exercise equipment. Business services. Some pets allowed. | 4 W. University Pkwy. 21218 | 410/235–5400 | fax 410/235–5572 | www.doubletreehotel.com | $109–$350 | AE, D, DC, MC, V.

Embassy Suites Hunt Valley. Just off I–83, this hotel is less than ¼ mi from the city's light rail system. It has a large tropical atrium, and rooms are all suites with balconies. The Inner Harbor is about 15 mi away. | 223 rooms. Restaurant, bar, room service. In-room data ports, cable TV, some in-room VCRs, refrigerators, some microwaves, some in-room hot tubs. 2 pools. Exercise equipment. Laundry facilities. Business services, free parking. Pets allowed. | 213 International Circle, Hunt Valley 21030 | 410/584–1400 | www.embassy-suites.com | $99–$229 | AE, D, DC, MC, V.

Holiday Inn Baltimore West. About 10 mi southwest from the Inner Harbor, this chain motel is close to the Baltimore Beltway. | 135 rooms. Restaurant, bar. In-room data ports, cable TV. Pool. Business services. Some pets allowed. | 1800 Belmont Ave. | 410/265–1400 or 800/465–4329 | fax 410/281–9569 | www.basshotels.com/holiday-inn | $69–$79 | AE, D, DC, MC, V.

Omni Inner Harbor. Baltimore's largest hotel has rooms in twin towers, and is 5 blocks east of the Inner Harbor. | 707 rooms in 2 buildings. Restaurant, bar. In-room data ports, minibars, refrigerators, cable TV. Pool. Gym. Video games. Business services, parking (fee). Pets allowed. | 101 W. Fayette St. 21201 | 410/752–1100 | fax 410/727–6223 | $169–$269 | AE, D, DC, MC, V.

Quality Inn. Within 4 blocks of Camden Yards and 1 mi of the Inner Harbor, this hotel is often packed with baseball fans coming in for a game at the stadium. | 52 rooms. Some in-room data ports, cable TV, some refrigerators, some microwaves. Outdoor pool. Pets allowed. | 1701 Russell St. | 410/727–3400 | fax 410/547–0586 | $79–$119 | AE, D, DC, MC, V.

Renaissance Harborplace. The hotel occupies a prime spot in the Inner Harbor. Rooms are light and cheerful. There is a coffee bar in the lobby and a shopping mall next door. | 622 rooms. Restaurant, bar, room service. In-room data ports, minibars, cable TV. Indoor pool. Hot tub. Exercise equipment. Shops. Business services, parking (fee). Pets allowed. | 202 E. Pratt St. 21202 | 410/547–1200 | fax 410/539–5780 | www.renaissancehotels.com/bwish | $199–$259 | AE, D, DC, MC, V.

★ **Tremont Plaza Hotel.** This 13-story brown-brick building was converted to a small European-style hostelry in 1985. The hotel is 5 blocks from the Inner Harbor. All rooms are suites with kitchens; the large suites provide comfort to couples and the business traveler. | 60 suites. Restaurant, bar, complimentary Continental breakfast. Cable TV. Business services, parking (fee). Some pets allowed. | 222 St. Paul Pl. 21202 | 410/727–2222 or 800/873–6668 | fax 410/244–1154 | www.tremontsuitehotels.com | $135–$155 | AE, D, DC, MC, V.

BETHESDA

Residence Inn Bethesda–Downtown. This 13-story all-suite hotel is in the center of town, 8 mi from Washington, D.C. Every room has its kitchen, as well as a coffee maker and a work desk. | 187 suites. Complimentary Continental breakfast. In-room data ports, kitchenettes, refrigerators, cable TV, TV in common area. Outdoor pool. Sauna. Golf courses. Exercise equipment. Laundry services. Business services, parking (fee). Some pets allowed (fee). | 7335 Wisconsin Ave., 20814 | 301/718–0200 or 800/331–3131 | fax 301/718–0679 | www.residenceinn.com | $89–$249 | AE, D, DC, MC, V.

BOWIE

Forest Hill Motel. This motel, 8 mi south of Bowie, is near the county courthouse and a handful of Upper Marlboro businesses. | 13 rooms. Some refrigerators. Some pets allowed. | 2901 U.S. 301, Upper Marlboro, 20772 | 301/627–3969 or 800/793–2828 | fax 301/627–4058 | $55 | AE, D, DC, MC, V.

CHESTERTOWN

Huntingfield Manor. Built in 1850, this B&B is in the center of 70 acres of farmland bordering the Eastern Shore. | 6 rooms, 1 cottage. Complimentary Continental breakfast. No room phones. Some pets allowed. | 4928 Eastern Neck Rd., Rock Hall 21661 | 410/639–7779 | fax 410/639–2924 | www.huntingfield.com | $95–$145 | AE, MC, V.

The Parker House. This 1876 farm house is in Chestertown's historic district, a few blocks from downtown. Guest rooms, with names like the Queen's Room and the Lincoln Room, are furnished with antiques. There is a sitting porch off the kitchen and flower gardens all around the one-acre plot. | 4 rooms. Complimentary Continental breakfast. TV in common area. Some pets allowed. | 108 Spring Ave. 21620 | 410/778–9041 | fax 410/778–7318 | parkerbb@dmv.com | $110–$125 | No credit cards.

CHEVY CHASE

Holiday Inn–Chevy Chase. Two blocks from the District's border, this 12-story hotel, built in 1975, is on tony Wisconsin Avenue amid world-renowned shops. | 213 rooms. Restaurant, bar, complimentary Continental breakfast. In-room data ports, cable TV. Pool. Gym. Business services. Some pets allowed. | 5520 Wisconsin Ave. 20815 | 301/656–1500 | fax 301/656–5045 | cornel@pop.net | www.basshotels.com/holiday-inn | $169 | AE, D, DC, MC, V.

COCKEYSVILLE

Chase Suites. Just 3 mi from the state fairgrounds and within 1 mi of restaurants and shops, this hotel's suites range from one room to two bedrooms. It serves a complimentary dinner Monday through Thursday. | 96 rooms, 24 suites. Complimentary Continental breakfast. In-room data ports, some kitchenettes, cable TV. Pool. Business services. Some pets allowed. | 10710 Beaver Dam Rd. | 410/584–7370 or 800/331–3131 | fax 410/584–7843 | $169 | AE, D, DC, MC, V.

Marriott Hunt Valley Inn. On 18 landscaped acres, this three-story hotel is just 3 mi from the light rail, which travels to downtown Baltimore. Rooms in this property, built in 1970, have easy chairs, ottomans, and floral bedspreads. | 390 rooms, 2 suites. Restaurant, bar, room service. In-room data ports, cable TV. Indoor pool, wading pool. Hot tub. Tennis. Exercise equipment. Laundry facilities. Business services, free parking. Some pets allowed. | 245 Shawan Rd., Hunt Valley, 21031 | 410/785–7000 | fax 410/785–0341 | www.marriott.com | $169 | AE, D, DC, MC, V.

COLUMBIA

Columbia Sheraton Hotel. Entertainment of all sorts is easily available when staying at this hotel across the street from the Columbia Mall and just 1 mi from the Merriweather Post Pavilion. It's also just 16 mi from BWI airport. | 288 rooms. Restaurant, bar. In-room data ports, refrigerators, cable TV. Pool. Business services. Some pets allowed. | 10207 Wincopin Cir. 21044 | 410/730–3900 or 800/638–2817 | fax 410/730–1290 | sales@ columbiainn | www.columbiainn.com | $99–$169 | AE, D, DC, MC, V.

CUMBERLAND

Holiday Inn. Built in 1972, this six-story hotel is in downtown Cumberland and within 1 mi of the train station and an antiques mall. | 130 rooms, 2 suites. Restaurant, bar. In-room data ports, room service, cable TV. Outdoor pool. Gym. Business services. Airport shuttle. Some pets allowed. | 100 S. George St. 21502 | 301/724–8800 | fax 301/724–4001 | www.basshotels.com/holiday-inn | $109–$159 | AE, D, DC, MC, V.

Oak Tree Inn. Five miles west of La Vale, this motel has a 24-hour diner and three meeting rooms. | 82 rooms. Restaurant. In-room data ports, microwaves, refrigerators, cable TV, VCRs. Laundry facilities. Pets allowed (fee). | 12310 Winchester Rd., La Vale 21502 | 301/729–6706 | www.hereintown.com | $69 | AE, D, DC, MC, V.

EASTON

Days Inn. Floor-to-ceiling windows brighten the lobby of this motel on a busy strip near shops and restaurants. | 80 rooms. Complimentary Continental breakfast. Some refrigerators, cable TV. Pool, wading pool. Some pets allowed. | 7018 Ocean Gateway (U.S. 50) 21601 | 410/822–4600 | fax 410/820–9723 | bsdiggs@ix.netcom.com | www.daysinn.com | $103–$115 | AE, D, DC, MC, V.

ELKTON

Knights Inn. You can walk to shops and restaurants from this economical in-town motel. | 119 rooms. Cable TV. Pool. Pets allowed. No smoking. | 262 Belle Hill Rd. 21921 | 410/392–6680 | fax 410/392–0843 | $49–$75 | AE, D, MC, V.

Sutton Motel. This family-owned motel is within 5 mi of Meadow Park. | 11 rooms. No room phones. Some pets allowed. | 405 E. Pulaski Hwy. (U.S. 40) | 410/398–3830 | $34–$36 | No credit cards.

Sinking Springs Herb Farm. This 130-acre farm is the home of the Bristoll Sycamore, a 400-year-old tree. It's immensely quiet, a truly romantic place to spend the night. The main entrance is on Elk Forest Road. | 1 room. Complimentary breakfast. Pets allowed (fee). | 234 Blair Shore Rd. 21921 | 410/398–5566 | www.cecilcounty.org | $93 | MC, V.

FREDERICK

Hampton Inn. This hotel 1 mi south of town is convenient to shopping plazas and restaurants. The health club across the street is free to guests. | 161 rooms, 2 suites. Restaurant, bar. Complimentary Continental breakfast. In-room data ports, cable TV. Pool. Exercise equipment. Pets allowed (fee). | 5311 Buckeystown Pike 21704 | 301/698–2500 | fax 301/695–8735 | $89 rooms, $150 suites | AE, D, DC, MC, V.

GAITHERSBURG

Comfort Inn–Shady Grove. Every room is different in this chain motel, which exhibits the work of local artists in the lobby. Restaurants and stores are close at hand, and a Washington subway stop is just a ½ mi away. | 127 rooms. Complimentary breakfast. In-room data ports, refrigerators, cable TV. Pool. Exercise equipment. Laundry facilities. Business services, free parking. Some pets allowed. | 16216 Frederick Rd. 20877 | 301/330–0023 | fax 301/258–1950 | www.comfortinn.com | $99–$119 | AE, D, DC, MC, V.

Hilton–Gaithersburg. Directly across from the Lake Forest Mall and near a busy commercial corridor, this rustic-looking hotel is geared toward business travelers. | 301 rooms. Restaurant, bar. In-room data ports, cable TV. Indoor pool. Exercise equipment. Business services. Some pets allowed. | 620 Perry Pkwy. 20877 | 301/977–8900 | fax 301/869–8597 | www.hilton.com | $99–$109 | AE, D, DC, MC, V.

Holiday Inn–Gaithersburg. This property on I–172 is near a busy shopping area. If you don't have time to check out the local scenery, don't worry. The rooms have panoramic paintings of local lakes and woods. | 301 rooms. Restaurant, bar, room service. In-room data ports, refrigerators, cable TV. Indoor pool. Hot tub. Exercise equipment. Video games. Laundry facilities. Business services. Some pets allowed. | 2 Montgomery Village Ave. 20879 | 301/948–8900 | fax 301/258–1940 | www.basshotels.com/holiday-inn | $99–$124 | AE, D, DC, MC, V.

GRANTSVILLE

Holiday Inn–Grantsville. A fireplace in the lobby and woodland scenes in the rooms give this place a woodsy charm much like the nearby state parks. | 100 rooms. Restaurant, bar. In-room data ports, cable TV. Pool. Sauna. Health club. Business services. Some pets allowed. | 2541 Chestnut Ridge Rd. 21536 | 301/895–5993 | fax 301/895–3410 | www. basshotels.com/holiday-inn | $59–$69 | AE, D, DC, MC, V.

HAGERSTOWN

Four Points by Sheraton. Just off exit 32 of I–70, this hotel—with contemporary stylings such as soft lighting, mirrors and tiled floors—is only 8 mi from the airport and Antietam. | 108 rooms. Restaurant, bar, complimentary Continental breakfast, room service. Cable TV. Pool. Exercise equipment. Business services, airport shuttle, free parking. Some pets allowed. | 1910 Dual Hwy. (U.S. 40) 21740 | 301/790–3010 | fax 301/790–0633 | www.sheraton.com | $89–$99 | AE, D, DC, MC, V.

Venice Inn. Convenient to downtown, shopping centers and restaurants, this property was remodeled in 1984 to slightly resemble a Venetian inn. The light-filled lobby is colorful with pillars that go to the second floor. | 222 rooms. Restaurant, bar, room service. Refrigerators, cable TV. Pool. Exercise equipment. Business services, free parking. Some pets allowed. | 431 Dual Hwy. (U.S. 40) 21740 | 301/733–0830 | fax 301/733–4978 | $60–$70 | AE, D, DC, MC, V.

LAUREL

Comfort Suites Laurel Lakes. Near restaurants, shopping centers, and movie theaters, this hotel has large rooms with pull-out sofas. | 119 suites. Complimentary Continental breakfast. Refrigerators, microwaves, cable TV. Indoor pool. Hot tub. Exercise equipment. Laundry facilities. Business services. Some pets allowed. | 14402 Laurel Pl. 20707 | 301/206–2600 | fax 301/725–0056 | www.comfortinn.com | $99–$129 | AE, D, DC, MC, V.

MCHENRY

Comfort Inn–Deep Creek Lake. Off U.S. 219 and about ¼ mi from Deep Creek Lake, this motel is just a short drive from area restaurants. Country furnishings give the rooms a cozy charm. | 76 rooms. Complimentary Continental breakfast. Some in-room hot tubs, cable TV. Some pets allowed. | 2704 Deep Creek Dr. 21541 | 301/387–4200 | fax 301/387–4204 | www.comfortinn.com | $60–$80 | AE, D, DC, MC, V.

Point View Inn. A private beach and dock on Deep Creek Lake make this old-fashioned, restful inn a perfect stopover for boaters. Antiques accent the small but homey rooms. | 19 rooms. Restaurant, bar, complimentary Continental breakfast. Cable TV. Pool. Some pets allowed (fee). | 21541 Deep Creek Dr. 21541 | 301/387–5555 | fax 301/387–5335 | $40–$85 | AE, MC, V.

NORTH EAST
Crystal Inn. This hotel sits at the top of Center Drive off I–95 north of town. Large windows, comfy chairs, and flowers welcome you to the lobby. The spacious rooms favor a burgundy color scheme and provide irons and ironing boards. | 92 rooms. Picnic area, complimentary Continental breakfast. In-room data ports, microwaves, refrigerators, cable TV, in-room VCRs. Indoor pool. Hot tub. Gym. Laundry facilities, laundry service. Business services. Pets allowed. | 1 Center Dr. 21901 | 410/287–7100 or 800/631–3803 | fax 410/287–7109 | www.crystalinns.com | $129 | AE, D, DC, MC, V.

OAKLAND
The Board Room Motel. The tiled bathrooms, mauve carpet, and tan painted walls lend a freshness to the guest rooms. A family restaurant and health club are adjacent to the motel. | 13 rooms. Some refrigerators, cable TV. Laundry facilities. Pets allowed (fee). | 12678 Garrett Hwy. 21550 | 301/334–2126 | $50–$55 | AE, D, DC, MC, V.

OCEAN CITY
Safari. Two yellow brick buildings, one with four floors and the other with three, make up this family-friendly motel on the boardwalk. | 46 rooms. Cable TV. Some pets allowed (fee). | 13th St., at the boardwalk 21842 | 410/289–6411 or 800/787–2183 | $135–$170 | Closed Nov.–Mar. | AE, D, DC, MC, V.

Sheraton Fontainebleau. This highrise hotel is on Ocean City's "Golden Mile." The rooms, some with ocean views, are done in floral patterns. | 250 rooms. 3 restaurants, bar. In-room data ports, some kitchenettes, microwaves, refrigerator, cable TV. Indoor pool. Beauty salon, hot tub. Gym, beach. Video games. Business services, airport shuttle. Some pets allowed (fee). | 10100 Coastal Hwy. | 410/524–3535 | fax 410/524–3834 | www.sheratonoc.com | $249–$309 | AE, D, DC, MC, V.

PIKESVILLE
Ramada Inn. A courtyard that runs both indoors and out distinguishes this motel from its run-of-the-mill brethren. Many of the large rooms have a pool view. This property is about 15 minutes by car to Baltimore's Inner Harbor. | 108 rooms. Restaurant, complimentary Continental breakfast. Pool. In-room data ports, refrigerators, cable TV. Business services. Some pets allowed. | 1721 Reisterstown Rd. 21208 | 410/486–5600 | fax 410/484–9377 | www.ramada.com | $79–$89 | AE, D, DC, MC, V.

POCOMOKE CITY
Days Inn. On a busy highway, this motel is near several restaurants. Inside the stucco building, the large rooms are furnished in a contemporary style. | 87 rooms. Complimentary Continental breakfast. In-room data ports, cable TV. Pool. Business services. Some pets allowed. | 1540 Ocean Hwy. (U.S. 13) 21851 | 410/957–3000 | fax 410/957–3147 | www.daysinn.com | $53–$79 | AE, D, DC, MC, V.

Quality Inn. This motel, 3 mi south of downtown Pocomoke, has large rooms with a muted beige-and-white color scheme. | 64 rooms. Pool, wading pool. In-room data ports, cable TV. Refrigerators, microwaves in some rooms. Business services. Some pets allowed. | 825

Ocean Hwy. (U.S. 13) | 410/957–1300 | fax 410/957–9329 | www.qualityinn.com | $67–$72 | AE, D, DC, MC, V.

ST. MARYS CITY

Days Inn. Rooms are standard, and the lobby is filled with plants. There's a movie theater next door, and shops in walking distance. | 165 rooms. Complimentary Continental breakfast. Refrigerators, cable TV. Pool. Laundry facilities. Some pets allowed. | 21847 Three Notch Rd., Lexington Park 20653; Rte. 235 | 301/863–6666 | fax 301/863–4691 | www.daysinn.com | $67–$71 | AE, D, DC, MC, V.

ST. MICHAELS

★ **Inn at Perry Cabin.** Built right after the War of 1812, this white colonial mansion is perched on the banks of the Miles River. Each room is distinct. Some have Laura Ashley fabrics and wallpaper, while others are furnished with English and early-American antiques. The hotel gets its name from Commodore Oliver Hazard Perry, the War of 1812 veteran who designed it after his own cabin on the USS Niagara. | 35 rooms, 6 suites. Restaurant, complimentary breakfast, afternoon tea, room service. In-room data ports, cable TV. Pool. Hot tub, sauna, massage. Tennis courts. Exercise equipment. No kids under 10. Some pets allowed. Business services, free parking. | 308 Watkins La. 21663 | 410/745–2200 or 800/722–2949 | fax 410/745–3348 | www.perrycabin.com | $295–$795 | AE, DC, MC, V.

SALISBURY

Comfort Inn. On the main road through the Delmarva Peninsula, this landscaped hotel is surrounded by shops and restaurants. | 96 rooms, 34 suites. Complimentary Continental breakfast. Some refrigerators, cable TV. Business services. Some pets allowed. | 2701 N. Salisbury Blvd. (U.S. 13) 21801 | 410/543–4666 | fax 410/749–2639 | www.comfortinn.com | $70–$140 | AE, D, DC, MC, V.

Howard Johnson. On busy U.S. 13, minutes from The Centre at Salisbury mall, this motel has standard rooms. | 123 rooms. Restaurant, complimentary Continental breakfast. Cable TV. Pool. Laundry facilities. Business services. Some pets allowed. | 2625 N. Salisbury Blvd. (U.S. 13) 21801 | 410/742–7194 | fax 410/742–5194 | www.hojosalisbury.com | $65–$120 | AE, D, DC, MC, V.

THURMONT

Super 8. Near state and national parks and 5 minutes from Mount St. Mary's College, this motel has basic rooms. | 46 rooms. In-room data ports, cable TV. Some pets allowed. | 300 Tippin Dr. 21788 | 301/271–7888 | $53–$68 | AE, D, DC, MC, V.

TOWSON

Ramada Inn. This two-story hotel off the Baltimore Beltway is less than 2 mi from Towson University. The rooms are furnished with modular, wood-veneer furniture, and the grounds here are well-kept. Restaurant, bar, room service. | 122 rooms. Some refrigerators, some microwaves, cable TV. Outdoor pool. Tennis courts. Laundry service. Business services. Pets allowed. | 8712 Loch Raven Blvd. 21286 | 410/823–8750 | fax 410/823–8644 | $52–$82 | AE, D, DC, MC, V.

WALDORF

Days Inn. Just off Rte. 301 this hotel is near shopping plazas. | 99 rooms. Complimentary Continental breakfast. In-room data ports, cable TV. Business services. Some pets allowed. | 11370 Days Ct. 20603 | 301/932–9200 | fax 301/843–9816 | www.daysinn.com | $55–$80 | AE, D, DC, MC, V.

Howard Johnson Express Inn. This single story hotel with pink interior is cozy, and you're ½ mi from restaurants and a shopping mall. | 109 rooms. Picnic area, complimentary Continental breakfast. In-room safes, cable TV. Pool. Business services. Some pets allowed. | 3125 S. Crain Hwy. (U.S. 301 and Rte. 228) 20602 | 301/932–5090 | fax 301/932–5090 | www.hojo.com | $64–$80 | AE, D, DC, MC, V.

WESTMINSTER

Best Western. A fireplace in the lounge makes this chain motel cozier than usual. Both Western Maryland College and a golf course are across the street; a shopping center and restaurants are next door. | 101 rooms. Complimentary Continental breakfast. Cable TV. Pool, hot tub. Business services. Some pets allowed. | 451 Western Maryland College Dr. 21158 | 410/857–1900 | fax 410/857–9584 | www.bestwesternwestminster.com | $69–$179 | AE, D, DC, MC, V.

Days Inn. Behind a shopping center, this three-story motel is in a busy commercial area just off Rte. 140. | 96 rooms. In-room data ports, some refrigerators, cable TV. Pool. Business services. Some pets allowed. | 25 S. Cranberry Rd. 21158 | 410/857–0500 or 800/336–DAYS | fax 410/857–1407 | www.daysinn.com | $65–$92 | AE, D, DC, MC, V.

Massachusetts

AMHERST

Lord Jeffery Inn. This rambling neo-Colonial inn overlooking the town common is at the edge of the Amherst College campus. Some of its rooms face the town common, while others face historic churches nearby, and some have balconies that overlook a garden; all are decorated with darker New England colors. Restaurants, bar. In-room data ports, cable TV. Pets allowed (fee). | 30 Boltwood Ave. | 413/253–2576 | fax 413/256–6152 | www.pinnacle-inns.com/lordjefferyinn | 48 rooms, 8 suites | $99–$189, $149–$189 suites | AE, DC, MC, V.

ANDOVER AND NORTH ANDOVER

Hawthorn Suites Andover. This extended-stay hotel caters to the business traveler with preferred pricing for 30-day stays and shuttle service to specific companies in Andover. Appetizers and fruit juices are served in the Hawthorn Room on Mondays through Thursdays. The property is just off exit 45 on Route 93. Complimentary breakfast. In-room data ports, kitchenettes, cable TV. Outdoor pool. Exercise room. Laundry facilities, laundry services. Business services. Pets allowed. | 4 Riverside Dr., Andover 01810 | 978/475–6000 or 800/527–1133 | fax 978/475–6639 | hawthorn.com | 84 rooms | $124–$159 studio, $134–$169 1–bedroom suite, $169–$209 2–bedroom suite | AE, D, DC, MC, V.

Wyndham Andover. This hotel is off Route 93, near Canobie Lake Park and Rockingham Park in New Hampshire. It has a marble lobby and the rooms have oak desks, which are ideal for business travelers. Behind the hotel there is a walking/bike trail. Restaurant, bar. In-room data ports, some refrigerators, cable TV. Indoor pool. Hot tub. Gym. Pets allowed. | 123 Old River Rd., Andover 01810 | 978/975–3600 or 800/WYNDHAM | fax 978/975–2664 | www.wyndham.com | 293 rooms | $79–$149 | AE, D, DC, MC, V.

AQUINNAH (MARTHA'S VINEYARD)

Duck Inn. The inn is named for the wild ducks that visit the 5½-acre property and also for the low spots in the house where you must duck to avoid bumping your head. The first floor of this 200-year-old farmhouse is built of granite; there's also a granite fireplace. Second-floor guest rooms have views of the ocean and Gay Head lighthouse. It's a short walk to the beach or to Gay Head cliff. Complimentary breakfast. No air-conditioning, cable

TV in 1 room. Hot tub, massage. Pets allowed in 1 guest room. | 160 State Rd. 02535 | 508/645–9018 | fax 508/645–2790 | 5 rooms | $85–$200 | Closed Jan.–Mar. | MC, V.

BOSTON

Boston Back Bay Hilton. A renovated hotel in Back Bay that is near Symphony Hall, Fenway Park, and one street over from Newbury Street, Boston's fashion and gallery row. The rooms overlook the downtown area, Fenway, or the Charles River. The hotel also has a sundeck. Restaurant, bar. In-room data ports, cable TV. Indoor pool. Gym. Business services. Some pets allowed. | 40 Dalton St. 02115–3123 | 617/236–1100 or 800/HILTONS | fax 617/867–6104 | www.bostonbackbay.hilton.com | 385 rooms, 9 suites | $215–$365, $450 suites, $1,000 3–bedroom suites | AE, D, DC, MC, V.

★ **Boston Harbor Hotel.** An archway framing a view of Boston Harbor is this hotel's most striking feature. Each guest room has a city or harbor view. The public areas are embellished by one of the nation's finest private antiquarian map collections. The hotel stands just in front of the Logan Airport water shuttle in Boston Harbor, just two blocks from the subway, and within walking distance of attractions such as the New England Aquarium. A chauffeured town car is offered to guests at no charge, based upon availability. 2 restaurants, bar with entertainment. In-room data ports, minibars, no-smoking floors, room service, cable TV. Indoor pool. Beauty treatments, Hot tub, message, spa. Gym. Business services. Parking (fee). Some pets allowed. | 70 Rowes Wharf 02110 | 617/439–7000 or 800/752–7077 | fax 617/345–6799 | www.bhh.com | 230 rooms, 26 suites | $405–$685, $495–$1,750 suites | AE, D, DC, MC, V.

THE COMMON DOG

Picture a cozy New England bed-and-breakfast, five handsome Cape Cod-style cottages, and an environment that encourages both relaxation and conviviality. Not for you—but for your dog. The Common Dog in Everett, Massachusetts, just ten minutes from downtown Boston, is an uncommon place to leave your dog. She can snooze the day away on a cedar-filled bed or curl up on an inviting sofa. A 5,000-sq ft yard is perfect for sunbathing or tag, and there are plenty of human buddies around to keep order, throw balls, rub tummies, and pull on the other end of a rope in a tug-of-war. Day school, training classes, and grooming services are available, and you can buy presents for your pet at the Barker's Boutique. If you're staying in a Boston hotel, Common Dog's familiar van will pick up your buddy at one of three regular stops: in Beacon Hill, outside the Bull & Finch, the bar made famous in the TV show "Cheers"; at Copley Square; and in the South End. The shuttle bus is included in the price and the dogs are seated and buckled in for the ride to Everett. Common Dog can board 30 dogs and has day care facilities for around 45. Call well in advance for reservations. Your dog will have to pass an informal interview and demonstrate good social skills, and you'll have to provide complete vaccination records. Contact: 22 Park Terr., Everett, MA 02149, 617/381-6363, www.commondog.com.

Colonnade Hotel. An independent European-style hotel in Back Bay with a modern decor and the only rooftop pool in Boston. Its restaurant, Brasserie Jo, is Boston's only authentic French-style brasserie. There is a subway stop near the hotel's front entrance. The hotel provides bathrobes and umbrellas to its guests. Restaurant, bar. In-room data ports, minibars, room service, cable TV. Pool (in season). Gym. Baby-sitting. Some pets allowed. | 120 Huntington Ave. 02116 | 617/424–7000 or 800/962–3030 | fax 617/424–1717 | www.colonnadehotel.com | 285 rooms, 12 suites | $225–$350, $450–$1,050 suites | AE, D, DC, MC, V.

Eliot Suite Hotel. This luxury all-suite property in Back Bay is on Boston's grandest street, Commonwealth Avenue. It has suites with marble baths and period furnishings as well as modern amenities including fax machines. Restaurant. In-room data ports, minibars, cable TV. Video games. Laundry services. Business services. Some pets allowed. Parking (fee). | 370 Commonwealth Ave. 02215 | 617/267–1607 or 800/44–ELIOT | fax 617/536–9114 | www.eliothotel.com | 16 rooms, 79 suites | $235–$295, $235–$395 suites | AE, DC, MC, V.

★ **Fairmont Copley Plaza.** This 1912 palatial hotel, in Boston's Back Bay, is a splendid example of French and Venetian Renaissance design. It has crystal chandeliers and mirrors, gilt coffered ceilings, and trompe l'oeil paintings. Every American president since William Taft has visited the hotel; more weddings have taken place in the Oval Room than in Trinity Church next door. The hotel is a member of Historic Hotels of America. Its neighbors in Copley Square include Hancock Tower, Trinity Church, and the Boston Public Library. Restaurant, bar with piano entertainment and jazz trio. In-room data ports, no-smoking floors, room service, cable TV. Barbershop, beauty salon. Gym. Shops. Business services. Some pets allowed. | 138 St. James Ave. 02116 | 617/267–5300 or 800/527–4727 | fax 617/247–6681 | boston@fairmont.com | www.fairmont.com | 379 rooms, 61 suites | $259–$349, $349–$1,500 suites | AE, DC, MC, V.

★ **Four Seasons Hotel Boston.** The decor of this luxury hotel captures Boston's old-world charm; its location in the Back Bay across from the Public Garden makes it convenient to every historic entertainment and cultural attraction in the city. Guests are offered town-car transportation to all downtown locations and special services such as twice-daily housekeeping. 2 restaurants, bar with entertainment, complimentary Continental breakfast, room service. In-room data ports, in-room safes, minibars, cable TV. Indoor pool. Hot tub, massage, spa. Health club. Laundry service. Business services. Some pets allowed. Parking (fee). | 200 Boylston St. 02116 | 617/338–4400 | fax 617/423–0154 | www.fourseasons.com | 288 rooms, 72 suites | $465–$505, $645–$1,950 1–bedroom suites, $2,300–$3,600 2–bedroom suites | AE, D, DC, MC, V.

Hilton Boston Logan Airport. This hotel offers shuttle service to airport terminals, the subway and the water shuttle. Restaurant, bar, snack bar, room service. In-room data ports, cable TV. Massage, sauna. Gym. Indoor pool. Shops. Business services. Airport shuttle. Pets allowed. | Logan Airport | 617/568–6700 | fax 617/568–6800 | www.hilton.com | 600 rooms, 4 suites | $380, $599 1–room suite, $750 2–room suite | AE, D, DC, MC, V.

Howard Johnson Hotel—Boston/Fenway. Next to Fenway Park, this hotel is ideal for baseball fans, and is close to Harvard Medical School and area colleges and universities. Rooms have queen- and king-size beds and some also have views of the ballpark. Restaurant, bar with entertainment. No-smoking rooms, cable TV. Pool. Business services. Free parking. Pets allowed. | 1271 Boylston St. 02215 | 617/267–8300 | fax 617/267–2763 | 94 rooms | $115–$199 | AE, D, DC, MC, V.

Howard Johnson Hotel—Boston/Kenmore. This central, Kenmore Square hotel is next to the Boston University campus, one block from the subway and two blocks from Fenway Park. Restaurant, 2 bars with entertainment. Cable TV. Indoor pool. Free parking. Pets allowed. | 575 Commonwealth Ave. 02215 | 617/267–3100 | fax 617/424–1045 | 179 rooms | $135–$235 | AE, D, DC, MC, V.

★ **The Ritz-Carlton, Boston.** A private club was originally planned for this Back Bay spot but the mayor persuaded the developer to build a deluxe hotel instead. Since its opening in 1927, this hotel has set the standard for elegance in Boston. Revered traditions include afternoon tea in the Lounge, gourmet cuisine in the original award-winning Dining Room, and dining and dancing to big band–era music on the Rooftop. New traditions include private dining in the Wine Cellar and Caviar Indulgence in the Lounge. Guest rooms have views of the Public Garden, Newbury Street, or Commonwealth Avenue. Suites have wood-burning fireplaces. 2 restaurants, bar, room service. In-room data ports, minibars, cable TV. Barbershop, massage, spa. Gym. Shops. Business services. Some pets allowed. | 15 Arlington St. 02117 | 617/536–5700 | fax 617/536–1335 | www.ritzcarlton.com | 275 rooms, 42 suites | $445, $545–$1,210 suites | AE, D, DC, MC, V.

Sheraton Boston Hotel. With more than 360,000 square ft of meeting space, the Sheraton in Back Bay is Boston's largest convention hotel. It is attached to the Hynes Convention Center and Prudential Center shopping mall. Its rooms have views of the city, the Charles River, or the pool. Restaurant, bars with entertainment. In-room data ports, cable TV. Indoor pool. Hot tub. Gym. Laundry service. Business services. Pets allowed. | 39 Dalton St. 02199 | 617/236–2000 | fax 617/236–1702 | www.sheraton.com | 1,071 rooms, 130 suites | $299–$349, $350–$1,800 suites | AE, D, DC, MC, V.

Swissôtel. Boston's only Swiss-owned hotel is in Downtown Crossing and has a traditional Boston look with fine art, antiques, crystal chandeliers, rich wood paneling, and marble accents throughout the property. There are Swiss touches, too, such as Swiss chocolates at check-in and muesli (cereal), Bundnerfleisch (air-dried beef), and a variety of Swiss wines served in the hotel restaurant. Restaurant, bar with entertainment. In-room data ports, no-smoking floors, room service, cable TV. Indoor pool. Hot tub, massage, sauna, steam room. Health club. Business services. Some pets allowed. | 1 Ave. de Lafayette 02111 | 617/451–2600 or 800/621–9200 | fax 617/451–2198 | www.swissotel.com | 501 rooms, 27 suites | $325–$425, $475–$2,200 suites | AE, D, DC, MC, V.

BOURNE (CAPE COD)

Bay Motor Inn. This motel features landscaped grounds with gardens, fresh-cut flowers in guest rooms (in season), and senior discounts. The town center, Buzzards Bay, the Cape Cod Canal, and the bike trail are within walking distance. Picnic area. Some kitchenettes, cable TV. Pool. Some pets allowed (fee). | 223 Main St. | 508/759–3989 | fax 508/759–3199 | www.capecod.com/baymotorinn | 17 rooms | $79–$110 | Closed Nov.–Mar. | AE, D, MC, V.

BRAINTREE

Days Inn. The three-story property offers typical accommodations with neat and comfortable rooms. The real attraction is the location at I–93, leading to Boston, and Route 3 to Plymouth and Cape Cod. It's a five-minute drive to the subway. A Boston sightseeing trolley makes daily pickups/drop-offs. Complimentary Continental breakfast. In-room data ports, some microwaves, some refrigerators, cable TV. Gym. Laundry facilities. Business services. Some pets allowed (fee). | 190 Wood Rd. | 781/848–1260 or 800/DAYS–INN | fax 781/848–9799 | 104 rooms, 2 suites | $89–$119, $109–$119 business class, $199 suites | AE, D, DC, MC, V.

Holiday Inn Express. This hotel is within a 20-minute drive from Boston and Plymouth, and 10 minutes south of Braintree. Discounts available to guests at local restaurants and attractions. Complimentary Continental breakfast. In-room data ports, some microwaves, some refrigerators, cable TV. Laundry service. Business services. Pets allowed (fee). | 909 Hingham St., Rockland 02370 | 781/871–5660 | fax 781/871–7255 | www.holiday-inn.com | 76 rooms, 5 minisuites | $114, $135 minisuites | AE, D, DC, MC, V.

BREWSTER (CAPE COD)

Greylin House. This Greek Revival house built in 1837 contains period reproductions along with the genuine articles. Breakfast often includes pastries made with fruits and berries grown on the property. The house is within walking distance of the beach and several good restaurants. Picnic area, complimentary breakfast. Some pets allowed (fee). No kids under 8. No smoking. | 2311 Main St. | 508/896–0004 or 800/233–6662 | fax 508/896–0005 | www.capecodtravel.com/greylin | 5 rooms | $85–$125 | Closed Dec.–Mar. | AE, D, MC, V.

High Brewster Inn. This 3-acre property, 2 mi from the center of town, consists of a house built in the 18th century and four cottages. The main inn contains antique furnishings, overlooks Lower Mill Pond, and is next to an old gristmill and herring run. Each cottage has a private yard and deck, living room with fireplace, kitchen, bedroom, and bath. Restaurant, complimentary Continental breakfast, room service. Some room phones. Some pets allowed (fee). No smoking. | 964 Satucket Rd. | 508/896–3636 or 800/203–2634 | fax 508/896–3734 | 2 rooms in main house, 2 cottages, 2 houses | $95–$115, $165–$220 cottages ($1,000–$1,400/wk) | Closed Jan.–Mar. | AE, MC, V.

BROOKLINE

Bertram Inn. This restored turn-of-the-century merchant's home features oak and cherry paneling, antiques, and fireplaces in two rooms. It has complimentary beverage and snack service. Dining room, complimentary Continental breakfast. In-room data ports, cable TV, in-room VCRs and movies. Free parking. Some pets allowed. No smoking. | 92 Sewall Ave. 02446 | 617/566–2234 or 800/295–3822 | fax 617/277–1887 | www.bertraminn.com | $169–$239 | 14 rooms | AE, MC, V.

BURLINGTON

Homestead Village Guest Studios. This budget-priced hotel for extended-stay visitors provides larger-than-average studio rooms without unnecessary frills. Each room has a fully stocked kitchen, including cookware and a coffeemaker. In-room data ports, kitchenettes, microwaves, refrigerators, cable TV. Laundry facilities, laundry service. Pets allowed (fee). | 40 South Ave. 01803 | 781/359–9099 | fax 781/359–9044 | www.stdyhsd.com | 140 rooms | $109 1–6 nights; $89 7–29 nights; $69 30 or more nights | AE, D, DC, MC, V.

Ramada Inn. You'll find clean, basic accommodations convenient to the sights of Boston, Salem, Lexington, and Concord, as well as corporate offices along Route 128. Restaurant, bar with entertainment. In-room data ports, cable TV. Pool. Gym. Business services. Local shuttle. Pets allowed. | 15 Middlesex Canal Park Rd., Woburn 01801 | 781/935–8760 or 800/2–RAMADA | fax 781/938–1790 | www.ramadawo.com | 195 rooms, 24 suites | $149–$169, $169–$189 executive room, $229–$259 suites | AE, D, DC, MC, V.

CAMBRIDGE

★ **Charles Hotel in Harvard Square.** This hotel features simple Shaker-style furniture. There are views of the Charles River, Harvard Square, and the Boston skyline from the top floor. The Regattabar features top jazz performers most evenings. 2 restaurants, bar with entertainment, room service. In-room data ports, minibars, cable TV. Indoor pool. Barbershop, beauty salon, hot tub, massage, spa. Gym. Shops. Laundry service. Business services, parking (fee). Some pets allowed. | 1 Bennett St. 02138 | 617/864–1200 or 800/882–1818 | fax 617/864–5715 | 296 rooms, 45 suites | $239–$439, $539 suites | AE, DC, MC, V.

Howard Johnson Cambridge. This moderately priced hotel is on the Charles River between Harvard and MIT, 3 mi from downtown Boston and a 10-minute walk to the subway. Inside this 16-story hotel are a Greek restaurant and a Japanese steak house. 2 restaurants, bar. In-room data ports, some refrigerators, cable TV. Indoor pool. Baby-sitting. Business services, free parking. Local shuttle. Pets allowed. | 777 Memorial Dr. 02139 | 617/492–7777 | fax 617/492–6038 | 205 rooms | $135–$245 | AE, D, DC, MC, V.

Residence Inn by Marriott. This property is designed for guests wishing to stay five nights or longer. It contains studio units and one- and two-bedroom suites with fully equipped kitchens, living rooms, bedrooms, and bathrooms; some have fireplaces. Complimentary Continental breakfast. In-room data ports, kitchenettes, cable TV. Indoor pool. Hot tub. Gym. Laundry facilities. Business services. Pets allowed (fee). | 6 Cambridge Center | 617/349–0700 or 800/331–3131 | fax 617/547–8504 | www.residenceinn.com | 221 suites | $169 | AE, D, DC, MC, V.

CENTERVILLE (CAPE COD)

Centerville Corners Motor Lodge. In the heart of Centerville Village, across the street from Four Seas Ice Cream Shop and a seven-minute walk from Craigville Beach. Guest rooms are decorated in typical Cape Cod fashion, with lots of blues and boats. Picnic area, complimentary Continental breakfast (in season). Cable TV. Indoor pool. Sauna. Pets allowed (fee). | 1338 Craigville Rd. 02632 | 508/775–7223 or 800/242–1137 | fax 508/775–4147 | www.centervillecorners.com | 48 rooms | $105–$140 | Closed Oct.–mid-Apr. | AE, D, MC, V.

CHICOPEE

Comfort Inn Parwick Center. This full-service chain is just a short distance from exit 5 of the Massachusetts Turnpike. Restaurant, bar with entertainment, complimentary Continental breakfast. Cable TV. Barbershop, beauty salon. Gym. Video games. Laundry facilities, laundry service. Business services. Pets allowed. | 450 Memorial Dr. 01020 | 413/739–7311 or 800/221–2222 | fax 413/594–5005 | www.bestlodging.com | 100 rooms | $49–$109 | AE, D, DC, MC, V.

Super 8 Chicopee Motor Lodge. This economic option is near I–91 and I–90. There's 24-hour coffee in the lobby. Complimentary Continental breakfast. Cable TV. Pool. Pets allowed. | 463 Memorial Dr. | 413/592–6171 | fax 413/598–8351 | 106 rooms | $52–$70 | AE, D, MC, V.

CONCORD

Best Western at Historic Concord. Some rooms in this renovated, moderately priced hotel overlook the pool and the landscaped grounds and gardens. It's a 10- to 15-minute walk to historic Concord center. Complimentary Continental breakfast. In-room data ports, cable TV. Pool. Hot tub. Gym. Laundry facilities. Business services. Pets allowed (fee). | 740 Elm St. | 978/369–6100 | fax 978/371–1656 | 106 rooms | $104–$119 | AE, D, DC, MC, V.

North Bridge Inn. This three-story gray-clapboard house at Concord's town center has suites equipped with kitchens, sitting areas, and work spaces. The family-friendly inn welcomes both children and pets. Complimentary breakfast. In-room data ports, kitchenettes, microwaves, refrigerators, cable TV, in-room VCRs. Pets allowed. No smoking. | 21 Monument St. 01742 | 978/371–0014 or 888/530–0007 | fax 978/371–6460 | www.northbridgeinn.com | 6 suites | $125–$250 | AE, MC, V.

DANVERS

Residence Inn by Marriott. This inn is a home away from home. Grocery-shopping services, daily newspapers, and summer barbecues on Wednesday evenings are included. The two-bedroom suites have living rooms with fireplaces, two bathrooms, and two TVs. Complimentary Continental breakfast, picnic area. In-room data ports, kitchenettes, microwaves, refrigerators, cable TV. Pool. Tennis courts. Gym. Laundry facilities, laundry service. Business services, free parking. Some pets allowed (fee). | 51 Newbury St. | 978/777–7171 or 800/331–3131 | fax 978/774–7195 | www.residenceinn.com | 72 1-bedroom suites, 24 2-bedroom suites | $119–$149 1–bedroom suites, $159–$179 2–bedroom suites | AE, D, DC, MC, V.

DEERFIELD

Motel 6. This economical motel, just off I–91, is 4 mi south of Deerfield, 5 mi from Deerfield Academy, and 10 mi from Amherst. There's free morning coffee, and no charge for local calls or HBO. Indoor pool. Laundry facilities. Some pets allowed. | 8 Greenfield

Rd., South Deerfield 01373 | 413/665–7161 or 800/466–8356 | fax 413/665–7437 | www.
motel6.com | 123 rooms | $54 | AE, MC, V.

DENNIS (CAPE COD)

Breakers Motel. You'll find standard rooms at this two-story motel that has its own private
beach on Nantucket Sound. It's within walking distance of restaurants and a 10-minute
drive to downtown Dennis Village. Complimentary Continental breakfast. Some kitch-
enettes, some microwaves, refrigerators, cable TV. Pool. Beach. Pets allowed. | 61 Chase
Ave., Dennisport 02639 | 508/398–6905 or 800/540–6905 (in MA) | fax 508/398–7360 |
www.capecodtravel.com/breakers | 40 rooms, 3 suites | $100–$200, $210–$350 suites | Closed
mid-Oct.–mid-Apr. | AE, MC, V.

EDGARTOWN (MARTHA'S VINEYARD)

Point Way Inn. Built in 1851, the former sea captain's home has a porch overlooking Main
Street, and a sculpture garden. Rooms have French doors, fireplaces, and balconies or
terraces. Here you're within walking distance of the harbor and downtown. To reach other
parts of the island, you can ride the island shuttle bus that stops across the street or
use the inn's courtesy vehicle. Complimentary breakfast. Cable TV. Local shuttle. Some
pets allowed. No smoking. | 104 Main St. 02539 | 508/627–8633 or 888/711–6633 | fax 508/
627–3338 | pointwayinn@vineyard.net | www.pointway.com | 12 rooms | $225–$375 | AE,
MC, V.

ESSEX

Essex River House Motel. This 1950s-style motel is patronized by families who come
back year after year. Its riverbank location offers views of the many egrets, cranes, and
herons who fish in the salt marsh and of the setting sun behind the little steepled
church. The motel is across the street from Woodman's restaurant and a five-minute walk
to other seafood restaurants, antiques shops, and Story's boatyard and shipbuilding
museum. Cable TV. Pets allowed. | 132 Main St. | 978/768–6800 | 15 rooms | $94 | Closed
Nov.–mid-Apr. | D, MC, V.

FALL RIVER

Quality Inn–Somerset. Equidistant from Fall River, Providence, and Newport, this inn makes
an ideal base for day trips to those popular destinations. Many rooms have water views.
Fishing enthusiasts can drop a line into a saltwater inlet next to the hotel grounds. There's
also a driving range and miniature golf nearby. About 10 minutes from Fall River. Complimentary Continental breakfast. In-room data ports, some in-room hot tubs, cable TV. Indoor
pool. Gym, volleyball. Laundry facilities. Business services. Pets allowed. | 1878 Wilbur Ave.,
Somerset 02725 | 508/678–4545 | fax 508/678–9352 | qualityinn@meganet.net | 106
rooms, 2 suites | $94–$119, $170–$180 suites | AE, D, DC, MC, V.

FALMOUTH (CAPE COD)

Mariner Motel. This traditional motel has all ground-level rooms. It has flower gardens in
the front and picnic tables and a field to the rear. It is less than ½ mi from the island ferry
and village shopping. Picnic area. Refrigerators, cable TV. Pool. Some pets allowed (fee).
No smoking. | 555 Main St. | 508/548–1331 or 800/233–2939 | fax 508/547–9470 | info@
marinermotel.com | www.marinermotel.com | 30 rooms | $89–$129 | AE, D, DC, MC, V.

FRAMINGHAM

Red Roof Inn Boston/Framingham. On the northeast edge of Framingham, the two-
story chain sits just off I–90 at exit 13, ½ mi from the Framingham Shoppers Mall. In-
room data ports, cable TV. Pets allowed. | 650 Cochituate Rd. 01701 | 508/872–4499 | fax
508/872–2579 | 170 rooms | $72–$105 | AE, D, MC, V.

GARDNER

Colonial Hotel and Conference Center. Just north of Route 2, on Gardner's eastern side, this two-story hotel sits on over 20 acres of forested land, insuring a tranquil and restful stay. Restaurant, bar, room service. Some refrigerators, some in-room hot tubs, cable TV. Pool. Hot tub. Laundry service. Business services. Pets allowed (fee). | 625 Betty Spring Rd. 01440 | 888/214–4991 or 978/630–2500 | fax 978/632–0913 | 112 rooms | $55–$250 | AE, D, MC, V.

GLOUCESTER

Cape Ann Motor Inn. The best feature of this wood-shingle three-story motel is its location—right on Long Beach. Rooms have balconies and views over the beach, sea, and twin lights of Thacher Island—plus double bed, sofa bed, ceiling fans, and sliding-glass doors that open onto a common deck leading to the beach. Complimentary coffee in the lobby. Complimentary Continental breakfast. No air-conditioning, some kitchenettes, cable TV. Beach. Pets allowed. | 33 Rockport Rd., 01930 | 978/281–2900 or 800/464–8439 | fax 978/281–1359 | www.capeannmotorinn.com | 29 rooms, 1 suite | $115–$130, $200 suite | AE, D, MC, V.

Manor Inn. This newly renovated inn on 5 landscaped acres gives you the feeling of seclusion, even though it's within walking distance of downtown Gloucester. Some rooms overlook the Anisquam River and salt marshes. Complimentary Continental breakfast. Cable TV. Pets allowed (fee). | 141 Essex Ave. | 978/283–0614 | 10 rooms in manor, 16 motel rooms | $89–$139 | AE, D, MC, V.

Ocean View Inn and Resort. This eight-building resort is on 5½ landscaped and garden-filled acres on Gloucester's rocky coastline. Most rooms have ocean views; some have wood-burning fireplaces and antiques. The oldest building is a 1907 English Tudor-style manor. There are also motel-style units and a Queen Anne–style cottage. Restaurants. Cable TV. 2 pools. Business services. Pets allowed. | 171 Atlantic Rd. | 978/283–6200 or 800/315–7557 | fax 978/283–1852 | oviar@shore.net | www.oceanviewinnandresort.com | 62 rooms in 6 buildings | $79–$265, $275 suites | AE, D, DC, MC, V.

GREAT BARRINGTON

Barrington Court Motel. All rooms in this two-story motel have new wallpaper and cherry furniture. Outside, the motel has nicely landscaped grounds and gardens, and is within walking distance of shops and restaurants. Complimentary Continental breakfast. Some kitchenettes, refrigerators, cable TV. Pool. Playground. Pets allowed (fee). | 400 Stockbridge Rd. | 413/528–2340 | 22 rooms, 3 suites | $125–$135, $225–$250 suites | AE, D, MC, V.

Briarcliff Motor Lodge. Approximately 1 mi north of the town center, this one-story motor inn is close to Tanglewood and the summer theaters, as well as to many of the area's antiques shops. Refrigerators, cable TV. Pets allowed. | 506 Stockbridge Rd. 01230 | 415/528–3000 | 16 rooms | $45–$175 | AE, D, DC, MC, V.

Race Brook Lodge. This 200-year-old New England barn 12 mi south of Great Barrington has been converted into a family-friendly lodge. Common rooms and guest suites have wood-beam ceilings and stenciled walls. Also in the lodge is the Horshoe Wine Bar. A brook flows through the grounds, and hiking trails lead to the summit of Mt. Everett (the state's second-highest peak) and Mt. Race, as well as to Race Brook Falls. It's at the base of the Taconic Mountain Range. Many antiques shops are nearby. Complimentary breakfast. No room phones, cable TV in common area. Some pets allowed (fee). No smoking. | 864 S. Under Mountain Rd., Sheffield 01257 | 413/229–2916 or 888/725–6343 | fax 413/229–6629 | info@rblodge.com | www.rblodge.com | 21 rooms (some with shower only) | $125–$175, $225 Brook House (sleeps 6) | AE, MC, V.

Turningpoint Inn. The six second-floor bedrooms are simply decorated at this 200-year-old inn, which was once a stagecoach stop. The two-bedroom cottage has a living room/kitchen and heated sun porch. The owner/chefs place as much emphasis on food as on accommodations—changing the breakfast menu daily and serving dinners to guests on weekends. Dining room, complimentary breakfast. No air-conditioning in some rooms, no cable TV in some rooms, no room phones. Some pets allowed. No smoking. | 3 Lake Buel Rd. 01230 | 413/528–4777 | 6 rooms (2 with shared bath), 1 two-bedroom cottage | $90–$150, $230 cottage | No credit cards.

GREENFIELD

★ **Brandt House.** This turn-of-the-century Colonial Revival house is on a quiet residential street a five-minute walk from downtown. The house contains antiques and feather beds as well as fireplaces and skylights in some rooms. There's a porch with a swing, a terrace, and 3½ acres of manicured lawns and gardens. The apartment has a full kitchen, hot tub, and loft bedroom, and is geared toward extended stays. Complimentary breakfast (Continental on weekdays). In-room data ports, some in-room hot tubs, cable TV, some in-room VCRs. Business services. Some pets allowed (fee). No smoking. | 29 Highland Ave. | 413/774–3329 or 800/235–3329 | fax 413/772–2908 | info@brandthouse.com | www. brandthouse.com | 8 rooms (2 with shared bath), 1 apartment | $125–$205; $300 apartment | AE, D, MC, V.

Candlelight Motor Inn. This one-story motel-style inn on the Mohawk Trail is near several private schools as well as scenic Shelburne Falls. There's golf and tennis nearby. Cable TV. Pool. Pets allowed (fee). | 208 Mohawk Tr. | 413/772–0101 or 888/262–0520 | fax 413/773–0886 | 56 rooms | $84–$96 | AE, D, DC, MC, V.

Old Tavern Farm. This inn—which was a stagecoach stop on the Post Road to Bennington, Vermont—has a Georgian Colonial center chimney, five Rumford fireplaces, and an 18th-century set-kettle in the kitchen (one of the earliers sinks). There's also a unique period ballroom with spring floor, vaulted ceiling, candle-lit chandeliers, and oil lamps. Pieces from the owner's extensive collection of Americana are on display, and there are two large formal parlor guest rooms with working wood-burning fireplaces, one with a reproduction queen-size, Queen Anne, four-poster bed and the other with a double-size four-poster canopy bed. Dining room, complimentary breakfast. No air-conditioning in some rooms, no room phones, no cable TV in some rooms, cable TV in common area. Some pets allowed. No smoking. | 817 Colrain Rd. 01301 | 413/772–0474 | fax 413/773–0377 | www.oldtavernfarm.com | 3 rooms | $110 | MC, V.

HADLEY

Howard Johnson Inn. Within a few miles of this hotel are the campuses of the University of Massachusetts and Hampshire College. Yankee Candle is 13 mi north. Rooms have private balconies or patios, and suites have hot tubs. Complimentary Continental breakfast. In-room data ports, some in-room hot tubs, cable TV. Pool. Gym. Laundry facilities. Business services. Pets allowed. | 401 Russell St. 01035 | 413/586–0114 or 800/654–2000 | fax 413/584–7163 | www.thhg.com | 100 rooms, 3 suites | $69–$129, $89–$149 suites | AE, D, DC, MC, V.

HARWICH (CAPE COD)

Barnaby Inn. This 200-year-old house is set back 150 ft from the road. It contains large wallpapered guest rooms with wall-to-wall carpeting and some four-poster beds. The two deluxe rooms have wood-burning fireplaces. Breakfast is delivered to each guest room. Complimentary Continental breakfast. Refrigerators, some in-room hot tubs, cable TV, no room phones. Some pets allowed. No smoking. | 36 Rte. 28, West Harwich 02671 | 508/432–6789 or 800/439–4764 | fax 508/430–1938 | www.barnabyinn.com | 4 standard rooms, 2 deluxe rooms, 1 cottage | $100 standard, $140 deluxe | MC, V.

Cape Cod Claddagh Inn. This inn resembles a small Irish manor, with lace curtains, Oriental rugs, crystal and china, and Irish art. A newer building with three guest rooms is decorated in a Colonial style and the main house is Victorian. There's Irish entertainment in the pub and a lobster bake by the pool on Sun. afternoons, with Irish and Caribbean music. Dining room, bar with entertainment, picnic area, bar, complimentary breakfast. Refrigerators, cable TV. Pool. Some pets allowed. | 77 Main St., West Harwich 02671 | 508/432–9628 or 800/356–9628 | fax 508/432–6039 | www.capecodcladdaghinn.com | 11 rooms, 4 suites | $95–$150 | AE, MC, V.

HYANNIS (CAPE COD)

Comfort Inn Hyannis. This renovated property is close to U.S. 6 but set back far enough from the road among the trees to be quiet. The three-story structure is on the side of a hill, and there are a couple of ponds nearby. Complimentary Continental breakfast. In-room data ports, cable TV. Indoor pool. Hot tub, sauna. Gym. Business services. Pets allowed (deposit). | 1470 Rte. 132 | 508/771–4804 | fax 508/790–2336 | www.comfortinn-hyannis.com | 104 rooms | $119–$169 | AE, D, DC, MC, V.

Simmons Homestead Inn. A 10-room main house, along with a restored barn with guest rooms and a two-bedroom suite, occupy 2 acres in a residential area about ½ mi from town and the beach. Each guest room has a different animal theme; some rooms have canopy beds and fireplaces. Abutting the property is a pond with a dock for fishing. Ten-speed mountain bikes, fishing poles, beach chairs, and towels are complimentary. Informal itinerary-planning services are offered during the evening social hour on the wraparound porch. Complimentary breakfast. No room phones, cable TV in common area. Fishing. Bicycles. Business services. Pets allowed (fee). | 288 Scudder Ave., Hyannis Port 02647 | 508/778–4999 or 800/637–1649 | fax 508/790–1342 | www.capecodtravel. com/simmonsinn | 14 rooms and 1 suite in 2 buildings | $160–$200, $300 suite | AE, D, MC, V.

IPSWICH

★ **Miles River Country Inn.** A 100-year-old formal secret garden, a 2-acre pond garden, and more than 170 species of birds roam the grounds of this 18th-century inn. The pastries served at breakfast are made with fresh fruit from the gardens, eggs from the inn's chickens, and honey from its bees. The innkeeper speaks Spanish and French. Complimentary breakfast. No room phones, cable TV in common area. Pets allowed. No smoking. | 823 Bay Rd., Hamilton 01936 | 978/468–7206 | fax 978/468–3999 | www.milesriver.com | 10 rooms in summer, 8 rooms in winter (4 with shared bath) | $95–$175 | AE, MC, V.

LAWRENCE

Hampton Inn Boston/North Andover. On the Lawrence–North Andover border, this hotel is close to I-495, major businesses, and restaurants. The commuter rail station is 3 mi away; the trip to Boston takes 50 minutes. Single, double, and king-size beds are available. Complimentary Continental breakfast. In-room data ports, cable TV. Gym. Some pets allowed. | 224 Winthrop Ave. 01843 | 978/975–4050 | fax 978/687–7122 | www.hamptoninn. com | 126 rooms | $89–$99 | AE, D, DC, MC, V.

LENOX

Walker House. This family-owned inn is on 3 landscaped and wooded acres in Lenox Village. Each guest room is named for a composer, there's a piano in the parlor, and films are shown on a 12-ft screen in the library. The country-home appeal and spacious common areas of Walker House make it a good choice for small reunions. Dining room, complimentary Continental breakfast. No room phones, TV in common area. Library. No kids under 12. Business services. Some pets allowed. No smoking. | 64 Walker St. | 413/637–1271 or 800/235–3098 | fax 413/637–2387 | phoudek@vgernet.net | www.walkerhouse.com | 8 rooms | $80–$200 | No credit cards.

LEXINGTON

Holiday Inn Express. This hotel, which caters to the business traveler, is in the high-tech district outside Boston. Complimentary Continental breakfast. In-room data ports, cable TV. Pool. Hot tub. Laundry facilities. Business services. Pets allowed (deposit). | 440 Bedford St. | 781/861–0850 or 800/HOLIDAY | fax 781/861–0821 | www.holiday-inn.com | 204 rooms, 28 suites | $129–$159, $149–$159 suites | AE, D, DC, MC, V.

LOWELL

Westford Regency Inn and Conference Center. Geared to the business traveler, this hotel close to Lowell has a bilevel convention center. The spacious rooms each include a sitting area and a work area with desk. Take exit 32 off I–495. 3 restaurants, bar with entertainment, room service. In-room data ports, some refrigerators, cable TV. Indoor pool. Beauty salon, hot tub, sauna, steam room. Health club, racquetball. Business services. Pets allowed (deposit). | 219 Littleton Rd., Westford 01886 | 978/692–8200 or 800/543–7801 | fax 978/692–7403 | www.westfordregency.com | 193 rooms, 15 suites | $89–$125, $135–$239 suites | AE, D, DC, MC, V.

LYNN

Diamond District Inn. This 1911 Georgian Revival inn is on the National Register of Historic Places. Rooms are furnished with antiques, and two suites have working fireplaces and private decks. The property is 300 ft from a sandy beach. Complimentary breakfast. In-room data ports, in-room hot tubs. Business services. Some pets allowed (fee). No smoking. | 142 Ocean St. 01902 | 781/599–4470 or 800/666–3076 | fax 781/595–2200 | diamonddistrict@msn.com | www.diamonddistrictinn.com | 11 rooms, 3 suites | $145–$200, $225–$260 suites | AE, D, DC, MC, V.

MARBLEHEAD

Seagull Inn. What a view! This blue-with-white-trim Colonial inn is on Marblehead Neck, less than a block from the ocean and 2½ blocks from the lighthouse. The house has four decks and a beautiful yard with swings, Adirondack chairs, and croquet. Bicycles and kayaks are available at no extra charge. The Lighthouse Suite has a private entrance, full kitchen, bedroom, living room, two TVs, two VCRs, and two decks, one with a hammock, chairs, and a panoramic view of the ocean. Complimentary Continental breakfast. In-room data ports, refrigerators, cable TV, in-room VCRs and movies. Bicycles. Pets allowed. No smoking. | 106 Harbor Ave. 01945 | 781/631–1893 | fax 781/631–3535 | host@seagullinn.com | www.seagullinn.com | 3 suites | $100–$200 | MC, V.

NANTUCKET

The Boat House. This adorable two-story former boathouse, complete with a fireplace, is only available for a party of two to four at once, so be sure to reserve well in advance. Cable TV, VCR. Laundry facilities. Pets allowed. | 15 Old North Wharf, 02554 | 508/228–9552 or 800/245–9552 | www.nantucket.net/lodging/greylady | 2 rooms | $100–$550 | AE, D, DC, MC, V.

Corkish Cottages. For perfect privacy and lots of room, consider a stay at this establishment, family-owned and -operated since the 1970s. It's 7 mi from town. Picnic area. Some kitchenettes, some microwaves, some refrigerators, cable TV, some in-room VCRs, TV in common area. Laundry facilities in cottages. Some pets allowed (fee). | 320 Polpis Rd., 02554 | 508/228–5686 | www.nantucket.net/lodging/corkishcottages | 4 cottages | $1,250–$2,800 weekly | No credit cards.

The Grey Lady. This charming guesthouse is in the historic district. Restaurants, shops, and the beach are within walking distance. Some kitchenettes, some refrigerators, cable TV, some in-room VCRs. Pets allowed. | 34 Center St., 02554 | 508/228–9552 or 800/245–9552 | www.nantucket.net/lodging/greylady | 8 rooms | $100–$550 | AE, D, DC, MC, V.

NEWBURYPORT

Morrill Place Inn. Period furnishings and four-poster canopy beds grace the guest rooms of this 23-room estate built in 1806. The lovely public rooms include an elegant dining room, the music room, winter and summer porches, and a terrace. Maudslay Park is nearby. Complimentary Continental breakfast. No air-conditioning, cable TV in common room. Pets allowed. | 209 High St. | 978/462–2808 or 888/594–4667 | fax 978/462–9966 | morrillpl@aol.com | 9 rooms (4 with shared bath) | $66–$125 | No credit cards.

The Windsor House in Newburyport. This 18th-century Federal mansion, complete with courtyard outside and a foot-thick firewall inside, was a wedding present for Jane Perkins and Lieutenant Aaron Pardee in 1786. Their master bedroom is now the bridal suite. Nearby is the Parker River Wildlife Refuge, and special birding packages are offered by the inn. There's also complimentary afternoon tea. Complimentary breakfast. In-room data ports, TV and VCR in common area. Business services. Some pets allowed. No kids under 8 (call for exceptions). No smoking. | 38 Federal St. | 978/462–3778 or 888–735–2969 | fax 978/465–3443 | windsorinn@earthlink.net | www.bbhost.com/windsorhouse | 4 rooms | $135 | AE, D, MC, V.

NEWTON

Boston Marriott Newton. This renovated hotel is an affordable alternative to Boston's more expensive properties. It's next to the Charles River at I–90 and Route 128/I–95, a 15-minute drive from downtown Boston. 3 restaurants, bar with entertainment, picnic area, room service. In-room data ports, cable TV. Outdoor and indoor pools. Barbershop, hot tub. Gym. Playground. Laundry facilities. Business services. Some pets allowed. | 2345 Commonwealth Ave. 02466 | 617/969–1000 | fax 617/527–6914 | www.marriott.com | 430 rooms, 4 suites | $159–$245, $350 suites | AE, D, DC, MC, V.

OAK BLUFFS (MARTHA'S VINEYARD)

Island Inn. On 7½ acres of landscaped grounds overlooking Nantucket Sound and a golf course, the inn offers the choice of a one- or two-bedroom suite, a condominium suite, or a cottage. Some units have water views. A bike path runs alongside the inn. There's a beach right next door and another 5 mi away. Picnic area. Kitchenettes, cable TV. Pool. 3 tennis courts. Playground. Laundry facilities. Business services. Pets allowed before Memorial Day and after Labor Day. | Beach Rd. 02557 | 508/693–2002 or 800/462–0269 | fax 508/693–7911 | innkeeper@islandinn.com | www.islandinn.com | 51 units | $85–$345 | Closed Dec.–Mar. | AE, D, DC, MC, V.

Martha's Vineyard Surfside Motel. Although the mid-town location makes for some noisy summer nights, this motel has spacious and bright rooms and fresh furnishings, albeit motel-style ones. Restaurant. Refrigerators, some in-room hot tubs, cable TV. Pets allowed (fee). | Oak Bluffs Ave. 02557 | 508/693–2500 or 800/537–3007 | fax 508/693–7343 | www.mvsurfside.com | 34 rooms, 4 suites | $140–$150 | AE, D, MC, V.

ORLEANS (CAPE COD)

Skaket Beach Motel. This one-story motel is in a quiet, wooded area near the intersection of Rte. 6A and U.S. 6, 1 mi from Cape Cod Bay and 2 mi from Nauset Beach. Blueberry and cranberry muffins from the owners' own recipe start every day. Complimentary Continental breakfast. Some kitchenettes, microwaves, refrigerators, cable TV. Outdoor pool. Laundry services. Free parking. Pets allowed (fee). | 203 Cranberry Hwy., Rte. 6A, 02653 |

508/255–1020 or 800/835–0298 | fax 508/255–6487 | www.skaketbeachmotel.com | 44 rooms, 2 suites | $53–$169 | AE, D, DC, MC, V.

PITTSFIELD

Heart of the Berkshires Motel. This basic motel is quiet and set back from the road. Just 2 mi from Hancock Shaker Village and a 15-minute drive from Tanglewood, it's also close to movie theaters. Cable TV. Some pets allowed. | 970 W. Housatonic St. 01201 | 413/443–1255 | 17 rooms | $199 | AE, D, MC, V.

PLYMOUTH

Foxglove Cottage. All the rooms in this restored 1820 structure feature queen- or king-size beds with Laura Ashley details. Expect to see foxes or coyotes from the deck of this pastoral, 4-acre property. Complimentary breakfast. No room phones, TV in common area. Some pets allowed. | 101 Sandwich Rd. 02360 | 508/747–6576 | fax 508/747–7622 | www.foxglove-cottage.com | 3 rooms | $90–$95 | No credit cards.

PROVINCETOWN (CAPE COD)

Bradford Gardens Inn. This multiple-building inn is popular with lesbians; however, all are welcome to stay and enjoy the inn's beautiful decor, including pine floors, antiques, and artwork. On the grounds are lush, extensive gardens. Many rooms have fireplaces. It's three blocks from the center of town and one block from the beach. Complimentary breakfast. Some microwaves, refrigerators, cable TV, in-room VCRs and movies. Some pets allowed. | 178 Bradford St. 02657 | 508/487–1616 or 800/432–2334 | fax 508/487–5596 | www.bradfordgardens.com | 8 rooms, 3 cottages, 2 town houses, 1 penthouse | $85–$155 | AE, MC, V.

Surfside Inn. Within walking distance of the center of town, this modern motel is right on the beach. Half the standard-issue rooms face the water; the others overlook the pool and Commercial Street. Pool. Pets allowed (fee). | 543 Commercial St. 02657 | 508/487–172 | fax 508/487–2087 | www.surfsideinn | 84 rooms | $129–$189 | Closed late Oct.–mid-Mar. | D, MC, V.

White Wind Inn. This large white Victorian inn is a Provincetown landmark at the start of the west end. The front porch is ideal for people-watching. Public rooms are decorated with antiques, chandeliers, art, and stained glass. The large guest rooms have high ceilings and four-poster beds; several rooms have water views and fireplaces. During the summer, the guests are mostly gay and lesbian. Picnic area, complimentary Continental breakfast. In-room data ports, refrigerators, cable TV. Some pets allowed. | 174 Commercial St. 02657 | 508/487–1526 or 888/449–WIND | fax 508/487–4792 | www.whitewindinn.com | 12 rooms (7 with shower only), 1 apartment | $120–$225 | AE, MC, V.

ROCKPORT

The Blueberry. Feel a part of the Hogan family as they share their home with you at this tiny bed-and-breakfast. Handmade quilts grace each room, and Mrs. Hogan's muffins have blueberries she picked herself. The Blueberry is in a residential area, but the yard adjoins woods with hiking trails. Guest rooms share a bath. Complimentary breakfast. Cable TV, no room phones. Pets allowed. No smoking. | 50 Stockholm Ave. 01966 | 978/546–2838 | members.aol.com/rockportBB | 2 rooms | $75 | No credit cards.

SALEM

Hawthorne Hotel. This Federal-style brick building next to Salem Common features local history exhibits. Restaurant, bar with entertainment, room service. In-room data ports, cable TV. Gym. Laundry service. Business services. Pets allowed (fee). | 18 Washington Sq. W | 978/744–4080 or 800/729–7829 | fax 978/745–9842 | www.hawthornehotel.com | 89 rooms, 6 suites | $132–$189, $295 suites | AE, D, DC, MC, V.

Salem Inn. There are three historic buildings here—the West House, built in 1834; the 1854 Curwen House; and the Peabody House (1874). Each has been gracefully restored, and furnished with antiques and period details. Enjoy breakfast on a brick patio in a rose garden. Complimentary Continental breakfast. Some kitchenettes, some in-room hot tubs, cable TV. Some pets allowed. | 7 Summer St. | 978/741–0680 or 800/446–2995 | fax 978/744–8924 | www.saleminnma.com | 28 rooms, 11 suites | $149–$219 suites | AE, D, DC, MC, V.

SANDWICH (CAPE COD)

Earl of Sandwich Motel. These Tudor-style buildings surround a duck pond and wooded lawn. Many rooms are rather dark, with ceiling beams, paneled walls, and quarry-tile floors, but they're spacious and have large windows. Pool. Pets allowed. | 378 Rte. 6A, East Sandwich, 02537 | 508/888–1415 or 800/442–3275 | fax 508/833–1039 | www.earlofsandwich. com | 24 rooms | $85–$109 | AE, D, DC, MC, V.

Sandwich Motor Lodge. Families are more than welcome at this quiet Route 6A motel about 1½ mi from the beach. Complimentary Continental breakfast. Some kitchenettes, some refrigerators, cable TV. 2 pools (1 indoor). Hot tub. Laundry facilities. Some pets allowed. | 54 Rte. 6A | 508/888–2275 or 800/282–5353 | fax 508/888–8102 | www.sandwichlodge.com | 34 rooms, 33 suites | $116–$170 suites. | AE, D, DC, MC, V.

Wingscorton Farm. Tucked away on a dirt road off busy Route 6A, this farmhouse was once a stop on the Underground Railroad. Since it's still a working farm, you'll see plenty of four-legged friends. Guest accommodations include three elegant suites with wide-planked floor boards and Oriental rugs, as well as a detached cottage and a fully-equipped stone carriage house. Complimentary Continental breakfast. Beach. Library. Pets allowed. No smoking. | 11 Wing Blvd, East Sandwich 02537 | 508/888–0534 | fax 508/888–0545 | 3 suites, 1 carriage house | $135; $175 carriage house | AE, MC, V.

SAUGUS

Colonial Traveler Motor Court. Family-owned and -operated, this brick motel has a one-story wing with parking outside the rooms, and a two-story wing with a parking lot. Breakfast is served in the coffee shop and there are nightclubs across the street. A bus to the T stops directly in front of the building. Restaurant, complimentary Continental breakfast. In-room data ports, some refrigerators, cable TV. Laundry facilities. Pets allowed. | 1753 Broadway 01906 | 781/233–6700 or 800/323–2731 | fax 781/231–8067 | www.roomsaver.com | 24 rooms | $89–$129 | AE, D, MC, V.

SHEFFIELD

Ivanhoe Country House. This 1780 Colonial home sits amidst 20 primarily wooded acres adjoining the Appalachian Trail. Rooms have some antiques, including old rag rugs. The owners deliver breakfast to your door, so you can crawl back under the covers to eat. Complimentary Continental breakfast. Some kitchenettes, some refrigerators, no room phones, no TV in some rooms. Outdoor pool. Some pets allowed (fee). No smoking. | 254 S. Undermountain Rd. 01257 | 413/229–2143 | 7 rooms, 2 suites | $110–$125 | No credit cards.

Racebrook Lodge. Originally a barn, this 1784 building has stenciled walls and a cathedral ceiling. Complimentary breakfast. No room phones, TV in common area. Pets allowed (fee). No smoking. | 864 S. Undermountain Rd. 01257 | 413/229–2916 | www.rblodge.com. | 19 rooms, 3 suites | $125–$225 | AE, MC, V.

SPRINGFIELD

Dave's Inn. This 1898 home, in the historic Crescent Hill section, is staffed by students from the Crescent Hill School of the Arts, who prepare meals. There is also a modern recording studio available, and professional musicians often rent the inn while recording albums. Complimentary breakfast. Some in-room hot tubs, cable TV, no room phones.

Pets allowed (fee). | 346 Maple St. 01105 | 413/747–8059 | fax 413/747–7609 | 6 rooms, 2 suites | $89–$13 | AE, D, MC, V.

Ramada Inn. This two-story chain was built in 1991, and has your basic modern motel conveniences. Complimentary Continental breakfast. In-room data ports, some in-room hot tubs, cable TV. Exercise equipment. Baby-sitting. Laundry service. Free parking. Pets allowed (fee). | 21 Baldwin St. 01089 | 413/781–2300 or 888/298–2054 | fax 413/732–1231 | 44 rooms, 4 suites | $59–$64; $120–$140 suites | AE, D, DC, V.

STURBRIDGE

Super 8 Motel. This straightforward motel is on Cedar Lake, 300 yards from Old Sturbridge Village. Some rooms have a view of the lake. Complimentary Continental breakfast. Cable TV. Pool. Pets allowed (fee). | 358 Main St. | 508/347–9000 or 800/800–8000 | fax 508/347–5658 | 58 rooms | $69–$120 | AE, D, DC, MC, V.

WALTHAM

Homestead Village Guest Studios. This new, extended-stay property has modern-looking studios with generic outdoor landscaping. Studios come with the latest business conveniences. In-room data ports, kitchenettes, cable TV. Laundry facilities. Pets allowed (fee). | 52 4th Ave. | 781/890–1333 or 888/STAYHSD | fax 781/890–1901 | www.stayhsd.com | 140 studios with bath | $99–$109 | AE, D, DC, MC, V.

Summerfield Suites by Wyndham. This tan stucco building encircles its heated outdoor pool. Each suite has a complete kitchen and cooking utensils, living room with pull-out sofa, bedroom(s) with king-size bed, and private bath(s) and vanity area. The front desk, on-site convenience store, and gym are open 24 hours. Complimentary breakfast. In-room data ports, kitchenettes, microwaves, refrigerators, cable TV, in-room VCRs. Outdoor pool. Hot tub. Gym. Laundry facilities, laundry service. Business services. Pets allowed. | 54 4th Ave. 02451 | 781/290–0026 | fax 781/290–0037 | www.summerfieldsuites.com | 85 1-bedroom suites, 51 2-bedroom suites | $239–$289 | AE, D, DC, MC, V.

The Westin Waltham–Boston. The business traveler will benefit from this hotel's proximity and convenient shuttle to many area businesses. It's also close to both Bentley and Brandeis. Restaurant, bar, room service. In-room data ports, cable TV. Indoor pool. Hot tub, sauna. Gym. Business services. Pets allowed. | 70 3rd Ave. | 781/290–5600 | fax 781/290–5626 | www.westin.com | 316 rooms, 30 suites | $249, $289 suites | AE, D, DC, MC, V.

WELLFLEET (CAPE COD)

★ **Surf Side Colony Cottages.** Scattered throughout a stand of scrub pine trees, some between the ocean and road, these 1950s-style cottages are a two-minute walk to Le Count Hollow Beach. The exterior of the units are retro Florida, but the interiors are Cape Cod classic, complete with knotty pine. Some have roof decks; all have fireplaces, indoor and outdoor showers, screened porches, and rattan furnishings. Picnic area. Kitchenettes. Laundry facilities. Pets allowed off-season (fee). No smoking. | Ocean View Dr. 02663 | 508/349–3959 | fax 508/349–3959 | www.capecod.net/surfside | 18 cottages | $750–$1350/wk (7–night minimum) | Closed Nov.–Mar. | MC, V.

WILLIAMSTOWN

Williams Inn. The owners manage this inn on the grounds of Williams College, and it's staffed by knowledgeable, longtime employees who help guests plan day trips. Bus tickets to Boston and New York are sold at the front desk; the bus stops out front. The lobby and living room with fireplace, herb and vegetable gardens, and bird feeders give the inn a country feeling. 2 restaurants, bar with entertainment, picnic area, room service. Cable TV. 1 indoor pool. Hot tub, sauna. Shop. Business services. Some pets allowed (fee). | Village Green, at U.S. 7 and Rte. 2 | 413/458–9371 or 800/828–0133 | fax 413/458–2767 | www.williamsinn.com | 103 rooms | $130–$180, $175–$200 suites | AE, D, DC, MC, V.

YARMOUTH (CAPE COD)

Cavalier Motor Lodge and Resort. This motel is less than a mile from the beach, within walking distance of restaurants and shops, and 6 mi from ferries. It features 4½ acres of landscaped grounds, where guests can play shuffleboard, volleyball, and bocce ball. There are also full kitchens in the cottages and family-friendly amenities. Some microwaves, refrigerators, cable TV. Indoor and outdoor pools. Hot tub, sauna. Putting green. Video games. Playground. Some pets allowed (fee). | 881 Main St. South Yarmouth | 508/394–6575 or 800/545–3536 | fax 508/394–6578 | 43 rooms, 22 cottages | $59–$99; cottages $650–$1050/wk | AE, D, DC, MC, V.

Colonial House Inn. This 1730s sea captain's mansion features many antiques and handmade afghans. It's 1 mi from a private beach and a 10-minute drive from Hyannis. Bar, 3 dining rooms, complimentary Continental breakfast. Cable TV. Indoor pool. Hot tub, massage. Business services. Some pets allowed (fee). | 277 Main St. (Rte. 6A), Yarmouth Port 02675 | 508/362–4348 or 800/999–3416 | fax 508/362–8034 | www.colonialhousecapecod.com | 21 rooms | $95–$125 | AE, D, MC, V.

Lane's End Cottage. Tucked at the end of a little dirt lane, this sweet cottage is filled with English antiques. From the library and common room to the tasteful guest rooms with feather comforters and firm mattresses, this homey place exudes the warm spirit of its innkeeper. Complimentary breakfast. Library. Pets allowed (off-season with prior notice). No smoking. | 268 Main St., Yarmouth Port 02657 | 508/362–5298 | 3 rooms | $120–$130 | No credit cards.

Village Inn. This old-fashioned hostelry, built in 1795 for a sea captain, still has the original wide plank floorboards and light fixtures. Rooms and in-room amenities vary considerably, from the tiny Wellfleet Room to the enormous Yarmouth Room with its own library and a fireplace in the bathroom. Pets allowed (fee) by arrangement. No smoking. | 92 Main St., Yarmouth Port 02657 | 508/362–3182 | 10 rooms | $75–$109 | MC, V.

Michigan

ALPENA

Fletcher Motel. This family-owned family-style motel is 1 mi north of downtown. Restaurant, bar, room service. Refrigerators, some in-room hot tubs. Cable TV. Indoor pool. Hot tub, sauna. Tennis. Some pets allowed. | 1001 U.S. 23 N 49707 | 517/354–4191 or 800/334–5920 | fax 517/354–4056 | www.fletchermotel.com | 96 rooms | $58–$64 | AE, D, DC, MC, V.

Holiday Inn. The indoor Holidome recreation center with pool and game room makes this a popular choice for families. It's 2 mi from Lake Huron and the city's well-known dive preserve. Restaurant, bar (with entertainment), room service. Cable TV. Indoor pool. Hot tub. Putting green. Exercise equipment. Laundry facilities. Business services. Some pets allowed. | 1000 U.S. 23 N 49707 | 517/356–2151 or 800/465–4329 | fax 517/356–2151 | www.basshotels.com/holiday-inn | 148 rooms | $64–$84 | AE, D, DC, MC, V.

ANN ARBOR

Motel 6. You'll be 1 mi from the Briarwood Mall and 3 mi from the U of M campus at this motel off I–94. Complimentary coffee. In-room data ports. Satellite TV. Pool. Some pets allowed. | 3764 S. State St. 48108 | 734/665–9900 | fax 517/463–2970 | www.motel6.com | 109 rooms | $45–$62 | AE, D, DC, MC, V.

Red Roof Inn. This budget hotel is on the north side of town. Cable TV. Some pets allowed. | 3621 Plymouth Rd. 48105 | 734/996–5800 or 800/733–7663 | fax 734/996–5707 | www.redroof.com | 108 rooms | $47–$73 | AE, D, DC, MC, V.

Residence Inn by Marriott. This extended-stay inn is a good bet if you're looking for a little extra room. Picnic area, complimentary Continental breakfast. Kitchenettes. Cable TV. Pool. Hot tub. Laundry facilities. Some pets allowed. | 800 Victors Way 48108 | 734/996–5666 | www.marriott.com | 114 suites | $99–$229 suites | AE, D, DC, MC, V.

BATTLE CREEK

Battle Creek Inn. A courtyard beckons lodgers to the putting green and outdoor pool. Furnished apartments and extended stay rates are available. Restaurant, bar, complimentary Continental breakfast, room service. Cable TV. 2 pools (1 indoor). Putting green. Exercise equipment. Video games. Laundry facilities. Business services. Some pets allowed.

| 5050 Beckley Rd. 49015 | 616/979–1100 or 800/232–3405 | fax 616/979–1899 | www.battlecreekinn.com | 212 rooms | $58–$73 | AE, D, DC, MC, V.

Days Inn. Downtown shopping, restaurants, and golf are within 4 mi of this single-story motel. Complimentary Continental breakfast. Some in-room hot tubs. Cable TV. Business services. Some pets allowed. | 4786 Beckley Rd. 49017 | 616/979–3561 or 800/388–7829 | fax 616/979–1400 | www.daysinn.com | 85 rooms | $49–$75 | AE, D, DC, MC, V.

BAY CITY
Holiday Inn. The city's shopping area is 5 mi away and the Saginaw River is 1 block from this hotel. Restaurant, bar, room service. Cable TV. Indoor pool. Hot tub, sauna. Laundry facilities. Business services. Some pets allowed. | 501 Saginaw St. 48708 | 517/892–3501 or 800/465–4329 | fax 517/892–9342 | www.basshotels.com/holiday-inn | 100 rooms | $79–$170 | AE, D, DC, MC, V.

BIRMINGHAM
Hamilton Hotel. If you're a video-game addict, you'll enjoy the Nintendo provided in every room of this European-style hotel downtown. Afternoon tea is served each day. Complimentary breakfast, room service. In-room data ports, some in-room safes, some minibars, some refrigerators. Cable TV. Exercise equipment. Laundry service. Business services. Pets allowed. | 35270 Woodward Ave. 48009 | 248/642–6200 | fax 248/642–6567 | www.hamilton-hotel.com | 64 rooms | $119–$250 | AE, D, DC, MC, V.

BREVORT
Chapel Hill Motel. You can rent a single room to a five-bedroom house at this 1950s motel, which was enlarged in the 1960s and again in the 1990s. Situated off the highway, it's also nice and quiet. TV. Pool. Some pets allowed. | 4422 W. U.S. 2, St. Ignace 49781 | 906/292–5534 | 26 rooms | $39–$54 | MC, V, D.

CADILLAC
Econo Lodge. Nestled between Lake Cadillac and Lake Mitchell, this budget chain hotel has some of the best views around. It's by two restaurants, 3 mi west of downtown on Rte. 55. In-room data ports, some kitchenettes, some microwaves, some refrigerators. Cable TV. Pets allowed. | 2501 Sunnyside Dr. 49601 | 231/775–6700 or 800/835–1934 | fax 231/775–8828 | www.econolodge.com | 29 rooms | $55–$110 | AE, D, DC, MC, V.

McGuire's Resort. At this 327-acre modern resort, the emphasis is on recreation, from golfing to skiing to volleyball. All rooms overlook Lake Cadillac, and suites have fireplaces and hot tubs. The resort is 1 mi south of town. Restaurant, bar. In-room data ports, some microwaves, some refrigerators, some in-room hot tubs. Indoor pool. Hot tub, sauna. 18-hole golf course, 9-hole golf course, putting green, 2 tennis courts. Basketball, hiking, volleyball. Cross-country skiing, sleigh rides, snowmobiling, tobogganing. Video games. Baby-sitting, children's programs (0–16). Laundry service. Pets allowed. | 7880 Mackinaw Trail 49601 | 231/775–9947 or 888/MCGUIRES | fax 231/775–9621 | www.mcguiresresort.com | 105 rooms, 15 suites | $129–$209 | AE, D, DC, MC, V.

Sun 'n Snow Motel. On Lake Mitchell, you'll have access to a private beach and cross-country skiing and biking trails at this motel. Cable TV. Beach. Business services. Some pets allowed. | 301 S. Lake Mitchell Dr. 49601 | 231/775–9961 or 231/477–9961 (reservations) | fax 231/775–3846 | www.cadillacmichigan.com/sunnsnowmotel/ | 29 rooms | $40–$79 | D, MC, V.

CHARLEVOIX
Lodge of Charlevoix. Downtown restaurants and shops are three blocks from this hotel. Cable TV. Pool. Business services. Some pets allowed (fee). | 120 Michigan Ave. 49720 | 231/547–6565 | fax 231/547–0741 | 40 rooms | $95–$155 | AE, DC, MC, V.

CHEBOYGAN

Birch Haus Motel. This family-owned motor lodge has bargain prices. The one-story building is nine blocks north of downtown on U.S. 23. Picnic area, complimentary Continental breakfast. Some refrigerators. Cable TV. Pets allowed. | 1301 Mackinaw Ave. 49721 | 231/627–5862 | birchhaus@webtv.net | www.cheboygan.com/lodging/birchhaus/index.phtml | 13 rooms | $40–$60 | AE, D, MC, V.

Days Inn. The Cheboygan County Historical Museum and Cheboygan Opera House are within 1 mi of this mid-downtown chain hotel. Cheboygan State Park is 5 mi away. Complimentary Continental breakfast. Refrigerators. Cable TV. Dock. Airport shuttle. Some pets allowed. | 889 S. Main St. (M–27) 49721 | 231/627–3126 or 800/388–7829 | fax 231/627–2889 | www.daysinn.com | 42 rooms | $48–$120 | AE, D, DC, MC, V.

CLARE

Crossroads Motel. A white picket fence surrounds this quaint blue motor lodge. It's four blocks south of downtown on Business Route U.S. 27. Picnic area. Refrigerators. Cable TV. Business services. Pets allowed. | 407 S. McEwan St. 48617 | 517/386–2422 or 800/386–3950 | fax 517/386–5387 | 9 rooms | $37–$55 | AE, D, DC, MV, V.

Doherty Hotel. Antiques decorate this gracious, old-fashioned downtown hotel. It houses a popular full-service dining room with hand-painted murals. Restaurant, bar (with entertainment), complimentary breakfast. Indoor pool. Hot tub. Business services, airport shuttle. Some pets allowed. | 604 McEwan St. (U.S. 27 Bus.) 48617 | 517/386–3441 or 800/525–4115 | fax 517/386–4231 | www.dohertyhotel.com | 158 rooms, 5 suites | $60–$136; $124–$136 suites | AE, D, DC, MC, V.

COLDWATER

Econo Lodge. This budget red-and-white motor lodge is 3 mi west of downtown in a peaceful country location. Complimentary Continental breakfast. In-room data ports, some kitchenettes, some refrigerators. Cable TV. Business services. Pets allowed. | 884 W. Chicago Rd. 49036 | 517/278–4501 or 800/553–2666 | fax 517/278–2099 | www.econolodge.com | 46 rooms | $45–$55 | AE, D, DC, MC, V.

Quality Inn Convention Center. This New Orleans-themed hotel has an indoor courtyard and a large convention center next door. Restaurant, bar (with entertainment), complimentary breakfast, room service. Some kitchenettes. Cable TV. Indoor pool. Hot tub. Video games. Business services. Some pets allowed. | 1000 Orleans Blvd. 49036 | 517/278–2017 or 800/228–5151 | fax 517/279–7214 | www.qualityinncoldwater.com | 123 rooms | $58–$125 | AE, D, DC, MC, V.

COPPER HARBOR

Minnetonka Resort. Accommodations are available in rustic cottages or in smaller, motel-style rooms. The Astor House Museum, which displays antique dolls, toys, and Native American artifacts, is on the grounds. Picnic area. No air-conditioning, some kitchenettes. Cable TV. Saunas. Some pets allowed. | 560 Gratiot St. 49918 | 904/672–1887 or 800/433–2770 | www.exploringthenorth.com | 26 rooms in 2 buildings, 12 cottages | $50–$96, $50–$95 cottages | Closed Nov.–Apr. | D, MC, V.

DEARBORN

Red Roof Inn. Ford Motor Co. world headquarters, Greenfield Village, Henry Ford Museum, and Fairlane Mall are within 3½ mi of this hotel that's 15 mi from Detroit sports venues and eateries. Complimentary Continental breakfast. Cable TV. Business services. Some pets allowed. | 24130 Michigan Ave. 48124 | 313/278–9732 or 800/733–7663 | fax 313/278–9741 | www.redroof.com | 111 rooms | $80 | AE, D, DC, MC, V.

DETROIT

Marriott Renaissance Center. In the middle of the huge Renaissance Center, this luxury chain hotel in downtown Detroit is a premier convention center. Popular with business travelers, it is one to six blocks to the financial district, the Detroit River, Belle Isle, shops, and golf courses. Restaurants, bar, room service. In-room data ports, some minibars. Cable TV. Indoor pool. Beauty salon. Gym. Business services. Some pets allowed. | 48243 Jefferson Ave., Renaissance Center 48226 | 313/568–8000 or 800/228–9290 | fax 313/568–8146 | www.marriott.com | 1,306 rooms, 50 suites | $85–$175 | AE, D, DC, MC, V.

Parkcrest Inn. One of the few lodging options in the eastern suburbs, this two-story motel is off I–94 in a residential area of Harper Woods. The formal rooms, with most of their original traditional furnishings, overlook a well-kept courtyard. Restaurant, bar, room service. Cable TV. Pool. Some pets allowed. | 20000 Harper Ave., Harper Woods 48225 | 313/884–8800 | fax 313/884–7087 | 47 rooms | $59–$68 | AE, D, DC, MC, V.

DOUGLAS

AmericInn. Less than a mile from downtown Douglas, this chain motel with six-inch concrete walls was built for quiet. Local artists display their works in its halls and lobby. Some suites have fireplaces. Some microwaves, some refrigerators, some in-room hot tubs. Cable TV. Indoor pool. Hot tub, sauna. Some pets allowed. | 2905 Blue Star Hwy. 49406 | 616/857–8581 | fax 616/857–3591 | americinn@americinn.com | www.americinn.com | 46 rooms | $69–$99, $160–$300 suites | AE, D, DC, MC, V.

ESCANABA

Super 8. This two-story motel is in a commercial area that's 2 mi north of downtown, yet close to city attractions and outdoor recreation. You can gamble at a casino 13 mi north, or ski at an area within 7 mi. Some in-room hot tubs. Cable TV. Some pets allowed. | 2415 N. Lincoln Ave. 49829 | 906/786–1000 or 800/800–8000 | fax 906/786–7819 | www.super8motels.com | 90 rooms | $60–$72 | AE, D, DC, MC, V.

FARMINGTON/FARMINGTON HILLS

Hilton. Modern furnishings abound at this seven-story hotel at I–275 and 8 Mile Road that's a choice for both business travelers and families. The hotel has a grand ballroom and amphitheater. Restaurant, bar, room service. In-room data ports, refrigerators (in suites). Cable TV. Pool. Hot tub. Exercise equipment. Business services. Some pets allowed. | 21111 Haggerty Rd., Novi 48375 | 248/349–4000 or 800/445–8667 | fax 248/349–4066 | www.hilton.com | 239 rooms | $85–$165 | AE, D, DC, MC, V.

Red Roof Inn. A busy corporate community and area shopping and restaurants are just 1–5 mi from this two-floor chain hotel. Cable TV. Some pets allowed. | 24300 Sinacola Ct., Farmington Hills 48335 | 248/478–8640 or 800/733–7663 | fax 248/478–4842 | www.redroof.com | 108 rooms | $58–$68 | AE, D, DC, MC, V.

FLINT

Super 8. In the Flint area's busiest commercial strip, this motel is off I–75 and Miller Road and 2 mi from downtown Flint. It has three floors. Cable TV. Some pets allowed. | 3033 Claude Ave. 48507 | 810/230–7888 or 800/800–8000 | fax 810/230–7888 | www.super8motels.com | 62 rooms | $37–$48 | AE, D, DC, MC, V.

FRANKENMUTH

Drury Inn. Though this four-story inn is in a commercial area 7 mi east of downtown, its Bavarian style is in keeping with the area's German theme. Cable TV. Indoor pool. Some pets allowed. | 260 S. Main St. 48734 | 517/652–2800 | fax 517/652–2800 | www.druryinn.com | 78 rooms | $60–$85 | AE, D, DC, MC, V.

Holiday Inn Express. You're 4 blocks from the factory outlets in Birch Run and 10 mi from Frankenmuth attractions when you stay in this motel that's ½ mi east of downtown Birch Run. Its three floors have modern furnishings. Game room. Cable TV. Indoor pool. Hot tubs. Some pets allowed. | 12150 Dixie Hwy., Birch Run 48415 | 517/624–9300 or 800/465–4329 | fax 517/732–9640 | www.bassbotels.com/holiday-inn | 95 rooms | $69–$129 | AE, D, DC, MC, V.

Super 8. This two-story chain motel is off I–75 on a busy commercial strip ¼ mi to the Birch Run outlet mall and fast-food restaurants. Cable TV. Some pets allowed. | 9235 E. Birch Run Rd. 48415 | 517/624–4440 or 800/800–8000 | fax 517/624–9439 | www. super8motels.com | 109 rooms | $38–$58 | AE, D, DC, MC, V.

FRANKFORT

Bay Valley Inn. This motel 1 mi south of town is in a former elementary school. Accommodations include a wide range of guest rooms, including whirlpool rooms, as well as a community room with a full kitchen and a pool table. Ski areas are 15 mi away. Picnic area, complimentary Continental breakfast. Refrigerators. Cable TV. Playground. Business services. Some pets allowed. | 1561 Scenic Hwy./Rte. 22 49635 | 231/352–7113 or 800/352–7113 | fax 231/352–7114 | 20 rooms | $60–$95, $119 penthouse | AE, D, MC, V.

Chimney Corners. Built in 1935, this old-fashioned, wood-construction resort fits in its wilderness setting. Furnishings are rustic, amenities are modern. Chimney Corners has been owned by the same family for four generations. Dining room, picnic area. No air-conditioning, some kitchenettes. Tennis. Beach, boating. Playground. Laundry facilities. Some pets allowed. | 1602 Crystal Dr./Rte. 22 49635 | 231/352–7522 | www.benzie.com/chimneycorners | 8 rooms in lodge, 7 apartments, 13 cottages | $40–$45 lodge rooms, $760–$795/wk apartments (minimum stay), $1,100–$1,300/wk cottages (minimum stay) | Closed Nov.–Apr. | No credit cards.

GAYLORD

Best Western Royal Crest. This two-story chain hotel is popular with skiers and golfers. It's right in town, within a commercial area off I–75 and U.S. 27. Complimentary Continental breakfast. Cable TV. Hot tub. Exercise equipment. Some pets allowed. | 803 S. Otsego Ave. 49735 | 517/732–6451 or 800/876–9252 | fax 517/732–7634 | www.bestwesternmichigan.com | 44 rooms | $69–$109 | AE, D, DC, MC, V.

Holiday Inn. This popular two-story Holidome hotel is three blocks from downtown restaurants and attractions and within 20 mi of canoeing and other area recreation. Rooms have traditional furnishings. Game room. Restaurant, bar, room service. Cable TV. Indoor pool. Hot tub. Exercise equipment. Laundry facilities. Business services. Some pets allowed. | 833 W. Main St. 49735 | 517/732–2431 or 800/465–4329 | fax 517/732–9640 | www.bassbotels.com/holiday-inn | 140 rooms | $74–$97 | AE, D, DC, MC, V.

GLADSTONE

Bay View Motel. A stunning view gives this inn between Escanaba and Gladstone its name. It's in a residential, 3-acre parklike area that's close to golf, cross-country ski trails, boat launches, and beaches. Two floors of traditional rooms. Picnic area. Some refrigerators. Cable TV. Indoor pool. Sauna. Playground. Business services. Some pets allowed. | 7110 U.S. 2/41 49837 | 906/786–2843 or 800/547–1201 | fax 906/786–6218 | 23 rooms | $36–$52 | AE, D, MC, V.

GRAND MARAIS

Walker's Harbor View Resort. Pretty scenery abounds at this resort on Lake Superior that has a beach and lots of trees. It's just ¼ mi from downtown. Rooms, some with lake views, have traditional furnishings. Restaurant, bar. No air-conditioning in some rooms. Cable

TV, some room phones. Indoor pool. Hot tub, sauna. Tennis. Beach. Playground. Laundry facilities. Business services. Some pets allowed. | M–77, Box 277 49839 | 906/494–2361 | fax 906/494–2371 | 41 rooms, 9 cottages | $49–$58, $268–$353 cottages | AE, D, MC, V.

GRAND RAPIDS

Exel Inn. In an adjacent suburb, this two-story motel is 2 mi from Kent County International Airport, 8 mi from Fredrick Meijer Gardens, and 10 mi south of Grand Rapids. Rooms are in the traditional style. Complimentary Continental breakfast. Some pets allowed. | 4855 28th St. SE, Kentwood 49512 | 616/957–3000 | www.exelinn.com | fax 616/957–0194 | 109 rooms | $48–$110 | AE, D, DC, MC, V.

Hawthorn Suites Hotel. This all-suites hotel geared to business travelers is 5 mi from downtown attractions and offices. In a suburban area, it has two floors of traditional suites. Complimentary Continental breakfast. Refrigerators. Cable TV. Business services. Some pets allowed. | 2985 Kraft Ave. SE 49512 | 616/940–1777 or 800/784–8371 | fax 616/940–9809 | 40 suites | $79–$94 suites | AE, D, DC, MC, V.

Holiday Inn North. Just 2 mi north of downtown, this seven-story brick hotel has a scenic view of the area. Restaurant, bar (with entertainment), picnic area. Cable TV. Indoor pool. Hot tub, sauna. Video games. Laundry facilities. Business services. Some pets allowed. | 270 Ann St. NW 49504 | 616/363–9001 or 800/465–4329 | fax 616/363–0670 | www.basshotels.com/holiday-inn | 164 rooms | $79–$99 | AE, D, DC, MC, V.

Red Roof Inn. Traditional rooms are in this two-story chain motel in a commercial area about 9 mi south of downtown. Cable TV. Business services. Some pets allowed. | 5131 28th St. SE 49512 | 616/942–0800 or 800/733–7663 | fax 616/942–8341 | www.redroof.com | 107 rooms | $45–$80 | AE, D, DC, MC, V.

Residence Inn by Marriott. Tudor-style suite accommodations are in this two-story hotel in a commercial area 8 mi southeast of downtown. Picnic area, complimentary Continental breakfast. Kitchenettes. Cable TV. Pool. Hot tub. Exercise equipment. Laundry facilities. Business services, airport shuttle. Some pets allowed. | 2701 E. Beltline SE 49546 | 616/957–8111 | fax 616/957–3699 | www.marriott.com | 96 suites | $104–$139 suites | AE, D, DC, MC, V.

GRAYLING

Holiday Inn. A family-focused hotel and convention center on wooded grounds, this two-floor chain hotel is 5 mi from cross country and downhill skiing and 1 mi from snowmobile trails. Restaurant, bar (with entertainment), picnic area, room service. Some refrigerators. Cable TV. Indoor pool, wading pool. Hot tub. Exercise equipment. Playground. Business services, airport shuttle. Some pets allowed. | 2650 I–75 Bus. Loop S | 517/348–7611 or 800/465–4329 | fax 517/348–7984 | www.basshotels.com/holiday-inn | 151 rooms | $69–$119 | AE, D, DC, MC, V.

North Country Lodge. This small motel in a wooded area ¼ mi north of Grayling is popular with snowmobilers, cross-country skiers, and canoeists. Fishing, swimming, and tubing are just 1 mi away. Half the rooms have a rustic, pine wood style, the other half are modern style. Some kitchenettes, some in-room hot tubs. Cable TV. Some pets allowed. | 617 I–75 Bus. Loop N | 517/348–8471 or 800/475–6300 | fax 517/348–6114 | 23 rooms | $38–$150 | AE, D, DC, MC, V.

Super 8. You only need to travel 3 mi to reach Grayling and all kinds of outdoor recreation when you stay at this year-round motel just off I–75 in a wooded area south of town. Fishing, canoeing, cross-country and downhill skiing, and snowmobiling are among your recreational options. The motel has two floors of rooms with traditional furnishings and standard amenities. Complimentary Continental breakfast. Cable TV. Laundry facilities. Some pets allowed. | 5828 Nelson A. Miles Pkwy. | 517/348–8888 or 800/800–8000 | fax 517/348–2030 | www.super8motels.com | 60 rooms | $48–$68 | AE, D, DC, MC, V.

HOUGHTON

Best Western King's Inn. In the heart of downtown, this five-story chain hotel is within a few blocks of shopping, city parks, and restaurants, and ¾ mi from Michigan Tech. Complimentary Continental breakfast. Cable TV. Indoor pool. Hot tub, sauna. Some pets allowed. | 215 Shelden Ave. 49931 | 906/482–5000 | fax 906/482–9795 | www.houghtonlodging.com | 69 rooms | $69–$81 | AE, D, DC, MC, V.

L'Anse Motel and Suites. This mom-and-pop motel 30 mi south of Houghton, near Baraga State Park and Lake Superior, is decidedly off the beaten path, but good for hikers and outdoor types. It's 4 mi from cross-country skiing and a half-hour to downhill skiing. Cable TV. Some pets allowed. | U.S. 41, Box 506, L'Anse 49946 | 906/524–7820 or 800/800–6198 | fax 906/524–7247 | 21 rooms | $29–$57 | D, DC, MC, V.

Super 8–Baraga. Across the street from a casino, this modern motel is 30 mi from Houghton. Complimentary Continental breakfast. Cable TV. Business services. Pets allowed. | 790 Michigan Ave., Baraga 49908 | 906/353–6680 or 800/800–8000 | fax 906/353–7246 | www.super8motels.com | 40 rooms | $45–$57 | AE, D, DC, MC, V.

IRON MOUNTAIN

Best Western Executive Inn. It's easy to get to this two-story brick chain hotel from U.S. 2. Shopping and fast-food dining are in the immediate area. Downtown Iron Mountain is a mile away, and it's about 5 mi to skiing. Complimentary Continental breakfast. Cable TV. Indoor pool. Some pets allowed. | 1518 S. Stephenson Ave. 49801 | 906/774–2040 or 800/780–7234 | fax 906/774–0238 | www.bestwestern.com | 57 rooms | $58–$68 | AE, D, DC, MC, V.

IRONWOOD

Davey's Motel. This two-story motel, which has a big cedar deck and many evergreens on two sides, is 12 mi from Lake Superior and 5 mi from the Wisconsin border. Some guest rooms have balconies, and all have pleasant views of the surrounding grounds. In-room data ports. Cable TV. Hot tub, sauna. Pets allowed. | 260 E. Cloverland Dr. (U.S. 2) 49938 | 906/932–2020 | fax 906/932–2020 | daveys@portup.com | www.westernup.com/daveys | 23 rooms | $36–$150 | AE, D, MC, V.

Super 8. Two restaurants are adjacent to this two-story chain hotel on U.S. 2. Some refrigerators. Cable TV. Some pets allowed. | 160 E. Cloverland Dr. 49938 | 906/932–3395 | fax 906/932–2507 | www.super8motels.com | 42 rooms | $56–65 | AE, D, DC, MC, V.

JACKSON

Holiday Inn. A Holidome entertainment/pool area draws families to this chain hotel 5 mi from Jackson. It's just off I–94. Restaurant, bar, room service. Cable TV. Indoor pool. Hot tub, sauna. Miniature golf, putting green. Laundry facilities. Business services. Some pets allowed. | 2000 Holiday Inn Dr. 49202 | 517/783–2681 | fax 517/783–5744 | www.basshotels.com/holiday-inn | 184 rooms | $89–$103 | AE, D, DC, MC, V.

Super 8. Several chain restaurants are next door to this two-story chain hotel, right off I–94 at exit 138, and 5 mi from Jackson. Some refrigerators. Cable TV. Some pets allowed. | 2001 Shirley Dr. 49202 | 517/788–8780 or 800/800–8000 | fax 517/788–8780 | www.super8motels.com | 54 rooms | $59–$69 | AE, D, DC, MC, V.

KALAMAZOO

Baymont Inn and Suites. Business travelers and convention-goers are the primary guests of this hotel, although it's also popular with parents visiting students at nearby Western Michigan University and Kalamazoo College. Complimentary Continental breakfast. In-room data ports. Cable TV. Laundry service. Business services. Pets allowed. | 2203 S. 11th

St. 49009 | 616/372–7999 or 800/301–0200 | fax 616/372–6095 | www.baymontinns.com | 70 rooms | $50–$71 | AE, D, DC, MC, V.

Holiday Inn–Airport. In a Kalamazoo industrial district, this chain hotel is 2 mi from the airport. Restaurant, bar, room service. Cable TV. 2 pools (1 indoor). Laundry facilities. Business services, airport shuttle. Some pets allowed. | 3522 Sprinkle Rd. 49002 | 616/381–7070 or 800/465–4329 | fax 616/381–4341 | www.basshotels.com/holiday-inn | 146 rooms | $69–$79 | AE, D, DC, MC, V.

Quality Inn and Suites. Southwestern adornments add a sunny touch to this chain hotel 5 mi west of downtown, off I–94 at exit 80. It's 3 mi to Wings Stadium, site of music concerts. Complimentary Continental breakfast. Cable TV. Pool. Business services, airport shuttle. Some pets allowed. | 3750 Easy St. 49002 | 616/388–3551 | fax 616/342–9132 | www.qualityinn.com | 122 rooms | $69–$120 | AE, D, DC, MC, V.

Red Roof Inn–West. Off U.S. 131 at exit 36-B, this two-story chain hotel is in a quiet residential area within a few miles of Kalamazoo colleges. Business services. Some pets allowed. | 5425 W. Michigan Ave. 49009 | 616/375–7400 or 800/733–7663 | fax 616/375–7533 | www.redroof.com | 108 rooms | $49–$59 | AE, D, DC, MC, V.

Residence Inn by Marriott. Large suites with kitchens are popular with families looking for a little more room and with long-term business travelers. Across the street from a golf course, this chain hotel in a residential area is 5 mi from downtown. Picnic area, complimentary light dinner Mon.–Thurs., complimentary breakfast. In-room data ports, kitchenettes. Cable TV. Pool. Hot tub. Exercise equipment. Laundry facilities. Business services, airport shuttle. Some pets allowed. | 1500 E. Kilgore Rd. 49001 | 616/349–0855 | fax 616/349–0855 | www.marriott.com | 83 suites | $119–$129 suites | AE, D, DC, MC, V.

Super 8. This three-story chain motel is 5 mi west of downtown Kalamazoo. Some refrigerators. Cable TV. Some pets allowed. | 618 Maple Hill Dr. 49009 | 616/345–0146 or 800/800–8000 | www.super8.com | 62 rooms | $55–$70 | AE, D, DC, MC, V.

LANSING AND EAST LANSING

Best Western Midway. Easy access to I–96 and a welcoming lobby with a fireplace are the main attractions at this basic hotel. Shopping is two blocks away and it's 15 mi to downtown Lansing. Restaurant, bar, room service. Cable TV. Indoor pool. Hot tub, sauna. Exercise equipment. Video games. Business services, airport shuttle. Some pets allowed. | 7711 W. Saginaw, Lansing 48917 | 517/627–8471 or 800/780–7234 | fax 517/627–8597 | www.bestwesternmichigan.com | 149 rooms | $78–$108 | AE, D, DC, MC, V.

Red Roof Inn–East. This two-story motel is north of the junction of I–496 and I–96 and 5 mi from downtown Lansing. Business services. Some pets allowed. | 3615 Dunckel Rd., Lansing 48910 | 517/332–2575 or 800/733–7663 | fax 517/332–1459 | www.redroof.com | 80 rooms | $56–$72 | AE, D, DC, MC, V.

LELAND

Falling Waters Lodge. This modern bed and breakfast has some of the best views of any accommodations in town. You can see Lakes Michigan and Leelanau, the Leland River, and a waterfall or two from any given guest room, and there are several waterfront decks. A penthouse room, accessible by a spiral staircase, is also available. Cable TV. Fishing. Pets allowed. | 200 W. Cedar St. 49654 | 231/256–9832 | fax 231/256–9832 | 11 rooms, 10 suites | $140–$225 | AE, D, MC, V.

LUDINGTON

Nader's Lakeshore Motor Lodge. The beach is 1 block away from this family-style motel with a main lodge and annex. It's 1 mi to downtown and the state park. The city's golf course, marina, and boat docks are nearby too. Picnic area. Some kitchenettes, refrigerators. Cable TV. Pool. Basketball. Some pets allowed. | 612 N. Lakeshore Dr. 49431 | 231/843–8757 or 800/968–0109 | www.t-one.net/~naders | 25 rooms | $75–$100 | Closed Dec.–Apr. | AE, D, DC, MC, V.

MACKINAC ISLAND

Mission Point Resort. Weekend sunset cruises and nightly movies are two favorite activities at this upscale family-style resort on 18 acres of lakefront outside of town. Guest rooms are decked out in a Ralph Lauren/lodge style. Lilac gardens surround the lodge. Bar, dining room, picnic area, room service. Cable TV. Pool. Hot tub. Exercise equipment. Boating, bicycles. Video games. Children's programs (4–12). Business services. Some pets allowed (fee). | 1 Lakeshore Dr. 49757 | 906/847–3312 or 800/833–7711 | fax 906/847–3833 | www.missionpoint.com | 242 rooms, 92 suites | $119–$359, $309–$409 suites | Closed Nov.–Apr. | AE, D, MC, V.

MACKINAW CITY

Beachcomber Motel. You can soak up sun on the sandy Lake Huron beach of this motel on a busy tourist strip. Picnic area. Cable TV. Beach. Some pets allowed. | 1011 S. Huron Ave. 49701 | 231/436–8451 | 22 rooms | $39–$125 | AE, D, MC, V.

Capri Motel. This small, independently run motel has basic guest rooms but a surprisingly charming lobby with antique-reproduction furniture and chintz swags on the windows. Cable TV. Pool. Pets allowed. | 801 S. Nicolet St. 49701 | 231/436–5498 | fax 231/436–7328 | 27 rooms | $69–$150 | AE, D, MC, V.

La Mirage Motel. This cozy, family-style inn is near the maritime museum and overlooks Mackinaw's largest lakeshore park and historic lighthouse. Refrigerators, some in-room hot tubs. Cable TV. Indoor pool. Hot tub, sauna. Beach. Some pets allowed. | 699 N. Huron Ave. 49701 | 231/436–5304 or 800/729–0998 | fax 231/436–5304 | www.lighthouseview-motel.com | 25 rooms | $35–$125 | Closed Nov.–Apr. | AE, D, DC, MC, V.

Motel 6. Basic lodgings are available at this chain motel one block from downtown. Some refrigerators. Cable TV. Indoor pool. Hot tub. Some pets allowed. | 206 Nicolet St. 49701 | 231/436–8961 or 800/388–9508 | fax 231/436–7317 | www.motel6.com | 53 rooms | $29–$58 | AE, D, DC, MC, V.

Parkside Inn–Bridgeside. A nice, friendly motel close to Colonial Michilimackinac State Park. Picnic area. Cable TV. Indoor pool. Hot tub. Game room. Some pets allowed. | 102 Nicolet St. 49701 | 231/436–8301 or 800/827–8301 | 44 rooms | $38–$110 | Closed Nov.–Apr. | AE, D, MC, V.

Quality Inn Beachfront. You get striking views of Mackinac Island and the Mighty Mac bridge at this chain hotel at the edge of town. The 270-ft private sandy beach is a family favorite. Picnic area. Some refrigerators. Cable TV. Indoor pool. Hot tub, sauna. Beach. Playground. Business services. Some pets allowed. | 917 S. Huron Ave. 49701 | 231/436–5051 | fax 231/436–7221 | 60 rooms | $24–$119 | AE, D, DC, MC, V.

Starlite Budget Inns. This no-frills motel is off the highway. Refrigerators. Cable TV. Pool. Playground. Some pets allowed. | 116 Old U.S. 31 49701 | 231/436–5959 or 800/288–8190 | fax 231/436–5101 | 33 rooms | $28–$89 | Closed Nov.–Apr. | AE, D, DC, MC, V.

Super 8. This year-round chain motel near the bridge is just a mile to area snowmobile trails. Cable TV. Indoor pool. Hot tub, sauna. Game room. Laundry facilities. Some pets allowed. | 601 N. Huron Ave. 49701 | 231/436–5252 or 800/800–8000 | fax 231/436–7004 | www.super8motels.com | 50 rooms | $32–$135 | AE, D, DC, MC, V.

Surf. Simple, family-style accommodations overlooking Lake Huron and within walking distance of ferries can be had here. There is a view of the bridge and the island. Refrigerators. Cable TV. Indoor pool. Hot tub. Beach. Playground. Business services. Some pets allowed. | 907 S. Huron Ave. 49701 | 231/436–8831 or 800/822–8314 | 40 rooms | $30–$85 | Closed Nov.–Apr. | AE, D, MC, V.

Waterfront Inn. Kids love the 600-ft private beach on Lake Huron, Mackinaw City's largest, at this independent motor inn. Picnic area. Cable TV. Pool. Hot tub. Beach. Playground. Some pets allowed. | 1009 S. Huron Ave. 49701 | 231/436–5527 or 800/962–9832 | 69 rooms | $28–$89 | AE, D, MC, V.

MANISTIQUE

Econo Lodge. The Lake Michigan boardwalk is across the street from this chain hotel. Complimentary Continental breakfast. Cable TV. Some pets allowed. | 209 E. Lake Shore 49854 | 906/341–6014 or 800/553–2666 | fax 906/341–2979 | www.econolodge.com | 31 rooms | $38–$66 | AE, D, DC, MC, V.

Holiday Motel. Schoolcraft County Airport is across the highway from these family-owned accommodations, 4 mi from town. Shuttles run from town to motel as well as to the casino, a mile away. The motel's 14 acres of evergreens are connected to snowmobile trails. Picnic area, complimentary Continental breakfast. No air-conditioning. Cable TV. Pool. Playground. Some pets allowed. | U.S. 2 49854 | 906/341–2710 | 20 rooms | $32–$49 | AE, D, MC, V.

MARQUETTE

Holiday Inn. Family-centered accommodations are available at this chain hotel. The rustic style includes a huge stone fireplace in the lobby. Restaurant, bar, picnic area, room service. Cable TV. Indoor pool. Hot tub, sauna. Cross-country and downhill skiing. Business services, airport shuttle. Some pets allowed. | 1951 U.S. 41 W 49855 | 906/225–1351 or 800/465–4329 | fax 906/228–4329 | www.basshotels.com/holiday-inn | 203 rooms | $75–$79 | AE, D, DC, MC, V.

Ramada Inn. Downtown recreation and shopping are near this comfortable chain hotel. Restaurant, bar, room service. Cable TV. Indoor pool. Hot tub, sauna. Laundry facilities. Business services, airport shuttle. Some pets allowed. | 412 W. Washington St./U.S. 41 Bus. 49855 | 906/228–6000 or 800/298–2054 | fax 906/228–2963 | www.ramada.com | 113 rooms | $77–$87 | AE, D, DC, MC, V.

MIDLAND

Best Western Valley Plaza. This popular chain hotel is a favorite of business travelers midweek and families on weekends. Restaurant, room service. In-room data ports. Cable TV. Indoor pool, lake, wading pool. Beach. Game room. Airport shuttle. Some pets allowed. | 5221 Bay City Rd. 48642 | 517/496–2700 | fax 517/496–9233 | www.bestwestern.com | 162 rooms | $62–$82 | AE, D, DC, MC, V.

Holiday Inn. Downtown Midland and the Soaring Eagle Casino aren't far from this chain hotel. Restaurant, bar (with entertainment), room service. In-room data ports, minibars. Cable TV. Indoor pool. Hot tub. Exercise equipment. Game room. Business services, airport shuttle. Some pets allowed. | 1500 W. Wackerly St. 48640 | 517/631–4220 or 800/465–4329 | fax 517/631–3776 | www.basshotels.com/holiday-inn | 236 rooms | $79–$140 | AE, D, DC, MC, V.

Ramada Inn Midland. In Midland's business district, this two-story chain hotel is north of U.S. 10 and 5 mi from Valley Plaza Convention Center. Restaurant, bar, complimentary Continental breakfast. In-room data ports, in-room safes, some in-room hot tubs. Cable TV. Pool. Gym. Laundry service. Business services. Pets allowed. | 1815 S. Saginaw Rd. 48640 | 517/631–0570 or 800/298–2054 | fax 517/631–0920 | www.ramada.com | 80 rooms | $55–$72 | AE, D, DC, MC, V.

MONROE

Comfort Inn. This three-floor chain hotel, west off I–75 N, exit 11, is next door to Horizon Outlet Mall. Complimentary Continental breakfast. In-room data ports, microwaves, refrigerators, some in-room hot tubs. Cable TV. Pool. Hot tub. Laundry service. Business services. Pets allowed. | 6500 E. Albain Rd. 48161 | 734/384–1500 | fax 734/384–1515 | www.choicehotels.com | 65 rooms | $74–$134 | AE, D, DC, MC, V.

Days Inn. Basic accommodations are available at this chain motor inn off I–75 near downtown and the Horizon Outlet Mall. Restaurant, bar, room service. In-room data ports. Cable TV. Indoor pool. Hot tub, sauna. Business services. Some pets allowed. | 1440 N. Dixie Hwy. (Rte. 50) 48162 | 734/289–4000 | fax 734/289–4262 | www.choicehotels.com | 115 rooms | $53–$65 | AE, D, DC, MC, V.

Holiday Inn. Native son General George Custer is honored in the rustic look and vintage Western photos of this hostelry. Restaurant, bar (with entertainment), room service. In-room data ports. Cable TV. Indoor pool. Hot tub, sauna. Game room. Some pets allowed. | 1225 N. Dixie Hwy. 48616 | 734/242–6000 | fax 734/242–0555 | www.basshotels.com/holiday-inn | 127 rooms | $69–$89 | AE, D, DC, MC, V.

MT. PLEASANT

Comfort Inn University Park. This comfortable facility next to Central Michigan University is also across the street from the Soaring Eagle Casino. It's within walking distance of restaurants. Complimentary Continental breakfast. In-room data ports. Cable TV, in-room VCRs (and movies). Indoor pool. Game room. Laundry facilities. Business services. Some pets allowed. | 2424 S. Mission St. 48858 | 517/772–4000 | fax 517/773–6052 | www.comfortinn.com | 138 rooms, 12 suites | $59–$150, $99–$195 suites | AE, D, DC, MC, V.

Fairfield Inn. Central Michigan University is across the street and the Soaring Eagle Casino is 4 mi from this hotel on parklike, well-landscaped grounds. Complimentary Continental breakfast. In-room data ports. Cable TV. Indoor pool. Game room. Laundry facilities. Business services. Some pets allowed. | 2525 University Park 48858 | 517/775–5000 | fax 517/773–1371 | www.labellemanagement.com | 74 rooms | $55–$90 | AE, D, DC, MC, V.

Holiday Inn. A wide range of facilities are available at this modern chain hotel that's 4 mi to Central Michigan University and a mile to the Soaring Eagle Casino. Restaurants, bar (with entertainment), room service. In-room data ports, some minibars, refrigerators, in-room hot tubs. Cable TV. 2 pools (1 indoor). Hot tub. Driving range, 36-hole golf course, putting green, tennis. Exercise equipment. Playground. Laundry facilities. Business services, airport shuttle. Some pets allowed. | 5665 E. Pickard Rd. 48858 | 517/772–2905 | fax 517/772–4952 | www.highresort.com | 184 rooms | $65–$150 | AE, D, DC, MC, V.

Super 8. Basic, no-frills accommodations are available at this motel just off U.S. 27. Complimentary Continental breakfast. Some refrigerators. Cable TV. Business services. Some pets allowed. | 2323 S. Mission 48858 | 517/773–8888 or 800/800–8000 | fax 517/772–5371 | www.super8motels.com | 143 rooms | $49–$90 | AE, D, DC, MC, V.

MUNISING

Alger Falls. Cozy, independently owned lodgings sit back from the road, surrounded by evergreens and trees. Picnic area. Cable TV. Snowmobiling. Some pets allowed. | E9427 M–28 49861 | 906/387–3536 | fax 906/387–3537 | www.algersfallsmotel.com | 17 rooms | $35–$64 | D, MC, V.

Best Western. Comfortable accommodations and on-site groomed snowmobile trails attract snowmobilers. Nearby cross-country ski trails include the Valley Spur ski area, 5 mi away. The motor inn is 4 mi out of town and surrounded by forest. Restaurant, bar, picnic area. Some refrigerators. Indoor pool. Hot tub, sauna. Snowmobiling. Business services. Some pets allowed. | M–28, Box 310 49895 | 906/387–4864 or 800/780–7234 | fax 906/387–2038 | www.bestwestern.com | 80 rooms | $55–$85 | AE, D, DC, MC, V.

Comfort Inn. Pictured Rock cruises and highways are near this chain hotel. Complimentary Continental breakfast. Cable TV, in-room VCRs (and movies). Indoor pool. Hot tub. Exercise equipment. Cross-country skiing. Laundry facilities. Business services. Some pets allowed. | M–28, Box 276 49895 | 906/387–5292 or 800/228–5150 | fax 906/387–3753 | www.choicehotels.com | 61 rooms | $55–$85 | AE, D, DC, MC, V.

Homestead Bed and Breakfast. This four-story 1890 house is on 25 wooded acres. The interior has Alaskan photos, masks, Russian dolls, and walrus ivory ornaments. A spacious porch overlooks the lawn and gardens. Breakfast is fresh fruit, bagels, and homemade muffins. Complimentary Continental breakfast. No TV in some rooms, TV in common area. Snowmobiling. Pets allowed. No smoking. | 713 Prospect St. 49862 | 906/387–2542 | 6 rooms (3 with private bath) | $65–$90 | MC, V.

Sunset Resort. This simple motel on Lake Superior is a favorite of families. Picnic area. No air-conditioning, some kitchenettes. Cable TV. Lake. Dock. Playground. Some pets allowed. | 1315 Bay St. 49825 | 906/387–4574 | 16 rooms, 5 suites | $35–$49, $55–$75 suites | Closed late Oct.–Apr. | MC, V.

Terrace Motel. Snowmobile trails begin at this motel two blocks from M–28, four blocks from Pictured Rocks Golf Course. Accommodations include one-, two-, and three-bedroom units. You can use a recreation room with billiards, a kitchen, and a sauna. Cable TV. Sauna. Pets allowed. | 420 Prospect St. 49862 | 906/387–2735 | fax 906/387–2754 | 18 rooms | $40–$52 | D, MC, V.

NEW BUFFALO

Comfort Inn. A pleasant breakfast room overlooks the courtyard of this chain hotel near beaches and shopping. Restaurant. Some in-room hot tubs. Cable TV. Gym. Game room. Laundry facilities. Business services. Some pets allowed. | 11539 O'Brien Ct. 49117 | 616/469–4440 | fax 616/469–5972 | www.choicehotels.com | 96 rooms | $59–$115 | AE, D, DC, MC, V.

NEWBERRY

Rainbow Lodge. Surrounded by state forests, this lodge, ¼ mi from Lake Superior, is popular with hunters and snowmobilers. The cafe is open during snowmobiling season. Restaurant. Some kitchenettes, some refrigerators. No room phones, no TV. Cross-country skiing. Pets allowed. | County Rd. 423 49868 | 906/658–3357 | 10 rooms, 2 cabins | $40–$80 | MC, V.

Zellar's Village Inn. Taquamenon Falls State Park is 30 mi from this small, independently owned motel right in the center of town. Restaurant, bar, room service. In-room data ports. Cable TV. Game room. Business services. Some pets allowed. | 7552 S. Newberry Ave. 49868 | 906/293–5114 | fax 906/293–5116 | 20 rooms | $50–$65 | AE, D, DC, MC, V.

PAW PAW

Quality Inn and Suites. Comfortable accommodations are at this two-story chain hotel built downtown in 1997. Some in-room hot tubs. Cable TV. Gym. Cross-country skiing. Game room. Laundry facilities. Business services. Some pets allowed. | 153 Ampey Rd. 49079 | 616/655–0303 or 800/228–5151 | fax 616/657–1015 | www.qualityinn.com | 49 rooms, 16 suites | $55–$100 | AE, D, DC, MC, V.

PETOSKEY

Econo Lodge. Comfortable lodgings are provided by this chain hotel on the outskirts of town near the junction of routes 31 and 131. Complimentary Continental breakfast. Cable TV. Indoor pool. Hot tub. Business services. Some pets allowed. | 1858 U.S. 131 S 49770 | 231/

348–3324 or 800/553–2666 | fax 231/348–3521 | www.econolodge.com | 60 rooms | $41–$110 | AE, D, DC, MC, V.

PLYMOUTH

Red Roof Inn. Basic budget lodgings are available at this chain hotel near restaurants and shopping. In-room data ports. Cable TV. Some pets allowed. | 39700 Ann Arbor Rd. 48170 | 734/459–3300 or 800/733–7663 | fax 734/459–3072 | 109 rooms | $43–$63 | www.redroof.com | AE, D, DC, MC, V.

Willow Brook Inn Bed and Breakfast. An acre of woods, gardens, and a brook surround this 1929 arts and crafts home. Breakfast, made to order and at the time you want, is served on a deck in summer, in the garden room in winter, or in your room. A guest area has a computer, microwave, and refrigerator with complimentary snacks and sodas. Complimentary breakfast. Some in-room hot tubs, in-room VCRs. TV. Pets allowed. No smoking. | 44255 Warren Rd., Canton 48187 | 734/454–0019 or 888/454–1919 | fax 734/451–1126 | wbibnb@earthlink.net | www.bbonline.com/mi/willow/index/html | 3 suites | $95–$125 | AE, MC, V.

PONTIAC

Hilton Suites. Roomy, suite-size accommodations are handy for business travelers and families. The hotel is near Daimler-Chrysler headquarters, the Silverdome, the Palace, and other Oakland County attractions. Restaurant, bar, complimentary breakfast, room service. In-room data ports, refrigerators. Cable TV, in-room VCRs (and movies). Indoor pool. Hot tub. Exercise equipment. Game room. Laundry facilities. Business services. Some pets allowed. | 2300 Featherstone Rd., Auburn Hills 48326 | 248/334–2222 | fax 248/334–2922 | www.hilton.com | 224 suites | $129–$149 suites | AE, D, DC, MC, V.

PORT AUSTIN

Lakeside Motor Lodge. In downtown, this motel sits directly on Lake Huron. The cottages have full kitchens, and rooms have views of the water. Some kitchenettes, some microwaves, some refrigerators. Cable TV. Pool. Boating, fishing. Playground. Pets allowed. | 8654 Lake St. 48467 | 517/738–5201 | 35 rooms, 15 cottages | $40–$90 | AE, MC, V.

PRESQUE ISLE

Northwood Shores Cabin Resort. These housekeeping cottages on the east shore of Grand Lake are 5 mi from Lake Huron. Some are no-smoking. No air conditioning. No room phones. Boating. Pets allowed. | 8844 E. Grand Lake Rd. 49777 | 989/595–6429 | pettalia@freeway.net | www.oweb.com/upnorth/northwood | 6 cabins, 3 two-level | $420–$520 per week | Closed Nov.–Apr. | V, MC.

ROMULUS

Baymont Inn Detroit Airport. Less than a mi from Detroit Metro Airport, this three-floor hotel is north of I–94, off of exit 198. Complimentary Continental breakfast. In-room data ports, some microwaves, some refrigerators. Cable TV. Business services. Airport shuttle. Pets allowed. | 9000 Wickham Rd. 48174 | 734/722–6000 | fax 734/722–4737 | feedback@baymontinns.com | www.baymontinns.com | 81 rooms | $89–$99 | AE, D, DC, MC, V.

Crowne Plaza. Its upscale accommodations and proximity to the airport are this hotel's two best selling points. Its welcoming lobby and dramatic, 11-story atrium, which some rooms overlook, are also big pluses. It's 2 mi north of Detroit Metro Airport in a commercial area. Restaurant, bar. In-room data ports, cable TV. Indoor pool. Hot tub. Exercise equipment. Business services, airport shuttle. Some pets allowed. | 8000 Merriman Rd. 48174 | 734/729–2600 or 800/227–6963 | fax 734/729–9414 | detroitcrown@cs.com | www.holidayinn.com.ru/crowneplaza | 365 rooms | $130–$150. | AE, D, DC, MC, V.

ROYAL OAK

Quality Inn Hazel Park. Two miles southeast of Royal Oak, this nine-floor hotel is off I–75 at the 9 Mile Road exit in Hazel Park. Some rooms have balconies overlooking the city. Restaurant, bar, room service. Some in-room hot tubs. Cable TV. Business services. Pets allowed. | 1 W. 9 Mile Rd., Hazel Park | 248/399–5800 | fax 248/399–2602 | www.qualityinn.com | 184 rooms | $66–$89 | AE, MC, V.

SAGINAW

Four Points by Sheraton. Country French describes this six-story hotel, which is ¾ mi from the Fashion Square Mall. Restaurant, bar, room service. Cable TV. Indoor-outdoor pool. Hot tub, sauna. Business services, airport shuttle. Some pets allowed. | 4960 Towne Centre Rd. 48604 | 517/790–5050 | fax 517/790–1466 | www.fourpoints.com | 156 rooms | $99–$129 | AE, D, DC, MC, V.

Super 8. This three-story budget motel is 2 blocks from the Fashion Square Mall. Cable TV. Some pets allowed. | 4848 Town Centre Rd. 48603 | 517/791–3003 | fax 517/791–3003 | www.super8.com | 62 rooms | $38–$52 | AE, D, DC, MC, V.

ST. IGNACE

Budget Host Golden Anchor. This hotel is 1 mi north of the Mackinac Bridge and a block from the ferries. Some rooms have private balconies or decks with stunning views of Lake Huron. The Huron boardwalk is within walking distance, as are shops, restaurants, the beach, and a museum. In-room data ports, some refrigerators, in-room hot tubs. Cable TV. Indoor pool. Hot tub. Playground. Business services. Some pets allowed. | 700 N. State St. 49781 | 906/643–9666 | fax 906/643–9126 or 800/872–7057 | stay@stignacebudgethost.com | www.stignacebudgethost.com | 56 rooms | $55–$170 (suites) | AE, D, DC, MC, V.

Howard Johnson Express. This two-story hotel on the southwest side of St. Ignace is ½ mi from the ferries and has a 24-hour shuttle to the Kewadin Casino in Sault Ste. Marie. You can rent one of the hotel's snowmobiles in winter. Complimentary Continental breakfast. Cable TV. Indoor pool. Hot tub. Video games. Laundry facilities. Some pets allowed. | 913 Boulevard Dr. 48671 | 906/643–9700 | fax 906/643–6762 | helmera@up.net | www.hojoexpress.net | 57 rooms | $89–$129 | AE, D, DC, MC, V.

ST. JOSEPH

Comfort Inn. This single-story chain motel is off I–94 in downtown Benton Harbor. Complimentary Continental breakfast. Some refrigerators. Cable TV. Indoor pool. Hot tub. Business services. Some pets allowed. | 1598 Mall Dr., Benton Harbor 49022 | 616/925–1880 | comfortinn@portup.com | www.comfortinn.com | 52 rooms | $73–$113 | AE, D, DC, MC, V.

Super 8. There's no-frills lodging at this three-story chain hotel on the outskirts of Benton Harbor. It's near Lake Michigan and I–94. Cable TV. Business services. Some pets allowed. | 1950 E. Napier Ave., Benton Harbor 49022 | 616/926–1371 | fax 616/926–1371, ext. 169 | 62 rooms | $39–$46 | AE, D, DC, MC, V.

SAULT STE. MARIE

Bambi Motel. Two miles from exit 392 off I–75, this motel is 1 mi south of the Soo Locks. Picnic area. Some refrigerators. Cable TV. Pool. Playground. Pets allowed. | 1801 Ashmun St. 49783 | 906/632–7881 or 800/289–0864 | www.saultstemarie.com/accom/bambi/bambi.htm | 25 rooms | $39–$65 | MC, V.

Budget Host Crestview Inns. You'll be close to attractions, restaurants, and shopping at this single-story motel downtown. In-room data ports. Cable TV. Some pets allowed. | 1200 Ashmun St. 49783 | 906/635–5213 or 800/955–5213 | fax 906/635–9672 | www.saultstemarie.com/accom/crestv/ | 44 rooms | $39–$59 | AE, D, DC, MC, V.

SOUTH HAVEN

Econo Lodge. A standard budget motel, this single-story, red-trimmed property is 1 mi from downtown South Haven. Bar. Cable TV. Indoor pool. Gym. Playground. Laundry facilities. Some pets allowed. | 09817 Rte. 140 49090 | 616/637–5141 | fax 616/637–1109 | 60 rooms | $55–$120 | AE, D, DC, MC, V.

SOUTHFIELD

Hilton Garden Inn. A business traveler's first choice, this 6-story hotel with nice amenities is off busy I–696 and the Lodge Freeway (U.S. 10). There are private sitting areas in the lobby, and a garden lounge, as well as a sun deck. The rooms have multiple phone lines. Restaurant, bar. In-room data ports. Cable TV. Indoor pool. Hot tub. Exercise equipment. Business services. Some pets allowed. | 26000 American Dr. 48034 | 248/357–1100 or 800/445–8667 | fax 248/799–7030 | www.hilton.com | 197 rooms | $120–$170 | AE, D, DC, MC, V.

Holiday Inn. This 16-story chain hotel in a circular glass tower is popular with business travelers. It has a Holidome recreation center, and is 2 mi from a shopping mall, 5 mi from the Detroit Zoo, and 15 mi from the Henry Ford Museum. Restaurant, bar, room service. Cable TV. Indoor pool. Beauty salon, hot tub. Video games. Laundry facilities. Some pets allowed. | 26555 Telegraph Rd. 48034 | 248/353–7700 | fax 248/353–8377 | gm201@:columbiasussex.com | www.basshotels.com/holiday-inn | 415 rooms | $75–$99 | AE, D, DC, MC, V.

TAWAS CITY AND EAST TAWAS

Aaron's Wooded Acres Resort. The homey cottages at this resort 4 mi north of town on Lake Huron have full kitchens; a sitting area with a fireplace; and one, two, or three bedrooms and are privately spaced around the 2½-acre grounds. You can go swimming in the lake or play darts and billiards in the game room. Picnic area. Some in-room hot tubs. Beach. Boating, fishing. Pets allowed. | 968 N. U.S. 23, East Tawas 48730 | 517/362–5188 | www.aaronswoodedacresresort.com | 11 cottages | $75–$95 | D, MC, V.

TRAVERSE CITY

Anchor Inn. You may feel nostalgic when you see the knotty pine furniture and quilts and dust ruffles on the beds in the rooms and cottages here. The one-, two-, and three-bedroom cottages have fireplaces and kitchens. Bring your own boat; there's plenty of parking. Enjoy the 100-ft water frontage on west Grand Traverse Bay. The inn is 2½ mi north of town. Picnic area. Some kitchenettes. Cable TV, room phones. Lake. Volleyball. Beach. Playground. Pets allowed. | 11998 S. West Bay Shore Dr. 49684 | 231/946–7442 | fax 231/929–2589 | anchorinn@aol.com | www.anchorinn.net | 6 rooms, 8 cottages | $59–$102, $118–$176 cottages | AE, D, MC, V.

Holiday Inn. On West Grand Traverse Bay, this four-story chain hotel has a private marina and beach. It's 1½ blocks from downtown. Restaurant, bar, room service. Some refrigerators. Cable TV. Indoor pool. Hot tub. Exercise equipment. Video games. Business services, airport shuttle. Some pets allowed. | 615 E. Front St. 49686 | 231/947–3700 | fax 231/947–0361 | sales@traverse-holidayinn.com | www.basshotels.com/holiday-inn | 179 rooms | $80–$142 | AE, D, DC, MC, V.

Main Street Inn. All rooms are on the street level at this motel close to a park, the beach on scenic Front Street, and the downtown area. Kitchenettes. Cable TV. Pool. Putting green. Laundry facilities. Business services. Some pets allowed. | 618 E. Front St. 49686 | 231/929–0410 or 800/255–7180 | fax 231/929–0489 | www.mainstreetinnusa.com | 95 rooms | $40–$90 | AE, D, DC, MC, V.

Traverse Bay Inn. One- and two-bedroom suites and studios are available at this small motel minutes from downtown. You can use one of the motel's bicycles to ride on the adjoining Traverse Area Recreational Bike Trail. Picnic area. Some refrigerators. Cable TV. Pool. Hot tub. Bicycles. Video games. Playground. Laundry facilities. Business services. Some pets allowed. | 2300 U.S. 31 N. 49686 | 231/938–2646 or 800/968–2646 | fax 231/938–5845 | fun@traversebay.com | www.traversebay.com | 24 studios and suites | $79 studios, $149–$209 suites | AE, D, MC, V.

TROY

Drury Inn. The Somerset Collection and Kmart headquarters are near this four-story chain hotel. It's a favorite of business travelers. Complimentary Continental breakfast. In-room data ports. Cable TV. Pool. Some pets allowed. | 575 W. Big Beaver Rd. 48084 | 248/528–3330 | fax 248/528–3330 | www.drury-inn.com | 153 rooms | $91–$108 | AE, D, DC, MC, V.

Hampton Inn. This chain hotel is in an upscale part of Madison Heights, and has four stories. Complimentary Continental breakfast. In-room data ports. Cable TV. Exercise equipment. Some pets allowed. | 32420 Stephenson Hwy., Madison Heights 48071 | 248/585–8881 | fax 248/585–9446 | www.hampton-inn.com | 124 rooms | $68–$85 | AE, D, DC, MC, V.

Holiday Inn. This four-story hotel is in southwest Troy just off I–75. It's close to shopping, restaurants, and the city's corporate parks. Restaurant, bar, room service. In-room data ports. Cable TV. Pool. Exercise equipment. Some pets allowed. | 2537 Rochester Ct. 48083 | 248/689–7500 or 800/465–4329 | fax 248/689–9015 | www.basshotels.com/holiday-inn | 153 rooms | $69–$119 | AE, D, DC, MC, V.

Marriott. A large atrium lobby and stylish rooms distinguish this 17-story hotel on Troy's west side. It is convenient to Troy corporate parks, restaurants, and shopping. Restaurant, bar. In-room data ports. Cable TV. Indoor pool. Hot tub. Exercise equipment. Business services. Some pets allowed. | 200 W. Big Beaver Rd. 48084 | 248/680–9797 or 800/228–9290 | fax 248/680–9774 | www.marriott.com | 350 rooms | $84–$174 | AE, D, DC, MC, V.

Northfield Hilton. This full-service hotel is off I–75 and near Somerset Collection, office parks, and restaurants. Restaurant, bar (with jazz entertainment, cigar bar), room service. In-room data ports, some refrigerators. Cable TV. Indoor pool. Sauna. Business services. Some pets allowed. | 5500 Crooks Rd. 48098 | 248/879–2100 or 800/445–8667 | fax 248/879–6054 | www.hilton.com | 191 rooms | $79–$159 | AE, D, DC, MC, V.

Red Roof Inn. This budget-minded, two-story chain hotel is on Troy's southwest side near Oakland University, site of the Meadow Brook Music Festival. In-room data ports. Cable TV. Some pets allowed. | 2350 Rochester Ct. 48083 | 248/689–4391 or 800/733–7663 | fax 248/689 4397 | www.redroof.com | 109 rooms | $51–$77 | AE, D, DC, MC, V.

Residence Inn by Marriott. Business travelers prefer this two-story, all-suite hotel just off I–75 because it's near many corporate complexes. Picnic area, complimentary Continental breakfast. In-room data ports, kitchenettes. Cable TV. Pool. Hot tub. Laundry facilities. Some pets allowed. | 2600 Livernois Rd. 48083 | 248/689–6856 | fax 248/689–3788 | www.marriothotels.com | 152 suites | $129–$179 | AE, D, DC, MC, V.

WAKEFIELD

Indianhead Mountain Resort. Several types of accommodations are available at this resort on 185 acres. You can stay in the main lodge, or rent a condo or a trailside chalet. Bar (with entertainment), dining room. Cable TV. Indoor pool. Hot tub. 9-hole golf course, tennis. Exercise equipment, hiking. Bicycles. Downhill skiing, sleigh rides. Children's programs (infants–17), playground. Business services. Some pets allowed. | 500 Indianhead Rd. 49968 | 906/229–5920 or 800/346–3426 | fax 906/229–5920 | info@indianheadmtn.com | www.indianheadmtn.com/lodging.html | 40 rooms, 60 condos, 43 chalets | $90–$164, $72–$152 condos, $122–$256 chalets | Closed mid-Apr.–June, Oct.–mid-Nov. | AE, D, MC, V.

Northwoods Motel. This no-frills place is right on the main highway, 2 mi west of town. The rooms are quiet and have two double beds. Some pets allowed. | 912 W. U.S. 2 49968 | 906/224–8631 | 16 rooms | $35–$42 | D, MC, V.

WARREN

Georgian Inn. Despite being along the busy Gratiot strip, this two-story hotel in Roseville has a quiet location and a peaceful courtyard. It's 6 mi from Warren. Restaurant, bar, room service. In-room data ports, some in-room hot tubs. Cable TV. Pool. Exercise equipment. Laundry facilities. Business services. Some pets allowed. | 31327 Gratiot Ave., Roseville 48066 | 810/294–0400 or 800/477–1466 | fax 810/294–1020 | www.thegeorgianinn.com | 111 rooms | $70–$76 | AE, D, DC, MC, V.

Homewood Suites. Apartment-style rooms are designed to make business travelers feel at home. This three-story hotel is 17 mi north of downtown Detroit. Complimentary Continental breakfast. In-room data ports, kitchenettes. Cable TV, in-room VCRs (and movies). Pool. Hot tub. Exercise equipment. Laundry facilities. Business services. Some pets allowed (fee). | 30180 N. Civic Center Dr. 48093 | 810/558–7870 or 800/225–5466 | fax 810/558–8072 | www.homewood-suites.com | 76 suites | $89–$169 | AE, D, DC, MC, V.

Motel 6. Rooms have either one king or two double-size beds in this motel in the heart of the business district. In-room data ports. Some pets allowed. | 8300 Chicago Rd. 48093 | 810/826–9300 | fax 810/979–4525 | 115 rooms | $42.95 | AE, D, DC, MC, V.

Red Roof Inn. This no-frills chain hotel just off I–696 at exit 20 has location going for it. It's 4 mi to the Detroit Zoo, 5 mi to the Michigan State Fairgrounds, and 20 mi to the Pontiac Silverdome and the Palace of Auburn Hills. In-room data ports. Cable TV. Business services. Some pets allowed. | 26300 Dequindre Rd. 48091 | 810/573–4300 | fax 810/573–6157 | www.redroof.com | 136 rooms | $45–$60 | AE, D, DC, MC, V.

Residence Inn by Marriott. One- and two-bedroom suites make this three-story hotel popular with business travelers. It's on the east side of Warren. Picnic area, complimentary Continental breakfast. In-room data ports, kitchenettes. Cable TV, in-room VCRs (and movies). Pool. Hot tub. Exercise equipment. Laundry facilities. Some pets allowed (fee). | 30120 Civic Center Dr. 48093 | 810/558–8050 | fax 810/558–8214 | www.marriotthotels.com | 133 suites | $79–$129 | AE, D, DC, MC, V.

Minnesota

AITKIN

Ripple River Motel and RV Park. The Ripple River flows just north of this motel, which sits on the southern edge of town. It is 10 mi from Lake Mille Lacs. Room access is via outside corridors. Complimentary Continental breakfast. Microwaves, refrigerators. Cable TV. Cross-country skiing, snowmobiling. Business services. Some pets allowed. | 701 Minnesota Ave. S 56431 | 218/927–3734 or 800/258–3734 | fax 218/927–3540 | jfkeimig@msn.com | www.ripplerivermotel.com | 29 rooms | $42–$75, $20 full RV hook-up | AE, D, MC, V.

ALBERT LEA

Bel Aire. Standing across the street from a shopping mall, this hotel is 1½ mi south of Albert Lea. Complimentary Continental breakfast. Cable TV. Pool. Playground. Some pets allowed. | 700 U.S. 69S | 507/373–3983 or 800/373–4073 | fax 507/373–5161 | 46 rooms | $35–$65 | D, MC, V.

Budget Host Albert Lea Inn. This budget inn is on the east edge of town, near several other accommodations. Restaurant, bar. Cable TV. Indoor pool. Hot tub. Video games. Laundry facilities. Business services. Some pets allowed. | 2301 E. Main St. | 507/373–8291 | fax 507/373–4043 | www.budgethost.com | 124 rooms | $59–$69 | AE, D, DC, MC, V.

Days Inn. The intersection of I–35 and I–90 is 1 mi north of this hotel. Restaurant, bar. In-room data ports. Cable TV. Indoor pool. Laundry facilities. Business services. Some pets allowed. | 2306 E. Main St. | 507/373–6471 | fax 507/373–7517 | 129 rooms | $59–$79 | AE, D, DC, MC, V.

Super 8. On the east edge of town, this hostelry stands among several restaurants and other accommodations. Some microwaves. Cable TV, in-room VCRs. Cross-country skiing. Business services. Pets allowed. | 2019 East Main St. 56007 | 507/377–0591 | www.super8hotels.com | 60 rooms | $37–$58 | AE, D, DC, MC, V.

ALEXANDRIA

Big Foot Resort. At the southwest corner of Lake Mary, this 19-acre resort has close to 1,000 ft of lakefront. Cabins sleep six and their patios and decks have lake views. No air-conditioning. Kitchenettes, refrigerators. No room phones. Basketball, volleyball. Beach, dock, boating. Playground. Some pets allowed. | 8231 State Hwy. 114 SW 56308 | 320/283–5533 or 888/239–2512 | fax 320/283–5040 | www.bigfootresort.com | 6 cabins | $90–$100 | MC, V.

Radisson Arrowwood. Directly on the shores of Lake Darling, 4 mi northwest of Alexandria, this rustic-but-modern resort hotel on 250 acres has lake-view balconies on most of its rooms. Bar, dining room, room service. In-room data ports, some microwaves, some refrigerators. Cable TV. 2 pools (1 indoor). Hot tub. 18-hole golf course, tennis. Health club. Beach, water sports, boating, bicycles. Ice-skating, cross-country skiing, sleigh rides, snowmobiling, tobogganing. Video games. Children's programs (5–12 yrs.), playground. Business services, airport shuttle. Pets allowed. | 2100 Arrowwood La. 56308 | 320/762–1124 or 800/333–3333 | fax 320/762–0133 | resort@rea-alp.com | www.radisson.com | 200 rooms, 24 suites | $149–$199, $225–$250 suites | AE, D, DC, MC, V.

ANOKA

Anoka Super 8. This two-story motel, built in 1990, is on the city's western edge, 1 mi from downtown. Complimentary Continental breakfast. Cable TV. Laundry services. Business services. Pets allowed. | 1129 W. Hwy. 10 55303 | 612/422–8000 or 800/800–8000 | fax 612/422–4892 | www.super8.com | 56 rooms | $67–$120 | AE, D, DC, MC, V.

AUSTIN

Holiday Inn. Both businesspeople and families enjoy this full-service hotel, right off I–90 (exit 178A), northwest of town. The main attraction is the Holidome, an indoor recreation area with three pools, a putting green, games, and a health club, among other diversions. 4 restaurants, bar (with entertainment), room service. In-room data ports, some refrigerators. Cable TV. 3 indoor pools, wading pool. Sauna. Putting green. Health club. Video games. Laundry facilities. Business services, airport shuttle. Some pets allowed. | 1701 4th St. NW | 507/433–1000 or 800/985–8850 | fax 507/433–8749 | hiata@clear.lakes.com | www.holiday-inn.com | 121 rooms, 11 suites | $89–$99, $119–$159 suites | AE, D, DC, MC, V.

BABBITT

Alder Place Inn. Built in the 1950s, this single-story inn sits on 2 acres, next to snowmobile, bicycle, and cross-country skiing trails. Rooms are done in gingham and prints with pine furnishings. The common area is a sunroom with a fireplace. Picnic area. Cable TV. Pets allowed (fee). | 13 Alder Rd. 55706 | 218/827–2220 | fax 218/827–2220 | 10 rooms | $34–$45 | AE, D, MC, V.

Timber Bay Lodge and Houseboats. A resort deep in the Superior National Forest, this hostelry has log-sided cabins with fireplaces, decks and views of Birch Lake. You can also rent houseboats. Cabin rates are based on a one-week stay, houseboat rates on a three-day rental. No air-conditioning, kitchenettes, some microwaves. Cable TV. Beach, marina, boating. Kids' programs. Some pets allowed. | 8347 Timber Bay Rd. | 218/827–3682 or 800/846–6821 | timber@uslink.net | www.timberbay.com | 12 cabins, 5 houseboats | $710–$1,185 cabins (1–wk rental), $160–$320 houseboats (3–day rental) | Closed Oct.–mid-May | D, MC, V.

BAUDETTE

Wigwam Resort. This resort fills a large wooded property along the Lake of the Woods at the mouth of the Rainy River. Wood paneling mixes with Native American motifs in the lodge rooms and cabins. Restaurant, 3 bars (live entertainment), picnic area. Some kitchenettes, some microwaves, some refrigerators, some in-room hot tubs. Cable TV, no room phones. Dock, boating, fishing. Pets allowed (fee). | 3502 Four Mile Bay Dr. NW 55623 | 218/634–2168 or 800/448–9260 | wigwam@wiktel.com | www.fishandgame.com/wigwam | 14 rooms, 12 cabins | $60–$75, $75 cabins | AE, D, MC, V.

BEMIDJI

Holiday Inn Express. Next to the Paul Bunyan Mall, this hotel, built in 1996, sits 1½ mi east of U.S. 71. In-room data ports, in-room hot tubs. Cable TV. Indoor pool. Hot tub, sauna. Video games. Laundry facilities. Business services. Pets allowed. | 2422 Ridgeway Ave. NW 56601 | 218/751-2487 or 800/617-4379 | fax 218/751-0771 | bjiex@paulbunyan.net | www.basshotels.com | 69 rooms | $63-$109 | AE, D, MC, V.

Northern Inn. Bemidji's only full-service hotel has the largest indoor recreational facility in northern Minnesota. Bemidji State Park is 5 mi away. Restaurant, bar, room service. In-room data ports. Cable TV. Indoor pool. Beauty salon, hot tub. Putting green. Exercise equipment. Laundry facilities. Business services, airport shuttle. Some pets allowed. | 3600 Moberg Dr. 56601 | 218/751-9500 | www.gphotels.com/northerninn | 123 rooms, 4 suites | $74-$79, $130 suites | AE, D, DC, MC, V.

Ruttger's Birchmont Lodge. Five generations of the same family have owned and operated this lodge, on 22 acres, including 1,700 ft of sandy beach on Lake Bemidji. Sports and recreation directors can help you choose between activities from waterskiing to movies. Bar, dining room. No air-conditioning in some rooms, in-room data ports, some kitchenettes, refrigerators. Cable TV. 2 pools (1 indoor). Hot tub. Tennis. Gym. Beach, dock, water sports, boating. Cross-country skiing. Children's programs (ages 4-12). Laundry facilities. Business services, airport shuttle. Some pets allowed. | 530 Birchmont Beach Rd. NE 56601 | 218/751-1630 or 888/788-8437 | rruttger@paulbunyan.net | www.ruttger.com | 28 rooms, 40 cottages | $62-$148, $152-$309 cottages | AE, D, MC, V.

BLOOMINGTON

Baymont Inn. Its location, about 2 mi from the Mall of America, makes this hotel an easy home base for shopping and dining excursions. Complimentary Continental breakfast. In-room data ports. Cable TV. Video games. Business services, airport shuttle. Some pets allowed. | 7815 Nicollet Ave. S 55420 | 612/881-7311 | fax 612/881-0604 | 190 rooms | $60-$74 | AE, D, DC, MC, V.

Best Western Thunderbird. A Native American theme extends throughout the hotel, with sculptures, paintings, draperies, and carpeting all reflecting the culture. The Mall of America is next door and you're at I-494, exit 2A. Restaurant, bar (with entertainment), room service. Microwaves, refrigerators. Cable TV. 2 pools (1 indoor). Hot tub. Exercise equipment. Business services, airport shuttle. Some pets allowed. | 2201 E. 78th St. 55425 | 952/854-3411 | fax 952/854-1183 | 263 rooms | $110-$115 | AE, D, DC, MC, V.

Residence Inn Bloomington. Each of the spacious suites here offers separate living and sleeping areas. It's ½ mi from the Mall of America. Complimentary breakfast. In-room data ports, kitchenettes, refrigerators. Cable TV, in-room VCRs (and movies). Pool. Hot tub. Exercise equipment. Laundry facilities. Business services, airport shuttle, free parking. Some pets allowed (fee). | 7850 Bloomington Avenue S, Minneapolis 55425 | 612/876-0900 | fax 612/876-0592 | www.residenceinn.com/MSPLL | 126 suites | $99-$179 | AE, D, DC, MC, V.

Select Inn. This hotel is along Bloomington's strip off I-494, exit 7A. Free shuttles take you to the Mall of America. Complimentary Continental breakfast. Cable TV. Indoor pool. Exercise equipment. Laundry facilities. Business services, airport shuttle. Some pets allowed (fee). | 7851 Normandale Blvd. 55435 | 952/835-7400 or 800/641-1000 | fax 952/835-4124 | 142 rooms | $52-$67 | AE, D, DC, MC, V.

BLUE EARTH

Budget Inn. Parking is in front of the rooms at this two-story motel 1 mi south of I-90, exit 119. Kitchenettes, microwaves, refrigerators. Cable TV. Laundry facilities. Free Parking. Small pets allowed. | Rte. 169 and 5th St. | 507/526-2706 | $35-$55 | MC, V.

BRAINERD

Country Inn. Downtown Brainerd is 1 mi east of this 2-story 1995 hotel, which has a fireplaced lobby with comfortable couches and high-backed chairs. Complimentary Continental breakfast. In-room data ports, microwaves, refrigerators, some in-room hot tubs. Cable TV. Indoor pool. Hot tub, sauna. Business services, free parking. Some pets allowed. | 1220 Dellwood Dr. N, Baxter 56425 | 218/828–2161 | fax 218/825–8419 | 56 rooms, 12 suites | $79–$89, $99–119 suites | AE, D, DC, MC, V.

Days Inn. This hotel rests nearly in the shadows of the amusement park landmarks Paul Bunyan and Babe the Blue Ox. Complimentary Continental breakfast. Cable TV. Business services. Some pets allowed. | 1630 Fairview Rd. | 218/829–0391 | fax 218/828–0749 | 59 rooms | $44–$79 | AE, D, DC, MC, V.

Days Inn–Nisswa. Convenient to golfers, this chain is ½ mi from The Pines, one of the state's finest championship golf courses. Complimentary Continental breakfast. Cable TV. Indoor pool. Hot tub. Laundry facilities. Some pets allowed (deposit). | 24186 N. Smiley Rd., Nisswa 56468 | 218/963–3500 | fax 218/963–4936 | 46 rooms | $60–$95 | AE, D, MC, V.

Ramada Inn. This full-service hotel is ½ mi south of town. Restaurant, bar, room service. In-room data ports. Cable TV. Indoor pool. Hot tub, sauna. Tennis. Laundry facilities. Business services, airport shuttle, free parking. Some pets allowed. | 2115 6th St. S (Rte. 371) | 218/829–1441 | fax 218/829–1444 | www.northernhospitality.com/ramadainn | 150 rooms | $73–$91 | AE, D, DC, MC, V.

CLOQUET

AmericInn. The Black Bear Casino and the popular Jay Cooke State Park, near Duluth, are each within 10 mi of this hotel. Complimentary Continental breakfast. Some refrigerators. Cable TV. Indoor pool. Hot tub, sauna. Business services. Some pets allowed. | 111 Big Lake Rd. | 218/879–1231 or 800/634–3444 | fax 218/879–2237 | www.AmericInn.com/minnesota/cloquet.html | 51 rooms | $55–$90 | AE, D, DC, MC, V.

CRANE LAKE

Borderland Lodge. Outdoor enthusiasts flock here for its central location: 2 mi from Voyageurs National Park, 3 mi from the Canadian border, and 1 mi from the Boundary Water Canoe Area Wilderness. Restaurant, bar. Pool, lake, wading pool. Hiking. Boating, fishing. Snowmobiling. Baby-sitting. Laundry facilities. Some pets allowed. | 7480 Crane Lake Rd. | 218/993–2233 or 800/777–8392 | fax 218/993–2495 | www.borderlandlodge.com | 14 cabins | $78–$480 | AE, D, MC, V.

CROOKSTON

Golf Terrace Motel. Standing next to a family-style restaurant and across the street from a bowling alley, the motel is on the north side of town on Rte. 2 (also called University Avenue), and one block from a nine-hole golf course, which offers guest privileges. Cable TV. Pets allowed. | 1731 University Ave. 56716 | 218/281–2626 | 17 rooms | $30–$40 | AE, D, MC, V.

DEER RIVER

Cutfoot Sioux Inn. The cabins at this resort in the Chippewa National Forest are close to the water, with no steep bank or steps to climb. Kitchenettes. Lake. Hiking. Beach, boating, fishing, bicycles. Snowmobiling. Baby-sitting, playground. Laundry facilities. Some pets allowed. | 44394 Rte. 46 | 218/246–8706 or 800/752–7357 | fax 218/246–8706 | www.cutfoot.com | 14 cabins | $65–$160 | D, MC, V.

DETROIT LAKES

Budget Host Inn. The 1950s-style motel is 1 mi from Sand Beach and 1½ mi from Detroit Lakes. Microwaves, refrigerators. Cable TV. Pets allowed. | 895 Hwy. E 56501 | 218/847–4454 | thiel@tekstar.com | www.BudgetHost.com | 24 rooms | $27–$64 | AE, D, MC, V.

DULUTH

Allyndale. The woodsy setting of this hotel, standing on 5 acres, features a children's playground. Picnic area. Microwaves, refrigerators. Cable TV. Snowmobiling. Playground. Some pets allowed. | 510 N. 66th Ave. W 55807 | 218/628–1061 or 800/806–1061 | 18 rooms, 3 suites | $38–$58, $70–$80 suites | AE, D, DC, MC, V.

Best Western Edgewater. Standing next to an outdoor recreation area with playground, miniature golf, and shuffleboard, this hotel is 2 mi from downtown Duluth. Complimentary Continental breakfast. In-room data ports, refrigerators. Cable TV. Indoor pool. Hot tub, sauna. Miniature golf. Video games. Playground. Business services, free parking. Some pets allowed. | 2400 London Rd. 55812 | 218/728–3601 or 800/777–7925 | fax 218/728–3727 | www.zmchotels.com | 281 rooms | $109–$139 | AE, D, DC, MC, V.

Days Inn. This is one of the most convenient hotels to the international airport, which is 5 mi away. Complimentary Continental breakfast. Cable TV. Business services. Some pets allowed. | 909 Cottonwood Ave. 55811 | 218/727–3110 | fax 218/727–3110, ext. 301 | 86 rooms | $59–$99 | AE, D, DC, MC, V.

Fitger's Inn. Lake Superior is visible from some rooms at this hostelry, which is 5 mi from downtown. Restaurant, bar (with entertainment), room service. In-room data ports, some in-room hot tubs. Cable TV. Exercise equipment. Business services. Some pets allowed. | 600 E. Superior St. 55802 | 218/722–8826 or 800/726–2982 | www.fitgers.com | 62 rooms, 20 suites | $80–$110, $135–$200 suites | AE, D, DC, MC, V.

Radisson. This unusual circular tower hotel is 5 blocks from the waterfront, and is topped with a revolving restaurant. Restaurant, bar. Cable TV. Indoor pool. Hot tub, sauna. Business services. Some pets allowed. | 505 W. Superior St. 55802 | 218/727–8981 | fax 218/727–0162 | www.radisson.com | 268 rooms | $80–$115 | AE, D, DC, MC, V.

ELK RIVER

AmericInn. This two-story, L-shape motel is one block from the Mississippi River. Complimentary Continental breakfast. Cable TV, in-room VCRs, TV in common area. Indoor pool. Hot tub, sauna. Some pets allowed (fee). | 17432 U.S. 10 | 612/441–8554 or 800/634–3444 | fax 612/441–8554 | www.AmericInn.com/minnesota/elkriver | 42 rooms | $70–$75 | AE, D, DC, MC, V.

Red Carpet Inn. Though not the most modern place in town, this two-building inn has helpful staff and a big back yard, is on the southern edge of the business district, and has a Chinese restaurant attached. Restaurant, complimentary Continental breakfast. Microwaves, refrigerators. Cable TV. Pool. Pets allowed (fee). | 17291 U.S. 10NW | 612/441–2424 | fax 612/241–9720 | www.redcarpetinn.com | 43 rooms | $45–59 | AE, D, DC, MC, V.

ELY

Budget Host. Standing in Superior National Forest, this hostelry is a main departure point for the Boundary Waters Canoe Area. Wood plank walls line the common areas and mounted fish and moose keep an eye on you. A snowmobile trail runs right by the motel, and the hotel's owner does guided fishing tours. Cable TV. Sauna. Business services, airport shuttle. Some pets allowed (fee). | 1047 E. Sheridan St. | 218/365–3237 | fax 218/365–3099 | stay@ely-motels.com | www.ely-motels.com | 17 rooms | $50–$65 | AE, D, DC, MC, V.

EVELETH

Eveleth Inn. The Hockey Hall of Fame is right next door to this facility. Restaurant, bar, room service. Some microwaves, some refrigerators. Cable TV. Indoor pool. Sauna. Laundry facilities. Business services. Some pets allowed. | Hat Trick Ave./U.S. 53 | 218/744–2703 | fax 218/744–5865 | 145 rooms | $62–$95 | AE, D, DC, MC, V.

Kokes Downtown Motel. Rooms in this two-level, 1950s-style motel have indoor or outdoor entrances. It's two blocks from the business district, 3 mi from the Laurentian Trail and Iron Trail system, and ½ mi from the U.S. Hockey Hall of Fame. Cable TV, room phones. Pets allowed. | 714 Fayal Rd. | 218/744–4500 or 800/892–5107 | fax 218/744–4500 | gkoke@yahoo.com | www.evelethmn.com/chamber/kokes | 14 rooms | $38–$48 | MC, V.

FAIRMONT

Holiday Inn of Fairmont. Renovated in 1998, all rooms have inside entrances. The property is 3½ mi from the airport at Route 15 and I-90, exit 102. A Torge's restaurant is on the premises. 2 restaurants, bar. In-room data ports. Cable TV. Pool, wading pool. Hot tub, sauna. Putting green. Health club. Video games. Laundry service. Airport shuttle. Pets allowed. | I-90 at Hwy. 15, 56031 | 507/238–4771 | fax 507/238–9371 | mntorges@frontiernet.com | www.torgersonproperties.com | 105 rooms, 2 suites | $84–$94, $99–$159 suites | AE, D, DC, MC, V.

Super 8. The motel is half a block from I-90, exit 102, within a block of restaurants. Complimentary Continental breakfast. Cable TV. Business services, airport shuttle. Pets allowed. | 1200 Torgerson Dr. 56031 | 507/238–9444 | fax 507/238–9371 | www.super8.com | 47 rooms | $45–$54 | AE, D, DC, MC, V.

FARIBAULT

AmericInn. You can relax in style here after a day of cruising the region. Complimentary breakfast. Microwaves, refrigerators, some in-room hot tubs. Cable TV. Pool. Sauna. Laundry service. Pets allowed. | 1801 Lavender Dr. 55021 | 507/334–9464 or 800/634–3444 | www.americinnfaribault.com | 61 rooms | $64–$69 | AE, D, DC, MC, V.

FERGUS FALLS

AmericInn Motel. Standing off I-94, at exit 54, this facility is also 1 mi from Otter Tail County trails. Some suites have microwaves, refrigerators, and hot tubs. Complimentary Continental breakfast. In-room data ports. Cable TV. Pool. Hot tub, sauna. Laundry service. Business services. Pets allowed. | 526 Western Ave. N | 218/739–3900 or 800/634–3444 | fax 218/739–3900 | www.americinn.com | 60 rooms, 9 suites | $56–$115, $74–$116 suites | AE, D, MC, V.

GLENWOOD

Green Valley Resort. Each bring-your-own-linens cabin has a picnic table on either a deck or a lawn. Campfire rings are available. Picnic area. Kitchenettes, no TV. Lake. Basketball. Beach, dock, boating. Playground. Laundry facilities. Pets allowed (fee). | 17632 N. Pelican Lake Rd. (3 mi west of Glenwood, Rte. 28 and N. Pelican Lake Rd.) 56334 | 320/634–4010 or 800/834–4010 | www.minnewaskamn.com/greenvalley | 12 cabins | $81–$160 | Oct. 15–May 1 | D, MC, V.

GRAND MARAIS

Best Western Superior Inn and Suites. Directly on Lake Superior, this hotel has rooms with your choice of lake-view balconies or outdoor, ground-floor access. The North Shore Corridor snowmobile trail system is right beside the property. Complimentary Continental breakfast. Refrigerators. Cable TV. Hot tub. Snowmobiling. Laundry facilities. Business services. Some pets allowed. | 1st Ave. E | 218/387–2240 or 800/842–8439 | fax 218/387–

2244 | bwsuperiorinn@lakesnet.net | www.bestwestern.com/superiorinn | 56 rooms, 10 suites | $79–$129, $109–$179 suites | AE, D, DC, MC, V.

Clearwater Canoe Outfitters and Lodge. Built in 1926, the log structure is a great starting point for canoe trips. Lakeside cabin, B&B, or suite accommodations are available. There is also a bunkhouse for 14, a tepee that sleeps six, or rustic Wyoming screenhouses for the intrepid. Canoe outfitter services are the focus and mainstay of the lodge. Cabin rates are based on a seven-day stay. Picnic area. No air-conditioning, microwaves. Sauna. Hiking. Beach, docks, boating. Bicycles. Playground. Some pets allowed. | 355 Old Rail La. | 218/388–2254 or 800/527–0554 | clearwater@canoe-bwca.com | www.canoe-bwca.com | 5 rooms, 6 cabins | $68–$100, $730–$770 cabins | Closed Oct.–May | D, MC, V.

Nor'wester Lodge. Operated by the same family who built the lodge in 1931, this small resort sits on the north shore of Poplar Lake, 30 mi up the Gunflint Trail from Grand Marais. Cabins are private, have decks and docks, are fully equipped, and can accommodate between two and ten people. You can also arrange for canoe expeditions, or short day trips. Rates are based on a one-week stay. Picnic area. No air-conditioning, kitchenettes, microwaves. TV in common area. Sauna. Beach, dock, water sports, boating. Cross-country skiing. Playground. Laundry facilities. Some pets allowed. | 7778 Gunflint Tr. | 218/388–2252 or 800/992–4386 | www.boreal.org/norwester | 7 cottages | $774–$1,134 | D, MC, V.

Super 8. This is the first hotel you come to as you approach Grand Marais from the south, and there are no lake views. It's a two-story establishment in two buildings. Complimentary Continental breakfast. In-room data ports, refrigerators. Cable TV. Hot tub, sauna. Laundry services. Business services. Some pets allowed. | 1711 Rte. 61W | 218/387–2448 or 800/247–6020 | fax 218/387–9859 | gmhotel@worldnet.att.com | 35 rooms | $45–$99 | AE, D, DC, MC, V.

GRAND RAPIDS

Budget Host. The downtown area is two blocks west of this motel. Picnic area. Cable TV. Playground. Business services, airport shuttle. Pets allowed. | 311 U.S. 2E | 218/326–3457 | fax 218/326–3795 | 34 rooms | $50–$69 | AE, D, DC, MC, V.

Country Inn. Opened in 1994, this inn is on the south edge of town next to the Judy Garland house. The handful of two-room suites are in a wing built in 2000. Complimentary Continental breakfast. Some refrigerators, some microwaves. Cable TV. Indoor pool. Hot tub. Exercise room. Some pets allowed. | 2601 U.S. 169S | 218/327–4960 | fax 218/327–4964 | www.countryinns.com | 46 rooms, 5 suites | $55–$73 | AE, D, DC, MC, V.

Judge Thwing House. You can experience living in "arts and crafts style" in this B&B, which was built during the movement's heyday. It's in a quiet valley surrounded by lakes and forested areas 1½ mi from town. Complimentary breakfast. Pets allowed. | 1604 County Rd. A 55744 | 218/326–5618 | fax 218/326–2019 | 4 rooms | $50–$60 | AE, D, MC, V.

Rainbow Inn. Built in the 1970s, this two-story hotel has direct access to a hiking trail. Restaurant, bar, in-room hot tubs. Cable TV. Pool. Hot tub, sauna. Pets allowed. | 1300 E. Rte. 169 55744 | 218/326–9655 | fax 218/326–9851 | 85 rooms, 6 suites | $39–$69, $75 suites | AE, D, DC, MC, V.

Sawmill Inn. This two-story, locally-owned inn is one block from the Judy Garland house. Restaurant, bar, room service. Cable TV. Indoor pool. Hot tub, sauna. Laundry facilities. Business services, airport shuttle. Pets allowed. | 2301 S. Pokegama Ave. | 218/326–8501 or 800/235–6455 | fax 218/326–1039 | 124 rooms, 10 suites | $75–$80, $108–$120 suites | AE, D, DC, MC, V.

GRANITE FALLS

Viking Motel. A locally owned, L-shape motel about 1 mi south of downtown, this is a 1-story drive-up, so it's good for folks who don't want to climb stairs. All beds are doubles.

Cable TV. Some pets allowed. | 1250 U.S. 212W | 320/564–2411 | 20 rooms | $28–$42 | AE, D, MC, V.

HIBBING

Super 8. Built in the early 1990s, this 2-story facility has a convenient highway location about 2 mi east of downtown, at the junction of Routes 169 and 37. Cable TV. Business services. Some pets allowed. | 1411 E. 40th St. | 218/263–8982 | www.super8.com | 49 rooms | $37–$53 | AE, D, DC, MC, V.

HINCKLEY

Days Inn. This 2-story member of the chain was built in 1991, and is about 1½ mi from the Hinckley Grand Casino, off exit 183 on I–35. The apartment suite can sleep five. Complimentary Continental breakfast. Some refrigerators. Cable TV. Indoor pool. Hot tub, sauna. Laundry facilities. Business services. Some pets allowed. | 104 Grindstone Ct. | 320/384–7751 | 69 rooms, 5 suites | $44–$85, $90–$135 suites | AE, D, DC, MC, V.

Holiday Inn Express. Built in 1994, this 2-story property is 1 mi from the casino, off I–35, exit 183, behind Tobie's restaurant. Complimentary Continental breakfast. Cable TV. Indoor pool. Hot tub, sauna. Some pets allowed (fee). | 604 Weber Ave. | 320/384–7171 | fax 320/384–7735 | 101 rooms | $69–$129 | AE, D, DC, MC, V.

Super 8. This 2-story motel is 12 mi north of Hinckley, in Finlayson, off I–35, exit 195. Complimentary Continental breakfast. Some in-room hot tubs. Cable TV. Hot tub. Game room. Laundry facilities. Business services. Some pets allowed. | 2811 Rte. 23, Finlayson | 320/245–5284 | fax 320/245–2233 | 30 rooms | $45–$57 | AE, D, DC, MC, V.

Waldheim Resort. Lodgings here are cedar cabins surrounded by pine trees, right on Big Pine Lake, 20 mi northwest of town. Each cabin has its own theme based on such northwoods animals as moose and wild boars, and is filled with wildlife pictures; floors are hardwood and furniture is made of logs. Tent and RV sites are also available. Kitchenettes. Lake. Beach, boating. Playground. Pets allowed (fee). | 906 Waldheim La. 55735 | 320/233–7405 | www.waldheimresort.com | 12 cabins | $110–$145 | No credit cards.

HUTCHINSON

Glencoe Castle Bed and Breakfast. This Queen Anne fieldstone home, 14 mi southeast of town, was built to woo a young woman into marriage (it worked). The three-story house, today a B&B, has unique parquet floors and stained-glass windows, as well as a fireplace, a parlor, and many interesting rooms. Complimentary breakfast. Some in-room hot tubs. TV in common area. Some pets allowed. | 831 13th St. E 55336 | 320/864–3043 or 800/517–3334 | www.glencoecastle.com | 3 rooms (2 with shared bath) | $70–$175 | AE, D, MC, V.

INTERNATIONAL FALLS

Budget Host Inn. Wood-paneled rooms have twin, double, queen-, and king-size beds. You can park at your door at this motel, which is in town, next door to restaurants and a movie theater. Picnic area. Cable TV. Playground. Pets allowed. | 10 Riverview Blvd. 56649 | 218/283–2577 | fax 218/285–3688 or 800/880–2577 | www.budgethost.com | 31 rooms | $41–$69 | AE, D, MC, V.

Days Inn. The gateway to Voyageurs National Park adjoins this two-story wood-and-cinderblock building 15 mi from the Canadian border. Complimentary Continental breakfast. Cable TV. Hot tub. Exercise equipment. Business services. Some pets allowed. | 2331 U.S. 53S | 218/283–9441 | fax 218/283–9441 | 58 rooms | $46–$70 | AE, D, DC, MC, V.

Holiday Inn. This log-sided hotel is next to the Rainy River. Restaurant, bar, room service. Some refrigerators, in-room data ports. Cable TV. Indoor pool, wading pool. Hot tub, sauna. Laundry facilities. Business services, airport shuttle. Some pets allowed. | 1500 U.S.

71 | 218/283–4451 | fax 218/283–3774 | 126 rooms, 12 suites | $74–$114, $85–$149 suites | AE, D, DC, MC, V.

Island View Lodge and Motel. Established in 1908, this two-story cedar lodge and cabins have a private beach on Rainy Lake. It's 12 mi east of International Falls, on Rte. 11. Restaurant, bar, picnic area. No air-conditioning in cottages, some kitchenettes. No TV in cottages. Beach, dock, boating. Snowmobiling on the lake. Airport shuttle. Some pets allowed. | 1817 Rte. 11E | 218/286–3511 or 800/777–7856 | iview@rainy-lake.com | www.rainy-lake.com | 9 rooms, 12 cabins | $85–$149 cottages, $65–$70 rooms in lodge | D, MC, V.

Northernaire Floating Lodges. Captain your own houseboat on Voyageur National Park's Rainy Lake. All "boatel houseboat" rentals include sunroofs, walkaround decks, and interiors with linens on the dining table and beds. Each boatel comes with a fishing boat. No air-conditioning. Kitchenettes. Water sports. Some pets allowed. | 2690 Rte. 94 | 218/286–5221 or 800/854–7958 | nhb@northernairehouseboats.com | www.northernaire-houseboats.com | 15 power-driven floating lodges on pontoon boats | $795–$2,100 (7–day stay) | Closed mid-Oct.–mid-May | MC, V.

JACKSON
Park-Vu Motel. Rooms have twin, double, and queen-size beds in this in-town motel. A picnic area and park are next door. Cable TV. Pets allowed. | 101 Third St. 56143 | 507/847–3440 | 18 rooms | $24–$47 | MC, V.

LAKEVILLE
Comfort Inn Lakeville. Some rooms at this hotel, 5 mi west of town, overlook a pond. Complimentary Continental breakfast. In-room data ports, microwaves, refrigerators. Cable TV. Indoor pool. Hot tub. Some pets allowed. | 10935 176th St. W 55044 | 952/898–3700 | fax 952/898–3827 | 56 rooms, 3 suites | $69.90–$89.90 | AE, D, DC, MC, V.

LE SUEUR
Beaver Dam Resort. These cabins stand 40 ft from the waters of Jefferson and German Lakes, 9 mi of town. Each has between one and four bedrooms, with double beds. Lake. Beach, boating, fishing. Some pets allowed. | County Rd. 13 56058 | 507/931–5650 | 12 cabins | $70–$132 | Closed Oct.–Apr. | D, MC, V.

Downtown Motel. The only motel downtown, this facility is part of a complex that also includes offices, a deli, a hospital clinic, and a bowling alley. Restaurant, bar. Kitchenettes, no-smoking rooms. Cable TV. Some pets allowed. | 510 N. Main St. | 507/665–6246 | fax 507/665–6246 | 39 rooms | $32–$41 | AE, D, DC, MC, V.

LITCHFIELD
Scotwood. This 1-story motel is on the east edge of town near a mall. Complimentary Continental breakfast. Indoor pool. Cable TV. Some pets allowed. | 1017 E. Frontage Rd. | 320/693–2496 or 800/225–5489 | 35 rooms | $45–$100 | AE, D, DC, MC, V.

LITTLE FALLS
Pine Edge Inn. A veranda faces the Mississippi at this downtown redbrick hotel. The high-ceilinged rooms have Victorian-style wallpaper and furniture. Restaurant, bar, room service. Cable TV. Pool. Playground. Business services. Some pets allowed. | 308 1st St. SE | 320/632–6681 or 800/344–6681 | fax 320/632–4332 | janders@upstel.net | www.pineedgeinn.com | 56 rooms | $35–$95 | AE, D, DC, MC, V.

LUTSEN
AmericInn. This 2-story cedar and stone building with a stone portico and columns was built in 1994. It's two blocks from the shore of Lake Superior; some rooms have limited

lake views. Snowmobile trail access is available from parking lot. Temperance State Park is 2 mi west, Cascade River State Park is 20 mi east, and Lutsen Mountains Ski Area is 9 mi east. Picnic area, complimentary Continental breakfast. Microwaves, some refrigerators, some in-room hot tubs. Cable TV. Indoor pool. Hot tub, sauna. Business services. Some pets allowed. | 7261 W. Hwy. 61, Tofte 55615 | 218/663–7899 | fax 218/663–7387 | www.AmericInn.com/minnesota/tofte-MN.html | 52 rooms | $59–$139 | AE, D, DC, MC, V.

Best Western Cliff Dweller. The unique feature of this 2-story wood building is that every room has a balcony overlooking Lake Superior. It is 5 mi south of Lutsen Mountains Ski Area between Tofte and Lutsen; restaurants are 5 mi north and south. Restaurant. In-room data ports. Cable TV. Business services. Some pets allowed. | 6452 Rte. 61 55615 | 218/663–7273 | gmhotel@worldnet.att.com | 22 rooms | $60–$99 | AE, D, DC, MC, V.

Bluefin Bay. These 2- and 3-story lakeside vacation homes along ½ mi of lake shore have vaulted ceilings and panoramic views. Although privately owned, they're often for rent. Lutsen Mountains Ski Area is 5 mi north. Restaurant, bar. No air-conditioning, many kitchenettes, many in-room hot tubs. Cable TV. 2 pools (1 indoor). Hot tub, massage. Exercise equipment. Game room. Kids' programs. Laundry facilities. Business services. Some pets allowed. | 7198 W. Hwy. 61, Tofte 55615 | 218/663–7296 or 800/258–3346 | fax 218/663–7130 | bluefin@boreal.org | www.bluefinbay.com | 16 rooms, 56 suites | $99–$189, $175–$420 suites | D, MC, V.

Chateau le Veaux. On a cliff over Lake Superior, this 2-story building has lake views from every room. Outdoors, a wooden deck built directly on boulders overlooks the Lake Superior shoreline. Lutsen Mountains Ski Area is 4 mi north. Kitchenettes. Cable TV. Indoor pool. Lake. Hot tub. Sauna. Hiking. Snowmobiling. Playground. Some pets allowed. | 6626 W. Rte. 61, Tofte 55615 | 218/663–7223 or 800/445–5773 | fax 218/663–7124 | www.boreal.org/chateau | 34 rooms | $69–$159 | AE, D, DC, MC, V.

Lutsen Resorts and Sea Villas. Started in 1885, added to in 1952, and rebuilt several times, this year-round resort is on Lake Superior, at the mouth of the Poplar River. The main lodge has pine paneling, handcarved beams of native timber, massive stone hearths, and a dining room. Lutsen Mountains Ski Area is across the street, and accommodations have ski-in, ski-out access. Bar, dining room. No air-conditioning. Cable TV. Indoor pool. Hot tub, sauna. 9-hole golf course, tennis. Playground. Some pets allowed. | 5700 Hwy. 61W 55612 | 218/663–7212 or 800/258–8736 | lutsen@lutsenresort.com | www.lutsenresort.com | 32 rooms in 1 lodge, 9 cabins, 47 sea villas, 12 condominium units | $33–$135 rooms in lodge, $125–$249 cabins, $80–$219 apartments | AE, D, DC, MC, V.

Mountain Inn. This 2-story wooden ski lodge, built in 1993, is in the woods 1½ mi from Lake Superior and 2 blocks from Lutsen Mountains Ski Area. Picnic area, complimentary Continental breakfast. Cable TV. Hot tub, sauna. Driving range, putting green. Business services. Some pets allowed. | 360 Ski Hill Rd. | 218/663–7244 or 800/686–4669 (reservations) | fax 218/387–2446 | 30 rooms | $99–$119 | AE, D, DC, MC, V.

Solbakken Resort. Accommodations here include rustic, knotty pine cabins (with decks and lake views), motel rooms, lodge suites, and luxurious lake houses which sleep eight to ten people. The main lodge is a 1930s log structure, and has a fireplace parlor with board games. The resort, 2 mi east of town, is open year-round. Some kitchenettes. Lake. Hot tub, sauna. Some pets allowed (fee). | 4874 Rte. 61W 55612 | 218/663–7566 | fax 218/663–7816 | www.solbakkenresort.com | 3 lodge suites, 6 rooms 6 cabins, 3 houses | $74–$93 rooms, $77–$114 cabins, $180–$227 houses | AE, MC, V.

LUVERNE

Hillcrest Motel. This simple, no-frills place is 1 mi from the center of town, off Rte. 71N. Twin and double beds are available. Cable TV. Some pets allowed (fee). | 210 W. Virginia St. 56156 | 507/283–2363 | 16 rooms | $28–$50 | AE, D, MC, V.

Super 8. This 2-story motel highway hotel is one of the last stops before the Iowa and South Dakota borders. Cable TV. Some pets allowed. | RR 2, Box 82C, Rte. 90 56156 | 507/283–9541 | 36 rooms | $41–$65 | AE, D, DC, MC, V.

MANKATO

Days Inn. This 2-story brick building has a walking path along the Minnesota River. Shopping is 3 mi east; Mankato State University is 5 mi south. Complimentary Continental breakfast. In-room data ports. Cable TV. Indoor pool. Hot tub. Business services. Some pets allowed. | 1285 Range St. 56001 | 507/387–3332 | 50 rooms | $40–$85 | AE, D, DC, MC, V.

Econo Lodge. Mankato State University is 2 mi of this motel on the north edge of town. It's also 2 mi north of the River Hill shopping mall and the Civic Center. Complimentary Continental breakfast. Cable TV. Hot tub, sauna. Business services. Free parking. Some pets allowed. | 111 W. Lind Ct. 56001 | 507/345–8800 | fax 507/345–8921 | 66 rooms | $36–$50 | AE, D, DC, MC, V.

Riverfront Inn. Some rooms at this 1-story motel have fireplaces. The property is $^3/_4$ mi north of downtown. In-room data ports, refrigerators. Cable TV. Business services. Some pets allowed. | 1727 N. Riverfront Dr. 56001 | 507/388–1638 | fax 507/388–6111 | 19 rooms | $30–$79 | AE, D, DC, MC, V.

MARSHALL

AmericInn. All rooms at this hostelry, directly in town, have queen-size beds, and some have fireplaces. Complimentary breakfast. Some microwaves, some refrigerators, some in-room hot tubs. Cable TV. Indoor pool. Laundry facilities. Some pets allowed. | 1406 E. Lyon St. 56258 | 507/537–9424 | www.gomarshall.net | 36 rooms | $69–$129 | AE, D, MC, V.

Best Western Marshall Inn. A 2-story brick building built in 1973, this property is on the edge of town, at the corner of Routes 19 and 23, across the street from Southwest State University. Restaurant, bar, room service. In-room data ports. Cable TV. Indoor pool. Hot tub, sauna. Business services, airport shuttle. Some pets allowed. | 1500 E. College Dr. 56258 | 507/532–3221 | fax 507/532–4089 | 100 rooms | $44–$61 | AE, D, DC, MC, V.

Comfort Inn. This 2-story motel is next to the university and next door to a restaurant. A downstairs lounge is available for group rentals. Complimentary Continental breakfast. In-room data ports. Cable TV. Indoor pool. Hot tub. Business services. Some pets allowed. | 1511 E. College Dr. | 507/532–3070 | fax 507/537–9641 | 49 rooms | $52–$95 | AE, D, DC, MC, V.

Super 8. This two-story building is surrounded by shops and restaurants, and within blocks of a 24-hour service station. Cable TV. Laundry facilities. Business services. Some pets allowed. | 1106 E. Main St. | 507/537–1461 | 50 rooms | $43–$51 | AE, D, DC, MC, V.

Traveler's Lodge. Marshall Square and Southwest State University are both across the street from this motel. Complimentary Continental breakfast. Cable TV. Business services, airport shuttle. Some pets allowed. | 1425 E. College Dr. | 507/532–5721 or 800/532–5721 | fax 507/532–4911 | 90 rooms | $34–$42 | AE, D, DC, MC, V.

MINNEAPOLIS

Baymont Inn. Downtown Minneapolis is 4 mi southeast of this three-story hotel next to Earle Brown's Bowling and within a few blocks of movie theaters and the Brookdale Shopping Center. You're 22 mi from the Minneapolis/St. Paul airport. Complimentary Continental breakfast. In-room data ports. Cable TV. Business services, free parking. Some pets allowed. | 6415 James Cir., Brooklyn Center 55430 | 763/561–8400 | fax 763/560–3189 | www.baymontinn.com | 99 rooms | $65–$84 | AE, D, DC, MC, V.

Best Western Kelly Inn. A theater in this two-story motel west of Minneapolis hosts off-Broadway productions and musicals. Restaurant, bar, room service. Cable TV. Indoor pool. Hot tub. Exercise equipment. Video games. Laundry facilities, laundry service. Business services, free parking. Some pets allowed. | 2705 Annapolis, Plymouth 55441 | 763/553–1600 | fax 763/553–9108 | www.bestwestern.com | 150 rooms | $69–$185 | AE, D, DC, MC, V.

Comfort Inn. This three-story hotel with beige stucco walls and white trim is off I–694, exit 34, 5 mi from downtown Minneapolis. Complimentary Continental breakfast. In-room data ports, some microwaves, some refrigerators. Cable TV. Hot tub, spa. Video games. Business services. Pets allowed. | 1600 James Cir. N, Brooklyn Center 55430 | 763/560–7464 | 60 rooms | $90 | AE, D, DC, MC, V.

Metro Inn. Centrally placed between downtown and the southern suburbs, this motel is about 10 mi west of the Mall of America. Cable TV. Some pets allowed (fee). | 5637 Lyndale Ave. S 55419 | 763/861–6011 | fax 763/869–1041 | 35 rooms | $35–$52 | AE, D, DC, MC, V.

Radisson–Metrodome. This hotel is 1 mi east of downtown on the University of Minnesota campus, in easy reach of the Northrop Auditorium, the Weisman Art Museum, the Williams Arena, the Aquatic Center, and other university landmarks. Restaurants, bar. In-room data ports. Exercise equipment. Business services. Some pets allowed. | 615 Washington Ave. SE 55414 | 763/379–8888 | fax 763/379–8436 | www.radisson.com | 304 rooms, 34 suites | $105–$120, $145–$350 suites | AE, D, DC, MC, V.

Regal Minneapolis. Nicollet Mall is the site of this hostelry, the closest hotel to the Minneapolis Convention Center. Restaurant, bars. In-room data ports. Cable TV. Indoor pool. Exercise equipment. Laundry facilities. Business services, airport shuttle. Some pets allowed. | 1313 Nicollet Mall 55403 | 763/332–6000 or 800/522–8856 | fax 763/359–2160 | www.regal/hotels.com | 325 rooms, 43 suites | $189–$205, $199–$365 suites | AE, D, DC, MC, V.

Super 8. This two-story brick building is 1 mi north of the Brookdale Mall off I–694, exit 34, and 5 mi northwest of downtown. Complimentary Continental breakfast. Cable TV. Business services. Some pets allowed (fee). | 6445 James Cir., Brooklyn Center 55430 | 763/566–9810 | fax 763/566–8680 | www.super8.com | 102 rooms | $73 | AE, D, DC, MC, V.

MOORHEAD

Red River Inn. Two stories of solid brick, the hotel is 2½ mi south of the University and College. All attractions in Moorhead and Fargo, North Dakota, are within a 15-minute drive. Restaurant, bar. Cable TV. Indoor pool. Sauna. Exercise equipment. Some pets allowed. | 600 30th Ave. S 56560 | 218/233–6171 or 800/328–6173 | fax 218/233–0945 | 173 rooms | $71–$78 | AE, D, DC, MC, V.

MORA

Ann River Swedish Motel. Quiet and seclusion are the key words at this single-story motel, even though it's right in town, about a mile from Mora's only stoplight. Complimentary Continental breakfast. No-smoking rooms, in-room hot tubs. Cable TV. Some pets allowed. | 1819 Rte. 65S | 320/679–2972 | fax 320/679–2973 | 23 rooms | $35–$95 | AE, D, MC, V.

Motel Mora. Built in 1965, this one-story brick motel includes a sun deck, and is on the south side of town. Picnic area. In-room data ports, some microwaves, some refrigerators. Cable TV. Business services. Some pets allowed (fee). | 301 Rte. 65S | 320/679–3262 or 800/657–0167 | fax 320/679–5135 | 23 rooms | $40–$52 | AE, D, DC, MC, V.

MORRIS

Best Western Prairie Inn. A wide expanse of lawn surrounds this two-story brick motel, which is four blocks from University of Minnesota–Morris, and 11 blocks from the Stevens County Museum. Restaurant, bar. Complimentary Continental breakfast Sun.–Thurs. Cable TV. Indoor pool, wading pool. Hot tub, sauna. Video games. Business services. Some pets allowed. | 200 Rte. 28E 56267 | 320/589–3030 or 800/535–3035 | fax 320/589–3030 | 90 rooms | $64 | AE, D, DC, MC, V.

NEW ULM

Budget Holiday. Sitting one block from the fairgrounds, this weathered motel has ground-floor and basement rooms. Microwaves and refrigerators available for rent. Cable TV. Business services. Some pets allowed. | 1316 N. Broadway 56073 | 507/354–4145 | fax 507/354–4146 | 44 rooms | $29–$40 | AE, D, MC, V.

Holiday Inn. A Holidome indoor recreation area is the highlight of this 1982 Tudor-style hotel 1 mi north of downtown. Restaurant, bar (with entertainment), room service. In-room data ports. Cable TV. Indoor pool. Hot tub, sauna. Exercise equipment. Video games. Business services, free parking. Pets allowed. | 2101 S. Broadway 56073 | 507/359–2941 and 877/359–2941 | fax 507/354–7147 | 126 rooms, 4 suites | $69–$89, $89–$129 suites | AE, D, DC, MC, V.

NORTHFIELD

Archer House. The front porch of this four-story redbrick 1877 colonial inn faces the town's main street. Room service. Some refrigerators, some in-room hot tubs. Cable TV. Laundry service. Free parking. Some pets. | 212 Division St. 55057 | 507/645–5661 or 800/247–2235 | fax 507/645–4295 | www.archerhouse.com | 18 rooms, 18 suites | $45–$55, $115–$140 suites | AE, D, MC, V.

College City Motel. This one-story motel is 1 mi north of town. Cable TV. Pets allowed. | 875 Rte. 3N 55057 | 507/645–4426 or 800/775–0455 | 24 rooms | $25–$55 | AE, D, MC, V.

Super 8. The two-story stucco highway hotel is 2 mi south of downtown. Cable TV. Some microwaves, some refrigerators. Business Services. Pets allowed. | 1420 Riverview Dr. 55057 | 507/663–0371 | fax 800/789–1331 | 40 rooms | $54–$70 | AE, D, DC, MC, V.

ONAMIA

Eddy's Lake Mille Lacs Resort. The spacious lobby has a fireplace and walls of varnished woods and exposed brick, and some rooms have hot tubs and gas or wood-burning fireplaces. Non-smoking rooms are available, and a free shuttle runs to Grand Casino Mille Lacs. Restaurant, bar. Some in-room hot tubs. Sauna, spa. Exercise equipment. Hiking, volleyball. Beach, dock, boating, fishing, bicycles. Baby-sitting, playground. Some pets allowed. | 41334 Shakopee Lake Rd. 56359 | 320/532–3657 or 800/657–4704 | fax 320/532–4483 | www.eddysresort.com | 80 rooms | $69–$129 | MAP | AE, D, DC, MC, V.

OWATONNA

Budget Host Inn. A 2-story brick motel 1 block from I–35, exit 42A, this facility is ½ mi from Owatonna and 6 mi from the Medford Outlet Center. Complimentary Continental breakfast. Cable TV. Laundry services. Small pets allowed (fee and with permission). | 745 State Ave. 55060 | 507/451–8712 | fax 507/451–4456 | 27 rooms | $65–$95 | AE, D, MC, V.

PINE RIVER

Travelodge. All the rooms in this two-story roadside motor lodge are no-frills rooms except for one: The Sleepy Bear room is decorated with a bear motif and equipped with a children's easy chair and free family videos. Room access is via outside corridors, and the location is ½ mi south of town between a meat market and a car dealership. Complimentary Continental breakfast. Cable TV. Hot tub, sauna. Laundry facilities. Pets allowed. | 2684 Rte. 371SW 56474 | 218/587–4499 | 30 rooms, 1 suite | $55–$73, $95–$105 suite | AE, D, DC, MC, V.

RED WING

Best Western Quiet House Suites. The Red Wing Pottery showroom is across the street from this white colonial-style hostelry, and the Mississippi River is 6 blocks east. In-room data ports, some refrigerators. Cable TV. Some in-room hot tubs. Indoor-outdoor pool. Hot tub. Exercise equipment. Some pets allowed. | 752 Withers Harbor Dr. 55066 | 651/388–1577 | fax 651/388–1150 | 51 rooms, 15 suites | $86–$169 | AE, D, DC, MC, V.

Days Inn. Colvill Park is across the street from this single-story motel. Cable TV. Indoor pool. Hot tub. Business services. Some pets allowed. | 955 E. 7th St. | 651/388–3568 | fax 651/385–1901 | 48 rooms | $58–$85 | AE, D, DC, MC, V.

REDWOOD FALLS

Comfort Inn. One mi north of downtown, this three-story, brick-and-stucco hotel runs a free shuttle to the Jackpot Casino 5 mi farther north. Complimentary Continental breakfast. Some in-room hot tubs. Hot tub, sauna. Some pets allowed (fee). | 1382 E. Bridge St. | 507/644–5700 or 800/569–1010 | fax 507/644–5722 | 105 rooms, 1 suite | $40–80 rooms, $120–$150 suite | AE, D, DC, MC, V.

ROCHESTER

AmericInn of Stewartville. This two-story hotel stands ½ mi south of I–90, exit 209A (Hwy. 63, Stewartville), 3 mi from the Rochester Airport. A large fireplace warms the lobby. Complimentary Continental breakfast. Cable TV. Business services. Some pets allowed. | 1700 2nd Ave. NW, Stewartville 55976 | 507/533–4747 | fax 507/533–4747 | www.AmericInn.com/minnesota/stewartville.html | 27 rooms | $40–$50 | AE, D, DC, MC, V.

Best Western. The Mayo Clinic is 3½ blocks southeast of this four-story hotel. An atrium surrounds its indoor pool–hot tub complex. Complimentary Continental breakfast. In-room data ports, microwaves, refrigerators. Cable TV. Indoor pool. Hot tub. Laundry facilities. Business services. Some pets allowed. | 20 5th Ave. NW 55901 | 507/289–3987, ext. 130 | fax 507/289–3987 | www.bestwestern.com | 63 rooms | $65–$85 | AE, D, DC, MC, V.

Best Western–Apache. A glass-and-wood atrium accents this hostelry next to the immense Apache Mall. Restaurant, bar, complimentary Continental breakfast, room service. In-room data ports. Cable TV. Indoor pool. Hot tub. Video games. Business services, airport shuttle. Some pets allowed. | 1517 16th St. SW 55902 | 507/289–8866, ext. 312 | fax 507/289–8866 | www.bestwestern.com | 149 rooms, 2 suites | $70–$80, $120 suites | AE, D, DC, MC, V.

Blondell Hotel. St. Mary's Hospital is across the street from this three-story, L-shape hotel. Restaurant, bar, room service. Cable TV. Laundry facilities. Business services. Some pets allowed. | 1406 2nd St. SW 55902 | 507/282–9444 or 800/441–5209 | fax 507/282–8683 | www.blondell.com | 58 rooms | $58 | AE, MC, V.

Days Inn. Two blocks from the Mayo Clinic, this hotel has a choice of European-theme rooms or B&B rooms. Restaurant. Some refrigerators. Cable TV. Laundry facilities. Some pets allowed. | 6 1st Ave. NW 55901 | 507/282–3801 | fax 507/282–3801 | www.daysinn.com | 71 rooms | $45–$69 | AE, D, DC, MC, V.

Days Inn–South. Three miles south of downtown, this two-story hostelry is at the intersection of Routes 52 and 63. Complimentary Continental breakfast. Cable TV. Business services, airport shuttle. Some pets allowed. | 111 28th St. 55901 | 507/286–1001 | www.daysinn.com | 128 rooms | $42–$62 | AE, D, DC, MC, V.

Executive Suites by Kahler. Nestled between a grocery store and the Galleria Mall, this nine-story hotel is also connected to the skyway–subway system. Restaurant, bar, complimentary Continental breakfast. In-room data ports, some refrigerators. Cable TV. Indoor pool. Hot tub. Exercise equipment. Laundry facilities. Business services, free parking. Some pets allowed. | 9 N.W. 3rd Ave. 55901 | 507/289–8646 | fax 507/282–4478 | www.kahler.com/executivesuites | 128 suites | $79–$109 | AE, D, DC, MC, V.

Holiday Inn–South. Across from the County Fairgrounds and Graham Arena, this two-story hotel is 1½ miles south of downtown. Restaurant, bar, room service. Some kitchenettes. Cable TV. Indoor pool. Laundry facilities. Business services, airport shuttle. Some pets allowed. | 1630 S. Broadway 55904 | 507/288–1844 | fax 507/288–1844 | www.kahler.com/holidayinn | 196 rooms | $62–$75 | AE, D, DC, MC, V.

Kahler Grand Hotel. Built in 1921, in the heart of downtown, this hotel is connected to the greater Kahler complex by a skywalk. From the domed, skylit pool to crystal chandeliers, every detail is lavish in this 12-story hostelry. Restaurant, bars (with entertainment). In-room data ports, refrigerators. Cable TV. Indoor pool. Hot tub, beauty salon. Exercise equipment. Business services, airport shuttle. Some pets allowed. | 20 2nd Ave. SW 55902 | 507/282–2581 or 800/533–1655 | fax 507/285–2775 | www.kahler.com/kahlergrand/index.html | 700 rooms, 26 suites | $59–$150, $350–$1,500 suites | AE, D, DC, MC, V.

Quality Inn and Suites. This 2-story hotel is part of a small cluster of similar hotels in a residential area, next to the Olmsted County Fairgrounds. Complimentary Continental breakfast. In-room data ports. Cable TV. Laundry facilities. Business services, airport shuttle. Some pets allowed. | 1620 1st Ave. SE 55904 | 507/282–8091 | fax 507/282–8091 | rochesterlodging.com/qualityinn | 41 rooms | $69–$165 | AE, D, DC, MC, V.

Ramada Limited. All rooms have microwaves and coffee makers at this 3-story hotel, 3 mi north of the Mayo Clinic complex. Restaurant. Some kitchenettes, microwaves, refrigerators. Cable TV. Indoor pool. Laundry facilities. Some pets allowed. | 435 16th Ave. NW 55901 | 507/288–9090, ext. 502 | fax 507/288–9090 | www.ramada.com | 120 rooms | $62–$125 | AE, D, DC, MC, V.

Red Carpet Inn. Each room has a dad-style recliner at this motel, ¾ mi north of downtown. Complimentary Continental breakfast. Some kitchenettes. Cable TV. Indoor pool. Laundry facilities. Business services. Some pets allowed. | 2214 S. Broadway 55904 | 507/282–7448 or 800–658–7048 | rochesterlodging.com/redcarpet | 34 rooms | $43–$53 | AE, D, MC, V.

Rochester Inn. Downtown is 2 mi north of this single-story, no-frills motel in a busy commercial area. Cable TV. Some pets allowed. | 1837 S. Broadway 55904 | 507/288–2031 | 27 rooms | $32–$40 | AE, D, DC, MC, V.

Super 8 South 1. This three-story 1980s hotel is on a commercial strip 1 mi south of downtown. In-room data ports. Cable TV. Sauna. Some pets allowed. | 1230 S. Broadway 55904 | 507/288–8288, ext. 350 | fax 507/288–8288 | rochesterlodging.com/super8s1 | 89 rooms | $52–$65 | AE, D, DC, MC, V.

ROSEAU

Evergreen Motel. Three single-story buildings make up the Evergreen, which is in the southwest corner of town. The original wood structure dates back to 1940. Kitchenettes. Cable TV. Some pets allowed. | 304 5th Ave. NW 56751 | 218/463–1642 | 34 rooms | $34–$37 | D, DC, MC, V.

ST. CLOUD

American Motel. On the southwest edge of St. Cloud, this 2-story motel is next door to a fast food restaurant. Complimentary Continental breakfast. In-room data ports, some kitchenettes, some in-room hot tubs. Cable TV. Indoor pool. Hot tub. Free parking. Pets allowed. | 4361 Clearwater Rd. 56301 | 320/253–6337 or 800/634–3444 | fax 320/253–6127 | 40 rooms, 5 suites | $61, $71 suites | AE, D, DC, MC, V.

Best Western Americana Inn and Conference Center. The Munsinger Gardens are three blocks from this 2-story hotel 1½ mi east of downtown. Restaurant, bar (with entertainment), room service. In-room data ports. Cable TV. Indoor pool. Hot tub, sauna. Business services.

Some pets allowed. | 520 S. Rte. 10 56304 | 320/252–8700 | fax 320/252–8700 | www.bestwestern.com | 63 rooms | $49–$104 | AE, D, DC, MC, V.

Best Western Kelly Inn. The Civic Center is right next door to this 6-story glass-and-brick hotel. Some rooms are poolside and others have views of the mighty Mississippi. Fireplace and Jacuzzi suites are available. Restaurant, bar. In-room data ports. Cable TV. Indoor pool, wading pool. Hot tub, sauna. Laundry facilities. Business services. Some pets allowed. | Rte. 23 at 4th Ave. S 56301 | 320/253–0606 | fax 320/202–0505 | www.bestwestern.com | 229 rooms | $59–$105 | AE, D, DC, MC, V.

Days Inn. A mile southeast of downtown, this two-story motel is 3 mi down Route 23 from the Crossroads Mall. Complimentary Continental breakfast. Cable TV. Indoor pool. Hot tub.. Business services. Some pets allowed. | 420 S.E. U.S. 10 | 320/253–0500 | www.daysinn.com/ctg/cgi-bin/DaysInn | 78 rooms | $41–$125 | AE, D, DC, MC, V.

Quality Inn Pool and Water Park. A 2½-story water slide and kiddie pool with fountain are right inside the hotel. All this fun is 3 mi from both St. Cloud State University and the Civic Center. Cable TV. Hot tub, sauna. Some pets allowed. | 70 37th Ave. S 56301 | 320/253–4444 | fax 320/259–7809 | www.qualityinn.com | 89 rooms | $50–$130 | AE, D, DC, MC, V.

Super 8. The Crossroads Mall is across the street from this two-story brick motel. Complimentary Continental breakfast. Cable TV. Business services. Some pets allowed. | 50 Park Ave. S 56301 | 320/253–5530 | fax 320/253–5292 | www.super8.com | 68 rooms | $36–$43 | AE, D, DC, V.

ST. PAUL

Best Western Kelly Inn. All six poolside video games thrill kids at this 10-story hotel across the street from the Minnesota Histories Center, between St. Paul Cathedral and the Capitol. Restaurant, bar, room service. In-room data ports, some microwaves. Cable TV. Indoor pool, wading pool. Hot tub, sauna. Video games. Business services. Some pets allowed. | 161 St. Anthony Blvd. 55103 | 651/227–8711 | fax 651/227–1698 | www.bestwestern.com | 126 rooms | $80–$195 | AE, D, DC, MC, V.

Best Western Maplewood Inn. St. Paul is 6 mi east of this two-story motel, which lies across the street from the Maplewood Mall. An in-house comedy club and poolside video games provide entertainment. Some rooms have Mississippi River views. Restaurant, bar (with entertainment), room service. In-room data ports. Cable TV. Indoor pool. Hot tub, sauna. Video games. Laundry facilities. Business services. Some pets allowed (fee). | 1780 E. County Rd. D, Maplewood 55109 | 651/770–2811 | www.bestwestern.com | 118 rooms | $74–$129 | AE, D, DC, MC, V.

Exel Inn. Five miles north of St. Paul, this 3-story motel is off of the White Bear Ave. exit of I–94. Complimentary Continental breakfast. In-room data ports, refrigerators. Cable TV. Laundry facilities. Business services. Some pets allowed. | 1739 Old Hudson Rd. 55106 | 651/771–5566 | fax 651/771–1262 | www.exelinns.com | 100 rooms | $44–$64 | AE, D, DC, MC, V.

Maplewood Super 8. Two blocks from the 3M world headquarters overlooking Tanner's Lake, this four-story chain hotel, built in 1986, is also 6 mi east of St. Paul. Take I–94, exit 51 (Century Avenue). Picnic area, complimentary Continental breakfast. In-room data ports. Cable TV. Laundry facilities. Business services, airport shuttle. Some pets allowed (fee). | 285 N. Century Ave., Maplewood 55119 | 651/738–1600 | fax 651/738–9405 | www.super8.com | 107 rooms, 3 suites | $47–$80, $127–$159 suites | AE, D, DC, MC, V.

Radisson Riverfront. From the 22nd-floor revolving restaurant atop this riverside hotel on the south edge of town, you can enjoy some of St. Paul's best views of the Mississippi. Also on site are a working carousel and poolside cabanas. Restaurant, bar. Some microwaves, in-room data ports, some refrigerators. Cable TV. Indoor pool. Exercise equipment. Business service. Some pets allowed.| 11 E. Kellogg Blvd. 55101| 651/292–1900 | fax 651/224–8999 | www.radisson.com | 475 rooms | $120–$155 | AE, D, DC, MC, V.

Red Roof Inn St. Paul/Woodbury. Ten miles east of St. Paul, at I–494, exit 59 (Valley Creek Road), you'll find this two-story, two-building motel. In-room data ports. Cable TV. Business services. Some pets allowed.| 1806 Wooddale Dr., Woodbury 55125| 651/738–7160 | fax 651/738–1869 | www.redroof.com | 108 rooms | $40–$70 | AE, D, DC, MC, V.

Wingate Inn–Oakdale. Five miles east of downtown St. Paul, this three-story hostelry is in the suburb of Oakdale, one mi from I–94. Restaurant, bar. Complimentary breakfast. In-room data ports. Cable TV. Hot tub. Exercise equipment. Video games. Laundry facility. Business services. Free parking. Pets allowed. | 970 Helena Ave. N 55128 | 651/578–8466 | fax 651/578–0763 | www.wingateinns.com | 83 rooms, 3 suites | $115–$125, $155 suites | AE, D, DC, MC, V.

SAUK CENTRE

Super 8. This 2-story motor hotel is in a rural area 2 mi south of Sinclair Lewis's Boyhood Home, and 1 mi north of I–94, exit 127 (Sauk Centre). Cable TV. Pool. Business services. Some pets allowed.| 322 12th St. S | 320/352–6581 | fax 320/352–6584 | www.super8.com | 38 rooms | $43–$62 | AE, D, DC, MC, V.

SPRING VALLEY

Super 8. Opened in June of 1999, rooms at this two-story motel have views of the rural countryside. Downtown Spring Valley is 1 mi south. Complimentary Continental breakfast. Some in-room hot tubs. Cable TV. Video games. Laundry facilities. Business services. Pets allowed.| 745 N. Broadway 55975 | 507/346–7788 | fax 507/346–7254 | www.super8.com | 36 rooms, 4 suites | $50–$70, $70–$85 suites | AE, D, DC, MC, V.

STILLWATER

Best Western Stillwater Inn. Standing in a commercial and recreational area 1½ mi south of downtown, this motel has a rustic, Scandinavian-style lobby with a fireplace. Complimentary Continental breakfast. In-room data ports, some in-room hot tubs. Cable TV. Hot tub. Exercise equipment. Business services. Some pets allowed. | 1750 Frontage Rd. W | 651/430–1300 | fax 651/430–0596 | www.bestwestern.com | 60 rooms | $55–$75 | AE, D, DC, MC, V.

TAYLORS FALLS

Springs Country Inn. The St. Croix River is visible from the upper floors of this inn, which is on the southwestern side of town. Restaurant, bar, complimentary Continental breakfast. In-room hot tubs. Cable TV. Business services. Some pets allowed (fee).| 361 Government St. | 651/465–6565 or 800/851–4243 | fax 651/822–4258 | 29 rooms | $45–$95 | AE, D, DC, MC, V.

THIEF RIVER FALLS

C'mon Inn. A residential area off Route 59, on the south end of town, is the setting for this small, two-story motel. Complimentary Continental breakfast. In-room data ports. Cable TV. Pool. Some in-room hot tubs. Business services. Some pets allowed.| 1586 U.S. 59S | 218/ 681–3000 or 800/950–8111 | fax 218/681–3060 | 44 rooms | $60–$99 | AE, D, MC, V.

Hartwood Motel. Seven blocks north of downtown, this single-story motel has been in business since the early 1950s. There is a café across the street. Cable TV. Pets allowed. | 1010 N. Main Ave. 56701 | 218/681–2640 | 34 rooms | $31–$38 | AE, D, DC, MC, V.

TOWER

Daisy Bay Resort. Each rustic lakeside cabin here has its own private dock. The resort is off Route 77, on Lake Vermilion. Kitchenettes. Cable TV. Lake. Hiking. Beach, dock, boating, fishing. Baby-sitting, playground. Some pets allowed. | 4070 Rte. 77 | 218/753–4958 or 800/449–8306 | www.lakevermilionresorts.com/daisy.html | 9 cabins | $65–$140 | AE, MC, V.

End of Trail Lodge. Trees and year-round recreational activities abound at this secluded resort, which has five log cabins on Lake Vermilion. Kitchenettes. Lake. Sauna. Beach, dock, boating, fishing. Some pets allowed. | 4284 End of Trail La. | 218/753–6971 or 800/353–0123 | www.endoftrail.com | 5 cabins | $130–$156 | AE, MC, V.

Glenwood Lodge. The only resort on the northeast section of Lake Vermilion, and one of the most isolated in the region, Glenwood has a lodge and cabins, as well as an on-site grocery and bait shop. Kitchenettes. Lake. Sauna. Hiking. Beach, dock, boating, fishing. Cross-country skiing, snowmobiling. Playground. Some pets allowed. | Rte. 408 | 218/753–5306 | www.GlenwoodLodge.com | 5 cabins | $290–$635 weekly | AE, D, DC, MC, V.

Marjo Motel. Built in 1957, this motel is ¼ mi west of the town center. West Two River, which leads to Lake Vermilion, flows next to the motel. No room phones. Cable TV. Pets allowed. | 712 Rte. 169 55790 | 218/753–4851 | 8 rooms | $40–$55.

TWO HARBORS

Country Inn by Carlson. This cozy 2-story motel is off Route 61, right in town, 1 mi west of Lake Superior. Restaurant, complimentary Continental breakfast. Some microwaves, some refrigerators. Cable TV. Pool. Hot tub, sauna. Laundry facilities. Business services. Some pets allowed (fee). | 1204 7th Ave. | 218/834–5557 or 800/456–4000 | fax 218/834–3777 | www.countryinns.com | 46 rooms | $70–$130 | AE, D, DC, MC, V.

Superior Shores. Standing in a woodsy area 1 mi north of town, this resort has full access to all Lake Superior recreational activities. Restaurant, bar. Some kitchenettes, microwaves, refrigerators. Cable TV, in-room VCRs (and movies). 3 pools. Hot tub, sauna. Tennis. Hiking. Business services. Some pets allowed. | 1521 Superior Shores Dr. | 218/834–5671 or 800/242–1988 | fax 218/834–5677 | supshores@norshor.dst.mn.us | www.superiorshores.com | 57 rooms, 47 suites, 42 apartments | $99–$169, $179–$329 suites, $179–$429 apartments | AE, D, MC, V.

VIRGINIA

Lakeshore Motor Inn. This small motel, right in town, has a lake in its backyard. Some in-room hot tubs. Cable TV. Some pets allowed. | 404 N. 6th Ave. | 218/741–3360 or 800/569–8131 | 18 rooms | $32–$89 | AE, D, DC, MC, V.

Ski View Motel. A golf course is next door to this motel on the north side of town. Complimentary Continental breakfast. Cable TV. Sauna. Some pets allowed. | 903 N. 17th St. | 218/741–8918 | 59 rooms | $30–$70 | AE, D, DC, MC, V.

WILLMAR

Colonial Inn. Across the street from several restaurants, this motel is on a lively thorough-fare two blocks south of downtown. In-room data ports, microwaves, refrigerators, some in-room hot tubs. Cable TV. Pets allowed. | 1102 S. 1st St. 56201 | 320/235–3567 or 800/396–4444 | 19 rooms, 3 suites | $42, $69–$89 suites | AE, D, MC, V.

Days Inn. The Civic Center is ¼ mi north of this stucco motel at the junction of routes 71 and 12 and the Route 23 bypass. Complimentary Continental breakfast. Some in-room hot tubs. Cable TV. Hot tub. Exercise equipment. Some pets allowed. | 225 28th St. SE | 320/231–1275 | www.torgersonproperties.com/daysinnwillmar/index.html | 59 rooms | $43–$54 | AE, D, DC, MC, V.

Holiday Inn. Visible from Highway 71, this 4–story hotel is 1 mi east of downtown. Restaurant, bar, room service. In-room data ports. Cable TV. Pool, wading pool. Hot tub. Business services. Some pets allowed. | 2100 U.S. 12E | 320/235–6060 | fax 320/235–4731 | www.TorgersonProperties.com | 98 rooms | $85–$95 | AE, D, DC, MC, V.

Super 8. This hotel is 1 mi from the Willmar lakes area, on the south edge of town. Cable TV. Business services. Some pets allowed. | 2655 1st St. S | 320/235–7260 | fax 320/235–5580 | www.super8.com | 60 rooms | $37–$55 | AE, D, MC, V.

WINONA

Best Western Riverport Inn. This full-service facility is right in town, at the junction of Highways 61 and 43. Restaurant, bar, complimentary Continental breakfast, room service. Some refrigerators. Cable TV. Pool. Hot tub. Some pets allowed (fee). | 900 Bruski Dr. | 507/452–0606 | fax 507/457–6489 | www.bestwestern.com | 106 rooms | $56–$99 | AE, D, DC, MC, V.

Sugar Loaf Motel. Surrounded by trees at the foot of one of the area's taller peaks, this single-story motel is 3 mi south of downtown. A snowmobiling/hiking trail starts on the property. Some microwaves, some refrigerators. Cable TV. Pets allowed (fee). | 1066 Homer Rd. 55987 | 507/452–1491 | fax 507/452–5334 | 20 rooms | $35–$75 | AE, D, DC, MC, V.

Mississippi

BILOXI

Breakers Inn. This inn, 3 mi from downtown and opposite a sandy beach, offers two-story condo-style rooms with kitchens. There is free shuttle service to casinos. | 47 rooms. In-room data ports, kitchenettes, microwaves, refrigerators, in-room laundry facilities. Cable TV. Pool, wading pool. Tennis. Playground. Business services. Some pets allowed. | 2506 Beach Blvd. 39531 | 228/388–6320 or 800/624–5031 | fax 228/388–7185 | $99–$150 | AE, D, DC, MC, V.

CLEVELAND

Cleveland Inn. This two-story motel is undergoing major renovations to modernize its facilities. The pleasant lounge is open from 4 to midnight. The motel is on the west side of U.S. 61, just south of downtown. | 119 rooms. Restaurant, bar, room service. In-room data ports, cable TV. Pool. Business services. Some pets allowed. | U.S. 61 | 662/846–1411 | fax 662/843–1713 | $50–$79 | AE, D, DC, MC, V.

COLUMBUS

Gilmer Inn. This three-story motel built in 1965 is in the center of the Columbus historic district. A nearby tunnel, now caved in, leads to the river and was used for transferring slaves and wounded Civil War soldiers. The Gilmer Inn is home to Lydia's Southern Cafe. | 64 rooms. Restaurant. Pool. Free parking. Some pets allowed (fee). | 321 Main St. 39701 | 662/328–0070 or 800/328–0722 | fax 662/328–1700 | $45 | AE, D, MC, V.

GRENADA

Best Western Motor Inn. This two-story motel has rooms with balconies. It's west of downtown, off I-55 at exit 206. | 61 rooms. Restaurant, complimentary breakfast, room service. In-room data ports, cable TV. Pool. Business services. Some pets allowed. | 1750 Sunset Dr. | 662/226–7816 or 800/528–1234 | fax 662/226–5623 | www.bestwestern.com | $55–$79 | AE, D, DC, MC, V.

GULFPORT

Red Creek. This three-story B&B was built in 1899 in a raised French cottage style, with a 64-ft front porch. The 11½-acre grounds are filled with fragrant magnolias and ancient live oak trees. There is also a vineyard and a racing stable (but no riding). Rooms are individually named and decorated in different period styles. Red Creek, 4 mi west of Gulfport, was the first B&B on the Gulf Coast. | 5 rooms. Complimentary Continental breakfast. No room phones. Business services. Some pets allowed. No smoking. | 7416 Red Creek Rd., Long Beach 39560 | 228/452–3080 or 800/729–9670 | www.redcreekinn.com | $65–$137 | No credit cards.

HATTIESBURG

Baymont Inn & Suites. This four-story hotel opened in 1999 in the center of town. All rooms and suites have coffee makers, and guests may use a nearby fitness center. | 74 rooms, 12 suites. Complimentary breakfast. Some in-room data ports, some microwaves, some refrigerators, cable TV. Pool. Pets allowed. | 123 Plaza Dr. 39402 | 601/264–8380 or 800/789–4103 | fax 601/264–6381 | www.baymontinns.com | $65, $80–$110 suites | AE, D, DC, MC, V.

Comfort Inn. This pleasant two-story chain hotel built in the 1970s, is less than a mile from the University of Southern Mississippi. | 119 rooms. Restaurant, bar (with entertainment), complimentary breakfast, room service. Cable TV. Pool. Laundry facilities. Business services. Some pets allowed. | 6595 U.S. 49 39401 | 601/268–2170 | fax 601/268–1820 | www.comfortinn.com | $55–$89 | AE, D, DC, MC, V.

HOLLY SPRINGS

Heritage Inn. Rooms at this motel have either a king-size or two double beds, and home-style southern cooking fills the restaurant's lunch buffet. The motel is less than 1 mi south of town on U.S. 78 where it meets Hwys. 7 and 4. | 48 rooms. Restaurant, bar. In-room data ports, cable TV. Outdoor pool. Pets allowed. | 120 Heritage Dr. 38635 | 662/252–1120 | $45–$50 | AE, D, DC, MC, V.

JACKSON

La Quinta North. The white and teal exterior is characteristic of the attractive motels in this chain. The motel is just east of Hwy. 51, 10 minutes from downtown and 20 minutes from the airport. | 145 rooms. Complimentary Continental breakfast. In-room data ports, cable TV. Pool. Laundry services. Business services. Some pets allowed. | 616 Briarwood Dr. 39236 | 601/957–1741 or 800/687–6667 | fax 601/956–5764 | www.laquinta.com | $54–$79 | AE, D, MC, V.

Crowne Plaza. In the heart of downtown, the largest hotel in Jackson provides top amenities, including a skywalk to a small shopping mall. In addition to the oversize guest rooms, there is a relaxed and warm atmosphere and a friendly hotel staff. | 354 rooms. Restaurant, bar. In-room data ports, some microwaves, some refrigerators, cable TV. Outdoor pool. Fitness center. Laundry services, business services. Some pets allowed. | 200 E. Amite St. 39201 | 601/969–5100 or 800/465–4329 | fax 601/969–9665 | www.crowneplaza.com | $100–$130 | AE, D, DC, MC, V.

Residence Inn by Marriott. This two-story hotel 1 mi from downtown is an excellent choice for an extended stay. One- and two-bedroom suites have full kitchens and daily housekeeping service. Some rooms have fireplaces. | 120 suites. Complimentary buffet breakfast, room service. In-room data ports, kitchenettes, microwaves, refrigerators, cable TV. Pool. Hot tub. Tennis. Playground. Laundry facilities. Business services. Some pets allowed. | 881 E. River Pl. 39202 | 601/355–3599 or 800/331–3131 | fax 601/355–5127 | www.residenceinn.com | $89–$129 | AE, D, DC, MC, V.

MCCOMB

Ramada Inn. Nicely landscaped grounds and a friendly staff greet you at this two-story motel 3½ mi from downtown. | 141 rooms, 2 suites. Restaurant, bar, room service. In-room data ports, cable TV. Pool. Laundry facilities. Business services. Some pets allowed. | 1900

Delaware Ave. 39648 | 601/684–6211 or 800/228–2828 | fax 601/684–0408 | www.ramada.com | $59–$79, $125 suites | AE, D, DC, MC, V.

MERIDIAN

Baymont Inn & Suites. This three-story hotel built in the 1980s is in a safe area near major restaurants, about 2½ mi from downtown. It's a good budget choice. | 102 rooms, 9 suites. In-room data ports, cable TV. Outdoor pool. Business services. Pet allowed. | 1400 Roebuck Dr. 39301 | 601/693–2300 or 800/301–0200 | fax 601/485–2534 | www.baymontinns.com | $54, $64–$74 suites | AE, D, DC, MC, V.

Holiday Inn Express. This basic chain motel is about 1 mi from downtown, off I–59 at exit 153. The Spanish-style building was built in the 1960s. It is set back from the road amid trees, giving it a country feeling. | 110 rooms. Complimentary Continental breakfast. In-room data ports, cable TV. Pool. Laundry facilities. Business services. Some pets allowed. | 1401 Roebuck Dr. 39301 | 601/693–4521 or 800/465–4329 | fax 601/693–4521 | www.holiday-inn.com | $60–$70 | AE, D, DC, MC, V.

NATCHEZ

Magnolia Hill Plantation Bed and Breakfast. This Greek Revival planter's cottage sits on a plot that includes 30 acres of old growth forest. You can hike, mountain bike, or ride horseback on the many trails, or fish for largemouth bass, bluegill, or catfish at one of the two ponds on the property. You can also attend the innkeepers' daily wine and cheese gathering, enlivened by their 500 bottle wine cellar. | 6 rooms. Complimentary breakfast. Some microwaves, some refrigerators, no TV in some rooms, TV in common area. Ponds, golf privileges, 9-hole golf course. Hiking, horseback riding. Fishing. Laundry service. Pets allowed. | 16 Wild Turkey Rd. 39120 | 601/445–2392 or 877/642–2392 | www.magnoliaplantation.com | $125–$150 | AE, D, MC, V.

Radisson Natchez Eola Hotel. An expertly restored early 20th-century hotel, the Natchez Eola is now grander than it was in its heyday. It's in the heart of the city's historic downtown area, only three blocks from the mighty Mississippi. Most rooms are small but some have spectacular views of the city and river. Julep's and Café Lasalle restaurants are featured here. The hotel is listed in the National Register of Historic Places. | 132 rooms. 3 restaurants, bar. Some refrigerators. Cable TV. Room service. Exercise equipment. Business services. Some pets allowed. | 110 N. Pearl St. 39120 | 601/445–6000 or 800/888–9140 | fax 601/446–5310 | www.radisson.com | $70–$150 | AE, D, DC, MC, V.

OCEAN SPRINGS

Ocean Springs Days Inn. Several local casinos run shuttles right to the door of this budget motel, which is a 10-minute drive to the Gulf of Mexico. | 58 rooms. In-room data ports, some microwaves, some refrigerators, some in-room hot tubs. Outdoor pool. Pets allowed. | 7305 Washington Ave. 39564 | 228/872–8255 | fax 228/872–8210 | www.daysinn.com | $60–$170 | AE, D, DC, MC, V.

OXFORD

Downtown Inn. This 1963 inn is a bit on the old side, but has a convenient location two blocks north of Courthouse Square. | 123 rooms. Restaurant, bar, room service. In-room data ports, cable TV. Outdoor pool. Laundry facilities. Business services, airport shuttle. Pets allowed. | 400 N. Lamar Blvd. 38655 | 662/234–3031 | fax 662/234–2834 | $60–$70 | AE, D, DC, MC, V.

Oliver-Britt House. This B&B is in a restored 1905 manor house. Rooms are small but comfortable. The house is conveniently located between the university and Courthouse Square. | 5 rooms. Complimentary breakfast. Cable TV, no room phones. Business services. Some pets allowed. | 512 Van Buren Ave. 38655 | 662/234–8043 | fax 662/281–8065 | $75–$150 | AE, D, MC, V.

PASCAGOULA

La Font Inn Resort. This 1963 two-story brick hotel 5 mi from downtown has a distinctive glass and metal pyramid. It is set on 9 acres of landscaped grounds, a few minutes from casinos, beaches, fishing, and golf courses. | 192 rooms. Restaurant, bar, room service. In-room data ports, some kitchenettes, refrigerators, cable TV. Pool, wading pool. Sauna, hot tub. Tennis courts. Exercise equipment. Playground. Laundry facilities. Business services. Some pets allowed. | 2703 Denny Ave., Pascagoula 39568-1028 | 228/762–7111 or 800/647–6077 (800/821–3668 within MS) | fax 228/934–4324 | www.lafont.com | $53–$79 | AE, D, DC, MC, V.

STARKVILLE

Ramada Inn. This two-story building three blocks from downtown was built in the 1960s, and recently renovated. | 142 rooms. Restaurant, bar, room service. Cable TV. Outdoor pool. Business services. Some pets allowed (fee). | 403 Hwy. 12 | 662/323–6161 or 800/228–2828 | fax 662/323–8073 | $69–$99 | AE, D, DC, MC, V.

TUPELO

Red Roof Inn. This two-story chain hotel 3 mi from downtown has standard facilities and rooms. | 100 rooms. In-room data ports, cable TV. Pool. Laundry facilities. Pets allowed. Business services. | 1500 McCullough Blvd. | 662/844–1904 or 800/733–7663 | fax 662/844–0139 | www.redroofinn.com | $39–$99 | AE, D, DC, MC, V.

VICKSBURG

Battlefield Inn. This Southern-style two-story motel, built in 1973, is next to Vicksburg National Military Park and Cemetery. You'll be greeted at the inn by talking parrots, as well as the human staff. | 117 rooms. Restaurant, bar (with entertainment), complimentary breakfast. In-room data ports, some refrigerators, room service, cable TV. Pool. Business services, airport shuttle. Pets allowed. | 4137 N. Frontage Rd. 39183 | 601/638–5811 and 800/359–9363 | fax 601/638–9249 | www.battlefieldinn.org | $55–$99 | AE, D, DC, MC, V.

★ **Duff Green Mansion.** One of Mississippi's oldest mansions, this B&B offers fireplaces in every room, antiques, Oriental rugs, and overstuffed furniture. This three-story brick mansion built in 1856 is an excellent example of Palladian architecture. The National Historic Landmark is in the historic district, eight blocks from downtown. | 7 rooms. Complimentary breakfast. Cable TV. Pool. Hot tub. Business services. Some pets allowed. | 1114 1st East St. 39180 | 601/638–6662 or 800/992–0037 | fax 601/661–0079 | www.duffgreenmansion.com | $95–$125 | AE, D, MC, V.

Holiday Inn. This hotel is across from Vicksburg National Military Park and Cemetery. | 173 rooms. Restaurant, bar, complimentary breakfast. In-room data ports, room service, cable TV. Indoor pool. Video games. Laundry facilities. Business services. Some pets allowed. | 3330 Clay St. 39180 | 601/636–4551 or 800/847–0372 | fax 601/636–4552 | www.holiday-inn.com | $56–$99 | AE, D, DC, MC, V.

WOODVILLE

Desert Plantation. This wooden Federal-style B&B, still part of a 1,000-acre working plantation, was built 1808–12. The home has period furnishings and antiques, including canopy beds. It's in a residential area 20 mi north of Woodville. | 4 rooms. Complimentary country breakfast. Pool. Some pets allowed. | 411 Desert La., St. Fancisville 39669 | 601/888–6889 | fax 601/888–7231 | www.desertplantation.com | $99–$125 | V.

Missouri

BETHANY

Family Budget Inn. This one-level inn is on a commercial strip just off I–35 at exit 92. Picnic area. Cable TV. Pool. Business services. Pets allowed. | 4014 Miller Rd. | 660/425–7915 | fax 660/425–3697 | 78 rooms | $40–$60 | AE, D, DC, MC, V.

BLUE SPRINGS

Ramada Limited. Spacious rooms overlook a small pond with a fishing beach at this resort-like hotel. Restaurant, complimentary Continental breakfast. Cable TV. Pool. Exercise room. Fishing. Laundry facilities. Pets allowed. | 1110 N. Rte. 7, 64014 | 816/229–6363 or 800/272–6232 | fax 816/228–7299 | www.ramada.com | 137 rooms | $50–$85 | AE, DC, MC, V.

BRANSON

Days Inn. Located in the heart of Branson's Theater District, this inn is within 1 mi of 15 theaters and is convenient to area shopping, dining, and attractions. Restaurant, complimentary Continental breakfast. Cable TV. Pool, wading pool. Hot tub. Playground. Business services. Pets allowed (fee). | 3524 Keeter St. | 417/334–5544 or 800/329–7466 | fax 417/334–2935 | www.daysinn.com | 425 rooms | $60–$130 | AE, D, DC, MC, V.

Settle Inn. The exterior of this inn is designed to bring Camelot to mind. Inside there are 32 theme rooms that range from Early England to Greek Mythology to the Wild West. Restaurant, bar, complimentary breakfast, room service. Cable TV. 2 pools. Hot tub, sauna. Gym. Video games. Laundry facilities. Business services. Pets allowed (fee). | 3050 Green Mountain Dr. | 417/335–4700 or 800/677–6906 | fax 417/336–1226 | www.bransonsettleinn.com | 300 rooms, 40 suites | $70–$130 | AE, D, MC, V.

Welk Resort Center and Champagne Theater. Rooms at the Welk Resort, which is 3 mi from Branson's theaters, have contemporary furnishings, country-style accents, and luxurious baths. The center is home to the Lawrence Welk Variety Show and its 20-piece orchestra. Restaurant, bar, complimentary Continental breakfast. Pool. Hot tub. Volleyball. Pets allowed. | 1984 Rte. 165, 65616 | 417/336–3575 or 800/505–9355 | fax 417/336–6573 | 160 rooms | $94–$99 | AE, D, MC, V.

CAMERON

Best Western Acorn Inn. This redbrick Colonial-style motel is $1/4$ mi from I-35 on U.S. 36 near the birthplace of Jesse James and several antiques malls. Complimentary Continental breakfast. In-room data ports, cable TV. Pool. Pets allowed. | I–35 and U.S. 36, 64429 | 816/632–2187 or 800/607–2288 | fax 816/632–2523 | www.bestwestern.com | 40 rooms | $51–$64 | AE, D, DC, MC, V.

Econo Lodge. This downtown chain hotel is within walking distance of Cameron's restaurants and shops. Complimentary Continental breakfast. Cable TV. Pool. Pets allowed. | 220 E. Grand | 816/632–6571 | 36 rooms | $35–$65 | AE, D, DC, MC, V.

CAPE GIRARDEAU

Drury Lodge. This chain motel just off I-55 at exit 96 about 10 minutes from downtown is especially proud of its restaurant, which is good enough to draw locals as well as guests. Restaurant, bar, complimentary breakfast, room service. Cable TV. Pool, wading pool. Gym. Playground. Business services. Some pets allowed. | 104 S. Vantage Rd. | 573/334–7151 or 800/325–8300 | fax 573/334–7151 | www.druryinn.com | 139 rooms | $68–$75 | AE, D, DC, MC, V.

Hampton Inn. Near the airport, 4 mi west of downtown, this chain motel is just across the street from several restaurants. Complimentary Continental breakfast. Cable TV. Business services. Some pets allowed. | 103 Cape West Pkwy. | 573/651–3000 or 800/426–7866 | fax 573/651–0882 | www.hamptoninn.com | 80 rooms | $60–$90 | AE, D, DC, MC, V.

Holiday Inn West Park. This chain hotel is 1 mi from the Southeast Missouri State University campus and a nearby mall. The hotel has several meeting rooms available to business travelers. Restaurant, bar, room service. In-room data ports, cable TV. 2 pools, wading pool. Sauna. Gym. Laundry facilities. Business services. Pets allowed. | 3257 William St. | 573/334–4491 or 800/465–4329 | fax 573/334–7459 | www.basshotels.com/holiday-inn | 186 rooms | $82–$88 | AE, D, DC, MC, V.

Pear Tree Inn. This chain hotel is within walking distance of a shopping mall and movie theater. Complimentary Continental breakfast. Cable TV. Pool, wading pool. Business services. Some pets allowed. | 3248 William St. | 573/334–3000 | 78 rooms | $55–$65 | AE, D, DC, MC, V.

Victorian Inn of Cape Girardeau. This motel is right off I-55 at exit 96 on a commercial strip with lots of chain restaurants. Despite its name it has a contemporary, not Victorian, look. Refrigerators, cable TV. 2 hot tubs. Pets allowed. | 3265 William St., 63701 | 573/651–4486 | fax 573/651–3970 | 133 rooms | $65–$95 | AE, D, DC, MC, V.

CARTHAGE

Econo Lodge. Some rooms have inside entrances, some outside entrances at this chain motel on a commercial street 1 mi from downtown. Complimentary Continental breakfast. Cable TV. Pool. Hot tub. Pets allowed (fee). | 1441 W. Central Ave. | 417/358–3900 | fax 417/358–6839 | 82 rooms | $52–$60 | AE, D, DC, MC, V.

CASSVILLE

Super 8 Motel. This two-story motel built in 1993 is 7 mi from the Roaring River State Park on Highway 37. Cable TV. Pool. Pets allowed. | 101 S. Hwy 37, 65625 | 417/847–4888 or 800/800–8000 | fax 417/847–4888 | www.super8.com | 46 rooms | $49–$56 | AE, D, DC, MC, V.

CHILLICOTHE

Best Western Inn. This chain hotel is set in a commercial area near several restaurants. Complimentary Continental breakfast. In-room data ports, refrigerators, cable TV. Pool.

Business services. Pets allowed (fee). | 1020 S. Washington St. | 660/646–0572 or 800/990–9150 | fax 660/646–1274 | www.bestwestern.com | 60 rooms, 6 suites in 2 buildings | $50–$85 | AE, D, DC, MC, V.

Grand River Inn. This brick hotel is within walking distance of several restaurants and shops including a Wal-Mart. Restaurant, bar, complimentary Continental breakfast, room service. In-room data ports, some refrigerators, cable TV. Pool. Hot tub, sauna. Business services. Some pets allowed. | 606 W. Business 36 | 660/646–6590 | 60 rooms, 5 suites | $58–$79, $83–$92 suites | AE, D, DC, MC, V.

Super 8 Motel. Built in 1995, this chain motel is off Highway 36 at the Industrial Road Exit. Complimentary Continental breakfast. Cable TV. Pets allowed. | 580 Old Highway 36 E, 64601 | 660/646–7888 or 800/800–8000 | fax 660/646–2531 | www.super8.com | 56 rooms | $50 | AE, D, DC, MC, V.

CLAYTON

Daniele. A steaming pot of coffee will be delivered to your room shortly after your wake-up call at this European-style hotel near Washington University. Rooms are furnished with antique reproductions. Restaurant, bar, complimentary Continental breakfast. In-room data ports, some refrigerators, cable TV. Pool. Business services, airport shuttle, free parking. Pets allowed. | 216 N. Meramac Ave. | 314/721–0101 or 800/325–8302 | fax 314/721–0609 | 82 rooms, 5 suites | $129, $250 1–bedroom suites, $500 2–bedroom suites, $800 3–bedroom suites | AE, D, DC, MC, V.

COLUMBIA

Columbia Dome. This chain hotel is a 10-minute drive from the University of Missouri. Restaurant, bar, room service. Cable TV. Pool. Hot tub. Gym. Some pets allowed. | 1612 N. Providence Rd., 65202 | 573/449–2491 | fax 573/874–6720 | 142 rooms | $80 | AE, D, DC, MC, V.

Holiday Inn Executive Center. This Holiday Inn claims to have the biggest hotel gym in the Midwest. Five miles from the University of Missouri, the hotel is just across the street from a shopping mall. Restaurant, bar, room service. In-room data ports, cable TV. 2 pools. Beauty salon, hot tub. Gym. Business services. Pets allowed. | 2200 I–70 Dr. SW, 65203 | 573/445–8531 or 800/465–4329 | fax 573/445–7607 | www.basshotels.com/holiday-inn | 311 rooms, 11 suites | $90, $135 suites | AE, D, DC, MC, V.

Travelodge. This chain motel is 4 mi from the University of Missouri and 2 mi from Boone County Fairgrounds. Complimentary Continental breakfast, picnic area. Some refrigerators, cable TV. Pool. Laundry facilities. Business services. Some pets allowed (fee). | 900 Vandiver Dr., 65202 | 573/449–1065 | fax 573/442–6266 | 164 rooms | $50–$70 | AE, D, DC, MC, V.

EXCELSIOR SPRINGS

Monterey Motel. This centrally located downtown motel was built in 1950 and has Spanish-style architecture and well-landscaped grounds. Cable TV. Pets allowed. | 217 Concourse | 816/630–0099 | fax 816/637–3171 | 56 rooms | $60 | AE, D, DC, MC, V.

FARMINGTON

Super 8 Motel. This basic motel, built in 1995, is on a commercial strip with several restaurants just off Highway 67 at Exit 32. Complimentary Continental breakfast. Cable TV. Pool. Pets allowed. | 930 Valley Creek Dr., 63640 | 573/756–0344 or 800/800–8000 | fax 573/760–0846 | www.super8.com | 60 rooms | $44–$52 | AE, D, DC, MC, V.

INDEPENDENCE

Howard Johnson. This 1960s HoJo is just minutes away from two local malls with several restaurant options and a 15-minute drive to either the Harry S Truman Library and Museum or the Worlds of Fun theme park. Complimentary Continental breakfast. In-room refrigerators, cable TV. 2 pools. Hot tub, 2 saunas. Business services. Pets allowed. | 4200 S. Noland Rd., 64055 | 816/373–8856 or 800/338–3752 | fax 816/373–3312 | 171 rooms, 2 suites | $80–$90 | AE, D, DC, MC, V.

Red Roof Inn. This chain hotel, built in 1975, is a 15-minute drive from Truman's home. Cable TV. Business services. Pets allowed. | 13712 E. 42nd Terrace, 64055 | 816/373–2800 or 800/RED–ROOF | fax 816/373–0067 | www.redroof.com | 108 rooms | $50–$75 | AE, D, DC, MC, V.

Serendipity Bed and Breakfast. Antique walnut furniture, antique rugs, and period lighting evoke the stately past of this three-story brick home built in 1887. Collections of Victorian children's books, toys, china, and glassware add to the flavor. An overnight stay comes with a 1920s car ride (weather permitting), and if you stay here you'll be just three blocks from the National Frontier Trails Center. Complimentary breakfast. TV. Laundry facilities. Pets allowed. | 116 S. Pleasant St., 64050 | 816/833–4719 or 800/203–4299 | fax 816/833–4719 | www.bbhost.com/serendipitybb | 6 rooms | $45–$85 | D, MC, V.

HANNIBAL

Travelodge. This older basic motel is the best economy value lodging in the area, and it's only four blocks from the historic district. Amenities include a grassy picnic area and barbecue grill. Complimentary Continental breakfast. Cable TV. Pool. Business services. Pets allowed. | 502 Mark Twain Ave. | 573/221–4100 | 42 rooms | $34–$75 | AE, D, DC, MC, V.

JEFFERSON CITY

Jefferson Inn. Floral wallpaper, lace curtains, and handsome antiques give this inn a Victorian flourish. Upon your arrival you will be served complimentary drinks and snacks in front of the common room's brick-and-marble fireplace. The inn is just six blocks from the capitol. Complimentary breakfast. Cable TV, in-room VCRs, some room phones. Hot tub. Pets allowed. No kids under 6. No smoking. | 801 High St., 65101 | 573/635–7196 or 800/530–5009 | jeffersoninn@aol.com | 4 rooms | $65–$125 | AE, D, MC, V.

Ramada Inn. This chain hotel is on a commercial strip about a five-minute drive from Jefferson City's business district and the State Capitol. Restaurant, bar (with entertainment), room service. Some refrigerators, cable TV. Pool. Gym. Business services, airport shuttle. Pets allowed. | 1510 Jefferson St., 65109 | 573/635–7171 or 800/272–6232 | fax 573/635–8006 | www.ramada.com | 233 rooms, 7 suites | $70–$140 | AE, D, DC, MC, V.

JOPLIN

Baymont Inn and Suites of Joplin. This hotel is just off I–44, 7 mi from downtown. It is surrounded by chain restaurants. In-room data ports, some microwaves, some refrigerators, some in-room hot tubs, cable TV. Pool. Hot tub. Gym. Pets allowed. | 3510 S. Range Line Rd., 64804 | 417/623–0000 or 800/301–0200 | 80 rooms | $62–$130 | AE, D, DC, MC, V.

Best Western Hallmark Inn. You can walk to several restaurants and area shops from this chain hotel, built in the 1970s. Offers standard, affordable rooms. In-room data ports, refrigerators available, cable TV. Pool. Playground. Business services, airport shuttle. Pets allowed. | 3600 Range Line Rd., 64804 | 417/624–8400 or 800/528–1234 | fax 417/781–5625 | www.bestwestern.com | 96 rooms | $40–$65 | AE, D, DC, MC, V.

Drury Inn. This chain hotel built in 1990 is on a commercial strip within walking distance of an antiques mall and approximately 20 mi from Precious Moments Chapel Center. Complimentary Continental breakfast. In-room data ports, some in-room refrigerators, cable TV. Pool. Hot tub. Business services. Some pets allowed. | 3601 Range Line Rd., 64804 | 417/781–8000 or 800/325–8300 | www.druryinn.com | 109 rooms | $55–$90 | AE, D, DC, MC, V.

Hampton Inn Joplin. Just ½ mi from I–44, this three-story chain hotel is in Joplin's commercial district, near the convention center. Restaurants and shops are within walking distance. Complimentary Continental breakfast. Some refrigerators, cable TV. Pool. Gym. Laundry service. Pets allowed. | 3107 E. 36th St., 64806 | 417/659–9900 or 800/426–7866 | fax 417/659–9901 | www.hamptoninn.com | 89 rooms | $75–$86 | AE, D, DC, MC, V.

Holiday Inn Hotel and Convention Center. This chain hotel is on a landscaped property on a commercial strip, and is just 3 mi from Missouri Southern State College. Restaurant, bar, room service. In-room data ports, cable TV. 2 pools. 2 hot tubs, sauna. Gym. Business services, airport shuttle. Some pets allowed. | 3615 Range Line Rd., 64804 | 417/782–1000 or 800/465–4329 | fax 417/623–4093 | www.basshotels.com/holiday-inn | 264 rooms, 8 suites | $65–$135 | AE, D, DC, MC, V.

Ramada Inn. Built in 1970 and renovated in 2000, this chain hotel is one of several on a commercial strip 2 mi southeast of downtown. Restaurant, bar, room service. In-room data ports, cable TV. 2 pools. Hot tub, sauna. Tennis court. Playground. Business services, airport shuttle. Pets allowed (fee). | 3320 Range Line Rd., 64804 | 417/781–0500 or 800/272–6232 | fax 417/781–9388 | www.ramada.com | 171 rooms | $54–$75 | AE, D, DC, MC, V.

Westwood. This wood-frame hotel is close to the hospital and 1 mi west of downtown. Cable TV. Pool. Laundry facilities. Pets allowed. | 1700 W. 30th St., 64804 | 417/782–7212 | fax 417/624–0265 | www.westwoodmotel.com | 33 rooms | $30–$45 | AE, D, MC, V.

KANSAS CITY

Baymont Inn. This chain hotel is close to Kansas City's business district and less than 20 minutes from the Kansas City International Airport. It has a homey atmosphere complete with a fireplace in the lounge. Complimentary Continental breakfast. In-room data ports, cable TV. Business services. Some pets allowed. | 2214 Taney, 64116 | 816/221–1200 | fax 816/471–6207 | www.baymontinn.com | 94 rooms, 8 suites | $70–$90 | AE, D, DC, MC, V.

Chase Suites at KCI. This all-suites hotel is 3½ mi from Kansas City International Airport. Complimentary Continental breakfast. In-room data ports, kitchenettes, cable TV. Pool, wading pool. Hot tub. Gym. Laundry facilities. Business services, airport shuttle, free parking. Some pets allowed (fee). | 9900 N.W. Prairie View Rd., 64153 | 816/891–9009 | fax 816/891–8623 | www.woodfinsuitehotels.com | 112 suites | $69–$139 | AE, D, DC, MC, V.

Marriott–Airport. This chain hotel is right at the airport, just ¼ mi from the terminals and 15 mi from downtown. Restaurant, bar, picnic area, room service. In-room data ports, cable TV. Pool. Hot tub, sauna. Gym. Laundry facilities. Business services, airport shuttle, free parking. Pets allowed. | 775 Brasilia Ave., 64153 | 816/464–2200 | fax 816/464–5915 | www.marriott.com | 382 rooms | $124 | AE, D, DC, MC, V.

Park Place. Some rooms in this 1970s motel in an industrial park a five-minute drive from Worlds of Fun theme park have views of a small lake. Restaurant, bar (with entertainment), complimentary Continental breakfast. In-room data ports, some refrigerators, cable TV. Indoor-outdoor pool. Gym. Business services, free parking. Some pets allowed. | 1601 N. Universal Ave., 64120 | 816/483–9900 or 800/821–8532 | fax 816/231–1418 | 227 rooms, 115 suites | $79–$89, $119 suites | AE, D, DC, MC, V.

Westin Crown Center. Just 1 mi from Worlds of Fun theme park and the Nelson-Atkins Museum of Art, this hotel is attached to the Crown Center shopping mall. Restaurants, bar (with entertainment), room service. In-room data ports, refrigerators, cable TV. Pool. Barbershop, beauty salon, hot tub. 2 tennis courts. Gym. Kids' programs (ages 6–12). Business services. Pets allowed. | 1 Pershing Rd., 64108 | 816/474–4400 or 800/228–3000 |

fax 816/391–4438 | www.westin.com | 725 rooms, 45 suites | $200–$245, $350–$400 1–bedroom suites, $500–$550 2–bedroom suites, $1,500 presidential suite | AE, D, DC, MC, V.

KIMBERLING CITY

Cove Resort. This resort on Table Rock Lake has both cottages and motel rooms. The cottages have fully equipped kitchens, and some of the wood-paneled motel rooms have views of the lake. There is a restaurant on the premises and one across the street. Restaurant, bar. Cable TV, no room phones. Pool. Dock, boating, fishing. Playground. Pets allowed (fee). | Hwy. 13, 65686 | 417/739–4341 or 800/739–COVE | candymnt@aol.com | www.tablerocklake.net/lodging/coveresort | 22 rooms, 16 cottages | $55 | AE, D, MC, V.

KIRKSVILLE

Budget Host Village Inn. This chain motel is just a two-minute walk from Truman State University. Cable TV. Business services. Some pets allowed. | 1304 S. Baltimore St. | 660/665–3722 | fax 660/665–8277 | 30 rooms | $48 | AE, D, DC, MC, V.

Kirksville Comfort Inn. This two-story hotel is on Highway 63, across the street from the Wal-Mart Super Center. Complimentary Continental breakfast. Some microwaves, some refrigerators, cable TV. Hot tub. Pets allowed. | 2209 N. Baltimore St./Hwy. 63, 63501 | 660/665–2205 or 800/228–5150 | fax 660/665–2205 | 47 rooms | $50–$75 | AE, D, DC, MC, V.

LAKE OZARK

Holiday Inn Sun Spree Resort. This large Lake of the Ozarks resort is next door to Port Arrowhead marina and 4 mi from town. Restaurant, bar, complimentary Continental breakfast, room service. In-room data ports, microwaves, cable TV. 3 pools. Hot tub. Miniature golf. Gym. Video games. Children's programs, playground. Laundry facilities. Business services. Pets allowed. | Business Rte. 54, Box 1930, 65049 | 573/365–2334 or 800/465–4329 | fax 573/365–6887 | www.funlake.com | 213 rooms | $125–$145 | AE, D, DC, MC, V.

LEBANON

Best Western Wyota Inn. This highway motel is 12 mi from Bennett Spring State Park. Restaurant, complimentary Continental breakfast. Cable TV. Pool. Laundry facilities. Some pets allowed. | 1225 Mill Creek Rd. | 417/532–6171 or 800/528–1234 | fax 417/532–6174 | www.bestwestern.com | 52 rooms | $55 | AE, D, DC, MC, V.

Quality Inn. This chain motel, built in 1984, is 2 mi from downtown. Restaurant, bar, complimentary Continental breakfast, room service. Cable TV. Pool. Laundry facilities. Business services. Pets allowed. | 2071 W. Elm St. | 417/532–7111 | fax 417/532–7005 | 82 rooms | $65 | AE, D, DC, MC, V.

Sand Spring Resort. This large tree-filled property provides opportunities for hiking, swimming, and enjoying nature. Because of its location adjacent to the Bennett Spring State Park and the Niangua River, the resort is also the perfect spot for fishing. Occasional fishing seminars are held at the resort. Restaurant. Some kitchenettes, some microwaves, some refrigerators, cable TV. Pool. Sauna. Hiking, boating, fishing. Pets allowed (fee). | Rte. 16, 65536 | 417/532–5857 or 800/543–FISH | www.sandspringresort.com | 52 rooms | $42–$67 | MC, V.

LEXINGTON

Lexington Inn. Built in 1969, this brick inn is 1 mi from Battle of Lexington State Historic site and Wentworth Military Academy. Restaurant, bar (with entertainment). Cable TV. Pool. Laundry facilities. Business services. Pets allowed (fee). | 1078 N. Outer Rd. W | 660/259–4641 or 800/289–4641 | 60 rooms | $45–$75 | AE, D, DC, MC, V.

MACON

Best Western Inn. This older chain hotel is across the street from Lake Longbranch and within walking distance of several antiques stores. In-room data ports, cable TV. Pool. Business services. Some pets allowed. | 28933 Sunset Dr. | 660/385–2125 or 800/528–1234 | www.bestwestern.com | 46 rooms | $55 | AE, D, DC, MC, V.

St. Agnes Hall Bed and Breakfast. This brick home was built in the 1840s and was once a girls' boarding school. The rooms are graced with family heirlooms and antiques, which accent the building's heritage. The grounds include period gardens and decks. Complimentary breakfast. No room phones. Hot tub. Pets allowed. No smoking. | 502 Jackson, 63552 | 660/385–2774 | fax 660/385–4436 | 3 rooms | $68–$95 | AE, D, MC, V.

MOBERLY

Ramada Inn of Moberly. One of the region's only full-service hotels, the Ramada is 1 ½ mi from downtown in a quiet commercial area. 2 restaurants, room service. Some refrigerators, cable TV. Pool. Hot tub. Airport shuttle. Pets allowed (fee). | 1200 Hwy. 24 E, 65270 | 660/263–6540 or 888/298–2054 | fax 660/263–0092 | www.the.ramada.com | 98 rooms | $69–$105 | AE, D, DC, MC, V.

MONROE CITY

Monroe City Inn. This hotel is within walking distance of several fast-food restaurants and is 1½ mi from a local golf course. It has a game room with video games, pool tables, and foozball. Cable TV. Pool. Hot tub. Some pets allowed (fee). | 3 Gateway Sq. | 573/735–4200 | fax 573/735–3493 | 47 rooms | $40–$55 | AE, D, DC, MC, V.

MOUND CITY

Audrey's Motel. Many people who come to view the area's wildlife stay at this low-key motel on Highway 59 North. Rooms have queen-size beds. Restaurants and shops are two blocks away. Complimentary Continental breakfast. Some microwaves, some refrigerators, cable TV. Pets allowed. | 1211 State St., 64470 | 660/442–3191 | 30 rooms | $40–$45 | AE, D, MC, V.

MOUNT VERNON

Budget Host Ranch. You can walk to several fast-food restaurants from this older chain motel. Picnic area. Cable TV. Pool. Some pets allowed. | 1015 E. Mount Vernon Blvd. | 417/466–2125 | fax 417/466–4440 | 21 rooms | $36–$52 | AE, D, MC, V.

NEVADA

Comfort Inn. This chain hotel is on a commercial strip along with a truck stop, a Wal-Mart, and a Burger King. Complimentary Continental breakfast. Cable TV. Some pets allowed (fee). | 2345 Marvel Dr. | 417/667–6777 or 800/221–2222 | fax 417/667–6135 | 46 rooms | $62 | AE, D, DC, MC, V.

Super 8. A standard chain motel within walking distance of a small restaurant. Complimentary Continental breakfast. Cable TV. Pool. Hot tub. Laundry facilities. Business services. Pets allowed. | 2301 E. Austin Blvd. | 417/667–8888 or 800/800–8000 | fax 417/667–8883 | www.super8.com | 60 rooms | $50 | AE, D, DC, MC, V.

NEW MADRID

Marston/New Madrid Super 8 Motel. This chain motel is in the middle of a cotton field just off I-55 at exit 40, 5 mi south of New Madrid. Cable TV. Business services. Pets allowed. | 501 S.E. Outer Rd., Marston, 63866 | 573/643–9888 or 800/800–8000 | fax 573/643–9025 | www.super8.com | 63 rooms | $41–$61 | AE, D, DC, MC, V.

OSAGE BEACH

SeaScape Resort. All the rooms in this lakefront resort have lakeview balconies and kitchenettes. Units have from one to four bedrooms, and the resort has a recreation room and a playground, which makes it a good place to bring the kids. Kitchenettes, refrigerators, cable TV, no room phones. Pool. Dock, fishing. Video games. Playground. Pets allowed. | 1359 SeaScape La., 65065 | 573/348–2620 | info@seascaperesort.net | www. seascaperesort.net | 23 rooms | $48–$75 | AE, D, MC, V.

POPLAR BLUFF

Drury Inn. This 1980s chain hotel is just 2 mi from Mark Twain National Forest. Convenient to local transportation and area attractions, including a museum and city parks. Complimentary breakfast. In-room data ports, cable TV. Indoor-outdoor pool. Business services. Some pets allowed. | 2220 Westwood Blvd. N (U.S. 67 N) | 573/686–2451 or 800/ 325–8300 | fax 573/686–2451 | www.druryinn.com | 78 rooms | $65–$71 | AE, D, DC, MC, V.

Ramada Inn. This chain hotel is less than a 30-minute drive from Wappapello Lake, and about 45 mi from Big Springs, one of the largest springs in the country. Restaurant, bar (with entertainment), complimentary breakfast, room service. Cable TV. Pool. Pets allowed. | 2115 N. Westwood Blvd. (U.S. 67 N) | 573/785–7711 or 800/272–6232 | fax 573/785–5215 | www.ramada.com | 143 rooms | $55 | AE, D, DC, MC, V.

ROLLA

Best Western Coachlight. This chain hotel is approximately 5 mi from the University of Missouri–Rolla campus and 2 mi from downtown. Complimentary Continental breakfast. In-room data ports, some refrigerators, cable TV. Pool. Playground. Pets allowed. | 1403 Martin Spring Dr. | 573/341–2511 or 800/528–1234 | fax 573/368–3055 | www.bestwestern.com | 88 rooms | $60 | AE, D, DC, MC, V.

Drury Inn. This chain hotel is just a block from the University of Missouri–Rolla. Complimentary Continental breakfast. Cable TV. Pool. Business services. Pets allowed. | 2006 N. Bishop Ave. | 573/364–4000 or 800/325–8300 | fax 573/364–4000 | www.druryinn.com | 86 rooms | $60–$75 | AE, D, DC, MC, V.

ST. CHARLES

New Motel 6 St. Charles. This chain motel is on a commercial strip 4 mi west of historic downtown St. Charles and within walking distance of several fast-food spots. Some refrigerators, cable TV. Pool. Pets allowed. | 3800 Harry S Truman Blvd., 63301 | 636/925–2020 or 800/843–5644 | fax 636/946–3480 | 109 rooms | $46–$50 | AE, D, DC, MC, V.

ST. JOSEPH

Drury Inn. This chain hotel is across the street from a mall and a 10-minute drive from the Pony Express Memorial and Jesse James's Home. Complimentary Continental breakfast. In-room data ports, cable TV. Pool. Gym. Business services. Pets allowed. | 4213 Frederick Blvd. | 816/364–4700 or 800/325–8300 | fax 816/364–4700 | www.druryinn.com | 134 rooms | $75 | AE, D, DC, MC, V.

Holiday Inn–Downtown. This older downtown hotel is within walking distance of restaurants and antiques shops and just 3 mi from the Pony Express Memorial and Jesse James's Home. Restaurant, bar, room service. Some refrigerators, cable TV. Pool. Hot tub, sauna. Business services. Pets allowed. | 102 S. 3rd St., 64501 | 816/279–8000 or 800/465–4329 | fax 816/279–1484 | www.basshotels.com/holiday-inn | 170 rooms, 5 suites | $78–$95, $135–$211 suites | AE, D, DC, MC, V.

Ramada Inn. This chain hotel is within walking distance of a strip mall and several restaurants and is 15 minutes away from area casinos. Restaurants, bar, complimentary Continental breakfast. Cable TV. Pool. Hot tub. Laundry facilities. Business services. Pets allowed. | 4016 Frederick Blvd. | 816/233–6192 or 800/272–6232 | fax 816/233–6001 | www.ramada.com | 163 rooms, 5 suites | $65–$90 | AE, D, DC, MC, V.

ST. LOUIS

Drury Inn. This chain hotel is just three blocks from Lambert–St. Louis International Airport, and approximately a 20-minute drive from St. Charles's historic district. There are several restaurants within walking distance. Complimentary Continental breakfast. In-room data ports, cable TV. Pool. Hot tub. Business services, airport shuttle, free parking. Some pets allowed. | 10490 Natural Bridge Rd., 63134 | 314/423–7700 or 800/325–8300 | fax 314/423–7700 | www.druryinn.com | 173 rooms, 10 suites | $93–$126 | AE, D, DC, MC, V.

Drury Inn-Convention Center. You can walk to the Gateway Arch or Laclede's Landing from this hotel which is adjacent to the convention center and stadiums in a historic building known as the Union Market in the mid-1800s when it was built. Complimentary Continental breakfast. In-room data ports, some microwaves, some refrigerators, cable TV. Pool. Hot tub. Business services, free parking. Some pets allowed. | 711 N. Broadway, 63102 | 314/231–8100 or 800/325–8300 | fax 314/621–6568 | www.druryinn.com | 178 rooms | $90–$125 | AE, D, DC, MC, V.

★ **Drury Inn Union Station.** Built as a YMCA in the early 1900s, this historic building with lead-glass windows and marble columns has charm and a great location across from Union Station. Restaurant, bar, complimentary Continental breakfast. In-room data ports, some refrigerators, cable TV. Pool. Hot tub. Gym. Laundry facilities. Free parking. Some pets allowed. | 201 S. 20th St., 63103 | 314/231–3900 or 800/325–8300 | fax 314/231–3900 | www.druryinn.com | 176 rooms, 20 suites | $125–$150 | AE, D, DC, MC, V.

AN ARTFUL TRIBUTE

The world's finest collection of art depicting dogs is the focal point of the American Kennel Club Museum of the Dog in St. Louis. You'll find everything from pre-Columbian pottery to paintings and photographs by famed 19th- and 20th-century artists such as Sir Edwin Landseer and William Wegman. An array of 19th-century dog collars is also here, along with silver trophies and tributes to such "Hall of Fame" dog stars as Lassie and Toto. There are special exhibits from time to time as well. Founded in New York by a group of people who loved dogs as much as they loved art, the American Kennel Club Museum of the Dog moved to St. Louis in 1987. Housed in the 1853 Jarville House, it overlooks Queeny Park about 20 minutes west of downtown St. Louis. In addition to seeing the paintings, drawings, and sculptures, you can also use the museum's reference collection of books and a complete library of AKC videos. Alas, dogs are not permitted in the museum. Contact: 1721 S. Mason Rd., St. Louis, MO 63131, 314/821–3647, www.akc.org/love/museum. Open Tues.–Sat. 9–5, Sun. noon-55. Admission: $3.

Hampton Inn. You can walk to the Gateway Arch from this downtown hotel. Restaurant, bar, complimentary Continental breakfast. In-room data ports, cable TV. Pool. Hot tub. Gym. Laundry facilities. Business services, free parking. Some pets allowed. | 2211 Market St., 63103 | 314/241–3200 or 800/426–7866 | fax 314/241–9351 | www.hamptoninn-suites.com | 229 rooms, 10 suites | $99–$139, $149–$159 suites | AE, D, DC, MC, V.

Holiday Inn–Airport West. This Holiday Inn is halfway between the airport and West Port Plaza, just 5 mi from each. Restaurant, bar, room service. In-room data ports, some refrigerators, cable TV. Pool. Hot tub. Gym. Video games. Laundry facilities. Business services, airport shuttle, free valet parking. Pets allowed. | 3551 Pennridge Dr., Bridgeton, 63044 | 314/291–5100 or 800/465–4329 | fax 314/291–1307 | www.basshotels.com/holiday-inn | 249 rooms | $110 | AE, D, DC, MC, V.

Holiday Inn–Forest Park. This chain hotel is on The Hill, 6 mi from the downtown area, and 1 mi south of Forest Park. Restaurant, bar, room service. In-room data ports, cable TV. Pool. Business services. Pets allowed. | 5915 Wilson Ave., 63110 | 314/645–0700 or 800/465–4329 | fax 314/645–0700 | www.basshotels.com/holiday-inn | 119 rooms | $95–$130 | AE, D, DC, MC, V.

Residence Inn by Marriott. You can walk to Westport Plaza from this chain hotel. Historic St. Charles and the airport are each less than 10 mi away. Complimentary Continental breakfast. In-room data ports, kitchenettes, microwaves, refrigerators, cable TV, in-room movies. Pool. Hot tub. Laundry facilities. Business services, airport shuttle. Some pets allowed (fee). | 1881 Craigshire Dr., 63146 | 314/469–0060 | fax 314/469–3751 | www.marriott.com | 128 suites | $99–$160 | AE, D, DC, MC, V.

Summerfield Suites. This West Port hotel 45 minutes west of downtown has seven different buildings as well as basketball and tennis facilities on its landscaped grounds. Picnic area, complimentary Continental breakfast. In-room data ports, microwaves, cable TV, in-room VCRs. Pool. Hot tub. Gym. Laundry facilities. Business services, airport shuttle, free parking. Some pets allowed (fee). | 1855 Craigshire Rd., 63146 | 314/878–1555 or 800/833–4353 | fax 314/878–9203 | 106 suites in 7 buildings | $139 1–bedroom suites, $159 2–bedroom suites | AE, D, DC, MC, V.

SEDALIA

Best Western State Fair Motor Inn. The state fairgrounds are just ½ mi from this motel. Restaurant, bar, room service. Cable TV. Pool, wading pool. Hot tub. Putting green. Gym. Video games. Laundry facilities. Business services, airport shuttle. Pets allowed. | 3120 S. Limit U.S. 65 | 660/826–6100 or 800/528–1234 | fax 660/827–3850 | www.bestwestern.com | 119 rooms | $50–$70 | AE, D, DC, MC, V.

SIKESTON

Best Western Coach House Inn. At the junction of I–55 and U.S 62 and just ½ mi from Lambert's Café and their famous "throwed rolls." Restaurant, bar (with entertainment), complimentary Continental breakfast, room service. In-room data ports, microwaves, refrigerators, cable TV. Pool. Gym. Video games. Laundry services. Business services. Some pets allowed. | 220 S. Interstate Dr. | 573/471–9700 or 800/528–1234 | fax 573/471–4285 | www.bestwestern.com | 63 suites | $70 | AE, D, DC, MC, V.

Drury Inn. This chain hotel off I–55 at exit 60 is in a commercial area with outlet shopping and restaurants within easy walking distance. Convenient also to Sikeston Memorial Airport. Complimentary Continental breakfast. Some microwaves, some refrigerators, cable TV. Indoor-outdoor pool. Hot tub. Business services. Some pets allowed. | 2602 E. Malone St. | 573/471–4100 or 800/325–8300 | fax 573/471–4100 | www.druryinn.com | 78 rooms | $75–$88 | AE, D, DC, MC, V.

SPRINGFIELD

Best Western Route 66 Rail Haven. This was the first Best Western in the United States when it opened in 1938 on attractively landscaped grounds on historic Route 66. Complimentary Continental breakfast. In-room data ports, some refrigerators, cable TV. Pool. Hot tub. Business services, free parking. Some pets allowed. | 203 S. Glenstone St., 65802 | 417/866–1963 or 800/528–1234 | www.bestwestern.com | 81 rooms, 12 suites | $65, $85–$105 suites | AE, D, DC, MC, V.

Clarion. A full-service hotel in the center of Springfield's entertainment and shopping district. Restaurant, bar, room service. In-room data ports, some refrigerators, cable TV. Pool. Business services, airport shuttle, free parking. Some pets allowed (fee). | 3333 S. Glenstone St., 65804 | 417/883–6550 | fax 417/887–1823 | 195 rooms | $70–$90 | AE, D, DC, MC, V.

GuestHouse Suites. This all-suites hotel on a quiet street within walking distance of local restaurants and shops is 2 mi from Southwest Missouri State University and 10 mi from Wilson's Creek National Battlefield. Picnic area, complimentary Continental breakfast. Kitchenettes, cable TV. Pool. Hot tub. Laundry facilities. Business services, free parking. Some pets allowed (fee). | 1550 E. Raynell Pl, 65804 | 417/883–7300 | fax 417/520–7900 | www.guesthouse3.com | 80 suites | $89 | AE, D, DC, MC, V.

Holiday Inn University Plaza and Convention Center. This downtown hotel has over 21,000 ft of meeting space in addition to its guest rooms. Restaurant, bar (with entertainment), room service. In-room data ports, some refrigerators, cable TV. 2 pools. Barbershop, beauty salon, hot tub. 2 tennis courts. Gym. Laundry facilities. Business services, airport shuttle. Some pets allowed. | 333 John Q. Hammons Pkwy., 65806 | 417/864–7333 or 800/465–4329 | fax 417/831–5893 | www.basshotels.com/holiday-inn | 271 rooms, 33 suites | $89–$99, $129–$143 suites | AE, D, DC, MC, V.

Ramada Inn. This chain hotel is on a commercial strip 5 mi from downtown. Restaurant, bar (with entertainment), complimentary breakfast. Some in-room data ports, some refrigerators, cable TV. Pool. Business services, airport shuttle. Pets allowed. | 2820 N. Glenstone St., 65803 | 417/869–3900 or 800/707–0326 | fax 417/865–5378 | www.ramada.com | 130 rooms | $75 | AE, D, DC, MC, V.

Sheraton Hawthorne Park. This chain hotel is on a commercial street near the Bass Pro Shop. Restaurant, bar. In-room data ports, cable TV. Indoor-outdoor pool. Hot tub, sauna. Laundry facilities. Business services, airport shuttle. Some pets allowed (fee). | 2431 N. Glenstone St., 65803 | 417/831–3131 or 800/325–3535 | fax 417/831–9786 | www.sheraton.com | 203 rooms | $104 | AE, D, DC, MC, V.

SULLIVAN

Budget Lodging. At the junction of I–44 and Route 47, 15 minutes from Meramec or Onondaga State Park and 20 minutes from Six Flags, this hotel aims to make you feel at home with lace curtains and flowers in the windows. Complimentary Continental breakfast. Cable TV. Pool. Laundry facilities. Business services. Pets allowed (fee). | 866 S. Outer Rd., St. Clair, 63077 | 636/629–1000 or 800/958–4354 | fax 636/629–1000 | www.stclairmo.com/budgetlodging | 68 rooms, 2 suites | $79, $129–$179 suites | AE, D, DC, MC, V.

Family Motor Inn. This four-building complex is 2 mi from downtown. Some kitchenettes, cable TV. Pool. Hot tub. Laundry facilities. Business services. Pets allowed (fee). | 209 N. Service Rd. | 573/468–4119 | fax 573/468–3891 | 63 rooms | $55 | AE, D, DC, MC, V.

VAN BUREN

Hawthorne Motel. This 1959 stucco motel, decorated in a country motif, is right in the center of downtown Van Buren. Cable TV. Pool. Pets allowed. | 1029 Business Hwy. 60, 63965 | 573/323–4274 | 26 rooms | $38–$58 | MC, V.

Smalley's Motel. Basic, comfortable rooms are available at this one-story motel in downtown Van Buren. Also, two- to six-hour tube floats on the Current River can be arranged. Cable TV. Pool. Picnic tables. Pets allowed. | 702 Main St., 63965 | 573/323–4263 or 800/727–4263 | dsmalley@semo.net | 18 rooms | $36 | AE, D, MC, V.

WAYNESVILLE

Best Western Montis Inn. This chain hotel is on a commercial strip 8 mi from downtown Waynesville. Complimentary Continental breakfast. Some kitchenettes, some microwaves, some refrigerators, cable TV. Pool. Laundry facilities. Business services. Some pets allowed. | 14086 Hwy. Z, St. Roberts, 65584 | 573/336–4299 or 800/528–1234 or 800/528–1234 | fax 573/336–2872 | www.bestwestern.com | 45 rooms | $55–$60 | AE, D, DC, MC, V.

Ramada Inn. This chain hotel is 2 mi from Waynesville's downtown just off I–44 at exit 161. Restaurant, bar. In-room data ports, some in-room hot tubs, cable TV. 2 pools. Beauty salon, hot tub. Gym. Video games. Business services. Pets allowed. | I–44, Exit 161 | 573/336–3121 or 800/272–6232 | fax 573/336–4752 | www.ramada.com | 82 rooms | $65–$105 | AE, D, DC, MC, V.

WENTZVILLE

Holiday Inn. This hotel is just off I–70 at exit 212 in an area of office buildings. Restaurant, bar. In-room data ports, room service, cable TV. Pool. Business services. Some pets allowed. | 900 Corporate Pkwy. | 636/327–7001 or 800/465–4329 | fax 636/327–7019 | www.basshotels.com/holiday-inn | 138 rooms | $80–$109 | AE, D, DC, MC, V.

WEST PLAINS

Ramada Inn. You can walk to Mark Twain National Forest from this hotel which is 1 mi outside town. Restaurant, bar, room service, cable TV. Pool. Laundry facilities. Business services. Pets allowed (fee). | 1301 Preacher Row | 417/256–8191 or 800/272–6232 | fax 417/256–8069 | www.ramada.com | 81 rooms | $57 | AE, D, DC, MC, V.

Montana

ANACONDA

Lodge at Skyhaven. Close to wilderness trails and fishing spots, this is a great base from which to venture afield. The rooms have views of the valley and mountains. No-smoking rooms. Cable TV. Pets allowed. | 1711 Rte. 48, next to airport | 406/563–8342 or 800/563–8089 | fax 406/563–3317 | www.skyhavenlodge.com | 10 rooms | $45 | AE, D, DC, MC, V.

BAKER

Roy's Motel. Clean rooms and information about local sights are offered at this affordable motel, which also has an RV campground. Hot tub. RV camping. Pets allowed. | 327 W. Montana Ave. | 406/778–3321 or 800/552–3321 | fax 406/778–2180 | 22 rooms | $40 | MC, V.

Sagebrush Inn. This attractive spot offers nicely decorated modern rooms and an older extension with lower prices. Pets allowed. | 518 W. Montana Ave. | 406/778–3341 or 800/638–3708 | fax 406/778–2753 | 40 rooms | $40–$50 | MC, V.

BIG SKY

Best Western–Buck's T-4 Lodge. Spacious rooms and a quiet mountain setting set this chain apart. Outdoor hot tubs add a touch of luxury. Restaurant, bar, complimentary Continental breakfast. No air-conditioning. Cable TV, some in-room VCRs. Laundry facilities. Business services. Pets allowed. | U.S. 191 | 406/995–4111 or 800/822–4484 | fax 406/995–2191 | www.buckst4.com | 75 rooms | $79–$154, $174–$214 suites | AE, D, DC, MC, V | Closed mid-Apr.–mid-May.

Comfort Inn at Big Sky. A Western-style hotel only 30 yards from the Gallatin River and 9 mi from Lone Peak. You can take the ski shuttle in winter. The indoor 90-foot waterslide is very popular year-round. All public areas are non-smoking; smoking rooms are available. Cable TV. Pool. Hot tub. Laundry services. Business services. Pets allowed in some rooms. | 47214 Gallatin Rd., Bigfork | 406–995–4552 | fax 406–995–2277 | 62 rooms, 1 with kitchen | $49–$129 | V, MC, AE, D.

BIG TIMBER

Super 8. Spacious rooms and convenience to the interstate make this a good place to stop if you're passing through. Complimentary Continental breakfast. Cable TV. Laundry facilities. Pets allowed (fee). | I–90 Exit 367 (Rte. 10) | 406/932–8888 | fax 406/932–4103 | 39 rooms | $58–$81 | AE, D, DC, MC, V.

BIGFORK

O'Duach'ain Country Inn. In a quiet logdepole-pine forest near Flathead Lake and the Swan River, this lovely property has two log buildings. Rooms and common spaces are furnished with Old West antiques and Navajo rug wall hangings. Complimentary breakfast. No air-conditioning, no room phones, no TV in rooms, TV in common area, in-room VCRs available. Hot tub. Some pets allowed. No smoking. | 675 Ferndale Dr. | 406/837–6851, 800/837–7460 for reservations | fax 406/837–0778 | knollmc@aol.com | 5 rooms, 1 guest house | $89–$129 | AE, D, MC, V.

Timbers. The rooms are contemporary and comfortable in this year-round establishment that's within walking distance of the village. Complimentary Continental breakfast. Cable TV. Pool. Hot tub, sauna. Laundry facilities. Pets allowed (fee). | 8540 Rte. 35 | 406/837–6200 or 800/821–4546 | fax 406/837–6203 | www.montanaweb.com/timbers | 40 rooms | $68 | AE, D, MC, V.

BILLINGS

Best Western. A round-the-clock restaurant next door and proximity to I–90 make this a good stop for last-minute or late arrivals. Complimentary Continental breakfast. Cable TV. Indoor pool. Hot tub, sauna. Laundry facilities. Business services. Some pets allowed. | 5610 S. Frontage Rd. | 406/248–9800 or 800/528–1234 | fax 406/248–2500 | www.bestwestern.com | 80 rooms, 12 suites | $72–$87 | AE, D, DC, MC, V.

Best Western Ponderosa Inn. You'll find comfortable modern rooms at this hotel in downtown Billings. All rooms are done in pastels, and the courtyard is pleasant. Restaurant, bar. Cable TV. Pool. Sauna. Exercise equipment. Laundry facilities. Business services. Airport shuttle. Some pets allowed. | 2511 First Ave. N | 406/259–5511 or 800/628–9081 | fax 406/245–8004 | www.bestwestern.com | 130 rooms | $70–$78 | AE, D, DC, MC, V.

Billings Inn. Located in the downtown medical corridor, this inn has basic, comfortable rooms. Complimentary Continental breakfast. Some refrigerators, some microwaves. Cable TV. Laundry facilities. Airport shuttle. Some pets allowed (fee). | 880 N. 29th St. | 406/252–6800 or 800/231–7782 | fax 406/252–6800 | tbi@wtp.net | 60 rooms | $53, $59 suites | AE, D, DC, MC, V.

Comfort Inn. The rooms are modern and modest and equipped for the handicapped. Complimentary Continental breakfast. Some refrigerators. Cable TV. Indoor pool. Hot tub. Business services. Some pets allowed. | 2030 Overland Ave. | 406/652–5200 or 800/221–2222 | www.comfortinn.com | 60 rooms | $59–$90, $69 suites | AE, D, DC, MC, V.

Days Inn. The rooms have been refurbished, and some have spas. If you need a different kind of scenery, you're only 2½ mi from Montana's largest shopping center. Complimentary Continental breakfast. Cable TV. Hot tub. Laundry facilities. Some pets allowed. | 843 Parkway La. | 406/252–4007 or 800/329–7466 | fax 406/896–1147 | www.daysinn.com | 63 rooms | $60, $130 suites | AE, D, DC, MC, V.

Hilltop Inn. The Western look prevails in the lobby and halls, and the rooms are modest, modern, and comfortable. Complimentary Continental breakfast. Some refrigerators, some microwaves. Cable TV. Laundry facilities. Pets allowed. | 1116 N. 28th St. | 406/245–5000 or 800/878–9282 | fax 406/245–7851 | hilltop@wtp.net | 45 rooms | $53, $69 suites | AE, D, DC, MC, V.

Quality Inn Homestead. A delightful outdoor sundeck and indoor swim center are the lures here. The rooms are contemporary in design and average in size. Restaurant, complimentary breakfast. Some refrigerators. Cable TV. Indoor pool. Hot tub, sauna. Laundry facilities. Airport shuttle. Pets allowed (fee). | 2036 Overland Ave. | 406/652–1320 or 800/228–5151 | fax 406/652–1320 | www.qualityinn.com | 119 rooms | $75–$79, $85 suites | AE, D, DC, MC, V.

Radisson Northern. The downtown location makes it easy for you to walk to shops, theaters, museums, and restaurants. The rooms are traditionally American in design and have recently been remodeled. Restaurant, bar. Some refrigerators. Cable TV. Exercise equipment. Business services. Airport shuttle. Some pets allowed. | 19 N 28th St. | 406/245–5121 or 800/333–3333 | fax 406/259–9862 | www.radisson.com | 160 rooms | $79–$99, $119 suites | AE, D, DC, MC, V.

Ramada Limited. The fireplace in the lobby gives a touch of Western charm. Contemporary design best describes the rooms, and two-room Jacuzzi suites are also available. Complimentary Continental breakfast. Cable TV. Pool. Exercise equipment. Playground. Business services. Some pets allowed. | 1345 Mullowney La. | 406/252–2584 or 800/272–6232 | fax 406/252–2584 | www.ramada.com | 116 rooms | $50–$69, $150 suites | AE, D, DC, MC, V.

Sheraton. This high-rise encloses a pleasant and large central courtyard. The downtown location is convenient, and the contemporary rooms are spacious. Restaurant, bar. Some refrigerators. Cable TV. Indoor pool. Hot tub. Exercise equipment. Video games. Business services. Airport shuttle. Some pets allowed. | 27 N. 27th St. | 406/252–7400 or 800/588–7666 | fax 406/252–2401 | www.sheraton.com/billings | 282 rooms | $99–$105, $145 suites | AE, D, DC, MC, V.

Super 8 Lodge. The rooms are standard and comfortable and rates are reasonable. Cable TV. Pets allowed (fee). | 5400 Southgate Dr. | 406/248–8842 or 800/800–8000 | fax 406/248–8842 | 115 rooms | $67–$75 | AE, D, DC, MC, V.

BOZEMAN

Bozeman's Days Inn and Conference Center. The contemporary rooms have been refurbished, and all have in-room data ports, especially convenient if you're attending a convention. The Gallatin Valley setting offers good views of surrounding mountains and forest. Complimentary Continental breakfast. Cable TV. Hot tub, sauna. Business services. Pets allowed (fee). | 1321 N. 7th Ave. | 406/587–5251 or 800/987–3297 | fax 406/587–5351 | 80 rooms | $88–$99 | AE, D, DC, MC, V.

Holiday Inn. Bozeman's largest full-service hotel has quiet, spacious, comfortable rooms. Restaurant, bar, picnic area, room service. Some refrigerators. Cable TV. Indoor pool. Hot tub. Exercise equipment. Laundry facilities. Business services. Airport shuttle. Pets allowed. | 5 Baxter La. | 406/587–4561 or 800/366–5101 | fax 406/587–4413 | www.bznholinn.com/ | 178 rooms | $99, $129–$149 suites | AE, D, DC, MC, V.

Holiday Inn Express. You get beautiful mountain views and standard contemporary rooms here. Skiing is close by, and you can relax in the cozy lobby after a day on the slopes. In-room data ports. Cable TV. Hot tub. Pets allowed. No smoking. | 6261 Jackrabbit La. | 406/388–0800 or 800/542–6791 | fax 406/388–0804 | www.holiday-inn.com | 67 rooms | $72–$82 | AE, D, DC, MC, V.

Ramada Limited. A 40-ft water slide and great views of the mountains are the lures at this chain establishment. The reasonably priced suites make it a good choice for families. Complimentary Continental breakfast. Cable TV. Indoor pool. Hot tub. Pets allowed. | 2020 Wheat Dr. | 406/585–2626 | fax 406/585–2727 | 50 rooms, shower only | $84, $99 suites | AE, D, DC, MC, V.

Royal 7 Budget Inn. Small and homey, this inn has Western furnishings and several fireplaces. The staff is friendly, and you can walk to downtown and the university. Picnic area, complimentary Continental breakfast. Cable TV. Hot tub. Playground. Business services. Pets allowed. | 310 N. 7th Ave. | 406/587–3103 or 800/587–3103 | www.avicom.net/royal7 | 47 rooms | $51, $69 suites | AE, D, DC, MC, V.

Sleep Inn. Five suites, good for families, augment the comfortable, standard contemporary rooms. You can ski at the Bridger Bow ski area, a 15-minute drive. Downtown Bozeman is 2 mi away. Complimentary Continental breakfast. Some refrigerators. Cable TV. Indoor pool. Hot tub, sauna. Pets allowed. | 817 Wheat Dr. | 406/585–7888 or 800/377–8240 | fax 406/585–8842 | www.sleepinn.com/hotel/MT410 | 56 rooms, shower only | $79–$99 | AE, D, DC, MC, V.

Western Heritage. Five blocks from downtown, this hotel has some suites with fireplaces and full kitchens as well as standard rooms. Complimentary Continental breakfast. Some in-room hot tubs. Cable TV. Steam room. Exercise equipment. Laundry facilities. Business services. Pets allowed. | 1200 E. Main St. | 406/586–8534 or 800/877–1094 | fax 406/587–8729 | www.avicom.net/westernheritage | 38 rooms | $78, $115–$125 suites | AE, D, DC, MC, V.

BUTTE

Comfort Inn. A TownHouse Inn of Montana, this place has some standard rooms equipped with the basics and some suites with microwaves, refrigerators, and hot tubs. Some rooms have in-room data ports. Complimentary Continental breakfast. Cable TV. Hot tubs. Exercise equipment. Laundry facilities. Business services. Airport shuttle. Pets allowed (fee). | 2777 Harrison Ave. | 406/494–8850 or 800/442–4667 | fax 406/494–2801 | 150 rooms | $80–$122 | AE, D, DC, MC, V.

Ramada Inn Copper King Park Hotel. You'll find lots of amenities here at the foot of the Rockies, as well as mountain views. Each room has a coffeemaker, direct-dial phone, data port, voice mail, an in-room safe, and heat and air conditioning controls. Restaurant, bar, room service. Cable TV. Indoor pool. Indoor tennis. Exercise equipment. Laundry facilities. Business services. Airport shuttle. Pets allowed. | 4655 Harrison Ave. S | 406/494–6666 or 800/332–8600 | fax 406/494–3274 | www.ramadainncopperking.com | 150 rooms. | $89–$94, $175 suites | AE, D, DC, MC, V.

War Bonnet Inn. This is a good place if you're here in the dead of winter—they have plug-in automobile block heaters. A newer facility, it also offers convention services. Room service. Cable TV. Indoor pool. Hot tub, sauna. Exercise equipment. Convention center. Airport shuttle. Pets allowed. | 2100 Cornell Ave. | 406/494–7800 or 800/443–1806 | fax 406/494–2875 | www.wbibutte.com | 131 rooms | $69, $99–$125 suites | AE, MC, V.

CHINOOK

Chinook Motor Inn. This two-story motel is on U.S. 2, the road to Glacier, a good place to stop if you want to take in some local history on your way to the park. Restaurant, bar. Cable TV. Pets allowed. | 100 Indiana Ave. | 406/357–2248 or 800/603–2864 | fax 406/357–2261 | www.chinookmotorinn.com | 38 rooms | $50–$60 | AE, D, MC, V.

CHOTEAU

Big Sky Motel. Small, cozy rooms and attentive management distinguish this clean downtown motel. Microwaves. Cable TV. Pets allowed (fee). | 209 S. Main Ave. | 406/466–5318 | fax 406/466–5866 | 13 rooms | $44–$55 | AE, D, MC, V.

COOKE CITY

High Country. In the Beartooth Mountains. Motel and cabins, some with kitchens and fireplaces. No air-conditioning, some kitchenettes, some refrigerators. Pets allowed. | U.S. 212 59020 | 406/838–2272 | 15 rooms, 4 kitchenettes | $47–$49, $67 kitchen suites | AE, D, DC, MC, V.

Soda Butte Lodge. Rooms of varying sizes, a sunken lobby with large fireplace, and spectacular views. Restaurant, bar. Cable TV. Pool. Hot tub. Pets allowed. | 209 U.S. 212 |

406/838–2251 or 800/527–6462 | fax 406/838–2253 | 32 rooms | $65–$70, $100 suites | AE, D, MC, V.

DEER LODGE

Super 8. A convenient downtown location is the draw at this basic modern motel. Cable TV. Pets allowed. | 1150 N. Main St. | 406/846–2370 | fax 406/846–2373 | 54 rooms | $64–$70, $80 suites | AE, D, DC, MC, V.

DILLON

Best Western Paradise Inn. The rooms are average in size, the furnishings are contemporary, the view is extraordinary. The reasonably priced suites are good for families. Restaurant, bar. Cable TV. Pool. Hot tub. Business services. Pets allowed. | 650 N. Montana St. | 406/683–4214 | fax 406/683–4216 | 65 rooms | $50–$54, $73–$83 suites | AE, D, DC, MC, V.

EAST GLACIER AREA

Bison Creek Ranch. The seven rustic cabins here are very close to Glacier National Park and have fantastic views of the mountains. Restaurant, complimentary Continental breakfast. No air-conditioning. Hiking. Pets allowed. | U.S. 2 | 406/226–4482 or 888/226–4482 | 7 rooms | $40–$60 | Closed Oct.–June | D, MC, V.

St. Mary Lodge and Resort. Choice is the lure here, with accommodations that range from lodge rooms to cabins to six new luxury cabins with park views. All lodge rooms have pine furniture and some have air-conditioning units (the only ones in Glacier). The two-bedroom cabins have kitchens and fireplaces. Restaurant, bar. Some air-conditioning. Laundry facilities. Pets allowed (fee). No smoking. | U.S. 89, St. Mary | 406/732–4431 or 208/726–6279; 800/368–3689 for reservations | fax 406/732–9265 | www.glcpark.com | 80 rooms, 62 with shower only | $75–$285 | Closed Oct.–Apr | AE, D, MC, V.

GARDINER

Absaroka. The spacious grounds of this lodging are directly on the Yellowstone River, and the large rooms have excellent river views. You can walk to shops and restaurants, as well as to fishing spots. Some kitchenettes. Cable TV. Pets allowed (fee). | U.S. 89 | 406/848–7414 or 800/755–7414 | fax 406/848–7560 | www.yellowstonemotel.com | 41 rooms | $90–$100 | AE, D, DC, MC, V.

Super 8. Some family rooms have kitchens at this hotel at the north entrance to Yellowstone and across from the river. Complimentary Continental breakfast. Cable TV. Indoor pool. Some pets allowed (fee). | U.S. 89 | 406/848–7401 or 800/800–8000 | fax 406/848–9410 | super8.com | 66 rooms | $89, $165 suites | AE, D, DC, MC, V.

GREAT FALLS

Comfort Inn. Across from the Holiday Village Mall, this three-story motel is convenient to shopping and restaurants. Complimentary Continental breakfast. Cable TV. Indoor pool. Hot tub. Business services. Pets allowed (fee). | 1120 Ninth St. S | 406/454–2727 or 800/228–5150 | www.comfortinn.com | 64 rooms | $64–$80, $90 suites | AE, D, DC, MC, V.

Holiday Inn. A seven-story atrium and indoor recreation facilities combine with contemporary furnishings to make this a good, standard hotel, which also has convention facilities. Restaurant, bar. Cable TV. Indoor pool. Hot tub, sauna. Business services. Airport shuttle. Some pets allowed. | 400 10th Ave. S | 406/727–7200 or 800/257–1998 | www.holiday-inn.com | 169 rooms | $71–$74, $100–$165 suites | AE, D, DC, MC, V.

HARDIN

Super 8. The museums are close to this modest, contemporary motel, and Little Bighorn Battlefield is about 13 mi away. Complimentary Continental breakfast. Cable TV. Laundry facilities. Pets allowed. | 201 14th St. W | 406/665–1700 or 800/800–8000 | fax 406/665–2746 | www.super8.com | 53 rooms | $52–$65 | AE, D, DC, MC, V.

HAVRE

Best Western Great Northern Inn. Spacious and close to restaurants, this inn has contemporary furnishings. Restaurant, bar, complimentary Continental breakfast. In-room data ports. Cable TV. Indoor pool. Laundry facilities. Airport shuttle. Some pets allowed. | 1345 1st St. | 406/265–4200 or 888/530–4100 | 65 rooms | $69–$79 | AE, D, DC, MC, V.

El Toro Inn. The Spanish design reflects the inn's name. Rooms come in various sizes, but all are spacious. The Amtrak Station is two blocks away. Complimentary Continental breakfast. Cable TV. Some pets allowed. | 521 1st St. | 406/265–5414 or 800/422–5414 | 41 rooms | $45–$49 | MC, V.

Townhouse Inn. Some rooms have Jacuzzis and some have been remodeled. You can also ask for a poolside room or one with a balcony. All are contemporary and comfortable and within walking distance of restaurants. Cable TV. Indoor pool. Hot tub. Gym. Laundry facilities. Airport shuttle. Some pets allowed. | 629 W. 1st St. | 406/265–6711 or 800/442–4667 | fax 406/265–6213 | www.townpump.com | 104 rooms | $84–$86 | AE, D, DC, MC, V.

HELENA

Barrister. Original antiques furnish the rooms of this Victorian-style house that has a large common area. Carved staircases, stained-glass windows, and five fireplaces add elegance. The wraparound porch is a nice place to sit and admire the garden. Complimentary evening wine and cheese. Complimentary breakfast. No room phones. Cable TV. Business services. Airport shuttle. Pets allowed. No smoking. | 416 N. Ewing St. | 406/443–7330 or 800/823–1148 | fax 406/442–7964 | 5 rooms | $90 | AE, MC, V.

Best Western Cavanaughs Colonial Hotel. Helena's largest hotel is a brick building with a Colonial theme. The rooms are spacious and modern, and there's a 15,000-square-ft meeting space. Restaurant, bar, room service. Some in-room hot tubs. Cable TV. 2 pools (1 indoor). Barber shop, beauty salon. Laundry facilities. Business services. Airport shuttle. Pets allowed. | 2301 Colonial Dr. | 406/443–2100 or 800/422–1002 | fax 406/442–0301 | www.bestwestern.com | 149 rooms | $89–$99 | AE, D, DC, MC, V.

Helena's Country Inn & Suites. Within walking distance of the Mall, State Capitol, and the Montana Historical Society Museum. Some of the comfortable rooms have fireplaces. The rates are extremely reasonable. Restaurant, bar, complimentary Continental breakfast. Cable TV. Indoor pool. Hot tub, sauna. Business services. Airport shuttle. Pets allowed. | 2101 11th Ave. | 406/443–2300 or 800/541–2743 in Montana | fax 406/442–7057 | 72 rooms | $49, $60–$70 suites | AE, D, DC, MC, V.

Holiday Inn Express. The reliably comfortable contemporary rooms are spacious and have in-room data ports for business travelers. Complimentary Continental breakfast. Some refrigerators. Cable TV. Exercise equipment. Business services. Some pets allowed. No smoking. | 701 Washington St. | 406/449–4000 or 800/465–4329 | fax 406/449–4522 | 75 rooms | $75 | AE, D, DC, MC, V.

Park Plaza. You can look out the window and see the gulch where the miners discovered gold. The renovated hotel is within walking distance from downtown, and the rooms are modern and of average size. Restaurant, bar. Cable TV. Business services, convention center. Airport shuttle. Pets allowed. | 22 N. Last Chance Gulch | 406/443–2200 or 800/332–2290 in Montana | fax 406/442–4030 | 71 rooms | $79–$89 | AE, D, DC, MC, V.

Shilo Inn. A newly remodeled chain lodging with contemporary design and furnishings. Complimentary Continental breakfast. Refrigerators. Cable TV, in-room VCRs (movies). Indoor pool. Hot tub. Sauna, steam room. Laundry facilities. Airport shuttle. Pets allowed. | 2020 Prospect Ave., (U.S. 12) | 406/442–0320 or 800/222–2244 | fax 406/449–4426 | www.shiloinns.com | 47 rooms, 3 kitchenettes | $89 | AE, D, DC, MC, V.

Super 8. Convenience is the selling point at this motel that is close to the Capitol, downtown, and the airport. Complimentary Continental breakfast. Cable TV. Pets allowed. | 2200 11th Ave. | 406/443–2450 or 800/800–8000 | fax 406/443–2450 | 102 rooms | $54–$66 | AE, D, DC, MC, V.

KALISPELL

Best Western Outlaw Inn. Close to Glacier National Park and Flathead Lake, this newer hotel is near eight golf courses. The furnishings are contemporary, and there's a large landscaped area around the motel. You can also raft, bicycle, and fish. Restaurant, bar, room service. Cable TV. 2 indoor pools. Barber shop, beauty salon, 4 hot tubs. Tennis. Exercise equipment, racquetball. Playground, laundry facilities. Business services. Pets allowed (fee). | 1701 U.S. 93 S | 406/755–6100 or 800/325–4000 | fax 406/756–8994 | www.cavanaughs.com | 220 rooms | $125 | AE, D, DC, MC, V.

Blue and White Motel. Basic and comfortable, the rooms here have modern furnishings. The Flathead Valley is the lure. Restaurant, bar, complimentary Continental breakfast. No-smoking rooms. Cable TV. Pool. Hot tub. Some pets allowed. | 640 E Idaho St. | 406/755–4311 or 800/382–3577 | fax 406/755–4330 | www.blu-white.com | 107 rooms | $52–$54 | MC, V.

Cavanaugh's at Kalispell Center. Attached to a downtown mall, this large, modern hotel has a strong Western style throughout. The location is convenient. Restaurant, bar, room service. Cable TV. Indoor pool. Barber shop, beauty salon, hot tubs. Exercise equipment. Business services. Some pets allowed. | 20 N. Main St. | 406/752–6660 or 800/325–4000 | fax 406/751–5051 | www.cavanaughs.com | 132 rooms, 14 suites | $135, $171–$205 suites | AE, D, DC, MC, V.

Hampton Inn. In-room hot tubs set this inn apart. The rooms have contemporary furnishings. Complimentary Continental breakfast. Cable TV, in-room VCRs. Indoor pool. Hot tub. Exercise equipment. Laundry facilities. Airport shuttle. Business services. Pets allowed. | 1140 U.S. 2 W | 406/755–7900 or 800/426–7866 | fax 406/755–5056 | www.hamptoninn.com | 120 rooms | $108 | AE, D, DC, MC, V.

Kalispell Grand. History is visible in the furnishings of this downtown hotel. The lobby ceiling is pressed tin and the staircase is golden oak. The walls are rich cherry-wood. Victorian in style, the rooms are spacious and comfortable. Restaurant, bar. Cable TV. Exercise equipment. Business services. Some pets allowed. | 100 Main St. | 406/755–8100 or 800/858–7422 | fax 406/752–8012 | www.kalispellgrand.com | 40 rooms, 38 with shower only | $75–$84, $115 suites | AE, D, DC, MC, V.

LEWISTOWN

Yogo Inn of Lewistown. The name comes from the yogo sapphires found nearby. This is where you pick up the Charlie Russell "Chew-Choo" dinner train. You can also take Western buggy rides, tours of historical ghost towns. Rooms are contemporary and comfortable, nothing fancy. Restaurant, bar. No-smoking rooms. Indoor-outdoor pool. Hot tub. Pets allowed. | 211 E Main St. | 406/538–8721 or 800/860–9646 | fax 406/538–8696 | www.yogo@lew.net | 122 rooms | $69–$79 | AE, D, MC, V.

LIBBY

Caboose Motel. Within walking distance of a shopping mall and a mile from the Amtrak Station, this motel has modest, modern furnishings and a very friendly staff. Complimentary Continental breakfast. No-smoking rooms. Pets allowed. | 714 W. 9th St. | 406/293–6201 or 800/627–0206 | fax 406/293–3621 | 28 rooms | $40–$60 | AE, MC, V.

Super 8. A good home base if you're going to explore the nearby Kootenai National Forest and within walking distance of the Kootenai River, this motel has standard-size rooms and contemporary furnishings. No-smoking rooms. Pool. Pets allowed. | 448 U.S. 2 W | 406/293-2771 or 800/800-8000 | fax 406/293-9871 | 42 rooms | $62-$74 | AE, D, MC, V.

LIVINGSTON

Chico Hot Springs. Two open-air hot-spring mineral pools are a welcome find if you've been hiking all day. The accommodations range from lodge rooms to cabins, and the hotel is set on 150 acres 30 mi from Yellowstone, in the foothills of the Absaroka Beartooth Mountains. Bar, dining room, picnic area. No air-conditioning, some refrigerators, some room phones. Pool. Massage. Exercise equipment, hiking. Bicycles. Fishing. Business services. Pets allowed (fee). | Old Chico Rd., Pray | 406/333-4933 or 800/468-9232 | fax 406/333-4694 | www.chicohotsprings.com | 49 lodge rooms, 29 motel units, 16 cottages | $45-$85, $189 cottages | AE, D, MC, V.

Paradise Inn. An indoor pool and some suites make this good for families. The rooms are contemporary in style and average in size. Restaurant, bar. Cable TV. Indoor pool. Hot tub. Pets allowed. | Rogers La. | 406/222-6320 or 800/437-6291 | fax 406/222-2481 | 43 rooms | $89, $125 suites | AE, MC, V.

MALTA

Great Northern Hotel. The downtown location makes for views of small-town street life. The comfortable rooms have modern furnishings, and you can eat at the steak house. Restaurant. Cable TV. Convention center. Pets allowed. | 2 1st Ave. E | 406/654-2100 or 888/234-0935 | fax 406/654-2622 | 29 rooms | $46 | AE, D, DC, MC, V.

MILES CITY

Best Western War Bonnet Inn. Many amenities are included at this standard contemporary chain accommodation with reasonable rates. Complimentary Continental breakfast. No-smoking rooms. Cable TV. Indoor pool. Hot tub, sauna. Pets allowed. | 1015 S. Haynes St. | 406/232-4560 or 800/528-1234 | fax 406/232-0363 | www.bestwestern.com | 54 rooms | $75-$99 | AE, D, DC, MC, V.

Rodeway Inn and Historic Olive Hotel. Built in 1899, the Olive Hotel is on the National Register of Historic Places. The style is traditional Old World, with original oak woodwork, stained-glass windows, and leaded-glass doors. You can walk to museums and the art center. Restaurant, bar. Cable TV. Pets allowed. | 501 Main St. | 406/232-2450 | fax 406/232-5866 | 59 rooms | $39-$50 | MC, V.

MISSOULA

4 B's Inn—North. Five miles from skiing and conveniently situated downtown, this inn has comfortable rooms and home-style dining. There are some suites that are ideal if you're traveling with a larger group. Refrigerators in suites. Cable TV. Hot tub. Laundry facilities. Pets allowed. | 4953 N. Reserve St. | 406/542-7550 or 800/272-9500 outside Montana | fax 406/721-5931 | www.bestinn.com | 67 rooms | $60 | AE, D, DC, MC, V.

4 B's Inn—South. This large convention facility has a convenient location and rooms with contemporary furnishings. Cable TV. Hot tub. Laundry facilities. Business services. Pets allowed. | 3803 Brooks St. | 406/251-2665 or 800/272-9500 | fax 406/251-5733 | www.bestinn.com | 91 rooms | $60-$63 | AE, D, DC, MC, V.

Doubletree Edgewater. Wood carvings and murals decorate the lobby, and the furnishings have a hint of Western style. On the Clark Fork River across from the university, this hotel also has most amenities you can think of and a good beef and seafood restaurant. Restaurant, bar, room service. In-room data ports, some refrigerators. Cable TV. Pool. Beauty salon, hot tub. Exercise equipment. Business services. Airport shuttle. Pets allowed. | 100 Madison St. | 406/728-3100 or 800/222-8733 | fax 406/728-2530 | 171 rooms | $99-$105, $120-$185 suites | AE, D, DC, MC, V.

Hampton Inn. Beautiful views of Lolo Peak and Snowbowl distinguish this newish hotel. The rooms are modern and comfortable. Complimentary Continental breakfast. Cable TV. Indoor pool. Hot tub. Exercise equipment. Business services. Airport shuttle. Pets allowed. | 4805 N. Reserve St. | 406/549–1800 or 800/426–7866 | fax 406/549–1737 | 60 rooms | $85–$89 | AE, D, DC, MC, V.

Holiday Inn—Parkside. You get panoramic mountain views from the atrium balconies and rooms. The patios have shaded tables. With in-room data ports, this is a good choice for business travelers. Restaurant, bar, room service. Cable TV. Indoor pool. Hot tub. Exercise equipment. Business services. Airport shuttle. Pets allowed. | 200 S. Pattee St. | 406/721–8550 or 800/399–0408 | fax 406/721–7427 | www.montana.com/parkside | 200 rooms | $99–$109, $129 suites | AE, D, DC, MC, V.

Orange Street Budget Motor Inn. The staff is pleasant, the rooms modest, and the location near downtown and restaurants. Complimentary Continental breakfast. Cable TV. Exercise equipment. Business services. Airport shuttle. Pets allowed. | 801 N. Orange St. | 406/721–3610 or 800/328–0801 | fax 406/721–8875 | 81 rooms | $53–$58 | AE, D, DC, MC, V.

Red Lion. The oversize rooms are useful if you're here for business. The design and furnishings are modern. Complimentary Continental breakfast. In-room data ports. Cable TV, in-room VCRs. Pool. Hot tub. Business services. Airport shuttle. Pets allowed. | 700 W. Broadway | 406/728–3300 or 800/547–8010 | fax 406/728–4441 | www.redlion.com | 76 rooms | $80–$84 | AE, D, DC, MC, V.

Super 8. At the south edge of town, this motel has standard and economical accommodations. Complimentary Continental breakfast. Cable TV. Pets allowed. | 3901 S. Brooks St. | 406/251–2255 or 800/800–8000 | fax 406/251–2989 | www.super8.com/ | 104 rooms | $52 | AE, D, DC, MC, V.

RED LODGE

Best Western Lupine Inn. Six blocks from downtown, this convenient hotel has standard contemporary rooms and some in-room hot tubs. Complimentary Continental breakfast. Some in-room hot tubs. Cable TV. Indoor pool. Hot tub. Exercise equipment. Video games. Playground. Laundry facilities. Business services. Some pets allowed. | 702 S. Hauser St. | 406/446–1321 or 888/567–1321 | fax 406/446–1465 | www.bestwestern.com | 46 rooms | $79, $85 suites | AE, D, DC, MC, V.

Chateau Rouge. These deluxe condos come with one or two bedrooms, full kitchens, and some fireplaces. The common area has a huge natural stone fireplace. Cable TV, in-room VCRs. Pool. Hot tub. Pets allowed. No smoking. | 1505 S. Broadway | 406/446–1601 or 800/926–1601 | fax 406/446–1602 | www.wtp.net/chateaurouge/ | 24 1-and 2-bedroom units | $68–$85 | AE, D, MC, V.

Comfort Inn. Mountain oak furniture lends warmth to this newer facility with family suites. Complimentary Continental breakfast. Cable TV. Indoor pool. Hot tub. Business services. Pets allowed (fee). | 612 N. Broadway | 406/446–4469 or 888/733–4661 | fax 406/446–4669 | www.wtp.net/comfortinn | 55 rooms | $80, $100–$129 suites | AE, D, DC, MC, V.

Super 8. You're only 1 mi from the Red Lodge Mountain ski area at this contemporary hotel with modern furnishings. It's on the Beartooth Highway (U.S. 212). Complimentary Continental breakfast. Some refrigerators, some in-room hot tubs. Cable TV. Indoor pool. Hot tub. Video games. Laundry facilities. Some pets allowed. | 1223 S. Broadway | 406/446–2288 or 800/813–8335 | fax 406/446–3162 | 50 rooms | $70–$90 | AE, D, DC, MC, V.

SEELEY LAKE

Emily A. If you want a classic Montana B&B experience, try this massive log lodge, with only 6 rooms in an 11,000-square-ft structure. A two-story stone fireplace, luxurious furnishings, and collections of Western art and sports memorabilia create a welcoming, spacious atmosphere. You can also stay in the original homestead cabin. The lovely grounds and private lake make this a popular wedding spot. Ducks, geese and deer like it, too. The proprietors are a doctor and a dietitian, so you can count on healthful but delicious breakfasts. Full breakfast. Boating. Fishing. Hiking trails. No smoking. Pets allowed with advance notice. | 5 miles north of town on Highway 83, just past mile marker 20 | 406/677–3474 or 800/977–4639 | fax 406/377–6474 | slk3340@blackfoot.net | www.theemilya.com | 6 plus cabin | $115 | MC, V.

Wilderness Gateway Inn. This attractive, well-maintained motel lies at the south end of town and derives its name from the three nearby wilderness areas. Hot tub. Pets allowed (fee). | Highway 83, south end of town | 406/677–2095 | fax 406/677–2095 | 19 | $56–$59 | D, MC, V.

THREE FORKS

Fort Three Forks. This newer hotel has Western-style furnishings, a friendly staff, and balconies that overlook the mountains. Complimentary Continental breakfast. Cable TV. Hot tub. Laundry facilities. Business services. Pets allowed (fee). | 10776 U.S. 287 | 406/285–3233 or 800/477–5690 | fax 406/285–4362 | www.fortthreeforks.com | 24 rooms | $50–$54 | AE, D, DC, MC, V.

WEST YELLOWSTONE

Days Inn. On the very quiet edge of town, this modest but modern motel is a good choice if you want to stay a bit away from the center of action. Complimentary Continental breakfast. Some refrigerators. Cable TV. Indoor pool. Hot tub. Business services. Pets allowed. | 301 Madison Ave. | 406/646–7656 or 800/548–9551 | fax 406/646–7965 | 45 rooms | $89–$110 | AE, D, DC, MC, V.

Kelly Inn. Large rooms, a lobby fireplace, and a Western-style interior make this newer hotel a pleasant place to stay. Complimentary Continental breakfast. Some refrigerators, microwaves. Cable TV. Indoor pool. Hot tub. Laundry facilities. Business services. Pets allowed. | 104 S. Canyon St. | 406/646–4544 or 800/259–4672 (reservations) | fax 406/646–9838 | www.wyellowstone.com/kellyinn | 78 rooms | $95–$109, $149 suites | AE, D, DC, MC, V.

WHITEFISH

Quality Inn Pine Lodge. The rustic log structure has Western-style furnishings and is less than 10 mi from Big Mountain. The in-room data ports are convenient for business travelers. Complimentary Continental breakfast. Microwaves, refrigerators (suites). Cable TV. Indoor pool. Hot tub. Exercise equipment. Laundry facilities. Business services. Airport shuttle. Some pets allowed. | 920 Spokane Ave. | 406/862–7600 or 800/305–7463 | fax 406/862–7616 | www.thepinelodge.com | 76 rooms, 25 suites | $100–$180 | AE, D, DC, MC, V.

Super 8. Proximity to both the Whitefish River and downtown make this modest and modern motel convenient. Cable TV. Hot tub. Some pets allowed (fee). | 800 Spokane Ave. | 406/862–8255 or 800/800–8000 | 40 rooms | $80 | AE, D, DC, MC, V.

Nebraska

AUBURN

Auburn Inn. This remodeled two-story, red brick motel, built in the late '70s, has kitch-enettes for your snacking after a visit to Indian Cave State Park, about 10 mi away. Complimentary Continental breakfast. Microwaves, refrigerators. Cable TV. Pets allowed (fee). | 517 J St. 68305 | 402/274–3143 or 800/272–3143 | fax 402/274–4404 | 36 rooms | $30–$50 | AE, D, DC, MC, V.

BEATRICE

Beatrice Inn. This brick structure with shake-shingle roof on Highway 77 across from the airport is within 10 mi of Homestead National Monument and Rock Creek Station State Historical Park. Truck parking and cold-weather hookups are available. Restaurant, bar. Cable TV. Pool. Laundry facilities. Pets allowed. | 3500 N. 6th St. | 402/223–4074 or 800/232–8742 | fax 402/223–4074 | 65 rooms | $29–$42 | AE, D, DC, MC, V.

Holiday Villa. You can can choose from the main three-story brick building or the 25 one-story stucco cabins at this complex on the north edge of town, about 5 mi northeast of Homestead National Monument and Rock Creek Station State Historical Park. Truck parking and cold-weather hookups are available. Some kitchenettes. Cable TV. Playground. Pets allowed. | 1820 N. 6th St. | 402/223–4036 | fax 402/228–3875 | 25 rooms, 25 cabins | $29–$41 | AE, D, DC, MC, V.

Victorian Inn. Right along Route 77, the exterior of this motor inn has a faintly Victorian look, but the interiors were planned for 20th-century road-travelers. Truck parking is available. Complimentary Continental breakfast. Cable TV. Pets allowed. | 1903 N. 6th St. | 402/228–5955 | fax 402/228–2020 | 44 rooms | $35–$55 | AE, D, DC, MC, V.

BLAIR

Rath Inn. After a day at Fort Atkinson State Historical Park, 7 mi away, you can return to this inn for a relaxing evening in the deck furniture on the covered front porch. This redbrick two-story building on the southern edge of town has a gently traditional look inside, and there is parking for trucks. Complimentary Continental breakfast. Refrigerators in suites. Pool. Pets allowed (fee). | 1355 Hwy. 30S | 402/426–2340 | fax 402/426–8703 | 32 rooms | $39–$60 | AE, D, DC, MC, V.

BRIDGEPORT

Bell Motor Inn. Handily next to a gas station and convenience store, this blond brick motel on Highway 385N is about 5 mi from the Courthouse and Jail Rocks and near the Platte River. Restaurant, bar. Cable TV. Pets allowed. | Hwy. 385N | 308/262–0557 | fax 308/262–0923 | 22 rooms | $35–$44 | AE, D, MC, V.

Bridgeport Inn. This single-story, family-run motel was built in 1930, but remodeled in 1997. It has a quiet, almost rural demeanor—you'll find lawn chairs for lounging on the front lawn and recliners and rocking chairs in the lobby. In-room data ports. Cable TV. Business services. Pets allowed (fee). | 517 Main St. 69336 | 308/262–0290 | sandmaur@hamilton.net | 12 rooms | $46.50 | AE, MC, V.

BROKEN BOW

Gateway Motel. This motel in a commercial area on Route 2 on the east end of town, has simple accommodations, but it is near Sylvester's Lounge, a local hang-out for the music on weekends. Cable TV. Sauna. Pets allowed. | 628 E. South E St. 68822 | 308/872–2478 | 23 rooms | $25–$40 | AE, D, DC, MC, V.

Wagon Wheel. This modest motel on Route 2, which is E Street, has been in town since the 1940s, but all the rooms have since been remodeled, and a sauna and heated pool have been added. Truck parking and RV hookups are available. The Broken Bow Municipal Airport is 5 mi away. Cable TV. Heated pool. Sauna. hot tub. Playground. Some pets allowed. | 1545 South E St. | 308/872–2433 or 800/770–2433 | 15 rooms | $23–$37 | AE, D, DC, MC, V.

William Penn Lodge. Rooms in this traditional, white clapboard motor inn on Route 2 have refrigerators for your cold snacks, and some have microwaves, too. You are near the Sandhills here, and the parking area has spaces for trucks, with cold-weather hookups. Refrigerators, some microwaves. Cable TV. Pets allowed. | 853 E. South E St. | 308/872–2412 | fax 308/872–6376 | 28 rooms | $35–$55 | AE, D, MC, V.

BROWNVILLE

Rock Port Inn Motel. Although it sits just off I–29 across the border in Missouri, about 7 mi from Brownville, this two-story, Colonial-style building is in a quiet rural area with a large lawn and trees out back. Inside, the lobby carries out the country feeling with lots of bird feeders and flowers. Some refrigerators, some microwaves. Cable TV. Pool. Laundry facilities. Pets allowed. | 1200 Hwy. 136W, Rock Port, MO 64482 | 660/744–6282 | 36 rooms | $43–$50 | AE, D, DC, MC, V.

CHADRON

Best Western West Hills Inn. The light and airy pale brick motel sits on a hill near the scenic Pine Ridge, 3 mi from the Fur Trade Museum. The rooms, in soft beiges and browns, have hot tubs, and many include two easy-curling chairs with a reading lamp. Complimentary Continental breakfast. Some microwaves, some refrigerators. Cable TV. Indoor pool. Hot tub. Exercise equipment. Laundry facilities. Pets allowed. | 1100 W. 10th St. | 308/432–3305 | fax 308/432–5990 | 66 rooms | $55–$115 | AE, D, DC, MC, V.

Economy 9. This modest one-story brick motel is at the junction of Highway 20 and Highway 385 in the north part of town, with a hot tub for easing sore muscles after a hike along the ridge. Cable TV. Hot tub. Pets allowed. | 1201 W. Highway U.S. 20 | 308/432–3119 | fax 308/432–3119 | 21 rooms | $30–$50 | AE, D, DC, MC, V.

Olde Main Street Inn. A three-generation female operation, this B&B, two blocks north of the town's single stoplight, dates to 1890. Built like a fort, the three-story brick structure was once headquarters for General Nelson Miles, who commanded U.S. Army troops at Wounded Knee in nearby South Dakota in 1891. Now a rustic country inn of suites and minisuites, it has a real well, a running fountain, a fireplace in the dining room, and preserved remnants of the original wallpaper. Truck parking and cold-weather hookups are available. Restaurant, bar, complimentary breakfast. Some rooms with shower only. Cable TV. Pets allowed. | 115 Main St. 69337 | 308/432–3380 | www.chadron.com/oldemain | 9 rooms | $30–$72 | AE, D, MC, V.

Super 8 Motel. If you've come from the east, you may want to reset watches. At this beige-and-stucco motel ½ mi east of the junction of Highways 20 and 385, you are definitely in the Mountain Time Zone. Renovated in 1996, it has some suites with recliners and coffeemakers. Truck parking and cold-weather hookups are available. Complimentary Continental breakfast. Cable TV. Indoor pool. Hot tub. Laundry facilities. Pets allowed. | 840 U.S. 20W 69337 | 308/432–4471 | fax 308/432–3991 | Super8chadron@aol.com | 45 rooms | $44–$64 | AE, D, DC, MC, V.

COLUMBUS

Johnnie's. Within walking distance of several restaurants and stores, this white brick motor inn has one section built in the 1950s and another added in the 1960s. It is 16 mi from Columbus and one block from Highway 15, with truck parking and cold-weather hookups. Cable TV. Some pets allowed. | 222 W. 16th St., Schuyler | 402/352–5454 | 30 rooms | $37–$45 | AE, D, DC, MC, V.

COZAD

Budget Host Circle S Motel. This motel option and its outdoor pool are just a just ¼ mi from exit 222 on I-80, and you'll find three restaurants within a quarter of a mile in the surrounding commercial area. It's also ¼ mi from the Robert Henri Museum and Pony Express station. Restaurant. Cable TV. Pool. Pets allowed. | 440 S. Meridian 69130 | 308/784–2290 or 800/237–5852 | fax 308/784–3917 | 49 rooms | $34–$48 | AE, D, MC, V.

CRAWFORD

Hilltop Motel. This small single-story motel on the south end of town is about 5 mi from the Fort Robinson State Park. Cable TV. Some pets allowed. | 304 McPherson St. 69339 | 308/665–1144 or 800/504–1444 | fax 308/665–1602 | 13 rooms | $35–$60 | D, MC, V.

FREMONT

Comfort Inn. This pale-toned two-story motel, 3 mi from Fremont Municipal Airport, takes a different tack inside, using lots of burgundy-colored fabrics. Suites also have sofabeds. Complimentary Continental breakfast. Some in-room data ports, microwaves, refriger-ators. Cable TV. Indoor pool. Hot tub. Business services. Pets allowed. | 1649 E. 23rd St. 68025 | 402/721–1109 | fax 402/721–1109 | 48 rooms | $50–$69 | AE, D, DC, MC, V.

Holiday Lodge. This brick motel has indoor and outdoor entrances to the rooms and a pleasant atrium and indoor pool for relaxing moments. Truck parking and cold-weather hookups are available. Restaurant, bar. Cable TV. Hot tub. Exercise equipment. Business services. Pets allowed. | 1220 E. 23rd St. 68025 | 402/727–1110 or 800/743–7666 | 100 rooms | $49–$70 | AE, D, DC, MC, V.

Super 8 Motel. Right beside the Platte River and a mall, this in-town motel helps you start the day with complimentary toast and coffee in the lobby. The free parking includes spaces for trucks and RVs. Bar. Cable TV. Pets allowed. | 1250 E. 23rd St./Hwy. 30, 68025 | 402/727–4445 or 800/800–8000 | fax 402/727–4445 | 43 rooms | $38–$66 | AE, D, DC, MC, V.

GERING

Circle S Lodge. Along the routes of the Oregon trail and the Pony Express, this 1950s brick motel on Route 92 offers ground-level rooms in a mostly commercial area about 8 mi from the Wildcat Hills Nature Center and Scotts Bluff National Monument. Truck parking is available. Cable TV. Pets allowed. | 400 M St. | 308/436–2157 | fax 308/436–3249 | 30 rooms | $34–$44 | AE, D, MC, V.

GOTHENBURG

Western Motor Inn. This two-story brick motor hotel off I–80 is surrounded by popular chain restaurants and about a mile from the Pony Express Station. If you're traveling with a child, you can arrange for a crib or roll-away bed. Some truck parking is available. Cable TV. Pets allowed. | 207 Lake Ave. | 308/537–3622 | fax 308/537–3650 | 26 rooms | $27–$49 | AE, D, MC, V.

GRAND ISLAND

Best Western Riverside Inn. With 10 meeting rooms, this two-story buff-colored brick motor hotel draws many group events. Off Highway 34E, it's about 2 mi from the interstate and a mile from the horse-racing at Fonner Park. In other leisure hours, you can cool off in the indoor pool or shape up at the fitness center. Most rooms have sofas, and guests receive a complimentary cocktail. Restaurant, bar, complimentary breakfast, room service. Cable TV. Hot tub. Laundry facilities. Business services, airport shuttle. Pets allowed. | 3333 Ramada Rd. 68801 | 308/384–5150 or 800/422–3485 | fax 308/384–6551 | 183 rooms | $52–$62 | AE, D, DC, MC, V.

Days Inn. Off Highway 281 on a side road, this northside motel is in a generally quite location, with a sauna and hot tub to help you refresh yourself after a long drive. The parking area includes spaces for trucks and cold-weather hookups. Complimentary Continental breakfast. Cable TV. Laundry facilities. Business services. Pets allowed. | 2620 N. Diers Ave. 68802 | 308/384–8624 | fax 308/384–1626 | 62 rooms | $40–$85 | AE, D, DC, MC, V.

Super 8 Motel. If you like to start the day with brisk exercise, you can trot along the lake behind this buff-colored motel in the south end of town—or do a few laps in the indoor pool. Truck/RV parking is available. Complimentary Continental breakfast. Cable TV. Hot tub. Pets allowed. | 2603 S. Locust St. 68801 | 308/384–4380 or 800/800–8000 | fax 308/384–5015 | 80 rooms | $43–$55 | AE, D, DC, MC, V.

HASTINGS

Super 8 Motel. Rooms in this buff-and-brown two-story motel have a quiet mix of pale walls and dark fabrics and include some "whirlpool suites." Just 26 mi from the Grand Island Airport and not far from the Hastings Convention Center, it is right off Highway 281, behind a Dairy Queen. Complimentary Continental breakfast. Cable TV. Pets allowed. | 2200 N. Kansas St. 68901 | 402/463–8888 or 800/800–8000 | fax 402/463–8899 | 50 rooms | $44–$54 | AE, D, DC, MC.

U.S.A. Inns. This motel option just off Highway 281 on the north side of town, built in the 1980s, is near the college and local attractions. Truck parking and cold-weather hookups are available. Some refrigerators. Cable TV. Pets allowed. | 2424 Osborne Dr. E | 402/463–1422 or 800/348–0426 | fax 402/463–2956 | 63 rooms | $41–$44 | AE, D, DC, MC, V.

KEARNEY

Best Western. About 7 mi from the Kearney Municipal Airport, this two-story white motel with crisp dark trim has a sauna and a heated outdoor pool—and hairdryers in the rooms if you need one after your swim or steam session. Truck and RV parking is available, with cold-weather hook-ups. Restaurant, complimentary breakfast. Cable TV. Indoor pool, wading pool. Hot tub, sauna. Exercise equipment. Business services, airport shuttle. Pets allowed. | 1010 3rd Ave. 68845-0967 | 308/237–5185 or 800/359–1894 | fax 308/234–1002 | 62 rooms | $72–$79 | AE, D, DC, MC, V.

Budget Motel South. This motel option is only about four blocks from I–80 exit 272. Within the surrounding 5 mi, you'll find many of the town's attractions as well as shopping. Truck parking is available. Cable TV. Indoor pool. Sauna. Laundry facilities. Pets allowed. | 411 S. 2nd Ave. | 308/237–5991 | fax 308/237–5991 | 69 rooms | $40–$70 | AE, D, DC, MC, V.

Holiday Inn. With 20,000 square ft of meeting space, this two-story motel caters to a lot of groups—but doesn't forget the families. In the indoor water recreation area, you'll find two 30-ft water slides into the pool, plus slides and a water cannon at the kids' pool (and hairdryers in the rooms). There is a complimentary shuttle to tourist attractions within 10 mi of the hotel, which covers most of the in-town sites. Truck parking with cold-weather hookups is available. Restaurant, bar, room service. In-room data ports. Cable TV. Hot tub. Exercise equipment, volleyball. Video games. Laundry facilities. Business services. Pets allowed. | 110 S. 2nd Ave. 68848 | 308/237–5971 | fax 308/236–7549 | 163 rooms | $69–$89 | AE, D, DC, MC, V.

Quality Inn. This modern stucco motel less than a block from I-80 is about 6 mi from the Fort Kearny State Historical Park, with the crane-viewing at the Hike/Bike Bridge in the State Recreation Area just a couple of miles beyond that, or a short 17-mi drive from all the collectibles at the Harold Warp Pioneer Village in Minden. Truck parking and cold-weather hookups are available. Restaurant, bar, complimentary Continental breakfast. Cable TV. Pool. Exercise room. Laundry facilities. Some pets allowed (fee). | 800 2nd Ave. 68848 | 308/234–2541 or 800/652–7245 | fax 308/237–4512 | 103 rooms | $45–$53 | AE, D, MC, V.

Ramada Inn. Remodeled in 2000, this casually modern motor hotel now has refrigerators and irons in the rooms. Just ½ mi from I-80, it is 2 mi from the Great Platte River Archway and a mile from the Trails and Rails Museum. Truck parking and cold-weather hookups are available. Restaurant, bar, complimentary Continental breakfast, room service. Refrigerators. Cable TV. Indoor pool, wading pool. Hot tub, sauna. Video games. Laundry facilities. Business services. Pets allowed. | 301 S. 2nd Ave. 68848 | 308/237–3141 or 800/652–1909 | fax 308/234–4675 | 209 rooms | $55–$85 | AE, D, DC, MC, V.

Western Inn South. Playing to its name both indoors and out, there is a wagon in front of this motel, and wood paneling and art with Old West themes in the lobby. Some rooms have kitchenettes, but the hotel provides a full hot breakfast from Oct. 15 to May 15. Truck parking with cold-weather hookups is available. Complimentary Continental breakfast. Some kitchenettes. Cable TV. Indoor pool. Hot tub, sauna. Pets allowed. | 510 S. 3rd Ave. | 308/234–1876 or 800/437–8457 | fax 308/237–2169 | 44 rooms | $39–$60 | AE, D, DC, MC, V.

KIMBALL

Days Inn. This compact sand-colored stucco motor hotel was remodeled, with all-new room furnishings, in 2000. A mile north of I-80 and next door to Kimball Event Center, it's also about 40 mi from the buffalo and elk herds at the Wildcat Hills Nature Center near Gering. Complimentary Continental breakfast. In-room data ports. Cable TV. Indoor pool. Pets allowed (fee). | 611 E. 3rd St. 69145 | 308/235–4671 or 800/329–7466 | fax 308/235–3557 | www.daysinn.com | 30 rooms | $46–$85 | AE, D, MC, V.

Super 8 Motel. This modest two-story motel built in 1990 at the I-80 junction with Route 71 helps you start the day with a free newspaper. It's about 8 mi from the Oliver Reservoir State Recreation Area—and only about 30 mi from Cabela's sporting goods store if you need to jaunt over to Sidney to stock up on new equipment. Truck and RV spaces are available. In-room data ports. Cable TV. Some pets allowed (fee). | 104 E. River Rd. 69145 | 308/235–4888 or 800/800–8000 | fax 308/235–2838 | 58 rooms | $52–$72 | AE, D, DC, MC, V.

LEXINGTON

Budget Host—Minute Man. On Highway 283, this one-story red brick-and-wood motel is only about 2 mi north of I-80, in an area where you'll find many dining options. Truck parking with cold-weather hookups is available. Cable TV. Pets allowed (fee). | 801 Plum Creek Pkwy. | 308/324–5544 or 800/973–5544 | 36 rooms | $34–$40 | AE, D, DC, MC, V.

1st Interstate Inn. Off exit 237 of I-80, this modest motel is only about 30–35 mi from several good crane-viewing sites near Kearney. If you follow 283 south of the interstate, you are also within minutes of the J-2 Eagle Viewing Facility. Truck parking is available. Complimentary Continental breakfast. Cable TV. Pool. Pets allowed. | 2503 S. Plum Creek Rd. | 308/324–5601 | fax 308/324–4284 | 52 rooms | $43–$58 | AE, D, DC, MC, V.

Gable View Inn. The building is modern, but the eight peaks of the roofline give it a slightly Victorian look. The small motel is only about a quarter of a mi from I–80 and within 10 mi of the Johnson Lake State Recreation Area. Truck parking is available. Cable TV. Pool. Pets allowed. | 2701 Plum Creek Pkwy. | 308/324–5595 or 800/341–8000 | fax 308/324–2267 | 24 rooms | $32–$40 | AE, D, MC, V.

LINCOLN

Best Western Villager Courtyard and Garden. Renovated in 1999, these five two-story wooden buildings are set in landscaped grounds with a wildflower garden, a heated pool, and walking paths. Downtown is 3 mi away. Restaurant, bar. Hot tub. Laundry facilities. Free parking. Pets allowed (fee). | 5200 O St. | 402/464–9111 or 800/356–4321 | fax 402/467–0505 | www.bestwestern.com | 193 rooms | $69–$84 | AE, D, DC, MC, V.

Chase Suites. The lobby of this complex on the east side of town has cathedral ceilings and a soaring stacked-stone fireplace where evening hospitality hour is held. Accommodations range from studio layouts to two-bedroom suites with fireplaces or lofts; all have separate breakfast areas. Picnic area, complimentary breakfast. Kitchens, microwaves. Cable TV. Pool. Hot tub. Tennis. Exercise equipment. Laundry facilities. Business services. Pets allowed (fee). | 200 S. 68th Pl. 68510 | 402/483–4900 or 800/331–3131 | fax 402/483–4464 | 120 suites | $102–$141 | AE, D, DC, MC, V.

Comfort Inn—Airport. The best way to reach this small two-story hotel a mile from the airport is through the parking lot of Perkins Restaurant. Rooms are basic but include hairdryers and irons and refreshing massage showerheads. Complimentary Continental breakfast. In-room data ports, microwaves, refrigerators. Cable TV. Indoor pool. Hot tub. Video games. Business services. Pets allowed. | 2940 N.W. 12th St. 68521 | 402/475–2200 or 800/228–5150 | fax 402/475–2200 | www.comfortinn.com | 67 rooms | $85 | AE, D, DC, MC, V.

Red Roof Inn. This hostelry, around the corner from the 27th Street exit off I–80, is 5 mi from the airport and 3 mi northwest of downtown Lincoln. Complimentary Continental breakfast. In-room data ports. Cable TV. Indoor pool. Hot tub. Pets allowed. | 64 rooms | 6501 North 28th St. 68504 | 402/438–4700 | fax 402/438–9007 | $50–$60 | AE, D, DC, MC, V.

MCCOOK

Best Western Chief. This two-story motel is only ½ mi from the Museum of High Plains and from the Heritage Hills Golf Course, consistently rated among the top public golf courses in the country. Truck and RV parking and cold-weather hookups are available. Restaurant, complimentary Continental breakfast. Cable TV. Indoor pool. Hot tub. Exercise equipment. Business services, airport shuttle. Pets allowed. | 612 W. B St. 69001 | 308/345–3700 | fax 308/345–7182 | 111 rooms | $54–$84 | AE, D, DC, MC, V.

Holiday Inn Express McCook. Downtown McCook is 2 mi from this hotel at the junction of Highways 6 and 34 with Highway 83, which has refrigerators in case you want to stock your own juice to have the minute you get up. Complimentary Continental breakfast. In-room data ports, refrigerators. Cable TV. Indoor pool. Hot tub, sauna, spa. Exercise equipment. Laundry facilities. Business services. Pets allowed. | 1 Holiday Bison Dr. 69001 | 308/345–4505 | fax 308/345–2990 | holiday@ocsmccook.com. | 50 rooms | AE, D, DC, MC, V.

Super 8 Motel. This one-story building, constructed in 1982, is at the junction of Highways 6 and 34, and only 10 blocks from downtown. The parking area has spaces for trucks and RVs. Cable TV. Pets allowed. | 1103 E. B St. | 308/345–1141 or 800/800–8000 | fax 308/345–1141 | 40 rooms | $34–50 | AE, D, DC, MC, V.

MINDEN

Harold Warp Pioneer Village Motel. Next door to Pioneer Village, the motel spreads through two two-story buildings built in the late 1970s. On the same site, there is a 135-space campground. The parking area includes spaces for trucks; cold-weather hookups are available. Admission to Pioneer Village is included in room rentals. Restaurant, bar. Cable TV. Pets allowed. | 224 E. Hwy. 6 | 800/445–4447 | fax 308/832–2750 | 90 rooms | $40–$47 | D, MC, V.

Home Comfort Bed and Breakfast. A mile north of Pioneer Village, this colonial-style house with a barn and outbuildings—and barnyard animals around the grounds—sits on 14 scenic acres. The house is decorated with an eclectic mixture of antique and modern furnishings. You can have dinner in the formal dining room and coffee in a smaller area that's is also used as a coffee house. Dining room, complimentary Continental breakfast. Pets allowed. No smoking. | 1523 N. Brown 68959 | 308/832–0533 or 888/969–2475. | 4 rooms | No credit cards.

NORFOLK

Ramada Inn. It may be steaming outside or streaming buckets, but you can find a nice oasis from any weather at the indoor tropical garden in this two-story motel at the intersection of Highways 81 and 275. Truck and RV parking is available, with cold-weather hookups. Restaurant, bar, room service. Cable TV. Indoor pool. Playground. Business services, airport shuttle. Some pets allowed. | 1227 Omaha Ave. 68701 | 402/371–7000 or 800/272–6232 | fax 402/371–7000 | 98 rooms | $65–$78 | AE, D, DC, MC, V.

NORTH PLATTE

Best Western Chalet Lodge. This two-story motel in a residential area is a mile from Buffalo Bill Ranch State Historical Park and 2 mi from the Factory Stores Outlet Mall. Many rooms have recliners, and all have in-room coffee. Cold-weather hookups are available. Complimentary Continental breakfast. Some refrigerators. Cable TV. Heated indoor pool. Pets allowed (fee). | 920 N. Jeffers St. 69101 | 308/532–2313 or 800/622–2313 | fax 308/532–8823 | 38 rooms | $50–$66 | AE, D, DC, MC, V.

Country Inn Motel. This two-story building is only a short walk from downtown, but if you've overdone on the walking—or hiking or golfing—you might try what the motel calls its therapy pool, with whirlpool, sauna, and hot tub. Truck parking is available, with cold-weather hookups. Some kitchenettes. Cable TV. Pool. Hot tub. Pets allowed. | 321 S. Dewey St. 69101-5422 | 308/532–8130 or 800/532–8130 | fax 308/534–0588 | 40 rooms | $40–$54 | AE, D, MC, V.

Motel 6. This motel with two floors, off I–80 at exit 177, is 5 mi from the Lincoln County Historical Museum and Buffalo Bill's Ranch. Cable TV. Indoor pool. Pets allowed. | 1520 S. Jeffers St. 69101 | 308/534–6200 | fax 308/532–5276 | 61 rooms | $56–$60 | AE, D, DC, MC, V.

Ramada Limited. At the junction of I–80 and Highway 83S, this two-story motel, renovated in 1998, is about 6 mi from Lee Bird Airport. If your morning minutes on the exercise machines leave you feeling wrung out, you can finish with a dip in the outdoor pool during summer months. The parking area includes spaces for trucks and RVs. In-room data ports. Cable TV. Pool. Hot tub. Exercise equipment. Laundry facilities. Pets allowed. | 3201 S. Jeffers St. 69101 | 308/534–3120 or 800/272–6232 | fax 308/532–3065 | 78 rooms | $64–$76 | AE, D, DC, MC, V.

Stanford Motel. A one-story building in a commercial area, this motel is just 10 blocks from downtown and about a mile from the Wild West Arena and Buffalo Bill Ranch State Historical Park. Truck parking and cold-weather hookups are available. Cable TV. Pets allowed. | 1400 E. 4th St. 69101 | 308/532–9380 or 800/743–4934 | fax 308/532–9634 | 32 rooms | $39–$44 | AE, D, MC, V.

Stockman Inn. This two-story building, renovated in 1999, is ½ mi from downtown and ½ mi north of I–80 and Hwy. 83. Room service is available, and there is a restaurant on the premises. The parking area has spaces for trucks, with cold-weather hookups. Restaurant, room service. Cable TV. Pool. Exercise equipment. Business services, airport van. Pets allowed. | 1402 S. Jeffers St. 69101 | 308/534–3630 or 800/624–4643 | fax 308/534–0110 | 140 rooms | $66 | AE, D, DC, MC, V.

Super 8. With Scout's Rest Ranch only 5 mi away, this two-story motel uses round wooden tables and frosted-glass lights in wagon-wheel fixtures to give an Old West feeling to its breakfast area off the lobby. Some whirlpool suites are available, along with truck and RV spaces with cold-weather hookups. Complimentary Continental breakfast. Cable TV. Exercise equipment. Laundry facilities. Pets allowed. | 220 Eugene Ave. 69101 | 308/532–4224 or 800/800–8000 | fax 308/532–4317 | 112 rooms | $58 | AE, D, DC, MC, V.

OGALLALA

Best Western Stagecoach Inn. When I–80 gets as far as this two-story white-columned motel at the junction with Route 61, you are in the Mountain Time Zone. By the river, the rust-colored building is 12 mi from Lake McConaughy's outdoor facilities and 2 mi from the Mansion on the Hill if you'd rather explore the finery of the past. Some family rooms are available. The parking area includes truck and RV spaces, with cold-weather hookups. Restaurant, bar. In-room data ports. Cable TV. Heated indoor pool. Hot tub. Exercise equipment. Playground. Laundry facilities. Business services, airport shuttle. Some pets allowed (fee). | 201 Stagecoach Trail 69153 | 308/284–3656 or 800/662–2993 | fax 308/284–6734 | 100 rooms | $50–$65 | AE, D, DC, MC, V.

Days Inn. This ranch-style motel has two floors and is a convenient resting place between fishing, boating, or jet skiing outings at Lake McConaughy, 9 mi away, or Lake Ogallala, 13 mi away. Complimentary Continental breakfast. In-room data ports, refrigerators. Cable TV. Pets allowed. | 601 Stagecoach Trail 69153 | 800/544–8313 or 308/284–6365 | fax 308/284–2351. | 31 rooms | AE, D, DC, MC, V.

Ramada Limited. Renovated in 1991, this two-story motor hotel and conference center near the Highway 29/61 junction helps you start the day with a free weekday newspaper and an iron, if you need to touch up your meeting clothes. The water sports at Lake McConaughy are about 10 mi away, as are several golf courses. Truck parking with cold-weather hookups is available. Restaurant, bar, complimentary Continental breakfast, room service. In-room data ports. Cable TV. Pool, wading pool. Gym. Laundry facilities. Business services. Pets allowed. | 201 Chuckwagon Rd. 69153 | 308/284–3623 or 800/573–7148 | fax 308/284–4949 | 152 rooms | $69 | AE, D, DC.

Super 8. This two-floor motel just off I–80 is 10 mi from all the goings-on at Lake McConaughy. The parking area includes spaces for trucks and RVs. Dining room. Cable TV. Laundry services. Pets allowed (fee). | 500 E. A South, 69153 | 308/284–2076 or 800/800–8000 | fax 308/284–2590 | 91 rooms | $55–$63 | AE, D, DC, MC, V.

OMAHA

Baymont Inns. This chain has many changes and renovations underway all around the country. This two-story outpost on the west side of town offers simple accommodations 15 mi from the SAC Museum and 3 mi from the shops of Oakview Mall. Cold-weather hookups are available. Complimentary Continental breakfast. In-room data ports. Cable

TV. Business services. Pets allowed. | 10760 M St. 68127 | 402/592–5200 or 800/428–3438 | fax 402/592–1416 | 97 rooms | $56–$74 | AE, D, DC, MC, V.

Best Inn. This three-story motel, at the junction of I–80 and Highway 50, is 3 mi from the Prairie Capital Convention Center and about 11 mi from the zoo. Bar, complimentary Continental breakfast. In-room VCRs. Hot tub. Exercise equipment. Laundry facilities. Free parking. Pets allowed (fee). | 9305 S. 145th St. 68138 | 402/895–2555 | fax 402/895–1565 | 56 rooms | $42–$56 | AE, D, DC, MC, V.

Best Western—Central. Set off by a swath of green lawns, this five-story white building was renovated in 1998–99. Just off I–80, it is also just down the street from the sports events at Aksarben Coliseum and has in-room movies. Truck parking is available. Restaurant, bar, room service. In-room data ports. Cable TV. Indoor pool. Hot tub, sauna. Laundry facilities. Business services, airport shuttle. Pets allowed. | 3650 S. 72nd St. 68124 | 402/397–3700 or 800/446–6242 | fax 402/397–8362 | 212 rooms | $79 | AE, D, DC, MC, V.

Clarion Hotel Carlisle. Sparkling chandeliers and cherrywood paneling help give a refined grace to the lobby of this three-story hotel about 3 mi from the stores of Regency Fashion Court. The spacious rooms include a full-sized desk. Truck parking is available. Restaurant, complimentary Continental breakfast, room service. In-room data ports. Cable TV. Indoor pool. Hot tub. Laundry facilities. Business services, airport shuttle. Some pets allowed (fee). | 10909 M St. 68137 | 402/331–8220 or 800/526–6242 | fax 402/331–8729 | 137 rooms | $89–$125 | AE, D, DC, MC, V.

Econo Lodge. The two-story lodging is 2 mi from I–80, about 2 mi from Westroads Mall, and five blocks from Nebraska Crossroads Mall. Free coffee is always available, along with truck and bus parking, and extended-stay rooms have microwaves and refrigerators. Restaurant. Some in-room hot tubs. Cable TV. Pool. Laundry facilities. Pets allowed. | 7833 W. Dodge Rd. 68124 | 402/391–7100 | fax 402/391–7100 | 48 rooms | $45–$100 | AE, D, DC, MC, V.

Embassy Suites. Although this seven-story building is next to the Old Market, it has an atrium and a courtyard for quiet moments away from the busy downtown scene, plus outdoor decks where you can work on your tan. Each suite has a separate bedroom and living room. Restaurant, bar, complimentary breakfast, room service. Cable TV. Microwave, refrigerator, in-room data ports. Indoor pool. Hot tub. Fitness center. Business services, airport shuttle. Pets allowed. | 555 S. 10th St. 68183 | 402/346–9000 or 800/362–2779 | fax 402/346–4236 | 249 suites | $129–$179 | AE, D, DC, MC, V.

Four Points Hotel Omaha. With a red roof topping its classically styled six stories, this hotel in southwest Omaha has minibars and coffeemakers in each room, as well as complimentary weekday newspapers. About 8 mi from Nebraska Crossroads Mall, it provides complimentary shuttles to the corporate/charter facilities at Millard Airport. Restaurant, room service. Cable TV. Heated indoor pool, wading pool. Hot tub, sauna. Gym. Laundry facilities. Business services. Pets allowed. | 4888 S. 118th St. 68137 | 402/895–1000 | fax 402/895–9247 | 163 rooms | $69–$129 | AE, D, DC, MC, V.

La Quinta. With crisp white exterior and refurbished guest rooms with dark wood furniture, this two-story motel on the northeast side of town is about 5 mi from the Children's Museum and 15 mi from downtown. Complimentary Continental breakfast. In-room data ports. Cable TV. Pool. Laundry facilities. Pets allowed. | 3330 N. 104th Ave. 68134 | 402/493–1900 or 800/687–6667 | fax 402/496–0757 | 129 rooms | $52–$59 | AE, D, DC, MC, V.

Marriott. This L-shape six-story hotel is 10 mi from the Old Market area and just across the street from the shopping at Regency Fashion Court. Restaurants, bar, room service. In-room data ports. Cable TV. Indoor-outdoor pool. Hot tub. Exercise equipment. Business services. Pets allowed. | 10220 Regency Cir. 68134 | 402/399–9000 | fax 402/399–0223 | 301 rooms, 4 suites | $109–$149 | AE, D, DC, MC, V.

Ramada-Central. At I–80 and 72nd St., this 10-floor motel draws a lot of group events to its 10 meeting rooms, and there's a concierge desk to help with special services. It's about 7 mi from the Joslyn and the Gerald Ford Birth Site, and 5 mi from the zoo. Restaurant, bar, room service. In-room data ports, some refrigerators, some microwaves. Cable TV. Indoor pool. Hot tub, sauna. Playground. Business services, airport shuttle. Pets allowed. | 7007 Grover St. 68106 | 402/397–7030 or 800/228–5299 | fax 402/397–8449 | 215 rooms | $79–$99 | AE, D, DC, MC, V.

O'NEILL

Elms Best Value Inn. This small one-story motel on Highway 20 is 29 mi from Ashfall Fossil Beds State Historical Park and 50 mi from the Fort Randall casino. Truck parking and cold-weather hookups are available. Cable TV. Playground. Pets allowed. | 414 E. Douglas St. 68763 | 402/336–3800 or 800/526–9052 or 888/315–2378 | fax 402/336–1419 | 21 rooms | $40–$45 | AE, D, MC, V.

Golden Hotel. This three-story hotel has seen many travelers since it was built in 1913. Renovated in 1998, each room has a different style of decorative theme. The Ashfall Fossil Beds are 29 mi away. Complimentary Continental breakfast. Some kitchenettes. Cable TV, in-room VCRs and movies. Beauty salon. Laundry facilities. Free parking. Some pets allowed. | 406 E. Douglas St. 68763 | 402/336–4436 or 800/658–3148 | fax 402/336–3549 | 24 rooms | $29–$50 | AE, D, MC, V.

RED CLOUD

Green Acres Motel. Made of brick and wood, this small one-floor motel, 1 mi from downtown Red Cloud and 1 mi from the Willa Cather girlhood home, has its own picnic area. Cable TV. Pets allowed (fee). | N. Hwy. 281 68970 | 402/746–2201 | 17 rooms | $40 | AE, D, MC, V.

ST. PAUL

Super 8. On the west edge of town on Highway 281, this two-floor motel built in 1996 is 3 blocks from downtown St. Paul. All rooms have electronic locks. Complimentary Continental breakfast. In-room data ports. Cable TV. Business services. Pets allowed. | 116 Howard Ave. 68873 | 308/754–4554 or 800/800–8000 | fax 308/754–5685 | 36 rooms | $37–$53 | AE, D, DC, MC, V.

SOUTH SIOUX CITY

Flamingo Inn. Like most of South Sioux City, this hotel is only a short drive from the boating facilities and events on the river. Historic 4th Street, across the bridge in Sioux City, Iowa, is less than 4 mi away. Complimentary Continental breakfast. In-room data ports. Cable TV. Pool. Hot tubs, sauna. Exercise equipment. Laundry services. Pets allowed. | 2829 Dakota Ave. 68776 | 402/494–8874 | 80 rooms | $40–$75 | AE, D, DC, MC, V.

Marina Inn. Most rooms in this two-building complex have patios or balconies, giving you a 24-hour view of river and Iowa skyline. Inside, you'll find an exercise room and indoor pool. Truck parking and cold-weather hookups are available. Restaurant, bar, room service. Cable TV. Indoor pool. Hot tub, sauna. Exercise equipment. Airport shuttle. Pets allowed. | 4th and B Sts. 68776 | 402/494–4000 or 800/798–7980 | fax 402/494–2550 | 182 rooms | $89–$104 | AE, D, DC, MC, V.

Travelodge. This two-story motel renovated in 1990 is a mile from downtown, close to the Missouri River and about two blocks from the convention center and a keno casino. There's in-room coffee, and a morning newspaper awaits in the lobby. Truck/RV parking spaces are available. Cable TV. Business services. Pets allowed. | 400 Dakota Ave. 68776 | 402/494–3046 or 800/578–7878 | fax 402/494–8299 | 61 rooms | $43–$48 | AE, D, DC, MC, V.

THEDFORD

Rodeway Inn. This modern, two-floor motel 1 mi east of Thedford uses part of its lobby to exhibit local artists' paintings, many of them depicting wildlife or local scenes. Complimentary Continental breakfast. In-room data ports, some microwaves, some refrigerators. Cable TV. Hot tubs. Laundry services. Pets allowed (fee). | Rte. 2 and Hwy. 83 69166 | 308/645–2284 | fax 308/645–2630 | rodeway@neb/sandhills.net | 42 rooms | $46–$67 | AE, D, DC, MC, V.

VALENTINE

Motel Raine. In the heart of Valentine off Highway 20, Motel Raine was built in the 1960s and renovated in the '90s. Truck parking and cold-weather hookups are available. Cable TV. Airport shuttle. Some pets allowed. | U.S. 20W | 402/376–2030 or 800/999–3066 | fax 402/376–1956 | 34 rooms | $46–$56 | AE, D, DC, MC, V.

Super 8. This one-story motel with dark detailing against a pale exterior, at the junction of Highways 20 and 83, is 15 mi from Smith Falls and the tubing and rafting on the Niobrara, and 3 blocks from downtown Valentine and the fun of the country music festival. Complimentary Continental breakfast. Cable TV. Pool. Hot tubs, sauna. Laundry services. Business services. Pets allowed. | 223 E. Hwy. 20 69201 | 402/376–1250 or 800/800–8000 | fax 402/376–1211 | 60 rooms | $70 | AE, D, MC, V.

Trade Winds Lodge. For guests who've had a successful day on lake or river, this quiet country lodge a mile southeast of Highways 20 and 83 on HC 37 has indoor fish-cleaning and freezer facilities. After the chores, there's a pool to try—and recliners and in-room movies for relaxing. Truck parking and cold-weather hookups are available. Cable TV. Pool. Airport shuttle. Pets allowed. | 402/376–1600 or 800/341–8000 or 888/315–3651 | fax 402/376–3651 | 32 rooms | $38–$61 | AE, D, DC, MC, V.

YORK

Best Western Palmer Inn. In a commercial area 1 mi south of York, this rusty-toned building sits in its space like a prairie hill at sunset–if prairie rises had white columned porticos. It's about 2 mi from the Palmer Museum and the York airport. The parking area includes truck and RV spaces and cold-weather hookups. Restaurant, complimentary Continental breakfast. Cable TV. Heated pool. Playground. Laundry facilities. Airport shuttle. Some pets allowed. | 2426 S. Lincoln Ave. 68467 | 402/362–5585 or 800/452–3185 | fax 402/362–6053 | 41 rooms | $45–$65 | AE, D, DC, MC, V.

Holiday Inn. Rooms in this two-story motel have hair dryers, irons, and whirlpool tubs. It's about 3 mi from York at the junction of I–60 and Highway 81 and 45 mi from the Lincoln airport. Van service is available through Eppley Express. Restaurant, bar, complimentary Continental breakfast, room service. Refrigerators. Cable TV. Indoor pool. Hot tub. Exercise equipment. Pets allowed (fee). | 4619 S. Lincoln Ave. 68467 | 402/362–6661 or 800/934–5495 | fax 402/362–3727 | 128 rooms | $44–$63 | AE, D, DC, MC, V.

Super 8. A skywalk joins together two separate buildings, one with two stories and one with three, at this hotel. Complimentary Continental breakfast. Cable TV. Indoor pool. Pets allowed. | 4112 South Lincoln Ave. 68467 | 402/362–3388 or 800/800–8000 | fax 402/362–3604 | 95 rooms | $30–$65 | AE, D, DC, MC, V.

Nevada

BATTLE MOUNTAIN

Best Western–Big Chief Motel. The largest and most modern motel in town, renovated, offers standard contemporary rooms. Rooms for guests with disabilities. Some kitchenettes with microwaves, some refrigerators. Cable TV. Pool. Laundry facilities. Pets allowed. | 58 rooms | 434 W. Front St. | 775/635–2416 or 800/528–1234 | fax 775/635–2418 | www.bestwestern.com | $37–$66 | AE, D, MC, V.

Comfort Inn. The rooms are standard and the amenities good. Complimentary Continental breakfast. Some refrigerators. Cable TV. Pool. Hot tub. Laundry facilities. Business services. Pets allowed (fee). | 72 rooms | 521 E. Front St. | 775/635–5880 | fax 775/635–5788 | $38–$54 | AE, D, DC, MC, V.

ELKO

Holiday Inn. The second-largest lodging in Elko has standard rooms and good amenities, plus a casino. Restaurant, bar, room service. No-smoking rooms. Cable TV. Indoor pool. Hot tub. Exercise equipment. Laundry facilities. Airport shuttle. Pets allowed. | 170 rooms | 3015 E. Idaho St. | 775/738–8425 or 800/465–4329 | fax 775/753–7906 | $64–$99 | AE, D, DC, MC, V.

Red Lion Inn & Casino. The largest and fanciest hotel in town has big rooms, a showroom, and lounge entertainment. Restaurant, bar. No-smoking rooms. Cable TV. Pool. Barbershop, beauty salon. Business services. Airport shuttle. Pets allowed. | 223 rooms | 2065 E. Idaho St. | 775/738–2111 or 800/545–0044 | fax 775/753–9859 | $79–$259 | AE, D, DC, MC, V.

Shilo Inn. Some of the accommodations here, the only all-suite lodging in Elko, have kitchenettes. Complimentary Continental breakfast. In-room data ports, some microwaves, no-smoking rooms, some refrigerators. Cable TV. Indoor pool. Hot tub, steam room. Exercise equipment. Laundry facilities. Business services. Airport shuttle. Pets allowed (fee). | 70 suites, 16 kitchenette units | 2401 Mountain City Hwy. | 775/738–5522 or 800/222–2244 | fax 775/738–6247 | $65–$125 | AE, D, DC, MC, V.

ELY

Hotel Nevada. One of the oldest hotel buildings in the state, the Nevada is in excellent shape. The hotel was built in 1908 at the main intersection downtown, and the rooms were renovated in 1997. You also get a casino and entertainment. Restaurant, bars, complimentary Continental breakfast. No-smoking rooms. Cable TV. Business services. Pets allowed. | 65 rooms | 501 Aultman St. | 775/289–6665 or 800/406–3055 | fax 775/289–4715 | $20–$69 | AE, D, DC, MC, V.

Jailhouse Motel & Casino. This modern motel at the main downtown intersection has a curious jailhouse theme: the rooms are referred to as "cells." Restaurant. No-smoking rooms. Cable TV. Pets allowed. | 47 rooms | 211 5th St. | 775/289–3033 or 800/841–5430 | fax 775/289–8709 | $40–$49 | AE, D, DC, MC, V.

Motel 6. The largest lodging in Ely is attractive because of its contemporary-style rooms with modern furnishing and its modest prices. Complimentary Continental breakfast. No-smoking rooms. Cable TV. Pool. Hot tub. Pets allowed. | 122 rooms | 770 Ave. O | 775/289–6671 or 800/466–8356 | fax 775/289–4803 | $28–$42 | AE, D, MC, V.

EUREKA

Jackson House Bed and Breakfast. Built in 1877, this venerable and still lovely downtown landmark was restored in 1994 with heavy wood, heavy quilts, and funky floors. You can see all the downtown action from the balcony. Bar. Pets allowed. | 9 rooms | 251 N. Main St. | 775/237–5577 | fax 775/237–5155 | $39–$59 | D, MC, V.

Sundown Lodge. A standard motel right downtown, this lodge is popular, and the rooms fill up fast. Reserve as far in advance as you can. Pets allowed. | 27 rooms | 60 N. Main St. | 775/237–5334 | fax 775/237–6932 | $31–$45 | MC, V.

FALLON

Bonanza Inn & Casino. This is where you stay if you want to be in the heart of the action, right downtown. Rooms can get noisy on the weekends. Restaurant, bar. Cable TV. Business services. Pets allowed (fee). | 74 rooms | 855 W. Williams Ave. | 775/423–6031 | fax 775/423–6282 | $40–$50 | AE, D, DC, MC, V.

HAWTHORNE

El Capitan Resort & Casino. Right in the center of downtown and across the street from the casino, this standard model is the place to stay to be in the middle of the action. Restaurant, bar. No-smoking rooms, refrigerators. Pool. Pets allowed. | 103 rooms | 540 F St. | 775/945–3321 | fax 775/324–6229 | $41 | AE, D, DC, MC, V.

Sand n Sage Lodge. One of the nicer hotels in Hawthorne. Some refrigerators. Cable TV. Some pets allowed. | 37 rooms | 1301 E. 5th St. | 775/945–3352 | $25–$40 | AE, D, MC, V.

LAS VEGAS

Alexis Park Resort. This sprawling, upscale low-rise business hotel is minutes from the airport and the Convention Center. All rooms are mini-suites, and there's no casino (an attractive feature to some). Restaurant, bar. In-room data ports, minibars, refrigerators, no-smoking rooms, some in-room hot tubs. Cable TV. 3 pools. Barbershop, beauty salon, hot tub. Putting green. Exercise equipment. Business services. Some pets allowed (fee). | 500 suites | 375 E. Harmon Ave. | 702/796–3300 or 800/582–2228 (outside NV) | fax 702/796–4334 | $99–$500 1–bedroom (under 12 free), $475–$1,000 2–bedroom (under 12 free) | AE, D, DC, MC, V.

Days Inn. Tennis and golf are nearby if you need a respite from the casino area and the Fremont Street Experience. The rooms are spacious and simple. Restaurant. No-smoking rooms, cable TV. Pool. Some pets allowed. | 147 rooms | 707 E. Fremont St. | 702/388–1400 or 800/325–2344 | fax 702/388–9622 | $35–$100 | AE, D, DC, MC, V.

Holiday Inn Crowne Plaza Suites. This non-casino hotel is a good place to stay if you're here on business other than gambling. The suites are large, and it's close to both the airport and the Convention Center. Restaurant, bar. In-room data ports, in-room safes, minibars, no-smoking floors. Cable TV. Pool. Hot tub. Exercise equipment. Business services. Airport shuttle. Pets allowed. | 201 suites | 4255 Paradise Rd. | 702/369–4400 or 800/227–6963 | fax 702/369–3770 | www.crowneplaza.com | $145–$185 | AE, D, DC, MC, V.

La Quinta. The location makes this motel popular with budget business travelers and university visitors. It's convenient to the airport, rental car companies, the Convention Center, and the university. Complimentary Continental breakfast. In-room data ports, no-smoking rooms, refrigerators, in-room hot tubs, cable TV. Pool. Laundry facilities. Business services. Airport and Strip shuttle. Some pets allowed. | 228 units, 171 kitchenettes | 3970 S. Paradise Rd. | 702/796–9000 | fax 702/796–3537 | $65–$109 | AE, D, DC, MC, V.

Residence Inn by Marriott. Great for business travelers and families, these apartment-like rooms all have eat-in kitchens and some have working fireplaces, in condolike units. The grounds and gardens are lush. Complimentary Continental breakfast. No-smoking rooms. Cable TV, in-room VCRs and movies. Pool. Hot tub. Laundry facilities. Business services. Airport shuttle. Some pets allowed (fee). | 192 kitchenette suites | 3225 Paradise Rd. | 702/796–9300 | fax 702/796–9562 | $79–$500 | AE, D, DC, MC, V.

Travelodge–Downtown. The name notwithstanding, this small, standard chain motel is not within walking distance of downtown. No-smoking rooms. Cable TV. Pool. Pets allowed. | 58 rooms | 2028 E. Fremont St. | 702/384–7540 | fax 702/384–0408 | $35–$85 | AE, D, DC, MC, V.

LAUGHLIN

Cottonwood Cove Resort And Marina. This is a full-scale resort facility right on Lake Mojave. The standard one-story motel is surrounded by pleasant grassy grounds. Restaurant, bar, picnic area. No-smoking rooms, some refrigerators. Cable TV. Beach, boating, jet skiing, waterskiing. Fishing. Pets allowed. | 24 rooms | 1000 Cottonwood Cove Rd. | 702/297–1464 | fax 702/297–1464 | $55–$95 | AE, D, MC, V.

LOVELOCK

Lovelock Inn. A modern motel right off the I–80 west exit, next to the museum and Chamber of Commerce. No-smoking rooms. Pool. Pets allowed. | 37 rooms | 55 Cornell Ave. | 775/273–2937 | fax 775/273–2242 | $42–$59 | MC, V.

Sturgeon's Ramada Inn. This is the largest lodging in Lovelock, right at the east I–80 exit. It offers a big casino (for Lovelock), a coffee shop and steakhouse, and remodeled rooms. Restaurant. No-smoking rooms. Pool. Pets allowed. | 74 rooms | 1420 Cornell Ave. | 775/273–2971 or 888/298–2054 | fax 775/273–2278 | $39–$105 | AE, D, MC, V.

MINDEN-GARDNERVILLE

Nenzel Mansion. A Southern Colonial–style house with 12-ft ceilings and a huge great room. The guest rooms are up a 25-step staircase. The hosts live on the third floor. Complimentary breakfast. No room phones. Cable TV in sitting room. Pets allowed. | 4 rooms, 2 share bath | 1431 Ezell St. | 775/782–7644 | $80–$110 | MC, V.

OVERTON

Echo Bay Resort and Marina. A bit of a trip from Overton (about 20 mi), but this resort is right on the best beach on Lake Mead. It is a small commercial operation and far enough away from Las Vegas to be relatively private and quiet. You can fish, swim, boat, and water- and jet-ski. The motel is right at marina. Restaurant, bar, picnic area. No-smoking rooms, some refrigerators. Cable TV. Beach, water sports, boating, fishing. Pets allowed. | 52 rooms | Northshore Rd. (Rte. 167) | 702/394–4000 or 800/752–9669 | fax 702/394–4182 | $69–$74 | AE, D, DC, MC, V.

RENO

Hampton Inn. One of the newer downtown high-rise hotels without a casino opened in 1996. It's connected to Harrah's casino, though. The rooms are modern, the location great, and the amenities the same as at the megaresort-casinos. Bar, complimentary Continental breakfast. In-room data ports, in-room safes, no-smoking rooms. Cable TV. Pool. Barbershop, beauty salon. Exercise equipment. Business services. Airport shuttle. Pets allowed. | 408 rooms | 175 E. 2nd St. | 775/788–2300 | fax 775/788–2301 | $62–$94 | AE, D, DC, MC, V.

Harrah's. Opened in 1937, this is the oldest casino in Reno and one of the oldest in the state. The snazzy joint covers nearly two blocks with three casinos and two hotel towers. New sports book, great buffet, and one of the few kids' arcades downtown. 4 restaurants, bar. No-smoking rooms. Cable TV. Pool. Hot tub, massage. Gym. Business services. Airport shuttle. Some pets allowed. | 958 rooms | 219 N. Center St. | 775/786–3232 or 800/427–7247 | fax 775/788–3274 | $54–$299 | AE, D, DC, MC, V.

La Quinta Inn–Airport. You're close to the airport and the interstate both at this standard motel, making it a good choice for those who don't plan a long stay in town. Complimentary Continental breakfast. No-smoking rooms. Cable TV. Pool. Business services. Airport shuttle. Pets allowed. | 130 rooms | 4001 Market St. | 775/348–6100 | fax 775/348–8794 | www.laquinta.com | $59–$85 | AE, D, DC, MC, V.

Rodeway Inn. Standard Travelodge motel, convenient for business travelers. Complimentary Continental breakfast. Microwaves in kitchenette units, no-smoking rooms. Cable TV. Pool. Hot tub, sauna. Laundry facilities. Business services. Airport shuttle. Pets allowed ($8 fee). | 210 rooms | 2050 Market St. | 775/786–2500 | fax 775/786–3884 | $39–$127 | AE, D, DC, MC, V.

Vagabond Inn. This motel at the south end of South Virginia Street is distinguished by its lack of a casino. Complimentary Continental breakfast. No-smoking rooms. Cable TV. Pool. Business services. Airport shuttle. Some pets allowed (fee). | 129 rooms | 3131 S. Virginia St. | 775/825–7134 | fax 775/825–3096 | www.vagabondinns.com | $50–$145 | AE, D, DC, MC, V.

STATELINE

★ **Harrah's.** The luxurious guest rooms here have private bars and two full bathrooms, each with a television and telephone. The 16th-floor Summit Restaurant is one of the best in the state. Lounge and showroom. 6 restaurants, bar, room service. No-smoking floors. Cable TV. Indoor pool. Barbershop, beauty salon, hot tub, massage. Exercise equipment. Business services. Pets allowed. | 532 rooms | U.S. 50 | 775/588–6611 or 800/648–3773 | fax 775/586–6607 | www.harrahstahoe.com | $169–$350 | AE, D, DC, MC, V.

TONOPAH

Best Western Hi Desert Inn. The most modern and most expensive motel in town, and one of the few with a pool. No-smoking rooms. Cable TV. Pool. Hot tub. Pets allowed. | 62 rooms | 320 Main St. (U.S. 95) | 775/482–3511 or 800/528–1234 | fax 775/482–3300 | $49–$65 | AE, D, DC, MC, V.

Silver Queen. The rooms at this downtown hotel are spacious and modestly priced, and you're in the heart of the historic mining town and within walking distance from the Convention Center. The staff is very friendly and will help guide you to the best local attractions. Restaurant, bar. No-smoking rooms. Cable TV. Pool. Pets allowed. | 85 rooms | 255 S. Main St. (U.S. 95) | 775/482–6291 | fax 775/482–3190 | $30–$40 | AE, D, DC, MC, V.

WINNEMUCCA

Best Western Gold Country Inn. The rooms are spacious here at the fanciest motel in town, and the most expensive. No-smoking rooms. Cable TV. Pool. Business services. Airport shuttle. Some pets allowed. | 71 rooms | 921 W. Winnemucca Blvd. | 775/623–6999 | fax 775/623–9190 | $75–$115 | AE, D, DC, MC, V.

Days Inn. Downtown, with modest rates, this motel is comfortable and predictable. No-smoking rooms. Cable TV. Pool. Pets allowed. | 50 rooms | 511 W. Winnemucca Blvd. | 775/623–3661 or 800/329–7466 | fax 775/623–4234 | $59–$69 | AE, D, DC, MC, V.

Red Lion Inn. This big motel is fronted by a mini-casino. the cutest little joint in town. Restaurant, bar. No-smoking rooms. Cable TV. Pool. Business services. Some pets allowed (fee). | 105 units | 741 W. Winnemucca Blvd. | 775/623–2565 or 800/633–6435 | fax 775/623–2527 | $79–$165 | AE, D, DC, MC, V.

Val-U Inn. This motel in the heart of downtown has modest rates and is one of the few with a sauna and steam room. Continental breakfast in lobby. No-smoking rooms. Cable TV. Pool. Sauna, steam room. Business services. Pets allowed (fee). | 80 rooms | 125 E. Winnemucca Blvd. | 775/623–5248 or 800/443–7777 | fax 775/623–4722 | $44–$75 | AE, D, DC, MC, V.

YERINGTON

Casino West. Considering the size of the town, this is a big motel. There's a casino across the street and bowling is one of the amenities. Restaurant, complimentary Continental breakfast. No-smoking rooms. Cable TV. Pool. Bowling. Pets allowed. | 79 rooms | 11 N. Main St. | 775/463–2481 or 800/227–4661 | fax 775/463–5733 | $40–$55 | AE, D, DC, MC, V.

New Hampshire

CENTER HARBOR

Meadows Lakeside Lodging. A motel on the shore of Lake Winnipesaukee. Picnic area. No room phones. Lake. Beach, dock, boating. Playground. Pets allowed (fee). | Rte. 25 03226 | 603/253–4347 | 39 rooms | $46–$119 | Closed Nov.–Apr. | AE, D, MC, V.

COLEBROOK

The Glen. This onetime fishing lodge, 29 mi north of Colebrook, on First Connecticut Lake still retains its outdoorsy, informal air. Now a B&B, the accommodations are rustic and simple with maple floors, antique chests, and individually decorated rooms. Cabins are well suited to families. Dining room, complimentary breakfast. Kitchenettes in some rooms, some refrigerators, no room phones, TV in common area. Lake. Dock, boating. Fishing. Ice-skating. Library. Pets allowed. | 77 The Glen Rd., Pittsburgh, 03592 | 603/538–6500 or 800/445–4536 | fax 603/538–7121 | 6 rooms, 10 cabins | $77–$96 | Closed mid-Oct.–mid-May | MAP | No credit cards.

Northern Comfort. Knotty-pine interiors and spacious well-maintained rooms in a hotel 1 mi south of Colebrook. No air-conditioning in some rooms, some kitchenettes, cable TV. Pool. Basketball. Playground. Pets allowed. | U.S. 3 03576 | 603/237–4440 | 19 rooms | $54–$72 | AE, D, MC, V.

CONCORD

Comfort Inn. Part of the chain that is close to downtown. Complimentary Continental breakfast. In-room data ports, some refrigerators, some in-room hot tubs, cable TV. Indoor pool. Hot tub, sauna. Business services. Free parking. Pets allowed (fee). | 71 Hall St. | 603/226–4100 or 800/228–5150 | fax 603/228–2106 | www.comfortinn.com | 100 rooms | $59–$130 | AE, D, DC, MC, V.

Holiday Inn. This modern member of the chain has clean rooms with standard furnishings. Restaurant, bar. In-room data ports, cable TV. Indoor pool. Hot tub, sauna. Exercise equipment. Laundry facilities. Business services. Free parking. Pets allowed. | 172 N. Main St., 03301 | 603/224–9534 | fax 603/224–8266 | hotelconc@aol.com | www.holidayinn. com/concordnh | 122 rooms | $105 | AE, D, DC, MC, V.

CONWAY

Albert B. Lester Memorial Hostel. If you're on a budget or are just looking for an interesting stay, this old farmhouse has bunkhouse dorms for up to 45 people and a community kitchen. Private rooms are available. Picnic area, complimentary Continental breakfast. No smoking, no room phones, TV in common area. Volleyball. Cross-country skiing. Pets allowed (fee). | 36 Washington St., Conway, 03818 | 603/447–1001 or 800/909–4776 | fax 603/447–1001 | hiconway@nxi.com | www.angel.net/~hostel | 34 bunks, 4 private rooms | $18 bunks, $45 private rooms | MC, V.

DIXVILLE NOTCH

Magalloway River Inn. This early 1800s outpost is right in the heart of moose country. Rooms are modest and simple, and reflect well the overall mood of the surroundings. The common areas are fixed with plants, knickknacks, and a warm, welcoming air. The larger rooms sleep up to four adults and are suitable for families. Complimentary breakfast. No air-conditioning, no smoking, no room phones, TV in common area. Hiking. Fishing. Cross-country skiing, snowmobiling. Pets allowed (no fee). | Rte. 16, Errol, 03579 | 603/482–9883 | www.magriverinn.com | 6 rooms | $65 | MC, V.

DURHAM

Hickory Pond Inn and Golf Course. A comfortable inn with a 9-hole golf course on the premises. Rooms are individually decorated. Complimentary Continental breakfast. No smoking, cable TV, in-room VCRs available. Golf. Cross-country skiing. Pets allowed. | 1 Stage-

MISS FELINE AMERICA

Your pussycat isn't pedigreed? No matter. She doesn't have to be a genuine Abyssinian or American bobtail, or even a Egyptian Mau or Turkish Van to take a prize at one of scores of cat shows held by local cat clubs, which are sponsored by the Cat Fanciers' Association (CFA), the International Cat Association (TICA), and the American Cat Fanciers' Association (ACFA), among other feline registries. Cat shows can be a rewarding experience for both of you. You get the chance to meet and mingle with hundreds of other cat-lovers and their furry, purry friends. And your pride-and-joy will have the chance to prance around and be admired by one and all. Almost any cat can be shown, whether in a breed class or in the household pet class. Your cat will be judged on her uniqueness, her stellar looks, her markings, and her sweet disposition. The only requirements are that she be in good health and have a friendly personality. To help her get acclimated to the strange smells, noises, and confusion in the show hall, bring familiar treats or toys. For more information, see the registries' Web sites at www.cfainc.org, www.tica.org, and www.acfacat.com. Magazines about cats, like *Cat Fancy* and *Cats*, also list scheduled shows.

coach Rd. | 603/659–2227 or 800/658–0065 | fax 603/659–7910 | www.hickorypond.com | 18 rooms (4 with shared bath) | $69–$99 | AE, MC, V.

ENFIELD

Mary Keane House. The views of Lake Mascoma and the adjoining 1,200 acres of field and woodlands add to this pleasant 1929 Victorian Inn with antique furnishings that is next door to the Shaker Museum. Complimentary breakfast. Some kitchenettes, some refrigerators, no smoking, cable TV, no room phones. Lake. Hiking, volleyball, beach, dock, boating. Fishing. Ice-skating. Pets allowed (fee). | 93 Chosen Vale La., 03748 | 603/632–4241 or 888/239–2153 | mary.keane.house@valley.net | www.marykeanehouse.com | 2 room, 2 suites | $95–$145 | AE, D, MC, V.

FRANCONIA

Horse & Hound. A cozy country inn not far from Cannon Mt. Restaurant, complimentary breakfast. No air-conditioning, no TV, TV in common area. Pets allowed (fee). | 205 Wells Rd. | 603/823–5501 or 800/450–5501 | 10 rooms (2 with shared bath) | $86 | Closed Apr. and Nov. | AE, D, DC, MC, V.

GORHAM

Gorham Motor Inn. Modern motel. Bar. Some refrigerators, cable TV. Pool. Some pets allowed (fee). | 324 Main St. | 603/466–3381 or 800/445–0913 | 39 rooms | $40–$86 | AE, D, MC, V.

Royalty Inn. A large, family-owned motor inn. Restaurant, bar. Some refrigerators, cable TV, in-room VCRs. 2 pools (1 indoor). Hot tub, sauna. Health club. Video games. Laundry facilities. Business services. Pets allowed (fee). | 130 Main St. | 603/466–3312 or 800/437–3529 | fax 603/466–5802 | innkeeper@royaltyinn.com | www.royaltyinn.com | 90 rooms | $58–$78 | AE, D, DC, MC, V.

Top Notch Motor Inn. Spacious motel-style accommodations in a clean, friendly, setting. There are larger rooms for families or groups. Refrigerators, cable TV. Outdoor pool. Hot tub. Laundry facilities. Pets allowed (deposit). | 265 Main St., (Rte. 16) 03581 | 603/466–5496 | www.top–notch.com | 36 rooms | $44–$89 | Closed mid-Oct.–mid.-May | MC, V.

HAMPTON

Hampton Falls Inn. A modern motel whose individually decorated rooms have views of the neighboring farmland from private balconies. Restaurant. In-room data ports, microwaves, refrigerators. Indoor pool. Hot tub. Video games. Laundry facilities. Business services. Pets allowed (free). | 11 Lafayette Rd., (U.S. 1), Hampton Falls, 03844 | 603/926–9545 or 800/356–1729 | www.hamptonfallsinn.com | 33 rooms, 15 suites | $99–$169 | AE, D, DC, MC, V.

HANOVER

Hanover Inn at Dartmouth College. This late-18th-century redbrick building feels very much a part of the college, which owns it. Restaurant, bar. Room service, cable TV, some in-room VCRs. Sauna. Driving range, putting green. Exercise equipment. Business services. Airport shuttle, parking (fee). Pets allowed. | Main and Wheelock Sts. | 603/643–4300 or 800/443–7024 | fax 603/646–3744 | hanover.inn@dartmouth.edu | www.dartmouth.edu/inn | 92 rooms, 22 suites | $250–$310 | AE, D, DC, MC, V.

INTERVALE

Swiss Chalets Village Inn. There's an alpine motif to this hostelry. Picnic area, complimentary Continental breakfast. Refrigerators, no smoking, some in-room hot tubs, cable TV, in-room VCRs (and movies). Pool. 2 hot tubs (1 outdoor). Video games. Pets allowed (fee). | Rte. 16A, 2½ mi north of North Conway Scenic Vista | 603/356–2232 or 800/831–2727 |

stay@swisschaletsvillage.com | www.swisschaletsvillage.com | 42 rooms | $49–$169 | AE, D, MC, V.

JACKSON

Dana Place Inn. A late-1800s colonial country inn at the base of Mt. Washington. The 300 acres are surrounded by the White Mountain National Forest and border the Ellis River. Rooms are individually designed and many have private patios and views of the gardens, river, or Presidential Range. Restaurant, bar, picnic area, complimentary breakfast. No smoking. Indoor pool. Hot tub. 2 tennis courts. Hiking. Fishing. Cross-country skiing. Library. Pets allowed. | Rte. 16 03846 | 603/383–6822 or 800/537–9276 | fax 603/383–6022 | contact@danaplace.com | www.danaplace.com | 35 rooms | $155–$225 | MAP | AE, D, DC, MC, V.

JAFFREY

Woodbound Inn. Open to the public since 1892 this full-service, four-season resort on 165 acres on Lake Contoocook has bed-and-breakfast, hotel-style, or cabin accommodations. Cabins are fully furnished and can sleep four to six adults and have fireplaces or woodstoves. Picnic area. Cable TV. Lake. 9-hole golf course, tennis. Hiking, volleyball, beach, water sports, boating. Fishing. Cross-country skiing. Some pets allowed. | 62 Woodbound Rd., Rindge, 03461 | 603/532–8341 or 800/688–7770 | fax 603/532–8341 | info@woodboundinn.com | www.woodboundinn.com | 36 rooms, 10 cabins | $50–$70 | AE, MC, V.

KEENE

Best Western Sovereign Hotel. A standard member of the chain with quiet, comfortable rooms. Restaurant, bar with entertainment, picnic area, complimentary breakfast. In-room data ports, some microwaves, some refrigerators, cable TV. Indoor pool. Video games. Business services. Pets allowed. | 401 Winchester St. | 603/357–3038 | fax 603/357–4776 | 131 rooms | $59–$140 | AE, D, DC, MC, V.

LITTLETON

Eastgate Motor Inn. A simple motel with large modern rooms just off I–93 Exit 41. Restaurant, bar, complimentary Continental breakfast. Cable TV. Pool, wading pool. Playground. Business services. Pets allowed. | 335 Cottage St. | 603/444–3971 | fax 603/444–3971 | www.eastgatemotorinn.com | 55 rooms | $50–$70 | AE, D, DC, MC, V.

LYME

Loch Lyme Lodge. Summer cabins flank the main lodge built in 1784 on 120 wooded acres with a pond. Cabins are open Memorial Day to Labor Day. Complimentary breakfast. No air-conditioning, some kitchenettes, some refrigerators, no room phones, no TV. Beach, boating. Playground. Pets allowed. | 70 Orford Rd. | 603/795–2141 or 800/423–2141 | www.dartbook.com | 4 rooms (with shared baths), 24 cabins | $68, $90 cabins | No credit cards.

MANCHESTER

Comfort Inn & Conference Center. A modern five-story hotel in downtown within walking distance to attractions. Complimentary Continental breakfast. In-room data ports, some refrigerators, cable TV. Indoor pool. Saunas. Exercise equipment. Laundry facilities. Business services. Airport shuttle. Pets allowed. | 298 Queen City Ave., 03102 | 800/228–5150 | 603/668–2600 | www.hotelchoice.com | 104 rooms | $65–$126 | AE, D, DC, MC, V.

Econo Lodge. A chain motel in a converted mill building overlooking the Merrimack River. Some microwaves, refrigerators, cable TV. Laundry facilities. Business services. Pets allowed (fee). | 75 W. Hancock St., 03102 | 603/624–0111 or 800/553–2666 | fax 603/623–0268 | 120 rooms | $40–$80 | AE, D, DC, MC, V.

MERRIMACK

Merrimack Days Inn. A simple, two-story member of the chain with standard furnishings. In-room data ports, cable TV, room phones. Laundry facilities. Business services. Pets allowed. | 242 Daniel Webster Hwy., 03054 | 603/429–4600 or 800/544–8313 (reservations) | fax 603/424–3804 | www.daysinn.com | 69 rooms | $55–$99 | AE, D, DC, MC, V.

Residence Inn by Marriott. A very comfortable all-suite hotel. Complimentary Continental breakfast. In-room data ports, kitchenettes, cable TV. Pool. Hot tub. Laundry facilities. Business services. Free parking. Pets allowed (fee). | 246 Daniel Webster Hwy., (Rte. 3) | 603/424–8100 or 800/331–3131 | fax 603/424–3128 | www.residenceinn.com/ashmh | 129 suites | $105–$155 | AE, D, DC, MC, V.

NASHUA

Holiday Inn. A nicely landscaped, standard member of the chain. Restaurant, bar with entertainment. Some kitchenettes, room service, cable TV. Pool. Exercise equipment. Laundry facilities. Business services. Free parking. Pets allowed. | 9 Northeastern Blvd., 03062 | 603/888–1551 | fax 603/888–7193 | www.holidayinn.com | 215 rooms, 34 suites | $69–$109, $109–$139 suites | AE, D, DC, MC, V.

Marriott. Chandeliers and Asian art add some panache to this large hotel. Restaurant, bar. In-room data ports, some refrigerators, room service, cable TV. Indoor pool. Hot tub. Health club. Playground. Business services. Pets allowed. | 2200 Southwood Dr., 03063 | 603/880–9100 or 800/228–9290 | fax 603/886–9489 | www.marriott.com | 245 rooms | $89–$119 | AE, D, DC, MC, V.

Red Roof Inn. A part of the chain that is located 50 ft off Highway 3. Picnic area. In-room data ports, cable TV. Laundry facilities. Business services. Pets allowed. | 77 Spit Brook Rd., 03060 | 603/888–1893 or 800/733–7663 | fax 603/888–5889 | 115 rooms | $49–$80 | AE, D, DC, MC, V.

NORTH CONWAY

Oxen Yoke Inn. Choose from motel, B&B, or cottage accommodations at this quiet colonial house and barn. Guests have access to all facilities at the Eastern Slope Inn. Complimentary breakfast. Some kitchenettes, some refrigerators, no smoking, some in-room hot tubs, cable TV. Video games. Library. Children's programs, playground. Pets allowed. | Kearsage St. 03860 | 603/356–6321 or 800/258–4706 | www.easternslopeinn.com | 15 rooms, 5 cottages | $80–$177 | AE, D, MC, V.

Stonehurst Manor. A stunning 1876 Victorian mansion inn 1.2 mi north of Conway catering to a mixed crowd of younger adventure/sports oriented travelers and romantic getaway seekers. Rooms are elegant and warm, with colonial furnishings and finished wood trim. Complimentary breakfast. Cable TV. Outdoor pool. Hot tub. Tennis. Hiking. Cross-country skiing. Pets allowed (fee). | Rte. 16 03860 | 603/356–3113 or 800/525–9100 | fax 603/356–3217 | smanor@aol.com | www.stonehurstmanor.com | 24 rooms (2 with shared bath) | $80–$140 | MAP | AE, MC, V.

PETERBOROUGH

Inn at Crotched Mountain. A cozy 1822 colonial farmhouse, 15 mi northeast of Peterborough, on 65 acres with nine fireplaces and views of the Piscatagoug Valley. Rooms are comfortable and filled with antiques or colonial reproductions; some have fireplaces. Restaurant, bar. Complimentary breakfast. No smoking, no room phones, TV in common area. Outdoor pool. Tennis. Hiking. Ice-skating. Cross-country skiing. Pets allowed. | 534 Mountain Rd., Francestown, 03043 | 603/588–6840 | fax 603/588–6623 | perry-inncm@

conknet.com | 13 rooms (5 with shared bath) | $100–$120 | Closed Apr. and Nov. | No credit cards.

PLYMOUTH

Susse Chalet. A member of the chain, 1 mi north of Portsmouth. Picnic area, complimentary Continental breakfast. In-room data ports, some refrigerators, cable TV, some in-room VCRs. Pool. Laundry facilities. Business services. Pets allowed. | U.S. 3 I–93 Exit 26 | 603/536–2330 | fax 603/536–2686 | 38 rooms | $62–$80 | AE, D, DC, MC, V.

PORTSMOUTH

Meadowbrook Inn. A sprawling, three-building complex with clean, quiet, modest rooms right off the highway. Complimentary Continental breakfast, restaurant, bar. Some microwaves, some refrigerators, cable TV. Outdoor pool. Laundry facilities. Pets allowed (no fee). | 549 Hwy. 1 Bypass, 03801 | 603/436–2700 or 800/370–2727 | fax 603/433–2700 | info@meadowbrookinn.com | www.meadowbrookinn.com | 122 rooms | $60–$89 | AE, D, MC, V.

SUGAR HILL

Hilltop Inn. Sparkling white turn-of-the-20th-century farmhouse filled with hand-pieced quilts and vintage furniture. Complimentary breakfast. No air-conditioning, room service, no smoking, no room phones, cable TV in common area. Pets allowed (fee). | Main St. (Rte. 117) | 603/823–5695 or 800/770–5695 | fax 603/823–5518 | aaa@hilltopinn.com | www.hilltopinn.com | 5 rooms, 1 cottage | $70–$150, $200–$250 cottage | D, MC, V.

Homestead Inn. Family antiques and heirlooms spanning seven generations fill this 1802 inn, one of the oldest family operated inns in America. Founded by Sugar Hill's first perma- nent settlers and constructed with material gathered from the property, including hand-hewn beams and hardwood floors, this inn gives an authentic look at early days of New England innkeeping. Rooms are filled with crafts and quilts and have views of the White Mountains. A two-bedroom 1917 stone-and-log chalet has a fireplace and kitchen and is suitable for families. Complimentary breakfast. No smoking, no room phones, TV in common area. Hiking. Cross-country skiing. Pets allowed. | 10 Sunset Hill Rd., 03585 | 603/823–5564 or 800/823–5564 | fax 603/823–9599 | homestead@together.net | www.thehomestead1802.com | 19 rooms (10 with shared bath), 1 cottage | $70–$125 | AE, D, MC, V.

SUNAPEE

Best Western Sunapee Lake Lodge. A standard, modern member of the chain, four minutes' walk from Mt. Sunapee State Park and ¼ mi from the Mt. Sunapee Ski area on Route 103. Restaurant, bar, complimentary Continental breakfast. In-room data ports, some microwaves, some refrigerators, cable TV. Indoor pool. Exercise equipment, volleyball. Ice- skating. Tobogganing. Laundry facilities. Business services. Pets allowed. | 1403 Rte. 103, 03255 | 603/763–2010 or 800/606–5253 | fax 603/763–3314 | info@sunapeelakelodge.com | www.sunapeelakelodge.com | 53 rooms, 2 suites | $99–$229 | AE, D, DC MC, V.

Burkehaven Motel. This motel is within walking distance of Sunapee Harbor and has rooms overlooking Mt. Sunapee. Some refrigerators. Pool. Hot tub. Tennis. Business services. Pets allowed. | 179 Burkehaven Hill Rd. | 603/763–2788 or 800/567–2788 | fax 603/763–9065 | www.burkehavenatsunapee.com | 10 rooms (all with showers only) | $74–$84 | AE, D, MC, V.

TAMWORTH

Chocorua Camping Village and Wabanaki Lodge. A 158-acre, full-service, lakeside property with camping sites and cottage accommodations. Primitive and full hookups are avail- able for RVs. The cottages are private, simple, and electricity-free. They also have outdoor toilets and sleep from four to eight adults. No vehicles are allowed in the cottage area, but the golf-cart shuttle will transport you and your bags. There is a rec hall, movie theater, and general store on the premise. Picnic area. No air-conditioning, no room phones, TV in common area. Pond. Hiking, beach, dock, boating. Fishing. Video games. Children's programs, laundry facilities. Pets allowed. | 893 White Mountain Hwy., (Rte. 16) | 603/323–8536 or 888/237–8642 | info@chocoruacamping.com | www.chocoruacamping.com | 175 sites, 6 cabins | $24–$34 camping, $69–$98 cottages | Closed Nov.–Apr. | MC, V.

WOLFEBORO

Museum Lodges. Private, fully equipped and furnished cottages on Lake Winnepesaukee in a relaxed, no-frills setting. Picnic area. No air-conditioning, kitchenettes, refrigerators, no room phones, no TV. Lake. Beach, dock, water sports, boating. Fishing. Ice-skating. Pets allowed (seasonally). | 32 Governor Wentworth Hwy. (Route 109), 03894 | 603/569–1551 | rsmuseum@worldpath.net | www.museumlodges.com | 10 cottages | $690–$940 wk | Closed mid-Oct.–mid-May | No credit cards.

New Jersey

ASBURY PARK

Berkeley-Carteret. This hotel, an elegant resort destination in the 1920s, '30s and '40s, is a reminder of Asbury Park in its heyday. It received a $20 million renovation in 1985 and its enviable location, right on the water, provides spectacular views from many rooms. Other views however, are not as appealing, such as the ones of stretches of abandoned buildings south of the hotel. The hotel has an interesting past, including having at one time been owned by the Mararishi Mahesh Yogi, who wanted to turn it into a transcendental meditation center (Asbury Park prevented this). The current owner has plans to restore it to its former grandeur, and help rejuvenate Asbury Park in the process. Restaurant, bar, complimentary Continental breakfast. Cable TV. Pool. Tennis court. Health club. Laundry service. Some pets allowed. | 1401 Ocean Ave. 07712 | 732/776–6700 or 800/776–6011 | fax 732/776–9546 | 246 rooms, 4 suites | $129–$159 rooms; $179–$219 suites | AE, D, DC, MC, V.

ATLANTIC CITY

Red Carpet Inn. Off the Garden State Parkway Exit 40, this two-story stucco motel is 6 mi from Atlantic City. Rooms are decorated with light, multicolored wallpaper and have views of the landscaped grounds. Complimentary Continental breakfast. Some microwaves, some refrigerators, some in-room hot tubs, cable TV, some in-room VCRs. Some pets allowed. | 206 E. White Horse Pkwy., Absecon, 08201 | 609/652–3322 | fax 609/652–9647 | 22 rooms | $30–$75 | AE, D, M, V.

BERNARDSVILLE

Somerset Hills. Nestled in the Watchung Mountains near the crossroads of historical Liberty Corner, 8 mi south of Bernardsville, this Colonial-style building has suites as well as regular rooms, and all rooms on the second floor have balconies overlooking a wildlife preserve. Restaurant, bar. In-room data ports, some kitchenettes, some microwaves, some in-room hot tubs, cable TV. Pool. Exercise equipment. Business services. Pets allowed. | 200 Liberty Corner Rd., Warren 07059 | 908/647–6700 or 800/688–0700 | fax 908/647–8053 | shhotel@aol.com | www.shh.com | 108 rooms, 3 suites | $135–$150; $150–$375 suites | AE, DC, MC, V.

BORDENTOWN

Days Inn. This two-story chain is 15 minutes from Great Adventure theme park. It prides itself on being family friendly and efficient. Restaurant, bar (with entertainment). Some refrigerators, cable TV. Pool. Laundry facilities. Business services. Pets allowed. | 1073 U.S. 206 | 609/298–6100 | fax 609/298–7509 | www.daysinn.com | 131 rooms | $45–$95 | AE, D, DC, MC, V.

BURLINGTON

Best Western Burlington Inn. You'll enjoy waking up to complimentary coffee and donuts in your room at this Best Western, 5 mi southeast of Burlington. Rooms are large, and there's a fireplace in the lobby. Restaurant, complimentary Continental breakfast. Some refrigerators, some in-room data ports, cable TV. Exercise room. Business services. Some pets allowed. | 2020 Rte. 541, Mt. Holly 08060 | 609/261–3800 or 800/780–7234 | fax 609/267–0958 | www.bestwestern.com | 64 rooms | $97–$111 | AE, D, DC, MC, V.

CAPE MAY

Marquis De Lafayette. There are two buildings that make up this property: a six-story building with regular hotel rooms and a three-story building with suites. The six-story structure houses the Pelican Club restaurant on the top floor. All rooms have ocean views. Restaurant, bar (with entertainment), complimentary breakfast. Some kitchenettes, cable TV. Pool. Sauna. Laundry facilities. Business services. Some pets allowed (fee). | 501 Beach Dr. | 609/884–3500 or 800/257–0432 | fax 609/884–3871 | 67 rooms, 6 suites | $129–$249; $219–$389 suites | AE, D, DC, MC, V.

CHERRY HILL

Hampton Inn. This four-story hotel is 15 mi from the Philadelphia International Airport and 9 mi from the city itself. Atlantic City and Six Flags Great Adventure are 40 mi and 25 mi away respectively. It's in a semi-residential area, about 5 mi south of Cherry Hill. Complimentary Continental breakfast. In-room data ports, cable TV. Pool. Business services. Pets allowed. | 121 Laurel Oak Rd. Voorhees, 08043 | 856/346–4500 | fax 856/346–2402 | 122 rooms | $99 | AE, D, DC, MC, V.

Holiday Inn. Take advantage of the hotel's facilities, and from May through September, consider picking a horse at the Garden State Race Track across the highway. This six-story hotel is in a commercial area. Restaurant, bar, room service. In-room data ports, cable TV. 2 pools, wading pool. Exercise equipment. Laundry facilities. Business services. Pets allowed. | Rte. 70 and Sayer Ave. 08002 | 856/663–5300 | fax 856/662–2913 | www.basshotels.com/holiday-inn | 186 rooms | $119 | AE, D, DC, MC, V.

Residence Inn by Marriott. This hotel was designed for extended business travel, but it is equally suited for tourists. Rooms are spacious and comfortable, with contemporary furnishings in subdued colors. Some rooms have fireplaces. You can get dinner delivered from local restaurants. Complimentary Continental breakfast. In-room data ports, kitchenettes, cable TV. Laundry facilities, laundry service. Business services. Pets allowed (fee). | 1821 Old Cuthbert Rd. 08034 | 609/429–6111 or 800/331–3131 | fax 856/429–0345 | www.marriott.com | 96 suites | $118–$179 | AE, D, DC, MC, V.

CLIFTON

Howard Johnson. This four-story chain hotel's location on Route 3 allows for convenient access to the New Jersey Turnpike and the Garden State Parkway. There's an IHOP on the premises, with a "grab and go" breakfast. Restaurant, bar, complimentary Continental breakfast. In-room data ports, cable TV. Pool. Business services. Some pets allowed. | 680 Rte. 3 W 07014 | 973/471–3800 | fax 973/471–2125 | www.hojo.com | 116 rooms | $89–$139 | AE, D, DC, MC, V.

ENGLEWOOD

Radisson Hotel Englewood. This full-service hotel is convenient to New York City, abundant shopping, and major highways. The rooms are spacious and suites are available. It's geared toward business travelers and tourists who want easy access to the city for less money than it would cost to stay there. In-room hot tubs. Pool. Health club. Business services, airport shuttle. Some pets allowed. | 401 Van Brunt St. 07631 | 201/871–2020 or 800/333–3333 | fax 201/871–7116 | www.radisson.com | 194 rooms | $119–$220 | AE, MC, D, DC, V.

FRENCHTOWN

Blackwell's National Hotel. Built in 1851, this is one of the oldest hotels in the country. Capitalizing on its long history, the owners have outfitted all the rooms with antique double beds and other period treasures. Downstairs, there's a cozy pub with a fireplace, the Rath Skeller. The upstairs restaurant and a bar, the Gibson, are open late. 2 restaurants. Cable TV. Pets allowed. | 31 Race St. 08825 | 908/996–4871 | www.frenchtown.com | 5 rooms | $50–$125 | AE, D, DC, MC, V.

HIGHTSTOWN

Ramada Inn. This four-story building with spacious rooms is just south of Hightstown, near a shopping mall. It's about 15 minutes by car to Princeton. Bar. Cable TV. Pool. Sauna. Exercise equipment. Laundry facilities. Business services. Pets allowed. | 399 Monmouth St., East Windsor | 609/448–7000 | fax 609/443–6227 | www.ramada.com | 200 rooms | $72–$129 | AE, D, DC, MC, V.

Town House. This reasonably-priced hotel, near New York City train service, caters to business travelers. Restaurant, bar (with entertainment), complimentary Continental breakfast. In-room data ports, refrigerators, some in-room hot tubs, cable TV. Pool, wading pool. Pets allowed. | 351 Franklin St. | 609/448–2400 or 800/922–0622 | fax 609/443–0395 | 104 rooms, 20 suites | $69–$99, $69–$119 suites | AE, D, DC, MC, V.

HOLMDEL

Wellesley Inn. This chain hotel is just 3 mi from the beach, Keansburg Amusement Park, and Keyport's Antique District. It's right across the Garden State Parkway from Holmdel, in the town of Hazlet. Complimentary Continental breakfast. Refrigerators, cable TV. Business services. Some pets allowed (fee). | 3215 Rte. 35, Hazlet 07730 | 732/888–2800 | fax 732/888–2902 | 89 rooms | $159 | AE, D, DC, MC, V.

HOPE

The Inn At Mill Race Pond. This unusual inn is actually a converted 18th century grist mill. It has 17 rooms and a number of nice amenities, such as a video and book library for guests to use free of charge. The rooms have queen-size beds, and are decorated in early-American Shaker style, with period antiques lending to their charm. Restaurant, complimentary breakfast. In-room data ports. Pond. Tennis. Library. Pets allowed. No smoking. | 113 Johnsonburg Road, Hope 07844 | 908/459–4884 or 800/746–6467 | millrace@epix.net | www.innatmillracepond.com | 17 rooms | $120–$170 | AE, D, DC, MC, V.

LAKEWOOD

Best Western Leisure Inn. This two-story hotel is 15 minutes by car from the beach, 20 minutes from two malls, and 30 minutes from Six Flags Great Adventure Theme Park. Locals describe it as a "friendly place." Restaurant, bar. In-room data ports, cable TV. Pool. Laundry facilities. Business services. Pets allowed. | 1600 Rte. 70 | 732/367–0900 | fax 732/370–4928 | 105 rooms | $95–$135 | AE, D, DC, MC, V.

LONG BEACH ISLAND

Engleside Inn. Pastel-color rooms have ocean views and private balconies at this beach-front inn, close to shops and restaurants. Some rooms have whirlpools and/or a heart-shape tub. Restaurant, bar. Some kitchenettes, refrigerators, cable TV, in-room VCRs (and movies). Pool. Business services. Some pets allowed. | 30 Engleside Ave., Beach Haven | 609/492–1251 or 800/762–2214 | fax 609/492–9175 | www.engleside.com | 72 rooms | $170–$328 | AE, D, DC, MC, V.

LYNDHURST

Novotel. Outlet shopping at the Meadowlands is close to this hotel, as is Giants Stadium and the Meadowlands racetrack. Or, catch a bus that stops at the corner of the hotel and take a 15-minute ride to New York City. Restaurant, bar (with entertainment). In-room data ports, refrigerators, cable TV. Pool. Hot tub, massage. Exercise equipment. Laundry facilities. Business services. Some pets allowed. | 1 Polito Ave. | 201/896–6666 or 800/668–6735 | meadmail@aol.com | 219 rooms | $109–$119 | AE, D, DC, MC, V.

MAHWAH

Sheraton Crossroads. A glass building with corporate offices and guest rooms make up this modern business-oriented hotel. Rooms are spacious, and some have mountain views. Others overlook the landscaped grounds, which include gardens, a fountain, and a fishpond. The Illusions nightclub plays disco favorites every night but Sunday. 2 restaurants, bar (with entertainment). Refrigerators, cable TV. Pool. Tennis. Exercise equipment. Shops. Business services. Some pets allowed. | Crossroads Corporate Center, Rte. 17 N 07495 | 201/529–1660 | fax 201/529–4709 | 228 rooms | $179–$215 | AE, D, DC, MC, V.

MATAWAN

Wellesley Inn. There are movie theaters, a water park, several amusement parks, and shopping near this well-situated three-story chain hotel, just east of Matawan. Complimentary Continental breakfast. Refrigerators, cable TV. Business services. Some pets allowed (fee). | 3215 Rte. 35, Hazlet 07730 | 732/888–2800 | fax 732/888–2902 | 89 rooms | $159 | AE, D, DC, MC, V.

MILLBURN

Holiday Inn Springfield. This four-story hotel is 4 mi from Millburn, 4 mi from Kean College and 5 mi from the Paper Mill Playhouse, an Equity Company with elaborately staged plays and musicals. Restaurant, bar. In-room data ports, cable TV. Pool. Exercise room. Laundry service. Business services. Pets (cats and dogs) allowed. | 304 Rte. 22 W, Springfield 07081 | 973/376–9400 or 800/465–4329 | fax 973/376–9534 | www.basshotels.com/holiday-inn | 195 rooms | $110–$112 | AE, MC, V.

MONTVALE

Marriott–Park Ridge. Renovated in 2000, this four-story Marriott less than 2 mi from Montvale has an atrium lobby and modern rooms. Its extensive grounds include a small lake. Restaurant. In-room data ports, cable TV. Pool. Hot tub. Exercise equipment. Business services. Some pets allowed. | 300 Brae Blvd., Park Ridge 07656 | 201/307–0800 | fax 201/307–0859 | www.marriott.com | 289 rooms | $99–$209 | AE, D, DC, MC, V.

MOUNT HOLLY

Best Western Burlington Inn. Located off the New Jersey Turnpike, this motel is between Mt. Holly and Burlington. It is 20 minutes by car from Six Flags Great Adventure Theme Park. There are meeting facilities and a comfortable lobby with a fireplace where coffee and donuts are served in the mornings. Restaurant. Cable TV. Exercise room. Some pets

allowed. | 2020 Rte. 541 08060 | 609/261–3800 or 800/780–7234 | fax 609/267–958 |
www.bestwestern.com | 61 rooms | $97–$111 | AE, D, DC, MC, V.

MOUNT LAUREL

Howard Johnson. This HoJos is right off the turnpike, near several fast-food restaurants.
Restaurant, bar. Cable TV. Pool. Sauna. Playground. Business services. Pets allowed. | Rte.
541 | 609/267–6550 | fax 609/267–2575 | 90 rooms | $75–$85 | AE, D, DC, MC, V.

NEW BRUNSWICK

Wellesley Inn. This three-story hotel is 10 minutes from Rutgers. There's a landscaped
approach to the hotel, with a fountain. Complimentary Continental breakfast. In-room
data ports, cable TV. Pets allowed. | 831 Rte. 1 08817 | 732/287–0171 or 800/444–8888 | fax
732/287–8364 | www.wellesleyinnandsuites.com | 100 rooms | $70 | AE, D, DC, MC, V.

NEWARK

Hilton Gateway. This modern hotel is connected to the PATH train, which takes visitors
to Manhattan in a matter of minutes. Suites have a wet bar and provide bathrobes, and
there's a nice outdoor pool. Restaurant, bar, room service. Cable TV. Pool. Exercise equip-
ment. Shops. Business services, airport shuttle. Some pets allowed. | Gateway Center,
Raymond Blvd. 07102 | 973/622–5000 | fax 973/824–2188 | www.hilton.com | 253 rooms |
$169–$249 | AE, D, DC, MC, V.

PARAMUS

Radisson. The Paramus Park Mall is directly behind this modern two-story hotel, and Sports-
world (with rides and games) is 10 minutes away by car. The hotel was renovated in 2000,
and the rooms have contemporary, streamlined furnishings in neutral colors. Restaurant, bar, room service. In-room data ports, refrigerators, cable TV. Laundry facilities.
Business services. Some pets allowed. | 601 From Rd. 07652 | 201/262–6900 | fax 201/262–
4955 | www.radisson.com | 119 rooms | $89–$169 | AE, D, DC, MC, V.

PARSIPPANY

Days Inn. Located at the junction of Interstates 80 and 287, this chain hotel is close to
area businesses as well as shopping. It was renovated in 1999 and has antique-style furnish-
ings. Cable TV. Laundry service. Pets allowed (fee). | 3159 Rte. 46 E 07054 | 973/335–0200
or 800/544–8313 | fax 973/263–3094 | 119 rooms | $69–$149 | AE, D, DC, MC, V.

Hilton. This huge Hilton has a well-tended front area with a fountain, a massive Grand
Ballroom, and a full business center. Restaurant, bar (with entertainment), room service.
In-room data ports, refrigerators (in suites), cable TV. Pool. Hot tub. Tennis. Exercise equip-
ment. Playground. Business services, airport shuttle. Some pets allowed. | 1 Hilton Ct. 07054
| 973/267–7373 | fax 973/984–6853 | www.hilton.com | 508 rooms, 5 suites | $89–$119
rooms; $109–$395 suites | AE, D, DC, MC, V.

Ramada Inn. This two-story hotel was built in 1970 and renovated in 1996. In Parsippany's
business district, it is close to all major highways, and adjacent to a 22,000-square-ft.
health club. There's also a poolside grill. In-room data ports, cable TV. Pool. Laundry
service. Pets allowed. | 949 Rte. 46 E 07054 | 973/263–0404 or 888/298–2054 | fax 973/
263–4057 | www.ramada.com | 72 rooms | $80–$105 | AE, D, DC, V.

PLAINFIELD

Holiday Inn. This three-story hotel in the business district of South Plainfield is 40
minutes by car from New York City and 15 minutes from shopping and movies at the
Menlo Park Mall. Restaurant, room service. In-room data ports, refrigerators, cable TV.
Pool. Hot tub. Exercise equipment. Laundry facilities. Business services. Some pets allowed.

| 4701 Stelton Rd., South Plainfield 07080 | 908/753–5500 | fax 908/753–5500 ext. 620 | 17 rooms | $69–$114 | AE, D, DC, MC, V.

Pillars Bed & Breakfast. This private and elegant Victorian mansion with stained-glass windows and fireplaces is surrounded by gardens. Large, luxurious suites have antique furnishings, canopy beds, and Stickley furniture. Other amenities include terry-cloth robes, turn-down service, and complimentary evening sherry. Complimentary breakfast. In-room data ports, cable TV, in-room VCRs. Some pets allowed. No kids 2yrs.–12yrs. No smoking. | 922 Central Ave. 07060 | 908/753–0922 or 888/–PILLARS | pillars2@juno.com | www.pillars2.com | 7 suites | $99–$165 | AE, MC, V.

PRINCETON

Novotel. You'll find this chain hotel in a corporate park overlooking woods, with a bright, remodeled lobby and café. Rooms were renovated in 2000. Restaurant, bar, room service. In-room data ports, cable TV. Pool, hot tub. Exercise equipment. Laundry facilities. Business services. Some pets allowed. | 100 Independence Way 08540 | 609/520–1200 | fax 609/520–0594 | 180 rooms | $69–$169 | AE, D, DC, MC, V.

Peacock Inn. Each room in this 1775 building, just three blocks from the Princeton University campus, is unique. All rooms have fireplaces and are done in period antiques. Complimentary breakfast. Cable TV. Business services. Pets allowed (fee). | 20 Bayard La. 08540 | 609/924–1707 | fax 609/924–0788 | http://peacockinn.tripod.com | 17 rooms (7 with shared bath) | $145–$165 | AE, MC, V.

Residence Inn by Marriott. Rent either a studio or bi-level suite, with a kitchen and a living area. Some have fireplaces and two bathrooms. Picnic area, complimentary Continental breakfast. Kitchenettes, microwaves, cable TV. Pool. Hot tub. Laundry facilities. Business services. Some pets allowed (fee). | 4225 U.S. 1 08543 | 732/329–9600 | fax 732/329–8422 | residenceinn.com/ttnpr | 208 suites | $79–$194 | AE, D, DC, MC, V.

RAMSEY

Best Western: The Inn at Ramsey. This hotel is near several Fortune 500 companies and adjacent to a shopping center and a multiplex cinema. Golf is available nearby. Restaurant, bar, complimentary Continental breakfast, room service. In-room data ports, some kitchenettes, cable TV, in-room VCRs. Hot tub, sauna. Laundry service. Business services. Pets allowed (fee). | 1315 Rte. 17 S 07446 | 201/327–6700 or 800/780–7234 | fax 201/327–6709 | www.bestwestern.com | 80 rooms | $89–$154 | AE, D, DC, MC, V.

Wellesley Inn. This three-story quiet, family-oriented hotel was renovated in 1997. Complimentary Continental breakfast. Refrigerators, cable TV. Business services. Some pets allowed (fee). | 946 Rte. 17 N 07446 | 201/934–9250 or 800/444–8888 | fax 201/934–9719 | 89 rooms | $74–$124 | AE, D, DC, MC, V.

SALEM

Brown's Historic Home Bed & Breakfast. This 1738 house has King of Prussia marble fireplaces and a lovely backyard with a waterfall and lily pond. Complimentary breakfast. Cable TV. Pets allowed. | 41-43 Market St. 08079 | 609/935–8595 | fax 609/935–8595 | 3 rooms | $55–$100 | AE, D, MC, V.

SECAUCUS

Radisson Suite. Accommodations are two-room suites here, and the music you hear on the way could be coming from the Radisson's banquet facility, frequently the site of wedding parties and other catered events. Renovations are scheduled for 2001. Restaurant, bar. In-room data ports, minibars, refrigerators, cable TV. Pool. Exercise equipment. Laundry facilities. Business services. Some pets allowed. | 350 Rte. 3 W 07094 | 201/863–8700 | fax 201/863–6209 | www.radisson.com | 151 suites | $149–$259 | AE, D, DC, MC, V.

SOMERS POINT

Residence Inn Atlantic City-Somers Point. This 120-suite hotel is near beaches, a health club, and four golf courses. Complimentary breakfast. In-room data ports, kitchenettes, cable TV. Pool. Laundry facilities, laundry service. Business services. Pets allowed (fee). | 900 Mays Landing Rd. 08244 | 609/927–6400 or 800/331–3131 | fax 609/926–0145 | www.residenceinn.com | 120 suites | $89–$99 | AE, D, DC, MC, V.

SOMERVILLE

Holiday Inn. Located 3 mi east of Somerville across from the Garden State Exhibit Center (and 15 minutes from Rutgers and several Fortune 500 companies), this Holiday Inn is geared toward the business traveler. The rooms have modular desks and rolling office chairs to make working more comfortable, and the hotel provides free access to a nearby health club. Restaurant, bar. In-room data ports, cable TV. Pool. Laundry service. Business services. Some pets allowed. | 197 Davidson Ave., South Bound Brook 08873 | 732/356–1700 or 800/465–4329 | fax 732/356–2355 | www.basshotels.com/holiday-inn | 284 rooms | $139–$159 | AE, MC, V.

SPRING LAKE

La Maison. Owned by a Francophile, this French country-style inn serves wine and cheese every afternoon. Sleep in under your duvet, or greet the morning with an elegant full breakfast including fresh-squeezed orange juice and cappuccino. Beach tags, towels, and chairs are available to guests. Rooms have outbound-only phones. Complimentary breakfast. Cable TV. Some pets allowed. No smoking. | 404 Jersey Ave. 07762 | 732/449–0969 or 800/276–2088 | fax 732/449–4860 | 5 rooms, 2 suites, 1 cottage | $145–$250 | AE, D, DC, MC, V.

TINTON FALLS

Red Roof Inn. This three-story chain hotel is 2 mi from downtown and convenient to area dining and attractions. It's about 35 mi from Newark International Airport. All rooms on the top two floors have balconies. The hotel was renovated in 1998. In-room data ports, cable TV. Some pets allowed. | 11 Centre Plaza 07724 | 732/389–4646 | www.redroof.com | fax 732/389–4509 | 119 rooms | $69–$99 | AE, D, DC, MC, V.

Residence Inn by Marriott. This chain hotel is 5 mi from the shore and approximately one hour by car from New York City. Great Adventure is about 40 mi away. Picnic area, complimentary Continental breakfast. In-room data ports, kitchenettes, microwaves, cable TV. Pool. Laundry facilities. Business services. Pets allowed. | 90 Park Rd. 07724 | 732/389–8100 | fax 732/389–1573 | 96 suites | $119–$139 | AE, D, DC, MC, V.

Sunrise Suites Tinton Falls. This three-story hotel is 1 mi from Eatontown Industrial Park, 6 mi from the shore, and close to several area restaurants. There is a complimentary cocktail hour evenings Monday-Thursday. Kitchenettes, cable TV. Pool. Spa. Exercise room. Laundry facilities, laundry service. Business services. Pets allowed. | 3 Centre Plaza 07724 | 732/389–4800 or 877/999–3223 | fax 732/389–0137 | www.summerfieldsuites.com | 96 suites | $149 | AE, D, DC, MC, V.

TOMS RIVER

Holiday Inn. This Holiday Inn is 2 mi from fishing and boating on Toms River. The modern rooms are "nothing fancy" but it's a decent place to spend the night, especially if you're traveling with your pet. Restaurant, bar (with entertainment), room service. Refrigerators, cable TV. Pool. Hot tub, sauna. Laundry facilities. Business services. Pets allowed. | 290 Rte. 37 E 08753 | 732/244–4000 | www.basshotels.com/holiday-inn | 123 rooms | $95–$115 | AE, D, DC, MC, V.

Howard Johnson. This two-story Hojo is down the street from the Ocean County Mall, the Seacourt Pavillion, and the Toys R Us plaza. Restaurant, bar. In-room data ports, cable TV. Pool. Business services. Some pets allowed (fee). | 955 Hooper Ave. 08753 | 732/244–1000 | fax 908/505–3194 | 96 rooms | $90–$110 | AE, D, DC, MC, V.

Pier One Motel & Restaurant. This motel is just over the bridge from Seaside Heights and the shore, but if you don't feel like venturing out it has its own private beach. Six Flags Great Adventure Theme Park is 13 mi west on Route 37, and on weekends there is live music in the motel lounge. Restaurant, bar. Cable TV. Beach. Pets allowed in winter only. | 3430 Rte. 37 E 08753 | 732/270–0914 | fax 732/270–9412 | 22 rooms | $65–$165 | AE, V.

TRENTON

Howard Johnson's Lawrenceville. This two-story motel was built in 1962 and renovated in 1996. It is near Princeton University (8 mi), Rider College (2 mi), Trenton College (4 mi), and Mercer County Park (3 mi). It's in Lawrenceville, less than 4 mi from downtown Trenton. Restaurant, bar, complimentary Continental breakfast. Cable TV. Pool. Business services. Some pets allowed. | 2995 Rte. 1, Lawrenceville 08648 | 609/896–1100 or 800/406–1411 | fax 609/895–1325 | www.hojo.com | 104 rooms | $70–$125 | AE, DC, D, MC, V.

UNION

Holiday Inn. This hotel, less than 4 mi from downtown Union, is 8 mi from Newark International Airport, 5 mi from Bowcraft Amusement Park, and 1 mi from a multiplex theater. You can work out at the nearby Bally's health club. Restaurant, bar. In-room data ports, cable TV. Pool. Exercise room. Laundry service. Business services. Some pets allowed. | 304 Rte. 22 W, Springfield 07081 | 973/376–9400 or 800/465–4329 | fax 973/376–9534 | www.basshotels.com/holiday-inn | 190 rooms | $112 | AE, D, DC, MC, V.

WALPACK CENTER

Columbia Day's Inn. Perfect for a budget-minded traveler who'll be out exploring most of the day, this motel offers a scenic view of the Delaware Water gap, clean rooms, and lots of nearby attractions. If you've exhausted the park's offerings, you can drive a few miles to "civilization," where the nearby Pocono and Shawnee resort areas have golfing, skiing and other activities. The restaurant is open 24 hours, and three local fast food spots are within walking distance. Restaurant. Business services. Some pets allowed. | Post Office Box 305, Columbia, NJ 07832; Exit 4 off Route 80. About 15–20 mi from Walpack | 908/496–8221 or 800/DAYS–INN | fax 908/496–4809 | www.daysinn.com | 35 rooms | $58–$62 | AE, D, DC, MC, V.

WAYNE

Howard Johnson. Although there's no restaurant in this two-story HoJo's, there are several within walking distance, including the Greenhouse Cafe. The hotel is scheduled for a complete overhaul in 2001. Complimentary breakfast. Some in-room data ports, some refrigerators, cable TV. Pool. Laundry facilities. Business services, airport shuttle. Some pets allowed. | 1850 Rte. 23 07470 | 973/696–8050 | fax 973/696–0682 | www.hojo.com | 149 rooms | $75–$105 | AE, D, DC, MC, V.

WOODBRIDGE

Woodbridge Days Inn. This two-story motel was built in 1963 and renovated in 1991. It is 3 mi from the Woodbridge Mall and Expo Hall. It's in Iselin, 2 mi west of downtown Woodbridge. Complimentary Continental breakfast, room service. Cable TV. Laundry service. Pets allowed. | Rte. 1 S, Iselin 08830 | 732/634–4200 or 800/544–8313 | fax 732/634–7840 | 76 rooms | $75–$130 | AE, DC, MC, V.

New Mexico

ALAMOGORDO

Best Western Desert Aire. This motel is an attractive adobe-and-brick building, with larger than average rooms. Complimentary Continental breakfast. Some microwaves, cable TV. Pool. Hot tub, sauna. Laundry facilities. Some pets allowed. | 1021 S. White Sands Blvd. | 505/437–2110 | fax 505/437–1898 | www.bestwestern.com | 100 rooms | $62–$109 | AE, D, DC, MC, V.

Holiday Inn Express. At this comfortable, two-story motel two blocks from the junction of highways 54 and 70, rooms are entered from an interior hallway, cutting down on noise. Complimentary Continental breakfast. In-room data ports, cable TV. Pool. Beauty salon. Laundry facilities, laundry service. Business services. Pets allowed. | 1401 S. White Sands Blvd. 88310 | 505/437–7100 or 800/465–4329 | fax 505/437–7100 | www.hiexpress.com | 108 rooms | $59–$75 | AE, D, DC, MC, V.

Satellite Inn. Medium-size budget motel on Alamogordo's main street. Some microwaves, refrigerators, cable TV, some in-room VCRs (and movies). Pool. Pets allowed. | 2224 N. White Sands Blvd. | 505/437–8454 or 800/221–7690 | fax 505/434–6015 | 40 rooms | $32–$46 | AE, D, DC, MC, V.

Super 8 Motel. This comfortable if spartan two-story motel on the northern edge of Alamogordo is located across the street from a shopping mall. Cable TV. Some pets allowed. Business services. | 3204 N. White Sands Blvd. 88310 | 505/434–4205 or 800/478–7378 | fax 505/434–4205 | www.super8.com | 57 rooms | $36–$60 | AE, D, DC, MC, V.

ALBUQUERQUE

Adobe and Roses B&B. You're "in the country" here, about 15 minutes from downtown Albuquerque, with a great view of the western slopes of the Sandia Mountains. Should you wish to fix your own breakfast in your room, 10% will be deducted. Complimentary breakfast. Kitchenettes, cable TV. Pets allowed. No smoking. | 1011 Ortega St. NW 87114 | 505/898–0654 | 1 room, 2 suites | $60–$95 (2–day minimum stay) | No credit cards.

Albuquerque I–40 Tramway Travelodge. This two-story budget motel was built in 1989. Complimentary Continental breakfast. Cable TV. Some pets allowed. | 13139 Central Ave. NE 87123 | 505/292–4878 | fax 505/299–1822 | www.travelodge.com | 41 rooms | $40–$60 | AE, D, DC, MC, V.

Amberly Suite Hotel. This full-service, all-suite hotel near Balloon Fiesta Park has spacious rooms with full kitchens. They will even do grocery shopping for you. Restaurant, bar, complimentary breakfast. In-room data ports, kitchenettes, microwaves, refrigerators, cable TV. Pool. Hot tub. Gym. Laundry facilities. Business services, airport shuttle. Pets allowed (fee). | 7620 Pan American Fwy. NE 87109 | 505/823–1300 or 800/333–9806 | fax 505/823–2896 | www.calav.com/amberley | $99–$138 | 170 suites | AE, D, DC, MC, V.

Best Western Inn at Rio Rancho. On 2 acres of manicured, well-landscaped grounds, this inexpensive, resort-style motel is 10 mi northwest of Albuquerque in Rio Rancho. Restaurant, bar (with entertainment), picnic area, room service. In-room data ports, some kitchenettes, some microwaves, refrigerators, cable TV, some in-room VCRs. Pool. Hot tub. Exercise equipment. Laundry facilities. Business services, airport shuttle. Some pets allowed (fee). | 1465 Rio Rancho Dr. 87124 | 505/892–1700 | fax 505/892–4628 | 121 rooms | $55–$67 | AE, D, DC, MC, V.

Brittania and W.E. Mauger Estate B&B. This redbrick Queen Anne Victorian is conveniently located downtown within walking distance of Old Town, making it popular with business-people and tourists alike. Complimentary breakfast. In-room data ports, refrigerators, cable TV. Laundry service. Business services. Pets allowed. | 701 Roma Ave. NW 87102 | 505/242–8755 or 800/719–9189 | fax 505/842–8835 | www.maugerbb.com | 8 rooms (with shower only) | $79–$189 | AE, D, DC, MC, V.

Casita Chamisa. In the village (now an Albuquerque suburb) of Los Ranchos, 15 minutes north of Old Town, this B&B is the former home of Jack Schaefer, author of the best-selling western *Shane*. The house sits atop an active archaeological site, and one of the owners is an archaeologist. Both units have fireplaces and access to a greenhouse, sundeck, and gardens. Complimentary Continental breakfast. Some kitchenettes. Pool. Hot tub. Pets allowed. | 850 Chamisal Rd. NW 87107 | 505/897–4644 | www.casitachamisa.com | 1 room, one 2-bedroom casita | $95 room, $135 casita | AE, MC, V.

Comfort Inn East. This basic, two-story, budget motel is 10 mi from the airport and just off Interstate 40. Restaurant, complimentary breakfast. Cable TV. Pool. Hot tub. Laundry facilities. Business services. Pets allowed (fee). | 13031 Central Ave. NE (I–40, exit 167) 87123 | 505/294–1800 | fax 505/293–1088 | www.comfortinn.com | 122 rooms | $52–$67 | AE, D, DC, MC, V.

Days Inn West. This basic two-story budget motel is 3 mi from Old Town. Complimentary Continental breakfast. Cable TV. Pool. Hot tub, sauna. Business services. Pets allowed (fee). | 6031 Iliff Rd. NW 87121 | 505/836–3297 | fax 505/836–1214 | www.daysinn.com | 81 rooms | $55–$80 | AE, D, DC, MC, V.

Hacienda Antigua. A lovely 200-year-old hacienda with kiva fireplaces and oriental rugs in the room and a warm beamed ceiling in the lobby. The large, landscaped courtyard has a pool. Complimentary breakfast. Refrigerators, no room phones, no TV, TV in common area. Pool. Hot tub. Business services. Some pets allowed. | 6708 Tierra Dr. NW 87107 | 505/345–5399 | fax 505/345–3855 | www.haciendantigua.com | 6 rooms | $100–$190 | MC, V.

Hampton Inn Albuquerque-North. This inexpensive southwestern-style motor inn is near the Balloon Fiesta Park. Complimentary Continental breakfast. In-room data ports, refrigerators, cable TV. Pool. Pets allowed. | 5101 Ellison NE 87109 | 505/344–1555 | fax 505/345–2216 | www.hamptoninn.com | 124 rooms | $64–$69 | AE, D, DC, MC, V.

Holiday Inn Express Albuquerque (I–40 Eubank). Simple clean rooms are offered in this mid-price limited-service motor hotel. Some rooms have balconies and views of the Sandia Mountains. Complimentary Continental breakfast. Some microwaves, some refrigerators, some in-room hot tubs, cable TV, some in-room VCRs. Pool. Hot tub, sauna. Gym. Laundry facilities. Pets allowed (fee). | 10330 Hotel Ave. NE 87123 | 505/275–8900 or 800/465–4329 | fax 505/275–6000 | www.basshotels.com/hiexpress | 104 rooms | $75–$100 | AE, D, DC, MC, V.

Inn at Paradise. Next to the first tee at the Paradise Hills Golf Club, this swank B&B atop West Mesa is a golfer's paradise. Rooms offer views of the mountains and are decorated with works and furnishings made by local artists and craftspeople. Complementary Continental breakfast. Cable TV. Spa. Library. Some pets allowed. No smoking. | 10035 Country Club La. NW 87114 | 505/898–6161 or 800/938–6161 | fax 505/890–1090 | www.innat-paradise.com | 16 rooms, 2 suites, 1 apartment | $55–$110 | AE, D, DC, MC, V.

La Quinta Inn Albuquerque Airport. This moderately priced motor hotel with large, comfortable rooms is ¼ mi from the Albuquerque airport. Complimentary Continental breakfast. In-room data ports, some microwaves, cable TV. Pool. Laundry facilities. Business services, airport shuttle. Some pets allowed. | 2116 Yale Blvd. SE 87106 | 505/243–5500 | fax 505/247–8288 | www.laquinta.com | 105 rooms | $69–$99 | AE, D, DC, MC, V.

Plaza Inn. Views of nightime Albuquerque are stunning from this attractive 5-story hotel, perched on a hill 2 mi from the airport. All of the rooms are decorated in south-western pastels and have private balconies. Restaurant, bar, complimentary Continental breakfast. Some refrigerators. Pool. Hot tub. Gym. Laundry facilities. Business services, airport shuttle. Pets allowed. | 900 Medical Arts Ave. NE 87102 | 505/243–5693 or 800/237–1307 | fax 505/843–6229 | www.plazainnabq.com | 120 rooms | $85–$130 | AE, D, DC, MC, V.

Radisson Inn Albuquerque Airport. This mid-price chain hotel built around a landscaped courtyard with a pool is 5 mi from the Albuquerque airport. Restaurant, bar, room service. In-room data ports, cable TV. Pool. Hot tub. Gym. Airport shuttle. Pets allowed. | 1901 University Blvd. SE 87106 | 505/247–0512 | fax 505/843–7148 | www.radisson.com | 148 rooms | $79–$119 | AE, D, DC, MC, V.

Ramada Inn East Albuquerque. This upscale motel complex consists of seven south-western-style buildings built around a courtyard. Restaurant, bar, room service. Cable TV. Pool. Hot tub. Video games. Laundry service. Business services, airport shuttle. Some pets allowed. | 25 Hotel Circle NE 87123 | 505/271–1000 | fax 505/291–9028 | www.ramada.com | 205 rooms | $65–$150 | AE, D, DC, MC, V.

ANGEL FIRE

Angel Fire Resort Hotel. Rooms in this modern resort hotel are large, and some have fireplaces. Suites have kitchenettes. Restaurant, bar. Some kitchenettes, refrigerators, cable TV. Pool. Hot tub, sauna. 18-hole golf course. Pets allowed. | N. Angel Fire Dr. 87710 | 505/377–6401 or 800/633–7463 | fax 505/377–4200 | 139 rooms, 16 suites, 18 condos | $80–$160 rooms, $125–$255 suites, $135–$345 condos | AE, D, DC, MC, V.

ARTESIA

Artesia Inn. This is a redbrick single-story motel on the outskirts of town on Highway 285 South. The southwestern-style rooms have a small dressing area next to the bathroom but are otherwise a bit cramped and unremarkable. Refrigerators, cable TV. Pool. Pets allowed. | 1820 S. 1st St. 88210 | 505/746–9801 or 800/682–4598 | fax 505/746–9801 | 33 rooms | $34–$52 | AE, D, DC, MC, V.

BELÉN

Casitas at Mountain View. Each of these cozy suites has a small living room, a kitchen, and small backyard. The walls are painted by a local artist, each with a unique border of flowers, plants, and trailing ivy. This family-run operation is at the southern end of town. Kitchenettes, refrigerators, cable TV. Some pets allowed. | 1304 S. Main St. 87002 | 505/861–1144 | 9 rooms | $39–$59 | AE, D, DC, MC, V.

CARLSBAD

★ **Best Western Stevens Inn.** Here you will find carefully landscaped grounds and attractively decorated, spacious rooms, offering a touch of elegance at bargain prices. Restaurant, bar (with entertainment), room service. Some refrigerators, cable TV, in-room VCRs (and movies). Pool. Playground. Business services. Pets allowed. | 1829 S. Canal St. | 505/887–2851 | fax 505/887–6338 | www.bestwestern.com | 204 rooms | $59–$85 | AE, D, DC, MC, V.

Continental Inn. This two-story brick motel is just south of Carlsbad. The rooms are simple, comfortable, and the grounds are well kept. In-room data ports, some refrigerators, cable TV. Pool. Business services, airport shuttles. Some pets allowed (fee). | 3820 National Parks Hwy. | 505/887–0341 | fax 505/885–1186 | 58 rooms | $35–$80 | AE, D, DC, MC, V.

Days Inn. This hotel is 2 mi southeast of the center of downtown. Rooms have southwestern decor, king-size beds, and sofa beds. Complimentary Continental breakfast. In-room data ports, cable TV. Pool. Hot tub. Business services, airport shuttle. Pets allowed. | 3901 National Parks Hwy. 88220 | 505/887–7800 or 800/329–7466 | fax 505/885–9433 | www.daysinn.com | 42 rooms, 8 suites | $55–$70 | AE, D, DC, MC, V.

Holiday Inn-Carlsbad. This southwestern-style, two-story chain motel in downtown Carlsbad has large, well-kept rooms opening onto exterior corridors. Restaurants, picnic area, room service. In-room data ports, some refrigerators, cable TV, some in-room VCRs (and movies). Pool. Hot tub. Gym. Playground. Business services. Pets allowed. | 601 S. Canal | 505/885–8500 or 800/472–9578 | fax 505/887–5999 | www.basshotels.com/holiday-inn | 100 rooms | $86–$115 | AE, D, DC, MC, V.

Quality Inn. One mile from the airport, this stone-face inn surrounds a landscaped patio with a pool and sundeck about as large as an aircraft hanger. Rooms are comfortable, with dull modern furnishings. Restaurant, bar with entertainment, complimentary breakfast. Some in-room data ports, cable TV. Pool. Hot tub. Video games. Laundry service. Airport shuttle. Some pets allowed. | 3706 National Parks Hwy. 88220 | 505/887–2861 or 800/321–2861 | fax 505/887–2861 | www.qualityinn.com | 120 rooms | $60–$70 | AE, D, DC, MC, V.

Stagecoach Inn. This family-oriented motor inn has basic rooms. Outside is a tree-shaded park with a playground and picnic area. Restaurant, complimentary Continental breakfast. Cable TV. Pool, wading pool. Hot tub. Laundry service. Some pets allowed. | 1819 S. Canal St. 88220 | 505/887–1148 | 57 rooms | $30–$46 | AE, D, DC, MC, V.

CHAMA

Elk Horn Lodge. This complex of rustic log cabins overlooks the Chama River. Some cabins have private porches. Restaurant, picnic area. Kitchenettes (in cottages), cable TV. Pets allowed. | 263 U.S. 84 | 505/756–2105 or 800/532–8874 | fax 505/756–2638 | www.elkhorn-lodge.net | 23 rooms, 10 cabins | $50–$72, $80–$125 cabins | AE, D, DC, MC, V.

The Lodge at Chama. An outdoor vacation can also be luxurious at this lodge and working ranch owned by the Jicarilla Apache tribe. Two miles south of Chama, on the Colorado border at elevations between 9,000 and 11,000 ft, this 32,000-acre ranch has 10 lakes and is nothing short of idyllic. Go horseback riding, trophy fishing, tour the ranch, or relax by the huge stone fireplace inside this high-class lodge furnished with leather couches and cowhide chairs. Restaurant, bar. In-room data ports, TV in some rooms. Hot tub, sauna. Some pets allowed. | 16253 Hwy. 84 S 87520 | 505/756–2133 | fax 505/756–2519 | www.lodgeatchama.com | 9 rooms, 2 suites | $225–$450, $550 suites | AP | D, MC, V.

River Bend Lodge. This comfortable yet simple lodge has one of the only hot tubs in town. Right on the Chama River, you can walk out your door and cast a fly. But be careful— you might surprise a black bear and her cub. Cabins are ideal for families, with two queen-size beds, and a double bed in the loft, and cooking facilities. Management here is especially sensitive and accommodating, particularly for groups or family reunions. Kitchenettes, refrigerators, cable TV. Hot tub. Some pets allowed. | Hwy. 84, 87520 | 505/756–2264 or 800/288–1371 | fax 800/288–1371 | www.chamaleisure.com | 15 rooms, 4 cabins | $53–$90, $100 cabins | AE, D, DC, MC, V.

Spruce Lodge. If you like roughing it but not too rough, these 12 little cabins beside the Rio Chama are the perfect balance of rustic but comfortable. You know you're away from it all when you can hear the river and the wind sifting through the pines. Some kitchenettes, cable TV. Some pets allowed. No smoking. | Hwy. 84/Hwy. 64 87520 | 505/756–2593 | 12 cabins | $47–$95 | Closed Nov.–Apr. | D, MC, V.

CHIMAYÓ

Casa Escondida. Intimate and serene, this adobe inn has sweeping views of the Sangre de Cristo range. Rooms are decorated with antiques, especially American Mission period pieces. Ask for the Sun Room, in the main house, which has a private patio with French doors, viga ceilings (with exposed wood beams), and a brick floor. The separate one-bedroom Casita Escondida has a kiva-style fireplace, tile floors, and a sitting area. Complimentary breakfast. Hot tub. Some pets allowed. | Country Rd. 0100 | 505/351–4805 or 800/643–7200 | fax 505/351–2575 | www.casaescondida.com | 8 rooms, 1 casita | $80–$140 | AE, MC, V.

CIMARRON

Kit Carson Motel. This serviceable motel is nothing special, but it will do the job if you are after shelter and a hot shower. Restaurant, bar. Cable TV. Some pets allowed. | 31039 U.S. 64 E 87714 | 505/376–2288 or 800/293–7961 | fax 505/376–9214 | 38 rooms | $54–$66 | AE, D, DC, MC, V.

CLAYTON

Best Western Kokopelli Lodge. When locals have out-of-town guests they can't put up for the night, they send them to this motel located 12 mi north of Clayton State Park. The pleasant lobby is full of fresh flowers and warmed with a gas stove. The rooms are spacious and clean. Complimentary Continental breakfast. Some in-room hot tubs, cable TV. Pool. Pets allowed. | 702 S. 1st St., 88415 | 505/374–2589 or 800/528–1234 | fax 505/374–2551 | www.bestwestern.com | 47 rooms, 6 suites | $57–$74 | AE, D, DC, MC, V.

CLOUDCROFT

Eagle Eyrie Vacation Manor. Built on Grand Avenue in 1897 by Major William H. Long, this 2,800-square-ft house has retained its rustic grandeur and is rented out as a complete unit. The stone fireplace and majestic staircase are the centerpieces of the large interior and are surrounded by antiques that hark back to another age. There are five bedrooms, two baths, and a full kitchen; it can sleep 16 people. Cable TV. Pets allowed. No smoking. | 609 Grand Ave. 88352 | 505/522–1787 | www.cloudcroft.com/eagle/index.htm | 1 house | $325 | AE, D, DC, MC, V.

CLOVIS

Bishops Inn. This clean southwestern motel has room entrances on an inside hallway. The rooms are mid-size but well appointed and colorful. Complimentary Continental breakfast. Cable TV, refrigerators, room phones. Pool. Hot tub. Some pets allowed. | 2920 Mabry Dr. 88101 | 505/769–1953 or 800/643–9239 | fax 505/762–8304 | 57 rooms | $33–$43 | AE, D, DC, MC, V.

Days Inn. Basic but reliable lodging near Clovis Community College. Cable TV. Pool. Business services. Pets allowed. | 1720 E. Mabry Dr. | 505/762–2971 | fax 505/762–2735 | www.daysinn.com | 94 rooms | $35–$57 | AE, D, DC, MC, V.

DEMING

Anselments Butterfield Stage Motel. These spacious rooms, the largest in town, are almost like suites, some equipped with up to four double beds. The 1960s motel-retro furniture is a treat for the nostalgic soul, and the neon sign out front is an original from 1963. The lobby is decked with an old-fashioned rifle, antique map of the United States, and an authentic Native American tomahawk. Refrigerators, cable TV, room phones. Laundry facilities. Some pets allowed. | 309 W. Pine St. 88030 | 505/544–0011 | fax 505/544–0614 | 13 rooms | $33–$56 | AE, D, DC, MC, V.

Deming Days Inn. This two-story motel, last remodeled in 1998, provides basic but comfortable rooms at reasonable prices. Restaurant, complimentary Continental breakfast. In-room data ports, some microwaves, refrigerators, cable TV. Pool. Some pets allowed. | 1601 E. Pine St. 88030 | 505/546–8813 | fax 505/546–7095 | www.daysinn.com | 57 rooms | $38–$53 | AE, D, DC, MC, V.

Grand Motor Inn. This budget motel on Deming's main street is located near the visitor center and golf club. Restaurant, bar, room service. In-room data ports, cable TV. Pool. Business services, airport shuttle. Pets allowed. | 1721 E. Spruce St. | 505/546–2631 | fax 505/546–4446 | 62 rooms | $32–$38 | AE, D, DC, MC, V.

Holiday Inn. This two-story motel offers standard-size rooms decorated in a southwestern style. Right off I-10 and 2 mi from downtown shops and restaurants, this is a good place for a short stop-over. Restaurant. In-room data ports, in-room safes, refrigerators, some in-room hot tubs, cable TV. Pool. Gym. Laundry facilities. Business services. Pets allowed. | I-10, exit 85 88031 | 505/546–2661 | fax 505/546–6308 | www.holiday-inn.com/demingnm | 116 rooms | $59–$99 | AE, D, DC, MC, V.

DULCE

Best Western Jicarilla Inn. A stucco building with great views of the Rocky Mountains, this motel also houses a large casino. It's the only lodging option in Dulce, $\frac{1}{4}$ mi from the reservation conference center and museum, and 25 mi from the Cumbres and Toltec Scenic Railroad in Chama. Restaurant, bar. Some refrigerators, cable TV. Airport shuttle. Some pets allowed. | Jicarilla Blvd. at U.S. 64 | 505/759–3663 | fax 505/759–3170 | 42 rooms | $65–$95 | AE, D, DC, MC, V.

ESPAÑOLA

Best Western Holiday Motel. On Highway 285 just south of town, this friendly motel has all rooms at the ground level so loading and unloading is a breeze. Its claim to fame was as the set for the grade-B movie *Vampires* starring James Woods. Some kitchenettes, cable TV. Pool. Some pets allowed. | 1215 S. Riverside Dr. 87532 | 505/753–2491 or 800/653–9847 | fax 505/753–0191 | www.bestwestern.com | 26 rooms | $40–$60 | AE, D, DC, MC, V.

Chamisa Inn. At the center of Española's main drag, this brick one-story motel offers clean, standard-sized rooms and friendly service. Its lounge hosts dancing to live Spanish, country, and rock music on Wednesday, Friday, and Saturday nights. Bar, complimentary Continental breakfast. Cable TV. Pool. Pets allowed (fee). | 920 Riverside Dr. N (Hwy. 68) 87533 | 505/753–7291 or 800/766–7943 | fax 505/753–1218 | 51 rooms | $54–$60 | AE, D, MC, V.

FARMINGTON

Best Western Inn & Suites. This is Farmington's largest hotel, with a covered courtyard featuring a large pool. Rooms are large, clean, and well kept. The Animas River Walk is just behind the hotel. Restaurant, bar, complimentary breakfast, room service. Some in-room data ports, some kitchenettes, some refrigerators, cable TV, some in-room VCRs (and movies). Pool. Hot tub, sauna. Gym. Video games. Laundry service. Business services, airport shuttle. Pets allowed. | 700 Scott Ave. 87401 | 505/327–5221 | fax 505/327–1565 | www.bestwestern.com | 194 rooms | $79 | AE, D, DC, MC, V.

Comfort Inn. Friendly and functional, this inexpensive motel offering basic, clean rooms is good for an overnight stay. Complimentary Continental breakfast. In-room data ports, some refrigerators, cable TV. Pool. Business services. Pets allowed. | 555 Scott Ave. 87401 | 505/325-2626 | fax 505/325-7675 | www.comfortinn.com | 60 rooms, 18 suites | $47-$69, $60-$66 suites | AE, D, DC, MC, V.

Holiday Inn. This moderately priced, two-story motel offers reliable lodgings with a large outdoor heated pool. Restaurant, bar, room service. Refrigerators, cable TV. Pool. Hot tub. Gym. Business services, airport shuttle. Pets allowed. | 600 E. Broadway 87499 | 505/327-9811 | fax 505/325-2288 | www.holiday-inn.com/farmingtonnm | 149 rooms | $55-$139 | AE, D, DC, MC, V.

La Quinta Inn Farmington. This modern, moderately priced two-story motor inn offers decent-size, well-kept rooms. Picnic area, complimentary Continental breakfast. In-room data ports, some refrigerators, cable TV. Pool. Video games. Laundry service. Pets allowed. | 675 Scott Ave. 87401 | 505/327-4706 | fax 505/325-6583 | www.laquinta.com | 106 rooms | $59-$74 | AE, D, DC, MC, V.

GALLUP

Best Western Inn and Suites. With nice-size rooms arranged around an enclosed courtyard that includes a heated pool, this is probably the best full-service hotel in Gallup. Restaurant, bar, complimentary breakfast, room service. In-room data ports, some microwaves, cable TV. Pool. Hot tub, sauna. Gym. Video games. Laundry. Some pets allowed. | 3009 W. U.S. 66 | 505/722-2221 | fax 505/722-7442 | www.bestwestern.com/gallupnm | 126 rooms | $64-$72 | AE, D, DC, MC, V.

EconoLodge. This basic but comfortable two-story motel is located on the west end of Gallup, beyond the municipal airport. Basic accommodations in a convenient location. Cable TV. Airport shuttle. Pets allowed (fee). | 3101 U.S. 66 W | 505/722-3800 | www.econolodge.com | 51 rooms | $39-$52 | AE, D, DC, MC, V.

El Rancho. This historic hotel, built in 1937, was a favorite stop for stars filming westerns in the area. Rooms are done up in Old West style, and some are quite large and have a certain nostalgic style, though others are more motel style. Bathrooms tend to be small. Restaurant, bar. Some kitchenettes, cable TV. Pool. Laundry facilities. Business services. Pets allowed. | 1000 U.S. Hwy. 66 E | 505/863-9311 or 800/543-6351 | fax 505/722-5917 | www.elranchohotel.com | $43-$76 | AE, D, MC, V.

Holiday Inn. This motel on the west end of Gallup, 2 mi east of the municipal airport, has a Holidome recreation area and is the largest hostelry in Gallup. Restaurant, bar, room service. In-room data ports, cable TV. Pool. Hot tub. Gym. Laundry service. Business services, airport shuttle. Pets allowed. | 2915 U.S. 66 W | 505/722-2201 | fax 505/722-9616 | www.holiday-inn.com/gallupnm | 212 rooms | $65-$73 | AE, D, DC, MC, V.

Sleep Inn. This quiet motel is just off exit 26 of I-40. You'll get a reasonably priced room with all the basics. Cable TV. Pool. Pets allowed. | 3820 E. Historic Rte. 66 87301 | 505/863-3535 | fax 505/722-3737 | www.sleepinn.com | 61 rooms | $39-$54 | AE, D, DC, MC, V.

GRANTS

Best Western Inn and Suites. Rooms are nicely kept and comfortably large; there is a central courtyard filled with attractive plants and a pool. Restaurant, bar, room service. Some refrigerators, cable TV. Pool. Hot tub, sauna. Gym. Video games. Laundry facilities. Business services. Some pets allowed. | 1501 E. Santa Fe Ave. | 505/287-7901 | fax 505/285-5751 | www.bestwestern.com | 126 rooms | $66-$97 | AE, D, DC, MC, V.

Holiday Inn Express. Just 1/4 mi off I-40, this limited-service motor hotel provides comfortable, moderately priced rooms. Complimentary Continental breakfast. Pool. Hot tub. Laundry service. Business services. Pets allowed. | 1496 E. Santa Fe Ave. (I-40, exit 85) 87020

| 505/285–4676 | fax 505/285–6998 | www.hiexpress/grantsnm | 58 rooms | $54–$70 | AE, D, DC, MC, V.

HOBBS

Best Inn. One of Hobbs's largest motels, it's popular with leisure and business travelers. Restaurant, bar (with entertainment). In-room data ports, room service, cable TV. Pool. Business services. Some pets allowed. | 501 N. Marland Blvd. | 505/397–3251 or 800/635–6639 | fax 505/393–3065 | 75 rooms | $39–$69 | AE, D, DC, MC, V.

Leawood Travelodge. This reasonably priced, one-floor motel is 7 mi from the Lea County Airport, offering basic rooms. Restaurant, complimentary breakfast. Cable TV. Pool. Business services. Pets allowed. | 1301 E. Broadway | 505/393–4101 or 888/532–9663 | fax 505/393–4101 | www.travelodge.com | 72 rooms | $40–$54 | AE, D, DC, MC, V.

LAS CRUCES

Days Inn. This economical chain motel tends to attract groups—it offers meeting rooms for 150—but it also offers simple, clean rooms at good prices. Restaurant, bar, room service. Some in-room data ports, some refrigerators, cable TV. Pool. Sauna. Laundry facilities. Business services. Some pets allowed (fee). | 2600 S. Valley Dr. 88005 | 505/526–4441 | fax 505/526–1980 | www.daysinn.com | 130 rooms | $45–$65 | AE, D, DC, MC, V.

Holiday Inn de las Cruces. The lushly planted, Spanish-style courtyard at this hotel is as open as a plaza in some Mexican towns; common areas are decorated with antiques. It's definitely not your typical Holiday Inn. Restaurant, bar, room service. Cable TV. Pool, wading pool. Video games. Laundry facilities. Business services, airport shuttle. Some pets allowed. | 201 E. University Ave. 88001 | 505/526–4411 | fax 505/524–0530 | www. holidayinnlc.com | 114 rooms | $59–$150 | AE, D, DC, MC, V.

★ **Inn of the Arts.** Built in 1890, this adobe hotel is furnished with antiques, and there's an art gallery on the property; each room is named for an artist. There are fireplaces in the suites. Picnic area, complimentary breakfast. Some kitchenettes, some microwaves, some refrigerators, cable TV, some in-room VCRs. TV in common area. Gym. Library. Business services. Pets allowed. | 618 S. Alameda 88005 | 505/526–3326 | fax 505/647–1334 | www.innofthearts.com | 21 rooms, 7 suites | $77–$125, $125–$175 suites | AE, D, DC, MC, V.

Las Cruces Hilton. This upscale, modern, seven-story hotel has a view of the city and the Organ Mountains, not to mention large rooms and a great deal of southwestern charm and elegance, with a fountain in the lobby and lots of Mexican tilework. Restaurant, bar (with entertainment), room service. In-room data ports, some refrigerators, cable TV, some in-room VCRs (and movies). Pool. Hot tub. Gym. Business services, airport shuttle. Pets allowed. | 705 S. Telshor Blvd. 88011 | 505/522–4300 | fax 505/522–7657 | lchilton@zianet.com | www.weblifepro.com/lchilton | 195 rooms, 7 suites | $77–$90, $120–$300 suites | AE, D, DC, MC, V.

T.R.H. Smith Mansion Bed and Breakfast. This historic B&B is located in the center of Las Cruces, yet offers a quiet retreat within its spacious and elegant domain. Each room has a regional theme to represent different parts of the world visited by the owner. Relax in the glass porch or enjoy a game of billiards. Complimentary Continental breakfast. In-room data ports. No TV, TV in common area. Some pets allowed. No smoking. | 909 N. Alameda Blvd., 88005 | 505/525–2525 or 800/526–1914 | fax 505/524–8227 | www.smith-mansion.com | 4 rooms | $70–$90 | AE, D, MC, V.

LAS VEGAS

Inn of Santa Fe Trail. All rooms face the courtyard of this lovely hacienda-style motel. The grounds are well manicured, the rooms simple and unfussy but clean and comfortable. Picnic area, complimentary Continental breakfast. In-room data ports, some microwaves, some refrigerators, cable TV, some in-room VCRs. Pool. Hot tub. Business services. Pets allowed. | 1133 Grand Ave. | 505/425–6791 or 888/448–8438 | fax 505/425–0417 | www.innonthesantafetrail.com | 33 rooms, 2 suites, 2 casitas | $64–$79 rooms, $105 suites, $140 casitas | AE, D, MC, V.

Plaza Hotel. This fully restored 1880 western Italianate hotel overlooks the downtown Las Vegas Plaza Park. Rooms continue the Victorian theme and are furnished with antiques and modern amenities. Interior rooms are quieter but have no views. Restaurant, bar. Cable TV. Business services, airport shuttle. Pets allowed (fee). | 230 Plaza | 505/425–3591 or 800/328–1882 | fax 505/425–9659 | www.lasvegasnewmexico.com/plaza | 36 rooms | $79–$129 | AE, D, DC, MC, V.

Regal Motel. This very basic budget motel offers clean, comfortable rooms on U.S. 85, Las Vegas's main north–south thoroughfare. Some pets allowed (fee). | 1809 N. Grand | 505/454–1456 | fax 505/454–1456 | 50 rooms | $30–$49 | AE, D, DC, MC, V.

Scottish Inn. This inexpensive budget motel is known for its clean, simple rooms. Cable TV. Some pets allowed. | 1216 N. Grand Ave. | 505/425–9357 | fax 505/425–9357 | 45 rooms | $28–$60 | AE, D, DC, MC, V.

Town House. This inexpensive, locally owned motel is well located in the center of Las Vegas, easily accessible to everything. Picnic area. Cable TV. Some pets allowed (fee). | 1215 N. Grand Ave. | 505/425–6717 or 800/679–6717 | fax 505–425–9005 | 42 rooms | $27–$44 | AE, D, DC, MC, V.

LORDSBURG

Days Inn and Suites. This two-story motel is a relatively new structure, built in 1998 in southwestern style. It's a convenient and inexpensive place to stop over. Complimentary Continental breakfast. In-room data ports, some microwaves, some refrigerators, cable TV. Pool. Hot tub. Gym. Pets allowed. | 1100 W. Motel Dr. 88045 | 505/542–3600 | www.daysinn.com | 44 rooms, 12 suites | $55–$62, $65–$72 suites | AE, D, DC, MC, V.

Holiday Inn Express. A pared-down version of the full-service Holiday Inns, this simple location still offers well-appointed rooms with two queen beds, a desk, chair, and dresser. For families, there are oversize rooms with a living area and queen sleeper. All of this is two blocks south of exit 22 on I–10. Complimentary Continental breakfast. In-room data ports, some kitchenettes, cable TV. Pool. Pets allowed. | 1408 S. Main St. 88045 | 505/542–3666 | fax 505/542–3665 | www.hiexpress.com | 40 rooms | $59–$79 | AE, D, DC, MC, V.

LOS ALAMOS

Best Western Hilltop House Hotel. This hotel and conference center within a few blocks of most of the town's major attractions, including the Los Alamos labs, has a magnificent view of the mountains. Its location makes it popular with both visiting scientists and tourists. Restaurant, complimentary Continental breakfast, room service. In-room data ports, some kitchenettes, some microwaves, some refrigerators, cable TV. Pool. Sauna. Gym. Laundry facilities, laundry service. Business services, airport shuttle. Pets allowed (deposit). | 400 Trinity Dr. (Hwy. 502) | 505/662–2441 or 800/462–0936 | fax 505/662–5913 | www.losalamos.com/hilltophouse | 98 rooms | $76–$275 | AE, D, DC, MC, V.

MESILLA

Best Western Mesilla Valley Inn. This pleasant, two-story motel built around a courtyard with a pool offers southwestern hospitality ½ mi from Mesilla Plaza. Restaurant, bar (with entertainment), room service. Some in-room data ports, some microwaves available, some refrigerators, cable TV. Pool. Hot tub. Video games. Laundry facilities, laundry service. Business services. Pets allowed. | 901 Avenida de Mesilla 88005 | 505/524–8603 or 800/528–1234 | fax 505/526–8437 | www.bestwestern.com | 152 rooms, 8 suites | $59, $69–$79 suites | AE, D, DC, MC, V.

PORTALES

Classic American Economy Inn. This inexpensive motel offering standard rooms is downtown, next to Eastern New Mexico University. Picnic area, complimentary Continental breakfast. In-room data ports, refrigerators, cable TV, some in-room VCRs. Pool. Playground. Laundry facilities. Airport shuttle. Pets allowed. | 1613 W. 2nd St. | 505/356–6668 or 800/901–9466 | fax 505/356–6668 | 40 rooms | $30–$50 | AE, D, DC, MC, V.

RATON

Budget Host Melody Lane Motel. This establishment is unpretentious but squeaky clean and affordable. Complimentary Continental breakfast. Refrigerators, cable TV. Some pets allowed. | 136 Canyon Dr. | 505/445–3655 or 800/421–5210 | fax 505/445–3461 | www.budgethost.com | 27 rooms | $36–$49 | AE, D, DC, MC, V.

El Portal. This downtown building was erected in 1885 as a livery stable but has been a hotel since 1912. For years a rowdy railroad hotel, the now more sedate establishment contains antiques throughout. It closely resembles the interior of the original, and ghosts allegedly abound, roaming the hallways. Restaurant. Some kitchenettes. Cable TV. Pets allowed. | 101 N. 3rd St. 87740 | 505/445–3631 or 888/362–7345 | 15 rooms, 39 apartments | $35–$55, $105–$245 weekly for apartments | MC, V.

Morning Star. This 1885 Victorian near downtown is also the home of the owner's antiques business. It's a relaxed and pleasant change from the strictly motel accommodations elsewhere. Snacks are served in the evening. Complimentary breakfast. No TV in rooms, TV in common area. Pets allowed. No smoking. | 301 S. 3rd St. 87740 | 505/445–1000 | 4 rooms (with shared baths), 1 suite (with private bath) | $50 | MC, V.

RED RIVER

Best Western River's Edge Lodge This small chain hotel is right on the Red River in the heart of town. Stores and restaurants are within walking distance. The lobby has a fireplace and an inviting common area. The winter offers ski-in/ski-out capabilities. The rooms are spacious, and some have balconies and full kitchens. Complimentary Continental breakfast, in-room data ports, some kitchenettes, microwaves, refrigerators, cable TV. Hot tub. Laundry facilities. Free parking. Pets allowed (fee). | 301 W. River St. | 505/754–1766 or 877/600–9990 | fax 505/754–2388 or 505/754–2408 | www.bestwestern.com | 31 rooms | $90–$120 | AE, D, DC, MC, V.

Tall Pine Resort. Surrounded by national forest and about 1½ mi into the mountains, the basic, well-spaced log cabins here are set in 40 acres of woods along the Red River and are perfect for those wanting peace, seclusion, and an outdoorsy setting. Picnic area. No air-conditioning, kitchenettes, no room phones. Playground. Pets allowed. | 1929 Hwy. 578 | 505/754–2241 or 800/573–2241 | fax 505/754–3134 | www.tallpineresort.com | 24 cabins | $75–$120 cabins | Closed Oct.–Apr. | MC, V.

Terrace Towers Lodge. This all-suite lodge offers a magnificent view of the Red River valley and spacious rooms. All units have a kitchenette or full kitchen, as well as a sleeper sofa, which makes them ideal for families. Hot tub. Kitchenettes, cable TV, some in-room VCRs (and movies). Playground. Laundry facilities. Pets allowed. | 712 W. Main St. | 505/754–2962 or 800/695–6343 | fax 505/754–2989 | www.redrivernm.com | 26 suites | $55–$160 | AE, D, MC, V.

ROSWELL

Best Western Sally Port Inn and Suites. This standard motel in the middle of town, close to the New Mexico Military Institute, is a favorite of the cadets' parents. Restaurant, bar, room service. In-room data ports, refrigerators, cable TV. Pool. Beauty salon, hot tub. Tennis. Gym. Laundry facilities. Business services, airport shuttle. Pets allowed. | 2000 N.

Main St. 88201 | 505/622–6430 | fax 505/623–7631 | www.bestwestern.com | $79–$119 | AE, D, DC, MC, V.

Budget Inn. A clean, no-frills motel, offering very basic rooms at reasonable prices two blocks north of the New Mexico Military Institute. Some microwaves, some refrigerators, cable TV. Pool. Hot tub. Some pets allowed (fee). | 2200 W. 2nd St. 88201 | 505/623–3811 or 800/806–7030 | fax 505/623–7030 | 29 rooms | $27–$45 | AE, D, MC, V.

Frontier. This is an older motel on the north side of town, but comfortable. Complimentary Continental breakfast. Some refrigerators, cable TV. Pool. Hot tub. Pets allowed. | 3010 N. Main St., at U.S. 70 88201 | 505/622–1400 or 800/678–1401 | fax 505/622–1405 | 38 rooms | $28–$40 | AE, D, DC, MC, V.

Ramada Inn. This is a comfortable, well-maintained chain hotel with large rooms near the golf course. Restaurant, complimentary breakfast. Cable TV. Pool. Business services, airport shuttle. Pets allowed. | 2803 W. 2nd St. 88201 | 505/623–9440 | fax 505/622–9708 | www.ramada.com | 61 rooms | $53–$70 | AE, D, DC, MC, V.

RUIDOSO

Best Western Swiss Chalet Inn. This charming, simple resort hotel in the mountains 3 mi north of Ruidoso, with sweeping forest views, looks like a Swiss chalet. It's a 16-minute drive from Ski Apache slopes. The on-premises restaurant serves German and American food. Restaurant, bar, complimentary breakfast, room service. Cable TV, some in-room VCRs (and movies). Pool. Hot tub, sauna. Laundry facilities. Business services. Some pets allowed. | 1451 Mechem Dr. | 505/258–3333 or 800/477–9477 | fax 505/258–5325 | www.ruidoso.net/swisschalet | 82 rooms | $68–$150 | AE, D, DC, MC, V.

High Country Lodge. Tucked beside a quiet mountain lake 5 mi north of Ruidoso, this mountain resort features large two-bedroom cabins, all with fully equipped kitchens and front porches, some with fireplaces. Picnic area. No air-conditioning, kitchenettes, cable TV. Pool. Hot tub, sauna. Tennis. Video games. Playground. Business services. Pets allowed (fee). | Hwy. 48, Alto 88312 | 505/336–4321 or 800/845–7265 | www.ruidoso.net/hcl | 32 two-bedroom cabins | $119 cabins | AE, D, DC, MC, V.

SANTA FE

Alexander's Inn. This B &B is an antiques-furnished, 1903 Craftsman-style house with a backyard garden, within walking distance of the Plaza. The inn also encompasses a seven-room adobe hacienda three blocks away and several cottages in the surrounding blocks. Some rooms have fireplaces. Complimentary Continental breakfast. No smoking, cable TV, no TV in some rooms. Hot tub. Business services. Some pets allowed. | 529 E. Palace Ave. 87501 | 505/986–1431 or 888/321–5123 | fax 505/982–8572 | www.collectorsguide.com/alexandinn | 18 rooms in 2 buildings, 7 cottages | $80–$175 | D, MC, V.

Best Western Santa Fe. The majority of regular rooms are fairly small at this chain motel built in 1990, but the more expensive doubles and all suites are larger; some have balconies. The motel is a 15-minute drive from the Plaza. Complimentary Continental breakfast. Some refrigerators, cable TV. Pool. Hot tub. Laundry facilities. Business services. Some pets allowed. | 3650 Cerrillos Rd. 87505 | 505/438–3822 | fax 505/438–3795 | 97 rooms | $45–$145 | AE, D, DC, MC, V.

Dunshee's. A mile from the Plaza, on *Acequia Madres*(Mother Ditch), which runs parallel to Canyon Road, this small B&B offers only two accommodations. The suite is in the restored adobe home of artist Susan Dunshee, the proprietor; the adobe casita is good for families. Both have fireplaces and are furnished with antiques. Complimentary Continental breakfast. Refrigerators, cable TV, room phones. Some pets allowed. No smoking. | 986 Acequia Madres 87501 | 505/982–0988 | www.bbhost.com/dunshee | 1 suite, 1 casita | $125 suite, $135 casita | MC, V.

El Paradero. An 1820 Spanish adobe in downtown Santa Fe with details from 1880 and 1912 remodelings. There are skylights, fireplaces, and many antiques, and some rooms have balconies. Complimentary breakfast. Some kitchenettes, cable TV in some rooms, no TV in some rooms, TV in common area. Library. Pets allowed (fee). No kids under 4. | 220 W. Manhattan 87501 | 505/988–1177 | www.elparadero.com | 12 rooms, 2 suites | $75–$140, $125–$140 suites | AE, MC, V.

Holiday Inn. This hotel is 5 mi from the Plaza. There's a four-story Holidome atrium. Restaurant, bar, room service. In-room data ports, some refrigerators, cable TV. Indoor-outdoor pool. Hot tub, sauna. Gym. Business services, airport shuttle. Some pets allowed. | 4048 Cerrillos Rd. 87505 | 505/473–4646 | fax 505/473–2186 | www.holiday-inn.com | 130 rooms | $89–$149 | AE, D, DC, MC, V.

★ **Inn of the Anasazi.** This boutique hotel one-half block off the Plaza was built in 1991, and though small has a feeling of grandeur and excellent service. Its restaurant is also one of the finest in Santa Fe. Restaurant. In-room safes, minibars, cable TV, in-room VCRs (and movies). Massage. Gym. Business services. Some pets allowed (fee). | 113 Washington Ave. 87501 | 505/988–3030 or 800/688–8100 | fax 505/988–3277 | www.innoftheanasazi.com | 59 rooms | $199–$429 | AE, D, DC, MC, V.

Inn of the Turquoise Bear. The former home of poet Witter Bynner, this 19th-century adobe offers simply furnished rooms that may have been slept in by D. H. Lawrence or Robert Oppenheimer. The terraced flower gardens offer a nice place to relax. Complimentary Continental breakfast. Cable TV. Library. Laundry facilities. Some pets allowed. No smoking. | 342 E. Buena Vista, 87501 | 505/983–0798 or 800/396–4104 | fax 505/988–4225 | www.turquoisebear.com | 8 rooms, 2 suites | $95–$195, $175–$195 suites | D, MC, V.

Inn on the Alameda. Some rooms in this inn, two blocks from the Plaza on the Santa Fe River, have kiva fireplaces and a balcony or other outdoor space. Bar, complimentary Continental breakfast. In-room data ports, cable TV, some in-room VCRs. Hot tub, massage. Gym. Library. Business services. Pets allowed (fee). | 303 E. Alameda 87501 | 505/984–2121 or 800/289–2122 | fax 505/986–8325 | www.inn-alameda.com | 69 rooms | $147–$334 | AE, D, DC, MC, V.

La Quinta Inn Santa Fe. Comfortable, basic three-story hotel, 3 mi from Interstate 25. Complimentary Continental breakfast. In-room data ports, some refrigerators, cable TV. Pool. Laundry service. Pets allowed. | 4298 Cerrillos Rd./Business Loop I–25 87505 | 505/471–1142 | fax 505/438–7219 | 130 rooms | $60–$110 | AE, D, DC, MC, V.

Madeleine Inn. Formerly the Preston House, this late-Victorian shingle-style mansion is four blocks east of the Plaza and filled with period antiques; there are fireplaces in some rooms. Complimentary Continental breakfast. No air-conditioning in some rooms. Business services. Some pets allowed. No smoking. | 106 Faithway St. 87501 | 505/982–3465 or 888/321–5123 | fax 505/982–8572 | 6 rooms, 2 cottages | $70–$165 | D, MC, V.

Motel 6 Santa Fe North. This well-maintained budget motel is 1½ mi from the Villa Linda Mall. Cable TV. Pool. Some pets allowed. | 3007 Cerrillos Rd., 87505 | 505/473–1380 or 800/466–8356 | fax 505/473–7784 | www.motel6.com | 104 rooms | $42–$54 | AE, D, MC, V.

Quality Inn. This is a convenient, economical choice 4 mi from I–25. Some refrigerators, cable TV. Pool. Tennis courts. Playground. Laundry facilities, laundry service. Business services, airport shuttle. Some pets allowed. | 3011 Cerrillos Rd. 87505 | 505/471–1211 | fax 505/438–9535 | www.qualityinn.com | 99 rooms | $55–$105 | AE, D, DC, MC, V.

Residence Inn by Marriott. This all-suite hotel 1½ mi from the Plaza has fantastic mountain views. All rooms have full kitchens. Picnic area, complimentary Continental breakfast. In-room data ports, kitchenettes, refrigerators, cable TV. Pool. Hot tub. Laundry facilities, laundry service. Business services, airport shuttle. Some pets allowed (fee). | 1698 Galisteo St. 87505 | 505/988–7300 | fax 505/988–3243 | www.marriott.com | 120 suites | $169–$209 suites | AE, D, DC, MC, V.

Steve's Santa Fe Inn. This hotel is 4 mi from the Plaza. Cable TV. Pool. Laundry service. Business services. Pets allowed. | 2907 Cerrillos Rd. 87505 | 505/471–3000 | fax 505/424–7561 | 265 rooms | $40–$90 | AE, D, DC, MC, V.

SANTA ROSA

Best Western Adobe Inn. This two-story motel offering larger-than-average-size rooms is built around a courtyard containing a large outdoor pool. Restaurant, complimentary Continental breakfast. In-room data ports, cable TV. Pool. Business services. Pets allowed. | 1501 Will Rogers Dr. (I–40, exit 275) | 505/472–3446 or 800/528–1234 | fax 505/472–5759 | www.bestwestern.com | 58 rooms | $38–$65 | AE, D, DC, MC, V.

Holiday Inn Express. This hotel has interior hallways and nice rooms. Cable TV. Pool. Hot tub, sauna. Laundry facilities. Business services. Pets allowed. | 3202 Will Rogers Dr. | 505/472–5411 or 800/465–4329 | fax 505/472–3537 | www.hiexpress.com | 100 rooms | $30–$70 | AE, D, DC, MC, V.

Ramada Limited Hotel. This is a two-story motel in the heart of Santa Rosa. The suites have microwaves and refrigerators. The indoor pool is a great place to relax. Complimentary Continental breakfast. Some microwaves, some refrigerators, cable TV. Pool. Hot tub. Gym. Laundry facilities. Free parking. Pets allowed (fee). | 1701 Will Rogers Dr. | 505/472–4800 or 800/272–6232 | fax 505/472–4809 | www.ramada.com | 60 rooms | $75 | AE, D, MC, V.

SILVER CITY

Econo Lodge Silver City This three-story chain motel is on a mesa overlooking Silver City and has a fountain courtyard. Some of the spacious rooms have spectacular views of town. Complimentary Continental breakfast. In-room data ports, some microwaves, some refrigerators, cable TV. Pool. Hot tub. Gym. Laundry facilities, laundry service. Pets allowed. | 1120 E. Hwy. 180 | 505/534–1111 or 800/553–2666 (central reservations) | fax 505/534–2222 | www.econolodge.com/hotel/nm014 | 62 rooms | $54–$61 | AE, D, DC, MC, V.

Holiday Motor Hotel. Many rooms at this two-story motel have views of the attractively landscaped lawn. Restaurant, room service. Cable TV. Pool. Business services, airport shuttle. Pets allowed. | 3420 Hwy. 180 E | 505/538–3711 or 800/828–8291 | www.holidayhotel.com | 79 rooms | $42–$48 | AE, D, DC, MC, V.

Super 8. This two-story motel is surrounded by juniper trees and piñons. Most rooms have double beds; five business minisuites have recliners, refrigerators, data ports, and coffeemakers. Complimentary Continental breakfast. In-room data ports, some refrigerators, cable TV, some in-room VCRs. Pets allowed (fee). | 1040 E. U.S. 180 | 505/388–1983 or 800/800–8000 | fax 505/388–1983 | www.super8.com | 69 rooms | $39–$52 | AE, D, DC, MC, V.

SOCORRO

Best Inn. This two-story chain motel is near Socorro's main street, 1 mi from New Mexico Tech. Restaurant, complimentary Continental breakfast. Microwaves, refrigerators, cable TV. Pool. Some pets allowed. | 507 N. California St. | 505/835–0230 | fax 505/835–1993 | www.bestinn.com | 41 rooms | $35–$55 | AE, D, DC, MC, V.

Econo Lodge. This motel has spacious rooms. All have a king- or a queen-size bed. Complimentary Continental breakfast. In-room data ports, microwaves, refrigerators, cable TV. Pool. Hot tub, sauna. Gym. Laundry facilities. Pets allowed. | 713 N. California | 505/835–1500 | www.econolodge.com | 64 rooms | $46–$58 | AE, D, DC, MC, V.

Holiday Inn Express. These rooms and suites are ample, quiet, and well maintained. The rooms have coffeemakers and a phone in the bathroom. The nice pool, hot tub, and other amenities set this specific property apart from the other chains in town. Complimentary Continental breakfast. In-room data ports, microwaves, refrigerators, cable TV, some in-room VCRs. Pool. Hot tub. Gym. Laundry service. Business services. Pets allowed (fee). | 1100 California NE | 505/838–0556 or 888/526–4657 | fax 505/838–0598 | www.hiexpress.com | 80 rooms | $79–$109 | AE, D, DC, MC, V.

TAOS

Adobe and Stars Inn. This impressive B&B offers spacious rooms, all with fireplaces, hot tubs or double showers, ceiling fans, and beamed ceilings. Large windows and decks enhance views of the surrounding Sangre de Cristo Mountains. Courtyard rooms have private entrances. Complimentary breakfast. No air-conditioning, TV in-room, VCRs (and movies), TV in common area. Some pets allowed. No smoking. | 584 Hwy. 150 | 505/776–2776 or 800/211–7076 | fax 505/776–2872 | www.taosnet.com/stars | 7 rooms (3 with shower only) | $115–$180 | AE, D, MC, V.

American Artists Gallery House. An unusual hotel with an art display and a quiet, secluded location. Complimentary breakfast. TVs in some rooms. No kids under 8. Some pets allowed. | 132 Frontier La. | 505/758–4446 or 800/532–2041 | fax 505/758–0497 | taoswebb.com/hotel/artistshouse | 10 rooms (5 with shower only) | $75–$150 | AE, MC, V.

Austing Haus. This large timber-frame building (the largest in the United States) is surrounded by national forest land, about 18 mi northeast of Taos. Especially popular with skiers due to its proximity to the Taos Ski Valley (1½ mi), but cheaper rates keep it popular in summer too. Dining room, complimentary Continental breakfast. No air-conditioning, cable TV. Hot tubs. Laundry facilities. Business services. Pets allowed. | 1282 Hwy. 150/Taos Ski Valley Rd. 87525 | 505/776–2649 or 800/748–2932 | fax 505/776–8751 | taoswebb.com/hotel/austinghaus | 24 rooms in 3 buildings | $120–$180 | Closed mid-Apr.–mid-May | AE, DC, MC, V.

El Pueblo Lodge and Condominiums. This property is on 3½ acres north of town, near Kit Carson Park. Rooms are offered in a 1950s-style motel around a courtyard, in a newer two-story building dating from 1972, and an even newer building, which has the nicest rooms. Condominium units are also available and are good for families; these can be rented by the unit or by the individual room. Some rooms have fireplaces. Complimentary Continental breakfast. In-room data ports, some kitchenettes, microwaves, refrigerators, cable TV. Pool. Hot tub. Pets allowed (fee). | 412 Paseo del Pueblo Norte | 505/758–8700 or 800/433–9612 | fax 505/758–7321 | www.taoswebb.com/hotel/elpueblo | 60 rooms | $70–$165 rooms, $115–$248 condos | AE, D, MC, V.

Fechin Inn. Located next door to the former home of Taos artist Nicolai Fechin, this luxury hotel built in 1996 is dominated by a handsome two-story lobby; the large rooms are decorated in southwestern style. Guests have free admission to the Fechin Institute, next door. Hot tub. Health club. Library. Business services. Pets allowed. | 227 Paseo del Pueblo Norte 87571 | 505/751–1000 or 800/811–2933 | fax 505/751–7338 | www.fechin-inn.com | 84 rooms | $109–$319 | AE, D, DC, MC, V.

Holiday Inn Don Fernando de Taos. There are fireplaces in some rooms in the pueblo-style hotel. Rooms are furnished with hand-carved New Mexican furnishings. A free shuttle takes guests to the town center. Restaurant, bar, room service. Cable TV, some in-room VCRs. Indoor-outdoor pool. Hot tub. Tennis. Business services, airport shuttle. Pets allowed. | 1005 Paseo del Pueblo Sur | 505/758–4444 | fax 505/758–0055 | www.taosweb.com/holidayinn | 124 rooms | $65–$149 | AE, D, DC, MC, V.

La Doña Luz Inn and Historic Bed & Breakfast. Spanish colonial furnishings, custom woodwork, elaborate carvings, and Native American artifacts and pottery add elegant and distinct touches to this 1802 hacienda-style inn. Many rooms have fireplaces and private hot tubs; ask about the guest room with the 100-mi view—its deck is the highest point in Taos. Right on the Plaza, this place is special without being horribly expensive. Picnic area, complimentary Continental breakfast. Some microwaves, cable TV, in-room VCRs (and movies), no room phones. Business services. Pets allowed (fee). | 114 Kit Carson

St. | 505/758–4874 or 800/758–9187 | fax 505/758–4541 | www.ladonaluz.com. | 15 rooms | $59–$199 | AE, D, MC, V.

Quality Inn. This motel is on busy Route 68, 2 mi south of the Plaza. Restaurant, bar, picnic area, room service. In-room data ports, some microwaves, refrigerators, cable TV, some in-room VCRs. Pool. Business services. Pets allowed (fee). | 1043 Camino del Pueblo Sur | 505/758–2200 or 800/845–0648 | fax 505/758–9009 | www.qualityinntaos.com | 99 rooms | $55–$175 | AE, D, DC, MC, V.

Sagebrush Inn. Many rooms in this 1929 pueblo-style adobe 3 mi south of the Plaza have fireplaces. Rooms are furnished with Native American crafts and southwestern antiques. Georgia O'Keeffe once lived in one of the third-floor rooms. Restaurant, bar (with entertainment), complimentary breakfast. Some refrigerators, cable TV. Pool. Hot tub. Business services. Pets allowed. | 1508 Paseo del Pueblo Sur | 505/758–2254 or 800/428–3626 | fax 505/758–5077 | www.sagebrushinn.com | 100 rooms | $65–$140 | AE, D, DC, MC, V.

Sun God Lodge. This adobe motel is on the main highway, 1½ mi from Taos Plaza. The well-priced rooms overlook a courtyard. There are several suites that have fireplaces and kitchenettes. Picnic area. Some in-room data ports, some kitchenettes, some microwaves, some refrigerators, cable TV, some in-room VCRs. Hot tub. Laundry facilities. Pets allowed (fee). | 919 Paseo del Pueblo Sur | 505/758–3162 or 800/821–2437 | fax 505/758–1716 | www.sungodlodge.com | 55 rooms | $55–$139 | AE, D, DC, MC, V.

TRUTH OR CONSEQUENCES

Ace Lodge. This small, quiet, and economical motel is in the heart of town. Restaurant, bar, picnic area. Cable TV. Pool. Playground. Airport shuttle. Some pets allowed. | 1302 N. Date St. (I–25 Business) | 505/894–2151 | 38 rooms | $33–$70 | AE, DC, MC, V.

Charles Motel and Bath House. Built in the 1940s, this hotel and spa was created as a place for relaxation. The apartment-style rooms are peaceful, and to help you center yourself, some rooms do not have phones for needless intrusions. This is a place to recuperate from the stress of life. Enjoy the massage therapy, reflexology, holistic healing, and wraps. Kitchenettes, refrigerators, cable TV, some room phones. Hot tub, massage, sauna, spa. Gym. Pets allowed. | 601 Broadway | 505/894–7154 or 800/317–4518 | www.globaldrum.com/sierra_newmexico/spa | 20 rooms | $35–$45 | AE, D, MC, V.

Quality Inn. This well-situated hotel 5 mi north of Truth or Consequences overlooks the lovely Elephant Butte Lake. Restaurant, bar, picnic area, room service. Cable TV. Pool, lake. Tennis court. Playground. Business services. Pets allowed. | Hwy. 195 at Warm Springs 87935 | 505/744–5431 | fax 505/744–5044 | 48 rooms | $69–$90 | AE, D, DC, MC, V.

TUCUMCARI

Budget Host Royal Palacio. This affordable small motel is on historic Route 66. Picnic area. Cable TV. Laundry facilities. Pets allowed. | 1620 E. Tucumcari Blvd. | 505/461–1212 | www.budgethost.com | 24 rooms | $20–$30 | AE, D, MC, V.

Comfort Inn. This modern two-story motel has mountain views, and it's right on historic Route 66. Complimentary Continental breakfast. Cable TV. Pool. Pets allowed. | 2800 E. Tucumcari Blvd. | 505/461–4094 or 800/228–5160 | fax 505/461–4099 | www.comfortinn.com | 59 rooms | $54–$66 | AE, D, DC, MC, V.

Days Inn–Tucumcari. This motel is 1 mi from the business district. The rooms are clean, quiet, and comfortable. The rates are reasonable. Complimentary Continental breakfast. Cable TV. Pets allowed. | 2623 S. 1st St. | 505/461–3158 or 800/544–8313 | fax 505/461–4871 | www.daysinn.com | 40 rooms | $45–$66 | AE, D, DC, MC, V.

Dream Catcher B&B. This mansion built in the 1900s has one suite with a queen bed and a private bath, four rooms that share a bath, and a third-floor sleeping dorm with three full beds and three twin beds, all of which share one bath. There's a large veranda for sipping tea and relaxing. Antiques fill the home, and it's your only nonchain choice in town. Picnic area, complimentary Continental breakfast. Some refrigerators, no room phones, no TV in some rooms, TV in common area. Library. Laundry facilities. Free parking. Pets allowed (fee). | 307 E. High St. | 505/461–2423 | 5 rooms (4 with shared bath), 1 dorm-style room (with shared bath) | $65 | MC, V.

Econo Lodge. This small and affordable motel is on historic Route 66. Cable TV. Business services. Pets allowed. | 3400 E. Tucumcari Blvd. | 505/461–4194 | fax 505/461–4911 | www.econolodge.com | 41 rooms | $40–$76 | AE, D, DC, MC, V.

Holiday Inn. This nice motor hotel is especially suited for the business traveler, with generous work desks and a place to hook up a laptop. Restaurant, bar, room service. In-room data ports, cable TV. Pool. Hot tub. Playground. Laundry facilities. Business services. Pets allowed. | 3716 E. Tucumcari Blvd. | 505/461–3780 or 800/335–3780 | fax 505/461–3931 | www.holiday-inn.com | 100 rooms | $45–$79 | AE, D, DC, MC, V.

Microtel Inn. This motel is right off of I–40. The rooms are comfortable and relatively spacious, basic accommodations that are centrally located. Complimentary Continental breakfast. In-room data ports, cable TV. Pool, hot tub. Pet allowed. | 2420 S. 1st St. | 505/461–0600 | 53 rooms | $50–$65 | AE, D, DC, MC, V.

Rodeway Inn West. This motel on historic Route 66 is in Tucumcari's main business district, on the west side of town. Complimentary Continental breakfast. Cable TV. Pool. Pets allowed (fee). | 1302 W. Tucumcari Blvd. | 505/461–3140 | fax 505/461–2729 | 61 rooms | $33 | AE, DC, MC, V.

New York

ALBANY

Howard Johnson Hotel. Some rooms at this chain hotel have desks, tables, and pull-out sofas. The hotel is 20 minutes from the Albany International Airport. Restaurant, complimentary Continental breakfast. In-room data ports, cable TV. Pool. Tennis. Gym. Business services, free parking. Some pets allowed. | 416 Southern Blvd. | 518/462–6555 | fax 518/462–2547 | 135 rooms | $82 | AE, D, DC, MC, V.

Mansion Hill Inn and Restaurant. This inn in the heart of downtown Albany was built in 1861 and has a central courtyard. Guest rooms are large and uncluttered, with antique reproduction pieces and tasteful watercolor prints. Restaurant, complimentary breakfast, room service. Cable TV. Free parking. Pets allowed. | 115 Philip St. 12202 | 518/465–2038 | fax 518/434–2313 | www.mansionhill.com | 8 rooms | $155–$175 | AE, D, DC, MC, V.

Marriott. You'll find rooms with pull-out couches, king-size beds, or two double beds at this chain hotel near I–87 and the Albany International Airport. Outside there's a patio and pool with a view. Two shopping malls are within 5 mi. Suites have meeting rooms. 2 restaurants, bar, complimentary Continental breakfast. In-room data ports, cable TV. 2 pools. Hot tub. Exercise equipment. Laundry facilities. Business services, airport shuttle, free parking. Pets allowed. | 189 Wolf Rd. 12205 | 518/458–8444 | fax 518/458–7365 | 359 rooms, 3 suites | $139–$184, $514–$678 suites | AE, D, DC, MC, V.

Ramada Inn of Albany. This hotel is 3 mi from downtown Albany and the state capitol building and 6 mi from Albany International Airport. Restaurant, bar, complimentary breakfast, room service. In-room data ports, cable TV. Pool. Beauty salon. Exercise equipment. Business services, airport shuttle, free parking. Pets allowed. | 1228 Western Ave. 12203 | 518/489–2981 | fax 518/489–8967 | ramadaonwestern@msn.com | www.sovereignhotels.com | 195 rooms | $98 | AE, D, DC, MC, V.

Ramada Limited. Basic lodging near the Albany International Airport is available in this chain motel. Complimentary Continental breakfast. Microwaves, refrigerators, some in-room hot tubs, cable TV. Exercise equipment. Business services. Pets allowed (deposit). | 1630 Central Ave. 12205 | 518/456–0222 | fax 518/452–1376 | ramada-albany@travelbase.com | 105 rooms | $74–$94 | AE, D, DC, MC, V.

ALEXANDRIA BAY

Northstar Resort Motel. This motel is only two blocks from downtown on an inlet. Some rooms have decks. Restaurant, bar. Some refrigerators, cable TV. Pool. Docks, boating. Playground. Pets allowed. | 116 Church St. 13607 | 315/482–9332 | fax 315/482–5825 | northstar@gisco.net | 66 rooms | $89–$119 | AE, D, MC, V.

AMHERST

Lord Amherst. This two-story hotel near the Buffalo Niagara International Airport has large spacious rooms done in colonial style, and bathrooms with double sinks. It's 2 mi from local restaurants and 20 mi from Niagara Falls. Restaurant, bar, complimentary breakfast. In-room data ports, cable TV. Pool. Exercise equipment. Laundry facilities. Business services. Some pets allowed. | 5000 Main St. 14226 | 716/839–2200, 800/544–2200 reservations | fax 716/839–1538 | 100 rooms | $72–$89 | AE, D, DC, MC, V.

Marriott. This 10-story hotel in the heart of Amherst's business district has a lobby with a marble finish and a restaurant that serves Tuscan food. Restaurant, bar. In-room data ports, microwaves, cable TV. Pool. Hot tub. Gym. Video games. Business services, airport shuttle. Some pets allowed. | 1340 Millersport Hwy. | 716/689–6900 | fax 716/689–0483 | www.marriotthotels.com/bufny/default.asp | 356 rooms | $80–$175 | AE, D, DC, MC,V.

Motel 6. There are few surprises at this standard-issue motel, which borders the campus of the University of Buffalo. Pets allowed. | 4400 Maple Rd. 14226 | 716/834–2231 | fax 716/834–0872 | 94 rooms | $54–$60 | AE, D, DC, MC, V.

Red Roof Inn. This hotel is 20 minutes from downtown Amherst by car and just a mile from the University of Buffalo. Rooms have video games. Cable TV. Business services. Some pets allowed. | 42 Flint Rd. 14226 | 716/689–7474 | 108 rooms | $60–$80 | AE, D, DC, MC, V.

AMSTERDAM

Best Western Amsterdam. This five-story chain hotel is about 8 mi from the Shrine of the North American Martyrs and 10 mi from Great Sacandage Lake and the surrounding parkland. Park and museum. Restaurant, bar. In-room data ports, cable TV. Pool. Shops. Business services. Some pets allowed. | 10 Market St. | 518/843–5760 | fax 518/842–0940 | 125 rooms | $70 | AE, D, DC, MC, V.

AUBURN

Days Inn. Renovated in 1996, this two-story hotel is less than ½ mi from both the William Seward House and the Auburn Family Restaurant. Days Inn gives out 10% discount coupons to nearby restaurants. It's next door to the YMCA. Complimentary Continental breakfast. In-room data ports, cable TV. Tennis. Gym. Laundry facilities. Business services. Pets allowed. | 37 William St. | 315/252–7567 | fax 315/252–7567 | 51 rooms | $39–$59 | AE, D, MC, V.

BATAVIA

Best Western. This chain hotel is 2 mi from the Genesee County Airport and 30 mi from the Buffalo International Airport. Restaurant, bar. In-room data ports, cable TV. Pool. Business services. Some pets allowed. | 8204 Park Rd. | 716/343–1000 | fax 716/343–8608 | 75 rooms | $80–$110 | AE, D, DC, MC, V.

Days Inn. This two-story hotel is a 45-min drive from Niagara Falls and Darien Lake. Complimentary Continental breakfast. Cable TV. Pool. Business services. Pets allowed. | 200 Oak St. | 716/343–1440 | fax 716/343–5322 | 120 rooms | $58 | AE, D, MC, V.

Holiday Inn. This link in the chain is a five-story building near Darien Lake and Batavia Downs thoroughbred racetrack. Restaurant, bar. In-room data ports, some refrigerators, cable TV. 2 pools. Exercise equipment. Business services. Some pets allowed. | 8250 Park Rd. | 716/344–2100 or 800/877–6145 | fax 716/344–0238 | 196 rooms | $84 | AE, D, DC, MC, V.

BATH

Caboose Motel. Sleep in an old railroad car at this motel, 12 mi from Bath. The "caboose" rooms are furnished with bunk beds and train seats. Caboose rooms are not available October–April. Restaurant, picnic area. In-room data ports, cable TV. Pool. Playground. Business services. Some pets allowed. | 8620 Rte. 415, Avoca, 14809 | 607/566–2216 | fax 607/566–3817 | 18 rooms, 5 caboose rooms | $45–$50 rooms, $75 caboose rooms | Closed Dec.–Mar. | MC, V.

Days Inn. This five-story downtown hotel is within walking distance of several restaurants. No-smoking rooms are available. Restaurant, bar. Cable TV. Pool. Laundry service. Business services. Pets allowed. | 330 W. Morris St. | 607/776–7644 | fax 607/776–7650 | 104 rooms | $75 | AE, D, DC, MC, V.

Super 8. This chain hotel is downtown. Guest rooms are spaced along two floors with interior corridors, and all are equipped with modern, modular furniture. Cable TV. Business services. Pets allowed. | 333 W. Morris St. 14850 | 607/776–2187 | fax 607/776–3206 | 50 rooms | $59–$62 | AE, D, MC, V.

BINGHAMTON

Comfort Inn. This hotel on a commercial strip in Nimmonsburg, a suburb north of Binghamton, is surrounded by restaurants. Complimentary Continental breakfast. In-room data ports, some microwaves, cable TV. Laundry facilities. Business services. Pets allowed. | 1156 Front St., Nimmonsburg, 13905 | 607/722–5353 | fax 607/722–1823 | www.macomfy@aol.com | www.comfortinn.com | 67 rooms | $80 | AE, D, DC, MC, V.

Grand Royale. This six-story inn is close to Binghamton University. Complimentary Continental breakfast. In-room data ports, cable TV. Business services. Some pets allowed (fee). | 80 State St. 13901 | 607/722–0000, 888/242–0323 reservations | fax 607/722–7912 | 55 rooms, 6 suites | $88 rooms, $158 suites | AE, D, DC, MC, V.

Holiday Inn–Arena. This high-rise hotel in Binghamton's business district overlooks the Chenango River and is across from the Broome County Arena. Restaurant, bar, room service. In-room data ports, some refrigerators, cable TV. Pool. Shops. Laundry facilities. Business services. Pets allowed (fee). | 2-8 Hawley St. 13901 | 607/722–1212 | fax 607/722–6063 | www.holiday-inn.com | 229 rooms, 11 suites | $90 rooms, $129 suites | AE, D, DC, MC, V.

Howard Johnson's. You'll find this Hojo on the northern end of Binghamton, just off the college campus, and within 2 mi of many restaurants. Complimentary Continental breakfast. Cable TV. Business services. Some pets allowed. | 690 Old Front St. 13905 | 607/724–1341 | fax 607/773–8287 | 107 rooms | $54 | AE, D, DC, MC, V.

BLUE MOUNTAIN LAKE

Mountain Motel. This motel is ¼ mi from Blue Mountain Lake and 1 mi from the Adirondack Museum. The 2 mini-suites have fully-equipped kitchenettes. Microwaves, kitchenettes, refrigerators, cable TV. Pets allowed. | Rtes. 28 and 30 | 518/352–7781 | 4 rooms, 2 suites | $45–$65 | MC, V.

BOLTON LANDING

House of Scotts. This inn with a beautiful view of Lake George is next to a public beach. Rooms have mission oak–style furniture. Restaurant. Cable TV. Pool. Some pets allowed. | 4943 Lake Shore Dr. | 518/644–9955 | 6 rooms | $60 | Closed Nov.–mid-Apr. | AE, D, MC, V.

BOONVILLE

Boonville Hotel. Built in 1860, this downtown hotel, with its 1940s cocktail lounge complete with copper ceilings and the original leather booths, is one of Boonville's long-standing landmarks. The bar is a popular tourist site, and the rooms are often rented out by groups of snowmobilers. The accommodations, which all overlook Water Street, are not exactly luxurious—they're comparatively small and all share a bathroom at the end of the hall. Pets allowed. | 103 Water St. 13309 | 315/942–2124 | fax 315/942–2124 | 8 rooms, shared bath | $40 | AE, D, MC, V.

Headwaters Motor Lodge. This two-story building just north of Boonville is near historic Constable Hall and the Old Canal Locks through which barges used to pass. Rooms have Colonial-style furniture. It's 6 mi from downhill and cross-country skiing. Complimentary Continental breakfast. In-room data ports, some kitchenettes, refrigerators, cable TV. Some pets allowed. | Headwaters Motor Lodge, Rte. 12 | 315/942–4493 | fax 315/942–4626 | 37 rooms | $50–$55 | AE, D, MC, V.

BUFFALO

Holiday Inn–Downtown. You'll find this Holiday Inn in historic Allentown across from the Wilcox Mansion, where Theodore Roosevelt was inaugurated. It's also near the downtown business district. Restaurant, bar, room service. In-room data ports, cable TV. Pool, wading pool. Laundry facilities. Business services, airport shuttle, free parking. Some pets allowed. | 620 Delaware Ave. 14202. | 716/886–2121 or 800/465–4329 | fax 716/886–7942 | www.basshotels.com/holiday-inn | 168 rooms | $76–$125 | AE, D, DC, MC, V.

Microtel Inn And Suites. A two-story hotel. Complimentary Continental breakfast. Cable TV. Some pets allowed. | 1 Hospitality Centre Way, Tonawanda 14150. | 716/693–8100 or 800/227–6346 | fax 716/693–8750 | 100 rooms | $50–$75 | AE, D, DC, MC, V.

CANANDAIGUA

Canandaigua Inn on the Lake. This resort is right on the lake and has sand beaches, a private boat dock, and several surrounding acres of cool green woodland. Entertainment is offered on weekends. Restaurant, bar, picnic area. In-room data ports, some refrigerators, some in-room hot tubs, cable TV. Pool. Exercise equipment. Business services. Pets allowed. | 770 S. Main St. 14424 | 716/394–7800 or 800/228–2801 | fax 716/394–5003 | 134 rooms, 44 suites | $65–$250 | AE, D, MC, V.

Econo Lodge. This two-story chain motel is within walking distance of Canandaigua Lake. Complimentary Continental breakfast. Refrigerators, cable TV. Laundry facilities. Business services. Some pets allowed. | 170 Eastern Blvd. 14424 | 716/394–9000 | fax 716/396–2560 | 65 rooms | $65–$85 | AE, D, DC, MC, V.

Finger Lakes Inn. Ten landscaped acres and a family activity center give you plenty of elbow room at this hotel. In addition to the standard rooms, there are special family minisuites which include two sleeping areas, one with two double beds and the other with a pull-out sofa bed. Picnic area, complimentary Continental breakfast. Some kitchenettes, some microwaves, some refrigerators, cable TV. Pool. Basketball, volleyball. Pets allowed. | 4343 Eastern Blvd., Rtes. 5/20 E 14424 | 716/394–2800 or 800/727–2775 | fax 716/393–1964 | relax@fingerlakesinn.com | www.fingerlakesinn.com | 124 rooms, 4 suites | $39–$118 | AE, D, DC, MC, V.

CANTON

Best Western University Inn. This rustic chain hotel is located next door to St. Lawrence University. Restaurant, bar. Refrigerators, cable TV. Pool. Golf. Cross-country skiing. Business services. Pets allowed. | 90 Main St. E | 315/386–8522 | fax 315/386–1025 | www.bwcanton.com | 98 rooms | $75–$95 | AE, D, DC, MC, V.

COLONIE

Inn at the Century. This hotel 10 mi from Albany has rooms done up in burgundy and green with cherry-wood furniture. There is also a nature trail on the property. Restaurant, bar, complimentary breakfast, room service. In-room data ports, some refrigerators, cable TV. Pool. Tennis. Exercise equipment. Business services. Some pets allowed. | 997 New Loudon Rd., Latham 12110 | 518/785–0931 | fax 518/785–3274 | 68 rooms | $119–$225 | AE, D, DC, MC, V.

Microtel Inn. This two-story motor lodge is ½ mi from the Albany International Airport and within walking distance of restaurants. In-room data ports, some refrigerators, cable TV. Business services. Some pets allowed. | 7 Rensselaer Ave., Latham, 12128 | 518/782–9161 or 800/782–9121 | fax 518/782–9162 | 100 rooms | $70–$90 | AE, D, DC, MC, V.

COOPERSTOWN

Aalsmeer Motel & Cottages. This 4½-acre wooded property has 300 ft of frontage on Otsego Lake, 7 mi from Cooperstown, is an inviting setting for outdoor activities. A shallow area is roped off for kids, and there's a dock and a float for swimming as well as enough sand for a castle or two, boat rentals, and fishing for lake trout, black bass, otsego bass, salmon, and panfish. Picnic area. Some kitchenettes, refrigerators, cable TV. Lake. Beach, dock, boating, fishing. Some pets allowed. | 7078 Rte. 80, 13326 | 607/547–8819 | www.cooperstown-chamber.org/aalsmeer | 8 rooms, 10 cottages | $55–$110 | D, MC, V.

CORNING

Best Western Lodge on the Green. This two-story chain hotel is on a 12-acre, parklike lot just west of Corning. You can go fishing next door. Restaurant, room service. In-room data ports, some kitchenettes, cable TV. Pool. Laundry service. Airport shuttle. Pets allowed. | 3171 Canada Rd., Painted Post, 14870 | 607/962–2456 or 800/528–1234 | fax 607/962–1769 | 135 rooms | $69–$104 | AE, D, DC, MC, V.

Econo Lodge. Roughly 10 mi west of Corning is this chain motel in the suburbs. Complimentary Continental breakfast. Some microwaves, some refrigerators, some in-room hot tubs, cable TV. Business services. Pets allowed (fee). | 200 Robert Dann Dr., Painted Post, 14870 | 607/962–4444 | fax 607/937–5397 | 61 rooms | $54–$125 | AE, D, MC, V.

Radisson-Corning. This three-story hotel is in downtown Corning. No-smoking rooms are available. Restaurant, bar (with entertainment), room service. Some kitchenettes, cable TV. Pool. Business services. Some pets allowed. | 125 Denison Pkwy. E 14830 | 607/962–5000 or 800/331–3920 | fax 607/962–4166 | radison@corningny.net | 177 rooms | $105–$169 | AE, D, MC, V.

DEPOSIT

Deposit Motel. One mile from the center of town, you'll find this quintessential country motel in the Catskill foothills. Pictures of farms and country landscapes surround you inside, while outside the Delaware River is only three blocks away. Rooms have two double beds. Pets allowed. | 44 Oak St., 13754 | 607/467–2998 | 12 rooms, 1 suite | $50–$65 | MC, V.

DIAMOND POINT

Trout Lake Club Resort. Some of the rustic, log cabin–style cottages at this family-oriented resort on the lake have fireplaces. You can go hiking nearby. Tennis. Beach, boating, fishing. Video games. Playground. Some pets allowed. | 1 Trout Lake Club Rd., 12824 | 518/644–3571 | 44 cabins | $390 (7–day minimum stay) | Closed Oct.–May | No credit cards.

DUNKIRK

Rodeway Inn. One mile from the center of town, this typical roadside accommodation is only a 2-minute drive from Lake Erie. Beds are double or queen size. Complimentary Continental breakfast. Pets allowed ($5 fee). | 310 Lake Shore Dr. | 888/310–5253 or 716/366–2200 | 48 rooms | $55 | AE, D, DC, MC, V.

Southshore Motor Lodge. Both rooms and cottages are available at this motel on 6 rural acres. Picnic area. Many kitchenettes, refrigerators, cable TV, some in-room VCRs. Pool. Playground. Some pets allowed. | 5040 W. Lake Shore Dr. | 716/366–2822 | 2 rooms, 6 suites, 12 cottages | $49–$115 | MC, V.

EAST HAMPTON

Bassett House–a Country Inn. Built in 1830 as a farmhouse, this Victorian inn is within walking distance of shops and restaurants. Rooms have eclectic antiques, and trees and gardens surround the house. Beds range from twin to queen-size. Some rooms have a fireplace. Complimentary breakfast. Some in-room hot tubs. Pets allowed ($20 fee). | 128 Montauk Hwy., 11937 | 631/324–6127 | fax 631/324–5944 | 12 rooms | $195–$275 | AE, D, MC, V.

Shady Pines Motel. East Hampton is a 5-minute drive from this two-story motel surrounded by trees. Cottages are also available and are great for families. Beds are either full or queen with patchwork quilts. Pool. Pets allowed. | 380 Montauk Hwy. 11937 | 631/537–9329 | fax 631/537–9328 | 12 rooms, 6 cottages | Call for room rates | Closed Jan.–Apr | AE, MC, V.

ELMIRA

Best Western Marshall Manor. This one-story chain motel is in a country setting 8 mi north of Elmira. Restaurant, bar, complimentary Continental breakfast. In-room data ports, microwaves, cable TV. Pool. Pets allowed. | 3527 Watkins Rd., Horseheads, 14845 | 607/739–3891 or 800/528–1234 | 40 rooms | $54–$70 | AE, D, DC, MC, V.

Coachman Motor Lodge. Each room at this motel 1½ mi from downtown Elmira has a separate living room. Picnic area. Kitchenettes, cable TV. Laundry facilities. Business services. Pets allowed. | 908 Pennsylvania Ave., Southport, 14904 | 607/733–5526 | fax 607/733–0961 | 18 rooms | $68–$95 | AE, D, MC, V.

Holiday Inn Riverview. This long brick building overlooks the river and is close to the city's downtown. Restaurant, bar (with entertainment). In-room data ports, microwaves, refrigerators, cable TV. 2 pools, wading pool. Exercise equipment. Laundry facilities. Business services, free parking. Pets allowed. | 760 E. Water St. 14901 | 607/734–4211 | fax 607/734–3549 | 150 rooms | $82–$110 | AE, D, DC, MC, V.

Howard Johnson. This two-story chain hotel, 4 mi north of Elmira, sits approximately 15 mi from the Corning Glass Center, and 25 mi from Watkins Glen State Park. Restaurant. In-room data ports, microwaves, cable TV. Pool. Free parking. Pets allowed. | 2671 Corning Rd., Horseheads, 14845 | 607/739–5636 or 888/895–1403 | fax 607/739–8630 | 76 rooms | $89 | AE, D, DC, MC, V.

ENDICOTT

Executive Inn. This hotel in a mostly residential neighborhood has simple rooms. Some kitchenettes, microwaves, cable TV in some rooms. Business services. Some pets allowed. | 1 Delaware Ave. | 607/754–7570 | 60 rooms, 40 suites | $54–$70 | AE, D, DC, MC, V.

FISHKILL

Wellesley Inn. Business travelers frequent this hotel at the intersection of I–84 and U.S. 9, less than a mile from the First Reformed Protestant Church and within 20 mi of the Westpoint historical area. Complimentary Continental breakfast. In-room data ports, some microwaves, cable TV. Pets allowed (fee). | 20 Schuyler Blvd., at Rte. 9 | 845/896–4995 or 800/444–8888 | fax 845/896–6631 | 82 rooms | $89–$125 | AE, D, DC, MC, V.

FREDONIA

Days Inn. This chain hotel offers standard rooms on the east side of town, just south of U.S. 20. Complimentary Continental breakfast. Cable TV. Free parking. Some pets allowed. | 10455 Bennett Rd. | 716/673–1351 | fax 716/672–6909 | 135 rooms | $55–$70 | AE, D, DC, MC, V.

FULTON

Fulton Motor Lodge. Some of the rooms at this two-story motel have river views. Refrigerators, cable TV. Pool. Exercise equipment. Business services, free parking. Pets allowed. | 163 S. 1st St. | 315/598–6100 or 800/223–6935 | fax 315/592–4738 | 70 rooms | $69–$79 | AE, D, DC, MC, V.

GARDEN CITY

Long Island Marriott. This 11-story chain hotel is near the Nassau Coliseum and offers 39 guest rooms specifically designed for the business traveller. Restaurant, bar, room service. In-room data ports, cable TV. Pool. Barbershop, beauty salon, hot tub, sauna. Gym. Shop. Business services. Some pets allowed. | 101 James Doolittle Blvd., Uniondale, 11553 | 516/794–3800 | fax 516/794–5936 | www.marriotthotels.com | 617 rooms | $135–$299 | AE, D, DC, MC, V.

GRAND ISLAND

Chateau Motor Lodge. This family-run lodge 5 mi from Niagara Falls is surrounded by trees and has a picnic area. Nearby restaurants are within walking distance. Beds are queen size. Pets allowed. | 1810 Grand Island Blvd. 14072 | 716/773–2868 | fax 716/773–5173 | 17 rooms | $69–$79 | AE, D, MC, V.

HERKIMER

Best Western–Little Falls. This chain motel is near the I–90 exit for Little Falls. Restaurant, bar. Cable TV. Video games. Business services. Pets allowed (fee). | 20 Albany St., Little Falls 13365 | 315/823–4954 | fax 315/823–4507 | lfbest@ntcnet.com | 56 rooms | $70–$80 | AE, D, DC, MC, V.

HILLSDALE

Linden Valley. All the rooms at this bed-and-breakfast have separate entrances and mountain views. The pond is great for swimming. Complimentary breakfast. Refrigerators, cable TV. Tennis. Beach. Some pets allowed. | Rte. 23 | 518/325–7100 | fax 518/325–4107 | 7 rooms (6 with shower only) | $115–$145 | AE, MC, V.

Swiss Hutte. This 1800s farmhouse is on 12 acres near the Catamount Ski area. Rooms have outdoor porches or balconies so you can enjoy the view. Restaurant, bar. Some refrigerators. Pool. Tennis. Business services. Some pets allowed. | Rte. 23 | 518/325–3333 | 8057@msn.com | www.swisshutte.com | 15 rooms | $110–$170 | MC, V.

HORNELL

Econo Lodge. A chain motel close to Alfred University and local hunting areas. Restaurant, bar, picnic area, complimentary breakfast. In-room data ports, cable TV. Business services. Pets allowed. | 7462 Seneca Rd. | 607/324–0800 | fax 607/324–0905 | 76 rooms | $60 | AE, D, MC, V.

HUDSON

St. Charles. This three-story Victorian hotel in downtown Hudson has rooms done up in green, burgundy, and mauve. Restaurant, bar (with entertainment), complimentary Continental breakfast. Cable TV. Business services. Pets allowed. | 16 Park Pl | 518/822–9900 | fax 518/822–0835 | 34 rooms, 6 suites | $79–109 rooms, $109 suites | AE, D, DC, MC, V.

HUNTER

Hunter Inn. This modern hotel is just ¾ mi from the Hunter Ski Resort. Most rooms have balconies and views of the mountains. Complimentary Continental breakfast. Cable TV. Hot tub. Exercise equipment. Video games. Business services. Pets allowed (fee). | Main

St. (Rte. 23A) | 518/263–3777 | fax 518/263–3981 | www.hunterinn.com | 41 rooms | $175–$235 | AE, D, MC, V.

ITHACA

Best Western University Inn. This modern hotel is ½ mi from Cornell University. Some rooms have fireplaces and cathedral ceilings. Complimentary Continental breakfast. In-room data ports, microwaves, cable TV, in-room VCRs (and movies). Pool. Business services, airport shuttle, free parking. Some pets allowed (fee). | 1020 Ellis Hollow Rd. 14850 | 607/272–6100 | fax 607/272–1518 | 94 rooms | $95–$199 | AE, D, DC, MC, V.

Columbia Bed and Breakfast. Four blocks from downtown, this B&B, designed and owned by an architect, is anything but conventional. Although the original building is Greek Revival from around 1830, it's filled with custom-designed furniture with lots of color in the rooms. Almost all the rooms have gas fireplaces, and works by local artists are displayed throughout. Breakfast is as creative as you'd expect, with dishes like savory French toast. Some pets allowed. | 529 S. Meadow St. 14850 | 607/273–3885 | fax 607/277–0758 | 7 rooms | $75.

Econo Lodge. Close to shopping malls and restaurants, this chain motel sits on Ithaca's northern end at the intersection of Route 13 and Triphammer Road. Complimentary Continental breakfast. In-room data ports, cable TV. Business services. Pets allowed (fee). | 2303 N. Triphammer Rd. 14850 | 607/257–1400 | fax 607/257–6359 | 72 rooms | $76–$102 | AE, D, MC, V.

Holiday Inn Executive Tower. The rooms have large windows at this downtown hotel across from Ithaca Commons. In addition to huge two-level penthouse suites, there are no-smoking rooms available. Restaurant, bar, room service. Cable TV. Pool. Exercise equipment. Business services, airport shuttle, free parking. Some pets allowed (fee). | 222 S. Cayuga St. | 607/272–1000 | fax 607/277–1275 | www.harthotels.com | 178 rooms | $99–109 | AE, D, MC, V.

La Tourelle Country Inn. Three miles from downtown is this three-story hotel in a commercial area. The rooms have dark Mexican wood or lighter, Haitian wood; some have fireplaces. Some refrigerators, some in-room hot tubs, cable TV. Tennis. Hiking. Business services. Some pets allowed. | 1150 Danby Rd. (Rte. 96B) 14850 | 607/273–2734 or 800/765–1492 | fax 607/273–4821 | 35 rooms | $125–$250 | AE, MC, V.

Ramada Inn–Airport. This two-story chain hotel is 1 mi from Cornell University and 4 mi from Ithaca College. Bar, room service. In-room data ports, microwaves, cable TV. Pool, wading pool. Exercise equipment. Video games. Business services, airport shuttle, free parking. Some pets allowed. | 2310 N. Triphammer Rd. | 607/257–3100 | fax 607/257–4425 | 120 rooms | $109–$139 | AE, D, DC, MC, V.

JAMESTOWN

Comfort Inn. This two-story chain hotel is just at the edge of town. Complimentary Continental breakfast. Some in-room hot tubs, cable TV. Business services. Some pets allowed. | 2800 N. Main St. | 716/664–592 or 800/453–7155 | fax 716/664–3068 | www.comfortinn.com | 101 rooms | $74–$139 | AE, D, DC, MC, V.

JOHNSTOWN

Holiday Inn. This two-story hotel is in a quiet, rural area accessible by exit 28 (Fultonville) off I-90. Once you exit, look for signs to Rte. 30A, which leads you to the hotel. Restaurant, bar (with entertainment), room service. In-room data ports, cable TV. Pool. Laundry facilities. Business services. Some pets allowed. | 308 N. Comrie Ave. 12095-1095 | 518/762–4686 | fax 518/762–4034 | jntny@telenet.net | 100 rooms | $65–$104 | AE, D, DC, MC, V.

KINGSTON

Holiday Inn. This two-story chain hotel is ¼ mi off the Kingston exit of I–87, and close to downtown. Restaurant, bar (with entertainment), room service. Cable TV. Pool, wading pool. Hot tub, sauna. Video games. Laundry facilities. Business services. Pets allowed. | 503 Washington Ave. | 845/338–0400 | holiday@mhb.net | 212 rooms | $99–$149 | AE, D, DC, MC, V.

The Rondout. This Colonial Revival home, built around 1906, is on 2 green and wooded acres with flower gardens, a hammock, and picnic tables. Inside are eclectic portraits, sculptures, and ceramics. No room phones. Some pets allowed. | 88 Westchester St. | 845/ 331–2369 | fax 845/331–9049 | www.pojonews.com/rondout | 4 rooms, two with private baths | $85–$115 | AE, MC, V.

Super 8. This chain motel, less than a mile from I–87's exit 19, is 10–15 minutes from the Senate House Museum. Cable TV. Laundry facilities. Business services. Some pets allowed. | 487 Washington Ave. | 845/338–3078, 800/800–8000 reservations | www.super8.com | 84 rooms | $55–$75 | AE, D, DC, MC, V.

LAKE GEORGE VILLAGE

Best Western of Lake George. This two-story chain motel is decorated in the Adirondack style. You'll find it just 1 mi from the Lake George beaches. Some in-room hot tubs, cable TV. 2 pools, wading pool. Hot tub. Business services. Some pets allowed. | Exit 21, off I–87 | 518/668–5701 | fax 518/668–4926 | reservations@bestwesternlakegeorge.com | www.bestwesternlakegeorge.com | 87 rooms | $79–$199 | AE, D, DC, MC, V.

LAKE PLACID

Art Devlin's Olympic. This hotel, named for the famous ski jumper, is three blocks from the Olympic Sports Complex. Complimentary Continental breakfast. Some in-room hot tubs, refrigerators, cable TV. Pool, wading pool. Airport shuttle. Pets allowed. | 350 Main St. | 518/523–3700 | 40 rooms | $48–$128 | AE, D, MC, V.

Best Western Golden Arrow. Rooms have two extra-long double beds at this chain hotel on the lake side of Main Street in the heart of the village. Sliding glass doors open onto private balconies or terraces. Restaurant, bar (with entertainment), picnic area, room service. In-room data ports, in room safes, refrigerators, cable TV. Pool, wading pool. Hot tub, sauna. Gym, racquetball. Boating. Shops. Baby-sitting. Business services, airport shuttle. Pets allowed (fee). | 150 Main St. | 518/523–3353 | fax 518/523–3353 | info@golden-arrow.com | www.golden-arrow.com | 130 rooms | $79–$159 | AE, D, DC, MC, V.

Howard Johnson. This hotel is made up of four buildings and lies ½ mi west of downtown. Restaurant, bar, picnic area. Cable TV. Pool. Hot tub. Tennis. Cross-country skiing. Pets allowed. | 90 Saranac Ave. | 518/523–9555 | fax 518/523–4765 | 92 rooms | $110–$180 | AE, D, DC, MC, V.

Interlaken. Chef/owner Kevin Gregg will treat you to a Victorian getaway with individually appointed rooms, and a five-course gourmet dinner. The honeymoon suite has a canopy bed and the dining room is panelled in walnut with original tin ceilings. Some rooms overlook the Adirondacks and some overlook the Interlaken's lush gardens. Restaurant, picnic area, complimentary breakfast. No air-conditioning, cable TV, no room phones. Some pets allowed. No kids under 5. | 15 Interlaken Ave. | 518/523–3180 or 800/ 428–4369 | fax 518/523–0117 | www.inbook.com | interlkn@northnet.org | 11 rooms | $140– $210 | AE, MC, V.

★ **Lake Placid Lodge.** Each of the unique rooms has a stone fireplace and rustic furniture made from twigs and birch bark at this lodge on 3 acres of land right on Lake Placid. Free-standing cabins are also available. Restaurant, bar, picnic area, complimentary breakfast. No air-conditioning in some rooms, in-room data ports, some refrigerators. Business services. Pets allowed (fee). No smoking. | Whiteface Inn Rd., off Rte. 86 | 518/523–2700 |

fax 518/523–1124 | www.lakeplacidlodge.com | 17 rooms (5 with shower only), 17 cabins| $300–$600, $475–$800 cabins | AE, MC, V.

Lake Placid Resort–Holiday Inn. This four-story hotel sits on a hilltop in the center of Lake Placid overlooking Mirror Lake. The more than 1,000 acres of grounds include 45 holes of golf, including both a links and a mountain golf course. In addition to standard rooms, there are chalets, lakeside condominiums, and special rooms with hot tubs and fireplaces available. 4 restaurants, bar, room service. In-room data ports, microwaves, refrigerators, some in-room hot tubs, cable TV. Pool. Hot tub, sauna. 2 golf courses, putting green, tennis. Gym. Beach. Playground. Business services. Pets allowed. | 1 Olympic Dr. | 518/523–2556, 800/874–1980 | fax 518/523–9410. | info@lpresort.com | www.lpresort.com | 199 rooms | $109–$249 | AE, D, DC, MC, V.

Ramada Inn. Many of the rooms at this three-story chain motel just off Main Street have views of the lake and mountains. Restaurant, bar. In-room data ports, cable TV. Pool. Hot tub. Exercise equipment. Business services. Some pets allowed. | 12 Saranac Ave. | 518/523–2587 | fax 518/523–2328 | www.ramadalp.com/ | 90 rooms | $75–$119 | AE, D, DC, MC, V.

Schulte's Family Lodge. The photographs on the walls of this motel's coffee shop were taken by Mr. Schulte, co-owner of the motel and an accomplished photographer. From December to March, the motel serves complimentary pastries. Picnic area. Kitchenettes (in cottages), some refrigerators, cable TV, some room phones. Pool. Playground. Some pets allowed. | Cascade Rd. (Rte. 73), near the airport | 518/523–3532 | 15 rooms, 15 cottages | $58–$92 rooms, $48–$95 cottages | AE, MC, V.

LIBERTY

Days Inn of Liberty. This renovated, brick, two-story motel built in the early 1990s is along a commercial strip surrounded by restaurants and one block from Route 17 and 1 mi from golf. Rooms are furnished with burgundy floral fabrics, dark wood, framed prints, and brass light fixtures. Bar, complimentary Continental breakfast. Cable TV. Pool. Video games. Laundry service. Business services. Pets allowed. | 25 Sullivan Ave. | 845/292–7600 | fax 845/292–3303 | www.daysinn.com | 120 rooms | $45–$95 | AE, D, DC, MC, V.

LIVERPOOL

Holiday Inn Syracuse/Liverpool. This six-story hotel is just 7 mi from Hancock International Airport in Syracuse and 10 mi from downtown Syracuse. Even closer is Onondaga Lake Park, which is just 1 mi away. Restaurant. In-room data ports. Cable TV. Pool. Hot tub, sauna. Exercise equipment. Laundry services. Business services, airport shuttle. Some pets allowed. | 441 Electronics Pkwy. 13088 | 315/457–1122 | fax 315/451–0675 | www.holiday-inn.com | 276 rooms | $150 | AE, D, DC, MC, V.

LOCKPORT

Best Western Lockport Inn. This two-story hotel is just 1 mi from historic locks on the Barge Canal and 15 mi from Buffalo International Airport. If you stay in the executive rooms, you'll get a complimentary Continental breakfast. Restaurant, bar. Cable TV. Pool. Sauna. Pets allowed (fee). | 515 S. Transit St. 14094 | 716/434–6151 | fax 716/434–5117 | www.bestwestern.com | 95 rooms | $89–$99 | AE, D, DC, MC, V.

LONG LAKE

Corner Motel. In a residential neighborhood southwest of Long Lake, this single-story motel is just a short jaunt on foot to the lake and a number of eateries. No air-conditioning, refrigerators. Cable TV. Pets allowed. | Rtes. 28 N/30 12847 | 518/624–3571 | fax 518/624–2344 | 6 rooms | $53 | AE, D, MC, V.

MALONE

Clark's Motel. This single-story motel, built in 1982, is within walking distance to one restaurant and is convenient to Route 11. For those looking for recreation, Titus Mountain is 3 mi to the east. Cable TV. Some pets allowed. | 42 E. Main St. 12953 | 518/483–0900 | 19 rooms | $49–$59 | AE, MC, V.

Econo Lodge. This chain motel consists of three buildings and some rooms feature balconies. Restaurant, complimentary Continental breakfast. Cable TV. Pool. Pets allowed. | 227 W. Main St. | 518/483–0500 | fax 518/483–4356 | www.econolodge.com | 38 rooms | $55–$65 | AE, D, MC, V.

Malone Super 8 Motel. This three-story motel, built in 1994, is next to a restaurant and 2 mi from a 36-hole golf course. In-room data ports. Cable TV, in-room VCRs (and movies). Pets allowed. | 17 Rockland St. 12953 | 518/483–8123 or 800/800–8000 | fax 518/483–8058 | www.super8.com | 44 rooms | $66 | AE, D, DC, MC, V.

MAMARONECK

Summerfield Suites Hotel. This four-story hotel is just 2 mi from Mamaroneck and a short drive to several restaurants and a mall. A complimentary shuttle to downtown White Plains is available. In-room data ports, kitchenettes, microwaves, refrigerators. Cable TV, in-room VCRs (and movies). Pool. Outdoor hot tub. Gym. Laundry services. Business services. Pets allowed (fee). | 101 Corporate Park Dr., Harrison 10528 | 914/251–9700 | fax 914/251–1699 | www.summerfieldsuites.com | 159 rooms | $149–$269 | AE, D, DC, MC, V.

MASSENA

St. Lawrence Hotel. Built in the late 1950s, this four-story hotel is just 7 mi from Robert Moses State Park. Live entertainment at the hotel's Smokey's Pubhouse on Friday and Saturday nights keeps the joint jumping. Restaurant, bar, dining room, room service. Cable TV. Laundry facilities. Business services. Pets allowed (fee). | 10 W. Orvis St. 13662 | 315/769–2441 | fax 315/769–9216 | www.stlawrence.com | 121 rooms | $45–$75 | AE, D, DC, MC, V.

MASTIC/MASTIC BEACH

Smith Point Motel. This L-shaped, one-story, beige building with a brown door is on the William Floyd Parkway, on the way to Smith Point Beach. Some microwaves, some refrigerators, cable TV. Business services. Some pets allowed. | 165 William Floyd Pkwy. 11967 | 631/281–8887 | fax 631/395–9584 | 21 rooms | $75 | AE, D, MC, V.

MEDINA

Dollinger's Courtyard. In a commercial area, this single-story motel is just 1 mi from a number of restaurants. Train buffs take note: the Medina Railroad Museum is close, too. Some microwaves, some refrigerators. Cable TV, in-room VCRs (and movies). Pets allowed (fee). | 11360 Maple Ridge Rd. 14163 | 716/798–0016 | fax 716/798–9113 | 18 rooms | $58 | AE, D, MC, V.

MIDDLETOWN

Super 8 Motel. This L-shaped two-story hotel offers newer accommodations that are near shopping and restaurants off Route 17. Complimentary Continental breakfast. Some in-room hot tubs. Pets allowed. | 563 Rte. 211 E | 845/692–5828 | www.super8.com | 82 rooms | $80 | AE, D, DC, MC, V.

MILLBROOK

Cottonwood Motel. This single-story motel is nestled in a sleepy, residential neighborhood. Stroll to the nearby restaurants or hop in the car to check out some of the antiques shops within 10 mi. Some refrigerators, some in-room hot tubs, cable TV. Business services. Pets allowed. | Rte. 44 12545 | 845/677–3283 | fax 845/677–3577 | 18 rooms, 1 cottage | $105–$145 rooms, $220 cottage | AE, MC, V.

Old Drovers Inn. Cattle herders (aka drovers) bringing in their stock to New York in the 18th century made a stopover at this inn 15 mi southeast of Millbrook. Today, it is one of the oldest continuously operating inns in the United States. Rooms are done in Victorian style and three still have fireplaces. The inn sits on 12 acres of land. Restaurant, complimentary breakfast. No room phones, no TV. Some pets allowed (fee). | Old Rte. 22, Dover Plains, 12522 | 845/832–9311 | fax 845/832–6356 | www.olddroversinn.com | Closed first 3 weeks Jan. | 4 rooms | $150 | DC, MC, V.

MONROE

James' Motel. This single-story motel is a short stroll to any of the several nearby restaurants. Some microwaves, some refrigerators, cable TV. Some pets allowed. | 370 Rte. 17M 10950 | 845/783–9651 | fax 845/783–5765 | 23 rooms | $55–$60 | AE, D, DC, MC, V.

MONTAUK

Oceanside Beach Resort. After a relaxing day at the beach, what could be better than a stroll to a nearby restaurant or a game of miniature golf? Many rooms have private balconies. Picnic area. Some kitchenettes, some microwaves, refrigerators. Cable TV. Pool. Beach. Some pets allowed. | 626 New Montauk Hwy. 11954 | 631/668–9825 | fax 631/668–2784 | obr@montaukmotel.com | www.montaukmotel.com | 30 rooms | $135–$225 | AE, D, MC, V.

MT. KISCO

Holiday Inn. Known as the "Hudson Valley country manor," this two-floor hotel has well-maintained rooms and offers pleasant amenities for both business and leisure travelers. Restaurant, bar (with entertainment), room service. In-room data ports, cable TV. Pool. Laundry facilities. Business services. Pets allowed. | 1 Holiday Inn Dr. | 845/241–2600 | fax 914/241–4742 | www.basshotels.com/holiday-inn | 122 rooms | $150–$170 | AE, D, DC, MC, V.

MT. TREMPER

La Duchesse Anne. This intimate B&B is surrounded by shade trees and filled with Victorian-style furnishings. Restaurant, bar, complimentary Continental breakfast. No room phones. Pets allowed. | 1564 Wittenberg Rd. 12457 | 845/688–5260 | fax 845/688–2438 | www.laduchesseanne.com | 10 rooms | $90 | AE, D, DC, MC, V.

NEW YORK CITY

The Carlyle. European tradition and Manhattan swank come together at New York's most lovable grand hotel. Everything about this Madison Avenue landmark suggests refinement, from the Mark Hampton–designed rooms, with their fine antique furniture and artfully framed Audubons and botanicals, to the first-rate service. Many guests head straight to the Bemelmans Bar, named after Ludwig Bemelmans, the illustrator who drew the beloved children's book *Madeline*; he created the murals here. Others come just to hear such singers as Barbara Cook or Bobby Short perform at the clubby Cafe Carlyle, the quintessential cabaret venue. Restaurant, bar, room service. In-room data ports, minibars, microwaves, some in-room hot tubs, cable TV, in-room VCRs (and movies). Massage. Gym. Laundry service. Business services. Some pets allowed. | 35 E. 76th St., between Madison and Park Aves. 10021 | 212/744–1600 or 800/227–5737 | fax 212/717–4682 | 196 rooms | $375–$650 | AE, DC, MC, V.

Four Seasons. An impressive soaring marble lobby, an elegant bar, spacious rooms, and panoramic city views make this one of the top choices in the city. There's a fax machine in every room. Restaurant, bar, room service. In-room data ports, minibars, cable TV, in-room VCRs. Massage. Gym. Business services. Some pets allowed. | 57 E. 57th St. 10022 |

212/758–5700 or 800/332–3442 | fax 212/758–5711 | www.fourseasons.com | 370 rooms, 61 suites | $585 rooms, $1,350 suites | AE, D, DC, MC, V.

Le Parker Meridien. A European ambience is created here with painted ceilings and classically appointed guest rooms. Great location near Carnegie Hall, 57th Street, and 5th Avenue shopping. The restaurant in the hotel specializes in wonderful breakfasts. Restaurant, bar, room service. In-room data ports, cable TV. Pool. Hot tub. Health club. Business services, parking ($39 per day). Small pets allowed. | 118 W. 57th St., between 6th and 7th Aves. 10019 | 212/245–5000 or 800/543–4300 | fax 212/708–7477 | www.parkermeridien.com | 700 rooms | $350–$450 | AE, D, DC, MC, V.

Manhattan Club. Guest rooms are spacious, understated, and elegant at this Midtown hotel, near Carnegie Hall, Lincoln Center, and the Museum of Modern Art. Microwaves, refrigerators, cable TV, in-room VCRs. Business services. Pets allowed (deposit). | 200 W. 56th St., at 7th Ave. 10019 | 212/707–5000 or 800/NYC–2121 | fax 212/707–5140 | www.manhattanclub.com | 165 suites | $350–$450 | AE, DC, MC, V.

Marriott La Guardia. This large, comfortable facility is convenient to La Guardia Airport and surrounding attractions. Among the closest are Queens Museum of Art (3 mi), Shea Stadium (2 mi), Yankee Stadium (7 mi), and Midtown Manhattan (6 mi). Restaurant, bar. In-room data ports, cable TV. Pool. Hot tub. Exercise equipment. Business services, airport shuttle. Pets allowed. | 102-05 Ditmars Blvd., East Elmhurst, Queens 11369 | 718/565–8900 | fax 718/898–4995 | www.marriotthotels.com/LGAAP | 436 rooms | $179 | AE, D, DC, MC, V.

The Mayflower. Some rooms have park views at this West Side hotel, directly across from Central Park. It's just three blocks away from Lincoln Center. Restaurant, bar. In-room data

CANINE COURT

Even in the world of dog parks, New York is a trendy place. When Canine Court opened in April 1998 in Van Cortlandt Park in the northern reaches of the Bronx, it was the first public dog agility course and playground in the country. Now there are others, but it's still pretty spectacular as dog play areas go with its 14,000 fenced square feet of playground and dog run. Van Cortlandt Park, with 1,146 acres of forest and wetlands, is one of the largest green spaces in New York City. It includes soccer and ball fields, a running track and hiking trails, and its golf course was the first public course built in the United States. If you or your friend long for some on-leash quality time, you can take to the trails. Stroll past Van Cortland House Museum, where George Washington headquartered—twice—during the Revolution. Or take a walk along the Cass Gallagher Nature Trail, the tracks of the Old Putnam Railroad line, which once lined New York and Boston, or along the Old Croton Aqueduct Trail, a path above the immense pipe that once brought New York City its water. There's also the John Kieran Nature Trail which encircles Van Cortland Lake—New York City's largest—where there's great bird-watching. You can reach it from Broadway or the Henry Hudson Parkway. Canine Court itself is near the equestrian facilities at the North End of the park's Parade Ground (at Broadway and Lakeview). There are dog events here throughout the year. Can't make it to the Bronx? The dog run in Washington Square Park, at West Fourth Street and Thompson Street in Greenwich Village, on the south side of the park, will show you a whole new side of the Big Apple as you mingle with the sophisticated Village crowd.

ports, cable TV. Exercise equipment. Business services, parking ($35 per day). Pets allowed. | 15 Central Park W, between W. 61st and 62nd Sts. 10023 | 212/265–0060 or 800/223–4164 | fax 212/265–5098 | www.mayflower.com | 365 rooms, 200 suites | $190–$400 rooms, $260–$400 suites | AE, D, DC, MC, V.

The Metropolitan. Located in a distinctive 1960s high-rise, this hotel provides basic amenities and convenience to Midtown. Restaurant, bar. In-room data ports, refrigerators, cable TV. Barbershop. Gym. Business services. Pets allowed. | 569 Lexington Ave., at E. 51st St. 10022 | 212/752–7000 or 800/836–6471 | fax 212/758–6311 | www.loewshotels.com | 722 rooms | $299–$369, rooms, $378–$1,000, suites | AE, D, DC, MC, V.

New York Palace. The reinvented Palace is one of New York's most upscale hotels. The rooms are plush and stylish in bright colors, with desks and electronic controls for lights and temperature control. Some suites have balconies, and many have views of nearby St. Patrick's Cathedral. The tower level on the uppermost floors offers 24-hour butler service. 2 restaurants, room service. In-room data ports, refrigerators (in suites), cable TV. Massage. Health club. Laundry service. Business services. Pets allowed. | 455 Madison Ave. 10022 | 212/888–7000 or 800/697–2522 | fax 212/303–6000 | hrihotel@haven.ios.com | www.newyorkpalace.com | 900 rooms, 104 suites | $475–$600 rooms, $900–$1,000 suites | AE, D, DC, MC, V.

Novotel. The seventh-floor Sky Lobby overlooks the lights of Times Square, and the hotel will assist guests in purchasing theater tickets for the many popular shows that are playing nearby. The white limestone building, built in 1984, has French-style rooms decorated with paintings and photographs. Restaurant, bar (with entertainment). In-room data ports, cable TV. Exercise equipment. Business services. Pets allowed. | 226 W. 52nd St., at Broadway

TAWNY'S TOURS

Susan and Art Zuckerman have been leading walking tours of New York City for many years. But they always missed taking their golden retriever, Tawny. So in 1998, they decided to stop leaving her at home when they set out for their extended walks, and they began offering dog-friendly tours. Susan, a history teacher, and Art, a computer expert, know and love New York and can tell endless colorful stories about its places and history. As pet owners, they also know where to find the most dog-friendly hotels and restaurants (and you usually stop for a meal on your tours). They know the best dog runs, too. And they're happy to plan a special tour of any length covering any part or aspect of the city that interests you. No dog surprises them: One guest arrived for a tour with a 165-lb. Newfoundland; he and Tawny literally blocked the sidewalk as they waited for their owners to eat. There's a $15 charge per person with a $50 minimum. Your dog and any children get to listen to the expert commentary for free. Book ahead: Tawny Tours, 81 Van Etten Blvd., New Rochelle NY 10804, 914/633-7397, www.zuckerman-familytravel.com.

10019 | 212/315–0100 or 800/221–3185 | fax 212/765–5369 | www.novotel.com | 480 rooms | $219–$339 | AE, D, DC, MC, V.

The Pierre. Run by the Four Seasons chain, the Pierre is the ultimate in elegance. Since the 1930s, it has occupied its 5th Avenue post with all the grandeur of a French château. The public areas drip with chandeliers, handmade carpets, and Corinthian columns. The king-size guest rooms are resplendent with traditional chintz fabrics and dark-wood furniture; bathrooms have Art Nouveau fixtures. Service is first rate. Restaurants, bar (with entertainment), room service. In-room data ports, minibars, cable TV. Barbershop, beauty salon, massage. Exercise equipment. Laundry service. Business services. Pets allowed. | 2 E. 61st St. 10021 | 212/838–8000 or 800/743–7734 | fax 212/940–8109 | www.fourseasons.com | 149 rooms, 53 suites | $430–$655 rooms, $695–$5,050 suites | AE, D, DC, MC, V.

Plaza Athénée. Based on the original Paris hotel, this version sports traditional French decor, with antique furniture in the rooms. Some suites have balconies. Restaurant, bar, room service. In-room data ports, refrigerators, cable TV. Exercise equipment. Laundry service. Business services. Pets allowed. | 37 E. 64th St. 10021 | 212/734–9100 or 800/447–8800 | fax 212/772–0958 | www.plaza-athenee.com | 124 rooms, 26 suites | $440–$600 rooms, $1,100–$3,600 suites | AE, D, DC, MC, V.

Royalton. The Philippe Starck–designed Royalton features sleek, contemporary rooms, some with fireplaces or balconies, and the Vodka Bar in the lobby attracts a fashionable crowd. The penthouse has a terrace. Restaurant, bar, room service. In-room data ports, minibars, refrigerators, cable TV, in-room VCRs (and movies). Exercise equipment. Business services. Some pets allowed. | 44 W. 44th St., between 5th and 6th Aves. 10036 | 212/869–4400 or 800/635–9013 | fax 212/869–8965 | 168 rooms | $315–$580 | AE, DC, MC, V.

THE SPA TREATMENT

Need a place to house your pet in the Big Apple? Want to pamper your pet as you would yourself? Check out the New York Dog Spa & Hotel in the Chelsea district, convenient to Greenwich Village, Gramercy Park, and midtown. Some pets come for the day; others for several, to be catered to by trained attendants, with private runs and cages as well as common areas to share with playmates, and several walks a day. You're free to bring along your pet's favorite toys, her bed, her blanket, and anything else to provide comfort in your absence. You can drop off Fido or Fifi as early as 7AM and return as late as 10PM. Having arranged in advance, your pet can also be treated as you might be at Elizabeth Arden farther uptown. They'll bathe her and blow-dry her hair, cut her nails and clean her ears—even give her a hot-oil treatment. Younger dogs can be enrolled in Puppy Class, given in conjunction with the Manhattan Dog Training and Behavior Center, which uses the Sirius Puppy Training Program. A veterinarian is on hand every day except Sunday, too, and the hotel's gift shop offers a nice selection of luxury shampoos, coats and sweaters, bowls, beds, and books (for you, not your dog). Rates depend on your dog's size and weight, beginning at around $26 for day care, around $45 for overnight boarding. Reserve ahead, and be prepared to provide your dog's medical and vaccination records. Contact: New York Dog Spa & Hotel, 145 West 18th St., New York NY 10011, 212/243-1199, www.nydogspa.com.

Soho Grand. The public spaces in this trendy SoHo hotel don't disappoint. There's a grand staircase leading to a hip lounge and the super-cool staff is dressed in black. The light-color rooms, however, are merely basic. There are terraces in the suites. Restaurant, bar. In-room data ports, minibars, cable TV. Massage. Exercise equipment. Business services. Pets allowed. | 310 W. Broadway 10013 | 212/965–3000 or 800/965–3000 (reservations) | fax 212/965–3200 | www.sohogrand.com | 369 rooms, 4 penthouse suites | $349–549 rooms, $1,299–$1699 suites | AE, D, DC, MC, V.

Surrey. This very private, sophisticated boutique hotel is just steps away from Central Park and major museums, and has one of the top restaurants in New York. Restaurant, bar, room service. In-room data ports, microwaves, cable TV, in-room VCRs (and movies). Exercise equipment. Laundry facilities. Business services. Small pets allowed ($300 deposit). | 20 E. 76th St. 10021 | 212/288–3700 | fax 212/628–1549 | www.mesuite.com | 130 rooms | $284–$325 | AE, DC, MC, V.

Wales. Set in an Uptown residential neighborhood convenient to Central Park and several major museums, this hotel has a restaurant known for brunch. The old English-style suites are big and very elegant. Restaurant, complimentary Continental breakfast and afternoon refreshments. Cable TV, in-room VCRs (and movies). Laundry service. Business services. Some pets allowed. | 1295 Madison Ave., between 92nd and 93rd Sts. 10128 | 212/876–6000 or 877/847–4444 (outside NYC) | fax 212/860–7000 | hotel-wales@aol.com | www.uniquehotels.com | 92 rooms, 40 suites | $269 rooms, $429 suites | AE, MC, V.

A WORLD OF DOG ART

Like horses, dogs have long fascinated artists. So too William Secord, the world authority on dogs in art. The founding director of the American Kennel Club's Museum of the Dog, now in St. Louis, he's the author of Dog Painting 1840-1940: A Social History of the Dog in Art and Dog Painting: The European Breeds. He opened an art gallery devoted to dog art and artifacts on New York City's Upper East Side in 1990. At first the gallery specialized in 19th-century dog paintings. The collection was international and included work by Sir Edwin Landseer, George Earl, Maud Earl, John Emms, and Arthur Wardle. Today, you'll also find works in bronze, antique walking sticks, terra-cottas, dog collars, porcelains, and various other collectible items, with prices ranging from around $1,000 and up, as well as work by 20th-century artists, modern masters Barrie Barnett and Christine Merrill, prints by Bert Cobb and Marguerite Kirmse, and drawings by Gladys Emerson Cook. Affenpinschers and Akitas, Australian cattle dogs and kelpies, Auvergne pointers and Basenjis, Basset hounds and bearded collies, bluetick coon hounds and border terriers, borzois and bouviers to Flandres, Tibetan terriers and wire-haired vizslas, weimareiners and Yorkshire terriers, there's scarcely a dog breed that has not made an appearance on Secord's walls. Books about dogs are also available, including Secord's own works and rare and out-of-print volumes that document the history of various breeds. Want to hang a painting of your own prize front and center in your living room? Commission a portrait by one of the living masters of dog and cat art. A gallery highlight is the Yellow Room, hung with dog paintings from floor to ceiling in the Victorian style. And, yes, your dog is welcome to visit, too. 52 East 76th St., New York NY 10021, 212/249-0075, 877/249-DOGS, www.dogpainting.com.

Westbury. British formality meets congeniality at the Forte Hotel chain's New York outpost. Leather banquettes look out on Madison Avenue at the clubby Polo Bar and Restaurant. Rooms and suites have a lived-in country-English look, with floral chintz, oriental rugs, and mahogany furnishings. Restaurant, bar, room service. In-room data ports, cable TV. Exercise equipment. Business services. Pets allowed. | 15 E. Madison Ave. 10021 | 212/535–2000 or 800/321–1569 | fax 212/535–5058 | 228 rooms, 52 suites | $325–$500 | AE, D, DC, MC, V.

NIAGARA FALLS

Best Western Summit Inn. This comfortable chain is in a quiet suburban setting just minutes from shopping and a casino. Restaurant, bar. Cable TV. Pool. Sauna. Business services. Pets allowed. | 9500 Niagara Falls Blvd. 14304 | 716/297–5050 | fax 716/297–0802 | www.bestwestern.com | 88 rooms | $89–$109 | AE, D, DC, MC, V.

Chateau Motor Lodge. This motel on Grand Island, 5 mi from the falls, offers affordable, basic rooms with contemporary furnishings. Some kitchenettes, microwaves, cable TV. Some pets allowed. | 1810 Grand Island Blvd., Grand Island 14072 | 716/773–2868 | fax 716/773–5173 | 17 rooms | $50–$80 | AE, D, MC, V.

Fallsview Travelodge Hotel. True to Niagara Falls's honeymoon tradition, some rooms have king-size beds and red, heart-shaped hot tubs. Just one block east of the falls, this property in a brown-brick building has some rooms with views of the upper Niagara River. Restaurant, bar. Some refrigerators, cable TV. Business services. Pets allowed. | 201 Rainbow Blvd. 14303 | 716/285–9321 or 888/515–6375 | fax 716/285–2539 | www.niagarafallstravelodge.com | 193 rooms | $89–$199 | AE, D, DC, MC, V.

NORTH CREEK

Black Mountain Ski Lodge. This family motel is located in a quiet country setting just minutes from Gore Mountain Ski Center. A dark-wood exterior and wood-paneling walls in the guest rooms give it a rustic chalet look. Restaurant. Some refrigerators, cable TV. Pool. Playground. Pets allowed. | 2999 Rte. 8 12853 | 518/251–2800 | www.blackmountainskilodge.com | 25 rooms | $41–$51 | AE, D, MC, V.

Garnet Hill Lodge and Crosscountry Ski Center. This rustic Adirondack inn overlooks mountains and a pristine private lake, and was built in the tradition of the Adirondack great camps, with hewn beams and posts and a front porch spanning the length of the house. Located 5 mi from Gore Mountain Ski Center, the lodge accommodates guests in five distinctive buildings. The Log House is an Adirondack lodge with a view of the lake and mountains, and a cozy fireplace area surrounded by sofas and rocking chairs. The Big Shanty is a turn-of-the-20th-century Adirondack house set on a hill above the lake. Curl up next to the stone fireplace, surrounded by shelves of old books and rustic yellow birch log pillars. Larger groups can be accommodated in the few guest rooms at The Birches (set in a grove of white birch trees), the Tea House, and the Ski Haus. Restaurant. TV in common room. Sauna. Tennis. Hiking, beach, boating, fishing, bicycles. Cross-country skiing. Business services. Pets allowed in Ski Haus. | 13th Lake Rd. 12856 | 518/251–2821 or 800/497–4207 | fax 518–251–3089 | garnet@netheaven.com | www.garnet-hill.com | 29 rooms (26 with bath) | $72–$125 | MC, V.

NORWICH

Howard Johnson Hotel. This chain hotel is located in the historic downtown area. Restaurant, bar. Some in-room hot tubs, some refrigerators, cable TV. Pool. Business services. Some pets allowed (fee). | 75 N. Broad St. 13815 | 607/334–2200 | fax 607/336–5619 | www.hojo.com | 83 rooms, 4 suites | $69–$99 rooms, $159 suites | AE, D, DC, MC, V.

NYACK

Nyack Motor Lodge. This two-floor local standby is across the street from the Palisades Mall and has been in business since 1975. At the junction off Rte. 303 and NY 59. Complimentary Continental breakfast. Cable TV. Pool. Pets allowed. | 110 Rte. 303, West Nyack 10994 | 845/358–4100 | fax 845/358–3938 | 125 rooms | $55–$70 | AE, DC, MC, V.

OGDENSBURG

Days Inn. This single-story member of the chain is at the junction of Rtes. 37 and 68, near the Frederic Remington Art Museum and the St. Lawrence River. Restaurant, bar. Cable TV. Pets allowed (fee). | 1200 Paterson St. 13669 | 315/393–3200 or 800/329–7466 | fax 315/393–6098 | dheren@bbs.tsf.com | www.daysinn.com | 29 rooms | $45–$75 | AE, D, DC, MC, V.

Ramada Inn/River Resorts of Ogdensburg. This two-story motel in downtown Ogdensburg was renovated in 1996. Boaters appreciate its 42-slip marina as well as its views of the Oswegatchie and St. Lawrence rivers. There's live entertainment or a DJ in the lounge on Friday and Saturday nights. Restaurant, bar with entertainment. Complimentary Continental breakfast, room service. Cable TV. Pool. Spa. Gym. Laundry facilities. Some pets allowed. | 119 W. River St. 13669 | 315/393–2222 or 888/298–2054 | fax 315/393–9602 | 76 rooms | $59–$129 | AE, MC, V.

Stone Fence Motel. This property has guest rooms in four buildings, all surrounded by the namesake stone wall. Two buildings have standard motel rooms, and one offers riverside rooms with large balconies overlooking the St. Lawrence. The fourth building has lofts with full kitchens that can sleep six–eight guests. Restaurant, picnic area. Cable TV. Pool. Hot tub, sauna. Tennis. Docks, boating. Laundry facilities. Pets allowed. | 7191 Riverside Dr. 13669 | 315/393–1545 or 800/253–1545 | fax 315/393–1749 | stonefence@1000islands.com | www.1000islands.com/stonefence | 31 rooms, 8 suites | $79–$135 | AE, D, DC, MC, V.

OLD FORGE

Best Western Sunset Inn. This property, 2 mi from public lakeside beaches and a water park, has standard, modern rooms. The lobby has hanging plants and Greek statues, and the pool has an attached sundeck. Picnic area. Cable TV. Pool. Hot tub, sauna. Tennis. Cross-country skiing, downhill skiing. Playground. Pets allowed. | 2752 Rte. 28 13420 | 315/369–6836 | www.bestwestern.com/best.html | 52 rooms | $79–$103 | AE, D, MC, V.

Clark's Beach Motel. Clark's is a popular destination for snowmobilers and has large, two-story, fully furnished family units with four double beds, a living and dining room, stocked kitchen, and private porches facing the lake. Double rooms are also available. A snowmobile trail is at the edge of the property, so on weekends it can get a little noisy. The lounge has magazines and games. Some kitchenettes, some microwaves, some refrigerators, cable TV. Indoor pool, lake. Hiking. Beach, dock, boating, fishing. Cross-country skiing, snowmobiling. Pets allowed. | Rte. 28 N 13420 | 315/369–3026 | 42 rooms | $52–$70 | MC, V.

Eagle Creek Cottages. Situated on eight private, wooded acres, these cottages (about 8 mi northeast of Old Forge), are named after trees—Balsam, Hemlock, Pine, and Spruce. Pillows, blankets, and cleaning supplies are available, but bring your own sheets, towels, and soap. Kitchens. Microwaves, refrigerators. Some pets allowed. | Kopps Rd. 13331 | 315/357–4134 | 4 cottages | $50–$80 | No credit cards.

Pine Knoll Motel. Set among pine trees, this motel overlooks Old Forge Lake and the Adirondack Mountains. Grocery stores, shops, restaurants, and churches are all within walking distance. Accommodations are in rooms or fully furnished cabins, some of which sleep up to seven. Golf, boat tours and rentals, hiking, and chairlift rides. Some kitchenettes, some refrigerators, cable TV. Lake. Tennis. Beach, dock. Pets allowed. | S. Shore Dr. 13420 | 315/369–6740 | 22 motel rooms, 3 cottages | $65–$74 rooms, $67–$80 cottages | MC, V.

ONEIDA

Governor's House Bed & Breakfast. This pristine four-story brick house was built in 1848 to be the state capitol. The town, however, lost out by one vote to Albany, and the building was used as a tourist house and private residence thereafter. Restored in 1995, the home now has spacious rooms furnished with period antiques and two parlors. You'll feel right at home using the fully stocked guest kitchen and large video library. Complimentary breakfast. Cable TV. Library. Laundry services. Some pets allowed. No smoking. | 50 Seneca Ave., Oneida Castle, 13421 | 315/363–5643 or 800/437–8177 | www.bbhost.com/govhouse | 5 rooms | $76–$155 | AE, D, MC, V.

ONEONTA

Holiday Inn. This hotel is near the interstate, about 10 mi east of the National Soccer Hall of Fame. Restaurant, bar (with entertainment), picnic area, room service. In-room data ports, microwaves, cable TV. Pool, wading pool. Video games. Laundry facilities. Some pets allowed. | Rte. 23 13820 | 607/433–2250 | fax 607/432–7028 | www.holiday-inn.com | 120 rooms | $139–$179 | AE, D, DC, MC, V.

Super 8. This chain motel is across from a movie theater and shopping mall, and approximately 1 mi from the National Soccer Hall of Fame, 2 mi from Hartwick College, and 2½ mi from the State University of Oneonta. Complimentary Continental breakfast. Cable TV. Laundry facilities. Business services. Some pets allowed. | 4973 Rte. 23 13820 | 607/432–9505 | www.super8.com | 60 rooms | $53–$107 | AE, D, DC, MC, V.

OWEGO

Sunrise Motel. This roadside motel offers affordable rooms 2 mi west of Owego. Rooms have two double or one queen-size bed, a round table, and a desk. There's a coffee shop on site. Picnic area. Cable TV. Some pets allowed. | 3778 Waverly Rd. 13872 | 607/687–5666 | 20 rooms | $49 | AE, D, MC, V.

PEEKSKILL

Peekskill Inn. This inn offers panoramic views of the Hudson River, and many of the rooms have outdoor terraces on which to enjoy the breathtaking scenery. Restaurant, bar, complimentary Continental breakfast, room service. Cable TV. Pool. Some pets allowed. | 634 Main St. 10566 | 914/739–1500 or 800/526–9466 | fax 914/739–7067 | www.peekskillinn.com | 53 rooms | $80–$93 | AE, D, DC, MC, V.

PENN YAN

Viking Resort. This resort about 6 mi south of Penn Yan is on the eastern shore of Keuka Lake, and has private docking facilities. It's home base for the *Viking Spirit* cruise, which takes visitors out on Keuka Lake. Three- and six-bedroom cottages are popular for family reunions. Picnic area. Some kitchenettes, refrigerators, cable TV. Pool. Hot tub. Beach, dock, boating. Pets allowed (fee). | 680 E. Lake Rd. 14527 | 315/536–7061 | fax 315/536–0737 | viking@vikingresort.com | www.vikingresort.com | 42 rooms, 35 apartments | $65–$140 rooms, $180–$212 apartments | Closed mid-Oct.–Apr. | No credit cards.

PLAINVIEW/OLD BETHPAGE

Residence Inn. Situated within 3 mi of major area businesses such as Lockheed Martin, Northrup/Grumman, and Lilco, this hotel is geared primarily toward business travelers. For recreation, a 9-hole golf course and tennis courts at Bethpage State Park are just ½ mi away. The ocean is about 10 mi away. Restaurant, bar, complimentary breakfast, room service. In-room data ports, some kitchenettes, cable TV, in-room VCRs. Pool. Hot tub, sauna.

Gym. Baby-sitting. Laundry facilities, laundry service. Business services. Pets allowed (fee). | 9 Gerhard Rd. 11803 | 516/433–6200 or 800/331–3131 | fax 516/433–2569 | 165 suites | $135–$214 | www.residenceinn.com | AE, MC, V.

PLATTSBURGH

Econo Lodge. This two-story motel is 1 mi from Lake Champlain and 5 mi from a snowmo-biling area and a golf course. For those looking for indoor entertainment, Champlain Centre Mall is just ½ mi away. Restaurant, bar, complimentary Continental breakfast. Cable TV. Pool. Business services. Pets allowed. | 528 Rte. 3 12901 | 518/561–1500 or 800/553–2666 | fax 518/563–3144 | www.econolodge.com | 98 rooms | $49–$57 | AE, MC, V.

Holiday Inn. This chain hotel is only 60 mi from Montreal at the intersection of I–87 and Route 3 at exit 37. Restaurant, bar, room service. In-room data ports, cable TV. Pool, wading pool. Hot tub. Exercise equipment. Video games. Business services. Some pets allowed. | 412 Rte. 3 12901 | 518/561–5000 | fax 518/562–2974 | www.holiday-inn.com | 102 rooms | $69–$79 | AE, D, DC, MC, V.

Inn at Smithfield. This Best Western hotel is located between two malls. Rooms have balconies, some with pool views. Some rooms have recliners. From the Adirondack Northway (I–87), take exit 37. Restaurant, bar, room service. In-room data ports, cable TV. Pool. Exercise equipment. Laundry facilities. Business services. Pets allowed. | 446 Rte. 3 12901 | 518/561–7750 | fax 518/561–9431 | www.bestwestern.com | 120 rooms | $66–$99 | AE, D, DC, MC, V.

POUGHKEEPSIE

Econo Lodge. This basic chain hotel is about a 10-minute drive to Vassar College, and good for folks coming for interviews or campus tours. Complimentary Continental breakfast. In-room data ports, some refrigerators, cable TV. Laundry facilities. Business services. Pets allowed. | 2625 South Rd. (U.S. 9) 12601 | 845/452–6600 | www.econolodge.com | 111 rooms | $100 | AE, D, DC, MC, V.

Holiday Inn Express. This chain hotel is in a residential area, 2 mi north of the commercial district. Complimentary Continental breakfast. Cable TV. Pool. Business services. Pets allowed. | 341 South Rd. (Rte. 9 and Sharon Dr.) 12601 | 845/473–1151 | fax 845/485–8127 | www.basshotels.com | 121 rooms | $109 | AE, D, DC, MC, V.

Poughkeepsie Travel Lodge. This two-story member of the chain is 2.2 mi from Vassar College. Restaurant, bar, picnic area. Some kitchenettes, refrigerators, cable TV. Pool. Tennis. Business services. Pets allowed. | 313 Manchester Rd. (Rte. 55) 12603 | 845/454–3080 or 800/578–7878 | fax 845/452–2516 | www.travelodge.com | 100 rooms | $45–$85 | AE, D, DC, MC, V.

QUOGUE/EAST QUOGUE

Inn at Quogue. The core of this inn was built in 1785 as a family residence, and it became a summer boardinghouse in 1871. The 15 rooms in the main house were recently renovated under the supervision of Ralph Lauren's design team. Beaches are nearby, and you can borrow towels and beach chairs from the inn. Restaurant, bar. Some kitchenettes, cable TV. Pool. Spa. Tennis. Beach. Bicycles. Baby-sitting. Pets allowed. | 47-52 Quogue St., Quogue 11959 | 631/653–6560 | fax 631/653–8026 | www.innatquogue.com | 67 rooms, 2 cottages | $200–$300 rooms, $550–$800 cottages | AE, D, MC, V.

ROCHESTER

Comfort Inn–West. This five-story brick hotel is located near Kodak Park, three major malls, and about 30 restaurants. Red Lobster, Bob Evans, Applebee's, Olive Garden adjacent. King suites and double rooms available. Continental breakfast. In-room data ports, some in-room hot tubs, cable TV. Barbershop, beauty salon. Baby-sitting. Business services. Some pets allowed. | 1501 Ridge Rd. W 14615 | 716/621–5700 or 800/892–9348 | fax 716/621–8446 | www.comfortinn.com | 83 rooms | $75–$140 | AE, D, DC, MC, V.

Econo Lodge–Brockport. This chain motel 15 mi west of Rochester has some connecting rooms and some efficiencies. Complimentary Continental breakfast. Some kitchenettes, some microwaves, cable TV. Pool. Playground, laundry facilities. Business services. Pets allowed. | 6575 4th Section Rd. (junction of Rtes. 19 and 31), Brockport, 14420 | 716/637–3157 | fax 716/637–0434 | www.econolodge.com | 39 rooms | $52–$90 | AE, D, DC, MC, V.

Econo Lodge–Rochester South. Some rooms at this three-story chain hotel off I–90 (exit 46) have king-size beds and in-room video games. Continental breakfast. Some in-room hot tubs, cable TV. Laundry facilities. Business services, airport shuttle. Some pets allowed. | 940 Jefferson Rd. 14623 | 716/427–2700 | fax 716/427–8504 | www.econolodge.com | 102 rooms | $58–$65 | AE, D, MC, V.

Four Points Sheraton. This downtown hotel overlooking the Genesee River has an enclosed skyway that connects you to the convention center. Rooms have double or king-size beds. Restaurant, bar, room service. In-room data ports, cable TV. Pool. Exercise equipment. Shops. Laundry facilities. Business services. Some pets allowed. | 120 E. Main St. 14604 | 716/546–6400 | fax 716/546–3908 | www.fourpoints.com | 466 rooms, 10 suites | $129–$149 | AE, D, MC, V.

Hampton Inn–South. This five-story chain hotel is 4 mi from downtown Rochester, 3 mi from the Rochester Institute of Technology, and 2 mi from the University of Rochester. Complimentary Continental breakfast. In-room data ports, cable TV. Business services. Some pets allowed. | 717 E. Henrietta Rd., off I–390, Brighton, 14623 | 716/272–7800 | fax 716/272–1211 | www.hamptoninn.com | 113 rooms | $75–$95 | AE, D, DC, MC, V.

Holiday Inn–Airport. This chain is right next to the airport and 4 mi from downtown. Restaurant, bar (with entertainment), room service. In-room data ports, cable TV. Pool. Hot tub. Exercise equipment. Laundry facilities. Business services, airport shuttle. Some pets allowed. | 911 Brooks Ave., Gates, 14624 | 716/328–6000 | fax 716/328–1012 | www.holiday-inn.com | 280 rooms | $89–$139 | AE, D, DC, MC, V.

Lodge at Woodcliff. Bi-level suites and rooms with king-size beds are available at this upscale lodge on a wooded hill in an Erie Canal community. The lodge also hosts special murder-mystery evenings. No-smoking rooms are available. Restaurant, bar. In-room data ports, refrigerators, minibars, cable TV. Indoor-outdoor pool. Sauna. 9-hole golf course, tennis. Laundry service. Pets allowed. | 199 Woodcliff Dr., Fairport, 14450 | 716/381–4000 or 800/365–3065 | fax 716/381–2673 | www.woodclifflodge.com | 232 rooms, 12 suites | $145 rooms, $175–$350 suites | AE, D, MC, V.

Marriott–Airport. This Marriott, 6 minutes from the airport and 10 minutes from downtown, is popular among business travelers. Restaurant, bar. In-room data ports, room service, cable TV. Pool. Hot tub. Exercise equipment. Business services, airport shuttle. Some pets allowed. | 1890 W. Ridge Rd., Greece, 14615 | 716/225–6880 | fax 716/225–8188 | 210 rooms | $130–$150 | AE, D, DC, MC, V.

Microtel. This chain hotel with compact rooms is 2 mi from the Rochester Institute of Technology. Cable TV. Business services. Some pets allowed. | 905 Lehigh Station Rd., Henrietta, 14467 | 716/334–3400 or 800/999–2005 | fax 716/334–5042 | www.microtelinn.com | 99 rooms | $56 | AE, D, DC, MC, V.

Ramada. This three-story hotel was fully renovated during its changeover to Ramada in 2000. Located 5 mi south of Rochester in the town of Henrietta, and about ½ mi from Marketplace Mall. Restaurant, bar, complimentary Continental breakfast. In-room data ports, room service, cable TV. Pool. Business services, airport shuttle. Some pets allowed. | 800 Jefferson Rd. 14623 | 716/475–9190 or 888/298–2054 | fax 716/424–2138 | 145 rooms | $76–$88 | AE, D, MC, V.

Red Roof Inn. Rooms have balconies at this chain hotel close to the intersection of Interstates 90 and 390 and 7 mi south of downtown Rochester. Some rooms have king-size beds and recliners. Cable TV. Business services. Pets allowed. | 4820 W. Henrietta Rd., Henrietta, 14467 | 716/359–1100 | fax 716/359–1121 | www.redroof.com | 108 rooms | $56–$76 | AE, D, DC, MC, V.

Residence Inn by Marriott. The studio and loft suites have fully equipped kitchens and some have fireplaces at this all-suite hotel south of Rochester. The penthouse suites have two king-size beds, two bathrooms, and pull-out couches. Complimentary Continental breakfast. In-room data ports, kitchenettes, cable TV. Pool. Hot tub. Laundry facilities. Business services, airport shuttle. Some pets allowed (fee). | 1300 Jefferson Rd., Henrietta, 14623 | 716/272–8850 | fax 716/272–7822 | www.residenceinn.com | 112 suites | $100–$145 | AE, D, DC, MC, V.

Trail Break Motor Inn. You'll find this no-frills motel in a residential area about 2 mi south of Rochester. Refrigerators, cable TV. Pets allowed. | 7340 Pittsford-Palmyra Rd., Fairport, 14450 | 716/223–1710 | fax 716/271–2147 | 32 rooms | $40–$59 | AE, D, MC, V.

Wellesley Inn–North. King-size beds are available at this hotel in a shopping and business district 3 mi northwest of Rochester. Complimentary Continental breakfast. In-room data ports, some refrigerators, cable TV. Business services. Some pets allowed. | 1635 W. Ridge Rd., Greece, 14615 | 716/621–2060 or 800/444–8888 | fax 716/621–7102 | www.wellesleyinnandsuites.com | 93 rooms (2 with shower only), 4 suites | $65–$90 | AE, D, DC, MC, V.

Wellesley Inn–South. This branch of the Wellesley is on the southern edge of the city, very close to the Erie Canal. Complimentary Continental breakfast. In-room data ports, cable TV. Business services. Some pets allowed. | 797 E. Henrietta Rd. (Rte. 15A), Brighton, 14623 | 716/427–0130 | fax 716/427–0903 or 800/444–8888 | www.wellesleyinnandsuites.com | 92 rooms, 4 suites | $70–$90 | AE, D, DC, MC, V.

ROCKVILLE CENTRE
Holiday Inn. Sandwiched between the Long Island Railroad Station and the ever-busy Sunrise Highway, this five-story standard member of the chain trades in peace and quiet for convenience and reliability. Restaurant, bar, room service. In-room data ports, some refrigerators, cable TV. Business services. Pets allowed ($15). | 173 Sunrise Hwy. 11570 | 516/678–1300 or 800/HOLIDAY | fax 516/465–4329 | www.holidayinn.com | 100 rooms | AE, D, DC, MC, V.

ROME
Beeches Paul Revere Lodge. This lodge is part of The Beeches estate which includes 52 landscaped acres, and the family that runs it has been in the hotel business since 1908. Rooms are done in French-country style. Restaurant. In-room data ports, refrigerators, cable TV. Pool. Business services. Some pets allowed (fee). | 7900 Turin Rd. 13340 | 315/336–1776 or 800/765–7251 | fax 315/339–2636 | www.thebeeches.com | 75 rooms | $69 | AE, D, DC, MC, V.

ROSCOE
Roscoe Motel. Some rooms have views of the water at this quiet motel along the Beaverkill River. Picnic area, complimentary Continental breakfast. Some refrigerators, cable TV. Pool. Pets allowed. | Old Rte. 17 12776 | 607/498–5220 | 18 rooms | $45–$60 | AE, MC, V.

SALAMANCA
Jefferson Inn of Ellicottville. This Victorian home with a wraparound Greek Revival porch is within walking distance of shops, restaurants, and bars in Ellicottville, 11 mi north of Salamanca. You can stay in B&B rooms, a luxury suite, or one of the two self-contained efficiency suites suitable for families with small children or pets. Complimentary break-

fast is included in bed-and-breakfast rooms only. Some kitchenettes, no TV in some rooms, TV in common area. Some pets allowed. No smoking. | 3 Jefferson St., Ellicottville 14731 | 716/699–5869 or 800/577–8451 | fax 716/699–5758 | jeffinn@eznet.net | www.thejeffersoninn.com | 5 rooms, 2 suites | $140 (2–night minimum stay) | AE, D, MC, V.

SARANAC LAKE

Adirondack Motel. Rooms at this two-story motel have views of Lake Flower. Standard rooms and suites with fireplaces are available, as well as efficiencies with kitchenettes. Picnic area, complimentary Continental breakfast. In-room data ports, some kitchenettes, refrigerators, cable TV. Dock, boating. Pets allowed. | 23 Lake Flower Ave. 12983 | 518/891–2116 or 800/416–0117 | fax 518/891–1405 | www.adirondackmotel.com | 14 rooms | $45–$150 | AE, D, DC, MC, V.

Lake Flower Inn. This small one-story motel on Lake Flower has lake access and is close to a public boat launch and snowmobiling trails. Some of the rooms have views of the water; the pool overlooks the lake. Picnic area. In-room data ports, cable TV. Pool. Dock. Some pets allowed. | 15 Lake Flower Ave. 12983 | 518/891–2310 or 888/628–8900 | 14 rooms | $42–$92 | MC, V.

Lake Side. Rooms have views of Lake Flower at this motel with a private swimming and picnic area. You can also fish or rent canoes and paddleboats and there is a 50-ft heated pool. No-smoking rooms are available. Picnic area. Cable TV. Pool. Beach, boating, fishing. Pets allowed. | 27 Lake Flower Ave. 12983 | 518/891–4333 | 22 rooms | $45–$89 | AE, D, DC, MC, V.

SARATOGA SPRINGS

Grand Union Motel. This one-story drive-up motel in a residential area was built in the 1950s and provides no-frills lodging. Picnic area. In-room data ports, cable TV. Pool. Pets allowed (fee). | 120 S. Broadway 12866 | 518/584–9000 | fax 518/584–9001 | www.grandunionmotel.com | 64 rooms | $69–106 | AE, MC, V.

Holiday Inn Saratoga. This four-story chain is in downtown Saratoga Springs. Restaurant, bar, room service. In-room data ports, some in-room hot tubs, cable TV. Pool. Gym. Laundry facilities. Business services. Pets allowed. | 232 Broadway 12866 | 518/584–4550 | fax 518/584–4417 | hisara@capital.net | www.hisaratoga.com | 168 rooms | $85–$129 | AE, D, DC, MC, V.

SCHENECTADY

Days Inn. This chain motel is downtown, within walking distance of Union College and Proctor's Theater. King-size beds are available. Complimentary Continental breakfast. In-room data ports, cable TV. Pets allowed. | 167 Nott Terr. 12308 | 518/370–3297 | fax 518/370–5948 | www.daysinn.com | 68 rooms | $80–$100 | AE, D, DC, MC, V.

Holiday Inn. This four-story chain hotel is in downtown Schenectady. King-size beds are available and the suites have wet bars, conference tables, and pull-out sofa beds. Restaurant, bar, room service. In-room data ports, cable TV. Pool. Hot tub. Exercise equipment. Airport shuttle. Some pets allowed. | 100 Nott Terr. 12308 | 518/393–4141 | fax 518/393–4174 | www.holiday-inn.com | 181 rooms, 3 suites | $84–$114 rooms, $159 suites | AE, D, DC, MC, V.

SHANDAKEN

Auberge des 4 Saisons. This charming French country inn with a wood-burning stove and noted restaurant is perched on a running stream. With its many activities on the grounds, including swimming, tennis, hiking, and fishing, it's more like a resort than just an inn. The rooms are country style, and many have balconies. Restaurant, bar, picnic area, complimentary breakfast. No air-conditioning, cable TV. Pool. Tennis. Hiking, fishing.

Playground. Some pets allowed. | 178 Rte. 42 | 845/688–2223 or 800/864–1877 | 30 rooms | $85 | AE, MC, V.

Margaretville Mountain Inn. Located on 6 country-farm acres, this bed-and-breakfast is a 1896 Queen Anne Victorian, situated atop Margaretville Mountain overlooking the Catskill Mountain State Park. Rooms are decorated in a Victorian style. Complimentary breakfast. Cable TV, no room phones. Playground. Some pets allowed (fee). No smoking. | Margaretville Mountain Rd., Margaretville 12455 | 845/586–3933 | www.catskill.net | 7 rooms | $65–$120 | AE, MC, V.

River Run Bed & Breakfast. This Queen Anne Victorian has wicker furniture and original stained glass from 1887. One suite is decorated with '50s memorabilia and has two bedrooms, two baths, and a full kitchen. Located 10 mi west of Shandaken. Dining room, picnic area. No air-conditioning, some kitchenettes, some in-room VCRs, no TV in some rooms, TV in common area. Library. Pets allowed. No smoking. | Main St., Fleischmanns 12430 | 845/254–4884 | www.catskill.net/riverrun | 8 rooms, 1 suite | $95–$120 | AC, MC, V.

SKANEATELES

Bird's Nest. Located about ½ mi east of the village on U.S. 20, this hotel is surrounded by 58 acres of countryside, with a pond for fishing and hiking trails. Picnic area. Some kitchenettes, some in-room hot tubs, refrigerators, cable TV. Pool. Some pets allowed. | 1601 E. Genesee St. | 315/685–5641 | www.skaneateles.com/birdsnest | 30 rooms | $49–$135 | D, MC, V.

SOUTHAMPTON

The Atlantic. This 1950s-style hotel has totally renovated deluxe rooms, and is about 4 mi from town center. Maple wood and stainless steel furniture give the rooms a streamlined clean look. Some kitchenettes, cable TV. Pool. Business services. Pets allowed. | 1655 Rte. 39 | 631/287–0908 | fax 631/283–4625 | 70 rooms | $180–$290 | AE, MC, V.

Bel-Aire Cove Motel. The quiet Bel-Aire Cove is right on the waters of Shinnecock Bay, 8 mi west of Southampton and 3 mi south of the Montauk Highway. Picnic area, complimentary Continental breakfast. Some kitchenettes, some microwaves, refrigerators, cable TV, room phones. Pool. Volleyball. Pets allowed. No smoking. | 20 Shinnecock Rd., Hampton Bays 11946 | 631/728–0416 | fax 631/728–9426 | www.bel-airecove.com | 19 rooms | $100–$150 | AC, D, DC, MC, V.

The Bentley. This modern mini-resort has some rooms overlooking the Peconic Bay. All suites have a private patio or deck. Set on 4½ acres, the property has a kidney-shaped pool with a large sunning deck and a tennis court. Picnic area, complimentary Continental breakfast. Kitchenettes, cable TV. Pool. Tennis. Laundry facilities. Business services. Pets allowed. | 161 Hill Station Rd. | 631/283–6100 | fax 631/283–6102 | 38 suites | $200–$390 | AE, D, DC, MC, V.

The Capri. This modest-yet-modern, privately-owned motel is 3 mi from the beach, and ½ mi from the downtown area. All guest rooms face the pool in the central courtyard of the property. Restaurant. Some refrigerators, cable TV. Pool. Business services. Pets allowed. | 281 Rte. 39A | 631/283–0908 | fax 631/283–6496 | 33 rooms | $140–$250 | AE, D, MC, V.

Southampton Village Latch Inn. Set on 5 acres near town and the beach, this hotel is owned and run by a collective of local artists, and the decor reflects their tastes. The rooms and suites are theatrically furnished with Burmese puppets, masks from New Guinea, African artifacts, and Tibetan rugs. Complimentary Continental breakfast. Some refrigerators, cable TV. Pool. Tennis. Business services. Pets allowed. | 101 Hill St. | 516/283–2160 or 800/545–2824 | fax 516/283–3236 | www.villagelatch.com | 72 rooms | $195–$550 | AE, D, MC, V.

SOUTHOLD

Santorini Beach. This hotel is on 17 acres of a private enclave with 800 ft of serene beach. All the rooms are furnished with European artwork and accessories. Restaurant, complimentary Continental breakfast. Cable TV, some room phones. Pool, wading pool. Basketball. Beach. Pets allowed. | 3800 Duck Pond Rd., Cutchogue 11935 | www.santorinibeach.com | 631/734–6370 | 45 rooms | $179–$345 | AE, D, MC, V.

SPRING VALLEY

Nanuet Inn. Located less than 2 mi outside of Spring Valley and just a few hundred yards off I–87 at exit 14. Cable TV, room phones. Pool. Laundry facilities. Pets allowed. | 260 W. Rte. 59, Nanuet 10954 | 845/623–0600 | 120 rooms | $125 | AE, D, DC, MC, V.

SUFFERN

Sheraton Crossroads Hotel. Party all night at the in-house dance club of this 22-floor hotel. It's 5 mi south of Suffern in Mahwah, New Jersey, and less than 1 mi from the New York State Thruway (I–87). 2 restaurants, bar, complimentary Continental breakfast, room service. In-room data ports, cable TV. Pool. Sauna. 2 tennis courts. Health club. Shop. Pets allowed. | 1 International Blvd., Mahwah, NJ 07495 | 201/529–1660 | fax 201/529–4709 | www.starwood.com | 221 rooms, 4 suites | $129–$179 | AE, D, DC, MC, V.

Wellesley Inn. This inn about 2 mi from the center of Suffern offers very basic rooms and limited services. It is near I–87 and I–287. Complimentary Continental breakfast. Microwaves, cable TV. Laundry services. Business services. Some pets allowed. | 17 N. Airmont Rd. | 845/368–1900 | fax 845/368–1927 | 95 rooms | $89–$99 | AE, D, DC, MC, V.

SYRACUSE

Cambridge Inn. Kids will love the outdoor minizoo here, with its peacocks, ostriches, pygmy goats, deer, and pheasants. Located 8 mi west of Syracuse in Camillus. Picnic area, complimentary Continental breakfast. Refrigerators. Cable TV. Pets allowed. | 2382 W. Genesee Tpk., Rte. 5 W, Camillus 13031 | 315/672–3022 | 10 rooms | $79–$89 | AE, D, MC, V.

Econo Lodge. Located approximately 4 mi from downtown Syracuse, this roadside lodge offers affordable rooms near exits for both I–90 and I–81. There are also five restaurants within walking distance. Complimentary Continental breakfast. In-room data ports, cable TV. Business services. Some pets allowed. | 401 7th North St., Liverpool 13088 | 315/451–6000 | fax 315/451–0193 | 83 rooms | $49–$79 | AE, D, DC, MC, V.

Embassy Suites. All the rooms in this quiet suburban five-story suite hotel overlook a garden atrium, which includes waterfalls and streams. It's close to downtown Syracuse. Restaurant, bar, complimentary breakfast. In-room data ports, kitchenettes, cable TV. Pool. Exercise equipment. Laundry facilities. Business services. Some pets allowed. | 6646 Old Collamer Rd., East Syracuse 13057 | 315/446–3200 | fax 315/437–3302 | 215 suites | $139 | AE, D, DC, MC, V.

Golden Tulip Genesee Inn Hotel. You'll be minutes from downtown Syracuse and Syracuse University at this modern hotel with huge arching windows. Rooms have Mission-style furniture. Restaurant, bar, room service. In-room data ports, cable TV. Business services. Pets allowed. | 1060 E. Genesee St. 13210 | 315/476–4212 or 800/365–HOME | fax 315/471–4663 | 96 rooms | $99 | AE, D, DC, MC, V.

Holiday Inn at Carrier Circle. This two-story hotel is built on a hill, 10 minutes by car from downtown Syracuse, near I–90, exit 35. The rooms are spacious. Restaurant, bar (with entertainment), room service. Cable TV. Pool. Hot tub. Exercise equipment. Business services. Some pets allowed. | 6555 Old Collamer Rd. S, East Syracuse 13057 | 315/437–2761 | fax 315/463–0028 | www.holiday-inn.com | 203 rooms | $109 | AE, D, DC, MC, V.

Holiday Inn at Farrell Road. This two-story hotel sits near the intersection of I–90 and I–690, about 10 mi from Syracuse University. Restaurant, bar (with entertainment), room service. In-room data ports, cable TV. Pool. Exercise equipment. Business services. Pets allowed. | 100 Farrell Rd. | 315/457–8700 | fax 315/457–2379 | www.holiday-inn.com | 152 rooms | $149 | AE, D, DC, MC, V.

Holiday Inn at Four Points. This eight-floor Holiday Inn is just south of I–90 at exit 37 and was completely renovated in 1998. Restaurant, bar (with entertainment). In-room data ports, room service. Cable TV. Pool. Hot tub. Exercise equipment. Video games. Business services. Pets allowed. | 441 Electronics Pkwy., Liverpool 13088 | 315/457–1122 | fax 315/451–1269 | www.holiday-inn.com | 280 rooms | $120 | AE, D, DC, MC, V.

John Milton Inn. Right off the Thruway at exit 35, this two-story motel sits northeast of Syracuse, near the airport. Complimentary Continental breakfast. Cable TV. Business services. Pets allowed. | 6578 Thompson Rd. 13206 | 315/463–8555 or 800/352–1061 | fax 315/432–9240 | 54 rooms | $40–$50 | AE, D, DC, MC, V.

Knights Inn. Stay here for spacious rooms just 5 mi from Syracuse University. Complimentary Continental breakfast. Some kitchenettes, cable TV. Business services. Some pets allowed. | 430 Electronics Pkwy., Liverpool 13088 | 315/453–6330 or 800/843–5644 | fax 315/457–9240 | 82 rooms | $50 | AE, D, DC, MC, V.

Red Roof Inn–Syracuse. You'll be close to the Syracuse State Fairgrounds here. Rooms are spacious and modern, and fast food is right outside your door. Cable TV. Business services. Pets allowed. | 6614 N. Thompson Rd. 13206 | 315/437–3309 | fax 315/437–7865 | www.redroof.com | 115 rooms | $60 | AE, D, DC, MC, V.

Residence Inn by Marriott. Built in 1991, this hotel is convenient to area attractions and dining. There are also several golf courses in the area and two restaurants within walking distance. All guest accommodations are suites, and there is an outdoor sports courtyard in the center of the hotel with a pool, tennis, basketball, and volleyball courts. Picnic area, complimentary Continental breakfast. Kitchenettes, cable TV. Pool. Hot tub. Tennis. Basketball, exercise equipment, volleyball. Laundry facilities. Business services. Pets allowed (fee). | 6420 Yorktown Cir., East Syracuse 13057 | 315/432–4488 | fax 315/432–1042 | 102 suites | $122 studio suites, $142 2–bedroom suites | AE, D, DC, MC, V.

Western Ranch Motor Inn. The restaurant serves home-cooked meals at this hotel about 6 mi west of downtown Syracuse. Restaurant. Some refrigerators, cable TV, room phones. Laundry facilities. Pets allowed. | 1255 State Fair Blvd. 13209 | 315/457–9236 | fax 315/457–9236 | 42 rooms | $59–$89 | AE, D, MC, V.

Wyndham Syracuse. Located in an East Syracuse business district, this hotel sits in front of a row of restaurants ranging from McDonalds to fine dining. Restaurant, bar (with entertainment), room service. In-room data ports, some refrigerators, cable TV. Indoor-outdoor pool. Hot tub. Exercise equipment. Laundry facilities. Business services, airport shuttle. Pets allowed. | 6301 Rte. 298, East Syracuse 13057 | 315/432–0200 | fax 315/433–1210 | www.wyndham.com | 248 rooms, 2 suites | $139 rooms, $275 suites | AE, D, DC, MC, V.

TICONDEROGA

Circle Court Motel. The Circle Court, situated at the top of Ticonderoga village, is within walking distance of the lakes and the river. There's also a public park nearby with waterfalls and springs. Refrigerators, cable TV. Pets allowed. | 440 Montcalm St. | 518/585–7660 | 14 rooms | $57–$62 | AE, MC, V.

TUPPER LAKE

Pine Terrace Motel and Resort. Located on Big Tupper Lake, this property consists of 20 cottages with pine-wood interiors. There is golf and hiking next door. Picnic area. No air-conditioning, some kitchenettes, refrigerators, cable TV. Pool, wading pool. Tennis. Boating.

Pets allowed. | 94 Moody Rd. | 518/359–9258 | fax 518/359–8340 | 20 cottages | $45–$75 | AE, DC, MC, V.

Sunset Park Motel. All rooms in this quiet motel overlook Tupper Lake. The motel is next to a park with basketball, tennis, and volleyball courts. Adirondack hiking and mountain-bike trails are also nearby. Picnic area. No air-conditioning, some kitchenettes, cable TV. Beach, dock, boating. Some pets allowed. | 71 De Mars Blvd. | 518/359–3995 | fax 518/359–9577 | sunsetpk@org.net | 11 rooms | $55–$70 | Closed Jan.–Apr. | AE, DC, MC, V.

UTICA

Best Western Gateway Adirondack Inn. Right off the Thruway exit 31, approximately 7 mi from the Oneida County Airport and 25 mi from downtown Utica, this two-story Best Western was built in 1960 in a business area. All rooms have double or king-size beds. Family suite available. Complimentary Continental breakfast. Cable TV. Exercise equipment. Video games. Business services. Some pets allowed. | 175 N. Genesee St. 13502 | 315/732–4121 | fax 315/797–8265 | 89 rooms, 1 suite | $109–$129 rooms, $139–$169 suite | AE, D, DC, MC, V.

Holiday Inn of Utica. Tucked off I–90 in the Utica Business Park, this hotel has a landscaped courtyard with an outdoor pool. Standard rooms include a desk, chair with reading light, and 25-inch color TV. The hotel is close to area attractions, including the Utica Zoo, the Saranac Brewery Tour Center, the Baseball Hall of Fame in Cooperstown, the Boxing Hall of Fame in Canastota, and the Adirondack Scenic Railroad in nearby Utica. Restaurant, bar (with entertainment), room service. In-room data ports, cable TV. Pool. Exercise equipment. Video games. Laundry facilities. Business services. Pets allowed. | 1777 Burrstone Rd., New Hartford | 315/797–2131 | fax 315/797–5817 | www.holiday-inn.com | 100 rooms | $110–$129 | AE, D, DC, MC, V.

Radisson–Utica Centre. This slightly upscale hotel is in the heart of downtown Utica, close to shopping, the Munson-Williams-Proctor Institute Museum, and the F. X. Matts Brewery. Relax next to the tropically landscaped indoor pool. Each room has double or king-size beds. Restaurant, bar (with entertainment). In-room data ports, refrigerators, cable TV. Pool. Barbershop, beauty salon, sauna. Exercise equipment, health club. Shops, video games. Business services. Some pets allowed. | 200 Genesee St. 13502 | 315/797–8010 | fax 315/797–1490 | www.radisson.com | 158 rooms | $119 | AE, D, DC, MC, V.

Red Roof Inn–Utica. A mile north of downtown Utica in a business area, this two-floor hotel is close to many restaurants. All rooms are furnished with either two full-size beds or a king-size bed. Cable TV. Business services. Some pets allowed. | 20 Weaver St. 13502 | 315/724–7128 | fax 315/724–7158 | www.redroof.com | 112 rooms | $65–$82 | AE, D, DC, MC, V.

VICTOR

Sunrise Hill Inn. This inn on 40 acres of open land (5 mi west of Victor) has a three-story building, housing the lobby and restaurant, and external corridors connecting separate buildings with guest rooms. Restaurant, bar. In-room data ports, cable TV. Pool. Business services. Some pets allowed. | 6108 Loomis Rd., Farmington 14425 | 716/924–2131 or 800/333–0536 | fax 716/924–1876 | www.e-localad.com/canandaigua/sunrisehill.html | 104 rooms | $40–$90 | AE, D, MC, V.

WATERLOO

Holiday Inn. This comfortable chain hotel is near an outlet mall and surrounded by a number of popular restaurants. Many rooms overlook a courtyard with a tennis court and heated swimming pool. King-size beds available. Restaurant, bar (with entertainment), room service. In-room data ports, cable TV. Pool. Hot tub. Tennis. Exercise equipment. Laundry facilities. Business services, free parking. Pets allowed. | 2468 Rte. 414 13165 | 315/539–5011 | fax 315/539–8355 | 147 rooms | $80–$159 | AE, D, MC, V.

Microtel Inn and Suites. This two-story hotel with inside corridors was built in 1999 and is situated between Waterloo and Seneca Falls. It's on Routes 5 and 20 near the intersection of Route 414. In-room data ports, cable TV. Free parking. Pets allowed. | 1966 Rtes. 5 and 20, Seneca Falls 13148 | 315/539–8438 | fax 315/539–4780 | 48 rooms, 21 suites | $65–$71 rooms, $73–$75 suites | AE, D, DC, MC, V.

WATERTOWN

Econo Lodge. Prefabricated, functional, and basic, this one-floor hotel is a study in bland corporate-chain American roadside accommodation. Picnic area, complimentary Continental breakfast. Refrigerators, cable TV. Pool. Laundry facilities. Pets allowed. | 1030 Arsenal St. 13601 | 315/782–5500 | fax 315/788–7608 | www.econolodge.com | econo@imc.net | 60 rooms | $63–$68 | AE, D, MC, V.

The Inn. This two-floor 1960s strip motel is notable for its spacious rooms that come with either two double or one queen-size bed. Cable TV. Pool. Video games. Laundry services. Pets allowed. | 1190 Arsenal St. 13601 | 315/788–6800 | fax 315/788–5366 | 96 rooms | $60–$70 | AE, D, MC, V.

Microtel Inn. This two-floor hotel is on the north side of Watertown, within shouting distance of the Thousand Islands. Rooms have queen-size beds only. Cable TV. Video games. Pets allowed. | 8000 Virginia Smith Dr. 13616 | 315/629–5000 and 800/447–9660 | fax 315/629–5393 | microtel@gisco.com | 100 rooms | $49 | AE, D, MC, V.

New Parrot Motel. This affordable motel is in a commercial area. Rooms are simple, with either a king-size bed or two doubles. Picnic area. Some refrigerators, cable TV. Pool. Pets allowed. | 19325 Washington St. 13601 | 315/788–5080 or 800/479–9889 | 26 rooms | $48–$68 | AE, D, MC, V.

WILLIAMSVILLE

Heritage House Country Inn. This two-story, Victorian-style inn has individually furnished rooms, some with king-size and four-post beds. Picnic area, complimentary Continental breakfast. Some kitchenettes, microwaves, some refrigerators, cable TV. Business services, airport shuttle, free parking. Some pets allowed. | 8261 Main St. 14221 | 716/633–4900 or 716/283–3899 (reservations) | fax 716/633–4900 | www.wnybiz.com/heritage | 53 rooms | $54–$100 | AE, D, DC, MC, V.

Residence Inn by Marriott. This two-story chain hotel near Dunlop and Dupont (10 mi from Lake Erie) specializes in extended-stay suite accommodation. Rooms in the suites have various combinations of double, queen-size, and king-size beds, and some have two levels, two baths, and pull-out beds. Complimentary Continental breakfast. In-room data ports, some kitchenettes, microwaves, cable TV. Pool. Exercise equipment. Laundry facilities. Business services, airport shuttle, free parking. Some pets allowed (fee). | 100 Maple Rd. 14221 | 716/632–6622 | fax 716/632–5247 | 112 suites | $120–$150 | AE, D, DC, MC, V.

WILMINGTON

Howard Johnson Resort Inn. This resort inn with mountain views on Lake Placid was the 1999 Howard Johnson Property of the Year. Many of the rooms have balconies and there are free rowboats, paddleboats, and canoes; a game room; and nature trails. Restaurant, picnic area. Pool. Hot tub. Golf privileges, tennis. Hiking, water sports, fishing. Pets allowed (fee). | 90 Saranac Ave., Lake Placid 12946 | 518/523–9555 or 800/858–4656 | hojolkpl@northnet.org | 92 rooms | $78–$150 | AE, D, DC, MC, V.

Hungry Trout Motor Inn. Rooms at this motel on the west branch of the Ausable River, close to Whiteface Mountain Ski Center, have mountain views. Two-room suites with kitchenettes are available. Restaurant. Cable TV. Pool, wading pool. Cross-country skiing. Playground. Pets allowed. | 12997 Rte. 86 | 518/946–2217 or 800/766–9137 | fax 518/946–7418 | www.hungrytrout.com | 22 rooms | $54–$139 | Closed Apr., Nov. | AE, D, DC, MC, V.

Ledge Rock at Whiteface Mountain. This upscale motel, named for the ledges on the mountain directly behind the building, is on 100 acres across the road from Whiteface Mountain. Rooms have mountain views, and two double or a queen-size bed. Picnic area. Some microwaves, some refrigerators, cable TV. Pool, pond, wading pool. Boating. Playground. Pets allowed. | Rte. 86, at Placid Rd. 12997 | 518/946–2302 or 800/336–4754 | fax 518/946–7594 | ledgerock@whiteface.net | 18 rooms | $50–$159 | AE, D, DC, MC, V.

Willkommen Hof B&B. The two-story European-style *gasthof*, or "guest house," was built in 1920 at the foot of Whiteface Mountain. There are rooms with private baths, shared baths, and a three-room suite. You'll also find a large cedar sauna, a year-round outdoor spa, and on-site bicycling and jogging trails. The breakfast includes apple pancakes and blintzes. Restaurant, complimentary breakfast. Hot tub. Hiking, fishing, cross-country skiing. Business services, free parking. Pets allowed (fee). | Rte. 86 12997 | 518/946–7669 or 800/541–9119 | www.lakeplacid.net/willkommenhof | 8 rooms (six with private bath), 1 suite | $58–$115 rooms, $125–$154 suite | MC, V.

North Carolina

ASHEVILLE

Comfort Inn River Ridge. Just 1 mi from the Blue Ridge Parkway and 3 mi from the Biltmore Estate, this hotel is housed in three separate 3-story buildings. Each room has a coffeemaker, iron, and ironing board. Hair dryers are also available. Rooms are neutral in color, and there is a two-room suite with a hot tub and kitchenette. Complimentary Continental breakfast. Some microwaves, some refrigerators. Pool. Hot tub. Hiking. Playground. Laundry facilities, laundry service. Business services. Pets allowed. | 800 Fairview Rd. | 828/298–9141 | fax 828/298–6629 | www.comfortinn.com | 178 rooms, 20 suites | $89–$139; $129–$159 suites | AE, D, DC, MC, V.

Dogwood Cottage. The veranda at this 1910 home is a great place to relax after a busy day of sightseeing. Though it's just 2 mi from downtown, this inn feels like it's in the country and affords a great view of the Blue Ridge Mountains. Complimentary breakfast. TV in common area. Pets allowed. | 40 N. Canterbury Rd. | 828/258–9725 | 4 rooms | $110–$125 | AE, MC, V.

Red Roof Inn. This motel sits in a residential area 6 mi from the Biltmore Estate and 5 minutes from the Blue Ridge Parkway. Business services. Some pets allowed. | 16 Crowell Rd. | 828/667–9803 | fax 828/667–9810 | www.redroof.com | 109 rooms | $30–$82 | AE, D, DC, MC, V.

BOONE

Scottish Inns. This bright two-story motel is off U.S. 321 at Rte. 105, two blocks from Appalachian State University. Restaurant, picnic area. Some kitchenettes, some microwaves, some refrigerators. Cable TV, in-room VCRs. Indoor pool. Sauna. Playground. Business services. Some pets allowed (fee). | 72 Blowing Rock Rd., 28607 | 828/264–2483 | www.boonelodging.com | 47 rooms | $43–$93 | AE, D, MC, V.

BURLINGTON

Burlington Comfort Inn. Burlington Manufacturers Outlet Center is within walking distance of this typical chain hotel on a main interstate highway. The two-story building is brick with outside entrances to the rooms. The rooms are in light and neutral colors. Complimentary Continental breakfast. Some refrigerators. Cable TV. Pool, wading pool.

Laundry facilities. Business services. Some pets allowed. | 978 Plantation Dr. | 336/227–3681 | fax 336/570–0900 | 127 rooms | $66 | AE, D, DC, MC, V.

CARY

La Quinta Inn and Suites. This might be the South, but inside this hotel it's the Southwest, with Mexican-influenced colors. The hotel is 1 mi from MacGregor Corporate Park and 16 mi from Research Triangle Park. There are no-smoking rooms. Complimentary Continental breakfast. In-room data ports, some microwaves, some refrigerators. Cable TV. Pool. Hot tub. Gym. Laundry service. Business services. Pets allowed. | 191 Crescent Commons | 919/851–2850 or 800/642–4258 | fax 919/851–0728 | 123 rooms, 5 suites | $65–$89 rooms, $105 suites | AE, D, DC, MC, V.

CASHIERS

High Hampton Inn and Country Club. On a 1,400-acre mountain estate stands this tranquil, rustic resort, established in 1924. It is the former hunting lodge of a Civil War general (Hampton), and some of the rooms have views of either a lake or the mountains. All meals are included in the rate. Kids' programs are available June through August and Thanksgiving weekend. Dining room, complimentary breakfast. No room phones, cable TV in common area. Two lakes. Driving range, 18-hole golf course, putting greens. Tennis courts. Exercise equipment. Hiking. Water sports. Bicycles. Library. Kids' programs (2–11). Laundry facilities. Business services. Airport shuttle. Some pets allowed. | 1525 Rte. 107 S | 828/743–2411 or 800/334–2551 | fax 828/743–5991 | www.highhamptoninn.com | 30 rooms; 90 rooms in 15 cottages | $172–$218 | Closed Dec.–mid-Apr. | AE, D, DC, MC, V.

Oakmont Lodge. This family resort is almost parklike: there's a pond right on the secluded property. Rooms are rustic and oversize. You'll find shops within walking distance, and waterfalls, horseback riding, and hiking are 3 mi away. Restaurant, picnic area, barbecue grills available. No air conditioning, some refrigerators. Cable TV. Pets allowed ($10 fee). | U.S. 63 | 828/743–2298 | fax 828/743–1575 | 20 rooms, 3 cabins | $55–$150 | AE, MC, V.

CEDAR ISLAND

Driftwood. This motel sits right on the beach, though not all rooms face the ocean. There is also a 65-site campground, 55 with hookups. Restaurant. Complimentary Continental breakfast. Cable TV, no room phones. Beach. Pets allowed. | Cedar Island Beach, Rte. 12 N | 252/225–4861 | fax 252/225–1113 | 37 rooms | $60–$70 | Closed mid-Jan.–mid-Mar. | AE, D, MC, V.

CHAPEL HILL

Joan's Place. Three miles south of downtown is this ranch house on a wooded property, where you can enjoy a wooden deck out back. Joan has lived in the area for 30 years and can advise you on activities and attractions. Complimentary Continental breakfast. Room phones, TV in common area. Some pets allowed. | 1443 Poinsett Dr. | 919/942–5621 | 2 rooms | $65–$75 | No credit cards.

Siena. The imported furniture and artwork remind you of the Italian Renaissance when you're in this first-class hotel. Out the window, you have a view of Chapel Hill. 15 minutes from airport; close to UNC. Restaurant, bar with entertainment, picnic area, complimentary breakfast. In-room data ports, some refrigerators. Cable TV. Laundry service. Business services. Airport shuttle. Some pets allowed ($50 fee). | 1505 E. Franklin St. | 919/929–4000 or 800/223–7379 | fax 919/968–8527 | 80 rooms, 12 suites | $169–$300 | AE, DC, MC, V.

CHARLOTTE

Bradley Motel. The NASCAR theme in the lobby, complete with old posters and other memorabilia, is appreciated by the truckers and construction workers who tend to land here. The motel is 1½ mi from the airport and 2 mi from the Coliseum, but about 25 minutes from Lowe's Motor Speedway. Family-owned and -operated since 1959. Cable TV. Some pets allowed. No-smoking rooms. | 4200 S. I–85 Service Rd. | 704/392–3206 | fax 704/392–5040 | 21 rooms | $31–$34 | AE, D, MC, V.

La Quinta–South. Just south of Charlotte, this hotel has bright, clean rooms and an inviting lobby area with fireplace. The hotel is 6 mi from the airport, 4 mi from the Coliseum, and 3 mi from shops and restaurants. Complimentary Continental breakfast. In-room data ports, some microwaves. Cable TV. Pool. Laundry service. Business services. Some pets allowed. | 7900 Nations Ford Rd. | 704/522–7110 | fax 704/521–9778 | www.laquinta.com | 118 rooms | $45–$76 | AE, D, DC, MC, V.

Red Roof Inn–Coliseum. This family-friendly hotel is 3 mi from Charlotte Coliseum. Rooms are cozy, with landscape paintings on the walls. Cable TV. Business services. Some pets allowed. | 131 Red Roof Dr. | 704/529–1020 | fax 704/529–1054 | 124@redroofinn.com | 115 rooms | $45–$55 | AE, D, DC, MC, V.

Residence Inn by Marriott–South. Suites have full-sized kitchens, and some rooms have fireplaces in this hotel catering to long-stay business travelers. Complimentary Continental breakfast. In-room data ports, kitchenettes, microwaves, refrigerators. Cable TV. Pool. Hot tub. Laundry facilities. Business services. Some pets allowed (fee). | 5816 Westpark Dr. | 704/527–8110 | fax 704/521–8282 | 116 suites | $99–$169 | AE, D, DC, MC, V.

Summerfield Suites. This standard, well-maintained chain hotel is 5 mi from Charlotte-Douglas International Airport and downtown Charlotte. Picnic area, complimentary breakfast. In-room data ports, kitchenettes. Cable TV, in-room VCRs. Pool. Hot tub. Exercise equipment. No-smoking floors. Business services, airport shuttle. Some pets allowed (fee). | 4920 S. Tryon St. | 704/525–2600 | fax 704/521–9932 | 135 suites | $89–$109 | AE, D, DC, MC, V.

CHEROKEE

Best Western–Great Smokies Inn. Across the street from the Great Smokies Convention Center is this hotel serving both business and leisure travelers. For business travelers, there are the usual amenities. For leisure travelers, there's a free shuttle to the casino. The log-cabin-style lobby has antique furniture and a fishing theme. Restaurant, room service. Cable TV. Pool, wading pool. Laundry facilities. Business services. Pets allowed ($10 fee). | U.S. 441 | 828/497–2020 or 800/528–1234 | fax 828/497–3903 | 152 rooms | $90 | AE, D, DC, MC, V.

CORNELIUS

Holiday Inn. The only full-service hotel in the area is only 500 ft from Lake Norman. Restaurant, bar, room service. Some microwaves, some refrigerators. Cable TV. Pool. Exercise equipment. Laundry facilities. Some pets allowed ($25 fee). | 19901 Holiday La. | 704/892–9120 | fax 704/892–3854 | 119 rooms | $80 | AE, D, DC, MC, V.

DUNN

Best Western Midway. Guest rooms all have desks; some have pool views. The affordable price is a big draw of this chain hotel. Restaurant. Cable TV. Pool, wading pool. Business services. Pets allowed ($5 fee). | 603 Springbranch Rd. | 910/892–2162 or 800/528–1234 | fax 910/892–3010 | 146 rooms | $40–$50 | AE, D, DC, MC, V.

Ramada Inn. This standard chain hotel is about eight blocks from the battlefield museum and golf courses. Restaurant, complimentary Continental breakfast. In-room data ports, some microwaves, some refrigerators. Cable TV. Pool. Laundry service. Business services. Pets allowed. | 1011 E. Cumberland St. | 910/892–8101 or 800/2RAMADA | 100 rooms | $48–$69 | AE, D, DC, MC, V.

DURHAM

Best Western Skyland Inn. Situated atop a hill, this chain motel is 5 mi from Duke University and 12 mi from the University of North Carolina at Chapel Hill. There is an adjacent restaurant, and golf and tennis facilities are also nearby. All rooms are on the ground floor and have their own entrances. Picnic area, complimentary Continental breakfast. In-room data ports, refrigerators. Cable TV. Pool. Playground. Business services, free parking. Pets allowed (fee). | 5400 U.S. 70, I–85 Exit 170 | 919/383–2508 | fax 919/383–7316 | www.bestwestern.com | 31 Northgate rooms | $58–$68 | AE, D, DC, MC, V.

Hawthorn Suites. A three-building complex 10 minutes from North Carolina Central University. The airport is 6 mi away. There are one- and two-bedroom suites available. Complimentary breakfast (full during week, Continental on weekends). In-room data ports, kitchenettes, microwaves. Cable TV. Pool. Laundry service. Business services, airport shuttle. Free parking. Pets allowed (fee). | 300 Meredith Dr. | 919/361–1234 | fax 919/361–1213 | www.citysearch.com/rdu/hawthornsuites or www.hawthorn.com | 100 suites in 3 buildings | $135–$169 | AE, D, DC, MC, V.

Red Roof Inn. This red brick chain motel is landscaped with trees and shrubs and is near a shopping mall. In-room data ports. Business services. Pets allowed (under 25 pounds). | 1915 N. Pointe Dr. | 919/471–9882 | fax 919/477–0512 | www.redroof.com | 117 rooms | $54–$58 | AE, D, DC, MC, V.

Wyndham Garden Hotel. Seven-story chain hotel 6 mi from the airport. If you like to luxuriate at bath time, this is the place to go: there are scented bath oils in every room. The flower-filled lobby is scented with aromatherapy oils, and also the place where, on Wednesdays, the house chef presents a free sampling of his creations. Restaurant, bar. In-room data ports. Cable TV. Pool. Hot tub. Exercise equipment. Business services, airport shuttle. Free parking. Pets allowed (fee). | 4620 S. Miami Blvd. | 919/941–6066 | fax 919/941–6363 | www.wyndham.com | 172 rooms | $125 | AE, D, DC, MC, V.

ELIZABETH CITY

Holiday Inn. This stucco-and-brick chain hotel is 2 mi from the waterfront, with landscaped grounds. Restaurant, bar, room service. In-room data ports. Cable TV. Pool. Laundry facilities. Business services. Pets allowed (fee). | 522 S. Hughes Blvd. | 252/338–3951 | fax 252/338–6225 | www.basshotels.com | 157 rooms | $64 | AE, D, DC, MC, V.

FAYETTEVILLE

Comfort Inn. Perennials, shrubs, and trees provide the backdrop for this red brick chain hotel with Shaker-shingled roof that stands on a strip with many other hotels and restaurants. It's 8 mi southeast of the airport and near the interstate, just off Exit 49. Complimentary breakfast. Some in-room data ports, refrigerators, microwaves. Cable TV. Outdoor pool. Exercise equipment. Shop. Business services, free parking. Pets allowed. | 1957 Cedar Creek Rd. | 910/323–8333 or 800/621–6596 | fax 910/323–3946 | www.comfortinn.com | 120 rooms | $65 | AE, D, DC, MC, V.

Days Inn. This stucco chain hotel is next to a Denny's restaurant, near I–95, and about 10 mi from shopping malls. The sofa-and-chair-filled lounge area allows you to sit and enjoy your morning coffee. Complimentary Continental breakfast. Some refrigerators. Cable TV. Outdoor pool. Pets allowed (fee). | 2065 Cedar Creek Rd. | 910/483–6191 | fax 910/483–4113 | www.daysinn.com | 122 rooms | $69 | AE, D, DC, MC, V.

Quality Inn Ambassador. This one-story chain hotel is 6 mi from shops and restaurants. Restaurant, picnic area. Some microwaves, some refrigerators. Cable TV. Outdoor pool. Playground. Business services. Pets allowed. | 2035 Eastern Blvd. | 910/485–8135 | fax 910/485–8682 | 62 rooms | $52–$62 | AE, D, DC, MC, V.

FONTANA DAM

Fontana Village Resort. On Fontana Lake, at the southern border of Great Smoky Mountains National Park, this secluded resort has three types of accommodations: rooms, cabins, and a hostel. Cabins have kitchenettes, and there's cable TV (except in some cabins). 3 restaurants. Some refrigerators. Some room phones. 3 pools (1 indoor). Hot tub. Miniature golf, lighted tennis court. Gym, hiking, horseback riding. Water sports, fishing, bicycles. Children's programs, 2 playgrounds. Laundry facilities. Pets allowed (fee). | Rte. 28 N | 800/849–2258 | fax 828/498–2209 | fontana@fontanavillage.com | www.fontanavillage.com | 84 rooms, 100 cabins; 16-bunk hostel | $49–$79 | AE, D, MC, V.

FRANKLIN

Colonial Inn. Several restaurants, as well as the Scottish Tartans Museum, are within 3 mi of this motel. Scenic waterfalls are 7 mi away. Complimentary Continental breakfast. Refrigerators. Cable TV. Outdoor pool. Laundry facilities. Free parking. Pets allowed. | 3157 Georgia Rd. | 828/524–6600 | fax 828/349–1752 | 42 rooms | $35–$65 | AE, D, MC, V.

Country Inn Town. All rooms are on the ground floor of this hotel set on a riverbank on 4½ acres of landscaped grounds. It's in the center of town and just a short walk from restaurants and shops. Cable TV. Outdoor pool. Pets up to 20 pounds allowed (fee). | 668 E. Main St. | 828/524–4451 or 800/233–7555 | fax 828/524–0703 | www.switchboard.com | 46 rooms in 2 buildings | $45–$98 | AE, D, MC, V.

Days Inn. All the rooms at this small motel are at ground level and have their own entrances. Some rooms have porches and rocking chairs, and there are restaurants within walking distance. Picnic area, complimentary Continental breakfast. Some microwaves, some refrigerators. Cable TV. Outdoor pool. Playground. Business services. Pets allowed (fee). | 1320 E. Main St. | 828/524–6491 | fax 828/369–9636 | www.daysinn.com | 41 rooms | $84–$95 | AE, D, DC, MC, V.

GOLDSBORO

Best Western Goldsboro Inn. This two-story hotel is 13 mi from Cliffs of the Neuse State Park. Restaurant, bar. Refrigerators, microwaves. Cable TV. Outdoor pool. Fitness center. Laundry facilities. Free parking. Pets allowed. | 801 U.S. 70 Bypass E | 919/735–7911 or 800/528–1234 | fax 919/735–5030 | www.bestwestern.com | 116 rooms | $51–$59 | AE, D, DC, MC, V.

Days Inn. This chain motel is within walking distance of restaurants, a 5-minute drive from the Berkeley Mall, and 5 mi from the center of town. Some in-room data ports, some refrigerators. Cable TV. Outdoor pool. Laundry facilities. Business services. Pets allowed (fee). | 2000 Wayne Memorial Dr. | 919/734–9471 | fax 919/736–2623 | www.daysinn.com | 121 rooms | $52–$57 | AE, D, DC, MC, V.

Ramada Inn. The Air Force base is 5 mi from here, and I–95 is 20 minutes away. Its wing-chair-stuffed lobby is a bit homier than most, a good place to sit and relax, watch TV, chat, and get acquainted with the 20-yr-old potted house plant. Restaurant, bar with entertainment. Some in-room data ports, some microwaves, some refrigerators. Cable TV. Outdoor pool. Laundry facilities. Business services. Some pets allowed (fee). | 808 W. Grantham St. | 919/736–4590. | fax 919/735–3218 | 128 rooms, 4 suites | $52 | AE, D, DC, MC, V.

GREENSBORO

Amerisuites. Within a 15-min drive of Haganstone Park, Greensboro Jaycee park, Bryan Park, and Carolyn Allen park, this chain hotel is also within walking distance of restaurants and shops and 1 mi from the Four Seasons Mall and the Greensboro Coliseum. Complimentary Continental breakfast. In-room data ports, microwaves, minibars, refrigerators. Cable TV, in-room VCRs. Outdoor pool. Exercise equipment. Laundry facilities. Business services, airport shuttle, free parking. Pets allowed. | 1619 Stanley Rd. | 336/852–1443 or

800/833–1516 | fax 336/854–9339 | www.amerisuites.com | 126 suites | $79–$114 | AE, D, DC, MC, V.

★ **Biltmore Greensboro Hotel.** Original architectural features like beveled-glass front doors, a walnut-paneled lobby, floor-to-ceiling windows, and a cage elevator, are just a few of the details that give period charm and character to this 1895 hotel in the heart of Greensboro's business district. Complimentary Continental breakfast. Minibars, refrigerators. Cable TV. Business services, airport shuttle. Some pets allowed. | 111 W. Washington St. | 336/272–3474 or 800/332–0303 | fax 336/275–2523 | members.aol.com/biltmorenc/ index.html | 25 rooms, 4 suites | $85–$95 | AE, D, DC, MC, V.

Motel 6. This two-story building is in a commercial area 9 mi from the Greensboro Coliseum Complex. There's a restaurant within a mile of the motel. Cable TV. Outdoor pool. Laundry facilities. Pets allowed. | 605 S. Regional Rd.; I–40 Exit 210 | 336/668–2085 or 800/ 466–8356 | fax 336/454–6120 | www.motel6.com | 125 rooms | $37–$40 | AE, D, MC, V.

Ramada Inn–Airport. A chain hotel, this spot is 5 mi from the airport and 10 mi from downtown. Restaurant, bar, room service. Indoor-outdoor pool. Sauna. Business services, airport shuttle, free parking. Pets under 15 pounds allowed. | 7067 Albert Pick Rd. | 336/ 668–3900 | fax 336/668–7012 | www.ramada.com | 168 rooms | $67–$79 | AE, D, DC, MC, V.

GREENVILLE

Red Roof Inn. This three-story motel is 2 mi south of downtown and 1 mi from several restaurants and a mall. Pitt County Greenville airport is 7 mi away. The on-site restaurant is a Bob Evans. Restaurant. In-room data ports, some microwaves, some refrigerators, cable TV. Outdoor pool. Business services. Some pets allowed. | 301 SE Greenville Blvd., 27858 | 252/756–2792 or 800/733–7663 | fax 252/321–0500 | www.redroof.com | 148 rooms | $36–$70 | AE, D, DC, MC, V.

HENDERSON

Quality Inn. This chain hotel is convenient to the lake, camping sites, and hiking. You can relax in the plant- and flower-filled lobby and watch a little TV. Restaurant, bar, complimentary breakfast. In-room data ports, some microwaves, some refrigerators. Cable TV. Pool, wading pool. Laundry service. Business services. Pets allowed (in carrier). | I–85 Tarham Road | 252/492–1126 | fax 252/492–2575 | 156 rooms | $60–$65 | AE, D, DC, MC, V.

HENDERSONVILLE

Comfort Inn. This chain hotel is a block from Blue Ridge Mall and 5 mi from the Carl Sandburg Home and Flat Rock Playhouse. The rooms are floral-themed, more elaborately than is typical for this level of chain hotel, and the building is constructed around the pool. Complimentary Continental breakfast. In-room data ports, some microwaves, some refrigerators, in-room hot tubs (in suites). Cable TV. Pool. Laundry services. Business services. Pets allowed (fee). | 206 Mitchell Dr. | 828/693–8800 | www.comfortinn.com | 85 rooms | $94– $135 | AE, D, DC, MC, V.

HICKORY

Red Roof Inn. This chain hotel is just a short drive from the main road, 1 mi from a shopping mall and movie cineplex, and 1½ mi from the Hickory Furniture Mart. There are plenty of restaurants nearby, and the rooms are enlivened by brightly colored bedspreads. In-room data ports, some microwaves, some refrigerators. Cable TV. Business services. Pets allowed. | 1184 Lenoir Rhyne Blvd. SE | 828/323–1500 | fax 828/323–1509 | www.redroof.com | 108 rooms | $45–$60 | AE, D, DC, MC, V.

HIGHLANDS

Mountain High. Mountain High is on a hilltop, with a front porch overlooking Main Street. The spacious double rooms contain antique furniture and ornate four-poster beds; the bath is oversized with marble floors and a Jacuzzi in the mountain brook superior rooms, where a fireplace and a balcony look out onto a small creek. Picnic area, complimentary Continental breakfast. Refrigerators, some in-room hot tubs. Cable TV. Business services. Pets allowed. | W. Main St. and 2nd Ave. | 828/526–2790 or 800/445–7293 (outside NC) | www.mountainhighinn.com | 55 rooms | $95–$165 | AE, D, MC, V.

KILL DEVIL HILLS

Budget Host Inn. Walk a block or two to ocean fishing, swimming, and restaurants. Complimentary breakfast, room service. Microwaves, refrigerators. Cable TV, phones. Free parking. Pets allowed (fee). | 1003 S. Croatan Hwy.; 1 mi south of Wright Brothers Memorial on U.S 158 Bypass | 252/441–2503 or 252/441–4671 | fax 252/441–4671 | www.budgethost.com | 40 rooms | $50–$150 | AE, D, MC, V.

Nags Head Beach Hotel. This beachside property is 1 mi from shops and restaurants, and is right across the street from the Wright Brother's Memorial. Complimentary Continental breakfast. Microwaves, refrigerators. Cable TV. Pool. Some pets allowed (fee). | 804 N. Virginia Dare Trail | 252/441–0411 | fax 252/441–7811 | 96 rooms | $99–$115 | AE, D, DC, MC, V.

Ramada Inn. The rooms in this oceanfront hotel include a private balcony. Restaurant, bar with entertainment. In-room data ports, microwaves, refrigerators, room service. Cable TV. Indoor pool, hot tub. Business services. Some pets allowed (fee). | 1701 S. Virginia Dare Trail | 252/441–2151 or 800/635–1824 | fax 252/441–1830 | www.ramadainnnagshead.com | 172 rooms | $158–$209 | AE, D, DC, MC, V.

MAGGIE VALLEY

Abbey Inn. Mountain and valley views from every room have brought guests back to this inn perched about 1,000 ft above Maggie Valley. The rooms are individually treated in a country theme. Picnic area. Some kitchenettes, some refrigerators. Cable TV. Pets allowed. | 6375 Soco Rd. | 828/926–1188 or 800/545–5853 | fax 828/926–2389 | tours@abbeyinn.com | www.abbeyinn.com | 20 rooms | $49–$89 | Closed Nov.–Mar. | AE, DC, MC, V.

MOREHEAD CITY

Dill House. Built in 1918, this residence of former Mayor George Dill is a few blocks from the waterfront, shops, and restaurants. The house has some of its original French doors, oriental carpets, and antiques. One of the rooms has a working fireplace. Dining room, complimentary breakfast. No air-conditioning in some rooms. Cable TV. Laundry facilities. Some pets allowed. No children under 10. | 1104 Arendell St. | 252/726–4449 | 2 rooms | $50–$125.

MORGANTON

Red Carpet Inn. This motel is near many restaurants and businesses in downtown Morgantown. Pets are allowed for a $5 fee, and you can rent videos at the front desk. Complimentary Continental breakfast. Some in-room microwaves, some in-room refrigerators. Cable TV, in-room VCRs. Outdoor pool. Pets allowed (fee). | 2217 S.Sterling St. 28655 | 828/437–6980 | 70 rooms | $48–$58 | AE, D,MC, V.

MOUNT AIRY

Comfort Inn. This motel is a few blocks from the shops and restaurants in Mount Airy. Complimentary Continental breakfast. Cable TV, room phones. Outdoor pool. Pets allowed. | 2136 Rockford St. | 336/789–2000 | 98 rooms | $60–$90 | AE, D, DC, MC, V.

OCRACOKE

Anchorage Inn. The four stories of this hotel overlook the Ocracoke Harbor. The beach is 2 mi away. Complimentary Continental breakfast. Cable TV. Pool. Some pets allowed. | Rte. 12 | 252/928–1101 | fax 252/928–6322 | www.theanchorageinn.com | 35 rooms | $114–$125 | D, MC, V.

RALEIGH

Best Western. Across the street from the Crabtree Mall, this motel is outside downtown Raleigh. Complimentary Continental breakfast. In-room data ports, microwaves, refrigerators. Cable TV, room phones. Pets allowed (fee). | 6619 Glenwood Ave. | 919/782–8650 | fax 919/782–8650 | www.bestwestern.com | 88 rooms, 2 suites | $78–$84 | AE, D, DC, MC, V.

Days Inn–Crabtree. This motel is 2 mi from the Crabtree Mall and 5 mi from the Raleigh Airport. A fitness club is across the street. Restaurant. Some microwaves, some refrigerators. Cable TV, room phones. Outdoor pool. Laundry facilities. Pets allowed. | 6329 Glenwood Ave. | 919/781–7904 | fax 919/571–8385 | www.daysinn.com | 122 rooms | $49–$79 | AE, D, DC, MC, V.

Holiday Inn Crabtree. Across the street from Crabtree Valley Mall, this 12-story hotel was refurbished in 1998. Complimentary breakfast, room service. In-room data ports, cable TV. Outdoor pool. Exercise center. Laundry facilities. Free parking. Pets allowed. | 4100 Glenwood Ave. | 919/782–8600 | 176 rooms | $69–$109 | AE, D, DC, MC, V.

Holiday Inn–Crabtree. This hotel is 8 mi from the airport and 2 mi from North Carolina State University. Some rooms have a Nintendo video game system. Restaurant, bar. In-room data ports. Cable TV. Pool. Exercise equipment. Laundry services. Business services, airport shuttle, free parking. Pets allowed. | 4100 Glenwood Ave. | 919/782–8600 | fax 919/782–7213 | www.basshotels.com | 176 rooms | $80–$120 | AE, D, DC, MC, V.

Holiday Inn–Downtown. Near the Crabtree Mall and many shops, restaurants and businesses in downtown Raleigh. Complimentary breakfast. In-room data ports. Cable TV, room phones. Health club. Laundry services. Pets allowed. | 320 Hillsborough St. | 919/782–8600 | fax 919/571–8385 | www.holiday-inn.com | 176 rooms | $109–$119 | AE, D, DC, MC, V.

Plantation Inn Resort. Spacious grounds, banquet facilities, and attractive landscaping make this a popular spot for weddings. Choose from king, queen, or twin beds in the guest rooms, they are appointed with a floral motif and oak furniture. 2 restaurants, bar, room service. In-room data ports, some refrigerators. Cable TV. Pool, lake, wading pool. Putting green. Fishing. Playground. Business services, airport shuttle. Some pets allowed (fee). | 6401 Capital Blvd. | 919/876–1411 or 800/521–1932 | fax 919/790–7093 | plan_inn@mindspring.com | www.plantationinnraleigh.com | 94 rooms | $58–$75 | AE, DC, MC, V.

ROCKY MOUNT

Bright Leaf Motel. In a quiet, rural area 10 mi outside downtown Rocky Mount, this one-story white brick motel has typical services and facilities. Cable TV, room phones. Pets allowed. | U.S. 301 S., Sharpsburg | 252/977–1988 | fax 252/977–3269 | 28 rooms | $40–$70 | AE, D, MC, V.

Comfort Inn. You can walk to restaurants next door to this five-story hotel that's 5 mi from the Children's Museum. You can also order room service from Coach's Sports Bar and Grill in the neighboring Holiday Inn. Complimentary Continental breakfast. Some in-room data ports. Cable TV. Pool. Exercise equipment. Laundry service. Business services, airport shuttle. Pets allowed. | 200 Gateway Blvd. | 252/937–7765 | fax 252/937–3067 | www.comfortinns.com | 125 rooms | $73–$90 | AE, D, DC, MC, V.

Holiday Inn–Dortches. In a quiet, secluded area and about 7 mi north of downtown, this two-story hotel has outside entrances. You can order room service from the hotel's restaurant. Restaurant, room service. In-room data ports, some microwaves, some refrigerators. Cable TV. Pool. Exercise equipment. Laundry facilities, laundry services. Business services. Pets allowed (fee). | 5350 Dortches Blvd. | 252/937–6300 or 800/HOLIDAY | fax 252/937–6312 | holiday-inn.com | 154 rooms | $62–68 | AE, D, DC, MC, V.

SMITHFIELD

Four Oaks Lodging. This motel is near the Tobacco Museum, Bentfield Battlegrounds, the outlet shopping mall, Atkinson Mill, the Benson Museum, and Benson State Park. You can swim in the pool at the Holiday Travel Park Camping Resort ½ mi from the motel. Cable TV. Pets allowed. | 4606 U.S. 301 S | 919/963–3596 | 15 rooms | $19–$52 | AE, D, DC, MC, V.

Log Cabin Motel. Poplar-wood furniture gives this motel its rustic charm. It is across from the outlet shopping mall and 5 mi from town. You can use the motel's private trout- and bass-stocked fishing pond. Restaurant, bar. Some microwaves, some refrigerators. Cable TV. Pond. Laundry facilities. Pets allowed (fee). | 2491 U.S. 70 | 919/934–1534 | fax 919/934–7399 | 61 rooms | $40–$42 | AE, D, MC, V.

SOUTHERN PINES

Days Inn. This one-story, peach-colored brick motel has golf packages for the Little River Golf Course, which is 5 mi away. Complimentary Continental breakfast. Some microwaves, some refrigerators. Cable TV, room phones. Outdoor pool. Pets allowed. | 1420 U.S. 1 S | 910/692–7581 | fax 910/692–7581 | www.daysinn.com | 120 rooms | $35–$70 | AE, D, DC, MC, V.

SOUTHPORT

Island Inn. One block from the ocean, this inn on Oak Island is just a few blocks from a few shops and restaurants and 2 mi from Southport. The one apartment in the facility has two bedrooms and cooking facilities. Refrigerators. Cable TV, room phones. Outdoor pool. Pets allowed. | 5611 E. Oak Island, Oak Island | 910/278–3366 | 18 rooms, 1 apartment | $40–$125 | AE, D, MC, V.

STATESVILLE

Best Western. This two-story motel is outside the business district, in a quiet area but less than a mile from I-77. It is 5 mi from JR Tobacco. Complimentary Continental breakfast. In-room data ports, some kitchenettes, some microwaves, some refrigerators, some in-room hot tubs. Cable TV, room phones. Outdoor pool. Health club. Laundry facilities, laundry service. Pets allowed (fee). | 1121 Moreland Dr. | 704/881–0111 | 69 rooms | $50–$109 | AE, D, DC, MC, V.

Red Roof Inn. There are three floors with exterior entrances at this motel just off I-77. Shops and restaurants are across the street. Cable TV. Pets allowed. | 1508 E. Broad St. | 704/878–2051 or 800/733–7663 | fax 704/872–3885 | www.redroof.com | 115 rooms | $46–$57 | AE, D, MC, V.

WILLIAMSTON

Holiday Inn. This chain hotel is 5 mi from the rodeos held at the Bob Martin Equestrian Center. Rooms are off-white with wood furniture. Restaurant, bar, room service. In-room data ports. Cable TV. Pool. Business services. Some pets allowed. | 101 East Blvd. | 252/792–3184 | fax 252/792–9003 | 100 rooms | $65 | AE, D, DC, MC, V.

WILMINGTON

Anderson Guest House. This is actually a 20-year-old detached carriage house behind a main house, which was built in 1851. There is a private patio looking over the garden, and a fireplace in each room. It is in downtown Wilmington, and just 10 mi from the beaches. Complimentary breakfast. Pets allowed. No kids under 18 years. No smoking. | 520 Orange St. | 910/343–8128 | 2 rooms | $90 | No credit cards.

Camellia Cottage B&B. This B&B is four blocks from Cape Fear River and 10 mi from the ocean. Complimentary breakfast. Some microwaves, some refrigerators. Cable TV, room phones. Laundry facilities. Pets allowed. No kids under 18 years. No smoking. | 118 South 4th St. | 910/763–9171 | www.capefearconventionsbureau.com | 3 rooms, 1 suite | $125–$150 | AE, MC, V.

Hampton Inn and Suites–Landfall Park. In this inn in the prestigious Landfall area of Wilmington, 1½ mi from the Wrightsville Beach drawbridge, you can relax in the rocking chairs on the veranda overlooking the courtyard or start your day with runs on the adjacent jogging trail. Golf packages. Bar, picnic area, complimentary Continental breakfast. In-room data ports, minibars and kitchenettes in suites, some microwaves, some refrigerators, some in-room whirlpools. Cable TV. Pool. Driving range, putting green. Exercise equipment. Laundry facilities. Business services. Some pets allowed. | 1989 Eastwood Rd. | 910/256–9600 | fax 910/256–1996 | www.landfallparkhotel.com | 120 rooms, 30 suites | $99–$129, $119–$399 suites | AE, D, DC, MC, V.

WINSTON-SALEM

Residence Inn by Marriott. If you—or your family—want to have munchies available at any hour, you can stock the kitchenettes for late-night snacking, or even a full-blown picnic outdoors. This spot is within walking distance of some restaurants, and movie theaters are less than a block away. Picnic area, complimentary Continental breakfast. Kitchenettes, microwaves, refrigerators. Pool. Hot tub. Laundry facilities. Free parking. Some pets allowed. | 7835 N. Point Blvd. | 336/759–0777 | fax 336/759–9671 | 88 suites | $94–$160 | AE, D, DC, MC, V.

WRIGHTSVILLE BEACH

Waterway Lodge. The Waterway Lodge complex at the Intracoastal Waterway drawbridge has one-bedroom condominiums, large hotel rooms, and an apartment. Each hotel room has a microwave oven, a refrigerator, and a coffeemaker. Larger units have full kitchens, plus sleeper sofas in condo living rooms. Cable TV. Pool. Business services. Some pets allowed ($15 fee). | 7246 Wrightsville Ave. | 910/256–3771 or 800/677–3771 | fax 910/256–6916 | www.waterwaylodge.com | 42 rooms | $90–$170 | AE, D, MC, V.

North Dakota

BISMARCK

Best Western Doublewood Inn. At I–94 and Hwy. 83, this two-story motel is ¼ mi from the State Capitol. Restaurant, bar, room service. In-room data ports, microwaves, refrigerators. Cable TV, some in-room VCRs. Indoor pool. Hot tub, sauna. Video games. Playground. Laundry services. Business services, airport shuttle, free parking. Pets allowed (fee). | 1400 E. Interchange Ave. 58501 | 701/258–7000 or 800/554–7077 | fax 701/258–2001 | www.bestwestern.com | 143 rooms | $73 | AE, D, DC, MC, V.

Comfort Inn. Poolside rooms have direct access to the courtyard in this hotel 2 mi north of downtown. The lounge and casino have a nightly happy hour. Complimentary Continental breakfast. Cable TV. Indoor pool. Hot tub. Game room. Laundry service. Business services, airport shuttle. Some pets allowed. | 1030 Interstate Ave. | 701/223–1911 or 800/228–5150 | fax 701/223–6977 | www.comfortinn.com | 148 rooms, 5 suites | $45–$50, $55 suites | AE, D, DC, MC, V.

Comfort Suites. A 92-ft water slide at its pool makes this hotel, 2 mi from downtown, popular with families. Complimentary Continental breakfast. In-room data ports, some in-room hot tubs. Cable TV. Indoor pool. Hot tub. Exercise equipment, gym. Laundry service. Business services, airport shuttle, free parking. Some pets allowed. | 929 Gateway Ave. | 701/223–4009 or 800/228–5150 | fax 701/223–9119 | www.comfortsuites.com | 60 suites | $50–$90 | AE, D, MC, V.

Radisson Inn. Many of the rooms here have large work areas and private patios overlooking the indoor pool. The hotel is across from Kirkwood Mall, 4 mi from the airport. Restaurant, bar, room service. In-room data ports, some in-room hot tubs. Cable TV. Indoor pool. Hot tub, sauna. Gym. Laundry service. Business services, airport shuttle. Some pets allowed. | 800 S. 3rd St. | 701/258–7700 or 800/333–3333 | fax 701/224–8212 | www.radisson.com | 298 rooms, 8 suites | $75–$90, $180–$195 suites | AE, D, DC, MC, V.

Super 8. This three-story hotel is at Exit 159 off I–94, a mile from the Capitol building. Room service. Cable TV. Laundry service. Business services, free parking. Some pets allowed. | 1124 E. Capitol Ave. | 701/255–1314 or 800/800–8000 | fax 701/255–1314 | www.super8.com | 61 rooms | $30–$55 | AE, D, DC, MC, V.

BOTTINEAU

Norway House. This large one-story motel is on the east edge of town, 1 block from the Tommy Turtle Park. Liquor store adjacent. Restaurant, bar, room service. Cable TV. Airport shuttle. Some pets allowed. | 1255 Rte. 5 NE | 701/228–3737 | fax 701/228–3740 | 46 rooms | $35–$41 | AE, D, MC, V.

BOWMAN

North Winds Lodge. Oak trim, brass, and soft color schemes distinguish the handful of newer rooms at this hostelry is on the edge of town, with views of the countryside. Some refrigerators. Cable TV. Pool. Laundry service. Business services. Some pets allowed. | 503 Rte. 85S | 701/523–5641 or 888/684–9463 | fax 701/528–5641 | 10 rooms | $40–$47 | AE, D, MC, V.

CARRINGTON

Chieftain Motor Lodge. A tall wooden Native American sculpture stands outside this two-story property. Inside, you can see Native American artifacts. The rooms are burgundy and dark green and there's a sports bar. Restaurant, bar, room service. In-room data ports, some microwaves, some refrigerators. Cable TV. Hot tub. Gym. Laundry facilities. Business services. Some pets allowed. | 60 Fourth Ave. S | 701/652–3131 | fax 701/652–2151 | 47 rooms, 1 suite | $47–$52, $86 suites | AE, D, MC, V.

Super 8. At Rte. 281/52, this two-story motel is three blocks from Main Street. Complimentary Continental breakfast. In-room data ports. Cable TV. Laundry facilities. Some pets allowed. | 101 4th Ave. S | 701/652–3982 or 800/800–8000 | fax 701/652–3984 | www.super8.com | 36 rooms, 4 suites | $34–$52, $80 suites | AE, D, MC, V.

CAVALIER

Cedar Inn. A dining room, lounge, and shop on the property here make this a convenient stopover point. It's 5 mi from Icelandic State Park. Dining room. In-room data ports, some microwaves, some refrigerators. Cable TV. Laundry facilities. Some pets allowed. | 502 Division Ave. S, 58220 | 701/265–8341 or 800/338–7440 | fax 701/265–4706 | 39 rooms, 1 suite | $46, $55 suite | AE, MC, V.

DEVILS LAKE

Comfort Inn. One mile outside of central Devils Lake, this hotel is on U.S. 2. Complimentary Continental breakfast. Microwaves, refrigerators. Cable TV. Indoor pool. Hot tub. Laundry facilities. Business services. Some pets allowed. | 215 U.S. 2E | 701/662–6760 or 800/266–3948 | fax 701/662–6760 | www.comfortinn.com | 82 rooms, 5 suites | $55–$76 | AE, D, MC, V.

Dakota Motor Inn. There's a small casino in the lounge at this two-story property with pastel rooms and local art. Restaurant, bar, complimentary Continental breakfast, room service. Cable TV. Indoor pool. Video games. Pets allowed. | Rte. 2E | 701/662–4001 or 888/662–7748 | fax 701/662–4003 | 80 rooms | $28–$54 | AE, D, MC, V.

Days Inn. Four miles from Devils Lake, this hotel attracts quite a few watersport enthusiasts. Complimentary Continental breakfast. Some microwaves, some refrigerators, some in-room hot tubs. Cable TV. Business services. Some pets allowed. | Junction of Rte. 2 and Rte. 20 58301 | 701/662–5381 or 800/329–7466 | fax 701/662–3578 | www.daysinn.com | 44 rooms | $55–$65 | AE, D, MC, V.

Super 8 Motel. Built in the 1980s and remodeled in 1998, this motel is on Hwy. 2, 8 mi northeast of downtown. Complimentary Continental breakfast. Cable TV. Indoor pool, hot tub. Pets allowed. | 1001 Hwy 2E 58301 | 701/662–8656 or 800/800–8000 | fax 701/662–8656 | www.super8.com | 39 rooms | $65 | AE, D, DC, MC, V.

DICKINSON

Comfort Inn. The indoor pool has a spiral waterslide. The hotel is on the north side of I-94, across from Prairie Hills Mall, 1½ mi outside downtown. Complimentary Continental breakfast. In-room data ports, kitchenettes. Cable TV. Indoor pool. Hot tub. Laundry facilities. Business services, airport shuttle. Some pets allowed. | 493 Elk Dr. | 701/264–7300 or 800/221–2222 | fax 701/264–7300 | www.comfortinn.com | 107 rooms, 10 suites | $72; $85–$105 suites | AE, D, MC, V.

Hartfiel Inn B&B. The suite in this 1980 downtown home has white furniture, navy walls, and wall-to-wall carpeting. French, German, and English rooms have hardwood floors with area rugs, black iron four poster or brass beds, and desks. The Common living room has a working fireplace. Breakfast, chosen from a menu, is from 5:30–11:30 in the formal dining room or on the tile terrace overlooking the lavish gardens with a waterfall, arbor, private hot tub cottage with stereo and a life-size statue of the goddess Hebe. Complimentary breakfast. Some in-room VCRs. Hot tub. Library. Some pets allowed. No smoking. | 509 3rd Ave. W 58601 | 701/225–6701 | fax 701/225–1184 | hartfielinn@goesp.com | 3 rooms (2 with shower only), 1 suite | $59–$68, $89 suite | MC, V.

Oasis Motel. This two-story brick and concrete motel is less than a block from the bus station and 1½ blocks from Dickinson State University. Furnishings are dark wood. For breakfast you'll receive a complimentary card for the nearby Donut Hole. Some microwaves, some refrigerators. Cable TV. Outdoor pool. Some pets allowed. | 1000 W. Villard St. 58601 | 701/225–6703 or 888/225–6703 | fax 701/225–6703 | 34 rooms | $46 | AE, D, DC, MC, V.

Travelodge. The huge lobby of this three-story motel, across from the Prairie Hills Mall, has a fireplace. A mezzanine overlooks the pool. Restaurant, bar, room service. Some refrigerators. Cable TV. Indoor pool. Hot tub, Sauna. Video games. Laundry facilities. Business services, airport shuttle. Some pets allowed. | 532 15th St. W | 701/227–1853 or 800/422–0949 | fax 701/225–0090 | www.travelodge.com | 149 rooms | $60–$64 | AE, D, DC, MC, V.

FARGO

Best Western Doublewood Inn. The hotel is 3 mi from downtown Fargo and two blocks from West Acres Mall. Restaurant, bar, room service. Microwaves, refrigerators, some in-room hot tubs. Cable TV. Indoor pool. Beauty salon, hot tub, sauna. Business services, airport shuttle. Some pets allowed. | 3333 13th Ave. S | 701/235–3333 or 800/528–1234 | fax 701/280–9482 | www.bestwestern.com | 162 rooms, 11 suites | $79–93, $115 suites | AE, D, DC, MC, V.

Best Western Kelly Inn. The kelly green exterior of this two-story hotel gives a splash of color to the neighborhood. In warm months, lounge around the hourglass-shaped outdoor pool. The property is next to a bingo parlor. North Dakota University, West Acres Mall, and Bonanzaville are less than 3 mi away. Restaurant, bar. Microwaves, refrigerators, some in-room hot tubs. Cable TV. 2 pools (1 indoor). Hot tub, sauna. Laundry facilities. Business services, airport shuttle, free parking. Some pets allowed. | 3800 Main Ave. | 701/282–2143 or 800/635–3559 | fax 701/281–0243 | www.bestwestern.com | 117 rooms, 16 suites | $69–$84, $108–$164 suites | AE, D, DC, MC, V.

Comfort Inn–East. This hotel is at the interstate, ½ mi from the Fargo Waterslide. Complimentary Continental breakfast. In-room data ports, microwaves, refrigerators. Cable TV. Indoor pool. Hot tub. Business services, free parking. Some pets allowed. | 1407 35th St. S | 701/280–9666 or 800/221–2222 | fax 701/280–9666 | www.comfortinn.com | 64 rooms | $72–$82 | AE, D, DC, MC, V.

Comfort Inn–West. Within ½ mi of West Acres shopping center, this hotel is within walking distance of restaurants, stores, and a movie theater, and is 5 mi from a miniature golf course. Complimentary Continental breakfast. In-room data ports, some microwaves, some refrigerators. Cable TV, some in-room VCRs. Indoor pool. Hot tub. Business services, free parking. Some pets allowed. | 3825 9th Ave. SW | 701/282–9596 or

800/221–2222 | fax 701/292–9596 | www.comfortinn.com | 42 rooms, 14 suites | $72–$82 | AE, D, DC, MC, V.

Comfort Suites. A maroon and emerald green is the outside color of this hotel next door to the Fargo Waterslide and 1 mi from a golf course and casino. Complimentary Continental breakfast. In-room data ports, microwaves, refrigerators. Cable TV. Indoor pool. Hot tub. Laundry service. Some pets allowed. | 1415 35th St. S | 701/237–5911 or 800/221–2222 | fax 701/237–5911 | www.comfortsuites.com | 66 rooms | $85–$100 | AE, D, DC, MC, V.

Country Suites by Carlson. West Acres Mall is four blocks from this two-story motel, with blonde wood in the lobby and rooms of pink and blue. Bar, complimentary Continental breakfast. In-room data ports, kitchenettes. Cable TV. Indoor pool. Hot tub. Exercise equipment. Business services, airport shuttle. Some pets allowed. | 3316 13th Ave. S | 701/234–0565 or 800/456–4000 | fax 701/234–0565 | www.fargoweb.com/countrysuites/ | 99 suites | $77–$160 | AE, D, DC, MC, V.

Holiday Inn. A pirate ship in the pool area has turned this hotel into a hot spot for families. Rooms have large desks for business travelers. It's at I–29 and I–94 and 4 mi from downtown. Restaurant, bar, room service. In-room data ports. Cable TV. Indoor and outdoor pools. Hot tub. Gym. Laundry facilities. Business services, airport shuttle. Some pets allowed. | 3803 13th Ave. S | 701/282–2700 or 800/465–4329 | fax 701/281–1240 | www.basshotels.com/holiday-inn | 302 rooms, 7 suites | $105–$130, $139–$159 suites | AE, D, DC, MC, V.

Holiday Inn Express. At West Acres shopping center, this four-story hotel is in the middle of a busy commercial strip. It's 4 mi from downtown. Complimentary Continental breakfast. In-room data ports. Cable TV. Indoor pool. Hot tub. Laundry facilities. Business services. Some pets allowed. | 1040 40th St. SW | 701/282–2000 or 800/465–4329 | fax 701/282–4721 | www.basshotels.com/holiday-inn | 71 rooms, 6 suites | $69–$80, $95–$115 suites | AE, D, DC, MC, V.

Kelly Inn–13th Avenue. A small pool gives kids and adults a chance to unwind at this hotel in the heart of the major shopping district. Complimentary Continental breakfast. Cable TV. Indoor pool. Hot tub, sauna. Laundry facilities. Business services, airport shuttle. Some pets allowed. | 4207 13th Ave. SW | 701/277–8821 or 800/635–3559 | fax 701/277–0208 | www.fargomoorhead.org | 46 rooms, 13 suites | $61–$69 | AE, D, DC, MC, V.

Radisson Hotel. From the restaurant on the second floor, you can see the city. The lobby's atrium extends to the third floor, with balconies overlooking it. A golf course and Yunker Children's Museum is 10 mi away. Restaurant, bar, room service. In-room data ports, some minibars, some in-room hot tubs. Cable TV. Hot tub, sauna. Exercise equipment. Business services, airport shuttle, free parking. Some pets allowed. | 201 N. 5th St. | 701/232–7363 or 800/333–3333 | fax 701/298–9134 | www.radisson.com | 151 rooms, 6 suites | $75–$115, $130–$155 suites | AE, D, DC, MC, V.

Ramada Plaza Suites. Families enjoy the 150-ft water slide at this six-story hotel, while locals prefer the hotel's restaurant, Basie's. The suites are furnished in mahogany and cherry wood. It's across the street from the West Acres Mall. Restaurant, bar, room service. In-room data ports, some in-room hot tubs. Cable TV. Indoor pool. Hot tub, sauna. Gym. Laundry services. Business services, free parking. Some pets allowed. | 1635 42nd St. SW | 701/277–9000 or 800/272–6232 | fax 701/281–7145 | www.ramadafargo.com | 67 rooms, 118 suites | $80–$105, $120–$315 suites | AE, D, DC, MC, V.

Sleep Inn. Cookies are offered each evening here, across the street from Fargo-Moorhead visitor center, and 1½ mi from the Roger Maris Museum. Complimentary Continental breakfast. In-room data ports. Cable TV. Indoor pool. Hot tub. Exercise equipment. Laundry services. Business services, free parking. Some pets allowed. | 1921 44th St. SW | 701/281–8240 or 800/905–7533 | fax 701/281–2041 | www.sleepinnfargo.com | 61 rooms | $62–$72 | AE, D, DC, MC, V.

Super 8 Motel and Suites. The Fargodome and the airport are within 5 mi of this two-story hotel. The suites have recliners. Complimentary Continental breakfast. In-room data ports. Cable TV. Indoor pool. Hot tub. Laundry facilities, laundry services. Business services, free parking. Some pets allowed. | 3518 Interstate Blvd. | 701/232–9202 or 800/800–8000 | fax 701/232–4543 | www.super8.com | 84 rooms, 25 suites | $34–$57; $47–$117 suites | AE, D, DC, MC, V.

GARRISON

Garrison Motel. Remodeled in 1997, this property, on the Lewis and Clark Trail, is 4 mi from Lake Sakakawea. Some microwaves, some refrigerators. Cable TV. Some pets allowed. | 539 4th Ave. SE | 701/463–2858 | 30 rooms | $41 | AE, D, MC, V.

GRAND FORKS

Comfort Inn. Built in the 1980s, the exterior of the hotel is a neutral stucco. It's in a commercial area 3 mi from downtown. Restaurants, shopping malls, and theaters are within five blocks. Complimentary Continental breakfast. Cable TV. Indoor pool. Hot tub. Laundry service. Business services. Some pets allowed. | 3251 30th Ave. S | 701/775–7503 or 800/228–5150 | fax 701/775–7503 | www.comfortinn.com | 58 rooms, 7 suites | $70; $80 suites | AE, D, DC, MC, V.

Country Inn and Suites By Carlson. This three-story inn is at Business Route 81, 10 minutes from downtown. Suites have fireplaces. A few blocks away, east and west, are Columbia Mall and Waterworld Waterslide Park. Complimentary Continental breakfast. In-room data ports. Cable TV, some in-room VCRs (and movie rentals). Indoor pool. Hot tub, sauna. Laundry facilities, laundry service. Business services. Some pets allowed. | 3350 32nd Ave. S | 701/775–5000 or 800/456–4000 | fax 701/775–9073 | 64 rooms, 25 suites | $60; $70 suites | AE, D, DC, MC, V.

Days Inn. This two-story inn, remodeled in 1999, is 2 mi from downtown and UND. Complimentary Continental breakfast. In-room data ports. Cable TV. Indoor pool. Hot tub, spa. Small pets allowed. Laundry service. Business services. | 3101 34th St. S | 701/775–0060 or 800/329–7466 | fax 701/775–0060 | www.daysinn.com | 52 rooms, 5 suites | $64, $74 suites | AE, D, DC, MC, V.

Econo Lodge. Built in 1982, this two-story hotel is 2 mi from downtown at the intersection of I–29 and Highway 2. You'll find an entrance to Turtle River State Park to the west. Complimentary Continental breakfast. In-room data ports. Cable TV. Business services. Some pets allowed. | 900 N. 43rd St. | 701/746–6666 or 800/553–2666 | fax 701/746–6666 | www.econolodge.com | 38 rooms, 6 suites | $47–$49, $52 suites | AE, D, DC, MC, V.

Fabulous Westward Ho Motel. Built in 1953, the two-story, wood-structured motel is part of a complex that has an entertainment center with with wagon wheels, red flocked wallpaper, and dark wood trim. Fast-food restaurants and car dealerships surround the motel, 3 mi from downtown. 3 restaurants, bar. In-room data ports. Cable TV. Outdoor Pool. Sauna. Business services. Some pets allowed. | 3400 Gateway Dr. 58208 | 701/775–5341 or 800/437–9562 | fax 701/775–3703 | 104 rooms, 4 suites | $50, $69 suites | AE, D, DC, MC, V.

Holiday Inn. A large block south of the University of North Dakota and across the railroad tracks, this 1950 hotel has shuttle services to UND, the medical park, and the airport. Restaurant, bar, room service. In-room data ports. Cable TV. Indoor pool, wading pool. Hot tub, sauna. Putting green. Gym. Video Games. Laundry facilities. Business services, airport shuttle. Some pets allowed. | 1210 N. 43rd St. | 701/772–7131 or 888/249–1464 | fax 701/780–9112 | www.basshotels.com/holiday-inn | 149 rooms, 1 suite | $76–$79, $135 suite | AE, D, DC, MC, V.

Select Inn. The hotel has three buildings, two are no smoking. Off I–29 at Exit 141, then east on Gateway Drive (Hwy. 2) and south on W. 42nd Street, the hotel is on the west side of the road, about 2 mi from the University and 3 mi from downtown. Complimentary Continental breakfast. In-room data ports. Cable TV. Laundry facilities. Business services. Pets allowed (fee). | 1000 N. 42nd St. | 701/775–0555 or 800/641–1000 | fax 701/775–9967 | www.selectinn.com | 119 rooms, 1 suite | $35–$45, $40 suite | AE, D, DC, MC, V.

JAMESTOWN

Comfort Inn. Built in the 1990s in a commercial area, the two-story, brick hotel is 1 mi from downtown and across the street from the National Buffalo Museum and its accompanying giant buffalo sculpture. Just north of I–94, off Hwy. 281 at Exit 258, this hotel has interior corridors. Restaurant, bar, complimentary Continental breakfast. In-room data ports. Cable TV. Indoor pool. Hot tub. Business services. Pets allowed (fee). | 811 20th St. SW | 701/252–7125 or 800/228–5150 | fax 701/252–7125 | www.comfortinn.com | 43 rooms, 9 suites | $64, $74 suites | AE, D, DC, MC, V.

Gladstone Select Hotel. In downtown, attached to the Gladstone Restaurant and one block from the Jamestown Mall and a few blocks from several local restaurants, the two-story hotel has nine theme suites. The Stadium Club room is surrounded with a grandstand mural and sports memorabilia, a large screen TV, and a grid-iron painted ceiling. You can enjoy a hearty breakfast, lunch and dinner at the Prairie Rose restaurant on site. If you venture north in the winter, the Gladstone has winter plug-ins for your vehicle. 2 Restaurants, bar, room service. In-room data ports. Cable TV. Indoor pool. Hot tub. Laundry facilities, laundry service. Business services, airport shuttle. Some pets allowed. | 111 2nd St. NE | 701/252–0700 or 800/641–1000 | www.selectinn.com | fax 701/252–0700 | 108 rooms, 9 suites | $54–$57, $86 suites | AE, D, DC, MC, V.

MANDAN

Best Western Seven Seas Motor Inn. This three-story hotel sits on the top of a hill, with views of Mandan and beyond. It was built in the 1970s and is in a commercial zone 2 mi from downtown and 4 mi from the region's largest shopping mall. There's nautical decor throughout, and also a casino. Restaurant, bar, room service. In-room data ports, kitchenettes. Cable TV. Indoor pool. Hot tub. Business services, free parking. Some pets allowed. | 2611 Old Red Trail | 701/663–7401 or 800/597–7327 | fax 701/663–0025 | www.bestwestern.com | 103 rooms, 4 suites | $67, $99 suites | AE, D, DC, MC, V.

MEDORA

AmericInn Motel and Suites. Glowing wood, stuffed animals, and western themes dominate this motel, the newest (1997) of Medora's lodgings. The two-story cement-block building is in a commercial area three blocks from downtown; restaurants and stores are nearby. Complimentary Continental breakfast. Cable TV. Indoor pool. Hot tub, sauna. Laundry facilities. Business services, free parking. Some pets allowed. | 75 E. River Rd. S | 701/623–4800 or 800/634–3444 | fax 701/623–4890 | www.americinn.com | 56 rooms, 8 suites | $60, $89–$120 suites | AE, D, DC, MC, V.

MINOT

★ **Best Western International Inn.** On a hilltop near the airport, this large, five-story hotel is within walking distance of several restaurants and 2 mi from downtown. The rooms are large, with contemporary furnishings. The hotel's restaurant has window seating overlooking the city. Restaurant, room service. Cable TV. Indoor pool. Beauty salon, hot tub. Some pets allowed. | 1505 N. Broadway 58703 | 701/852–3161 or 800/735–4493 | fax 701/838–5538 | www.bestwestern.com | 266 rooms, 4 suites | $62–$75, $125 suites | AE, D, DC, MC, V.

Best Western Kelly Inn. This two-story stucco hotel was built in 1992 in a commercial area. It's within walking distance of the Dakota Square Mall, the town's major shopping district, and restaurants, and is 3 mi from downtown. Complimentary Continental breakfast, bar. In-room data ports. Cable TV. Indoor pool. Hot tub. Video games. Business services, free parking. Some pets allowed. | 1510 26th Ave. SW | 701/852–4300 or 800/735–5868 | fax 701/838–1234 | www.bestwestern.com | 80 rooms, 20 suites | $59, $80–$125 suites | AE, D, DC, MC, V.

Comfort Inn. The hotel was built in 1989 in a commercial area next to the Dakota Square Mall, the major shopping mall of Minot, and near theaters and restaurants. Complimentary Continental breakfast. In-room data ports. Cable TV. Indoor pool. Hot tub. Video games. Laundry facilities, laundry service. Business services, free parking. Some pets allowed. | 1515 22nd Ave. SW | 701/852–2201 or 800/228–5150 | fax 701/852–2201 | www.comfortinn.com | 140 rooms, 12 suites | $58–$75, $70–$95 suites | AE, D, DC, MC, V.

Days Inn. One of several hotels near the city's main shopping area, Dakota Square Mall, this is also near U.S. 2 and U.S. 83. The two-story brick hotel was built in 1982. Complimentary Continental breakfast. Cable TV. Indoor pool. Hot tub, sauna. Video games. Laundry facilities. Business services, free parking. Some pets allowed. | 2100 4th St. SW | 701/852–3646 or 800/329–7466 | fax 701/852–0501 | www.daysinn.com | 81 rooms, 1 suite | $40–$59, $75 suite | AE, D, DC, MC, V.

Holiday Inn Riverside. This huge, seven-story hotel, built in 1983, is 15 blocks from downtown. The hotel is in a commercial neighborhood, but nearby houses give it a residential look. Within 1 mi there's a mall and zoo, and the state fairgrounds are right across the street. In the center of the hotel is an enormous atrium that overlooks a lounge and seating area. Restaurant (*see* Ground Round Bar and Grill), bar, room service. In-room data ports. Cable TV. Indoor pool. Beauty salon, hot tub, sauna. Video games. Laundry service. Business services, airport shuttle. Some pets allowed. | 2200 Burdick Expressway E | 701/852–2504 or 800/468–9968 | fax 701/852–2630 | www.basshotels.com/holiday-inn | 170 rooms, 3 suites | $89, $200 suite | AE, D, DC, MC, V.

Super 8. This hotel is two blocks from the airport on the north end of town, is close to Minot University and 1 mi from downtown. Cable TV. Laundry facilities. Business services, free parking. Some pets allowed. | 1315 N. Broadway | 701/852–1817 or 800/800–8000 | fax 701/852–1817 | www.super8.com | 60 rooms | $30–$35 | AE, D, DC, MC, V.

NEW ROCKFORD

Bison Lodge. Built in 1959 and remodeled in 1994, this motel is on the south end of the strip, about eight blocks east of New Rockford center, off Hwy. 281. A small motel with parking out front and restaurants and gas stations nearby, the furnishings are sturdy oak, with rooms in mauve and teal colors. There are five additional units in a hunter's lodge with kitchenettes and game cleaning facilities. Complimentary Continental breakfast. Cable TV. Some pets allowed. | 222 First St. S, 58356 | 701/947–5947 | fax 701/947–5059 | 13 rooms | $34 | AE, D, MC, V.

NEW TOWN

Four Bears Casino and Lodge. This small, two-story brick motel is next to the casino and has a great view of Lake Sakakawea. It was built in 1996 and is 4 mi west of downtown, off Hwy 23. You can go fishing in a nearby park. Restaurant, bar. In-room data ports. Cable TV. Video games. Laundry facilities. Business services, free parking. Some pets allowed. | HC3 Box 2A 58763 | 701/627–4018 or 800/294–5454 | fax 701/627–4012 | 40 rooms | $55 | AE, D, MC, V.

PEMBINA

Forestwood Inn. This 1984 two-story wood and brick hotel is five blocks from downtown. Rooms are furnished in deep earth tones. In-room data ports. Cable TV. Hot tub. Some pets allowed. | 504 Sunset Ave., Walhalla 58282 | 701/549–2651 | 28 rooms, 1 suite | $33–$44, $71 suite | AE, D, DC, MC, V.

Red Roost Motel. You can spot this 1960s motel downtown by its bright red exterior, trimmed with white. Cable TV. Some pets allowed. | 203 Stutsman | 701/825–6254 | 9 rooms | $33 | No credit cards.

RUGBY

Econo Lodge. There are gas stations, a store, and restaurants within a mile of this two-story brick hotel on Highway 2. Restaurant, bar. Cable TV. Indoor pool. Hot tub. Video games. Business service. Some pets allowed. | Hwy. 2E south of the intersection with Hwy. 3 58368 | 701/776–5776 or 800/424–4777 | fax 701/776–5156 | www.econolodge.com | 59 rooms, 1 suite | $40–$55, $90 suite | AE, D, DC, MC, V.

Hillman Inn & Campground. A 1960s motel at U.S. 2 and Route 3, built of cement block with brown and beige colors. Complimentary Continental breakfast. Some refrigerators. Cable TV. Laundry facilities. Pets allowed. | U.S. 2 and Rte. 3 58368 | 701/776–5272 | fax 701/776–2300 | 39 rooms in 2 buildings (showers only) | $44 | D, MC, V.

VALLEY CITY

Super 8. The Winter Show Arena, Baldhill Dam, and downtown are all within one mile of this two-story 1977 motel. In-room data ports. Cable TV. Business services. Some pets allowed. | 822 11th St. SW | 701/845–1140 or 800/800–8000 | fax 701/845–1145 | www.super8.com | 30 rooms | $35–$41, $41–$51 deluxe rooms | AE, D, DC, MC, V.

WASHBURN

Scot Wood Motel. On the Lewis and Clark trail, this 1970s two-story brick motel is six blocks from downtown, three blocks from the Lewis and Clark Center, and 3 mi from Fort Mandan. There's coffee all day and a microwave in the lobby. A Dakota Farms Restaurant is next door. Cable TV. Pets allowed (fee). | 1323 Frontage Rd. 58577 | 701/462–8191 | fax 701/462–3795 | 24 rooms | $35–$48 | AE, D, DC, MC, V.

WILLISTON

El Rancho Motor Hotel. This Southwestern-style motel is six blocks from downtown and is well known for its restaurant. Restaurant, bar. In-room data ports. Cable TV. Laundry service. Some pets allowed. | 1623 2nd Ave. W | 701/572–6321 or 800/433–8529 | fax 701/572–6321 | 91 rooms | $52–$58 | AE, D, DC, MC, V.

Ohio

AKRON

Hilton Inn-West. With two swimming pools, a shopping mall across the street, and downtown Akron just 5 mi away, this hotel might be an option if you're traveling with the family. Guest rooms are spare and furnished with unassuming wood-veneer pieces. Restaurant, bar, room service. In-room data ports, some refrigerators. Cable TV. 2 pools (1 indoor). Exercise equipment. Laundry facilities. Business services. Airport shuttle. Free parking. Some pets allowed. | 3180 W. Market St. | 330/867–5000 or 800/445–8667 | fax 330/867–1648 | awhilton@aol.com | www.hilton.com | 204 rooms | $109 | AE, D, DC, MC, V.

Holiday Inn-South. This two-story stucco lodging 8 mi from downtown Akron was built in 1973 and has been renovated several times since. There's nightly entertainment in the hotel bar if you don't feel like venturing out into the city. Restaurant, bar, complimentary Continental breakfast. Cable TV. Pool. Business services. Airport shuttle. Free parking. Some pets allowed. | 2940 Chenoweth Rd. | 330/644–7126 or 800/465–4329 | fax 330/644–1776 | www.holiday-inn.com | 131 rooms | $79–$89, hot tub rooms $109 | AE, D, DC, MC, V.

Red Roof Inn. Restaurants and shops surround this two-story suburban motel roughly 10 mi south of downtown Akron. The exterior is stucco on a brick foundation, and guest rooms are simply furnished with basic wood-veneer pieces. Cable TV. Some pets allowed. | 99 Rothrock Rd. | 330/666–0566 or 800/843–7663 | fax 330/666–6874 | www.redroof.com | 108 rooms | $39–$49 | AE, D, DC, MC, V.

ALLIANCE

Comfort Inn. Adjacent to an Alliance's small downtown shopping mall, this five-story lodging was built in 1989 and is popular with parents who are in town to visit students at Mount Union. Guest rooms are basic and uncluttered with the usual modular-type furniture. There are several sit-down, family-style restaurants in the adjacent mall, as well as within a few blocks of the hotel. Complimentary Continental breakfast. Cable TV. Indoor pool. Hot tub. Exercise equipment. Laundry facilities. Business services. Some pets allowed (fee). | 2500 W. State St. | 330/821–5555 or 800/228–5150 | fax 330/821–4919 | www.comfortinn.com | 113 rooms | $99 | AE, D, DC, MC, V.

ATHENS

Days Inn. This motel's rural location, just off Route 78 about 4 mi from the downtown area, affords pleasant views from the guest rooms and a quiet respite from urban distractions. A nearby driving range and putting course make it a favorite of golfers. Complimentary Continental breakfast. Cable TV. Business services. Some pets allowed (fee). | 330 Columbus Rd. | 740/592–4000 or 800/325–2525 | fax 740/593–7687 | www.daysinn.com | 60 rooms | $75 | AE, D, DC, MC, V.

BEACHWOOD

Hilton Cleveland-East. This large hotel, a Marriott-turned-Hilton at U.S. 422 and I–272, has equipped all its rooms with Sony Playstations and the Movie Channel. Restaurant, bar, room service. Some refrigerators. Cable TV. Indoor-outdoor pool. Hot tub, sauna. Exercise equipment. Video games. Laundry facilities. Business services. Some pets allowed (fee). | 3663 Park East Dr. | 216/464–5950 or 800/445–8667 | fax 216/464–6539 | www.hilton.com | 403 rooms | $109–$159 | AE, D, DC, MC, V.

Residence Inn By Marriott–Cleveland-Beachwood. This four-story brick hostelry in the Beachwood business district is comfortable for a longer stay; it's an all-suites property with studios and one- and two-bedroom units. Complimentary Continental breakfast. In-room data ports, refrigerators, microwaves. Cable TV. Pool. Tennis court. Exercise equipment. Video games. Laundry service, laundry facility. Pets allowed (fee). | 3628 Park East Dr. | 216/831–3030 or 800/331–3333 | fax 216/831–3232 | www.marriot.com | 174 rooms, 46 two-bedroom units | Studios $149, one–bedroom units $159, two–bedroom units, $205 | AE, D, DC, MC, V.

BELLEFONTAINE

Comfort Inn. The two-story motel was built in 1989 and is about 2 mi from the downtown area. A dozen or so restaurants are within a 5 mi radius of the motel, as are ski slopes and golf courses. Bar with entertainment, complimentary Continental breakfast. In-room data ports, microwaves, some refrigerators. Cable TV. Pool. Exercise equipment. Laundry facilities. Some pets allowed (fee). | 260 Northview Dr. | 937/599–6666 or 800/228–5150 | fax 937/599–2300 | www.comfortinn.com | 80 rooms | $71–$115 | AE, D, DC, MC, V.

BRECKSVILLE

Hilton Cleveland South. Comfortably removed from the bustle and hurry of Cleveland proper, this two-story hotel's exterior is reminiscent of the English countryside's exposed-timber cottages. Downtown Cleveland is about 12 mi away, or you can go the other direction and explore Brecksville. Restaurant, room service. In-room data ports. Cable TV. Indoor-outdoor pool. Tennis. Exercise equipment. Playground. Business services. Airport shuttle. Some pets allowed. | 6200 Quarry La., Independence | 216/447–1300 or 800/445–8667 | fax 440/642–9334 | www.hilton.com | 195 rooms | $105 | AE, D, DC, MC, V.

CAMBRIDGE

Best Western. Right off I–70, this motel is just minutes away from the Cambridge Glass Museum and Salt Fork State Park. The two-story brick building is in a largely commercial area that includes a score of restaurants, a large discount store, and several small shopping plazas. Bar. Cable TV. Pool. Business services. Some pets allowed. | 1945 Southgate Pkwy. | 740/439–3581 or 800/528–1234 | fax 740/439–1824 | www.bestwestern.com | 95 rooms | $65 | AE, D, DC, MC, V.

Holiday Inn. Strategically located at the junction of I–70 and I–77, this hotel is a pretty good bet if you're just passing through the area. There's a multiscreen movie theater right across the street, and two major shopping malls within 30 minutes of the hotel. If you've come to explore, downtown Cambridge is only 2 mi away. Restaurant, bar, room service. Cable TV. Pool. Laundry facilities. Business services. Some pets allowed. | 2248 Southgate Pkwy. | 740/432–7313 | fax 740/432–2337 | www.holiday-inn.com | 109 rooms | $69–$99 | AE, D, DC, MC, V.

CANTON

Holiday Inn-North Canton. This newly renovated member of the familiar hotel chain is across the street from the Beldon Village Mall, a popular shopping area, and is less than a quarter mile from I–77. Restaurant, bar with entertainment, room service. In-room data ports. Cable TV. Pool. Business services. Airport shuttle. Some pets allowed. | 4520 Everhard Rd. NW | 330/494–2770 or 800/465–4329 | fax 330/494–6473 | www.holiday-inn.com | 194 rooms | $149 | AE, D, DC, MC, V.

CHILLICOTHE

Comfort Inn. This Comfort Inn, just 1 mi north of Chillicothe, is close to the Hopewell Culture National Historic Park. Weekends are hopping at the hotel bar, where bands perform on Friday and Saturday nights. Bar with entertainment, complimentary Continental breakfast. Cable TV. Pool. Some pets allowed. Business services. | 20 N. Plaza Blvd. | 740/775–3500 | fax 740/775–3588 | 106 rooms, 8 suites | $80, $95 suites | AE, D, DC, MC, V.

Days Inn. This standard hotel is on the north edge of Chillicothe, close to the Adena State Memorial and the Franklin House. Cable TV. Pool. Business services. Some pets allowed. | 1250 N. Bridge St. | 740/775–7000 | fax 740/773–1622 | www.daysinn.com | 42 rooms | $59 | AE, D, DC, MC, V.

CINCINNATI

Amerisuites. Spacious rooms and an array of business amenities are featured at this six-story hotel 15 mi northeast of downtown Cincinnati. Complimentary Continental breakfast. In-room data ports, refrigerators, microwaves. Cable TV, in-room VCRs. Pool. Exercise equipment. Laundry facilities. Business services. Free parking. Some pets allowed. | 11435 Reed-Hartman Hwy., Blue Ash | 513/489–3666 or 800/833–1516 | fax 513/489–4187 | www.amerisuites.com | 127 suites | $149 | AE, D, DC, MC, V.

Garfield Suites Hotel. This contemporary hotel with a glass greenhouse lobby is across the street from Piatt Park. Many of its suites have balconies. It's three blocks from the center of town. Restaurant, bar, room service. Kitchenettes, microwaves, in-room safes. Cable TV. Exercise equipment. Laundry facilities. Business services. Some pets allowed (fee). Parking $5 per day, $17 per valet. | 2 Garfield Pl | 513/421–3355 or 800/367–2155 | fax 513/421–3729 | 150 suites | $165–$185 suites, $175–$200 2–bedroom suites, $425–$1,200 penthouse suites | AE, D, DC, MC, V.

Homewood Suites by Hilton. This three-story hotel caters to business travelers. Suites are exceptionally large, modern, and pleasantly furnished in dark wood furniture; some have fireplaces. The hotel is 15 mi north of Cincinnati in Sharonville, a ¼ mi from Exit 44 of I-275. Complimentary Continental breakfast. In-room data ports, some kitchenettes. Cable TV. Pool. Exercise room. Laundry service. Business services. Some pets allowed (fee). | 2670 E. Kemper Rd., Sharonville | 513/772–8888 | fax 513/772–8737 | www.homewood/suites.com | 111 suites | $109–$149 | AE, D, DC, MC, V.

Quality Hotel and Suites Central. This eight-story property is just a few blocks away from Xavier University and 7 mi north of downtown Cincinnati. It's attached to a popular seafood restaurant. Restaurant, bar, room service, picnic area, complimentary Continental breakfast. In-room data ports, some microwaves, some refrigerators. Cable TV. Pool. Business services. Airport shuttle. Some pets allowed. | 4747 Montgomery Rd., Norwood | 513/351–6000 or 800/292–2079 | fax 513/351–0215 | www.qualityinn.com | 148 rooms, 14 suites | $95, $110 suites | AE, D, DC, MC, V.

Red Roof Inn. This two-story hotel in Sharonville, about 15 mi north of downtown Cincinnati, is easily identified by the chain's signature red roof. The king rooms have large-screen

TVs. Cable TV. Business services. Free parking. Some pets allowed. | 11345 Chester Rd., Sharonville | 513/771–5141 or 800/843–7663 | fax 513/771–0812 | www.redroofsharonville.com | 108 rooms | $64 | AE, D, DC, MC, V.

Residence Inn by Marriott. All rooms are suites in this two-story hostelry designed for extended stays. It's made up of several two-story buildings, each with eight units ranging from studios to penthouse apartments; each has a fireplace. It's in Sharonville, one of the fastest-growing suburbs of Cincinnati, next to the Tri-County Mall. Picnic area, complimentary Continental breakfast. Kitchenettes, microwaves. Cable TV. Pool, hot tub. Laundry facilities. Business services. Free parking. Some pets allowed (fee). | 11689 Chester Rd., Sharonville | 513/771–2525 or 800/331–3131 | fax 513/771–3444 | www.marriott.com | 144 suites | $99–$149 | AE, D, DC, MC, V.

Super 8 Motel. This two-story, red-brick budget motel is a short walk from the popular Tri-County Mall. It is also close to the Sharonville Convention Center. Complimentary Continental breakfast. Cable TV. Pool. Laundry facilities. Free parking. Business services. Some pets allowed. | 11335 Chester Rd., Sharonville | 513/772–3140 or 800/800–8000 | fax 513/772–1931 | www.super8motels.com | 144 rooms | $81 | AE, D, DC, MC, V.

Woodfield Suites. Just off I–75 in Sharonville, this all-suites hotel has spacious rooms and attractive cherry furnishings. Complimentary cocktails are served in the evening. Restaurants, a shopping mall, the Cincinnati Zoo, and the Riverfront Stadium are within 10 mi of the property. Complimentary Continental breakfast. In-room data ports, some kitchenettes, microwaves, refrigerators, in-room hot tubs (in some suites). Cable TV. Indoor pool, hot tub. Exercise equipment. Playground. Laundry facilities. Business services. Free parking. Some pets allowed. | 11029 Dowlin Dr., Sharonville | 513/771–0300 or 800/338–0008 | fax 513/771–6411 | www.woodfieldsuites.com | 151 suites | $99–$189 | AE, D, DC, MC, V.

CLEVELAND

Cleveland Airport Marriott. Almost half of the rooms at this nine-story hotel are designed for business travelers and have work stations. Guests in concierge rooms have access to a private lounge. It's 2 mi from the airport and 7 mi from downtown. Restaurant, bar. In-room data ports. Cable TV. Indoor pool. Hot tub. Exercise equipment. Laundry facilities. Business services. Airport shuttle. Some pets allowed (fee). Free parking. | 4277 W. 150th St. | 216/252–5333 or 800/228–9290 | fax 216/251–1508 | www.marriott.com | 371 rooms, 4 suites in 2 buildings | $139–$159 | AE, D, DC, MC, V.

Comfort Inn-Cleveland Airport. This four-story brick hotel is off I–71, near restaurants and stores. It was a Choice Hotels Gold Award winner from 1994-1999. Complimentary breakfast. Cable TV, in-room movies. Pool. Business services. Airport shuttle. Some pets allowed. Free parking. | 17550 Rosbough Dr., Middleburg Heights | 440/234–3131 or 800/228–5150 | fax 440/234–6111 | www.comfortinn.com | 136 rooms | $108 | AE, D, DC, MC, V.

Edgewater Estates I and II. This 1920s English Tudor is directly across the street from Edgewater State Park, a three-minute drive from downtown. The guest rooms, furnished with period antiques, look out on either the gardens of the estate or Lake Erie. There are two kitchens (one for you to share with the rest of the guests) and two dining rooms. Complimentary breakfast. Some microwaves, some refrigerators. Hiking. Beach, dock, swimming and water sports, boating, fishing. Laundry facilities. Airport shuttle. Pets allowed. | 9803–5 Lake Ave. | 216/961–1764 | fax 216/961–7043 | lopezgayle@hotmail.com | www.bedandbreakfast.com/bbc/p616727.asp | 5 rooms | $110–$135 | AE, D, MC, V.

Embassy Suites. This all-suites hotel in a 13-story, brick-and-stone, early 1900s building is in downtown's Reserve Square. The two-room suites have a bedroom with two double beds or a king-sized bed, and a living room with a sofa bed. Connecting units are available. Restaurant, bar, complimentary breakfast. In-room data ports, minibars, microwaves. Cable TV. Indoor pool. Tennis. Exercise equipment. Laundry facilities.

Some pets allowed. | 1701 E. 12th St. | 216/523–8000 or 800/362–2779 | fax 216/523–1698 | www.embassysuites.com | 268 suites | $129–$199 | AE, D, DC, MC, V.

Red Roof Inn. The three-story stucco motel built in 1980 is 4 mi from the airport. The bright rooms with slate gray carpet have lounge chairs. Several restaurants and stores are nearby. Cable TV. Some pets allowed. Free parking. | 17555 Bagley Rd., Middleburg Heights | 440/243–2441 or 800/843–7663 | fax 440/243–2474 | www.redroof.com | 117 rooms | $65 | AE, D, DC, MC, V.

Residence Inn-Cleveland Airport. Some rooms have fireplaces at this all-suites, three-story hotel built in 1992. All rooms have a desk and one or two queen-sized beds. It's 4 mi from the airport. Picnic area, complimentary full breakfast. Kitchenettes, microwaves. Cable TV. Pool. Hot tub. Exercise equipment. Laundry facilities. Business services. Airport shuttle. Some pets allowed (fee). Free parking. | 17525 Rosbough Dr., Middleburg Heights | 440/234–6688 | fax 440/234–3459 | www.residenceinn.com | 158 suites | $79, $179 suites | AE, D, DC, MC, V.

★ **Ritz-Carlton, Cleveland.** This seven-story grand luxury hotel in the Tower City Center blends modern elegance with a touch of Victorian charm. The bright guest rooms have work desks and marble baths. It opened in 1991. Tea is served in the lobby in the afternoon. Restaurant, bar with entertainment, room service. In-room data ports. Cable TV. Indoor pool. Hot tub, massage. Exercise equipment. Business services. Some pets allowed. | 1515 W. Third St. | 216/623–1300 or 800/241–3333 | fax 216/623–0515 | www.ritzcarlton.com | 208 rooms, 21 suites | $209, $339 suites | AE, D, DC, MC, V.

COLUMBUS

Amerisuites. This six-story all-suites property built in 1994 has a lovely lobby with a polished marble floor. It's 20 minutes north of downtown at the junction of I–270 and Route 23 N, at the border of Worthington. Complimentary Continental breakfast. In-room data ports, microwaves, refrigerators. Cable TV, in-room VCR. Pool. Exercise equipment. Laundry facilities. Business services. Airport shuttle. Free parking. Some pets allowed. | 7490 Vantage Dr. | 614/846–4355 or 800/833–1516 | fax 614/846–4493 | www.amerisuites.com | 126 suites | $109 suites | AE, D, DC, MC, V.

Best Western-East. This motel was built in 1980 and is 15 minutes from the Columbus airport and 20 minutes east of downtown. Restaurant, bar, room service. In-room data ports. Cable TV. Pool. Business services. Airport shuttle. Free parking. Some pets allowed. | 2100 Brice Rd., Reynoldsburg | 614/864–1280 or 800/528–1234 | fax 614/864–1280, ext. 388 | www.bestwestern.com | 143 rooms | $61 | AE, D, DC, MC, V.

Columbus Marriott-North. This nine-story brick hotel is in the suburbs 20 minutes north of downtown at I–71 Exit 117. A number of rooms are specially equipped for business travelers; a full business center is in the lobby. Restaurant, bar, room service. In-room data ports. Cable TV. Indoor-outdoor pool. Hot tub. Exercise equipment. Game room. Laundry facilities. Business services. Airport shuttle. Free parking. Pets allowed (fee). | 6500 Doubletree Ave. | 614/885–1885 or 800/228–9290 | fax 614/885–7222 | www.marriott.com | 300 rooms, 7 suites | $139, $275 suites | AE, D, DC, MC, V.

Doubletree Guest Suites–Columbus. This 10-story stone-faced hotel is on the river, within walking distance of the Convention Center. The well-appointed one-bedroom suites have wet bars; some have river views. Restaurant, bar. In-room data ports, refrigerators, wet bars. Cable TV. Business services. Some pets allowed (fee). | 50 S. Front St. | 614/228–4600 or 800/528–0444 | fax 614/228–0297 | www.doubletree.com | 194 suites | $119–$139 | AE, D, DC, MC, V.

Holiday Inn-Airport. You'll think you're already in the tropics in the atrium lobby of this three-story airport motel, with tropical plants and a resident parrot. The glass-enclosed indoor recreation center is a big draw. It's 2 mi from the Columbus airport and 5 mi from downtown. Restaurant, bar, room service. In-room data ports. Cable TV. Indoor pool. Hot tub. Exercise equipment. Laundry facilities. Business services. Airport shuttle. Some pets allowed. | 750 Stelzer Rd. | 614/237–6360 or 800/465–4329 | fax 614/237–2978 | www.holiday-inn.com | 236 rooms in 3 buildings | $89 | AE, D, DC, MC, V.

Holiday Inn-City Center. This chain's 12-story downtown Columbus property is a few blocks from the Capitol and the City Center Mall. Rooms have desks and beds with wooden headboards. Restaurant, bar. Cable TV. Pool. Business services. Airport shuttle. Some pets allowed (fee). | 175 E. Town St. | 614/221–3281 or 800/465–4329 | fax 614/221–2667 | www.holiday-inn.com | 240 rooms | $145 | AE, D, DC, MC, V.

Holiday Inn-Columbus/Worthington Area. This six-story hotel, built in 1988, has an atrium lobby with a classical Italian theme. If you're in town on business, you can request a room with a desk and a second phone line. It's 10 mi north of downtown on the I–270 beltway, near Worthington's restaurants and retail stores. Restaurant, bar, room service. In-room data ports, refrigerators (in suites). Cable TV. Indoor pool. Exercise equipment. Laundry facilities. Business services. Airport shuttle. Free parking. Some pets allowed. | 175 Hutchinson Ave. | 614/885–3334 or 800/465–4329 | fax 614/846–4353 | www.holiday-inn.com | 316 rooms, 6 suites | $109, $205 suites | AE, D, DC, MC, V.

Holiday Inn-East. This 12-story brick hotel dating from the 1970s is near I–70 Exit 107. It's 8 mi from the Columbus airport and 8 mi from downtown. Some guest rooms have a sleeper sofa. Restaurant, bar. In-room data ports. Cable TV. Indoor pool, wading pool. Exercise equipment. Playground. Business services. Airport shuttle. Pets allowed. | 4560 Hilton Corporate Dr. | 614/868–1380 or 800/465–4329 | fax 614/863–3210 | www.holiday-inn.com | 278 rooms | $99–$129 | AE, D, DC, MC, V.

Lenox Inn. All rooms have double beds at this two-story motor hotel that opened in 1975. It's 20 minutes east of downtown. Restaurant, bar, room service. In-room data ports. Cable TV. Pool. Business services. Airport shuttle. Free parking. Some pets allowed (fee). | I–70E at Rte. 256, Reynoldsburg | 614/861–7800 or 800/821–0007 | fax 614/759–9059 | 151 rooms | $71 | AE, D, DC, MC, V.

Ramada Plaza. This six-story brick-faced hotel built in 1970 was totally remodeled in 2000. The restaurant serves American regional cuisine; the lounge has a DJ and dancing. Restaurant, bar with entertainment. In-room data ports. Cable TV. 2 pools (1 indoor), wading pool. Hot tub. Exercise equipment. Video games. Business services. Airport shuttle. Free parking. Some pets allowed. | 4900 Sinclair Rd. | 614/846–0300 or 800/272–6232 | fax 614/847–1022 | www.ramadaplaza.com | 268 rooms | $99 | AE, D, DC, MC, V.

Red Roof Inn-Columbus North. This two-story early '70s brick motel is within walking distance of Sam's Diner and 8 mi north of downtown. Rooms are basic. Cable TV. Business services. Some pets allowed. Free parking. | 750 Morse Rd. | 614/846–8520 or 800/843–7663 | fax 614/846–8526 | www.redroof.com | 107 rooms | $58 | AE, D, DC, MC, V.

Trueman Club Hotel. Each evening, there's a manager's reception with complimentary hors d'oeuvres at this hotel, which is 12 mi north of downtown. Bar, complimentary Continental breakfast. Some refrigerators. Cable TV. Indoor pool. Hot tub. Exercise equipment. Laundry facilities. Business services. Airport shuttle. Pets allowed. | 900 E. Dublin-Granville Rd. | 614/888–7440 or 800/477–7888 | fax 614/888–7879 | redroof.com | 182 rooms, 16 suites | $91, $129 suites | AE, D, DC, MC, V.

Woodfin Suites. This two-story, all-suites brick-faced complex opened in 1990. Many of the one- and two-bedroom suites have fireplaces. You can rent a video from the hotel's library to watch in your room. It's 20 minutes from downtown. Complimentary breakfast. In-room data ports, kitchenettes, microwaves. Cable TV, in-room VCRs, and movies. Pool. Hot tub. Laundry facilities. Business services. Free parking. Some pets allowed (fee). | 4130 Tuller Rd., Dublin | 614/766–7762 or 800/237–8811 | fax 614/761–1906 | www.woodfinsuiteshotels.com | 88 suites | $150–$189 | AE, D, DC, MC, V.

Wyndham Dublin. The rooms in this three-story stucco hotel are spacious; they have a large work area and a long phone cord, making it easy to get your work done. Some rooms have skylights and balconies. It's 25 minutes northwest of downtown. 2 restaurants, bar. In-room data ports, room service. Cable TV. Indoor pool. Sauna. Business services. Free parking. Some pets allowed (fee). | 600 Metro Place N, Dublin | 614/764–2200 or 800/ 996–3426 | fax 614/764–1213 | www.wyndham.com | 217 rooms, 5 suites | $129, $349 suites | AE, D, DC, MC, V.

CONNEAUT

Conneaut Days Inn. This no-frills chain is within minutes of Lake Erie. The two-story stucco building, erected in 1975, is off Highway 90 at exit 241. Restaurant, complimentary Continental breakfast. Some microwaves, some refrigerators. Cable TV. Pool. Pets allowed. | 600 Days Blvd. | 440/593–6000 or 800/325–2525 | fax 440/593–6416 | www.daysinn.com | 104 rooms | $85–$150 | AE, D, DC, V.

DAYTON

Best Western Executive Hotel. This two-story chain is 5 mi southeast of the airport, right off I–75. Lush greenery covers the lobby, which has an overhead skylight. Rooms range from standard rooms with twin beds to executive whirlpool suites. Kids under 12 stay free. Restaurant, bar. In-room data ports, some microwaves, some refrigerators, some in-room hot tubs. Cable TV. Indoor pool. Sauna. Gym. Laundry facilities, laundry service. Business services. Airport shuttle. Some pets allowed. | 2401 Needmore Rd. | 937/278–5711 or 800/ 528–1234 | fax 937/278–6048 | www.bestwestern.com | 231 rooms | $79–$119 | AE, D, DC, MC, V.

Crowne Plaza Dayton. Connected to the downtown Dayton Convention Center, this 14-story hotel has bright rooms with wood desks and armoires. Each has two doubles or a king-size bed. Restaurant, bar with entertainment, room service. Cable TV. Pool. Hot tub. Exercise equipment. Business services. Some pets allowed. | 33 E. 5th St. | 937/224–0800 or 800/227–6963 | fax 937/224–3913 | www.crowneplaza.com | 284 rooms | $99, $249– $349 suites | AE, D, DC, MC, V.

Dayton Days Inn Wright-Patterson A.F.B./Museum. This two-story chain, right off Route 4, is almost a bed-and-breakfast, with a Bob Evans restaurant right outside your door. One room is fully handicapped-accessible. Smoking and no-smoking rooms are available. In-room data ports, some microwaves, some refrigerators. Laundry facilities. Pets allowed. | 1891 Hersham Rd. | 937/236–8083 or 800/325–2525 | fax 937/236–8083 | www.daysinn.com | 47 rooms | $56 | AE, D, DC, MC, V.

Hampton Inn. This three-story brick motel built in 1995 is 25 minutes east of downtown, off I–675. Complimentary Continental breakfast. In-room data ports, refrigerators (in suites). Cable TV. Indoor pool. Hot tub. Business services. Free parking. Some pets allowed. | 2550 Paramount Pl., Fairborn | 937/429–5505 or 800/426–7866 | fax 937/429–6828 | www.hampton-inn.com | 63 rooms, 8 suites | $84, $93 suites | AE, D, DC, MC, V.

Homewood Suites Fairborn. The roomy suites at this Hilton-owned property, 1 mi from Wright Patterson Air Force Base, have kitchens and separate living areas and bedrooms. Some have fireplaces. The two- and three-story buildings were built in 1990. It's 20 minutes from downtown. Picnic area, complimentary Continental breakfast. In-room data ports, microwaves, refrigerators. Cable TV, in-room VCRs, and movies. Pool. Hot tub. Exercise equipment. Laundry facilities. Business services. Free parking. Some pets allowed. | 2750 Presidential Dr., Fairborn | 937/429–0600 or 800/225–5466 | fax 937/429–6311 | www.homewoodsuites.com | 128 suites in 3 buildings | $119 suites | AE, D, DC, MC, V.

Howard Johnson. This two-story hacienda-style motor inn is 6 mi north of downtown and 5 mi south of the airport. Rooms have two doubles or a king-size bed. Bar, complimentary Continental breakfast. Cable TV. Pool. Laundry facilities. Business services. Airport shuttle. Free parking. Some pets allowed (fee). | 7575 Poe Ave. | 937/454–0550 or 800/654–4656 | fax 937/454–5566 | www.hojo.com | 121 rooms | $60–$70 | AE, D, DC, MC, V.

Marriott. This hotel five minutes from downtown is one of Dayton's largest lodging properties. Rooms have two doubles or a king-sized bed. Guests in concierge rooms have access to a private lounge. The six-story white concrete building opened in 1982. Restaurant, bar with entertainment, room service. In-room data ports. Cable TV. Indoor-outdoor pool. Hot tub. Exercise equipment. Laundry facilities. Business services. Free parking. Some pets allowed. | 1414 S. Patterson Blvd. | 937/223–1000 or 800/228–9290 | fax 937/223–7853 | www.marriott.com | 399 rooms | $129 | AE, D, DC, MC, V.

Ramada Inn–North Airport. This two-story accommodation is 20 minutes north of Dayton, directly off I–75. The area is rich with restaurants. Complimentary Continental breakfast, restaurant, room service. In-room data ports, some refrigerators. Pool. Laundry facilities, laundry service. Business services. Airport shuttle. Small pets allowed. | 4079 Little York Rd. | 937/890–9500 or 800/228–2828 | fax 937/890–8525 | www.ramada.com/ramada.html | 136 rooms | $65–$135 | AE, D, DC, MC, V.

Red Roof Inn-North. This two-story motel built in the mid-'70s is 7 mi from downtown. Cable TV. Business services. Some pets allowed. | 7370 Miller La. | 937/898–1054 or 800/843–7663 | fax 937/898–1059 | www.redroof.com | 109 rooms | $55 | AE, D, DC, MC, V.

DELAWARE

Days Inn. This hotel, which is 16 mi east of Delaware, gives guests free access to a nearby community pool and fitness center. Picnic area, complimentary Continental breakfast. In-room data ports, some kitchenettes, some in-room hot tubs. Cable TV. Business services. Some pets allowed. | 16510 Square Dr., Marysville | 937/644–8821 or 877/644–8821 | www.daysinn.com | 74 rooms | $69–$99 | AE, D, DC, MC, V.

Travelodge. This hotel is in front of the Delaware County Fairgrounds on State Route 23N Restaurant. Cable TV. Business services. Some pets allowed (fee). | 1001 U.S. 23N | 740/369–4421 or 800/255–3050 | fax 740/362–9090 | www.travelodge.com | 35 rooms | $52 | AE, D, DC, MC, V.

ELYRIA

Camelot Inn. This low-budget, no-frills mom-and-pop hotel, right off Route 57, has been under new management since 1999. Rooms come with two twin beds or one queen bed. Some pets allowed. | 550 Griswold Rd. | 440/324–3232 | fax 440/324–3232, ext. 103 | 27 rooms | $40 | AE, D, DC, MC.

Comfort Inn. This two-story hotel on the north side of town is opposite the Midway Mall. Complimentary Continental breakfast. Some microwaves, some refrigerators, some in-room hot tubs. Cable TV. Laundry facilities, laundry service. Pets allowed (fee). | 739 Leona St. | 440/324–7676 or 800/228–5150 | fax 440/324–4046 | www.comfortinn.com | 66 rooms, 9 suites | $79 | AE, D, DC, MC, V.

FINDLAY

Ramada Inn Findlay. This two-story chain, with outside room access, is just 3 mi from the University of Findlay, right off Interstate 75, exit 159. There are three meeting rooms on-site. Restaurant, room service. Pool. Laundry service. Business services. Pets allowed (fee). | 820 Trenton Ave. | 419/423–8212 or 800/228–2828 | fax 419/423–8217 | www.ramada.com/ramada.html | 140 rooms | $55–$71 | AE, D, DC, MC, V.

FREMONT

Fremont Travelodge. This two-story motel is 4 mi south of the Ohio Turnpike. There are a surprising number of amenities, considering the low rates, including recliner chairs in every room. In-room data ports, some microwaves, some refrigerators. Cable TV. Pool. Pets allowed. | 1750 Cedar St. | 419/334–9517 or 800/255–3030 | fax 419/334–9517 | www.travelodge.com | 50 rooms | $39–$71 | D, DC, MC, V.

GALLIPOLIS

Holiday Inn Gallipolis-Point Pleasant. Just 10 mi east of the Bob Evans Farm at the junction of Ohio Route 7 and U.S. 35 stands this two-story chain hotel. The guest rooms include a desk, reclining chair, and entertainment center. There is a 2,000-square-ft meeting room, which can be divided into three parts. Restaurant. In-room data ports. Pool. Business services. Pets allowed. | 577 Rte. 7 N | 740/446–0090 or 800/465–4329 | fax 740/446–0090 | kilgore@zoomnet.net | www.basshotels.com | 100 rooms | $69 | AE, D, DC, MC, V.

William Ann Motel. Three-quarters of a mile from downtown, this is one of the few motels in Gallipolis. It's privately owned; you'll get donuts and coffee in the morning. Some microwaves, some refrigerators. Cable TV. Business services. Some pets allowed. | 918 2nd Ave. | 740/446–3373 | fax 740/446–1337 | 50 rooms | $45 | AE, MC, V.

GNADENHUTTEN

Best Western Country Inn. The Country Inn has efficiency suites and double rooms, each in an Early American style. It is 8 mi east of Gnadenhutten, just off Route 250 and right behind Ike's Family Restaurant. There is a laundromat in the strip mall across the street. Kids under 18 stay free. Complimentary Continental breakfast. In-room data ports, some kitchenettes. Business services. Pets allowed (fee). | 111 McCauley Dr., Uhrichsville | 740/922–0774 or 800/528–1234 | fax 740/922–2270 | www.bestwestern.com | 48 rooms | $75–$82 | AE, D, DC, MC, V.

HAMILTON

The Hamiltonian. This six-story hotel is on Great Miami River in downtown Hamilton. There's a concierge level with extra amenities. It houses a popular restaurant, Alexander's Grill, and a sports lounge. Guests can use the nearby fitness club. Restaurant, bar, room service. In-room data ports. Cable TV, in-room movies. Pool. Business services. Some pets allowed. | 1 Riverfront Plaza | 513/896–6200 or 800/522–5570 | fax 513/896–9463 | www.brilyn.com | 120 rooms, 4 suites | $81–$89, $149 suites | AE, D, DC, MC, V.

White Rose Bed and Breakfast. Built in 1905, this two-story home is in Hamilton's historic German Village. There are flood marks on the second floor from the 1913 flooding of the Miami River. The home's proximity to the river affords many scenic views. You can borrow bikes, and after a long day of touring, you can relax in the outdoor Jacuzzi on the back porch. Rooms blend antiques with more modern furnishings. All rooms have private baths, though one upstairs bedroom has a downstairs bath. A full breakfast is served on weekends, and a Continental breakfast on weekdays. Some room phones, TV in common area. Outdoor hot tub. No kids under 12. Small pets allowed. | 116 Buckeye St. | 513/863–6818 | wrose@fuse.net | www.bbonline.com/oh/whiterose | 3 rooms | $65–$75 | No credit cards.

KENT

Holiday Inn. It's 3 mi to Kent State University and golfing from this hotel. In season, you can enjoy the pool and hot tub with a cabana bar. Restaurant, bar, room service. Cable TV. Pool. Hot tub. Exercise equipment. Video games. Laundry facilities, laundry service.

Business services. Some pets allowed. | 4363 Rte. 43 | 330/678-0101 or 800/465-4329 | fax 330/677-5001 | www.holiday-inn.com | 150 rooms | $79-$119 | AE, D, DC, MC, V.

LANCASTER

Best Western. The River Valley Mall is directly across the street from this hotel. Free passes to the local YMCA fitness center are available. Restaurant, bar, room service. Some refrigerators. Cable TV. Pool. Putting green. Laundry facilities, laundry service. Business services. Airport shuttle. Some pets allowed. | 1858 N. Memorial Dr. | 740/653-3040 or 800/528-1234 | fax 740/653-1172 | www.bestwestern.com | 168 rooms | $65 | AE, D, DC, MC, V.

Knights Inn. You can park right at the door at this one-story motel a mile from the River Valley Mall. Complimentary Continental breakfast. Some kitchenettes. Cable TV. Business services. Some pets allowed. | 1327 River Valley Blvd. | 740/687-4823 or 800/843-5644 | fax 740/687-4823 | www.knightsinn.com | 60 rooms | $62 | AE, D, DC, MC, V.

LIMA

Holiday Inn Lima. The hotel has an interior, four-story, glass-enclosed tropical atrium, with a pool and hot tub. You can ask for a room with an outside view or one with a balcony overlooking the atrium. It's 5 mi from downtown Lima and 3 mi from the Allen County Fairgrounds, at I-75 and Route 309. Restaurant, bar with entertainment, room service. In-room data ports. Cable TV. Indoor pool. Hot tub, sauna. Exercise equipment. Video games. Playground. Laundry facilities. Business services. Some pets allowed. | 1920 Roschman Ave. | 419/222-0004 or 800/465-4329 | fax 419/222-2176 | www.holiday-inn.com | 150 rooms | $110 | AE, D, DC, MC, V.

LOGAN

Inn at Cedar Falls. You can stay in the lodge, a refurbished barn whose rooms are furnished with primitive antiques, or in one of the 19th-century cabins, which sleep up to four. Each cabin was moved from other parts of the country and decorated with antiques picked personally by the innkeeper. Homemade granola is always served; other breakfast fare includes omelets, french toast, and crepes. Dining room, complimentary breakfast. Some kitchenettes, some in-room hot tubs. No room phones. No TV. Some pets allowed. No smoking. | 21190 Rte. 374 | 740/385-7489 or 800/65-FALLS | fax 740/385-0820 | 8 rooms, 5 cabins | Lodge, $65-$100; cabins, up to $240 | AE, D, MC, V.

Old Man's Cave Chalets. These cabins, 11 mi south of Logan, are tucked in the woods and have private porches, hot tubs, and full kitchens. They range in size from two-person A-frame cottages to large lodges that can sleep up to 20 people or more. Kitchenettes, microwaves, refrigerators. In-room hot tubs. Cable TV, in-room VCRs. Pool. Tennis. Some pets allowed. | 18905 Rte. 664 S | 470/385-6517 or 800/762-9396 | www.oldmanscavechalets.com | 30 cabins, 4 lodges | Cabins and suites, $99-$205; lodges, $399-$775 | AE, D, MC, V.

MANSFIELD

Best Value Inn. Right off I-71 and Route 30, this chain property is close to several restaurants and stores. Restaurant, bar, room service. Cable TV. Pool. Business services. Some pets allowed. | 880 Laver Rd. | 419/589-2200 | fax 419/589-5624 | 101 rooms | $75 | AE, D, DC, MC, V.

Comfort Inn North. On the north side of Mansfield in the Carousel District, this property is about 20 minutes away from the Clear Fork Ski Area. A restaurant is next door. Bar, complimentary Continental breakfast, room service. In-room data ports, refrigerators (in suites). Cable TV. Indoor pool. Hot tub, sauna. Laundry facilities. Business services. Some pets allowed. | 500 N. Trimble Rd. | 419/529-1000 or 800/918-9189 | fax 419/529-2953 | www.christopherhotels.com | 114 rooms, 22 suites | $70, $79 suites | AE, D, DC, MC, V.

Knights Inn. Rooms are in four buildings at this one-story motel next to a restaurant and near area shopping. Complimentary Continental breakfast, room service. Cable TV, in-room VCRs and movies. Pool. Laundry service. Business services. Some pets allowed. | 555 N. Trimble Rd. | 419/529–2100 or 800/843–5644 | fax 419/529–6679 | www.christopherhotels.com | 110 rooms | $50 | AE, D, DC, MC, V.

Mansfield/Ontario Hampton Inn. This hotel is 3 to 4 mi from Kingwood Center, the Carousel District, and downtown Mansfield; 8 mi west of I–71 on Route 30. Complimentary Continental breakfast. Some microwaves, some refrigerators. Cable TV, in-room movies. Indoor pool. Hot tub. Pets allowed in some rooms. | 1051 N. Lexington Spring Mill Rd. | 419/747–5353 or 800/426–7866 | www.hampton-inn.com | 62 rooms | $69 | AE, D, DC, MC, V.

Travelodge. Right at the entrance to the Clear Fork Ski Area, this hotel is for skiers who like to be near the slopes. There's a 24-hour restaurant next door. Complimentary Continental breakfast. Some microwaves, some refrigerators. Cable TV. Pool. Business services. Some pets allowed (fee). | 90 Hanley Rd. | 419/756–7600 or 800/255–3050 | www.travelodge.com | 46 rooms | $75 | AE, D, MC, V.

MARIETTA

Best Western. The hotel is on the banks of the Muskingum River, and you can enjoy a picnic overlooking the water. Picnic area, complimentary Continental breakfast. Refrigerators. Cable TV. Dock. Laundry service. Business services. Some pets (fee). | 279 Muskingum Dr. | 740/374–7211 or 800/528–1234 | www.bestwestern.com | 47 rooms | $72 | AE, D, DC, MC, V.

Econo Lodge. Some rooms at this two-story hotel, situated right behind a public golf course, have river views. You can drive right up to your room. Picnic area, complimentary Continental breakfast. Cable TV. Pool. Pets allowed (fee). | 702 Pike St. | 740/374–8481 or 800/446–6900 | www.hotelchoice.com | 48 rooms | $60 | AE, D, MC, V.

Knights Inn. The convenient location off I–77, front-door parking, and a restaurant next door that delivers directly to your room make this a good stopping point. In-room data ports, some kitchenettes. Cable TV. Pool. Business services. Pets allowed (fee). | 506 Pike St. | 740/373–7373 or 800/526–5947 | fax 740/374–9466 | www.christopherhotels.com | 111 rooms | $65–$95 | AE, D, DC, MC, V.

MARION

Comfort Inn. This hotel near the Harding Home entices you with an indoor heated pool and hot tub. It's in a prime business and shopping area and within walking distance of three restaurants. Complimentary Continental breakfast. Refrigerators (in suites). Cable TV. Indoor pool. Hot tub. Laundry service. Some pets allowed. | 256 James Way | 740/389–5552 or 800/228–5150 | www.comfortinn.com | 56 rooms, 4 suites | $67, $76 suites | AE, D, DC, MC, V.

Travelodge. The first-floor rooms of this two-story hostelry next to Route 23 have outside access; you enter second-floor rooms through the lobby. A restaurant is next door. Complimentary Continental breakfast. In-room data ports. Cable TV. Pool. Business services. Some pets allowed. | 1952 Marion-Mount Gilead Rd. | 740/389–4671 or 800/578–7878 | www.travelodge.com | 46 rooms | $54 | AE, D, DC, MC, V.

MASON

Days Inn Kings Island. Just minutes away from Paramount's Kings Island and The Beach Waterpark, this establishment is popular with families visiting the area. Complimentary Continental breakfast. Cable TV. Pool. Video games. Playground. Business services.

Some pets allowed. | 9735 Mason-Montgomery Rd. | 513/398–3297 or 800/325–2525 | www.travelweb.com/daysinn.html | 124 rooms | $109 | AE, D, DC, MC, V.

Quality Inn-Kings Island. Just off I–71, this hotel offers easy-off, easy-on access to the interstate. Plus it's just minutes away from Paramount's Kings Island and the Beach Waterpark. A Chinese restaurant is on the premises. Restaurant, complimentary Continental breakfast, room service. In-room data ports. Cable TV. Pool. Playground. Business services. Some pets allowed. | 9845 Escort Dr. | 513/398–8015 or 800/228–5151 | fax 513/398–0822 | www.qualityinn.com | 104 rooms | $99 | AE, D, DC, MC, V.

MENTOR

Ramada Inn. This upscale hotel in Willoughby, about 5 mi south of Mentor, has two pools and a picnic area complete with a cabana. Restaurant, bar, picnic area, room service. In-room data ports, some refrigerators. Cable TV. 2 pools (1 indoor), wading pool. Sauna. 2 tennis courts. Exercise equipment. Video games. Laundry facilities, laundry service. Business services. Pets allowed (fee). | 6051 SOM Center Rd., Willoughby | 440/944–4300 or 800/228–2828 | fax 440/944–5344 | www.ramada.com/ramada.html | 146 rooms | $99 | AE, D, DC, MC, V.

MIAMISBURG

Homewood Suites Hotel by Hilton. The interior of this all-suite hotel, built in 1999, is indeed homey. It's 10 minutes from downtown Dayton and across the road from the Dayton Mall. Take Exit 44 off I–75, or Exit 2 off I–675. Complimentary Continental breakfast. In-room data ports, kitchenettes, microwaves, refrigerators. Cable TV, free VCRs. Pool. Gym. Balls, board games. Gift/snack shop, video games. Laundry facilities, laundry service. Business services. Pets allowed (fee). | 3100 Contemporary La. | 937/432–0000 or 800/225–5466 | www.welcomehomewood.com | 96 rooms in 2 towers | $135 | AE, D, DC, MC, V.

Knights Inn. A 24-hour restaurant just steps away is one of the conveniences available at this budget hotel. Complimentary Continental breakfast. Some kitchenettes, some refrigerators. Cable TV. Pool. Some pets allowed. | 185 Byers Rd. | 937/859–8797 or 800/843–5644 | fax 937/859–5254 | www.christopherhotels.com | 100 rooms | $56 | AE, D, DC, MC, V.

Red Roof Inn-Dayton South. Proximity to I–75, two family-style eateries just steps away and nearby stores make this a popular place to stay. In-room data ports, some refrigerators. Cable TV. Business services. Pets allowed. | 222 Byers Rd. | 937/866–0705 or 800/843–7663 | fax 937/866–0700 | www.redroof.com | 107 rooms | $55 | AE, D, DC, MC, V.

Residence Inn by Marriott. Roomy accommodations are the hallmark of this all-suites hotel. Some rooms have fireplaces. The hotel hosts a complimentary social hour weeknights with snacks and beverages pool-side during the summer. You can use the sport court, complete with tennis and basketball. Picnic area, complimentary Continental breakfast. In-room data ports. Cable TV. Pool. Hot tub. Tennis, basketball. Laundry facilities, laundry service. Business services. Some pets allowed. | 155 Prestige Pl | 937/434–7881 or 800/331–3131 | fax 937/434–9308 | www.marriott.com | 96 suites | $97–$125 1–bedroom suites, $120–$150 2–bedroom suites | AE, D, DC, MC, V.

MIDDLETOWN

Manchester Inn and Conference Center. This hostelry in downtown Middletown hosts most of the city's banquets and receptions. Restaurant, bar with entertainment, room service. In-room data ports, some refrigerators. Cable TV, some in-room VCRs. Laundry service. Business services. Some pets allowed. | 1027 Manchester Ave. | 513/422–5481 or 800/523–9126 (reservations) | fax 513/422–4615 | www.manchesterinn.com | 78 rooms | $80–$133 | AE, D, DC, MC, V.

MOUNT VERNON

Dan Emmett House Hotel. Built in 1996, this modern hotel in downtown Mount Vernon is close to many antique stores and a bike trail. Restaurant, bar, picnic area, complimentary full breakfast on weekdays, complimentary Continental breakfast on weekends. In-room data ports, kitchenettes, microwaves, refrigerators, hot tubs in some rooms. Cable TV. Indoor pool. Exercise bike. Laundry facilities. Pets allowed (fee). | 150 Howard St. | 740/392–6886 or 800/480–8221 | 59 rooms | $65 | AE, D, DC, MC, V.

NEW PHILADELPHIA

Holiday Inn. This two-story hotel, off I–77, was built in 1996. Restaurant, bar. Some refrigerators, some in-room hot tubs. Cable TV. 2 pools (1 indoor). Hot tub. Exercise equipment. Business services. Some pets allowed. | 131 Bluebell Dr. | 330/339–7731 or 800/465–4329 | fax 330/339–1565 | www.holidayinn.com | 107 rooms | $79 | AE, D, DC, MC, V.

Schoenbrunn Inn. Amish quilts decorate the beds and locally made pieces fill the rooms in this modern motel done in Amish country style. It's 1½ mi from downtown, off I–77 Exit 81. Suites with kitchenettes are across the street. Bar. Complimentary Continental breakfast. In-room data ports. Some microwaves, some refrigerators, some in-room hot tubs. Cable TV. Indoor pool. Hot tub. Exercise equipment. Laundry facilities. Pets allowed (fee). | 1186 W. High Ave. | 330/339–4334 or 800/929–7799 | 60 rooms, 6 suites | $72–$80 | AM, D, DC, MC, V.

NEWARK

Cherry Valley Lodge. A real family inn, a lake, well-tended acreage, and lots of extras put this lodge at the top of the list of area hostelries. The hotel has complimentary bikes and has 22 mi of paths. If that's not enough activity, there's volleyball, shuffleboard, basketball, and croquet. Restaurant, bar, room service. In-room data ports. Cable TV, in-room VCRs and movies. 2 pools (1 indoor), lake. Hot tub. Basketball, exercise equipment, volleyball, bicycles. Baby-sitting, playground. Laundry service. Business services. Pets allowed (fee). | 2299 Cherry Valley Rd. | 740/788–1200 or 800/788–8008 | fax 740/788–8800 | www.cherryvalleylodge.com | 200 rooms | $149–$159 | AE, D, DC, MC, V.

PAINESVILLE

Rider's 1812 Inn. The inn, built in 1812, was originally a resting point for stagecoaches passing through; it was later part of the Underground Railroad. Rooms are furnished with some 19th-century antiques. Restaurant, complimentary breakfast, room service. Cable TV. Business services. Airport shuttle. Some pets allowed. | 792 Mentor Ave. | 440/354–8200 | 10 rooms | $109 | AE, D, MC, V.

PIQUA

Ramada Inn Limited. This modern motel is across the road from the Miami Valley Center Mall and next to the Hollow Park, which has a stream, trail, and softball field. It's off I–75 Exit 82. Complimentary Continental breakfast. In-room data ports, some refrigerators, some microwaves, some in-room hot tubs. Cable TV, in-room movies. Indoor pool. Spa. Laundry facilities. Business services. Pets allowed (fee). | 950 E. Ash St. | 937/615–0140 or 800/228–2828 | www.ramada.com/ramada.html | 70 rooms | $64–$70 | AE, D, DC, MC, V.

PORT CLINTON

Country Hearth Inn. This modern hotel on the shores of Lake Erie is off State Route 2, 10 minutes from Clinton Bay and 20 minutes from Cedar Point Amusement Park. Complimentary Continental breakfast. In-room data ports, in-room safes, some in-room microwaves and refrigerators. Cable TV. Pool. Laundry facilities. Pets allowed. | 1815 E. Perry St. | 419/732–2111 or 800/282–5711 | 66 rooms | $106 | AE, D, DC, MC, V.

PORTSMOUTH

Best Western Inn. This two-story chain motel is just 2 mi north of downtown and five minutes from golf, fitness center, and tours. Restaurant, bar, complimentary Continental breakfast, room service. Some in-room data ports, some refrigerators. Cable TV. Pool. Laundry facilities. Pets allowed. | 3762 U.S. 23 | 740/354–2851 or 800/528–1234 | fax 740/354–2851 | www.bestwestern.com | 100 rooms | $53–$75 | AE, D, DC, MC, V.

Ramada Inn. Near downtown Portsmouth, this motel is accessible to area attractions. Restaurant, complimentary Continental breakfast, room service. Some refrigerators. Cable TV. Indoor pool, wading pool. Hot tub. Business services. Some pets allowed. | 711 2nd St. | 740/354–7711 or 800/228–2828 | fax 740/353–1539 | www.ramada.com/ramada.html | 119 rooms | $89 | AE, D, DC, MC, V.

ST. CLAIRSVILLE

Knights Inn. A few of the rooms in this motel, which is near local restaurants, are equipped with hot tubs. In-room data ports, some kitchenettes, some microwaves, some in-room hot tubs. Cable TV. Pool. Business services. Some pets allowed. | 51260 National Rd. | 740/695–5038 or 800/835–9628 | fax 740/695–3014 | www.christopherhotels.com | 104 rooms | $69 | AE, D, DC, MC, V.

Super 8. This three-story chain motel is downtown off Route 70 near several restaurants. Cable TV. Pets allowed. | 68400 Matthew Dr. | 740/695–1994 or 800/848–8888 | www.super8motels.com | 62 rooms | $35–$60 | AE, D, MC, V.

SANDUSKY

Clarion Inn. This hotel is across the street from the Sandusky Mall and within minutes of the area's tourist major attractions. Restaurant, bar with entertainment, room service. In-room data ports. Cable TV. Indoor pool. Hot tub. Exercise equipment. Video games. Business services. Some pets allowed. | 1119 Sandusky Mall Blvd. | 419/625–6280 or 800/252–7466 | www.clarioninn.com | fax 419/625–9080 | 143 rooms | $109 | AE, D, DC, MC, V.

Radisson Harbour Inn. Most of the rooms at this hotel have breathtaking views of the waterfront of Sandusky Bay. Restaurant, bar with entertainment, room service. In-room data ports. Cable TV. Indoor pool. Hot tub. Exercise equipment. Video games. Kids' programs. Laundry facilities. Business services. Airport shuttle. Some pets allowed. | 2001 Cleveland Rd. | 419/627–2500 or 800/333–3333 | fax 419/627–0745 | www.radisson.com | 237 rooms, 49 suites | $135, $189–$209 suites | AE, D, DC, MC, V.

SIDNEY

Holiday Inn. A pool and restaurant make this a good stopping point for families with young children. Restaurant, bar, room service. In-room data ports, microwaves (in suites). Cable TV. Pool. Exercise equipment. Laundry facilities. Business services. Some pets allowed. | 400 Folkerth Ave. | 937/492–1131 or 800/465–4329 | fax 937/498–4655 | www.holidayinn.com | 134 rooms, 5 suites | $69, $74 suites | AE, D, DC, MC, V.

STEUBENVILLE

Holiday Inn. A number of restaurants and shops are within minutes of this hotel. Restaurant, bar, room service. In-room data ports. Cable TV. Pool. Laundry facilities. Business services. Some pets allowed. | 1401 University Blvd. | 740/282–0901 or 800/465–4329 | fax 740/282–9540 | www.holidayinn.com | 120 rooms | $79 | AE, D, DC, MC, V.

TOLEDO

Clarion Westgate. A landscaped enclosed courtyard keeps this hotel's lobby open and airy. Restaurant, bar, room service. In-room data ports. Cable TV. Indoor pool. Hot tub. Exercise equipment. Video games. Business services. Free parking. Some pets allowed. | 3536

Secor Rd. | 419/535–7070 or 800/252–7466 | fax 419/536–4836 | www.clarioninn.com | 305 rooms | $99 | AE, D, DC, MC, V.

Comfort Inn Westgate. This two-story motel off I–475 in Toledo is smaller and less expensive than the Clarion Westgate next door, though you can use that hotel's indoor pool. Picnic area, complimentary Continental breakfast. Cable TV. Some pets allowed. | 3560 Secor Rd. | 419/531–2666 or 800/228–5150 | fax 419/531–4757 | www.comfortinn.com | 70 rooms | $89 | AE, D, DC, MC, V.

Days Inn. A number of restaurants and stores surround this motel, which is just off I–80/90 in Maumee, about 10 mi southwest of Toledo. Complimentary Continental breakfast. Some kitchenettes, some microwaves, some refrigerators. Cable TV. Pool. Business services. Free parking. Some pets allowed. | 150 Dussel Dr., Maumee | 419/893–9960 or 800/325–2525 | fax 419/893–9559 | www.daysinn.com | 120 rooms, 6 suites | $89 | AE, D, DC, MC, V.

Holiday Inn. This is a full-service hotel with indoor pool, restaurant, and beauty salon among the on-site conveniences. Restaurant, bar, room service. In-room data ports. Cable TV. Indoor pool. Beauty salon. Exercise equipment. Business services. Airport shuttle. Some pets allowed. | 2340 S. Reynolds Rd. | 419/865–1361 or 800/465–4329 | fax 419/865–6177 | www.holidayinn.com | 218 rooms | $89 | AE, D, DC, MC, V.

Quality Hotel. The Olympic-size indoor pool, hot tub, and playground are appealing to families with children. Business travelers like the business services, modem links, and airport shuttle. Restaurant, bar. In-room data ports. Cable TV. Indoor pool. Hot tub. Playground. Business services. Airport shuttle. Free parking. Some pets allowed. | 2429 S. Reynolds Rd. | 419/381–8765 | fax 419/381–0129 | 246 rooms | $69–$89 | AE, D, DC, MC, V.

Radisson Hotel Toledo. This 15-story hotel is connected to the Seagate Convention Center, and all rooms have views of the river. Restaurant, bar, room service. In-room data ports. Cable TV. Sauna. health club. Laundry facilities. Pets allowed. | 101 N. Summit St. | 419/241–3000 or 800/333–3333 | www.radisson.com | 399 rooms | $109–$149 | AE, D, MC, V.

Studio Plus-Toledo. This hotel is a home away from home, with a complete kitchen and even a barbecue pit for each unit. It's 12 mi from the downtown area and 8 mi from the airport. In-room data ports. Cable TV. Pool. Exercise room. Laundry service. Pets allowed (fee). | 540 W. Dussel Dr. | 419/244–5676 | 73 rooms | $59 | AE, D, MC, V.

Toledo Hawthorne Hotel & Suites. This 19-story hotel has a restaurant and bar on the top floor, overlooking the city. It's connected to the SeaGate Convention Center. Complimentary Continental breakfast. In-room data ports, some refrigerators. Cable TV. Indoor pool. Business services. Pets allowed. | 141 N. Summit St. | 419/242–8885 or 800/527–1133 | 168 rooms, 30 suites | $89–$130 | D, MC, V.

VANDALIA

Park Inn International. This single-story inn is directly across from the Dayton International Airport, a half mile from the center of Vandalia. Complimentary Continental breakfast. Some kitchenettes, some microwaves, some refrigerators. Cable TV. Pool. Gym. Laundry facilities. Pets allowed (fee). Airport shuttle. | 75 Corporate Center Dr. | 937/898–8321 or 800/437–7275 | fax 937/898–6334 | www.parkinn.com | 97 rooms | $60 | AE, D, DC, MC, V.

VERMILION

Vermilion Holiday Inn Express. Rooms are decorated in peach and green at this hotel built in 1997; those in the back overlook a cornfield. It's 1½ mi south of downtown. Complimentary Continental breakfast. In-room data ports, some in-room hot tubs. Cable TV. Pool. Hot tub. Gym. Pets allowed. | 2417 Rte. 60 | 440/967–8770 or 800/465–4329 | fax 440/967–8772 | www.hiexpress.com | 50 rooms, 16 suites | $139, $159 suites | AE, D, DC, MC, V.

WAPAKONETA

Holiday Inn. This hotel next to the Neil Armstrong Museum is a convenient place to cap off a day of space exploration. Restaurant, bar, complimentary Continental breakfast, room service. In-room data ports. Cable TV. Pool. Exercise equipment. Laundry facilities. Business services. Some pets allowed. | 1510 Saturn Dr. | 419/738–8181 or 800/465–4329 | fax 419/738–6478 | www.holidayinn.com | 99 rooms | $69 | AE, D, DC, MC, V.

WARREN

Best Western-Downtown. In the heart of downtown, this motel is within minutes of Warren attractions and points of interests. Complimentary Continental breakfast. Some refrigerators. Cable TV. Pool. Business services. Some pets allowed. | 777 Mahoning Ave. | 330/392–2515 or 800/528–1234 | fax 330/392–7099 | www.bestwestern.com | 73 rooms | $99 | AE, D, DC, MC, V.

Park Hotel. This family-run motel is set in a late 19th-century brick building and has clean and comfortable rooms. Families with children are welcome. Restaurant. Cable TV. Business services. Airport shuttle. Some pets allowed. | 136 N. Park Ave. | 330/393–1200 or 800/397–7275 | fax 330/399–2875 | 66 rooms | $77–$109 | AE, D, DC, MC, V.

WASHINGTON COURT HOUSE

Knights Inn. This motel is just off U.S. 62 near Washington Square Shopping Plaza. Cable TV. Some pets allowed. | 1820 Columbus Ave. | 740/335–9133 or 800/843–5644 | fax 740/333–7938 | 56 rooms | $48–$56 | AE, D, MC, V.

WAUSEON

Best Western Del Mar. This single-story hotel was refurbished in 2000; you can borrow a video from their library to watch in your room. A variety of restaurants and stores surround this property, which is a mile north of downtown Wauseon. Complimentary Continental breakfast. Refrigerators. Cable TV. Pool. Playground. Some pets allowed. | 8319 U.S. 108 | 419/335–1565 or 800/528–1234 | fax 419/335–1828 | www.bestwestern.com | 39 rooms, 9 suites | $75 | AE, D, DC, MC, V.

WOOSTER

Econo Lodge. An indoor pool, hot tub, and picnic tables are nice features for families. Picnic area, complimentary Continental breakfast. Cable TV. Indoor pool. Hot tub. Laundry facilities. Business services. Some pets allowed. | 2137 Lincoln Way E | 330/264–8883 or 800/248–8341 | fax 330/264–8883, ext. 301 | www.hotelchoice.com | 98 rooms | $84 | AE, D, DC, MC, V.

Wooster Inn. The College of Wooster owns this hotel on the school's campus. Restaurant, picnic area. Cable TV. Driving range, nine-hole golf course, putting green. Business services. Some pets allowed. | 801 E. Wayne Ave. | 330/264–2341 | fax 330/264–9951 | 15 rooms | $99 | Closed Jan. 2–9, Dec. 25, 26 | AE, D, DC, MC, V.

Wooster Super 8. This single-story motel is surrounded by shops, restaurants, and nightlife venues a half mile south of downtown. The Metroplex Convention Center is also nearby. Complimentary Continental breakfast. In-room data ports. Cable TV. Pets allowed (fee). | 969 Timken Rd. | 330/264–6211 or 800/800–8000 | fax 330/264–6211 | www.super8.com | 43 rooms | $48–$60 | AE, D, DC, MC, V.

YOUNGSTOWN

Best Western Meander Inn. Several restaurants and stores surround the motel. More than a dozen businesses are within walking distance. Restaurant, bar. Complimentary Continental breakfast, room service. Cable TV. Pool. Laundry facilities. Some pets allowed. | 870

N. Canfield-Niles Rd. | 330/544-2378 or 800/528-1234 | fax 330/544-7926 | www.bestwestern.com | 57 rooms | $89 | AE, D, DC, MC, V.

ZANESVILLE

Comfort Inn. The suites at this two-story hotel near restaurants and pottery shops has nice suites with whirlpools and refrigerators. Complimentary Continental breakfast. Cable TV. Indoor pool. Hot tub. Exercise equipment. Laundry facilities. Business services. Pets allowed (fee). | 500 Monroe St. | 740/454-4144 or 800/228-5150 | www.comfortinn.com | 93 rooms, 20 suites | $69 | AE, D, DC, MC, V.

Holiday Inn Conference Center. This motel is off I–70 in a quiet, rural area, 5 mi from Zanesville Restaurant, bar, room service. In-room data ports. Cable TV. Indoor pool. Hot tub. Exercise equipment. Playground. Laundry facilities. Business services. Some pets allowed. | 4645 E. Pike | 740/453-0771 or 800/465-4329 | www.holidayinn.com | 130 rooms, 4 suites | $69 | AE, D, DC, MC, V.

Super 8 Zanesville. This hotel is in a gleaming white, three-story building, reminiscent of the Tudor style, right off I–70 at exit 152. Downtown Zanesville is 2 mi away and Dillon Lake is 8 mi away. Complimentary Continental breakfast. Cable TV. Pets allowed. | 2440 National Rd. | 740/455-3124 or 800/800-8000 | www.super8.com | 62 rooms | $45–$65 | AE, D, DC, MC, V.

Oklahoma

ADA

Economy Inn. This centrally located light-blue roadside motel is adjacent to a restaurant, and within walking distance of a laundromat and bowling alley. Some microwaves, some refrigerators, cable TV, pool, business services, pets allowed (fee). | 1017 N. Broadway 74820 | 580/332–3883 | fax 580/332–3884 | 46 rooms | $28–$45 | AE, D, DC, MC, V.

ALTUS

Best Western. Chain-hotel accommodations 2 mi west of Altus and 1 mi north of the Air Force base. Complimentary Continental breakfast, in-room data ports, some refrigerators, cable TV, in-room VCRs (and movies), indoor-outdoor pool, sauna, laundry facilities, business services, pets allowed. | 2804 N. Main St. 73521 | 580/482–9300 | fax 580/482–2245 | 100 rooms | $54 | AE, D, DC, MC, V.

Days Inn. Some rooms display the work of local artists in this motel 2 mi from downtown Altus. Complimentary Continental breakfast, cable TV, business services, pets allowed. | 3202 N. Main St. 73521 | 580/477–2300 | fax 580/477–2379 | 36 rooms | $49 | AE, D, DC, MC, V.

Falcon Inn. Rooms at this off-white and brick two-story motel are basic, but each is equipped with a refrigerator, the attached restaurant (and lounge) serves three meals a day, and the price speaks for itself. It's 5 mi from Altus Air Force Base. Restaurant, bar, picnic area, some microwaves, refrigerators, cable TV, pool, laundry facilities, business services, pets allowed (fee). | 2213 Falcon Rd. 73521 | 580/482–0400 or 888/283–4450 | fax 580/482–1884 | 60 rooms | $27 | AE, D, MC, V.

Ramada Inn. This two-story hotel is ½ mi from the Air Force base. Restaurant, bar, refrigerators, room service, cable TV, pool, business services, pets allowed (fee). | 2515 E. Broadway, 73521 | 580/477–3000 | fax 580/477–0078 | 121 rooms, 12 suites | $59, $104 suites | AE, D, DC, MC, V.

ALVA

Ranger Inn. This one-story brick-and-siding building is ½ mi from Northwestern Oklahoma State University. Microwaves, cable TV, pets allowed. | 420 E. Oklahoma Blvd. | 580/327–1981 | fax 580/327–1981 | 41 rooms | $42–$46 | AE, D, DC, MC, V.

Vista Motel. Rooms are fairly spacious in this yellow brick motel (built in 1949 with a mineral shingle roof) on the far west side of town. A city pool is about 1 mi away. In-room data ports, cable TV, business services, pets allowed. | 1330 Oklahoma Blvd. | 580/327–3232 or 800/322–1821 | fax 580/327–5591 | 20 rooms | $30–$40 | AE, D, DC, MC, V.

ARDMORE

Dorchester Inn. Rooms are clean and quiet in this downtown motel, 2 blocks from the Greater Southwest Historical Museum. Restaurant, complimentary Continental breakfast, refrigerators, cable TV, pets allowed. | 2614 W. Broadway | 580/226–1761 | fax 580/223–3131 | 50 rooms | $40 | AE, D, DC, MC, V.

Holiday Inn. This two-story hotel is 18 mi from Turner Falls and 12 mi from Lake Murray. Restaurant, in-room data ports, cable TV, pool, wading pool, gym, playground, laundry facilities, business services, pets allowed. | 2705 Holiday Dr. | 580/223–7130 | fax 580/223–7130 | 171 rooms | $69 | AE, D, DC, MC, V.

Lake Murray. In Lake Murray State Park, this state-owned lodge aims for the flavor of a country inn, with fluffy floral comforters and oak armoires. Bar, dining room, room service, cable TV, pool, 18-hole golf course, miniature golf, tennis, water sports, children's programs, playground, business services, airport shuttle, pets allowed. | 3310 S. Lake Murray Dr. #12A, Ardmore, 73401 | 580/223–6600 or 800/654–8240 | fax 580/223–6154 | 49 rooms, 3 suites, 81 cottages | $55, $150 suites, $48 cottages | AE, D, DC, MC, V.

ATOKA

Best Western Atoka Inn. This motel is on the south end of Atoka off Rtes. 69 and 75. It's two mi from the Confederate Memorial Museum and Information Center and 15 mi from McGee Creek State Park. Restaurant, cable TV, pool, business services, pets allowed. | 2101 S. Mississippi Ave. | 580/889–7381 | fax 580/889–6695 | bestwest@texomaonline.com | 54 rooms | $59 | AE, D, DC, MC, V.

Brandenburg's Motel. This L-shaped white and blue roadside motel is right off I–75 in the middle of town, a stone's throw from restaurants, the courthouse, and police station. Nightly or weekly rates are offered, and truck parking is available. Some microwaves, some refrigerators, cable TV, pool, pets allowed (fee). | 102 S. Mississippi Ave. 74525 | 580/889–3363 | 25 rooms | $30–$35 | AE, MC, V.

BARTLESVILLE

Best Western Weston Inn. This three-story hotel is 15 blocks from downtown Bartlesville, in Oklahoma Green Country. Restaurant, room service, microwaves, some refrigerators, in-room hot tubs, cable TV, pool, laundry facilities, business services, pets allowed. | 222 S.E. Washington Blvd. 74006 | 918/335–7755 or 800/336–2415 | fax 918/335–7763 | 111 rooms | $45–$80 | AE, D, DC, MC, V.

Holiday Inn. This full-service hotel with three banquet rooms is next to a bowling alley and one mi from the Washington Boulevard mall. Restaurant, bar, room service, in-room data ports, some kitchenettes, cable TV, pool, exercise equipment, laundry facilities, business services, pets allowed. | 1410 S.E. Washington Blvd. 74006 | 918/333–8320 | fax 918/333–8979 | www.holiday-inn.com | 104 rooms | $66 | AE, D, DC, MC, V.

Super 8. You can ask for a room with a recliner or sofa at this beige-and-turquoise brick hotel. It's one block or less from a handful of restaurants, and less than one mi from downtown. In-room data ports, in-room hot tubs, cable TV, pets allowed. | 211 S.E. Washington Blvd. 74006 | 918/335–1122 or 800/800–8000 | fax 918/335–1708 | 40 rooms | $45–$47 | AE, D, DC, MC, V.

BROKEN BOW

Hochatown Resort Cabins. Each of this resort's cabins is on an acre or two of land, amid 197,000 acres of timberland in a pristine wilderness area. There is easy access to Beavers Bend Resort Park, where you can hike, bike, canoe, and fish. Some in-room hot tubs, cable TV, in-room VCRs, some room phones, 18-hole golf course, hiking, boating, bicycles, some pets allowed (fee). | U.S. 259, 6½ mi north of Broken Bow | 580/494–6521 | 51 cabins | $125 | AE, D, MC, V.

Microtel Inn. Built in 2000, this homey, two-story hotel has rooms that are more spacious than most for this price, and breakfast is available as early as 5 AM. It's about 10 mi south of Broken Bow Lake. Complimentary Continental breakfast, in-room data ports, some kitchenettes, some microwaves, some refrigerators, cable TV, laundry facilities, business services, pets allowed (fee). | 1701 S. Park Dr. 74728 | 580/584–7708 or 888/771–7171 | fax 580/584–7709 | www.microtelinn.com | 43 rooms | $45–$78 | AE, D, DC, MC, V.

Whip-Poor-Will Resort. Log cabins, ranging from cozy one-room models to larger family-size units, are equipped with full kitchens and fireplaces. The resort also has a fishing pond, an ice-cream parlor, and canoe rentals. Picnic area, kitchenettes, cable TV, pond, horseback riding, boating, fishing, pets allowed. | HC 75, 2 mi north of Broken Bow | 580/494–6476 | okresort.com | 17 cabins | $55–$155 | AE, D, DC, MC.

CHICKASHA

Best Western Inn. This is Chickasha's only full-service hotel, and it's conveniently located at Exit 80 off I–44. Some rooms have framed prints on the wall. Restaurant, room service, refrigerators, cable TV, pool, hot tub, sauna, gym, business services, pets allowed. | 2101 S. 4th St. 73018 | 405/224–4890 | fax 405/224–3411 | www.bestwestern.com/innchickasha | 154 rooms | $60 | AE, D, DC, MC, V.

Days Inn. This two-story motel is 1 mi from a golf course. Restaurant, room service, in-room data ports, some refrigerators, cable TV, pool, business services, pets allowed. | 2701 S. 4th St. 73018 | 405/222–5800 | 106 rooms | $55 | AE, D, DC, MC, V.

Deluxe Inn. There's nothing out of the ordinary about this turquoise-and-ivory, two-story hotel, but it's right off the highway and less than a block from a handful of restaurants. In-room data ports, some microwaves, some refrigerators, cable TV, pool, laundry facilities, pets allowed. | 728 S. Fourth St. | 405/222–3710 | 54 rooms | $37 | AE, D, DC, MC, V.

CLAREMORE

Best Western Will Rogers Inn. Rooms are spacious in this motel four mi from the Will Rogers Museum and two mi from the Expo Center, where most rodeos are held. Bar, microwaves, refrigerators, cable TV, pool, laundry facilities, pets allowed. | 940 S. Lynn Riggs Blvd. | 918/341–4410 or 800/644–WILL (reservations) | fax 918/341–6045 | 52 rooms | $59–$75 | AE, D, DC, MC, V.

Days Inn. Opened in 1995, this two-story motel has a Southwestern feel, with a terra-cotta–colored stucco exterior and tile floors in the lobby and breakfast area. Health club privileges are available at a club about three blocks from the motel. Complimentary Continental breakfast, in-room data ports, some refrigerators, cable TV, pool, laundry service, business services, pets allowed. | 1720 S. Lynn Riggs Blvd. | 918/343–3297 or 877/343–3297 | fax 918/343–9434 | daysinnc@swbell.net | www.daysinn.com | 58 rooms | $48–$75 | AE, D, DC, MC, V.

CLINTON

Best Western Tradewinds. This one-story motel on legendary Route 66 was a stopover for Elvis Presley when he traveled from Memphis to Las Vegas. Restaurant, cable TV, pool, hot tub, pets allowed (fee). | 2128 Gary Blvd. | 580/323–2610 | 81 rooms | $58 | AE, D, DC, MC, V.

Red Roof Inn. Opened in 1999, this two-story tan stucco hotel off I–40, Exit 65, is built around a grassy exterior courtyard and is within walking distance of the Route 66 Museum, shopping, restaurants, and public tennis courts. Restaurant, bar, complimentary breakfast, room service, in-room data ports, some microwaves, some refrigerators, cable TV, pool, exercise equipment, video games, laundry facilities, business services, pets allowed (fee). | 2140 Gary Blvd. | 580/323–2010 or 800/734–7663 | fax 580/323–7552 | io561@redroof.com | www.redroof.com | 100 rooms | $50–$54 | AE, D, DC, MC, V.

TraveLodge. The Oklahoma Route 66 Museum is only 1½ blocks from this one-story motel. Complimentary Continental breakfast, cable TV, pool, pets allowed (fee). | 2247 Gary Blvd. | 580/323–6840 | 71 rooms | $43–$47 | AE, D, DC, MC, V.

DAVIS

Arbuckle Mountain Motel. Rooms are clean and homey and the staff are friendly in this attractive two-story motel at the foot of the Arbuckle Mountains. It's less than 1 mi from Arbuckle Wilderness and 2 mi from Turner Falls Park. Some kitchenettes, some refrigerators, cable TV, hot tub, pets allowed (fee). | U.S. 77, 3 mi south of Davis | 580/369–3347 | 32 rooms | $52–$65 | AE, D, DC, MC, V.

DUNCAN

Chisholm Suite Hotel. This four-story all-suites hotel is right off the highway, in the middle of town. It's the tallest building in sight, and the nicest place to stay in Duncan. Each room has ample space, and living areas include couches that pull out to an additional queen-size bed. Complimentary Continental breakfast, in-room data ports, microwaves, refrigerators, some in-room hot tubs, cable TV, in-room VCRs, pool, exercise equipment, business services, pets allowed (fee). | 1204 U.S. 81N 73533 | 580/255–0551 | fax 580/255–9132 | 60 suites | $67–$108 | AE, D, MC, V.

Duncan Inn. Rooms are spacious in this one-story motel 3 mi from downtown. Restaurant, cable TV, pool, laundry facilities, pets allowed. | 3402 N. U.S. 81 | 580/252–5210, ext. 336 | fax 580/252–5210 | 92 rooms | $30–$34 | AE, D, DC, MC, V.

Holiday Inn. A small mall is across the highway from this motel built in the 1960s. The Chisolm Trail Museum is 2 mi away. Restaurant, bar, picnic area, room service, in-room data ports, cable TV, pool, wading pool, business services, pets allowed. | 1015 N. U.S. 81 | 580/252–1500 | fax 580/255–1851 | ducokhi@starcom.net | www.holiday-inn.com | 138 rooms | $65 | AE, D, DC, MC, V.

DURANT

Best Western Markita Inn. This two-story motel is 16 mi from Lake Texoma. Restaurant, picnic area, room service, some refrigerators, cable TV, pool, business services, some pets allowed. | 2401 W. Main St. | 580/924–7676 | fax 580/924–3060 | 62 rooms | $55–$65 | AE, D, DC, MC, V.

Comfort Inn and Suites. On the west end of town just off U.S. 69/I–75, this hotel is a convenient choice for those passing through. The Continental breakfast is better than most. Complimentary Continental breakfast, in-room data ports, some microwaves, some refrigerators, some in-room hot tubs, cable TV, pool, putting green, laundry facilities, business services, pets allowed (fee). | 2112 W. Main St. 74701 | 580/924–8881 or 800/228–5150 | fax 580/924–0955 | 62 rooms | $69–$89 | AE, D, DC, MC, V.

EDMOND

Howard Johnson Inn. Rooms surround a plant-filled atrium and open onto a pool and dining area in this two-story hotel. Expect excellent rates and amenities, larger-than-average rooms, and many areas for business meetings or conferences. Restaurant, bar, complimentary breakfast, room service, in-room data ports, some microwaves, some refrigerators, cable TV, pool, hot tub, sauna, driving range, exercise equipment, laundry facilities, laundry service, business services, pets allowed. | 2606 Rte. 66E 73644 | 580/225–3111 or 800/446–4656 | fax 580/225–1531 | 72 rooms | $35–$90 | AE, D, DC, MC, V.

TraveLodge. Twelve-foot-wide parking spaces and clean, reasonably priced rooms can be found in this single-story motel. Kids may enjoy the "Sleepy Bear Room", where furnishings are embellished with the familiar TraveLodge mascot. Picnic area, in-room data ports, some microwaves, some refrigerators, cable TV, driving range, miniature golf, laundry service, business services, pets allowed. | 301 Sleepy Hollow Ct | 580/243–0150 or 877/243–0150 | fax 580/243–0152 | fhunt@itlnet.net | www.travelodge.com | 44 rooms | $32–$65 | AE, D, DC, MC, V.

EL RENO

Best Western Hensley's. This hotel is on 8 acres of landscaped grounds, and an RV park and gas station are on the property. It's within 3 mi of Lake El Reno, the historic downtown area, and a golf course. Restaurant, complimentary Continental breakfast, cable TV, pool, business services, pets allowed. | 2701 S. Country Club Rd. | 405/262–6490 | fax 405/262–7642 | bestwestern.com | 60 rooms | $53 | AE, D, DC, MC, V.

Comfort Inn. A handful of restaurants is less than a block away, and a golf course and Lake El Reno are both less than 1 mi from this three-story motel. Complimentary Continental breakfast, in-room data ports, some microwaves, some refrigerators, some in-room hot tubs, cable TV, some in-room VCRs, pool, hot tub, sauna, exercise equipment, business services, pets allowed. | 1707 S.W. 27th St. 73036 | 405/262–3050 or 800/228–5150 | fax 405/262–5303 | 30 rooms, 31 suites | $46–$55, $58–$81 suites | AE, D, DC, MC, V.

ELK CITY

Days Inn. Local shopping is just a few miles away from this two-story stucco motel. Complimentary Continental breakfast, kitchenettes (in suites), some refrigerators, cable TV, pool, business services, pets allowed. | 1100 Rte. 34 73644-9752 | 580/225–9210 | fax 580/225–1278 | 132 rooms, 4 suites | $40–$50, $55–$95 suites | AE, D, DC, MC, V.

Holiday Inn. A full-service hotel, this is a highly ranked hotel in the state and the nation for customer satisfaction. The Holidome has entertainment and fitness opportunities, and a waterfall, gazebo, and karaoke bar are on site. Restaurant, bar, complimentary breakfast, room service, in-room data ports, cable TV, pool, hot tub, sauna, miniature golf, exercise equipment, video games, business services, some pets allowed. | 101 Meadow Ridge 73644 | 580/225–6637 | holidayinnelk@itlnet.net | 147 rooms, 4 suites | $65, $80–$120 suites | AE, D, DC, MC, V.

Quality Inn. This motel is within walking distance of a number of restaurants. Complimentary Continental breakfast, cable TV, pool, hot tub, business services, pets allowed. | 102 Hughes Access Rd. | 580/225–8140 | fax 580/225–8233 | 50 rooms | $45 | AE, D, DC, MC, V.

ENID

Holiday Inn. Rooms are modern in this chain hotel, and the courtyard is filled with trees and foliage. Restaurant, bar, room service, cable TV, pool, exercise equipment, business services, pets allowed. | 2901 S. Van Buren Ave. 73703 | 580/237–6000, ext. 177 | fax 580/237–6000 | www.holiday-inn.com | 100 rooms | $59 | AE, D, DC, MC, V.

Ramada Inn. This two-story hotel is in the center of town, about 1 mi from the Museum of the Cherokee Strip. The indoor pool is surrounded by lush greenery and flowers. Restaurant, bar, room service, microwaves, cable TV, 2 pools, hot tub, sauna, gym, laundry facilities, pets allowed (fee). | 3005 W. Owen K. Garriott Rd. 73703 | 580/234–0440 | fax 580/233–1402 | 125 rooms | $45–$69 | AE, D, DC, MC, V.

EUFAULA

Days Inn of Eufaula. This single-story redbrick motel is less than 1 mi from Eufaula Lake, and a couple of restaurants are adjacent. Complimentary Continental breakfast, in-room data ports, cable TV, business services, pets allowed (fee). | U.S. 69, 5 mi north of Eufaula 74426 | 918/689–3999 | fax 918/689–5800 | 40 rooms | $56–$62 | AE, D, DC, MC, V.

Lakeview Landing and RV Park. Rooms have pastel hues and modern furnishings in this pink brick motel, built in 2000. Some rooms have a view of Eufaula Lake, and two have two queen-size beds and an adjoining kitchenette. Some kitchenettes, some microwaves, some refrigerators, cable TV, lake, hiking, boating, fishing, pets allowed (fee). | Junction of Rtes. 9 and 9A, 3 mi east of Eufaula 74432 | 918/452–2736 | 12 rooms | $44–$78 | AE, D, MC, V.

GROVE

Hickory Inn Motel. This buff brick U-shaped motel with white and brass trim has clean rooms, most with one king- or two queen-size beds. It's less than 1 mi from Grand Lake O' the Cherokees, and 1½ mi south of downtown Grove via U.S. 59. Some microwaves, some refrigerators, cable TV, pool, lake, boating, fishing, laundry facilities, pets allowed (fee). | 2320 S. Main St. 74344 | 918/786–9157 | fax 918/786–6192 | gse@greencis.net | 37 rooms | $40–$50 | MC, V.

GUTHRIE

Best Western Territorial Inn. This hotel is backed by a wooded area and has oak furniture throughout. It's 30 minutes north of Oklahoma City, and 4–5 mi from museums, antique shops, malls, and restaurants. Restaurant, bar, complimentary Continental breakfast, cable TV, pool, pets allowed. | 2323 Territorial Dr. | 405/282–8831 | www.bestwestern.com | 84 rooms | $57–$65 | AE, D, DC, MC, V.

GUYMON

Ambassador Inn. This motel was built in 1978 and sits in a quiet neighborhood at the end of town, across from a movie theater and 1 mi from a golf course. Restaurant, bar with dancing, cable TV, pool, business services, pets allowed. | U.S. 64N at 21st St. | 580/338–5555 | fax 580/338–1784 | 70 rooms | $53 | AE, D, DC, MC, V.

Econo Lodge. Affordable accommodations near area restaurants and golf. Cable TV, business services, pets allowed. | 923 U.S. 54 E | 580/338–5431 | fax 580/338–0554 | 40 rooms | $42 | AE, D, DC, MC, V.

Super 8. The larger, executive rooms have recliners and more amenities in this two-story motel on the northeast end of town. The large parking lot has truck parking. Complimentary Continental breakfast, in-room data ports, some microwaves, some refrigerators, cable TV, some in-room hot tubs, laundry facilities, business services, pets allowed. | 1201 Rte. 54E | 580/338–0507 or 800/800–8000 | 59 rooms | $40–$88 | AE, D, DC, MC, V.

HOMINY

Budget Z Motel. The largest of this motel's modest rooms has two queen-size beds, a pull-out, full-size futon, and a separate living area. There's plenty of parking space, a restaurant is across the street, and a movie theater, roller rink, and Keystone Lake are each less than 2 mi away. Picnic area, some microwaves, some refrigerators, cable TV, playground, business services, pets allowed. | 1209 W. Caddo St., Cleveland 74020 | 918/358–3591 | fax 918/358–2441 | 20 rooms | $37–$50 | AE, D, DC, MC, V.

LAWTON

Days Inn. This two–story motel is about ¼ mi from shops and restaurants. Complimentary Continental breakfast, some refrigerators, cable TV, 2 pools, hot tub, business services, airport shuttle, pets allowed. | 3110 N.W. Cache Rd. 73505 | 580/353–3104 or 800/241–3952 | fax 580/353–0992 | 96 rooms | $48 | AE, D, DC, MC, V.

Ramada Inn. This chain hotel has a lovely courtyard, pool, and patio. A huge park with a new bike track is across the street and shopping is within 5 to 10 minutes. Restaurant, bar, room service, cable TV, pool, business services, pets allowed. | 601 N. 2nd St. 73507 | 580/355–7155 | fax 580/353–6162 | 98 rooms | $44–$54 | AE, D, DC, MC, V.

MCALESTER

Best Western Inn of McAlester. You can curl up in comfortable wing-back chairs or spread out your work on large desks at this hotel. For relaxation, you can swim in the Olympic-size swimming pool. Restaurant, complimentary Continental breakfast, some refrigerators, cable TV, pool, business services, pets allowed. | 1215 George Nigh Expressway 74501 | 918/426—0115 | fax 918/426–3634 | 61 rooms | $52 | AE, D, DC, MC, V.

Days Inn. Try a room facing the indoor pool at this motel 5 mi north of the Municipal Airport. Restaurant, bar, room service, some refrigerators, cable TV, in-room VCRs (and movies), pool, hot tub, business services, pets allowed. | 1217 George Nigh Expressway | 918/426–5050 | 100 rooms | $54–$69 | AE, D, DC, MC, V.

Holiday Inn Express Hotel and Suites. Built in 1999, this all-suites hotel is a welcome addition in a town that hasn't had a new hotel since the 1960s. Rooms have two data ports, and some have special filtration systems that rid the air of allergens. Restaurant, complimentary Continental breakfast, in-room data ports, microwaves, refrigerators, some in-room hot tubs, cable TV, pool, hot tub, exercise equipment, laundry facilities, business services, pets allowed (fee). | 650 S. George Nigh Expressway | 918/302–0001 | fax 918/302–0002 | express@gxmi.com | 80 suites | $79–$129 suites | AE, D, DC, MC, V.

Ramada Inn. The indoor recreation dome has something for everyone—from fitness buffs to those looking for personal pampering. Extensive renovations conducted in 1997–98 added more in-room amenities. Restaurant, bar, room service, in-room data ports, refrigerators, cable TV, pool, hot tub, sauna, miniature golf, gym, video games, laundry facilities, business services, pets allowed. | 1500 George Nigh Expressway 74502 | 918/423–7766 | fax 918/426–0068 | 161 rooms | $48–$65 | AE, D, DC, MC, V.

MIAMI

Best Western Inn of Miami. This one-story stucco motel is surrounded by lush landscaped grounds. Restaurant, bar, room service, refrigerators, cable TV, pool, airport shuttle, pets allowed. | 2225 E. Steve Owens St. | 918/542–6681 | fax 918/542–3777 | www.bestwestern.com | 80 rooms | $59–$69 | AE, D, DC, MC, V.

Townsman Motel. This simple redbrick two-story motel is 2 mi west of the I–44 Turnpike gate. The Miami Golf and Country Club is 3 mi away, and adjacent Taylor Park has a playground. Restaurant, bar, room service, cable TV, laundry facilities, laundry service, pets allowed. | 900 E. Steve Owens Blvd. | 918/542–6631 | 72 rooms | $32–$46 | AE, D, MC, V.

MUSKOGEE

Ramada Inn. This hotel's atrium has a pool, exercise equipment, and games. A golf course is five mi away. Restaurant, bar (with entertainment), microwaves, room service, cable TV, in-room VCRs, pool, hot tub, sauna, exercise equipment, video games, business services, pets allowed. | 800 S. 32nd St. 74401 | 918/682–4341 | fax 918/682–7400 | 135 rooms, 7 suites | $59, $95–$135 suites | AE, D, DC, MC, V.

TraveLodge. This motel is 1 mi west of Muskogee. Bar, in-room data ports, cable TV, pool, business services, pets allowed. | 534 S. 32nd St. 74401 | 918/683–2951 | 104 rooms | $50–$85 | AE, D, DC, MC, V.

NORMAN

Days Inn. This motel is between two car lots on the interstate service road. It's ½ mi from shopping and dining, and just 3½ mi from the University of Oklahoma. Some refrigerators, cable TV, pool, business services, pets allowed. | 609 N. Interstate Dr. | 405/360–4380 | fax 405/321–5767 | 72 rooms | $45–$60 | AE, D, DC, MC, V.

Guest Inn. This west side lodging just 3 mi from the University of Oklahoma has motel-style rooms you can drive up to, as well as a main building with hotel rooms. It's within walking distance of shopping and dining, and a courtyard has grills for your personal use. Restaurant, picnic area, room service, microwaves, refrigerators, cable TV, in-room VCRs, pool, video games, laundry facilities, business services, pets allowed. | 2543 W. Main St. | 405/360–1234 or 800/460–4619 | www.telepath.com/weblynx/norman | 110 rooms | $52 | AE, D, DC, MC, V.

La Quinta. Rooms are cheerful and soundproof in this chain hotel just off I–35. It's on the south end of town, 3 mi from the University of Oklahoma. Complimentary Continental breakfast, in-room data ports, some microwaves, some refrigerators, cable TV, pool, hot tub, exercise equipment, laundry facilities, laundry service, business services, pets allowed. | 930 Ed Noble Pkwy. 73072 | 405/579–4000 or 800/687–6667 | fax 405/579–4001 | 117 rooms | $89–$129 | AE, D, DC, MC, V.

Residence Inn by Marriott. The University of Oklahoma is only 3 mi from this Marriott, designed for extended-stay visitors. At least three golf courses are within 5 mi of the property and major restaurants are within 1 mi. Complimentary Continental breakfast, in-room data ports, microwaves, cable TV, pool, hot tub, tennis, laundry facilities, business services, some pets allowed. | 2681 Jefferson St. | 405/366–0900 | fax 405/360–6552 | 126 suites | $89–$109 suites | AE, D, DC, MC, V.

OKLAHOMA CITY

The Biltmore. Built in the early 1980s, this hotel is the largest in the state. It's on the west side of the city, 5 mi north of the Will Rogers World Airport, about 4½ mi from downtown, and within walking distance of many restaurants. Each of the three buildings in the complex has a tree- and flower-filled courtyard. 2 restaurants, 3 bars (with entertainment), room service, in-room data ports, microwaves, some in-room hot tubs, cable TV, in-room VCRs, 4 pools, barber shop, hot tub, tennis, exercise equipment, business services, airport shuttle, pets allowed, free parking. | 401 S. Meridian Ave. | 405/947–7681 | fax 405/947–4253 | 509 rooms | $59–$69 | AE, D, DC, MC, V.

Days Inn–Northwest. As the name implies, this two-story motel is in the northwest part of the city. It's within walking distance of fast-food restaurants. Restaurant, bar, room service, some refrigerators, some in-room hot tubs, cable TV, pool, laundry facilities, airport shuttle, free parking, pets allowed. | 2801 N.W. 39th St. | 405/946–0741 | fax 405/942–0181 | gertysocks@msn.com | www.daysinn.com | 117 rooms | $56–$156 | AE, D, DC, MC, V.

Embassy Suites. This hotel is 10 mi from downtown and 2 mi from the Will Rogers World Airport. The two-room suites have a living area with a couch and a wet bar. Restaurant, bar, complimentary breakfast, room service, in-room data ports, microwaves, refrigerators, cable TV, pool, hot tub, exercise equipment, business services, airport shuttle, pets allowed, free parking. | 1815 S. Meridian Ave. | 405/682–6000 | fax 405/682–9835 | www.embassy.com | 236 suites | $99–139 suites | AE, D, DC, MC, V.

Fifth Seasons Hotel. Oversized rooms and a lovely atrium area with pool, restaurant, and fountain make this a popular choice for business and leisure travelers. Restaurant, bar, complimentary breakfast, minibars, refrigerators, cable TV, pool, laundry facilities, business services, airport shuttle, pets allowed, free parking. | 6200 N. Robinson Ave. | 405/843–5558 or 800/682–0049 (excluding OK) or 800/522–9458 (OK) | fax 405/840–3410 | 202 rooms, 27 suites | $65–$105, $85–$150 suites | AE, D, DC, MC, V.

Hawthorne Suites. This all-suites hotel is in the middle of downtown. It's two blocks from the Penn Square shopping mall, and 2½ mi from the Oklahoma City Zoo, Firefighters Museum, National Softball Hall of Fame, and the National Cowboy Hall of Fame. All of the suites have spacious living and sleeping areas and are appointed with polished wood furniture. Restaurant, bar (with entertainment), complimentary Continental breakfast, room service, in-room data ports, microwaves, refrigerators, cable TV, pool, business services, airport shuttle, pets allowed, free parking. | 1600 Richmond Sq. | 405/840–1440 or 800/843–1440 | fax 405/843–4272 | 51 suites | $74 suites | AE, D, DC, MC, V.

Holiday Inn Airport. Rooms surround an atrium with recreational facilities in this two-story hotel 2½ mi north of the airport. Some rooms open onto an interior corridor. Restaurant, bar, room service, in-room data ports, some microwaves, cable TV, pool, hot tub, sauna, exercise equipment, video games, laundry facilities, laundry service, business services, pets allowed (fee). | 2101 S. Meridian St. 73108 | 405/681–1674 or 800/622–7666 | fax 405/681–1674 | holokc@ionet.net | www.holiday-inn.com/okc-airport | 236 rooms, 10 suites | $87, $135 suites | AE, D, DC, MC, V.

Howard Johnson. This two-story hotel is 3 mi from the state fairgrounds and 7 mi from downtown. Complimentary Continental breakfast, some kitchenettes, microwaves, some refrigerators, cable TV, pool, laundry facilities, business services, free parking, pets allowed. | 4017 N.W. 39th Expressway | 405/947–0038 | fax 405/946–7450 | www.hojo.com | 105 rooms | $55 | AE, D, DC, MC, V.

Howard Johnson Express Inn. These chain accommodations are within 5 minutes of downtown, the Will Rogers World Airport, and area attractions. There are plenty of restaurants within walking distance as well. Complimentary Continental breakfast, microwaves, refrigerators, cable TV, pool, gym, laundry facilities, business services, pets allowed, free parking. | 400 S. Meridian Ave. | 405/943–9841 | fax 405/942–1869 | 96 rooms | $49–$65 | AE, D, DC, MC, V.

La Quinta Oklahoma City Airport. A beautiful courtyard with a gazebo, pool, and landscaping is the centerpiece of this hotel 4 mi from the state fairgrounds and 20 minutes from the Myriad Convention Center. Restaurant, bar, complimentary Continental breakfast, room service, in-room data ports, microwaves, refrigerators, cable TV, in-room VCRs, pool, wading pool, business services, airport shuttle, pets allowed, free parking. | 800 S. Meridian Ave. | 405/942–0040 | fax 405/942–0638 | 168 rooms | $69 | AE, D, DC, MC, V.

Motel 6 Oklahoma City Airport. Rooms are basic and inexpensive, and you can usually park in front of your door in this two-story, tan brick motel. It's 3½ mi north of the airport, within walking distance of many restaurants, and around the corner from recreational facilities and White Water Bay water park. In-room data ports, cable TV, pool, laundry facilities, business services, pets allowed. | 820 S. Meridian St. 73108 | 405/946–6662 | fax 405/946–4058 | www.motel6.com | 128 rooms | $46 | AE, D, DC, MC, V.

Marriott. This elegant, 16-story hotel 5 mi from downtown is lit with chandeliers and has lots of plants in the foyer. Restaurants and shopping are less than 1 mi away. Restaurant, bar (with entertainment), room service, in-room data ports, cable TV, pool, exercise equipment, laundry facilities, business services, pets allowed, free parking. | 3233 NW Expwy. (Rte. 3) | 405/842–6633 | fax 405/840–5338 | www.marriott.com | 354 rooms | $129–$139 | AE, D, DC, MC, V.

Residence Inn by Marriott. This complex consists of 17 two-story buildings. It's 5 mi from downtown and within 1 mi of the Oklahoma City Zoo and White Water Bay. Picnic area, complimentary Continental breakfast, in-room data ports, microwaves, refrigerators, cable TV, in-room VCRs (and movies), pool, hot tub, laundry facilities, business services, airport shuttle, free parking, pets allowed. | 4361 W. Reno Ave. | 405/942–4500 | fax 405/942–7777 | www.residenceinn.com | 135 suites | $105–$135 suites | AE, D, DC, MC, V.

Willow Way Bed and Breakfast. All guest rooms in this English Tudor country house have period antiques. One room is actually a converted greenhouse. Grounds include two fish ponds and a walking path. Complimentary breakfast, no TV in rooms, TV in common area, some pets allowed. | 27 Oakwood Dr. | 405/427–2133 | 3 rooms | $70–$175 | MC, V.

OKMULGEE

Best Western. Built in 1999, this strip motel is 2 mi north of town. Restaurant, bar (with entertainment), in-room data ports, refrigerators, cable TV, pool, gym, business services, pets allowed. | 3499 N. Wood Dr. | 918/756–9200 | www.bestwestern.com | 50 rooms, 6 suites | $49–$55 | AE, D, DC, MC, V.

Henryetta Inn and Dome. Built in 1987, this domed, skylit hotel 11 mi south of Okmulgee is 3 blocks from Henryetta's Main St. A movie theater is $1/2$ mi away. Restaurant, bar, room service, cable TV, pool, gym, racquetball, laundry facilities, business services, pets allowed. | 810 E. Trudgeon, Henryetta 74437 | 918/652–2581 | 84 rooms | $67–$78 | AE, D, DC, MC, V.

PAULS VALLEY

Days Inn. Built in 1985, this two-story motel is 2 mi out of town, at I–35 and Rte. 19. Complimentary Continental breakfast, cable TV, pets allowed. | 3203 W. Grant Ave. | 405/238–7548 | fax 405/238–1262 | 54 rooms | $70 | AE, D, DC, MC, V.

Sands Inn. This single-story motel less than 1 mi from town has a barbeque joint right in the lobby. 2 restaurants, some kitchenettes, cable TV, pool, laundry facilities, pets allowed (fee). | 3006 W. Grant | 405/238–6415 | fax 405/238–7213 | 54 rooms | $38 | AE, D, DC, MC, V.

PAWNEE

Pecan Grove Motel. Built in 1995, this motel has rooms with king-size or double beds. It's two blocks from the town square and courthouse, and within walking distance of shops and restaurants. Cable TV, laundry facilities, pets allowed (fee). | 609 4th St. | 918/762–3061 | 16 rooms | $38 | AE, D, MC, V.

PERRY

Best Western Cherokee Strip Motel. Built in 1963, this single-story motel is right off I–35, just 2 mi west of Perry. Restaurant, bar, cable TV, in-room VCRs, pool, pets allowed. | 2819 U.S. 77 W | 580/336–2218 | fax 580/336–9753 | www.bestwestern.com | 90 rooms | $48 | AE, D, DC, MC, V.

Perry Days Inn. A restaurant, convenience store, and gas station are across the street from this motel right off I–35, Exit 186. The parking lot can accommodate anything from big rig trucks to motorcycles. Complimentary Continental breakfast, cable TV, laundry services, pets allowed. | Jct. I–35 and Fir Ave. | 580/336–2277 | fax 580/336–2086 | www.daysinn.com | 40 rooms | $48 | AE, D, DC, MC, V.

PONCA CITY

Days Inn. This 1975 motel is on the north side of town, within walking distance of some restaurants and stores. Complimentary Continental breakfast, microwaves, cable TV, pets allowed. | 1415 E. Bradley St. | 580/767–1406 | fax 580/762–9589 | 59 rooms | $54 | AE, D, DC, MC, V.

Rose Stone Bed and Breakfast Inn. Built in 1950, this B&B is housed in a former commercial building. Complimentary breakfast, in-room data ports, some microwaves, some refrigerators, no smoking, cable TV, in-room VCRs (and movies), laundry service, business services, pets allowed. | 120 S. 3rd St. | 580/765–5699 or 800/763–9922 | 25 rooms, 3 suites | $49–$59 | AE, D, DC, MC, V.

Super 8 Ponca City. This modest, single-story motel has few amenities, but it's clean and centrally located. If you're in the region for golf or fishing, save money by staying here; weekly rates are available upon request. Complimentary Continental breakfast, cable TV, hot tub, pets allowed (no fee). | 301 S. 14th St. | 580/762–1616 | fax 580/762–8777 | www.super8.com | 40 rooms | $38 | AE, D, DC, MC, V.

PRYOR

Days Inn. Green County is known for fishing. Anglers staying at this bungalow-style hotel set among sweeping lawns have their pick of three bountiful lakes; Ft. Gibson, Grand, and Hudson are all within a 20 minute drive. Restaurant, some microwaves, refrigerators, cable TV, pool, laundry services, pets allowed. | Jct. U.S. 69S and Rte. 69A | 918/825–7600 | www.daysinn.com | 55 rooms | $52 | AE, D, DC, MC, V.

Pryor House Motor Inn. This 1990s brick motel is in the center of town, within walking distance of a few shops and restaurants. Complimentary Continental breakfast, cable TV, pool, pets allowed. | 123 S. Mill St. | 918/825–6677 | 35 rooms | $46 | AE, DC, MC, V.

SALLISAW

Best Western Blue Ribbon Motor Inn. This 1970s motel is in the center of town, 3 mi from golf and 18 mi from fishing at Lake Tenkiller. Restaurant, some refrigerators, cable TV, 2 pools, hot tub, exercise equipment, laundry facilities, pets allowed. | 706 S. Kerr Blvd. | 918/775–6294 | www.bestwestern.com | 81 rooms | $54 | AE, D, DC, MC, V.

Days Inn. This motel is on the south side of town. It's within 2 mi of restaurants, and 10 mi from a golf course. Some kitchenettes, some refrigerators, cable TV, pets allowed. | 1700 W. Cherokee St. | 918/775–4406 | fax 918/775–4406 | 33 rooms | $45–$65 | AE, D, DC, MC, V.

Econo Lodge. This modestly priced, no-frills motor inn is 1 mi from the golf course, 2 mi from the cinema, and 8 mi from boating and fishing. Complimentary Continental breakfast, cable TV, laundry facilities, pets allowed (fee). | 2403 E. Cherokee | 918/775–7981 | fax 918/775–7981 | www.econolodge.com | 40 rooms | $36 | AE, D, DC, MC, V.

Golden Spur Motel. Clean, modern rooms are available at this motel, just a couple of miles from the area racetrack and the Cherokee Indian Museum. Fishing at Kerr and Tenkiller lakes is a popular pastime with guests. Cable TV, pool, pets allowed. | 601 S. Kerr Blvd. | 918/775–4443 | 29 rooms | $32 | AE, D, DC, MC, V.

Sallisaw Super 8 Motel. Horse-racing enthusiasts can visit Blue Ribbon Downs, just 2 mi from this duplex motel, while others may choose to take advantage of the fishing, hiking, scuba diving, and more at Tenkiller Lake, "Oklahoma's Clearwater Wonderland," which is 12 mi from the motel. Complimentary Continental breakfast, cable TV, pool, pets allowed. | 924 Kerr Blvd. | 918/775–8900 | fax 918/775–8901 | www.super8.com | 97 rooms | $40 | AE, D, DC, MC, V.

SHAWNEE

Best Western Cinderella. About 30 mi from Oklahoma City and the Will Rogers World Airport, this hotel is 1 mi from the Oklahoma Exposition Center and the Mabee-Gerrer Museum of Art, and 3 mi from the Shawnee Mall. Restaurant, bar, room service, cable TV, pool, hot tub, laundry facilities, business services, pets allowed. | 623 Kickapoo Spur 74801 | 405/273–7010 | www.bestwestern.com | 92 rooms | $57–$68 | AE, D, DC, MC, V.

Hampton Inn Shawnee. Built in 1996, this three–story motor lodge is right off I–40 Exit 185. Complimentary Continental breakfast, some kitchenettes, some refrigerators, cable TV, hot tub, pool, pets allowed (fee). | 4851 N. Kickapoo | 405/275–1540 | 64 rooms | $56 | AE, D, DC, MC, V.

Ramada Inn. This two-story hotel just off I–40 is in a commercial area on the north end of town. It's adjacent to both Oklahoma Baptist University and St. Gregory's University, and it's ¼ mi from a shopping mall. Restaurant, bar (with entertainment), room service, in-room data ports, minibars, cable TV, pool, video games, laundry facilities, business services, pets allowed. | 4900 N. Harrison St. 74801 | 405/275–4404 | fax 405/275–4998 | 106 rooms | $60–$75 | AE, D, DC, MC, V.

STILLWATER

Best Western. Oklahoma State University is just ¼ mi from this three-story hotel. The modern-style building has a glass facade. Restaurant, bar, room service, in-room data ports, some refrigerators, cable TV, pool, video games, laundry facilities, business services, some pets allowed. | 600 E. McElroy St. | 405/377–7010 | fax 405/743–1686 | 122 rooms | $65 | AE, D, DC, MC, V.

Holiday Inn. Oklahoma State University is less than 10 minutes away from this two–story hotel in the southwest corner of town. Restaurant, bar, room service, cable TV, pool, hot tub, exercise equipment, video games, laundry facilities, pets allowed. | 2515 W. 6th St. | 405/372–0800 | fax 405/377–8212 | www.holiday-inn.com | 141 rooms | $74–$87 | AE, D, DC, MC, V.

TAHLEQUAH

Fin and Feather. Family-owned and -operated since 1960, this resort 1 mi from Lake Tenkiller specializes in family reunions and retreats. The grounds are littered with lush greenery and rolling hills. Dining rooms, picnic area, some kitchenettes, refrigerators, cable TV, in-room VCRs (and movies), pool, pond, wading pool, hot tub, miniature golf, tennis, basketball, volleyball, playground, laundry facilities, business services, some pets allowed. | Rte. 10 off Rte. 100 | 918/487–5148 | fax 918/487–5025 | www.finandfeatherresort.com | 82 rooms | $67–$74 | Closed Oct.–Easter | AE, D, MC, V.

MarVal Resort. Tent campsites and fully equipped cabins are available on this 105-acre property in the foothills of the Oklahoma Ozarks. Cable TV (in cabins), no room phones, pool, pond, miniature golf, basketball, volleyball, fishing, children's programs (ages 2–17). Pets allowed (fee). | Rte. 100, 40 mi north of Tahlequah | 918/489–2295 | www.marval-resort.com | 17 cabins | $47 cabins | D, MC, V.

Tenkiller Lodge. This luxurious lodge 4 mi out of town is the premiere destination for sportsmen and families coming to enjoy the namesake lake. Spacious guest rooms have handmade log furniture and modern amenities. Just past the heated pool and pavilion is the magnificent lake—"Oklahoma's Clearwater Wonderland"—with all the fishing, swimming, hiking, and recreation you could ask for. In-room data ports, cable TV, pool, pets allowed. | Jct. Rte. 82 S. and Indian Rd. | 918/453–9000 | 25 rooms | $70 | AE, D, DC, MC, V.

TULSA

Best Western Glenpool. This one-story motel is less than 2 mi from downtown Tulsa and the airport, as well as many area attractions. Complimentary Continental breakfast, in-room data ports, microwaves, refrigerators, cable TV, pool, laundry facilities, business services, pets allowed. | 14831 S. Casper, Glenpool 74033-0520 | 918/322–5201 | fax 918/322–9604 | www.bestwestern.com | 64 rooms | $70 | AE, D, DC, MC, V.

Best Western Trade Winds Central Inn. Most rooms have exterior entrances in this two-story motel off I–44. It's 15 minutes from downtown Tulsa and within 1 mi of two golf courses. Restaurant, bar (with entertainment), complimentary Continental breakfast, room service, in-room data ports, in-room hot tubs, cable TV, in-room VCRs (and movies), pool, laundry facilities, business services, airport shuttle, some pets accepted. | 3141 E. Skelly Dr. 74105-6375 | 918/749–5561 | fax 918/749–6312 | www.bestwestern.com | 167 rooms | $69 | AE, D, DC, MC, V.

Doubletree Downtown. Right in the middle of downtown Tulsa's business district, this hotel is within sight of a number of malls, boutiques, and art galleries. Well-appointed guest rooms have spacious work areas. Restaurant, bar (with entertainment), in-room data ports, microwaves, cable TV, in-room VCRs, pool, hot tub, exercise equipment, business services, airport shuttle, pets allowed (fee). | 616 W. 7th St. | 918/587–8000 | fax 918/587–1642 | www.doubletreehotels.com | 417 rooms | $119 | AE, D, DC, MC, V.

Doubletree Hotel at Warren Place. Public areas are furnished with classic period pieces, and rooms have tranquil, sandy color schemes and textured wall treatments. 2 restaurants, bar, room service, in-room data ports, refrigerator, cable TV, in-room VCRs, pool, hot tub, exercise equipment, business services, airport shuttle, pets allowed. | 6110 S. Yale Ave. | 918/495–1000 | fax 918/495–1944 | www.doubletreehotels.com | 370 rooms | $119 | AE, D, DC, MC, V.

Guest House Suites Plus. Bi-level suites have a living room on the first level and a loft bedroom on the second. All kitchens are fully equipped. Picnic area, complimentary Continental breakfast, in-room data ports, kitchenettes, microwaves, cable TV, in-room VCRs, pool, hot tubs, laundry facilities, business services, airport shuttle, some pets allowed. | 8181 E. 41st St. | 918/664–7241 | fax 918/622–0314 | 135 suites | $75–$109 | AE, D, DC, MC, V.

Hawthorn Suites. All suites have two large rooms, a fireplace, and well-lit desks. The hotel is a stone's throw away from two highways (I–44 and Rte. 51), and the Woodland Hills Mall is just 3 mi away. Complimentary breakfast, some kitchenettes, microwaves, cable TV, pool, hot tub, laundry facilities, business services, airport shuttle, some pets allowed. | 3509 S. 79th E. Ave. | 918/663–3900 | fax 918/663–0548 | www.hawthorn.com | 131 suites | $99–189 suites | AE, D, DC, MC, V.

Holiday Inn–East/Airport. The courtyard has a recreation center and grills in this hotel 15 minutes from the downtown Tulsa area. Restaurant, bar, room service, in-room data ports, microwaves, cable TV, pool, video games, playground, business services, airport shuttle, pets allowed. | 1010 N. Garnett Rd. | 918/437–7660 | fax 918/438–7538 | www.holiday-inn.com | 158 rooms | $84 | AE, D, DC, MC, V.

Holiday Inn Select. Rooms are spacious at this hotel less than 5 mi from a water park, a horse-racing track, and the Tulsa Drillers Stadium. Restaurant, bar, room service, cable TV, pool, exercise equipment, laundry facilities, business services, airport shuttle, pets allowed (fee). | 5000 E. Skelly Dr. | 918/622–7000 | fax 918/664–9353 | hiseltulsa@aol.com | 294 rooms, 13 suites | $99, $159–$225 suites | AE, D, DC, MC, V.

La Quinta Inn. This hotel is far enough from the city's main commercial strip to be quiet and relaxing, but close enough (10 minutes or less) to the zoo, the convention center, and the downtown area to still make you feel a part of the action. Complimentary Continental breakfast, in-room data ports, cable TV, pool, business services, airport shuttle, some pets allowed. | 35 N. Sheridan Rd. | 918/836–3931 | fax 918/836–5428 | 93 rooms, 8 suites | $62, $75–$85 suites | AE, D, DC, MC, V.

Sheraton. Built in 1983, rooms in this 11–story hotel have wooden furniture and framed art-prints on the wall. Three major shopping malls are within 5 mi. Restaurant, bar, room service, in-room data ports, cable TV, in-room VCRs (and movies), indoor-outdoor pool, hot tub, sauna, laundry facilities, business center, exercise equipment, airport shuttle, some pets allowed. | 10918 E. 41st St. | 918/627–5000 | fax 918/627–4003 | www.sheraton.com/tulsa | 325 rooms, 5 suites | $74–$129, $450–$500 suites | AE, D, DC, MC, V.

VINITA

Holiday Motel. This two-story strip motel in the center of town was built in the 1970s. Cable TV, pool, pets allowed. | 519 S. Wilson St. | 918/256–6429 | 25 rooms | $40 | AE, D, MC, V.

WAURIKA

A-OK Motel. This modest, single-story motel is the only place in town to rest your head. Cable TV, pets allowed. | Jct. U.S. 81 and U.S. 70 | 580/228–2337 | 32 rooms | $35 | AE, D, MC, V.

WEATHERFORD

Best Western Mark Motor Hotel. This two–story motel is four blocks from a city park, 12 blocks from Southwestern Oklahoma State University, and 15 mi from the Oklahoma Route 66 Museum. Complimentary Continental breakfast, in-room data ports, refrigerators, cable TV, in-room VCRs, pool, business services, pets allowed. | 525 E. Main St. 73096 | 580/772–3325 | fax 580/772–8950 | www.bestwestern.com | 63 rooms | $59 | AE, D, DC, MC, V.

WOODWARD

Northwest Inn. This is the only lodging in town with a swimming pool. Rooms have cherry-wood furniture, and golf, parks, and museums are within 1–2 mi. Restaurant, bar (with entertainment), room service, some in-room data ports, some refrigerators, cable TV, pool, laundry facilities, exercise equipment, video games, business services, pets allowed. | U.S. 270 and 1st St. | 580/256–7600 or 800/727–7606 | fax 580/254–2274 | www.shinc.com | 124 rooms | $57–$64 | AE, D, DC, MC, V.

Super 8. The rooms at this 2–story motel have plenty of space, but are otherwise unremarkable. Boiling Springs State Park is a 15 minute drive away. Complimentary Continental breakfast, picnic area, cable TV, pool, business services, pets allowed (fee). | 4120 Williams Ave. | 580/254–2964 | fax 580/254–2964 | 60 rooms | $42 | AE, D, MC, V.

Oregon

ALBANY

Best Western Pony Soldier Motor Inn. Rooms at this basic motel face an attractive court-yard with a pool. It's close to golf, tennis, shopping, and restaurants. | 72 rooms. Complimentary Continental breakfast, in-room data ports, microwaves, refrigerators, cable TV, pool, hot tub, exercise equipment. Pets allowed. | 315 Airport Rd. SE 97321 | 541/928–6322 or 800/634–7669 | fax 541/928–8124 | $74–$90 | AE, D, DC, MC, V.

Budget Inn. There's nothing fancy here, but it's a good choice if you prefer an inexpensive alternative. | 48 rooms. Cable TV, laundry facilities. Pets allowed. | 2727 Pacific Blvd. SE 97321 | 541/926–4246 | fax 541/926–5208 | $40–$45. | AE, D, DC, MC, V.

Hawthorne Inn and Suites. A fireplace and antiques in the lobby welcome you to the rustic interior of the Hawthorne Inn. Quite a variety of amenities are available and it's near both the airport and the fairgrounds. | 50 rooms. Complimentary buffet breakfast, cable TV, pool, hot tub, exercise equipment, laundry facilities, business services. Pets allowed. | 251 Airport Rd. SE 97321 | 541/928–0921 | fax 541/928–8055 | $69–$139 | AE, D, DC, MC, V.

ASHLAND

Best Western Bard's Inn. This Best Western, in a beautiful rose garden setting, is only one block from downtown. Rooms have views of the surrounding mountains. | 92 rooms, 7 suites. Refrigerators, some in-room hot tubs, cable TV, pool, hot tub, cross-country and downhill skiing, business services, airport shuttle. Pets allowed (fee). | 132 N. Main St. 97520 | 541/482–0049 | fax 541/488–3259 | $98–$134, $138–$175 suites | AE, D, DC, MC, V.

Cedarwood Inn. All the rooms at this motel in a residential area 2 mi from downtown have queen- or king-size beds. Courtyard rooms have semi-private patios or decks. | 64 rooms (14 with shower only). Picnic area, some kitchenettes, cable TV, 2 pools, cross-country and downhill skiing, business services. Some pets allowed. | 1801 Siskiyou Blvd. 97520 | 541/488–2000 or 800/547–4141 (for reservations) | fax 541/482–2000 | $68–$134 | AE, D, DC, MC, V.

Knights Inn. You'll find clean, comfortable rooms with king- or queen-size beds at this chain property located 2 mi from downtown. | 40 rooms. Restaurant, bar, cable TV, pool, hot tub. Some pets allowed (fee). | 2359 Hwy. 66 97520 | 541/482–5111 or 800/547–4566 (for reservations) | $53–$74 | AE, D, DC, MC, V.

Rodeway Inn. This modern hotel is across from Southern Oregon State College. | 64 rooms. Cable TV, pool, cross-country and downhill skiing, business services. Some pets allowed (fee). | 1193 Siskiyou Blvd. 97520 | 541/482–2641 | fax 541/488–1656 | $72–$82 | AE, D, DC, MC, V.

Windmill Inn of Ashland. The Oregon Shakespeare Festival box office is 3 mi from this hotel where the rooms are plush and comfortable. | 159 rooms, 72 suites. Complimentary Continental breakfast, microwaves (in suites), refrigerators (in suites), pool, beauty salon, hot tub, tennis, cross-country and downhill skiing, exercise equipment, laundry facilities, airport shuttle. Pets allowed. | 2525 Ashland St. 97520 | 541/482–8310 or 800/547–4747 | fax 541/488–1783 | info@windmillinns.com | www.windmillinns.com/ | $99–$109, $119 suites | AE, D, DC, MC, V.

ASTORIA

Bayshore Motor Inn. The rooms in this motel are housed either in a two-story or newer four-story building. Set on the riverbank, it is close to Astoria's historic district. | 76 rooms. Complimentary Continental breakfast, no air-conditioning in some rooms, cable TV, pool, hot tub, laundry facilities, business services. Some pets allowed (fee). | 555 Hamburg Ave. 97103 | 503/325–2205 or 800/621–0641 | fax 503/325–5550 | $64–$128 | AE, D, DC, MC, V.

Crest Motel. This is an older, no-frills motel on 2½ acres overlooking the mouth of the Columbia River. There is a large backyard where you can watch the river traffic. | 40 rooms. Free Continental breakfast, no air-conditioning, some refrigerators, cable TV, hot tub, laundry facilities, business services. Pets allowed. | 5366 Leif Erickson Dr. 97103 | 503/325–3141 or 800/421–3141 | $52–$89 | AE, D, DC, MC, V.

Red Lion Inn. Many of the rooms, decorated in earth tones, have views of the Columbia River, the marina, and Astoria Bridge. This dependable chain's Astoria property is on the river bank and 8 blocks from the City Center. | 124 rooms. Restaurant, bar with entertainment, room service, cable TV, business services, airport shuttle. Some pets allowed (fee). | 400 Industry St. 97103 | 503/325–7373 | fax 503/325–5786 | $124 | AE, D, DC, MC, V.

Shilo Inn. This Shilo property is 1 mi south of town near the Pacific. | 63 rooms. Restaurant, bar, complimentary breakfast, some kitchenettes, microwaves, refrigerators, room service, cable TV, pool, hot tub, exercise equipment, laundry facilities, business services, airport shuttle. Pets allowed (fee). | 1609 E. Harbor Dr., Warrenton 97146 | 503/861–2181 | fax 503/861–2980 | $79–$119 | AE, D, DC, MC, V.

BAKER CITY

Bridge Street Inn. The rooms at this downtown motel are clean and good value. | 40 rooms. Complimentary Continental breakfast, some microwaves, refrigerators, cable TV. Pets allowed. | 134 Bridge St. 97814 | 541/523–6571 or 800/932–9220 | fax 541/523–9424 | reservations@bridgestreetinn.com | www.bridgestreetinn.com | $31–$50 | AE, D, MC, V.

Eldorado Inn. This small motel has clean rooms and low rates. | 56 rooms. Restaurant, cable TV, pool, hot tub, business services. Pets allowed (fee). | 695 E. Campbell St. 97814 | 541/523–6494 or 800/537–5756 | fax 541/523–6494 | $45–$54 | AE, D, DC, MC, V.

Quality Inn. The rooms here are basic but clean. | 54 rooms. Complimentary Continental breakfast, some refrigerators, cable TV. Pets allowed (fee). | 810 Campbell St. 97814 | 541/523–2242 | fax 541/523–2242, ext. 400 | $42–$62 | AE, D, DC, MC, V.

BANDON

Sunset Motel. Many rooms at this rustic property have decks with ocean views; some are oceanfronts, some have fireplaces. Beach houses are also available. | 58 rooms; 5 beach houses. Restaurant, some kitchenettes, cable TV, hot tub, laundry facilities, business services, airport shuttle. Some pets allowed (fee). | 1755 Beach Loop Rd. 97411 | 541/347–2453 or 800/842–2407 | fax 541/347–3636 | sunset@harborside.com | www.sunsetmotel.com | $52–$110, $155–$165 beach houses | AE, D, DC, MC, V.

BEAVERTON

Greenwood Inn. This suburban hotel, built in 1974, is in a quiet residential area, 1 mi from downtown. The grounds of this contemporary two-story building are beautifully landscaped with lots of flowers and trees. | 250 rooms. Restaurant, bar with entertainment, in-room data ports, some kitchenettes, some refrigerators, room service, cable TV, 2 pools, hot tub, laundry facilities, business services. Pets allowed (fee). | 10700 S.W. Allen Blvd. 97005 | 503/643–7444 or 800/289–1300 | fax 503/626–4553 | www.greenwoodinn.com | $79–$99 | AE, D, DC, MC, V.

BEND

Best Western Entrada Lodge. Next to the Deschutes National Forest and 1 mi from the Deschutes River, this Best Western property in southwest Bend is surrounded by pine trees. | 79 rooms. Complimentary Continental breakfast, in-room data ports, cable TV, pool, hot tub, cross-country and downhill skiing, business services. Pets allowed (fee). | 19221 Century Dr. 97702 | 541/382–4080 | $59–$99 | AE, D, DC, MC, V.

Best Inn & Suites. You can walk from here to a pub next door, restaurants, and all the bargains at Prime Outlets, and it's only five minutes to the High Desert Museum. There's a fireplace and complimentary coffee in the lobby at this friendly place, and the sauna is open 24 hours. The mural of a lake scene in the pool area was painted by a local artist. | 59 rooms, 6 suites. Complimentary breakfast, in-room data ports, some kitchenettes, some microwaves, some refrigerators, some in-room hot tubs, cable TV, pool, hot tub, sauna, gym, laundry facilities, laundry service, business services. Some pets allowed. | 61200 S. Hwy. 97 97702 | 541/388–2227 or 800/237–8466 | fax 541/388–8820 | $50–$59 | AE, D, DC, MC, V.

Cimarron Motor Inn—North. This late 1970s motel in central Bend has comfortable rooms with king-size beds. It is close to the downtown commercial area. | 60 rooms. Complimentary Continental breakfast, some microwaves, cable TV, pool, cross-country and downhill skiing, business services. Some pets allowed (fee). | 201 N.E. Third St. 97701 | 541/382–8282 or 800/304–4050 | fax 541/388–6833 | $45–$74 | AE, D, DC, MC, V.

Hampton Inn. You'll find contemporary rooms at this property set on three landscaped acres close to downtown Bend. | 99 rooms. Complimentary Continental breakfast, in-room data ports, cable TV, pool, hot tub, business services. Pets allowed. | 15 N.E. Butler Market Rd. 97701 | 541/388–4114 | fax 541/389–3261 | www.hamptoninn.com | $74–$89 | AE, D, DC, MC, V.

Red Lion Inn—North. This is a small two-story building with limited services, just 5 minutes walk from downtown. Red Lion's rooms are comfortable in a quiet area that caters to both families and businesspeople. | 75 rooms. Restaurant, in-room data ports, cable TV, pool, hot tub, business services. Pets allowed. | 1415 N.E. Third St. 97701 | 541/382–7011 | fax 541/382–7934 | $54–$79 | AE, D, DC, MC, V.

Riverhouse Motor Inn. Rooms at this motel on the Deschutes River are spacious with contemporary oak furniture. Some of the rooms have fireplaces while many have river views. It is a cut or two above what you'd expect given its very reasonable rates. | 220 rooms, 29 suites. Restaurant, in-room data ports, some kitchenettes, some microwaves, room service, cable TV, in-room VCRs (movies), 2 pools, driving range, 18-hole golf course, putting green, exercise equipment, laundry facilities, business services. Pets allowed. | 3075 N. U.S. 97 97701 | 541/389–3111 or 800/547–3928 | fax 541/389–0870 | $77–$209, $114–$209 suites | AE, D, DC, MC, V.

Shilo Inn Suites Hotel. On the Deschutes River and across from the Bend River Mall, this Shilo was recently remodeled. | 151 rooms. Bar, complimentary breakfast buffet, some kitchenettes, microwaves, refrigerators, cable TV, 2 pools, exercise equipment, cross-country and downhill skiing, laundry facilities, business services, airport shuttle. Pets allowed (fee). | 3105 O.B. Riley Rd. 97701 | 541/389–9600 | fax 541/382–4310 | $99–$139 | AE, D, DC, MC, V.

BURNS

Days Inn. This is the closest hotel to the downtown area. The two-story stucco building was built in 1959 and has a courtyard filled with trees and plants. | 52 rooms. Cable TV, pool, gym, business services. Pets allowed. | 577 W. Monroe 97720 | 541/573–2047 | fax 541/573–3828 | www.daysinn.com | $41–$85 | AE, D, DC, MC, V.

CANNON BEACH

Hallmark Resort. Large suites with fireplaces and great views make this triple-decker oceanfront resort a good choice for families or couples looking for a romantic splurge. The rooms, all with oak-tile baths, have soothing color schemes. The least expensive units do not have views. | 131 rooms, 63 suites; 4 cottages. Some kitchenettes, refrigerators, cable TV, some in-room hot tubs, 2 pools, hot tub, exercise equipment, laundry facilities, business services, airport shuttle. Pets allowed (fee). | 1400 S. Hemlock 97110 | 503/436–1566 or 800 888/448–4449 | fax 503/436–0324 | $174–$269 | AE, D, DC, MC, V.

Surfsand Resort. Many of the bright, modern rooms at this resort, within walking distance of downtown, have views of Haystack Rock and the Pacific Ocean; some are oceanfront. Many rooms have fireplaces. | 86 rooms; 5 cottages. Restaurant, bar, no air-conditioning, some kitchenettes, refrigerators, some in-room hot tubs, cable TV, in-room VCRs (movies), pool, hot tub, beach, laundry facilities, airport shuttle. Pets allowed (fee). | Ocean and Gower St. 97110 | 503/436–2274 or 800/547–6100 | fax 503/436–9116 | www.surfsand.com | $129–$309, $285–$375 cottages | AE, D, DC, MC, V.

CAVE JUNCTION

Country Hills Resort. A motel, cabins, camping in tents, and RV parking are all available at this resort 12 mi from the Oregon Caves. A golf course is nearby. | 11 rooms. Complimentary Continental breakfast, some kitchenettes, laundry facilities. Pets allowed. | 7901 Caves Hwy. 97523 | 541/592–3406 or 800/99–RVING | mike@crater-lake.com | $42–$59 | AE, D, MC, V.

COOS BAY

Red Lion Inn. This motel is on the bay, six blocks north of the city center and boardwalk. There is a putting green on the grounds. | 143 rooms. Restaurant, bar with entertainment, in-room data ports, room service, cable TV, pool, business services. Some pets allowed. | 1313 N. Bayshore Dr. 97420 | 541/267–4141 | fax 541/267–2884 | $65–$99 | AE, D, DC, MC, V.

CORVALLIS

Shanico Inn. This three-story quiet motel is 1 mi from downtown and close to the Oregon University campus. It's set on 1 acre of property with a picnic area and plenty of benches to sit on. The rooms are basic, but functional. | 76 rooms. Complimentary Continental breakfast, pool. Some pets allowed. | 1113 N.W. 9th St. 97330 | 541/754–7474 or 800/432–1233 | fax 541/754–2437 | shanicoinn@aol.com | $53–$60 | AE, D, DC, MC, V.

COTTAGE GROVE

Best Western Village Green. This chain hotel was originally built in the 1950s as a resort on 16 acres of property. Situated in a business area of Cottage Grove, it's a five-minute drive to downtown. It's close to the covered bridges and about 20 mi from Eugene. The rooms are clean and comfortable. | 96 rooms. Restaurant, bar, some refrigerators, cable TV, pool, hot tub, tennis, playground, laundry facilities, business services. Pets allowed. | 725 Row River Rd. 97424 | 541/942–2491 | fax 541/942–2386 | www.bestwestern.com | $69–$79 | AE, D, DC, MC, V.

Holiday Inn Express. Contemporary accommodations are available at this hotel just off the freeway. Built in 1993, it is right next door to a golf course. | 41 rooms. Pool, hot tub, coin laundry, tennis courts, laundry/valet, business services. Pets allowed (fee). | 1601 Gateway Blvd., 97424 | 541/942–1000 or 800/465–4329 | www.holidayinn.com | $68–$110 | AE, D, DC, MC, V.

DEPOE BAY
Surfrider Oceanfront Resort. There are six buildings on five landscaped acres, 2 mi from the center of Depoe Bay. Every room has an oceanfront deck and direct access to the beach. The resort is close to whale watching and you can enjoy bald eagles nesting within view of the lodging. | 50 rooms. Restaurant, bar, no air-conditioning, some kitchenettes, some in-room hot tubs, cable TV, pool, hot tub, airport shuttle. Pets allowed. | 3115 N.W. Highway 101 97341 | 541/764–2311 or 800/662–2378 | fax 541/764–2634 | stay@surfriderresort.com | www.surfriderresort.com | $80–$137 | AE, D, DC, MC, V.

EUGENE
Best Western New Oregon. The plush furnishings and comprehensive amenities at this midsize motel near the University of Oregon come as a bit of a surprise, given the property's price range. Some rooms overlook a creek. | 129 rooms. In-room data ports, refrigerators, cable TV, pool, hot tub, exercise equipment, laundry facilities, business services. Some pets allowed (fee). | 1655 Franklin Blvd., 97403 | 541/683–3669 | fax 541/484–5556 | neworegon@aol.com | $65–$125 | AE, D, DC, MC, V.

Campus Inn. Walk to shopping and Autzen Stadium from this hotel which is in the heart of downtown Eugene. The rooms are bright and clean. | 58 rooms. Complimentary Continental breakfast, in-room data ports, cable TV. Pets allowed (fee). | 390 E. Broadway 97401 | 541/343–3376 or 800/888–6313 | eugene@campus-inn.com | www.campus-inn.com | $62–$96 | AE, D, DC, MC, V.

Eugene Hilton. Location, amenities, and service make this downtown hotel Eugene's most convenient and comfortable. Sliding glass doors in each of the rooms open out to the city. The Hilton and its extensive convention facilities adjoin Eugene's Hult Center for the Performing Arts. Downtown shopping, the Willamette River, and more than 30 restaurants are within easy walking distance. | 272 rooms. Restaurant, bar with entertainment, some refrigerators, cable TV, pool, hot tub, exercise equipment, business services, airport shuttle. Some pets allowed (fee). | 66 E. Sixth Ave. 97401 | 541/342–2000 | fax 541/302–6660 | $100–$175 | AE, D, DC, MC, V.

Eugene Travelodge. This chain property is within walking distance of the University of Oregon campus and within 1 mi of Hult Center and downtown Eugene. | 60 rooms, 4 suites. Complimentary Continental breakfast, in-room data ports, refrigerators (in suites), cable TV, hot tub, sauna, business services. Some pets allowed. | 1859 Franklin Blvd. 97403 | 541/342–6383 | $51, $75 suites | AE, D, DC, MC, V.

Holiday Inn. Rooms at this chain motel 3 mi from downtown Eugene are plain but comfortable. | 58 rooms. Complimentary Continental breakfast, in-room data ports, cable TV, pool, exercise equipment, laundry facilities, business services. Pets allowed (fee). | 3480 Hutton St., Springfield 97477 | 541/746–8471 | fax 541/747–1541 | $70–$76 | AE, D, DC, MC, V.

Red Lion Inn. You'll find larger than standard rooms at this hotel, which is 3 mi from the Lane County Fairgrounds and across the street from a shopping center. | 137 rooms.

Restaurant, bar with entertainment, in-room data ports, room service, cable TV, pool, hot tub, exercise equipment, business services, airport shuttle. Some pets allowed. | 205 Coburg Rd. 97401 | 541/342–5201 | fax 541/485–2314 | $59–$110 | AE, D, DC, MC, V.

Shilo Inn. You'll find Shilo's consistently dependable, comfortable, cozy rooms at this location 3½ mi northeast of Eugene. It is right next to 3 golf courses and 3½ blocks from Gateway Mall. | 140 rooms. Restaurant, bar, complimentary Continental breakfast, some kitchenettes, some microwaves, room service, cable TV, pool, laundry facilities, business services, airport shuttle. Some pets allowed (fee). | 3350 Gateway St., Springfield 97477 | 541/747–0332 | fax 541/726–0587 | $89–$109 | AE, D, DC, MC, V.

★ **Valley River Inn.** Eugene's only four-star hotel, and one of only a few in the state of Oregon, is set on the picturesque bank of the Willamette River. Rooms have an outdoor patio or balcony, some have river or pool views. Concierge rooms on the third floor have access to a private lounge that serves a complimentary happy hour buffet with open bar. The Valley River Center, the largest shopping center between Portland and San Francisco, is across the parking lot. | 257 rooms. Restaurant, bar with entertainment, in-room data ports, room service, cable TV, pool, wading pool, hot tub, gym, business services, airport shuttle, free parking. Some pets allowed. | 1000 Valley River Way 97401 | 541/687–0123 or 800/543–8266 | fax 541/683–5121 | reserve@valleyriverinn.com | www.valleyriverinn.com | $150–$180 | AE, D, DC, MC, V.

FLORENCE

Money Saver. This two-story motel is 2 mi from the beach in a commercial neighborhood. | 40 rooms. No air-conditioning, cable TV. Some pets allowed (fee). | 170 U.S. 101 97439 | 541/997–7131 | $60–$80 | AE, D, MC, V.

GLENEDEN BEACH

Salishan. Nestled on a 700-acre hillside forest preserve on the Oregon coast, Salishan comprises multiple buildings connected by bridges and walkways. Views of the ocean, forest, and golf course are available and there is a self-guided nature trail. The rooms feature gas fireplaces and art work by Oregon artists. | 205 rooms. Restaurant, bar with entertainment, refrigerators, room service, cable TV, pool, hot tub, driving range, 18-hole golf course, putting green, tennis, gym, shops, library, business services. Some pets allowed (fee). | 7760 U.S. 101 97388 | 541/764–2371 or 800/452–2300 | fax 541/764–3681 | www.salishan.com | $249–$349 | AE, D, DC, MC, V.

GOLD BEACH

Shore Cliff Inn. The rooms are bright, but the decor is a bit dated. The inn is right on the beach and most rooms have oceanfront views. | 40 rooms. Some kitchenettes, cable TV. Pets allowed. | 29346 Ellensburg Ave. (U.S. 101) 97444 | 541/247–7091 | $50–$70 | AE, MC, V.

GRANTS PASS

Best Western Inn at the Rogue. Best Western's newer Grants Pass property is across from the Rogue River and has the relaxed feeling of a lodge. Fishing and white-water rafting are minutes away. Some rooms have river views. | 54 rooms. Bar, complimentary Continental breakfast, minibars, microwaves, some refrigerators, some in-room hot tubs, cable TV, pool, hot tub, exercise equipment, laundry facilities, business services. Some pets allowed (refundable fee). | 8959 Rogue River Hwy. 97527 | 541/582–2200 | fax 541/582–1415 | www.bestwestern.com | $85–$95 | AE, D, DC, MC, V.

Comfort Inn. It's only 1 mi to the Rogue River. | 59 rooms. Complimentary Continental breakfast, some refrigerators, cable TV, pool. Pets allowed. | 1889 N.E. Sixth St. 97526 | 541/479–8301 | fax 541/955–9721 | www.comfortinn.com | $40–$55 | AE, D, DC, MC, V.

Hawthorne Inn & Suites. This three-story hotel has some standard rooms and some with country-style quilts, light bed frames, and night stands. | 28 rooms, 31 suites. Complimentary breakfast, cable TV, some kitchenettes, pool, some hot tubs, sauna, air-conditioning. Pets allowed. | 243 N.E. Morgan La. 97526 | 541/472–1808 | $62–$78 | AE, D, DC, MC, V.

Holiday Inn Express. This four-story hotel is in a quiet neighborhood. It is very close to the Rogue River and within walking distance of restaurants and movie theaters. | 80 rooms. Complimentary Continental breakfast, in-room data ports, cable TV, pool, hot tub, laundry facilities, business services. Some pets allowed (fee). | 105 N.E. Agness Ave. 97526 | 541/471–6144 | fax 541/471–9248 | www.holiday-inn.com | $81–$91 | AE, D, DC, MC, V.

Redwood Motel. This motel is in a park-like setting that is filled with a wide variety of flora, which are all identified with markers. The rooms are bright and comfortable. | 28 rooms. Picnic area, complimentary Continental breakfast, some kitchenettes, some microwaves, some refrigerators, some in-room hot tubs, cable TV, pool, playground, laundry facilities. Some pets allowed (fee). | 815 N.E. Sixth St. 97526 | 541/476–0878 | fax 541/476–1032 | info@redwoodmotel.com | www.redwoodmotel.com | $66–$97 | AE, D, DC, MC, V.

Riverside Inn Resort and Conference Center. This large resort on the Rogue River covers three city blocks. The rooms are cozy and decorated with fabrics highlighting Pacific Northwest themes. Almost all rooms overlook the river. Hellgate Jetboat Excursions depart from a nearby dock May–Sept. | 174 rooms. Restaurant, bar, some in-room hot tubs, cable TV in-room, 2 pools, hot tubs, business services. Some pets allowed (fee). | 971 S.E. Sixth St. 97526 | 541/476–6873 or 800/334–4567 | fax 541/474–9848 | riverinn@budget.net | www.riverside-inn.com | $88–$98 | AE, D, DC, MC, V.

Royal Vue. Every room in this hotel, which is close to I–5, has a patio or a balcony. Restaurants and shopping are nearby. | 60 rooms. Restaurant, bar with entertainment, refrigerator, room service, cable TV, pool, hot tub, laundry facilities. Pets allowed. | 110 N.E. Morgan Lane 97526 | 541/479–5381 or 800/547–7555 (outside Oregon), 800/452–1452 | $48–$53 | AE, D, DC, MC, V.

Shilo Inn. This modern motel in a residential neighborhood, 2 mi from the city center and 3 mi from the Rogue River, provides comfortable convenient lodging. | 70 rooms. Continental breakfast, cable TV, pool. Pets allowed (fee). | 1880 N.W. Sixth St. 97526 | 541/479–8391 | fax 541/474–7344 | grantspass@shiloinns.com | $84–$105 | AE, D, DC, MC, V.

HERMISTON

Oxford Inn. Right in the center of town, this hotel is close to area restaurants and shops. The rooms are clean, basic, and inexpensive. | 90 rooms. Restaurant, complimentary Continental breakfast, some kitchenettes, pool. Pets allowed. | 655 N First 97838 | 541/567–7777 | fax 541/567–3085 | $42 | AE, D, DC, MC, V.

HOOD RIVER

Columbia Gorge Hotel. Situated next to the top of a waterfall overlooking the Columbia River Gorge, this small hotel in a restored 1920s building has a "jazz age" atmosphere and formal manicured gardens. There is windsurfing nearby. | 40 rooms. Restaurant, bar, complimentary Continental breakfast, no air-conditioning, cable TV, business services. Pets allowed. | 4000 Westcliff Dr. | 541/386–5566 or 800/345–1921 | fax 541/387–5414 | cghotel@gorge.net | www.columbiagorgehotel.com | $179–$279 | AE, D, DC, MC, V.

Inn of the White Salmon. This quiet, cozy, European-style two-story brick inn was built in 1937. It is filled with antiques and original art. | 16 rooms, 5 suites. Complimentary breakfast, hot tub. Pets allowed. | 172 W. Jewett, White Salmon, WA 98672 | 509/493–2335 or 800/972–5226 | innkeeper@gorge.net | www.innofthewhitesalmon.com | $99, $109–$129 suites | AE, D, DC, MC, V.

Vagabond Lodge. This motel is on five acres of quiet, wooded grounds at the edge of the Columbia River Gorge cliffs. The decor is simple. Most rooms have views of the river, some have fireplaces. Ponderosa pines tower 110 ft over the courtyard. | 42 rooms, 7 suites in 5 buildings. Picnic area, some kitchenettes, some in-room hot tubs, cable TV, playground. Pets allowed. | 4070 Westcliff Dr. | 541/386–2992 | fax 541/386–3317 | $52–$72, $85 suites | AE, DC, MC, V.

JACKSONVILLE

Jacksonville Inn. This small 1863 vintage inn is filled with period antiques. A block away are three larger and more luxurious cottages with fireplaces. | 8 rooms; 3 cottages. Restaurant, bar, complimentary breakfast, in-room data ports, microwaves, refrigerators, some in-room hot tubs, cable TV, shops, business services, airport shuttle. Some pets allowed (refundable fee). | 175 E. California St. | 541/899–1900 or 800/321–9344 (for reservations) | fax 541/899–1373 | www.jacksonvilleinn.com | $115–$150, $210–$245 cottages | AE, D, DC, MC, V.

Stage Lodge. In the heart of historic Jacksonville and close to the Britt Festival, this bed and breakfast is plush and modern with fireplaces in the rooms. | 27 rooms, 2 suites. Complimentary Continental breakfast, microwaves, some refrigerators, cable TV. Some pets allowed (fee). | 830 N. 5th St. | 541/899–3953 or 800/253–8254 | www.stagelodge.com | $65–$140, $125–$145 suites | AE, D, DC, MC, V.

JOHN DAY

Dreamers Lodge. This hotel in the center of town has the closest access to the John Day Fossil Beds. The rooms are homey, comfortable, and spacious. There is fishing and golf nearby. | 25 rooms. Refrigerators, cable TV, cross-country skiing, business services, airport shuttle. Pets allowed. | 144 N. Canyon Blvd. | 541/575–0526 or 800/654–2849 | fax 541/575–2733 | $46–$54 | AE, D, DC, MC, V.

KLAMATH FALLS

Best Western Klamath Inn. You will be staying right on Klamath Lake at this property, which is within 1 mi of the Jefferson Square Mall and only ¼ mi from the fairgrounds. The back of the inn has tables and chairs for outdoor relaxing. | 52 rooms. Complimentary Continental breakfast, in-room data ports, microwaves, refrigerators, some in-room hot tubs, cable TV, pool. Some pets allowed. | 4061 S. Sixth St. 97603 | 541/882–1200 | fax 541/882–2729 | www.bestwestern.com | $63–$68 | AE, D, DC, MC, V.

Cimarron Motor Inn. This is the largest lodging facility in Klamath Falls. It's near restaurants and shopping. | 163 rooms. Complimentary Continental breakfast, microwaves, refrigerators, cable TV, pool, business services. Pets allowed (fee). | 3060 S. Sixth St. 97603 | 541/882–4601 or 800/742–2648 | fax 541/882–6690 | $54–$64 | AE, D, DC, MC, V.

Quality Inn. This chain hotel is in city center and within walking distance to many area attractions. | 80 rooms, 4 suites. Complimentary Continental breakfast, in-room data ports, microwaves, some in-room hot tubs, cable TV, pool, laundry facilities, business services. Some pets allowed. | 100 Main St. 97601 | 541/882–4666 or 800/732–2025 | fax 541/883–8795 | $59–$60, $63–$79 suites | AE, D, DC, MC, V.

Shilo Inn Suites. This all-suites hotel overlooks the Cascades and Upper Klamath Lake. Most of the rooms have a view of the lake. It's 2 mi to the center of town. | 143 suites. Restaurant, bar, complimentary Continental breakfast, in-room data ports, room service, microwaves, refrigerators, cable TV, in-room VCRs (movies), pool, hot tub, gym, laundry facilities, business services, airport shuttle. Some pets allowed (fee). | 2500 Almond St. 97601 | 541/885–7980 | fax 541/885–7959 | $99–$125 suites | AE, D, DC, MC, V.

Super 8. This lodging is close to local restaurants. | 61 rooms. In-room data ports, cable TV, hot tub, laundry facilities. Pets allowed. | 3805 U.S. 97 N 97601 | 541/884–8880 | fax 541/884–0235 | $50–$67 | AE, D, DC, MC, V.

LA GRANDE

La Grande Howard Johnson. This hotel, 1 mi from downtown, is close to the university and area restaurants. It is also within a one-hour drive of all area parks and recreation facilities. | 146 rooms. Refrigerators, complimentary Continental breakfast, in-room data ports, cable TV, pool, hot tub, gym, laundry facilities, business services. Pets allowed. | 2612 Island Ave. 97850 | 541/963–7195 | fax 541/963–4498 | $67–$77 | AE, D, DC, MC, V.

LAKE OSWEGO

Crowne Plaza. Rooms are modern with all the amenities. There is a complimentary van service within a 5-mi radius. | 161 rooms. Restaurant, bar, room service. Pool, hot tub, exercise equipment, business services, free parking. Pets allowed. | 14811 S.W. Kruse Oaks Blvd. 97035 | 503/624–8400 | fax 503/684–8324 | thecrowne@aol.com | www.crowneplaza.com | $154–$280 | AE, D, DC, MC, V.

Residence Inn by Marriott—South. This all-suites property is within walking distance of neighborhood restaurants. The units all have fireplaces and full kitchens. | 112 suites. Picnic area, complimentary Continental breakfast, cable TV, pool, hot tub, laundry facilities, business services. Pets allowed (fee). | 15200 S.W. Bangy Rd., Lake Oswego 97035 | 503/684–2603 | fax 503/620–6712 | $120–$175 suites | AE, D, DC, MC, V.

LAKEVIEW

Lakeview Lodge Motel. Basic accommodations are to be found in this secluded area surrounded by hills and mountains. The rooms have beautiful views of the mountains. | 40 rooms. Cable TV, hot tub, exercise equipment, cross-country and downhill skiing. Pets allowed. | 301 North G St. 97630 | 541/947–2181 | fax 541/947–2572 | bobkings@triax.com | $44–$50 | AE, D, DC, MC, V.

LINCOLN CITY

Coho Inn. Close to the center of the city, in a residential neighborhood, all the rooms overlook the ocean. | 50 rooms. No air-conditioning, some kitchenettes, cable TV, hot tub, business services. Some pets allowed (fee). | 1635 N.W. Harbor Ave. 97367 | 541/994–3684 or 800/848–7006 | fax 541/994–6244 | $107–$177 | AE, D, MC, V.

Shilo Inn—Oceanfront Resort. This beachfront motel is very popular because of its convenient location next door to the Chinook Winds Casino. The room are furnished simply, but the newer building has suites with fireplaces and ocean views. | 247 rooms. Bar, picnic area, some kitchenettes, some microwaves, some refrigerators, room service, cable TV, pool, hot tub, exercise equipment, laundry facilities, business services, airport shuttle. Some pets allowed (fee). | 1501 N.W. 40th Place 97367 | 541/994–3655 | fax 541/994–2199 | $125–$169 | AE, D, DC, MC, V.

MADRAS

Sonny's. This medium-size motel has basic accommodations. It is on the highway, about 12 mi from the lake and water ski resort areas. | 44 rooms, 2 suites. Restaurant, bar, complimentary Continental breakfast, some microwaves, some in-room hot tubs, pool, hot tub, laundry facilities, business services. Pets allowed (fee). | 1539 S.W. U.S. 97 | 541/475–7217 or 800/624–6137 | fax 541/475–6547 | www.sonnysmotel.com | $55–$58, $90–$110 suites | AE, D, DC, MC, V.

MAUPIN

Oasis Resort. The small cabins are very basic at this property on the south side of the river. They also operate rafting excursions and a river shuttle. | 11 cabins. Restaurant, rafting, swimming, fishing. Pets allowed. | 609 Hwy. 197 | 541/395–2611 | www.deschutesriveroasis. com | $35–69 | MC, V.

MCMINNVILLE

★ **Flying M Ranch.** Decorated in a style best described as Daniel Boone eclectic, the log lodge is the centerpiece of the 625-acre Flying M Ranch, perched above the steelhead-filled Yamhill River. Choose between somewhat austere cabins (the cozy Honeymoon Cabin is the nicest) or riverside hotel units. | 28 rooms in lodge; 8 cabins. Bar with entertainment, dining room, picnic area, some kitchenettes, some in-room hot tubs, some room phones, no TV in some rooms, TV in common area, pond, tennis, hiking, horseback riding, fishing, cross-country skiing, snowmobiling, laundry facilities, business services. Pets allowed. | 23029 N.W. Flying M Rd., Yamhill 97148 | 503/662–3222 | fax 503/662–3202 | $60, $85–$200 cabins | AE, D, DC, MC, V.

Paragon. This motel is located near the Spruce Goose Museum and a golf course. | 55 rooms. Complimentary Continental breakfast, refrigerators, cable TV, pool, laundry facilities, business services. Pets allowed (fee). No smoking. | 2065 S. Rte. 99 W | 503/472–9493 or 800/525–5469 | fax 503/472–8470 | $45–$57 | AE, D, DC, MC, V.

MEDFORD

Best Inn. This no-frills hotel is less than ½ mi from Highway 5 and has two meeting rooms. | 112 rooms. Complimentary Continental breakfast, coin laundry, exercise equipment, pool, cable TV, air-conditioning. Some pets allowed. | 1015 S. Riverside Dr. 97501 | 541/773–8266 | $75–$102 | AE, D, DC, MC, V.

Best Western Pony Soldier. Rooms at this motel face the pool. | 74 rooms. Complimentary Continental breakfast, in-room data ports, microwaves, refrigerators, cable TV, pool, hot tub, cross-country and downhill skiing, laundry facilities, airport shuttle. Some pets allowed. | 2340 Crater Lake Hwy. 97504 | 541/779–2011 or 800/634–7669 | fax 541/779–7304 | $85–$95 | AE, D, DC, MC, V.

Cedar Lodge Motor Inn. This centrally located motor inn is two blocks from the movie theater and within walking distance of restaurants. | 79 rooms. Bar, complimentary Continental breakfast, some microwaves, refrigerators, cable TV, pool, cross-country and downhill skiing. Some pets allowed. | 518 N. Riverside Ave. 97501 | 541/773–7361 or 800/ 282–3419 | fax 541/776–1033 | www.oregonfishing.com | $40–$45 | AE, D, DC, MC, V.

Horizon Motor Inn. This large motel is close to shopping as well as downhill and cross-country skiing. | 129 rooms. Restaurant, bar, some microwaves, cable TV, pool, hot tub, airport shuttle. Pets allowed (fee). | 1154 E.Barnett Rd. 97504 | 541/779–5085 or 800/452–2255 | www.horizoninns.com | $79–$145 | AE, DC, MC, V.

Red Lion Inn. Right in downtown Medford, this popular chain hotel is close to local entertainment and 1 mi from the closest shopping mall. | 186 rooms. Restaurant, bar with entertainment, dining room, in-room data ports, room service, cable TV, 2 pools, cross-country and downhill skiing, laundry facilities, business services, airport shuttle. Pets allowed (fee). | 200 N. Riverside Ave. 97501 | 541/779–5811 | fax 541/779–7961 | $79–$89. | AE, D, DC, MC, V.

Reston Hotel. This is a business hotel with 10,000 square ft of meeting, exhibit, and banquet space. The rooms are comfortable and spacious. It is only ½ mi to local shopping and restaurants. | 164 rooms. Restaurant, bar, cable TV, pool, business services, airport shuttle. Some pets allowed (fee). | 2300 Crater Lake Hwy. 97504 | 541/779–3141 or 800/779–7829 | fax 541/779–2623 | sales@restonhotel.com | www.restonhotel.com | $72 | AE, D, DC, MC, V.

Rogue River Guest House. The wide front porch of the 1890s farmhouse 12 mi north of town looks out to fir, catalpa, and holly trees. This is one of the few bed and breakfasts that welcome children, and business travelers will find a small office at their disposal. | 3 rooms. Complimentary breakfast, cable TV in some rooms, business services. No in-room phones. Pets allowed. | 41 Rogue River Hwy., Gold Hill 97525 | 541/855–4485, 877/764–8322 | $100–$150.

Windmill Inn. Rooms at this pleasant inn are plush and comfortable. Complimentary hot beverage, juice, muffin, and newspaper are delivered to your door in the morning. | 123 rooms. Complimentary Continental breakfast, cable TV, pool, hot tub, bicycles, library, business services, airport shuttle. Pets allowed. | 1950 Biddle Rd. 97504 | 541/779–0050 or 800/547–4747 | www.windmillinns.com | $84 | AE, D, DC, MC, V.

MOUNT HOOD NATIONAL FOREST

Mt. Hood Inn. The Mount Hood National Forest is right outside the east windows of this comfortable contemporary inn. Rooms facing the southwest have a remarkable view of the Ski Bowl, which is just across the street. Accommodations come in various sizes, from spacious standards to king-size suites. Among the amenities are complimentary ski lockers and a ski tuning room. | 56 rooms, 4 suites. Picnic area, complimentary Continental breakfast, some refrigerators, some in-room hot tubs, cable TV, hot tub, cross-country and downhill skiing, laundry facilities, business services. Pets allowed (fee). | Box 400, Government Camp Loop, Government Camp 97028 | 503/272–3205 or 800/443–7777 | fax 503/272–3307 | $129–$159, $154–$164 suites | AE, D, DC, MC, V.

NEWBERG

Shilo Inn. In the heart of the wine country, this all-minisuites property looks out into the commercial neighborhood from the front, while the rooms in back overlook a quiet residential neighborhood. | 60 rooms. Complimentary Continental breakfast, microwaves, refrigerators, pool, hot tub, exercise equipment, laundry facilities, business services, airport shuttle. Pets allowed (fee). | 501 Sitka Ave. 97132 | 503/537–0303 | fax 503/537–0442 | $69–$79 | AE, D, DC, MC, V.

NEWPORT

Shilo Inn Ocean Front Resort. On a bluff overlooking the beach, this resort is 2 mi from the center of downtown Newport. | 179 rooms. Restaurant, bar with entertainment, some kitchenettes, microwaves, refrigerators, in-room VCRs, room service, 2 pools, beach, laundry facilities, business services, airport shuttle. Some pets allowed (fee). | 536 S.W. Elizabeth St. 97365 | 541/265–7701 | fax 541/265–5687 | $145–$199 | AE, D, DC, MC, V.

Whaler. All rooms at this motel have ocean views; some have fireplaces. Set in a residential area across from the city park and the beach, it's a short walk to the Yaquina Bay Lighthouse. | 73 rooms. Complimentary Continental breakfast, some microwaves, some refrigerators, cable TV, laundry facilities, airport shuttle. Some pets allowed. | 155 S.W. Elizabeth St. 97465 | 541/265–9261 or 800/433–9444 | fax 541/265–9515 | $95–$105 | AE, D, DC, MC, V.

NORTH BEND

Bay Bridge. This small motel is on Pacific Bay with views of the bay. The rooms are simple and basic. | 16 rooms. Some kitchenettes, some refrigerators, cable TV. Some pets allowed (fee). | 33 U.S. 101 97459 | 541/756–3151 or 800/557–3156 | $39–$65 | AE, D, DC, MC, V.

ONTARIO

Best Western Inn and Suites. This inn is right on the freeway, near the Snake River and close to area shopping. The rooms are typical of Best Western style—they are comfortable and spacious. | 61 rooms, 12 suites. Complimentary Continental breakfast, some minibars, refrigerators (in suites), cable TV, pool, hot tub, exercise equipment, laundry facilities. Some pets allowed (fee). | 251 Goodfellow St. 97914 | 541/889–2600 | fax 541/889–2259 | www.bestwestern.com | $56–$76, $95–$165 suites | AE, D, DC, MC, V.

Holiday Motel. The basic budget accommodations here are convenient to restaurants and fishing. It is five blocks from the Snake River. | 72 rooms. Restaurant, cable TV, pool, business services. Pets allowed. | 615 E. Idaho Ave. 97914 | 541/889–9188 | fax 541/889–4303 | $38–$59 | AE, D, DC, MC, V.

OREGON CITY

Rivershore Hotel. All rooms overlook the Willamette River and have decks with patio furniture. It is close to shopping and restaurants. | 120 rooms. Restaurant, bar, room service, cable TV, pool, hot tub. Some pets allowed (fee). | 1900 Clackamette Dr. 97045 | 503/655–7141 or 800/443–7777 | fax 503/655–1927 | $54–$142 | AE, D, DC, MC, V.

PACIFIC CITY

Inn at Cape Kiwanda. All the rooms at this three-story inn built in 1998 on the Three Capes Scenic Loop have gas fireplaces, minibars, and a view of the ocean. | 35 rooms. Exercise room, coin laundry, data ports. Pets allowed. No smoking. | 33105 Cape Kiwanda Drive, 97135 | 503/965–7001 | fax 503/965–7002 | www.innatcapekiwanda.com | $99–$219, suites $199–$279 | AE, D, DC, MC, V.

Inn at Pacific City. Walk to the beach and restaurants from this ground-level inn on the Nestucca River. | 16 rooms. Kitchettes with microwaves, refrigerators. Pets allowed (fee). | 35215 Brooten Road, Box 1000, 97135 | 503/965–6366 or 888/722–2489 | fax 503/965–6812 | $37–$69, suites $59–$95 | AE, D, DC, MC, V.

PENDLETON

Chaparral. Affordable accommodations 1 mi from downtown, this lodging is visible from the highway and in front of the Pendleton Forest Service. | 51 rooms. Some kitchenettes, cable TV. Pets allowed (fee). | S.W. 620 Tutuilla Rd. 97801 | 541/276–8654 | fax 541/276–5808 | $36–$57 | AE, D, DC, MC, V.

Tapadera Inn. This centrally located inn, convenient to shopping and restaurants, has basic, affordable rooms. | 47 rooms. Restaurant, bar, room service, cable TV, pool, hot tub, business services. Pets allowed (fee). | 105 S.E. Court Ave. 97128 | 541/276–3231 or 800/722–8277 | fax 541/276–0754 | $41–$63 | AE, D, DC, MC, V.

PORTLAND

5th Avenue Suites. The 1912 Lipman Wolfe Department Store building reopened as a boutique hotel in 1997. It is designed to look like a turn-of-the-20th-century, American country home. A tall vestibule with a marble mosaic floor leads to the art-filled lobby. Curtained sliding doors divide the 10-story property's 550-square-ft suites. The large bathrooms are stocked with every amenity. | 221 rooms, 139 suites. Restaurant, bar, complimentary Continental breakfast, in-room data ports, refrigerators, cable TV, in-room VCRs (movies), exercise equipment, business services. Some pets allowed. | 506 S.W. Washington 97206 | 503/222–0001 or 800/711–2971 | fax 503/222–0004 | $160–$180, $180–$275 suites | AE, D, DC, MC, V.

The Benson. Portland's grandest hotel was built in 1912. The hand-carved Russian Circassian walnut paneling and the Italian white-marble staircase are among the noteworthy design touches in the public areas. In the guest rooms expect to find small crystal chandeliers, inlaid mahogany doors, and the original ceilings. | 286 rooms, 44 suites. Restaurant, bar with entertainment, in-room data ports, minibars, room service, cable TV, exercise equipment, business services, airport shuttle. Pets allowed (fee). | 309 S.W.

Broadway 97205 | 503/471–3920 | fax 503/226–4603 | $140–$225, $199–$275 suites | AE, D, DC, MC, V.

Days Inn—North. Set in a commercial neighborhood, this inn is convenient to the Expo Center and the Portland International Raceway. Many rooms have views of Mt. Hood. | 213 rooms. Complimentary Continental breakfast, in-room data ports, cable TV, laundry facilities, business services, airport shuttle. Pets allowed (fee). | 9930 N. Whitaker Rd. 97217 | 503/289–1800 or 800/833–1800 | fax 503/289–3778 | $65–$85 | AE, D, DC, MC, V.

Doubletree—Columbia River. On Hayden Island between Portland and Vancouver, Wash., this Doubletree is convenient to downtown and the airport. Rooms are decorated in earth tones and many have riverfront views. | 351 rooms. Restaurants, bars with entertainment, in-room data ports, some refrigerators, room service, some in-room hot tubs, cable TV, pool, beauty salon, putting green, business services, airport shuttle. Pets allowed (fee). | 1401 N. Hayden Island Dr. 97217 | 503/283–2111 | fax 503/283–4718 | $109–$139 | AE, D, DC, MC, V.

Doubletree—Jantzen Beach. On the banks of the Columbia River, there is a beautiful rose garden around the pool. | 320 rooms. Restaurant, bar with entertainment, room service, some in-room hot tubs, cable TV, pool, hot tub, tennis, exercise equipment, dock, business services, airport shuttle. Pets allowed (fee). | 909 N. Hayden Island Dr. 97217 | 503/283–4466 | fax 503/283–4743 | $119–$129 | AE, D, DC, MC, V.

★ **Doubletree—Lloyd Center.** This busy, well-appointed, business-oriented hotel maintains a huge traffic in meetings and special events. The public areas are a tasteful mix of marble, rose-and-green carpet, and antique-style furnishings. The large rooms have views of the mountains or the city center. Lloyd Center and the MAX light rail are across the street; the Oregon Convention Center is a five-minute walk away. | 382 rooms, 17 suites. Restaurant, bar with entertainment, refrigerators, some in-room hot tubs, cable TV, pool, exercise equipment, business services, airport shuttle. Pets allowed. | 1000 N.E. Multnomah St. 97232 | 503/281–6111 | fax 503/284–8553 | $139–$149, $269–$575 suites | AE, D, DC, MC, V.

Imperial Hotel. This restored downtown hotel preserves its historic charm with a lobby that has the original columns and moldings dating from 1908. There is some antique furniture in the lobby; however, the rooms are standard. It's conveniently located near restaurants, entertainment, and the MAX light rail. The Typhoon! Thai restaurant is off the lobby. | 136 rooms. Restaurant, in-room data ports, cable TV. Pets allowed (fee). | 400 S.W. Broadway 97205 | 503/228–7221 or 800/452–2323 | fax 503/223–4551 | $85–$125 | AE, D, DC, MC, V.

Hawthorne Inn and Suites This hotel is close to the airport and restaurants. | 71 rooms, 23 suites. Complimentary Continental breakfast, in-room data ports, some refrigerators, cable TV, pool, hot tub, exercise equipment, laundry facilities, business services. Some pets allowed. | 2323 N.E. 181st Ave. Gresham 97230 | 503/492–4000 | fax 503/492–3271 | $73–$83, $90–$130 suites | AE, D, DC, MC, V.

Mallory Hotel. The years have been kind to this 1920s-vintage hotel eight blocks from the downtown core. Its gilt-ceiling lobby has fresh white paint and floral carpeting; crystal chandeliers and a leaded-glass skylight hark back to a more genteel era. The rooms are old-fashioned but clean and cheerful and have been refurbished; corner suites and rooms on the east side of the building have impressive skyline views. The staff is friendly and knowledgeable. | 131 rooms, 10 suites. Restaurant, bar, some refrigerators, cable TV, business services. Pets allowed (fee). | 729 S.W. 15th Ave. 97205 | 503/223–6311 or 800/228–8657 | fax 503/223–0522 | $75–$140, $140 suites | AE, D, DC, MC, V.

Mark Spencer. Located near Portland's gay bar district and Powell's City of Books, the world's largest bookstore, the Mark Spencer offers one of the best values in town. The rooms are clean and comfortable. It's also near the MAX light rail and Jake's seafood restaurant. There is a rooftop garden. | 101 rooms. Complimentary Continental breakfast, kitchenettes, cable TV, laundry facilities, business services. Pets allowed (fee). | 409 S.W. 11th Ave. 97205 | 503/224–3293 or 800/548–3934 | fax 503/223–7848 | mspencer@ipinc.net | www.markspencer.com | $79–$129 | AE, D, DC, MC, V.

Marriott. The large rooms here are decorated in off-whites; the best ones look east to the Willamette and the Cascades. Champions Lounge, filled with sports memorabilia, is a singles' hot spot on weekends. It's near the MAX light rail. | 503 rooms. Restaurant, bar with entertainment, some, refrigerators, cable TV, pool, hot tub, exercise equipment, laundry facilities, business services. Pets allowed. | 1401 S.W. Naito Pkwy. 97201 | 503/226–7600 | fax 503/221–1789 | www.marriott.com | $114–$159 | AE, D, DC, MC, V.

Riverplace. This luxury resort is right on the Portland waterfront. The hotel, which has a decidedly European feel, overlooks the marina and the surrounding Riverplace neighborhood. All the rooms have beautiful wood paneling and some have fireplaces. | 84 rooms, 16 suites. Restaurant, bar with entertainment, complimentary Continental breakfast, in-room data ports, minibars, some refrigerators, room service, cable TV, hot tub, shops, business services. Parking (fee). Some pets allowed (fee). | 1510 S.W. Harbor Way 97201 | 503/228–3233 or 800/227–1333 | fax 503/295–6161 | www.riverplacehotel.com | $219, $219–$499 suites | AE, D, DC, MC, V.

Sheraton Four Points. This hotel is decorated in a classic European style and is conveniently located downtown, close to shopping and restaurants. Guests receive complimentary access to a nearby health club. | 139 rooms, 1 suite. Restaurant, bar, room service, business services, parking (fee). Some pets allowed (fee). | 50 S.W. Morrison St. 97204 | 503/221–0711 or 800/899–0247 | fax 503/274–0312 | $90–$170, $200–$250 suite | AE, D, DC, MC, V.

Shilo Inn—Washington Square. This motel just south of Portland is next to Washington Square Mall. The rooms are modern and have in-room first-run movies. | 77 rooms. Complimentary Continental breakfast, some kitchenettes, cable TV, exercise equipment, laundry facilities, business services. Pets allowed (fee). | 10830 S.W. Greenburg Rd., Tigard 97223 | 503/620–4320 | fax 503/620–8277 | $69–$89 | AE, D, DC, MC, V.

Super 8. An inexpensive option if you need to stay on the far south side of the metropolitan area. | 72 rooms. Cable TV, laundry facilities, business services. Pets allowed (fee). | 25438 S.W. Parkway Ave., Wilsonville 97070 | 503/682–2088 | fax 503/682–0453 | $43–$61 | AE, D, DC, MC, V.

Sweetbrier Inn. This inn is approximately 10 mi south of Portland. The large rooms feature traditional-style furniture and have views of a garden with tall firs. | 100 rooms, 32 suites. Restaurant, bar with entertainment, picnic area, in-room data ports, refrigerators (in suites), room service, cable TV, pool, playground, business services. Pets allowed (fee). | 7125 S.W. Nyberg, Tualatin 97062 | 503/692–5800 or 800/551–9167 | fax 503/691–2894 | www.sweetbrierinn.com | $75–$115, $120 suites | AE, D, DC, MC, V.

REDMOND

Redmond Inn. Nearby outdoor activities include horseback riding, skiing, fishing, swimming, and golf or if you prefer to stay closer to home there is a patio by the pool. Just three blocks from the center of town, this inn is convenient to both restaurants and sights. | 46 rooms. Complimentary Continental breakfast, kitchenettes, microwaves, refrigerators, cable TV, pool. Some pets allowed (fee). | 1545 U.S. 97 S 97756 | 541/548–1091 or 800/833–3259 | $40–$57 | AE, D, DC, MC, V.

REEDSPORT

Anchor Bay Inn. Right in the center of Reedsport, this motel has easy access to the dunes. Elk viewing is only 4 mi away. | 21 rooms. Complimentary Continental breakfast, some kitchenettes, some microwaves, some cable TV, pool, laundry facilities, business services. Some pets allowed (fee). | 1821 Winchester Ave. 97467 | 541/271–2149 or 800/767–1821 | fax 541/271–1802 | anchorbay@presys.com | $55–$69 | AE, D, MC, V.

Best Western Salbasgeon Inn. This chain property is a few feet away from the tranquil Schoelfield River, yet close to area shopping and dining. Some of the immaculately kept rooms have river views and fireplaces. | 56 rooms, 9 suites. Complimentary Continental breakfast, some kitchenettes, minibars, refrigerators, cable TV, pool, hot tub, exercise equipment, laundry facilities, business services. Pets allowed (fee). | 1400 Highway Ave. 97467 | 541/271–4831 | fax 541/271–4832 | $79–$88, $75–$125 suites | AE, D, DC, MC, V.

Salbasgeon Inn of the Umpqua. In the heart of fishing country, this inn takes its name from salmon, striped bass, and sturgeon. It overlooks the Umpqua River and all rooms have river views. | 12 rooms. Picnic area, some kitchenettes, cable TV, putting green. Some pets allowed (fee). | 45209 Rte. 38 97467 | 541/271–2025 | Redel@salbasgeon.com | www.inn-net.com/umpqua.htm | $68–$98 | AE, D, DC, MC, V.

ROSEBURG

Best Western Garden Villa. This Best Western is next to Garden Valley Shopping Center and 6 mi from Wildlife Safari. There is a walking trail just across the street. | 122 rooms. Complimentary Continental breakfast, cable TV, pool, exercise equipment, laundry facilities. Some pets allowed. | 760 N.W. Garden Valley Blvd. 97470 | 541/672–1601 | fax 541/672–1316 | $69–$89 | AE, D, DC, MC, V.

Windmill Inn. Rooms at this pleasant inn are plush and comfortable. Complimentary hot beverage, juice, muffin, and newspaper are delivered to your door in the morning. | 128 rooms. Restaurant, bar, complimentary Continental breakfast, in-room data ports, cable TV, pool, hot tub, exercise equipment, laundry facilities, business services, airport shuttle, free parking. Some pets allowed. | 1450 Mulholland Dr. 97470 | 541/673–0901 or 800/547–4747 | www.windmillinns.com | $70–$90 | AE, D, DC, MC, V.

SALEM

Phoenix Inn. This quiet all-suites hotel is just 5 mi from downtown Salem. | 89 suites. Complimentary Continental breakfast, refrigerators, some in-room hot tubs, cable TV, pool, hot tub, exercise equipment, laundry facilities, business services. Some pets allowed (fee). | 4370 Commercial St. SE 97302 | 503/588–9220 or 800/445–4498 | fax 503/585–3616 | $69–$79 suites | AE, D, DC, MC, V.

Red Lion Inn—Salem. The chief virtue of this clean, functional hotel is its location, about five minutes from the Capitol. | 150 rooms. Restaurant, bar with entertainment, room service, cable TV, pool, hot tub, exercise equipment, laundry facilities, business services, free parking. Pets allowed (fee). | 3301 Market St. 97301 | 503/370–7888 | fax 503/370–6305 | $72–$89 | AE, D, DC, MC, V.

Tiki Lodge. This inexpensive motel has simple rooms and is located near a golf course. | 50 rooms (20 with shower only). Cable TV, pool, playground, business services. Pets allowed. | 3705 Market St. 97301 | 503/581–4441 | fax 503/581–4442 | $33–$49 | AE, D, DC, MC, V.

SEASIDE

Best Western Ocean View Resort. Many rooms at this motel on the beach have ocean-view rooms. | 104 rooms, 20 suites. Restaurant, bar, no air-conditioning, in-room data ports, some kitchenettes, some refrigerators, room service, pool, hot tub, laundry facilities, business services. Some pets allowed (fee). | 414 N. Promenade 97138 | 503/738–3334 | fax 503/738–3264 | $70–$99, $160–$325 suites | AE, D, DC, MC, V.

Convention Center Inn. Two-bedroom suites are available at this motel on the Necanicum River a few blocks from the Promenade. | 48 rooms. Complimentary Continental breakfast, some kitchenettes, some refrigerators, cable TV, pool, hot tub, laundry facilities, business services. Pets allowed (fee). | 441 2nd Ave. | 503/738–9581 or 800/699–5070 | fax 503/738–3212 | $99–$149 | AE, D, DC, MC, V.

THE DALLES

Lone Pine Village. This property on the Columbia River has simple, comfortable rooms and is right on the eastern edge of town, next to I–84. Many rooms have views of the river. | 57 rooms. Bar, complimentary Continental breakfast, microwaves, refrigerators, some in-room hot tubs, pool, hot tub, driving range, exercise equipment, laundry facilities, business services, airport shuttle. Some pets allowed (fee). | 351 Lone Pine Dr. 97058 | 541/298–2800 or 800/955–9626 | fax 541/298–8282 | $67–$78 | AE, D, DC, MC, V.

Quality Inn. This chain motel is close to shopping and 2 mi from downtown. The rooms are standard but comfortable and placed in three buildings. Cousin's Restaurant is located here. | 85 rooms. Restaurant, in-room data ports, some kitchenettes, cable TV, pool, hot tub, laundry facilities, business services. Pets allowed (fee). | 2114 W. 6th St. 97058 | 541/298–5161 | fax 541/298–6411 | $60–$73 | AE, D, DC, MC, V.

TILLAMOOK

Marclair Inn. This family-owned hotel is set on a landscaped garden abloom with flowers. It is located 2½ miles from the Air Museum and within walking distance of restaurants. | 47 rooms. Restaurant, some kitchenettes, hot tub, pool. Pets allowed. | 11 Main Ave. 97141 | 503/842–7571 or 800/331–6857 | $60–$103 | AE, D, MC, V.

Shilo Inn. Shilo's Tillamook outpost is less than 1 mi from the Tillamook Cheese Factory and close to shopping. The rooms are standard for this chain. One suite is a full-size apartment. | 101 rooms. Complimentary full breakfast, some kitchenettes, restaurant, refrigerators, cable TV, pool, hot tub, exercise equipment, laundry facilities, business services. Some pets allowed (fee). | 2515 N. Main St. 97112 | 503/842–7971 | fax 503/842–7960 | $89–$129 | AE, D, DC, MC, V.

TROUTDALE

Phoenix Inn—Troutdale. This all-minisuites motel near the mouth of the Columbia River Gorge has rooms with pretty views of the garden. | 73 rooms. Bar, complimentary Continental breakfast, cable TV, pool, hot tub, exercise equipment, business services, airport shuttle. Pets allowed (fee). | 477 N.W. Phoenix Dr. 97060. | 503/669–6500 or 800/824–6824 | fax 503/669–3500 | $61–$75 | AE, D, DC, MC, V.

WARM SPRINGS

Kah-Nee Tah. Located in a remote desert spot in the middle of the Warm Springs Reservation, Kah-Nee Ta is perfect for a quick getaway from Portland. In addition to the hotel and casino, which has 300 slots, blackjack, and poker, there's also an RV park and Spa Wanapine, which offers aromatherapy, massage, reflexology, facials, and manicures. Mineral hot springs bubbling up from the desert floor fill baths and pools. If you like to rough it, check into one of the wood-frame, canvas-covered, unfurnished tepees. Kayak float trips can be arranged. | 139 rooms in lodge, 31 apartments, 20 tepees. Bars, dining room, some in-room hot tubs, cable TV, 2 pools, hot tubs, spa, driving range, 18-hole golf course, putting green, tennis, gym, hiking, boating, bicycles, video game room. Pets allowed. | 100 Main St. 97761 | 541/553–1112 or 800/554–4786 | fax 541/553–1071 | $129–$219, $229–$259 apartments, $70 tepees | AE, D, DC, MC, V.

YACHATS

Adobe Motel. The knotty-pine rooms in this unassuming resort motel on the ocean are on the small side, but are warm and inviting. High-beam ceilings and picture windows frame majestic views. Many of the rooms have wood-burning fireplaces. | 84 rooms, 10 suites. Restaurant, bar, some kitchenettes, refrigerators, in-room hot tubs (in suites), cable TV, in-room VCRs, hot tub, exercise equipment, business services. Some pets allowed (fee). | 1555 U.S. 101 97498 | 541/547–3141 or 800/522–3623 (western U.S.) | fax 541/547–4234 | $58–$75, $150–$175 suites | AE, D, DC, MC, V.

Fireside Motel. The west building faces the ocean and every room has a spectacular view. Some units have gas fireplaces. | 43 rooms; 3 cottages. Refrigerators, some in-room hot tubs, cable TV. Some pets allowed (fee). | 1881 U.S. 101 N 97498 | 541/547–3636 or 800/336–3573 | fax 541/547–3152 | $50–$95, $115 cottages | D, MC, V.

Shamrock Lodgettes. This property is on the beach. The quarters here are mostly individual log cabins, although there are some buildings with more than one unit. The grounds are beautifully and elaborately landscaped; some people come just to walk through the gardens. All rooms have ocean or Yachats River views. | 19 rooms, 11 cottages. Kitchenettes (in cottages), refrigerators, some in-room hot tubs, cable TV. Some pets allowed (fee). | 105 Highway 101 97498 | 541/547–3312 or 800/845–5028 | fax 541/547–3843 | www.beachesbeaches.com | $75–$100, $99–$118 cottages | AE, D, DC, MC, V.

Pennsylvania

ALLENTOWN

Allenwood. Built in 1962 out of cinder block and wood, this small motel in west Allentown is 2 mi from Dorney Park. It is one story high with outside room entrances and some studio units. Microwaves, refrigerators. Cable TV. Some pets allowed. | 1058 Hausman Rd. 18104 | 610/395–3707 | fax 610/530–8166 | 21 rooms | $50–$120 | AE, D, MC, V.

Holiday Inn Express. Completely renovated in 1999, this relatively small hotel was built in 1980 and is in the heart of downtown. It has four stories with interior corridors and it's only 8 mi from Dorney Park. Complimentary Continental breakfast. In-room data ports. Cable TV. Business services. Some pets allowed (fee). | 1715 Plaza La. 18103 | 610/435–7880 | fax 610/432–2555 | www.humphreyhospitality.com | 82 rooms | $79–$110 | AE, D, DC, MC, V.

Howard Johnson Inn and Suites. This hotel is on a busy commercial strip, close to local highways. It was built in 1989 and has two floors with interior corridors and elevators. Complimentary breakfast. Indoor pool. Hot tub. Some pets allowed ($30 deposit). | 3220 Hamilton Blvd. 18103 | 610/439–4000 | fax 610/438–8947 | www.hojo.com | 58 rooms | $62–$140 | AE, D, DC, MC, V.

Sheraton Inn Jetport. This full-service, three-story hotel is next to the airport in the Lehigh Valley Industrial Park, about 5 mi from both Allentown and Bethlehem. Restaurant, bar (with entertainment), room service. In-room data ports. Cable TV. Indoor pool. Hot tub, sauna. Exercise equipment. Business services, airport shuttle. Some pets allowed. | 3400 Airport Rd. 18103 | 610/266–1000 | fax 610/251–5717 | www.sheraton.com | 147 rooms, 30 suites | $99–$119, $119–$145 suites | AE, D, DC, MC, V.

ALTOONA

Motel 6. Large rooms have king and queen beds at a reasonable price. This one-story motel was built in 1987 and is only 7 mi from Horseshoe Curve. Outdoor pool. Laundry facilities. Pets allowed (no fee). | 155 Sterling St. 16602 | 814/946–7601 | fax 814/946–5162 | www.motel6.com | 112 rooms | $50–$55 | AE, D, DC, MC, V.

Ramada. The only full-service hotel in town, this three-story chain hotel offers ski packages to Blue Knob Ski Area (20 mi southwest of town). It is only 2 mi from downtown, 3 mi from the Railroader's Memorial Museum, and 10 mi from Horseshoe Curve. 3 Restaurants, bar, complimentary Continental breakfast, room service. In-room data ports. Cable TV. Indoor pool, wading pool. Hot tub. Gym. Business services, airport shuttle. Some pets allowed. | 1 Sheraton Dr. 16601 | 814/946–1631 | fax 814/946–0785 | www.ramada.com | 215 rooms | $75–$90 | AE, D, DC, MC, V.

BEAVER FALLS

Conley's Motor Inn. Just off Exit 2 of the Pennsylvania Turnpike, this two-story, budget motel is 3 mi outside of Beaver Falls. You're just a 20-mi drive away from Pittsburgh. Restaurant, bar. Some kitchenettes, refrigerators. Cable TV. Spa. Business services. Some pets allowed. | 7099 Rte. 18 15010 | 724/843–9300 or 800/345–6819 | fax 724/843–9039 | 58 rooms in 2 buildings | $55–$60 | AE, D, DC, MC, V.

Holiday Inn. Only 4 mi from downtown Beaver Falls, this midpriced, two-story chain hotel is near Exit 2 of the Pennsylvania Turnpike. It is 18 mi from New Castle and within 5 mi of Geneva College. Restaurant, bar, room service. In-room data ports. Indoor pool. Hot tub, sauna. Video games. Business services. Some pets allowed. | 7195 Eastwood Rd. 15010 | 724/846–3700 | fax 724/846–7008 | www.crownamericanhotels.com | 156 rooms | $89–$104 | AE, D, DC, MC, V.

BEDFORD

Best Western Bedford Inn. Only 3 mi from Old Bedford Village and downtown Bedford, this medium-sized, full-service motel is near Exit 11 of the Pennsylvania Turnpike. The one-story building is designed around a central courtyard. Rooms are in both a one- and two-story building. Restaurant, bar. Cable TV. Pool. Exercise equipment. Video games. Some pets allowed (fee). | 4517 Business 220 15522 | 814/623–9006 | fax 814/623–7120 | www.bestwestern.com/best.html | 105 rooms in 2 buildings | $54–$65 | AE, D, DC, MC, V.

Econolodge. Built in the late 1960s, this relatively modern, two-story motel has interior corridors and is 2 mi from Old Bedford Village and 25 mi from Blue Knob Ski Resort. A small, budget motel that's easily accessible from Exit 11 of the Pennsylvania Turnpike. Bar. Cable TV. Some pets allowed. | 141 Hillcrest Dr. 15522 | 814/623–5174 | fax 814/623–5455 | www.econolodge.com/hotel/pa182 | 32 rooms | $42–$65 | AE, D, DC, MC, V.

Quality Inn. Less than ½ mi from Old Bedford Village, this reasonably priced motel is near fishing in Blue Knob State Park (15-min drive), golfing, and 20 mi from Blue Knob Ski Resort. The two-story inn with interior corridors underwent a major renovation in 1990. Restaurant, bar. Cable TV. Pool. Business services. Some pets allowed. | 4407 Business Rte. 220, 15522 | 814/623–5188 | fax 814/623–0049 | www.qualityinn.com | 66 rooms, 2 suites in 3 buildings | $60–$69, $80 suites | AE, D, DC, MC, V.

BETHLEHEM

Comfort Inn. A standard, budget-oriented motel just off U.S. 22. Built in 1984, this two-story inn with interior corridors is 6 mi north of downtown Bethlehem. Bar (with entertainment), complimentary Continental breakfast. Cable TV, in-room VCRs (and movies). Business services, free parking. Some pets allowed. | 3191 Highfield Dr. 18020 | 610/865–6300 | fax 610/865–5074 | www.comfortinnbethlehem.com | 116 rooms | $75–$95 | AE, D, DC, MC, V.

BLOOMSBURG

Econo Lodge at Bloomsburg. This motel sits on the edge of a mall parking lot that also connects to a truck stop at Rte. 80. Cable TV. Business services. Pets allowed ($10). | 189 Columbia Mall Dr. 17815 | 570/387–0490 | fax 570/387–0893 | www.econolodge.com | 80 | $65–$119 | AE, D, DC, MC, V.

Inn at Turkey Hill. Built in 1839, this homestead has elegant rooms and pretty, landscaped grounds. The privately owned home was turned into an inn in 1984 and includes a gazebo and pond. It is 5 mi south of downtown Bloomsburg. Bar, dining room, complimentary breakfast, room service. In-room data ports, some in-room hot tubs. Cable TV. Business services, airport shuttle. Some pets allowed (fee). | 991 Central Rd. 17815 | 570/387–1500 | fax 570/784–3718 | www.innatturkeyhill.com | 23 rooms, 2 suites | $95–$100, $150–$190 suites | AE, D, DC, MC, V.

Inn of Buckhorn. Just off Exit 34 of I–80, right near Columbia Mall, this moderately sized, two-story hotel is about 2 mi from the middle of downtown Bloomsburg. Bar. Business services. Some pets allowed. | 5 Buckhorn Rd. 17815 | 570/784–5300 | fax 570/387–0367 | www.pavisnet.com/innatbuckhorn | 120 rooms in 2 buildings | $55–$68 | AE, D, DC, MC, V.

Magee's Main Street. Originally built in 1855 and purchased by James Magee in 1911, this small, two story hotel is right in the heart of downtown Bloomsburg, 1 mi from the Bloomsburg Fairgrounds. Bar, dining room, complimentary breakfast. Cable TV. Business services. Some pets allowed. | 20 W. Main St. 17815 | 570/784–3200 or 800/331–9815 | fax 570/784–5517 | www.magees.com | 43 rooms, 5 suites | $70–$90, $84 suites | AE, D, DC, MC, V.

BREEZEWOOD

Ramada Inn. A full-service, two-story hotel that was remodeled in 1981. It is in the scenic mountains of south central Pennsylvania, giving you easy access to many outdoor activities year-round. Restaurant, bar, picnic area, room service. In-room data ports. Cable TV. Indoor pool. Hot tub, sauna. Exercise equipment. Playground. Business services. Some pets allowed. | 16602 Lincoln Hwy. 15533 | 814/735–4005 | fax 814/735–3228 | www.bedford.net/ramada | 125 rooms, 6 suites | $49–$89, $129–$169 suites | AE, D, DC, MC, V.

Wiltshire Motel. Popular because of the low prices, often traveling workers live here. No on-premise facilities, but the owner will point out the local laundromat or store. Some pets allowed. | 140 Breezewood Rd. 15533 | 814/735–4361 | 12 | $41–$44 | AE, D, MC, V.

BROOKVILLE

Days Inn. Off Exit 13 of I–80, this affordable, three story motel is 16 mi from Cook Forest State Park, but only 1 mi from historic Brookville. Bar. Cable TV. Pool. Spa. Video games. Laundry facilities. Business services. Some pets allowed. | 230 Allegheny Blvd. 15825 | 814/849–8001 | fax 814/849–9647 | www.daysinn.com | 124 rooms | $50–$70 | AE, D, DC, MC, V.

Golden Eagle Inn. This budget hotel has some unique style with its wooden paneling and white-wash walls. A short drive into town, or to the Cook Forest State Park. 1 restaurant. Complimentary Continental breakfast. Some pets allowed. | 250 W. Main St. 15825 | 814/849–7344 | fax 814/849–7345 | budgethost.com | 29 | $34–$60 | AE, D, MC, V.

Holiday Inn Express. Only 1 mi from historic Brookville, this budget chain hotel is near Exit 13 of I–80 and it's only 30 mi to the Smicksburg Amish community. Originally built in 1969, this three-story hotel was renovated 2 years ago. It has an interior corridor but no elevators. Complimentary Continental breakfast. Cable TV. Laundry facilities. Business services. Some pets allowed (fee). | 235 Allegheny Blvd. 15825 | 814/849–8381 | fax 814/849–8386 | www.basshotels.com/hiexpress | 68 rooms, 2 suites | $60–$75, $89–$99 suites | AE, D, DC, MC, V.

CAMP HILL

Radisson Penn Harris. Constructed in the late 1960s but furnished in a Colonial style, this two-story chain hotel is 1 mi from downtown Camp Hill. It's also about 5 mi from Exit 17 of the Pennsylvania Turnpike, 20 mi west of Hershey, and 40 mi from Gettysburg. Restaurant, bar, room service. In-room data ports. Cable TV. Pool. Exercise equipment. Business services, airport shuttle, free parking. Some pets allowed. | 1150 Camp Hill Bypass 17011 | 717/763–7117 or 800/333–3333 | fax 717/763–4518 | www.radisson.com | 250 rooms, 6 suites | $89–$135, $195–$395 suites | AE, D, DC, MC, V.

CANADENSIS

Merry Inn. When proprietor Chris Huggard suggested the name for this inn he did not know that, as a child, his wife Meredyth was known as Merry. The name, and the irony, has become part of the legend of this blue-and-white inn in the Pocono Mountains. Full breakfast. Cable TV, in-room VCR. Hot tub. Some pets allowed. No smoking. | Rte. 390 18325; I–80 to exit 52 which will put you on 447. Follow 447 to 390 | 570/595–2011 or 800/858–4182 | Merryinn@ezaccess | www.pbcomputerconsulting.com/themerryinn | 6 rooms | $95 | MC, V.

CARLISLE

Clarion Hotel and Convention Center. A full-service, one-story hotel that was renovated in 1999. It's about 4 mi from downtown and Dickinson College and 2 mi to Carlisle Barracks. Restaurant, bar, room service. In-room data ports, refrigerators, cable TV. Indoor pool, wading pool. Hot tub, sauna. Exercise equipment. Business services, airport shuttle, free parking. Some pets allowed. | 1700 Harrisburg Pike/U.S. 11 17013 | 717/243–1717 or 800/692–7315 | fax 717/243–6648 | sales@clarioncarlisle.com | 273 rooms | $75–$85 | AE, D, DC, MC, V.

Holiday Inn. Built in 1983, this moderately priced, two-story chain hotel is at Exit 17 of I–81. It's about 2 mi from downtown Carlisle, the Carlisle Fairgrounds, and the Army War College. Restaurant, bar, room service. In-room data ports, cable TV. Pool. Gym. Laundry facilities. Business services, free parking. Some pets allowed. | 1450 Harrisburg Pike/U.S. 11 17103 | 717/245–2400 | fax 717/245–9070 | www.lodgingincarlisle.com | 100 rooms | $89–$99 | AE, D, DC, MC, V.

Pheasant Field. This Federal redbrick farmhouse, built in 1800, across the street from a three-acre pond, used to be on a pheasant farm (the present owners are hoping to re-introduce the birds to the area). Its summer kitchen, once separate because of heat and in case of fire, has a hiding place that was used for the underground railroad. Full breakfast. Cable TV, room phones. Some pets allowed. No kids under 8. No smoking. | 150 Hickorytown Rd. 17013 | 717/258–717 or 877/258–0717 | fax 717/258–0717 | pheasant@pa.net | www.pheasantfield.com/ | 5 rooms | $85–110 | AE, MC, V.

Quality Inn. An affordable, two-story motel with interior corridors is at Exit 17 of I–81. It's close to the Carlisle Fairgrounds, Dickinson University, and the Army War College. It is 4 mi from downtown Carlisle and about 30 mi from Gettysburg and Hershey. Bar, complimentary Continental breakfast. Cable TV. Pool, wading pool. Laundry facilities. Business services, free parking. Some pets allowed. | 1255 Harrisburg Pike/U.S. 11 17013 | 717/243–6000 | fax 717/258–4123 | www.qualityinn.com | 96 rooms | $65–$125 | AE, D, DC, MC, V.

CHADDS FORD

Brandywine River Hotel. This small, two-story hotel was built in 1985 and has a Victorian interior, including some rooms with fireplaces. It is close to the Art History Museum and Gardens, right in downtown Chadds Ford. Complimentary Continental breakfast. Refrigerators (in suites). Cable TV. Exercise equipment. Shops. Business services. Some pets allowed. | Routes 1 and 100 19317 | 610/388–1200 | fax 610/388–1200 | www.virtualcities.com/pa/brh.htm | 40 rooms, 10 suites, 1 cottage | $125–$169, $149–$169 suites | AE, D, DC, MC, V.

Pennsbury Inn. Originally built in 1714 this inn, on land purchased from William Penn's commissioners, was later enlarged by a stone and brick addition and later still with a clapboard extension. Visitors claim to have seen the ghost of Joseph Lancaster, the first innkeeper, around the coachmen's quarters and there is a trap door entrance to the basement hiding a stop on the underground railroad. Full breakfast. In-room data ports. Cable TV, room phones. Library. Some pets allowed. No kids under 12. No smoking. | 883 Baltimore Pike 19317 | 610/388–1435 | fax 610/388–1436 | www.bbchannel.com/bbc/ph601510.asp | 7 rooms | $150–225 | AE, DC, MC, V.

CHAMBERSBURG

Days Inn. An affordable, three-story motel that is at Exit 6 of I–81. Built in 1984, it's less than 2 mi from downtown with Whitetail Ski Resort less than 25 mi away. Complimentary Continental breakfast. Cable TV. Some pets allowed. | 30 Falling Spring Rd. 17201 | 717/263–1288 | fax 717/263–6514 | www.daysinn.com | 99 rooms | $55–$70 | AE, D, DC, MC, V.

Penn National Inn. The Federal-style manor house, built around 1850, provides Georgian period charm, but most guest rooms are in a 1989 addition. It's only 10 mi southeast of Chambersburg. Restaurant, complimentary breakfast. Refrigerators. Cable TV. Pool. Driving range, 18-hole golf course, putting green, tennis courts. Playground. Some pets allowed. | 3809 Anthony Hwy., Mont Alto 17237 | 717/352–2400 or 800/231–0080 | fax 717/352–3926 | www.penngolf.com | 40 rooms in 2 buildings | $100–$120 | AE, D, MC, V.

Quality Inn. This full-service hotel is near Exit 5 of I–81. The two-story building was built in 1984 and is 5 mi north of downtown Chambersburg. Restaurant, bar, room service. Some in-room data ports. Cable TV. Pool. Exercise equipment. Business services, free parking. Some pets allowed. | 1095 Wayne Ave. 17201 | 717/263–3400 | fax 717/263–8386 | www.qualityinn.com | 139 rooms, 32 suites | $70–$75, $97 suites | AE, D, DC, MC, V.

Travelodge. Only 1 mi from downtown Chambersburg, this afforable, three-story motel at Exit 6 of I–81 was built in 1964 and all of its rooms were remodeled in 2000. It is within 25 mi of Gettysburg and 33 mi of Carlisle. Restaurant, bar, room service. Cable TV. Some pets allowed. | 565 Lincoln Way East/U.S. 30 17201 | 717/264–4187 | fax 717/264–2446 | www.travelodge.com | 49 rooms | $55–$65 | AE, D, DC, MC, V.

CLARION

Days Inn. A full-service hotel with two floors and interior corridors. It is at Exit 9N of I–80. Built in 1983, this hotel is 22 mi from Cook Forest State Park and only 1 mi from downtown Clarion. Restaurant, bar (with entertainment), complimentary Continental breakfast, room service. Cable TV. Pool. Laundry facilities. Business services. Some pets allowed. | Rte. 68 and I–80 16214 | 814/226–8682 | fax 814/226–8372 | www.daysinn.com | 150 rooms, 1 suite | $60–$70, $100 suite | AE, D, DC, MC, V.

Super 8. This midpriced motel is near Exit 9 of I–80. Its rooms are all on one floor with exterior corridors. It's only 1 mi from downtown and 22 mi from Cook Forest State Park. Complimentary Continental breakfast. In-room data ports, some kitchenettes. Cable TV. Outdoor pool. Some pets allowed. | Rte. 3 at Rte. 68 16214 | 814/226–4550 | fax 814/227–2337 | www.super8.com | 99 rooms, 2 suites | $60–$66, $150 suites | AE, D, DC, MC, V.

CLEARFIELD

Christopher Kratzer House. The oldest house in Clearfield, built in 1828, this yellow with green shutters classic Revival mansion is full of antiques and artwork by co-owner Ginny Baggett. There are views of the river and park. The house has white picket fences, a big yard, and large old trees. It is near shops, a public library, restaurants, a movie theater, and the Clearfield County Historical Museum. The B&B is 3 mi south of I–80. Full breakfast. Cable TV, room phones. Some pets allowed. | 101 E. Cherry St. 16830 | 814/765–5024 or 888/252–2632 | fax / | bbagget@uplink.net | www.virtualcities.com/pa/kratzerhouse.htm | 3 rooms, 2 with bath | $65–85 | D, MC, V.

Days Inn. An affordable chain motel near Exit 19 of I–80, 2 mi from downtown Clearfield and less than 5 mi from Moshannon State Forest. The two-story building with interior corridors was built in the late 70s. There are shopping outlets less than a mile away. Bar, complimentary Continental breakfast. In-room data ports. Pool. Exercise equipment. Business services. Some pets allowed. | R.R. 1 16830 | 814/765–5381 | fax 814/765–7885 | www.daysinn.com | 118 rooms, 4 suites | $55–$85, $65–$95 suites | AE, D, DC, MC, V.

CONNELLSVILLE

Melody Motor Lodge. A one-story motel with exterior corridors has some of the lowest rates in the region. It's only 4 mi from downtown and 15 mi from Fallingwater. Bar, picnic area. Cable TV. Some pets allowed. | 1607 Morrell Ave./U.S. 119 15425 | 724/628–9600 | 46 rooms | $40–$50 | AE, D, MC, V.

CORAOPOLIS

Clarion-Royce. Only 16 mi from downtown Coraopolis, this upscale, nine-story hotel is 5 mi from the airport and 10 mi to downtown Pittsburgh. Restaurant, bar (with entertainment). In-room data ports. Cable TV. Pool. Exercise equipment. Business services, airport shuttle. Some pets allowed. | 1160 Thorn Run Rd. Ext. 15108 | 412/262–2400 | fax 412/264–9373. www.lodgian.com | 193 rooms | $79–$149 | AE, D, DC, MC, V.

Embassy Suites. A waterfall and river run through the center atrium of this hotel within the Cherrington Corporate Center and next to Pittsburgh International Airport. Restaurant, bar, complimentary breakfast. Cable TV, in-room VCRs. Indoor pool. Hot tub, sauna. Gym. Shops. Laundry facilities, laundry service. Business services, airport shuttle. Pets allowed. | 550 Cherrington Pkwy. | 412/269–9070 or 800/EMBASSY | fax 412/262–4119 | www.embassy-suites.com | 223 suites | $109–$189 | AE, D, DC, MC, V.

Hampton Inn–Northwest. You can take advantage of the affordable rates at this five-story chain motel, 13 mi from downtown Coraopolis. It's 13 mi northwest of Pittsburgh's Golden Triangle and 7 mi from the airport. Complimentary Continental breakfast. Cable TV. Business services, airport shuttle, free parking. Some pets allowed. | 1420 Beers School Rd. 15108 | 412/264–0020 | fax 412/264–3220 | www.hamptoninn.com | 129 rooms | $69–$79 | AE, D, DC, MC, V.

La Quinta. Another affordable three-story chain motel, 2 mi from downtown Coraopolis. It's 7.5 mi to the airport, 15 mi to downtown Pittsburgh, and a short drive to two malls. Complimentary Continental breakfast. In-room data ports. Cable TV. Pool. Exercise equipment. Laundry facilities. Business services, airport shuttle, free parking. Some pets allowed. | 1433 Beers School Rd. 15108 | 412/269–0400 | fax 412/269–9258. www.laquinta.com | 128 rooms | $69–$89 | AE, D, DC, MC, V.

Pittsburgh Airport Marriott. It's the tallest building in the area, with views of the Ohio River from its 14 floors. This upscale, full-service hotel is 5 mi from downtown Coraopolis and 7 mi from the airport. Restaurant, bar. In-room data ports, some refrigerators. Cable TV. Indoor-outdoor pool. Hot tub, sauna. Exercise equipment. Business services, airport shuttle. Some pets allowed. | 777 Aten Rd. 15108 | 412/788–8800 | fax 412/788–6299. www.marriott.com | 314 rooms | $89–$179 | AE, D, DC, MC, V.

Red Roof Inn. Convenient to the airport (4 mi), this 3-story motel has reasonable rates. It's also within 5 mi of three golf courses: Montour Heights, Bon Air, and Scally's. Cable TV. Laundry facilities. Business services, airport shuttle, free parking. Some pets allowed. | 1454 Beers School Rd. 15108 | 412/264–5678 | fax 412/264–8034 | www.redroof. com | 119 rooms | $47–$63 | AE, D, DC, MC, V.

DENVER

Black Horse Lodge. Five two- and single-story buildings stand on 10 acres of landscaped property only 3 mi from Denver. This full-service hotel, built in 1959, is at Exit 21 of the Pennsylvania Turnpike and its rooms were remodeled many times since. Restaurant, bar, picnic area, complimentary breakfast. Some refrigerators. Cable TV. Pool. Playground. Laundry facilities. Business services. Some pets allowed. | 2180 N. Reading Rd., Denver 17517 | 717/336–7563 | fax 717/336–1110. www.blackhorselodge.com | 74 rooms | $79–$189 | AE, D, DC, MC, V.

DOWNINGTOWN

Best Western–Exton Hotel and Conference Center. Only 4 mi from town, this hotel is off U.S. Highway 30, in the center of Chester County. Built in the 1970s, the 5-story hotel is less than 5 mi from Marsh Creek State Park and 15 mi from Valley Forge National Historic Park. Restaurant, bar (with entertainment), picnic area, room service. In-room data ports, refrigerators, cable TV. 2 pools. Laundry facilities. Business services, airport shuttle, free parking. Pets allowed. | 815 N. Pottstown Pike, Exton 19341 | 610/363–1100 | fax 610/524–2329 | www.bestwestern.com | 225 rooms | $99–$109 | AE, D, DC, MC, V.

DOYLESTOWN

Best Western. Full-service, 3-story hotel at Exit 31 of the Northeast Extension of the Pennsylvania Turnpike for convenient access to Philadelphia. Built in 1975, it's 15 mi to Doylestown's Mercer Mile. Restaurant, bar (with entertainment), room service. In-room data ports, cable TV. Pool. Exercise equipment. Business services, airport shuttle, free parking. Pets allowed. | 1750 Sumneytown Pike, Kulpsville 19443 | 215/368–3800 | fax 215/368–7824 | www.bestwestern.com | 183 rooms | $89–$99 | AE, D, DC, MC, V.

DU BOIS

Holiday Inn. At Exit 16 of I–80, this midpriced, 2-story chain hotel is 5 mi to Du Bois Mall and 4 mi to downtown. Restaurant, bar, room service. In-room data ports, cable TV. Pool, wading pool. Laundry facilities. Business services, airport shuttle. Pets allowed. | Rte. 219 and I–80 15801 | 814/371–5100 | fax 814/375–0230 | www.holiday-inn.com | 160 rooms | $80–$90 | AE, D, DC, MC, V.

Ramada Inn. A large lobby with a fireplace highlights this midpriced, 3-story chain hotel. Built in 1973, this hotel is off Exit 17 of I–80. Restaurant, bar (with entertainment), room service. Cable TV. Indoor pool. Business services, airport shuttle. Pets allowed. | Rte. 255 N and I–80 15801 | 814/371–7070 | fax 814/371–1055 | www.ramada.com | 96 rooms | $65–$80 | AE, D, DC, MC, V.

ERIE

Vineyard Bed and Breakfast. You can watch beautiful sunsets over Lake Erie from this farmhouse, built in 1900 and remodeled into a bed and breakfast in 1993. Rooms have private baths. Complimentary breakfast. Pets allowed. | 10757 Sidehill Rd. 16428 | 814/725–5307 or 888/725–8998 | www.lakeside.net/vineyardbb | 5 rooms | $65–$75 | AE, D, MC, V.

GETTYSBURG

Home Sweet Home Motel. You can walk to the Battlefield Visitors Center from this motel or take advantage of its free shuttle service. Complimentary Continental breakfast. Cable TV, room phones. Some pets allowed (fee). | 593 Steinwehr Ave. 17325 | 717/334–3916 or 800/440–3916 | 40 rooms | $65 | AE, D, MC, V.

GREENSBURG

Four Points by Sheraton. This hotel is near Exit 7 of the Pennsylvania Turnpike. Restaurant, bar with entertainment. Some refrigerators, cable TV. Indoor pool. Gym, volleyball. Business services, airport shuttle. Pets allowed (fee). | 100 Sheraton Dr./U.S. 30 E 15601 | 724/836–6060 | fax 724/834–5640 | www.sheraton.com | 146 rooms | $80–$95 | AE, D, DC, MC, V.

HARMONY

Zelienople Motel. About ¼ mi out of town on 6 acres of open land, this old brick ranch-style motel offers quiet and simple lodging. There's a creek on the property. Cable TV. Pets allowed (fee). | 238 Perry Hwy. 16037 | 724/452–7900 | fax 724/452–7900 | 27 rooms | $40–$60 | AE, D, DC, MC, V.

HARRISBURG

Baymont Inn. Midway betwen Harrisburg and Hershey, this hotel is 12 mi from Hershey Park Chocolate World and outlets and 8 mi from Penn National Race Track. Rooms have cream colored walls, with dark green drapes and spreads. Restaurants within 1 mi. Complimentary Continental breakfast. In-room data ports, some microwaves, some refrigerators, cable TV. Laundry facilities. Business services. Pets allowed. | 200 N. Mountain Rd. 17112 | 717/540–9339 | fax 717/540–9486 | www.baymontinn.com | 67 rooms | $75–$85 | AE, D, DC, MC, V.

Best Western Harrisburg–Hershey Hotel and Suites. This hotel is near Exit 26B of I–81, between Harrisburg and Hershey. It is near downtown Harrisburg and the center of Hershey. Restaurant, bar. In-room data ports, some refrigerators, some microwaves, cable TV. Indoor pool. Hot tub, sauna. Exercise equipment. Laundry facilities. Business services. Pets allowed. | 300 N. Mountain Rd. 17112 | 717/652–7180 | fax 717/541–8991 | www.bestwestern.com | 101 rooms | $89–$95 | AE, D, DC, MC, V.

Comfort Inn. You receive complimentary passes to a nearby gym and all rooms have coffee makers and irons at this hotel near Exit 29 of I–83. Complimentary Continental breakfast. Some microwaves, some refrigerators, cable TV. Outdoor pool. Laundry facilities. Business services, airport shuttle. Pets allowed. | 4021 Union Deposit Rd. 17109 | 717/561–8100 | fax 717/561–1357 | www.comfortinn.com | 115 rooms | $89–$119 | AE, D, DC, MC, V.

Holiday Inn. This chain hotel is near Harrisburg Airport and downtown Harrisburg. Restaurant, bar (with entertainment), picnic area, room service. In-room data ports, some microwaves, some refrigerators, cable TV. Indoor pool. Hot tub. Exercise equipment. Video games. Laundry facilities. Business services, airport shuttle, free parking. Pets allowed (fee). | 148 Sheraton Dr., New Cumberland 17070 | 717/774–2721 | fax 717/774–2485 | www.holiday-inn.com | 196 rooms | $109–$129 | AE, D, DC, MC, V.

Marriott. This hotel at I–283/83 and Route 441 is a 10-min drive to downtown. Restaurant, bar (with entertainment), complimentary Continental breakfast, room service. In-room data ports, cable TV. Indoor-outdoor pool. Hot tub. Exercise equipment. Video games. Laundry service. Business services, airport shuttle, free parking. Pets allowed ($50 fee). | 4650 Lindle Rd. 17111 | 717/564–5511 | fax 717/564–6173 | www.marriott.com | 348 rooms | $90–$169 | AE, D, DC, MC, V.

Red Roof Inn. This midsize motel is near downtown and 15 mi from Hershey. In-room data ports, cable TV. Pets allowed. | 400 Corporate Circle 17110 | 717/657–1445 | fax 717/657–2775 | www.redroof.com | 110 rooms | $55–$70 | AE, D, DC, MC, V.

Wyndham Garden. You can get freshly baked cookies, coffee, and a newspaper in your room, and even a choice of foam or feather pillows at this downtown hotel near Exit 1 of I–283/83, 9 mi from Hershey. Restaurant, bar, room service. In-room data ports, some microwaves, some refrigerators, cable TV. Pool. Hot tub, sauna. Exercise equipment. Laundry facilities, laundry service. Business services, airport shuttle, free parking. Pets allowed. | 765 Eisenhower Blvd. 17111 | 717/558–9500 | fax 717/558–8956 | www.travelweb.com | 167 rooms | $99–$129 | AE, D, DC, MC, V.

HAZLETON

Ramada Inn. You can see a spectacular view of Hazelton from this motel, less than a mile from downtown and close to ski resorts and golf courses. Restaurant, bar, room service. In-room data ports, cable TV. Pool. Business services. Laundry services. Pets allowed. | Rte. 309 18201 | 570/455–2061 | fax 570/455–9387 | 107 rooms | $65–$70 | AE, D, DC, MC, V.

HERSHEY

Holiday Inn Harrisburg-Hershey. Near Hershey Park and Penn Down Race Track, and 10 mi from downtown Harrisburg, this modern stucco hotel is designed to accommodate families and business travelers. Restaurant, bar (with entertainment), room service. In-room data ports, cable TV. 2 pools, wading pool. Hot tub. Exercise equipment. Shops. Laundry facilities. Business services, airport shuttle, free parking. Pets allowed. | 604 Station Rd., Grantville 17028 | 717/469–0661 | fax 717/469–7755 | info@stayholiday.com | www. stayholiday.com | 195 rooms | $139–$199 | AE, D, DC, MC, V.

HUNTINGDON

Huntingdon Motor Inn. In a quiet residential neighborhood, this two-story brick motel is a short car ride from most Huntingdon attractions. Bar. In-room data ports, cable TV. Gym. Business services. Pets allowed. | Junction of Rte. 22 and 26, Rd. #1 16652 | fax 814/643–1331 | www.huntingdon.net/lodging.htm | 48 rooms | $50–$65 | AE, D, DC, MC, V.

INDIANA

Best Western University Inn. One mile from Indiana University's campus and the Jimmy Stewart Museum and birthplace, this Best Western is 5 mi from several golf courses, downtown shops, two local malls, and 9 mi from Yellow Creek State Park. Restaurant, bar, room service. In-room data ports, cable TV. Pool. Pets allowed ($15 fee). | 1545 Wayne Ave. 15701 | 724/349–9620 | fax 724/349–2620 | www.bestwestern.com | 107 rooms | $70–$80 | AE, D, DC, MC, V.

Holiday Inn. A modern two-story stucco building, this hotel is 1 mi from downtown and a short drive from the Jimmy Stewart Museum, Indiana University of Pennsylvania, Challenger Raceway, Yellow Creek State Park, Blue Spruce County Park, Saltsburg Canal, Smicksburg Amish Village, Windgate Vineyards, Indiana Mall, and Punxsutawney. Restaurant, bar (with entertainment), complimentary breakfast, room service. In-room data ports, cable TV. Indoor pool. Hot tub, sauna. Miniature golf. Business services. Pets allowed. | 1395 Wayne Ave. 15701 | 724/463–3561 | fax 724/463–8006 | 159 rooms | $89–$99 | AE, D, DC, MC, V.

JOHNSTOWN

Comfort Inn. The Johnstown Flood Museum is 5.2 mi northwest of this two-story stucco motel. Picnic area, complimentary Continental breakfast. In-room data ports, refrigerators, cable TV, in-room VCRs (and movies). Indoor pool. Hot tub. Exercise equipment. Laundry facilities. Business services, airport shuttle. Pets allowed (fee). | 455 Theatre Dr. 15904 | 814/266–3678 | fax 814/266–9783 | www.comfortinn.com | 117 rooms, 27 suites | $65–$70, $95 suites | AE, D, DC, MC, V.

Holiday Inn–Downtown. This six-story hotel made of mostly brick is downtown and within walking distance of the central park, Cambria County Community College, shopping, the Johnstown Flood Museum, and Inclined Plane Railway. Restaurant, bar. In-room data ports, cable TV. Indoor pool. Hot tub, sauna. Exercise equipment. Business services, airport shuttle. Pets allowed. | 250 Market St. 15901 | 814/535–7777 | fax 814/539–1393 | www.holidayinn.com | 164 rooms | $82–$99 | AE, D, DC, MC, V.

Sleep Inn. In the business district, this three-story motel is 5 mi northwest of the Johnstown Flood Museum. Complimentary Continental breakfast. In-room data ports, cable TV. Business services, airport shuttle. Pets allowed (fee). | 453 Theatre Dr. 15904 | 814/262–9292 | fax 814/262–0486 | www.sleepinn.com | 62 rooms (59 with shower only) | $60–$65 | AE, D, DC, MC, V.

Towne Manor Motel. Built in the 1940s, this two-story downtown motel is next to a park, a stadium, and the Inclined Plane Railway. Different sizes of rooms and suites are available, with some for a family of four. Complimentary Continental breakfast. Cable TV. Pets allowed. | 155 Johns St. 15901 | 814/536–8771 | 55 rooms | $30–$60. | AE, D, DC, MC, V.

KING OF PRUSSIA

Fairfield Inn–Valley Forge. Across the street from the King of Prussia malls, this five-story hotel is next to a health club, which guests are allowed to use. Complimentary Continental breakfast. Cable TV. Indoor pool. Laundry service. Pets allowed. | 258 Mall Blvd. 19406 | 610/337–0700 or 800/228–2800 | fax 610/337–7027 | www.fairfieldinn.com | 80 rooms | $79 | AE, D, DC, MC, V.

KUTZTOWN

Die Bauerei. This restored red-brick 1867 farmhouse (bauerei means farmhouse in the Pennsylvania-German dialect), is 2 mi northwest of Kutztown University. Filled with Pennsylvania Dutch quilts and artwork, it has a walk-in fireplace. Complimentary breakfast. Some room phones, no TV in some rooms. Pets allowed. No smoking. | 187 Sharadin Rd. 19530 | 610/894–4854 | bauerei@juno.com | www.bauerei.com | 5 rooms (4 with bath) | $85 | AE, MC, V.

LANCASTER

★ **Best Western Eden Resort Inn.** In the heart of Dutch Country, this two-level modern brick lodging has a detailed garden and lawn. Restaurant, bar (with entertainment), room service. In-room data ports, cable TV. 2 pools (1 indoor). Hot tub. Tennis. Exercise equipment. Playground. Business services, airport shuttle. Pets allowed. | 222 Eden Rd. 17601 | 717/569–6444 | fax 717/569–4208 | eden@edenresort.com | www.edenresort.com | 276 rooms, 42 suites | $159 | AE, D, DC, MC, V.

Hotel Brunswick. In historic downtown Lancaster, this full-service hotel is in a large 10-story brick building on a city street corner. It's within walking distance of the famous Central Market, Fulton Opera House, and numerous shops and art galleries. Complimentary enclosed parking is provided in the adjacent parking deck. | 222 rooms. Restaurant, bar (with entertainment). Cable TV. Indoor pool. Exercise equipment. Laundry facilities. Business services. Some pets allowed. | Corner of Chestnut and Queen St. 17603 | 717/397–4801 or 800/233–0182 | fax 717/397–4991 | hblanc@lancnews.info.net | www.hotelbrunswick.com | $80–$95 | AE, D, DC, MC, V.

Ramada Inn. Built in 1967, this one-level brick hotel is directly across from Dutch Wonderland Family Park. The Strasburg Railroad is 5 mi away and Hershey Park and Chocolate World, 40 mi. | 166 rooms. Picnic area. In-room data ports, refrigerators, cable TV. 2 pools (1 indoor). Sauna. Driving range, putting green, Tennis courts. Video games. Playground. Laundry facilities. Business services. Airport shuttle. Some pets allowed. | 2250 Lincoln Hwy. E 17602 | 717/393–5499 | fax 717/293–1014 | www.ramada.com/ramada.html | $90–$129 | AE, D, DC, MC, V.

LEBANON

Quality Inn. This red-brick four-building complex, housing the Lebanon Tourist Bureau, was renovated in 1999. It's 12 mi east of Hershey Park. Restaurant, bar, room service. In-room data ports, some microwaves, some refrigerators, cable TV. Outdoor pool. Laundry service. Pets allowed (fee). | 625 Quentin Rd. 17042 | 800/626–8242 | fax 717/273–4882 | 130 rooms | $79–$110 | AE, D, DC, MC, V.

LEWISTOWN

Clarion Inn. Built in 1960, this two-story chain motel is 3 mi outside of Lewistown and 30 minutes west of State College. | 119 rooms. Restaurant, bar. In-room data ports, room service, cable TV. Pool. Some pets allowed. | 13015 Ferguson Valley Rd., Burnham 17009 | 717/248–4961 | fax 717/242–3013 | $69 | AE, D, DC, MC, V.

LIGONIER

Colonial House. The least-lacy B&B in the state, this three-story red-brick house, built in 1906, was restored and renovated in 1999. It has four rocking chairs, complete with afghans, on the front porch, which is comfortable enough—say those who've spent some time there—to serve as an extra bedroom. Dining room. Complimentary breakfast. Cable TV. No room phones. Pets allowed. No kids under 16. No smoking. | 231 W. Main St. | 724/238–6804 | www.colhouse.helicon.net | 4 rooms (sharing 2 baths) | $85 | No credit cards.

LOCK HAVEN

Best Western. One mile from the Piper Aviation Museum, this three-story brick hotel is 12 blocks from Lehigh University. Complimentary Continental breakfast. In-room data ports, some microwaves, some refrigerators, cable TV. Gym. Laundry facilities. Business services. Pets allowed (fee). | 101 E. Walnut St. 17745 | 570/748–3297 | fax 570/748–5390 | www.bestwestern.com/lockhaven | 67 rooms | $90 | AE, D, DC, MC, V.

MANHEIM

Rodeway Inn Penn's Woods. Formerly a Friendship Inn, this hotel is ½ mi north of Manheim on I–72, less than ½ mi north of the Mount Hope Winery. Picnic area. Indoor pool. Volleyball. Pets allowed (fee). | 2931 Lebanon Rd. | 717/665–2755 / | fax 717/664–2513 | www.choicehotels.com | 43 rooms | $70 | AE, D, MC, V.

MANSFIELD

Comfort Inn. Built in 1991, this hotel is within 15 mi of most local attractions, and its location on a hill gives it a gorgeous view of the mountains and Mansfield College. Complimentary Continental breakfast. Cable TV. Exercise equipment. Business services. Pets allowed (fee). | 300 Gateway Dr. | 570/662–3000 | fax 570/662–2551 | www.comfortmansfield.com | 100 rooms | $77–$105 | AE, D, DC, MC, V.

West's Deluxe Motel. This one-story red-brick motel is 3½ mi south of downtown Mansfield, next to West's restaurant (not related, but recommended). Picnic area. Refrigerators, cable TV. Outdoor pool. Pets allowed. | R.R. 1, Rte. 15 16933 | 570/659–5141 or 800/995–9378 | fax 570/659–5851 | www.westsdeluxe.com | 20 rooms | $50 | AE, D, MC, V.

MEADVILLE

Days Inn. This motel is at Exit 36A of I–79, 30 min from the Grove City outlets. Restaurant, bar. Cable TV. Indoor pool. Hot tub. Laundry facilities. Business services. Pets allowed. | 18360 Conneaut Lake Rd. 16335 | 814/337–4264 | fax 814/337–7304 | www.daysinn.com | 163 rooms | $77–$86 | AE, D, DC, MC, V.

MECHANICSBURG

Holiday Inn–West. Pillars and a canopy surrounded by flowers and shrubs frame the entrance of this motel, 2 mi west of Harrisburg. Restaurant, bar (with entertainment), picnic area, room service. Some in-room hot tubs, cable TV. Indoor-outdoor pool. Miniature golf. Exercise equipment. Laundry facilities. Business services. Pets allowed (fee). | 5401 Carlisle Pike 17055 | 717/697–0321 | fax 717/697–7594 | www.holiday-inn.com | 218 rooms | $110–$125 | AE, D, DC, MC, V.

MEDIA

Media Inn. After a fire destroyed the original Media Inn in the 1950s, this red-brick two-story building went up directly across the street. It's on the edge of downtown. Complimentary Continental breakfast. Some kitchenettes, cable TV, room phones. Pets allowed. | 435 E. Baltimore Pk. 19063 | 610/566–6500 | fax 610/566–4173 | www.mediainn.com | 39 rooms | $69–$74 | AE, D, DC, MC, V.

MERCER

Howard Johnson. Eight miles from Grove City factory outlets, this motel is popular with families visiting the area. The lobby is full of Amish furniture. Restaurant, bar, room service. Some in-room data ports, cable TV. Pool. Exercise equipment. Playground. Laundry facilities. Business services. Pets allowed. | 835 Perry Hwy. | 724/748–3030 | fax 724/748–3484 | www.hojo.com | 102 rooms | $78–$90 | AE, D, DC, MC, V.

MILFORD

Best Western Inn at Hunts Landing. Sitting atop 30 acres and overlooking the Delaware River, this hotel has its own stocked trout pond. Restaurant, bar. In-room data ports, some in-room hot tubs, cable TV. Indoor pool. Sauna. Video games. Laundry facilities. Business services. Pets allowed (fee). | 120 Rte. 6/209, Matamoras 18336 | 570/491–2400 | fax 570/491–5934 | www.bestwesternpa.com | 108 rooms | $119–$129 | AE, D, DC, MC, V.

Myer Motel. This motel boasts "All the luxury of home but in a country-style cottage." Although all the cottages have wraparound porches out front, each one has a different color scheme and individualized touches. The cottages are on 4 acres with blue spruce and white pine trees lining the courtyard. Picnic area. Some kitchenettes, refrigerators, cable TV. Pets allowed. | 600 Rte. 6/209 18337 | 570/296–7223 or 800/764–6937 | www.myermotel.com | 19 cottages | $60–$80 cottages | AE, D, DC, MC, V.

MONROEVILLE

William Penn Motel. The rooms in this 1950s motel are furnished with early-American oak or maple wood pieces, with landscape pictures on the walls. The block-long Miracle Mile Shopping Center is across the street. Complimentary Continental breakfast. Cable TV, some in-room VCRs. Pets allowed. | 4139 William Penn Hwy. 15146 | 412/373–0700 | fax 412/372–3814 | www.williampennmotel.com | 22 rooms | $52–$56 | AE, D, DC, MC, V.

NEW HOPE

Aaron Burr House. Hardwood floors, tall arched windows, and a screened-in patio accent this circa-1854 bed-and-breakfast. Complimentary breakfast. TV in common area. Business services. Pets allowed. No smoking. | 80 W. Bridge St./Chestnut St. | 215/862–2570 | fax 215/862–3937 | www.new-hope-inn.com/aaron | 6 rooms, 2 suites | $90–$195, $150–$255 suites | MC, V.

Best Western New Hope Inn. This motel is a few minutes from New Hope and 30 min from Sesame Place. Restaurant, bar. Cable TV. Pool. Exercise equipment. Tennis. Playground. Laundry facilities. Business services. Pets allowed. | 6426 Lower York Rd./US 202 18938 | 215/862–5221 or 800/467–3202 | fax 215/862–5847 | www.bwnewhope.com | 152 rooms | $73–$100 | AE, D, DC, MC, V.

Cordials Bed and Breakfast. Themed rooms in this white clapboard building vary from Gay '90s furnishing to art deco styles with burgundy, white, black, and gold coloring. From each room, you can access either a private balcony or deck overlooking large pines, hemlocks, annual flowers, and statuary. Wine and cheese are served on weekends. Dining room, complimentary Continental breakfast. Refrigerators, cable TV, in-room VCRs (and movies). Pool. Pets allowed. No kids under 16. No smoking. | 143 Old York Rd. 18938 | 215/862–3919 or 877/219–1009 | fax 215/862–3917 | www.cordialsbb.com | 6 rooms | $120–$130 (2–night minimum stay on weekend; 3–night minimum stay on holiday weekend) | AE, MC, V.

★ **Wedgwood Inn.** Three buildings, two Victorians and an 1840 Federal manor, make up this bed-and-breakfast. All buildings were renovated in 2000. There are Victorian antiques, flowers, original art, and Wedgwood china, and it's on 2 parklike acres with gazebos and wicker-sealed porches. Picnic area, complimentary breakfast. Some in-room hot tubs, some room phones. Business services. Pets allowed. No smoking. | 111 W. Bridge St. | 215/862–

3996 | fax 215/862–3936 | www.new-hope-inn.com | 19 rooms, 6 suites | $90–$195, $150–$255 suites | MC, V.

NEW STANTON

New Stanton Motel. Rooms here have brown and gold carpeting and floral or solid-colored bedspreads with coordinated curtains. About 15 rooms have queen-size beds. The motel is in a commercial area three blocks from fast food restaurants. Laundry facilities. Pets allowed. No kids under 21. | 116 W. Pennsylvania Ave. 15672 | 724/925–7606 | 34 rooms | $25–$28 | AE, D, MC, V.

NORTH EAST

Vineyard Bed and Breakfast. Vineyards, orchards, and Lake Erie are all in view of this 1900 country home, in a quiet rural area. A vine motif is present throughout the house; the blue concord suite even has vines draped over sheer-white curtains. Other rooms have pillows and wallpaper with grape designs to bring out the mauve, green, and cranberry color schemes. The owners make homemade juice from their own grapes. Dining room, complimentary breakfast. Cable TV, some room phones. Pets allowed. No smoking. | 10757 Sidehill Rd. 16428 | 814/725–8998 or 888/725–8998 | www.lakeside.net/vineyardbb | 5 rooms | $65–$75 | AE, D, MC, V.

PHILADELPHIA

Best Western–Center City. This chain hotel has reasonable rates and a location less than four blocks from the museums on Benjamin Franklin Parkway. It's 2 mi from Center City attractions. Restaurant, bar. In-room data ports, cable TV. Exercise equipment. Pool. Business services, free parking. Pets allowed. | 501 N. 22nd St. 19130 | 215/568–8300 | fax 215/557–0259 | www.bestwesternpa.com | 183 rooms | $107–$154 | AE, D, DC, MC, V.

Comfort Inn. This motel is north of Philadelphia city limits, and 5 mi from the Northeast Philadelphia Airport. Bar (with entertainment), complimentary Continental breakfast. In-room data ports, some in-room hot tubs, cable TV. Exercise equipment. Laundry services. Business services. Pets allowed. | 3660 Street Rd., Bensalem 19020 | 215/245–0100 | fax 215/245–1851 | www.comfortinn.com | 141 rooms | $95–$160 | AE, D, DC, MC, V.

★ **Four Seasons Hotel Philadelphia.** Considered the city's finest, this hotel has one of the city's best restaurants (The Fountain), luxuriously appointed guest rooms, and a stunning location on Logan Circle across from Swann Fountain. Restaurant, bar (with entertainment), room service. In-room data ports, minibars, cable TV. Indoor pool. Hot tub, massage. Gym. Laundry service. Business services. Pets allowed. | 1 Logan Sq. 19103 | 215/963–1500 | fax 215/963–9506 | www.fourseasons.com/locations/philadelphia | 365 rooms | $335–$470 | AE, D, DC, MC, V.

Hilton–Philadelphia Airport. This hotel has a unique pool just off the lobby. Many of the guest rooms are oversized. It's 1 mi to Philadelphia International Airport. Restaurant, bar, room service. In-room data ports, cable TV. Indoor pool. Hot tub. Exercise equipment. Laundry service. Business services, airport shuttle. Pets allowed. | 4509 Island Ave. 19153 | 215/365–4150 | fax 215/937–6382 | 330 rooms | $125–$205 | AE, D, DC, MC, V.

Philadelphia Marriott. This 23-story convention hotel—the biggest in Pennsylvania—takes up an entire city block. A short walk takes you to the Franklin Institute, Penn's Landing, or the Liberty Bell. Restaurant, bar, room service. In-room data ports, some refrigerators, cable TV. Indoor pool, wading pool. Beauty salon, hot tub. Exercise equipment. Laundry facilities. Business services, parking (fee). Pets allowed. | 1201 Market St. 19107 | 215/625–2900 | fax 215/625–6000 | 1,408 rooms, 76 suites | $129–$290, $350–$1100 suites | AE, D, DC, MC, V.

★ **The Rittenhouse Hotel.** This small luxury hotel has condominium residences on other floors of the building. It takes full advantage of its Rittenhouse Square location and boasts some of the city's most plush guest rooms, with marble bathrooms and mahogany accents. Restaurants, bar (with entertainment), room service. In-room data ports, minibars, cable TV. Indoor pool. Beauty salon, massage. Gym. Laundry service. Business services. Pets allowed. | 210 W. Rittenhouse Sq. 19103 | 215/546–9000 or 800/635–1042 | fax 215/732–3364 | www.rittenhousehotel.com | 98 rooms; 28 suites | $345–$410, $575–$1500 suites | AE, D, DC, MC, V.

Sheraton Rittenhouse Square Hotel. The first "environmentally smart" facility from Starwood Hotels and Resorts Worldwide, this hotel has eco-friendly features such as fresh, filtered air, organic cotton linens, and a bamboo garden designed to oxygenate air in the lobby. The panoramic views of Rittenhouse Square and the city skyline are another draw. From here, you only have to take a quick walk to Restaurant Row and the Franklin Institute. Restaurants, bar, room service. In-room data ports, minibars, some refrigerators, cable TV. Massage. Gym. Business services. Pets allowed. | 227 S. 18th St. 19103 | 215/546–9400 or 800/854–8002 | www.sheratonphiladelphia.com | 193 rooms | $129–$200 | AE, D, DC, MC, V.

Sheraton Society Hill. This neo-Colonial hotel, with a four-story atrium and traditionally furnished rooms, is in the heart of the city's historic district. Restaurant, bar, room service. In-room data ports, minibars, some refrigerators, cable TV. Indoor pool, wading pool. Hot tub, massage, sauna. Gym. Business services. Pets allowed. | 1 Dock St. 19106 | 215/238–6000 | fax 215/922–2709 | www.sheraton.com | 362 rooms; 17 suites | $189–$299 | AE, D, DC, MC, V.

The Warwick. First opened in 1924, this 23-story hotel in English Renaissance style has completed a thorough renovation, which added a new restaurant and made guest rooms from former apartments. The hotel is across the street from Rittenhouse Square. 3 Restaurants, 2 bars. In-room data ports, cable TV. Beauty salon. Exercise equipment. Business services. Pets allowed. | 1701 Locust St. 19103 | 215/735–6000 or 800/523–4210 (outside PA) | fax 215/790–7766 | www.warwickhotels.com/phil | 550 rooms; 17 suites | $189–$269 | AE, D, DC, MC, V.

PITTSBURGH

AmeriSuites–Pittsburgh Airport. All of the rooms here are two-room suites. Besides the extra room, business suites have an oversized desk, ergonomic desk chair, and an overstuffed chair with ottoman. AmeriSuites can provide you with free van service within 5 mi of the hotel. Complimentary Continental breakfast. In-room data ports, kitchenettes, microwaves, refrigerators, cable TV, in-room VCRs (and movies). Pool. Gym. Laundry service. Business services, airport shuttle, free parking. Pets allowed. | 6011 Campbells Run Rd. 15205 | 412/494–0202 or 800/833–1516 | fax 412/494–0880 | www.amerisuites.com | 128 suites | $79–$89 | AE, D, DC, MC, V.

Clarion Hotel. Standard rooms here have wood furnishings and colorful carpeting and bedspreads, while business class rooms have an extra large desk and an ergonomic office chair. During evenings the bar has a DJ, live band, karaoke, or comedy. 17 mi northeast of downtown. Restaurant, bar (with entertainment), picnic area, room service. Some in-room data ports, some microwaves, some refrigerators, cable TV. Pool. Gym. Video games. Laundry facilities, laundry service. Business services, free parking. Pets allowed. | 300 Tarentum Bridge Rd., New Kensington 15068 | 724/335–9171 | fax 724/335–6642 | 115 rooms | $60–$70 | AE, DC, MC, V.

Doubletree. This hotel has an atrium-style lobby and a convenient downtown location across from the convention center. Restaurant, bar, room service. In-room data ports, refrigerators, cable TV. Indoor pool. Hot tub. Gym. Shops. Business services. Pets allowed. | 1000 Penn Ave. 15222 | 412/281–3700 | fax 412/227–4500 | www.doubletree.com | 616 rooms | $155–$225 | AE, D, DC, MC, V.

Hampton Inn–Greentree. For affordable rates 3 mi west of downtown, try this motel. Picnic area, complimentary Continental breakfast. In-room data ports, cable TV. Business services, airport shuttle, free parking. Pets allowed. | 555 Trumbull Dr. 15205 | 412/922–0100 | fax 412/921–7631 | www.hamptoninn.com | 135 rooms | $94–$109 | AE, D, DC, MC, V.

Hawthorn Suites. An all-suites hotel, it's 4 mi from downtown, off Exit 4 of I–279. You can get a spacious suite with separate living and sleeping areas nearly twice the size of a traditional hotel room. Picnic area, complimentary breakfast. Microwaves, refrigerators, cable TV. Pool. Hot tub. Business services, airport shuttle. Pets allowed (fee). | 700 Mansfield Ave. 15205 | 412/279–6300 or 800/527–1133 | fax 412/279–4993 | www.hawthorn.com | 151 suites | $99–$129 | AE, D, DC, MC, V.

Hilton Pittsburgh & Towers. Overlooking Point State Park is a large, elegant hotel. Its grand ballroom is the largest in Pittsburgh, and has a view of three rivers and Mt. Washington. Restaurant, 2 bars (with entertainment). In-room data ports, minibars, refrigerators, cable TV. Beauty salon. Exercise equipment. Business services, airport shuttle. Pets allowed. | 600 Commonwealth Pl., Gateway Center 15222 | 412/391–4600 | fax 412/594–5161 | www.hilton-pit.com | 713 rooms | $189–$264 | AE, D, DC, MC, V.

Holiday Inn Greentree–Central. This hotel is 3 mi west of downtown, and 1 mi to Parkway Center mall. Restaurant, bar (with entertainment), room service. In-room data ports, cable TV. Pool. Exercise equipment. Business services, airport shuttle, free parking. Pets allowed. | 401 Holiday Dr. 15220 | 412/922–8100 | fax 412/922–6511. www.holiday-inn.com | 200 rooms | $110–$150 | AE, D, DC, MC, V.

Holiday Inn–Monroeville. This hotel is ¼ mi from the turnpike and 12 mi east of downtown. Restaurant, bar, room service. In-room data ports, cable TV. Outdoor pool. Exercise equipment. Laundry facilities. Business services, free parking. Pets allowed. | 2750 Mosside Blvd., Monroeville 15146 | 412/372–1022 | fax 412/373–4065 | www.holiday-inn.com | 188 rooms | $79–$139 | AE, D, DC, MC, V.

Holiday Inn, North Hills. In a wooded area 6 mi from downtown, 1 mi from the Ross Park Mall's restaurants and shopping, is this hotel. Restaurant, bar (with entertainment), room service. In-room data ports, some refrigerators, cable TV. Pool. Laundry facilities. Business services, free parking. Pets allowed. | 4859 McKnight Rd. 15237 | 412/366–5200 | fax 412/366–5682 | www.holiday-inn.com | 147 rooms | $85–$139 | AE, D, DC, MC, V.

Holiday Inn–Parkway East. This hotel is 8 mi east of downtown, and 4 mi from Monroeville Mall and Expo Mart. Restaurant, bar (with entertainment), room service. Some refrigerators, cable TV. Indoor pool. Laundry facilities. Business services, free parking. Pets allowed. | 915 Brinton Rd. 15221 | 412/247–2700 | fax 412/371–9619. | www.holiday-inn.com | 180 rooms | $109–$139 | AE, D, DC, MC, V.

Holiday Inn–Pittsburgh South. Right across from South Hills Village Mall is this hotel, 8 mi south of downtown. Restaurant, bar (with entertainment), room service. In-room data ports, cable TV. Pool. Video games. Business services, airport shuttle, free parking. Pets allowed. | 164 Fort Couch Rd. 15241 | 412/833–5300 | fax 412/831–8539 | www.holiday-inn.com | 210 rooms | $89–$120 | AE, D, DC, MC, V.

MainStay Suites. In addition to bedrooms, about half of the suites here have a separate living area with a full kitchen. The other half of the suites are studio apartments with large workspaces, ergonomic desk chairs, and two-line speaker phones. Picnic area, complimentary Continental breakfast. In-room data ports, kitchenettes, cable TV. Exercise equipment. Laundry facilities, laundry service. Business services, free parking. Pets allowed. | 1000 Park Lane Drive 15275 | 412/490–7343 | fax 412/788–6097 | 100 suites | $80–$105 | AE, D, DC, MC, V.

Morning Glory Inn. This 1862 brick Italian Victorian townhouse is in the Southside Historical District, just over a mile from Pittsburgh's downtown. Its garden room is bright, with pink lattice and floral wallpaper, a white wicker bed and chair, and a walnut rocker. Other rooms have earth-tone, floral, or yellow-striped wallpaper. You can find clawfoot tubs in two of the rooms and a canopy bed in one. Dining room. In-room data ports, cable TV. Laundry facilities. Pets allowed. No smoking. | 2119 Sarah St. 15203 | 412/431–1707 | fax 412/431–6106 | www.morningglorybedandbreakfast.com | 5 rooms | $140–$180; 2–night minimum on selected weekends | AE, D, MC, V.

Radisson Greentree. If you want to be right near the heart of the city, this hotel is 3 mi west of downtown. Restaurant, bar (with entertainment), room service. In-room data ports, some minibars, cable TV. 3 pools (1 indoor). Beauty salon, hot tub. Exercise equipment. Business services, airport shuttle, free parking. Pets allowed. | 101 Marriott Dr. 15205 | 412/922–8400 or 800/525–5902 | fax 412/922–7854 | www.radisson.com | 465 rooms | $89–$139 | AE, D, DC, MC, V.

Ramada Inn–Pittsburgh East. A hillside hotel that caters especially to business travelers, it's situated east of downtown off I–376. Restaurant, bar (with entertainment), room service. In-room data ports, cable TV. Indoor pool. Hot tub, sauna. Tennis. Business services, airport shuttle, free parking. Pets allowed. | 699 Rodi Rd. 15235 | 412/244–1600 or 800/272–6232 | fax 412/829–2334 | www.ramada.com | 152 rooms | $79–$140 | AE, D, DC, MC, V.

Red Roof Inn. Affordable rates are the earmark of this motel, 11 mi west of downtown and 5 mi from Pittsburgh International Airport. Cable TV. Business services. Pets allowed. | 6404 Steubenville Pike/Rte. 60 15205 | 412/787–7870 | fax 412/787–8392 | www.redroof.com | 120 rooms | $53–$65 | AE, D, DC, MC, V.

Westin William Penn. The grande dame of Pittsburgh hotels boasts a stately lobby with crystal chandeliers and ornate moldings, and guest rooms with marble baths. The hotel is considered a landmark. Restaurant, bar (with entertainment), room service. Cable TV. Exercise equipment. Business services, airport shuttle. Pets allowed (fee). | 530 William Penn Pl. 15219 | 412/281–7100 | fax 412/553–5252 | www.westin.com | 595 rooms | $99–$3,000 | AE, D, DC, MC, V.

PORT ALLEGANY

The Poet's Walk Bed and Breakfast. This 1948 white-clapboard Cape Cod has six guest rooms—one in the basement, four on the second floor, and one in the attic, which is the only room with air-conditioning and cable TV. The rooms are plainly furnished with no common design, except that three of them have queen-size beds. The neighborhood is residential and you can stroll 2½ acres of lawn with several large trees. Dining room, complimentary breakfast. No air-conditioning in some rooms, no room phones, no TV in some rooms. Pets allowed. No smoking. | 428 Arnold Ave. 16743 | 814/642–2676 | 6 rooms | $65 | MC, V.

POTTSTOWN

Comfort Inn. This motel is about 1 mi from Pottsgrove Manor. Complimentary Continental breakfast, room service. In-room data ports, some refrigerators, cable TV. Pool. Laundry facilities. Business services. Pets allowed. | Rte. 100 and Shoemaker Rd., 19464 | 610/326–5000 | fax 610/970–7230 | www.pottstownpacomfortinn.com | 151 rooms | $89–$119 | AE, D, DC, MC, V.

Days Inn. This two-story motel is at the end of downtown and close to highways. Complimentary Continental breakfast. Some microwaves, some refrigerators, cable TV. Pets allowed (fee). | 29 High St. 19464 | 610/970–1101, 800/329–7466 | fax 610/327–8643 | www.daysinn.com | 59 rooms | $39–$69 | AE, D, DC, MC, V.

Holiday Inn Express. This midpriced hotel caters mostly to business travelers. Complimentary Continental breakfast. In-room data ports, some refrigerators, cable TV. Pool. Business services, free parking. Pets allowed. | 1600 Industrial Hwy./U.S. 422 | 610/327–3300 | fax 610/327–9447 | www.hiexpottstownpa.com | 120 rooms | $79–$135 | AE, D, DC, MC, V.

QUAKERTOWN

Rodeway Inn. This motel is at Exit 32 of the PA Turnpike Extension (U.S. 476). Complimentary Continental breakfast. In-room data ports, some microwaves, some in-room hot tubs, cable TV. Pets allowed. | 1920 Rte. 663 | 215/536–7600 | fax 215/536–5922 | www.rodewayinn. com | $50–$139 | AE, D, DC, MC, V.

READING

Best Western Dutch Colony Inn. This motel is 3 mi from downtown Reading. Restaurant, bar, room service. Cable TV. Pool. Laundry facilities. Business services, free parking. Pets allowed. | 4635 Perkiomen Ave. 19606 | 610/779–2345 or 800/828–2830 | fax 610/779–8348 | www.bestwestern.com | 71 rooms | $65–$90 | AE, D, DC, MC, V.

Econo Lodge Outlet Village. This chain motel has reasonable rates and is ½ mi from the outlet malls. Complimentary Continental breakfast. Some microwaves, refrigerators, cable TV. Exercise equipment. Laundry facilities. Business services. Pets allowed (fee). | 635 Spring St., Wyomissing 19610 | 610/378–5105 | fax 610/373–3181 | www. econolodgewyomissing.com | 84 rooms | $54–$150 | AE, D, MC, V.

Holiday Inn. A chain hotel, it's at Exit 22 of the PA Turnpike. Restaurant, bar, room service. In-room data ports, some refrigerators, cable TV. Indoor pool. Hot tub. Exercise equipment. Business services. Pets allowed. | 230 Cherry La./Rte. 10, Morgantown 19543 | 610/286–3000 | fax 610/286–0520 | www.holiday-inn.com | 192 rooms | $99–$119 | AE, D, DC, MC, V.

Inn at Reading. This sprawling motel is 10 minutes away from most outlet shopping. Restaurant, bar (with entertainment), picnic area, room service. In-room data ports, cable TV. Outdoor pool. Exercise equipment. Business services, airport shuttle, free parking. Pets allowed. | 1040 Park Rd., Wyomissing 19610 | 610/372–7811 or 800/383–9713 | fax 610/372–4545 | www.innatreading.com | 250 rooms | $89–$139 | AE, D, DC, MC, V.

Ramada Inn at the Outlets of Reading. This is a two-story chain motel. Some microwaves, some refrigerators, cable TV. Outdoor pool. Pets allowed (fee). | 2545 N. 5th St. 19635 | 610/929–4741 or 800/272–6232 | fax 610/929–5237 | 139 | $59–$79 | AE, D, DC, MC, V.

Sheraton Reading. The hotel is made up of two sections, with luxury rooms housed in a five-story tower. Restaurant, bar (with entertainment), room service. In-room data ports, cable TV. Indoor pool. Hot tub. Putting green. Exercise equipment. Business services, airport shuttle, free parking. Pets allowed (fee). | 1741 Papermill Rd. 19610 | 610/376–3811 | fax 610/375–7562 | www.sheraton.com | 255 rooms | $89–$149 | AE, D, DC, MC, V.

SCRANTON

Days Inn. This chain motel is at Exit 55A off I–81. Complimentary Continental breakfast. Refrigerators, cable TV. Business services, free parking. Pets allowed (fee). | 1226 O'Neill Hwy., Dunmore 18512 | 570/348–6101 | fax 570/348–5064 | www.daysinn.com | 88 rooms | $65–$100 | AE, D, DC, MC, V.

EconoLodge Scranton. This is a two-story hotel, 2 mi from skiing, 10 min from Steamtown and the coal mines. Complimentary Continental breakfast. In-room data ports, some in-room hot tubs. Pets allowed (fee). | 1175 Kane St. 18505 | 570/348–1000 or 800/553–2666 | fax 570/348–0683 | 64 rooms | $30–$95 | AE, D, DC, MC, V.

Holiday Inn–East. A chain hotel, it's at Exit 1 of I–380. Restaurant, bar, room service. In-room data ports, cable TV. Pool. Exercise equipment. Video games. Business services, free parking. Pets allowed (fee). | 200 Tigue St., Dunmore 18512 | 570/343–4771 | fax 570/343–5171 | www.holiday-inn.com | 139 rooms | $89–$149 | AE, D, DC, MC, V.

SHAMOKIN DAM

Inn at Shamokin Dam. This is a good-sized motel with affordable rates. Restaurant, bar. In-room data ports, cable TV. Pool. Business services. Pets allowed. | Rte. 11 and U.S. 15 | 570/743-1111 | fax 570/743-1190 | 131 rooms | $45-$75 | AE, D, DC, MC, V.

SHARTLESVILLE

Dutch Motel. This one-story motel is at the foot of the Blue Mountains, near the highway, restaurants, and 25 mi from the Reading outlets. Cable TV. Pets allowed (fee). | 1 Motel Dr. 19554 | 610/488-1479 | 14 rooms | $35-$50 | AE, D, MC, V.

SOMERSET

Dollar Inn. Affordable rates are the draw of this small motel. Some refrigerators, cable TV. Business services. Pets allowed (fee). | 1146 N. Center Ave. | 814/445-2977 | fax 814/443-6205 | 16 rooms | $50-$70 | AE, D, DC, MC, V.

The Inn at Georgian Place. Oak paneling, ornate fireplaces, a marble foyer, and chandeliers with gold leaf nearly drip elegance. This inn is 20 min from Hidden Valley Resort, and 40 min from Fallingwater. Individual, unique rooms are in Georgian style. Restaurant, complimentary breakfast, room service. Cable TV, in-room VCRs (and movies). No kids under 5. Pets allowed. | 800 Georgian Place Dr. | 814/443-1043 | fax 814/443-6220 | www.somersetcounty.com/theinn | 11 rooms | $95-$185 | AE, D, DC, MC, V.

Knights Inn. Hidden Valley Resort is 11 mi from this motel, and Fallingwater is 40 mi away. Some kitchenettes, cable TV. Pool. Laundry facilities. Business services. Pets allowed. | 585 Ramada Rd. | 814/445-8933 or 800/843-5644 | fax 814/443-9745 | www.knightsinn.com | 112 rooms | $50-$70 | AE, D, DC, MC, V.

Ramada Inn. This motel is at Exit 10 of the PA Turnpike. Restaurant, bar (with entertainment), room service. Cable TV. Indoor pool. Hot tub, sauna. Video games. Business services, free parking. Pets allowed. | 215 Ramada Rd. | 814/443-4646 | fax 814/445-7539 | www.ramada.com | 152 rooms | $64-$125 | AE, D, DC, MC, V.

STATE COLLEGE

Nittany Budget Motel. Geared for the business traveler who still wants a homey touch, this motel has workstations and modems in all rooms and an on-site beer shop and restaurant. Restaurant, complimentary Continental breakfast. In-room dataports, refrigerators, cable TV. Pets allowed (fee). | 2070 Cato Ave. 16801 | 814/238-0015 | fax 814/238-0035 | 150 rooms | $40-$63. | AE, D, DC, MC, V.

Days Inn–Penn State. The hotel is one block from the center of Penn State campus. Restaurant, bar (with entertainment), complimentary Continental breakfast, room service. In-room data ports, cable TV. Indoor pool. Gym. Video games. Business services, airport shuttle, free parking. Pets allowed (fee). | 240 S. Pugh St. 16801 | 814/238-8454 | fax 814/234-3377 | www.daysinn.com | 184 rooms | $79-$125 | AE, D, DC, MC, V.

Ramada Inn. Here are standard chain accommodations, 2 mi from the Penn State campus and 1½ mi from downtown shopping. Restaurant, bar. In-room data ports, room service, cable TV. 2 pools. Exercise equipment. Video games. Laundry facilities. Business services. Pets allowed. | 1450 S. Atherton St./US 322 Business 16801 | 814/238-3001 | fax 814/237-1345 | www.ramadasc.com | 28 rooms | $85-$225 | AE, D, DC, MC, V.

The Queen: A Victorian Bed and Breakfast. This 1890s Queen Anne-style home in a National Historic Registered residential neighborhood in Bellefonte, 13 mi northeast of State College, has one room filled with Victorian ladies' undergarments, dressing screen, and a fireplace, a two-room turret suite with hunting and fishing memorabilia and a fireplace, and an efficiency apartment. There is also a turn-of-the-century player piano. | 1 room, 2 suites. Complimentary breakfast. Some in-room TVs, TV in common room. Pets

allowed. | 176 E. Lynn St., Bellefonte 16823 | 814/355–7946 | fax 814/357–8068 | www.
bellefonte.com/queen | $75–$155 | AE, D, MC, V.

STRASBURG
Historic Strasburg Inn. You can enjoy the petting zoo, carriage rides, and hot air balloon
rides at this sprawling 58-acre property. It's a three-level country-style brick building made
of brick that dates to 1793, when the Washington House began serving travelers on the
square in Strasburg. Several well-known patrons enjoyed its special hospitality, including
J.P. Morgan, William Astor, and Sir Thomas Lipton. Guest registers bearing their signa-
tures are on display in the Washington House lobby. Restaurant, bar, complimentary breakfast. Cable TV. Pool. Hot tub. Exercise equipment. Playground. Business services. Pets
allowed (fee). | 1 Historic Dr. (Rte. 896) 17579 | 717/687–7691 or 800/872–0201 | fax 717/687–
6098 | www.800padutch.com/strasinn.html | 101 rooms in 5 buildings | $129–$139 | AE,
D, DC, MC, V.

STROUDSBURG
Budget. Take Exit 51 off I–80 to reach this motel. Restaurant, bar. In-room data ports, cable
TV. Video games. Business services. Pets allowed (fee). | I–80, Exit 51, E. Stroudsburg 18301
| 570/424–5451 or 800/233–8144 | fax 570/424–0389 | www.budmotel.com | 115 rooms | $55–
$80 | AE, D, DC, MC, V.

TOWANDA
Towanda Motel. A small two-story motel, this is a low-cost alternative to the large resorts
in the area. Some rooms have whirlpool tubs. Restaurant, bar. Cable TV. Pool. Business
services. Pets allowed. | 383 York Ave./U.S. 6 18848 | 570/265–2178 | fax 570/265–9060 | 48
rooms | $50–$70 | AE, D, MC, V.

UNIONTOWN
Holiday Inn. This midpriced, two-story chain hotel is in downtown Uniontown. Restau-
rant, bar (with entertainment), room service. In-room data ports, cable TV. Indoor pool.
Hot tub, sauna. Gym. Miniature golf. Tennis. Volleyball. Video games. Business services,
free parking. Pets allowed. | 700 W. Main St. 15401; U.S. 40 | 724/437–2816 or 800/258–7238
| fax 724/437–3505 | www.holiday-inn.com | 174 rooms, 4 suites | $89–$99, $150 suites |
AE, D, DC, MC, V.

Lodge at Chalk Hill. Each room has a private deck in this lakeside, medium-size inn. It's
on 37 acres, 5 mi east of Uniontown. Picnic area, complimentary Continental breakfast.
Some kitchenettes, cable TV. Business services. Pets allowed (fee). | U.S. 40 E, Chalk Hill
15421; Rte. 40 E | 724/438–8880 or 800/833–4283 | fax 724/438–1685 | www.
thelodgeatchalkhill.com | 60 rooms, 6 suites | $78–$84, $153–$179 suites | AE, D, MC, V.

WARREN
Holiday Inn. Only 2 mi from downtown, this inn is partially surrounded by the Allegheny
Mountains. Rooms have double beds, and some have hot tubs. Restaurant. In-room data
ports, cable TV. Indoor pool. Sauna. Health club. Pets allowed. | 210 Ludlow St. 16365 | 814/
726–3000 | fax 814/726–3720 | holinwrn@penn.com | www.users.penn.com-holinwrn |
112 rooms | $80.

WASHINGTON
Holiday Inn–Meadow Lands. Next to the Meadows Racetrack, this six-story hotel is 30
mi south of Pittsburgh. Restaurant, bars (with entertainment), room service. In-room data
ports, cable TV. Pool. Hot tub. Exercise equipment. Business services, airport shuttle. Pets
allowed. | 340 Race Track Rd. 15301; Intersection of I-70 and I-79 | 724/222–6200 | fax 724/
228–1977 | www.holiday-inn.com | 138 rooms | $89–$119 | AE, D, DC, MC, V.

Motel 6. This one-story motel has affordable rates and is 6 blocks from Washington Jefferson College. Cable TV. Pool. Laundry facilities. Pets allowed. | 1283 Motel 6 Dr.; I-70 to exit 7A | 724/223–8040 or 800/466–8356 | fax 724/228–6445 | www.motel6.com | 102 rooms | $45–$60 | AE, D, DC, MC, V.

Red Roof Inn. This two-story motel is 2 mi from the Pennsylvania Trolley Museum. Cable TV. Pets allowed. | 1399 W. Chestnut St. 15301 | 724/228–5750 | fax 724/228–5865 | www.redroof.com | 110 rooms | $45–$55 | AE, D, DC, MC, V.

WELLSBORO

Canyon Motel. This frame, two-story motel, on 4 acres in the center of town, is 10 mi west of the Pennsylvania Grand Canyon. The motel has special ski packages. Some rooms have Jacuzzi baths and oversized bathrooms. Picnic area. In-room data ports, refrigerators, microwaves, cable TV, in-room VCRs (and movies). Pool. Spa. Gym. Playground. Business services. Pets allowed. | 18 East Ave. 16901 | 570/724–1681 or 800/255–2718 | fax 570/724–5202 | www.canyonmotel.com | 25 rooms, 6 suites | $55, $60–$80 suites | AE, D, DC, MC, V.

Terrace Motel Choose from an efficiency unit or a fully equipped cabin for an extended stay, or a suite or a room for a shorter visit. | 15 rooms. Pets allowed. | Rr 7 16901 | 570/724–4711 | $49–$55 | AE, D, MC, V.

WEST MIDDLESEX

Holiday Inn. This midpriced, three-story brick hotel is at Exit 1N off I–80. Restaurant, bar (with entertainment), room service. In-room data ports, cable TV. Pool. Video games. Playground. Laundry facilities. Business services. Pets allowed. | 3200 S. Hermitage Rd., Hermitage | 724/981–1530 | fax 724/981–1518 | www.holiday-inn.com | 180 rooms | $80 | AE, D, DC, MC, V.

Radisson Hotel Sharon. A two-story hotel at exit 1 N on I–80, this hotel has two 2-floor suites. The building exterior is white brick trimmed in black. Restaurant, bar (with entertainment), room service. Some refrigerators, in-room hot tubs, cable TV. Indoor pool. Hot tub. Exercise equipment. Game room. Laundry facilities. Business services. Pets allowed. | Rte. 18 | 724/528–2501 | fax 724/528–2306 | www.radisson.com | 153 rooms, 5 suites | $90–$100, $150–$250 suites | AE, D, DC, MC, V.

WHITE HAVEN

Ramada Inn. A snowman-shaped indoor swimming pool and indoor miniature golf make this hotel, built in 1974, unique. Some rooms have Jacuzzi baths. Restaurant, bar, picnic area, room service. Some refrigerators, cable TV. Indoor pool. Sauna. Miniature golf. Basketball, hiking, volleyball. Video games. Laundry facilities. Business services, airport shuttle. Pets allowed (fee). | Rte. 940, Lake Harmony 18624; I-80 to Rte. 940 | 570/443–8471 | fax 570/443–0326 | www.ramada.com | 136 rooms, 2 suites | $95–$125, $145–$200 suites | AE, D, DC, MC, V.

WILKES-BARRE

Best Western Genetti. This brick, seven-story hotel is in the downtown area. The front entrance is landscaped. Restaurant, bar, room service. Cable TV. Pool. Laundry facilities. Business services, free Parking. Pets allowed (fee). | 77 E. Market St. 18701; Exit 46, I-81 | 717/823–6152 or 800/833–6152 | fax 717/820–8502 | www.bestwestern.com | 72 rooms, 16 suites | $79–$89, $135 suites | AE, D, DC, MC, V.

Holiday Inn. In the downtown area on the business route, all rooms open to the outdoors. The motel is connected to a restaurant. Restaurant, bar, room service. In-room data ports, cable TV. Pool, wading pool. Exercise equipment. Laundry services. Business services, free parking. Pets allowed. | 880 Kidder St. 18702; Rte. 115 and Rte. 315 | 570/824–8901 or

888/466–9272 | fax 570/824–9310 | www.holiday-inn.com | 167 rooms, 14 suites | $75–$119, $129–$139 suites | AE, D, DC, MC, V.

WILLIAMSPORT

Econo Lodge - Williamsport. This two-story motel is 2 mi east of Lycoming College. All rooms have outside entrances. The motel is attached to a steakhouse. Restaurant, bar (with entertainment), complimentary Continental breakfast. Cable TV, in-room VCRs (and movies). Exercise equipment. Business services, free parking. Pets allowed. | 2401 E. 3rd St.; Rte. 220 | 570/326–1501 | fax 570/326–9776 | 99 rooms | $50–$60 | AE, D, DC, MC, V.

Genetti Hotel. This historical 10-story hotel in downtown was built in 1922. There are whirlpool baths in some rooms, and some rooms are poolside. Restaurant, bar (with entertainment). Some refrigerators, cable TV. Pool. Beauty salon. Exercise equipment. Laundry facilities. Business services, airport shuttle, free parking. Pets allowed. | 200 W. 4th St. 17704; Rte. 15 to Business District exit | 570/326–6600 or 800/321–1388 | fax 570/326–5006 | www.genetti.com | 206 rooms, 42 suites | $50–$115, $86–$125 suites | AE, DC, MC, V.

Holiday Inn. The hotel is 5 mi from downtown. There are two stories and rooms have outside entrances. Suites have Jacuzzi baths. Restaurant, bar, room service. In-room data ports, cable TV. Pool. Laundry facilities. Business services, free parking. Pets allowed. | 1840 E. 3rd St./U.S. 220 | 570/326–1981 or 800/369–4572 | fax 570/323–9590 | www.holiday-inn. com | 157 rooms, 2 suites | $65–$80, $130–$139 suites | AE, D, DC, MC, V.

Radisson Hotel Williamsport. The hotel is in the downtown center. It's a five-story building with a driveway and free parking. Restaurant, bar (with entertainmnent), room service. Some refrigerators, some in-room hot tubs, cable TV. Indoor pool. Business services, airport shuttle. Pets allowed. | 100 Pine St.; I–80/Rte. 15 | 570/327–8231 | fax 570/322–2957 | www.radisson.com | 145 rooms, 2 suites | $79–$119, $159 suites | AE, D, DC, MC, V.

WILLOW GROVE

Days Inn. One mile from Willow Grove, rooms here are spacious, with a king-size bed or two doubles. Some rooms overlook a wooded area in back. Suites have hot tubs. Complimentary breakfast. In-room data ports. Exercise equipment. Laundry service, laundry facility. Business service, airport shuttle. Pets allowed. | 245 Easton Rd. 19090 | 215/674–2500 | fax 215/674–0879 | www.thedaysinn.com/horsham06707 | 168 rooms, 3 suites | $109–$129 | AE, D, DC, MC, V.

Homestead Village. Half a mile from I-611, this three-story hotel offers accomodation mostly for corporations and business people. Within walking distance of restaurants and half a mile from downtown, it can arrange guest passes to a nearby gym. In-room data ports. 1 shop. Laundry facilities. Pets allowed. | 537 Drescher Rd. 19090 | 215/956–9966 | fax 215/956–9002 | www.stayhsd.com | 116 rooms, 21 suites | $89–$109 | AE, D, DC, MC, V.

YORK

Holiday Inn–Arsenal Road. A two-story building with outside entrances, this hotel is 3 mi from downtown. Restaurant, bar, room service. In-room data ports, cable TV. Pool. Laundry facilities. Business services, airport shuttle. Pets allowed. | 334 Arsenal Rd. 17402; I-83 to Rte. 30 | 717/845–5671 | fax 717/845–1898 | www.holiday-inn.com | 100 rooms | $79–$109 | AE, D, DC, MC, V.

Holiday Inn–East. The West Manchester Mall and the Holidome, an inside recreation center, are part of this two-story hotel, 1 mi west of downtown. Restaurant, bar, room service. Cable TV. 2 pools (1 indoor). Hot tub. Miniature golf. Exercise equipment. Playground. Business services, free parking. Pets allowed. | 2000 Loucks Rd. 17404; Rte. 30 to Rte. 74 W | 717/846–9500 | fax 717/764–5038 | www.holiday-inn.com | 180 rooms | $84–$102 | AE, D, DC, MC, V.

Rhode Island

BLOCK ISLAND

Blue Dory Inn. This romantic seaside inn with Victorian charm was built in 1897. A deck in back overlooks the ocean. Rooms have antique furnishings with flowery wallpapers. Complimentary Continental breakfast. Some kitchenettes, some microwaves, some refrigerators. Beach. Pets allowed. | Dodge St. | 401/466–2254 | fax 401/466–9910 | www.bluedoryinn.com | 12 rooms, 3 suites, 4 cottages | $165–$225, $275–$495 suites, $165–$365 cottages | AE, D, MC, V.

BRISTOL

Joseph Reynolds House Inn. A night at this 1693, red-clapboard inn includes a lesson in Colonial history: George Washington and Thomas Jefferson planned the Revolutionary War Battle of Rhode Island here with the Marquis de Lafayette. The Marquis' room is period-accurate, with a 17th-century marbelized fireplace. Some of the other rooms have four-poster beds. Complimentary breakfast. Some kitchenettes, no room phones, cable TV in some rooms, some in-room VCRs. Business services. Pets allowed. | 956 Hope St. | 401/254–0230 or 800/754–0230 | fax 401/254–2610 | reynoldsbb@aol.com | 3 rooms, 2 suites | $95–$115, rooms; $165–$175 suites | AE, D, DC, MC, V.

Swanson House. Enjoy beautiful views of gardens and Narragansett Bay from this three-room suite that can sleep up to five people, in a 1930s colonial-style house. There's a veranda with a wisteria covered pergola in the back, and the property has 1½ landscaped acres, a short walk from downtown. Complimentary Continental breakfast. Pets sometimes allowed. No smoking. | 150 Ferry Rd. 02809 | 401/254–5056 | 1 3-room suite | $110–$130 | No credit cards.

GALILEE

Lighthouse Inn of Galilee. Across the street from the Block Island ferry dock and 300 yards from sandy Salty Brine Beach lies this very basic, 1970s, two-story motel with outside entrances. Kids love the large indoor pool and huge activity area around it. Restaurant, bar. Some in-room hot tubs, cable TV. Indoor pool. Saunas. Gym. Laundry facilities. Pets allowed (fee). | 307 Great Island Rd. 02882 | 401/789–9341 or 800/336–6662 | fax 401/789–1590 | 100 rooms | $105–$150 | Closed Nov.–Apr. | D, MC, V.

KINGSTON

The Kings' Rose B&B. On the National Historic Register, this spacious 1933 Colonial Revival house ½ mi east of Kingston Village and URI is on 2¼ acres of gardens with fish and reflecting pools. The large rooms are done in Williamsburg colors and wallpapers, and the furnishings are antiques and family pieces, with a writing table and easy chair in each room. The common area downstairs features an honor bar for guests. You get a menu of breakfast choices. Complimentary breakfast. No air-conditioning in some rooms, some room phones, no TV in some rooms, TV in common area. 1 tennis court. Library. Pets allowed. No kids under 8. No smoking. | 1747 Mooresfield Rd., (Rte. 138), South Kingstown 02879 | 401/783–5222 or 888/230–ROSE | fax 401/783–9984 | www.virtualcities.com/ons/ri/s/ris8701.htm | 4 rooms, 1 suite | $120–$150 | No credit cards.

MIDDLETOWN

Howard Johnson Lodge. This chain option is 2 mi from downtown Newport and within walking distance of shops and restaurants. It offers a free shuttle to Newport on summer evenings. Restaurant, complimentary Continental breakfast. Some microwaves, some refrigerators, cable TV. Indoor pool. Sauna, hot tub, spa. Tennis courts. Business services. Free parking. Pets allowed. | 351 W. Main Rd. 02842 | 401/849–2000 | fax 401/849–6047 | 155 rooms | $99–$189 | AE, D, DC, MC, V.

Newport Ramada Inn. The inn is ½ mi from the naval base and 3 mi north of Newport. Children under 18 stay free. Restaurant, bar. In-room data ports, microwaves, refrigerators, cable TV. Indoor pool. Exercise equipment. Laundry facilities. Business services. Pets allowed (fee). | 936 W. Main Rd. 02840 | 401/846–7600 | fax 401/849–6919 | www.ramadainnnewport.com | 134 rooms, 15 suites | $129–205, $179–$239 suites | AE, D, DC, MC, V.

NARRAGANSETT

Larchwood Inn. A Colonial and a Victorian house face each other across Wakefield's main street that is less than 1 mi south of Narragansett. The inn offers a range of accommodations. The gardens are beautiful, ancient trees dot the 3 ½ acre property, and antiques are sprinkled throughout. Restaurant, bar. No air-conditioning in some rooms, some room phones, TV in common area. Pets allowed. | 521 Main St., Wakefield, South Kingston 02879 | 401/783–5454 or 800/275–5450 | fax 401/783–1800 | www.xpos.com/larchwoodinn | 18 rooms (7 with shared bath) | $65–$140 | AE, D, DC, MC, V.

NEWPORT

Sanford-Covell Villa Marina. This impressive waterfront Victorian home with a majestic, 35-ft entrance hall was built in 1869 by architect William Ralph Emerson. A saltwater pool, dock with seating, and wraparound porch adds to the inn's charm, as do original details like parquet floors, walnut wainscoting, and frescoes. The porch swing was featured on *This Old House*. Complimentary Continental breakfast. No air-conditioning, no room phones, no TV. Heated pool. Laundry facilities. Some pets allowed. No smoking. | 72 Washington St. | 401/847–0206 | fax 401/848–5599 | www.sanford-covell.com | 5 rooms (2 with shared bath) | $160–$295 | AE, DC, MC, V.

PORTSMOUTH

Founder's Brook Motel. This motel is near the junction of Routes 138 and 24. The suites are separate from the motel, in country-style cabins. Picnic area. Some kitchenettes, some in-room hot tubs, cable TV. Laundry facilities. Pets allowed (fee). | 314 Boyd's La. 02871 | 401/683–1244 or 800/334–8765 | fax 401/683–9129 | 8 rooms, 24 suites | $69–$119, $89–$139 suites | AE, D, DC, MC, V.

PROVIDENCE

The Biltmore. Built in 1922, this hotel has an art deco facade with an exterior glass elevator that offers sweeping views of Providence. The staff is very attentive, and the rooms are elegant and spacious. Restaurant, bar, room service. In-room data ports, cable TV. Beauty salon. Gym. Laundry service. Business services. Parking (fee). Pets allowed. | 11 Dorrance St., Kennedy Plaza 02903 | 401/421–0700 or 800/294–7709 | fax 401/455–3050 | www.providencebiltmore.com | 278 rooms, 21 suites | $130–$260, $160–$375 suites | AE, D, DC, MC, V.

C. C. Ledbetter Bed & Breakfast. A downtown location, a most cheerful C. C. herself, and the charm of this 1770 mansard-roof home make this a special place to stay. The garden has two hammocks and blooms with roses, lilies, and peonies. Its proximity to Brown and RISD makes it a favorite for visiting parents. Complimentary Continental breakfast. Cable TV, no room phones. Free parking. Pets allowed. No smoking. | 326 Benefit St. 02903 | 401/351–4699 | 4 rooms (2 with shared bath) | $95–$110 | MC, V.

Providence Marriott. A full-service hotel in downtown Providence with all the modern conveniences. The restaurant, Bluefin Grille, serves local seafood with a French flair. Restaurant, bar with entertainment, room service. In-room data ports, cable TV. Indoor-outdoor pool. Hot tub, sauna. Exercise equipment. Laundry service. Business services, airport shuttle. Pets allowed. Free parking. | 1 Orms St. 02904 | 401/272–2400 | fax 401/273–2686 | www.marriott.com | 346 rooms, 5 suites | $159–$199, $375 suites | AE, D, DC, MC, V.

★ **The Westin Providence.** The 25-story Westin towers over Providence's downtown and features a wine cellar in its Agora Restaurant. There's a skywalk connecting it to the convention center. Restaurants, bars, room service. In-room data ports, minibars, some refrigerators, cable TV. Indoor pool. Hot tub, massage, sauna. Health club. Laundry service. Business center. Parking (fee). Some pets allowed. | 1 W. Exchange St. 02903 | 401/598–8000 or 888/625–5411 | fax 401/598–8200 | www.westin.com | 341 rooms, 23 suites | $249–$329, $324–$400 suites | AE, D, DC, MC, V.

WARWICK

Comfort Inn Airport. This chain option caters to business travelers as it is close to downtown Providence and T. F. Green Airport. Complimentary Continental breakfast. In-room data ports, some refrigerators, some in-room hot tubs, cable TV. Hot tub. Business services, airport shuttle. Some pets allowed. | 1940 Post Rd. 02886 | 401/732–0470 or 800/228–5150 | fax 401/732–4247 | www.comfortinn.com | 200 rooms | $159–$179 | AE, D, DC, MC, V.

Mainstay Suites. This all-suite hotel ½ mi from the airport has modern rooms in a variety of configurations. Some have lounges, some pull-out couches, all have queen-sized beds. Complimentary Continental breakfast. In-room data ports, kitchenettes, microwaves, refrigerators, cable TV. Hot tub. Gym. Laundry facilities, laundry service. Pets allowed (fee). | 268 Metro Center Blvd. 02886 | 401/732–6667 or 800/660–MAIN | fax 401/732–6668 | www.mainstaysuites.com | 94 suites | $99–$189 | AE, D, DC, M, V.

Motel 6. Frugal travelers favor this price-conscious chain that provides basic motel amenities. It is 2 mi north of the airport and has a 24 hour Bickford's Restaurant. Restaurant, bar. In-room data ports, cable TV. Outdoor pool. Laundry facilities. Some pets allowed. | 20 Jefferson Blvd. 02888 | 401/467–9800 | fax 401/467–6780 | www.motel6.com | 123 rooms in 2 buildings | $69–$85 | AE, D, DC, MC, V.

Residence Inn by Marriott. The Marriott, 15 minutes from downtown Providence, caters to business travelers and families, with rooms and kitchen suites at moderate prices. Complimentary Continental breakfast. In-room data ports, cable TV. Indoor pool. Hot tub. Baby-sitting, playground. Laundry service. Business services. Pets allowed. | 500 Kilvert St. 02886 | 401/737–7100 | fax 401/739–2909 | www.residenceinn.com | 96 kitchen suites | $119–$189 | AE, D, DC, MC, V.

WESTERLY

The Villa. This Italian-style villa has a beautiful garden and is ideal for a romantic getaway. Some rooms have whirlpools and fireplaces. Picnic area, complimentary Continental breakfast. Refrigerators, some room phones, some in-room hot tubs, cable TV. Pool. Hot tub. Business services. Some pets allowed. No smoking. | 190 Shore Rd., at Rte. 1 A 02891 | 401/596–1054 or 800/722–9240 | fax 401/596–6268 | www.thevillaatwesterly.com | 6 suites | $130–$245 | AE, MC, V.

South Carolina

ALLENDALE

Executive Inn. This L-shape motel serves tourists, business people, and—as the parking facilities for large trucks indicates—truckers. Cable TV, room phones. Pets allowed (fee). | 671 N. Main St., 29810 | 803/584–2184 | fax 803/584–2184 | 65 rooms | $35–$50 | AE, D, DC, MC, V.

ANDERSON

Anderson Hotel. This former Holiday Inn 4 mi from downtown was built in 1962 but it's still a good bet for simple, reasonably priced rooms. Restaurant, bar (with entertainment), room service. In-room data ports. Cable TV. Pool. Laundry facilities. Business services. Some pets allowed. | 3025 N. Main St., 29621 | 864/226–6051 | fax 864/964–9145 | 130 rooms | $59–$99 | AE, D, DC, MC, V.

BEAUFORT

Howard Johnson Express Inn. Large trees shade the white stucco building surrounded by greenery and on the edge of the marsh. Rooms overlook the river, and sunlight streams in through the large windows. The hotel is 5 mi from beaches and 5 mi from Parris Island. Complimentary Continental breakfast. Microwaves, refrigerators. Cable TV. Pool. Fishing. Business services. Pets allowed. | 3651 Trask Pkwy. (Hwy. 21), 29902 | 843/524–6020 or 800/406–1411 | fax 843/524–2070 | 63 rooms | $75 | AE, D, DC, MC, V.

CAMDEN

Camden B&B. Working fireplaces and Belgian stained-glass windows decorate this original Federal-style home, surrounded by acres of pine forest. Complimentary breakfast. In-room data ports, microwaves, refrigerators. Cable TV, in-room VCRs, room phones. Pets allowed. No smoking. | 127 Union St., 29020 | 803/432–2366 | fax 803/432–9767 | jerixon@tech-tech.com | www.camdenscbandb.com | 1–3 bedroom suite; 2 cottages | $85–$109 | AE, D, DC, MC, V.

Colony Inn. Rooms in the two two-story brick buildings of this mom-and-pop hotel 1½ mi from downtown have either interior or exterior entrances. The building with interior entrances is entirely non-smoking and without pets. Restaurant. Cable TV. Pool.

Some pets allowed. | 2020 W. DeKalb St., 29020 | 803/432–5508 or 800/356–9801 | fax 803/432–0920 | 53 rooms | $55 | AE, D, DC, MC, V.

Travelodge. This motel is in Lugoff, 5 mi south from Camden on I-20 and next to a number of restaurants. Complimentary Continental breakfast. In-room data ports, microwaves, refrigerators. Cable TV, room phones. Outdoor pool. Pets allowed (fee). | 928 Hwy. 1S, Lugoff, 29078 | 803/438–4961 | fax 803/438–4961 | www.travelodge.com | 83 rooms | $49–$59 | AE, D, DC, MC, V.

CHARLESTON

Days Inn–Airport. This two-story chain hotel is ½ mi the from Charleston Coliseum and about 10 mi from beaches. Restaurant. Some refrigerators. Cable TV. Pool. Playground. Laundry facilities. Business services. Free Parking. Some pets allowed (fee). | 2998 W. Montague Ave., North Charleston, 29418 | 843/747–4101 or 800/544–8313 | fax 843/566–0378 | 147 rooms | $37–$89 | AE, D, DC, MC, V.

Hampton Inn–Riverview. Some rooms in this five-floor cement high-rise overlook the pool and small gardens. The hotel is next to the Ripley Light Marina, about 2 mi from the Charleston Museum, the Citadel, and downtown Charleston. 12 mi northwest of Charleston International Airport. Complimentary Continental breakfast. In-room data ports. Cable TV. Pool. Laundry facilities. Business services, parking (fee). Some pets allowed. | 11 Ashley Pointe Dr., 29407 | 843/556–5200 | fax 843/571–5499 | 175 rooms | $89–$109 | AE, D, DC, MC, V.

Indigo. The 1850s Greek Revival Jasmine House Inn and carriage house comprise this hotel nestled in the heart of Charleston's historic district. Period-correct fabrics, antique reproductions, and queen-size beds furnish the rooms, and plants fill the lush courtyard. Complimentary Continental breakfast. In-room data ports. Cable TV. Business services, free parking. Some pets allowed (fee). | 1 Maiden La., 29401 | 843/577–5900 or 800/845–7639 | fax 843/577–0378 | indigoinn@awod.com | www.aesir.com/indigoinn | 40 rooms | $189–$225 | AE, D, DC, MC, V.

La Quinta Inn Charleston. Red tile roofing and teal trim on a white stucco building are the trademark style of this budget hotel. Some rooms have walk-on porches. Picnic area, complimentary Continental breakfast, room service. In-room data ports, refrigerators. Cable TV. Pool. Business services, free parking. Some pets allowed. | 2499 La Quinta La., North Charleston, 29420 | 843/797–8181 | fax 843/569–1608 | www.laquinta.com | 122 rooms, 2 suites | $59–$69, $89 suites | AE, D, DC, MC, V.

Red Roof Inn. This white stucco and stone building with triangular slanted roofs is convenient to restaurants and shopping, 12 mi from the Citadel, and 21 mi from Fort Sumter. You enter rooms on both floors from exterior corridors. Cable TV. Microwaves, refrigerators. Laundry facilities. Free parking. Some pets allowed. | 7480 Northwoods Blvd., North Charleston, 29406 | 843/572–9100 or 800/RED–ROOF (733–7663) | fax 843/572–0061 | 109 rooms | $57 | AE, D, DC, MC, V.

Red Roof Inn. This particular branch of the budget chain sits at the foot of Cooper River Bridge, 5 mi from the historic district and 9 mi from the Isle of Palms. Rooms on two floors have exterior entrances. Cable TV. Pool. Free parking. Some pets allowed. | 301 Johnnie Dodds Blvd., Mt. Pleasant, 29464 | 843/884–1411 or 800/RED–ROOF (733–7663) | fax 843/971–0726 | 124 rooms | $65–$90 | AE, D, DC, MC, V.

CHERAW

Cheraw State Park. For instant access to hiking, canoeing, biking, and kayaking, you can stay in the fully furnished cabins in South Carolina's oldest and largest state park. There are also equestrian trails and golf. Kitchens, microwaves, refrigerators. Golf privileges. Hiking, horseback riding. Boating. Pets allowed. | 100 State Park Rd., 29520 | 800/868–9630 or 843/537–2215 | fax 843/537–1009 | 8 cabins | $65 for up to 4 people | D, DC, MC, V.

Days Inn. Although not particularly distinctive, this chain hotel is just 2 mi from golf courses and tennis courts and 1 mi from restaurants and shopping. Complimentary Continental breakfast. In-room data ports, some microwaves, refrigerators, some in-room hot tubs. Cable TV, room phones. Outdoor pool. Pets allowed (fee). | 820 Market St., 29520 | 800/329–7466 or 843/537–5554 | fax 843/537–4110 | www.daysinn.com | 55 rooms | $45–$55 | AE, D, DC, MC, V.

Inn Cheraw. A little balcony greets you at the entrance of this simple, affordable accommodation about two blocks from the downtown historic area and near restaurants and shops. Restaurant, complimentary Continental breakfast. Refrigerators. Cable TV, in-room VCRs. Free parking. Some pets allowed. | 321 Second St., 29520 | 843/537–2011 or 800/535–8709 | fax 843/537–0227 | 50 rooms | $40–$70 | AE, D, DC, MC, V.

CHESTER

Executive Inn. With a fishing camp next to it, this two-building motel seems particularly suited to fishermen. There are two restaurants across the street. Complimentary Continental breakfast. In-room data ports, some kitchenettes, some in-room hot tubs. Cable TV, room phones. Outdoor pool. Pets allowed (fee). | 1632 J.A. Cochran Bypass, 29706 | 803/581–2525 | fax 803/581–4171 | 45 rooms, 2 suites | $43–$75 | AE, D, MC, V.

CLEMSON

Lake Hartwell Inn. Though 1½ mi from the downtown area and within walking distance of some restaurants, this lakeside hotel has a quiet, laid-back feel to it. Restaurant, bar, complementary buffet breakfast. In-room data ports. Cable TV. Pool. Laundry facilities. Business services. Some pets allowed. | 894 Tiger Blvd., 29633 | 864/654–4450 | fax 864/654–8451 | 219 rooms | $65 | AE, D, DC, MC, V.

COLUMBIA

Days Inn–Columbia. About a 15-min drive from Ft. Jackson, Williams–Brice Stadium, malls, and restaurants is this chain hotel, with extra parking for trucks. Complimentary Continental breakfast. In-room data ports. Cable TV, room phones. Outdoor pool. Free parking. Pets allowed (fee). | 133 Plumbers Rd., 29203 | 803/754–4408 | fax 803/786–2821 | www.daysinn.com | 42 rooms | $45 | AE, D, DC, MC, V.

Governor's House Hotel. This elegant mansion has nine guest bedrooms or suites, each with private baths and hardwood floors. The Grand Rooms have 12' ceilings, a fireplace, and a private verandah. The Roofscape Rooms have a view of historic Charleston. The Kitchen House Suites have a separate living room, private porch, whirlpool, wet bar, and an original 1760 fireplace. The State Capitol is right across the street. 2 restaurants, complimentary Continental breakfast. In-room data ports, some microwaves, refrigerators, some hot tubs. Cable TV, room phones. Outdoor pool. Free parking. Pets allowed (fee). | 1301 Main St., 29201 | 803/779–7790 | fax 803/779–7856 | 9 rooms | $59–$119, $139–$189 suites | AE, D, DC, MC, V.

Ramada Plaza Hotel. This chain hotel is within 8 mi of movie theaters, the shopping mall, and restaurants. Restaurant, bar, service. In-room data ports, microwaves, refrigerators in suites. Cable TV. Pool. Hot tub. Exercise equipment. Business services, free parking. Some pets allowed. | 8105 Two Notch Rd., 29223 | 803/736–5600 | fax 803/736–1241 | www.ramada.com | 186 rooms | $89 | AE, D, DC, MC, V.

Residence Inn by Marriott. Fireplaces distinguish most of the rooms in this chain hotel. Complimentary Continental breakfast. In-room data ports, kitchenettes, microwaves. Cable TV. Pool. Hot tub. Exercise equipment. Laundry facilities. Business services, free parking. Some pets allowed. | 150 Stoneridge Dr., 29210 | 803/779–7000 or 800/331–3131 | fax 803/779–0408 | 128 suites | $114 | AE, D, DC, MC, V.

EDGEFIELD

Pleasant Lane Acres B&B. Trees line the driveway up to this 120-yr-old renovated farm house, which sits on 50 acres of land. Hard pine floors, antique heirlooms, and fireplaces romantically furnish the rooms, making this an ideal retreat for couples. There is a fishing pond on the land, as well as miles of bike trails; you can get a picnic to go if you plan to explore the area. Complimentary breakfast. Microwaves, refrigerators. Cable TV. Laundry facilities. Pets allowed. No kids. No smoking. | 318 Pleasant Lane Rd., 29824 | 888/ 771–3161 or 803/637–9387 | fax 803/637–9387 | pleasantlaneacresbb@jetbinn.net | www.bbonline.com/sc/pleasantlane | 3 rooms | $135–$150 | Closed Mon.–Wed. | No credit cards.

FLORENCE

Days Inn. The rooms have exterior entrances at this standard two-story chain hotel 3 mi from downtown area. Complimentary Continental breakfast. Some microwaves, some refrigerators, some in-room hot tubs. Cable TV. Pool. Hot tub. Exercise equipment. Business services. Some pets allowed. | 2111 W. Lucas St., 29501 | 843/665–4444 | fax 843/665–4444 | 103 rooms | $63 | AE, D, DC, MC, V.

Ramada Inn. The commercial area of shopping malls and restaurants is 4 mi from this two-story chain hotel with simple rooms, some of which have exterior entrances. Restaurant, bar (with entertainment), room service. Microwaves. Cable TV. Pool. Hot tub. Exercise equipment. Business services. Some pets allowed. | 2038 W. Lucas St., 29501 | 843/669– 4241 | fax 843/665–8883 | 179 rooms | $69 | AE, D, DC, MC, V.

Red Roof Inn. You can get budget accommodations across from the local shopping center. Some of the rooms have exterior entrances. Cable TV. Business services. Some pets allowed. | 2690 David McLeod Blvd., 29501 | 843/678–9000 | fax 843/667–1267 | 112 rooms | $48–$57 | AE, D, DC, MC, V.

Swamp Fox Inn. This standard motel has two double beds in each room. Restaurant. Cable TV, room phones. Outdoor pool. Pets allowed. | I–95 and U.S. 76, 29501 | 843/665–0803 | fax 843/665–0803 | 60 rooms | $24–$28 | AE, D, DC, MC, V.

FOLLY BEACH

Holliday Inn of Folly Beach. This family-owned inn caters to families seeking rest and relaxation. Surfing, fishing, and kayaking are 1 block away. Kitchenettes, microwaves, refrigerators. Cable TV, room phones. Outdoor pool. Pets allowed (fee). | 116 West Ashley St., 29439 | 800/792–5270 or 843/588–2191 | fax 843/588–6645 | inn108@aol.co | www. hollidayinnfollybeach.com | 14 rooms | $95–$150 | AE, D, MC, V.

GEORGETOWN

Mansfield Plantation. The original house and slave cabins are among the 11 buildings that remain on this 460-acre former rice plantation. Four-poster rice beds and 19th-century oil paintings decorate the guest rooms in the 1930s schoolhouse and renovated servants' quarters, all of which have private entrances. Complimentary breakfast. Boating, bicycles. Some pets allowed. | 1776 Mansfield Rd., 29440 | 843/546–6961 or 800/355–3223 | fax 843/ 546–5235 | www.bbonline.com/sc/mansfield | 8 rooms | $95–$135 | No credit cards.

GREENVILLE

AmeriSuites. Three miles from downtown Greenville, 4 mi from Bob Jones University, and 15 mi from Furman University, this hotel is also convenient to downtown restaurants and shopping. Complimentary Continental breakfast. In-room data ports, kitchenettes, microwaves, refrigerators. Cable TV, in-room VCRs, room phones. Outdoor pool. Exercise equipment. Free parking. Pets allowed (fee). | 40 West Orchard Park Dr., 29615 | 800/833–

1516 or 864/232–3000 | fax 864/271–4388 | www.amerisuites.com | 128 suites | $59–$89 | AE, D, DC, MC, V.

Crowne Plaza Greenville. This hotel is 5 mi from downtown Greenville, 8 mi from the airport, the Roper Mt. Science Center, and the Greenville Braves Ball Park. The rooms contain a hair dryer, iron, and ironing board. Restaurant, bar, room service. In-room data ports. Cable TV, room phones. Pool. Exercise equipment. Free parking. Pets allowed (fee). | 851 Congaree Rd., 29607 | 800/465–4329 or 864/297–6300 | fax 864/234–0747 | www.basshotels.com | 208 rooms | $129–$139 | AE, D, DC, MC, V.

GuestHouse International Suites Plus. The cozy and intimate suites here are within ½ mi from various shops and eateries. Complimentary Continental breakfast. Kitchenettes. Cable TV. Pool. Hot tub. Business services. Some pets allowed (fee). | 48 McPrice Ct, 29615 | 864/297–0099 | fax 864/288–8203 | 96 suites | $99–$129 | AE, D, DC, MC, V.

La Quinta. The Mediterranean decor matches the Spanish name of this two-story chain hotel. It's 7 mi from the airport. Complimentary Continental breakfast. Cable TV. Pool. Laundry facilities. Business services, free parking. Some pets allowed. | 31 Old Country Rd., 29607 | 864/297–3500 | fax 864/458–9818 | www.laquintainn.com | 122 rooms | $59–$66 | AE, D, DC, MC, V.

Microtel Inn Greenville. One of the many budget options in Greenville, this motel is in the shopping district. Complimentary Continental breakfast. In-room data ports, some microwaves. Cable TV, room phones. Free parking. Pets allowed (fee). | 20 Interstate Ct., 29615 | 864/297–7866 | fax 864/297–7883 | 122 rooms | $32–$42 | AE, D, DC, MC, V.

Travelodge. Five miles from downtown Greenville is this two-story hotel, which has special access for people with disabilities. In-room data ports, some microwaves, some refrigerators. Cable TV, room phones. Outdoor pool. Free parking. Pets allowed (fee). | 1465 S. Pleasantburg Dr., 29605 | 800/578–7878 or 864/277–8670 | fax 864/422–8960 | www.travelodge.com | 100 rooms | $39–$65 | AE, D, DC, MC, V.

HARTSVILLE

Nealcrest Farm B&B. Handmade quilts cover four-poster beds in spacious rooms with hardwood floors. The 47 acres of this property include a small kennel. Complimentary breakfast. Cable TV. Pool. Business services. Some pets allowed (fee). | 1248 Windfall Farm La., 29550 | 843/383–6677 | fax 843/383–4009 | 3 rooms, 1 apartment | $60–$80 | MC, V.

HILTON HEAD ISLAND

Comfort Inn and Suites. This resort-style hotel on a seven-acre park with a lagoon opens a water park during the summer. It's across from the beach and 1 block from tennis courts. Restaurant, dining room, picnic area, complimentary Continental breakfast. In-room data ports, in-room safes, some microwaves, some refrigerators. Cable TV, room phones, TV in common area. Outdoor pool, wading pool. Golf privileges, miniature golf. Video games. Laundry facilities. Business services. Pets allowed (fee). | 2 Tanglewood Dr., 29928 | 843/842–6662 or 800/228–5150 | fax 843/842–6664 | www.comfortinn.com/hotel/sc173 | 153 rooms | $139–$179 | AE, D, DC, MC, V.

Howard Johnson. The rooms come with balconies at this two-story standard. It's 15 mi from Savannah Airport. Restaurant. Cable TV. Pool, wading pool. Business services. Some pets allowed (fee). | I–95, junction Hwy. 17, Hardeeville (24 mi east of Hilton Head) 29927 | 843/784–2271 | fax 843/784–2271 | 128 rooms | $40–$45 | AE, D, DC, MC, V.

Motel 6. Two blocks south of Shelter Cove Marina you'll find clean rooms typical of this chain. You can take advantage of the outdoor pool or walk to the beach. Some kitchenettes, some microwaves, some refrigerators. Cable TV, room phones. Outdoor pool. Laundry facilities. Pets allowed. | 830 William Hilton Pkwy., 29928 | 843/785–2700 or 800/466–8356 | fax 843/842–9543 | 116 rooms | $66–$76 | AE, D, DC, MC, V.

KIAWAH ISLAND

Holiday Inn Riverview. Although in Charleston, you have direct access to all the barrier islands and a complimentary shuttle to the area's attractions, as well as all the amenities. The restaurant and bar on the top floor have nice views of the Ashley River and Charleston Harbor. Restaurant, bar, dining room, room service. In-room data ports, some kitchenettes, some refrigerators. Cable TV, some in-room VCRs, room phones, TV in common area. Outdoor pool. Golf privileges. Gym. Laundry facilities, laundry service. Business services. Pets allowed. | 301 Savannah Hwy., 29407 | 843/556–7100 or 800/465–4329 | fax 843/556–6176 | www.holiday-inn.com | 181 rooms | $109–$139 | AE, D, DC, MC, V.

MURRELLS INLET

Barnacle Inn. The friendly staff and ocean view at this small motel keep the regulars coming back year after year. You can walk a half-mile to the center of town or across the street to fish at the Garden City Pier. Picnic area. Some kitchenettes, microwaves, refrigerators. Cable TV, some in-room VCRs, room phones. Outdoor pool. Laundry facilities. Pets allowed. | 215 S. Waccamaw Dr., 29575 | 843/651–2828 or 800/272–4222 | fax 843/651–2828 | 27 rooms, 3 apartments | $80 rooms, $108 apartments; 2–night minimum on weekends | AE, D, DC, MC, V.

MYRTLE BEACH

Royal Inn. Surrounded by palm trees and across the street from the city park, this motel is four blocks from the Pavilion in a quiet neighborhood. Only couples and families may stay in its rooms and 2- and 3-bedroom suites. Picnic area. Some kitchenettes, refrigerators. Cable TV, room phones. 2 pools (1 indoor). Laundry facilities. Free Parking. Some pets allowed. | 1406 N. Chester St., 29577 | 843/448–7743 | 32 rooms, 8 suites | Rooms $67–$77, suites $85–$105 | Closed Dec.–Feb. | D, MC, V.

St. John's Inn. The rooms at this hotel across the street from the beach are decorated in bright colors and some have balconies. Restaurant. Kitchenettes, refrigerators. Cable TV. Pool. Hot tub. Some pets allowed. | 6803 N. Ocean Blvd., 29572 | 843/449–5251 or 800/845–0624 | fax 843/449–3306 | www.stjohnsinn.com/vacation.html | 90 rooms | $33–$105 | AE, D, MC, V.

Stardust Motel. The rooms are clean and comfortable at this motel four blocks from the Pavilion and a short walk to the beach. Some kitchenettes, some microwaves, refrigerators. Cable TV, room phones. Outdoor pool. Laundry facilities. Some pets allowed. | 501 5th Avenue N, 29577 | 843/448–6717 | fax 843/626–8729 | 24 rooms | $68–$103 | MC, V.

NEWBERRY

Best Western Newberry Inn. The nearby lake draws people who like to fish, and since 1965, travelers have been staying at this chain motel off I–26 (Exit 74) and near the Newberry Opera House and Japanese Garden. Complimentary Continental breakfast. Some microwaves, some refrigerators. Cable TV, room phones. Outdoor pool. Pets allowed (fee). | 11701 S. Carolina Hwy., 29108 | 803/276–5850 or 800/528–1234 | fax 803/276–9851 | 113 rooms | $42–$55 | AE, D, DC, MC, V.

Days Inn. This standard chain motel is close to I–385 and Hwy. 56 as well as restaurants and shopping. Complimentary Continental breakfast. Some refrigerators. Cable TV. Pool. Exercise equipment. Laundry facilities. Some pets allowed. | 12374 Hwy. 56, North Clinton, 20 mi north of Newberry on Hwy. 56 29325 | 864/833–6600 | fax 864/833–6600 | 54 rooms, 4 suites | $45–$85 | AE, D, DC, MC, V.

ROCK HILL

Days Inn Charlotte South/Carowinds. This chain hotel is ½ mi from Paramount's Carowinds amusement park and 3 mi from restaurants and shopping. Paintings of Carolina scenery decorate the rooms' walls. Complimentary Continental breakfast. Cable TV, in-room VCRs (and movies). Pool. Some pets allowed. | 3482 U.S. 21, Fort Mill, 29715 | 803/548–8000 | fax 803/548–6058 | www.daysinn.com | 119 rooms | $35–$75 | AE, D, DC, MC, V.

Holiday Inn. Pastel-shaded bedspreads and walls decorate the rooms at this standard chain hotel, which is close to the bus station, shopping areas, and movie theatres. Restaurant, bar, complimentary breakfast. In-room data ports. Cable TV. Pool. Laundry facilities. Business services, airport shuttle. Some pets allowed. | 2640 Cherry Rd., 29730 | 803/329–1122 | fax 803/329–1072 | www.holiday-inn.com | 125 rooms | $89 | AE, D, DC, MC, V.

Ramada Plaza Hotel Carowinds. Rooms with pull-out sofas distinguish this otherwise typical chain hotel across the street from the amusement park and within 2 mi of restaurants. Restaurant, bar, complimentary Continental breakfast. In-room data ports. Cable TV. Pool. Gym. Laundry facilities. Business services, airport shuttle. Some pets allowed. | 225 Carowinds Blvd., Fort Mill, 29715 | 803/548–2400 | fax 803/548–6382 | www.ramada.com | 205 rooms, 3 suites | $71–$105 rooms, $125–$145 suites | AE, D, DC, MC, V.

SANTEE

Days Inn. A fishing area and three golf courses next door make this typical chain hotel somewhat distinctive. Some rooms have lawn views, and the state park is 7 mi away. Restaurant, complimentary breakfast. Cable TV. Pool. Playground. Laundry service. Business services. Some pets allowed (fee). | 9074 Old Hwy. 6, 29142 | 803/854–2175 | fax 803/854–2835 | www.daysinn.com | 119 rooms | $50–$55 | AE, D, DC, MC, V.

SPARTANBURG

The Jameson Inn. The cathedral ceiling, glass foyer, and Old English lobby furniture make this chain hotel distinct. Maroon and green floral prints decorate the rooms and you can walk next door to restaurants. Picnic area, complimentary Continental breakfast. In-room data ports, some microwaves, some refrigerators, some in-room hot tubs. Cable TV, room phones, TV in common area. Outdoor pool. Gym. Some pets allowed. | 115 Rogers Commerce Blvd., 29316 | 864/814–0560 or 800/526–3766 | fax 864/814–0620 | 42 rooms | $56 | AE, D, DC, MC, V.

Main Street Motel. You can check into a clean, quiet room at this family run hotel, in operation since the 1950s. Free coffee is available in the foyer in the morning, and reception is open 24 hours. Cable TV, room phones. Pets allowed (fee). | 700 W. Main St., 29301 | 864/583–8471 | 33 rooms | $45 | MC, V.

Quality Hotel and Conference Center. The University of South Carolina Spartanburg is only 1 mi away from this hotel, and there are many restaurants nearby. Restaurant, bar. In-room data ports, cable TV. Pool. Exercise equipment. Business services. Some pets allowed. | 7136 Asheville Hwy., 29303 | 864/503–0780 | fax 864/503–0780 | 143 rooms | $79–$149 | AE, D, DC, MC, V.

SUMTER

Ramada Inn. Like the many chain hotels in the area, little distinguishes this one, though the rooms are clean and simple. Restaurant, bar, complimentary breakfast buffet, room service. In-room data ports, refrigerators. Cable TV. Pool. Business services. Some pets allowed. | 226 N. Washington St., 29150 | 803/775–2323 | fax 803/773–9500 | ramadagolf@aol.com | www.ramadagolf.com | 125 rooms in 2 buildings | $59–$109 | AE, D, DC, MC, V.

WALTERBORO

Best Western of Walterboro. Dark woodwork and floral patterns decorate the rooms at this motel chain, playing on a "Southern hospitality" theme. There are restaurants within walking distance; the motel is off I–95 at Exit 53. Restaurant, complimentary Continental breakfast. Cable TV, room phones, TV in common area. Outdoor pool. Exercise equipment. Pets allowed (fee). | 1428 Sniders Hwy., 29488 | 843/538–3600 or 800/528–1234 | fax 843/538–3600 | www.bestwestern.com | 112 rooms | $50–$70 | AE, D, DC, MC, V.

Holiday Inn. This chain hotel is near the historic district and within 2 mi of the museum; downtown is 3 mi away. Restaurant, room service. Cable TV. Pool, wading pool. Business services. Some pets allowed. | 1286 Sniders Hwy., 29488 | 843/538–5473 | fax 843/538–5473 | www.basshotels.com/holiday-inn | 171 rooms | $49–$69 | AE, D, DC, MC, V.

South Dakota

ABERDEEN

AmericInn. Spacious guest rooms are a mainstay in this brick hostelry. Two guest suites have fireplaces of their own. This location, next to Lakewood Mall on Hwy. 12, is 1 mi from the airport and the Swisher Field Sport Complex. Complimentary Continental breakfast. In-room data ports, some kitchenettes, some microwaves, some refrigerators, in-room hot tubs. Cable TV. Indoor pool. Spa, steam room. Airport shuttle. Pets allowed (fee). | 310 Centennial St. 57401 | 605/225-4565 or 800/634-3444 | fax 605/229-3792 | www.americinn.com | 64 rooms | $54-$156 | AE, D, MC, V.

Best Western Ramkota. This hotel off Hwy. 281 is set between two golf courses on the northeast edge of town. It is also convenient to bowling. Restaurant, bar, picnic area, room service. Cable TV. Indoor pool, wading pool. Hot tub, sauna. Video games. Laundry service. Business services, airport shuttle. Pets allowed. | 1400 8th Ave. NW 57401 | 605/229-4040 | fax 605/229-0480 | ramkotaabr@dtgnet.com | 154 rooms | $69 | AE, D, DC, MC, V.

Ramada Inn. At this hotel just 1½ mi from the airport you will find clean, comfortable rooms and a relaxing whirlpool tub. Restaurant, bar, complimentary Continental breakfast, room service. Cable TV. Indoor pool. Hot tub. Exercise equipment. Video games. Business services, airport shuttle. Pets allowed. | 2727 6th Ave. SE 57401 | 605/225-3600 | fax 605/225-6704 | 152 rooms | $69 | AE, D, DC, MC, V.

Super 8. This motel on the east side of town has standard chain rooms, but this is the original, first-ever Super 8. A mall and dining are nearby. Complimentary Continental breakfast. In-room data ports, some microwaves, some refrigerators. Cable TV. Indoor pool. Sauna. Exercise equipment. Laundry facilities. Airport shuttle. Pets allowed. | 2405 6th Ave. SE 57401 | 605/229-5005 | 108 rooms | $51-$53 | AE, D, DC, MC, V.

White House Inn. A distinctive landmark in the area and just 5 blocks from Main St., this modern concrete-and-steel inn has quiet, spacious rooms. Complimentary Continental breakfast. In-room data ports. Cable TV. Laundry facilities. Business services. Pets allowed. | 500 6th Ave. SW 57401 | 605/225-5000 or 800/225-6000 | fax 605/225-6730 | 96 rooms | $42-$44 | AE, D, MC, V.

BADLANDS NATIONAL PARK

Badlands Budget Host Motel. Every room in this motel has views of the Badlands National Forest, which is 1 mi away. You can have breakfast and dinner on the premises or walk over to a nearby restaurant. Restaurant, room service. Outdoor pool, wading pool. Video games. Playground. Laundry facilities. Pets allowed. | Rte. 377, Interior | 605/433–5335 or 800/388–4643 | 21 rooms | $50 | Closed Oct.–Apr. | MC, V.

★ **Cedar Pass Lodge and Restaurant.** Cedar Pass has spacious individual log cabins with views of the Badlands peaks, each with two beds. There's a gift shop with local crafts, including turquoise and beadwork. You'll find hiking trails that run next to the cabins. Restaurant, picnic area. Hiking. Some pets allowed. | 1 Cedar St., Interior | 605/433–5460 | fax 605/433–5560 | 24 cabins | $45 | Closed Nov. 1–Apr. 14 | AE, DC, MC, V.

BELLE FOURCHE

Ace Motel. Economical rooms one block off the highway in a quiet location are what you'll find here. Children under 12 stay free. Some microwaves, some refrigerators. Cable TV. Some pets allowed. | 109 6th Ave. | 605/892–2612 | 15 rooms | $28–$48 | D, MC, V.

Motel 6. This chain motel's rooms have blue decor and tiled bathrooms. The motel is 10 blocks from downtown and next door to a family-style restaurant. It's also convenient to many attractions, such as Mount Rushmore (about 1 hr), a golf course, the Black Hills Passion Play (a summer event similar to the European Passion plays), and gaming and skiing in Deadwood (about ½ hr). Kids 17 and under stay free. Cable TV. Indoor pool. Hot tub. Laundry facilities. Some pets allowed. | 1815 5th Ave. | 605/892–6663 | fax 605/892–6638 | 51 rooms | $66 | AE, D, MC, V.

BERESFORD

Crossroads. The rooms are large and on the ground floor, with individual parking spaces outside. Truck parking is available. The town of Beresford is small but has all essential facilities, and there is a restaurant within walking distance. Children under 12 stay free. Cable TV. Some pets allowed (fee). | I–29 and Rte. 46 | 605/763–2020 | fax 605/763–2504 | 20 rooms | $34–$38 | AE, D, DC, MC, V.

Super 8 Motel. This single-story motel built in 1998 is near downtown and I–29. Complimentary Continental breakfast, room service. In-room data ports, some refrigerators, some microwaves. Cable TV. Indoor pool. Spa. Exercise equipment. Laundry facilities. Pets allowed (fee). | 1410 W. Cedar 57004 | 605/763–2001 or 800/800–8000 | fax 605/763–2001 | www.super8.com | 35 rooms. 3 whirlpool suites | $60–$110 | AE, D, DC, MC, V.

BROOKINGS

Brookings Inn. This clean and quiet facility is 1 mi from a golf course and South Dakota State University. Restaurant, bar (with entertainment), picnic area, room service. Cable TV. Indoor pool. Hot tub, sauna. Miniature golf. Exercise equipment. Video games. Laundry facilities. Business services, airport shuttle. Some pets allowed. | 2500 E. 6th St. | 605/692–9471 | fax 605/692–5807 | 125 rooms | $62 | AE, D, DC, MC, V.

Staurolite Inn and Suites. Staurolite is less than 1 mi from South Dakota State University and 2 blocks from McCrory Gardens. The rooms are spacious, and some have private patios or balconies, or outside entrances. The restaurant is self-service. Children under 18 stay free. Restaurant, bar (with entertainment), room service. In-room data ports, some microwaves, some refrigerators. Cable TV. Indoor pool, wading pool. Hot tub. Video games. Laundry facilities. Business services, airport shuttle. Some pets allowed. | 2515 E. 6th St. | 605/692–9421 | 102 rooms | $55–$67 | AE, D, DC, MC, V.

Super 8 Motel. This motel built in 1995 is just 2 mi from South Dakota State University. It's at Exit 132 off I–29 east on Hwy. 14. Three rooms with whirlpool are available. Complimentary Continental breakfast. Some microwaves, some refrigerators. Cable TV. Outdoor pool. Video games. Laundry facilities. Pets allowed. | 3034 LeFevre Dr. 57006 | 605/692–6920 or 800/800–8000 | fax 605/692–6920, Ext. 401 | www.super8.com | 67 rooms | $40–$80 | AE, D, DC, MC, V.

CHAMBERLAIN

Cedar Shore Resort. This independent resort and campground built in 1995 is 2 mi from downtown right along the Missouri River. All rooms have decks or balconies. The lobby and atrium have a contemporary design, with 30 ft ceilings and original South Dakota artwork. Conference center. Restaurant, bar, dining room, room service. In-room data ports, some microwaves, some refrigerators. Cable TV. Indoor pool. Hot tub, sauna. Tennis court. Basketball, exercise equipment, hiking, horseback riding, volleyball. Water sports, fishing. Laundry facilities. Pets allowed (fee). | 3.5 mi from Exit 260 off I–90; 1500 Shoreline Dr., Ocoma 57365 | 605/734–6376, 888/697–6363 | fax 605/734–6854 | info@cedarshore.com | www.cedarshore.com | 99 rooms, 8 suites | $89–$99 | AE, D, DC, MC, V.

Comfort Inn. Built in 1976, this Comfort Inn is on service road I–92 between Crowcreek and Loperool casinos. Hunting, fishing, and boating are available nearby. Cable TV. Hot tub. Pets allowed (fee). | 203 E. Hwy. 16 57325 | 605/734–4222 or 800/228–5151 | fax 605/734–4222 | www.comfortinn.com | 35 rooms | $59–$159 | AE, D, DC, MC, V.

Oasis Inn. The rooms are standard, but some of them come with views of the Missouri River. In fact, this hotel is well located for fishing and water sports and is within walking distance of several restaurants. Bar, picnic area, complimentary Continental breakfast. In-room data ports. Cable TV. Outdoor hot tub, sauna. Playground. Laundry facilities. Pets allowed. | Rte. 16 | 605/734–6061 or 800/635–3559 (in SD) | fax 605/734–4161 | 68 rooms | $70–$79 | AE, D, DC, MC, V.

River View Inn. The rooms are standard but they overlook the river. The inn is near fishing and water activities. From here you can visit the Indian museum, just 1 mi away. Cable TV. Indoor pool. Hot tub, sauna. Laundry facilities. Pets allowed (fee). | 128 N. Front St. | 605/734–6057 | 29 rooms | $50–$72 | Usually closed Nov.–Mar. | AE, D, MC, V.

Super 8. This standard Super 8 accommodation has clean, economical rooms and sits on a hill overlooking the Missouri River. A deck with tables and chairs makes a nice spot to enjoy the view. Complimentary Continental breakfast. Cable TV. Pool. Hot tub, sauna. Video games. Laundry facilities. Pets allowed. | Lakeview Heights and Main St. | 605/734–6548 | 56 rooms | $61 | AE, D, MC, V.

CUSTER

Bavarian Inn. This looks just like a traditional German resort nestled in the pines; some rooms have views of the Black Hills, and all upstairs rooms open onto balconies with seating areas. The inn is less than 1 mi from downtown. Special rates are available for families with children under 12. Restaurant, bar. Cable TV. 2 pools (1 indoor). Hot tub, sauna. Tennis. Video games. Playground. Some pets allowed. | U.S. 16/385 N 57730 | 605/673–2802 or 800/657–4312 | fax 605/673–4777 | www.custer-sd.com/bavariansd.com/bavarian | 64 rooms | $80–$83 | AE, D, DC, MC, V.

Blue Bell Lodge and Resort. This hideaway retreat in Custer State Park has a western flavor. The modern hand-crafted log cabins have fireplaces, a lodge, and a conference center. There is a campground on the premises, and hayrides and cookouts are part of the entertainment. A stable offers trail rides and overnight pack trips on old Indian trails. Restaurant, bar, picnic area. No air-conditioning, some kitchenettes, some refrigerators. Cable TV, some room phones. Hiking, horseback riding. Playground. Laundry facilities. Some pets allowed. | 605/255–4531 or 800/658–3530 | fax 605/255–4706 | e-mail@custer-resorts.com | www.custerresorts.com | 29 cabins | $87–$170 (2–8 people) | Closed Oct.–Mother's Day | AE, D, MC, V.

Legion Lake Resort. This is a family-oriented rustic lakeside lodge with cabins surrounded by a pine forest in Custer State Park (which has an entrance fee). Restaurant. No air-conditioning. Some kitchenettes. No room phones. Hiking. Beach, boating, bicycles. Playground. Pets allowed. | HC 83 57730 | 605/255–4521 or 800/658–3530 | fax 605/255–4753 | e-mail@custerresorts.com | www.custerresorts.com | 25 cabins | $75–$120 | Closed Oct.–Mother's Day | AE, D, MC, V.

State Game Lodge and Resort. Once the summer White House for Presidents Coolidge and Eisenhower, this stately stone-and-wood lodge has well-appointed rooms and pine-shaded cabins. There are also Jeep rides into the buffalo area. Restaurant, bar, picnic area. No air-conditioning in some rooms, kitchenettes (in some cabins). Cable TV, some room phones. Hiking. Some pets allowed. | HC 83 57730 | 605/255–4541 or 800/658–3530 | fax 605/255–4706 | e-mail@custerresorts.com | www.custerresorts.com | 7 lodge rooms, 40 motel rooms, 33 cabins | $75–$215 lodge rooms, $89–$132 motel rooms, $75–$315 cabins | Closed Oct.–Mother's Day | AE, D, MC, V.

DEADWOOD

Days Inn Deadwood Gulch Resort. Pine-clad hills and a creek await you at this family-style resort, which also has a casino and a deck with a view of the mountains. It's about 1 mi from town, and a trolley stops in front of the hotel to take you to various sites in Deadwood. There is nearby hiking, horseback riding, fly-fishing, biking, and snowmobiling on the Mickelson Trail. Restaurant, bar. Cable TV. Pool. Hot tub. Hiking. Bicycles. Some pets allowed (fee). | Hwy. 85 S 57732 | 605/578–1294 or 800/695–1876 | fax 605/578–2505 | www.deadwoodgulch.com | 98 rooms | $109 | AE, D, DC, MC, V.

Franklin Hotel. Built in 1903, the imposing Franklin Hotel in the heart of Deadwood has housed many famous guests, including John Wayne, Teddy Roosevelt, and Kevin Costner. The original banisters, ceilings, and fireplace add character. A casino is in the hotel. Restaurant, bar (with entertainment). Room service. Cable TV. Business services. Some pets allowed. | 700 Main St. | 605/578–2241 or 800/688–1876 | fax 605/578–3452 | franklin@deadwood.net | www.deadwood.net/franklin | 81 rooms | $92 | AE, D, DC, MC, V.

HILL CITY

Best Western Golden Spike Inn. Only minutes from Mount Rushmore and Crazy Horse and 1½ blocks from the Mickelson Trail, the Golden Spike offers comfortable lodging and several rooms with views of the mountains. The pool is the ideal place to relax—it's in a room with wood walls and pine pillars. A garden with scattered tables, an espresso bar, and a gift shop are part of the hotel complex. Restaurant. Cable TV. Indoor pool. Hot tub. Exercise equipment. Bicycles. Video games. Laundry facilities. Some pets allowed. | 106 Main St. | 605/574–2577 or 800/528–1234 | fax 605/574–4719 | 62 rooms | $117 | Closed Nov. 21–Mar. | AE, D, DC, MC, V.

Lodge at Palmer Gulch. In an idyllic mountain valley near Mount Rushmore, the lodge is shadowed by the massive granite ramparts of Harney Peak. With its pools, waterslide, outdoor activities, and children's programs of movies and other entertainment, this is a great place for families. A free shuttle takes you to Mount Rushmore and Crazy Horse. Camping is allowed on the premises. Restaurant, picnic area. No air-conditioning in some rooms. Some kitchenettes. Cable TV, some room phones. 2 outdoor pools. Hot tub, sauna. Miniature golf. Basketball, horseback riding, volleyball. Video games. Children's programs, playground. Pets allowed. | 12620 Hwy. 244 | 605/574–2525 or 800/562–8503 | fax 605/574–2574 | palmerkoa@aol.com | www.travelsd.com | 62 rooms, 30 cabins | $113 | Closed Oct. 15–Apr. 15 | AE, D, MC, V.

HOT SPRINGS

Comfort Inn. Near the main highway, U.S. 385, and three blocks from downtown, this hotel offers easy access to the Mueller Civic Center. Family suites are available, and some rooms have views of a small river. Complimentary Continental breakfast. Microwaves, refrigerators. Some in-room hot tubs. Cable TV. Indoor pool. Hot tub. Gym. Laundry facilities. Business services. Pets allowed. | 737 S. 6th St. | 605/745–7378 or 800/228–5150 | fax 605/745–3240 | 51 rooms, 9 suites | $109, $129 suites | AE, D, MC, V.

Super 8 Motel. This typical Super 8 accommodation is next to the Mammoth Site and about 1 mi from the Hot Springs restaurants. Many rooms have a view of the Black Hills, and several large family-size rooms are available. Complimentary Continental breakfast. Some microwaves, some refrigerators. Cable TV. Video games. Laundry facilities. Pets allowed. | 800 Mammoth St. | 605/745–3888 or 800/800–8000 | fax 605/745–3385 | www.super8.com | 48 rooms | $92 | AE, D, MC, V.

HURON

Crossroads Hotel and Convention Center. Within walking distance of Huron's business district, the hotel proudly displays the locally sculpted *Spirit of Dakota* on its front lawn. 2 restaurants, bar, room service. In-room data ports, some refrigerators. Cable TV. Indoor pool. Hot tub, sauna. Business services, airport shuttle. Pets allowed. | 100 4th St. 57350 | 605/352–3204 | fax 605/352–3204 | 100 rooms | $57–$75 | AE, D, DC, MC, V.

Dakota Inn. Totally remodeled in 1997, this inn stands next to the city park and a scenic bike path. A restaurant is within walking distance. Guide services for pheasant hunting are available. Complimentary Continental breakfast. In-room data ports. Cable TV. Pool. Bowling. Business services. Pets allowed. | 924 4th St. and Hwy. 14E 57350 | 605/352–1400 or 800/933–6626 | fax 605/352–1400 | $65 | AE, D, MC, V.

Holiday Inn Express. This facility on the south end of Huron offers clean, comfortable rooms at a moderate price; all the rooms come equipped with irons, ironing boards, and hairdryers. Several restaurants are within walking distance. Huron is known as the "Pheasant Capital of the World," and this hotel fills up a year in advance for the hunting season. Complimentary Continental breakfast. In-room data ports, in-room safes. Some in-room hot tubs. Cable TV. Sauna. Exercise room. Laundry facilities. Pets allowed. | 100 21st St. SW 57350 | 605/352–6655 or 800/465–4329 | fax 605/353–1213 | 60 rooms, 8 suites | $70, $89–$125 suites | AE, D, DC, MC, V.

KEYSTONE

Best Western Four Presidents. In the shadow of Mount Rushmore in downtown Keystone, this hotel's rooms have been remodeled. You can walk to the city park and dining. Complimentary Continental breakfast. Some in-room hot tubs. Cable TV. Pets allowed. | 250 Winter St. | 605/666–4472 | fax 605/666–4574 | 33 rooms, 1 suite | $84–$94, $135 suite | All but 3 rooms closed Nov.–Apr. | AE, D, DC, MC, V.

Buffalo Rock Lodge B&B. A large, native rock fireplace surrounded by hefty logs adds to the rustic quality of this lodge decorated with Western artifacts. There's an extensive view of Mt. Rushmore from an oversize deck surrounded by plush pine forests filled with wildflowers. Complimentary Continental breakfast. In-room hot tubs. Hiking. Fishing. Pets allowed. | On Playhouse Rd., 5 mi east of Keystone 57751 | 605/666–4781 or 888/564–5634 | 3 rooms | $125–$150 | DC, MC, V.

Kelly Inn. This family favorite 2½ mi from downtown has extra large guest rooms, including family rooms with bunk beds and rooms for people with disabilities. Complimentary Continental breakfast. Some microwaves, some refrigerators. Cable TV. Hot tub. Exercise equipment. Laundry facilities. Business services. Pets allowed. | 320 Old Cemetery Rd. | 605/666–4483 or 800/635–3559 | fax 605/666–4883 | www.blackhills.com/kellyinn | 44 rooms | $90–$100 | Closed Nov.–Mar. | AE, D, DC, MC, V.

Mt. Rushmore White House Resort. This independent, two-story motel built around 1985 is near downtown, 30 mi off of I–90. You're minutes from Crazy Horse Memorial, 1880 Train, cave touring, amusement parks, helicopter rides, and recreational activities. Some kitchenettes, some refrigerators. Cable TV. Outdoor heated pool. Pets allowed (fee). | 115 Swanzey St. 57751 | 605/666–4929 or 800/456–1878, 800/504–3210 | fax 605/666–4805 | info@mtrushmoreresorts.com | www.mtrushmoreresorts.com | 70 rooms | $59–$99 | DC, MC, V.

Powder House Lodge. In the pines off U.S. 16A, this lodge has rustic cabins and a friendly staff. The lodge caters to family vacations with its outdoor heated pool, access to hiking trails, nearby stables, playground, and proximity to Mount Rushmore. Restaurant. Cable TV. Outdoor pool. Playground. Pets allowed. | 24127 Hwy. 16A | 605/666–4646 or 800/321–0692 | 37 rooms, 12 cabins | $80–$90 | Closed Sept.–mid-May | AE, D, MC, V.

LEAD

Deer Mountain B&B. This is a log home B&B with a ski resort right next door. You can relax by the fireplace or enjoy a game of pool in the billiards room. After complimentary hors d'oeuvres or dessert at night you can rest your muscles in the indoor hot tub. Deer Mountain is 3 mi south of Lead next to Deer Mountain Ski Resort and 5 minutes away from skiing, snowmobiles, and sleigh rides. Complimentary breakfast. TV in common area. Hot tub. Hiking. Pets allowed (fee). | HC 37 57754 | 605/584–2473 | fax 605/584–3045 | vonackerman@dtgnet.com | www.bbonline.com/sd/deermtn/ | 4 rooms (2 with shared bath) | $65–$85 | D, MC, V.

White House Inn. This white hotel, more than a decade old, offers economy lodging with direct access to snowmobile and hiking trails and close proximity to ski resorts. There's free transportation to Deadwood's main street and the casinos. Complimentary Continental breakfast. Some microwaves, some refrigerators, some in-room hot tubs. Cable TV. Hot tub. Snowmobiling. Business services. Pets allowed (fee). | 395 Glendale Dr. | 605/584–2000 or 800/654–5323 | 71 rooms, 17 suites | $75–$90, $75–$120 suites | AE, D, DC, MC, V.

LEMMON

Prairie Motel. This motel off U.S. 12 is within 15 min of the petrified wood park, fishing on Shade Hill Lake, and a restaurant. Some microwaves, refrigerators. Cable TV. Pets allowed. | 115 10 St. E 57638 | 605/374–3304 | 13 rooms | $30–$60 | AE, D, MC, V.

MADISON

Lake Park. Only minutes from pheasant hunting, lake recreation, and gambling, this all-ground-level motel offers trailer and camper parking and hookups. Some rooms have views of a garden, and one has an in-room hot tub. There is a restaurant behind the hotel. Refrigerators. Cable TV. Pool. Hot tub. Pets allowed. | 1515 N.W. 2nd St. | 605/256–3524 | 37 rooms | $40–$50 | AE, D, MC, V.

Super 8. This motel is about 1 mi from Prairie Village, an outdoor campground, and outdoor museum, and five blocks from Dakota State College. It's also next to the city park, which has a pool and tennis court that you're welcome to use as a hotel guest. A restaurant is next door. Complimentary Continental breakfast. Cable TV. Pets allowed (fee). | Junction Hwy. 34 and 81 | 605/256–6931. | www.super8.com | 34 rooms | $47 | AE, D, DC, MC, V.

MILBANK

Lantern Motel and Supper Club. All rooms are ground level at this clean, quiet motel with soft water, winter hookups, and truck parking. The motel is 5 blocks from downtown. Restaurant, complimentary Continental breakfast. Cable TV. Sauna. Pets allowed. | 1010 S. Dakota St. | 605/432–4591 or 800/627–6075 | fax 605/432–4986 | 30 rooms | $40 | AE, D, MC, V.

MISSION

Antelope Country Inn. This inn at the I–83 and 1883 junction is within 3 mi of the Prairie Hills Golf Club. Restaurant. Cable TV. Laundry facilities. Pets allowed. | 175 Adam St. 57555 | 605/856–2371 | 12 rooms | $35–$60 | AE, MC, V.

MITCHELL

Corn Palace Motel. This single-story motel has efficiencies and cabins; it's just a block off I–90, Exit 332. It's near the famous Corn Palace—the world's biggest bird feeder, built to celebrate the area's fertile farmland. Complimentary Continental breakfast. Some kitchenettes. Cable TV. Laundry facilities. Pets allowed. | 902 S. Burr St. 57301-4527 | 605/996–5559 | 50 rooms | $45–$95 | AE, MC, V.

Der Rumboly Platz Country B&B Hunting and Horse Camp. This is a fourth-generation working horse farm 10 mi outside of town. You can take a horseback ride or a stroll in the countryside. Der Rumboly, which was built in the late 1800s, has 7 bedrooms. In the informal kitchen/dining room that overlooks the property, you can sample German pancakes and Belgian waffles. Horseback riding. Laundry facilities. Pets allowed. | 40732 266th St., Ethan 57334 | 605/227–4385 | 7 rooms | $50 | No credit cards.

EconoLodge. This standard chain motel is just ½ mi from I–90. Complimentary Continental breakfast. Cable TV. Business services. Some pets allowed (fee). | 1313 S. Ohlman St. 57301 | 605/996–6647 | fax 605/996–7339 | 44 rooms | $58–$77 | AE, D, MC, V.

Flavia's Place B&B. This Italian Revival–style house, 2 blocks from downtown Mitchell, dates from 1882. The private baths all have the original red clawfoot bath tubs. Flavia's caters to hunters. Lunch and dinner are served by prior arrangement. Full complimentary breakfast. Pets allowed. No smoking. | 515 E. 3rd St. 57334 | 605/995–1562 | 4 rooms (3 with shared bath) | $60–$90 | AE, DC, MC, V.

Holiday Inn. This is the largest hotel in the area and a convenient and quiet location not far from I–90, close to gasoline and retail services. An 18-hole miniature golf course is on the premises, and there is a patio off the bar. Restaurant, bar, room service. In-room data ports. Cable TV. Indoor pool, wading pool. 2 hot tubs, sauna. Miniature golf. Laundry facilities. Business services, airport shuttle. Some pets allowed (fee). | 1525 W. Havens St. 57301 | 605/996–6501 | fax 605/996–3228 | 153 rooms | $80–$100 | AE, D, DC, MC, V.

Motel 6. Economy rooms near I–90 with coffee available in the morning. Several restaurants are just a short drive away. Pool. Pets allowed. | 1309 S. Ohlman St. 57301 | 605/996–0530 | fax 605/995–2019 | 96 rooms | $40 | AE, D, DC, MC, V.

Siesta. An economy motel with clean rooms and complimentary coffee near a restaurant and small shopping center and about 1 mi from downtown Mitchell. In-room data ports. Cable TV. Pool. Pets allowed. | 1210 W. Havens St. 57301 | 605/996–5544 or 800/424–0537 | fax 605/996–4946 | www.siestamotel.com | 22 rooms | $38–$58 | AE, D, MC, V.

MOBRIDGE

Best Value Wrangler Motor Inn. Just 5 mi from the Sitting Bull Monument, very near the Klein Museum, and alongside the Lewis and Clark trails, this is a convenient spot to stay. The motel caters to hunters and fishermen. Many of the rooms have balconies overlooking the Missouri River and Lake Oahe. Restaurant, bar, room service. Some microwaves, some refrigerators. Cable TV. Indoor pool. Hot tub. Exercise equipment. Video games. Business services, airport shuttle. Pets allowed. | 820 W. Grand Crossing | 605/845–3641 or 800/341–8000 | fax 605/845–3641 | 61 rooms | $56–$61 | AE, D, DC, MC, V.

Super 8. This standard chain is on the banks of the Missouri River, convenient to Lake Oahe and about 1 mi from downtown Mobridge. Some rooms have river views. Cable TV. Pets allowed. | 1301 W. Grand Crossing | 605/845–7215 | fax 605/845–5270 | 30 rooms | $51 | AE, D, DC, MC, V.

PIERRE

Best Western Kings Inn. Two blocks from the Missouri River and the capitol building, the 2-floor chain stands in the heart of the downtown area. Restaurant, bar, room service. Some refrigerators. Cable TV. Hot tub, sauna. Business services. Pets allowed. | 220 S. Pierre St. | 605/224–5951 | fax 605/224–5301 | 104 rooms | $55–$58 | AE, D, MC, V.

Best Western Ramkota Inn RiverCentre. Next to the RiverCentre convention complex, this hotel overlooks the Missouri River. Some rooms open onto the indoor pool. Restaurant, bar, room service. Some refrigerators. Cable TV. Indoor pool, wading pool. Hot tub. Laundry facilities. Business services, airport shuttle. Pets allowed. | 920 W. Sioux Ave. | 605/224–6877 | fax 605/224–1042 | ramkota@dtgnet.com | www.bestwestern.com | 151 rooms | $69–$200 | AE, D, DC, MC, V.

Capitol Inn. On one of the city's main thoroughfares, this 2-story hotel is 2 blocks east of the capitol and surrounded by restaurants and shopping. Some refrigerators. Cable TV. Pool. Business services. Pets allowed. | 815 E. Wells Ave. | 605/224–6387 or 800/658–3055 | fax 605/224–8083 | 86 rooms | $33–$39 | AE, D, DC, MC, V.

Days Inn. The 3-floor hotel sits 3 blocks from the Missouri River on U.S. 14. Complimentary coffee and fresh cookies are provided each afternoon in the lobby. Complimentary Continental breakfast. Cable TV. Business services. Pets allowed. | 520 W. Sioux Ave. | 605/224–0411 | fax 605/224–0411 | www.daysinn.com | 81 rooms | $55–$80 | AE, D, DC, MC, V.

Super 8. Near the convention center and the Discovery Museum, this 3-story motor lodge sits on U.S. 14. Complimentary Continental breakfast. Some in-room data ports. Cable TV. Laundry facilities. Business services. Pets allowed. | 320 W. Sioux Ave. | 605/224–1617 | www.super8.com | 78 rooms | $32–$65 | AE, D, DC, MC, V.

PLATTE

King's Inn. The single-story, exterior corridor motel sits in the heart of town, on the main thoroughfare. If you catch a fish or pheasant, you can freeze it for free. Complimentary Continental breakfast. Cable TV. Hot tub. Playground. Pets allowed. | 221 E. 7th St. | 605/337–3385 or 800/337–7756 | ben@kingsinnmotel.com | www.kingsinnmotel.com | 36 rooms | $41–$62 | AE, D, MC, V.

RAPID CITY

Fair Value Inn. One mile north of downtown, this 2-story motel sits just south of I–90 at exit 59. Cable TV. Pets allowed. | 1607 LaCrosse St. 57701 | 605/342–8118 | 25 rooms | $45–$65 | AE, D, DC, MC, V.

Ramada Inn. This 4-floor hotel sits just south of I–90 at exit 59. Bar. Some refrigerators. Cable TV. Indoor pool. Business services. Pets allowed. | 1721 LaCrosse St. 57701 | 605/342–1300 | fax 605/342–1300 | www.ramada.com | 139 rooms | $109–$179 | AE, D, DC, MC, V.

Super 8. This 3-story brick and stucco hotel is just north of I–90 at exit 59, about ½ mi from the Rushmore Mall. Complimentary Continental breakfast. Cable TV. Laundry facilities. Business services. Pets allowed. | 2124 LaCrosse St. 57701 | 605/348–8070 | fax 605/348–0833 | 119 rooms | $66–$76 | AE, D, DC, MC, V.

SIOUX FALLS

Baymont Motel. Just west of I–29 at exit 77, this 3-floor hotel sits 3 blocks from the Empire Mall. Complimentary Continental breakfast. Some refrigerators. Cable TV. Indoor pool. Hot tub. Some pets allowed. | 3200 Meadow Ave. 57106 | 605/362–0835 | budgetel.com | 82 rooms | $74–$84 | AE, D, DC, MC, V.

Best Western Ramkota Inn. The Dakotas' largest convention center, this 2-story hotel sits just east of I–29 at exit 81, next to the Sioux Falls Regional Airport. Restaurant, bar. Room service. Cable TV. 2 pools, wading pool. Hot tub, sauna. Playground. Laundry facilities. Business services, airport shuttle. Some pets allowed. | 2400 N. Louise Ave. 57107 | 605/336–0650 | fax 605/336–1687 | www.bestwestern.com | 226 rooms | $89–$99 | AE, D, DC, MC, V.

Budget Host Plaza Inn. Three mi north of downtown, this single-story hotel is off I–229 at exit 6. Cable TV. Pool. Pets allowed. | 2620 E. 10th St. 57103 | 605/336–1550 or 800/283–4678 | fax 605/339–0616 | 38 rooms | $39–$41 | AE, D, DC, MC, V.

Comfort Inn. This 2-story chain hotel, east of I–29 at exit 77, stands ½ mi north of the Empire Mall. Complimentary Continental breakfast. Some refrigerators. Cable TV. Indoor pool. Hot tub. Some pets allowed. | 3216 S. Carolyn Ave. 57106 | 605/361–2822 | www.choicehotels.com | 65 rooms | $49–$99 | AE, D, DC, MC, V.

Comfort Suites. Across from the Empire Mall, this 3-floor chain hotel sits just south of the Comfort Inn, off I–29 at exit 77. Complimentary Continental breakfast. Cable TV. Indoor pool. Hot tub. Business services. Pets allowed. | 3208 S. Carolyn Ave. 57106 | 605/362–9711 | www.choicehotels.com | 61 rooms | $75 | AE, D, DC, MC, V.

Exel Inn. Near the Sioux Falls Arena, a sports and concert venue, this 2-floor hotel is 2 mi west of downtown. Complimentary Continental breakfast. Some in-room hot tubs. Cable TV. Laundry facilities. Some pets allowed. | 1300 W. Russell St. 57104 | 605/331–5800 | fax 605/331–4074 | 104 rooms | $39–$59 | AE, D, DC, MC, V.

Kelly Inn. East of I–29 (at exit 81), this 2-floor chain is 4 mi from the Sioux Falls Regional Airport. Cable TV. Hot tub, sauna. Laundry facilities. Airport shuttle. Some pets allowed. | 3101 W. Russell St. 57104 | 605/338–6242 or 800/635–3559 | fax 605/338–5453 | 43 rooms | $62–$75 | AE, D, DC, MC, V.

Motel 6. Less than 1 mi from the Sioux Empire Arena, this 2-story motel sits east of I–29 at exit 81. Cable TV. Pool. Business services. Some pets allowed. | 3009 W. Russell St. 57104 | 605/336–7800 | fax 605/330–9273 | www.motel6.com | 87 rooms | $40–$48 | AE, D, DC, MC, V.

Ramada Inn Convention Center. This 2-floor hotel, sitting just south of the Sioux Falls Regional Airport, has a large indoor recreation center, including a video casino and a comedy club. Restaurant, bar (with entertainment), room service. In-room data ports. Cable TV. Indoor pool. Hot tub, sauna. Putting green. Laundry facilities. Business services, airport shuttle. Some pets allowed. | 1301 W. Russell St. 57104 | 605/336–1020 | fax 605/336–3030 | www.ramada.com | 200 rooms | $80–$90 | AE, D, DC, MC, V.

Select Inn. This 2-story chain hotel is just west of I–29 at exit 77. Complimentary Continental breakfast. Cable TV. Pets allowed. | 3500 S. Gateway Blvd. 57106 | 605/361–1864 | fax 605/361–9287 | www.selectinn.com | 100 rooms | $42–$45 | AE, D, DC, MC, V.

Super 8. The 3-story hotel sits just south of the Sioux Falls Regional Airport. Restaurant. In-room data ports. Cable TV. Business services. Pets allowed. | 1508 W. Russell St. 57104 | 605/339–9330 | www.super8.com | 95 rooms | $39–$50 | AE, D, DC, MC, V.

SISSETON

Holiday Motel. On the eastern edge of town, this single-story hotel is 1 block from a restaurant. Cable TV. Some pets allowed. | Hwy. 10 E | 605/698–7644 or 800/460–9548 | 19 rooms | $37–$40 | AE, D, DC, MC, V.

Viking Motel. This family-run hotel is 20 mi from Roy Lake and Sica Hollow state parks. Cable TV. Some pets allowed. | Hwy. 10 W 57262 | 605/698–7663 | 24 rooms | $37–$43 | MC, V.

SPEARFISH

Comfort Inn. Built in 1997, this 2-story hotel is right off exit 14 on I–90. There is a restaurant next door. Complimentary Continental breakfast. Cable TV. Indoor pool. Hot tub. Laundry facilities. Some pets allowed. | 2725 1st Ave. | 605/642–2337 | fax 605/642–0866 | 40 rooms | $75–$99 | AE, D, DC, MC, V.

Kelly Inn. I–90 is 1 block away and downtown's main strip is 4 blocks to the west. There is a restaurant next door. Some in-room hot tubs. Cable TV. Hot tub, sauna. Laundry facilities. Pets allowed. | 540 E. Jackson | 605/642–7795 or 800/635–3559 | fax 605/642–7751 | 50 rooms | $70–$85 | AE, D, DC, MC, V.

STURGIS

Super 8. Off exit 30 on I–90, this 3-story motel is $\frac{1}{2}$ mi east of downtown. Cable TV. Hot tub. Exercise equipment. Laundry facilities. Pets allowed. | I–90 | 605/347–4447 | fax 605/ 347–2334 | 59 rooms | $37–$77 | AE, D, DC, MC, V.

WALL

Best Western Plains. This hotel is 7 mi from Badlands National Park and 4 blocks from downtown. There is a restaurant 1½ blocks away. Cable TV. Pool. Business services. Pets allowed. | 712 Glenn St. | 605/279–2145 or 800/528–1234 | fax 605/279–2977 | 74 rooms, 8 suites | $69–$105, $120–$145 suites | AE, D, DC, MC, V.

WATERTOWN

Travel Host. This 2-story motel is 1 mi south of downtown. There is a supper-only restaurant across the street and a 24-hour cafe 3 blocks away. Complimentary Continental breakfast. Cable TV. Pets allowed. | 1714 9th Ave. SW | 605/886–6120 or 800/658–5512 | fax 605/ 886–5352 | 29 rooms | $39–$45 | AE, D, DC, MC, V.

WINNER

Buffalo Trail. This single-story motel on the Oyate Trail is in the heart of South Dakota's prime pheasant hunting area. Downtown is 1 mi away. Picnic area, complimentary Continental breakfast. In-room data ports. Cable TV. Pool. Driving range, putting green. Pets allowed. | 1030 W. 2nd St. | 605/842–2212 | fax 605/842–3199 | 31 rooms | $44–$99 | AE, D, DC, MC, V.

YANKTON

Best Western Kelly Inn. This 2-story hotel on the east side of town is 2 mi from the Dakota Territorial Capitol. Complimentary Continental breakfast. Some refrigerators. Cable TV. Indoor pool, wading pool. Hot tub. Exercise equipment. Cross-country skiing. Video games. Business services. Pets allowed. | 1607 Hwy. 50 E | 605/665–2906 | fax 605/665–4318 | 119 rooms, 4 suites | $69–$89, $150–$250 suites | AE, D, DC, MC, V.

Comfort Inn. The Yankton Mall is across the street from this 2-story motel on the north side of town. There are many places to eat within a 3-block radius. Complimentary Continental breakfast. In-room data ports. Cable TV. Hot tub. Business services. Some pets allowed. | 2118 Broadway | 605/665–8053 | fax 605/665–8165 | 45 rooms | $56 | AE, D, DC, MC, V.

Tennessee

BOLIVAR
Super 8 Motel. Off U.S. 64 west, right downtown, this motel is typical of the chain. Complimentary Continental breakfast. Microwaves, refrigerators, cable TV. Pool. Pets allowed (fee). | 916 W. Market St. 38008 | 901/658–7888 | fax 901/658–2794 | www.super8.com | 28 rooms | $50–60 | AE, D, DC, MC, V.

CARYVILLE
Budget Host Inn. This one-story, drive-up motel is across the highway from Cove Lake. Prices are among the most reasonable in the area. Cable TV. Laundry service. Some pets allowed. | 115 Woods Ave. 37714 | 423/562–9595 | fax 423/566–0515 | members.nbci.com/bhinn | 22 rooms | $25–$37 | AE, D, MC, V.

CELINA
Cedar Hill. Approximately 4 mi north of Celina, this wooded resort overlooks Dale Hollow Lake, offering great opportunities for fishing and other water-related activities. Boats rentals are available, and there's a grocery store within walking distance. Restaurant. Some kitchenettes, some cable TV, no room phones. Pool. Water sports, boating, fishing. Some pets allowed. | 2371 Cedar Hill Rd. 38551 | 931/243–3201 or 800/872–8393 | 14 rooms, 37 cottages | $52; $107 cottages | MC, V.

CHATTANOOGA
Best Inn. This property is conveniently located 3 mi from the Hamilton Place Mall—the largest shopping mall in Tennessee, with about 100 stores, 135 restaurants, and four movies theaters. Just 10 mi west of downtown. Complimentary Continental breakfast. Cable TV. Pool. Some pets allowed (fee). | 7717 Lee Hwy. | 423/894–5454 | fax 423/499–9597 | 64 rooms | $59 | AE, D, DC, MC, V.

Days Inn–Airport. These conveniently located accommodations are just 2 mi south of Hamilton Place Mall, 5 mi south of the airport, and 15 mi east of downtown. Complimentary Continental breakfast. Cable TV. Indoor pool. Hot tub. Some pets allowed (fee). | 7725 Lee Hwy. | 423/899–2288 | www.daysinn.com | 80 rooms | $45 | AE, D, MC, V.

King's Lodge. Rooms with balconies are available at this reasonably priced hotel. It's about 4 mi west of the incline chair lift up Lookout Mountain, about 5 mi west of Hamilton Place Mall, and many restaurants are within a 2-mi radius. Restaurant, bar. Refrigerators, room service, cable TV. Pool. Business services. Some pets allowed. | 2400 West Side Dr. | 423/698–8944 or 800/251–7702 | fax 423/698–8949 | 180 rooms, 20 suites | $45; $75 suites | AE, D, DC, MC, V.

La Quinta. This stucco-clad hotel is about 15 minutes northeast of downtown, just ½ mi east of a mall and 4 mi north of the airport. Complimentary Continental breakfast. Some refrigerators, cable TV. Pool. Some pets allowed. | 7015 Shallowford Rd. | 423/855–0011 | fax 423/855–0011, ext. 72 | 132 rooms, 4 suites | $68; $92 suites | AE, D, DC, MC, V.

Lookout Lake Bed & Breakfast. This B&B 5 mi west of downtown has a 9-acre, private lake for fishing. Guests may also relax in the living room with its TV and video library, in the solarium, in the well-stocked library, or while playing the inn's grand piano. Complimentary breakfast. Some in-room hot tubs, cable TV. Lake. Fishing. No smoking. Pets allowed. | 3408 Elder Mountain Rd. | 423/821–8088 | 8 | $110–$160 | MC, V.

Red Roof Inn–Chattanooga Airport. Restaurants and shopping are within walking distance of this standard chain motel. The airport is 4 mi northwest and downtown is 11 mi west of the inn. Cable TV. Some pets allowed. | 7014 Shallowford Rd. | 423/899–0143 | fax 423/899–8384 | 112 rooms | $56 | AE, D, DC, MC, V.

Super 8. This standard member of the Super 8 chain is about 2 mi west of Ruby Falls and Rock City tourist attractions. Restaurants are within a 4 mi radius. Picnic area. Cable TV. Laundry facilities. Some pets allowed. | 20 Birmingham Hwy. | 423/821–8880 | 73 rooms | $70 | AE, D, DC, MC, V.

CLARKSVILLE

Days Inn. This standard two-floor chain motel is remarkably quiet despite its location on Route 76, approximately 7 mi south of downtown. Complimentary Continental breakfast. Cable TV. Pool. Business services. Some pets allowed. | 1100 Connector Rd. 37043 | 931/358–3194 | fax 931/358–9869 | 81 rooms | $450 | AE, D, DC, MC, V.

Hachland Hill Inn. This downtown brick bed-and-breakfast, built in 1795, is furnished with antiques and handmade quilts. Rooms have private baths and fireplaces. There are also cedar cottages tucked away in nearby woods on the inn's 3-acre grounds. Restaurant. No TV in some rooms. Library. Some pets allowed. | 1601 Madison St. | 931/647–4084 | 7 rooms, 3 cottages | $95 | AE.

Heritage. This basic motel is conveniently located on U.S. 79, 5 mi north of downtown. Some rooms have views of the countryside. Complimentary breakfast. Cable TV. Pool. Video games. Business services. Some pets allowed. | 3075 Wilma Rudolph Blvd. 37040 | 931/645–1400 | fax 931/551–3917 | Travel@knightwave.com | 127 rooms | $50–$70 | AE, D, DC, MC, V.

Quality Inn. Predictable accommodations in downtown Clarksville, near restaurants and antiques shops. Bar, complimentary Continental breakfast. Some microwaves, cable TV. Indoor pool. Hot tub, sauna. Laundry facilities. Business services. Some pets allowed. | 803 N. 2nd St. 37040 | 931/645–9084 | fax 931/645–9084, ext. 340 | 129 rooms; 9 suites | $56; $89 suites | AE, D, DC, MC, V.

Red Roof Inn. These well-serviced accommodations are about 7 mi north of town, near several restaurants off I–24. There are honeymoon suites and business king suites with in-room data ports. There is also a dry-cleaning pickup service. Complimentary Continental breakfast. Some microwaves, some refrigerators, cable TV, some in-room VCRs. Pool. Laundry facilities. Some pets allowed. | 197 Holiday Dr. 37040 | 931/905–1555 | www.redroof.com | 61 rooms | $45–$100 | AE, D, DC, MC, V.

Riverview Inn. This riverfront lodging, convenient to Clarksville's River District, is also near a shopping mall and within walking distance of restaurants and pubs. Restaurant, bar. In-room data ports, some microwaves, cable TV. Indoor pool. Some pets allowed. Free parking. | 50 College St. 37040 | 931/552–3331 | fax 931/647–5005 | 154 rooms, 11 suites | $54–$85 | AE, D, DC, MC, V.

CLEVELAND

Baymont Inn. Fifteen minutes southeast of downtown Cleveland, this stucco motel is also conveniently within a mile of several restaurants. Complimentary Continental breakfast. Cable TV. Pool. Laundry facilities. Business services. Some pets allowed. | 107 Interstate Dr. NW 37312 | 423/339–1000 | fax 423/339–2760 | www.baymontinn.com | 102 rooms, 14 suites | $63, $70 suites | AE, D, DC, MC, V.

Holiday Inn–North. Enjoy mountain views from this two-story motel, just 2½ mi north of downtown Cleveland. White-water rafting and Red Clay State Historic Park are also easily accessible from this convenient location off I–75. Restaurant, room service. Cable TV. Pool. Business services. Some pets allowed. | 2400 Executive Park Dr. 37312 | 423/472–1504 | fax 423/479–5962 | 145 rooms | $75 | AE, D, DC, MC, V.

Lincoln Swiss House. This standard motel 3 mi north of town is near several restaurants. Some kitchenettes, cable TV. Some pets allowed. | 2597 Georgetown Rd. 37311 | 423/479–3720 | 25 rooms | $29.95–$39.95 | AE, D, MC, V.

Ocoee Mist Farm. This outdoorsy B&B, shadowed by the Chilhowee Mountain, is in Benton, 13 mi east of Cleveland. There are water sports at nearby Lake Ocoee, and the hosts lead llama hikes in the neighboring Cherokee National Forest. Animal lovers will enjoy the many permanent residents of the farm. Complimentary breakfast. Refrigerators, cable TV, in-room VCRs. Hot tub. Pets allowed. | 377 Parksville Rd., Benton 37307 | 423/338–6818 | fax 423/338–6710 | http://ivillage.bbchannel.com/bbc/p614485.asp | 4 rooms | $75–$89 | AE, D, MC, V.

Quality Inn Chalet. You can walk to area restaurants from this conveniently located chain motel or drive less than 3 mi west to reach downtown Cleveland. Restaurant. Some refrigerators, cable TV. Pool, wading pool. Laundry facilities. Some pets allowed. | 2595 Georgetown Rd. 37311 | 423/476–8511 | 97 rooms | $59 | AE, D, DC, MC, V.

COLUMBIA

James K. Polk Motel. The lobby of this locally-owned motel 2 mi north of town features historical pictures and literature about the area, once the president's home. Rooms with three beds are available. Some refrigerators, cable TV. Pool. Pets allowed for a fee. | 1111 Nashville Hwy. 38401 | 931/388–4913 | 50 rooms | $32.85–$42.95 | AE, D, MC, V.

Ramada Inn. Sitting on a major thoroughfare, this two-story brick motel, 4 mi north of downtown and its restaurants and shops, is surprisingly quiet. Restaurant, bar, room service. Cable TV. Pool. Some pets allowed. | 1208 Nashville Hwy. 38401 | 931/388–2720 | fax 931/388–2360 | 155 rooms | $59; $80 suite | AE, D, DC, MC, V.

COOKEVILLE

Alpine Lodge and Suites. This quiet, secluded property is off Highway 70 N 4 mi east of town. Restaurant, picnic area, complimentary Continental breakfast. In-room data ports, refrigerators, some in-room hot tubs, cable TV, some in-room VCRs. Pool, wading pool. Hot tub. Laundry facilities. Business services. Some pets allowed (fee). | 2021 E. Spring St. 38506 | 931/526–3333 | fax 931/528–9036 | 88 rooms, 26 suites | $50 rooms, $60–$70 suites | AE, D, DC, MC, V.

Best Western Thunderbird. This motel, three blocks from I–40, sits 2 mi south of downtown. Its two buildings have outside entrances. Complimentary Continental breakfast. Cable

TV. Pool. Business services. Some pets allowed. | 900 S. Jefferson Ave. 38501 | 931/526–7115 | 276 rooms, 15 suites | $49; $75 suites | AE, D, DC, MC, V.

Econo Lodge. These standardized accommodations are 2 mi south of downtown, near area restaurants and shopping. Complimentary Continental breakfast. Some refrigerators, cable TV. Pool. Business services. Some pets allowed (fee). | 1100 S. Jefferson Ave. 38501 | 931/528–1040 | fax 931/528–5227 | 70 rooms | $56 | AE, D, DC, MC, V.

Hampton Inn. Area shopping and restaurants are not far from this representative of the popular hotel chain, 2 mi south of downtown. Tennessee Tech, city parks, and golf courses are also nearby. Cable TV. Pool. Hot tub. Gym. Some pets allowed. | 1025 Interstate Dr. 38501 | 931/520–1117 or 800/426–7866 | 65 rooms | $75 | AE, D, DC, MC, V.

Holiday Inn. A movie theater, shopping mall, and plenty of restaurants are within walking distance of this chain hotel 2 mi south of the downtown area. Restaurant, bar, room service. In-room data ports, cable TV. Indoor/outdoor pool. Hot tub. Exercise equipment. Video games. Business services. Some pets allowed. | 970 S. Jefferson Ave. 38501 | 931/526–7125 | fax 931/372–8508 | www.basshotels.com | 200 rooms, 3 suites | $75 | AE, D, DC, MC, V.

CROSSVILLE

Days Inn. This stucco standard, 3 mi north of downtown, sits near shopping and restaurants. An outlet mall is 1½ mi to the north, just off I–40. Complimentary Continental breakfast. Cable TV. Pool. Business services. Some pets allowed. | 105 Executive Dr. 38555 | 931/484–9691 or 800/626–9432 | 61 rooms | $70 | AE, D, DC, MC, V.

Heritage Inn. This motor lodge sits 1 mi north of downtown, off I–40, on what locals call Restaurant Row. The newly renovated rooms are a good bet at budget prices. Cable TV. Pool. Some pets allowed. | 2900 N. Main St. 38555 | 931/484–9505 or 800/762–7065 | 64 rooms | $47.50 | AE, D, DC, MC, V.

Ramada Inn. This old-fashioned motor inn, atop a mountain, near the Obed River, sits about 4½ mi north of Crossville center and 8 mi north of the entrance to Cumberland Mountain State Park. Antique and gift shops are within walking distance. Restaurant, room service. Cable TV. Pool. Some pets allowed. | 4083 U.S. 127 38555 | 931/484–7581 or 800/228–2828 | 130 rooms | $84 | AE, D, DC, MC, V.

DICKSON

Comfort Inn. This recently remodeled motel provides standard chain accommodations. It's 5 mi south of downtown, off I–40. Cable TV. Pool. Hot tub. Some pets allowed. | 2325 Rte. 46 S 37055 | 615/446–2423 or 800/228–5150 | 50 rooms | $66 | AE, D, DC, MC, V.

The Inn on Main Street. Enjoy the nostalgic atmosphere of this 1903 bed-and-breakfast, far from the bustle of highways and fast-food joints, on old Main Street next to the town hall. Antiques, crafts, and specialty stores are within walking distance. Complimentary breakfast. Cable TV. Some pets allowed. | 112 S. Main St. 37055 | 615/441–5821 | www.bbonline.com/tn/innmain/ | 4 rooms | $95 | AE, D, MC, V.

Quality Inn–Dickson. Comfortable rooms at affordable prices are the draw at this chain motel located just off I–40, 4 mi south of downtown. The indoor heated pool is open 24 hours. Complimentary Continental breakfast. Cable TV. Pool. Some pets allowed. | 1025 E. Christi Dr. 37055 | 615/441–5252 or 888/375–5522 | 46 rooms | $44 | AE, D, DC, MC, V.

ELIZABETHTON

Doe River Inn. You can sit in the sunroom or on the patio of this Victorian B&B, enjoying the view of the Doe River and watching the ducks walk right up to the door. Both guest rooms have private bathrooms with old-fashioned claw-foot tubs. It's two blocks from the town's famous covered bridge and antique stores and cafés. Complimentary Continental breakfast. Cable TV, in-room VCRs. Fishing. Laundry facilities. Pets allowed. No smoking. | 217 Academy St. 37643 | 423/543–1444 | mary@doeriverinn.com | 2 rooms | $85 | MC, V.

FRANKLIN

Amerisuites–Cool Springs. This all-suites property is across from a large mall and not far from I–65, 5 minutes north of downtown. Complimentary breakfast. Kitchenettes, cable TV. Pool. Gym. Some pets allowed. | 650 Bakers Bridge Ave. 37067 | 615/771–8900 or 800/834–1516 | 128 suites | $87 | AE, D, DC, MC, V.

Best Western Franklin Inn. At Exit 65, off I–65, this two-story hotel sits on Franklin's eastern edge, on a commercial strip, within walking distance from many restaurants. Restaurant, complimentary Continental breakfast. In-room data ports, cable TV. Pool. Business services. Some pets allowed. | 1308 Murfreesboro Rd. 37064 | 615/790–0570 | fax 615/790–0512 | www.bestwestern.com | 142 rooms | $65–$75 | AE, DC, MC, V.

GATLINBURG

Alto. Floor-to-ceiling sliding glass doors with views of the mountains distinguish this motor lodge from others in the area. Discerning budget travelers appreciate the accommodations for the price. Picnic area. Refrigerators, cable TV. Pool, wading pool. Playground. Some pets allowed. | 404 Airport Rd. | 865/436–5175 or 800/456–4336 | fax 865/430–7342 | 21 rooms | $40 | AE, D, MC, V.

Bon Air Mountain Inn. Three buildings and a chalet are part of this property in downtown Gatlinburg, near movie theaters and plenty of restaurants. Refrigerators, some in-room hot tubs, cable TV. Pool. Business services. Some pets allowed. | 950 Parkway 37738 | 865/436–4857 or 800/848–4857 | fax 865/436–8942 | www.smokeymountainresort.com | 75 rooms; 1 chalet | $89.65; $169.65 chalet | AE, D, DC, MC, V.

★ **Holiday Inn Sunspree.** This family-friendly hotel has a Holidome that houses electronic space games, Ping-Pong, and other amusements. There's a general store and a pizza place on-site. The hotel is two blocks from downtown and within walking distance of the ski tramway. Restaurant, bar, picnic area, room service. In-room data ports, refrigerators, cable TV. 3 pools (2 indoor), wading pool. Hot tubs. Exercise equipment. Children's programs. Laundry facilities. Business services. Some pets allowed. | 520 Airport Rd. 37738 | 865/436–9201 | fax 865/436–7974 | 400 rooms | $130 | AE, D, DC, MC, V.

HARROGATE

Ramada. At the crossroads of two U.S. highways and three states, this standard hotel offers an exceptional mountain view from its elevated location. Within walking distance of town, the hotel is also just 3 mi south of Cumberland Gap National Historic Park. Restaurant, bar, room service. Cable TV. Pool. Laundry facilities. Some pets allowed (fee). | U.S. 25E and U.S. 58, Cumberland Gap 37724 | 423/869–3631 | fax 423/869–5953 | ramadainn@wwgap.net | 150 rooms | $71 | AE, D, DC, MC, V.

HURRICANE MILLS

Best Western. For those who don't want to lose time getting on and off the interstate, this hotel is ideally situated, right on I–40, 7 mi south of the center of Loretta Lynn's Ranch. The property is landscaped with trees and flowers. Some refrigerators, cable TV. Pool. Hot tub. Playground. Laundry facilities. Some pets allowed. | 15542 Rte. 13 S 37078 | 931/296–4251 | fax 931/296–9104 | www.bestwestern.com | 89 rooms | $50–$70 | AE, D, DC, MC, V.

Holiday Inn Express–Hurricane Mills–Waverly. This two-story hotel is conveniently located 6 mi south of Loretta Lynn's Ranch and less than a mile north of I–40. In-room data ports, some microwaves, some refrigerators, some in-room hot tubs, cable TV. Pool. Laundry facilities. Pets allowed (fee). | 15368 Rte. 13 S 37078 | 931/296–2999 | fax 931/296–2999 | 50 rooms | $62–$73 | AE, D, DC, MC, V.

JACKSON

Best Western Old Hickory Inn. Across from Casey Jones Village's shops and museum, this hotel offers easy on and off access to I–40, 2 mi north of town. Also nearby are a bowling alley, go-karting, and a mall. Restaurant, bar with entertainment, room service, complimentary Continental breakfast. Cable TV. Pool, wading pool. Business services. Some pets allowed. | 1849 U.S. 45 S Bypass 38305 | 901/668–4222 | fax 901/664–8536 | www. bestwestern.com | 141 rooms | $49–$60 | AE, D, DC, MC, V.

Garden Plaza Hotel. This five-story chain hotel provides convenient accommodations, just 4 mi north of downtown and within walking distance of Casey Jones Village. Restaurant, bar, room service. Cable TV. Pool. Hot tub. Gym. Some pets allowed. | 1775 U.S. 45 S Bypass 38305 | 901/664–6900 or 800/3–GARDEN | 168 rooms | $69–$89 | AE, D, DC, MC, V.

JELLICO

Best Western Holiday Plaza Motel. This two-story chain motel sits at the base of the Cumberland Mountains, just off I–75, 2 miles west of Indian State Park. Cable TV. Pool. Pets allowed. | 5th St.(U.S.25W) off I–75 (Exit 160) 37766 | 423/784–7241 | fax 423/784–5657 | 50 rooms | $47–$57 | AE, D, DC, MC, V.

JOHNSON CITY

Comfort Inn. Just off I–181 at Exit 31, this two-story hotel is 2 mi east of Cherokee National Forest and next door to a golf course. Complimentary Continental breakfast. Microwaves, refrigerators, some in-room hot tubs, cable TV. Laundry service. Pets allowed (fee). | 1900 S. Roan St. 37604 | 423/928–9600 | fax 423/928–0046 | 143 rooms | $56–$109 | AE, D, DC, MC, V.

Days Inn. These are the largest hotel rooms in the city, and they're conveniently located on I–181, a five-minute walk to malls, and a five-minute drive south to downtown. The grounds include gardens, a courtyard, and an outdoor pool. Restaurant, bar, room service. Refrigerators, cable TV. Pool. Laundry facilities. Business services. Some pets allowed. | 2312 Brown's Mill Rd. 37601 | 423/282–2211 | fax 423/282–6111 | 102 rooms | $45–$50 | AE, D, DC, MC, V.

Garden Plaza. This five-story hotel is 1 mi off I–181 and 2 mi north of downtown. For fitness-minded travelers, a complimentary shuttle is offered to a local health club. Restaurant, bar, complimentary Continental breakfast, room service. Cable TV. Indoor/outdoor pool. Business services, airport shuttle. Some pets allowed. | 211 Mockingbird La. 37604 | 423/929–2000 or 800/342–7336 | 186 rooms | $85–$100 | AE, D, DC, MC, V.

Red Roof Inn Johnson City. About 3 mi north of downtown, just off I–181 at Exit 35, this three-story motel is adjacent to the Johnson City Mall. In-room data ports, cable TV. Business services. Pets allowed. | 210 Broyles St. 37601 | 423/282–3040 | fax 423/283–0673 | 115 rooms | $57–$75 | AE, D, MC, V.

KINGSPORT

Cleek's Motel. If you don't mind spartan rooms, you can save a buck at this tiny cinderblock property, 6 mi northeast of town. Cable TV. Pets allowed ($10). | 2760 E. Stone Dr. 37660 | 423/288–9996 | no fax | 15 rooms | $34 | No credit cards.

KNOXVILLE

Baymont. Conveniently located hotel, 20 minutes west of downtown, is near restaurants, a movie theater, an antiques mall, and other shopping. Complimentary Continental breakfast. Some refrigerators, cable TV. Pool. Exercise equipment. Laundry facilities. Business services. Some pets allowed. | Campbell Lakes Dr. | 865/671–1010 | fax 865/675–5039 | 98 rooms | $61–$85 | AE, D, DC, MC, V.

Best Western Highway Host. This member of the popular lodging chain is 15 minutes north of downtown and less than 20 mi from two major shopping malls and the airport. Several restaurants are within walking distance. Restaurant, bar. Cable TV. Indoor pool. Hot tub. Video games. Laundry facilities. Business services. Free parking. Some pets allowed. | 118 Merchants Dr. | 865/688–3141 | fax 865/687–4645 | 213 rooms | $59–$92 | AE, D, DC, MC, V.

Budget Inn. There's a park one block away and restaurants within walking distance from this chain hotel, which is 15 mi west of downtown. Restaurant, bar. Room service, cable TV. Indoor pool. Business services. Some pets allowed. | 323 Cedar Bluff Rd. | 865/693–7330 | fax 865/693–7383 | 178 rooms | $52–$68 | AE, D, DC, MC, V.

Days Inn. This no-frills hotel is conveniently located in downtown Knoxville. Cable TV. Business services. Some pets allowed (fee). | 1706 W. Cumberland Ave. | 865/521–5000 | www.daysinn.com | 119 rooms | $55–$65 | AE, D, DC, MC, V.

Days Inn. This typical chain motel (with external entrances) is 12 mi east of downtown restaurants and shopping. Complimentary breakfast. Cable TV. Pool. Some pets allowed (fee). | 200 Lovell Rd. | 865/966–5801 | fax 865/966–1755 | www.daysinn.com | 120 rooms | $43–$75 | AE, D, DC, MC, V.

Holiday Inn West. In a residential neighborhood 4 mi west of downtown but east of Knoxville's suburban commercial center, this Holiday Inn offers a cozy family atmosphere and rooms overlooking a courtyard. The restaurant is cafeteria-style, but there are numerous eateries within 3 mi. The hotel is only minutes from the biggest mall in town and two movie theaters. Restaurant, bar with entertainment, picnic area, room service. Cable TV. Pool. Hot tub. Laundry facilities. Business services. Some pets allowed. | 1315 Kirby Rd. | 865/584–3911 | fax 865/588–0920 | www.holiday-inn.com | 240 rooms | $80–$119 | AE, D, DC, MC, V.

Howard Johnson Plaza. This four-story standby is on I-75, across from a mall in West Knoxville. Guests enjoy live music in the lobby on weekend evenings. Restaurant, bar with entertainment, room service. In-room data ports, cable TV. Pool. Business services. Some pets allowed (fee). | 7621 Kingston Pike | 865/693–8111 | fax 865/690–1031 | www.hojo.com | 162 rooms | $59–$79 | AE, D, DC, MC, V.

★ **Hyatt Regency.** The eight-story atrium lobby adds to the sleek, modern feel of this full-service hotel. It's situated on a hill overlooking the Tennessee River. Restaurants, bar. Cable TV. Pool. Beauty salon. Exercise equipment. Playground. Business services, airport shuttle. Some pets allowed (fee). | 500 Hill Ave. SE | 865/637–1234 | fax 865/637–1193 | 385 rooms, 20 suites | $130–$160; $175–$425 suites | AE, D, DC, MC, V.

La Quinta Inn. Surrounded by restaurants and other hotels, this five-story La Quinta, off I-75, is also about 8 mi from a shopping mall and movie theater. Just 15 minutes north of downtown. Complimentary Continental breakfast. In-room data ports, cable TV. Pool. Some pets allowed. | 5634 Merchants Center Blvd. | 865/687–8989 | fax 865/687–9351 | www.laquinta.com | 123 rooms | $49–$75 | AE, D, DC, MC, V.

La Quinta Motor Inn. Guests can enjoy area attractions, restaurants, and shopping from this West Knoxville base camp less than 2 mi from almost everything. Complimentary Continental breakfast. In-room data ports, cable TV. Pool. Laundry facilities. Business services. Some pets allowed. | 258 Peters Rd. N | 865/690–9777 | fax 865/531–8304 | www.laquinta.com | 130 rooms | $58–$78 | AE, D, DC, MC, V.

Maplehurst Inn. From the outside, this house built in 1917 doesn't look like much, but it's regal inside. Floral quilts cover handcarved walnut and cherry beds, and there is a pre–World War I Baldwin piano. It's in downtown Knoxville within a ten block walk of museums, restaurants, and the Tennessee River Boat. Complimentary breakfast. Some in-room hot tubs, cable TV. Some pets allowed. | 800 W. Hill Ave. | 865/523–7773 or 800/451–1562 | www.maplehurstinn.com | 11 rooms | $89–$149 | MC, V.

Masters Manor Inn. The first thing you'll see upon entering this 1894 manor, now a B&B, is an ornate staircase with a sturdy bannister. Rooms have huge windows and four-poster beds. The sprawling front porch is a great place to sit and gaze at the magnolia tree on the property. Complimentary breakfast. Cable TV. Laundry facilities. Pets allowed. No smoking. | 1909 Cedar La. | 865/219–9888 or 877/866–2667 | fax 865/219–9811 | www.mastersmanor.com | 6 rooms | $100–$150 | AE, MC, V.

Microtel of Knoxville. This no-frills three-story motel 15–20 minutes east of downtown has an elevator. In-room data ports, cable TV. Pets allowed ($10 deposit). | 309 N. Peters Rd. | 865/531–8041 | fax 865/539–1792 | 105 rooms | $44 | AE, D, DC, MC, V.

Red Roof Inn. These chain accommodations are in a commercial area, about 5 mi north of downtown and 10 mi northwest of the zoo. In-room data ports, cable TV. Business services. Some pets allowed. | 5640 Merchants Center Blvd. | 865/689–7100 | fax 865/689–7974 | www.redroof.com | 84 rooms | $36–$64 | AE, D, DC, MC, V.

Red Roof Inn–West. Standard accommodations off I-40, 12 mi west of downtown. Convenient to restaurants and malls. In-room data ports, cable TV. Business services. Some pets allowed. | 209 Advantage Pl. | 865/691–1664 | fax 865/691–7210 | www.redroof.com | 115 rooms | $34–$70 | AE, D, DC, MC, V.

Super 8. Area attractions, restaurants, and a large shopping mall are not far from this two-story chain motel in West Knoxville. Cable TV. Pool, wading pool. Hot tub. Exercise equipment. Business services. Some pets allowed. | 6200 Paper Mill Rd. | 865/584–8511 | www.super8.com | 139 rooms | $54–$95 | AE, D, DC, MC, V.

LEBANON

Comfort Inn. The rooms here are basic, but six restaurants are within walking distance and hotel amenties are plentiful. Located in South Lebanon. Complimentary Continental breakfast. Some microwaves, some refrigerators, cable TV. Outdoor pool. Hot tub, sauna. Health club. Business services. Pets allowed ($5). | 829 S. Cumberland St. 37087 | 615/444–1001 | fax 615/444–1002 | 76 rooms | $69–$89 | AE, D, DC, MC, V.

Days Inn. Right off I-40 and only five blocks south of downtown, this no-frills motor lodge is in a good location for those passing through Lebanon. Complimentary Continental breakfast. Some refrigerators, cable TV. Pool. Laundry facilities. Business services. Some pets allowed. | 914 Murfreesboro Rd. 37087 | 615/444–5635 | 52 rooms | $42–$60 | www.daysinn.com | AE, D, DC, MC, V.

Hampton Inn. This property is just off I-40, near gas stations and convience stores. It's a short drive to downtown Lebanon. Guests especially enjoy relaxing in the sauna and hot tub. Complimentary Continental breakfast. Cable TV. Pool. Exercise equipment. Business services. Some pets allowed. | 704 S. Cumberland St. 37087 | 615/444–7400 | fax 615/449–7969 | www.hampton-inn.com | 80 rooms, 6 suites | $55–$90; $105–$125 suites | AE, D, DC, MC, V.

MANCHESTER

Hampton Inn. The rooms here have sturdy hardwood furniture and cheery floral borders on the walls. Only ½ mi from downtown. Complimentary Continental breakfast. In-room data ports, some microwaves, some refrigerators, some in-room hot tubs, cable TV. Outdoor pool. Laundry services. Business services. Pets allowed (fee). | 33 Paradise St. 37355 | 931/728–3300 | fax 931/728–0159 | www.hampton-inn.com | 64 rooms, 8 suites | $75, $95 suites | AE, D, DC, MC, V.

Super 8. Blues and greens are accented with floral patterns in the decor of this standard chain motel, 1½ mi from downtown. Complimentary Continental breakfast. Cable TV. Pool. Some pets allowed. | 2430 Hillsboro Hwy. | 931/728–9720 | www.super8.com | 50 rooms | $31–$45 | AE, D, DC, MC, V.

MCMINNVILLE

Best Western–McMinnville Inn. Many of the rooms in this downtown motel—decorated in burgundy and hunter green—have views of the Smoky Mountains. The Race Car Café is next door. Complimentary Continental breakfast. Some kitchenettes, some microwaves, some in-room hot tubs, cable TV. Outdoor pool. Laundry services. Pets allowed (fee). | 2545 Sparta St. 37110 | 931/473–7338 | fax 931/473–1052 | www.bestwestern.com | 49 rooms | $50–$65 | AE, D, DC, MC, V.

MEMPHIS

Comfort Inn–Poplar East. This Comfort Inn is on I-240 at Exit 24E. It's near a mall and several restaurants, 15 minutes east of downtown. The neighborhood is predominantly a business area. Complimentary Continental breakfast, room service, cable TV. Pool. Exercise equipment. Airport shuttle. Some pets allowed (fee). | 5877 Poplar Ave. | 901/767–6300 | fax 901/767–0098 | www.comfortinn.com | 126 rooms | $59–$79 | AE, D, DC, MC, V.

King's Cottage Bed and Breakfast Inn. The owners are devout Christians, and calligraphy of Bible scriptures can be found in each room. The 1910 stucco-and-brick inn is comfortably cluttered, and the rooms have silk drapes and white bedding accented with roses. It's in the Evergreen District. Complimentary Continental breakfast. Cable TV, in-room VCRs. Pets allowed (fee). No smoking. | 87–89 Clark Pl. | 901/722–8686 | www.thekingscottage.com | 2 rooms | $128 | AE, D, MC, V.

La Quinta Inn. This is the first representative of the chain built around 1980, just 2 mi east of downtown. The rooms have abstract Mexican motifs. Complimentary breakfast. Cable TV. Outdoor pool. Business services. Some pets allowed. | 42 S. Camilla St. | 901/526–1050 | fax 901/525–3219 | www.laquinta.com | 128 rooms, 2 suites | $55–$60 | AE, D, DC, MC, V.

Marriott Memphis–Downtown. Relax and listen to the grand piano that's played in the greenery-filled lobby of this sophisticated high-rise. The nineteen-story hotel is next to the downtown Convention Center. Restaurant, bar. In-room data ports, some refrigerators, cable TV. Indoor pool. Hot tub, sauna. Exercise equipment. Shops. Business services. Parking (fee). Some pets allowed. | 250 N. Main St. | 901/527–7300 | fax 901/526–1561 | www.marriott.com | 402 rooms | $139–$144 | AE, D, DC, MC, V.

Red Roof Inn–South. Cozy rooms with burgundy accents are close to shopping and the airport. The hotel is a 10-minute drive south from the Overton Park area. In-room data ports, cable TV. Some pets allowed. | 3875 American Way | 901/363–2335 | fax 901/363–2822 | www.redroofinn.com | 109 rooms | $39–$50 | AE, D, DC, MC, V.

Residence Inn by Marriott. These small apartment-style lodgings in the business district, catering chiefly to business people, are near several restaurants, 20 mi east of downtown. Complimentary Continental breakfast. Kitchenettes, microwaves, refrigerators, cable TV. Pool. Hot tub. Laundry facilities. Business services. Some pets allowed (fee). | 6141 Poplar Pike | 901/685–9595 | fax 901/685–1636 | www.marriott.com | 105 suites | $109–$154 | AE, D, DC, MC, V.

Studio 6–Memphis. This extended-stay property offers suites near restaurants and the mall. It's 15 minutes east of the airport and 20 minutes east of downtown. Kitchenettes, microwaves, refrigerators, cable TV. Pool. Hot tub. Laundry facilities. Business services. Some pets allowed (fee). | 4300 American Way | 901/366–9333 or 800/456–4000 | fax 901/366–7835 | 51 rooms, 67 suites | $55, $59 suites | AE, D, DC, MC, V.

MONTEAGLE

Best Western Smoke House. Enjoy home-smoked meats at this small resort, on top of Monteagle Mountain. The lodging is set on 25 acres and offers access to 200 mi of local hiking trails. The Hideaway Cabins have hot tubs, and also rockers on a long porch. There are laundry facilities across the street. Located 4 mi from the University of the South campus.

Restaurant, room service. Some in-room hot tubs. Cable TV. Pool. Tennis. Playground. Business services. Some pets allowed. | 850 Main St. 37356 | 931/924–2091 or 800/489–2091 | www.bestwestern.com | 99 rooms; 12 cabins | $68–$85, $141 cabins | AE, D, MC, V.

MORRISTOWN

Holiday Inn of Morristown Conference Center. You can enjoy a relaxed atmosphere and friendly southern hospitality at this chain hotel near I–81 in the south part of town. The rooms are pleasantly decorated in hues of burgundy and green. Restaurant. Cable TV. 2 pools, wading pool. Exercise equipment. Business services. Some pets allowed. | 5435 S. Davy Crockett Pkwy. 37813 | 423/587–2400 | fax 423/581–7344 | www.basshotels.com | 112 rooms | $62–$105 | AE, D, DC, MC, V.

MURFREESBORO

Garden Plaza. There's a large atrium lobby and garden at this hotel, directly off I–24. Rooms are tastefully decorated in deep reds and greens. It's within walking distance of shopping and restaurants. Restaurant, bar, room service. Some minibars, refrigerators, cable TV. Indoor-outdoor pool. Hot tub. Some pets allowed. | 1850 Old Fort Pkwy. 37129 | 615/895–5555 or 800/342–7336 | fax 615/895–5555, ext. 165 | 170 rooms | $55–$89, $139 suites | AE, D, DC, MC, V.

Hampton Inn. This hotel within the Mursfreeboro city limits is near shopping, restaurants, and Middle Tennessee State University. There's a casual lobby filled with couches and TV. Complimentary Continental breakfast. Cable TV, in-room VCRs. Pool. Business services. Some pets allowed. | 2230 Armony Dr. 37129 | 615/896–1172 | fax 615/895–4277 | www.hamptoninn.com | 119 rooms | $54–$70 | AE, D, DC, MC, V.

Howard Johnson. This comfortable motel with large rooms is directly off I–40 in Murfreesboro. Restaurant, complimentary Continental breakfast. Some refrigerators, some microwaves, some in-room hot tubs. Cable TV. Pool. Laundry facilities, laundry service. Business services. Some pets allowed (fee). | 2424 S. Church St. 37130 | 615/896–5522 or 800/406–1411 | fax 615/890–0024 | www.hojo.com | 80 rooms | $30–$89 | AE, D, DC, MC, V.

Quality Inn Murfreesboro. The rooms are modest and generic, but you can walk to shops and restaurants, including Demo's and Shoney's, just 3 blocks away. The hotel was built in 1996 and is in a residential neighborhood. Complimentary Continental breakfast. Some microwaves, some refrigerators, some in-room hot tubs, Cable TV. Outdoor pool. Tennis. Pets allowed (fee). | 118 Westgate Blvd. 37130 | 615/848–9030 | fax 615/896–3470 | www.qualityinn.com | 78 rooms | $40–$100 | AE, D, DC, MC, V.

Ramada Limited. Lush greenery welcomes guests to the lobby of this Ramada. It's near restaurants and shopping, and the hotel offers a discount to neighboring Ponderosa restaurant. Complimentary Continental breakfast. Cable TV. Pool, wading pool. Business services. Some pets allowed. | 1855 S. Church St. 37130 | 615/896–5080 | www.ramada.com | 81 rooms | $30–$85 | AE, D, DC, MC, V.

Wingate Inn. This classy hotel is situated between two malls. The rooms feature dark-wood furniture and four-poster beds. Complimentary Continental breakfast. In-room data ports, in-room hot tubs, some minibars, cable TV. Pool. Hot tub. Exercise equipment. Business services. Laundry facilities. Some pets allowed. | 165 Chaffin Pl. 37129 | 615/849–9000 or 800/228–1000 | fax 615/849–9066 | www.wingateinns.com | 86 rooms; 2 suites | $89–$12, $125–$250 suites | AE, D, DC, MC, V.

NASHVILLE

Amerisuites. This hotel offers contemporary, clean suites, and is near suburban Brentwood, a mall, and Restaurant Row. It's also 5 mi south of downtown Nashville, and within 5 mi of both the 100 Oaks Mall and the Galleria Mall. Complimentary Continental breakfast. Kitchenettes, refrigerators, cable TV, in-room VCRs and movies. Pool. Exercise equipment. Laundry facilities. Business services, free parking. Some pets allowed (fee). | 202 Summit View Dr., Brentwood | 615/661–9477 | fax 615/661–9936 | www.amerisuites.com | 126 suites | $74–$150 suites | AE, D, DC, MC, V.

Baymont Inn. This Baymont is near a mall and countless restaurants, and is 14 mi north of Nashville. Complimentary Continental breakfast. Cable TV. Pool. Business services, free parking. Some pets allowed. | 120 Cartwright Ct., Goodlettsville | 615/851–1891 | fax 615/851–4513 | 100 rooms, 30 suites | $55–$70, $79–$120 suites | AE, D, DC, MC, V.

Crocker Springs Bed and Breakfast. When you stay at this 1880s farmhouse, 4 mi off I-24 and 14 mi from downtown Nashville, you'll have a delightful view of the owners' 58-acre spread. The rooms have pine floors and pitched pine ceilings. Stefanie's Quilt Room has a full-size feather bed, Todd's Paisley Room has a decorative queen-size iron bed, and the Rose Room includes an antique iron day bed, a queen-size bed, and a claw foot bathtub with shower. The Blue Sitting Room has a fireplace and TV. Complimentary breakfast. No room phones, TV in common area. Pond. Hiking, fishing. Some pets allowed. No smoking. | 2382 Crocker Springs Rd. | 615/876–8502 or 800/373–4911 | fax 615/876–4083 | www.bbonline.com/tn/crockersprings | 3 rooms | $100–$200 | AE, D.

Daisy Hill Bed and Breakfast. It's cozy here when you sit out on the brick patio and survey the owners' gardens. This 1925 Tudor Revival home is on the National Register of Historic Places. Each room design is on a national theme: French country, Scottish Highlands, and Norwegian. Complimentary breakfast. No room phones, TV in common area. Pets allowed. No kids under 12. No smoking. | 2816 Blair Blvd. | 615/297–9795 | www.bbonline.com/tn/daisyhill | 3 rooms | $95–$130 | AE, MC, V.

Embassy Suites. This hotel is among office buildings in a business district 8 mi east of downtown and 2 mi south of the airport. The interior atrium has waterfalls, plants, and flowers. Restaurant, bar, complimentary breakfast, room service. Minibars, refrigerators, microwaves, cable TV. Indoor pool. Hot tub. Exercise equipment. Video games. Laundry services. Business services, airport shuttle. Some pets allowed (fee). | 10 Century Blvd. | 615/871–0033 or 800/362–2779 | fax 615/883–9245 | www.embassysuites.com | 296 suites | $129–$169 suites | AE, D, DC, MC, V.

Hillsboro House Bed and Breakfast. Built in 1904, this Victorian home is just four blocks from Vanderbilt University in the Belmont–Hillsboro area. The rooms combine English country touches like gingham with contemporary furniture. You can stroll through the herb garden. Complimentary breakfast. Cable TV. Some pets allowed. No smoking. | 1933 20th Ave. S | 615/292–5501 or 800/228–7851 | www.bbonline.com/tn/hillsboro | 3 rooms | $110 | AE, D, MC, V.

Hilton Suites–Brentwood. Conveniently located accommodations 20 minutes from downtown Nashville. There's a complimentary shuttle to Brentwood-area restaurants, and a two-hour beverage reception each evening. Restaurant, bar, complimentary breakfast, room service. Minibars, refrigerators, cable TV, in-room VCRs. Indoor pool. Hot tub. Exercise equipment. Laundry service. Business services. Some pets allowed. | 9000 Overlook Blvd., Brentwood | 615/370–0111 or 800/774–1500 | fax 615/370–0272 | www.hilton.com | 203 suites | $125–$165 | AE, D, DC, MC, V.

La Quinta. This newly renovated hotel is centrally located—4 mi north of downtown and 10 minutes from the airport. It's close to the Country Music Hall of Fame and Opryland, and a perfect place for spotting the stars who stay across the street in the Regal Maxwell Hotel. Complimentary Continental breakfast. Microwaves, cable TV. Pool. Laundry facilities. Business services. Some pets allowed. | 2001 Metrocenter Blvd. | 615/259–2130 | fax 615/242–2650 | www.laquinta.com | 120 rooms | $67–$89 | AE, D, DC, MC, V.

La Quinta Inn. This is the first La Quinta in Nashville, built around 1980. This facility is surrounded by hospitals, but downtown is just 2 mi away. The rooms have abstract Mexican motifs. Complimentary Continental breakfast. Cable TV. Outdoor pool. Business services. Some pets allowed. | 42 S. Camilla St. | 901/526–1050 | fax 901/525–3219 | www.laquinta.com | 128 rooms, 2 suites | $55–$60 | AE, D, DC, MC, V.

Loews Vanderbilt Plaza. A pristine, white lobby and top-notch service are the first things guests encounter at this quiet, European-style luxury hotel, across the street from Vanderbilt University and 1 mi from Music Row. Guest rooms are elegant with dark-cherry furniture and skyline views. Musicians play nightly in the piano bar. 2 restaurants, bar (with entertainment), room service. In-room data ports, minibars, microwaves, cable TV. Beauty salon. Exercise equipment. Shops. Business services. Some pets allowed. | 2100 West End Ave. | 615/320–1700 | fax 615/320–5019 | www.loewsvanderbilt.com | 327 rooms, 13 suites | $184–$249, $450–$975 suites | AE, D, DC, MC, V.

Ramada Inn Suites–South. In between the airport and Opryland, this quiet hotel features a sparkling atrium lobby with live plants native to the South. The hotel was renovated in 1998. Complimentary Continental breakfast. Kitchenettes, refrigerators, microwaves, cable TV. Pool. Exercise equipment. Laundry facilities. Business services, airport shuttle. Laundry services. Free parking. Some pets allowed. | 2425 Atrium Way | 615/883–5201 or 888/298–2054 | fax 615/883–5594 | www.ramada.com | 120 suites | $83–$137 suites | AE, D, DC, MC, V.

Ramada Limited. Newly renovated rooms in mauve hues are open to the outside. Directly off I–40 in a suburb of Nashville, this hotel is 10 mi from downtown and Music Row. Complimentary Continental breakfast. Cable TV. Pool. Business services. Some pets allowed (fee). | 5770 Old Hickory Blvd., Hermitage | 615/889–8940 | fax 615/871–4444 | www.ramada.com | 100 rooms | $35–$70 | AE, D, DC, MC, V.

Red Roof Inn. This casual motor inn is near a few restaurants, groceries, and convience stores, 6½ mi from the Grand Ole Opry. Cable TV. Airport shuttle. Some pets allowed. | 510 Claridge St. | 615/872–0735 | fax 615/871–4647 | www.redroof.com | 120 rooms | $40–$56 | AE, D, DC, MC, V.

Red Roof Inn. This newly remodeled hotel is within walking distance of 12 different restaurants, 1 mi from the Grand Ole Opry, the Opry Mills Mall, and the Factory Outlet Mall. The lobby is furnished with comfortable wing-back chairs. Cable TV. Pool. Some pets allowed. | 2460 Music Valley Dr. | 615/889–0090 | fax 615/889–0086 | www.redroof.com | 86 rooms | $70–$85 | AE, D, DC, MC, V.

Red Roof Inn–South. This hotel is off I–65 at Exit 69, 5 mi from downtown, 9 mi from the Country Music Hall of Fame, 13 mi from Opryland, and near restaurants. Cable TV. Some pets allowed. | 4271 Sidco Dr. | 615/832–0093 | fax 615/832–0097 | www.redroof.com | 85 rooms | $45–$70 | AE, D, DC, MC, V.

Regal Maxwell House. Expect Southern hospitality in a contemporary environment at this large, contemporary hotel just off I–265. It's just 2 minutes from downtown, 15 minutes from the Opry, and 1⅓ mi from a golf course. Rooms are spacious, and are decorated in rose or beige floral prints. Restaurant, bar. Cable TV. Pool. Hot tub. Tennis. Exercise equipment. Business services. Pets allowed. | 2025 Metrocenter Blvd. | 615/259–4343 | www.maxwellhotel.com | 285 rooms, 4 suites | $119–$148, $175–$350 suites | AE, D, DC, MC, V.

Residence Inn by Marriott. This hotel underwent renovations in 2000. Many rooms have fireplaces, and the large suites include second-story lofts. It's 15 mi east of downtown and 4 mi south of Opryland Spring House golf course. Complimentary Continental breakfast. Kitchenettes, refrigerators, microwaves, cable TV. Pool. Hot tub. Laundry facilities, laundry services. Business services. Pets allowed. | 2300 Elm Hill Pike | 615/889–8600 | fax 615/871–4970 | www.residenceinn.com | 168 suites | $72–$159 | AE, D, DC, MC, V.

Sheraton–Music City. This Georgian-style member of the popular Sheraton chain is set on 23 landscaped acres atop a hill. The semiformal decor makes for a casual, comfortable atmosphere. It's 2 mi north of the airport and 10 mi east of downtown. Restaurant, bar with entertainment. Some refrigerators, cable TV. Indoor-outdoor pool, wading pool. Beauty salon, hot tub. Tennis. Gym. Business services, airport shuttle. Some pets allowed. | 777 McGavock Pike | 615/885–2200 | fax 615/231–1134 | www.sheraton.com | 392 rooms, 20 suites | $139–$179, $150–$550 suites | AE, D, DC, MC, V.

Super 8. This no-frills hotel is off I–65 and near various restaurants. It's 5 mi west of downtown, 10 mi from Opryland, and 3 mi from Vanderbilt University. Complimentary Continental breakfast. Cable TV. Business services. Some pets allowed. | 412 Robertson Ave. | 615/356–0888 or 800/800–8000 | fax 615/356–0888, ext. 118 | www.super8.com | 73 rooms | $42–$62, $52–$77 suites | AE, D, DC, MC, V.

Union Station. This hotel is in a renovated historic train station (1897) and has an amazing 128-panel stained-glass roof in the lobby. The building is a Romanesque landmark, with limestone walls that are 4 ft thick in some spots. During World War II the dining room served as a USO canteen. Two blocks from Music Row. Restaurant, bar. Cable TV. Tennis. Business services. Airport shuttle. Some pets allowed. | 1001 Broadway | 615/726–1001 or 800/331–2123 | fax 615/248–3554 | www.grandheritage.com | 124 rooms, 12 suites | $125–$275, $205–$305 suites | AE, D, DC, MC, V.

Wilson Inn. Atop a small hill off Briley Parkway, this hotel is 3 mi north of the airport and 7 mi south of downtown. Complimentary Continental breakfast. Some minibars, refrigerators, cable TV. Business services. Airport shuttle. Some pets allowed. | 600 Ermac Dr. | 615/889–4466 or 800/945–7667 | fax 615/889–0464 | 94 rooms, 16 suites | $65, $89 suites | AE, D, DC, MC, V.

NORRIS

Holiday Inn Express. Burgundy and hunter green are the color scheme in these rooms, which come with conveniences like in-room coffeemakers. Several restaurants are in the neighborhood, directly off I–75 at the Route 61 exit. Complimentary Continental breakfast. In-room data ports, some minibars, some microwaves, some refrigerators, some in-room hot tubs. Cable TV. Outdoor pool. Laundry facilities. Business services. Pets allowed (fee). | 141 Buffalo Rd. 37716 | 865/457–2233 | fax 865/457–2233 | www.hiexpress.com | 29 rooms, 22 suites | $70–$100 | AE, D, DC, MC, V.

OAK RIDGE

Comfort Inn. Guest rooms with dark cherry furniture are near restaurants and the Oak Ridge Mall. The hotel is near the Tinseltown 14-screen movie theater, and 1 mi from central Oak Ridge. Complimentary Continental breakfast. Refrigerators (in suites), cable TV. Pool. Laundry facilities. Business services. Some pets allowed. | 433 S. Rutgers Ave. 37830 | 865/481–8200 | fax 865/483–6142 | www.comfortinn.com | 102 rooms, 20 suites | $71–$81, $71–$91 suites | AE, D, DC, MC, V.

Days Inn. This member of the popular chain is located in downtown Oak Ridge, just blocks from a variety of restaurants. Complimentary Continental breakfast. Refrigerators, cable TV. Pool. Playground. Business services. Some pets allowed. Free parking. | 206 S. Illinois Ave. 37830 | 865/483–5615 | fax 865/483–5615 | www.daysinn.com | 80 rooms | $35–$57 | AE, D, DC, MC, V.

Garden Plaza Hotel. Rooms are larger than the average hotel room, and business people are the most frequent guests. The hotel is in the heart of downtown, five minutes from anywhere in Oak Ridge, and within walking distance to the Civic Center. Restaurant, bar, room service. Some minibars, some refrigerators, cable TV. Indoor-outdoor pool. Hot tub. Business services. Some pets allowed. | 215 S. Illinois Ave. 37830 | 865/481–2468 or 800/342–7336 | fax 865/481–2474 | 168 rooms | $79–$109 | AE, D, DC, MC, V.

Ridge Inn Plaza. This inexpensive motel is located within a half mile of shops. A Mexican restaurant shares the same lot. Microwaves, refrigerators. Cable TV. Outdoor pool.

Business services. Pets allowed (fee). | 1590 Oak Ridge Tpke. 37830 | 865/482–9968 | fax 865/482–9834 | 49 rooms | $37 | AE, D, DC, MC, V.

PARIS

Mansard Island Resort and Marina. This property is on the shores of Kentucky Lake adjacent to the Tennessee National Wildlife Refuge. You can enjoy wildlife, fishing and boating during your stay. Just 12 mi north of Paris. Microwaves, refrigerators, cable TV. Pool. Volleyball. Dock, water sports, boating, fishing. Playground. Laundry facilities. Pets allowed (fee). | 60 Mansard Island Dr., Springville 38256 | 901/642–5590 | fax 901/642–3120 | www.mansardisland.com | 40 rooms in 6 cottages, 8 apartments, 7 town houses, and 4 mobile homes | $63 1–bedroom town houses, $88 2–bedroom town houses, $78 apartments, $70 cottages | AE, D, MC, V.

PIGEON FORGE

Grand Resort Hotel and Convention Center. This is the largest, and one of the more upscale, hotels in Pigeon Forge. It sits at the foot of the Smoky Mountains. Fireplaces warm some rooms. Floral patterns ornament some rooms, others are done in light colors or pastels. Restaurant, complimentary Continental breakfast. Room service, cable TV. Pool. Hot tub. Business services. Some pets allowed. | 3171 Parkway 37863 | 865/453–1000 or 800/362–1188 | fax 865/428–3944 | www.lodging4u.com/pf/grand/default.html | 425 rooms | $70–$100 | AE, D, DC, MC, V.

Heartlander Country Resort. Rooms at this hotel located at the northern tip of Pigeon Forge have inside access and some mountain views. All rooms have private balconies. Complimentary Continental breakfast. Cable TV. 2 pools (1 indoor). Hot tub. Video games. Business services. Some pets allowed. | 2385 Parkway 37862 | 865/453–4106 | fax 865/429–0159 | 160 rooms | $59–$119 | AE, D, DC, MC, V.

ROGERSVILLE

Holiday Inn Express. You'll be served late-afternoon seasonal refreshments which include iced-tea and cookies in the summer, and soup, crackers, hot cider, and cocoa in the winter. Board games and checkers are available at the front desk. The hotel is in the commercial area of town just 2 mi south of downtown. View the Appalachian Mountains from all rooms. Ten second-story rooms allow smoking. Complimentary Continental breakfast. Microwaves, refrigerators, some in-room hot tubs, cable TV. Outdoor pool. Laundry service. Some pets allowed (fee). | 7139 Rte. 11W 37857 | 423/272–1842 or 800/HOLIDAY | fax 423/272–1634 | www.hiexpress.com | 43 rooms | $70 | AE, D, DC, MC, V.

SAVANNAH

Savannah Motel. This downtown property is within 2 blocks of restaurants and shops. Some microwaves, some refrigerators, cable TV. Pets allowed (fee). | 105 Main St. 38372 | 901/925–3392 | 20 rooms | $30–$40 | AE, D, MC, V.

Shaws Komfort Motel. Personalized service and newly furnished rooms are the draws at this motel located on U.S. 64. Its highway location makes it especially convenient to Shiloh National Park and Pickwick Landing State Resort Park. Restaurant. Cable TV. Some pets allowed. | 2302 Wayne Rd. 38372 | 901/925–3977 | 31 rooms | $29–$36 | AE, D, DC, MC, V.

SHELBYVILLE

Super 8 Shelbyville. This conveniently located motor lodge is in downtown Shelbyville, directly on U.S. 231. It's just 2 mi west of the Calsonic Arena. There are restaurants nearby. Restaurant. Cable TV. Pool. Some pets allowed (fee). | 317 N. Cannon Blvd. 37160 | 931/684–6050 or 800/684–0466 | fax 931/684–2714 | 72 rooms | $55 | AE, D, DC, MC, V.

SWEETWATER

Budget Host. Located off I-75, 6 mi northwest of the Lost Sea, this hotel offers clean, comfortable rooms facing the interstate. Some refrigerators, cable TV. Laundry facilities. Some pets allowed (fee). | 207 Rte. 68 37874 | 423/337-9357 | fax 423/337-7436 | www.budgetinn.com | 61 rooms | $34-$44 | AE, D, DC, MC, V.

Comfort Inn. This member of the popular lodging chain enjoys a peaceful setting 2½ mi from I-75, and 4 mi east of the Lost Sea. There's a pond and picnic area on the grounds. Downtown Sweetwater and local restaurants are nearby. Some rooms have balconies overlooking the duck pond. Complimentary Continental breakfast, picnic area. Microwaves, refrigerators, cable TV. Pool, wading pool. Business services. Some pets allowed. | 731 S. Main St. 37874 | 423/337-6646 | fax 423/337-5409 | www.comfortinn.com | 60 rooms | $32-$65 | AE, D, DC, MC, V.

TIPTONVILLE

Bluebank Resort. This small resort located on the shores of Reelfoot Lake offers fishing and hunting packages. The lodge houses a common room with pool tables and a lakeside deck with tables. Some rooms have fireplaces and balconies overlooking the lake. Cabins house from 2 to 16 people. Choose from between three types of lodgings: the Hunter's Lodge is located on the lake, with kitchen, picnic area, and private fishing; the Marina Lodge is surrounded by a boardwalk deck; the Resort Lodging is the main inn, with restaurant and golfing nearby. Restaurant. Kitchenettes, cable TV. Pool. Hot tub. Some pets allowed. | 813 Lake Dr. 38079 | 901/253-6878 or 901/253-8976 | www.bluebankresort.com | 18 rooms, 2 suites, 13 cabins | $85-$95, $135 suites, $60-$365 cabins | AE, D, DC, MC, V.

Blue Basin Cove Bed and Breakfast. Couples and families come to this B&B on Reelfoot Lake, 5 mi east of Tiptonville, to go fishing for crappie March through June; there's a boat and bait shop on the property. Bald eagles are the main attraction in winter. Two buildings have units that sleep up to six people. Complimentary breakfast. Some kitchenettes, refrigerators. Cable TV, no room phones. Dock, fishing. Pets allowed. | Off Rte. 213, R.D. 1 38079 | 901/253-9064 | www.bluebasin.com | 5 rooms | $65 | AE, MC, V.

Boyette's Resort. Across the street from the Reelfoot Lake visitor's center, this complex has cottages that are rustic with cyprus walls and knotty pine cabinets; all have screened-in porches. Restaurants are less than a mile away. Some kitchenettes. Cable TV. Outdoor pool. Pets allowed. | Rte. 213, R.D. 1, Box 1230 38079 | 901/253-6523 | www.lakereelfoot.net | 16 rooms, 3 1-bedroom cottages, 10 2-bedroom cottages, 4 family houses | $40 rooms | AE, D, MC, V.

Cypress Point Resort. This resort is on the shores of Reelfoot Lake, just 3 mi east of Tiptonville, and offers four-day fishing packages. The two buildings are surrounded by cypress trees. Cabins have screened-in porches. Restaurant. Kitchenettes, cable TV. Pool. Some pets allowed. | Rte. 1 38079 | 901/253-6654 or 901/253-6659 | www.cypresspointresort.com | 25 rooms | $69-$89 | AE, D, DC, MC, V.

TOWNSEND

Best Western Valley View Lodge. These standard chain accommodations are set on 17 lawnlike acres enclosed by white fences. Great Smoky Mountains National Park is just 3 mi to the south. Rooms with fireplaces are available. Picnic area, complimentary Continental breakfast. Some minibars, refrigerators, cable TV. 3 pools (1 indoor). Hot tubs. Business services. Some pets allowed. | 7726 Lamar Alexander Pkwy. 37882 | 865/448-2237 | fax 865/448-9957 | www.valleyviewlodge.com | 138 rooms, 12 cabins, 4 guesthouses | $46-$89, $119-$131 cabins, $95-$110 guesthouses | AE, D, DC, MC, V.

Texas

ABILENE

Best Inn. This two-story, mid-size hotel has a garden courtyard on its grounds. A restaurant is behind the property. Cable TV, pool, laundry facilities, business services, airport shuttle, some pets allowed (fee). | 1625 Rte. 351 79601 | 915/673–5271 | fax 915/673–8240 | 163 rooms | $49–$59 | AE, DC, MC, V.

Budget Host. The airport and two universities are 10 mi from this motel. Restaurant, room service, cable TV, pool, wading pool, business services, some pets allowed. | 3210 Pine St. 79601 | 915/677–2683 | fax 915/677–8211 or 888/672–5293 | 100 rooms | $35–$55 | AE, D, DC, MC, V.

Clarion Hotel and Conference Center. This three-story hotel has a variety of meeting rooms in which business travelers can hold court. A number of fast food restaurants are 4 blocks away. Restaurant, bar, room service, some microwaves, cable TV, 2 pools, wading pool, hot tub, sauna, laundry facilities, business services, some pets allowed. | 5403 S. 1st St. 79605 | 915/695–2150 | fax 915/698–6742 | 176 rooms, 5 suites | $44–$64, $60–$69 suites | AE, D, DC, MC, V.

Embassy Suites. A shopping mall is across the street from this full-service, all-suites hotel. A hot, made-to-order breakfast is available daily, and an open bar is scheduled nightly. Restaurant, bar, complimentary breakfast, room service, in-room data ports, microwaves, refrigerators, cable TV, pool, hot tub, sauna, steam room, laundry facilities, laundry service, business services, pets allowed. | 4250 Ridgemont Dr. | 915/698–1234 or 800/362–2779 | fax 915/698–2771 | mburke@embassyabilene.com | www.embassyabilene.com | 176 suites | $86–$150 | AE, D, DC, MC, V.

La Quinta. This two-story hotel is 8 mi from the airport. Complimentary Continental breakfast, cable TV, pool, some pets allowed. | 3501 W. Lake Rd. 79601 | 915/676–1676 | fax 915/672–8323 | www.laquinta.com | 106 rooms | $49–$90 | AE, D, DC, MC, V.

Quality Inn. The civic center is across the street from this two-story motel, and the airport is 15 mi away. Restaurant, bar, complimentary breakfast, room service, cable TV, pool, business services, airport shuttle, some pets allowed. | 505 Pine St. 79601 | 915/676–0222 or 800/221–0222 | fax 915/676–0513 | 118 rooms | $49–$65 | AE, D, DC, MC, V.

Royal Inn. This single-story motel was built in the 1940s. It's less than 1 mi from Dyess Air Force Base. Restaurant, bar, room service, cable TV, pool, business services, some pets allowed (fee). | 5695 S. 1st St. 79605 | 915/692–3022 or 800/588–4386 | fax 915/692–3137 | 150 rooms | $25–$48 | AE, D, DC, MC, V.

ALICE

Days Inn. Built in the mid 1970s, this two-story motel is within 5 mi of two golfing facilities. Restaurant, complimentary Continental breakfast, room service, in-room data ports, cable TV, pool, golf, laundry service, business services, pets allowed. | 555 N. Johnson St. 78332 | 361/664–6616 or 800/544–8313 | fax 361/664–8016 | www.daysinn.com | 97 rooms | $40–$50 | AE, D, DC, MC, V.

AMARILLO

Best Western Amarillo Inn. A two-story hotel with brown brick and cream trim, you can park in front of your door on the first floor, and second floor rooms are accessed from an interior corridor via staircase. Rooms are neutrally colored, with Southwestern-style art on the walls. Medi Park is within walking distance, with two small lakes and a walking trail. Restaurant, complimentary breakfast, room service, in-room data ports, some microwaves, some refrigerators, cable TV, pool, laundry facilities, laundry service, business services, pets allowed (fee). | 1610 Coulter St. 79106 | 806/358–7861 or 800/528–1234 | fax 352–7287 | 103 rooms | $69–$89 | AE, D, DC, MC, V.

Hampton Inn. This two-story hotel is 3 mi south of historic Route 66. The Amarillo Zoo is 10 mi to the north and the Amarillo Museum of Art is only 5 mi away. Complimentary Continental breakfast, cable TV, pool, business services, pets allowed. | 1700 I–40E, 79103 | 806/372–1425 | fax 806/379–8807 | www.hamptoninn.com | 116 rooms | $59–$89 | AE, D, DC, MC, V.

Ramada Inn West. Guest rooms are in either a three-story atrium or a two-story wing. Rooms off the enclosed atrium are close to the pool and airy restaurant. The hotel is about 4 mi west of downtown. Restaurant, complimentary breakfast, in-room data ports, some minibars, some microwaves, some in-room hot tubs, cable TV, pool, hot tub, spa, laundry facilities, laundry service, business services, pets allowed (fee). | 6801 I–40W 79106 | 806/358–7881 or 800/858–2223 | fax 806/358–1726 | 148 rooms, 32 suites | $69–$109, $89–$109 suites | AE, D, DC, MC, V.

ANGLETON

Ramada Inn. This two-story mid-1970s redbrick hotel is in nearby Lake Jackson, 15 mi south of Angleton via U.S. 288 to U.S. 332. Conveniences include a complimentary lunch buffet and five meeting rooms. Restaurant, bar, complimentary Continental breakfast, room service, some microwaves, some refrigerators, cable TV, pool, exercise equipment, laundry service, business services, pets allowed (fee). | 925 U.S. 332W, Lake Jackson 77566 | 979/297–1161 or 800/544–2119 | fax 979/297–1249 | www.ramadainnlakejacksontx.com | 144 rooms | $90–$155 | AE, D, DC, MC, V.

ARLINGTON–GRAND PRAIRIE

Hawthorn Suites. All rooms have either a private patio or balcony. Some kitchenettes, microwaves, cable TV, pool, exercise equipment, laundry facilities, business services, some pets allowed (fee). | 2401 Brookhollow Plaza Dr. 76006 | 817/640–1188 or 800/527–1133 | fax 817/649–4720 | www.hawthorn.com | 26 rooms, 130 suites | $75–$79, $149 suites | AE, D, DC, MC, V.

Residence Inn by Marriott. All rooms have separate living areas, making it a fine choice for extended stays or families. Complimentary Continental breakfast, in-room data ports, refrigerators, kitchenettes, cable TV, hot tub, exercise equipment, pool, tennis, laundry facilities, laundry service, business services, pets allowed. | 1050 Brookhollow Plaza Dr., Arlington 76006 | 817/649–7300 or 800/331–3131 | fax 817/649–7600 | residenceinn. com/DALAR | 114 suites | $85–$160 suites | AE, D, DC, MC, V.

ATHENS

Motel 6. Rooms have exterior corridor entrances in this two-story motel 2 mi north of downtown. Ground-floor rooms have front parking spaces. A popular fish hatchery with picnic facilities is 5 mi away. In-room data ports, cable TV, pool, business services, pets allowed. | 205 Dallas Hwy. 175 75751 | 903/675–7511 | fax 903/675–8833 | 70 rooms | $37–$56 | AE, D, DC, MC, V.

AUSTIN

Days Inn University/Downtown. Its downtown location puts this two-story motel just blocks from the University of Texas. Complimentary Continental breakfast, microwaves, refrigerators, cable TV, pool, pets allowed. | 3105 I–35N 78722 | 512/478–1631 or 800/725–7666 | fax 512/236–0058 | 61 rooms | $64–$89 | AE, D, DC, MC, V.

Doubletree Guest Suites. The State Capitol building, which is just across the street, is visible from many rooms in this all-suites hotel. The University of Texas is just 2 mi away. Restaurant, bar, room service, in-room data ports, microwaves, refrigerators, cable TV, pool, sauna, exercise equipment, laundry facilities, laundry service, business services, parking (fee), pets allowed (fee). | 303 W. 15th St. 78701 | 512/478–7000 or 800/424–2900 | fax 512/478–5103 | www.doubletree.com | 189 suites | $125–$250 suites | AE, D, DC, MC, V.

Drury Inn. A mall and a restaurant are across the street from this four-story hotel. Austin's downtown area is 5 mi away, and the airport is 12 mi away. Complimentary Continental breakfast, in-room data ports, some microwaves, cable TV, pool, exercise equipment, laundry facilities, business services, free parking, some pets allowed. | 6711 I–35N 78752 | 512/467–9500 | fax 512/467–9500 | 224 rooms | $73–$85 | AE, D, DC, MC, V.

Exel Inn. This three-story hotel is 3 mi from Austin's downtown and 5 mi from the Governor's mansion. Complimentary Continental breakfast, cable TV, pool, video games, laundry facilities, some pets allowed. | 2711 I–35S 78741 | 512/462–9201 | fax 512/462–9371 | 89 rooms | $59–$79 | AE, D, DC, MC, V.

Four Seasons. Built along the shoreline, this luxury hotel has views of beautiful sunsets over Town Lake. Restaurant, bar, room service, in-room data ports, some microwaves, cable TV, pool, hot tub, massage, gym, business services, parking (fee), some pets allowed. | 98 San Jacinto Blvd. 78701 | 512/478–4500 | fax 512/478–3117 | www.fourseasons.com | 291 rooms | $235–$350 | AE, DC, MC, V.

Hawthorn Suites–South. Numerous restaurants are less than 1 mi from this two-story hotel, 4 mi south of downtown Austin. Picnic area, complimentary Continental breakfast, kitchenettes, microwaves, cable TV, pool, hot tub, laundry facilities, business services, free parking, pets allowed (fee). | 4020 I–35S 78704 | 512/440–7722 | fax 512/440–4815 | www.hawthorn.com | 120 suites | $149–$179 suites | AE, D, DC, MC, V.

Hilton–North. Austin's downtown area, a mall, and a theater are within 4 mi of this nine-story hotel. Restaurant, bar, room service, in-room data ports, cable TV, pool, exercise equipment, business services, free parking, some pets allowed (fee). | 6000 Middle Fiskville Rd. 78752 | 512/451–5757 | fax 512/467–7644 | 7416162@compuserv.com | 189 rooms | $79–$199 | AE, D, DC, MC, V.

Holiday Inn–South. This five-story hotel is just 5 mi from downtown Austin and the State Capitol Building. Be sure to reserve in advance if you want a poolside suite. Restaurant, bar, room service, in-room data ports, refrigerators, cable TV, pool, hot tub, exercise equipment, laundry facilities, business services, airport shuttle, pets allowed. | 3401 I–35S

78741 | 512/448–2444 | fax 512/448–4999 | www.holiday-inn.com | 190 rooms, 20 suites | $84, $114 suites | AE, D, DC, MC, V.

La Quinta–Capitol. Restaurants and the State Capitol building are two blocks from this four-story hotel. In-room data ports, cable TV, pool, business services, pets allowed, parking (fee). | 300 E. 11th St. 78701 | 512/476–1166 or 800/687–6667 | fax 512/476–6044 | www.laquinta.com | 145 rooms | $69–$109 | AE, D, DC, MC, V.

La Quinta–North. This two-story motel is less than 1 mi from a mall and restaurants. In-room data ports, cable TV, pool, business services, some pets allowed. | 7100 I–35N 78752 | 512/452–9401 | fax 512/452–0856 | www.laquinta.com | 115 rooms | $69–$125 | AE, D, DC, MC, V.

La Quinta/Round Rock. The downtown area is about 12 mi from this three-story motel. A 24-hour restaurant is 2 blocks away. Complimentary Continental breakfast, in-room data ports, some microwaves, cable TV, pool, hot tub, exercise equipment, some pets allowed. | 2004 I–35N, Round Rock 78681 | 512/255–6666 | fax 512/388–3635 | www.laquinta.com | 116 rooms | $77–$84 | AE, DC, MC, V.

Motel 6–Austin North. Truck parking is available at this two-story motel in northern Austin. A bowling alley is within walking distance. Cable TV, pool, free parking, pets allowed. | 9420 I–35N 78753 | 512/339–6161 | fax 512/339–7852 | 158 rooms | $49 | AE, D, DC, MC, V.

Motel 6–North Central. Several restaurants are less than 2 mi from this two-story motel. Cable TV, pool, pets allowed. | 8010 I–35N 78753 | 512/837–9890 | fax 512/339–3045 | 111 rooms | $49 | AE, D, DC, MC, V.

Quality Inn–Airport. The airport is 15 mi from this motel. Sixth Street, where there are numerous bars and restaurants, is just 2 mi away. Complimentary Continental breakfast, cable TV, pool, free parking, pets allowed (fee). | 909 E. Koenig La. 78751 | 512/452–4200 | fax 512/374–0652 | 91 rooms | $59–$69 | AE, D, DC, MC, V.

Red Lion. A mall and shopping plaza are 2 mi from this seven-story hotel. A number of restaurants are within two blocks. Restaurant, bar, room service, in-room data ports, some refrigerators, cable TV, pool, hot tub, exercise equipment, laundry facilities, business services, free parking, pets allowed. | 6121 I–35N 78752 | 512/323–5466 | fax 512/453–1945 | 300 rooms | $99 | AE, D, DC, MC, V.

Red Roof Inn. This four-story motel is 1½ mi from a shopping mall. Pool, free parking, pets allowed. | 8210 I–35N 78753 | 512/835–2200 | fax 512/339–9043 | www.redroof.com | 143 rooms | $46–$56 | AE, D, DC, MC, V.

Renaissance. An imposing atrium lobby is filled with plants, birds, statues, and tiki bells. Restaurant, bar (with entertainment), in-room data ports, some microwaves, cable TV, 2 pools, hot tub, exercise equipment, business services, free parking. Some pets allowed. | 9721 Arboretum Blvd. 78759 | 512/343–2626 | fax 512/346–7953 | www.renaissancehotels.com | 478 rooms, 16 suites | $189, $240–$325 suites | AE, D, DC, MC, V.

BANDERA

Hackberry Lodge Bed and Breakfast. All but one of the guest rooms in this turn-of-the-20th-century home are two-bedroom suites. Help yourself to whatever you crave from the summer kitchen, then relax on one of the porches or the hammock. Breakfast is served in the garden, and you can request a five-course dinner in the dining room. Dining room, complimentary breakfast, microwaves, cable TV, no room phones, library, business services, pets allowed, no kids, no smoking. | 1005 Hackberry St. 78003 | 830/460–7134 | fax 830/460–7500 | www.hackberrylodge.com | 7 suites | $95–$155 suites | MC, V.

BAYTOWN

Holiday Inn Express. The Houston airport is one hour from this three-story motel, and a shopping mall and steak house are across the Interstate. Cable TV, pool, pets allowed. | 5222 I–10E, 77521 | 281/421–7200 | fax 281/421–7209 | www.holidayinn.com | 62 rooms | $49–$75 | AE, D, DC, MC, V.

La Quinta. Right off I-10, this two-story hotel is across the highway from the San Jacinto Mall. You can request a free pass for use at a gym 2 mi away. Complimentary Continental breakfast, some microwaves, some refrigerators, cable TV, pool, laundry service, business services, pets allowed. | 4911 I–10E 77521 | 281/421–5566 or 800/687–6667 | fax 281/421–4009 | 130 rooms | $60–$75 | AE, D, DC, MC, V.

Motel 6. This two-story motel is within walking distance of several restaurants and is 4 mi from a shopping mall. Cable TV, pool, pets allowed. | 8911 Rte. 146 77520 | 281/576–5777 | fax 281/576–2351 | 124 rooms | $35–$40 | AE, D, DC, MC, V.

BEAUMONT

Best Western–Beaumont Inn. The airport is 20 mi from this two-story motel, and a shopping mall is within walking distance. Several restaurants are within three blocks. Complimentary Continental breakfast, in-room data ports, some refrigerators, cable TV, pool, laundry facilities, business services, some pets allowed. | 2155 N. 11th St. 77703 | 409/898–8150 | fax 979/898–0078 | 152 rooms | $54–$72 | AE, D, DC, MC, V.

Best Western–Jefferson Inn. Several restaurants are within walking distance of this two-story motel, and a shopping mall is 3 mi away. Complimentary Continental breakfast, in-room data ports, some kitchenettes, some refrigerators, cable TV, pool, laundry facilities, business services, some pets allowed. | 1610 I–10S 77707 | 409/842–0037 or 800/528–1234 | fax 979/842–0057 | 120 rooms | $67 | AE, D, DC, MC, V.

Holiday Inn–Beaumont Plaza. A three-story waterfall is in the lobby of this eight-story hotel. The convention center is next door. Restaurant, bar, in-room data ports, some refrigerators, cable TV, pool, hot tub, exercise equipment, business services, airport shuttle, pets allowed (fee). | 3950 I–10S 77705 | 409/842–5995 | fax 409/842–0315 | www.holidayinn.com | 253 rooms, 80 suites | $90, $113 suites | AE, D, DC, MC, V.

Holiday Inn–Midtown. This six-story hotel is 2 mi from Beaumont's downtown area and a shopping mall. Restaurant, bar, room service, in-room data ports, cable TV, pool, laundry facilities, business services, airport shuttle, some pets allowed. | 2095 N. 11th St. 77703 | 409/892–2222 | fax 409/892–2231 | hi-beaumont@bristolhotels.com | www.holiday-inn.com | 190 rooms | $69–$99 | AE, D, DC, MC, V.

La Quinta. This motel is within walking distance of several restaurants, 2 mi from a shopping mall, and 8 mi from the airport. Complimentary Continental breakfast, in-room data ports, cable TV, pool, business services, some pets allowed. | 220 I–10N 77702 | 409/838–9991 | fax 405/832–1266 | www.laquinta.com | 122 rooms | $57–$63 | AE, D, DC, MC, V.

Scottish Inns. This two-story motel is 2 mi from a shopping mall and across the Interstate from a number of chain restaurants. Cable TV, pool, some pets allowed. | 2640 I–10E 77703 | 409/899–3152 | fax 409/895–0228 | 118 rooms | $35 | AE, D, MC, V.

BIG BEND NATIONAL PARK

Chisos Mining Co. Motel. This mom-and-pop motel's bright colors and rustic decor make it stand out from its desert setting. Cable TV, some pets allowed. | Box 228, Terlingua 79852 | 915/371–2254 | fax 915/371–2430 | 20 rooms, 10 cabins | $56 room, $56 cabin | AE, D, MC, V.

Chisos Mountains Lodge. Though Big Bend National Park has hundreds of campsites, this is the only hotel; it's therefore often booked months in advance. Although it isn't fancy, most rooms have private balconies and spectacular views of the mountains and the desert floor. Dining room, no air-conditioning in some rooms, no room phones, no TV, pets allowed. | From the Alpine/Study Butte entrance, follow Basin Rd. 22 mi east to its end 79834 | 915/477–2291 | fax 915/477–2352 | www.chisosmountainslodge.com | 72 rooms (6 with shower only) | $70–$81 | AE, D, DC, MC, V.

BIG SPRING

Econolodge. Rooms have exterior access in this two-story motel 1 mi north of downtown Big Spring via Rte. 87. Complimentary Continental breakfast, in-room data ports, some microwaves, some refrigerators, cable TV, pool, exercise equipment, business services, pets allowed. | 804 I–20W 79720 | 915/263–5200 | fax 915/263–5457 | 50 rooms | $55–$65 | AE, D, DC, MC, V.

BRAZOSPORT

La Quinta. This two-story motel is less than 1 mi from several restaurants, and 2 mi from a mall and a theater. Complimentary Continental breakfast, in-room data ports, cable TV, pool, exercise equipment, some pets allowed. | 1126 Rte. 332W, Clute 77531 | 979/265–7461 | fax 979/265–3804 | www.laquinta.com | 135 rooms | $49–$65 | AE, D, DC, MC, V.

Ramada Inn. The waters of the Gulf are about 10 mi from this two-story hotel. It's within walking distance of several restaurants and 2 mi from a mall. Restaurant, bar, room service, cable TV, pool, some pets allowed. | 925 Rte. 332W, Lake Jackson 77566 | 979/297–1161 | fax 979/297–1249 | ramadainn@computron.net | www.ramada.com | 144 rooms | $117 | AE, D, DC, MC, V.

BROWNSVILLE

Four Points by Sheraton. Both the Gladys Porter Zoo and a 10-screen movie theater are within 5 mi of this two-story hotel. The Brownsville/South Padre Island International Airport is 7 mi away. Restaurant, bar (with entertainment), room service, in-room data ports, hot tub (in suites), refrigerators, cable TV, 2 pools, hot tub, business services, some pets allowed. | 3777 N. Expressway 78520 | 956/547–1500 | fax 956/350–4153 | www.sheraton.com | 141 rooms | $99–$109 | AE, D, DC, MC, V.

Holiday Inn Fort Brown. This two-story hotel is two blocks from the International Gateway Bridge. Restaurant, bar (with entertainment), room service, in-room data ports, cable TV, pool, business services, some pets allowed. | 1900 E. Elizabeth St. 78520 | 956/546–2201 | fax 956/546–0756 | www.holidayinn.com | 168 rooms | $72–$95 | AE, D, DC, MC, V.

Motel 6. Several restaurants and a mall are within walking distance of this motel. Cable TV, pool, pets allowed. | 2255 N. Expressway Feeder Rd. | 956/546–4699 | fax 956/546–8982 | www.motel6.com | 190 rooms | $36–$47 | AE, D, DC, MC, V.

BRYAN/COLLEGE STATION

Hilton. This 11-story hotel is the only full-service accommodation in the Bryan/College Station area. As with most hotels in the area, it's close to Texas A&M University—about 1½ mi west via University Dr. E. Restaurant, bar, complimentary Continental breakfast, in-room data ports, some microwaves, some refrigerators, some in-room hot tubs, some in-room VCRs, pool, outdoor hot tub, exercise equipment, laundry service, business services, pets allowed. | 801 University Dr. E, College Station 77840 | 979/693–7500 or 800/445–86 | fax 979/260–6720 | www.hiltoncs.com | 250 rooms, 53 suites | $89–$185, $109–$260 suites | AE, D, DC, MC, V.

La Quinta. This two-story motel is across the street from Texas A&M University and 5 mi from Easterwood Airport. Picnic area, complimentary Continental breakfast, in-room data ports, cable TV, pool, airport shuttle, pets allowed. | 607 Texas Ave. S 77840 | 979/696–7777 | fax 979/696–0531 | www.laquinta.com | 176 rooms | $69–$79 | AE, D, DC, MC, V.

Manor House. All rooms have exterior access in this two-story motel 6 mi from Easterwood Airport. Complimentary Continental breakfast, in-room data ports, refrigerators, cable TV, pool, airport shuttle, pets allowed (fee). | 2504 Texas Ave. S, College Station 77840 | 979/764–9540 or 800/231–4100 | fax 979/693–2430 | 115 rooms | $51–$79 | AE, D, DC, MC, V.

BURNET

Canyon of the Eagles Lodge. On Lake Buchanan in a 940-acre nature park, this out-of-the-way place has 2 mi of trails, a 5-mi beach, a general store, and an astronomical observatory. Bird-watchers might spot a bald eagle, black-capped vireo, and golden-cheeked warbler. Guest rooms have porches, most of which are equipped with rocking chairs. Restaurant, bar, in-room data ports, some microwaves, some refrigerators, pool, hiking, beach, boating, fishing, business services, pets allowed (fee). | 16942 Ranch Rd. 2341 78611 | 512/756–8787 or 800/977–0081 | fax 512/715–9819 | www.canyonoftheeagles.com | 64 rooms | $87–$127 | AE, MC, V.

CANTON

Best Western Canton Inn and Good Sam RV Park. An RV park with full hookups is on site at this two-story chain hotel. Restaurant, picnic area, complimentary Continental breakfast, cable TV, pool, laundry facilities, some pets allowed. | 2521 N. Trade Days Blvd. | 903/567–6591 or 800/528–1234 | 82 rooms | $59–$89 | AE, D, MC, V.

Ramada Limited Suites. This small, two-story, all-suites hotel opened in 1997. It's at the junction of Rte. 19 and I–20. Restaurant, complimentary Continental breakfast, cable TV, pool, hot tub, pets allowed. | 3001 N. Trade Days Blvd. | 903/567–0455 | www.ramada.com | 40 rooms | $110–$125 | AE, D, MC, V.

CASTROVILLE

Alsatian Inn. This two-story motel overlooks town. Cable TV, pool, some pets allowed. | 1650 U.S. 90 W | 830/538–2262 or 800/446–8528 | 40 rooms | $45–$60.

CHILDRESS

Econolodge. This two-story motel is within walking distance of stores and restaurants. Restaurant, cable TV, pool, business services, pets allowed. | 1612 Avenue F NW 79201 | 940/937–3695 or 800/542–4229 | fax 940/937–6956 | 28 rooms | $38–$49 | AE, D, DC, MC, V.

Holiday Inn Express. This two-story hotel has a semi-circular drive covered by a large, looming carport. Both the carport and main building are topped with squarish cupolas that are easily seen from the road. In-room data ports, safes, refrigerators, cable TV, pool and hot tub, exercise equipment, laundry, business services, pets allowed. | 2008 Ave. F NW | 940/937–3434 | fax 940/937–2270 | 52 | $55–$70 | AE, D, DC, MC, V.

CLARENDON

Bar H Dude Ranch. Guests at this all-inclusive 1,500-acre working ranch sleep in bunk houses—five bunks to a room—ride horses, and help with ranch chores daily. Restaurant, no room phones, no TV, TV in common area, pool, hiking, horseback riding, volleyball, laundry facilities, pets allowed. | Rte. 3257 and Rte. N | 806/874–2634 or 800/627–9871 | fax 806/874–3679 | 17 rooms (with shared bath) | $130 | AP | AE, D, MC, V.

Western Skies. Greenbelt Lake is 3 mi from this motel built in the mid-1950s. Cable TV, pool, playground, business services, some pets allowed. | 800 W. 2nd St. | 806/874–3501 | fax 806/874–5303 | 23 rooms | $35–$45 | AE, D, MC, V.

CLEBURNE

Comfort Inn. Built in July 2000, this is the newest hotel in town. Complimentary Continental breakfast, in-room data ports, microwaves, refrigerators, some in-room hot tubs, cable TV, pool, exercise equipment, laundry facilities, laundry service, business services, pets allowed (fee). | 2117 N. Main St. 76031 | 817/641–4702 or 800/228–5150 | fax 817/641–4336 | www.comfortinn.com | 36 rooms, 18 suites | $69–$89, $89–$120 suites | AE, D, DC, MC, V.

Days Inn. This motel is within walking distance of restaurants and just 2 mi from the Cleburne airport. It's comprised of one two-story building, and two one-story buildings. Cable TV, pool, pets allowed. | 101 N. Ridgeway Dr. (Rte. 67 Business) 76031 | 817/645–8836 | fax 817/645–4813 | 45 rooms | $45–$69 | AE, D, MC, V.

COMANCHE

Days Inn. This two-story motel is within walking distance of a mall and restaurants. In-room data ports, cable TV, pool, hot tub, exercise equipment, laundry facilities, business services, pets allowed (fee). | 515 E. Commerce St., Brownwood 76801 | 915/646–2551 | fax 915/643–6064 | 140 rooms | $50–$75 | AE, D, DC, MC, V.

Guest House at Heritage Hill. This 1930s ranch house with a full kitchen is on a 120-acre working cattle and goat ranch just outside of town. See armadillos, turkeys, and white-tail deer, and observe the panoramic sweep of stars in the night sky from your private porch. The single-story home has antique furnishings from the 1920s and 1930s, with a few Victorian-style details thrown in—like the claw-foot tubs in two of the three bathrooms. Microwave, refrigerator, cable TV, in-room VCR, pond, hiking, fishing, business services, pets allowed. | Rte. 36, 2½ mi east of Comanche | 915/356–3397 | fax 915/356–2308 | perkinshhp@itexas.net | 4 rooms | $100 | No credit cards.

CORPUS CHRISTI

Drury Inn. The Corpus Christi International Airport is 3 mi from this motel, and popular attractions such as the Texas State Aquarium and the USS *Lexington* Museum on the Bay are just 5 mi away. Complimentary Continental breakfast, in-room data ports, refrigerators (in suites), cable TV, pool, business services, airport shuttle, pets allowed. | 2021 N. Padre Island Dr. 78408 | 361/289–8200 | www.drury-inn.com | fax 361/289–8200 | 105 rooms | $64–$80 | AE, D, DC, MC, V.

Fortuna Bay. This stunning, Spanish Mission–style B&B sits at the intersection of five canals on North Padre Island, facing the Gulf of Mexico. Whitewashed walls and terra-cotta tiles provide a distinct Caribbean flavor. You can fish right off the back deck, or head over to the nearby country club for golf, tennis, or fine dining. Corpus Christi's shopping district is 20 minutes away, as is a gorgeous white sand beach. Kids are allowed with prior arrangement only. In-room data ports, kitchenettes, cable TV, golf privileges, beach, dock, fishing, some pets allowed, no smoking. | 15405 Fortuna Bay Dr. | 361/949–7554 | 5 suites | $110 | No credit cards.

Holiday Inn–Emerald Beach. This downtown hotel is on the bay and overlooks Emerald Beach. It's comprised of one seven-story building and one five-story building. Restaurant, bar, room service, in-room data ports, cable TV, pool, wading pool, hot tub, exercise equipment, beach, playground, business services, pets allowed, airport shuttle. | 1102 S. Shoreline Blvd. 78401 | 361/883–5731 | fax 361/883–9079 | www.holiday-inn.com | 368 rooms | $125–$149 | AE, D, DC, MC, V.

Knolle Farm Bed and Breakfast. This B&B is on a working cattle ranch. Anglers can capture their own dinner in the fully stocked tank, and hunters can participate in a guided dove, goose, duck, or pheasant hunt. You can also bird-watch, go horseback riding, or enjoy a full picnic served on the banks of the Nueces River, which flows through the property.

Picnic areas, some kitchenettes, cable TV, pond, horseback riding, fishing, laundry service, some pets allowed, no smoking. | 13016 Rte. 70, Mathis 78368 | 361/547–2546 | fax 361/547–3934 | knollefarm@thei.net | 6 rooms, 1 suite | $75–$100, $150–$250 suites | AE, D, MC, V.

La Quinta North. The Corpus Christi International Airport is within 6 miles of this two-story motel, and the downtown area is 4 mi away. Restaurant, complimentary Continental breakfast, in-room data ports, cable TV, pool, business services, pets allowed. | 5155 I–37N 78408 | 361/888–5721 | fax 361/888–5401 | www.laquinta.com | 121 rooms | $65–$76 | AE, D, DC, MC, V.

Monterrey Motel. This is the closest motel to the Padre Island National Seashore and it is across the street from the Bob Hall Pier. There are a few restaurants less than 2 mi away. Some kitchenettes, some refrigerators, cable TV, some pets. | 15705 South Padre Island Dr., Corpus Christi 78418 | 361/949–8137 | fax 361/949–8137 | 24 rooms | $35–$75 | AE, D, MC, V.

Motel 6–Corpus Christi East. This two-story motel is 3 mi from a shopping mall and 10 mi from the beach. Cable TV, pool, laundry facilities, pets allowed. | 8202 S. Padre Island Dr. 78412 | 361/991–8858 | fax 361/991–1698 | 126 rooms | $38–$50 | AE, D, DC, MC, V.

Motel 6–Corpus Christi Northwest. This two-story motel is 5 mi from the Texas State Aquarium and 24 mi from the beach. Cable TV, pool, laundry facilities, pets allowed. | 845 Lantana St. 78408 | 361/289–9397 | fax 361/289–0280 | 124 rooms | $35–$40 | AE, D, DC, MC, V.

Western Isles Motel. This one-story motel is 13 mi from Padre Island National Seashore, and a 20-minute drive from downtown Corpus Christi. Some kitchenettes, some refrigerators, some microwaves, cable TV, pets allowed. | 15378 South Padre Island Dr., Corpus Christi 78418 | 361/949–8111 | fax 361/949–1768 | 22 rooms | $49–$69 | AE, D, MC, V.

DALHART

Dalhart Days Inn. The Dalhart airport is 6 mi from this two-story motel. Complimentary Continental breakfast, cable TV, pool, hot tub, business services, some pets allowed. | 701 Liberal St. 79022 | 806/244–5246 | fax 806/249–0805 | 40 rooms | $52–$99 | AE, D, DC, MC, V.

Dalhart Super 8. This motel is six blocks east of the town's major intersection at U.S. 54 and U.S. 87. The largest room right over the lobby has a pullout couch, a king-size bed, and a recliner. A steakhouse is within walking distance. Complimentary Continental breakfast, in-room data ports, cable TV, hot tub, sauna, pets allowed (fee). | Box 1325, Denver St./Rte. 54E 79022 | 806/249–8526 or 800/800–8000 | fax 806/249–5119 | 45 rooms | $52–$62 | AE, D, DC, MC, V.

DALLAS

Best Western Dallas North. The Dallas/Ft. Worth International Airport is 12 mi from this hotel, and attractions within 5–10 minutes include the Galleria mall, West End Historic District, and the Dallas Arboretum. Restaurant, bar, room service, in-room data ports, cable TV, pool, hot tub, laundry facilities, business services, airport shuttle, free parking, some pets allowed. | 13333 N. Stemmons Fwy. 75234 | 972/241–8521 | fax 972/243–4103 | www.bestwestern.com | 185 rooms | $59–$69 | AE, D, DC, MC, V.

Best Western Park Suites Hotel. This hotel aims to offer luxurious, spacious rooms for extended-stay travelers, business travelers, or large families. The Dallas/Ft. Worth International Airport is 35 mi away. Bar, complimentary Continental breakfast, in-room data ports, microwaves, refrigerators, some in-room hot tubs, cable TV, pool, hot tub, exercise equipment, laundry facilities, business services, free parking, some pets allowed (fee). | 640 E. Park Blvd., Plano 75074 | 972/578–2243 | fax 972/578–0563 | www.bestwestern.com | 84 suites | $55–$95 suites | AE, D, DC, MC, V.

Crowne Plaza–North Dallas/Addison. This four-story hotel is 15 mi from downtown Dallas and 17 mi from Dallas/Ft. Worth International Airport. 2 restaurants, room service, in-room data ports, some microwaves, refrigerators, cable TV, pool, hot tub, exercise equipment, laundry facilities, business service, airport shuttle, free parking, some pets allowed (fee). | 14315 Midway Rd. 75001 | 972/980–8877 | fax 972/788–2758 | www.bristolhotels.com | 429 rooms | $69–$159 | AE, D, DC, MC, V.

Crowne Plaza Suites Dallas. This 10-story all-suites hotel with 14 meeting rooms is a good choice for business travelers. It's 18 mi from the Dallas/Ft. Worth International Airport, 15 mi from downtown Dallas, and 15 mi from the convention center. Restaurant, bar, room service, in-room data ports, microwaves, refrigerators, cable TV, 2 pools, hot tub, exercise equipment, laundry facilities, business services, free parking, pets allowed (fee). | 7800 Alpha Rd. 75240 | 972/233–7600 | fax 972/701–8618 | www.bristolhotels.com | 295 rooms | $79–$159 | AE, D, DC, MC, V.

Hampton Inn–West End. This downtown hotel is connected to the Underground Tunnel, where you'll find numerous shops and restaurants. The tunnel also connects the buildings of downtown Dallas. The Dallas/Ft. Worth International Airport is 18 mi away. Complimentary Continental breakfast, in-room data ports, cable TV, pool, barbershop, exercise equipment, laundry facilities, business services, parking (fee), pets allowed (fee). | 1015 Elm St. 75202 | 214/742–5678 | fax 214/744–6167 | www.hamptoninn.com | 311 rooms | $70–$119 | AE, D, DC, MC, V.

Harvey Hotel–Dallas. Dallas's downtown area is just 15 minutes away from this three-story hotel. Restaurant, bar, in-room data ports, room service, cable TV, pool, business services, free parking, pets allowed (fee). | 7815 L.B.J. Fwy. 75240 | 972/960–7000 or 800/922–9222 | fax 972/788–4227 | 313 rooms | $89–$109 | AE, D, DC, MC, V.

Harvey Hotel–Plano. This three-story hotel is across the street from a shopping mall and within walking distance of several restaurants. Restaurants, bar, room service, in-room data ports, some refrigerators, cable TV, pool, hot tub, exercise equipment, laundry facilities, business services, free parking, pets allowed (fee). | 1600 N. Central Expressway, Plano 75074 | 972/578–8555 | fax 972/578–9720 | 279 rooms | $110–$120 | AE, D, DC, MC, V.

Hawthorn Suites at Market Center. This all-suites hotel is 3 mi from Love Field airport, 10 mi from downtown Dallas, and 12 mi from Dallas/Ft. Worth International Airport. Complimentary breakfast, in-room data ports, kitchenettes, cable TV, pool, laundry facilities, business services, airport shuttle, free parking, some pets allowed (fee). | 7900 Brookriver Dr. 75247 | 214/688–1010 or 800/527–1133 | fax 214/638–5215 | www.hawthorn.com | 97 suites | $80–$115 suites | AE, D, DC, MC, V.

Hotel Crescent Court. The centerpiece of the Crescent Complex (which includes office buildings, shops, and galleries), this hotel is on the edge of Dallas's central business district and uptown art scene. Each room has French doors, a vanity, and a down-feather love seat. Suites are either one- or two-story, and may have spiral staircases and hardwood floors. Restaurant, bar, room service, in-room data ports, refrigerators, cable TV, pool, hot tub, gym, shops, business services, airport shuttle. Parking (fee), some pets allowed (fee). | 400 Crescent Ct. 75201 | 214/871–3200 or 800/654–6541 | fax 214/871–3272 | www.rosewood-hotels.com | 178 rooms, 40 suites | $360–$490 rooms, $445–$2,000 suites | AE, D, DC, MC, V.

La Quinta Inn–East. This limited-service hotel is about 5 mi from a mall and many restaurants. Complimentary Continental breakfast, in-room data ports, cable TV, pool, business services, free parking, some pets allowed. | 8303 E. R. L. Thornton Freeway (I–30) | 214/324–3731 | fax 214/324–1652 | www.laquinta.com | 102 rooms | $49–$99 | AE, D, DC, MC, V.

La Quinta Northwest–Farmers Branch. This two-story hotel is 10 mi from Love Field airport and 5 mi from the Galleria mall. Complimentary Continental breakfast, in-room data ports, some microwaves, cable TV, pool, business services, airport shuttle, free parking, some pets allowed. | 13235 Stemmons Freeway N 75234 | 972/620–7333 | fax 972/484–6533 | www.laquinta.com | 121 rooms | $52–$57 | AE, D, DC, MC, V.

Motel 6–Dallas Addison. This two-story motel is less than 1 mi from several restaurants, a movie theater, and shopping. Cable TV, pool, laundry facilities, free parking, pets allowed. | 4325 Beltline Rd. 75244 | 972/386–4577 | fax 972/386–4579 | 161 rooms | $44–$50 | AE, D, DC, MC, V.

Motel 6–Dallas Forest Plains North. Downtown Dallas is 7 mi from this motel, and Six Flags Over Texas (in Arlington) is 24 mi away. Cable TV, pool, laundry facilities, free parking, pets allowed. | 2753 Forest Ln. 75234 | 972/620–2828 | fax 972/620–9061 | 100 rooms | $40–$46 | AE, D, DC, MC, V.

Motel 6–Dallas Forest Plains South. This motel is 3 mi from the Galleria mall, 8 mi from the Love Field airport, and 12 mi from Dallas/Ft. Worth International Airport. Cable TV, pool, laundry facilities, free parking, pets allowed. | 2660 Forest La. 75234 | 972/484–9111 | fax 972/484–0214 | 117 rooms | $40–$46 | AE, D, DC, MC, V.

Motel 6–Dallas Southwest. The Ballpark in Arlington is 13 mi away, and downtown Dallas is 10 mi away. Cable TV, pool, laundry facilities, free parking, pets allowed. | 4220 Independence Dr. 75237 | 972/296–3331 | fax 972/709–9438 | 129 rooms | $35–$50 | AE, D, DC, MC, V.

Radisson Hotel and Suites. Most of the suites are poolside in this eight-story hotel. Love Field airport is 6 mi from this hotel, and Dallas/Ft. Worth International Airport is 14 mi away. Restaurant, bar, in-room data ports, cable TV, some kitchenettes, some microwaves, some refrigerators, pool, hot tub, exercise equipment, laundry facilities, business services, airport shuttle, free parking, some pets allowed (fee). | 2330 W. Northwest Hwy. 75220 | 214/351–4477 | fax 214/351–2364 | www.radisson.com | 145 rooms, 36 suites | $109 rooms, $119–$139 suites | AE, D, DC, MC, V.

Ramada Plaza Hotel Downtown Convention Center. This twelve-story hotel, within walking distance of the Convention Center, is also the closest to Fair Park, and provides free van transportation within 5 mi of the hotel. All rooms have private balconies, and the restaurant and bar have a great view of the downtown skyline. Restaurant, bar, room service, in-room data ports, cable TV, pool, barbershop, beauty salon, spa, golf, tennis, gym, laundry facilities, laundry service, shops, business services, baby-sitting, pets allowed, free parking. | 1011 S. Akard St. | 214/421–1083 or 888/298–2054 | fax 214/428–6827 | www.ramada.com | 238 rooms | $79–$150 | AE, D, DC, MC, V.

Ramada Texas Stadium/Love Field. A 12-story, full-service high-rise hotel on Rte. 183, Texas Stadium is 1 mi away, and Love Field airport is 7 mi away. Restaurant, bar, some refrigerators, cable TV, pool, tennis, exercise equipment, video games, business services, airport shuttle, free parking, some pets allowed. | 1055 Regal Row 75247 | 214/634–8550 | fax 214/634–8418 | www.ramada.com | 322 rooms | $69–$85 | AE, D, DC, MC, V.

Residence Inn by Marriott–Market Center. This all-suites hotel is 3 mi from Love Field airport and 15 minutes from numerous restaurants. Picnic area, complimentary Continental breakfast, kitchenettes, cable TV, pool, hot tub, exercise equipment, laundry facilities, business services, free parking, pets allowed (fee). | 6950 N. Stemmons St. 75247 | 214/631–2472 | fax 214/634–9645 | www.marriotthotels.com | 142 suites | $119–$149 suites | AE, D, DC, MC, V.

Residence Inn by Marriott–North Central. This all-suites hotel off I–75 is within 1 block of several restaurants and a movie theater, and 4 mi from the Galleria mall. Complimentary Continental breakfast, in-room data ports, kitchenettes, microwaves, refrigerators, cable TV, pool, hot tub, laundry facilities, business services, free parking, some pets allowed (fee). | 13636 Goldmark Dr. 75240 | 972/669–0478 | fax 972/644–2632 | 70 suites | $99–$179 suites | AE, D, DC, MC, V.

Sleep Inn. Several restaurants and three shopping malls are less than 2 mi from this motel. Complimentary Continental breakfast, in-room data ports, cable TV, pool, business services, free parking, pets allowed. | 4801 W. Plano Pkwy., Plano 75093 | 972/867–1111 | fax 972/612–6753 | 104 rooms | $49–$89 | AE, D, DC, MC, V.

DEL RIO

Best Western Inn. This two-story motel is within walking distance of restaurants, and offers extra perks like cherry wood furniture in the rooms, and complimentary cocktails every evening. Complimentary breakfast, in-room data ports, cable TV, pool, hot tub, laundry facilities, business services, pets allowed (fee). | 810 Ave. F 78840 | 830/775–7511 | fax 830/774–2194 | 62 rooms | $69 | AE, D, DC, MC, V.

Holiday Inn Express. Boat hook-ups are available in the parking lot for those on their way to or from Lake Amistad. Complimentary Continental breakfast, pool, pets allowed. | 3616 Ave. F | 830/775–2933 or 888/775–2933 | fax 830/775–2466 | www.holiday-inn.com | $48–$65 | AE, D, DC, MC, V.

La Quinta. This two-story motel is one block from several restaurants and ½ mi from a shopping mall. Complimentary Continental breakfast, in-room data ports, cable TV, pool, laundry facilities, pets allowed. | 2005 Ave. F 78840 | 830/775–7591 | fax 830/774–0809 | www.laquinta.com | 101 rooms | $55–$70 | AE, D, DC, MC, V.

Ramada Inn. Numerous fast food places are within walking distance of this two-story hotel. A mall is two blocks away. Restaurant, bar, room service, refrigerators, cable TV, in-room VCRs (and movies), pool, hot tub, sauna, exercise equipment, laundry facilities, business services, some pets allowed. | 2101 Ave. F 78840 | 830/775–1511 | fax 830/775–1476 | www.ramada.com | 155 rooms | $66–$137 | AE, D, DC, MC, V.

DENTON

La Quinta. Families will feel at home at this comfortable, basic, two-story chain hotel, which 1 mi from the University of North Texas and 7 mi from Texas Women's University. Complimentary Continental breakfast, in-room data ports, cable TV, pool, business services, pets allowed. | 700 Fort Worth Dr. 76201 | 940/387–5840 | fax 940/387–2493 | www.laquinta.com | 99 rooms | $65 | AE, D, DC, MC, V.

Radisson. This upscale hotel is country-western in style and is an ideal place to stay for sports enthusiasts, especially Monday Night Football watchers. Restaurant, bar, room service, cable TV, pool, driving range, 18-hole golf course, putting green, exercise equipment, business services, some pets allowed. | 2211 I–35E, North 76205 | 940/565–8499 | fax 940/387–4729 | www.radisson.com | 150 rooms | $99–$189 | AE, D, DC, MC, V.

DUMAS

Best Western Windsor Inn. This two-story motel is within blocks of numerous fast food restaurants, and 1 mi from the Moore County Historical Museum. The Amarillo International Airport is 45 minutes away. Complimentary Continental breakfast, some refrigerators, cable TV, pool, hot tub, laundry facilities, exercise equipment, some pets allowed (fee). | 1701 S. Dumas Ave. | 806/935–9644 | fax 806/935–9730 | 57 rooms | $69–$79 | AE, D, DC, MC, V.

Konakai Dumas Inn. This hotel has a tropical-theme atrium and is 3 blocks from a shopping center. Restaurant, room service, in-room data ports, cable TV, pool, hot tub, exercise equipment, video games, business services, pets allowed. | 1712 S. Dumas Ave. | 806/935–6441 | fax 806/935–9331 | 102 rooms | $55–$75 | AE, D, DC, MC, V.

Super 8. This motor inn allows truck parking and is within walking distance of shopping and restaurants. Complimentary Continental breakfast, refrigerators, cable TV, business services, some pets allowed (fee). | 119 W. 17th St. | 806/935–6222 | fax 806/935–6222 | 30 rooms | $60 | AE, D, DC, MC, V.

EAGLE PASS

Best Western. Eat and shop in the area, or drive 3 mi to the Mexican border. In-room data ports, microwaves, refrigerators, cable TV, pool, business services, some pets allowed. | 1923 Loop 431 78852 | 830/758–1234 | fax 830/758–1235 | 40 rooms, 14 suites | $77–$83, $83 suites | AE, D, DC, MC, V.

Holly Inn. This motel is within walking distance of restaurants and shopping, and it's 7 mi from Kickapoo Lucky Eagle Casino. Complimentary Continental breakfast, cable TV, outdoor pool, microwaves, refrigerators, laundry facilities, pets allowed. | 2423 E. Main St. 78852 | 830/773–9261 | fax 830/773–1619 | 70 rooms | $40–$48 | AE, D, DC, MC, V.

La Quinta. A shopping mall is 1½ mi away, and the Mexican border is 2½ mi away. Complimentary Continental breakfast, in-room data ports, microwaves, cable TV, pool, pets allowed. | 2525 Main St. 78852 | 830/773–7000 | fax 830/773–8852 | www.laquinta.com | 130 rooms | $65–$80 | AE, D, DC, MC, V.

EASTLAND

Super 8. This motel is within walking distance of many restaurants and shopping, including an antiques market. Complimentary Continental breakfast, in-room data ports, some microwaves, some refrigerators, some in-room hot tubs, cable TV, pool, pets allowed. | 3900 I–20E | 254/629–3336 | fax 254/629–3338 | 30 rooms | $49–$69 | AE, D, DC, MC, V.

EDINBURG

Echo Hotel and Conference Center. Set on 16 immaculately landscaped acres, this four-story hotel is surrounded by palm and mesquite trees and is within walking distance of golfing. Restaurant, room service, pool, exercise equipment, playground, laundry, business services, airport shuttle, pets allowed. | 1903 S. Closner | 956/383–3823 | fax 956/381–5913 | echohotel@aol.com | 122 rooms | $60–$92 | AE, D, DC, MC, V.

EL PASO

Baymont Inn and Suites–El Paso West. This chain is 7 mi from downtown, right on the Mexico border. Complimentary Continental breakfast, in-room data ports, pool, video games, laundry facilities, free parking, pets allowed. | 7620 Mesa St. | 915/585–2999 | fax 915/585–1667 | www.baymontinn.com | 102 rooms, 4 suites | $49–$96 | AE, D, DC, MC, V.

Camino Real. Built in 1912, this elegant, brick downtown hotel with commanding views of the city is listed on the National Register of Historic Places. The jewel of the lobby is the dark-wood circular Dome Bar, which sits under a superb Tiffany skylight. 3 restaurants, bar (with entertainment), in-room data ports, room service, cable TV, pool, exercise equipment, business services, free parking, airport shuttle, some pets allowed (fee). | 101 S. El Paso St. 79901 | 915/534–3000 or 800/769–4300 | fax 915/534–3024 | www.caminoreal.com | 395 rooms | $135–$150 | AE, D, DC, MC, V.

Comfort Inn. All rooms in this three-story hotel open onto the street. It's 12 mi from downtown, 5 mi from the airport, and as a guest, you'll have free access to a nearby Gold's Gym. Complimentary Continental breakfast, in-room data ports, some microwaves, some refrigerators, cable TV, pool, hot tub, laundry facilities, airport shuttle, free parking, pets allowed (fee). | 900 N. Yarbrough Dr. 79915 | 915/594–9111 | fax 915/590–4364 | www.comfortinn.com | 195 rooms, 5 suites | $59–$74 | AE, D, DC, MC, V.

Embassy Suites. Three mi from the Mexican border and 2.5 mi from the airport. Complimentary breakfast, room service, in-room data ports, microwaves, refrigerators, cable TV, pool, hot tub, golf privileges, tennis, health club, video games, baby-sitting, laundry facilities, business services, airport shuttle, free parking, some pets allowed (fee). | 6100 Gateway E 79905 | 915/779–6222 | fax 915/779–8846 | www.embassysuites.com | 185 suites | $79–$114 | AE, D, DC, MC, V.

Hawthorne Suites. Fifteen mi from downtown El Paso, this hotel is within walking distance of restaurants and shopping. Complimentary Continental breakfast, in-room data ports, pool, laundry facilities, airport shuttle, free parking, some pets allowed. | 6789 Boeing | 915/778–6789 | fax 915/778–2288 | www.hawthorn.com | 191 suites | $95–$129 | AE, D, DC, MC, V.

Hilton–Airport. This chain property has a convenient walkway that connects to the airport. Restaurant, bar, complimentary Continental breakfast, room service, in-room data ports, cable TV, pool, barbershop, beauty salon, hot tub, gym, business services, airport shuttle, free parking, pets allowed. | 2027 Airway Blvd. 79925 | 915/778–4241 | fax 915/772–6871 | www.hilton.com | 272 rooms | $75–$147 | AE, D, DC, MC, V.

Holiday Inn–Sunland Park. Located at the foothills of the Franklin Mountains, 5 mi from downtown. Restaurant, bar, room service, some microwaves, room service, cable TV, pool, wading pool, hot tub, gym, business services, airport shuttle, free parking, some pets allowed. | 900 Sunland Park Dr. 79922 | 915/833–2900 | fax 915/833–6338 | www.holiday-inn.com | 178 rooms | $69–$98 | AE, D, DC, MC, V.

Howard Johnson. Three mi from the airport, 8 mi from downtown. There's a 24-hour International House of Pancakes on site and a shopping mall across the street. In-room data ports, some refrigerators, cable TV, pool, wading pool, gym, laundry facilities, business services, airport shuttle, free parking, pets allowed. | 8887 Gateway W 79925 | 915/591–9471 | fax 915/591–5602 | www.hojoelpaso.com | 140 rooms | $57–$69 | AE, D, DC, MC, V.

La Quinta–Airport. This chain motel is 2 mi from the airport. In-room data ports, cable TV, pool, business services, airport shuttle, free parking, pets allowed. | 6140 Gateway E 79905 | 915/778–9321 | fax 915/778–9321 | www.laquinta.com | 121 rooms | $49–$70 | AE, D, DC, MC, V.

Marriott. Convenient to the airport. Restaurant, bar, room service, in-room data ports, cable TV, pool, hot tub, exercise equipment, laundry facilities, shops, business services, airport shuttle, free parking, pets allowed. | 1600 Airway Blvd. 79925 | 915/779–3300 | fax 915/772–0915 | www.marriott.com | 296 rooms | $89–$149 | AE, D, DC, MC, V.

Quality Inn. For those who want to visit Ciudad Juárez, this is a good choice. The El Paso–Juárez Trolley stops right out front. Restaurant, bar (with entertainment), room service, in-room data ports, cable TV, pool, wading pool, business services, airport shuttle, free parking, pets allowed. | 6201 Gateway W 79925 | 915/778–6611 | fax 915/779–2270 | www.qualityinn.com | 307 rooms | $48–$52 | AE, D, DC, MC, V.

Ramada Inn. All rooms have either a courtyard or mountain view at this two-story motel 1 mi from the University of Texas at El Paso. Restaurant, bar, complimentary Continental breakfast, room service, in-room data ports, some refrigerators, cable TV, pool, hot tub, laundry facilities, business services, free parking, pets allowed (fee). | 500 Executive Ctr. | 915/532–8981 | fax 915/577–9997 | www.ramada.com | 99 rooms | $69–124 | AE, D, MC, V.

FORT STOCKTON

Atrium Inn. Just ½ mi from town, this hotel has the only heated pool in the area. Tropical plants and a rock fountain in the lobby give the inn its name. Bar, complimentary Continental breakfast, some microwaves, some refrigerators, cable TV, indoor pool, exercise equipment, business services, pets allowed. | 1305 N. Hwy. 285 | 915/336–6666 | fax 915/336–5777 | 85 rooms | $69–$119 | AE, D, DC, MC, V.

Best Western Swiss Clock Inn. This motel is within walking distance of shopping and restaurants. Lounge in the garden under the shade of mulberry trees. Restaurant, room service, cable TV, pool, business services, pets allowed. | 3201 W. Dickinson St. | 915/336–8521 | fax 915/336–6513 | 112 rooms | $45–$60 | AE, D, DC, MC, V.

La Quinta. This motel is right on the highway and has truck parking available. Complimentary Continental breakfast, cable TV, pool, business services, some pets allowed. | 2601 I–10W | 915/336–9781 | fax 915/336–3634 | 97 rooms | www.laquinta.com | $52–$69 | AE, D, DC, MC, V.

FORT WORTH

American Inn. Just an exit away from the mall and restaurants. Complimentary Continental breakfast, in-room data ports, some microwaves, cable TV, pool, laundry facilities, business services, some pets allowed. | 7301 W. Fwy. 76116 | 817/244–7444 | fax 817/244–7902 | 118 rooms | $59–$99 | AE, D, DC, MC, V.

Green Oaks Park Hotel. This two-story hotel is next to the Naval Air Station, Carswell Joint Reserve Base, and several restaurants. Restaurant, bar (with entertainment), room service, in-room data ports, cable TV, 2 pools, 18-hole golf course, exercise equipment, business services, pets allowed (fee). | 6901 W. Fwy. 76116 | 817/738–7311 or 800/433–2174 (outside TX) or 800/772–2341 (TX) | fax 817/377–1308 | greenoak@onramp.net | 284 rooms in 5 buildings | $79–$150 | AE, D, DC, MC, V.

La Quinta–West. This motel is 10 mi west of downtown Fort Worth. Complimentary Continental breakfast, in-room data ports, cable TV, pool, some pets allowed. | 7888 I–30W 76108 | 817/246–5511 | fax 817/246–8870 | www.laquinta.com | 106 rooms | $49–$60 | AE, D, DC, MC, V.

Motel 6–Forth Worth East. Shops and fast-food restaurants are within walking distance of this motel. Cable TV, pool, some pets allowed. | 1236 Oakland Blvd. 76103 | 817/834–7361 | fax 817/834–1573 | 244 rooms | $36–$48 | AE, D, DC, MC, V.

Motel 6–Fort Worth South. This motel is 3 mi from a shopping mall and restaurants. Cable TV, pool, some pets allowed. | 6600 S. Fwy. 76134 | 817/293–8595 | fax 817/293–8577 | 279 rooms | $46 | AE, D, DC, MC, V.

Residence Inn by Marriott. This hotel is 1 mi south of I–30, and just 3 mi from downtown Fort Worth. Picnic area, complimentary breakfast, in-room data ports, kitchenettes, microwaves, refrigerators, cable TV, pool, hot tub, laundry facilities, business services, free parking, pets allowed (fee). | 1701 S. University Dr. 76107 | 817/870–1011 | fax 817/877–5500 | www.marriotthotels.com | 120 suites | $105–$175 suites | AE, D, DC, MC, V.

FREDERICKSBURG

Best Western Sunday House. Farmers coming into town during the last century used to spend the night in their "Sunday house" before returning to the outlying communities. Today, this Best Western has its own log cabin Sunday house on the premises—it's now used as the lobby and fireplace area. Restaurant, in-room data ports, cable TV, pool, business services, some pets allowed. | 501 E. Main St. 78624 | 830/997–4484 | fax 830/997–5607 | 124 rooms | $65–$130 | AE, D, DC, MC, V.

Comfort Inn. This standard motel is 9 blocks from downtown, within walking distance of shopping and restaurants. Picnic area, complimentary Continental breakfast, cable TV, pool, tennis, some pets allowed. | 908 S. Adams 78624 | 830/997–9811 | fax 830/997–2068 | 46 rooms | $64–$69 | AE, D, DC, MC, V.

Dietzel Motel. Only 1 mi from downtown and next to Friedrich's Bavarian Restaurant, weary truckers and business travelers tend to put up at this privately owned motel. Picnic area, cable TV, pool, some pets allowed ($5 fee). | 1141 West U.S. Hwy. 290 78624 | 830/997–3330 | fax 830/997–3330 | 20 rooms | $42–$62 | AE, D, MC, V.

Frontier Inn Motel. This independent motel has friendly service, and it's only ¼ mi from Main St. It also has an RV park. Cable TV, some kitchenettes, some microwaves, some refrigerators, laundry facilities, pets allowed ($5 fee). | 1704 U.S. 290 W | 830/997–4389 | fax 830/997–1500 | 13 rooms | $36–$58 | AE, D, DC, MC, V.

Peach Tree Inn. This motel is prettily situated around a grassy courtyard with a waterfall fountain and large pecan trees and is within walking distance of the Nimitz museum, restaurants, and shopping. Picnic area, complimentary Continental breakfast, some microwaves, refrigerators, cable TV, pool, business services, playground, some pets allowed. | 401 S. Washington (U.S. 87S) 78624 | 830/997–2117 or 800/843–4666 | fax 830/997–0827 | www.thepeachtreeinn.com | 34 rooms, 10 suites | $30–$98 | AE, D, MC, V.

FRITCH
Lake Town Inn. This motel is within walking distance of a grocery, 1 mi from the Lake Meredith Center, and 15 mi from the Huchinson County Historical Museum and Alibates Flint Quarries. Truck parking available. Cash only. Cable TV, pets allowed. | 205 East Broadway | 806/857–3191 | 20 rooms | $40 | No credit cards.

GAINESVILLE
Gainesville Bed & Bath. The cheapest overnight stay in Gainesville, the small, affordable rooms available in this motel are only 2 mi from the town center, restaurants, and shopping. Cable TV, laundry facilities, pets allowed. | 2000 I–35N | 940/665–5555 | fax 940/612–3003 | 22 rooms | $37 | AE, D, MC, V.

GALVESTON
Hotel Galvez. With a view of the Gulf, this turn-of-the-20th-century Spanish-style villa is decorated with 1930s furnishings. Once called the "Queen of the Gulf," the Hotel Galvez has a rich history of hosting families, celebrities, and Galvestonians for vacations and special celebrations. Restaurant, bar (with entertainment), in-room data ports, refrigerators (in suites), cable TV, pool, wading pool, hot tubs, business services, pets allowed. | 2024 Seawall Blvd. 77550 | 409/765–7721 or 800/392–4285 | fax 409/765–5780 | www.wyndham.com | 228 rooms | $139–$239 | AE, DC, MC, V.

La Quinta. This La Quinta is just five blocks away from Stewart Beach, 7 mi from the State Park, and 4 mi from Moody Gardens. Complimentary Continental breakfast, in-room data ports, cable TV, pool, business services, some pets allowed. | 1402 Seawall Blvd. 77550 | 409/763–1224 | fax 409/763–1224 | www.laquinta.com | 117 rooms | $62–$139 | AE, D, DC, MC, V.

GEORGETOWN
Comfort Inn. Decorated in a Southwestern style, this Comfort Inn is on the south end of town, 2 mi from historic Georgetown and 6 mi from Lake Georgetown. Complimentary Continental breakfast, cable TV, pool, some pets allowed. | 1005 Leander Rd. 78628 | 512/863–7504 | fax 512/819–9016 | www.comfortinn.com | 55 rooms | $54–$80 | AE, D, DC, MC, V.

Days Inn. Standard chain accommodations close to shopping area and restaurants. Cable TV, pool, some pets allowed. | 209 I–35N, exit 262 78628 | 512/863–5572 | fax 512/869–5301 | www.daysinn.com | 55 rooms | $44–$75 | AE, D, DC, MC, V.

GOLIAD
Budget Inn. This motel has reasonable prices and is easy to find, at the intersection of U.S. 77A and U.S. 59. Microwaves, refrigerators, cable TV, pets allowed (fee). | 124 S. Jefferson St. 77963 | 361/645–3251 | fax 361/645–2714 | www.budgetinns.com | 17 rooms | $35–$38 | AE, D, DC, MC, V.

GONZALES
Texas Lexington. This three-story motel is on U.S. 90, and has very affordable rates. Cable TV, some pets. | U.S. 90A E 78629 | 830/672–2807 | fax 830/672–7941 | 30 rooms | $45 | AE, MC, V.

GRAHAM

Gateway Inn. This well-kept motel, located southeast of downtown, was remodeled in 2000 with a southwestern decor. Restaurant, cable TV, pool, laundry facilities, airport shuttle, some pets allowed (fee). | 1401 Rte. 16S 76450 | 940/549–0222 | fax 940/549–4301 | 77 rooms | $48–$60 | AE, D, DC, MC, V.

GRANBURY

Classic Inn. This is a no-frills one-story motel. Complimentary Continental breakfast, microwaves, refrigerators, cable TV, pool, some pets allowed. | 1209 N. Plaza Dr. | 817/573–8874 | fax 817/573–8874 | 42 rooms | $45–$54 | AE, D, DC, MC, V.

Days Inn. Standard chain accommodations last renovated in 1996. Restaurant, cable TV, pool, laundry facilities, business services, pets allowed. | 1339 N. Plaza Dr. 76048 | 800/858–8607 | fax 817/573–7662 | 67 rooms | $49–$79 | AE, D, DC, MC, V.

Lodge of Granbury. Set on a lake providing great views, the Lodge's condominium suites feature one or two bedrooms with living areas, complete kitchens, woodburning fireplaces, and private balconies. Picnic area, microwaves, refrigerators, cable TV, pool, hot tub, business services, pets allowed. | 401 E. Pearl St. 76048 | 817/573–2606 | fax 817/573–2077 | 48 suites | $89–$109 suites | AE, D, DC, MC, V.

Plantation Inn. Overlooking Lake Granbury, this motel is 1 mi from the center of town. Complimentary Continental breakfast, in-room data ports, microwaves, cable TV, pool, wading pool, some pets allowed. | 1451 E. Pearl St. 76048 | 817/573–8846 or 800/422–2402 | fax 817/579–0917 | planinn@hcnews.com | www.plantationinngranbury.com | 53 rooms | $60–$90 | AE, D, DC, MC, V.

GRAPEVINE

Embassy Suites Outdoor World. This full-service, 12-story, all-suites hotel was built in 1999. Suites have separate living and sleeping areas, a dining table/work desk, and pullout sofa. The corner suites on the 12th floor are pricier, but have cathedral ceilings and private, covered balconies. It's across the street from the Grapevine Mills mall. Restaurant, bar, complimentary breakfast, room service, in-room data ports, minibars, microwaves, refrigerators, some in-room data ports, cable TV, pool, sauna, exercise equipment, video games, laundry facilities, laundry service, business services, airport shuttle, free parking, pets allowed. | 2401 Bass Pro Dr. 76051 | 972/724–2600 or 800/362–2779 | fax 972/724–2670 | www.embassyoutdoorworld.com | 329 suites | $109–$350 | AE, D, DC, MC, V.

GREENVILLE

Best Western Inn. This Best Western has easy access to Lake Tawakoni. Bar, complimentary Continental breakfast, cable TV, pool, laundry facilities, business services, free parking, pets allowed. | 1216 I–30 W 75401 | 903/454–1792 | fax 903/454–1792 | www.bestwestern.com | 99 rooms | $54–$70 | AE, D, DC, MC, V.

Motel 6. This two-story motel is 16 mi from the Texas International Speedway. Cable TV, pool, laundry facilities, some pets. | 5109 I–30 75401 | 903/455–0515 | fax 903/455–8314 | www.motel6.com | 94 rooms | $41 | AE, D, DC, MC, V.

Ramada Inn. Standard chain accommodations. Cable TV, pool, hot tub, laundry facilities, business services, free parking, some pets allowed. | 1215 I–30 75402 | 903/454–7000 | www.ramada.com | 138 rooms | $49–$69 | AE, D, DC, MC, V.

GROESBECK

Limestone Inn. You'll be sure to get a good night's sleep at this inn—the Limestone is located in a rural, quiet neighborhood. However, you'll still find a restaurant within walking distance. Cable TV, pets allowed. | 300 S. Ellis St. 76642 | 254/729–3017 | 75 rooms | $40 | AE, D, DC, MC, V.

GUADALUPE MOUNTAINS NATIONAL PARK

Best Western Cavern Inn. Thirty-five miles northeast of Guadalupe National Park, this is the closest lodging facility to the park. All rooms at this single-story motel are quite spacious. 2 restaurants, cable TV, 2 pools, 2 spas, video games, pets allowed. | 17 Carlsbad Caverns Hwy., White's City, NM 88268 | 505/785–2291 | fax 505/785–2283 | www.bestwestern. com | 63 rooms | $84 | AE, D, DC, MC, V.

HARLINGEN

Harlingen Super 8 Motel. This three-story motel was built in 1995. Both South Padre Island and Gladys Porter Zoo are 35 mi away. Complimentary Continental breakfast, refrigerators, microwaves, cable TV, pool, laundry services, pets allowed (fee). | 1115 S. U.S. 83 78550 | 956/412–8873 | fax 956/412–8873 | www.super8.com | 55 rooms | $55–$60 | AE, D, DC, MC, V.

La Quinta. This La Quinta is 7 mi from the Iwo Jima Memorial and Museum. Complimentary breakfast, in-room data ports, cable TV, pool, laundry facilities, business services, airport shuttle, free parking, pets allowed. | 1002 U.S. 83S 78552 | 956/428–6888 | fax 956/425–5840 | www.laquinta.com | 130 rooms | $59–$79 | AE, D, DC, MC, V.

HENDERSON

Best Western of Henderson. This two-story motel is 3 mi from the Depot Museum and Children's Discovery Center, and 19 mi from Gregg County Airport. Cable TV, pool, laundry facilities, pets allowed. | 1500 Rte. 259S 75654 | 903/657–9561 | fax 903/657–9183 | 130 rooms | $50–$60 | AE, D, DC, MC, V.

HILLSBORO

Ramada Inn. Standard chain accommodations. Cable TV, pool, business services, some pets allowed. | 254/582–3493 | fax 254/582–2755 | www.ramada.com | 94 rooms | $45–$50 | AE, D, DC, MC, V.

HOUSTON

Days Inn West. This two-story motel is near Bush Intercontinental Airport and Hobby Airport. Many restaurants and shops are within 1 mi. There is a tennis facility and fitness center less that 5 mi away. Restaurant, complimentary Continental breakfast, in-room data ports, some refrigerators, some microwaves, some in-room hot tubs, cable TV, pool, business services, pets allowed (fee). | 9535 Katy Fwy. 77024 | 713/467–4411 | fax 713/467–3647 | www.daysinn.com | 160 rooms, 4 suites | $39–$54, $99 suites | AE, D, DC, MC, V.

Doubletree at Allen Center. This hotel is right in the middle of downtown and is within walking distance of the Theater District, Bayou Place, Enron Field, and the George R. Brown Convention Center. Guest rooms offer views of Sam Houston Park and the Memorial Park greenbelt, the downtown skyline, or the Allen Center Courtyard. Restaurants, bar (with entertainment), in-room data ports, cable TV, exercise equipment, business services, some pets allowed. | 400 Dallas St. 77002 | 713/759–0202 | fax 713/752–2734 | www. doubletree.com | 341 rooms | $89–$215 | AE, D, DC, MC, V.

Doubletree Guest Suites. This luxury, all-suites hotel is one block west of the Galleria and within 10 minutes of downtown. Restaurant, bar, in-room data ports, kitchenettes, refrigerators, room service, cable TV, pool, hot tub, exercise equipment, business services, laundry facilities, some pets allowed. | 5353 Westheimer Rd. 77056 | 713/961–9000 | fax 713/877–8835 | www.doubletree.com | 335 suites | $155–$165 suites | AE, D, DC, MC, V.

Drury Inn and Suites–Houston West. Located throughout mid-America, this motel chain is into free stuff. Look for free breakfast, free evening beverages and snacks, free HBO, and free local calls. This motel is far from downtown (12 mi) but convenient to the Energy Corridor. Complimentary Continental breakfast, in-room data ports, some microwaves, cable TV, indoor pool, hot tub, pets allowed, free parking. | 1000 Rte. 6N 77079 | 281/558–7007 | fax 281/558–7007 | www.drury-inn.com | 120 rooms | $59–$89 | AE, D, DC, MC, V.

Drury Inn and Suites–Near the Galleria. Adjacent to the Galleria, this Drury is 6 mi from downtown and 8 mi from the Medical Center. Complimentary Continental breakfast, in-room data ports, some microwaves, cable TV, pool, hot tub, business services, pets allowed, free parking. | 1615 W. Loop 610S 77027 | 713/963–0700 | fax 713/963–0700 | www.drury-inn.com | 134 rooms | $87–$107 | AE, D, DC, MC, V.

Fairfield Inn by Marriott at the Galleria. Mere feet from the Galleria, this Fairfield Inn is 6 mi from the Medical Center and 6 mi from downtown. Bar; complimentary Continental breakfast, in-room data ports, room service, cable TV, pool, wading pool, hot tub, exercise equipment, laundry facilities, business services, pets allowed. | 3131 West Loop S 77027 | 713/961–1690 | fax 713/627–8434 | 107 rooms | $59–$84 | AE, D, DC, MC, V.

Four Seasons Hotel–Houston Center. With its skyline view, impressive lobby, and huge rooms, business travelers are made very comfortable in this luxury hotel situated in the middle of downtown. You can get a gourmet meal at the Deville restaurant located on the premises and can do a little window shopping (or more) across the street at The Park Shops Downtown mall. Restaurant, bar (with entertainment), in-room data ports, minibars, some microwaves, room service, cable TV, pool, beauty salon, hot tub, massage, gym, business services, valet parking, parking (fee), pets allowed. | 1300 Lamar St. 77010 | 713/650–1300 or 800/332–3442 | fax 713/276–3393 | www.fshr.com | 426 rooms | $155–$175, $195–$215 suites | AE, DC, MC, V.

Hampton Inn–I–10 East. On the east side of the loop, this Hampton Inn is convenient to Jacinto City, Channelview, and the Port of Houston and is 8 mi from downtown. Complimentary Continental breakfast, in-room data ports, some refrigerators, cable TV, pool, laundry facilities, business services, valet parking, free parking, pets allowed. | 828 Mercury Dr. 77013 | 713/673–4200 | fax 713/674–6913 | www.hamptoninn.com | 90 rooms | $69–$77 | AE, D, DC, MC, V.

Holiday Inn–International Airport. This Holiday Inn is 1 mi south of Bush Intercontinental Airport and 18 mi from downtown. Restaurant, bar, in-room data ports, some microwaves, room service, cable TV, pool, wading pool, tennis, exercise equipment, laundry facilities, business services, airport shuttle, valet parking, free parking, pets allowed (fee). | 15222 J.F.K. Blvd. 77032 | 281/449–2311 | fax 281/449–6726 | www.holiday-inn.com | 402 rooms | $79–$149 | AE, D, DC, MC, V.

Hyatt Regency–Houston Airport. Set in a wooded complex known as the World Houston Business Development, this hotel is 1 mi from Houston's Bush Intercontinental Airport. Restaurant, bar, in-room data ports, cable TV, pool, hot tub, exercise equipment, business services, airport shuttle, pets allowed (fee). | 15747 J.F.K. Blvd. 77032 | 281/987–1234 | fax 281/590–8461 | www.hyatt.com | 314 rooms | $69–$195 | AE, D, DC, MC, V.

La Quinta–Greenway Plaza. Greenway Plaza's La Quinta is close to the Compaq Center and the Galleria. Complimentary Continental breakfast, cable TV, pool, laundry facilities, some pets allowed. | 4015 Southwest Fwy. 77027 | 713/623–4750 | fax 713/963–0599 | www.laquinta.com | 131 rooms | $75–$95 | AE, D, DC, MC, V.

La Quinta–Wilcrest. This La Quinta is in western Houston and is within 5 mi of the Energy Corridor and 17 mi from downtown. Complimentary Continental breakfast, in-room data ports, cable TV, pool, laundry facilities, pets allowed. | 11113 Katy Fwy. 77079 | 713/932–0808 | fax 713/973–2352 | www.laquinta.com | 176 rooms | $55–$65 | AE, D, DC, MC, V.

Lovett Inn. Once the home of Houston mayor and Federal Court Judge Joseph C. Hutcheson, this historic home is in the heart of the Montrose-Museum District. Each room has a distinct aesthetic quality: Room 5 is flowery and romantic, while Room 10 is Art Deco and modern. Most of the rooms overlook the inn's finely landscaped grounds and pool. Complimentary Continental breakfast, some refrigerators, some microwaves, some in-room hot tubs, cable TV, pool, spa, some pets, no smoking. | 501 Lovett Blvd. 77006 | 713/522–5224 or 800/779–5224 | fax 713/528–6708 | www.lovettinn.com | 4 rooms, 2 suites, 2 cottages | $75–$85, $115–$150 suites/cottages | AE, D, DC, MC, V.

Marriott–Westside. This property is convenient to the Energy Corridor and is within 3 mi of the Memorial City and Town & Country malls. Restaurant, bar (with entertainment), in-room data ports, cable TV, pool, hot tub, tennis, exercise equipment, business services, pets allowed (fee). | 13210 Katy Fwy. 77079 | 281/558–8338 | fax 281/558–4028 | www.marriott.com | 400 rooms | $75–$169 | AE, D, DC, MC, V.

Radisson Hotel and Conference Center. Only 1 mi from Hobby Airport, this 10-story atrium hotel has one of the largest conference facilities in South Houston. Complimentary transportation is available for the Almeda Mall and a golf course, both 3 mi away. Restaurant, bar (with entertainment), in-room data ports, cable TV, indoor pool, hot tub, exercise equipment, business services, airport shuttle, some pets allowed. | 9100 Gulf Fwy. 77017 | 713/943–7979 | fax 713/943–2160 | www.radisson.com | 288 rooms | $119–$129 | AE, D, DC, MC, V.

Red Lion. This outpost is adjacent to the Galleria and 8 mi from downtown. Restaurant, bar, in-room data ports, cable TV, pool, hot tub, exercise equipment, business services, pets allowed (fee), airport shuttle. | 2525 West Loop S 77027 | 713/961–3000 | fax 713/961–1490 | www.redlion.com | 319 rooms | $89–$140 | AE, D, DC, MC, V.

Red Roof Inn. In western Houston, this motel is 20 mi from downtown and 15 mi from the Galleria. In-room data ports, cable TV, business services, pets allowed. | 15701 Park Ten Pl. 77084 | 281/579–7200 | fax 281/579–0732 | 123 rooms | $32–$50 | AE, D, DC, MC, V.

RUNNING FOR FUN

One of the biggest pets-and-humans fun runs in the country takes place on a Sunday in late in March every year in Houston. Sponsored by the local Humane Society, this K-9 Fun Run has grown to around 8,000 people and more than 2,500 of their four-legged best friends since it was started in 1982. A competitive 1-mi run and two non-competitive events, a 1-mi jog and a 1-mi walk, the focal points of the day. These wind up with a party, and booths offer pet-related products, giveaways, and lots of food. There's a Doggy Costume Contest, divided into several categories (you can participate, too), and the Houston Humane Society's annual SpokesDog and SpokesCat are announced. (Judging and choice of the SpokesCat is done in advance to prevent any feline horror at the proximity of so many pooches.) All events take place downtown in Sam Houston Park. Register in advance—the charge is higher on the big day. Contact the Houston Humane Society, 14700 Almeda Rd., Houston TX 77053, 713/434–5535 or 713/434–5555, www.houstonhumane.org.

Renaissance. At first glance, this tower in an office complex may seem all business, but it's attached to Greenway Plaza shops, which include the Landmark Greenway Cinema. The rooms, all the way up to the top of the tower, are gracious and offer expansive views of the city. The Renaissance is close to the Compaq Center and the Galleria. Restaurant, bar, in-room data ports, some refrigerators, room service, cable TV, pool, exercise equipment, business services, valet parking, parking (fee), some pets allowed. | 6 Greenway Plaza E 77046 | 713/629–1200 | fax 713/629–4702 | www.renaissancehotels.com | 389 rooms | $144–$179 | AE, D, DC, MC, V.

Residence Inn by Marriott–Astrodome. Designed for people on longer stays, this motel is close to the Medical Center and 1.5 mi from the Astrodome. Bar, picnic area, complimentary Continental breakfast, in-room data ports, kitchenettes, cable TV, pool, hot tub, business services, valet parking, free parking, pets allowed (fee). | 7710 S. Main St. 77030 | 713/660–7993 | fax 713/660–8019 | 285 suites | $89–$199 suites | AE, D, DC, MC, V.

Residence Inn by Marriott–Clear Lake. With larger than average rooms, the Residence Inn chain is designed for longer-staying guests. This motel is located 2 mi from Clear Lake and 3 mi from the Space Center. Complimentary Continental breakfast, in-room data ports, kitchenettes, microwaves, cable TV, pool, exercise equipment, laundry facilities, business services, pets allowed (fee). | 525 Bay Area Blvd. 77058 | 281/486–2424 | fax 281/488–8179 | 110 rooms | $124–$145 | AE, D, DC, MC, V.

Robin's Nest Bed and Breakfast. This 1898 Victorian home is one-and-a-half miles south of downtown Houston. Most of the artwork and the furnishings in the house come from the various foreign countries that owner Robin Smith visited during her work with the U.S. Foreign Service. Antiques and hardwood floors decorate the rooms. Complimentary breakfast, cable TV, library, some pets, no smoking. | 4104 Greeley St. 77006 | 713/528–5821 | fax 713/521–2154 | www.therobin.com | 4 rooms | $110–$120 | AE, D, MC, V.

Sheraton Houston Brookhollow. In northwest Houston, this Sheraton is within 25 mi of both Bush Intercontinental and Hobby Airports. Restaurant, bar, in-room data ports, room service, cable TV, pool, hot tub, exercise equipment, some pets allowed. | 3000 N. Loop W 77092 | 713/688–0100 or 800/688–3000 | fax 713/688–9224 | www.sheraton.com | 382 rooms | $119–$139 | AE, D, DC, MC, V.

Westin Oaks. Rooms and suites at this 18-story hotel are oversized and elegantly decorated in cream and white. The hotel is within the Galleria in uptown Houston, near to many museums, shops, and the theater district. There is also an outdoor jogging track. 2 restaurants, bar, in-room data ports, cable TV, pool, exercise facility, laundry services, business services, pets allowed. | 5011 Westheimer 77056 | 713/960–8100 | fax 713/960–6554 | www.westin.com | 395 rooms, 11 suites | $99–$109, $205–$750 suites | AE, D, DC, MC, V.

HUNTSVILLE

Best Western Sam Houston Inn. This quaint, two-story inn prides itself on providing a warm, small-town feel and attentive service. Most rooms have king-size beds. There are many shops and restaurants in the vicinity, as well as a cocktail lounge on the premises. Visit the Huntsville State Amusement Park or Sam Houston State University, both 2 mi away. Complimentary Continental breakfast, cable TV, pool, business services, pets allowed. | 613 I–45 77340 | 936/295–9151 | fax 936/295–9151 | www.bestwestern.com | 72 rooms | $55 | AE, D, DC, MC, V.

La Quinta. This La Quinta is near the Westhills Mall, a movie theater, and plenty of restaurants. Complimentary Continental breakfast, some refrigerators, cable TV, pool, wading pool, pets allowed. | 124 I–45N | 409/295–6454 | fax 409/295–9245 | 120 rooms | $65–$75 | AE, D, DC, MC, V.

Motel 6. This budget motel is at the intersection of I–45 and U.S. 90, off Exit 116. Both the Sam Houston Memorial Park and the State University are 3 mi away; Huntsville State

Park is 6 mi away. Cable TV, pool, laundry facilities, some pets allowed. | 1607 I–45 77340 | 936/291–6927 | fax 936/291–8963 | www.motel6.com | 122 rooms | $39 | AE, D, DC, MC, V.

University Hotel. This hotel is situated on the Sam Houston State University campus and is close to movies, shopping, and restaurants. Microwaves, no smoking, cable TV, some pets allowed. | 1610 Ave. H 77341 | 409/291–2151 | fax 409/294–1683 | 95 rooms | $37–$42 | AE, DC, MC, V.

IRVING

Courtyard Las Colinas. This four-story hotel is off of U.S. 114, about 4 mi from Hyatt Bear Creek Golf Course and 3 mi from Texas Stadium. A variety of restaurants and shops are within walking distance. Restaurant, bar, in-room data ports, cable TV, pool, exercise equipment, laundry services, laundry facilities, business services, some pets. | 1151 West Walnut Hill 75038 | 972/550–8100 | fax 972/550–0764 | www.courtyard.com | 147 rooms, 13 suites | $122, $155 suites | AE, D, DC, MC, V.

Drury Inn. This chain motel is 1 mi from the Dallas/Ft. Worth International Airport, 6 mi from Texas Stadium, and 6 mi from University of Dallas at Irving. Complimentary Continental breakfast, in-room data ports, cable TV, pool, business services, airport shuttle, some pets allowed. | 4210 W. Airport Fwy. 75062 | 972/986–1200 | fax 972/986–1200 | www.druryinn.com | 129 rooms | $75–$87 | AE, D, DC, MC, V.

★ **Four Seasons Resort and Club (Dallas at Las Colinas).** This luxury resort is set on 400 rolling acres. Rooms have balconies that overlook the Tournament Players Course golf course, where the Professional Golfers' Association's GTE Byron Nelson Classic is held. 3 restaurants, room service, in-room data ports, minibars, cable TV, 4 pools, barbershop, beauty salon, hot tub, massage, driving range, 18-hole golf course, 2 putting greens, 12 tennis courts, gym, baby-sitting, children's programs (6 months–8), business services, some pets allowed. | 4150 N. MacArthur Blvd. 75038 | 972/717–0700 | fax 972/717–2550 | www.fourseasons.com | 345 rooms, 12 suites | $305–$510, $650–$1200 suites | AE, DC, MC, V.

La Quinta–Dallas/Fort Worth. This two-story motel is in a commercial area. There is a 24-hour restaurant right next door and there are many others within a two-block radius. Complimentary Continental breakfast, in-room data ports, cable TV, pool, business services, airport shuttle, pets allowed. | 4105 W. Airport Fwy. 75062 | 972/252–6546 | fax 972/570–4225 | www.laquinta.com | 169 rooms | $59–$80 | AE, D, DC, MC, V.

Marriott–DFW Airport. This 20-story hotel is 1 mi from the Dallas/Ft. Worth International Airport and 3 mi from the Grapevine Mills mall. Restaurants, bar, in-room data ports, some refrigerators, cable TV, pool, hot tub, exercise equipment, laundry facilities, business services, airport shuttle, some pets allowed. | 8440 Freeport Pkwy. 75063 | 972/929–8800 | fax 972/929–6501 | www.marriott.com | 491 rooms | $69–$179 | AE, D, DC, MC, V.

Sheraton Grand Hotel DFW Airport. You'll find this 10-story hotel off of U.S. 114 (the Esters Blvd. exit), just 1½ mi from the Dallas airport and 15 mi from downtown Dallas. The hotel accommodates several conventions per year, and plenty of business travelers, with 23 meeting rooms, a huge conference center, and exhibit facilities; service here is very professional. Restaurant, bar, in-room data ports, cable TV, pool, indoor hot tub, sauna, exercise equipment, business services, airport shuttle, pets allowed (fee). | 4440 W. John Carpenter Fwy. 75063 | 972/929–8400 | fax 972/929–4885 | www.sheraton.com | 297 rooms, 3 suites | $82–$140, $250 suites | AE, D, DC, MC, V.

Wilson World. This full-service hotel with gift shop is 1 mi south of Dallas/Ft. Worth International Airport. Restaurant, bar, in-room data ports, microwaves, cable TV, indoor pool, hot tub, exercise equipment, business services, airport shuttle, some pets allowed. | 4600 W. Airport Fwy. 75062 | 972/513–0800 | fax 972/513–0106 | 200 rooms, 96 suites | $89–$119, $99–$119 suites | AE, D, DC, MC, V.

JASPER

Best Western Inn of Jasper. This motel is on U.S. 190, three blocks west of the intersection of U.S. 190 and U.S. 96. There are shops and restaurants less than 1 mi from the motel, and the Martin Dies Park and lake is 12 mi away. Complimentary Continental breakfast, cable TV, outdoor pool, outdoor hot tub, pets allowed. | 205 W. Gibson St. 75951 | 409/384–7767 | fax 409/384–7665 | www.bestwestern.com | 59 rooms | $51–$63 | AE, D, DC, MC, V.

Jasper Days Inn. Constructed in the early 80s, this two-story inn is off U.S. 96 and just minutes from downtown. There are several restaurants within walking distance. Cable TV, pool, laundry services, some pets. | 1730 S. Wheeler St. 75951 | 409/334–6816 | fax 409/384–6085 | www.daysinn.com | 31 rooms | $38–$46 | AE, D, DC, MC, V.

Ramada Inn. There are plenty of restaurants and even a movie theater close by this standard Ramada facility near the airport. Restaurant, bar, in-room data ports, some refrigerators, cable TV, pool, laundry facilities, business services, pets allowed. | 239 E. Gibson St. 75951 | 409/384–9021 | fax 409/384–9021, ext. 309 | 100 rooms | $55–$58 | AE, D, DC, MC, V.

JOHNSON CITY

Save Inn Motel. There is a restaurant adjacent to this two-story motel. The Exotic Resort Zoo is just 4 mi away. Restaurant, complimentary Continental breakfast, cable TV, pool, pets allowed (fee). | 107 U.S. 281 78636 | 830/868–4044 | fax 830/868–7888 | 53 rooms | $36–$46 | AE, D, MC, V.

Zoo Exotic Resort B&B. Enjoy the company of friendly wild animals roaming around this B&B in the Zoo Exotic Resort. There is a fence around the area and even along a walkway to the fishpond, so you can fish without visits from some of the larger animals. You can cook what you catch in the barbecue pit. Rooms overlook the lake and have polished wooden walls, large plants, and basic, comfortable furniture. Complimentary Continental breakfast, some kitchenettes, no room phones, no TV, pool, outdoor hot tub, fishing, pets allowed, no smoking. | 235 Zoo Trail 78636 | 830/868–4357 | www.zooexotics.com | 3 cabins | $100–$120 | AE, D, MC, V.

KERRVILLE

Best Western Sunday House Inn. This chain hotel is near the River Hills mall, a movie theater, and lots of restaurants. Quiet and comfortable with friendly service and great accommodations. Restaurant, bar, cable TV, pool, pets allowed (fee). | 2124 Sidney Baker St. 78028 | 830/896–1313 | fax 830/896–1336 | www.bestwestern.com | 97 rooms | $64–$84 | AE, D, DC, MC, V.

Econolodge. This native limestone hotel, handsomely surrounded by native plants and shrubs, sits in the middle of town, near Shriner College and several restaurants. It's two blocks off I–10, exit 508. Restaurant, bar, complimentary Continental breakfast, cable TV, pool, wading pool, laundry facilities, pets allowed (fee), free parking. | 2145 Sidney Baker St. 78028 | 830/896–1711 | fax 830/257–4375 | www.hc.net/econo | 102 rooms | $59–79 | AE, DC, MC, V.

Holiday Inn–Y. O. Ranch Hotel and Conference Center. This hotel has Western accents and Mexican tile floors. Restaurant, bar, room service, in-room data ports, refrigerators, cable TV, pool, wading pool, hot tub, tennis, business services, airport shuttle, pets allowed. | 2033 Sidney Baker St. 78028 | 830/257–4440 | fax 830/896–8189 | www.holidayinn.com | 200 rooms | $79–$119 | AE, D, DC, MC, V.

Inn of the Hills. The balconies in many of the rooms here overlook the Guadalupe River. The inn has a convenient location at the west end of town near a shopping center and restaurants. Restaurant, bar (with entertainment), room service, in-room data ports, some kitchenettes. microwaves, cable TV, 5 pools (2 indoor), wading pool, barbershop, beauty salon, hot tub, playground, laundry facilities, free parking, pets allowed. | 1001 Junction

Hwy. 78028 | 830/895–5000 or 800/292–5690 | fax 830/895–6091 | www.innofthehills.com | 228 rooms | $70–$360 | AE, D, DC, MC, V.

Lamb Creek Inn Bed and Breakfast. This lovely inn is surrounded by over 100 acres of rolling hills. Lamb Creek runs through the property and goats, sheep, and other animals roam the fields. Rooms and cottages are all elegantly furnished with antiques and queen- or king-size beds. You'll find a library, a video and book store, and an antique shop on the grounds. Complimentary Continental breakfast, kitchenettes, microwaves, refrigerators, no room phones, no TV, some pets allowed, no smoking. | 6121 Medina Hwy. 78028 | 830/792–5262 | www.lambcreekinn.com | 5 rooms, 2 cottages | $159 | MC, V.

KILLEEN

Holiday Inn Express. This two-story motel is on U.S. 190, 3 mi from downtown Killeen, and 12 mi from Fort Hood. The Texas Roadhouse restaurant is nearby. Bar, complimentary Continental breakfast, in-room data ports, some refrigerators, some microwaves, cable TV, business services, pets allowed. | 1602 E. Central Texas Expressway (U.S. 190) 76541 | 254/554–2727 | fax 254/554–9980 | www.hiexpress.com | 68 rooms | $61–$65 | AE, D, DC, MC, V.

La Quinta. You can enjoy this hotel for its Mediterranean Spanish feel and beautifully landscaped grounds, all convenient to Fort Hood and the Killeen Mall. Rooms are modern and well equipped. Restaurant, complimentary Continental breakfast, in-room data ports, cable TV, pool, airport shuttle, free parking, pets allowed. | 1112 S. Hood St. 76541 | 254/526–8331 | fax 254/526–0394 | 105 rooms | $59–$72 | AE, D, DC, MC, V.

Ramada Inn Fort Hood/Killeen. You'll find this large, standard inn on manicured grounds near U.S. 190 and U.S. 195. The entrance to the east gate of Fort Hood is less than 1 mi away, and there are several restaurants within walking distance, as well as one on the premises. Restaurant, bar, room service, complimentary breakfast, in-room data ports, cable TV, pool, laundry services, business services, airport shuttle, some pets allowed. | 1100 S. Fort Hood Rd. 76541 | 254/634–3101 | fax 254/634–8844 | www.ramada.com | 164 rooms | $43–$77 | AE, D, DC, MC, V.

KINGSVILLE

B-Bar-B Ranch. Originally part of the historic King Ranch, this ranch-house-turned-lodge has kept its rustic feel, down to the Old West-style rooms. You can arrange to go hunting for quail, turkey, or nilgai, or go bird watching. Complimentary breakfast, some in-room hot tubs, pool, outdoor hot tub, fishing, some pets allowed, no kids, no smoking. | 325 E. CR 2215 78363 | 361/296–3331 | fax 361/296–3337 | bbarb@rivnet.com | www.b-bar-b.com | 15 rooms, 1 suite | $85, $125 suite | D, MC, V.

Best Western Kingsville Inn. For large rooms at a reasonable rate, this Best Western is the perfect choice. The King Ranch Museum and Texas A&M University are both 1 mi away. Complimentary Continental breakfast, some microwaves, some refrigerators, in-room data ports, cable TV, pool, outdoor hot tub, laundry services, business services, some pets allowed. | 2402 East King Ave. 78363 | 361/595–5656 | fax 361/595–5000 | www.bestwestern.com | 50 rooms | $53–$59 | AE, D, DC, MC, V.

Quality Inn. This chain motel is close to the Southgate Mall, movie theaters, a restaurant, and local museums. Standard but comfortable chain accommodations. Complimentary Continental breakfast, refrigerators, cable TV, pool, wading pool, exercise equipment, business services, pets allowed. | 221 S. Hwy. 77 Bypass 78363 | 361/592–5251 | fax 361/592–6197 | 117 rooms | $50–$55 | AE, D, DC, MC, V.

LA GRANGE

Oak Motel. This small motel is within walking distance of downtown shops and restaurants. Cable TV, some pets allowed. | 227 S. Jefferson St. 78945 | 979/968–3133 | www.oakmotel.8m.com | 18 rooms | $39–$45 | AE, D, DC, MC, V.

LAREDO

Best Western Fiesta Inn. This motel is 3 mi from Texas A&M University. | 150 rooms. Complimentary Continental breakfast, some refrigerators, cable TV, pool, laundry facilities, business services, airport shuttle, some pets allowed. | 5240 San Bernardo 78041 | 956/723–3603 | fax 956/724–7697 | $69–$73 | AE, D, DC, MC, V.

Family Gardens Inn. This lovely complex has a number of facilities and special services to keep you and your family entertained, and its pricing encourages extended visits. There are grills available in the picnic area for outdoor cooking, and there's evening entertainment accessible both at the inn and in nearby Laredo. Picnic area, complimentary Continental breakfast, in-room data ports, some microwaves, refrigerators, cable TV, pool, spa, exercise equipment, video games, playground, laundry facilities, airport shuttle, pets allowed (fee). | 5830 San Bernardo Ave. 78041 | 956/723–5300 | www.familygardens.com | 192 rooms | $54–$61 | MAP | AE, D, DC, MC, V.

Holiday Inn Civic Center. This stunning 14-story hotel is only 2 mi from the Mexican border. There is live entertainment in the lounge Thurs., Fri., and Sat. nights. Restaurant, bar (with entertainment), in-room data ports, cable TV, pool, outdoor hot tub, sauna, exercise equipment, laundry services, business services, airport shuttle, pets allowed. | 800 Garden St. 78040 | 956/727–5800 | fax 956–727–0278 | www.holiday-inn.com | 200 rooms, 3 suites | $98, $170 suites | AE, D, DC, MC, V.

Motel 6–Laredo South. A mall is across the highway from this two–story motel, and the Mexican border is 3 mi away. Cable TV, pool, pets allowed. | 5310 San Bernardo Ave. 78041 | 956/725–8187 | fax 956/725–0424 | 94 rooms. | $40–$45 | AE, D, DC, MC, V.

Motel 6–North. Rooms have either indoor or outdoor access. Restaurants are within walking distance. Cable TV, pool, laundry facilities, pets allowed. | 5920 San Bernardo Ave. 78041 | 956/722–8133 | fax 956/725–8212 | 109 rooms | $39–$45 | AE, D, DC, MC, V.

Red Roof Inn. Rooms have interior entrances at this four-story motel close to Laredo Community College, Seven Flags over Texas, and shopping. Cable TV, pool, laundry facilities, pets allowed. | I–35 at Calton Rd. 78041 | 800/843–7663 | fax 956/712–4337 | 150 rooms | $40–$68 | AE, D, DC, MC, V.

Rio Grande Plaza. Overlooking the Rio Grande River, this 15-story hotel has unique round architecture. All rooms have floor-to-ceiling, wall-to-wall views of the city or of the Rio Grande and Old Mexico. Close to shopping, museums, and restaurants. Restaurant, bar, in-room data ports, cable TV, gym, laundry facilities, business services, airport shuttle, pets allowed. | 1 S. Main Ave. 78040 | 956/722–2411 | fax 956/722–4578 | 207 rooms | $110–$125 | AE, D, DC, MC, V.

LONGVIEW

La Quinta Inn. This hotel is near the convention center, mall, and LeTourneau University. Complimentary Continental breakfast, in-room data ports, cable TV, pool, business services, free parking, some pets allowed. | 502 S. Access Rd. 75602 | 903/757–3663 | fax 903/753–3780 | 105 rooms | $55–$80 | AE, D, DC, MC, V.

Motel 6. This motel is off of I–20 and about 1 mi from LeTourneau University. Cable TV, pool, laundry facilities, pets allowed. | 110 S. Access Rd. 75603 | 903/758–5256 | fax 903/758–0711 | 86 rooms | $33–$49 | AE, D, DC, MC, V.

Travelodge. Restaurant, in-room data ports, cable TV, pool, laundry facilities, airport shuttle, pets allowed. | 3304 S. Eastman Rd. 75602 | 903/758–0711 | fax 903/758–0711 | 86 rooms | $33–$49 | AE, D, DC, MC, V.

LUBBOCK

Holiday Inn–Civic Center. This Holiday Inn stands beside the Lubbock Civic Center and is close to Texas Tech University and the Lubbock International Airport. It is one of the largest hotels in Lubbock, and is within walking distance of restaurants. Restaurant, bar, some kitchenettes, cable TV, indoor pool, hot tub, exercise equipment, laundry facilities, business services, airport shuttle, pets allowed. | 801 Avenue Q 79401 | 806/763–1200 | fax 806/763–2656 | www.holidayinn.com | 295 rooms | $76–$90 | AE, D, DC, MC, V.

Holiday Inn–Park Plaza. This full-service hotel in southwest Lubbuck boasts a popular restaurant, a lounge in its tropical atrium, and more than 25,000 square ft of meeting space. Restaurant, bar, room service, in-room data ports, cable TV, pool, wading pool, laundry facilities, business services, airport shuttle, some pets allowed. | 3201 South Loop 289S 79423 | 806/797–3241 | fax 806/793–1203 | www.holiday-inn.com | 202 rooms | $69–$108 | AE, D, DC, MC, V.

La Quinta Inn. This motel is down the street from the Civic Center. Complimentary Continental breakfast, in-room data ports, cable TV, pool, business services, pets allowed. | 601 Ave. Q 79401 | 806/763–9441 | fax 806/747–9325 | 137 rooms | $62–$69 | AE, D, DC, MC, V.

Residence Inn by Marriott. This hotel is 10 minutes from Lubbock International Airport, 6 mi from downtown, 8 mi from the Buddy Holly Center, and 4 mi from Texas Tech University. Picnic area, complimentary Continental breakfast, in-room data ports, kitchenettes, refrigerators, cable TV, pool, hot tub, tennis, laundry facilities, business services, airport shuttle, free parking, pets allowed. | 2551 S. Loop 289 79423 | 806/745–1963 | fax 806/748–1183 | www.residenceinn.com | 80 suites | $97–$135 suites | AE, D, DC, MC, V.

LUFKIN

Best Western Expo Inn. This hotel is on Loop 287 and U.S. 59N, and it's only 15 minutes from any part of town. You'll find Dude's Lounge, with live entertainment, on the premises and a 24-hour restaurant next door. Fishing, golfing and a zoo are all within 10 mi. Complimentary Continental breakfast, room service, in-room data ports, cable TV, pool, laundry facilities, business services, pets allowed (fee). | 4200 N. Medford Dr. 75901 | 409/632–7300 | fax 409/632–8094 | www.bestwestern.com | 83 rooms | $67 | AE, D, DC, MC, V.

Days Inn. This Days Inn is near Angelina Junior College, Angelina County Airport, Lufkin Mall, and some restaurants. Restaurant, bar, complimentary Continental breakfast, room service, some refrigerators, some in-room hot tubs, cable TV, pool, wading pool, laundry facilities, business services, some pets allowed. | 2130 S. 1st St. | 409/639–3301 | fax 409/634–4266 | 126 rooms | $38–$80 | AE, D, DC, MC, V.

Holiday Inn. This is a two-story hotel located near the Lufkin mall, Angelina Junior College, United Pentecostal Campgrounds, and Crown Colony Country Club. Restaurant, bar, room service, in-room data ports, some minibars, some refrigerators, cable TV, pool, laundry facilities, business services, airport shuttle, free parking, pets allowed (fee). | 4306 S. 1st St. | 409/639–3333 | fax 409/639–3382 | www.holidayinn.com | 102 rooms | $66–$73 | AE, D, DC, MC, V.

La Quinta Inn. This motel is 6 mi from the Angelina County airport. Complimentary Continental breakfast, in-room data ports, cable TV, pool, business services, free parking, some pets allowed. | 2119 S. 1st St. 75901 | 409/634–3351 | fax 409/634–9475 | 106 rooms | $49–$89 | AE, D, DC, MC, V.

MARBLE FALLS

Best Western Marble Falls Inn. A good base for exploring, this two-story hotel resides on the Texas Wildflower/Bluebonnet Trail. Before you head out, enjoy breakfast before a stone fireplace in the lobby. Complimentary Continental breakfast, some microwaves, some refrigerators, in-room data ports, cable TV, pool, outdoor hot tub, exercise equipment, laundry facilities, business services, some pets. | 1403 Rte. 281N 78654 | 830/693–5122 | fax 830/693–3108 | www.bestwestern.com | 61 rooms | $65–$99 | AE, D, DC, MC, V.

MARFA

Arcon Inn Bed and Breakfast. This two-story, yellow Victorian adobe home is located in the historic district. Guests can relax on the patio or on the front porch swing. Rooms are decorated with European and Latin American antiques. Complimentary breakfast, no room phones, TV in common area, some pets allowed, no smoking. | 215 N. Austin, 79843 | 915/729–4826 | fax 915/729–3391 | 3 rooms, 1 cottage | $75–$95 | AE, D, DC, MC, V.

MARSHALL

Guest Inn. This motel is near a mall and plenty of restaurants are less than a mile away. Complimentary Continental breakfast, some refrigerators, cable TV, pool, free parking, pets allowed. | 4911 E. End Blvd. 75672 | 903/927–1718 | fax 903/927–1747 | 46 rooms | $51–$95 | AE, D, DC, MC, V.

Motel 6. This motel is 16 mi from Caddo State Park and 20 mi from Lake O' the Pines. Cable TV, pool, laundry facilities, pets allowed. | 300 I–20E 75670 | 903/935–4393 | fax 903/935–2380 | 121 rooms | $41 | AE, D, DC, MC, V.

MCALLEN

Airport International Inn. This inn is across the street from McAllen Miller International Airport and minutes away from the international bridge to Mexico. Rooms are spacious. Cable TV, some pets allowed. | 817 Bales Rd. 78503 | 956/682–3111 | fax 956/682–3245 | 63 rooms | $35–$40 | AE, D, MC, V.

Drury Inn. This three-story motel is ½ mi from a mall, movie theater, hospital, and Miller International Airport. Complimentary Continental breakfast, in-room data ports, some refrigerators, cable TV, pool, business services, some pets allowed. | 612 W. U.S. 83 78501 | 956/687–5100 | fax 956/687–5100 | www.druryinn.com | 89 rooms | $75–$86 | AE, D, DC, MC, V.

Hampton Inn. This inn is close to the airport and has four stories with room entrances from the inside. Complimentary Continental breakfast, in-room data ports, cable TV, pool, business services, pets allowed. | 300 W. U.S. 83 78501 | 956/682–4900 | fax 956/682–6823 | www.hampton-inn.com | 91 rooms | $73–$77 | AE, D, DC, MC, V.

Holiday Inn Civic Center. Remodeled in early 2000, this two-story Holiday Inn hosts many conventions and sees a lot of business travelers. There are two malls within 1 mi and a golf course only 7 mi away. Restaurant, bar, in-room data ports, some microwaves, some refrigerators, cable TV, outdoor pool, indoor pool, indoor hot tub, sauna, exercise equipment, laundry services, business services, airport shuttle, some pets. | 200 U.S. 83W 78501 | 956/686–2471 | fax 956/682–7609 | www.holiday-inn.com | 173 rooms | $68–$85 | AE, D, DC, MC, V.

La Quinta Motor Inn. Scenic South Padre Island is 30 minutes away from this inn. It is within walking distance of the Plaza mall. Bar, complimentary Continental breakfast, in-room data ports, cable TV, pool, business services, airport shuttle, pets allowed. | 1100 S. 10th St. 78501 | 956/687–1101 | fax 956/687–9265 | 120 rooms | $73–$110 | AE, D, DC, MC, V.

Motel 6. This motel is 3 mi from McAllen Park. Cable TV, pool, laundry facilities, pets allowed. | 700 U.S. 83W 78501 | 956/687–3700 | fax 956/630–3180 | 93 rooms | $38–$44 | AE, D, DC, MC, V.

MIDLAND

Best Inn and Suites. This motel is about 10 mi from the Confederate Air Force and American Airpower Heritage Museum. Complimentary Continental breakfast, cable TV, indoor pool, hot tub, exercise equipment, business services, airport shuttle, some pets allowed. | 3100 W. Wall St. | 915/699–4144 | fax 915/699–7639 | www.bestwestern.com | 137 rooms | $49–$69 | AE, D, DC, MC, V.

Hampton Inn Midland. This hotel is located in a residential neighborhood in the north-west part of Midland. The Confederate Air Force and American Airpower Heritage Museum is 10 mi away. Complimentary Continental breakfast, in-room data ports, some microwaves, some refrigerators, cable TV, outdoor pool, indoor hot tub, laundry services, business services, pets allowed. | 3904 W. Wall St. 79703 | 915/694–7774 | fax 915/694–0134 | www.hamptoninn.com | 110 rooms, 6 suites | $55, $70 suites | AE, D, DC, MC, V.

Hilton Midland & Towers. This 11-story hotel is in the heart of downtown Midland. It's 15 minutes from the Midland International Airport, and the Midland Convention Center is across the street. Two restaurants, bar, complimentary Continental breakfast, in-room data ports, some kitchenettes, some refrigerators, some in-room hot tubs, cable TV, outdoor pool, outdoor hot tub, exercise equipment, laundry services, business services, airport shuttle, some pets. | 117 W. Wall St. 79701 | 915/683–6131 | fax 915/683–0958 | www.hilton.com | 242 rooms, 7 suites | $69–$109, $125–$145 suites | AE, D, DC, MC, V.

Holiday Inn. This two-story hotel is on landscaped grounds. It has over 30,000 square ft of meeting space. Restaurant, bar, room service, cable TV, indoor pool, hot tub, exercise equipment, laundry facilities, business services, airport shuttle, pets allowed. | 4300 W. Wall St. 79703 | 915/697–3181 | fax 915/694–7754 | www.holidayinn.com | 252 rooms, 31 suites | $72–$107, $79–$130 suites | AE, D, DC, MC, V.

La Quinta. This hotel is about 10 mi from Midland International Airport. Complimentary Continental breakfast, in-room data ports, cable TV, pool, laundry facilities, business services, pets allowed. | 4130 W. Wall St. 79703 | 915/697–9900 | fax 915/689–0617 | 146 rooms | $49–$65 | AE, D, DC, MC, V.

Midland Days Inn. Rooms are spacious in this three-story motel. There is a 24-hour restaurant across the street. Restaurant, complimentary Continental breakfast, kitchenettes, microwaves, refrigerators, cable TV, pool, outdoor hot tub, business services, pets allowed (fee). | 1003 South Midkiff Ave., Midland 79701 | 915/697–3155 | fax 915/699–2017 | www.daysinn.com | 177 rooms | $50–$67 | AE, D, DC, MC, V.

Motel 6. This motel is 6½ mi from the Confederate Air Force Museum. Pool, laundry facilities, pets allowed. | 1000 S. Midkiff Rd. 79701 | 915/697–3197 | fax 915/697–7631 | 87 rooms | $27–$31 | AE, D, DC, MC, V.

MONAHANS

Best Western Colonial Inn. This single-story motel is 3 mi from the Million Barrel Museum and 6 mi from Monahans Sandhills State Park. Restaurant, some in-room data ports, pool, some pets allowed. | 702 W. I–20 79756 | 915/943–4345 | fax 915/943–3627 | www.bestwestern.com | $48–$51 | AE, D, DC, MC, V.

MOUNT PLEASANT

Best Western Mt. Pleasant Inn. This two-story motel was renovated in 1997, and is 2 mi from the bus terminal. Complimentary Continental breakfast, in-room data ports, microwaves, refrigerators, some in-room hot tubs, cable TV, outdoor pool, outdoor hot tub, laundry facilities, business services, pets allowed (fee). | 102 E. Burton Rd. 75455 | 903/577–7377 | fax 903/577–0401 | www.bestwestern.com | 41 rooms, 15 suites | $66, $76–$109 suites | AE, D, DC, MC, V.

NACOGDOCHES

Fredonia. Built in the 1950s, this six-story, full-service hotel is one block from historic downtown Nacogdoches. It has a redbrick and iron exterior with New Orleans–style furnishings. Restaurant, complimentary breakfast, in-room data ports, cable TV, pool, business services, pets allowed. | 200 N. Fredonia St. 75961 | 936/564–1234 | fax 936/564–1234, ext. 240 | www.fredoniahotel.com | 113 rooms | $150–$163 | AE, D, DC, MC, V.

NEW BRAUNFELS

Holiday Inn. Business travelers and vacationing families alike feel at home in this comfortable, two-story, full-service chain hotel. Restaurant, bar, room service, in-room data ports, cable TV, pool, wading pool, exercise equipment, laundry facilities, business services, pets allowed (fee). | 1051 I–35E 78130 | 830/625–8017 | fax 830/625–3130 | www.holidayinn.com | 140 rooms | $79–$99 | AE, D, DC, MC, V.

New Braunfels Super 8 Motel. Built in 1996, this two-story motel with spacious rooms is in the middle of Texas Hill Country. Shopping is a mile away, and recreational activities within 3 mi. Complimentary Continental breakfast, in-room data ports, some microwaves, some refrigerators, cable TV, pool, outdoor hot tub, spa, laundry services, some pets. | 510 S. State Hwy. 46, New Braunfels 78130 | 830/629–1155 | fax 830/629–1155 | www.super8.com | 36 rooms, 14 suites | $54–$99, $59–$119 suites | AE, D, DC, MC, V.

Rodeway Inn. This motel is 3 mi from Gruene and the Schlitterbahn Water Park. There are a number of fast-food and fine dining restaurants next-door. Complimentary Continental breakfast, in-room data ports, cable TV, pool, outdoor hot tub, business services, some pets. | 1209 I–35E, New Braunfels 78130 | 830/629–6991 | fax 830/629–0754 | www.choicehotels.com | 130 rooms | $69–$89 | AE, D, DC, MC, V.

ODESSA

Best Western Garden Oasis. Rooms overlook the pool and a garden atrium in this motel 3 mi from the heart of town. Restaurant, room service, cable TV, pool, hot tub, sauna, laundry facilities, business services, airport shuttle, some pets allowed. | 110 I–20W, at Grant Ave. 79761 | 915/337–3006 or 877/574–9231 | fax 915/332–1956 | www.bestwestern.com | 118 rooms | $60–$68 | AE, D, DC, MC, V.

Holiday Inn Centre. This is one of the largest hotels in Odessa. It's on I–20, just a few minutes from Odessa College. Restaurant, bar, room service, in-room data ports, microwaves (in suites), cable TV, 2 pools, hot tub, putting green, exercise equipment, laundry facilities, business services, airport shuttle, some pets allowed. | 6201 I–20E 79760 | 915/362–2311 | fax 915/362–9810 | www.holiday-inn.com | 245 rooms, 36 suites | $74–$83 | AE, D, DC, MC, V.

La Quinta. Rooms with balconies and lots of light are available at this hotel 1 mi from the University of Texas, Permian Basin campus. Complimentary Continental breakfast, picnic area, cable TV, pool, business services, some pets allowed. | 5001 I–20E 79761 | 915/333–2820 | fax 915/333–4208 | www.laquinta.com | 122 rooms | $62–$69 | AE, D, DC, MC, V.

Motel 6. An economical option just south of town with basic amenities. | 95 rooms. Cable TV, pool, laundry facilities, some pets allowed. | 200 I–20E Service Rd. 79766 | 915/333–4025 | fax 915/333–2668 | www.motel6.com | $28–$32 | AE, D, DC, MC, V.

Odessa Days Inn. This three-story motel is on the outskirts of town. The Globe Theater is only 4 mi away and there are restaurants within walking distance. Complimentary Continental breakfast, in-room data ports, some microwaves, some refrigerators, cable TV, outdoor pool, business services, pets allowed. | 3075 E. Business Loop 20, Odessa 79761 | 915/335–8000 | fax 915/335–9562 | www.daysinn.com | 94 rooms, 2 suites | $46–$48, $52 suites | AE, D, DC, MC, V.

ORANGE

Best Western Inn. This basic chain property is just ½ mi from downtown. There's a casual restaurant next door. In-room data ports, some refrigerators, cable TV, pool, some pets allowed. | 2630 I–10 | 409/883–6616 | fax 409/883–3427 | www.bestwestern.com | 60 rooms | $55–$66 | AE, D, DC, MC, V.

Days Inn Orange. This motel is across the street from a 24-hour restaurant, and a casino is a 25-minute drive away. Complimentary Continental breakfast, cable TV, laundry services, some pets allowed. | 401 27th St., Orange | 409/883–9981 | fax 409/883–7902 | www.daysinn.com | 53 rooms | $38 | AE, D, DC, MC, V.

Holiday Inn Express. Off I–10, this two-story motel is within walking distance of a few fast-food restaurants. The Piney Woods Country Winery is only 2 mi away. Complimentary Continental breakfast, in-room data port, some microwaves, some refrigerators, cable TV, pool, laundry services, business services, pets allowed (fee). | 2900 I–10, Orange | 409/988–0110 | fax 409/988–0105 | www.holiday-inn.com | 97 rooms | $79 | AE, D, DC, MC, V.

Motel 6. Several restaurants and a tasty waffle shop are within walking distance of this basic two-story motel, 4½ mi from the center of Orange. Cable TV, pool, some pets allowed. | 4407 27th St. | 409/883–4891 | fax 409/886–5211 | www.motel6.com | 126 rooms | $27–$32 | AE, D, MC, V.

Ramada Inn. You'll find basic rooms and a casual restaurant at this chain hotel just off 16th St. in the heart of town. Restaurant, bar (with entertainment), in-room data ports, some microwaves, refrigerators, room service, cable TV, pool, wading pool, business services, pets allowed. | 2610 I–10 | 409/883–0231 or 800/635–5312 | fax 409/883–8839 | 125 rooms | $60–$135 | AE, D, DC, MC, V.

PADRE ISLAND

Holiday Inn SunSpree Resort. The only full-service beachfront property on the north end of Padre Island, this six-story hotel has a marine motif complete with aquariums in the lobby. The rooms are spacious; many have balconies and gulf views. Restaurant, bar (with entertainment), picnic area, room service, in-room data ports, microwaves, refrigerators, cable TV, 2 pools, hot tub, sauna, golf privileges, exercise equipment, beach, bicycles, video games, playground, business services, pets allowed (fee). | 15202 Windward Dr. | 361/949–8041 | fax 361/949–9139 | www.northpadreholidayinn.com or www.holiday-inn.com | 149 rooms | $119–$209 | AE, D, DC, MC, V.

PALESTINE

Best Western Palestine Inn. This motel is 3 mi from the center of town. Restaurant, in-room data ports, cable TV, pool, playground, business services, pets allowed. | 1601 W. Palestine Ave. 75801 | 903/723–4655 or 800/523–0121 | fax 903/723–2519 | www.bestwestern.com | 66 rooms | $44–$55 | AE, D, DC, MC, V.

PARIS

Comfort Inn. This reliable chain property (2½ mi from downtown) offers proximity to family restaurants and local businesses. Complimentary Continental breakfast, cable TV, pool, business services, some pets allowed. | 3505 NE Loop 286 | 903/784–7481 | fax 903/784–0231 | www.comfortinn.com | 62 rooms | $55–$65 | AE, D, DC, MC, V.

Holiday Inn. The on-site Denny's is open 24 hours a day. Restaurant, in-room data ports, room service, cable TV, pool, gym, laundry facilities, business services, pets allowed. | 3560 NE Loop 286 75460 | 903/785–5545 | fax 903/785–9510 | www.holiday-inn.com | 114 rooms, 10 suites | $79 | AE, D, DC, MC, V.

PECOS

Best Western Swiss Clock Inn. This Swiss-theme Best Western is just off I–20, right next to Maxey Park. The attached Alpine Inn restaurant serves German and Southwest dishes. Restaurant, bar, in-room data ports, room service, cable TV, pool, business services, laundry services, some pets allowed. | 900 W. Palmer Rd. 79772 | 915/447–2215 | fax 915/447–4463 | www.bestwestern.com | 103 rooms | $56–$62 | AE, D, DC, MC, V.

Motel 6. This bargain motel is 2 mi south of town at the junction of I–20 and Rte. 285. Cable TV, pool, laundry facilities, some pets allowed. | 3002 S. Cedar St. 79772 | 915/445–9034 or 800/332–5255 | fax 915/445–2005 | www.motel6.com | 96 rooms | $29–$37.95 | AE, D, DC, MC, V.

Quality Inn. Basic accommodations are available here, 3 mi from the West of the Pecos Museum and the Buck Jackson Memorial Rodeo. Restaurant, bar, in-room data ports, room service, cable TV, pool, business services, pets allowed. | 4002 S. Cedar St. 79772 | 915/445–5404 | fax 915/445–2484 | www.qualityinn.com | 96 rooms | $45–$61 | AE, D, DC, MC, V.

Town and Country Motel. This one-story motel is just outside of Pecos, off Hwy. 20. Cable TV, refrigerators, pets allowed (fee). | 2128 W. Hwy. 80 79772 | 915/445–4946 | 35 rooms | $30–$35 | AE, D, MC, V.

PLAINVIEW

Best Western–Conestoga. There's a 24-hour restaurant on the premises and shopping nearby. Restaurant, bar, complimentary Continental breakfast, in-room data ports, some refrigerators, cable TV, pool, business services, some pets allowed. | 600 N. I–27 79072 | 806/293–9454 | www.bestwestern.com | 82 rooms | $56–$100 | AE, D, DC, MC, V.

Days Inn. One block east of I–27, on U.S. 70, this one-story hotel is within walking distance of shopping and several restaurants, including the Cotton Patch Cafe. Complimentary Continental breakfast, cable TV, pool, laundry facilities, pets allowed (fee). | 3600 Olton Rd. (U.S. 70) | 806/293–2561 | fax 806/293–2561 | 48 rooms | $45–$65 | AE, D, DC, MC, V.

PLANO

Comfort Inn. You'll find king-size beds and some connecting rooms in this hotel, which is less than a block east of U.S. 75. Complimentary Continental breakfast, cable TV, pool, laundry facilities, pets allowed (fee). | 621 Central Pkwy. E | 972/424–5568 | fax 972/881–7265 | bobbiedill@yahoo.com | www.comfortinn.com/hotel/tx299 | 102 rooms | $52–$65 | AE, D, DC, MC, V.

Harvey Hotel. A conveniently located full-service hotel. A mall and restaurants are within walking distance. Restaurant, bar, cable TV, pool, business services, pets allowed. | 1600 N. Central Expressway 75074 | 972/578–8555 | fax 972/578–9720 | 279 rooms | $110–$120 | AE, D, DC, MC, V.

Holiday Inn. This hotel is on the north side of town, near several restaurants and a mall. Restaurant, bar, cable TV, pool, business services, pets allowed. | 700 E. Central Pkwy. 75074 | 972/881–1881 | fax 972/422–2184 | www.holiday-inn.com | 160 rooms | $89–$109 | AE, D, DC, MC, V.

La Quinta Inn and Suites. In addition to its basic accommodations, La Quinta also offers special rooms for extended stays. Complimentary Continental breakfast, in-room data ports, some microwaves, some refrigerators, cable TV, pool, spa, video games, laundry facilities, business services, some pets allowed. | 4800 W. Plano Pkwy. 75093 | 972/599–0700 or 800/NU–ROOMS | www.laquinta.com | fax 972/599–1361 | 121 rooms, 8 suites | $59–$99 | AE, D, DC, MC, V.

Motel 6. A low-priced option right off I–75. Cable TV, pool, laundry facilities, pets allowed. | 2550 N. Central Expressway 75074 | 972/578–1626 | fax 972/423–6994 | www.motel6.com | 118 rooms | $41–$48 | AE, D, DC, MC, V.

Red Roof Inn. This is an economical choice located at the busy intersection of I–75 and Parker Rd. Cable TV, some pets allowed. | 301 Ruisseau Dr. | 972/881–8191 or 800/843–7663 | fax 972/881–0722 | www.redroof.com | 123 rooms | $40–$70 | AE, D, DC, MC, V.

Sleep Inn. This hotel is 5 mi south of a business hub, Legacy Park. Over 20 restaurants are within a 1-mi radius, and guests have free access to an off-site health club. Complimentary Continental breakfast, cable TV, pool, pets allowed (fee). | 4801 W. Plano Pkwy. | 972/867–1111 | fax 972/612–6753 | www.choicehotels.com/hotel/tx338 | 102 rooms | $65–$79 | AE, D, DC, MC, V.

Super 8. Drive right up to your door—this motel is right off the highway. Complimentary Continental breakfast, cable TV, business services, some pets allowed. | 1704 N. Central Expressway 75074 | 972/423–8300 or 800/800–8000 | www.super8.com | fax 972/881–7744 | 102 rooms | $52–$63 | AE, D, DC, MC, V.

PORT ARANSAS
Days Inn. This basic chain property is 7 mi from Port Aransas. Complimentary Continental breakfast, in-room data ports, refrigerators, cable TV, pool, exercise equipment, business services, some pets allowed. | 410 Goodnight Ave, Aransas Pass 78336 | 361/758–7375 | fax 361/758–8175 | www.daysinn.com | 32 rooms, 18 suites | $65–$105 | AE, D, DC, MC, V.

PORT ARTHUR
Comfort Inn. Constructed in 1997, this sparkling Comfort Inn sits right on U.S. 69. Complimentary Continental breakfast, microwaves, refrigerators, some in-room hot tubs, cable TV, pool, outdoor hot tub, gym, pets allowed (fee). | 8040 Memorial Blvd. (U.S. 69) | 409/729–3434 | fax 409/729–3636 | 43 rooms | $65–$75 | AE, D, DC, MC, V.

Holiday Inn Park Central. There's a golf course next door, and rooms overlook the pool, courtyard, or dining patio. Restaurant, bar, in-room data ports, microwaves, room service, cable TV, pool, business services, airport shuttle, some pets allowed. | 2929 Jimmy Johnson Blvd. 77642 | 409/724–5000 | fax 409/724–7644 | www.holiday-inn.com | 164 rooms | $72–$84 | AE, D, DC, MC, V.

Ramada Inn. This basic motel is just 1 mi from the city center. Restaurant, bar, some refrigerators, room service, cable TV, pool, wading pool, tennis, business services, airport shuttle, some pets allowed. | 3801 Rte. 73 77642 | 409/962–9858 | fax 409/962–3685 | www.ramada.com | 125 rooms | $59–$155 | AE, D, DC, MC, V.

PORT LAVACA
Days Inn. Amenities are plentiful at this choice 1 mi from Lighthouse Beach. Restaurant, bar, complimentary Continental breakfast, in-room data ports, some refrigerators, cable TV, pool, laundry facilities, business services, pets allowed. | 2100 N. Rte. 35 | 361/552–4511 | fax 361/552–4511 | www.daysinn.com | 99 rooms | $59–$63 | AE, D, DC, MC, V.

QUANAH
Casa Royale Inn. This modern hotel sits 1 mi west of the center of Quanah. Spanish-style architecture and a warm brick lobby add distinction to comfort. Cable TV, pool, hot tub, playground, pets allowed. | 1500 W. 11th St. | 940/663–6341 | 40 rooms | $47 | AE, D, DC, MC, V.

RICHARDSON
Hawthorn Suites. Special corporate rates and a location just off I–75 accommodate the business traveler. Complimentary Continental breakfast, in-room data ports, microwaves, refrigerators, cable TV, pool, hot tub, exercise equipment, laundry service, business services, airport shuttle, pets allowed (fee). | 250 Municipal Dr. 75080 | 972/669–1000 | fax 972/437–4146 | www.hawthorn.com | 72 suites | $89–$102 suites | AE, D, DC, MC, V.

ROCKPORT

Best Western Inn by the Bay. This quiet property is just ½ mi from the gulf and 1 mi from the Fulton Mansion. Restaurant, complimentary breakfast, some refrigerators, cable TV, pool, laundry facilities, business services, pets allowed. | 3902 N. Hwy. 35, Fulton 78358 | 361/729–8351 or 800/235–6076 | fax 361/729–0950 | www.bestwestern.com | 72 rooms | $54–$66 | AE, D, DC, MC, V.

SAN ANGELO

Best Western Inn of the West. A local theater, which hosts a variety of plays, is 10 blocks from this two-story motel. Restaurant, room service, in-room data ports, cable TV, pool, business services, some pets allowed. | 415 W. Beauregard Ave. 76903 | 915/653–2995 | fax 915/659–4393 | www.bestwestern.com | 75 rooms | $45–$50 | AE, D, DC, MC, V.

Holiday Inn–Convention Center. The new San Angelo Museum of Fine Arts is only 2 blocks from this full-service hotel. Restaurant, bar, some microwaves, some refrigerators, cable TV, pool, hot tub, business services, some pets allowed. | 441 Rio Concho Dr. 76903 | 915/658–2828 | fax 915/658–8741 | www.holidayinn.com | 148 rooms | $79–$98 | AE, D, DC, MC, V.

Inn of the Conchos. This is the first hotel in San Antonio that you'll reach when traveling south on U.S. 87. The Crossroads Club in the lobby has entertainment on the weekends. Bar, room service, cable TV, pool, some pets allowed. | 2021 N. Bryant 76903 | 915/658–2811 | fax 915/653–7560 | www.inn-of-the-conchos.com | 125 rooms | $49–$54 | AE, D, DC, MC, V.

La Quinta. A seven-screen multiplex is adjacent to this two-story motel. Complimentary Continental breakfast, in-room data ports, cable TV, pool, business services, some pets allowed. | 2307 Loop 306 76904 | 915/949–0515 | fax 915/944–1187 | www.laquinta.com | 170 rooms | $49–$89 | AE, D, DC, MC, V.

Motel 6. There are fast food restaurants within a block, Concho Lake is 10 mi away. | 106 rooms. Cable TV, pool, some pets allowed. | 311 N. Bryant Ave. 76903 | 915/658–8061 | fax 915/653–3102 | $28–$32 | AE, D, DC, MC, V.

Super 8. The unusual Spanish-style architecture of this hotel distinguishes it from other Super 8s. Food and entertainment are just outside: La Scala restaurant is in the hotel parking lot and Santa Fe Junction, a country-western nightclub, is across the street. Complimentary Continental breakfast, cable TV, pool, hot tub, pets allowed (fee). | 1601 S. Bryant Blvd. | 915/653–1323 | fax 915/658–5769 | 81 rooms | $47 | AE, D, DC, MC, V.

SAN ANTONIO

Comfort Inn Airport. This chain hotel is near the airport and designed to please the business traveler. There are many bars and nightclubs in the area, including the Far West Rodeo. Complimentary Continental breakfast, in-room data ports, cable TV, pool, business services, airport shuttle, pets allowed (fee). | 2635 Loop 410 78217 | 210/653–9110 | fax 210/653–8615 | 203 rooms | $69–$79 | AE, D, DC, MC, V.

Drury Inn and Suites. The interior of this hotel is both modern and rustic with a large fountain in the lobby. The Henry B. Gonzales Convention Center is 6 mi away and the airport is nearby. There's also the convenience of an Applebee's restaurant next door. Complimentary Continental breakfast, in-room data ports, microwaves, refrigerators, cable TV, pool, hot tub, business services, airport shuttle, some pets allowed. | 95 NE Loop 410 78216 | 210/366–4300 | fax 210/308–8100 | www.drury-inns.com | 289 rooms | $75–$112 | AE, D, DC, MC, V.

Executive Guesthouse. This hotel strives to make its corporate guests feel at home while they're away on business. It's convenient to Fiesta Texas, the airport, and Northstar Mall and within walking distance of several restaurants. Complimentary breakfast, some in-room hot tubs, in-room data ports, microwaves, refrigerators, cable TV, indoor pool, exercise equipment, airport shuttle, valet parking, free parking, some pets allowed (fee). | 12828 U.S. 281N 78216 | 210/494–7600 or 800/362–8700 | fax 210/545–4314 | 124 rooms | $99–$109 | AE, D, DC, MC, V.

Hawthorn Suites. The Malibu Miniature Golf course nearby also has go-carts and arcade games. Farther east on I–10, Dave and Buster's lounge has music on weekends and a pool table, and across the street from the hotel there is a 24-screen multiplex and shopping center. Picnic area, complimentary breakfast, in-room data ports, kitchenettes, microwaves, cable TV, pool, hot tub, laundry facilities, business services, valet parking, free parking, some pets allowed (fee). | 4041 Bluemel Rd. 78240 | 210/561–9660 | fax 210/561–9663 | www.hawthorn.com | 128 suites | $79–$169 suites | AE, D, DC, MC, V.

Hilton Palacio del Rio. This is a towering complex with a central location downtown on the River Walk. It is the only hotel with extended balconies that overlook the river. It is across the street from the River Center Mall, the Alamo, and the Convention Center. Restaurant, bars with entertainment, in-room data ports, microwaves, cable TV, pool, hot tub, exercise equipment, business services, valet parking, parking (fee), some pets allowed. | 200 S. Alamo St. 78205 | 210/222–1400 | fax 210/270–0761 | www.hilton.com | 481 rooms | $100–$289 | AE, D, DC, MC, V.

Holiday Inn Crockett Hotel. Built in 1909 and listed on the National Register of Historic Places, this hotel is a relic of turn-of-the-20th-century San Antonio. You'll find traditional American food and a view of passing horse-drawn carriages in its Landmark Restaurant. Take in the city from the seventh-story sundeck or relax to nightly piano music in the central atrium. Restaurant, bar, room service, in-room data ports, cable TV, pool, outdoor hot tubs, laundry service, parking (fee), some pets allowed (fee). | 320 Bonham St. | 210/225–6500 or 800/292–1050 | fax 210/225–6251 | crockett.sales@gal-tex.com | 206 rooms | $79–$139 | AE, D, MC, V.

Holiday Inn Market Square. This Spanish-style hotel is two blocks away from a bustling shopping area, the Market Square. Inside the hotel, a game room will keep you entertained with pool, video games, and a full-swing golf simulator. Restaurant, bar, room service, cable TV, outdoor pool, outdoor hot tub, gym, video games, laundry facilities, free parking, pets allowed (fee). | 318 W. Durango | 210/225–3211 | fax 210/225–1125 | hi-sanantonio@bristolhotels.com | www.holiday-inn.com | 317 rooms | $70–$140 | AE, D, DC, MC, V.

Holiday Inn–River Walk. This modernized hotel has views of the San Antonio River. The rooms are contemporary and elegant, although the lobby has more of a Southwestern theme. It's 1 block from the Hard Rock Café. In-room data ports, refrigerators (in suites), room service, cable TV, pool, hot tub, exercise equipment, business services, some pets allowed. | 217 N. St. Mary's St. 78205 | 210/224–2500 or 800/445–8475 | fax 210/223–1302 | www.holidayinn.com | 313 rooms | $129–$179 | AE, D, DC, MC, V.

La Mansion del Rio. This hotel on the river is conveniently located on River Walk, nicely furnished, and has good service and a very pleasant staff. Restaurants, bar (with entertainment), in-room data ports, minibars, room service, cable TV, pool, business services, airport shuttle, pets allowed. | 112 College St. 78205 | 210/225–2581 or 800/323–7500 | fax 210/226–0389 | www.lamansion.com | 337 rooms | $214–$324 | AE, D, DC, MC, V.

La Quinta–Ingram Park. This chain hotel is 20 minutes from downtown San Antonio and welcomes families as well as business travelers. Complimentary Continental breakfast, in-room data ports, microwaves (in suites), refrigerator, cable TV, pool, some pets allowed. | 7134 Loop I–410 78238 | 210/680–8883 | fax 210/681–3877 | www.laquinta.com | 195 rooms | $85–$95 | AE, D, DC, MC, V.

La Quinta–Market Square. Market Square is across the street from the hotel, and the 600-ft Tower of Americas (commanding views of the area) is 1 mi away. Complimentary Continental breakfast, in-room data ports, cable TV, pool, business services, valet parking, free parking, some pets allowed. | 900 Dolorosa St. 78207 | 210/271–0001 | fax 210/228–0663 | 124 rooms | $105–$115 | AE, D, DC, MC, V.

Marriott Plaza. This hotel and resort is set on 6 acres and is known for the exotic birds and peacocks which roam the grounds. It's across from the HemisFair and 1 block from the Convention Center and the River Walk. This is a full-service hotel with many amenities to please executives in town during the week or families on vacation. Restaurant, bar (with entertainment), in-room data ports, room service, cable TV, pool, hot tub, massage, tennis court, exercise equipment, bicycles, business services, some pets allowed. | 555 S. Alamo St. 78205 | 210/229–1000 | fax 210/229–1418 | www.plazasa.com | 252 rooms | $95–$219 | AE, D, DC, MC, V.

Marriott Rivercenter. This large hotel has over 80,000 square ft of meeting space and a 40,000-square-ft Grand Ballroom. It is 1 block from the San Antonio Zoo and 5 minutes from The Alamo, the Convention Center and 10 minutes from the airport. Restaurant, bar, in-room data ports, some refrigerators, room service, cable TV, pool, barbershop, beauty salon, hot tub, driving range, putting green, exercise equipment, business services, valet parking, parking (fee), pets allowed. | 101 Bowie St. 78205 | 210/223–1000 | fax 210/223–6239 | 1,000 rooms | $91–$219 | www.marriott.com | AE, D, DC, MC, V.

Marriott Riverwalk. This hotel has a Southwestern theme. Half of the rooms have balconies facing the River Walk. There are 10,000 square ft of Grand Ballroom space. Restaurant, bar (with entertainment), in-room data ports, refrigerators, room service, cable TV, pool, hot tub, exercise services, valet parking, parking (fee), pets allowed. | 711 E. River Walk 78205 | 210/224–4555 | fax 210/224–2754 | 500 rooms | $199–$244 | AE, D, DC, MC, V.

Pear Tree Inn. Next to this traditionally decorated Pear Tree you'll find Jim's Restaurant, and across the freeway, Texas Land and Cattle and Red Lobster. The airport is also convenient. Complimentary Continental breakfast, in-room data ports, some microwaves, cable TV, pool, laundry facilities, business services, airport shuttle, some pets allowed. | 143 Loop 410 78216 | 210/366–9300 | 125 rooms | $66–$76 | AE, D, DC, MC, V.

Radisson Downtown Market Square. This upscale, full-service hotel with a Southwestern theme is in the heart of San Antonio's commercial district. It's a few blocks from the River Walk, across from UTSA College and 2 blocks from Market Square. Restaurant, bar, refrigerators (in suites), cable TV, pool, hot tub, exercise equipment, laundry facilities, business services, pets allowed. | 502 W. Durango St. | 210/224–7155 | fax 210/224–9130 | 250 rooms | $139–$169 | AE, D, DC, MC, V.

Red Roof Inn. This chain hotel is close to the airport, shopping, and restaurants. Complimentary Continental breakfast, in-room data ports, cable TV, business services, airport shuttle, pets allowed. | 333 Wolfe Rd. 78216 | 210/340–4055 | fax 210/340–4031 | 135 rooms | $68–$84 | AE, D, DC, MC, V.

Residence Inn by Marriott. Some of the amenities at this Marriott make it an excellent choice for families visiting the River Walk area. Complimentary Continental breakfast, in-room data ports, kitchenettes, microwaves, refrigerators, cable TV, pool, hot tub, exercise equipment, laundry facilities, business services, pets allowed (fee). | 425 Bonham Ave. 78205 | 210/212–5555 | fax 210/212–5554 | 220 suites | $159 suites | AE, D, DC, MC, V.

SAN MARCOS

Best Western. This property was built in the late 1990s and the contemporary feeling reflects this. There is an interesting combination of things to do near this hotel: Shop for bargains at the Outlet Mall or take a tour of the caves in nearby Wonder World. Complimentary Continental breakfast, in-room data ports, some refrigerators, microwaves, cable TV, pool, wading pool, laundry facilities, business services, some pets allowed. | 917 I-35N | 512/754–7557 | fax 512/754–7557 | www.bestwestern.com | 51 rooms | $59–$89 | AE, D, DC, MC, V.

Howard Johnson. This two-story motel is on the expressway and close to all area attractions. Complimentary Continental breakfast, in-room data ports, cable TV, pool, business services, pets allowed. | 1635 Aquarena Springs Dr. 78666 | 512/353–8011 | fax 512/396–8062 | 100 rooms | $39–$90 | AE, D, DC, MC, V.

La Quinta. Near this La Quinta there are movie theaters, outlet malls, and the famous glass-bottom boat at the Aqua-Marina. It is also very close to the Wonder World Cave and South West Texas State University. Complimentary Continental breakfast, in-room data ports, some refrigerators, cable TV, pool, some pets allowed. | 1619 I–35N 78666 | 512/392–8800 | fax 512/392–0324 | www.laquinta.com | 117 rooms | $79–$89 | AE, D, DC, MC, V.

SEGUIN

Best Western. A mile and a half west of the fairgrounds and less than a mile from downtown, this hotel puts you in striking distance of all of Seguin's attractions. Two restaurants are on the same lot as the hotel. Complimentary Continental breakfast, cable TV, pool, pets allowed (fee). | 1603 I–10, Highway 46 | 830/379–9631 | fax 830/379–9631 | 80 rooms | $90–$130 | AE, D, DC, MC, V.

SHAMROCK

Best Western Irish Inn. The name of this two-story motel honors the heritage of the postmaster who founded Shamrock. There is shopping within walking distance. Restaurant, in-room data ports, cable TV, in-room VCRs (and movies), pool, hot tub, laundry facilities, business services, pets allowed. | 301 I–40E | 806/256–2106 | fax 806/256–2106 | www.bestwestern.com | 157 rooms | $54–$59 | AE, D, DC, MC, V.

Econo Lodge. One mile east of town, this motel is on historic Route 66, 2 blocks off of I–40. You can get hearty biscuits and gravy with your complimentary breakfast and free admission at a local golf course. Complimentary Continental breakfast, cable TV, pool, pets allowed (fee). | 1006 E. 12th St. | 806/256–2111 | fax 806/256–2302 | 72 rooms | $35–$80 | AE, D, DC, MC, V.

Western Motel. This family run motel is right off Rte. 66. The rooms are comfortably and traditionally furnished and the price is right. Restaurant, cable TV, pool, pets allowed. | 104 E. 12th St. | 806/256–3244 | fax 806/256–3244, ext. 128 | 24 rooms | $34–$38 | AE, D, DC, MC, V.

SHERMAN

La Quinta Inn and Suites. This hotel is 2 mi north of downtown Sherman and steps away from many familiar chain restaurants. Each room features an entertainment system with pay-per-view movies and pay-per-play Nintendo games. Complimentary Continental breakfast, in-room data ports, some microwaves, some refrigerators, cable TV, pool, outdoor hot tub, gym, laundry facilities, laundry service, pets allowed. | 2912 U.S. 75N | 903/870–1122 | fax 903/870–1132 | 115 rooms | $69–$79 | AE, D, DC, MC, V.

SMITHVILLE

Pine Point Inn. This small motel, built in 1998, is on the highway 2 mi from Smithville and 2 blocks from the hospital. Complimentary Continental breakfast, cable TV, pool, outdoor hot tub, pets allowed (fee). | 1503 Dorothy Nichols Lane (U.S. 71) | 512/360–5576 | fax 512/360–5576 | 34 rooms | $55–$65 | AE, D, MC, V.

SNYDER

Beacon Lodge and RV Campground. A complete renovation in 1999 restored the Beacon to its original 1950s state, without sacrificing modern innovations. Old Coca-Cola memorabilia adorns the lobby and Elvis posters dress up some bedrooms. The hotel, on 6 acres of land, has grills available for all guests. Picnic area, complimentary Continental breakfast, some microwaves, some refrigerators, cable TV, laundry facilities, pets allowed. | 1900 E. U.S. 180 | 915/573–8526 | fax 915/573–4731 | 36 rooms | $38–$52 | AE, MC, V.

Purple Sage. A purple sage bush is just outside the front door of this family-owned friendly inn. Furnished in a traditional style, it is within walking distance of Snyder Coliseum, and Western Texas College is 5 mi away. Picnic area, complimentary Continental breakfast, refrigerators, cable TV, pool, playground, business services, pets allowed. | 1501 E. Coliseum Dr. 79549 | 915/573–5491 or 800/545–5792 | fax 915/573–9027 | 45 rooms | $34–$53 | AE, D, DC, MC, V.

SONORA

Best Western Sonora Inn. This hotel welcomed its first guests in May 2000 and is in pristine condition. It is within walking distance of several restaurants and less than a mile from the center of town. Complimentary Continental breakfast, some refrigerators, some microwaves, cable TV, pool, laundry facilities, pets allowed (fee). | 270 U.S. 277N | 915/387–9111 | 48 rooms | $56–$73 | AE, D, DC, MC, V.

Days Inn Devil's River. Sonora Caverns are 15 mi from this two-story motel. Restaurant, cable TV, pool, laundry facilities, business services, some pets allowed (fee). | 1312 N. Service Rd. 76950 | 915/387–3516 | fax 915/387–2854 | 99 rooms | $39–$58 | AE, D, DC, MC, V.

SOUTH PADRE ISLAND

Best Western Fiesta Isles. A horseshoe-shape hotel on a channel of Laguna Madre Bay. There is a kite shop, T-shirt vendor, and other tourist shopping opportunities nearby. Many kitchenettes, cable TV, pool, hot tub, pets allowed. | 5701 Padre Blvd. 78597 | 956/761–4913 | fax 956/761–2719 | www.bestwestern.com | 58 rooms | $69–$79 | AE, D, DC, MC, V.

Days Inn. This chain hotel offers an inexpensive way to be close to the gulf beach area, bars, and restaurants. Refrigerators, cable TV, pool, hot tub, laundry facilities, pets allowed (fee). | 3913 Padre Blvd. 78597 | 956/761–7831 | fax 956/761–2033 | 57 rooms | $55–$75 | AE, D, DC, MC, V.

Howard Johnson's. Opened in 2000, this sparkling hotel is half a block from the beach in both directions. Bayside rooms on upper floors have a view of the water, and, from certain balconies, you can see South Padre Island's weekly fireworks display. Start the night out with a cocktail at the pool-side lounge where you can also enjoy live music on weekends. Bar, complimentary Continental breakfast, microwaves, refrigerators, cable TV, pool, outdoor hot tub, gym, laundry facilities, pets allowed (fee). | 1709 Padre Blvd. | 956/761–5658 | fax 956/761–5520 | 89 rooms | $99–$156 | AE, D, DC, MC, V.

STEPHENVILLE

Best Western Cross Timbers. This motel is less than a mile west of downtown Stephenville. A 24-hour restaurant serving breakfast, sandwiches, and burgers, is on the same lot, and a 24-hour Walmart is a few blocks away. Complimentary Continental breakfast, microwaves, refrigerators, cable TV, pool, laundry facilities, some pets allowed. | 1625 S. Loop | 254/968–2114 | fax 254/968–2299 | 50 rooms | $53–$69 | AE, D, DC, MC, V.

Days Inn. Two restaurants are across the street, and a neighborhood park is 2 blocks away from this motel. In-room data ports, cable TV, pool, business services, some pets allowed (fee). | 701 S. Loop 76401 | 254/968–3392 | fax 254/968–3527 | 60 rooms | $45–$75 | AE, D, DC, MC, V.

Holiday Inn. A movie theater is across the street and a bowling alley is 4 mi away. Restaurant, in-room data ports, room service, cable TV, pool, business services, pets allowed. | 2865 W. Washington St. | 254/968–5256 | fax 254/968–4255 | www.holidayinn.com | 100 rooms | $64–$69 | AE, D, DC, MC, V.

Inn of Stephenville. This motel, built in 1997, is 1½ mi west of Tarleton State University. It is also across the street from the Bosque River Shopping Center. Complimentary Continental breakfast, microwaves, refrigerators, some in-room hot tubs, cable TV, pool, outdoor hot tub, some pets allowed. | 2925 W. Washington | 254/965–7162 | fax 254/965–7913 | 51 rooms | $64 | AE, D, DC, MC, V.

Texan Motor Inn. Truck parking is available at the one-story motel. Restaurants are next door and a shopping center is within walking distance. Complimentary Continental breakfast, cable TV, business services, some pets allowed (fee). | 3030 W. Washington St. 76401 | 254/968–5003 | fax 817/968–5060 | 30 rooms | $45–$65 | AE, D, MC, V.

SULPHUR SPRINGS

Comfort Suites Inn. At this three-story, all-suites hotel, just off of I-30 East, several room configurations are available. You can have a king-size bed or two queens for your bedroom, and the convertible sofa in your sitting room folds out to sleep additional guests. Two televisions in each suite. Complimentary Continental breakfast, microwaves, refrigerators, cable TV, pool, gym, laundry facilities, some pets allowed. | 1521 Industrial Dr. E | 903/438–0918 | fax 903/438–0329 | 60 suites | $74 | AE, D, DC, MC, V.

Holiday Inn. This newly remodeled hotel is just five minutes from Cooper Lake and Lake Fort. The dairy museum is less than 10 minutes away, and the Heritage Center is nearby. Restaurant, bar, in-room data ports, some refrigerators, room service, cable TV, pool, laundry facilities, free parking, some pets allowed. | 1495 E. Industrial Ave. 75482 | 903/885–0562 | fax 903/885–0562 | www.holidayinn.com | 98 rooms | $54–$64 | AE, D, DC, MC, V.

SWEETWATER

Holiday Inn. Across the expressway from this Holiday Inn you can enjoy steaks and barbecued food at Bucks. Sweetwater Lake is less than 10 mi away. Restaurant, some refrigerators, room service, cable TV, pool, playground, laundry facilities, business services, pets allowed. | 500 N.W. Georgia St. 79556 | 915/236–6887 | fax 915/236–6887 | www.holidayinn.com | 110 rooms | $59–$99 | AE, D, DC, MC, V.

Motel 6. If you're looking to pull off the highway and get a good night's rest without spending a fortune, look no further. Truck parking available. Cable TV, pool, laundry facilities, pets allowed. | 510 N.W. Georgia St. 79556 | 915/235–4387 | fax 915/235–8725 | 79 rooms | $30–$43 | AE, D, DC, MC, V.

Ramada Inn. This chain hotel is within easy access of I-20. You'll find hearty American food at the hotel restaurant, and drinks and entertainment at the Sunday House lounge. You are welcome to act out your country-star dreams at the Sunday House's lively weekly karaoke night. Restaurant, bar, room service, cable TV, pool, pets allowed. | 701 S.W. Georgia | 915/235–4853 | fax 915/235–8935 | 131 rooms | $51 | AE, D, DC, MC, V.

TEMPLE

Holiday Inn Express. About ½ mi north from the center of town, this hotel can be easily reached from I-35. You'll find many fast food and restaurant chains nearby. Complimentary Continental breakfast, microwaves, refrigerators, cable TV, pool, gym, laundry facilities, some pets allowed. | 1610 W. Nugent Ave. | 254/770–1100 or 877/732–3320 | fax 254/770–1500 | 61 rooms | $72–$199 | AE, D, DC, MC, V.

Inn at Scott and White. This motel is part of Scott and White hospital and is near Belton Lake and several restaurants. It's also just 10 mi from a popular shopping mall. Restaurant, some refrigerators, room service, cable TV, pool, business services, free parking, some pets allowed. | 2625 S. 31st St., Belton 76504 | 254/778–5511 | fax 254/773–3161 | 129 rooms | $56–$74 | AE, D, DC, MC, V.

La Quinta. Temple High School is across the street from this traditionally decorated chain hotel. You'll find friendly service and great accommodations here. A family restaurant is directly behind. The more adventurous can drive a few miles to Stampede, a dance club. Continental breakfast, cable TV, pool, business services, some pets allowed. | 1604 W. Barton Ave. 76504 | 254/771–2980 | fax 254/778–7565 | 106 rooms | $69–$90 | AE, D, DC, MC, V.

Luxury Inn. This modernized hotel has a quiet and relaxing atmosphere. It's so comfortable that many locals stay here as well. There is entertainment every night except Sunday in Drake's Lounge. Restaurant, bar, picnic area, in-room data ports, cable TV, pool, exercise room, laundry facilities, business services, free parking, some pets allowed. | 802 N. General Bruce Dr., 76504 | 254/778–4411 | fax 254/778–8086 | 132 rooms | $48–$62 | AE, D, DC, MC, V.

Travel Lodge. Just off I–35 (exit 302), this large, two-story motel is near many area restaurants. Complimentary Continental breakfast, microwaves, refrigerators, cable TV, pool, gym, laundry facilities, some pets allowed. | 802 N. Bruce St. | 254/778–4411 | fax 254/778–8086 | 132 rooms | $48–$58 | AE, D, DC, MC, V.

TEXARKANA

Four Points Sheraton Hotel. This hotel is 15 minutes from the airport and 15 minutes from downtown. Complimentary donuts and coffee are served during the week. There is a restaurant, the Garden Room, in the hotel, and your room key gains you entry to the club adjacent to the hotel, where you can hear live music most nights of the week. Restaurant, bar, room service, in-room data ports, cable TV, pool, indoor hot tub, gym, laundry service, business services, airport shuttle, pets allowed (fee). | 5301 N. Stateline Ave. | 903/792–3222 | fax 903/793–3930 | 147 rooms | $80 | AE, D, DC, MC, V.

La Quinta. This La Quinta is on the Arkansas border and has a country-style relaxing atmosphere, but if you're eating at the nearby Denny's or at the Waffle House, you're in Texas. Complimentary Continental breakfast, in-room data ports, cable TV, pool, airport shuttle, pets allowed. | 5201 State Line Ave. 75503 | 903/794–1900 | fax 903/792–5506 | 130 rooms | $57–$67 | AE, D, DC, MC, V.

Ramada Inn. Just off I–30, this hotel is easy to find and it has much to offer: the restaurant serves a bountiful Southern buffet at lunchtime, you can sing karaoke at the bar two nights a week, and you can exercise for free at a nearby health club. Antiques decorate this Ramada Inn's unusual lobby. Restaurant, bar, room service, in-room data ports, cable TV, pool, pets allowed (fee). | 2005 Mall Dr. | 903/794–3131 | fax 903/793–0606 | 98 rooms | $51 | AE, D, DC, MC, V.

TEXAS CITY

La Quinta. The NASA Space Center is 15 mi from this chain hotel, but if you want to fish off the world's largest fishing pier, you need only drive 5 minutes into town. This chain hotel's great service and comfortable accommodations are well known. Complimentary Continental breakfast, cable TV, pool, laundry facilities, business services, pets allowed. | 1121 Rte. 146N 77590 | 800/687–6667 | fax 409/945–4412 | 121 rooms | $49–$89 | AE, D, DC, MC, V.

Ramada Inn. With the Mall of the Mainland across the street, and the Gulf Greyhound racing park nearby, this hotel is a good choice for outlet shoppers and dog-race gamblers alike. There's live music in the hotel bar on weekends. Restaurant, bar, cable TV, pool, outdoor hot tub, laundry service, pets allowed (fee). | 5201 Gulf Fwy | 409/986–9777 | fax 409/986–5295 | 150 rooms | $59–$99 | AE, D, DC, MC, V.

THREE RIVERS

Best Western. Sparkling interiors reflect a southwestern influence in this Best Western, opened in 1998. There's a laundromat next door and a Mexican restaurant a block away. Complimentary Continental breakfast, some microwaves, some refrigerators, cable TV, pool, pets allowed (fee). | 900 N. Harbor Ave. | 361/786–2000 | fax 361/786–1022 | 38 rooms | $60 | AE, D, DC, MC, V.

TYLER

Days Inn. This two-story motel is ½ mi from a zoo and next door to a restaurant. Restaurant, complimentary Continental breakfast, some refrigerators, room service, cable TV, pool, barbershop, beauty salon, exercise equipment, laundry facilities, business services, free parking, pets allowed. | 3300 Mineola 75702 | 903/595–2451 | fax 903/595–2261 | 139 rooms | $45–$60 | AE, D, DC, MC, V.

Holiday Inn–Southeast Crossing. You will find contemporary architecture inside and outside of this Holiday Inn, on the southeast side of town around the corner from a bowling alley and near many shopping centers. Don't forget to save time to admire the landscaping. It's 10 minutes from Lake Tyler and within walking distance of area restaurants. Restaurant, in-room data ports, room service, cable TV, pool, laundry facilities, business services, airport shuttle, free parking, pets allowed. | 3310 Troup Hwy. 75701 | 903/593–3600 | fax 903/533–9571 | www.holidayinn.com | 160 rooms | $69–$78 | AE, D, DC, MC, V.

La Quinta. This modernized hotel is close to downtown Tyler, a selection of steakhouses and fast-food restaurants, and bargain shopping outlets. Complimentary Continental breakfast, in-room data ports, cable TV, pool, airport shuttle, free parking, some pets allowed. | 1601 W. Southwest Loop 323 75701 | 903/561–2223 | fax 903/581–5708 | www.laquinta.com | 130 rooms | $69–$79 | AE, D, DC, MC, V.

Radisson. Completely modernized, the rooms are traditionally decorated. The more expensive restaurants and shopping opportunities are 10 mi south on the loop, but there is fast food and a movie theater close to this Radisson. It's also close to the Caldwell Zoo and the downtown square. Restaurant, complimentary Continental breakfast, refrigerators, microwaves, in-room safes, in-room data ports, cable TV, pool, business services, airport shuttle, some pets allowed. | 2843 N.W. Loop 323 75702 | 903/597–1301 | fax 903/597–9437 | 139 rooms | $69–$79 | AE, D, DC, MC, V.

Residence Inn by Marriott. This updated Marriott offers upscale accommodations for visitors intending to spend more than a night or two in the area. It is across the road from restaurants. Picnic area, complimentary Continental breakfast, in-room data ports, cable TV, pool, hot tub, laundry facilities, business services, airport shuttle, free parking, pets allowed (fee). | 3303 Troup Hwy. 75701 | 903/595–5188 | fax 903/595–5719 | 128 kitchen suites | $86–$125 | AE, D, DC, MC, V.

Travel Inn. This chain hotel is perfect for tourists on a budget or business travelers looking for no-frills accommodations. Cable TV, pool, business services, pets allowed (fee). | 3209 W. Gentry Pkwy. 75702 | 903/593–0103 | fax 903/593–0103 | 50 rooms | $35–$39 | AE, D, DC, MC, V.

UVALDE

Best Western Continental Inn. This motel is on U.S. 90, within walking distance of downtown. You can cook any fish you catch in one of Uvalde's famous clear-running rivers in the barbecue pit located behind the motel. Truck parking is available. Picnic area, cable TV, pool, pets allowed. | 701 E. Main St. | 830/278–5671 | fax 830/278–6351 | 87 rooms | $58 | AE, D, DC, MC, V.

Holiday Inn. Near Garner State Park, you will find clean and modern rooms at this hotel. There's a jukebox in this hotel's lounge, The Corral Club, or you can drive a mile east to the six-screen Forum Theater. Restaurant, bar, room service, cable TV, pool, laundry facilities, free parking, some pets allowed. | 920 E. Main St. | 830/278–4511 | fax 830/591–0413 | www.holidayinn.com | 150 rooms | $59–$65 | AE, D, DC, MC, V.

VAN HORN

Best Western Inn of Van Horn. At this Western style hotel you will have privileges at a nearby golf course and the world's largest telescope is a little over an hour away. Restaurant, complimentary Continental breakfast, cable TV, pool, business services, some pets allowed. | 1705 Broadway, 79855 | 915/283–2410 | fax 915/283–2143 | www.bestwestern.com | 60 rooms | $55–$60 | AE, D, DC, MC, V.

Days Inn of Van Horn. This motel has the unusual benefit of a peaceful setting—in back, you'll find a shady wooded area with a picnic table. A quarter mile off of I–10, the motel is within walking distance of several Van Horn eateries. Picnic area, complimentary Continental breakfast, some microwaves, some refrigerators, cable TV, pool, pets allowed (fee). | 600 E. Broadway | 915/283–1007 | fax 915/283–1189 | 58 rooms | $45–$55 | AE, D, DC, MC, V.

Ramada Inn. Stay at this Ramada by night and take day trips to the caverns up north or to Big Bend National Park 100 mi south. This is 78 mi from Marfa "ghost lights." Pool, wading pool, laundry facilities, business services, some pets allowed. | 200 Golf Course Dr. 79855 | 915/283–2780 | fax 915/283–2804 | 98 rooms | $38–$58 | AE, D, DC, MC, V.

VERNON

Best Western Village Inn. This motor lodge is near the many restaurants along U.S. 287. Also, the restaurant on the premises, Norman's Catfish, will deliver to your room. Restaurant, bar, complimentary Continental breakfast, room service, cable TV, pool, laundry service, some pets allowed. | 1615 U.S. 287 | 940/552–5417 or 800/600–5417 | rogers@chipshot.net | www.bestwestern.com/villageinnvernon | 46 rooms | $53 | AE, D, DC, MC, V.

Days Inn. On the highway (with truck parking available) and a few restaurants in the area. This is 5 minutes from downtown and 2 mi from the museum. Cable TV, pool, business services, pets allowed. | 3110 Frontage Rd. 76384 | 940/552–9982 | fax 940/552–7851 | 50 rooms | $47–$53 | AE, D, DC, MC, V.

Green Tree Inn. This is a privately owned, recently modernized and updated motel less than 5 minutes from Vernon Regional Junior College (visit their museum on the history of Vernon). Complimentary Continental breakfast, in-room data ports, cable TV, pool, pets allowed. | 3029 Morton St. 76384 | 940/552–5421 or 800/600–5421 | fax 940/552–5421 | 30 rooms | $39–$45 | AE, D, DC, MC, V.

VICTORIA

Hampton Inn. This privately owned hotel is modern and comfortable. It is just 5 minutes from shopping, restaurants, and museums in the historical downtown area. Complimentary Continental breakfast, in-room data ports, cable TV, pool, business services, airport shuttle, free parking, pets allowed. | 3112 Houston Hwy. 77901 | 361/578–2030 | fax 361/573–1238 | 102 rooms | $63–$83 | AE, D, DC, MC, V.

Holiday Inn. A mainly corporate hotel that gives business travelers access to Union Carbide, BP Chemical, Dupont, and other plants in the area. It is near such historical sites as Riverside Park and the Texas Zoo, and is 12 mi from the Rose Garden, golfing, and playground area. Restaurant, bar, in-room data ports, room service, cable TV, pool, hot tub, exercise equipment, game room, video games, laundry facilities, business services, airport shuttle, free parking, pets allowed. | 2705 E. Houston Hwy., 77901 | 361/575–0251 | fax 361/575–8362 | www.holidayinn.com | 226 rooms | $70 | AE, D, DC, MC, V.

La Quinta. A strong Southwestern feeling greets you at this La Quinta which is close to several restaurants, the Victoria Mall, and movie theaters. Complimentary Continental breakfast, in-room data ports, cable TV, pool, business services, pets allowed. | 7603 N. Navarro Hwy. 77904 | 361/572–3585 | fax 361/576–4617 | 130 rooms | $49–$89 | AE, D, DC, MC, V.

Ramada Inn. This is a typical Ramada offering Texas hospitality to business travelers. Century Lanes Bowling is near the hotel, and guests can go dancing at the West Key Lounge or Cactus Canyon further down "the strip." It's not far from the OK Corral for more dancing and music. Restaurant, bar, in-room data ports, room service, cable TV, pool, hot tub, sauna, business services, airport shuttles, pets allowed. | 3901 Houston Hwy. 77901 | 361/578–2723 | fax 361/578–2723 | 126 rooms | $49–$59 | AE, D, DC, MC, V.

WACO

Best Western Old Main Lodge. This motel is filled with Western furnishings. It is near Baylor University, the Texas Sports Hall of Fame, and the Dr. Pepper Museum. The Brazos River and other tourist attractions are close by. Some microwaves, cable TV, pool, business services, free parking, some pets allowed. | I–35 at 4th St. 76703 | 254/753–0316 | fax 254/753–3811 | www.bestwestern.com | 84 rooms | $64–$83 | AE, D, DC, MC, V.

Holiday Inn. This four-story hotel, built in the 70s, is ½ mi south of Baylor University and the Texas Sports Hall of Fame. Restaurant, lounge, room service, cable TV, outdoor pool, gym, laundry facilities, airport shuttle, pets allowed (fee). | 1001 Martin Luther King, Jr. Blvd. | 254/753–0261 | fax 254/753–0227 | 171 rooms | $82–$92 | AE, D, DC, MC, V.

La Quinta Motor Inn. This contemporary chain motel is near Baylor University. It is within blocks of the Texas Ranger Hall of Fame, the Texas Sports Hall of Fame, and area restaurants. Complimentary Continental breakfast, in-room data ports, cable TV, pool, business services, free parking, some pets allowed. | 1110 S. 9th St., 76706 | 254/752–9741 | fax 254/757–1600 | 102 rooms | $72–$79 | AE, D, DC, MC, V.

WEATHERFORD

Best Western Santa Fe Inn. This hotel, off of I–20 at exit 409, has Spanish-style architecture, with Spanish tiles that continue the motif indoors. A restaurant on the premises serves Mexican and American food, but you won't find alcohol in this dry county. Restaurant, some refrigerators, some microwaves, cable TV, outdoor pool, laundry facilities, pets allowed (fee). | 1927 Santa Fe Dr. | 817/594–7401 | fax 817/594–5542 | 45 rooms | $59 | AE, D, DC, MC, V.

WICHITA FALLS

La Quinta. The Wichita Falls Arts and Science Museum and Midwestern University are close to this renovated La Quinta. Area restaurants are a pleasant walk away. Complimentary Continental breakfast, in-room data ports, cable TV, pool, laundry facilities, business services, free parking, pets allowed. | 1128 Central Fwy. N 76305 | 940/322–6971 | fax 940/723–2573 | 139 rooms | $49–$65 | AE, D, DC, MC, V.

Motel 6. There is a mall beside this modern chain motel called the Skies Center which also has a multiplex. It is 1 mi from The Falls where you can enjoy the park and man-made waterfall. It's also 2 mi from Sheppard Air Force Base. Restaurant, cable TV, pets allowed. | 1812 Maurine St. 76304 | 940/322–8817 | fax 940/322–5944 | 82 rooms | $43–$47 | AE, D, DC, MC, V.

Ramada Limited. This two-story hotel is 2 mi north of downtown and the airport, and is close to many area restaurants. Complimentary breakfast, some refrigerators, some microwaves, cable TV, pool, laundry facilities, laundry service, free parking, pets allowed (fee). | 3209 NW U.S. 287 | 940/855–0085 | fax 940/855–0040 | www.ramadawichitafalls.com | 59 rooms | $45–$64 | AE, D, DC, MC, V.

Trade Winds Motor Hotel. This motor lodge focuses primarily on extended-stay clientele. No matter the length of your visit, however, you will surely appreciate the large swimming pool and the hotel's proximity to the convention center and antique district. A bar on the premises, the Windjammer Lodge, once functioned as a private club and is now open to the public. Complimentary Continental breakfast, some refrigerators, some microwaves, cable TV, pool, laundry facilities, free parking, pets allowed (fee). | 1212 Broad St. | 940/723–8008 | fax 940/723–5160 | msallis@wf.net | www.bcscenter.com/tradewinds | 150 rooms | $35–$50 | AE, D, MC, V.

Utah

BEAVER

Best Western Butch Cassidy Inn. Brick, with white trim and surrounded by flowers and shrubbery, this downtown, one-story motel has better-than-average services and amenities. Restaurant. In-room data ports. Cable TV. Pool. Hot tub, sauna. Business services. Some pets allowed. | 24 rooms | 161 S. Main St. | 435/438–2438 | fax 435/438–1053 | $45–$55 | AE, D, DC, MC, V.

Best Western Paradise Inn. Large family suites are available at this one-story motel, and the location, right off I–15, is convenient for stopovers. Cable TV. Indoor pool. Hot tub, exercise room. Some pets allowed. | 50 rooms, 3 suites | 300 W. 1451 N | 435/438–2455 or 877/233–9330 | fax 435/438–2455 | $59, $77 suites | AE, D, DC, MC, V.

BLANDING

Best Western Gateway Inn. The downtown location is convenient and you get free movies in every room here. Cable TV. Pool. Pets allowed. | 60 rooms | 86 E. Center St. | 435/678–2278 | fax 435/678–224 | $60–$85 | AE, MC, V.

BRIGHAM CITY

Howard Johnson Inn. You're not far from the I–15/U.S. 89 split, and within walking distance to restaurants and historic buildings. Complimentary Continental breakfast. Cable TV. Indoor pool. Hot tub. Business services. Some pets allowed. | 44 rooms | 1167 S. Main St. | 435/723–8511 | fax 435/723–8511 | www.hojo.com | $50–$65 | AE, D, DC, MC, V.

BRYCE CANYON NATIONAL PARK

Best Western Ruby's Inn. The closest accommodation outside the park, this large two-story inn has spacious rooms and a comfortable lobby. It's a good place to stay if you like organized activities such as chuckwagon cookouts, trail rides, and helicopter and ATV tours. Restaurant, picnic area. Cable TV, in-room VCRs and movies. 2 indoor pools. Cross-country skiing. Laundry facilities. Business services. Pets allowed (fee). | 368 rooms | Rte. 63, 1 mi off Rte. 12 | 435/834–5341 or 800/468–8660 | fax 435/834–5265 | jean@rubysinn.com | www.rubysinn.com | $65–$95 | AE, D, DC, MC, V.

Bryce View Lodge. Next to the Bryce Canyon National Park entrance, this motel has reasonable rates, and you can use the pool and other amenities at the mammoth Ruby's Inn next door. 2 restaurants. Cable TV. Pool access. Laundry facilities. Pets allowed. | 160 rooms | Rte. 63 | 435/834–5180 or 888/279–2304 | fax 435/834–5181 | $55 | AE, D, DC, MC, V.

CEDAR CITY

Rodeway Inn. Downtown and within walking distance of the Utah Shakespearean Festival, this is a convenient place whose rates are lower than those of other chains. Cable TV. Pool. Sauna. Business services. Airport shuttle. Pets allowed. | 48 rooms | 281 S. Main St. | 435/586–9916 | www.hotelchoice.com | $60–$75 | AE, D, DC, MC, V.

FILLMORE

Best Western Paradise Inn. The largest property in town also has good amenities and a downtown location. Restaurant. Cable TV. Pool. Hot tub. Business services. Pets allowed. | 80 rooms | 1025 N. Main St. | 435/743–6895 | fax 435/743–6892 | www.bestwestern.com | $50–$60 | AE, D, DC, MC, V.

GREEN RIVER

Book Cliff Lodge. Rooms at this basic downtown motor inn are larger than average, and children can try the on-site mini-golf course. Restaurant. Cable TV. Outdoor heated pool. Pets allowed. | 99 rooms | 395 E. Main St. | 435/564–3406 | fax 435/564–8359 | $60–$70 | AE, D, DC, MC, V.

HEBER CITY

Danish Viking Lodge. A simple but solid favorite for families and Park City skiers more interested in value than resort-town atmosphere. | 34 rooms, 3 kitchenettes. Microwaves, refrigerators. Cable TV. Pool. Hot tub, sauna. Playground. Laundry facilities. Some pets allowed. | 989 S. Main St. | 435/654–2202 or 800/544–4066 (except Utah) | fax 435/654–2770 | $50–$65 | AE, D, DC, MC, V.

KANAB

Holiday Inn Express. The spacious rooms here have views of the coral cliffs right behind the inn. Numerous conveniences like in-room ironing boards, curling irons, dryers, and work desks with lamps are nice pluses. Continental breakfast. In-room data ports. Cable TV. Outdoor heated pool. Hot tub. Laundry facilities. Pets allowed in some rooms. | 71 rooms | 815 E. U.S. 89 | 435/644–8888 or 800/574–4061 | fax 435/644–8880 | $89 | AE, D, DC, MC, V.

Parry Lodge. The lobby of this Colonial-style building, constructed in 1929, is lined with photos of movie stars who stayed here while filming in the area, including Ronald Reagan and Barbara Stanwyk. Some of the spacious rooms have plaques over the doors to tell you who stayed here before you. The lodge barn, which housed Victor Mature's camels during the making of *Timbuktu*, is now a playhouse, where old-time Western melodramas are performed in summer. Restaurant. Cable TV. Pool. Laundry facilities. Business services. Pets allowed. | 89 rooms | 89 E. Center St. | 435/644–2601 or 800/748–4104 | fax 435/644–2605 | $45–$75 | AE, D, MC, V.

MOAB

Pack Creek Ranch. With neither in-room telephones nor televisions, peace and quiet are the lures here. The log building has open-beamed ceilings inside. Some of the spacious, one- to four-bedroom cottages have kitchens. Restaurant, picnic area. No room phones. Pool. Hot tub, sauna, massage. Hiking. Cross-country skiing. Pets allowed. | 10 1-, 2-, 3-, and 4-bedroom cottages | La Sal Mountain Loop Rd. | 435/259–5505 | fax 435/259–8879 |

www.packcreekranch.com | $135–300 per cabin (with breakfast) Apr.–Oct.; $100–$200 (no meals) Nov.–Mar. | AE, D, MC, V | AP.

OGDEN

Days Inn. Many amenities and a downtown location near restaurants and shopping, plus modest rates, are the distinguishing characteristics of this chain property. Complimentary Continental breakfast. In-room data ports. Cable TV. Indoor pool. Hot tub. Exercise equipment. Laundry facilities. Business services. Some pets allowed. | 108 rooms | 3306 Washington Blvd. | 801/399–5671 | fax 801/621–0321 | www.daysinn.com | $69–$79 | AE, D, DC, MC, V.

Radisson Suite Hotel. Totally restored, this downtown historic building was once the Hotel Ben Lomond and is on the National Register of Historic Places. Now part of the Radisson group, it has spacious and elegantly appointed rooms and suites furnished with reproductions of antiques. It's close to stores, offices, and restaurants. Restaurant, complimentary breakfast buffet. Refrigerators, microwaves in suites. Cable TV. Exercise equipment. Laundry facilities. Business services. Some pets allowed. | 144 rooms, 122 suites | 2510 Washington Blvd. | 801/627–1900 | fax 801/393–1258 | $150–$175 | AE, D, DC, MC, V.

PARK CITY

Best Western Landmark Inn. Right off I-80, near a cluster of popular factory outlet stores, this inn is a little less pricey than most Park City hotels. Pleasantly furnished rooms, a relaxing poolside area, and a recreation area make this a good bet for stopovers and families. Restaurant, Continental breakfast. In-room data ports, refrigerators. Cable TV. Indoor pool. Hot tub. Exercise room. Laundry facilities. Some pets allowed (fee). | 92 rooms, 14 suites | 6560 N. Landmark Dr. | 435/649–7300 or 800/548–8824 | fax 435/649–1760 | $169, $199–$375 suites | AE, D, DC, MC, V.

PAYSON

Comfort Inn. Right on Main Street, this inn gives you easy access to the Mt. Nebo Scenic Byway and the Uinta National Forest. Complimentary Continental breakfast. Cable TV. Indoor pool. Hot tub. Exercise equipment. Laundry facilities. Business services. Pets allowed (fee). | 62 rooms, 6 kitchenettes (no equipment) | 830 N. Main St. | 801/465–4861 | fax 801/465–4861 | www.comfortinn.com | $70–$85 | AE, D, DC, MC, V.

PROVO

Best Inn & Suites. Next to the BYU campus, this chain inn is convenient to museums and shopping. Complimentary Continental breakfast. In-room data ports, some microwaves, refrigerators. Cable TV. Indoor pool. Hot tub. Laundry facilities. Business services. Some pets allowed. | 101 rooms, 6 suites | 1555 N. Canyon Rd. | 801/374–6020 | fax 801/374–0015 | www.comfortinn.com | $69–$129 | AE, D, DC, MC, V.

Days Inn. Close to three major shopping areas, this chain property offers comfortable, contemporary rooms. Restaurant, complimentary Continental breakfast. Some in-room data ports, some microwaves, refrigerators. Cable TV. Pool. Business services. Some pets allowed. | 49 rooms | 1675 N. 200 W | 801/375–8600 | fax 801/374–6654 | www.daysinn.com | $50–$75 | AE, D, DC, MC, V.

RICHFIELD

Romanico Inn. Some of the spacious rooms here have three beds, some have refrigerators and microwaves, and there's a lawn with picnic tables. In a quiet area on the outskirts of town, this is a good place to stay if you're traveling with children or pets. Some microwaves and refrigerators. Cable TV. Hot tub. Laundry facilities. Pets allowed. | 29 rooms | 1170 S. Main St. | 435/896–8471 | $50–$65 | AE, D, DC, MC, V.

ROOSEVELT

Frontier Motel. The restaurant at this downtown motel is the most popular in town, and you're close to shops. A golf course is 1/2 mi away. Conference room. Restaurant. Some kitchenettes, cable TV. Pool. Hot tub. Business services. Pets allowed. | 54 units, 2 kitchenettes | 75 S. 200 E | 435/722–2201 | fax 435/722–2212 | $50–$75 | AE, D, DC, MC, V.

ST. GEORGE

Travelodge Motel. This modest-sized chain establishment has red-rock views from most rooms and is very close to golf. Some refrigerators. Cable TV. Pool. Business services. Pets allowed. | 40 rooms | 175 N. 1000 E | 435/673–4621 | fax 435/674–2635 | www.travelodge.com | $60–$75 | AE, D, DC, MC, V.

SALINA

Scenic Hills Motel. Simple, inexpensive lodging off the highway. Restaurant. Air-conditioning. Cable TV, some room phones. Pool. Business services. Pets allowed. | 67 rooms | 75 E. 1500 S | 435/529–7483 | fax 435/529–3616 | $52 | AE, D, DC, MC, V.

SALT LAKE CITY

Best Western-Salt Lake Plaza. Within walking distance of shopping, restaurants, Temple Square, and the Delta Center, this is a good place to stay if you are interested in the city's history and culture. Restaurant, room service. In-room data ports, some refrigerators. Cable TV. Pool. Hot tub. Exercise equipment. Laundry facilities. Business services. Airport shuttle. Pets allowed (fee). | 226 rooms | 122 W. South Temple St. | 801/521–0130 | fax 801/322–5057 | sales@plaza-hotel.com | www.plaza-hotel.com | $80–$125 | AE, D, DC, MC, V.

Chase Suite Hotel. These airy and spacious suites have vaulted ceilings, fireplaces, full kitchens, and sitting areas. Each suite has two telephones, two TVs, plus high-speed Internet access and free videos. Only 30 minutes from most ski facilities, the hotel can be an alternative to pricey all-suite lodging at the resorts. Conference rooms. Full breakfast. Microwaves. Cable TV, in-room VCRs. Outdoor pool. Hot tub. Airport shuttle. Pets allowed. | 150 suites | 765 E. 400 S | 801/532–5511 | fax 801/531–0416 | $159 | AE, D, DC, MC, V.

Comfort Inn Airport. The furnishings make this new facility a more upscale property than many in this chain. Restaurant. Some microwaves, refrigerators. Cable TV. Pool. Hot tub. Business services. Airport shuttle. Pets allowed (fee). | 154 rooms | 200 N. Admiral Byrd Rd. | 801/537–7444 or 800/535–8742 | fax 801/532–4721 | www.comfortinn.com | $85–$130 | AE, D, MC, V.

Days Inn Airport. Halfway between downtown and the airport, this renovated hotel has good amenities for both families and business travelers. Complimentary Continental breakfast. In-room data ports, some refrigerators and microwaves. Cable TV. Indoor pool. Business services. Airport shuttle. Pets allowed. | 110 rooms | 1900 W. North Temple | 801/539–8538 | www.daysinn.com | $75 | AE, D, DC, MC, V.

Hampton Inn Salt Lake City–North. This is a good alternative to pricier downtown lodgings yet still within easy reach of Salt Lake City. Eight miles north of downtown, the five-story hotel is close to businesses and restaurants. Complimentary Continental breakfast. In-room data ports. Cable TV. Indoor pool. Hot tub. Laundry facilities. Business services. Airport shuttle. Pets allowed. | 60 rooms | 2393 S. 800 W, Woods Cross | 801/296–1211 | fax 801/296–1222 | www.cottontree.net/hampton | $75–$95 | AE, D, DC, MC, V.

La Quinta. A bit south of the city, this is one of the first South Valley motels, although remodeling and new furnishings keep it fresh. The building has a Spanish Mission look, with a red-tile roof over the entry. Rooms are spacious, with large TVs and desks with data ports. Continental breakfast. In-room data ports. Cable TV. Pool. Hot tub. Laundry facilities. Business services. Pets allowed. | 121 rooms | 7231 S. Catalpa Rd., Midvale | 801/566–3291 | fax 801/562–5943 | www.laquinta.com | $60 | AE, D, DC, MC, V.

Ramada Inn–Downtown. The spacious rooms with work areas, a large pool in a courtyard, proximity to the convention center, and modest rates make this a good value. Restaurant, room service. In-room data ports. Cable TV. Indoor pool. Hot tub. Exercise equipment. Laundry facilities. Business services. Airport shuttle. Some pets allowed. | 160 rooms | 230 W. 600 S | 801/364–5200 | fax 801/364–0974 | www.ramadainnslc.com | $60–$85 | AE, D, DC, MC, V.

SPRINGDALE

Cliffrose Lodge & Gardens. A riverfront property on five acres of landscaped lawns and gardens with views of Zion Canyon, the lodge has contemporary rooms and a lot of space for children to run around in. Cable TV. Pool. Playground. Pets allowed (fee). | 36 rooms | 281 Zion Park Blvd. | 435/772–3234 or 800/243–8824 | fax 435/772–3900 | cliffrose@infowest.com | www.cliffrose.com | $109–$145 | AE, D, MC, V.

VERNAL

Weston Lamplighter Inn The simply furnished rooms are larger than average, and the family suites accommodate groups of up to six. In central Vernal, the motel is within walking distance of area shops, theaters, restaurants, and attractions. Restaurant. Some microwaves and refrigerators. Cable TV. Pool. Some pets allowed. | 88 rooms, 6 suites | 120 E. Main St. | 435/789–0312 | fax 435/781–1480 | $40–$50 | AE, DC, MC, V.

Vermont

ARLINGTON

Cutleaf Maples Motel. Near the Battenkill River, golf, and tennis courts, this Victorian motel offers clean, affordable accommodations. A wraparound porch has been converted into a lounge and contains a fireplace and web-TV. A full breakfast is available for an extra charge. Cable TV. Pets allowed. | Rte. 7A | 802/375–2725 | cutleafsandy@webtv.net | www.virtualvermont.com/cutleafmaples | 9 rooms | $55–$75 | AE, D, MC, V.

BARNARD

The Inn at Chelsea Farm. Surrounded by beautiful formal gardens and adjacent to a lush forest, this bed-and-breakfast is a rural oasis. The rooms overlook meadows where pet sheep graze. Complimentary breakfast. No air-conditioning, no smoking, no room phones, TV in common area. Hiking. Pets allowed. | Rte. 12 | 802/234–9888 | fax 802/234–5629 | emmy@sover.net | www.innatchelseafarm.com | 3 rooms | $95–$130 | AE, MC, V.

BARRE

Autumn Harvest Inn. Standing atop a knoll 7 mi southwest of Barre, this inn overlooks a 46-acre workhorse farm, the valley, and the surrounding mountains. Five rooms are part of the original farmhouse and feature wide-board wooden floors. A porch graces the front of the inn and the living room has a brick fireplace. Restaurant, bar. No smoking. Cable TV, in-room VCRs. Pond. Horseback riding. Cross-country skiing. Pets allowed. | Clark Rd., Williamstown | 802/433–1355 | fax 802/433–5501 | autumnharv@aol.com | central-vt.com/web/autumn | 18 rooms | $89 | AE, MC, V.

BENNINGTON

The Fife 'n Drum Motel. Picnic areas, lawns, and a playground surround this affordable motor lodge with views of the majestic Green Mountains. The proprietors speak German and manufacture small clocks that they sell in a gift shop adjacent to the motel. Some microwaves, refrigerators, no smoking, cable TV. Pool. Pets allowed (fee). | 693 Rte. 7 S | 802/442–4074 or 802/442–4730 | fax 802/442–8471 | toberua@sover.net | www.sover.net/~toberua | 18 rooms | $95 | AE, D, MC, V.

Serenity. Cottages with inviting porches, 7 mi north of Bennington. Picnic area. Cable TV, refrigerators. Pets allowed. | 4379 Rte. 7A, Shaftsbury | 802/442–6490 or 800/644–6490 | www.thisisvermont.com/pages/serenity | 8 units (all with shower only) | $55–$75 | Closed Nov.–Apr. | AE, DC, MC, V.

BRANDON

Moffett House. A handsome Victorian home on Brandon's finest residential street. Complimentary breakfast. No air-conditioning in some rooms, no smoking, some in-room hot tubs, no room phones. Pets allowed (fee). | 69 Park St. | 802/247–3843 or 800/394–7239 | 6 rooms (3 with shared bath) | $90–$200 | Closed Apr. | MC, V.

BRATTLEBORO

Quality Inn. A representative of the reliable chain, convenient to the Interstate. Restaurant, bar. In-room data ports, room service, cable TV. 2 pools (1 indoor). Hot tub, sauna. Business services. Pets allowed. | 1380 Putney Rd., (Rte. 5 N) | 802/254–8701 | fax 802/257–4727 | 104 rooms | $129 | AE, D, DC, MC, V.

BURLINGTON

Best Western Windjammer Inn and Conference Center. A handy chain option for airport travelers. The Windjammer restaurant is on site. Restaurant, complimentary Continental breakfast. Cable TV. Pool. Hot tub. Exercise equipment. Laundry facilities. Business services. Airport shuttle. Pets allowed (fee). | 1076 Williston Rd. | 802/863–1125 | fax 802/658–1296 | www.bestwestern.com | 173 rooms | $89–$179 | AE, D, DC, MC, V.

Days Inn. An expanded chain representative, directly opposite St. Michael's College, 7 mi northeast of town. Complimentary Continental breakfast. Refrigerators, some in-room hot tubs, cable TV. Indoor pool. Business services. Pets allowed (fee). | 23 College Pkwy., Colchester, 05446 | 802/655–0900 | fax 802/655–6851 | www.daysinn.com | 73 rooms | $69–$125 | AE, D, DC, MC, V.

Hampton Inn and Conference Center. A large, full-service hotel just off Interstate 89 on Burlington's northern outskirts. You'll need to drive to downtown from here. Restaurant, complimentary Continental breakfast. In-room data ports, some refrigerators, cable TV, some in-room VCRs. Indoor pool. Hot tub. Exercise equipment. Laundry facilities. Business services. Airport shuttle. Pets allowed. | 42 Lower Mountain View Dr., Colchester, 05446 | 802/655–6177 | fax 802/655–4962 | www.hampton-inn.com | 188 rooms | $94–$109 | AE, D, DC, MC, V.

Holiday Inn. One of the area's largest hotels is 1½ mi from the city, halfway between downtown and the airport. Restaurant, bar with entertainment. In-room data ports, room service. Cable TV. 2 pools (1 indoor). Sauna. Exercise equipment. Business services. Airport shuttle. Pets allowed. | 1068 Williston Rd., S. Burlington, 05403 | 802/863–6363 | fax 802/863–3061 | www.holiday-inn.com/hotels/btvvt | 174 rooms | $100 | AE, D, DC, MC, V.

Residence Inn by Marriott. A chain option that is near the airport and Interstate 89 and is popular with business travelers. It's a 10-minute drive to downtown. Some rooms with fireplaces. Complimentary Continental breakfast. In-room data ports, kitchenettes, cable TV. Indoor pool. Hot tub. Exercise equipment. Playground. Laundry facilities. Business services. Airport shuttle, free parking. Pets allowed (fee). | One Hurricane La., Williston, 05495 | 802/878–2001 | 96 suites | $159–$175 | AE, D, DC, MC, V.

Sheraton Hotel and Conference Center. The area's largest hotel is 1½ mi east of Burlington and frequently hosts major functions. Restaurant, bar with entertainment, room service. In-room data ports, some refrigerators, cable TV, some in-room VCRs. Indoor pool. Hot tub. Gym. Video games. Business services. Airport shuttle. Pets allowed. | 870 Williston

Rd., S. Burlington, 05403 | 802/865-6600 | fax 802/865-6670 | www.sheraton.com/
burlington | 309 rooms | $145-$195 | AE, D, DC, MC, V.

CRAFTSBURY COMMON

Craftsbury Outdoor Center. Lakes and hills surround this haven for outdoor enthusiasts.
The center has terrific cross-country skiing on its 160 km (99 mi) of trails, which also go
through the local farmland. Dining room, complimentary breakfast. No air-conditioning,
no smoking, no room phones, TV in common area. Tennis court. Hiking, beach, boating.
Bicycles, ice-skating. Cross-country skiing. Library. Pets allowed (in cottages only). | Lost
Nation Rd. | 802/586-7767 or 800/729-7751 | fax 802/586-7768 | crafts@sover.net |
www.craftsbury.com | 29 rooms (26 share bath), 3 cottages, 2 efficiencies | $118-$215 | AP
| MC, V.

Inn on the Common. Set on 10 acres, this picturesque Federal-style inn has tastefully
appointed rooms with handcrafted country furnishings and quilts. Five-course dinners
are served at communal tables in the dining room, overlooking the gardens. Excellent
cross-country skiing is available. Dining room, complimentary breakfast. Pool. Tennis court.
Library. TV in common area. Pets allowed (fee). | N. Craftsbury Rd. 05827 | 802/586-9619
or 800/521-2233 | fax 802/586-2249 | 16 rooms | $250-$300 | MAP | AE, MC, V. .

DORSET

Barrows House. This antiques-filled inn sprawls over nine buildings and 11 acres. Some
rooms have fireplaces. Restaurant, bar, picnic area. Some kitchenettes, some refrigerators, some in-room VCRs, no room phones, TV in some rooms. Pool. Sauna. Tennis. Bicycles.
Cross-country skiing, downhill skiing. Library. Business services. Pets allowed. | Rte. 30,
at corner of Dorset Hollow Rd. | 802/867-4455 or 800/639-1620 | fax 802/867-0132 |
www.barrowshouse.com | 28 rooms in 9 houses | $90-$265 including dinner | MAP | AE,
D, MC, V.

FAIRLEE

Silver Maple. You can stay in a knotty pine-paneled cottage or in the main late-18th-century
inn in this hotel 1 mi from Lake Morey. Complimentary Continental breakfast. No air-condi-
tioning, no room phones, no TV in some rooms. Pets allowed. | 520 U.S. Rte. 5 S | 802/333-
4326 or 800/666-1946 | www.silvermaplelodge.com | 8 rooms (2 with shared bath), 8
cottages | $56-$86 | AE, D, MC, V.

ISLAND POND

Quimby Country. A Northeast Kingdom tradition since 1894, this inn feels like an old-
time fishing lodge where hearty meals attract loyal family clientele. The hotel is on 650
acres tucked deep in the woods overlooking Forest Lake, 20 mi north of Island Pond, with
larger Great Averill Pond nearby. No room phones. Lake. Tennis. Hiking, boating. Fishing.
Children's programs (ages 5 and up). Pets allowed. | Rte. 114, Forest Lake Rd., Averill | 802/
822-5533 | fax 802/822-5537 | 20 cabins | $111-$126 (adults), $63-$74 (ages 9-16), $49-$52
(ages 3-8) | Closed Oct.-mid-May | AP | No credit cards.

JEFFERSONVILLE

Deer Run Motor Inn. In a rural wooded area, this property has clean, comfortable accommodations in a scenic landscape. The backyard area has room for picnicking and lounging
as well as a swing set for the kids. Refrigerators, cable TV. Pool. Playground. Pets allowed.
| Rte. 15 | 802/644-8866 or 800/354-2728 | 25 rooms | $70 | AE, D, MC, V.

KILLINGTON

Val Roc. An inexpensive option for overnight travelers who don't need one of the full-
service resorts up on the mountain. Picnic area, complimentary Continental breakfast.

No air-conditioning in some rooms, some kitchenettes, refrigerators, cable TV, some in-room VCRs. Pool. Hot tub. Tennis. Pets allowed. | 8006 Rte. 4 | 802/422–3881 or 800/238–8762 | www.valroc.com | 24 rooms | $59–$99 | AE, DC, MC, V.

LUDLOW

Cavendish Pointe Hotel. This hotel, 2½ mi east of Ludlow, has a living room with a two-story fireplace and numerous antiques. The indoor pool provides a source of relaxation year-round. Rooms have views of the lovely Okemo Mountain. Restaurant, bar. Refrigerators, no smoking, cable TV. Hiking. Cross-country skiing. Video games. Business services. Pets allowed. | Rte. 103, Cavendish | 802/226–7688 or 800/438–7908 | cavpnt@ludl.tds.net | www.okemo-cavendishpointe.com/contact.html | 70 rooms | $108–$199 | AE, D, MC, V.

Combes Family Inn. This 1850 farmhouse anchors 50 acres of woods and fields 4 mi north of Ludlow. As its name implies, the lodging has a homey feel, from the country antiques right down to the home-cooked meals. Three of the rooms are large enough to accommodate families. Dining room, picnic area, complimentary breakfast. No air-conditioning in some rooms, room service, no room phones, TV in common area. Cross-country skiing. Pets allowed. | 953 E. Lake Rd. | 802/228–8799 or 800/822–8799 | billcfi@ludl.tds.net | www.combesfamilyinn.com | 11 rooms | $60–$134 | AE, D, MC, V.

LYNDONVILLE

Old Cutter Inn. A Swiss chef runs this inn 7 mi northeast of town with one of the Northeast Kingdom's most esteemed kitchens in an old farmhouse. Dining room, picnic area. No smoking, no TV in rooms, TV in common area. Pool. Cross-country skiing. Pets allowed. | 143 Pinkham Rd. | 802/626–5152 | fax 802/626–5152 | www.pub.com/cutter.htm | 9 rooms, 1 suite | $56–$70, $96–$150 suite | Closed Apr., Nov. | MAP | MC, V.

MANCHESTER AND MANCHESTER CENTER

Brittany Motel. This tidy, little, independently owned motel at the base of Mt. Equinox offers warm, cozy rooms and friendly service. Picnic area. Refrigerators, cable TV. Some pets allowed. | 1056 Main St. (Rte. 7A), Manchester Center | 802/362–1033 | fax 802/362–0551 | www.thisisvermont.com/brittany | 12 rooms | $68–$83 | AE, D, MC, V.

Mt. Tabor Inn and Restaurant. This inn 10 mi north of Manchester is directly across from the Green Mountains National Forest and has spectacular views of the nearby mountains. The spacious, individually decorated rooms are bright and sunny, each with a mountain view. Restaurant. Cable TV, no room phones. Some pets allowed. | Rte. 7, Mt. Tabor | 802/293–5907 or 877/658–2267 | mttaborinn@aol.com | www.mttaborinn.com | 12 rooms | $85 | AE, D, DC, MC, V.

MARLBORO

Colonel Williams Inn. The rooms in this 1796 white clapboard inn, originally built as part of a sheep farm, have wide-plank wood floors and antique furniture. Four of them also have wood-burning fireplaces. The innkeepers are New England Culinary Institute graduates and prepare delicious breakfasts and dinners. Restaurant, bar, complimentary breakfast. No air-conditioning in some rooms, some kitchenettes, some refrigerators, no smoking, no room phones, TV in common area. Pond. Fishing. Ice-skating. Cross-country skiing. Pets allowed (in efficiencies). | Rte. 9 | 802/257–1093 | fax 802/257–4460 | colwminn@sover.net | www.colonelwilliamsinn.com | 9 rooms, 4 efficiencies | $100–$140 | AE, D, MC, V.

Whetstone Inn. Stagecoaches once halted at this 1700s inn in the heart of Marlboro village. There are fireplaces in the public rooms. Restaurant, picnic area. No air-conditioning, some kitchenettes, some refrigerators. Pond. Pets allowed. | South Rd. | 802/254–2500 | www.whetstone | 11 rooms (3 with shared bath) | $60–$80 | No credit cards.

MIDDLEBURY

Middlebury Inn. One of Vermont's most distinguished small hotels, the inn has been a fixture of this town since the early 19th century. The best rooms are on upper floors of the main building, facing west. Lunch is served on the porch in summer. Restaurants, bar, complimentary Continental breakfast. Cable TV. Business services. Pets allowed (fee). | 14 Court House Sq. | 802/388–4961 or 800/842–4666 | fax 802/388–4563 | midinnut@sover.net | www.middleburyinn.com | 66 rooms, 9 suites | $86–$195, $195–$355 suites | AE, D, DC, MC, V.

Sugarhouse Motel. When it's warm enough, this motel allows you to build a campfire on the front lawn and cook your dinner on it. Standing on the crest of a hill, it affords beautiful views of the sunrise and sunset across the mountains. Prices are very reasonable during nonpeak times. Microwaves, refrigerators, no smoking, cable TV. Pets allowed (fee). | Rte. 7 | 802/388–2770 or 800/784–2746 | fax 802/388–8616 | ars@together.net | 14 rooms | $99 | MC, V.

MONTGOMERY CENTER

Hazen's Notch Bed-and-Breakfast. This renovated red clapboard farmhouse in the middle of the Green Mountains has scenic views of the surrounding mountain meadows and forests. The property is only steps away from hiking, biking, and cross-country skiing trails. Complimentary breakfast. No air-conditioning, no smoking, no room phones, TV in common area. Pond. Library. Pets allowed. | Rte. 58/Hazen's Notch Rd. | 802/326–4708 |

CAMP GONE TO THE DOGS

Do George and Gracie run the other way from you when you call? You may want to take them to Camp Gone to the Dogs. Every year, more than 400 dog lovers and more than 500 dogs do just that, coming from as far away as Australia and Japan to Marlboro College in Marlboro, Vermont, in June and July, and to the Mountaineer Inn in Stowe, Vermont, every fall, for a week with Honey Loring. At these camps, which she has been directing since 1990, she puts you through your paces, and there's plenty of fun for all as dogs get obedience and agility training from top instructors, dashing through tunnels and over (and around) obstacle courses, learning to track by following a scent, playing with Frisbees, freestyle dancing, tricks and games, and much more, all in a non-competitive atmosphere. At the Marlboro session there are some 50 events each day, where you'll learn about herding, hunting, Tellington Touch, competition obedience, and other topics; there's even a dog costume contest and a dog kissing contest. Of the many events, the funniest and everybody's favorite is the "hot dog retrieve!" Reserve well ahead—the camps have been featured on national television shows and in national magazines, and are extremely popular. Some people even come without their dogs, and many return year in and year out. The single all-inclusive price runs around $800–$1,200. Contact: Camp Gone to the Dogs, Box 600, Putney, VT 05346, 802/387–5673, www.campgonetothedogs.com.

hazens@together.net | www.pbpub.com/hazensnotch.htm | 3 rooms | $60–$70 | No credit cards.

MONTPELIER

Econo Lodge Montpelier. This motel just off Interstate 89 has clean rooms with a full range of modern amenities. Some microwaves, some refrigerators, no smoking, cable TV. Pets allowed. | 101 Northfield St. | 802/223–5258 or 800/553–2666 | fax 802/223–0716 | 54 rooms | $98 | AE, D, DC, MC, V.

NEWFANE

Four Columns Inn. This Greek Revival mansion dating from 1830 faces Newfane's much-photographed green. It is filled with antique furniture. Dining room, bar, complimentary breakfast. No smoking, cable TV in lounge, no TV in rooms. Pool. Business services. Pets allowed. | 21 West St. | 802/365–7713 | fax 802/365–0022 | www.fourcolumnsinn.com | 15 rooms, 4 suites | $140–$175, $195–$270 suites | AE, D, MC, V.

NEWPORT

Inn at the Hill/Top of the Hills Motel and Inn. The individually appointed rooms of this late Victorian house share a country motif. A full range of modern amenities complements these rustic charms and makes the inn a comfortable and relaxing retreat. Complimentary Continental breakfast. Cable TV, in-room VCRs. Laundry facilities. Business services. Pets allowed ($10 fee). | 1724 E. Main St. | 802/334–6748 or 800/258–2748 | fax 802/334–1463 | iath@together.net | www.innatthehill.com | 15 rooms | $65–$75 | AE, D, MC, V.

NORTH HERO

Shore Acres Inn and Restaurant. At this inn, lawns sweep down to Lake Champlain, and you can contemplate the sweeping views from sparkling white Adirondack chairs. The restaurant is known for steak, chops, and seafood. Restaurant, bar. No air-conditioning in some rooms, some refrigerators, cable TV. Golf course, 2 tennis courts, croquet. Pets allowed. | 237 Shore Acres Dr. | 802/372–8722 | www.shoreacres.com | 23 rooms | $87–$129 | Closed mid-Oct.–mid-Apr. | D, MC, V.

PERU

Johnny Seesaw's. This snug, log lodge was a dance hall in the 1920s. It has long been a favorite with skiers who gather around the big circular fireplace. The cottages also have fireplaces. Restaurant, complimentary breakfast. Some refrigerators, some room phones. Pets allowed. | Rte. 11, Peru | 802/824–5533 | fax 802/824–5533 | gary@jseesaws.com | www.jseesaw.com | 8 rooms, 8 suites, 4 cottages | $160, $170 suites, $190 cottages | Closed mid-Apr.–late May | D, MC, V.

PUTNEY

Putney Inn. This post-and-beam farmhouse, built in the 1750s by one of the first settlers of the area, houses a restaurant and public rooms. The guest rooms in annex are furnished with Queen Anne reproductions. The 13-acre site has Connecticut River valley views. The restaurant is highly regarded. MAP available off-season. Restaurant, bar. Cable TV. Pets allowed. | 57 Putney Landing Rd. | 802/387–5517 or 800/653–5517 | fax 802/387–5211 | putneyinn@sover.net | www.putneyinn.com | 25 rooms | $88–$158 | MAP | AE, D, MC, V.

RANDOLPH

Three Stallion Inn. This inn on 1,300 acres is perfect for outdoor enthusiasts; the property's 50 km (30 mi) of trails pass through woods, streams, and meadows. The rooms are adorned with floral pattern wallpaper and bedcovers that complement the rural landscape seen from the windows. The inn is just off Interstate 89 at Exit 4. Complimentary Continental breakfast. No air-conditioning, no smoking, no room phones, TV in common area. Pool. Hot tub, sauna. Tennis courts. Gym, hiking. Fishing. Cross-country skiing. Pets allowed (fee). | Green Mountain Stock Farm | 802/728–5575 or 800/424–5575 | fax 802/728–4036 | tsi@quest-net.com | www.3stallionsinn.com | 15 rooms | $147 | Closed 1 wk in Apr. and 1 wk in Nov. | AE, D, MC, V.

RUTLAND

Holiday Inn Center of Vermont. This is Rutland's largest hotel, just south of downtown, off the busy Route 7 strip. Restaurant, bar with entertainment. In-room data ports, room service, cable TV. Indoor pool. Hot tub. Gym. Laundry facilities Business center. Airport shuttle. Some pets allowed (fee). | 476 U.S. Rte. 7 S | 802/775–1911 | fax 802/775–0113 | www.holidayinn-vermont.com | 150 rooms | $119–$299 | AE, D, DC, MC, V.

Howard Johnson Inn. A standard chain entry on busy Route 7 just south of downtown. Complimentary Continental breakfast. Cable TV, some in-room VCRs. Indoor pool. Sauna. Video games. Laundry facilities. Some pets allowed. | 378 S. Main St. | 802/775–4303 | fax 802/775–6840 | 98 rooms | $64–$149 | AE, D, DC, MC, V.

ST. ALBANS

Cadillac. A traditional, independent motel just south of downtown St. Albans. It is surrounded by 3½ acres of landscaped grounds and has a rock garden and a waterfall. Restaurant, picnic area. Refrigerators, cable TV. Pool. Pets allowed. | 213 S. Main St. | 802/524–2191 | fax 802/527–1483 | www.motel-cadillac.com | 54 rooms, 5 suites, 1 honeymoon suite | $55–$70, $75–$85 suites | AE, D, DC, MC, V.

Econo Lodge in St. Albans. This chain motel provides warm, inviting accommodations at affordable prices. Some rooms are handicapped accessible and pets are allowed in other rooms. Complimentary Continental breakfast. Refrigerators, cable TV. Pets allowed (fee). | 287 S. Main St. | 802/524–5956 or 800/55–ECONO | fax 802/524–5956 | econolake@aol.com | www.econolodge.com/hotel/vt022 | 29 rooms | $99 | AE, D, DC, MC, V.

ST. JOHNSBURY

Injun Joe Court. Tidy cabins in a scenic location on Joe's Pond, 10 mi west of St. Johnsbury. Kitchenettes. Beach, boating. Fishing. Pets allowed. | 3251 Rte. 2, West Denvill, 05873 | 802/684–3430 | 15 cabins | $40–$48 cabins | Closed mid-Oct.–mid-May | MC, V.

SPRINGFIELD

Holiday Inn Express. A smaller, no-frills representative of the chain that's just off Interstate 91 at Exit 7. Restaurant, bar, picnic area, complimentary Continental breakfast. In-room data ports, microwaves, some refrigerators, cable TV. Indoor pool. Exercise equipment. Business services. Pets allowed. | 818 Charlestown Rd. | 802/885–4516 | fax 802/885–4595 | hixpress@aol.com | 88 rooms | $125 | AE, D, DC, MC, V.

STOWE

Commodores Inn. A big, modern motel just south of Stowe village. Restaurant, complimentary Continental breakfast (off season). In-room data ports, some refrigerators, cable TV, some in-room VCRs. 2 pools (1 indoor), wading pool. Hot tubs. Exercise equipment. Video games. Business services. Pets allowed (fee). | 823 S. Main St. | 802/253–7131 or 800/447–8693 | fax 802/253–2360 | www.commodoresinn.com | 50 rooms | $112–$138 | AE, D, DC, MC, V.

Foster's Place. An affordable lodge on 18 acres with spectacular views of Mt. Mansfield. It has numerous amentities—not only is there a swimming pool, there is also a swimming hole and trout stream. In winter, the property's proximity to the ski resort is an added bonus. No smoking, no room phones, TV in common area. Pool. Spa. Hiking, volleyball. Fishing. Video games. Laundry facilities. Pets allowed (fee). | Rte. 108/4986 Mountain Rd. | 802/253–9404 or 800/330–4880 | fax 802/253–4470 | info@fosters-place.com | www.fosters-place.com | 32 rooms (6 with private bath), 3 houses | $39–$55 | AE, MC, V.

Green Mountain Inn. This 1833 inn, filled with antiques, is right in the center of Stowe and has a year-round heated outdoor pool. Rooms are in the main inn and an annex. Dining room, bar. Cable TV, in-room VCRs (and movies). Pool. Hot tub, massage. Exercise equipment. Business services. Pets allowed. | 18 Main St. | 802/253–7301 or 800/786–9346 | fax 802/253–5096 | grnmtninn@aol.com | www.greenmountaininn.com | 54 rooms, 24 suites, 1 house | $115–$209, $179 suites, $200 carriage house | AE, D, MC, V.

Innsbruck Inn. This mountainside inn with European flair, 4 mi west of Stowe has private accommodations in the chalet in addition to rooms in main lodge. Restaurant, bar, picnic area. Some kitchenettes, refrigerators, cable TV, some in-room VCRs. Pool. Hot tub. Exercise equipment. Cross-country skiing. Video games. Business services. Pets allowed (fee). | 4361 Mountain Rd. | 802/253–8582 or 800/225–8582 | fax 802/253–2260 | www.innsbruckinn.com | 28 rooms | $74–$169 | AE, D, MC, V.

Miguel's Stowe Away. Wide-planked floors and barn-board walls original to the 18th-century structure mix with a subtle Southwestern influence to give this lodging its unique charm. Restaurant, bar, complimentary breakfast. No smoking, cable TV, no room phones. Pool. Hot tub. Pets allowed. | 3148 Mountain Rd. | 802/253–7574 or 800/245–1240 | fax 802/253–5192 | www.miguels.com | 6 rooms | $80 | AE, D, DC, MC, V.

Mountain Road Resort. Small, well-appointed resort tucked away on flower-filled property, 1 mi north of Stowe. The French pétanque court is an unusual offering. It is the French equivalent to bocce ball, played on a flat, hard, gravel surface with metal and wood balls. Picnic area. Some kitchenettes, some microwaves, refrigerators, some in-room hot tubs, cable TV, in-room VCRs available. 2 pools (1 indoor). Hot tub. Tennis. Exercise equipment. Bicycles. Playground. Laundry facilities. Business services. Pets allowed (fee). | 1007 Mountain Rd. | 802/253–4566 or 800/367–6873 | fax 802/253–7397 | stowevt@aol.com | www.stowevtusa.com | 30 rooms, 7 suites, 7 apartments | $95–$189, $189–$380 suites, $179–$235 apartments | AE, D, DC, MC, V.

Notch Brook Condominium. This 16-acre compound with spectacular Mt. Mansfield views has a range of accommodations including three-bedroom apartments. There are fireplaces in some units. Complimentary Continental breakfast (in season). No air-conditioning, some kitchenettes, cable TV. Pool. Saunas. Tennis. Laundry facilities. Business services. Pets allowed (fee). | 1229 Notch Brook Rd. | 802/253–4882 or 800/253–4882 | fax 802/253–4882 | nbrook@sover.net | www.stoweinfo.com/saa/notchbrook | 49 rooms | $76–$195 | AE, DC, MC, V.

Riverside Inn. This inn, originally an 18th-century farmhouse, provides clean, tidy, and affordable accommodations next to a golf course and the Trapp Family Lodge. Ten rooms are in the main house and another six are part of a more recently built motel-style lodging. The common room has books and a fireplace. No air-conditioning in some rooms, no smoking, cable TV, some room phones, TV in common area. Hiking. Fishing. Cross-country skiing. Pets allowed. | 1965 Mountain Rd. | 802/253–4217, 800/966–4217, or 800/548–7568 | fax 802/253–4117 | rivinn@aol.com | www.gostowe.com/saa/riverside | 16 rooms (6 with shared bath) | $59–$89 | AE, MC, V.

Stowe Inn and Tavern at Little River. This inn is just a short walk from downtown, Mountain Road shops, and recreation path. Restaurant, bar, complimentary Continental breakfast. Some kitchenettes, some refrigerators, cable TV. Pool. Hot tub. Business services. Pets allowed. | 123 Mountain Rd. | 802/253–4836, 800/227–1108 eastern U.S | fax 802/253–7308 | www.stoweinn.com | 43 rooms | $99–$130 | AE, MC, V.

STRATTON MOUNTAIN

Liftline Lodge. Right at the Stratton slopes, this European-style chalet is a perfect place for skiers. Rooms are appointed with fine furnishings, richly colored carpets, fireplaces, stoves, and refrigerators. Restaurant. No air-conditioning in some rooms, in-room data ports, cable TV, some in-room VCRs. 2 outdoor pools. Hot tubs, saunas. Driving range, putting green. Exercise equipment. Business services. Pets allowed. | Stratton Mountain Rd., Stratton | 802/297-6100 or 800/787-2886 | fax 802/297-2949 | www.stratton.com | 77 rooms | $75–$150, $150–$300 apartments | AE, MC, V.

VERGENNES

Basin Harbor Club. A tidy and genteel traditional summer resort that sprawls away from its waterfront on Lake Champlain. There are fine views along the footpaths that meander among the cottages and to the main lodge and various sports facilities. A lovely place. Dining room, bar. Some refrigerators, TV in common area. Outdoor heated pool. Massage. 18-hole golf course, putting green, tennis. Gym, hiking, beach, dock, boating. Bicycles. Children's programs (ages 3–13). Laundry facilities. Business services. Airport shuttle. Pets allowed. | Basin Harbor Rd. | 802/475-2311 or 800/622-4000 | fax 802/475-6545 | res@basinharbor.com | www.basinharbor.com | 40 rooms, 77 cottages | $210–$270, $305–$425 cottages | Closed mid-Oct.–mid-May | MAP | MC, V.

WAITSFIELD

Millbrook Inn. Wide, worn pink plank floors greet you as you enter this Cape-style farmhouse. Rooms are individually appointed with period furniture, antique objets d'art, and handmade quilts. The price of the rooms includes breakfast and dinner during the peak seasons. Restaurant, complimentary breakfast. No air-conditioning, no smoking, no room phones, no TV. No kids under 6. Pets allowed. | Rte. 17/533 McCullough Hwy. | 802/496-2405 or 800/477-2809 | fax 802/496-9735 | millbrkinn@aol.com | www. millbrookinn.com | 7 rooms | $120–$140 | AE, MC, V.

WARREN

Golden Lion Riverside Inn. A motel on the ski area access road with a private river beach. Picnic area, complimentary breakfast. No air-conditioning, some kitchenettes, cable TV. Pets allowed. | 731 Rte. 100 | 802/496-3084 | fax 802/496-7438 | gldnlion@madriver.com | www.madriver.com/lodging/goldlion | 15 rooms | $49–$98 | AE, D, MC, V.

Powderhound Inn. A 19th-century farmhouse at the intersection of Route 100 and the Sugarbush Access Road, two of the main drags through the area. All guest quarters are apartments. Restaurant (in season only), picnic area. No air-conditioning, kitchenettes, cable TV. Pool. Hot tub. Tennis. Pets allowed (fee). | Rte. 100 | 802/496-5100 or 800/548-4022 | fax 802/496-5163 | www.powderhoundinn.com | 44 apartments | $70–$145 | AE, D, MC, V.

WATERBURY

Black Bear Inn. This mountaintop inn is in Bolton, 7 mi west of Waterbury. It is decorated with teddy bears of all shapes and sizes. Many of the rooms have gas fireplaces and balconies. Some have hot tubs. Restaurant, complimentary breakfast. No smoking, some in-room hot tubs, cable TV, no room phones. Pool. Hot tub. Tennis courts. Hiking. Pets allowed. | Bolton Access Rd., Bolton | 802/434-2126 or 800/395-6335 | fax 802/434-5161 | blkbear@wcvt.com | www.blkbearinn.com | 24 rooms | $135 | MC, V.

Holiday Inn. A full-service chain that is right off Interstate 89 and near Ben and Jerry's and Cold Hollow Cider Mill. Restaurant, bar with entertainment, picnic area, room service. In-room data ports, cable TV, some in-room VCRs. Pool. Sauna. Tennis. Video games. Laundry facilities. Business services. Pets allowed. | 45 Blush Hill Rd. | 802/244–7822 | fax 802/244–7822 | 79 rooms | $79–$109 | AE, D, DC, MC, V.

Old Stagecoach Inn. This 1820s inn is in the center of town. Antiques from America and abroad fill the rooms and common areas, giving the inn an authentic country flavor. The more inexpensive rooms share a bath. Dining room, bar, complimentary breakfast. No air-conditioning in some rooms, some kitchenettes, some refrigerators, no smoking, some room phones, TV in common area. Library. Pets allowed (fee). | 18 N. Main St. | 802/244–5056 or 800/262–2206 | fax 802/244–6956 | lodging@oldstagecoach.com | www.oldstagecoachinn.com | 8 rooms (3 share bath), 3 efficiencies | $55–$200 | AE, D, MC, V.

WHITE RIVER JUNCTION

Best Western at the Junction. A representative of the chain that is convenient to Interstates 89 and 91. Some microwaves, cable TV. Indoor pool, wading pool. Hot tub. Exercise equipment. Playground. Laundry facilities. Pets allowed (fee). | 306 N. Hartland Rd. | 802/295–3015 | fax 802/296–2581 | bestwesternjunct@cgnetworks.net | www.bestwestern.com | 112 rooms | $69–$139 | AE, D, DC, MC, V.

Ramada Inn. A full-service chain operation near Interstate 89 and Interstate 91. Restaurants, bar with entertainment. Room service, cable TV. Indoor pool. Hot tub. Putting green. Exercise equipment. Downhill skiing. Video games. Business services. Pets allowed. | 259 Holiday Dr. | 802/295–3000 | fax 802/295–3774 | 136 rooms | $135 | AE, D, MC, V.

WINDSOR

Mill Brook Bed-and-Breakfast. This 1878 farmhouse is directly across from the Mt. Ascutney ski slopes. The four sitting rooms and bedrooms have antiques and contemporary furnishings and are ornamented with such architectural details as scrolling on the baseboards. There's a gazebo next to the brook that provides a quiet, secluded place for lounging. Picnic area, complimentary breakfast. No air-conditioning, no smoking, no room phones, no TV. Hot tub. Volleyball. Fishing. Pets allowed (fee). | Rte. 44, Brownsville | 802/484–7283 | millbrook@outboundconnection.com | 2 rooms, 3 suites | $79–$129 | AE, MC, V.

WOODSTOCK

Kedron Valley Inn. There are fireplaces and woodstoves in some of the rooms at this riding-happy inn 5 mi south of Woodstock. The rooms also have queen-size canopy beds and gorgeous quilts. Restaurant, bar. No air-conditioning in some rooms, no room phones. Pond. Business services. Pets allowed. | Rte. 106, South Woodstock | 802/457–1473 or 800/836–1193 | fax 802/457–4469 | kedroninn@aol.com | www.innformation.com/vt/kedron | 28 rooms | $120–$230 | Closed Apr. | MAP | D, MC, V.

Three Church Street. The unique charms of this Georgian mansion include a 19th-century music room, adorned with chandeliers, couches, and a Steinway. Although the inn is in the middle of the village, the porch overlooks the Ottauquechee River and Mount Tom. Rooms have such details as four-poster beds and antiques. Complimentary breakfast. No smoking, no room phones, no TV in some rooms, TV in common area. Pets allowed. | 3 Church St. | 802/457–1925 | fax 802/457–9181 | 3chrch@aol.com | www.scenesofvermont.com/3church | 11 rooms | $80–$115 | MC, V.

Village Inn of Woodstock. Brass beds, wicker furniture, and Laura Ashley prints fill the rooms of this Victorian country inn. Two common areas provide room for watching TV or relaxing next to a fire. A shaded perennial garden occupies the backyard where you can relax and enjoy the afternoon. Complimentary breakfast. No smoking, some in-room hot tubs, no room phones, no TV in some rooms, TV in common area. Pets allowed.

| 41 Pleasant St. | 802/457–1255 or 800/722–4571 | fax 802/457–3109 | villageinn@aol.com
| www.villageinnofwoodstock.com | 8 rooms | $130–$240 | AE, D, MC, V.

Winslow House. This secluded farmhouse built in 1872 once presided over a dairy farm that reached down to the banks of the Ottauquechee River. Guest quarters are uncommonly spacious, with separate sitting rooms and attractive antiques. Complimentary breakfast. Refrigerators, no smoking, cable TV. Cross-country skiing, downhill skiing. Pets allowed. | 492 Woodstock Rd., 05091 | 802/457–1820 | fax 802/457–1820 | www.pbpub.com/winslowhouse | 5 rooms | $115–$150 | D, DC, MC, V.

Virginia

ALEXANDRIA

Alexandria Suites. Choose from studios, one-, and two-bedroom units, all with full kitchens. Though designed for corporate travelers, it's also a comfortable option for families. Take Exit 3A off I–395. Complimentary breakfast. Kitchenettes, microwaves, refrigerators, cable TV. Pool. Gym. Laundry facilities, laundry service. Business services, free parking. Pets allowed. | 420 N Van Dorn St. 22304 | 703/370–1000 or 800/368–3339 | fax 703/370–1000 | alexandriasuites@erols.com | www.alexandriasuites.com | 185 suites | $89–$173 | AE, D, DC, MC, V.

Alexandria Travelodge. A convenient choice if you're traveling in or out of Reagan National Airport, this two-story chain, renovated in 1999, is 1½ mi south of the airport. In-room data ports, some microwaves, some refrigerators, cable TV. Pets allowed. | 700 N. Washington St. 22314 | 703/836–5100 | fax 703/519–7015 | 40 rooms | $55–$95 | AE, D, MC, V.

Best Western Old Colony Inn. The only thing "old colony" about this Best Western is its location not far from Alexandria's Old Town. The courtyard rooms are bright and have pleasant views. Complimentary Continental breakfast. In-room data ports, cable TV. Pool. Business services. Airport shuttle. Free parking. Some pets allowed (fee). | 615 1st St. 22314 | 703/739–2222 | fax 703/549–2568 | www.bestwestern.com | 151 rooms | $90–$105 | AE, D, DC, MC, V.

Comfort Inn Gunston Corner. Five miles south of Mount Vernon (Exit 163, I–95), this motor lodge is in a quiet, residential neighborhood close to Grist Mill Historical Park. Rooms face the pool and residential neighborhood. Complimentary Continental breakfast. Cable TV. Pool. Business services. Some pets allowed (fee). | 8180 Silverbrook Rd., Lorton, 22079 | 703/643–3100 | fax 703/643–3175 | www.ci.gunstun.com | 129 rooms | $80–$90 | AE, D, DC, MC, V.

Comfort Inn–Mt. Vernon. This two-floor, suburban Comfort Inn is just off the Capital Beltway, a mammoth-laned expressway that zips Washington-area commuters from home to work (when they're not sitting in traffic). Rooms are predictably characterless. Complimentary Continental breakfast. In-room data ports, microwaves, cable TV. Pool. Business services. Free parking. Some pets allowed. | 7212 Richmond Hwy./U.S. 1 22306 | 703/765–9000 | fax 703/765–2325 | www.comfortinn.com | 92 rooms | $65–$85 | AE, D, DC, MC, V.

Doubletree Guest Suites. Five miles from Old Town, this all-suite hotel is a converted apartment complex in a residential area near the Metro and shopping at Landmark Mall. Rooms view the Potomac and courtyard. Restaurant, bar, complimentary Continental breakfast. In-room data ports, kitchenettes, microwaves, cable TV. Pool. Exercise equipment. Laundry facilities. Business services. Pets allowed (fee). | 100 S. Reynolds St. 22304 | 703/370–9600 | fax 703/370–0467 | www.doubletreehotels.com | 225 suites | $109–$119 | AE, D, DC, MC, V.

Econo Lodge Old Town. In the heart of Old Town, the budget choice is close to historical sites, shopping, and dining. The motel is housed in a multileveled stone building in a more commercial area of Old Town. Cable TV. Business services. Airport shuttle. Some pets allowed. | 700 N. Washington St. 22314 | 703/836–5100 | fax 703/519–7015 | www.choicehotels.com | 39 rooms | $65 | AE, D, DC, MC, V.

Executive Club Suites. This all-suites, luxury complex on the north end of Old Town Alexandria has apartment-style units, furnished with rich Queen Anne reproductions and complete with cookware and dinnerware in the kitchenettes. Picnic area, complimentary Continental breakfast. In-room data ports, kitchenettes, microwaves, cable TV. Exercise equipment, gym, health club, sauna. Pool. Laundry facilities. Business services. Airport shuttle. Parking (fee). Some pets allowed. | 610 Bashford La. 22314 | 703/739–2582 or 800/535–2582 | fax 703/548–0266 | www.dcexeclub.com | 78 suites | $179–$199 | AE, D, DC, MC, V.

Hampton Inn–Olde Towne. This chain hotel in a bland stone multiple-level building is convenient to both I–95 and 395. Rooms are comfortable and bright. Restaurant, bar. In-room data ports, room service, some in-room hot tubs, cable TV. Indoor pool. Beauty salon. Exercise equipment. Business services. Airport shuttle. Free parking. Some pets allowed. | 5821 Richmond Hwy./U.S. 1 22303 | 703/329–1400 | fax 703/329–1424 | www.hojo.com | 156 rooms | $99–$109 | AE, D, DC, MC, V.

Holiday Inn Select Old Town. This high-end Holiday Inn is across the street from Alexandria's town hall in the Old Town and is within convenient walking distance to the Metro and the waterfront. The lobby is elegantly put together in mahogany with chandelier lighting. Rooms are colonial-themed with a long list of amenities. Every Sunday there is a colorful market on the town square across the street. Restaurant, bars, complimentary Continental breakfast. In-room data ports, in-room safes, some in-room kitchenettes, minibars, microwaves, cable TV, some in-room VCRs. Indoor pool. Barbershop, beauty salon. Exercise equipment. Laundry facilities. Business services. Airport shuttle. Some pets allowed. | 480 King St. 22314 | 703/549–6080 or 800/368–5047 | fax 703/684–6508 | othismta@erols.com | www.hiselect.com | 227 rooms | $169–$190 | AE, D, DC, MC, V.

Radisson Hotel–Old Town. Convenient to monuments and museums, the 12-floor high-rise has rooms with gorgeous views of the low-slung Washington D.C. skyline. Rooms are conservative in darker-hued colors. Restaurant, bar. In-room data ports, microwaves, cable TV. Pool. Business services. Airport shuttle. Some pets allowed. | 901 N. Fairfax St. 22314 | 703/683–6000 | fax 703/683–7597 | www.ramada.com | 253 rooms | $159–$249 | AE, D, DC, MC, V.

Red Roof Inn. This three-floor motor lodge with exterior corridors is less than a mile from the Capital Beltway, the traffic artery that encircles Washington. Rooms are simply furnished in conservative colors. In-room data ports, cable TV. Laundry facilities. Business services. Free parking. Some pets allowed. | 5975 Richmond Hwy./U.S. 1 22303 | 703/960–5200 | fax 703/960–5209 | www.redroofinn.com | 115 rooms | $59–$79 | AE, D, DC, MC, V.

Sheraton Suites. In the heart of Old Town, the distinctive U-shaped, 10-floor building that houses this hotel is high enough that the upper rooms have decent views of the Washington skyline. Rooms are bright with prominent windows. Restaurant, bar, complimentary Continental breakfast. In-room data ports, refrigerators, cable TV. Indoor pool. Hot tub. Exercise equipment. Business services. Airport shuttle. Some pets allowed. | 801 N. St. Asaph St. 22314 | 703/836–4700 | fax 703/548–4514 | www.ittsheraton.com | 247 suites | $99–$139 | AE, D, DC, MC, V.

ARLINGTON

Best Western Key Bridge. A half-block from the Rosslyn Metro station, this hotel, housed in a high-rise building, is within walking distance to Georgetown and only a short Metro ride away from Washington, D.C.'s numerous museums and cultural attractions. Restaurant. Some microwaves, cable TV. Pool. Exercise equipment. Business services. Some pets allowed. | 1850 N. Fort Myer Dr. 22219 | 703/522–0400 | fax 703/524–5275 | www.bestwestern.com | 178 rooms | $139 | AE, D, DC, MC, V.

Doubletree–Reagan National Airport. The Pentagon, National Airport, and shops are all close to this gigantic hotel. The rooms are designed in warm beige and neutral hues and have large windows. Restaurant, bar with entertainment. In-room data ports, some microwaves, cable TV. Indoor pool. Sauna. Business services. Airport shuttle. Free parking Some pets allowed. | 300 Army-Navy Dr. 22202 | 703/416–4147 | fax 703/416–4126 | www.doubletreehotels.com | 632 rooms, 265 suites | $100–$149, $200–$400 suites | AE, D, DC, MC, V.

Executive Club Suites. In a residential area, this all-suites hotel has a columned entrance and chandeliers. The otherwise conservatively furnished suite rooms are lightened by large windows. Picnic area, complimentary Continental breakfast. Kitchenettes, microwaves, refrigerators, cable TV. Exercise equipment. Pool. Hot tub. Laundry facilities. Business services. Airport shuttle. Free parking. Some pets allowed (fee). | 108 S. Courthouse Rd. 22204 | 703/522–2582 or 877/316–2582 | fax 703/486–2694 | www.dcexeclub.com | 74 suites | $159–$179 suites | AE, D, DC, MC, V.

Holiday Inn National Airport. Just ½ mi from the airport, this Holiday Inn has rooms dressed in dark drapery to keep out the distant roar of landing jets. Restaurant, bar. In-room data ports, cable TV. Pool. Business services. Airport shuttle. Some pets allowed. | 2650 Jefferson Davis Hwy./U.S. 1 22202 | 703/682–7200 | fax 703/684–3217 | www.holiday-inn.com | 280 rooms | $114–$180 | AE, D, DC, MC, V.

Holiday Inn Rosslyn Westpark. Not just another link in the national chain, this high-rise hotel overlooks the Potomac River in the commercial Rosslyn area of Arlington. Rooms, brightly festooned in rose and green, have large windows, and views of D.C. and the Potomac. One block from the Rosslyn Metro Station. Restaurant, bar. In-room data ports, some refrigerators, cable TV. Indoor pool. Exercise equipment. Laundry facilities. Business services. Some pets allowed. | 1900 N. Ft. Myer Dr. 22209 | 703/807–2000 | fax 703/522–7480 | www.holiday-inn.com | 306 rooms | $120–$140 | AE, D, DC, MC, V.

Hyatt Arlington. This hotel near Key Bridge and next to the Metro is another elegant high-rise that forms the futuristic skyline just across the Potomac from D.C. With low-lighting and deep dark furniture, the rooms are enlivened by the appointment of flowers and plants. Restaurant, bars. In-room data ports, cable TV. Exercise equipment. Business services. Some pets allowed. | 1325 Wilson Blvd. 22209 | 703/525–1234 | fax 703/525–1476 | www.hyatt.com | 302 rooms | $129–$230 | AE, D, DC, MC, V.

Marriott Crystal Gateway. The eighteen floors of this asymmetrically designed, luxury high-rise hotel have bright rooms with fresh flowers and wall art. Restaurant, bar. In-room data ports, cable TV. Indoor-outdoor pool. Hot tub. Exercise equipment. Business services. Airport shuttle. Some pets allowed. | 1700 Jefferson Davis Hwy./U.S. 1 22202 | 703/920–3230 | fax 703/271–5212 | www.marriott.com/marriott/wasgw | 697 rooms, 17 suites | $119–$209, $199–$300 suites | AE, D, DC, MC, V.

Quality Hotel Courthouse Plaza. Two blocks from Courthouse Metro, the property has a movie theater on premises and an urban garden with flowers and flower bushes. Rooms have lots of lighting and walk-out balconies overlooking the gardens. Restaurant, bar. In-room data ports, cable TV. Pool. Exercise equipment. Laundry facilities. Business services. Some pets allowed. | 1200 N. Courthouse Rd./U.S. Route 50 22201 | 703/524–4000 or 888/987–2555 | fax 703/522–6814 | www.qualityhotelarlington.com | 391 rooms | $90–$120 | AE, D, DC, MC, V.

Virginian Suites. Atop a hill one block from the Iwo Jima Memorial, this 10-story hotel has rooms, studios, and one-bedroom suites, all with full kitchens and dishwashers. In-room data ports, kitchenettes, microwaves, refrigerators, cable TV. Gym. Laundry service. Business services. Pets allowed. | 1500 Arlington Blvd. 22209 | 703/522–9600 or 800/275–2866 | fax 703/525–4462 | www.virginiansuites.com | 262 rooms | $118–$135 | AE, D, DC, MC, V.

ASHLAND

Comfort Inn. In downtown Ashland, this relaxed hotel is close to Randolph-Macon University. Rooms are brightly lit and look out on the neighborhood. Complimentary Continental breakfast. Some refrigerators, cable TV. Pool. Exercise equipment. Laundry facilities. Business services. Some pets allowed. | 101 Cottage Green Dr. | 804/752–7777 | fax 804/798–0327 | www.comfortinn.com | 126 rooms | $59–$79 | AE, D, DC, MC, V.

Sky Chalet Mountain Top Lodge. Opened in 1937, this rustic lodge sits on 14 acres atop Supin Lick Ridge, with magnificent views of the surrounding mountains. Accommodations are spartan but comfortable, with living room fireplaces warming some suites, and decks to take in the scenery. Complimentary Continental breakfast. Some kitchenettes, no air-conditioning, no room phones, no TV. Hiking. Some pets allowed. | 280 Sky Chalet La. 22810 | 540/856–2147 or 877/TOP–VIEW | fax 540/856–2436 | 5 suites | $34–$79 | D, DC, MC, V.

BASYE

Best Western Shenandoah Valley. The colonial-styled two-story hotel near Bryce Resort has a large front lawn, blue and red roof and an old cannon on the front lawn. Large windows frame the bright, simple rooms. Restaurant, bar. Cable TV. Pool, wading pool. Tennis. Playground. Business services. Some pets allowed. | 250 Conicksville Rd., Mt. Jackson, 22842 | 540/477–2911 | fax 540/477–2392 | www.bestwestern.com | 98 rooms | $54–$65 | AE, D, DC, MC, V.

Widow Kip's. This quaint country house, has a shrub-lined walkway, and is peaceful and sunny. The country-style rooms have dark wood furniture, lace canopies, flowers, and lots of quilts and plaids. Picnic lunches are available. Complimentary breakfast. No smoking, TV only in common area, cable TV, no room phones. Pool. Bicycles. Some pets allowed. | 355 Orchard Dr., Mt. Jackson, 22842 | 540/477–2400 or 800/478–8714 | widokips@shentel.net | www.widowkips.com | 5 rooms; 2 cottages | $70–$90, $90–$95 cottages | MC, V.

BIG STONE GAP

Country Inn Motel. The 1950s era brick motel with exterior corridors is near Jefferson National Forest, on the outskirts of town. Rooms are basic and bright with pictures adorning the walls and lamps by the bedside. Cable TV. Business services. Some pets allowed. | 627 Gilley Ave. 24219 | 540/523–0374 | fax 540/523–5043 | 42 rooms | $45–$51 | AE, D, DC, MC, V.

BLACKSBURG

Comfort Inn. This bright and roomy hotel conveniently close to Interstate 81 is not far from Virginia Tech. Complimentary Continental breakfast. In-room data ports, cable TV. Pool. Exercise equipment. Business services. Some pets allowed. Free parking. | 3705 S. Main St. 24060 | 540/951–1500 | fax 540/951–1530 | www.comfortinn.com | 80 rooms | $62–$72 | AE, D, DC, MC, V.

Days Inn. This two-floor hotel with exterior corridors prides itself for its "southern hospitality." The hotel is in a commercial area, eight mi south of Blacksburg, 15 minutes from Virginia Tech. Rooms are basic, and neutral colored. Across the street is a Cracker Barrel restaurant. Complimentary Continental breakfast. In-room data ports, cable TV. Pool.

Playground. Some pets allowed. | U.S. 11, Christiansburg, 24073 | 540/382–0261 | fax 540/382–0365 | 122 rooms | $56–$64 | AE, D, DC, MC, V.

Ramada Inn Limited. This hotel has a drive-thru entrance and the Ramada signature white tower. Rooms are simple with scenic view of the hotel's parking lot. 2 mi from the Virginia Tech campus. Restaurant, bar. Room service, cable TV. Pool, wading pool. Laundry facilities. Cross-country skiing. Business services. Some pets allowed. Free parking. | 3503 Holiday La. 24060 | 540/951–1330 | fax 540/951–4847 | www.ramada.com | 98 rooms | $50–$125 | AE, D, DC, MC, V.

BLUE RIDGE PARKWAY
Waynesboro/Afton Mountain Holiday Inn. Atop Afton Mountain, this three-story, white-brick hotel has breathtaking views of the Rockfish Valley below. The hotel stands at the northern end of the Blue Ridge Parkway, near the junction of Skyline Drive. Restaurant, bar, room service. Cable TV. Pool. Business services. Pets allowed. | Junction of I–64 (Exit 99) and U.S. 250 22980 | 540/942–5201 or 800/465–4329 | fax 540/943–8746 | 118 rooms | $73–$91 | AE, D, DC, MC, V.

BRISTOL
Econo Lodge Bristol. A two-story chain option that's 2½ mi south of I–381 at Exit 3. The Omelet Shoppe, open 24 hours, is next door. Some microwaves, some refrigerators, cable TV. Pets allowed. | 912 Commonwealth Ave. 24201 | 540/466–2112 | 48 rooms | $33–$56 | AE, D, DC, MC, V.

Holiday Inn Bristol. This 10-story hotel is just off I–81 at Exit 7, on the northeast side of town. The hotel caters to businesses, with conference facilities and meeting rooms. Restaurant, bar, room service. In-room data ports, some kitchenettes, some microwaves, cable TV. Pool. Hot tub. Gym. Laundry service. Business services. Pets allowed. | 3005 Linden Dr. 24202 | 540/466–4100 or 888/466–4141 | fax 540/466–4103 | 226 rooms | $74–$189 | AE, D, DC, MC, V.

La Quinta Inn Bristol. The inn in a white stone building has comfortable rooms dressed in a conservative blue and green color scheme and floral and stripe prints. Complimentary breakfast. Pool. Some pets allowed. | 1014 Old Airport Rd. | 540/669–9353 | fax 540/669–6974 | www.laquinta.com | 123 rooms | $52 | AE, D, DC, MC, V.

Red Carpet Inn. This redbrick hotel is in a valley and has a courtyard. Rooms are comfortable, and have sliding glass doors to balconies that overlook the courtyard. Cable TV. Pool. Business services. Some pets allowed. | 15589 Lee Hwy. 24202 | 540/669–1151 | 60 rooms | $46 | AE, D, DC, MC, V.

Super 8. A member of the budget chain, this three-floor hotel in a commercial area has simple modest rooms. Just minutes from downtown Bristol. Picnic area. Some microwaves, refrigerators, cable TV. Business services. Some pets allowed. | 2139 Lee Hwy, Exit 4000 24201 | 540/466–8800 | fax 540/466–8800 | www.super8.com | 62 rooms | $37–$120 | AE, D, DC, MC, V.

BROOKNEAL
Comfort Suites Hotel. Conservative, quaintly well-appointed rooms are offered at the chain hotel, almost 27 mi west of Brookneal. Complimentary Continental breakfast. Some in-room hot tubs, cable TV. Business services. Some pets allowed. | 1558 Main St., Altavista, 24517 | 804/369–4000 | fax 804/369–4007 | www.comfortsuites.com | 65 suites | $68–$90 | AE, D, DC, MC, V.

CAPE CHARLES
Pickett's Harbor. On Chesapeake Bay, the inn offers 27 acres of private beach. The rooms, which are furnished with antiques, all face the bay. Complimentary breakfast. No TV in

rooms. Beach. Fishing. Some pets allowed. | 28288 Nottingham Ridge La. 23310 | 757/331–2212 | pickharb@aol.com | 6 rooms | $110–$150 | No credit cards.

CHARLOTTESVILLE

Best Western Cavalier Inn. Convenient to the University of Virginia campus, this hotel is just three blocks from Barracks Road Shopping Center. The comfortable lobby has a library with many books to choose from and a large overstuffed chair, and the rooms are just as relaxed. For two-day stays, inquire about the Getaway plan. Cable TV. Pool. Business services. Airport shuttle. Some pets allowed. Free parking. | 105 Emmet St. 22903 | 804/296–8111 | fax 804/296–3523 | www.bestwestern.com | 118 rooms | $69–$99 | AE, D, DC, MC, V.

Best Western–Mount Vernon. This large motel has six two-bedroom suites available, and large rooms. Easy access to Monticello and the University of Virginia. Cable TV. Pool, wading pool. Business services. Some pets allowed. | 1613 Emmet St. 22901 | 804/296–5501 | fax 804/977–6249 | www.bestwestern.com | 110 rooms | $56–$68 | AE, D, DC, MC, V.

Days Inn. This chain hotel has a landscaped courtyard, which some of the more comfortable rooms face. Conveniently close to the University of Virginia and the interstate.Restaurant, bar. In-room data ports, room service, cable TV. Outdoor pool, wading pool. Sauna. Exercise equipment. Business services. Airport shuttle. Some pets allowed. Free parking. | 1600 Emmet St. 22901 | 804/293–9111 | fax 804/977–2780 | 129 rooms | $70–$80 | AE, D, DC, MC, V.

Knights Inn. On Route 29, a main commercial thoroughfare, this popular one-floor motel is quite close to shops and restaurants. Rooms are relaxed and well-appointed, with private entries. Some kitchenettes, cable TV. Pool. Business services. Some pets allowed. | 1300 Seminole Trail 22901 | 804/973–8133 | fax 804/973–1168 | www.knightsinnofcharlottesville.com | 115 rooms | $49–$68 | AE, D, DC, MC, V.

Omni. The sleek ultramodern architecture of this hotel cuts a rakish knife-like pose among the buildings making up the low skyline of the pedestrian Downtown Mall. In the lobby, true to form, there is a fairly flamboyant seven-story gardened atrium. Rooms are well-apportioned (the standard size being 250 square feet), and modern. Restaurant, bar. Cable TV. In-room data ports. 2 pools (1 indoor). Hot tub. Massage. Exercise equipment. Business services. Some pets allowed. | 235 W. Main St. 22902 | 804/971–5500 | fax 804/979–4456 | www.omnihotels.com | 204 rooms | $124–$169 | AE, D, DC, MC, V.

University Econo Lodge. A popular choice for parents of students at the University of Virginia, this chain motel is across the street from the school's sports arena, and fills up on weekends and when football games are played. Some microwaves, some refrigerators, cable TV. Pets allowed ($5). | 400 Emmet St. 22903 | 804/977–5591 | 60 rooms | $60–$75 | AE, D, DC, MC, V.

CHESAPEAKE

Red Roof Inn Chesapeake. A half mile north of Greenbrier Mall, this two-story, moderately priced chain lodging stands near I-64 at Exit 289–A. Some in-room data ports, some microwaves, some refrigerators, cable TV. Pets allowed. | 724 Woodlake Dr. 23320 | 757/523–0123 | fax 757/523–4763 | 108 rooms | $41–$53 | AE, D, DC, MC, V.

Super 8 Motel Churchland. This two-story, Tudor-style chain motel sits just off I-664, Exit 8B. In-room data ports, some refrigerators, cable TV. Pets allowed. | 3216 Churchland Blvd. 23321 | 757/686–8888 | fax 757/686–8888, ext. 403 | 59 rooms | $41–$75 | AE, D, DC, MC, V.

Wellesley Inn. This modern corporate chain hotel has coffee makers in all the rooms, and love seats and pull-out sofas in some rooms. The hotel is 10 minutes from the beach, and within walking distance to several malls and a supermarket. Complimentary Continental breakfast. Microwaves, refrigerators, cable TV. Pool. Laundry facilities. Business services. Pets allowed (fee). Free parking. | 721 Conference Center Dr. 23320 | 757/366–0100 | fax 757/366–0396 | 106 rooms; 16 suites | $89–$149 | AE, D, DC, MC, V.

CHINCOTEAGUE

Lighthouse Inn. This modest, two-story motel has screened-in patios and is within walking distance of downtown, and just minutes from NASA's Wallops Flight Facility Visitors Center. Picnic area. Refrigerators, microwaves, cable TV. Pool. Hot tub. Some pets allowed (fee). | 4218 Main St. | 757/336–5091 | 17 rooms | $69–$89 | Closed Dec.–Feb. | MC, V.

CLIFTON FORGE

Longdale Inn. This dusty-rose, gingerbread-trimmed Victorian inn is listed on the National Register of Historic Places. Built in 1873 for the Firmstone family and the Board of Directors of the Longdale Iron Works, it has been an inn since 1938 and was restored in 1989 and 1991. Rooms come in a variety of styles from Victorian to Southwestern to European, and period antiques populate the nooks and corners of the inn. Picnic area, complimentary breakfast. No air-conditioning, no smoking, no TV in rooms, no room phones, TV and VCR in common area. Playground. Business services. Some pets allowed. | 6209 Longdale Furnace Rd. | 540/862–0892 | fax 540/862–3554 | www.bbonline.com/va/longdale | 10 rooms (3 with shower only, 4 with shared bath), 2 suites | $80–$100, $130 suites | AE, D, MC, V.

COVINGTON

Best Western–Mountain View. The chain hostelry is close to the interstate. Rooms are painted in comfortable colors and sufficiently furnished. Restaurant, bar, complimentary breakfast, room service. In-room data ports, some refrigerators, cable TV. Pool, wading pool. Business services. Pets allowed (fee). Free parking. | 820 E. Madison St./U.S. 60 | 540/962–4951 | fax 540/965–5714 | www.bestwestern.com | 79 rooms | $74–$99 | AE, D, DC, MC, V.

Budget Inn Motel. How many chain motels let you cast a line into a quiet stretch of river looping through the backyard? This two-story lodging sits on the western edge of town, along the Jackson River and adjacent to the James Burke House Eatery. Room service. Some in-room data ports, microwaves, refrigerators, cable TV. Fishing. Laundry service. Business services. Pets allowed ($10). | 420 N. Monroe Ave. 24426 | 540/962–3966 | 30 rooms | $70 | AE, D, DC, MC, V.

Comfort Inn. Two miles southeast of Covington, this Comfort Inn has beautiful mountain views from its rooms and facilities. coffee makers and irons are in every rooms. Restaurant, bar. Complimentary Continental breakfast. Some refrigerators, cable TV. Pool. Hot tub. Business services. Pets allowed (fee). | 203 Interstate Dr. | 540/962–2141 | fax 540/965–0964 | www.comfortinn.com | 98 rooms, 32 suites | $72–$74, $81 suites | AE, D, DC, MC, V.

Knights Court. A comfortable small, standard hotel, with easy interstate access. Rooms are coordinated in dark muted colors. Complimentary Continental breakfast. Some kitchenettes, microwaves, refrigerators, cable TV. Some pets allowed. | 908 Valley Ridge Rd. | 540/962–7600 | fax 540/965–4926 | 72 rooms | $57–$65 | AE, D, DC, MC, V.

Milton Hall Bed and Breakfast. Built in 1874 out of solid brick, this Gothic Victorian inn has period antiques, reproduction furniture, and fireplaces to warm yourself. The building is on 44 acres and has lush gardens for wandering. Adjacent is the George Washington National forest. Complimentary breakfast. TV in rooms, common area, common area phone. Some pets allowed. No smoking. | 207 Thorny La. | 540/965–0196 | www.miltonhall.com | 6 rooms (3 with shower only), 1 suite | $100–$150 suite | MC, V.

CULPEPER

Comfort Inn. In downtown Culpeper, this fully-carpeted hotel has coffee makers in every room, and some king-size beds and nonsmoking rooms available. Rooms are conservatively furnished. Complimentary Continental breakfast. In-room data ports, cable TV. Pool. Business services. Pets allowed (fee). | 890 Willis La. | 540/825–4900 | fax 540/825–4904 | www.comfortinn.com | 49 rooms | $60–$85 | AE, D, DC, MC, V.

Graves' Mountain Lodge. This family-run resort lodge is on a peaceful, 135-year-old working farm with apple orchards and cattle, six mi west of Culpeper next to Shenandoah National Park. With many different lodgings to choose from, you can stay in anything from a motel-like room to a rustic log cabin by a running river, to a renovated one-room schoolhouse. Box lunches are available. Dining room, picnic area. Pool. Tennis. Playground, laundry facilities. Business services. Some pets allowed. | Rte. 670, Syria, 22743 | 540/923–4231 | fax 540/923–4312 | www.gravesmountain.com | 48 rooms; 13 cottages | $132–$195, $110–$230 cottages | Closed Dec.–mid-Mar. | AP | D, MC, V.

DANVILLE

Stratford Inn. This brown-brick hotel, built in the 1970s, has a variety of room layouts, from rooms with king-size beds and hot tubs to more standard accommodations. All rooms are comfortable and plainly furnished. Restaurant, bar, complimentary breakfast. Room service, cable TV. Pool, wading pool. Hot tub. Exercise equipment. Laundry facilities. Business services, conference center. Some pets allowed. Free parking. | 2500 Riverside Dr./U.S. 58 24540 | 804/793–2500 or 800/326–8455 | fax 804/793–6960 | www.stratford-inn.com | 152 rooms, 5 suites | $55–$65, $85–$150 suites | AE, D, DC, MC, V.

EMPORIA

Brunswick Mineral Springs. A 1,200-foot driveway with stone columns off U.S. 58 leads you to a huge oak grove and plantation house built in 1785, 20 minutes west of Emporia. The three guest suites are named in honor of people who were laid to rest in the adjacent family cemetery. Enjoy your breakfast on the glassed-in porch; dinner is served with china and crystal in the formal dining room. Dining room, complimentary breakfast, complimentary dinner. Cable TV, no TV in some rooms, TV in common area. Hiking. Library. Laundry service. Some pets allowed (fee). No children under 18. | 14910 Western Mill Rd., Lawrenceville 23868 | 804/848–4010 | fax 804/848–9110 | nanny@jnent.com | www.brunswickmineralspring.com | 3 rooms | $105–$125 | No credit cards.

Comfort Inn. This chain hotel is 1.4 mi outside of Emporia (Exit 8, I–95). Rooms are furnished in standard corporate hostelry style. Complimentary Continental breakfast. In-room data ports, cable TV. Pool. Playground. Fishing. Business services. Some pets allowed. | 1411 Skipper's Rd. 10960 | 804/348–3282 | fax 804/348–3282 | www.comfortinn.com | 96 rooms | $49–$60 | AE, D, DC, MC, V.

Hampton Inn. The chain hotel is northwest of the Emporia, adjacent to a Shoney's Restaurant, the Sadlers Truck Plaza and a Cactus Steakhouse. Rooms painted in neutral tones are comfortably equipped with desks, and depending on the room, easy chairs and sofas. Nearby is the Interstate–95 and U.S. Route 58 interchange. Complimentary Continental breakfast. Some microwaves, refrigerators, cable TV. Pool. Some pets allowed. | 1207 W. Atlantic St. 10960 | 804/634–9200 | fax 804/348–0071 | www.hampton-inn.com | 115 rooms | $62–$70 | AE, D, DC, MC, V.

FAIRFAX

Holiday Inn Fair Oaks Mall. Adjacent to Fair Oaks Mall, this large hotel has an enclosed garden-like atrium. Rooms either have exterior windows or balconies that open up to the atrium, and are all well-appointed with a reasonable list of amenities. Restaurant, bar with entertainment. In-room data ports, cable TV. Indoor pool. Exercise equipment. Video games. Laundry facilities. Business services. Airport shuttle. Some pets allowed. | 11787 Lee Jackson Hwy. 22033 | 703/352–2525 | fax 703/352–4471 | www.holiday-inn.com | 312 rooms | $129–$195 | AE, D, DC, MC, V.

Homestead Village Guest Studios. This hotel caters to the business traveler on an extended visit. The burgundy-, green-, and beige-toned rooms each have a fully stocked kitchenette that's set off from the carpeted living area with a tile floor. In-room data ports, kitchenettes, microwaves, refrigerators, cable TV, some in-room VCRs, room phones. Laundry facilities, laundry service. Pets allowed (fee). | 8281 Willow Oaks Corporate Dr. 22031 | 703/204-0088 or 888/782-9473 | fax 703/204-2741 | 130 rooms | $89-$109 | AE, D, DC, MC, V.

Wellesley Inn. This white stone hotel was built in 1980. The muted tones, sofas, and chairs in the lobby create a peaceful place to relax, read, or wait for friends. Each room is equipped with a coffee maker and hair dryer. Dining room, complimentary Continental breakfast. In-room data ports, some microwaves, some refrigerators, cable TV, room phones, TV in common area. Laundry service. Some pets allowed (fee). | 10327 Lee Hwy. 22030 | 703/359-2888 or 800/444-8888 | fax 703/385-9186 | www.wellesleyinnandsuites.com | 82 rooms | $114 | AE, D, DC, MC, V.

FARMVILLE

Super 8. Popular with construction workers and parents of university students, this chain hotel is located five minutes from Farmville's business district. The lobby has a love seat and breakfast bar that's open until 11AM. Complimentary Continental breakfast. Some microwaves, some refrigerators, cable TV, room phones. Pets allowed. | Hwy. 15, at Hwy. 460 23901 | 804/392-8196 | 42 rooms | $70 | AE, D, DC, MC, V.

FREDERICKSBURG

Best Western. This red-brick chain hotel opened in April, 2000. All rooms have hair dryers and coffee makers. A sports bar, restaurant, and lounge are nearby. Complimentary Continental breakfast. In-room data ports, some microwaves, some refrigerators, cable TV, room phones, TV in common area. Outdoor pool. Laundry facilities, laundry service. Some pets allowed. | 2205 William St. 22401 | 540/371-5050 or 800/937-8376 | fax 540/373-3496 | 107 rooms | $75 | AE, D, DC, MC, V.

Best Western Central Plaza. The motor lodge is between the Spotsylvania Mall and Central Park, two mi from historic Fredericksburg, and a mile from Mary Washington College. Rooms, painted light colors, are made comfortable with floral arrangements. Complimentary Continental breakfast. Cable TV. Laundry facilities. Business services. Some pets allowed. Free parking. | 3000 Plank Rd. 22401 | 540/786-7404 | fax 540/785-7415 | www.bestwestern.com | 76 rooms | $40-$82 | AE, D, DC, MC, V.

Days Inn–North. This two-story hotel has exterior room entrances, and is quite close to Fredericksburg's historic district. Easy interstate access is also a plus. Complimentary Continental breakfast. Cable TV. Pool. Business services. Pets allowed (fee). | 14 Simpson Rd. 22406 | 540/373-5340 | fax 540/373-5340 | 120 rooms | $30-$70 | AE, D, DC, MC, V.

Dunning Mills. Near a quiet wooded area, this all-suite motel added a new non-smoking building with ten suites in September, 2000. Every suite at Dunning Mills has a full kitchen with a sitting area. Hang out in the lobby on the comfy sofa and read a paperback from the library, or play a board game and socialize with other guests. The outdoor picnic area has barbecues. Picnic area, complimentary Continental breakfast. In-room data ports, kitchens, microwaves, refrigerators, some in-room hot tubs, cable TV, room phones, TV in common area. Outdoor pool. Library. Laundry facilities. Pets allowed (fee). | 2305C Jefferson Davis Hwy. 22401 | 540/373-1256 | fax 540/599-9041 | www.dunningmills.com | 54 rooms | $118 | AE, D, DC, MC, V.

Econo Lodge Central. You'll find this chain hotel off I-95 at Exit 130B, near the Spotsylvania Mall. There are places to eat nearby. Complimentary Continental breakfast. Cable TV, room phones. Pets allowed. | 2802 Plank Rd. 22401 | 540/786-8379 or 800/553-2666 | fax 540/786-8811 | 96 rooms | $50 | AE, D, MC, V.

Hampton Inn. This two-story hotel with exterior room entrances is located at the intersection of Route 3 and I–95. Rooms are plainly furnished. Mary Washington College is nearby. Complimentary Continental breakfast. In-room data ports, cable TV. Pool. Laundry facilities. Business services. Some pets allowed. | 2310 William St. 22401 | 540/371–0330 | fax 540/371–1753 | www.hampton-inn.com | 166 rooms | $60–$90 | AE, D, DC, MC, V.

Ramada Inn–South. This hotel has a large lobby with high ceilings from which the state flag hangs. Rooms either face the hotel atrium or the exterior. The hotel is easily accessible from Interstate–95. Restaurant, bar with entertainment. In-room data ports, room service, cable TV. Pool. Hot tub. Exercise equipment. Video games. Laundry facilities. Business services. Some pets allowed. Free parking. | 5324 U.S. 1 22408 | 540/898–1102 | fax 540/898–2017 | 196 rooms | $62–$75 | AE, D, DC, MC, V.

Ramada Inn–Spotsylvania Mall. The chain facility is close to the shopping mall and 2 mi from Mary Washington College. Rooms have exterior entrances and are plainly furnished. In-room data ports, cable TV. Pool. Business services. Some pets allowed. Free parking. | 2802 Plank Rd. 22404 | 540/786–8361 | fax 540/786–8811 | www.ramada.com | 129 rooms | $60–$72 | AE, D, DC, MC, V.

Roxbury Mill. Dating back to 1723, this old gristmill on the river, 13 mi south of Fredericksburg, is decorated with family antiques, including two beds from the 1850s. The house is on 3.9 wooded acres that stretch down to the river. One of the three rooms is a 900-square-foot suite with its own kitchen and a deck overlooking the waterfall. Complimentary breakfast. One kitchenette, refrigerators, cable TV, some room phones, no TV in some rooms. Pond. Hiking. Fishing. Laundry facilities. Some pets allowed. No smoking. | 6908 Roxbury Mill Rd., Thornburg, 22553 | 540/582–6611 | members.aol.com/roxburymill | 3 rooms | $95–$150 | AE, D, MC, V.

HAMPTON

Arrow Inn. The property sits just off I-64 and U.S. 134, next to Langley Air Force Base. Basic efficiencies and kitchenettes provide you with simple comforts. Kitchenettes, refrigerators, some microwaves, cable TV. Laundry facilities. Business services. Pets allowed (fee). | 7 Semple Farm Rd. 23666 | 757/865–0300 or 800/833–2520 | fax 757/766–9367 | mb@arrowinn.com | www.arrowinn.com | 81 rooms | $40–$61 | AE, D, DC, MC, V.

Days Inn. Just off I–64 at Exit 263, this chain hotel has a restaurant on the premises. You can walk to the Coliseum; a five-minute drive will take you to Buckroe Beach or the Langley Speedway. Restaurant. Some microwaves, some refrigerators, cable TV, room phones. Outdoor pool. Laundry facilities, laundry service. Pets allowed (fee). | 1918 Coliseum Dr. 23666 | 757/825–4810 or 800/325–2525 | fax 757/827–6503 | 144 rooms | $60–$85 | AE, D, DC, MC, V.

Hampton Inn. The inn is ½ mi away from the Hampton Coliseum and the Hampton Mall. Rooms have jewel tones and contemporary oak furnishings. Complimentary Continental breakfast. In-room data ports, cable TV. Business services. Some pets allowed. | 1813 W. Mercury Blvd. 23666 | 757/838–8484 | fax 757/826–0725 | www.hamptoninn.com | 132 rooms | $79–$89 | AE, D, DC, MC, V.

HARRISONBURG

Days Inn. Adjacent to James Madison University, this hotel is only six blocks from downtown. You can enjoy the neutral colors and a room with a king-size bed and wet bar. Easy access to I-81 provides quick entry to local sights. Complimentary Continental breakfast. Cable TV. Outdoor pool. Hot tub. Laundry Services. Business services, free parking. Pets allowed (fee). | 1131 Forest Hill Rd. | 540/433–9353 | fax 540/433–5809 | 89 rooms | $50–$75 | AE, D, DC, MC, V.

Econo Lodge. This two-story motel is 1 mi from James Madison University and I-81. The Valley View Mall is within view. Complimentary Continental breakfast. Some in-room hot tubs, cable TV. Outdoor pool. Business services. Some pets allowed. | 1703 E. Market St. | 540/433–2576 | fax 540/433–2576, ext. 240 | www.choicehotels.com | 89 rooms | $55–$85 | AE, D, DC, MC, V.

Four Points by Sheraton. The large stone fireplace in the lobby roars on cold winter days. The Valley View Mall and James Madison University are both only 1 mi away. Restaurant, bar with entertainment, room service. In-room data ports, cable TV. Indoor pool, wading pool. Hot tub. Exercise room. Business services. Free parking. Some pets allowed. | 1400 E. Market St. | 540/433–2521 | fax 540/434–0253 | www.sheraton.com | 140 rooms | $79–$109 | AE, D, DC, MC, V.

Howard Johnson. Just east of I-81, dogwoods, pine trees, and flowering annuals, beautiful in late spring, color the long front lawn. James Madison University is ¼ mi away across the interstate to the west. Restaurant. Cable TV. Outdoor pool, wading pool. Business services. Some pets allowed. | 605 Port Republic Rd. | 540/434–6771 | fax 540/434–0153 | www.hojo.com | 134 rooms | $45–$70 | AE, D, DC, MC, V.

Village Inn. Family owned, this countryside motel is ¼ mi south of the Rockingham County Fairgrounds. Rooms have outside entrances and decks. Restaurant, picnic area. Some in-room hot tubs, cable TV. Pool. Playground. Business services. Some pets allowed. | Rte. 11 | 540/434–7355 or 800/736–7355 | fax 540/434–7355 | 36 rooms, 1 suite | $47–$57, $60 suite | AE, D, DC, MC, V.

HOT SPRINGS

Roseloe. This family-owned motel is 3 mi north of Hot Springs and 2 mi south of Warm Springs. All rooms view the Allegheny mountains as this motel sits in the midst of the mountains themselves. Some rooms have patios. Kitchenettes, refrigerators, cable TV. Business services. Pets allowed (fee). | U.S. 220 | 540/839–5373 | 20 rooms | $48–$55 | AE, D, DC, MC, V.

Vine Cottage Inn. Built in 1894, this inn has been a bed and breakfast since 1904. Leisure and business travelers mingle in the large living room or out on the wraparound porch. Lakes for fishing and canoeing and hiking trails are nearby. The 15 rooms, each uniquely decorated, some with shared baths, can sleep one to five people. Dining room, complimentary breakfast. No air-conditioning, cable TV, no room phones, no TV, TV in common area. Pets allowed (fee). | Rte. 220 24445 | 540/839–2422 | 15 rooms | $65–$90 | AE, D, DC, MC, V.

IRVINGTON

Hope and Glory Inn. This Victorian inn, built in 1890 and once an elementary school, is near the Chesapeake Bay. Hollyhocks and roses bloom in the English garden; cottages have private patio gardens. All rooms are unique and furnished with antiques. Complimentary breakfast. No smoking, phones in cottages only, no TV in rooms, TV in common area. Boating. Fishing. Bicycles. Kids allowed in cottages only. Business services. Some pets allowed. | 634 King Carter Dr. 22480 | 804/438–6053 or 800/497–8228 | fax 804/438–5362 | www.hopeandglory.com | 7 rooms, 4 cottages | $110–$195, $145–$195 cottages | AE, MC, V.

Tides Lodge Resort and Country Club. Opened in 1947, this popular golf and water-sports resort is on the Chesapeake Bay. Rooms are done in tartan plaids and have a woodsy, rustic look. You can sign up for bay cruises at the front desk. Bar, dining room. Refrigerators, cable TV. Exercise room, game room, 2 pools. Driving range, putting greens, tennis courts. Marina, boating. Bicycles. Kids' programs, playground, laundry facilities. Business services. Some pets allowed (fee). | 1 St. Andrews La. 22480 | 804/438–6000 or 800/248–4337 | fax 804/438–5950 | www.thetides.com | 60 rooms | $238–$302 | Closed Dec.–late Mar. | MAP | D, MC, V.

KEYSVILLE

Sheldon's. Family-owned and -operated since 1940, this hotel is in a rural setting. All rooms have outside entrances and picture-postcard views of open fields, an old farmhouse, and a big red barn. Restaurant. Some microwaves, cable TV. Business services. Some pets allowed. | 1450 Four Locust Highway | 804/736–8434 | fax 804/736–9402 | 40 rooms | $40–$70 | AE, D, MC, V.

LEESBURG

Colonial. This redbrick inn is in the heart of the downtown historic district. Early-American furniture, hardwood floors, and fireplaces give each room a special warmth. Restaurant, picnic area, complimentary breakfast. Room service, some in-room hot tubs, cable TV. Library. Airport shuttle. Some pets allowed. | 19 S. King St. 20175 | 703/777–5000 or 800/392–1332 | fax 703/777–7000 | saeidi@aol.com | 10 rooms | $78–$120 | AE, D, DC, MC, V.

Days Inn. The location is convenient—it's near Prosperity Shopping Center, just off of Rte. 15, and less than 1 mi from Leesburg. Complimentary Continental breakfast. Cable TV. Laundry facilities. Business services. Some pets allowed (fee). | 721 E. Market St. 20175 | 703/777–6622 | fax 703/777–4119 | 81 rooms | $65 | AE, D, DC, MC, V.

Milltown Farms. Like every house in Waterford, this 1765 log and stone home is on the National Historic Registry. Set on a 300-acre farm, the inn is decorated with antiques from the 1600s and a piece dating back to the Ming Dynasty. Two rooms have fireplaces; one has a private entrance. Dining rooms, complimentary breakfast. Some refrigerators. No room phones, no TV. Hiking. Some pets allowed. No smoking. | 14163 Milltown Rd., Waterford 20197 | 540/882–4470 or 888/747–3942 | www.milltownfarms.com | 5 rooms | $100–$135 | AE, D, DC, MC, V.

LEXINGTON

Best Western Inn at Hunt Ridge. The spacious rooms are decorated with Shaker-style furniture. Restaurant, bar. In-room data ports, microwaves (in suites), refrigerators, room service, cable TV. Indoor-outdoor pool. Laundry facilities. Business services. Some pets allowed. | 112 Willow Springs Rd. | 540/464–1500 | fax 540/464–1500 | 100 rooms, 10 suites | $74–$86, $90–$149 suites | AE, D, DC, MC, V.

Comfort Inn. This chain hotel is near the Virginia Horse Center. Rooms on the top floor of the four-story building have views of the mountains. Complimentary Continental breakfast. Cable TV. Indoor pool. Laundry facilities. Business services. Some pets allowed. | U.S. 11 S | 540/463–7311 | fax 540/463–4590 | 80 rooms | $60–$90 | AE, D, DC, MC, V.

Days Inn Keydet-General. This mid-sized hotel is set on a hill 1 mi east of historic downtown Lexington. The rooms have mountain views. Complimentary Continental breakfast, picnic area. Some kitchenettes, some refrigerators, cable TV. Business services. Some pets allowed. | 325 W. Midland Trail | 540/463–2143 | fax 540/463–2143 | 63 rooms | $50–$75 | AE, D, DC, MC, V.

Holiday Inn Express. Restaurants and stores are within easy walking distance of this hotel, which is about three mi north of Lexington. Rooms have queen beds. Picnic area, complimentary Continental breakfast. In-room data ports, cable TV. Pool. Laundry facilities. Business services. Some pets allowed. | U.S. 11 | 540/463–7351 | fax 540/463–7351 | 72 rooms | $64–$96 | AE, D, DC, MC, V.

Howard Johnson. The motel is in a commercial district about 5 mi north of downtown Lexington. Rooms have mountain views. Restaurant. Cable TV. Pool. Laundry facilities. Business services. Some pets allowed. | U.S. 11 N | 540/463–9181 | fax 540/464–3448 | 100 rooms | $55–$75 | AE, D, DC, MC, V.

Hummingbird Inn. First built in 1780 and expanded in 1853, this Carpenter Gothic Victorian villa is at the edge of the George Washington National Forest. Most rooms have canopy beds, and three rooms have working fireplaces. Verandas overlook the gardens. Picnic area, complimentary breakfast. No smoking, some in-room hot tubs, no room phones, no TV in rooms, TV in common room. Business services. No kids under 12. Pets allowed (fee). | 30 Wood La., Goshen 24439 | 540/997–9065 or 800/397–3214 | fax 540/997–0289 | hmgbird@cfw.com | www.hummingbirdinn.com | 5 rooms | $85–$135 | AE, D, MC, V.

Ramada Inn. Built in 1993, this contemporary hotel has large rooms and easy access to the interstate. Restaurant, bar, room service. Cable TV. Indoor pool. Business services. Some pets allowed. | U.S. 11 N | 540/463–6400 | fax 540/464–3639 | www.ramada.com | 80 rooms | $60–$68 | AE, D, DC, MC, V.

Wattstull. This family-owned motel is near the Natural Bridge. Rooms have wood-beamed ceilings and outside entrances. Restaurant. TV. Pool, wading pool. Some pets allowed. | U.S. 11, Buchanan, 24066 | 540/254–1551 | 26 rooms | $44–$50 | MC, V.

LURAY

Best Western Intown. Rooms at this centrally located, two-story motor inn have separate outside entrances. Restaurant. Room service, cable TV. Pool. Playground. Business services. Pets allowed (fee). | 410 W. Main St./U.S. 211 Business | 540/743–6511 | fax 540/743–2917 | 40 rooms | $50–$105 | AE, D, DC, MC, V.

Days Inn. Three miles from the Luray Caverns and 7 mi from the entrance to Shenandoah National Park, this chain hotel offers mountain views in almost all of its rooms. Thirteen of the rooms are decorated with antiques collected by the former owner. You can picnic and play horseshoes out back. Restaurant, bar with entertainment, picnic area, room service. In-room data ports, some in-room hot tubs, cable TV, room phones, TV in common area. Outdoor pool, wading pool. Miniature golf. Hiking. Pets allowed (fee). | 138 Whispering Hill Rd. 22835 | 540/743–4521 | fax 540/743–6863 | 101 | $64–$89 | AE, D, DC, MC, V.

Little Inn at the Kite Hollow. You'll have pretty views of the surrounding area from this guest house perched on a hill. The cows may come up to the fence while you're relaxing in the outdoor hot tub. Inside you'll find a pool table, a sunroom, and a sitting room with a piano and Oriental rug. Dining room, complimentary breakfast. Refrigerators, cable TV, room phones. Outdoor hot tub. Pets allowed (fee). | 340 Taylor Dr., Stanley 22851 | 540/778–2758 | info@kitehollow-b-b.com | www.kitehollow-b-b.com | 2 rooms | $55–$85 | No credit cards.

Mimslyn Inn. This reconstructed former girls' school is in the center of downtown Luray. Rooms look out over the town and mountains. Restaurant, room service. Cable TV. Business services. Some pets allowed. | 401 W. Main St./U.S. 211 Business | 540/743–5105 or 800/296–5105 | fax 540/743–2632 | www.svta.com/mimslyn/virginia | 49 rooms (2 with shower only), 11 suites | $84–$95, $99–$139 suites | AE, D, DC, MC, V.

LYNCHBURG

Budget Inn. This chain motel is close to historical sites and parks, including Appomattox Court House National Historic Park. Some microwaves, refrigerators, cable TV. Pool. Business services. Some pets allowed. | 714 W. Confederate Blvd./U.S. 460 Business | 804/352–7451 | fax 804/352–2080 | 20 rooms | $45–$50 | AE, D, MC, V.

Holiday Inn Select. Near downtown shops and the commercial area, this chain provides live piano music by the fountain in the marble-floored lobby during Sunday brunch. Some rooms have Murphy beds. Restaurant, bar. In-room data ports, refrigerators, cable TV. Pool. Exercise equipment. Business services. Airport shuttle. Some pets allowed. | 601 Main St. 24504 | 804/528–2500 | fax 804/528–4782 | basshotels.com/holiday-inn | 243 rooms | $69–$79 | AE, D, DC, MC, V.

MANASSAS

Best Western Battlefield Inn. A mile from Manassas National Battlefield Park and 2 mi from Nissan Pavilion Amphitheater. The grounds include a courtyard with rose garden. Restaurant, bar with entertainment, picnic area, complimentary Continental breakfast, room service. In-room data ports. Some microwaves. Cable TV. Outdoor pool. Exercise equipment. Laundry facilities. Business services. Free parking. Pets allowed (fee). | 10820 Balls Ford Rd. 20109 | 703/361–8000 | fax 703/361–8000 | www.bestwestern.com | 121 rooms | $89 | AE, D, DC, MC, V.

Red Roof Inn Manassas. This motel is off I–66 1 mi from Manassas National Battlefield Park. In-room data ports. Cable TV. Business services. Pets allowed. | 10610 Automotive Dr. 20109 | 703/335–9333 | fax 703/335–9342 | www.redroof.com | 119 rooms | $84.99 | AE, D, DC, MC, V.

MARION

Best Western Inn. The property is 5 mi from Hungry Mother State Park and close to I-81. Restaurant, bar, complimentary Continental breakfast, room service. In-room data ports, microwaves, refrigerators, cable TV. Outdoor pool. Laundry service. Free parking. Pets allowed. | 1424 N. Main St. | 540/783–3193 | fax 540/783–3193 | www.bestwestern.com | 80 rooms | $69–$73 | AE, D, DC, MC, V.

MARTINSVILLE

Best Western Martinsville Inn. Just off Business Route 220, this hotel is 2 mi from the Virginia Museum of Natural History and 5 mi from Martinsville Speedway. Restaurant, bar, room service. In-room data ports, microwaves, refrigerators, cable TV. Outdoor pool. Exercise equipment. Laundry service. Free parking. Pets allowed. | 1755 Virginia Ave. 24112 | 540/632–5611 or 800/388–3934 | fax 540/632–1168 | www.bestwestern.com | 97 rooms | $59–$65 | AE, D, DC, MC, V.

Dutch Inn. This motel, five mi northwest of Martinsville, is easy to spot—there's a giant windmill replica on the front of the building. Restaurant, bar, room service. In-room data ports, refrigerators, cable TV. Pool, hot tub, sauna. Exercise equipment. Free parking. Pets allowed. | 2360 Virginia Ave., Collinsville, 24078 | 540/647–3721 or 800/800–3996 | fax 540/647–4857 | sgrodens@neocomm.net | www.dutchinn.com | 148 rooms | $75 | AE, D, DC, MC, V.

MCLEAN

Holiday Inn. You'll find this standard hotel chain 1 mi from Tysons Corner Center and Galleria. Restaurant, bar with entertainment. In-room data ports, cable TV. Indoor pool. Hot tub, sauna. Exercise equipment. Airport shuttle. Pets allowed. | 1960 Chain Bridge Rd. 22102 | 703/893–2100 | fax 703/356–8218 | www.holiday-inn.com | 316 rooms | $89–$189.95 | AE, D, DC, MC, V.

MONTROSS

Days Inn on the Potomac. This two-story motel is by the beach 4 mi from the George Washington Birthplace National Monument. Complimentary Continental breakfast. Some microwaves, refrigerators; cable TV. Pool. Baby-sitting, laundry service. Business services, free parking. Pets allowed. | 30 Colonial Ave., Colonial Beach 22443 | 804/224–0404 | fax 804/224–0404 | 60 rooms | $67–$87 | AE, D, DC, MC, V.

NEWPORT NEWS

Comfort Inn. This property is next to the Patrick Henry Mall. Guest privileges at Bally Total Fitness Club, across the street, are available. Complimentary Continental breakfast, room service. In-room data ports, some microwaves, some refrigerators, cable TV. Pool. Laundry facilities. Business services. Airport shuttle. Free parking. Pets allowed. | 12330 Jefferson Ave. 23602 | 757/249–0200 | fax 757/249–4736 | www.comfortinn.com | 124 rooms | $94–$99 | AE, D, DC, MC, V.

Days Inn. This motel is 5 mi from Newport News Park, 6 mi from the Mariners Museum, and 8 mi from Busch Gardens in Williamsburg. Restaurant, picnic area, complimentary Continental breakfast. In-room data ports, some microwaves, some refrigerators, cable TV. Outdoor pool. Playground. Laundry services. Business services. Free parking. Pets allowed (fee). | 14747 Warwick Blvd. 23602 | 757/874–0201 | fax 757/874–0201 | 112 rooms | $65 | AE, D, DC, MC, V.

NORFOLK

Clarion–James Madison Hotel. Persian carpets, oak paneling and mirrors give this 1902 hotel the air of a turn-of-the-century hunt club. The lobby has soft light and elegant furnishings. Rooms are snug, with antique reproduction quilts on the beds, and a blend of traditional and contemporary furniture. Antique Alley is 1 mi from the hotel. Restaurant, bar, room service. In-room data ports, some refrigerators, cable TV. Exercise equipment. Video games, laundry facilities, laundry service. Business services. Parking (fee). Pets allowed. | 345 Granby St. | 757/622–6682 | fax 757/623–5949 | www.clarionhotel.com/hotelva332 | 124 rooms | $89–$119 | AE, D, DC, MC, V.

Econo Lodge Oceanview. The ocean beach, complete with fishing pier, is across the street. Complimentary Continental breakfast. Some kitchenettes, refrigerators, cable TV. Exercise equipment. Laundry facilities. Business services. Pets allowed. | 9601 4th View St. 23503 | 757/480–9611 | fax 757/480–1307 | www.choicehotels.com | 71 rooms | $70–$80 | AE, D, DC, MC, V.

Marriott Norfolk Waterside. The hotel is 2 blocks from Waterside Festival Marketplace and Nauticus. Some rooms have river views. Restaurant, bar, room service. In-room data ports, some refrigerators, cable TV. Indoor pool. Hot tub, sauna. Health club. Laundry facilities, laundry services. Business services. Parking (fee). Pets allowed (fee). | 235 E. Main St. 23510 | 757/627–4200 | fax 757/628–6466 | www.marriott.com | 404 rooms | $139–$179 | AE, D, DC, MC, V.

Page House Inn. This Georgian revival-style brick mansion was carefully transformed into a bed-and-breakfast with beautiful turn-of-the-20th-century antiques, china, and fine art. A sitting room/library and a rooftop patio are available for guest use, as is the stocked guest refrigerator. Rooms have four-poster beds with down comforters, some have soaking or whirlpool tubs. Suites also have fireplaces. The inn is in a residential area, next door to the Chrysler Museum. The waterside area is less than a mile away. Complimentary breakfast, room service. In-room data ports, some refrigerators, some in-room hot tubs, cable TV. Laundry service. Business services. Free parking. Pets allowed (fee). No kids under 12. No smoking. | 323 Fairfax Ave. 23507 | 757/625–5033 or 800/599–7659 | fax 757/623–9451 | innkeeper@pagehouseinn.com | www.pagehouseinn.com | 7 rooms, 3 suites | $122–$147, $152–$200 suites, $200–$300 yacht | AE, MC, V.

Quality Inn Lake Wright Resort. This lodge is 3mi from the Botanical Gardens, 4 mi from Oceanview Beach, and 6 mi from Waterside, Nauticus, and other downtown waterfront sites. Restaurant, bar, complimentary breakfast. In-room data ports, refrigerators, cable TV. Outdoor pool. Barbershop, beauty salon. Driving range, 18-hole golf course, putting green. Laundry facilities. Business services. Airport shuttle. Free parking. Pets allowed (fee). | 6280 Northampton Blvd. 23502 | 757/461–6251 | fax 757/461–5925 | www.lakewrighthotel.com | 149 rooms, 4 suites | $89–$99, $125–$250 suites | AE, D, DC, MC, V.

Radisson Hotel Norfolk. This 12-story, modern lodging has a futuristic exterior with a circular drive. Guest rooms have lots of blonde wood and large windows. Restaurant, bar. Cable TV, in-room VCRs. Pool. Beauty salon. Gym. Pets allowed. | 700 Monticello Ave. | 757/627–5555 | fax 757/627–5921 | www.radisson.com | 339 rooms | $119–$139 | AE, D, DC, MC, V.

ORANGE

Willow Grove Inn. An encampment site during the Revolutionary War, this restored plantation house, built in 1778, sits on 37 acres. Antiques and heirloom furnishings are found throughout and a piano graces the parlor. Some guest rooms have fireplaces and/or private verandas. Prices include full breakfast and dinner; box lunches are available. Restaurant, bar, complimentary breakfast. No smoking, no TV. Some in-room hot tubs. Business services. Some pets allowed. | 14079 Plantation Way 22960 | 540/672–5982 or 800/949–1778 | fax 540/672–3674 | www.willowgroveinn.com | 5 rooms, 5 cottages | $225–$330, $275–$330 cottages | MAP | AE, D, MC, V.

PETERSBURG

Best Western. This three-story motel is just off I–95 South Exit 52 (I–95 North Exit 50D) and I–85 Exit 69. Restaurant, bar, complimentary Continental breakfast. In-room data ports, microwaves, refrigerators, cable TV, some in-room hot tubs. Outdoor pool. Video games. Laundry facilities. Business services. Free parking. Pets allowed (fee). | 405 E. Washington St. | 804/733–1776 | fax 804/861–6339 | www.bestwestern.com | 120 rooms | $57–$67 | AE, D, DC, MC, V.

Comfort Inn. This motel is ¹/₂ mi from the Softball Hall of Fame and 5 mi from the battlefields and the Quartermaster Museum. Restaurant, complimentary Continental breakfast. Some kitchenettes, microwaves, refrigerators, cable TV. Outdoor pool. Laundry facilities. Pets allowed. | 11974 S. Crater Rd.23805 | 804/732–2900 | fax 804/732–2900 | www.comfortinn.com | 96 rooms | $74.95–$79.95 | AE, D, DC, MC, V.

Days Inn Fort Lee/South. I–95 Exit 45 and the I–295 interchange are less than ¹/₂ mi from this large two-story hostelry, set on 30 acres of green land. Victorian-style furnishings add flair to guest rooms. Restaurant, bar. In-room data ports, some kitchenettes, microwaves, refrigerators, cable TV. Pool, wading pool. Barbershop, beauty salon. Putting green. Tennis. Exercise equipment. Playground, shopping, laundry services. Business services. Pets allowed. Free parking. | 12208 S. Crater Rd. 23805 | 804/733–4400 | fax 804/861–9559 | 155 rooms | $59–$79 | AE, D, DC, MC, V.

Quality Inn Steven Kent. This motel is 2 mi from the Softball Hall of Fame and 4 mi from the Civil War battlefields. Restaurant, bar, picnic area. In-room data ports, some microwaves, some refrigerators, cable TV. Outdoor pool, wading pool, sauna. Miniature golf, tennis, basketball. Playground, laundry facilities. Business services. Pets allowed. | 12205 S. Crater Rd. 23805 | 804/733–0600 | fax 804/862–4549 | 136 rooms | $54–$70 | AE, D, DC, MC, V.

PORTSMOUTH

Holiday Inn Old Town–Portsmouth. This 30-year-old, 4-story hotel is on the waterfront at the Elizabeth River. Some rooms have river views. Restaurant, bar, room service. In-room data ports. Cable TV. Pool. Exercise equipment. Dock, marina. Laundry facilities. Business services. Some pets allowed (fee). | 8 Crawford Pkwy. 23704; Interstate 264, Exit Crawford Parkway | 757/393–2573 | fax 757/399–1248 | www.holiday-portsmouth.com | 268 rooms | $95–$115 | AE, D, DC, MC, V.

RADFORD

Best Western Radford Inn. The 2-story chain hotel off U.S. 81 at Exit 109 has two double beds or a single king-size bed. Restaurant. Cable TV. Indoor pool, wading pool. Hot tub. Exercise equipment. Business services. Some pets allowed. | 1501 Tyler Ave. | 540/639–3000 | fax 540/639–3000, ext. 412 | www.bestwestern.com | 72 rooms | $64–$85 | AE, D, DC, MC, V.

Executive. This two-story hotel in the Radford University area has some in-room balconies. Refrigerators, some microwaves. Cable TV. Some pets allowed (fee). | 7498 Lee Hwy. (Rte.

11) | 540/639–1664 or 888/393–8483 reservations | fax 540/633–1737 | 26 rooms (13 with shower only) | $50–$85 | AE, D, MC, V.

REEDVILLE

Morris House. In the heart of town, this Queen Anne Victorian (1895) was built by one of Reedville's founders. The inn is furnished with antiques, and has a wraparound porch and suites with hot tubs and fireplaces. Every room has a view of the water. Complimentary breakfast. Cable TV. Dock. Some pets allowed in cottage. | 826 Main St. | 804/453–7016 | fax 804/453–9032 | morrishs@crosslink.net | www.eaglesnest.net/morrishouse | 2 rooms, 2 suites, 1 cottage | $80–$125, $125–$150 suites, $170 cottage | MC, V.

RESTON

Hilton. This Hilton is just 2 mi from Dulles International Airport and 6 mi from the town center. The executive level has extra amenities, including living rooms. Most rooms have double beds or a single king. Restaurant, bars with entertainment. In-room data ports. Some refrigerators. Room service. Cable TV. 2 pools (1 indoor). Barbershop. Beauty salon. Tennis courts. Exercise equipment, basketball, racquetball. Business services. Airport shuttle. Some pets allowed. | 13869 Park Center Rd., Herndon 22171 | 703/478–2900 or 800/445–8667 | fax 703/834–1996 | www.hilton.com | 301 rooms | $105–$165 | AE, D, DC, MC, V.

Holiday Inn. Most rooms in this two-story chain hotel have double beds or a single king-size. Restaurant, bar with entertainment. In-room data ports. Room service. Cable TV. Indoor pool. Hot tub. Exercise equipment. Laundry facilities. Business services. Airport shuttle. Free parking. Some pets allowed. | 1000 Sully Rd., Sterling, 20166 | 703/471–7411 | fax 703/834–7558 | www.holiday-inn.com | 296 rooms | $169 | AE, D, DC, MC, V.

Holiday Inn Express. This four-story budget offshoot of the chain is near the airport, and has double beds or a single king. From Rt. 495, take Exit 12 to Dulles Access. Complimentary Continental breakfast. Some microwaves, cable TV. Exercise equipment. Business services. Airport shuttle. Free parking. Some pets allowed. | 485 Elden St., Herndon, 20170 | 703/478–9777 | fax 703/471–4624 | disales@bfsaulco.com | www.holiday-inn.com | 115 rooms | $139 | AE, D, DC, MC, V.

Residence Inn by Marriott. This chain hotel, 2 mi from the downtown shopping area, has 21 separate buildings, all two stories high. Picnic area. Complimentary Continental breakfast. In-room data ports. Kitchenettes. Microwaves. Cable TV. Pool. Hot tub. Tennis court. Playground. Laundry facilities. Business services. Free parking. Some pets allowed (fee). | 315 Elden St., Herndon, 20170 | 703/435–0044 | fax 703/437–4007 | www.marriott.com | 168 rooms | $159–$209 | AE, D, DC, MC, V.

Westfields Marriott. 15 minutes from downtown shopping, this hotel has three stories and some balconies. Picnics and box lunches can be arranged. Restaurant, bar with entertainment, picnic area. In-room data ports. Minibars. Room service. Cable TV. 2 pools (1 indoor). Hot tub, massage. Tennis court. Basketball, gym, hiking, bicycles. Business services. Airport shuttle. Free parking. Some pets allowed. | 14750 Conference Center Dr., Chantilly, 20151 | 703/818–0300 | fax 703/818–3655 | www.marriott.com | 340 rooms | $119–$264 | AE, D, DC, MC, V.

RICHMOND

Holiday Inn–Airport. The hotel occupies two buildings—one a tower building with six floors, the other with three floors—near Richmond International Airport, 12 mi east of the city. Built in 1974. The rooms come with double beds and a table and two chairs. Restaurant, bar. In-room data ports, microwaves, room service, cable TV. Pool. Business services. Airport shuttle. Some pets allowed. | 5203 Williamsburg Rd., Sandston, 23150 | 804/222–6450 | fax 804/226–4305 | www.holiday-inn.com | 230 rooms | $99 | AE, D, DC, MC, V.

Holiday Inn Richmond Central. You're paying for location when you book a room at this two-building complex: It's smack in the center of town. Some rooms have balconies, and there is a courtyard in the back. Restaurant. Cable TV. In-room data ports. Picnic area. Outdoor pool. Exercise facility. Laundry Service. Pets allowed. | 3207 North Blvd. 23230 | 804/359–9441 or 800/465–4329 | fax 804/359–3207 | 184 rooms | $89 | AE, D, DC, MC, V.

Knight's Inn. This two-story building has Romanesque columns fronting a large lawn. Though 8 mi south of downtown Richmond, the hotel is nonetheless near shopping centers and restaurants. Rooms are unadorned and basic. Restaurant. Cable TV. In-room data port. Refrigerator. Microwave. Outdoor Pool. Pets ok. | 9002 Brook Rd. 23060 | 804/266–2444 | fax 804/261–5834 | www.knightsinn.com. | 63 rooms | $44–$64 | AE, V, MC, DC, D.

La Quinta. The three-story hacienda-style hotel has a bell tower and outdoor entrances to the rooms. It's convenient to shopping—about 10 mi south of downtown. It has standard rooms with double beds. Complimentary Continental breakfast. In-room data ports, cable TV. Pool. Business services. Free parking. Some pets allowed. | 6910 Midlothian Pike/U.S. 60 W 23225 | 804/745–7100 | fax 804/276–6660 | www.laquinta.com | 130 rooms | $60–$67 | AE, D, DC, MC, V.

Red Roof Inn. This two-story chain hotel has standard rooms with double beds or a single king. Some refrigerators, cable TV. Business services. Some pets allowed. | 4350 Commerce Rd. 23234 | 804/271–7240 | fax 804/271–7245 | www.redroofinn.com | 108 rooms | $50–$70 | AE, D, DC, MC, V.

Residence Inn by Marriott. The apartment-style motel is about 10 mi west of downtown. Many rooms have fireplaces and double beds or a single king. Picnic area, complimentary Continental breakfast. In-room data ports, kitchenettes, microwaves, cable TV. Pool. Laundry facilities. Business services. Free parking. Some pets allowed (fee). | 2121 Dickens Rd. 23230 | 804/285–8200 | fax 804/285–2530 | www.marriott.com | 80 suites | $124–$164 | AE, D, DC, MC, V.

Wyndham Garden Hotel–Richmond Airport. This hotel has four stories and standard rooms with double beds. Restaurant, bar. In-room data ports, room service, cable TV. Pool. Barber shop, beauty salon, hot tub. Exercise equipment. Business services. Airport shuttle. Free parking. Some pets allowed. | 4700 S. Laburnum Ave. | 804/226–4300 | fax 804/226–6516 | www.wyndham.com | 155 rooms, 4 suites | $125–$149 | AE, D, DC, MC, V.

ROANOKE

AmeriSuites Roanoke/Valley View Mall. This six-story chain hotel is near Valley View Mall and the Roanoke Regional Airport. Many restaurants are within walking distance, and the hotel is less than five mi to downtown Roanoke. Rooms are very clean, though unexceptional. Complimentary Continental breakfast. Picnic Area. Kitchenettes. Cable TV. Indoor pool. Exercise equipment. Airport Shuttle. Pets allowed. | 5040 Valley View Blvd. 24012 | 540/366–4700 or 800/833–1516 | fax 540/366–1157 | 128 rooms | $89–$139 | AE, D, DC, MC, V.

Clarion-Airport. This four-story hotel, near the Roanoke Regional Airport, has standard rooms with double beds or a single king. Restaurant, bar, picnic area. In-room data ports, some microwaves, refrigerators, room service, cable TV. Indoor-outdoor pool. Hot tub. Tennis court. Exercise equipment. Business services. Airport shuttle. Free parking. Some pets allowed. | 2727 Ferndale Dr. 24017 | 540/362–4500 | fax 540/362–4506 | www.roanokeclarion.com | 154 rooms | $100–$110 | AE, D, DC, MC, V.

Holiday Inn–Tanglewood. This five-story chain hotel is convenient to Tanglewood Mall. Restaurant, bar. In-room data ports, room service, cable TV. Pool. Business services. Airport shuttle. Some pets allowed (fee). Free parking. | 4468 Starkey Rd. SW 24014 | 540/774–4400 | fax 540/774–1195 | www.holiday-inn.com | 196 rooms | $67–$102 | AE, D, DC, MC, V.

Ramada Inn. Close to the Roanoke River, this chain hotel has four stories, outdoor entrances, and standard-size rooms, most with double beds. Restaurant, bar, complimentary Continental breakfast. In-room data ports, cable TV. Pool. Laundry facilities. Business services. Some pets allowed. | 1927 Franklin Rd. SW 24014 | 540/343–0121 | fax 540/342–2048 | www.ramada.com | 126 rooms | $45–$85 | AE, D, DC, MC, V.

Rodeway Inn. This two-story stucco building is within walking distance to the Roanoke Civic Center, and to the downtown shops, restaurants, and Farmers' Market. Complimentary Continental breakfast. In-room data ports. Some microwaves. Refrigerators. Cable TV. Laundry facilities. Pets allowed. | 526 Orange Avenue NE 24016 | 540/981–9341 or 800/424–4777 | fax 540/345–8477 | VA248@apluslodging.com | www.choicehotels.com | 102 rooms | $30–$60 | AE,D, DC, MC V.

Travelodge-North. All rooms in this chain option are at ground level, with outdoor entrances and parking in front. The rooms have double beds. The location makes for easy interstate access; it's about 10 mi north of Roanoke. Complimentary Continental breakfast. Some kitchenettes, cable TV. Pool. Playground. Business services. Some pets allowed (fee). | 2619 Lee Hwy. S, Troutville 24175 | 540/992–6700 | fax 540/992–3991 | 108 rooms | $44–$55 | AE, D, DC, MC, V.

Wyndham Hotel. This hotel is on 12 acres, with two tower buildings—one eight stories, the other seven stories—and some balconies, 2 mi from the municipal airport. It has standard-size rooms, most with double beds. Restaurant, bars. Some refrigerators, room service, cable TV. 2 pools (1 indoor). Hot tub. Tennis court. Exercise equipment. Business services. Airport shuttle. Some pets allowed (fee). | 2801 Hershberger Rd. NW 24017 | 540/563–9300 | fax 540/366–5846 | www.wyndham.com | 320 rooms | $79–$145 | AE, D, DC, MC, V.

SALEM

Quality Inn. This chain option has two stories with balconies, mountain views, and standard rooms with double beds. Restaurant, bar, picnic area, complimentary Continental breakfast, cable TV. Pool. Putting green. Exercise equipment. Playground, laundry facilities. Business services. Airport shuttle. Some pets allowed. | 179 Sheraton Dr. | 540/562–1912 | fax 540/562–0507 | 120 rooms | $57–$72 | AE, D, DC, MC, V.

SCHUYLER

High Meadows. You can lodge in Victorian- and Federal-style buildings at this working vineyard, 13 mi east of Schuyler. The surrounding 50 acres are dotted with gardens and ponds. Some rooms have fireplaces and private decks. The dining room is open Thursday through Sunday; supper baskets are available Monday through Wednesday. Dining room, complimentary breakfast. Some in-room hot tubs. Some pets allowed. No smoking. | 55 High Meadows La., Scottsville 24590 | 804/286–2218 or 800/232–1832 | fax 804/286–2124 | www.highmeadows.com | 9 rooms, 2 suites, 3 cottages | $89–$145, $119–$135 suites, $135–$195 cottages | DC, D, MC, V.

SOUTH BOSTON

Best Western Howard House Inn. This hotel is in town, right off U.S. 360 and ¼ mi from U.S. 58. Restaurant, complimentary Continental breakfast. In-room data ports, cable TV. Pool. Business services. Some pets allowed. | 2001 Seymour Dr. | 804/572–4311 | fax 804/572–2740 | www.bestwestern.com | 52 rooms | $59–$73 | AE, D, DC, MC, V.

Super 8. This budget motel is on U.S. 58. Cable TV. Some pets allowed. | 1040 Bill Tuck Hwy. | 804/572–8868 | fax 804/572–8868 | www.super8.com | 58 rooms | $46–$50 | AE, D, DC, MC, V.

SOUTH HILL

Best Western. This property is in town, at the intersection of I-85 and U.S. 58. Restaurant, complimentary Continental breakfast, bar. Cable TV. Pool, wading pool. Game room, video games. Laundry facilities. Airport shuttle. Free parking. Some pets allowed (fee). | 911 E. Atlantic St. | 804/447-3123 | fax 804/447-4237 | www.bestwestern.com | 151 rooms | $65-$80 | AE, D, DC, MC, V.

Econo Lodge. The chain hotel is on the east edge of town, near I-85. Some microwaves, refrigerators. Business services. Some pets allowed. | 623 Atlantic St. | 804/447-7116 | fax 804/447-6985 | www.choicehotels.com | 53 rooms | $50-$70 | AE, D, DC, MC, V.

SPRINGFIELD

Comfort Inn. The chain hotel is next to the Springfield Mall. Complimentary Continental breakfast. In-room data ports, cable TV. Business services. Free parking. Some pets allowed. | 6560 Loisdale Ct. | 703/922-9000 | fax 703/971-6944 | www.comfortinn.com | 112 rooms | $79-$95 | AE, D, DC, MC, V.

Hampton Inn. The motel is next door to the Springfield Mall. Complimentary Continental breakfast. Cable TV. Pool. Free parking. Some pets allowed. | 6550 Loisdale Ct. | 703/924-9444 | fax 703/924-0324 | www.hampton-inn.com | 153 rooms | $99-$109 | AE, D, DC, MC, V.

Motel 6. This four-story brick building is less than a five-minute drive from the Springfield Mall, restaurants, Brookfield Park, and grocery stores. Rooms are standard, chain-motel style: It used to be a Ramada Inn, and not much has changed. Cable TV. In-room data ports. Laundry service. Pets allowed. | 6868 Springfield Blvd. 22150 | 703/644-5311 | fax 703/644-1077 | www.motel6.com | 190 rooms | $58-$70 | AE, D, DC, MC, V.

STAUNTON

Ashton Country House Bed and Breakfast. An 1860s Greek Revival home on 25 acres of farmland, the Ashton's interior is completely furnished with antiques and reproductions. About 1½ mi from downtown Staunton, there are porches overlooking the Blue Ridge Mountains, and fireplaces in every room. Complimentary breakfast. Cable TV. VCRs. Pets allowed. | 1205 Middlebrook Ave. 24401 | 540/885-7819 or 800/296-7819 | fax 540/885-6029 | ashtonhouse@aol.com | www.bbhost.com/ashtonbnb | 6 rooms | $70-$125 | AE, D, DC, MC, V.

Comfort Inn. This chain motel is 3 mi from town, along I-81. Complimentary Continental breakfast. Some refrigerators, cable TV. Pool. Business services. Some pets allowed. | 1302 Richmond Ave. | 540/886-5000 | fax 540/886-6643 | www.comfortinn.com | 98 rooms | $65-$110 | AE, D, DC, MC, V.

Econo Lodge-Hessian House. The property is 8 mi south of town, along I-81. Picnic area, complimentary Continental breakfast. Refrigerators, cable TV. Pool, wading pool. Playground. Some pets allowed (fee). | 3554 Lee Jackson Hwy. | 540/337-1231 | fax 540/337-0821 | www.choicehotels.com | 32 rooms | $45-$75 | AE, D, MC, V.

Twelfth Night Inn. Built at the turn of the century, in the Prairie style, the inn has a wrap-around veranda and a landscaped garden in the back. Each room is Shakespearean-themed, with antiques and reproductions to match. It's also right downtown, within walking distance of most attractions, restaurants, and shops. Complimentary breakfast. Cable TV. Pets allowed ($10 extra). No kids under 10. | 402 Beverley Street 24401 | 540/885-1733 | fax 540/885-4213 | stay@12th-night-inn.com | www.12th-night-inn.com | 1 single, 2 suites | $75-110 | AE, D, MC, V.

STRASBURG

Budget Inn. Three miles south of downtown Strasburg, the hotel was built in 1933. Rooms in the one-story brick building are basic and serviceable. Cable TV. Pets allowed. | 2899 Old Valley Pike 22657 | 540/465–5298 | fax 540/465–5165 | 14 rooms | $50 | AE, MC, V.

Hotel Strasburg. This restored Victorian is furnished with antiques from the Strasburg Emporium, the town's vast antiques market, and nearly all are for sale. There are 21 rooms in the main hotel and four suites in each of the two adjacent houses. The hotel is 2 mi from I-81. Dining room, picnic area, complimentary Continental breakfast. In-room data ports, some in-room hot tubs, cable TV, room phones. Pets allowed. | 2133 Holliday St. 22657 | 540/465–9191 or 800/348–8327 | fax 540/465–4788 | www.hotelstrasburg.com | 21 rooms, 8 suites (17 with shower only) | $79–$175 | AE, D, DC, MC, V.

SUFFOLK

Holiday Inn. The hotel is 5 mi west of town at the intersection of U.S. 58 and U.S 460 west. Restaurant. Cable TV. Pool. Business services. Some pets allowed. | 2864 Pruden Blvd. | 757/934–2311 | fax 757/539–5846 | www.holiday-inn.com | 100 rooms | $69–$109 | AE, D, DC, MC, V.

SURREY

Surrey Country Inn. A small, 2-story brick hotel in the middle of town, the Surrey has a family-owned and -operated restaurant in the front. Complimentary breakfast. No in-room TVs or phones. One room set aside for pets. | 11865 Rolfe Hwy. 23883 | 757/294–3389 | 11 rooms | $49–$99 | AE, MC, V.

TRIANGLE

Quality Inn. Just off I-95, the property is close to Prince William Forest Park. Complimentary Continental breakfast. Some microwaves, refrigerators, cable TV, some in-room hot tubs. Pool. Game room. Video games. Laundry facilities. Business services. Some pets allowed. | 1109 Horner Rd., Woodbridge | 703/494–0300 | fax 703/494–5644 | www.qualityinn.com | 94 rooms | $70–$85 | AE, D, DC, MC, V.

Ramada Inn–Quantico. Despite the building's romanesque arches and columns, and the courtyard out back, rooms at this two-story stucco hotel are basic, with very little to differentiate them from any other Ramada Inn room. But the location is a plus; from here, you can walk to downtown Triangle. Restaurant. Lounge. Picnic Area. In-room data ports. Cable TV. Pool. Exercise facilities. Laundry facilities. Pets allowed. | 4316 Inn St. 22172 | 703/221–1181 or 800/2RAMADA | fax 703/221–6952 | www.ramadaquantico.com | 139 rooms | $55–$85 | AE, D, MC, V.

TYSONS CORNER

Best Western Tysons Westpark. It's ½ mi from Tysons Corner Center and 2 mi from Wolf Trap Farm. Restaurant, bar. In-room data ports, microwaves, cable TV, in-room movies. Indoor pool, hot tub, sauna. Exercise equipment. Pets allowed (fee). | 8401 Westpark Dr. 22102 | 703/734–2800 | fax 703/821–8872 | www.bestwestern.com | 301 rooms, 14 suites | $89, $189 suites | AE, D, DC, MC, V.

Hilton McLean Tysons Corner. Built in 1987 this nine-story hotel has a glass atrium with lots of marble and greenery. There's ample parking for RVs and trucks. Restaurant, bar, complimentary Continental breakfast. In-room data ports, minibars, cable TV. Indoor pool. Spa. Exercise equipment. Laundry services. Business services. Pets allowed ($50 nonrefundable deposit). | 7920 Jones Branch Dr., McLean, 22102 | 703/847–5000 | fax 703/761–

5100 | www.hilton.com | 449 rooms, 9 suites | $80–$235 rooms, $325–$1150 suites. Kids under 18 stay free | AE, D, DC, MC, V.

Marriott Residence Inn Tysons Corner. The utilitarian suites (some bi-level) are large enough for some families. Complimentary Continental breakfast. Outdoor pool. Hot tub. Basketball, volleyball. Laundry services. Business services. Pets allowed ($150 deposit and $5/night). | 8616 Westwood Center Dr., Vienna, 22182 | 703/893–0120 | fax 703/790–8896 | www.marriott.com | 96 suites | $190–$260 | AE, D, DC, MC, V.

VIRGINIA BEACH

Days Inn–Oceanfront. All rooms face the ocean at this waterfront motel. Restaurant, bar. In-room data ports, some microwaves, room service, cable TV. Pool. Hot tub. Beach. Laundry facilities. Business services. Some pets allowed (fee). | 32nd St. and Atlantic Ave. | 757/428–7233 | fax 757/491–1936 | www.daysinnoceanfront.com | 121 rooms | $135–$215 | AE, D, DC, MC, V.

WARM SPRINGS

Anderson Cottage. A restored former tavern that was built in the 1790s, the inn has mountain views and rooms with antiques and fireplaces. Complimentary breakfast. No TV in rooms. Nearby downhill skiing. Some pets allowed in cottage. No kids under 6. | 312 Old Germantown Rd. | 540/839–2975 | www.bbonline.com/va/anderson | 2 rooms, 2 suites (1 with shared bath); 1 cottage | $60–$70; $80–$100 suites; $125 cottage | Open year-round | No credit cards.

Three Hills Inn. This country inn built in 1913 by Mary Johnson, author of "To Have and To Hold," is on the National Register of Historic Places; the 40-acre property is surrounded by wide lawns and boxwood gardens atop Warm Springs Mountain. Rooms have individualized interiors, with antique furniture. Complimentary breakfast. No TV in rooms, TV in common area. Some pets allowed. Conference center. | U.S. 220 | 540/839–5381 | fax 540/839–5199 | www.3hills.com | 13 rooms | $69–$179 | D, MC, V.

WARRENTON

Comfort Inn. The inn is ¼ mi north of town on U.S. 29 and U.S. 15. Complimentary Continental breakfast. In-room data ports, refrigerators, some in-room hot tubs; cable TV. Pool. Exercise equipment. Laundry facilities. Business services. Some pets allowed (fee). | 7379 Comfort Inn Dr. | 540/349–8900 | fax 540/347–5759 | www.comfortinn.com | 97 rooms | $59–$150 | AE, D, DC, MC, V.

WATERFORD

George's Mill Farm Bed and Breakfast. This massive stone house, dating from the 1860s, is run by descendants of the original owners. The floors are pine, and some of the antiques have been here since the place was built. The 200-acre property lies between the Shenandoah and Potomac rivers, in the Short Hill Mountains. 10 mi north of Waterford off Rte. 287. Complimentary breakfast. No room phones, TV in common area. Pond. Fishing. Pets allowed (no fee). No smoking. | 11867 Georges Mill Rd., Lovettsville, 20180 | 540/822–5224 | www.georgesmill.com | 4 rooms | $85–$115 | No credit cards.

Milltown Farms Inn. The common areas in this 1765 log-and-stone home tend toward colonial elegance, whereas the private rooms are more spare, with exposed log walls and four-poster beds. The inn sits at the end of a dirt road in the middle of 300 acres of rolling hills. Complimentary breakfast. No room phones, no TV. Pets allowed (in one room). Kids allowed (with advance notice). No smoking. | 14163 Milltown Rd. 20197 | 540/882–4470 or 888/747–3942 | www.milltownfarms.com | 5 rooms | $115–$135 | AE, D, DC, MC, V.

WAYNESBORO

Comfort Inn. The property is in town about 3 mi south of I–64. Microwaves, cable TV. Pool, wading pool. Business services. Free parking. Some pets allowed. | 640 W. Broad St. | 540/942–1171 | fax 540/942–4785 | www.comfortinn.com | 75 rooms | $59–$79 | AE, D, DC, MC, V.

Days Inn. The chain hotel is 2 mi south of town, just off I–64. Picnic area. Cable TV. Pool. Business services. Free parking. Some pets allowed (fee). | 2060 Rosser Ave. | 540/943–1101 | fax 540/949–7586 | 98 rooms | $69–$85 | AE, D, DC, MC, V.

WEST POINT

Hewick Plantation. Since 1678, ten generations of Robinsons have lived in this impressive manor house on an old tobacco plantation. Today, 45 of the 66 acres are used for growing corn, wheat, and soy. The brick house, a state and national registered landmark, has eight fireplaces, a dining room and parlor decorated with 18th-century antiques, and two rooms with private baths. The house is 15 mi east of West Point, off Rte. 17. Dining room, complimentary Continental breakfast. Cable TV, some room phones. Some pets allowed. No kids under 12. | Intersection of Hwy. 602 and 615, Urbanna, 22480 | 804/758–4214 | fax 804/758–3115 | www.hewick.com | 2 rooms | $99–$135 | AE, MC, V.

WHITE POST

Battletown Inn. The early 1900s furniture in this inn is for sale; honeymooners have been known to buy the bed in their room. The inn dates from 1809, and you can dine on the patio. Complimentary Continental breakfast. Cable TV, no room phones. Pets allowed (no fee). No smoking. | 102 W. Main St., Berryville 22611 | 540/955–4100 | fax 540/955–0127 | www.battletown.com | 12 rooms | $95–$120 | AE, D, DC, MC, V.

WILLIAMSBURG

Heritage Inn. This motel is 1 mi west of the historic district, and 3 mi from I–64. Cable TV. Pool. Business services. Some pets allowed. | 1324 Richmond Rd. | 757/229–6220 or 800/782–3800 | fax 757/229–2774 | www.heritageinnwmsb.com | 54 rooms | $42–$84 | AE, D, DC, MC, V.

Quarterpath Inn. This inn is next to a public park on the edge of the historic district. Some in-room hot tubs, cable TV. Pool. Business services. Some pets allowed. | 620 York St. | 757/220–0960 or 800/446–9222 | fax 757/220–1531 | www.hotelroom.com/virginia/wmquar | 130 rooms | $55–$69 | AE, D, MC, V.

WINCHESTER

Best Western Lee–Jackson Motor Inn. The hotel is located next to a regional mall, race tracks, and entertainment. Restaurant, bar, picnic area. Some refrigerators, room service, cable TV. Pool. Laundry facilities. Business services. Airport shuttle. Some pets allowed. | 711 Millwood Ave. 22601 | 540/662–4154 | fax 540/662–2618 | www.bestwestern.com | 140 rooms | $52–$56 | AE, D, DC, MC, V.

Days Inn. This hotel is within 2 mi of the historic and business districts, and there's a city bus stop in front. Rooms are small and simple. Restaurant. Outdoor pool. Laundry facilities. Small pets allowed ($5 fee). | 2951 Valley Ave. 22601 | 800/325–2525 or 540/667–1200 | fax 540/667–7128 | www.daysinn.com | 66 rooms | $50–$69 | AE, D, DC, MC, V.

Travelodge. This chain hotel offers easy interstate access with its location at the intersection of Interstate 81, 50 East and E22 South. Complimentary Continental breakfast. In-room data ports, some kitchenettes, some in-room hot tubs, cable TV. Pool. Laundry facilities. Business services. Some pets allowed. | 160 Front Royal Pike 22602 | 540/665–0685 | fax 540/665–0689 | www.travelodge.com | 157 rooms | $53–$75 | AE, D, DC, MC, V.

WISE

Bedrock Inn. This Blue Ridge Mountains inn has a country setting and gardens; its interior is filled with antiques. Rooms overlook a tennis court and deck. Complimentary breakfast. No TV in rooms; TV in common area. Tennis courts. Business services. Pets allowed. | U.S. 460, Pounding Mill, 24637 | 540/963–9412 | fax 540/322–3617 | bedrock@netscape.net | www.symweb.com/bedrock/index.html | 3 rooms, 2 suites | $75–$100 | AE, MC, V.

WOODSTOCK

Budget Host Inn. This chain hotel is right on Main Street (US Route 11) in Woodstock. Restaurant, picnic area. Cable TV. Pool. Laundry facilities. Business services. Some pets allowed. | 1290 S. Main St., Woodstock | 540/459–4086 | fax 540/459–4043 | www.budgethost.com | 43 rooms | $40–$47 | AE, D, DC, MC, V.

Washington

ABERDEEN

Guest House International Suites and Inn. The hotel overlooks the Wishkah River and is directly adjacent to the Wishkah mall and the city center. | 60 rooms. Complimentary Continental breakfast, in-room data ports, microwaves, refrigerators, cable TV, in-room VCRs, pool, hot tub, gym, laundry facilities, business services. Pets allowed. | 701 E. Heron St. 98520 | 360/537–7460 or 800/21–GUEST | fax 360/537–7462 | gha08@aol.com | www.guesthouse.net | $78–$140 | AE, D, MC, V.

Red Lion Inn. This hotel is right in the heart of downtown. | 67 rooms. Complimentary Continental breakfast, cable TV. Pets allowed. | 521 W. Wishkah 98520 | 360/532–5210 | fax 360/533–8483 | $55–$109 | AE, D, DC, MC, V.

ANACORTES

Albatross. This 1927 Cape Cod–style house sits across the street from the marina and only two blocks away from Washington Park. The rooms each have their own character. The Scarlett O'Hara Room has lace curtains and genuine plantation furnishings, while Monet's Garden is named for the views it affords of the backyard garden. | 4 rooms. Complimentary breakfast, no room phones, TV in common area. Pets allowed. No kids under 5, no smoking. | 5708 Kingsway W | 360/293–0677 or 800/622–8864 | fax 360/299–2262 | albatros@cnw.com | www.cnw.com/~albatros | $85–$95 | AE, D, MC, V.

Anacortes Inn. This small motel is 2 mi from the city center and next door to a pretty park with old trees. The rooms have views of the water. | 44 rooms. Some kitchenettes, microwaves, refrigerators, cable TV, pool, business services. Pets allowed (fee). | 3006 Commercial Ave. 98221 | 360/293–3153 or 800/327–7976 | fax 360/293–0209 | $50–$100 | AE, D, DC, MC, V.

BELLEVUE

Candlewood Suites. Although this is primarily an extended-stay hotel, you might find its location—less than a mile from exit 11 off I–90—convenient. | 126 rooms. Kitchenettes, microwaves, refrigerators, cable TV, in-room VCRs, gym, laundry service. Pets allowed (fee). | 15805 S.E. 37th St. 98006 | 425/373–1212 | fax 425/373–1500 | www.candlewoodsuites.com | $115–$135 | AE, D, DC, MC, V.

Residence Inn by Marriott. This residential-style hotel is designed for longer stays and is also perfect for entertaining clients. | 120 suites. Picnic area, complimentary Continental breakfast, in-room data ports, microwaves, refrigerators, cable TV, pool, laundry facilities, business services. Shuttle service, free parking. Pets allowed (fee). | 14455 N.E. 29th Place 98007 | 425/882–1222 or 800/331–3131 | fax 425/885–9260 | $125–$170 suites | AE, D, DC, MC, V.

BELLINGHAM

Anderson Creek Lodge. Eight miles northeast of downtown, the 65 acres of this property are split between woods and pastures filled with llamas. The rooms have hand-carved furniture, exposed beams, and stained-glass windows. Each overlooks the garden and landscaped grounds that surround the lodge. Hikes are conducted on a regular basis throughout the year. Although the property's seclusion is suitable for romantic getaways, the lodge can also accommodate families. | 3 rooms. Complimentary breakfast, no air-conditioning, cable TV, in-room VCRs, no room phones, outdoor hot tub, hiking, business services. Pets allowed. No smoking. | 5602 Mission Rd. 98226 | 360/966–0598 | AndersonCreek@ compuserve.com | www.andersoncreek.com | $85 | MC, V.

Best Western Lakeway Inn. This chain hotel is 3 mi from the Alaska Ferry Terminal and historic Fairhaven. | 132 rooms. Restaurant, bar with entertainment, room service, cable TV, indoor pool, beauty salon, hot tub, gym, laundry facilities, business services, airport shuttle, free parking. Some pets allowed (fee). | 714 Lakeway Dr. 98226 | 360/671–1011 | fax 360/676–8519 | $79–$99 | AE, D, DC, MC, V.

Days Inn. This hotel is centrally located and caters to business travelers and families. | 70 rooms. Complimentary Continental breakfast, some refrigerators, cable TV, pool, hot tub, laundry facilities. Pets allowed (fee). | 125 E. Kellogg Rd. 98226 | 360/671–6200 | fax 360/671–9491 | $45–$125 | AE, D, DC, MC, V.

Travelers Inn. This motel is near the Belli-Fair Mall and caters to families. | 124 rooms. Some refrigerators, microwaves, cable TV, pool, hot tub, laundry facilities, business services. Some pets allowed. | 3750 Meridian St. 98225 | 360/671–4600 | fax 360/671–6487 | $45–$75 | AE, D, DC, MC, V.

Val-U-Inn. This family motel, just off I–5, is close to downtown and only 25 mi south of the Canadian border. | 82 rooms. Complimentary Continental breakfast, some refrigerators, cable TV, hot tub, laundry facilities, business services. Airport and ferry terminal shuttles, free parking. Pets allowed (fee). | 805 Lakeway Dr. 98226 | 360/671–9600, 800/ 443–7777 | fax 360/671–8323 | $47–$75 | AE, D, DC, MC, V.

BLAINE

Inn at SemiAhMoo. A sprawling country resort on a sandy peninsula, 15 minutes from downtown Blaine. | 198 rooms, 14 suites. Bar with entertainment, dining rooms, snack bar, in-room data ports, room service, cable TV, indoor-outdoor pool, beauty salon, hot tub, spa, driving range, 18-hole golf course, putting green, tennis, gym, marina, water sports, boating, bicycles, video games and pool table, laundry facilities, business services. Pets allowed (fee). | 9565 Semiahmoo Pkwy. 98230 | 360/371–2000 | fax 360/371–5490 | www.semiahmoo.com | $179–$219 rooms, $239–$279 suites | AE, D, DC, MC, V.

BREMERTON

Illahee Manor Bed and Breakfast. This 1920s manor sits directly on the bay and has its own private beach. The 6 acres of woods, orchards, and gardens on which the manor sits are also home to miniature deer and llamas. The bedrooms are all large; some have fireplaces and balconies, those in the manor's turret have wraparound windows. | 5 rooms, 2 cabins. Restaurant, complimentary breakfast, room service, some microwaves, refrigerators, some in-room hot tubs, cable TV, in-room VCRs, pond. Pets allowed. | 6680 Illahee Rd. NE

98311 | 360/698–7555 or 800/693–6680 | fax 360/698–0688 | innkeeper@illaheemanor.com | www.illaheemanor.com | $115–$195 rooms, $175–$225 cabins | AE, D, MC, V.

Oyster Bay Inn. Most rooms at this inn have beautiful panoramic views of the bay. Stroll down the back lawn to see the bay up close. The rooms are well maintained and appointed with many modern amenities. | 76 rooms. Restaurant, bar (with entertainment), complimentary Continental breakfast, some kitchenettes, microwaves, refrigerators, cable TV. Pets allowed (fee). | 4412 Kitsap Way 98312 | 360/377–5510 or 800/393–3862 | kangmail@email.msn.com | www.oysterbaymotel.com | $68 | AE, D, DC, MC, V.

CATHLAMET

Nassa Point Motel. Three mi east of Cathlamet, at the base of an evergreen-covered hill, this small roadside motel is a favorite with fishermen who choose the lodging for its proximity to the Columbia River across the street. Wind surfing and swimming are also possible 2 mi east. The rooms are appointed with simple, basic furnishings and amenities. | 6 rooms. No air-conditioning, kitchenettes, refrigerators, no room phones. Pets allowed. | 851 E. State Rte. 4 98612 | 360/795–3941 | $40 | MC, V.

CENTRALIA

Ferryman's Inn. Just off I–5 at exit 82, this two-story motel is located between the Riverside Park, behind which the Skookumchuk River flows, and Borst Park, adjacent to the Chehalis River. Try for an upstairs room. | 84 rooms. Complimentary Continental breakfast, no smoking rooms, pool, spa. Pets allowed. | 1003 Eckerson Rd. 98532 | 360/330–2094 | $48–$55 | AE, D, DC, MC, V.

Inn of Centralia. Only steps away from factory outlet stores and the antique malls, this hotel sits conveniently close to I–5, less than two blocks from exit 82. The rooms are modern and well-maintained. | 88 rooms. Complimentary Continental breakfast, picnic area, some refrigerators, some in-room hot tubs, cable TV, pool. Pets allowed (fee). | 702 Harrison Ave. 98531 | 360/736–2875 | fax 360/736–2651 | $59–$64 | AE, D, DC, MC, V.

CHEHALIS

Parkplace Inn and Suites. Just off I–5 at exit 76, this chain has rooms with views of Mt. Rainier. Three blocks away is a park with a playground for kids. | 61 rooms. Complimentary Continental breakfast, in-room data ports, refrigerators, microwaves, cable TV, pool, hot tub, gym, laundry services, business services. Pets allowed (fee). | 201 S.W. Interstate Ave. 98532 | 360/748–4040 or 877/748–0008 | www.bestwester.com | $64–$118 | AE, D, DC, MC, V.

CHENEY

Rosebrook Inn. Visiting parents tend to stay at this motel, which is just seven blocks from Eastern Washington University. The rooms are given a country touch with lace curtains and flowery wallpaper. | 12 rooms. Picnic area, microwaves, refrigerators, cable TV. Pets allowed. | 304 W. 1st St. 99004 | 509/235–6538 or 888/848–9853 | fax 509/235–9229 | rosebinn@worldnet.att.net | $64 | AE, D, DC, MC, V.

Willow Springs Motel. This small motel is in a quiet neighborhood close to Eastern Washington University and 12 mi from Spokane. | 44 rooms. Complimentary Continental breakfast on weekends, some kitchenettes, air-conditioning, cable TV, laundry facilities. Pets allowed (fee). | 5 B St. 99004 | 509/235–5138 | fax 509/235–4528 | $39–$54 | AE, D, DC, MC, V.

CLE ELUM

Cascade Mountain Inn. This affordable lodging is located in the downtown area, near exit 84 off I–90. The rooms are all spacious and, with the many amenities, give a home-away-from-home comfort. | 43 rooms. Complimentary Continental breakfast, kitchenettes, microwaves, refrigerators, some in-room hot tubs, cable TV. Pets allowed. | 906 E. 1st St. 98922 | 509/674–2380 or 888/674–3975 | fax 509/674–7099 | $50–$60 | AE, D, DC, MC, V.

COLVILLE

Benny's Colville Inn. This is a comfortable family motel nestled in a pristine valley between the Kettle and Selkirk Mountain ranges. | 105 rooms. Restaurant, no-smoking rooms, pool, hot tub, gym. Pets allowed. | 915 S. Main | 509/684–2517 or 800/680–2517 | fax 509/684–2546 | www.colvilleinn.com | $40–$125 | AE, D, MC, V.

Comfort Inn. Majestic mountains look down on this chain hotel. You cannot forget you are near the forest with the enormous amount of wildlife around the hotel. | 53 rooms. Complimentary Continental breakfast, in-room data ports, cable TV, pool, hot tub, laundry service. Pets allowed. | 166 N.E. Canning Dr. 99114 | 509/684–2010 or 800/228–5150 | fax 509/684–1918 | comfortinn@coville.com | www.comfortinn.colville.com | $56–$125 | AE, D, DC, MC, V.

COPALIS BEACH

Echoes of the Sea. Sitting on 8 acres of wooded land just north of Copalis, this motel is only a short walk to the beach. A recreation room provides space to relax and play billiards or ping-pong. The property also contains a number of campsites. | 8 rooms. Picnic area, no air-conditioning, cable TV, hiking, gift shop. Pets allowed (fee). No smoking. | 3208 Rte. 109 98535 | 360/289–3358 or 800/578–ECHO | $55–$90 | AE, D, MC, V.

Iron Springs Resort. This long-established resort with a loyal following is right on the beach. | 28 rooms. Pool. Pets allowed (fee). | 3707 Rte. 109 98535 | 360/276–4230 | fax 360/276–4365 | $66–$104 | AE, D, MC, V.

COULEE DAM

Coulee House. This is a great spot for viewing the laser light show at the Grand Coulee Dam. The casino is across the street. | 61 rooms. Some kitchenettes, some refrigerators, cable TV, pool, hot tub, laundry facilities, business services. Pets allowed. | 110 Roosevelt Way 99116 | 509/633–1101 or 800/715–7767 | fax 509/633–1416 | $64–$120 | AE, D, DC, MC, V.

DAYTON

Purple House Bed and Breakfast. This Queen Anne Italianate-style house was built in 1882 by a pioneer physician. Today a mixture of European art and Chinese collectibles adorn the interior. The bedrooms are individually appointed with a tasteful selection of Victorian antiques. Afternoon pastries and tea are presented in the parlor. | 4 rooms. Complimentary breakfast, TV in common area, pool. Pets allowed. No kids under 16. No smoking. | 415 Clay St. 99328 | 509/382–3159 or 800/486–2474 | fax 509/382–3159 | $85–$125 | MC, V.

Weinhard Hotel. Built in the late 1800s as a saloon and lodge by the nephew of beer baron Henry Weinhard, this hotel was lovingly restored (with modern amenities added) a few years ago. The rooms are furnished with period antiques, and there's a pleasant roof garden for catching the breezes. The dining room is open from mid-morning through dinner, Thursday–Monday. | 15 rooms. Dining room, complimentary Continental breakfast, no-smoking rooms. Pets allowed. | 235 E. Main St. 99328 | 509/382–4032 | fax 509/382–2640 | $75–$125 | AE, MC, V.

EDMONDS

Edmonds Harbor Inn. A country inn in the city with luxurious rooms, but, alas, no water views. It is near the Kingston ferry terminal and the marina. | 60 rooms. Dining room, complimentary Continental breakfast, no-smoking rooms. Pets allowed (fee). | 130 W. Dayton 98020 | 425/771–5021 or 800/441–8033 | fax 425/672–2880 | www.nwcountryinns.com/harbor | $79–$135 | MC, V.

ELLENSBURG

Best Western Ellensburg Inn. A comfortable freeway motel that's a favorite with traveling salesmen, families, and visiting college professors. | 105 rooms. Restaurant, bar with entertainment, room service, cable TV, indoor pool, wading pool, hot tub, exercise equipment, business services, free parking. Pets allowed (fee). | 1700 Canyon Rd. 98926 | 509/925–9801 | fax 509/925–2093 | $54–$77 | AE, D, DC, MC, V.

ENUMCLAW

Best Western Park Center Hotel. This is a comfortable motel only 7 mi away from a recreation area, including Mud Mountain Dam, which also makes it ideal for families. | 40 rooms. Restaurant, bar picnic area, in-room data ports, microwaves, some refrigerators, room service, cable TV, hot tub, business services. Pets allowed (fee). | 1000 Griffin Ave. 98022 | 360/825–4490 | fax 360/825–3686 | $69–$78 | AE, D, DC, MC, V.

EVERETT

Holiday Inn Hotel and Conference Center. Upscale business travelers' hotel convenient to all area activities. | 249 rooms. Restaurant, no-smoking rooms, pool, gym. Pets allowed (fee). | 101 128th St. SE | 425/337–2900 | fax 425/337–0707 | $95–$129 | AE, D, DC, MC, V.

FORKS

Forks Motel. Forks's largest motel has guest rooms, small suites, larger suites with two bedrooms and full kitchens and a single suite with a hot tub. Each year a portion of the motel is renovated. | 73 rooms. No air-conditioning in some rooms, some kitchenettes, cable TV, pool, wading pool, laundry facilities, business services. Pets allowed. | 351 S. Forks Ave. 98331 | 360/374–6243 or 800/544–3416 | fax 360/374–6760 | www.forksmotel.com | $54–$135 | AE, D, DC, MC, V.

Hoh Humm Ranch Bed and Breakfast. This B&B sits on a 200-acre ranch 20 mi south of Forks. The simple, comfortable rooms overlook the valley and river below. Kids love the llamas, deer, and goats that are raised on the ranch. | 4 rooms. Complimentary breakfast, no air-conditioning, no room phones, TV in common area. Pets allowed. No smoking. | 171763 Hwy. 101 98331 | 360/374–5337 | fax 360/374–5344 | hohhumm@olypen.com | www.olypen.com/hohhumm | $35–$55 | No credit cards.

Kalaloch Lodge. This venerable, weather-beaten lodge is on the wild outer coast of the national park, with rustically simple, no-frills accommodations. But the isolated beach is worth the lack of amenities. There is a convenience store on the property, with a gas station. | 10 rooms, 4 suites; 4 cabins; 10 rooms, 2 suites in lodge. Restaurant, bar, no air-conditioning, some kitchenettes, some refrigerators, no room phones. Pets allowed (fee). | 157151 U.S. 101 98331 | 360/962–2271 | fax 360/962–3391 | www.visitkalaloch.com | $122–$140, $120–$225 suites, $135–$225 cabins | AE, MC, V.

Miller Tree Inn Bed and Breakfast. Originally a farmhouse, this B&B is bordered on two sides by pasture land. The inn's many windows make the rooms bright, cheerful places to relax amid the assortment of antiques, knick-knacks, and quilts. A porch and back deck allow for summer lounging. | 7 rooms. Complimentary breakfast, no air-conditioning, no room phones, no TV in some rooms, TV in common area, hot tub. Pets allowed. No smoking. | 654 E. Division St. 98331 | 360/374–6806 or 800/943–6563 | fax 360/374–6807 | info@millertreeinn.com | www.millertreeinn.com | $75–$135 | MC, V.

GOLDENDALE

Ponderosa Motel. This 2-story motel in the heart of the city sits just a ¼ mi north of Highway 97 at exit 142. Restaurants and shops are all within easy walking distance. | 28 rooms. Some kitchenettes, cable TV, business services. Pets allowed (fee). | 775 E. Broadway St. 98620 | 509/773–5842 | fax 509/773–4049 | $40–$65 | AE, D, DC, MC, V.

ILWACO

Eagle's Nest Resort. Just ½ mi east of Ilwaco, this resort sits on 94 acres of wooded land. The accommodations vary from cedar cottages to parked trailers. The cottages have full kitchens, though the cabins and trailers are simpler. | 5 cottages, 3 cabins. Restaurant, no air-conditioning, some kitchenettes, some microwaves, some refrigerators, some in-room hot tubs, cable TV, pool, hot tub, miniature golf, basketball, volleyball, shops, video games, playground. Pets allowed. | 700 W. North Head Rd. 98624 | 360/642–8351 | fax 360/642–8402 | eaglenr@pacifier.com | www.eaglesnestresort.com | $100–$125 | D, MC, V.

KENNEWICK

Best Western Kennewick Inn. One of Kennewick's newest lodgings, this chain motel is conveniently close to I–82, to the city's shopping and restaurants, and to an 18-hole golf course. | 87 rooms. In-room data ports, microwaves, refrigerators, some in-room hot tubs, cable TV, pool, hot tub, sauna, gym, laundry services, business services. Pets allowed (fee). | 4001 W. 27th Ave. 99337 | 509/586–1332 | fax 509/586–0263 | www.bestwestern.com | $74 | AE, D, DC, MC, V.

Cavanaugh's at Columbia Center. This comfortable conference and convention hotel is next to a major regional shopping mall. | 161 rooms. Restaurant, bar with entertainment, room service, cable TV, pool, hot tub, gym, business services, airport shuttle. Pets allowed (fee). | 1101 N. Columbia Center Blvd. 99336 | 509/783–0611 or 800/325–4000 | fax 509/735–3087 | $60–$125 | AE, D, DC, MC, V.

Nendels Inn. This is a two-story family motel in the center of town. | 106 rooms. Some kitchenettes, some refrigerators, cable TV, pool, business services. Pets allowed (fee). | 2811 W. 2nd 99336 | 509/735–9511 or 800/547–0106 | fax 509/735–1944 | $43–$63 | AE, D, DC, MC, V.

Tapadera Inn. This budget motel is within walking distance of movie theaters and restaurants. | 61 rooms. Restaurant, complimentary Continental breakfast, some refrigerators, cable TV, pool. Pets allowed (fee). | 300 N. Ely 99336 | 509/783–6191 | fax 509/735–3854 | $38–$56 | AE, D, DC, MC, V.

KIRKLAND

Best Western Kirkland Inn. Sitting conveniently at exit 20A off I–405, this chain hotel is only 1 mi from shopping, dining, and Lake Washington. | 110 rooms. Complimentary Continental breakfast, some microwaves, some refrigerators, some in-room hot tubs, cable TV, pool, hot tub, laundry facilities. Pets allowed. | 12223 N.E. 116th St. 98034 | 425/822–2300 or 800/332–4200 | fax 425/889–9616 | www.bestwestern.com | AE, D, DC, MC, V.

LA CONNER

Heron. This B&B, in a Victorian house, has a stone fireplace in the parlor. The rooms are spacious, and the homemade breads and muffins served with breakfast are scrumptious. | 9 rooms, 3 suites. Complimentary breakfast, no air-conditioning, hot tub. Some pets allowed (fee). | 117 Maple Ave. 98257 | 360/466–4626 | fax 360/466–3254 | $100, $125–150 suites | AE, MC, V.

LEAVENWORTH

Der Ritterhof Motor Inn. Deluxe motel with a vaguely Bavarian theme. All of the rooms enjoy views of the mountains. | 51 rooms. Picnic area, some kitchenettes, cable TV, pool, hot tub, putting green, business services. Pets allowed (fee). | 190 U.S. 2 98826 | 509/548–5845 or 800/255–5845 | fax 509/548–4098 | $76–$98 | AE, MC, V.

Evergreen Inn. Built in the 1930s as a roadside inn, the lodging is popular for its proximity to downtown (only one block) and for its distance from the highway. A sun deck and balconies, some of which are private, have views of the surrounding Cascades. | 40 rooms. Complimentary Continental breakfast, in-room data ports, some minibars, some in-room hot tubs, cable TV, outdoor hot tub. Pets allowed. No smoking. | 1117 Front St. 98826 | 509/548–5515 or 800/327–7212 | fax 509/548–6556 | info@evergreeninn.com | www.evergreeninn.com | $65–$135 | AE, D, DC, MC, V.

Oysterville Guest House. Nestled in the north end of Oysterville, this peaceful, private cottage has three bedrooms, a wood burning stove, and panoramic views of Willapa Bay. | 3 rooms. Kitchenettes, microwaves, refrigerators, cable TV, in-room VCRs, laundry facilities. Pets allowed. No smoking. | Territory Rd., Oysterville 98624 | 206/726–8004 | ligre@ willapabay.org | $125 | No credit cards.

LONG BEACH

Anchorage Motor Court. This beachfront motel with fireplaces and free firewood in the rooms overlooks the dunes and the distant ocean. | 10 rooms. No air-conditioning, kitchenettes, cable TV, playground. Some pets allowed (fee). | 2209 Boulevard N | 360/642–2351 or 800/646–2351 | $60–$120 | AE, D, MC, V.

Breakers. Rather generic condominiums in a splendid location next to the dunes and beach, with great views of the surf and ocean. It is next to a public golf course. | 116 rooms. No air-conditioning, some kitchenettes, some refrigerators, cable TV, indoor pool, hot tub, business services. Pets allowed (fee). | 210 26th St. N 98631 | 360/642–4414 or 800/219–9833 | fax 360/642–8772 | breakerslongbeach.com | $59–$200 | AE, D, MC, V.

Chautauqua Lodge. Conference resort bordering the dunes. | 180 rooms. Restaurant, bar, no air-conditioning, some kitchenettes, refrigerators, indoor pool, hot tub, sauna, game room, laundry facilities, business services. Pets allowed (fee). | 304 14th St. NW 98361 | 360/642–4401 or 800/869–8401 | fax 360/642–2340 | $55–$160 | AE, D, DC, MC, V.

Edgewater Inn. A very plain motel in a great spot on the beach with an ocean view. Boardwalk nearby, as well as bike and hiking trails, and horseback riding. | 84 rooms. Cable TV. Some pets allowed (fee). | 409 10th St. SW 98631 | 360/642–2311 or 800/561–2456 | fax 360/642–8018 | $49–$104 | AE, D, DC, MC, V.

Historic Sou'wester Lodge. Built in 1892 as a summer retreat for a timber baron and U.S. Senator, this lodge sits directly adjacent to dunes that lead to the ocean. Rooms are eclectically appointed in what is described by the proprietor as "early Salvation Army beach decor." In the mornings you are invited to make your own breakfast in the lodge's kitchen. The parlor is frequently the setting for soirées, discussions, theater performances, and chamber music concerts. | 6 suites, 4 cabins, 10 trailers. No air-conditioning, no room phones, no TV in some rooms. Pets allowed. No smoking. | Beach Access Rd. 38th Place, Seaview 98644 | 360/642–2542 | info@souwesterlodge.com | www.souwesterlodge.com | $39–$129 | D, MC, V.

Our Place at the Beach. Comfortable dune-front hostelry within easy walking distance of the beach, and all the area restaurants and shops. | 25 rooms. Picnic area, some kitchenettes, refrigerators, 2 hot tubs, sauna, gym, business services. Pets allowed (fee). | 1309 South Blvd. 98631 | 360/642–3793 or 800/538–5107 | fax 360/642–3896 | www.ohwy.com/ wa/ourplace | $49–$63, cabins $80 | AE, D, DC, MC, V.

Shaman. A plain but very comfortable motel off the beaten path near the dunes and beach. One of the better local low-budget choices. | 42 rooms. No air-conditioning, some kitchenettes, some refrigerators, cable TV, pool, business services. Some pets allowed (fee). | 115 3rd St. SW 98631 | 360/642–3714 or 800/753–3750 | fax 360/642–8599 | www. shamanmotel.com | $79–$104 | AE, D, DC, MC, V.

LONGVIEW

Patrician Inn and Suites. The lobby's many antiques give this quiet hotel, located 3 mi from the highway, a comfortable homey feel. There are guest rooms, mini-suites, and one larger suite with a hot tub. | 50 rooms. Complimentary Continental breakfast, no-smoking rooms, pool, hot tub. Pets allowed (fee). | 723 7th Ave. | 360/414–1000 | fax 360/414–1076 | $65–$79 | AE, D, DC, MC, V.

MARYSVILLE

Best Western Tulalip Inn. This chain motel sits across the road from the Tulalip Casino and Bingo, just off I–5 at exit 199. Restaurants and shops are nearby. | 69 rooms. Restaurant, complimentary Continental breakfast, room service, some microwaves, some refrigerators, some in-room hot tubs, cable TV, pool, spa, laundry services, business services. Pets allowed. | 6128 33rd Ave. NE 98271 | 360/659–5688 or 800/481–4804 | fax 360/659–5688 | $69–$103 | AE, D, DC, MC, V.

Village Motor Inn. Small, personal service is the hallmark of this comfortable 3-story motel in central Marysville. | 45 rooms, 6 suites. Complimentary Continental breakfast, in-room data ports, cable TV, business services, free parking. Some pets allowed (fee). | 235 Beach Ave. 98270 | 360/659–0005 | fax 360/658–0866 | $52–$130, $95–$130 suites | AE, D, DC, MC, V.

MOCLIPS

Hi-Tide Ocean Beach Resort. At this typical beach town resort all the rooms have great ocean views. | 25 suites. No air-conditioning, kitchenettes, cable TV, business services. Pets allowed (fee). | 4890 Railroad Ave. 98562 | 360/276–4142 or 800/662–5477 (WA) | fax 360/276–0156 | $95–$169 suites | D, MC, V.

Moonstone Beach Motel. Each room of this small motel, which sits directly on the beach, has an unbeatable view of the ocean. Some rooms have full kitchens and open onto the beach itself. | 8 rooms. No air-conditioning, some kitchenettes, some microwaves, some refrigerators, cable TV, no room phones. Pets allowed. | 4849 Pacific Ave. 98562 | 888/888–9063 | $65–$85 | AE, MC, V.

Sandpiper Beach Resort. The resort sits 3 mi south of Moclips directly on a secluded beach. The clean, contemporary suites have fireplaces, exposed wood ceilings, and sliding glass doors that lead to a porch overlooking the beach and ocean. | 31 suites. No air-conditioning, kitchenettes, microwaves, refrigerators, no room phones, no TV. Pets allowed (fee), no smoking. | 4159 Rte. 109, Pacific Beach 98571 | 360/276–4580 or 800/56–PIPER | esandpiper@hotmail.com | www.sandpiper-resort.com | $85–$130 | MC, V.

MOSES LAKE

Best Value El Rancho Motel. Commercial travelers' and family motel. | 20 rooms. Some kitchenettes, refrigerators, cable TV, pool. Some pets allowed. | 1214 S. Pioneer Way 98837 | 509/765–9173 or 888/315–BEST (2378) | fax 509/765–1137 | www.bestvalueinn.com | $32–$60 | AE, D, DC, MC, V.

Best Western Hallmark Inn. This comfortable waterfront motel overlooks the lake and fields and hills to the west. | 161 rooms. Restaurant, bar with entertainment, refrigerators, room service, cable TV, pool, wading pool, hot tub, sauna, tennis, dock, laundry facilities, business services, airport shuttle, free parking. Some pets allowed. | 3000 Marina Dr. 98837 | 509/765–9211 | fax 509/766–0493 | $64–$140 | AE, D, DC, MC, V.

Interstate Inn. Off I–90 at exit 176, this two-story motel sits just 1 mi east of Moses Lake State Park. | 30 rooms. Some refrigerators, cable TV, indoor pool, hot tub, sauna, business services. Pets allowed. | 2801 W. Broadway 98837 | 509/765–1777 | fax 509/766–9452 | $45–$54 | AE, D, DC, MC, V.

Moses Lake Travelodge. This chain hotel, at the center of downtown, is close to restaurants and shopping. A park directly adjacent to the hotel allows room for outdoor relaxation. | 40 rooms. Microwaves, refrigerators, cable TV, pool, spa. Pets allowed (fee). | 316 S. Pioneer Way 98837 | 509/765-8631 or 800/578-7878 | fax 509/765-3685 | www.travelodge.com | $59-$75 | AE, D, DC, MC, V.

MT. RAINIER NATIONAL PARK

Randle Motel. There are basic accommodations at this motor inn that sits in the center of Randle, adjacent to restaurants and stores. The rooms are all furnished with double beds. | 10 rooms. No air-conditioning, no room phones. Pets allowed. | 9780 Hwy. 12, Randle 98377 | 360/497-5346 | $35-$45 | MC, V.

MOUNT VERNON

Best Western College Way Inn. Comfortable off-freeway inn near the Skagit River. It's centrally located, with easy access to several restaurants. | 66 rooms. Complimentary Continental breakfast, no air-conditioning, in-room data ports, some kitchenettes, some refrigerators, cable TV, pool, hot tub, business services. Pets allowed (fee). | 300 W. College Way | 360/424-4287 | fax 360/424-6036 | $73-$91 | AE, D, DC, MC, V.

Best Western Cotton Tree Inn. Plain but comfortable off-freeway motel that's not far from the casinos. | 120 rooms. Bar, complimentary Continental breakfast, in-room data ports, some refrigerators, cable TV, pool, laundry facilities, business services, free parking, pets allowed (fee). | 2300 Market St. 98273 | 360/428-5678 | fax 360/428-1844 | www. cottontree.net | $79-$89 | AE, D, DC, MC, V.

NEAH BAY

Silver Salmon Resort Motel. Sitting in the center of Neah Bay and across from the Marina, this motel is only a hop, skip, and a jump away from restaurants and shopping; the beach is a block from your door. Rooms are appointed with basic furnishings. | 11 rooms. Picnic area, no air-conditioning, some kitchenettes, some microwaves, some refrigerators, no room phones, no TV, shop. Pets allowed. | 1280 Bayview Ave. 98357 | 360/645-2388 or 888/ 713-6477 | silvsalm@centurytell.net | www.silversalmonresort.com | $51.50-$62 | Dec.- Feb. | D, MC, V.

Tyee Motel. A plain motel in a rather plain Indian village on a gorgeous coastline. | 41 rooms. RV park. Pets allowed. | Bayview Ave. 98357 | 360/645-2223 | $42-$108 | Closed Labor Day-mid-Apr. | MC, V.

NEWPORT

Golden Spur Motor Inn. This two-story motel sits just west of downtown on Highway 2. Renovated in 1999, the rooms are clean and well-maintained. | 24 rooms. Restaurant, bar, some kitchenettes, some microwaves, refrigerators, cable TV. Pets allowed (fee). | 924 W. Hwy. 2 99156 | 509/447-3823 | users.rightathome.com/~goldspur | $45-$68 | AE, D, MC, V.

Newport City Inn. Small-town motel within walking distance of restaurants in downtown Newport. | 13 rooms. No-smoking rooms. Some pets allowed (fee). | 220 N. Washington 99156 | 509/447-3463 | fax 509/447-2168 | $52-$58 | AE, MC, V.

NORTH CASCADES NATIONAL PARK

Salmonberry Way Bed and Breakfast. This Victorian road house from the early 1900s stands on 8 acres of wilderness, next to the Skagit River, just 4 mi west of the park. The hiking here is unbeatable. Rooms are appointed with antiques that evoke bygone days when gold miners would stay at this road house on their way prospecting. | 2 rooms. Complimentary breakfast, no room phones, no TV. Pets allowed. No smoking. | 61008 S.R. 20, Marblemount 98267 | 360/873-4016 | $49-$59 | No credit cards.

OAK HARBOR

Best Western Harbor Plaza. This three-story highway motel is 1 mi from the city beach and recreation area. | 80 rooms. Lounge, complimentary Continental breakfast, in-room data ports, microwaves, refrigerators, cable TV, pool, hot tub, gym, business services, free parking. Some pets allowed (fee). | 33175 SR. 20 98277 | 360/679–4567 | fax 360/675–2543 | $80–$129 | AE, D, DC, MC, V.

OCEAN SHORES

Grey Gull. A post-modernist beach resort within walking distance of restaurants and shops. Trails from the hotel lead down to the beach. All rooms have ocean views and fireplaces. | 34 suites, 36 apartments. No air-conditioning, kitchenettes, refrigerators, cable TV, pool, hot tub, sauna, laundry facilities, business services. Some pets allowed (fee). | 651 Ocean Shores Blvd. 98569 | 360/289–3381 or 800/562–9712 (WA) | www.thegreygull.com | $110–$125 studios, $120–$275 suites | AE, D, DC, MC, V.

Polynesian Resort. Only a short stroll through the dunes separates you from the beach when you stay at this resort, complete with modern amenities. The upper floors have views of the water and most rooms come with a fireplace and full kitchen. | 71 rooms. Restaurant, picnic area, kitchenettes, microwaves, refrigerators, cable TV, pool, spa, sauna, basketball, volleyball, beach. Pets allowed. | 615 Ocean Shores 98569 | 360/289–3361 or 800/562–4836 | $79–$320 | AE, D, DC, MC, V.

OLYMPIA

Best Western Tumwater. This faux-brick, mission-style motel is next to golf and tennis and ½ mi from Tumwater Falls. It's also 1 mi from the Olympia and Miller Brewing Co. | 89 rooms. Complimentary Continental breakfast, in-room data ports, refrigerators, microwaves, cable TV, gym, hot tub, sauna, laundry facilities, business services. Some pets allowed (fee). | 5188 Capitol Blvd. S., Tumwater 98501 | 360/956–1235 | fax 360/956–1235, ext. 277 | $70–$83 | AE, D, DC, MC, V.

OLYMPIC NATIONAL PARK

Lake Crescent Lodge. Sitting directly on the lake 21 mi west of Port Angeles and surrounded by tall firs and hemlocks, the main building harkens back to 1916 when it served as a tavern. A stuffed elk head hangs above the huge stone fireplace in the antiques-filled lobby. The simple pine furniture of the cedar-paneled guest rooms gives them a spartan flavor. Making up for this, however, are the wonderful mountain and water views from the bedroom windows. | 52 rooms. Restaurant, no air-conditioning, no room phones, no TV. Pets allowed. No smoking. | 416 Lake Crescent Rd., Port Angeles 98363 | 360/928–3211 | www.olypen.com/lakecrescentlodge | $66.50–$141.50 | AE, D, DC, MC, V.

Sol Duc Hot Springs. This rustic resort, 12 mi off Hwy. 101, has had some ups-and-downs, but is currently on the upswing again. Great location in the park and great hot springs. | 32 cottages. Dining room, picnic area, no air-conditioning, some kitchenettes, 4 pools, wading pool, massage. Pets allowed. | Soleduck Rd. and Hwy. 101 98362 | 360/327–3583 | fax 360/327–3593 | $98–$118 cottages | Closed Oct.–Mar. | AE, D, MC, V.

OMAK

Omak Inn. Located just off I–97, this motel—built in 1995—is close to restaurants and shopping. A small patio and expansive lawn behind the pool allow for relaxing in the summer. | 49 rooms. Complimentary breakfast, in-room data ports, some microwaves, some refrigerators, some in-room hot tubs, cable TV, pool, hot tub, gym, laundry facilities, business services. Pets allowed (fee). | 912 Koala Dr. 98841 | 509/826–3822 or 800/204–4800 | fax 509/826–2980 | dlawver@northcascades.net | www.omakinn.com | $62 | AE, D, MC, V.

ORCAS ISLAND

Deer Harbor Inn. The original log lodge, which was built in 1915, no longer houses guests, but is now used as the inn's dining room. Today you can stay in a 1987 log lodge or in one of four cottages that stands in the center of an orchard. The lodge rooms have peeled-log furniture, quilts, and balconies from which to view the meadows, water, and inquisitive wildlife. | 8 rooms, 4 cottages. Restaurant, complimentary Continental breakfast, no air-conditioning, some kitchenettes, some microwaves, refrigerators, no room phones, no TV in some rooms. Pets allowed. No smoking. | 33 Inn La., Deer Harbor 98243 | 360/376–4110 | fax 360/376–2237 | stay@deerharborinn.com | www.deerharborinn.com | $119–$299 | AE, MC, V.

OTHELLO

Mar Don Resort. Sitting along the shores of the Potholes Reservoir, the 25 rooms of this facility provide an escape from the modern world. There are lots of activities to pursue around the lake, including numerous water sports and hikes. The rooms have basic furnishings, 10 have cooking facilities and six overlook the reservoir. | 25 rooms. Restaurant, picnic area, some kitchenettes, some microwaves, some refrigerators, no room phones, no TV, hiking, volleyball, beach, dock, boating, fishing. Pets allowed (fee). | 8198 Hwy. 262 SE 99344 | 509/346–2651 or 509/765–5061 or 800/416–2736 | www.mardonresort.com | $40–$75 | D, MC, V.

PASCO

Doubletree Hotel. This large hotel has all the amenities, plus it is close to the airport. | 269 rooms, 10 suites. 2 Restaurants, bar with entertainment, in-room data ports, some refrigerators, room service, cable TV, 2 Pools, hot tub, gym, business services, airport shuttle, free parking. Pets allowed. | 2525 N. 20th St. 99301 | 509/547–0701 | fax 509/547–4278 | $75–$115, $125–$200 suites | AE, D, DC, MC, V.

PORT ANGELES

Flagstone Motel. Many of the small but well-maintained rooms of this motel have views of Mount Olympia and the surrounding Olympic Mountains. The motel is just off Highway 101 and is only a short way from the harbor. | 45 rooms. No air-conditioning, some microwaves, some refrigerators, cable TV, pool, sauna. Pets allowed. | 415 E. 1st St. 98362 | 360/457–9494 | $65 | AE, D, DC, MC, V.

Red Lion. This is a big resort hotel on the harbor, next to the Victoria ferry landing. | 187 rooms. Restaurant, no air-conditioning, cable TV, pool, hot tub, business services. Pets allowed. | 221 N. Lincoln 98362 | 360/452–9215 | fax 360/452–4734 | $59–$155 | AE, D, DC, MC, V.

Uptown Inn. South of town, at the green edge of the Olympic Mountain foothills, this inn offers views of the mountains, as well as the harbor. | 51 rooms. Complimentary Continental breakfast, no air-conditioning, some kitchenettes and microwaves, refrigerators, cable TV. Some pets allowed (fee). | 101 E. 2nd St. 98362 | 360/457–9434 or 800/858–3812 | fax 360/457–5915 | $69–$169, depending on views | AE, D, DC, MC, V.

PORT LUDLOW

Heron Beach Inn. Despite the fact that this is a comfortable and luxurious inn with a great location, it has never quite attracted the following it deserves. Nor has its restaurant helped, though it has been called the best dining room along the inland waters. Hence several name changes, designed to attract a strangely reluctant clientele. Perhaps it's because urban folks in western Washington still think of Port Ludlow as a grimy mill town, and don't recognize the changes the place has undergone. As it is, many zip by on their way to Port Townsend, leaving this area a quiet backwater. | 37 rooms, 3 suites. Restaurant, complimentary Continental breakfast, no air-conditioning, in-room data ports, refrigerators, in-room VCRs (movies), business services. Some pets allowed (fee). No smoking. | 1 Heron Rd. 98365 | 360/437–0411 | fax 360/437–0310 | www.heronbeach.com | $165, $165–$450 suites | AE, D, DC, MC, V.

PORT TOWNSEND

Bishop Victorian Guest Suites. This English inn built in 1890 was an office and warehouse building. At the west end of town, near the boatyards, you would be hard pressed today to see even a passing resemblance to its former incarnation. Nor should you care; just enjoy it as it is today: comfortable, warm and inviting. | 14 suites (8 with shower only). Complimentary Continental breakfast, no air-conditioning, kitchenettes, in-room data ports, some microwaves, refrigerators, cable TV, business services. Some pets allowed (fee). No kids under 12. No smoking. | 714 Washington St. 98368 | 360/385–6122 or 800/824–4738 (reservations) | fax 360/379–1840 | www.bishopvictorian.com | $99–$179 suites | AE, D, MC, V.

Palace Hotel. This 1889 inn in the heart of downtown Port Townsend occupies an old brick building that was once a bordello. | 17 rooms. Complimentary Continental breakfast, no air-conditioning, some refrigerators, cable TV, no room phones, laundry facilities. Pets allowed (fee). | 1004 Water St. 98368 | 360/385–0773 or 800/962–0741 | fax 360/385–0780 | palace@olympus.net | www.olympus.net/palace | $65–$189 | AE, D, MC, V.

Swan Hotel. Encircled by verandas and with a widow's walk on top, this comfortable inn has all the views you might possibly want. | 4 suites, 4 cottages, 1 penthouse loft. In-room data ports, kitchenettes (in suites, cottages), refrigerators, cable TV, business services, local airport shuttle. Some pets allowed (fee). No smoking. | 222 Monroe St. 98368 | 360/385–1718 or 800/776–1718 (reservations) | fax 360/379–1010 | swan@waypt.com | www.theswanhotel.com | $105–155 suites, $105–$135 cottages, $175–$500 penthouse | AE, DC, MC, V.

Tides Inn. Sitting directly on the beach, this inn also has views of the surrounding Olympic and Cascade mountains. The rooms have contemporary furniture that works with the pine walls and ceilings. Some rooms have decks that stretch over the water; the suites all have fireplaces, hot tubs, and views of the bay and mountains. The inn is close to the historic downtown area, restaurants, and shopping. | 21 rooms, 21 suites. Complimentary Continental breakfast, some kitchenettes, some microwaves, some refrigerators, some in-room hot tubs, cable TV, in-room VCRs, hot tub. Pets allowed. | 1807 Water St. 98368 | 360/385–0595 or 800/822–8696 | fax 360/379–1115 | www.tides-inn.com | $85–$140 | AE, D, MC, V.

PULLMAN

Country Bed and Breakfast. This 1893 farmhouse sits approximately 5½ mi south of Pullman, surrounded by junipers and flowering trees. Although the B&B's interior with cherry paneling might appear a bit suburban, the warm hospitality of its owners makes a visit here a thoroughly enjoyable experience. | 7 rooms (4 with private bath). Complimentary Continental breakfast, no air-conditioning in some rooms, no room phones, TV in common area, hot tub. Pets allowed. No smoking. | 2701 Staley Rd. 99163 | 509/334–4453 | fax 509/332–5163 | mtenwick@aol.com | $50–$100 | D, MC, V.

Holiday Inn Express. This motel caters to the business traveler and is close to the Washington State University campus. | 130 rooms. Restaurant, complimentary Continental breakfast, some no-smoking rooms, pool, hot tub, gym. Airport shuttle. Pets allowed. | S.E. 1190 Bishop Blvd. 99163 | 509/334–4437 | fax 509/334–4447 | $79–$99 | AE, D, DC, MC, V.

QUINCY

Sun Downer Motel. Renovated in 1999, the motel has rooms that contain a full range of modern amenities and are conveniently close to local restaurants (only one block away).

The motel is located on Highway 28. | 24 rooms. Refrigerators, microwaves, cable TV, pool. Pets allowed. | 414 F St. SE, 98848 | 509/787–3587 | fax 509/787–3485 | $55–$72 | AE, D, DC, MC, V.

Traditional Inns. This motel caters to families and is close to the concert series at the Gorge. | 24 rooms. Refrigerators, microwaves, cable TV, laundry facilities. Pets allowed (fee). | 500 S.W. F Street, off of Rte. 28 | 509/787–3525 | fax 509/787–3528 | $66 | AE, D, DC, MC, V.

REPUBLIC

K-Diamond-K Guest Ranch. This guest ranch, set on 1,400 acres, offers a great way of experiencing the Old West in beautiful surroundings. Join in the ranch activities or relax and enjoy the views. B&B also available. | 4 rooms. Dining room, complimentary breakfast, no-smoking rooms. Pets allowed. | 15661 Hwy. 21 99166 | 509/775–3536 or 888/345–5355 | fax 509/775–3536 | www.kdiamondk.com | $65–$115 | No credit cards.

Northern Inn. The motel's fort-like structure includes a tower and a covered walkway that provides access to each room. Fossils and historical pictures adorn the walls of the lobby where local crafts are sold and where there is an espresso coffee shop. Rooms are appointed with contemporary furnishings and many amenities. | 23 rooms. Complimentary Continental breakfast, in-room data ports, microwaves, refrigerators, cable TV, hot tub, sauna. Pets allowed. | 852 S. Clark Ave. 99166 | 509/775–3371 or 888/801–1068 | fax 509/775–2089 | www.northern-inn.com | $53 | AE, D, DC, MC, V.

RICHLAND

Hampton Inn Richland. This enormous chain hotel stretches along the west shore of the Columbia River adjacent to a park and a riverfront promenade. Many of the rooms have spectacular views of the river; some have balconies. | 130 rooms. Complimentary Continental breakfast, microwaves, refrigerators, some in-room hot tubs, cable TV, pool, gym, laundry service, business services, airport shuttle. Pets allowed. | 486 Bradley Blvd. 99352 | 509/943–4400 or 800/HAMPTON | www.northwestinns.com/richland.html | $79–$89 | AE, D, DC, MC, V.

Red Lion Hotel. Hotel overlooking Columbia River at the southern end of Hanford Reach, the last free-flowing stretch of the river between Bonneville Dam and the Canadian border. Ask for a room with a river view. The hotel borders a greenbelt park on the river and has easy access to levee trails. | 149 rooms. Restaurant, bar, room service, gym, pool, local airport shuttle, free parking. Pets allowed. | 802 George Washington Way | 509/946–7611 | fax 509/943–8564 | $74–$84 | AE, D, DC, MC, V.

Shilo Inn Rivershore. This hotel borders the Columbia River above the mouth of the Yakima. It has easy access to riverside trails with a park upriver and downriver. | 150 rooms, 13 suites. Restaurant, bar, some kitchenettes, refrigerators (in suites), cable TV, room service, pool, wading pool, hot tub, gym, laundry facilities, business services, airport shuttle, free parking. Pets allowed (fee). | 50 Comstock St. 99352 | 509/946–4661 | fax 509/943–6741 | $59–$129, $109–$169 suites | AE, D, DC, MC, V.

RITZVILLE

Best Inn and Suites Heritage Inn. Comfortable business travelers' and family motel. | 52 rooms, 2 suites. Complimentary Continental breakfast, cable TV, pool, hot tub, laundry facilities, business services. Pets allowed. | 1513 Smitty's Blvd. 99169 | 509/659–1007 | fax 509/659–1025 | $69–$89, $129–$159 suites | AE, D, DC, MC, V.

SAN JUAN ISLANDS

Tucker House. A comfortable B&B in a turn-of-the-20th-century home, 2 blocks from the ferry terminal and a park. | 6 rooms, 2 suites, 3 cottages. Picnic area, complimentary breakfast and afternoon snacks, no air-conditioning, some kitchenettes, microwaves, some refrigerators, cable TV, some in-room hot tubs, hot tub. Some pets allowed (fee). No kids under 18 (except in cottages). No smoking. | 260 B St., Friday Harbor 98250 | 360/378–2783 or 800/965–0123 (reservations) | fax 360/378–6241 | www.tuckerhouse.com | $115–$175 rooms, $120–$165 cottages | MC, V.

SEATTLE

Alexis Hotel. Hard to believe that this charming small hotel was once a parking garage. It's near Pioneer Square and the waterfront. Each room is individually decorated, and the hotel has permanent and rotating art collections. Complimentary wine tastings in the evenings. | 65 rooms, 44 suites. Restaurant, bar, cafe, in-room data ports, minibars, some refrigerators, room service, in-room hot tubs (in suites), cable TV and movies, bookstore, massage, gym, sauna, business services. Pets allowed (fee). | 1007 1st Ave. 98104 | 206/624–4844 or 800/264–8482 | fax 206/621–9009 | www.alexishotel.com | $225–$245, $365–$450 suites | AE, D, DC, MC, V.

Beech Tree Manor. This inn was built in 1902 and is well appointed in the manner of an English home. | 7 rooms (2 with shared bath). Complimentary breakfast, no air-conditioning, cable TV in sitting room, no room phones, business services. Pets allowed. No smoking. | 1405 Queen Anne Ave. N 98109 | 206/281–7037 | fax 206/284–2350 | $89–$129 | MC, V.

Hawthorne Inn and Suites. This modern hotel is downtown, catering mainly to families and business travelers. | 54 rooms, 18 suites. Complimentary breakfast, in-room data ports, cable TV, some refrigerators (in suites), hot tub, sauna, gym, laundry facilities, business services, free parking. Pets allowed. | 2224 8th Ave. 98121 | 206/624–6820 | fax 206/467–6926 | $89–$134, $175 suites | AE, D, MC, V.

Hotel Monaco. A modern, very comfortable downtown hotel with whimsical yet elegant decor. The rooms are surprisingly cozy for such a splashy place. Offers a special "goldfish service"—guests can request a pet goldfish in their room during their stay. | 144 rooms, 45 suites. Restaurant, bar, in-room data ports, minibars, refrigerators, room service, some in-room hot tubs, cable TV, stereos, some VCRs, massage, gym, business services, valet parking (fee), pets allowed. | 1101 4th Ave. 98101 | 206/621–1770 or 800/945–2240 (reservations) | fax 206/621–7779 | www.monaco-seattle.com | $230–$240, $295–$890 suites | AE, D, DC, MC, V.

Pensione Nichols. Only a block away from Pike Place Market, the downtown setting gives this B&B an authentic Seattle air. Enclosed balconies, full kitchens, private baths, and large living rooms are features of the second-story suites. Rooms on the third floor mostly have skylights rather than windows and have a mixture of antique and contemporary furnishings. | 10 rooms share 4 baths, 2 suites. Complimentary Continental breakfast, no air-conditioning in some rooms, some kitchenettes, some microwaves, some refrigerators, some room phones, no TV. Pets allowed. No smoking. | 1923 1st Ave. 98101 | 206/441–7125 or 800/440–7125 | www.seattle-bed-breakfast.com | $105–$190 | AE, D, DC, MC, V.

Residence Inn Seattle–Lake Union. This extended residence hotel sits directly on splendid Lake Union. Perfect for families, all the rooms have a living room and full kitchen. The lobby is part of a seven-story atrium, complete with waterfall and many areas to relax. | 234 suites. Complimentary Continental breakfast, room service, in-room data ports, kitchenettes, microwaves, refrigerators, cable TV, pool, spa, sauna, gym, business services. Pets allowed (fee). | 800 Fairview Ave. N, 98109 | 206/624–6000 or 800/331–3131 | fax 206/223–8106 | www.marriott.com | $200–$300 | AE, D, DC, MC, V.

Sorrento. Comfortable old hotel built in 1909 to look as authentically Italian as possible. It is on First Hill and overlooks downtown and Elliott Bay. Offers wine tasting and coffee service in the evenings. | 34 rooms, 42 suites. Restaurant, bar, in-room data ports, minibars, many cable TVs, massage, gym, business services. Pets allowed. | 900 Madison St. 98104 | 206/622–6400 or 800/426–1265 (outside WA) | fax 206/343–6155 | www.hotelsorrento.com | $230–$250, $270–$500 suites | AE, D, DC, MC, V.

SEATTLE-TACOMA INTERNATIONAL AIRPORT AREA

Best Western Executel. Business travelers' hotel located about 10 mi from the airport and minutes away from area attractions and major corporations. | 116 rooms. Restaurant, bar, in-room data ports, room service, cable TV, pool, hot tub, business services, airport shuttle, free parking. Pets allowed (fee). | 31611 20th Ave. S, Federal Way 98003 | 253/941–6000 | fax 253/941–9500 | executel@ricochet.net | $99–$179 | AE, D, DC, MC, V.

La Quinta. This 6-story hotel is close to the airport and offers the personal service that is the hallmark of this chain. | 143 rooms. Complimentary Continental breakfast, in-room data ports, cable TV, pool, hot tub, exercise equipment, gym, laundry facilities, business services, airport shuttle. Some pets allowed. | 2824 S. 188th St., Seattle 98188 | 206/241–5211 | fax 206/246–5596 | $79–$129 | AE, D, DC, MC, V.

Marriott Sea-Tac. Big, splashy airport hotel with 21,000-square-ft atrium with trees, plants, totem poles, and a waterfall. | 459 rooms. Restaurant, bar, in-room data ports, room service, cable TV, indoor pool, hot tub, spa, gym, game room with video games, business services, airport shuttle, free parking. Pets allowed (fee). | 3201 S. 176th St., Seattle 98188 | 206/241–2000 | fax 206/248–0789 | $79–$159 | AE, D, DC, MC, V.

Seattle Airport Hilton. Prize-winning modern hotel in garden setting, with large ballroom and conference center. It's a 30-minute drive to downtown Seattle. | 398 rooms. Restaurant, bar, in-room data ports, room service, cable TV, pool, hot tub, exercise equipment, business services, laundry facilities, airport shuttle. Pets allowed. | 17620 International Blvd., Seattle 98188 | 206/244–4800 | fax 206/248–4495 | debra_noonan@hilton.com | www.hilton.com | $119–$179 | AE, D, DC, MC, V.

Westcoast Sea-Tac Hotel. This hotel usually has a special "park and fly" deal—if you spend a night or two (depending on how long you're planning to be gone), you can park your car for free while you're away, and take the hotel shuttle to the terminal and back. The hotel itself is convenient to shopping and restaurants and all rooms have Nintendo systems. | 146 rooms. Restaurant, bar, room service, cable TV, some refrigerators, pool, hot tub, gym, business services, airport shuttle, free parking. Pets allowed. | 18220 International Blvd., Seattle 98188 | 206/246–5535 or 800/426–0670 | fax 206/246–9733 | $89–$130 | AE, D, DC, MC, V.

SEDRO WOOLLEY

Skagit Motel. Basic but comfortable family motel. | 46 rooms. Some kitchenettes, cable TV, no-smoking rooms. Pets allowed. | 1977 Rte. 20 98284 | 360/856–6001 | $45–$50 | AE, D, DC, MC, V.

SEQUIM

Groveland Cottage. A country inn with a cozy library/sitting room. A Victorian farmhouse built in 1886, this B&B features stained glass windows, and a mix of period furnishings and modern pieces. | 4 rooms, 1 cottage. Picnic area, complimentary breakfast, no air-conditioning, cable TV, VCRs (movies), some in-room hot tubs, kitchen in cottage, library, business services. Pets allowed. No kids under 12. No smoking. | 4861 Sequim-Dungeness Way, Dungeness | 360/683–3565 or 800/879–8859 (reservations) | fax 360/683–5181 | www.sequimvalley.com | $80–$110 | AE, D, MC, V.

Sequim Bay Lodge. Comfortable lodge just off of the highway, near a wooded area. | 54 rooms (1 with shower only). Picnic area, complimentary Continental breakfast, no air-conditioning in some rooms, refrigerators (in suites), cable TV, pool, putting green, business services. Pets allowed (fee). | 268522 U.S. 101 | 360/683–0691 | fax 360/683–3748 | $79–$91 | AE, D, DC, MC, V.

SHELTON

Shelton Inn Motel. Six blocks west of Hwy. 3, this two-story motel is in the middle of town, surrounded by shops. | 30 rooms. Restaurant, cable TV, some no-smoking rooms, pool. Pets allowed (fee). | 628 W. Railroad Ave. 98584 | 360/426–4468 | fax 360/426–7927 | $52–$54 | AE, MC, V.

Shelton's Super 8 Motel. Located on Shelton's upcoming eastern side, this motel stands near new restaurants and new shops. | 38 rooms. Refrigerators, cable TV. Pets allowed (fee). No smoking. | 2943 Northview Circle 98584 | 360/426–1654 or 800/800–8000 | fax 360/426–1847 | $60–$70 | AE, D, DC, MC, V.

SKYKOMISH

Skykomish Hotel. Once a hotel for railroad crews, this rustic lodging sits directly on the railroad tracks. As the fog rolls in, you might feel a slight chill; be warned the hotel is said to be the residence of a ghost, Mary, who was murdered in room 32 in 1920. | 22 rooms. Restaurant, no air-conditioning, cable TV, no room phones. Pets allowed. | 102 Railroad Ave. E, 98288 | 360/677–0309 | $35 | No credit cards.

SNOHOMISH

Snohomish Grand Valley Bed and Breakfast. This country Victorian home overlooks the Snohomish valley. The comfortable rooms are decorated with antiques. Outside are large gardens and inside there is a fireplace in the living room. | 2 rooms. Complimentary breakfast, cable TV, no-smoking rooms. Some pets allowed. | 88816 E. Lowell Larimer Rd., Snohomish 98296 | 360/568–8854 | fax 360/568–1919 | $75–125 | MC, V.

SNOQUALMIE

★ **Kimball Creek Inn.** Secluded on a quiet country road, the inn (formerly the Old Honey Farm Inn) sits on 4 acres of meadows through which Kimball Creek runs. The rooms of this contemporary, New England–style house are appointed with antiques and a variety of collectibles. The inn is near Snoqualmie Falls and has wonderful views. | 10 rooms. Complimentary breakfast, no air-conditioning, some in-room hot tubs, cable TV no room phones. Pets allowed. No smoking. | 9050 384th Ave. SE 98065 | 425/888–9399 | $79–$155 | MC, V.

Salish Lodge and Spa. It's the location that makes this lodge, which was used in filming the TV series *Twin Peaks*, at the crest of spectacular 268-ft Snoqualmie Falls, special. The lodge has the occasional antique; most rooms have a view of the Snoqualmie Valley, a few have views of the river, and even fewer have a view of the falls. | 87 rooms. 2 Restaurants, bar, in-room data ports, minibars, refrigerators, room service, in-room hot tubs, cable TV, in-room VCRs, spa, gym, cross-country and downhill skiing, library, business services. Some pets allowed (fee). | 6501 Railroad Ave., 98065 | 425/888–2556 or 800/826–6124 | fax 425/888–2533 | www.salishlodge.com | $249–$999 | AE, D, DC, MC, V.

SOAP LAKE

Notaras Lodge. The rooms at this well-known three-building lodge on the shores of Soap Lake are individually decorated. Water from the lake is piped into the bathrooms (bring lots of room freshener). | 14 rooms. Restaurant, picnic area, microwaves, refrigerators, some in-room hot tubs, cable TV. Pets allowed (fee). | 231 Main St. 98851 | 509/246–0462 | fax 509/246–1054 | $65–$125 | MC, V.

SPOKANE

Best Western Thunderbird Inn. This hotel is seven blocks from Riverfront Park, the Opera House, and the Convention Center. It is easily accessible to I–90. | 89 rooms. Complimentary Continental breakfast, in-room data ports, cable TV, pool, business services. Pets allowed (fee). | W. 120 3rd Ave. 99204 | 509/747–2011 | fax 509/747–9170 | $59–$74 | AE, D, DC, MC, V.

Best Western Trade Winds North. Comfortable business travelers' and family hotel. Three mi from Riverfront Amusement Park, 2 mi from Expo '74 Site and Gonzaga University. | 63 rooms. Complimentary Continental breakfast, cable TV, indoor pool, laundry facilities, business services. Some pets allowed (fee). | N. 3033 Division St. 99207 | 509/326–5500 | fax 509/328–1357 | $64–$70 | AE, D, DC, MC, V.

Budget Inn. Business travelers' hotel near hospitals. | 153 rooms, 15 suites. Minibar in suites, cable TV, pool, laundry facilities, business services, airport shuttle. Pets allowed. | E. 110 4th Ave. 99202 | 509/838–6101 | fax 509/624–0733 | $59–$69, $79–$84 suites | AE, D, DC, MC, V.

Cavanaugh's River Inn. Luxurious hotel overlooking the Spokane River east of Riverfront Park, in the heart of downtown. | 245 rooms, 2 suites. Restaurant, bar with entertainment, room service, cable TV, 2 pools, wading pool, hot tub, sauna, tennis, business services, airport shuttle, free parking. Some pets allowed. | N. 700 Division St. 99202 | 509/326–5577 or 800/843–4667 | fax 509/326–1120 | $99–$119, $190–$240 suites | AE, D, DC, MC, V.

Comfort Inn Spokane Valley. Comfortable business travelers' and family hotel, just off of the freeway. | 63 rooms, 13 suites. Complimentary Continental breakfast, some refrigerators, cable TV, pool, hot tub, laundry facilities, business services, free parking. Some pets allowed (fee). | N. 905 Sullivan Rd. 99037 | 509/924–3838 | fax 509/921–6976 | $59–$99, $89–$150 suites | AE, D, DC, MC, V.

Doubletree Hotel–Spokane City Center. This hotel is near the Convention Center and the Opera House. | 373 rooms, 4 suites. 2 restaurants, bar with entertainment, in-room data ports, cable TV, room service, gym, pool, business services, airport shuttle. Pets allowed (fee). | N. 322 Spokane Falls Ct. 99201 | 509/455–9600 | fax 509/455–6285 | $109–$155, $209–$500 suites | AE, D, DC, MC, V.

Doubletree Hotel–Spokane Valley. This hotel is 11 mi east of the downtown area. Across the freeway is the Spokane Valley Mall. | 236 rooms. 2 restaurants, bar with entertainment, some refrigerators, room service, cable TV, pool, barbershop, beauty salon, hot tub, gym, airport shuttle, free parking. Some pets allowed. | N. 1100 Sullivan Rd. 99220 | 509/924–9000 | fax 509/922–4965 | $79–$118 | AE, D, DC, MC, V.

Hotel Lusso. Italian marble tile ornaments many of the floors, archways, and fountains that fill the elegant lobby at this hotel. Guest rooms are appointed with European furnishings and contain many modern amenities. Each evening the hotel hosts a complimentary wine and cheese social. | 48 rooms. Restaurant, bar, room service, complimentary Continental breakfast, in-room data ports, minibars, some in-room hot tubs, cable TV. Pets allowed. No smoking. | 808 W. Sprague St. 99201 | 509/747–9750 | fax 509/747–9751 | www.fugazzi.com | $250–$460 | AE, D, DC, MC, V.

Love's Victorian Bed and Breakfast. Built in 1986, the turret, gabled roofs, and wraparound porch make this B&B a splendid example of Victorian architecture. The house sits 15 mi north of Spokane on 5 acres, surrounded by exquisitely maintained gardens and lawns. The guest rooms are appointed with antiques such as the Turret Suite's 1840s high oak bed which is accessed by a small stool. | 3 rooms. Complimentary breakfast, cable TV, in-room VCRs. Pets allowed. No smoking. | 31317 Cedar Rd., Deer Park 99006 | 509/276–6939 | lovesbandb@juno.com | www.bbhost.com/lovesvictorian | $75–$125 | MC, V.

Motel 6. Comfortable budget hotel off of freeway, close to restaurants and shops. | 92 rooms. Cable TV, business services. Some pets allowed. | 1919 Hutchinson Rd. 99212 | 509/926–5399 | fax 509/928–5974 | $45–$65 | AE, D, DC, MC, V.

Ramada Inn. Business travelers' hotel, right across from the airport. | 168 rooms. Restaurant, bar with entertainment, room service, cable TV, 2 pools (1 indoor), hot tub, gym, business services, airport shuttle, free parking. Pets allowed. | 8909 Airport Rd. 99219 | 509/838–5211 | fax 509/838–1074 | $65–$95 | AE, D, DC, MC, V.

Shangri-La Motel. Business travelers' and family motel far enough off the highway to escape the noise of the traffic and trains. | 20 rooms, 8 apartments. Picnic area, complimentary Continental breakfast, some kitchens, some refrigerators, microwaves, cable TV, pool, playground, business services, airport shuttle, free parking. Some pets allowed. | W. 2922 Government Way 99204 | 509/747–2066 or 800/234–4941 | fax 509/456–8696 | $47–$76 | AE, D, DC, MC, V.

Shilo Inn. Comfortable family and business travelers' motel with friendly staff. | 105 rooms. Restaurant, bar, complimentary breakfast, in-room data ports, refrigerators, microwaves, room service, cable TV, indoor pool, gym, business services, airport shuttle. Pets allowed (fee). | 923 E. 3rd Ave. 99202 | 509/535–9000 or 800/222–2244 (res) | fax 509/535–5740 | $69–$99 | AE, D, DC, MC, V.

STEVENSON

Carson Mineral Hot Springs Resort. This resort stands in a secluded woodsy area 4 mi east of Stevenson. The mineral-laden waters have been an attraction since the early part of the 20th century when the bathhouses and cabins were built. The rooms are spartan and rustic; the cabins have a few more amenities. | 9 rooms (all with shared bath), 12 cabins. Restaurant, no air-conditioning, no room phones, no TV, massage, 18-hole golf course, hiking. Pets allowed (fee). No smoking. | 372 St. Martin's Springs Rd., Carson 98610 | 509/427–8292 or 800/607–3678 | fax 509/427–7242 | www.ohwy.com/wa/c/carminhs.htm | $35–$60 rooms and cabins | MC, V.

SUNNYSIDE

Sun Valley Inn. Comfortable downtown family motel. | 40 rooms. No-smoking rooms, pool. Pets allowed. | 724 Yakima Valley Hwy. | 509/837–4721 | $39–$60 | AE, D, MC, V.

TACOMA

Best Western Executive Inn. This modern four-story hotel is 4 mi east of downtown Tacoma. | 138 rooms. Restaurant, bar, in-room data ports, some refrigerators, room service, cable TV, pool, hot tub, business services, airport shuttle. Some pets allowed (fee). | 5700 Pacific Hwy E, Fife 98424 | 253/922–0080 | fax 253/922–6439 | $85–$145 | AE, D, DC, MC, V.

Best Western Tacoma Inn. Comfortable business travelers' motel 5 minutes from the Air Force base. | 149 rooms. Restaurant, bar with entertainment, in-room data ports, some kitchenettes, some refrigerators and microwaves, room service, cable TV, pool, putting green, gym, playground, laundry facilities, business services, free parking. Some pets allowed (fee). | 8726 S. Hosmer St. 98444 | 253/535–2880 | fax 253/537–8379 | $79–$99 | AE, D, DC, MC, V.

Days Inn. Budget travelers' motel. | 123 rooms. In-room data ports, cable TV, pool, business services, free parking. Pets allowed (fee). | 6802 Tacoma Mall Blvd. 98409 | 253/475–5900 | fax 253/475–3540 | $67–$129 | AE, D, DC, MC, V.

La Quinta. Freeway hotel, close to the Tacoma Dome, and about 10 minutes from downtown. | 157 rooms, 2 suites. Restaurant, bar, complimentary Continental breakfast, in-room data ports, room service, cable TV, pool, hot tub, gym, laundry facilities, business services, free parking. Some pets allowed. | 1425 E. 27th St. 98421 | 253/383–0146 | fax 253/627–3280 | $72–$103 | AE, D, DC, MC, V.

Shilo Inn. Comfortable family motel with friendly staff. Located near the Tacoma Dome and many restaurants. | 132 rooms. Complimentary Continental breakfast, in-room data ports, some kitchenettes, microwaves, refrigerators, cable TV, pool, hot tub, gym, laundry facilities, business services, free parking. Pets allowed (fee). | 7414 S. Hosmer St. 98408 | 253/475–4020 | fax 253/475–1236 | $85–$109 | AE, D, DC, MC, V.

TOPPENISH

Comfort Inn–Zillah. Business travelers' and family motel that serves complimentary cookies and milk in the evenings. | 40 rooms. Complimentary Continental breakfast, cable TV, pool, hot tub. Pets allowed (fee). | 911 Vintage Valley Pkwy. Zillah 98953 | 509/829–3399 | fax 509/829–3428 | $76 | AE, D, MC, V.

Ox Bow Motor Inn. This two-story indoor corridor motor inn sits at the junction of I–97 and Highway 22. There are restaurants and shopping within one block of the motel. | 44 rooms. Some kitchenettes, microwaves, refrigerators, cable TV. Pets allowed (fee). | 511 S. Elm St. 98948 | 509/865–5800 or 888/865–5855 | fax 509/865–3623 | $32–$49 | AE, D, DC, MC, V.

TWISP

Idle-A-While Motel. Comfortable family motel. | 25 rooms. Cable TV, hot tub. Pets allowed (fee). | 505 N. Rte. 20 98856 | 509/997–3222 | fax 509/997–2105 | $55–$71 | AE, D, MC, V.

VANCOUVER

Best Inn and Suites. Budget travelers' motel located close to the Columbia Gorge and the Vancouver waterfront. Ask about their special "Evergreen Rooms," which feature extra-clean facilities, such as purified water and air filters. | 118 rooms. Restaurant, complimentary Continental breakfast, cable TV, pool, hot tub, business services, airport shuttle, free parking. Pets allowed (fee). | 221 N.E. Chkalov Dr. 98684 | 360/256–7044 or 800/426–5110 | fax 360/256–1231 | $52–$139 | AE, D, DC, MC, V.

Ferryman's Inn. Just west of I–5, at exit 4, this two-story blue with red-brick motel is 2 mi north of Vancouver. | 134 rooms. Complimentary Continental breakfast, some kitchenettes, cable TV, pool, laundry facilities, business services. Pets allowed (fee). | 7901 N.E. 6th Ave. 98665 | 360/574–2151 | fax 360/574–9644 | $54–$68 | AE, D, DC, MC, V.

Homewood Suites Portland-Vancouver. Near the banks of the Columbia River, this hotel sits close to Highway 14 and is especially well-suited to those staying longer than a single night. The outdoor barbecue grills and picnic area are a perfect place to relax. | 104 rooms. Picnic area, complimentary breakfast, in-room data ports, kitchenettes, microwaves, refrigerators, cable TV, pool, hot tub, tennis court, basketball, gym, shop, laundry services, business services. Pets allowed. | 701 S.E. Columbia Shores Blvd. 98661 | 360/750–1100 or 800/CALL–HOME | fax 360/750–4899 | kimw@pacifier.com | www.homewood-suites.com | $129–$179 | AE, D, DC, MC, V.

Shilo Inn–Downtown Vancouver. In the heart of downtown, this hotel is close to the Vancouver National Historic Site and is directly off I–5. There are several restaurants within walking distance. | 118 rooms. Complimentary Continental breakfast, some microwaves, some refrigerators, cable TV, pool, hot tub, sauna, steam room, gym, laundry service, business service. Pets allowed (fee). | 401 E. 13th St. 98660 | 360/696–0411 or 800/222–2244 | fax 360/750–0933 | vancouver@shiloinns.com | www.shiloinns.com | $79–$95 | AE, D, DC, MC, V.

Shilo Inn–Hazel Dell. Comfortable motel. One of the early Shilo Inns that helped make this regional chain's reputation for comfort and friendly service throughout the Northwest. It is close to the Clark County Fairgrounds. | 66 rooms. Complimentary Continental breakfast, some kitchenettes, refrigerators, microwaves, cable TV, indoor pool, hot tub, sauna, steam room, laundry facilities, business services, airport shuttle, free parking. Pets allowed (fee). | 13206 Hwy. 99 98686 | 360/573–0511 | fax 360/573–0396 | $79–$109 | AE, D, DC, MC, V.

WALLA WALLA

Best Western Walla Walla Suites Inn. The inn's location 1 mi from wineries and from Whitman College make this a very convenient place to stay while touring in the area. | 78 suites. Complimentary Continental breakfast, refrigerators, microwaves, coffee makers in each room, indoor pool, spa, business services. Some pets allowed (fee). | 7 E. Oak St. 99362 | 509/525–4700 | fax 509/525–2457 | $59–$100 suites | AE, D, DC, MC, V.

Hawthorne Inn and Suites. In downtown Walla Walla, next door to restaurants and shopping, this hotel sits right off Highway 12 at the 2nd Avenue exit. Hot baked cookies are served in the evenings. | 61 rooms. Complimentary Continental breakfast, some refrigerators, cable TV, pool, business services. Some pets allowed. | 520 N. 2nd Ave. | 509/525–2522 | fax 509/522–2565 | $69–$189 | AE, D, DC, MC, V.

WENATCHEE

Red Lion Hotel–Wenatchee. Right in the heart of Wenatchee, this Red Lion is a 15-minute drive from Pangborn Airport. | 149 rooms. Restaurant, bar with entertainment, in-room data ports, room service, cable TV, pool, business services, airport shuttle. Pets allowed. | 1225 N. Wenatchee Ave. 98801 | 509/663–0711 | fax 509/662–8175 | $69–$89 | AE, D, DC, MC, V.

Warm Springs Inn Bed and Breakfast. Roses planted along the driveway lead you to this 1917 mansion that sits amid gardens and trees on 10 acres. Individually appointed, the rooms are filled with a tasteful selection of art and antiques and overlook the gardens and lawns. | 5 rooms. Complimentary breakfast, cable TV, no room phones, hot tub. Pets allowed. No smoking. | 1611 Love La. 98801 | 509/662–8365 or 800/543–3645 | fax 509/663–5997 | warmsi@warmspringsinn.com | www.warmspringsinn.com | $85–$110 | AE, D, MC, V.

Westcoast Wenatchee Center. Comfortable business travelers' and family vacation motel near the riverfront park and downtown. | 147 rooms. Restaurant, bar with entertainment, cable TV, pool, hot tub, exercise equipment, downhill skiing, business services, airport shuttle. Pets allowed (fee). | 201 N. Wenatchee Ave. 98801 | 509/662–1234 | fax 509/662–0782 | $99–$200 | AE, D, DC, MC, V.

WESTPORT

Harbor Resort. From the windows of your room you might spy a whale—that's how close you are to the water. Rooms are all located on the second story and are appointed with contemporary furnishings. | 7 rooms, 7 cottages. Some kitchenettes, some microwaves, some refrigerators, cable TV. Pets allowed (fee). | Float 20 98595 | 360/268–0169 | fax 360/268–0338 | www.harborresort.com | $59–$65 rooms, $99–$120 cottages | AE, D, MC, V.

WHIDBEY ISLAND

Harbour Inn. Twenty mi south of Coupeville in Freeland, this pleasant family motel has a convenient in-town location, but is set on 2 acres of land and is a short walk to the city beach. | 20 rooms. Complimentary Continental breakfast, no air-conditioning, refrigerators, cable TV. Some pets allowed (fee). | 1606 E. Main 98249 | 360/331–6900 | fax 360/331–6900 | harborinn@whidbey.com | $64–$90 | AE, MC, V.

WINTHROP

Virginian Resort. Comfortable riverfront log lodge and restaurant. Though it is on the highway, at night you'll only hear the river flowing over the rocks. | 37 rooms. Restaurant, pool, hot tub. Pets allowed. | 808 N. Cascades Hwy. 98862 | 800/854–2834 | fax 509/996–2483 | $50–$95 | D, MC, V.

Winthrop Inn. Comfortable family motel with a large lawn and trees, far enough off the highway that it is quiet. On 4½ acres near the river's edge. | 30 rooms. Picnic area, complimentary Continental breakfast, pool, hot tub, cable TV, microwaves, refrigerators, cross-country and downhill skiing, playground, business services. Some pets allowed (fee). | 950 Hwy. 20 98862 | 509/996–2217 or 800/444–1972 | fax 509/996–3923 | $55–$100 | AE, D, DC, MC, V.

YAKIMA

Apple Country Bed and Breakfast. From the windows of this 1911 Victorian, which sits in the middle of a working ranch, you can spy quail, pheasants, gophers, and even coyotes. The rooms, with a mixture of antiques and contemporary furnishings, have spectacular views of the valley. | 3 rooms. Complimentary breakfast, cable TV, some in-room VCRs, laundry facilities. Pets allowed. No smoking. | 4561 Old Naches Hwy. 98937 | 509/972–3409 or 877/788–9963 | fax 509/965–1591 | apple@yvn.com | $65–$90 | D, MC, V.

Cavanaugh's. Freeway motel that can be noisy at times. | 171 rooms. Restaurant, bar, complimentary Continental breakfast, in-room data ports, some kitchenettes, some refrigerators, room service, cable TV, pool, laundry facilities, business services. Pets allowed. | 9 N. 9th St. 98901 | 509/452–6511 | fax 509/457–4931 | $65–$95 | AE, D, DC, MC, V.

Cavanaugh's at Yakima Center. Convention hotel next to convention center and a few blocks from a major shopping mall. The restaurant is not up to the quality of the lodging. | 153 rooms, 5 suites. Restaurant, bar with entertainment, some refrigerators, room service, cable TV, 2 pools, business services, airport shuttle, free parking. Pets allowed (fee). | 607 E. Yakima Ave. 98901 | 509/248–5900 | fax 509/575–8975 | $87–$105, $150–200 suites | AE, D, DC, MC, V.

Doubletree Inn Hotel. Business travelers' and family vacation hotel (some westside families come here just to get out of the rain and to soak up some sun by the pool). | 208 rooms, 6 suites. Restaurant, bar with entertainment, in-room data ports, some refrigerators, room service, cable TV, 2 pools, hot tub, business services, free parking. Pets allowed (fee). | 1507 N. 1st St. 98901 | 509/248–7850 | fax 509/575–1694 | $89–$135; $225 suites | AE, D, DC, MC, V.

Quality Inn. This 2-story motel is across from the Valley Mall. It's known for its reliable service to families and business travelers. | 85 rooms. Complimentary Continental breakfast, cable TV, pool, laundry facilities, business services, free parking. Pets allowed. | 12 Valley Mall Blvd. 98903 | 509/248–6924 | fax 509/575–8470 | $59–$88 | AE, D, DC, MC, V.

Red Lion Inn. Stay eight blocks north of downtown Yakima at this spacious hotel. Mt. Rainier is a one-hour drive away. | 58 rooms. Cable TV, pool, business services. Some pets allowed. | 818 N. 1st St. 98901 | 509/453–0391 | fax 509/453–8348 | $54–$99 | AE, D, DC, MC, V.

West Virginia

BECKLEY

Best Western Four Seasons Inn. One-half mi from I–77 Exit 44 (Harper Rd. exit), this two-story motel is 1 mi from the Tamarack craft center. Cable TV. Sauna, spa. Some pets allowed. | 1939 Harper Rd. (Rte. 3) 25801 | 304/252–0671 | fax 304/252–3951 | 80 rooms | $59–$64 | AE, D, DC, MC, V.

Comfort Inn. This Tudor-style chain is ¾ mi from downtown Beckley and ¾ mi from the Tamarack craft center. Complimentary Continental breakfast. Microwaves, refrigerators. Cable TV. Exercise equipment, health club. Laundry facilities. Business services. Some pets allowed. | 1909 Harper Rd. (Rte. 3) 25801 | 304/255–2161 | fax 304/255–2161 | www.comfortinn.com | 130 rooms in 2 buildings | $49–$109 | AE, D, DC, MC, V.

BLUEFIELD

Country Chalet. In a secluded rural setting with mountain views, this three-story, shake cedar A-frame has floor-to-ceiling windows, a deck, and a stone fireplace. The chalet is off I–77 at Exit 1 (Bluefield ext.). Permission is required to bring kids under 12. Complimentary breakfast. Some pets allowed. No smoking. | New Hope Rd., Box 176B 24701 | 304/487–2120 | www.countrychalet.com | 2 rooms | $40–$70 | No credit cards.

Holiday Inn. Seven miles off I–77 Exit 1 (Bluefield exit), this two-story motel has mountain views, a stone fireplace in the lobby, and a "picture window" skylight in the cafe. Restaurant. In-room data ports. Cable TV. Pool. Sauna. Some pets allowed. | U.S. 460/52 Bypass 24701 | 304/325–6170 | fax 304/323–2451 | www.holiday-inn.com | 118 rooms | $79 | AE, D, DC, MC, V.

BUCKHANNON

Centennial Motel. This one-story brick motel in downtown Buckhannon has views of the nearby mountains. The motel is within 1 block of several restaurants, on the city's main commercial strip. Some refrigerators, cable TV. Some pets allowed. | 22 N. Locust St. 26201 | 304/472–4100 | fax 304/472–9158 | 26 rooms | $53 | AE, D, DC, MC, V.

A Governor's Inn. Daniel Farnsworth, the state's second governor, built this brick Victorian mansion in 1863; today, the house is a bread-and-breakfast with a landscaped courtyard and a wraparound veranda in downtown Buckhannon. Some in-room hot tubs.

Cable TV, in-room VCRs. Baby-sitting. Some pets allowed. No smoking. | 76 E. Main St. 26201 | 304/472–2516 | fax 304/472–1613 | 6 rooms (1 with shared bath) | $69–$125 | AE, MC, V.

CHARLES TOWN

Turf. Originally built in 1955, this two-story brick motel is next to the Charles Town Races racetrack, and 5 mi east of Harper's Ferry. Although basic, rooms are ultra-clean, and have framed fabric wall-hangings. Restaurant, bar, room service. Some refrigerators, some in-room hot tubs. Cable TV. Pool. Business services. Some pets allowed (fee). | 608 E. Washington St. | 304/725–2081 or 800/422–8873 | fax 304/728–7605 | 46 rooms, 3 suites | $66, $80–$155 suites | AE, D, DC, MC, V.

CHARLESTON

Holiday Inn—Charleston House. In the downtown business district and 5 mi from the airport, this 12-story hostelry has a restaurant and bar on the top floor with views of the city. Restaurant, bar, dining room. In-room data ports. Cable TV. Pool. Beauty salon. Exercise equipment. Business services, airport shuttle. Some pets allowed. | 600 Kanawha Blvd. | 304/344–4092 | fax 304/345–4847 | www.holiday-inn.com | 256 rooms | $99–$125 | AE, D, DC, MC, V.

Red Roof Inn. This chain is 5 mi from the State Capitol Complex off I–64 Exit 95 (MacCorkle Ave. exit) in Kanawha City. Cable TV. Business services. Some pets allowed. | 6305 MacCorkle Ave. SE | 304/925–6953 | fax 304/925–8111 | i0059@redroof.com | www.redroof.com | 108 rooms | $43 | AE, D, DC, MC, V.

CLARKSBURG

Greenbrier Motel. This colonial-style motel is 3/4 mi off U.S. 50 and 12 mi east of historic Fort New Salem in a commercial area just outside downtown Clarksburg. Standard-sized rooms are clean and comfortable, and the inn is within 3 blocks of several restaurants. Restaurant. Room service. Cable TV, in-room VCRs. Hot tub, sauna. Some pets allowed. | 200 Buckhannon Pike 26301 | 304/624–5518 | fax 304/624–5510 | 50 rooms | $49 | AE, D, DC, MC, V.

FAIRMONT

Red Roof Inn. Easy to spot with its trademark red roof, this two-story motel is off I–79 Exit 132 (South Fairmont exit), about 5 mi from downtown. The motel is in a commercial area, across the street from a shopping plaza, within 3 blocks of several restaurants, and 1½ mi from Morris Park. Cable TV. Business services. Pets allowed. | 50 Middletown Rd. 26554 | 304/366–6800 | fax 304/366–6812 | www.redroof.com | 108 rooms | $46–$66 | AE, D, DC, MC, V.

HILLSBORO

The Current Bed and Breakfast. Built on the Greenbrier River Trail in 1905, this cozy farmhouse with a 4-acre pasture can accommodate both you and your horses. Country-style antiques fill the guest rooms, and beds are draped with handmade quilts. Kids allowed by permission. The inn is 5 mi southeast of Hillsboro, off Denmar Rd. Cable TV, no room phones. Hot tub. Some pets allowed. | Beard Post Office Rd. 24946 | 304/653–4722 | www.currentbnb.com | 6 rooms (some with private baths) | $60–$85 | MC, V.

HUNTINGTON

Red Roof Inn. Five miles from the Huntington Mall, the Civic Center, and the Blenko Glass Factory, and not far from nearly all of Huntington's major tourist attractions, this two-story white stucco motel is between Huntington and Barboursville near I–64. Cable TV.

Business services. Some pets allowed. | 5190 U.S. 60 E 25705 | 304/733–3737 | fax 304/733–3786 | www.redroof.com | 108 rooms | $55 | AE, D, DC, MC, V.

Travelodge Uptowner Inn. In the heart of downtown Huntington, next to Marshall University, this concrete and stucco building has an enclosed central corridor lined with smoked glass. Restaurant, bar, room service. In-room data ports. Cable TV. Pool, wading pool. Exercise equipment. Business services. Some pets allowed. | 1415 4th Ave. 25701 | 304/525–7741 or 800/828–9016 (reservations) | fax 304/525–5599 | 138 rooms | $65 | AE, D, DC, MC, V.

LEWISBURG

Brier Inn. Directly off I–64 Exit 169 (Roenceverte exit), this hostelry is not fancy; parking is available for 18-wheel trucks. Restaurant, bar (with entertainment), room service. In-room data ports. Cable TV. Pool. Business services. Some pets allowed (fee). | 540 N. Jefferson St. | 304/645–7722 | fax 304/645–7865 | 162 rooms | $47 | AE, D, DC, MC, V.

Days Inn. This one-story chain is only ½ mi from downtown restaurants. Because of its hilltop location above I–64, every room has scenic views. Cable TV. Business services, airport shuttle. Some pets allowed (fee). | 635 N. Jefferson St. | 304/645–2345 or 800/325–2525 | fax 304/645–5501 | 26 rooms | $110 | AE, D, DC, MC, V.

Embassy Inn. This two-story brick building is in downtown Lewisburg; rooms have wood paneling and flowered bedspreads. There is a private outdoor patio, and the inn is surrounded by restaurants. Complimentary Continental breakfast. In-room data ports. Microwaves, refrigerators. Cable TV. Outdoor hot tub. Laundry facilities. Pets allowed (fee). | 107 West Fair St. 24901 | 304/645–7070 or 800/260–8641 | fax 304/645–3383 | www.embassyinn.com | 32 rooms | $40–$55 | MC, V.

Fort Savannah Inn. This three-story hostelry is in the heart of historic Lewisburg. The inn is on a quiet street, 1 block from several historic sites, and 3 mi from Lost World Caverns. Restaurant, room service. Cable TV. Pool. Business services, airport shuttle. Some pets allowed (fee). | 204 N. Jefferson St. | 304/645–3055 or 800/678–3055 | 67 rooms | $70 | AE, D, DC, MC, V.

MARLINTON

Marlinton Motor Inn. This property, composed of two brick buildings in a rural area just outside Marlington, is nestled in the Allegheny Mountains, and surrounded by fields and woods. There are restaurants ½ mi away. Restaurant, bar, room service. Outdoor pool. Some pets allowed. | HC 69, Box 25 24954; Rte. 219, 4 mi north of Marlinton | 304/799–4711 | 70 rooms in 2 buildings | $59 | AE, D, DC, MC, V.

MARTINSBURG

Holiday Inn. About ½ mi off I–81 exit 13 (King St. exit) near downtown Martinsburg, this five-story brick hotel is in a commercial area 1½ mi from War Memorial Park. The Victorian-style interior was renovated in 2000. Restaurant. In-room data ports, some refrigerators. Cable TV. 2 pools (1 indoor). Hot tub. Tennis. Gym. Business services. Some pets allowed. | 301 Foxcroft Ave. 25401 | 304/267–5500 | fax 304/264–9157 | 120 rooms | $79–$89 | AE, D, DC, MC, V.

Knights Inn. In a commercial area ¼ mi from Martinsburg, this hostelry is on 1 acre surrounded by trees and flowers. The motel is 10 mi from Antietam Battlefield, and Harpers Ferry is approximately 20 mi away. Some kitchenettes, microwaves, refrigerators. Cable TV. Business services. Some pets allowed. | 1599 Edwin Miller Blvd. 25401 | 304/267–2211 | fax 304/267–9606 | 59 rooms | $50 | AE, D, DC, MC, V.

Super 8. This three-story chain is in a commercial area in Martinsburg off I–81 Exit 16 E(Queen St. exit). The inn is 1 block from a steak house, within 5 blocks of several other restaurants, and 2 mi from the Martinsburg Mall. Complimentary Continental breakfast. Cable TV. Some pets allowed. | 1602 Edwin Miller Blvd. | 304/263–0801 | 43 rooms | $56 | AE, D, DC, MC, V.

MORGANTOWN

Applewood Bed & Breakfast. This post-and-beam house was built on the second highest peak in Monongahela County. You can explore the 35 acres of grounds or warm up by the huge stone fireplace. Cherrywood furnishings are in the common areas and the guest rooms. The inn is 4 mi outside of Morgantown. Complimentary breakfast. Cable TV, VCR. Outdoor pool. Hot tub. Pets allowed. | 1749 Smithtown Rd. 26508 | 304/296–2607 | www.appelwood.com | 3 rooms | $55–$75 | MC, V.

Econo Lodge—Coliseum. This two-story chain is in a commercial area 1 mi outside of Morgantown in Star City, next to the WVU Coliseum and the WVU Evansdale Campus. Complimentary Continental breakfast. Cable TV. Business services. Some pets allowed. | 3506 Monongahela Blvd. | 304/599–8181 | fax 304/599–8187 | 72 rooms | $66 | AE, D, DC, MC, V.

Friends Inn. This inn is in a rural area, close to the WVU stadium and within view of the WVU Medical Center. Cable TV. Business services. Some pets allowed. | 452 Country Club Rd. | 304/599–4850 or 888/811–4850 | fax 304/599–4866 | www.friendsinn.com | 42 rooms in 2 buildings | $53 | AE, D, MC, V.

Holiday Inn. This chain hotel is 4 mi from Morgantown Mall and the WVU campus, and 1 mi from the WVU Medical Center. Restaurant, bar, room service. Cable TV. Pool. Business services. Some pets allowed. | 1400 Saratoga Ave. 26505 | 304/599–1680 | fax 304/598–0989 | 147 rooms | $79 | AE, D, DC, MC, V.

NITRO

Ramada Limited. In a rural community, this Victorian-style Ramada is about 30 mi from both Huntington and Charleston, off I–64 Exit 34 (Hurricane exit). Picnic area, complimentary Continental breakfast. Some refrigerators. Cable TV. Pool. Business services. Some pets allowed (fee). | 419 Hurricane Creek Rd., Hurricane 25526 | 304/562–3346 | fax 304/562–7408 | 147 rooms | $49–$64 | AE, D, DC, MC, V.

PETERSBURG

Smoke Hole Lodge Bed & Breakfast. A remote 1,500-acre tract in West Virginia's famed Smoke Hole Gorge is home to this lodge, which prides itself on being a wilderness retreat. The grounds are made up of several different farmholdings, and each of the guest rooms is unique, though all have a rustic country appeal, with antiques, handmade quilts, and some four-poster beds. Complimentary breakfast. Cable TV. Pets allowed. | Rte. 28 S 26847 | 304/242–8377 or 304/257–1539 | 7 rooms | $90–$165 | No credit cards.

PRINCETON

Days Inn. In a commercial area between Bluefield and Beckley and surrounded by trees and flowers, this two-story motel is 19 mi from the Winterplace Ski Resort. Complimentary Continental breakfast. Cable TV. Indoor pool. Hot tub. Business services. Some pets allowed. | 347 Meadowfield La. 24740 | 304/425–8100 | fax 304/487–1734 | 122 rooms | $69 | AE, D, DC, MC, V.

Sleep Inn. This three-story hotel is off I–77 Exit 9 (Princeton exit). It is 2 mi from downtown and 15 mi southeast of the Mercer County Airport. Complimentary Continental breakfast. In-room data ports. Cable TV, room phones. Indoor pool. Hot tub. Pets allowed. | 1015 Oakvale Rd. 24740 | 304/431–2800 | fax 304/425–7693 | 81 rooms | $45–$95 | AE, D, DC, MC, V.

RICHWOOD

Four Seasons Lodge. Overlooking Rudolph Falls and at the edge of the Monongahela National Forest, this two-story motel has rooms with wooded views. The innkeepers can help you arrange mountain biking, fishing, cross-country skiing, or kayaking trips during your stay. The motel is 1 mi east of downtown. Complimentary Continental breakfast. Cable TV. Bicycles. Pets allowed. | Marlinton Rd. (Rte. 39/Rte. 55) 24740 | 800/829–4605 | fax 304/846–2170 | 27 rooms, 2 suites | $50–$76 rooms, $125 suites | AE, D, DC, MC, V.

SALEM

Old Salem Bed & Breakfast. The president of Salem-Teikyo University (then known as Salem College) built this two-story downtown building in 1889. The university is two blocks away. There are several restaurants within a few blocks of the B&B. Dining room, complimentary breakfast. Cable TV. Pets allowed. No smoking. | 117 W. Main St. 26426 | 304/782–1227 | 5 rooms | $50 | AE, D, MC, V.

SHEPHERDSTOWN

Mecklenberg Inn. Each room in this Revolutionary War–era downtown inn (built while George Washington was president) has a theme. The Lincoln room, for example, has a fireplace and is filled with Victorian furniture; the country room has an antique bed with a rope box spring. There is live entertainment in the English-style pub. Bar, complimentary breakfast. No TV in some rooms. Pets allowed. No smoking. | 128 E. German St. 25443 | 304/876–2126 | 4 rooms, 1 suite | $75 rooms, $130 suite | MC, V.

SUMMERSVILLE

Best Western Summersville Lake. This three-story motel in a commercial area is 2 mi from Summersville Lake and 4 mi from the airport. Restaurant, bar, complimentary Continental breakfast, room service. Cable TV. Business services. Some pets allowed. | 1203 Broad St. off Rte. 19 26651 | 304/872–6900 | fax 304/872–6908 | 59 rooms | $47–$53 | AE, D, DC, MC, V.

Sleep Inn Summersville. This two-story hotel is in a shopping complex on the east side of town, near a medical clinic and several restaurants. Restaurant, picnic area, complimentary Continental breakfast. In-room data ports, cable TV, in-room VCRs (and movies). Outdoor pool. Kids' programs, playground. Laundry facilities. Business services. Pets allowed. | 701 Professional Park Dr. 26651 | 304/872–4500 | fax 304/872–0288 | 97 rooms | $79–$199 | AE, D, DC, MC, V.

WEBSTER SPRINGS

Mineral Springs Motel. You'll have scenic views from any room in this two-story motel near the Elk River, high in the Appalachians. Get a room in the front and you'll have a view of mountains; get one in the back and you'll have one of the mountains and the river too. Air-conditioning, cable TV. Pets allowed (fee). | 1 Spring St. 26288 | 304/847–5305 | 23 rooms | $42 | AE, D, DC, MC, V.

WESTON

Comfort Inn. Right off Exit 99 on I–79 and 3 mi east of town, this two-story hostelry is near shopping and 4 mi north of Stonewall Jackson Lake State Park. The hotel is renovated every winter. Restaurant, bar. Cable TV. Pool. Some pets allowed. | I–79 and U.S. 33 E 26452 | 304/269–7000 | 60 rooms | $59–$61 | AE, D, DC, MC, V.

WHEELING

Days Inn. Just to make a point, there's an 18-wheeler truck in the lobby of this chain motel 5 mi west of downtown Wheeling, off I–70 Exit 11 (Dallas Pike). The hotel is near a commercial area. Bar, complimentary Continental breakfast. Some in-room hot tubs. Cable TV.

Pool. Business services. Some pets allowed. | Exit 11 and E. Ih 70, Triadelphia 26059 | 304/547–0610 | fax 304/547–9029 | 106 rooms | $47–$55 | AE, D, DC, MC, V.

Holiday Inn Express. There are mountain views from some of the rooms at this two-story motel 8 mi east of town. Complimentary Continental breakfast. In-room data ports, some in-room hot tubs. Cable TV. Outdoor pool. Laundry facilities, laundry service. Business services, free parking. Pets allowed (fee). | Rte. 1 26059 | 304/547–1380 or 800/422–7829 | fax 304/547–9270 | 116 rooms, 1 suite | $70 rooms, $109 suite | AE, D, DC, MC, V.

WHITE SULPHUR SPRINGS

Old White. Off I–64, this motel is ½ mi east of town and 1½ mi east of the Greenbrier. To get there traveling on I–64 West, take Exit 181 to I–60 West ¼ mi from the exit; traveling I–64 East, take Exit 175 to I–60 East 4½ mi from the exit. Cable TV. Pool. Some pets allowed. | 865 E. Main St. (Rte. 60) 24986 | 304/536–2441 or 800/867–2441 | fax 304/536–1836 | 26 rooms | $45 | AE, D, DC, MC, V.

Wisconsin

ALGOMA

Algoma Beach Motel. On the edge of town in a quiet residential neighborhood, this motel has simply furnished lakeshore rooms and condo units; all have water views that are especially beautiful at sunrise. You can grill out on the private beach, have a bonfire, or take a stroll down the town boardwalk. Picnic area. Some kitchenettes, cable TV. Beach. Some pets allowed. | 1500 Lake St., 54201 | 920/487–2828 | 28 rooms, 4 condos | $70–$119 rooms, $219 condos | AE, D, DC, MC, V.

APPLETON

Best Western Midway Hotel. This hotel is surrounded by lakes, parks, and golf courses and is just 5 mi from the airport. It has a domed atrium filled with tropical plants and a pub and restaurant popular with locals. Complimentary breakfast weekdays. Restaurant, bar, room service. In-room data ports, cable TV. Pool. Hot tub. Gym. Business services, airport shuttle. Some pets allowed. | 3033 W. College Ave. (Rte. 125) 54915 | 920/731–4141 | fax 920/731–6343 | www.bestwestern.com | 105 rooms | $82–$122 | AE, D, DC, MC, V.

Exel Inn. This chain hotel is in the heart of the city just two blocks from Fox Valley Mall. There is one whirlpool suite. Complimentary Continental breakfast. In-room data ports, microwaves, refrigerators, some in-room hot tubs, cable TV. Gym. Business services. Some pets allowed. | 210 N. Westhill Blvd. 54914 | 920/733–5551 | fax 920/733–7199 | www.exelinns.com | 105 rooms | $58–$95 | AE, D, DC, MC, V.

Ramada Inn. This modern hotel, 1 mi from downtown, has an Aztec motif throughout from its stone exterior to its large outdoor mural; western art and cacti accent the lobby. Bar, complimentary breakfast. Some refrigerators, cable TV, in-room VCRs and movies available. Pool. Hot tub. Gym. Laundry facilities. Business services, airport shuttle. Some pets allowed. | 200 N. Perkins St. | 920/730–0495 | fax 920/730–2957 | www.ramada.com | 91 rooms | $70–$115 | AE, D, DC, MC, V.

Road Star Inn. This inn on the outskirts of town—part of a local chain—is just a block from U.S. 41. Pets may stay in smoking rooms only. Complimentary Continental breakfast. Cable TV. Pets allowed. | 3623 W. College Ave. (Rte. 125) | 920/731–5271 or 920/731–5271 | fax 920/731–0227 | 102 rooms | $42–$63 | AE, D, MC, V.

ASHLAND

Best Western Holiday House. This modern hotel on the shore of Lake Superior overlooks Chequamegon Bay. 2 restaurants, bar. Cable TV. Pool. Hot tub, sauna. Business services. Some pets allowed. | 30600 U.S. 2 | 715/682–5235 | fax 715/682–4730 | www.bestwestern.com | 65 rooms | $69–$99 | AE, D, DC, MC, V.

Super 8. This modern brick motel is across the road from Lake Superior, and about ½ mi from downtown on a busy shop-lined street. In-room data ports, microwaves available, cable TV. Pool. Hot tub. Laundry facilities. Business services. Some pets allowed. | 1610 Lake Shore Dr. | 715/682–9377 | fax 715/682–9377 | www.super8.com | 70 rooms | $63–$86 | AE, D, DC, MC, V.

BAILEYS HARBOR

Journey's End Motel. This small motel built in the early 1980s is tucked away ½ mi from the harbor on 3½ acres of rolling, landscaped grounds. You can picnic, grill out, or have a bonfire and enjoy the quiet countryside. Refrigerators, cable TV. Some pets allowed. | 8271 Journey's End La., 54202 | 920/839–2887 | 10 rooms | $60–$72 | MC, V.

BARABOO

Spinning Wheel. This modern brick-and-wood motel is on the east side of town in a residential neighborhood not far from Highway 33. Cable TV. Some pets allowed (fee). | 809 8th St. | 608/356–3933 | 25 rooms | $63–$69 | AE, D, MC, V.

BAYFIELD

Super 8. All rooms have indoor entrances, and some rooms have a view of the water at this standard chain hotel with a brick exterior. Bar, complimentary Continental breakfast. Cable TV. Hot tub, sauna. Video games. Business services. Some pet allowed (fee). | Harbor View Dr., Washburn 54814 | 715/373–5671 | fax 715/373–5674 | www.super8.com | 35 rooms | $79–$85 | AE, D, DC, MC, V.

Winfield Inn. Set on 4½ acres overlooking Lake Superior, this inn has two separate buildings, a sundeck, and extensive gardens. No air-conditioning in some rooms, kitchenettes in apartments, cable TV. Pets allowed. | 225 E. Lyndee Ave. | 715/779–3252 | fax 715/779–5180 | www.winfieldinn.com | 25 rooms, 6 apartments | $59–$145 | AE, D, MC, V.

BEAVER DAM

Grandview Motel. This no-frills, mom-and-pop roadside motel had a grand view when it was first built in the 1940s, but in the years since then a quiet, residential neighborhood has grown up around it. Cable TV. Some pets allowed. | 1510 N. Center St. 53916 | 920/885–9208 | fax 920/887–8706 | 22 rooms | $30–$40 | AE, D, MC, V.

BELOIT

Comfort Inn. This two-story modern motel is right off Interstate 90 on a commercial strip. Complimentary Continental breakfast. Refrigerator in suites, cable TV, in-room VCRs available. Pool. Hot tub. Business services. Pets allowed. | 2786 Milwaukee Rd. | 608/362–2666 | fax 608/362–2666 | 56 rooms, 16 suites | $66–$75 | AE, D, DC, MC, V.

BLACK RIVER FALLS

Days Inn. This contemporary brick-and-stucco hotel in a wooded area has access to snowmobile trails directly from the grounds. Complimentary Continental breakfast. In-room data ports, cable TV, in-room VCRs available. Pool. Hot tub, sauna. Video games. Laundry facilities. Business services. Some pets allowed. | 919 Rte. 54 E | 715/284–4333 or 800/356–8018 | fax 715/284–9068 | 86 rooms | $55–$85 | AE, D, DC, MC, V.

Best Western Arrowhead Lodge. This three-story hotel has a Native American motif, with arrowhead effects on the walls outside and in. You can get to county snowmobile and the hotel's nature/fitness trails right from the grounds. Restaurant, bar (with entertainment Sat.). In-room data ports, cable TV, in-room VCRs available. Pool. Hot tub, sauna. Playground. Business services. Pets allowed. | 600 Oasis Rd. | 715/284–9471 or 800/284–9471 | fax 715/284–9664 | www.bestwestern.com | 144 rooms, 30 suites | $52–$190 | AE, D, DC, MC, V.

BOULDER JUNCTION

White Birch Village. This modern cottage complex is in Northern Highland State Forest 8 mi southeast of Boulder Junction. Each cottage has a fireplace and some have views of the lake. No air-conditioning, kitchenettes, TV in common room. Beach, dock, boating, fishing, bicycles. Playground. Laundry facilities. Business services. Pets allowed. | 8764 Rte. K | 715/385–2182 | fax 715/385–2537 | www.whitebirchvillage.com | 11 cottages | $600–$1,050 per week (7–day minimum stay) | No credit cards | Closed mid-Oct.–May.

Zastrow's Lynx Lake Lodge. This lodge in the woods on Lynx Lake 9 mi north of Boulder Junction has a knotty-pine interior. Two of the cottages have fireplaces. Weekly rates in season. Bar, dining room, complimentary breakfast and dinner in season. No air-conditioning, some kitchenettes, cable TV. Beach, boating, fishing, bicycles. Playground. Business services, airport shuttle. Pets allowed. | Rte. B, Presque Isle 54512 | 715/686–2249 or 800/882–5969 | fax 715/686–2257 | 11 cottages | $325 with 2 meals a day (7–day minimum stay) | D, MC, V | Closed Mar.–Apr. and late Oct.–late Dec.

CEDARBURG

Best Western Quiet House and Suites. A modern hotel in a rural setting 5 mi southeast of Cedarburg. The lobby has a large fireplace and a display of geese figurines. Complimentary Continental breakfast. In-room data ports, some in-room hot tubs, cable TV. Indoor-outdoor pool. Hot tub. Gym. Business services. Pets allowed (fee). | 10330 N. Port Washington Rd., Mequon 53092 | 262/241–3677 | fax 262/241–3707 | www.quiethouse.com | 55 rooms | $111–$190 | AE, D, DC, MC, V.

Breeze Inn to the Chalet. The four buildings of this motel, in a residential area 10 mi southeast of Cedarburg, were built to look like Swiss chalets with peaked roofs and wraparound porches. Restaurant, bar. Refrigerators, cable TV. Business services. Some pets allowed. | 10401 N. Port Washington Rd., Mequon 53092 | 262/241–4510 | fax 262/241–5542 | breezemeasap@worldnet.att.net | 41 rooms | $68–$175 | AE, D, DC, MC, V.

CHIPPEWA FALLS

Americinn. This hotel is in a residential neighborhood on the south side of town, 2 mi from downtown and the zoo. The cozy lobby has a sunroom and a brick fireplace. Complimentary Continental breakfast. In-room data ports, some microwaves, some refrigerators, cable TV. Pool. Hot tub. Business services. Pets allowed (deposit). | 11 W. South Ave. 54729 | 715/723–5711 | fax 715/723–5254 | 62 rooms | $65–$73 | AE, D, DC, MC, V.

Glen Loch. Rooms have outdoor entrances at this simple motel on 3½ acres in a commercial neighborhood at the north end of town. Picnic area. Cable TV. Pets allowed. | 1225 Jefferson Ave. | 715/723–9121 | 19 rooms | $26–$75 | AE, MC, V.

Indianhead Motel. On a bluff overlooking downtown, this dark brown, rustic building is independently owned. All rooms are at ground level. Some microwaves, some refrigerators, cable TV. Pets allowed. | 501 Summit Ave. | 715/723–9171 or 800/341–8000 | fax 715/723–6142 | dixie2@ecol.net | www.cvol.net/~dixie2 | 27 rooms | $55–$70 | AE, D, DC, MC, V.

Park Inn International. This large dark-brown downtown hotel has a big-screen TV in a common area. Restaurant, bar, room service. Cable TV. Pool. Hot tub. Business services.

Some pets allowed. | 1009 W. Park Ave. | 715/723–2281 or 800/446–9320 | fax 715/723–2283 | 67 rooms | $85–$120 | AE, D, DC, MC, V.

EAGLE RIVER

Days Inn. This large colonial-style brick hotel is backed by trees with a field on one side; there are large windows in the lobby. Snowmobile trails lead directly to the hotel. Complimentary Continental breakfast. Some refrigerators, some in-room hot tubs, cable TV. Pool. Hot tub, sauna. Laundry facilities. Business services. Some pets allowed. | 844 Railroad St. N | 715/479–5151 or 800/356–8018 | fax 715/479–8259 | www.americanheritageinn.com | 93 rooms | $75–$84 | AE, D, DC, MC, V.

Gypsy Villa. This resort, 3 mi south of Eagle River, is spread over 2 mi and each villa has lots of space including 200 ft or more of private lake frontage, with a private swimming beach and pier. Most units are on Cranberry Island, in the middle of Cranberry Lake, one of the Chain of 28 Lakes. Maid service costs $20 a day. Picnic area. No air-conditioning in some rooms, kitchenettes, some in-room hot tubs, no room phones, cable TV in some rooms, in-room VCRs available. Wading pool. Hot tub. Tennis. Gym. Beach, dock, boating, fishing, bicycles. Playground. Laundry facilities. Business services. Pets allowed. | 950 Circle Dr. | 715/479–8644 or 800/232–9714 | fax 715/479–8780 | www.falmonoid.com/gypsy/gypsy.htm | 21 cottages, 6 apartment suites | $657–$1,957 for cottages (1–week minimum), $79–$99 for suites | AE, D, MC, V.

White Eagle Motel. This motel and its outdoor pool overlook the Eagle River, which flows into the Chain of 28 Lakes. There are woods with snowmobiling trails behind the building. Picnic area. No air-conditioning, cable TV. Pool. Hot tub, sauna. Driving range. Boating. Pets allowed. | 4948 Rte. 70 W | 715/479–4426 or 800/782–6488 | fax 715/479–3570 | www.whiteeaglemotel.com | 22 rooms | $60–$65 | D, MC, V.

EAU CLAIRE

Comfort Inn. This two-story brick motel is in a commercial area 10 mi from downtown. Complimentary Continental breakfast. In-room data ports, cable TV. Pool. Business services. Pets allowed. | 3117 Craig Rd. | 715/833–9798 | fax 715/833–9798 | 56 rooms | $54–$99 | AE, D, DC, MC, V.

Exel Inn. Three miles from downtown, this simple brick motel is surrounded by businesses. Complimentary Continental breakfast. 1 in-room hot tub, cable TV. Gym. Laundry facilities. Business services. Pets allowed. | 2305 Craig Rd. | 715/834–3193 | fax 715/839–9905 | 100 rooms | $47–$59 | AE, D, DC, MC, V.

Green Tree Inn and Suites. This mom-and-pop motel downtown has some permanent residents and many families return year after year. You can walk to the university, shopping, and dining. Complimentary Continental breakfast. Some kitchenettes, cable TV. Pets allowed. | 516 Galloway St. | 715/832–3411 | 20 rooms, 12 suites | $26–$40 | AE, D, DC, MC, V.

Maple Manor. This small, cozy brick motel is 3 mi north of Interstate 94 in a commercial area. Restaurant, bar, picnic area, complimentary breakfast. Some refrigerators, cable TV. Pets allowed. | 2507 S. Hastings Way | 715/834–2618 or 800/624–3763 | fax 715/834–1148 | www.mapleman@aol.com | 36 rooms | $35–$60 | AE, D, DC, MC, V.

Quality Inn. A large fireplace greets you in the lobby of this brick-accented hotel with two wings and a center courtyard with a pool. It is on a busy shopping strip. Restaurant, bar (with entertainment), complimentary breakfast, room service. In-room data ports, cable TV, in-room VCRs available. 2 pools. Hot tub, sauna. Business services. Pets allowed. | 809 W. Clairemont Ave. | 715/834–6611 | fax 715/834–6611 | www.qualityinn-eauclaire.com | 120 rooms | $59–$119 | AE, D, DC, MC, V.

Road Star Inn. This large white modern motor hotel within Eau Claire's city limits is part of a local chain. Complimentary Continental breakfast. Some refrigerators, cable TV. Some pets allowed. | 1151 W. MacArthur Ave. | 715/832–9731 or 800/445–4667 | fax 715/832–0690 | 62 rooms | $41–$47 | AE, D, DC, MC, V.

EGG HARBOR

Alpine Resort. This resort sits on 300 acres on the Green Bay shore. Built in 1921, the lodge has original birch-bark wallpaper, as well as two large lobbies and screened porches. Restaurant, bar, picnic area. Kitchenettes (in cottages and homes), microwaves available, some refrigerators, no room phones. Pool. 27-hole golf course, putting green, tennis. Basketball, beach. Children's programs (ages 3–8), playground. Business services. Some pets allowed. | 7715 Alpine Rd. | 920/868–3000 | alpine@mail.wiscnet.net | www.alpineresort.com | 41 motel rooms, 5 suites, 20 cottages, 12 homes | $77–$101 rooms, $101 suites, $110–$162 cottages, $134–$288 homes | AE, D, MC, V | Closed late Oct.–mid-May.

ELLISON BAY

Harbor House. This hotel's main building is a turn-of-the-20th-century mansion with a lake view, beach access, a charming porch with lattice work, and many period furnishings. A new Scandinavian Country wing overlooks the town's quaint fishing harbor and bluffs, and is perfect for sunset views. The Lighthouse Suite, in a newly constructed 35-ft lighthouse, is a two-room suite with a fireplace and a hot tub. Picnic area, complimentary Continental breakfast. Microwaves available, refrigerators, no room phones. Hot tub, sauna. Playground. Some pets allowed. No smoking. | 12666 Rte. 42 | 920/854–5196 | fax 920/854–9717 | www.door-county-inn.com | 7 rooms, 6 suites, 2 cottages | $60–$150 | AE, MC, V.

FOND DU LAC

Days Inn. This simple, two-story motel 3 mi from downtown in a commercial area has a TV room in addition to its lobby. Complimentary Continental breakfast. In-room data ports, cable TV. Video games. Business services. Pets allowed. | 107 N. Pioneer Rd. | 920/923–6790 | fax 920/923–6790 | 59 rooms | $52–$75 | AE, D, DC, MC, V.

Holiday Inn. This homey, antiques-decorated motel is 3 mi from downtown and just across the street from a golf course. There's live entertainment in the bar on weekends. Restaurant, bar, room service. In-room data ports, microwaves available, cable TV, in-room VCRs available. Pool. Hot tub. Putting green. Gym. Laundry facilities. Airport shuttle. Pets allowed. | 625 W. Rolling Meadows Dr. | 920/923–1440 | fax 920/923–1366 | www.holiday-inn.com | 139 rooms | $99–$170 | AE, D, DC, MC, V.

Stretch, Eat & Sleep Motel. The name says it all at this basic drive-to-your-door motel at the 24-hour truck-stop restaurant just off Highway 41 a mile from a mall. Restaurant. Cable TV. Pets allowed. | Pioneer Rd. | 920/923–3131 | 35 rooms | $26–$59 | D, MC, V.

GLENDALE

Exel Inn–Northeast. This modern hotel off Interstate 43 is 5 mi from downtown Milwaukee on a street lined with hotels and fast food restaurants. There's a game room with ping-pong and air hockey. Complimentary Continental breakfast. In-room data ports, some microwaves, some in-room hot tubs, cable TV. Laundry facilities. Business services, free parking. Some pets allowed. | 5485 N. Port Washington Rd. | 414/961–7272 | fax 414/961–1721 | www.exelinns.com | 125 rooms | $65–$75 | AE, D, DC, MC, V.

GREEN BAY

Baymont Inn. This modern motel is in a commercial area a mile from the Bay Park Square Mall and 8 mi from downtown. Complimentary Continental breakfast. Microwaves available, cable TV, in-room VCRs and movies available. Business services. Some pets allowed. | 2840 S. Oneida St. | 920/494–7887 | fax 920/494–3370 | www.baymontinns.com | 78 rooms | $76–$82 | AE, D, DC, MC, V.

Days Inn. This modern hotel is next to Port Plaza and right on the Fox River. Rooms have river views. Restaurant, bar. In-room data ports, microwaves available, cable TV. Pool. Business services, free parking. Pets allowed. | 406 N. Washington St. | 920/435–4484 | fax 920/435–3120 | 98 rooms | $70–$115 | AE, D, DC, MC, V.

Exel Inn. This brick motel is in a commercial area 1½ mi from Bay Park Square Mall and 7 mi from downtown. Complimentary Continental breakfast. In-room data ports, cable TV. Business services, free parking. Some pets allowed. | 2870 Ramada Way | 920/499–3599 | fax 920/498–4055 | 105 rooms | $49–$85 | AE, D, DC, MC, V.

Holiday Inn–City Centre. This seven-story hotel with a cement façade is on the banks of the Fox River, near the center of downtown. The lobby and rooms have a nautical motif and the hotel has a marina on the river. Restaurant, bar (with entertainment weekends), room service. Cable TV. Pool. Hot tub, sauna. Laundry facilities. Business services, free parking. Some pets allowed. | 200 Main St. | 920/437–5900 | fax 920/437–1199 | 146 rooms | $109–$129 | AE, D, DC, MC, V.

Road Star Inn. This small, homey motel 2½ mi from downtown in a commercial neighborhood is part of a local chain. Complimentary Continental breakfast. Some refrigerators, cable TV. Free Parking. Pets allowed. | 1941 True La. | 920/497–2666 or 800/445–4667 | fax 920/497–4754 | 63 rooms | $45–$51 | AE, D, DC, MC, V.

Sky-Lit Motel. This small motel 3 mi from downtown on the edge of a residential neighborhood has front parking and outside entrances to rooms. Picnic area. Some kitchenettes, microwaves and refrigerators available, cable TV. Laundry facilities. Free parking. Some pets allowed. | 2120 S. Ashland Ave. | 920/494–5641 | fax 920/494–4032 | 24 rooms | $35–$60 | D, MC, V.

Super 8. This modern motel is 3 mi from the Packers' Lambeau Field and the airport and 6 mi from downtown. The lobby has a homey feel and there's parking for semi trucks out back. Complimentary Continental breakfast. Microwaves available, cable TV, in-room VCRs available. Hot tub, sauna. Laundry facilities. Business services, free parking. Pets allowed. | 2868 S. Oneida St. | 920/494–2042 | fax 920/494–6959 | www.super8.com | 84 rooms | $67–$73 | AE, D, DC, MC, V.

HAYWARD

Americinn. This brick motel is on the edge of town. The large lobby has a fireplace and there's a game room with a pool table. Picnic area, complimentary Continental breakfast. Microwaves, refrigerators, some in-room hot tubs, cable TV, in-room VCRs available. Pool. Hot tub, sauna. Business services. Some pets allowed (fee). | 15601 U.S. 63 N | 715/634–2700 or 800/634–3444 | fax 715/634–3958 | 42 rooms | $81–$96 | AE, D, DC, MC, V.

Country Inn and Suites. This large hotel, 1 mi outside downtown Hayward in a suburban residential area, sports a Northwoods motif—with rustic furniture, deer antlers, and fish paintings on the walls, and a fireplace in the lobby. Restaurant, bar, complimentary Continental breakfast, room service. In-room data ports, microwaves, refrigerators, some in-room hot tubs, cable TV. Pool. Hot tub. Video games. Business services. Some pets allowed. | 10290 Rte. 27 S | 715/634–4100 | fax 715/634–2403 | 58 rooms, 8 suites | $73–$83 rooms, $113–$123 suites | AE, D, DC, MC, V.

Northwoods Motel. This cozy ranch-style motel is surrounded by woods 2 mi north of downtown. Rooms are large and one has a full kitchen. Cable TV. Pets allowed. | 9854 N. Rte. 27 | 715/634–8088 or 800/232–9202 | 9 rooms | $46–$75 | AE, D, DC, MC, V.

HUDSON

Best Western Hudson House Inn. This large colonial-style motel is in a commercial area 2 mi from the center of town. Restaurant, bar (with entertainment), complimentary Continental breakfast, room service. In-room data ports, cable TV. Pool. Beauty salon, hot tub, sauna. Gym. Business services. Some pets allowed. | 1616 Crest View Dr. 54016 | 715/386–2394 | fax 715/386–3167 | www.bestwestern.com | 102 rooms | $72–$81 | AE, D, DC, MC, V.

JANESVILLE

Best Western Janesville Motor Lodge. A fireplace will greet you in the lobby of this motel on a commercial strip right off Interstate 90 at exit 171 E. Restaurant, bar, complimentary Continental breakfast, room service. Cable TV. Pool. Hot tub. Gym. Business services, airport shuttle. Pets allowed. | 3900 Milton Ave. | 608/756–4511 or 800/334–4271 | fax 608/756–0025 | www.bestwestern.com | 105 rooms | $59–$89 | AE, D, DC, MC, V.

KENOSHA

Baymont Inn. This hotel is 4 mi from downtown, across from an outlet mall at the junction of Interstate 94 and Rte. 50. Complimentary Continental breakfast. In-room data ports, cable TV. Business services. Pets allowed. | 7540 118th Ave. | 262/857–7911 | fax 262/857–2370 | www.baymontinn.com | 95 rooms | $64–$84 | AE, D, DC, MC, V.

Knights Inn. This standard motel is in a commercial area 5 mi from downtown. Several outlet stores are within walking distance. Some kitchenettes. Pets allowed. | 7221 122nd Ave. | 262/857–2622 | fax 262/857–2375 | 113 rooms | $58–$76 | AE, D, DC, MC, V.

Southport B&B. This white colonial house is just two blocks from Lake Michigan and seven blocks north of downtown. It has a small porch and rooms are simple, comfortable, and wheelchair accessible. Complimentary Continental breakfast. Microwaves, refrigerators, in-room hot tubs, cable TV. Pets allowed. No smoking. | 4405 7th Ave. 53140 | 262/652–1951 | 2 rooms | $55–$60 | AE, D, DC, MC, V.

LA CROSSE

Radisson. Many rooms in this eight-story hotel have views of the Mississippi River. The large lobby has marble floors; paintings depict the riverfront during the 1900s. Restaurant, bar (with entertainment), complimentary Continental breakfast. Cable TV. Pool. Hot tub. Gym. Business services, airport shuttle. Pets allowed. | 200 Harborview Plaza | 608/784–6680 or 800/333–3333 | fax 608/784–6694 | www.radisson.com | 170 rooms | $109–$169 | AE, D, DC, MC, V.

LAC DU FLAMBEAU

Dillman's Bay. This resort on a 15-acre peninsula in White Sand Lake has striking views and offers lakeside cottages or motel accommodations. From mid-May to mid-October two or three different workshops in subjects ranging from painting and wood carving to personal growth or corporate training are offered each week. No air-conditioning, some kitchenettes, TV in common area, no TV in some rooms. Tennis. Hiking, beaches, dock, water sports, boating, fishing, bicycles. Playground. Pets allowed. | 3285 Sand Lake Lodge La. | 715/588–3143 | fax 715/588–3110 | www.dillmans.com | 17 rooms, 18 cottages | $89–$150 | MC, V | Closed Nov.–Apr.

LADYSMITH

Best Western El Rancho. This hotel is on 20 acres of woods and fields just about a mile outside of town and in winter there are groomed trails for cross-country skiing. Some rooms have outside entrances, others are off interior hallways. Restaurant, bar. Cable TV. Cross-country skiing. Business services. Pets allowed. | 8500 W. Flambeau Ave. | 715/532–6666 | fax 715/532–7551 | www.bestwestern.com | 27 rooms | $63–$70 | AE, D, DC, MC, V.

LAKE GENEVA

Roses Bed-and-Breakfast. This secluded colonial, a block from Lake Geneva, has a casual, English-country look. The main level has a wraparound porch, large windows, and an outdoor deck. Complimentary breakfast. Cable TV. Some pets allowed. No smoking. | 429 S. Lake Shore Dr. | 262/248–4344 or 888/767–3262 | fax 262/248–5766 | www.rosesbnb.com | 5 rooms | $110–$155 | D, MC, V.

LAND O' LAKES

Sunrise Lodge. This resort on Lac Vieux Desert just north of Land O' Lakes has modern cottages of varying sizes spread along the lakefront and interspersed with fragrant evergreen trees. The resort offers swimming and fishing in the warmer months, and snowmobiling, cross-country skiing, and ice-fishing when things get chilly. The main building houses a restaurant, recreation room with board games, a pool table, and books. Restaurant, picnic area. No air-conditioning in some rooms, kitchenettes, refrigerators, TV in common area. Miniature golf, tennis. Beach, boating, fishing, bicycles. Cross-country skiing. Kids' programs (ages 3–16), playground. Business services, airport shuttle. Pets allowed. | 5894 W. Shore Dr. | 715/547–3684 or 800/221–9689 | fax 715/547–6110 | www.sunriselodge.com | 21 cottages | $90–$300 | AP | D, MC, V.

MADISON

Baymont Inn and Suites. This two-story modern inn has a cozy lobby with a seating area. A big-screen TV is in the lounge. Bar, complimentary Continental breakfast. Refrigerator in suites, cable TV. Pool. Hot tub. Exercise equipment. Laundry facilities. Business services, airport shuttle, free parking. Some pets allowed. | 8102 Excelsior Dr. | 608/831–7711 | fax 608/831–1942 | www.baymontinn.com | 129 rooms, 14 suites | $92–$104 rooms, $104–$125 suites | AE, D, DC, MC, V.

Best Western West Towne Suites. This modest motel has an unexpectedly elaborate lobby with vaulted ceilings, artwork, large plants, and a crystal chandelier. Complimentary breakfast. In-room data ports, microwaves available, refrigerators, cable TV. Exercise equipment. Laundry facilities. Business services. Pets allowed. | 650 Grand Canyon Dr. | 608/833–4200 | fax 608/833–5614 | www.bestwestern.com | 101 suites | $62–$105 | AE, D, DC, MC, V.

The Edgewater. This 9-story, blond-brick hotel was built in 1949 right downtown on the edge of Lake Monona. Most rooms have a view of the lake, and some have a view of the Capitol. Crystal chandeliers and polished oak embellish the lobby. State Street's shops and restaurants are only 4 blocks away, and you can relax on the hotel's private pier in fine weather. Restaurant, bar, room service. Some microwaves, cable TV. Massage. Business services, airport shuttle. Some pets allowed. | 666 Wisconsin Ave. | 608/256–9071 or 800/922–5512 | fax 608/256–0910 | www.gowisconsin.com/edgewater | 116 rooms | $98–$295 | AE, DC, MC, V.

Exel Inn. This colonial-style motel on the east side of Madison has a small, standard lobby. Guest rooms are equipped with faux-walnut wood-veneer furniture, and there are unobtrusive watercolor prints on the walls. Complimentary Continental breakfast. In-room data ports, microwaves available, some refrigerators. Exercise equipment. Laundry facilities. Business services. Some pets allowed. | 4202 E. Towne Blvd. | 608/241–3861 | fax 608/241–9752 | 102 rooms | $42–$75 | AE, D, DC, MC, V.

Ivy Inn. A fireplace dominates the lobby of this colonial-style, redbrick hotel in central Madison, and the University of Wisconsin campus is directly across the street. Restaurant, bar. Cable TV. Business services, free parking. Pets allowed. | 2355 University Ave. | 608/233–9717 | fax 608/233–2660 | 57 rooms | $60–$90 | AE, DC, MC, V.

Residence Inn by Marriott. This inn is made up of 10 simply styled brick buildings that look like condos with a gatehouse in the center. All rooms are suites, with private entries.

The gatehouse has a fireplace, TV, and a dining area. Restaurant, picnic area, complimentary Continental breakfast. Kitchenettes, microwaves, cable TV, in-room VCRs. Pool. Hot tub. Exercise equipment. Laundry facilities. Free parking. Some pets allowed. | 501 D'Onofrio Dr. | 608/833-8333 | fax 608/833-2693 | www.residenceinn.com | 80 suites | $120-$150 | AE, D, DC, MC, V.

Select Inn. This motel has a large modern lobby with a cozy fireplace. Complimentary Continental breakfast. Some minibars, some refrigerators, cable TV. Hot tub. Business services. Pets allowed (deposit). | 4845 Hayes Rd. | 608/249-1815 or 800/641-1000 | fax 608/249-1815 | www.selectinn.com | 97 rooms | $39-$89 | AE, D, DC, MC, V.

Woodfield Suites. This modern, 4-story redbrick hotel is about 10 mi from the downtown area and the university campus, in a largely commercial suburban division surrounded by popular chain restaurants and mini-malls. Complimentary cocktails are served every evening. Kids can have fun with the indoor play equipment and pinball machines. Four restaurants are located within 1 mi. Complimentary Continental breakfast. In-room data ports, refrigerators, cable TV, in-room VCRs available. 2 pools. Hot tub. Gym. Video games. Laundry service. Business services, airport shuttle, free parking. Pets allowed. | 5217 Terrace Dr. | 608/245-0123 or 800/338-0008 | fax 608/245-1644 | www.woodfield-suites.com | 120 rooms | $99-$145 | AE, D, DC, MC, V.

MANITOWISH WATERS

Great Northern Motel. Mounted animals and animal heads are everywhere at this motel on San Domingo Lake 3 mi northwest of Manitowish Waters. Restaurant, bar, complimentary Continental breakfast. No air-conditioning, cable TV. Pool. Hot tub, sauna. Beach. Video games. Business services. Pets allowed. | 5720 N. U.S. 51, Mercer 54547 | 715/476-2440 | fax 715/476-2205 | www.mercerwi.com | 80 rooms | $59-$69 | D, MC, V.

MANITOWOC

Inn on Maritime Bay. This modern, redbrick building on Lake Michigan has an atrium lobby with lofty, vaulted ceilings, partial glass walls, and a panoramic view of Lake Michigan. Most guest rooms also have views of the water, and Manitowoc's famous Maritime Museum is only a few blocks away. Several restaurants and lounges are also in the immediate vicinity. Restaurant, bar, room service. In-room data ports, microwaves available, refrigerators, cable TV. Pool. Hot tub, sauna. Business services, airport shuttle, free parking. Some pets allowed. | 101 Maritime Dr. | 920/682-7000 or 800/654-5353 | fax 920/682-7013 | 107 rooms | $75-$185 | AE, D, DC, MC, V.

MARINETTE

Super 8. A small lobby with a TV and seating area greet you as you enter this modest chain property, which is on the outskirts of town. Complimentary Continental breakfast. Cable TV. Hot tub, sauna. Business services. Some pets allowed. | 1508 Marinette Ave. | 715/735-7887 | fax 715/735-7455 | www.super8.com | 68 rooms | $38-$51 | AE, D, DC, MC, V.

MAUSTON

Woodside Ranch Resort. This ranch-style resort on 1,400 acres is on the side of a hill with woods behind it. The land in front runs directly downhill to the Lemonweir River. Many accommodations are log cabins, and there is a petting zoo on-site. There is a social director on the property who coordinates group activities and social opportunities for guests to get to know each other and take full advantage of the resort's facilities. Bar (with entertainment), dining room, picnic area. No room phones, TV in common area. Pool, wading pool. Sauna. Tennis. Hiking, horseback riding. Boating, fishing. Sleigh rides. Video games. Kids' programs (ages infant–12), playground. Laundry facilities. Pets allowed. | W. 4015 Rte. 82 | 608/847-4275 or 800/626-4275 | www.woodsideranch.com | 14 rooms, 23 cabins | $275 (2–night minimum stay) | D, MC, V.

MENOMONEE FALLS

Super 8. This is a modern stucco motel, surrounded by parking, in a rural area. Complimentary Continental breakfast. Cable TV. Pool. Hot tub. Laundry facilities. Business services. Pets allowed (deposit). | N96 W17490 County Line Rd., Gemantown 53022 | 262/255–0880 | fax 262/255–7741 | www.super8.com | 100 rooms | $49–$69 | AE, D, DC, MC, V.

MENOMONIE

Bolo Country Inn. This inn and its restaurant have a black-labrador dog theme, right down to the artwork on the walls and the black lab-emblazoned carpeting. The inn is in a mostly rural area just outside of town. Restaurant, bar, picnic area, complimentary Continental breakfast. Cable TV. Pets allowed. | 207 Pine Ave. | 715/235–5596 | fax 715/235–5596 | 25 rooms | $49–$79 | AE, DC, MC, V.

MILWAUKEE

Baymont Inn and Suites. This three-story white brick building off U.S. 45 at exit 46 is near a shopping center and several restaurants. Complimentary Continental breakfast. In-room data ports, some microwaves, cable TV. Business services, free parking. Some pets allowed. | 5442 N. Lovers Lane Rd. (Rte. 100) | 414/535–1300 | fax 414/535–1724 | www.baymontinns.com | 140 rooms | $77–$87 | AE, D, DC, MC, V.

Exel Inn–South. This motel is just a five-minute drive from the airport, right off Interstate 94 at the College Avenue Exit (Number 319). Complimentary Continental breakfast. In-room data ports, some microwaves, cable TV. Laundry facilities. Business services, free parking. Some pets allowed. | 1201 W. College Ave. | 414/764–1776 | fax 414/762–8009 | www.exelinns.com | 110 rooms | $47–$69 | AE, D, DC, MC, V.

Hotel Wisconsin. Built in 1913, this 11-story downtown hotel is the second oldest in Milwaukee. The interior includes oak paneling, stained glass, fancy glasswork bearing a badger emblem, and a grandfather clock that is original to the hotel. Restaurant. Some microwaves, some refrigerators, cable TV. Video games. Laundry facilities. Business services, free parking. Pets allowed. | 720 N. Old World 3rd St. | 414/271–4900 | fax 414/271–9998 | 234 rooms | $69–$149 | AE, D, DC, MC, V.

Red Roof Inn. This standard chain motel has outdoor entries, and is about 2 mi from downtown. Cable TV. Business services, free parking. Pets allowed. | 6360 S. 13th St., Oak Creek 53154 | 414/764–3500 | fax 414/764–5138 | 108 rooms | $59–$79 | AE, D, DC, MC, V.

MINOCQUA

Aqua Aire. Within walking distance of downtown, this simple motel on Lake Minocqua overlooks the beach and the tennis and volleyball courts at Lake Minocqua Park. Picnic area. Refrigerators, cable TV. Docks. Business services. Some pets allowed. | 806 U.S. 51 N | 715/356–3433 | fax 715/356–3433 | 10 rooms (shower only) | $59–$79 | MC, V.

Best Western Lakeview Motor Lodge. Some rooms have lake views in this chalet-style motel on Lake Minocqua. The motel maintains a stretch of private beach for sunbathing and swimming, as well as a lakeside boardwalk and several piers for docking boats and fishing. Downtown Minocqua is only a half-block away, with plenty of shopping and dining opportunities. Picnic area, complimentary Continental breakfast. Some in-room hot tubs, cable TV. Dock. Business services. Pets allowed. | 311 E. Park Ave. 54568 | 715/356–5208 | fax 715/356–1412 | www.bestwestern.com | 41 rooms | $86–$116 | AE, D, DC, MC, V.

NEENAH

Parkway. This hotel's two red-and-white buildings are 2 mi southwest of downtown on a commercial strip that's also home to a bowling alley and several fast-food restaurants. Picnic area, complimentary Continental breakfast. Cable TV. Pool. Playground. Some pets allowed. | 1181 Gillingham Rd. | 920/725–3244 | 19 rooms (8 with showers only) | $35–$90 | AE, D, MC, V.

NEW GLARUS

Chalet Landhaus. These two enormous Swiss-style chalets have huge pine beams, riotous flowerboxes, whitewashed walls, and acres of hardwood inside. Downtown New Glarus is only a couple of blocks away. Restaurant. Some in-room hot tubs, cable TV. Business services. Pets allowed. | 801 Hwy. 69 | 608/527–5234 | fax 608/527–2365 | landhaus@madison.tds.net | www.chaletlandhaus.com | 67 rooms, 6 suites | $76–$145 | AE, D, MC, V.

Swiss-Aire. Red and white flowers bloom in window boxes and in jumbo whiskey barrels outside this basic motel on Highway 69. A bike trail crosses the property. Picnic area, complimentary Continental breakfast. Cable TV. Pool. Pets allowed. | 1200 Hwy. 69 | 608/527–2138 or 800/798–4391 | swissaire@mail.tdsnet.com | 26 rooms | $51–$65 | D, MC, V.

OSHKOSH

Howard Johnson. This standard motel occupies a spot on a strip of similar establishments and popular chain restaurants close to Whittman Regional Airport. Parking is sheltered by a carport. Bar. Cable TV. Pool. Hot tub. Business services. Some pets allowed. | 1919 Omro Rd. | 920/233–1200 | fax 920/233–1135 | 100 rooms | $70–$75 | AE, D, DC, MC, V.

Park Plaza Hotel. The restaurant and lounge at this downtown hotel overlook the Fox River. The lobby has a glass atrium with tropical plants and several seating areas. Some rooms have water views, as well. Restaurant, bar. In-room data ports, microwaves available, some refrigerators, cable TV, in-room VCRs available. Pool. Hot tub. Gym. Business services, airport shuttle. Some pets allowed. | 1 N. Main St. | 920/231–5000 | fax 920/231–8383 | relax@parkinn.com | www.parkinn.com | 179 rooms | $79–$135. | AE, D, DC, MC, V.

PARK FALLS

Boyd's Mason Lake Resort. This century-old resort 5 mi south of Park Falls consists of cabins with access to four private lakes on a 2,600-acre private estate. The lakes are professionally managed for muskies, walleyes, and bass. There's a three- to five-night minimum stay, depending upon the time of year. TV in common area. Hiking, beach, boating, fishing, bicycles. Pets allowed. | Box 57, Fifield 54524 | 715/762–3469 | 18 cabins | $80 | May–mid-Oct. | AP | No credit cards.

Buckhorn Retreat. The former 1920s Buckhorn Tavern is now a vacation cottage on 30 acres in the heart of Chequamegon National Forest 11 mi east of Park Falls. There's plenty of country charm and a sprinkling of antiques throughout. The Great Room has a gas fireplace and the kitchen is fully equipped. Kitchenette, cable TV, no phone. Hiking, fishing, biking. Cross-country skiing, snowmobiling. Laundry service. Some pets allowed. No smoking. | 344 Division St., Eisenstein 54552 | 715/762–2086 (days) or 715/762–3132 (evenings) | fax 715/762–4544 | www.parkfalls.com/buckhornretreat | 1 cottage | $85–$115 (2–night minimum stay) | D, MC, V.

Cry of the Loon Resort. The two- and three-bedroom cabins at this small resort 18 mi northeast of Park Falls all face the sandy shoreline of the Turtle Flambeau Flowage and have knotty-pine interiors and gas-log fireplaces. Picnic area. Kitchenettes. Lake. Boating, fishing. Some pets allowed (fee). | 6505 O'Meara Rd., Butternut 54514 | 715/476–2502 | 4 cabins | $500 (7–night minimum stay in summer) | MC, V.

Double E Resort. A 14-ft boat is supplied with each cabin at this family resort backed by white birch trees near the Chequamegon National Forest and 3 mi from Turtle Flambeau Flowage fishing area. Kitchenettes. Beach, boating. Some pets allowed. | 1610 N. Double EE Rd. | 715/583–4477 | www.lodging.org | 4 cabins | $385–$395 (7–day minimum stay) | D | Closed Nov.–Apr.

Flambeau Resort. Rustic but modern wood cabins built in the 1940s are nestled amid birch and pine trees in the Chequamegon National Forest within 200 ft of the south fork of the Flambeau River. Each rental comes with a boat. Golfing is nearby. Restaurant, bar. Hiking, boating, fishing, bicycles. Snowmobiling. Video games. Playground. Pets allowed. | N15355 East Rd. | 715/762–2178 or 715/762–4757 | 7 cabins | $150 (2–night minimum stay) | MC, V.

Moose Jaw Resort. Twenty miles east of Park Falls, on Round Lake (part of the Pike-Round Chain of Lakes), in the heart of the Chequamegon National Forest. The main lodge was built in 1887, at the height of northern Wisconsin's logging days. Today the resort is updated and has modern amenities. A big-screen TV is in the dining room. Cabins, some log, have screened porches, and a boat or canoe is included with each rental. Restaurant, bar, picnic area. Kitchenettes. Basketball, volleyball, beach, boating, fishing. Snowmobiling. Playground. Pets allowed. | N15098 Shady Knoll Rd. 54552 | 715/762–3028 | 7 cabins | $300–$525 (7–day minimum stay) | MC, V.

PLATTEVILLE

Governor Dodge Motor Inn. White pillars and a canopy accent the front of this motel five blocks from the University of Wisconsin–Platteville. Restaurant. Cable TV, in-room VCRs available. Pool. Hot tub. Gym. Business services. Some pets allowed. | U.S. 151 W | 608/348–2301 | fax 608/348–8579 | 74 rooms | $65–$77 | AE, D, DC, MC, V.

Super 8. This two-story white brick building overlooking the Platte River is nearly the length of a football field. Many guest rooms have views of the river flowing by. Complimentary Continental breakfast. Some refrigerators, cable TV. Hot tub, sauna. Laundry facilities. Business services. Pets allowed (fee). | 100 Rte. 80/81 south | 608/348–8800 | fax 608/348–7233 | www.super8.com | 73 rooms | $58–$75 | AE, D, DC, MC, V.

PORT WASHINGTON

Best Western Harborside Motor Inn. Located downtown, this is a standard brick hotel. Bar. Some in-room hot tubs, cable TV. Pool. Hot tub, sauna. Dock. Video games. Business services, free parking. Pets allowed. | 135 E. Grand Ave. | 262/284–9461 | fax 262/284–3169 | www.bestwestern.com | 96 rooms | $99–$119 | AE, D, DC, MC, V.

PORTAGE

Ridge Motor Inn. On the north side of town, this brick motel with a large, modern lobby is within walking distance to strip malls and restaurants. Restaurant, bar, room service. Some kitchenettes, cable TV, in-room VCRs and movies. Pool. Hot tub, massage. Gym, volleyball. Video games. Laundry facilities. Business services. Pets allowed. | 2900 New Pinery Rd. | 608/742–5306 | fax 608/742–5306 | 113 rooms, 9 suites | $49–$99 | AE, D, DC, MC, V.

PRAIRIE DU CHIEN

Best Western–Quiet House and Suites. Light gray-blue siding and stone masonry cover this two-story motel. Inside, a country Victorian motif prevails—you'll find Amish pieces and refurbished antiques including an old dry sink. Many rooms have a theme—there's a Mississippi riverboat room, a dairy state/barn room, and an Art Deco room. In-room data ports, kitchenettes (in suites), some in-room hot tubs, cable TV. Pool. Hot tub. Gym. Business services. Pets allowed. | Rtes. 18 and 355 | 608/326–4777 | fax 608/326–4787 | www.bestwestern.com | 42 rooms, 2 suites | $93–$111 | AE, D, DC, MC, V.

Holiday Motel. This bluish-gray motel in a long building dating from 1954 has outside room entrances and a small lobby. Cable TV. Business services. Some pets allowed. | 1010 S. Marquette Rd. | 608/326–2448 or 800/962–3883 | fax 608/326–2413 | 18 rooms | $55–$75 | AE, D, MC, V.

Prairie Motel. Three separate brick and stucco buildings make up this single-story motel on the south end of town. A miniature golf course is about 2 blocks away; a bowling alley and a movie theater are also nearby. Picnic area. Some refrigerators, cable TV. Pool. Playground. Pets allowed. | 1616 S. Marquette Rd. | 608/326–6461 or 800/526–3776 | 32 rooms | $65–$75 | D, MC, V.

PRAIRIE DU SAC
Prairie Garden Bed-and-Breakfast. This wood-and-brick farmhouse is set high on a hill and is shaded by lovely mature trees. Inside are cathedral ceilings and a stone fireplace. This B&B is a block from Lake Wisconsin and less than a mile and a half from downtown Prairie du Sac. Complimentary full breakfast. Cable TV. Some pets allowed. No smoking. | W13172 Rte. 188, Lodi 53555 | 608/592–5187 or 800/380–8427 | fax 608/592–5853 | prairiegarden@bigfoot.com | www.prairiegarden.com | 4 rooms | $55–$115 | MC, V.

RACINE
Days Inn. This two-story motel is on the Root River, in a quiet wooded area on the northeast side of town. There's a fireplace in the lobby. Restaurant, bar, picnic area, room service. In-room data ports, in-room hot tubs (in suites), cable TV. Pool. Laundry facilities. Business services, free parking. Pets allowed. | 3700 Northwestern Ave. | 262/637–9311 | fax 262/637–4575 | 109 rooms, 3 suites | $49–$69 | AE, D, DC, MC, V.

Knights Inn. In all four single-story buildings here, you can park in front of your room and enter directly from the parking lot. The motel, built in the late 1980s, is in a commercial area with restaurants and two shopping malls nearby. Complimentary Continental breakfast. Cable TV, in-room VCRs and movies available. Pets allowed. | 1149 Oakes Rd. | 262/886–6667 or 800/843–5644 | fax 262/886–6667, ext. 136 | 107 rooms | $45–$57 | AE, D, DC, MC, V.

RHINELANDER
Americinn. Flower beds and a putting green front this motel. A deer-antler chandelier hangs in the colonial-style lobby. Complimentary Continental breakfast. Some refrigerators, cable TV, in-room VCRs available. Pool. Hot tub, sauna. Laundry facilities. Business services. Pets allowed. | 648 W. Kemp St. | 715/369–9600 | fax 715/369–9613 | 52 rooms (3 with shower only), 10 suites | $70 | AE, D, DC, MC, V.

Best Western Claridge. This two-story brick motel in close to the courthouse and downtown shopping. Out front is a trout pond, inside a fireplace adorns the lobby. Restaurant, bar, room service, cable TV. Pool. Hot tub. Gym. Laundry facilities, laundry service. Business services, airport shuttle. Pets allowed. | 70 N. Stevens St. | 715/362–7100 | fax 715/362–3883 | www.claridge-bestwestern.com | 81 rooms, 4 suites | $66 | AE, D, DC, MC, V.

Holiday Acres. One thousand acres surround this rustic two-story wood-and-brick lodge and its cottages on Lake Thompson just 4 mi east of Rhinelander. Some cottages are more modern than others; all come with their own parking and boat, and some have screened-in porches. There are cross-country ski trails on the property. Bar, dining room, picnic area, room service. Kitchenettes in cottages, cable TV, in-room VCRs and movies available. Pool. Tennis. Beach, water sports, boating, bicycles. Cross-country skiing, snowmobiling. Playground. Business services, airport shuttle. Pets allowed. | 4060 S. Shore Dr. | 715/369–1500 or 800/261–1500 | fax 715/369–3665 | hacres@newnorth.net | www.holidayacres.com | 28 lodge rooms, 28 cottages | $94 | AE, D, DC, MC, V.

RICE LAKE
Currier's Lakeview. This chalet-style motel is on a wooded 4-acre peninsula on Rice Lake, next to a 10-acre park. Each room is different, and all have themed decor such as fishing, logging, and hummingbird haven. Picnic area, complimentary Continental break-

fast. Some kitchenettes, refrigerators, cable TV. Beach, dock, boating. Snowmobiling. Airport shuttle. Pets allowed. | 2010 E. Sawyer St. | 715/234–7474 or 800/433–5253 | www.wisconsintourism.com | 19 rooms | $53–$104 | AE, D, MC, V.

SAYNER

Froelich's Sayner Lodge. For rustic comfort and tranquility, stay at this 1920 lakeside lodge. The main house has cathedral ceilings with floor-to-celing windows. The cottages have lake views and most also have a screened-in porch. Bar. No air-conditioning, no room phones. Pool. Tennis. Hiking, boating, fishing. Playground. Pets allowed. | 3221 Plum Lake Dr. | 715/542–3261 or 800/553–9695 | www.saynerlodge.com | 11 lodge rooms, 20 cottages | $65–$190 | MC, V | Closed Nov.–May.

Plum Gate Resort. Choose from six renovated cottages with one to three bedrooms, most with views of Plum Lake. Some cottages with fireplaces can be used year-round. The resort is within walking distance of restaurants, library, the city park, and tennis and basketball courts. Full kitchens, TV. Beach, boating, fishing, bicycles. Pets allowed. | 3047 Plum Lake Dr. 54560 | 715/542–2224 | fax 715/542–3722 | www.innline.com | 6 cottages | $50–$85 per night, $315–$675 per week | No credit cards.

SHEBOYGAN

Baymont Inn. Just west of town, this standard brick hotel is painted white with green shutters and is near restaurants and shopping malls. Complimentary Continental breakfast. Cable TV. Business services. Some pets allowed. | 2932 Kohler Memorial Dr. | 920/457–2321 | fax 920/457–0827 | www.baymontinn.com | 96 rooms | $70–$100 | AE, D, DC, MC, V.

Best Value Inn This quiet motel in a rural area 6 mi south of town has two sections with either outside or inside entrances to rooms. Each room is decorated differently; one is furnished with antiques. Picnic area, complimentary Continental breakfast. Some microwaves, refrigerators, cable TV. Business services. Some pets allowed. | 3900 Motel Rd. | 920/458–8338 or 800/341–8000 | fax 920/459–7470 | www.imalodging.com | 32 rooms | $47–$64 | AE, D, DC, MC, V.

SISTER BAY

Century Farm Motel. Located on a country farm just 2 mi south of the heart of Sister Bay, this motel is actually four separate cottages. Refrigerators. Pets allowed. | 10068 Hwy. 57 54234 | 920/854–4069 | 4 cottages | $45–$60 | No credit cards | Closed mid-Oct.–mid-May.

Edge of Town. Two buildings make up this quiet and homey motel at the north edge of town. Behind the building is a waterfall and lawn furniture with umbrellas for summertime relaxing. Microwaves, refrigerators, cable TV, no room phones. Some pets allowed. | 11092 Rte. 42 | 920/854–2012 | 9 rooms | $67 | D, MC, V.

SPARTA

Best Nights Inn. This inn, in a residential area near the center of town, consists of four single-story buildings. Refrigerators, cable TV. Pets allowed. | 303 W. Wisconsin St. | 608/269–3066 | fax 608/269–3175 | www.Bestnightsinn.bizonhe.net | 28 rooms | $32–$82 | AE, D, DC, MC, V.

Country Inn. With its big first-floor porch, this wood motel looks like a very large country house. The country-style lobby has a green-tile gas fireplace, hardwood floors, country wreaths, and stenciling. Bar, complimentary Continental breakfast. Some refrigerators, cable TV. Pool. Hot tub. Laundry facilities. Business services. Pets allowed. | 737 Avon Rd. | 608/269–3110 or 800/456–4000 | fax 608/269–6726 | 61 rooms | $79–$81 | AE, D, DC, MC, V.

Heritage Motel. This L-shape wood-sided motel with parking in front is on the west side of town; restaurants are nearby. Cable TV. Pool. Hot tub. Pets allowed. | 704 W. Wisconsin St. | 608/269–6991 or 800/658–9484 | 22 rooms | $40–$42 | AE, D, MC, V.

SPOONER

Green Acres. This motel is in a quiet area at the south edge of town set back from the highway on 5 landscaped acres dotted with mature trees and flower beds. All rooms get bright morning sunshine. Picnic areas. Microwaves available, cable TV. Playground. Business services. Some pets allowed (fee). | N. 4809 U.S. 63 south | 715/635–2177 | 21 rooms | $49–$89 | AE, D, MC, V.

STEVENS POINT

Baymont Inn. This modern building on the east side of town is near a mall, the university, the municipal airport, and golf. Complimentary Continental breakfast. In-room data ports, cable TV. Pool. Laundry facilities. Business services. Pets allowed. | 4917 Main St. | 715/344–1900 | fax 715/344–1254 | 74 rooms | $44–$79 | AE, D, DC, MC, V.

Holiday Inn. On the north side of town, this six-story hotel is centered around a glass-enclosed holidome filled with trees and plants. A six-story tower is at one side of the lobby. Restaurant, bar (with entertainment), room service. In-room data ports, cable TV, in-room VCRs and movies. Pool. Hot tub. Exercise room. Laundry facilities. Business services, airport shuttle, free parking. Pets allowed. | 1501 N. Point Dr. | 715/341–1340 | fax 715/341–9446 | www.basshotels.com/holiday-inn | 295 rooms | $109–$168 | AE, D, DC, MC, V.

Point Motel. This modern stone structure built in 1970 is on a city lot, with parking, trees, bushes, and flower beds in front. Complimentary Continental breakfast. Cable TV, in-room VCRs available. Pets allowed (fee). | 209 Division St. | 715/344–8312 | 44 rooms | $36–$50 | AE, D, DC, MC, V.

STURGEON BAY

Holiday Motel. Built in the 1950s, this white motel with red awnings in the downtown historic district has flowers out front in summer. Complimentary Continental breakfast. Microwaves available, refrigerators, cable TV, VCR and movies available in common area. Business services. Some pets allowed. | 29 N. 2nd Ave. | 920/743–5571 | 18 rooms | $50–$69 | AE, D, DC, MC, V.

SUPERIOR

Best Western Bay Walk Inn. This colonial-style building is in a residential area about ½ mi from Lake Superior. Brick pillars support an entry portico, and a fireplace and sofas make the lobby comfortable. Complimentary Continental breakfast. Some refrigerators, cable TV, in-room VCRs and movies available. Pool. Hot tub, sauna. Video games. Laundry facilities. Business services. Some pets allowed. | 1405 Susquehanna | 715/392–7600 | fax 715/392–7680 | 50 rooms | $55–$81 | AE, D, DC, MC, V.

Best Western Bridgeview Motor Inn. This brownstone building dating from 1966 is at the foot of a bridge as you enter the north side of town. There is a restaurant next door. Complimentary Continental breakfast. Some microwaves, some refrigerators, cable TV. Pool. Hot tub, sauna. Laundry facilities. Business services. Pets allowed. | 415 Hammond Ave. | 715/392–8174 | fax 715/392–8487 | 96 rooms | $60–$100 | AE, D, DC, MC, V.

THREE LAKES

Oneida Village Inn. This modern two-story building in downtown Three Lakes has a cathedral ceiling in the dining room where dinner and Sunday brunch are served. The game room has air hockey and pool tables. Restaurant, bar. Cable TV. Video games.

Business services. Pets allowed. | 1785 Superior St. | 715/546–3373 or 800/374–7443 | fax 715/546–8060 | ovi@newnorth.net | www.wisvacations.com | 47 rooms | $49–$80 | AE, D, DC, MC, V.

TOMAH

Budget Host Daybreak. This rustic cedar hotel is made up of three separate buildings. Rooms are individually decorated to pay tribute to famous Wisconsinites, such as Frank Lloyd Wright and Laura Ingalls Wilder. Inside you'll find their photos and objects common to their personalities. The hotel is next to snowmobile trails and a municipal park. Microwaves and refrigerators available, cable TV. Business services. Small pets allowed. | 215 E. Clifton St. | 608/372–5946 | fax 608/372–5947 | 32 rooms | $63–$73 | AE, D, MC, V.

Comfort Inn. On the north side of town, this two-story brick motel is just off the highway near a truck stop and other hotels and businesses. Complimentary Continental breakfast. Refrigerators in suites, cable TV. Pool. Hot tub. Business services. Pets allowed. | 305 Wittig Rd. | 608/372–6600 | fax 608/372–6600 | 44 rooms, 8 suites | $53–$80 | AE, D, DC, MC, V.

Lark Inn. At this inn on 4 acres on the north side of town you can stay in historic 1920s log cabins with cathedral ceilings, or in the main building. Restaurant, picnic area, room service. Some kitchenettes, microwaves, refrigerators, cable TV, in-room VCRs and movies available. Laundry facilities. Pets allowed. | 229 N. Superior Ave. | 608/372–5981 or 800/447–5275 | fax 608/372–3009 | www.larkininn.com | 25 rooms, 5 cabins | $69–$81 | AE, D, DC, MC, V.

Super 8. This T-shape building, on the east side of town, has parking spaces for large trucks. Complimentary Continental breakfast. Some refrigerators, cable TV. Laundry facilities. Business services. Pets allowed (deposit). | 1008 E. McCoy Blvd. | 608/372–3901 | fax 608/372–5792 | www.super8.com | 65 rooms | $57–$67 | AE, D, DC, MC, V.

WAUKESHA

Select Inn of Waukesha. This chalet-style motel on the south side of town has themed suites including the Gallery Room which has an art gallery, and the Tackle Box Room complete with a canoe and fishing rods. Complimentary Continental breakfast. Refrigerators (in some suites). Business services. Pets allowed (deposit). | 2510 Plaza Ct. | 262/786–6015 or 800/641–1000 | fax 262/786–5784 | 91 rooms, 9 suites | $56–$70 | AE, D, DC, MC, V.

WAUSAU

Baymont Inn. Two miles from downtown, on the western edge of Wausau, this inn has a country decor, with quilts in the rooms. There's a landscaped lawn and the lobby has a breakfast area. Several restaurants are within 5 blocks of the inn. *USA Today* newspaper is complimentary. Complimentary Continental breakfast. In-room data ports, cable TV. Pool. Business services. Pets allowed. | 1910 Stewart Ave. 54401 | 715/842–0421 | fax 715/845–5096 | www.baymontinn.com | 95 rooms | $62–$65 | AE, D, DC, MC, V.

Best Western Midway Hotel. This standard motel 5 mi south of town, in Rib Mountain, has a small, contemporary lobby with a polished-rock floor and leather furniture. Shuttles run to the Rib Mountain Ski Area. Restaurant, bar, picnic area, room service. In-room data ports, cable TV. Pool. Hot tub, sauna. Playground. Business services, airport shuttle. Pets allowed (fee). | 2901 Martin Ave., Rib Mountain | 715/842–1616 | fax 715/845–3726 | 99 rooms | $80–$95 | AE, D, DC, MC, V.

Exel Inn. This brick motel is near the center of town near Highway 51 and has a view of Rib Mountain. Complimentary Continental breakfast. Cable TV. Video games. Laundry facilities. Business services. Pets allowed. | 116 S. 17th Ave. | 715/842–0641 | fax 715/848–1356 | 122 rooms | $48–$52 | AE, D, DC, MC, V.

Rib Mountain Inn. This chalet-style inn is at the base of Rib Mountain, just a 15-minute walk from skiing. Picnic areas, complimentary Continental breakfast. Refrigerators, some in-room hot tubs, cable TV, in-room VCRs and movies. Hot tub, sauna. Driving range. Business services. Pets allowed. | 2900 Rib Mountain Way | 715/848–2802 | fax 715/848–1908 | 16 rooms, 4 villas, 4 apartments | $78–$114 rooms, $148–$219 villas, $250–$308 apartments | AE, D, DC, MC, V.

Super 8. This standard motel on the west side of town is near the business district and within walking distance of restaurants. Complimentary Continental breakfast. Cable TV. Pool. Hot tub. Business services. Pets allowed. | 2006 Stewart Ave. | 715/848–2888 | fax 715/842–9578 | www.super8.com | 88 rooms | $69 | AE, D, DC, MC, V.

WAUWATOSA

Exel Inn–West. This simple modern hotel is across the street from the zoo and 2 mi from large shopping malls. Complimentary Continental breakfast. Cable TV. Business services. Some pets allowed. | 115 N. Mayfair Rd. (U.S. 100) | 414/257–0140 | fax 414/475–7875 | 123 rooms | $56–$80 | AE, D, DC, MC, V.

WISCONSIN DELLS

International Motel. This modern motel is made up of three Miami-stone buildings. Picnic area. Refrigerators available, cable TV. Pool, wading pool. Playground. Some pets allowed. | 1311 E. Broadway | 608/254–2431 | www.dells.com/international/index.html | 45 rooms | $50–$80 | AE, D, DC, MC, V | Closed early Nov.–Apr.

Wyoming

AFTON

Best Western Hi Country Inn. You get the convenience of downtown and are only 2 mi from the Periodic Spring. In winter, you can cross-country ski nearby. No air-conditioning. Cable TV. Pool in summer. Hot tub. Some pets allowed. | 689 S. Washington St. | 307/886–3856 | fax 307/885–9318 | 30 rooms | $50–$65 | AE, D, DC, MC, V.

Corral. The large backyard doubles as a children's play area, and the individual log cabins in downtown Afton let you have both rustic touches and downtown convenience. Picnic area. No air-conditioning, some refrigerators. Cable TV. Some pets allowed. | 161 Washington St. (U.S. 89) | 307/886–5424 | 15 rooms (2 with kitchenettes) | $40–$80 | Closed winter | AE, D, DC, MC, V.

Lazy B Motel. Not every motel offers lodgings for your horse. This is one of them. The 1960s style roadside motel has large grassy common areas with deer statuettes, and wonderful views of the surrounding mountains. Picnic area, grill. Cable TV. Playground. Pets allowed. | 219 Washington St. (U.S. 89) | 307/885–3187 | fax 307/885–3035 | 24 rooms, 1 suite | $54, $100 suite | AE, D, DC, MC, V.

Three Rivers Motel. Families may appreciate the kitchenettes in every room of this downtown motel, which has contemporary, L-shaped rooms. Pets allowed. | 60 Main St. | 307/654–7551 | threeriv@cyberhighway.net | www.wy-biz.com/3riversmotel/ | 23 rooms with kitchenettes | $50–$60 | AE, D, MC, V.

ALPINE

Royal Resort. Only 8 mi from the Snake River, this resort makes a great headquarters for virtually any outdoor sport. The design and furnishings, both in the lobby and in the rooms, may remind you of a Bavarian lodge. The small market also has a gas station. Restaurant, bar. Some minibars, some refrigerators. Cable TV, some in-room VCRs. Hot tub. Exercise room. Horseback riding. Cross-country skiing, snowmobiling. RV spaces. Playground. Small pets allowed. | U.S. 26 and 89 | 307/654–7545 ext. 331; 800/343–6755 (outside WY) | fax 307/654–7546 | www.royal-resort.com | 45 rooms | $50–$100 | AE, D, DC, MC, V.

BUFFALO

Canyon Motel. An airport shuttle and three rooms with kitchenettes are added conveniences at this contemporary motel on the west side of Buffalo on U.S. 16, near the Bighorn Mountains. Picnic area. Cable TV. Airport shuttle. Pets allowed. | 997 Fort St. | 307/684–2957 or 800/231–0742 | 18 rooms, 3 with kitchenettes | $50–$80 | AE, D, MC, V.

Comfort Inn. Several blocks from downtown, this hotel was built in 1995 and has rooms priced to fit any budget. Complimentary Continental breakfast. Cable TV. Hot tub. Some pets allowed. | 65 U.S. 16 E | 307/684–9564 or 800/228–5150 | fax 307/684–9564 | 41 rooms | $39–$119 | AE, D, DC, MC, V.

CowboyTown Motel. The individual cabin units have front porches, and the bright rooms have king-size beds and Western-style furnishings. Cable TV. Outdoor hot tub. Pets allowed. No-smoking rooms. | 181 U.S. 16 E | 307/684–0603 or 888/323–2865 | fax 307/684–0605 | 4 rooms, 8 cabins, 2 kitchenettes | $62 rooms and cabins, $58–$88 kitchenettes | D, MC, V.

Crossroads HoJo Inn. Near the Bighorn Mountains and I–25, this large, modern hotel has spacious rooms and convenient access to the interstate. Restaurant, bar, complimentary breakfast. Pool. Hot tub. Pets allowed (fee). | 75 N. Bypass | 307/684–2256 | fax 307/684–2256 | 60 rooms | $79–$104 | AE, D, DC, MC, V.

Ranch at Ucross. This converted old ranch home is a good place for business retreats, with full meeting facilities and cabins that have great views. Restaurant, bar, complimentary breakfast. Pool. Tennis. Fishing. Cross-country skiing, snowmobiling. Business services. Pets allowed. | 2673 U.S. 14 E, Ucross | 307/737–2281 or 800/447–0194 | fax 307/737–2211 | blair@wavecom.net | www.innsite.com/inns/A002021.html | 31 rooms, 4 suites | $109–$159 | MC, V.

Wyoming Motel. Some extra-large rooms and some with kitchenettes make this a good stopping place for families on the road. The motel is near the intersection of I–90, I–25, and U.S. 16. Restaurant, picnic area. Cable TV. Pool. Hot tub. Pets allowed. | 610 E. Hart St. | 800/666–5505 | fax 307/684–5442 | wyomotel@vcn.com | 27 rooms, 5 with kitchenettes | $62–$67, $129–$145 large family rooms | AE, D, DC, MC, V.

Z-Bar Motel. At the base of the Bighorn Mountains, these clean, quiet cabins sit in a huge shaded yard with tables and barbecue grills. Some kitchenettes are available—ideal if you are traveling with pets or children. Picnic area. Refrigerators. Cable TV. Pets allowed. | 626 Fort St. | 307/684–5535 or 888/313–1227 | fax 307/684–5538 | 4 rooms, 22 cabins | $50–$63 rooms and cabins | AE, D, DC, MC, V.

CASPER

Econolodge. Formerly the Kelly Inn, this contemporary hotel is near I–25 and the Casper Events Center. Cable TV. Hot tub. Laundry facilities. Pets allowed. | 821 N. Poplar | 307/266–2400 or 800/635–3559 | fax 307/266–1146 | 103 rooms | $46–$65 | AE, D, DC, MC, V.

Hampton Inn. Business travelers will appreciate the in-room data ports and other business services at this modern and comfortable hotel near I–25 and the Casper Events Center. Complimentary Continental breakfast. In-room data ports. Cable TV. Pool. Sauna. Business services. Airport shuttle. Pets allowed (fee). | 400 W. F St. | 307/235–6668 | fax 307/235–2027 | 122 rooms | $75–$95 | AE, D, DC, MC, V.

Holiday Inn. On the river, next to I–25 and several blocks from downtown Casper, this circular hotel has a lot of greenery in the public spaces and contemporary rooms, plus a terraced room that faces the river. Restaurant, bar, picnic area, room service. In-room data ports. Cable TV. Indoor pool. Hot tub. Exercise equipment. Video games. Laundry facilities. Business services. Airport shuttle. Some pets allowed. | 300 W. F St. | 307/235–2531 | fax 307/473–3400 | 200 rooms | $89–$109 | AE, D, DC, MC, V.

Radisson. This large facility has everything under one roof. The rooms are large and decorated in muted blue, green, and mauve. Restaurant, bar, coffee shop, room service. Some in-room hot tubs. Cable TV. Indoor pool. Beauty salon, hot tub. Cross-country and downhill skiing. Airport shuttle. Pets allowed. | 800 N. Poplar St. | 307/266–6000 | fax 307/473–1010 | 228 rooms | $69–$79 | AE, D, DC, MC, V.

CHEYENNE

Best Western Hitching Post Inn. State legislators frequent this hotel near the capitol. The Hitch, as locals call it, books country-western performers in its lounge. It has dark-wood walls and an elegance not found in many of the lodging properties in Wyoming. Restaurants, bar with entertainment, room service. In-room data ports, refrigerators. Cable TV. 2 pools (1 indoor). Hot tub. Exercise equipment, gym. Playground. Laundry facilities. Business services. Airport shuttle. Pets allowed. | 1700 W. Lincolnway (U.S. 30) | 307/638–3301 | fax 307/778–7194 | 166 rooms | $63–$179 | AE, D, DC, MC, V.

Comfort Inn. This modern hotel is on the west side of town near I–80 and I–25. The rooms have contemporary furnishings and handicapped facilities. Complimentary Continental breakfast. Cable TV. Pool. Laundry facilities. Business services. Pets allowed. | 2245 Etchepare Dr. | 307/638–7202 | fax 307/635–8560 | 77 rooms | $79–$99 | AE, D, DC, MC, V.

La Quinta. The design and furnishings are Spanish style and the hotel is near the I–80 and I–25 interchange. You can rent video games. Complimentary Continental breakfast. In-room data ports. Cable TV. Pool. Some pets allowed. | 2410 W. Lincolnway (U.S. 30) | 307/632–7117 | fax 307/638–7807 | 105 rooms | $69–$72 | AE, D, DC, MC, V.

CODY

Best Western Sunset Motor Inn. This inn sits on a large grassy property with shade trees and has an enclosed play area for children. Numerous amenities, clean rooms, a downtown location, and a quiet and relaxed atmosphere make this a favorite with families. Restaurant. Cable TV. 2 pools. Hot tub. Exercise room. Playground. Coin laundry. Some pets allowed. | 1601 8th St. | 307/587–4265 or 800/624–2727 | fax 307/587–9029 | 116 rooms, 4 suites | $119, $145–$165 suites | AE, D, DC, MC, V.

Elephant Head. Buffalo Bill's niece built these cabins, which have been modernized but retain their original charm. The resort is only 11 mi from Yellowstone, and is convenient to the Buffalo Bill Reservoir. You get to watch Western movies nightly. Restaurant, bar, picnic area. No air-conditioning. Playground. Pets allowed. | 1170 Yellowstone Hwy., Wapiti | 307/587–3980 | fax 307/527–7922 | www.elephantheadlodge.com | 12 cabins | $75–$150 | AE, D, MC, V | Closed Sept.–May.

Kelly Inn. The handcrafted wooden bears that inhabit the entrance and the lobby are one eye-catching element at this inn. The view from the rooms is another. On the hill above Cody's main business district and near the airport, the place has southwestern-style furnishings. Cable TV. Hot tub. Laundry facilities. Business services. Pets allowed. | 2513 Greybull Hwy. | 307/527–5505 or 800/635–3559 | fax 307/527–5001 | 50 rooms | $99–$105 | AE, D, DC, MC, V.

Shoshone Lodge. The cabins are basic, but the location is scenic, on Grinnell Creek about 5 mi east of Yellowstone National Park. Restaurant. No air-conditioning, no room phones. Cross-country and downhill skiing. Laundry facilities. Pets allowed. | 349 Yellowstone Hwy. | 307/587–4044 | fax 307/587–2681 | 16 cabins, 3 kitchenettes (no equipment) | $80 | AE, D, MC, V.

Yellowstone Valley Inn. Only 32 mi from Yellowstone's main east entrance, this sprawling and peaceful property offers basic accommodations in a mountain setting. Campsites are also available, and some of the rooms are in duplex cabins. Restaurant, bar, picnic area. No room phones. Coin laundry. Pets allowed. | 3324 Yellowstone Park Hwy., 18 mi west of Cody | 307/587–3961 or 877/587–3961 | fax 307/587–4656 | 18 rooms, 18 cabin rooms | $83–$85 | AE, D, MC, V.

DOUGLAS

Best Western Douglas Inn. The atrium lobby with a cathedral ceiling and fireplace makes for an impressive entrance. The location is convenient, next to I–25 on the north side of town and close to the Wyoming State Fairgrounds and the main tourist attractions. Restaurant, bar, room service. Cable TV. Indoor pool. Hot tub. Exercise equipment. Video games. Laundry facilities. Business services. Some pets allowed. | 1450 Riverbend Dr. | 307/358–9790 | fax 307/358–6251 | 116 rooms | $79 | AE, D, DC, MC, V.

DUBOIS

Super 8. On the north side of town, this motel was renovated in 1998 and has modern furnishings. It is near the National Bighorn Sheep Interpretive Center. Cable TV. Hot tub. Pets allowed. | 1414 Warm Springs Dr. | 307/455–3694 | fax 307/455–3640 | 32 rooms | $70 | AE, D, DC, MC, V.

ENCAMPMENT

Riverside Garage and Cabins. These modern, woodsy log cabins are close to the river, and a garage and gas station with food and drinks are also on the property. Cabins vary in size. Pets allowed. | 108 E. Riverside Ave., Riverside | 307/327–5361 | 8 cabins | $32–$85 | AE, D, MC, V.

EVANSTON

Super Budget Inn. Right off I–80, the clean rooms, reasonable rates, and basic amenities make this a great place for a stopover. Bar, dining room. Pool. Pets allowed. | 1936 Harrison Dr. | 307/789–2810 | fax 307/789–5506 | 115 rooms | $65 | AE, D, DC, MC, V.

Weston Plaza Hotel. Numerous amenities make for a comfortable stay at this basic but attractive 3-story hotel-style inn. Most of the rooms have new furniture, and some have microwaves and refrigerators. On the first I–80 exit east of Utah. Restaurant, bar, Continental breakfast, dining room. Pool. Hot tub. Laundry facilities. Pets allowed. | 1983 Harrison Dr. | 307/789–0783 | fax 307/789–3353 | 101 rooms | $55 | AE, D, DC, MC, V.

GILLETTE

Ramada Limited. Minutes from downtown and area attractions, rooms at this clean, dependable motor inn are spacious and comfortable. Continental breakfast. Cable TV. Outdoor pool. Hot tub. Pets allowed (fee). | 608 East 2nd St. | 307/682–9341 or 888/298–2054 | fax 307/682–9341 | 76 rooms | $75 | AE, D, DC, MC, V.

Thunder Basin Hotel. Travelers with a yen for exercise will appreciate the gym and the indoor pool big enough for swimming. Rooms at this former Holiday Inn are decorated in soft teal and mauve. Some have in-room data ports. Restaurant, bar with entertainment, room service. Cable TV. Indoor pool. Hot tub. Gym. Video games. Laundry facilities. Business services. Airport shuttle. Pets allowed. | 2009 S. Douglas Hwy. | 307/686–3000 | fax 307/686–4018 | 158 rooms | $90–$94 | AE, D, DC, MC, V.

GRAND TETON NATIONAL PARK

Colter Bay Village. On Jackson Lake at Colter Bay, this is one of the park's cheaper lodgings, with cabins, tent cabins, and an RV park. The views are outstanding. Tent cabins have woodburning stoves, picnic tables, fee showers, and double-decker bunks (no bedding). You can rent sleeping bags, cots, and blankets. 2 restaurants, picnic area, snack bar. No air-conditioning, no room phones. Horseback riding, boating. Shops. Airport shuttle. Some pets allowed. | U.S. 89/191/287 | 307/543–3100 or 800/628–9988 (reservations) | fax 307/

543–3046 | www.gtlc.com | 166 cabins, some with shower only, some share bath; 66 tent cabins; 113 RV spaces | $66–$120 | AE, DC, MC, V | Closed early Oct.–late May.

Hatchet Resort. Some units sleep up to 12 at this log-style motel about 10 mi south of the south gate to Grand Teton and 35 mi from Yellowstone. Ownership changed in 1999. Restaurant, picnic area. No air-conditioning. Pets allowed (fee). No smoking. | 19980 E. U.S. 89 | 307/543–2413 | fax 307/543–2034 | www.hatchetresort.com | $90–$99 | D, MC, V.

Signal Mountain Lodge. The lodge-style cabins have a sofa bed in the living room, useful if you're traveling with a family. One-room units have refrigerators and fireplaces and are on the waterfront. Two-room units have kitchenettes. All have views of the Grand Tetons and some of Jackson Lake. Bring your own utensils. Restaurant, bar. No air-conditioning, some microwaves. Marina, boating. Fishing. Some pets allowed. | Teton Park Rd., Moran | 307/543–2831 | fax 307/543–2569 | www.signalmtnlodge.com | 79 cabins, 30 with kitchenettes | $80–$175 | AE, D, MC, V.

GREEN RIVER

Oak Tree Inn. A completely no-smoking facility, this two-story inn was built in 1997. If you're a photographer, you can shoot the distinctive surrounding rock formations. Flaming Gorge is 20 mi away. Restaurant. Some refrigerators. Cable TV. Pets allowed. No smoking. | 1170 W. Flaming Gorge Way | 307/875–3500 | fax 307/875–4889 | 192 rooms | $65–$100 | AE, D, DC, MC, V.

Sweet Dream Inn. Some large suite-style rooms will sleep up to five people at this locally owned motel. The larger rooms have microwaves, refrigerators, and Jacuzzis. Restaurant, bar. Pets allowed. | 1416 Uinta Dr. | 307/875–7554 | 30 rooms | $68–$89 | AE, D, MC, V.

GREYBULL

Yellowstone Motel. The motel is small but rooms are large, with colorful furnishings. Cable TV. Pool. Pets allowed. | 247 Greybull Ave. | 307/765–4456 | fax 307/765–2108 | 35 rooms | $63 | AE, D, MC, V.

JACKSON

Friendship Inn-Antler Inn. Just one block from the town square, this inn is basic and contemporary in style. Cable TV. Hot tub. Exercise equipment. Some pets allowed. | 43 W. Pearl St. | 307/733–2535 or 800/522–2406 | fax 307/733–4158 | 104 rooms, 2 suites | $66–$110 | AE, D, DC, MC, V.

Pony Express. A standard locally owned and operated motel on the west side of town, this is good for those who want to get an early start for the Tetons. South-facing rooms have mountain views, and service is friendly. Cable TV. Outdoor pool. Pets allowed. | 1075 W. Broadway | 307/733–2658 or 800/526–2658 | fax 307/733–2658 | 24 rooms | $70–$125 | D, MC, V.

Quality 49er. Suitable for families or business travelers, this hotel has 30 new fireplace suites, several conference rooms, and a 40-person outdoor hot tub. Near the town square, it's within easy walking distance of shopping and restaurants. Complimentary Continental breakfast. Some in-room hot tubs, microwaves, refrigerators. Cable TV. Hot tub. Exercise equipment. Some pets allowed. | 330 W. Pearl St. | 307/733–7550 or 800/451–2980 | fax 307/733–2002 | townsquareinns@wyoming.com | www.townsquareinns.com | 148 rooms | $70–$225 | AE, D, DC, MC, V.

Snow King Resort. Ski-in, ski-out to Snow King Mountain, which rises above this resort. The layout is multilevel and widely spread out, with many steps and ramps for people with disabilities. A free shuttle takes you to the Jackson Hole ski area. Restaurant, bar, room service. Cable TV. Pool. Barbershop, beauty salon, hot tubs. Exercise equipment. Cross-country and downhill skiing. Video games. Laundry facilities. Business services. Airport shuttle. Some pets allowed. | 400 E. Snow King Ave. | 307/733–5200 or 800/522–5464 | fax 307/733–4086 | snowking@wyoming.com | www.snowking.com | 204 rooms | $90–$200 | AE, D, DC, MC, V.

Wyoming Inn. The reception desk in the lobby of this inn, one of the finest in Jackson, has a carving of two large bighorn sheep facing off. The rooms, done in soft blues and greens, have comfortable sitting areas, desks, and in-room data ports. Some have gas fireplaces and Jacuzzis. You can raft, go horseback riding, and hike in summer and snowmobile in winter. Complimentary Continental breakfast. Some refrigerators. Cable TV. Hot tubs. Business services. Airport shuttle. Pets allowed. No smoking. | 930 W. Broadway | 307/734–0035 or 800/844–0035 | fax 307/734–0037 | 73 rooms, 4 with kitchenettes | $249–$259 | AE, D, MC, V.

KEMMERER

Bon Rico. Nothing fancy, but the motel rooms here, 12 mi south of Kemmerer on U.S. 189, are available throughout the summer at budget rates. The restaurant and bar are open year-round. Restaurant, bar. Cable TV. Pets allowed. | U.S. 189 | 307/877–4503 | 24 rooms | $25–$39 | Closed Nov.–Mar. | MC, V.

Fairview Motel. The rooms here are exceptionally large and comfortable, with good views. The film star Mel Gibson once spent several nights here while in the area fishing. In-room data ports, some microwaves, refrigerators. Cable TV. Airport shuttle. Business services. Pets allowed. | 61 Rte. 30 | 307/877–3938 or 800/247–3938 | fax 307/877–3938 ext. 2 | www.wy-biz.com/fairviewmotel.com | 61 rooms | $44–$50 | AE, D, MC, V.

LANDER

Budget Host Pronghorn. The sculpture garden that spreads through Lander starts at this convenient downtown motel. Some rooms have kitchens. Restaurant, complimentary Continental breakfast. Some refrigerators. Cable TV. Hot tub. Laundry facilities. Some pets allowed. | 150 E. Main St. | 307/332–3940 | fax 307/332–2651 | pronghorn@wyoming.com | www.wyoming.com/~thepronghorn | 54 rooms | $55–$79 | AE, D, DC, MC, V.

LARAMIE

Best Western Foster's Country Inn. At the intersection of I–80 and Rtes. 130/230, this hotel has full services, including a convenience store, filling station, restaurant, and bar. The lobby and halls are rustic Western knotty pine, and the rooms are standard contemporary. Restaurant, bar. Cable TV. Indoor pool. Hot tub. Airport shuttle. Pets allowed. | 1561 Snowy Range Rd. | 307/742–8371 | fax 307/742–0884 | 112 rooms | $64–$96 | AE, D, DC, MC, V.

Econo Lodge. The rooms are both extra-large and cozy, with burgundy and forest-green comforters. Some have coffemakers. Some refrigerators. Cable TV. Indoor pool. Pets allowed. | 1370 McCue St. | 307/745–8900 | fax 307/745–5806 | econol@trib.com | 51 rooms | $54–$100 | AE, D, DC, MC, V.

First Inn Gold. Right off I–80, this standard motel has appealing, spacious rooms, numerous amenities, and efficient service at reasonable rates. Great if you want to get an early start. Restaurant, bar, Continental breakfast. Cable TV. Pool. Hot tub. Pets allowed (fee). | 421 Boswell St. | 307/742–3721 or 800/642–4212 | fax 307/742–5473 | 80 rooms | $69 | AE, D, DC, MC, V.

Holiday Inn. Some of the rooms have in-room data ports in this standard contemporary hotel. An enclosed wing houses 32 of the rooms. Restaurant, bar, room service. Cable TV. Indoor pool. Hot tub. Laundry facilities. Airport shuttle. Pets allowed. | 2313 Soldier Springs Rd. | 307/742–6611 | fax 307/745–8371 | 100 rooms | $75–$85 | AE, D, DC, MC, V.

LOVELL

Cattleman Motel. Clean, simple Western-style rooms have lodgepole furniture at this basic one-story motel near the center of town. The rates are reasonable and the service is good. Continental breakfast. Cable TV. Hot tub. Pets allowed. | 470 Montana Ave. | 307/548–2296 or 888/548–2296 | fax 307/548–2483 | 13 rooms | $46 | AE, D, MC, V.

Horseshoe Bend Motel. Western-style and contemporary Western furnishings characterize this small in-town motel with modest rates. Cable TV. Pool. Pets allowed. | 375 E. Main St. | 307/548–2221 | fax 307/548–2131 | hsbmotelja@tctwest.net | 22 rooms, 5 with kitchenettes | $39–$49 | AE, D, DC, MC, V.

MEDICINE BOW

Loghorn Lodge. Off the beaten path, about 18 mi east of Medicine Bow, this is a quiet and cozy place to stay. In the spring, lilac bushes bloom around these rustic, individual cabin-style rooms, which are basic, comfortable, clean, and affordable. Restaurant. TVs. Pets allowed. | 362 N. 4th St., Rock River | 307/378–2567 | fax 307/378–2567 | 8 rooms | $34 | D, MC, V.

Trampas Lodge. Rooms at this motel have no fancy decorations but are clean and affordable. Pets allowed. | Lincoln Hwy. | 307/379–2280 | 20 rooms | $31–$36 | MC, V.

NEWCASTLE

Flying V Cambria Inn. Completed in 1928, this European manor-style inn began as a resort for the then-booming mining town of Cambria. The mine went bust, and the inn was used as a Bible school, cattle ranch, and casino before evolving into this bed-and-breakfast with individually decorated rooms and spacious common areas. Nestled in the Black Hills 8 mi north of Newcastle, the inn is quiet, down-home, and relaxed. Some shared baths. Full breakfast, restaurant, bar. Some pets allowed. | 23726 U.S. 85 | 307/746–2096 | www.trib.com/~flyingv | 7 rooms | $79 | D, MC, V.

Fountain Motor Inn. Ponds and fountains on the 20 landscaped acres around this inn set it apart, as does the pool. Apartment-style accommodations and campsites are also available. Restaurant. Some rooms with kitchenettes. Cable TV. Pool. Some pets allowed. | 2 Fountain Plaza | 307/746–4426 or 800/882–8858 | fax 307/746–3206 | 80 rooms | $70 | AE, D, DC, MC, V.

Four Corners Store, Diner & Country Inn. Four Corners serves as the diner, general store, inn, and church. It's a popular spot with rooms for all budgets. Restaurant. Pets allowed. | 24713 U.S. 85 N, Four Corners | 307/746–4776 | 9 rooms | $35–$100.

PINEDALE

Best Western Pinedale Inn. The inn is on the north side of town, within walking distance of shops and restaurants. The rooms are modest and contemporary. Complimentary Continental breakfast. Some refrigerators. Cable TV. Indoor pool. Hot tub. Exercise equipment. Pets allowed. | 850 W. Pine St. | 307/367–6869 | fax 307/367–6897 | 58 rooms | $99 | AE, D, DC, MC, V.

Window on the Winds B&B. This comfortable log home gets its name from huge windows that offer stunning views of the Gros Ventre Range, the Wind River Mountains, and Gannett Peak, the state's highest point. All of the rooms have lodgepole-pine beds, jewel- or earth-toned southwestern quilts and rugs, and mountain views. Children and pets are welcome at this family-oriented, homey place. Full breakfast, dining room. Hot tub. Pets allowed. | 10151 U.S. 191 | 307/367–2600 or 888/367–1345 | fax 307/367–2395 | www.windowonthewinds.com | 4 rooms (2 with shared bath) | $75–$95 | AE, D, DC, MC, V.

POWELL

Lamplighter Inn. Near downtown and renovated in 1999, this hotel has reasonably priced rooms done in blue, mauve, rose, and cream. Many are no-smoking. Restaurant, bar. Pets allowed. | 234 E. 1st St. | 307/754–2226 | fax 307/754–2229 | 20 rooms | $49 | AE, D, DC, MC, V.

Super 8. This standard Super 8 is close to downtown and caters to varied budgets. Cable TV. Pets allowed. | 845 E. Coulter Dr. | 307/754–7231 | 35 rooms | $40–$73 | AE, D, DC, MC, V.

RAWLINS

Cottontree Inn. This is Rawlins's finest motel, with spacious guest rooms and inviting public areas where you'll find easy chairs to relax in. Restaurant, bar. In-room data ports. Cable TV. Indoor pool. Hot tub, sauna. Business services. Pets allowed. | 23rd and Spruce | 307/324–2737 | fax 307/324–5011 | cotton@trib.com | 122 rooms | $74 | AE, D, DC, MC, V.

Days Inn. On the east side of town near the junction of I–80 and U.S. 287, you'll find average-size, contemporary rooms, some equipped for the handicapped. Restaurant, bar, room service. In-room data ports. Cable TV. Pool. Laundry facilities. Business services. Pets allowed. | 2222 E. Cedar St. | 307/324–6615 | fax 307/324–6615 | 118 rooms | $66 | AE, D, DC, MC, V.

Weston Inn. At the eastern edge of town, off I–80, this standard motel has affordable rooms that come in a variety of sizes, and is a good place for stopovers. Continental breakfast, bar. Cable TV. Pool. Small pets allowed. | 1801 E. Cedar St. | 307/324–2783 | fax 307/328–1011 | 132 rooms | $54 | AE, D, DC, MC, V.

RIVERTON

Holiday Inn. Blue, green, and mauve carpets and bedspreads furnish the rooms here, and the walls are hung with Western and Native American paintings. Restaurant, bar, room service. Cable TV. Indoor pool. Beauty salon, hot tub. Laundry facilities. Airport shuttle. Pets allowed. | 900 E. Sunset | 307/856–8100 | fax 307/856–0266 | 121 rooms | $69–$89 | AE, D, DC, MC, V.

Roomers. This quaint motor inn is housed in an older, restored brick building on Riverton's main thoroughfare. The Early American–style rooms, although smaller than average, are filled with personal touches like quilts, extra pillows, and wallpaper borders. Most rooms have refrigerators and microwaves. Cable TV. Pets allowed (fee). | 319 N. Federal Blvd. | 307/857–1735 or 888/857–4097 | 13 rooms | $35–$40 | AE, D, DC, MC, V.

Sundowner Station. The furnishings are modern and the rooms of average size, but this hotel strives for a home away from home style. The courtyard and waterfall are soothing, and shopping centers are close on the east side of the city. Restaurant, bar. Cable TV. Sauna. Airport shuttle. Pets allowed. | 1616 N. Federal | 307/856–6503 or 800/874–1116 | fax 307/856–6503 | 60 rooms | $55–$60 | AE, D, DC, MC, V.

ROCK SPRINGS

Comfort Inn. On the west side of the city, near the shopping mall and Western Wyoming Community College, this hostelry offers good amenities and varied furnishings. Complimentary Continental breakfast. In-room data ports. Cable TV. Pool. Hot tub. Exercise equipment. Playground. Laundry facilities. Business services. Pets allowed (fee). | 1670 Sunset Dr. | 307/382–9490 | fax 307/382–7333 | 103 rooms | $62–$68 | AE, D, DC, MC, V.

Days Inn. This standard chain motel is right off I–80 and has a bright lobby and breakfast nook area. Rooms have modern amenities, and an otherwise neutral color scheme is splashed with bright pinks, mauves, and teals. Continental breakfast. In-room data ports, microwave, refrigerator. Cable TV. Outdoor pool. Laundry facilities. Pets allowed. | 1545

Elk St. | 307/362–5646 or 800/544–8313 | fax 307/382–9440 | www.daysinn.com | 107 rooms | $50–$70 | AE, D, DC, MC, V.

Elk Street Motel. An older mom-and-pop establishment, this eclectic motor inn is convenient to I–80 and has rooms with microwaves and refrigerators. The decor is Early American. Rates are affordable and the service is friendly and casual. Microwaves, refrigerators. Cable TV. Some pets allowed. | 1100 Elk St. | 307/362–3705 | 18 rooms | $36 | MC, V.

Holiday Inn. A good place for a convention, this hotel is on the west side of town near a shopping mall and I–80. Rooms have coffeemakers and two-line phones with modems. Convention facilities can handle up to 600 people. Restaurant, bar, room service. Cable TV. Indoor pool, wading pool. Hot tub. Laundry facilities. Business services. Airport shuttle. Pets allowed. | 1675 Sunset Dr. | 307/382–9200 | fax 307/362–1064 | 114 rooms | $75–$79 | AE, D, DC, MC, V.

Ramada Limited. The basic rooms are decorated in soft tones in this hotel on the western side of the city. The rooms are large, and there is a lot of space outside for children to play in. Complimentary Continental breakfast. In-room data ports. Cable TV. Pool. Gym. Business services. Pets allowed. | 2717 Dewar Dr. | 307/362–1770 | fax 307/362–2830 | 130 rooms | $70–$75 | AE, D, DC, MC, V.

SARATOGA

Hacienda Motel. A two-story adobe motor inn at the southern edge of Saratoga, this one has larger-than-average rooms and a lobby adorned with Native American crafts and blankets. Kitchenettes are available. In-room data ports. Cable TV. Pets allowed. | Rte. 130 S | 307/326–5751 | 32 rooms | $64 | AE, D, DC, MC, V.

Riviera Lodge. On the North Platte River and two blocks north of downtown businesses, shops, and restaurants, this standard motor inn sits in a shaded park. Some rooms have balconies that overlook the river, and condominiums come with full kitchens. Conference room. Picnic area. Cable TV. Pets allowed. | 104 E. Saratoga St. | 307/326–5651 | fax 307/326–5651 | 29 rooms, 2 condos | $42–$90, $150 condos | AE, D, MC, V.

SHERIDAN

Holiday Inn. Five minutes from downtown Sheridan, this hotel is decorated in Western style throughout. The lobby has a four-story atrium with a waterfall and lots of plants. Raquet ball courts are a nice extra. Restaurant, bar, picnic area, room service. In-room data ports, some refrigerators. Cable TV. Indoor pool. Beauty salon, hot tub. Putting green. Exercise equipment. Laundry facilities. Business services. Airport shuttles. Pets allowed. | 1809 Sugarland Dr. | 307/672–8931 | fax 307/672–6388 | 212 rooms | $79–$119 | AE, D, DC, MC, V.

Mill Inn Motel. An old mill by a bridge is incorporated into this motel, which has large guest rooms with pastel spreads, drapes, and rugs. The offices of *American Cowboy* magazine are upstairs, and the walls in the lobby and breakfast room are decorated with Western art prints, boots, saddles, and the like. Complimentary Continental breakfast. Gym. Pets allowed. | 2161 Coffeen Ave. | 307/672–6401 | 45 rooms | $72–$102 | AE, D, MC, V.

SUNDANCE

Sundance Mountain Inn. This one-story ranch-style motor inn is convenient to I–90 and across the street from area restaurants. Clean, basic rooms, friendly service, and a comfortable poolside area make this a nice place to stay. Continental breakfast. Cable TV. Indoor pool. Hot tub. Laundry facilities. Pets allowed. | 26 Rte. 585 | 307/283–3737 or 888/347–2794 | fax 307/283–3738 | www.sundancewyoming.com/sundancemountaininn.htm | 42 rooms | $79–$89 | AE, D, MC, V.

THERMOPOLIS

Holiday Inn of the Waters. The rooms are standard here, but the extra amenities and proximity to the mineral springs set it apart. You can soak year-round in the outdoor mineral hot tub and swim in the pool in summer. A complete health club is nearby, as well as a hiking and jogging trail and a water slide. Special winter lodging-meal-activity packages. Restaurant, bar, room service. In-room data ports, no-smoking rooms. Pool (summer). Outdoor hot tub, massage, sauna, spa, steam room. Health club. Hiking. Laundry service. Pets allowed. | Hot Springs State Park | 307/864–3131 | 80 rooms | $99 | AE, D, DC, MC, V.

WHEATLAND

Best Western Torchlite Motor Inn. You're right next to I–25 at this inn with a homey lobby and refrigerators in the rooms. Restaurant. Refrigerators. Cable TV. Gym. Business services. Airport shuttle. Pets allowed. | 1809 N. 16th | 307/322–4070 | fax 307/322–4072 | 50 rooms | $56 | AE, D, DC, MC, V.

WORLAND

Settlers Inn. The rooms here are spacious with contemporary furnishings. Also, the inn is conveniently near to downtown. Continental breakfast. Business services. Pets allowed. | 2200 Big Horn Ave. | 307/347–8201 | fax 307/347–9323 | 44 rooms | $54 | AE, D, DC, MC, V.

Worland Days Inn. All the larger-than-average, clean, earth-toned rooms are on the ground level at this reliable motor inn, which is within walking distance of a handful of restaurants. Continental breakfast. Cable TV. Laundry facilities. Airport shuttle. Small pets allowed. | 500 N. 10th St. | 307/347–4251 or 800/544–8313 | fax 307/347–6500 | 42 rooms | $56 | AE, D, DC, MC, V.

YELLOWSTONE NATIONAL PARK

Yellowstone Park Campgrounds. You can choose from multiple camping options throughout Yellowstone, including Fishing Bridge RV Park and developed campgrounds at Bridge Bay, Canyon, Grant Village, and Madison. There are numerous backcountry campsites and some suitable for people with disabilities. Campgrounds generally open in May or June and close in September or October. Due to the presence of bears, food-storage regulations are strictly enforced; at Fishing Bridge RV Park only hard-sided vehicles are allowed. Some campgrounds have coin-operated showers and laundry facilities. Flush toilets. Some pets allowed. | 307/344–7311 | fax 307/344–7456 | www.amfac.com. or www.travelyellowstone.com/ | $15–$27 | AE, D, DC, MC, V | Closed Nov.–early May.

Pet Resources

By Andrea Arden

National Pet Resources

Air Transport Association of America. This organization sets the guidelines for pet air travel. | 1301 Pennsylvania Ave. NW, Suite 1100, Washington, D.C. | 202/626–4000 | ata@air-transport.org.

American Animal Hospital Association (AAHA). This is an association of more than 16,000 veterinary care providers founded in 1933. You can call them for veterinary referrals; their web site is full of lots of tips on pet health and safety. | Box 150899, Denver, CO; 12575 W. Bayaud Ave., Denver, CO | 303/986–2800 or 800/252–2242 | www.healthypet.com.

American Boarding Kennels Association. Referrals for boarding kennels are available from this association. | 4575 Galley Rd., #400A, Colorado Springs, CO | 719/591–1113 | www.abka.com.

American Cat Association. This is the oldest registry for purebred cats in the US. Call for some basic tips on cat health or referrals to cat breeders. | 8101 Katherine Ave., Panorama City, CA | 818/782–6080.

American Cat Fancier's Association. This cat association and registry provides information about domesticated cats, purebred and non-purebred, and sponsors shows and awards for outstanding cats. | Box 203, Point Lookout, MO | 417/334–5430 | www.acfacat.com.

American Humane Association. This is a national federation of concerned individuals and agencies dedicated to the prevention of cruelty, neglect, abuse and exploitation of animals. Contact them for information on how to report any of the above. | 63 Inverness Dr. E, Englewood, CO | 800/227–4645 | www.americanhumane.org.

American Kennel Club. A national registry for purebred dogs, the AKC offers free brochures on traveling with your dog as well as free packets on responsible dog ownership. The library in New York is full of great resources about dogs. | 51 Madison Ave., New York, NY | 212/696–8336 or 212/696–8245 | www.akc.org.

American Veterinary Medical Association. This association can provide veterinarian referrals from a list that includes more than 50,000 vets in the US. | 930 N. Meacham Rd., Schaumburg, IL | 800/233–2862 in IL; 800/248–2862 | www.avma.org.

Animal and Plant Health Inspection Service,U.S. Department of Agriculture Inquiries regarding airline reimbursements, pets lost in transport or mistreatment of animals by airline personnel should be directed here. | 12th & Independence Ave., SW, Washington, D.C. | APHIS.Web@usda.gov | www.aphis.usda.gov.

Animal Behavior Systems. ABS offers a collar that stops barking using an innovative and humane method. When the dog barks a small squirt of citronella is automatically emitted. The dog eventually associates barking with this unpleasant smell and barks less frequently. They also offer a shampoo that aids in the reduction of nonseasonal hair shedding. One of their best products is a very effective clean-up aid called Petzorb. | 591–F Breckenridge Pkwy., Tampa, FL | 800/233–2862 in IL; 800/248–2862 | www.animalbehaviorsystems.com.

Association of Pet Dog Trainers. If you are interested in learning more about dog training, this is the group to contact. The APDT can refer you to trainers and to educational seminars and conferences about dogs and dog training throughout the US. Their web site is clear and informative. | 66 Morris Ave., Suite 2A, Springfield, NJ | 800/PET–DOGS | www.apdt.com.

Canadian Cat Association. This is the registry body for purebred cats in Canada. The Canadian Cat Association offers a magazine for members that includes tips on cat care. | 83 Kennedy Rd. S, Unit 18, Brampton, Ontario, Canada | 905/459–1481 | www.cca-afc.co.

Canadian Veterinary Medical Association. This is a good source for veterinary referrals if you are traveling in Canada. | 339 Booth St., Ottawa, Ontario, Canada | 613/236–1162 | www.cvma-acmv.org.

Cherry Brook. Cherry Brook is a wholesale pet-supply catalog. | Rt. 57, Box 15, Broadway, NY | 800/524–0820 or 908/689–7979 | www.cherrybrook.com.

Chicago Veterinary Medical Association. Call to hear pre-recorded information from vets who are members of the association. Topics discussed include veterinary and training tips. | Box 5017, Oak Brook, IL | 630/325–1231 | www.chicagovma.org.

Cool Paw Productions. This mail-order catalog offers dog boots to protect your dog's paws from hot, burning sidewalks or rough terrain for about $25. | 708 E. Solana Dr., Tempe, AZ | 800/650–PAWS.

Delta Society. This organization promotes all aspects of the human and companion animal bond. It includes pet partners therapy programs and service-animal training and education. | 289 Perimeter Rd. E, Renton, WA | 425/226–7357 | www.petsforum.com/deltasociety.

Doggone Good! Doggone Good! is a mail-order catalog of dog travel and gift items, including collapsible bowls. | 6429 Pelham Ct, San Jose, CA | 800/660–2665 | www.doggone.com.

Good Dog! These consumer magazines for dog and cat owners cover health, behavior and nutrition. Exclusive product test reports look at everything for your pet. There are six issues a year. | Box 10069, Austin, TX | 800/968–1738 | www.doggone.com.

Help 4 Pets. Help 4 Pets services include a national vet referral system and 24-hour pet-recovery system. The more pets you register, the lower the registration fees. Help 4 Pets is endorsed by the Los Angeles SPCA. | 800/HELP–4–PETS (435-7473) | www.help4pets.com.

Humane Society of the United States. Contact this organization for information regarding the humane treatment of animals. | 2100 L St. NW, Washington, D.C. | 202/452–1100 | www.hsus.org.

In the Company of Dogs. This free catalog offers a wide selection of unique gift items for dog lovers. | Box 7071, Dover, DE | 800/662–5616 | www.inthecompanyofdogs.com.

James & Kenneth Publishers. This publisher is a great source for cutting-edge books and videos on cat and dog training and behavior. | 2140 Shattuck Ave., #2406, Berkeley, CA | 800/784–5531 or 510/547–4582.

JB Wholesale. Call to request a free wholesale pet-supply catalog. | 5 Raritan Rd., Oakland, NJ | 800/526–0388 | www.JBPet.com.

K9 Cruiser. This is a wonderful device designed to make taking your pet along on bike rides a safe and fun prospect. If you intend to go biking with your dog at home or while traveling, the K9 Cruiser is indispensable. | 4640 Desoto St., San Diego, CA | 800/592–7847.

Meblo. This company carries some quality products for traveling with your pet in the car. The Deluxe Travelbed covers the entire backseat and acts as a barrier to keep your dog out of the front seat. | Box 322, Redwood Valley, CA | 800/776–3256 | www.meblo.com.

National Animal Poison Control Center. This center provides twenty-four-hour service for emergency calls; major credit cards are accepted. Be prepared to give relevant information regarding your pet, and if possible, the suspected poison. The 900 number should be used if you don't have a credit card and for non-emergency question regarding poisons. The charge for all calls is $30. | 1717 Thilo Rd., Suite #36, Urbana, IL | 800/548–2423 for emergencies; 900/680–0000 for non–emergencies | www.napcc.aspca.org.

National Dog Registry. The NDR was established in 1966 and currently has over 4 million registered pets. NDR members' dogs are registered with a tattooed number or with an implanted microchip. There is a one-time fee of $38, which covers any pet you ever own. NDR has phones staffed 365 days a year, 24 hours a day. | Box 116, Woodstock, NY | 800/NDR–DOGS (548–2423) | www.natldogregistry.com.

Pet Affairs. This company sells a harness that converts to a seatbelt. The device clips into the seatbelt holder of your car. | 691 E. 20th St., Building 111, Tucson, AZ | 800/777–9192.

Pet Assure. Pet assure is a membership savings program for pet owners. Members save 25 percent at the vet, an average of 50 percent off supplies and products and 10 to 50 percent off services such as training, grooming, boarding and pet-sitting. They also offer a lost-pet recovery program for members. Members can use any veterinarian in the network. There are currently approximately a thousand vets in over 30 US states in addition to vets overseas. Fees are lower if you register more than one pet. Discounts are available for groups and corporations for employees. | 10 S. Morris St., Dover, NJ | 888/789–PETS (7387) | www.petassure.com.

Pet Finders. Pet Finders finds homes for neglected and homeless pets. They're essentially an adoption service that places over a thousand pets per year, including dogs, cats, rabbits, guinea pigs, lizards, snakes, parrots, birds, goats, chickens, horses, and ponies. | Box 276796, Sacramento, CA | 530/647–9447 | www.petfinders.org.

R.C. Steele. R.C. Steele provides a catalog full of wholesale pet- and animal-care supplies. | 1989 Transit Way, Box 910, Brockport, NY | 888/839–9420 | www.rcsteele.com.

Roger's Visionary Pet Products. They have a nice product called soft store that is a convenient way to carry pet food and keep it fresh. | Box 5150, Stateline, NV | 800/364–4537 | www.rogerspet.com or www.3whost.com/roger.

Tattoo-A-Pet International. Tattoo-a-pet has been in business since 1972 and has more than 2 million registered pets. They charge a one-time fee of $25 to register any pet(s) you have in your lifetime. Their phones are staffed 365 days a year, 24 hours a day. | 6571 S.W. 20th Ct, Ft. Lauderdale, FL | 800/TAT–TOOS (828–8667) or 954/581–5834 | www.tattoo-a-pet.com.

Notes

Notes

Notes

Notes

Notes

Notes

Notes

Notes

Notes

Notes

Notes

Notes